ANTHROPOLOGICAL THEORY

An Introductory History

Second Edition

R. Jon McGee
Richard L. Warms

Southwest Texas State University

Mayfield Publishing Company

Mountain View, California
London • Toronto

To our guys: Jake McGee and
Benjamin and Nathan Warms

Library of Congress Cataloging-in-Publication Data
McGee, R. Jon
    Anthropological theory : an introductory history /
R. Jon McGee, Richard L. Warms—2nd ed.
        p.   cm.
    Includes bibliographical references and index.
    ISBN 0-7674-1166-8
    1. Anthropology—Philosophy.   2. Anthropology—
    Methodology.
I. Warms, Richard L.   II. Title.
GN33.M33   1999
301'.01—dc21   99-17966
                                                       CIP

Manufactured in the United States of America
10   9   8   7   6   5   4   3

Mayfield Publishing Company
1280 Villa Street
Mountain View, CA 94041

Sponsoring editor, Janet M. Beatty; production editor,
Julianna Scott Fein; manuscript editor, Judith Brown;
design and art manager, Jean Mailander; text designer,
Wendy LaChance; cover designer, Joan Greenfield;
illustrator, Joan Carol; manufacturing manager, Randy
Hurst. The text was set in 10/11.5 Fairfield Medium by
ColorType and printed on acid-free 50# OPC Opaque
Smooth by Custom Printing Company.

Preface

*T*heory is the core of anthropology. Theorists determine the types of questions anthropologists ask and the sort of information they collect. Without a solid understanding of the history of theory, anthropological data remains a collection of exotic ethnographic vignettes. Students face two choices, then, if they wish to understand the theoretical perspectives that ultimately drive ethnographic fieldwork: they can read classic theoretical articles or they can read someone's interpretations of those articles. For readers who are not well versed in anthropological theory, neither choice is ideal. We created this volume to provide a more accessible means of introducing students to the past century and a half of theorizing in anthropology.

We believe that it is essential for students to read original essays by the field's important thinkers. Reading original works promotes depth of understanding and opens possibilities of analysis that even the best books describing the history of theory can never provide. What better introduction to Herbert Spencer can there be than actually reading Spencer? Yet many students find reading original essays extremely demanding. The language is sometimes difficult, and the intellectual disputes, references to other thinkers, and historical context are often obscure. Sitting down to read an essay by Spencer is, for many, an arduous task. We have attempted to make the task less onerous by providing detailed commentary, in close proximity to difficult passages in the original essay, that illuminates obscure references, arcane language, and unfamiliar contexts.

We have assembled an exceptional collection of essays by some of the most important thinkers in anthropology. We have favored essays that provide vivid ethnographic examples of theoretical positions over those that are simply declarations of theory. The collection begins in the mid-nineteenth century and ends in the 1990s. It is divided into chapters encompassing well-known theoretical positions that are represented by authors generally considered to be the outstanding spokespersons for their points of view.

We have provided extensive support material to help students understand these 40 essays. Each of the 13 chapters begins with a brief introductory essay to acquaint readers with some of the most important proponents of the school of thought, the problems they set out to solve, the methods they used, and the dilemmas they faced. Extensive editorial footnotes that provide additional information to help the reader actively understand and interpret the reading accompany each essay. In addition to providing definitions, translations of foreign phrases, and historical information, the notes help students trace the intellectual connections among thinkers both inside and outside of anthropology. The notes are designed to inform, raise interesting questions, and foster further creative and original thought. They make essential but sometimes difficult information accessible to students and provide some interesting little-known background details. Anthropological theory, even that of a century ago, is alive and vital. We hope our commentary helps readers see it that way.

No book of theory and commentary can ever be entirely without bias, but we have tried to come as close to this ideal as we can. In our introductions and commentary, we point to both the strengths and weaknesses of each theoretical position. Though astute readers will realize our likes and dislikes, we do not intend to promote one theory at the expense of another. In fact, we come from quite different theoretical perspectives: McGee's interests tend to the symbolic and interpretive side of anthropology and Warms generally favors positivist and materialist approaches. Every introductory essay and note in this volume was written and rewritten by both of us; obviously, we have sympathies for the opposing position and have been willing to accept substantial criticism of ideas we hold dear.

For us, editing this volume continues to be an exciting process of discovery and interpretation. Research, careful reading, discussion, and argumentation as well as the comments of numerous reviewers and readers of the first edition have greatly deepened our understanding of the works of the great thinkers in anthropology. Writing this book has forced us to rethink what we believed we knew, and in the process we have become far better scholars of theory. Selecting these essays and writing the introductions and commentary for them continues to be profoundly rewarding for us. We hope that reading the essays and our comments will be as productive for students and colleagues.

NEW IN THE SECOND EDITION

Preparing the second edition has given us a chance to reconsider both our selection of essays, the notes we wrote as commentary to the essays, and our introductions. We have made substantial improvements in all three of these, incorporating new information and bringing a wider selection of authors and opinions to the volume.

Most notably, this edition includes four new essays. A fifth essay has been moved to a new position. We have expanded the chapter on Materialism to include Bourgois' essay "From Jíbaro to Crack Dealer," a compelling example of contemporary Marxist analysis. We have substantially altered the chapter on Anthropology and Gender to better reflect different positions in that theoretical perspective. We have chosen Leacock's "Interpreting the Origins of Gender Inequality" to represent a Marxist approach to gender stratification and Stoler's "Making Empire Respectable" to reflect an approach focusing on the different ways in which race, class, and gender structure cultural institutions. You may have noticed that we have also moved Ortner's essay "Is Female to Male as

Nature is to Culture?" to the Structuralism chapter. It is an outstanding example of this school of thought. Finally, we have added D'Andrade's "Moral Models in Anthropology" to the Postmodernism and Its Critics chapter. There are now numerous critiques of specific aspects of postmodern theory. We have chosen this essay because it provides a thoughtful analysis of some of the assumptions underlying postmodern thought.

We have, additionally, revisited all of our introductions and footnotes. We have updated and revised many of these in light of new material that has come to our attention and to redress some issues that were omitted from the first edition. For example, the introduction to Culture and Personality now includes much more information on Margaret Mead, and the introduction to Historical Particularism examines Boas' censure by the American Anthropological Association. The roles Weber and Durkheim played in anthropological theory are described in greater detail and the contributions of European thinkers, such as Gramsci and Foucault, are given much more coverage. We have gone over each of our footnotes, correcting and revising them according to the information that we have gathered since the publication of the first edition. We have also tried to improve the index, increasing the level of detail and making the book a more useful research tool.

We have been particularly gratified by the reactions of readers of the first edition. We have received many letters and e-mails from all over the United States, Canada, and Europe. Many people have sent thoughtful commentary and recommendations. We have been able to incorporate some of these into this edition. We deeply regret that editorial constraints and issues of timing have prevented us from including more of your suggestions. We look forward to being able to act upon them in the future. Keep those cards and letters coming!

ACKNOWLEDGMENTS

Writing this book has involved the labor, support, and forbearance of many people. First and foremost, we would like to thank our families, Karen, Benjamin, and Nathan Warms and Stacie and

Jacob McGee. Without their support, this project would have been impossible.

We also thank our professors at Rice and Syracuse, both for what they taught us and for what they left us to discover on our own. We hope they will view this work with approving eyes (but we're sure they won't be pleased by all that they find).

We are indebted to the many scholars who reviewed and commented on this book in various stages of preparation. Our work has benefited greatly from their comments and our ideas were altered by their insights. We deeply appreciate their advice even though we were not always able to follow it. We would particularly like to thank John H. Bodley, Washington State University; Daniel L. Boxberger, Western Washington University; Castle McLaughlin, Peabody Museum, Harvard University; Mary Jo Schneider, University of Arkansas–Fayetteville; and Christopher P. Tourney, University of Kentucky.

The comments of students in our history and anthropological thought classes have also been invaluable. Our students have often shed new light on old issues and forced us to look at problems in new ways. We are thankful for the help we received from the Anthropology Department staff at Southwest Texas and extend our thanks to them, particularly our Administrative Assistant Sharan Smith. We would also like to thank our student assistants Glenda Gaunt, Cara Laubach, Jennifer Pennington, A. C. White, and Elizabeth Airhart for their time and patience.

Finally, we are grateful to the people at Mayfield, particularly Jan Beatty, for her consistent backing of our work, Star MacKenzie for her help with acquiring permissions to reprint articles, production editor Julianna Scott Fein, and our copyeditor Judith Brown. Their knowledge, editing skills, and many superb suggestions have contributed greatly to this work.

Contents

Part Three
Theory at Mid-Century

Part Four
Recent Trends in Anthropological Theory

Introduction

$\mathcal{A}$nthropology is concerned with understanding the "other." Typically anthropologists study the behavior, beliefs, and lifestyles of people in other cultures. Some examine current cultures; others study the remains of past societies to re-create the lives of people who disappeared long ago; yet others study primates to see what our closest relatives can tell us about being human. What unites this diverse work is a common ground in some fundamental theoretical ideas concerning biological evolution and social behavior.

We team-teach a course on theory in cultural anthropology at Southwest Texas State University. Each fall, as the semester begins, we face the same issues: some students want to know why the theory course is required, and others worry about reading original works by authors and delving into a subject that seems esoteric. Because both matters are important, we have chosen to begin this book by telling you why we think theory is essential in anthropology, and why it is valuable to read original works rather than predigested theoretical summaries.

WHY STUDY THEORY?

Theory is critical because, while anthropologists collect data through fieldwork, data in and of themselves are meaningless. Whether stated explicitly or assumed, theories are the tools anthropologists use to give meaning to their data. Anthropologists' understanding of the artifacts they collect or the events they record in the field is derived from their theoretical perspective. A wink and an eyelid twitch look identical to an observer, but one carries information ("I'm kidding," "you're cute," "that's OK"), while the other signi-

fies nothing more than dust in someone's eye. So, to paraphrase Clifford Geertz, a famous cultural anthropologist, how does one differentiate between winks and eyelid twitches? Anthropologists distinguish the two through their understanding of the context in which the action occurs. Theories guide that understanding. They are the tools anthropologists use to sort significant from meaningless information. In fact, one's choice of theory largely determines the data to be collected in the first place. A structuralist interested in the unconscious meaning of mythology will probably not spend too much time studying subsistence patterns. An economic anthropologist might well ignore ritual and religion. Without theory, one cannot do anthropology.

Although this is a book about theory in sociocultural anthropology, the different branches of anthropology have always freely borrowed ideas from each other and from other sciences. In the nineteenth century, Herbert Spencer, a sociologist, and Charles Darwin, a naturalist, greatly influenced each other's work. Sigmund Freud was well versed in nineteenth-century ethnological studies, and his work is imbued with ideas taken from anthropology; anthropology, in turn, has been greatly influenced by his theories. Sociobiologists study human behavior in terms of evolutionary biology and cultural adaptations. Symbolic anthropologists and postmodernists rely on tools developed in the study of literature. Contemporary archaeology relies, in part, on theoretical developments in cultural anthropology in the 1940s and 1950s. In the course of their research, anthropologists today delve into biology, geology, psychology, history, literature, physics, chemistry, medicine, and other subjects.

1

Modern anthropology is built on the work of earlier generations of theorists. Indeed, anthropologists today ask many of the same questions that occupied scholars in the nineteenth and early twentieth centuries. Nineteenth-century theories continue to resonate in popular culture. Have you ever heard the phrase "survival of the fittest," for example? It was coined by Herbert Spencer in the middle part of the nineteenth century. Do you think that technology is a measure of a society's development? Then you will be comfortable reading Lewis Henry Morgan's *Ancient Society* first published in 1877. To fully comprehend anthropological writing, you must appreciate the history of the ideas that inform it. These are, ultimately, the principles upon which current work is based.

Anthropological theory is also important because it helps us think about who and what we are as human beings. It does this by forcing us to consider the ways in which we understand the "other." At its most basic level, anthropology asks how we are to understand other people in the world—those who look different than we do and have different languages and customs (what anthropologists have come to call different cultures). Are such people inferior to us, superior to us, or just different? Are their cultures unchanging, following their own paths of evolution, or bound to ours in a grand evolutionary scheme? How should we behave toward such people?

At a second level, anthropology forces us to consider the otherness of nature itself. It forces us to ask if we, as human beings, are fundamentally part of the natural world. If so, perhaps we can be studied by the scientific methods and principles used by biologists, physicists, and other scholars in the traditional physical sciences. Alternatively, are human beings sufficiently different from the rest of the world that studying them with these methods will permit only trivial and confusing results? If that is true, the skills needed might be creative insight, imaginative interpretation, and soul-borne empathy—analytic tools traditionally associated with the arts and humanities.

A final level of discourse deals with the otherness of culture itself. By directing us, sometimes only implicitly, to the comparison of cultures, anthropology ultimately points toward the study of universal human nature. If we could strip away the cultural clothing of all peoples, would we be left with some set of basic principles or underlying essence? Would this be equivalent to finding untrammeled human nature before us in the buff? If so, how are we to understand human culture? Is it that which permits the full and satisfying expression of human nature, or that which prevents human nature from destroying human society?

At some level, all theory in anthropology, whether written in the eighteenth, nineteenth, or twentieth centuries, addresses these essential questions. Sometimes, individual theorists take extreme postures and score telling points against those who hold alternative positions. However, no definitive conclusion has ever been reached on any of these issues. Perhaps these questions are ultimately unanswerable by their very nature. However, the fact that no authoritative conclusion has been reached does not lessen the importance of the debate, for how we answer these questions has practical applications in our world. The answers determine our understanding of ourselves and our behavior toward other individuals and groups. In a world of instantaneous communication and virtually unlimited capacity for violence, in a world of ethnic strife and national warfare, surely these are among the most important questions that face us.

WHY READ ORIGINAL WORKS?

We believe it is important to read original works for several reasons. First, commentary on a theory cannot replace the original work because commentators unavoidably (and frequently quite intentionally) place their own interpretations on the material. For instance, Robert Lowie's 1937 *History of Ethnological Theory* and Marvin Harris' 1968 *The Rise of Anthropological Theory* are both comprehensive summaries of anthropological theory, but they provide strikingly different perspectives on the field.

Second, part of the importance of classic works in theory is their subtlety and complexity. The creation of theory is part of an ongoing dialogue with earlier thinkers, and these essays (and many others) are a portion of that dialogue. As our understanding changes, we return to these old writings, where we find insights that advance our thinking or perceive errors against which we react. Through this process, new theory is generated. When works are summarized or when we read only analyses, the theoretical dialogue is flattened, simplified, and ultimately impoverished. In this volume, we provide what we believe is accurate and fairly sophisticated commentary on the essays we present, but reading such analysis cannot replace careful reading of the original text. As new insights are made, many of our notes may become dated and stale. The essays themselves have a much longer shelf life.

Finally, a firsthand reading of the original sources helps one avoid inaccuracies. In preparing this text, we have run across numerous cases where the popularly accepted information passed to us by our professors or found in textbooks was incorrect. Some of the folk wisdom of anthropology consists of half-truths or is frankly inaccurate. We bring this up not to point fingers or assign blame, but to suggest that reading original sources can serve as a partial corrective for this problem.

USING THIS TEXTBOOK

This book is designed to help you understand where some of the great minds in anthropology have been before you and to help you formulate your theoretical position in the field today. It is a historical overview of some of the principal developments in culture theory since the 1850s. The book is different from others because it contains our introductions and paragraph-by-paragraph comments to inform your reading and raise interesting points or questions.

Theory texts are problematic because their contents tend to become accepted doctrine. Readers and critics suppose that the authors of such a text have chosen to present those pieces universally considered the most important works in the field. When the editors of such a volume have the audacity to write detailed comments on the essays they have chosen, they seem to elevate the texts they chose to scripture and their work to Talmudic authority. Should you entertain these notions, let us disabuse you of them. No group of professional anthropologists, however small, will agree

on a single set of critical essays. We have selected what we feel are representative articles by individuals traditionally associated with particular theories and works that seem to us to be good examples of theories in practice. We will gladly agree with anyone who claims that better works can be found, but we insist that this will always be the case. An enormous corpus of work in anthropology now exists. We believe that the best way to study anthropological theory is to read as widely as possible. No collection of essays, however artfully chosen, will be able to substitute for years of reading in the field, and that is what is ultimately required for a solid background in theory.

You will find that our commentary on the texts varies from extremely straightforward definitions and explanations to fairly elaborate speculation on the motives of authors and influences upon them. Although it is almost impossible to entirely eliminate mistakes, we have checked our work carefully; when we point to a fact, you may be reasonably certain that it is correct. However, please remember that our interpretations are just that, our interpretations. They are meant to guide your reading, stimulate discussion, call your attention to certain ideas, and get you to think about different issues. You are invited to disagree with them and propose alternatives. If you read through this book and find nothing with which to disagree, you are not reading carefully enough or critically enough.

While our likes and dislikes may become apparent to the conscientious reader, we do not intend to promote any particular viewpoint to the exclusion of others. In fact, we come from very different theoretical perspectives (McGee tends to the interpretive-symbolic side of anthropology, Warms to the positivist-materialist). We have tried to present the key strengths and weaknesses of each position, but we frequently differ in our interpretations of theory and amuse our students by arguing about them.

In short, while we hope that scholars will agree with most of what we have written, we have tried to write at least something bound to offend your theoretical sensibilities, no matter who you are. You are invited to disagree with the text and debate us about it if you wish. We can be contacted by e-mail at RW04@swt.edu for Warms or

RM08@swt.edu for McGee or by traditional mail at the Department of Anthropology, Southwest Texas State University, San Marcos, Texas 78666. If, by chance, you reach the end of the book without finding something to offend you, you may contact us at one of the addresses above, and we will try to remedy that situation as well.

THE ARRANGEMENT OF ESSAYS AND THE NOTATIONAL SYSTEM

The arrangement of essays within a reader presents a surprising number of problems. Should they be arranged strictly chronologically or by intellectual association or descent? If the text is to be divided into sections, what about those authors who do not quite fit? One reviewer of this book felt that placing postmodernism as the final section proved that our intention was to promote the postmodern position. We assure you, this is not the case. We have chosen to arrange the theories in a rough chronological order to show readers the progression of ideas in cultural anthropology and to demonstrate the relationship between concepts. We have divided our chronology into named sections. Each begins with an introduction describing the theorists represented in the section and the principal ideas presented in their work. However, our scheme is not entirely consistent. Different schools of thought often overlap both intellectually and chronologically. Freud's speculations on anthropology, for example, were largely based on nineteenth-century evolutionary assumptions even though they were written in the early decades of the twentieth century. Exploiting these inconsistencies and thinking about other possible arrangements of the text

may prove an intellectually useful experience. New arrangements may provide new insights.

Space limitations and, occasionally, copyright regulations have forced us to make difficult decisions about the essays we have reprinted. Several entire essays included in earlier drafts of the book have been removed from the final form. More importantly, we have, in many cases, eliminated fairly large passages of those essays that we have retained. In some instances, we have also chosen to remove some lengthy sets of footnotes or endnotes. These are not decisions we took lightly, nor do they indicate that we believe the notes and passages removed were of no importance. It was simply a question of choosing between removing notes and passages or losing several entire essays. While there are good intellectual reasons for selecting either of these options, we believe that most readers are better served by the first. In doing this editing, we have tried to preserve a sense of the original by including notes telling the reader exactly how much text was removed and briefly summarizing the content of the lost passage. We also note how many footnotes appeared in those passages, which allows readers to see the subjects about which the authors wrote notes and those they did not and gives a feel for the frequency and pacing of notes.

Each essay in the volume is accompanied by our notes, which appear as footnotes and are numbered with Arabic numerals. Footnotes or endnotes created by the original authors are indicated by lowercase letters and appear as endnotes to the essays. Where authors have provided references in their work, they appear at the end of the essay. Our own references appear in the Bibliography at the end of the volume.

Nineteenth-Century Evolutionism

In the English-speaking world, the word *anthropologist* first appeared in print in 1805 (Kuklick 1991:6). It was another seventy-nine years before the first university position in anthropology was created. The discipline of anthropology, however, did not just appear, but rather combined two long-existing streams of thought. The first was the study of what we have come to call cultural differences among societies, and the second dealt with the biological origins of humans and other species. In Europe, both of these areas have been the subject of investigation and speculation for much of the past millennium. While it is far beyond the scope of this text to analyze all the antecedents of anthropology, we will briefly review some of the principal developments that led to it before exploring evolutionary and anthropological thinking in the nineteenth century.

It is probably fair to say that wherever literate civilizations came into contact with members of different societies, something like ethnographic writing occurred. For example, ancient authors such as Herodotus, a Greek historian of the fifth century B.C.E., offered readers fanciful descriptions of other societies. In the fourteenth century, Ibn Khaldun, a Tunisian politician and historian, wrote the *Muqaddimah*, or *Introduction to History*, in which he proposed to create a science for studying "human society and its own problems vis the social transformations that succeed each other in the nature of society" (quoted in Lacoste 1984:169).

In Europe there was a long tradition of interest in the exotic. Writings such as *The Wonders of the East* and *The Travels of Marco Polo* had fascinated Europeans. Until the fifteenth century, however, Europe remained relatively isolated and provincial. Then, developments in sailing technology and advances in weaponry allowed Europeans to expand their influence across the globe. For the first time, they were in frequent contact with people from societies radically different from their own. This confrontation raised a host of philosophical problems. Were these other people human in the same way that Europeans were? Did their societies function according to brute natural law, or were they moral beings possessed of a free will? How were social differences to be explained?

Degenerationism provided an early explanation of cultural diversity. Degenerationists held that there was a biblical cause for variation in human society. In this view, prior to the destruction of the Tower of Babel, all people belonged to a single civilization. When God destroyed the Tower, creating differences in language and dispersing the people, some degenerated, losing their civilization and eventually becoming savages.

Progressivism was an alternative view of social life. Progressivists believed that, rather than deteriorating from a previously civilized condition, societies had started out primitive but were progressing toward a more advanced state. One proponent of this approach was the British philosopher John Locke (1632–1704). In his *Essay Concerning Government* (1939 [1690]), Locke proposed that the human mind was a blank slate and that knowledge and reason were derived from experience. The corollary of this was that different sorts of experiences would provide different sorts of ideas. Consequently, individuals growing up in different societies would have varied experiences, and the differences between human societies could thus be explained.

The idea that people had progressed rather than degenerated became popular as scientific investigation and empirical observation increasingly yielded both academic and commercial results. By the beginning of the Industrial Revolution, few Europeans doubted that humankind was making progress, and Europeans generally believed that they were the most advanced of all people.

With the general idea of progress firmly entrenched, philosophers devised various schemes to explain the nature and course of this social evolution. Their goal was generally to construct a universal history of humankind that moved from a primitive past to the development of European nations. One of the most influential of these works was Edward Gibbon's (1737–1794) *The History of the Decline and Fall of the Roman Empire* (orig. 1776–1788), but there were others as well. Italian philosopher Giambattista Vico (1668–1744), in his 1725 work *The New Science,* attempted to write a universal history of humanity. Vico believed that human nature was shaped by history and hence changed over time. Thus he thought that history was a better guide than the natural sciences to understanding humanity. French statesman Anne-Robert-Jacques Turgot (1727–1781) published his *Plan for Two Discourses on Universal History* in 1750. He submitted that, after the biblical flood, humans had passed through stages of savagery and barbarism to agricultural- and urban-based civilization. One last example of this perspective is *Sketch for a Historical Picture of the Progress of the Human Mind,* written by the French mathematician and philosopher Marie Jean Antoine Nicolas Caritat, the Marquis de Condorcet (1743–1794). In this work, written in 1794 while he was in hiding from his radical revolutionary enemies, Condorcet proposed a ten-stage scheme describing human progress from early tribal society through the founding of the French Republic and on to a future in which human society was perfected. These ideas played pivotal roles in much of later sociocultural evolutionary thinking (Stocking 1987:15).

The European expansion into different parts of the world that began in the fifteenth century had a profound effect on the natural sciences as well as philosophy. Explorers' accounts of the flora and fauna of these new lands challenged the biblical view of life, which had been based largely on the story of the flood. Long before Darwin, naturalists began to try to account for the plant and animal distribution and variation they were now confronted with, which could not be explained in biblical terms.

The foundation of biological-evolutionary speculation was laid down in the descriptive writings of seventeenth-century naturalists such as Gilbert White (1720–1793) and John Ray (1627–1705), who attempted to classify and describe the diversity of life-forms they observed (Eiseley 1961). Ray influenced Carolus Linnaeus (1707–1778), best known for his taxonomic categorization of life-forms presented in *Systema Naturae* in 1735. Previously, the naming of plants and animals had been confused. Linnaeus's taxonomic system provided a systematic, organized framework for the classification of life-forms that was necessary for the scientific investigation of biological evolution to take place.

One aspect of Linnaean thought was belief in the immutability of species. That is, Linnaeus, along with most scholars, believed that life-forms were created by God as they were and could not change. The task of biology was to name and classify them. However, challenges to this position were developed by a number of scholars. For example, in *Telliamed: or Discourses Between an Indian Philosopher and a French Missionary on the Diminution of the Sea, the Formation of the Earth, the Origin of Men and Animals, etc.,* a book widely read in the mid-eighteenth century, Benoit de Maillet (1656–1738) outlined a scheme for biological evolution. He speculated that the age of the earth was much greater than popularly believed, recognized that fossils were the remains of life-forms, and suggested that some of these fossils represented extinct species (Eiseley 1961:29).

Another naturalist, second in importance only to Linnaeus, was Georges Louis Leclerc, Comte de Buffon (1707–1788). In his forty-four-volume *Natural History* (1752–1799), he outlined an evolutionary theory that he called "degeneration" but which contained many of the elements that Darwin used in his theory of natural selection over 100 years later. Some of Buffon's key observations were that there was physical variation within species; that different animals had underlying structural similarities; that life multiplied faster than its food supply, promoting a struggle for existence; and that some life-forms had become extinct.

Jean Lamarck (1744–1829) and Charles Darwin's grandfather, Erasmus Darwin (1731–1802), were two great evolutionists of the late eighteenth century, and their work exerted a profound influence on the development of later evolutionary theory. Although they held similar views, Lamarck's theories were more systematically presented, and his work is better known today. Lamarck believed that changes in geographic and climatic areas placed pressures on plant and animal life. Over long periods of time, these pressures resulted in the transformation of life-forms. In this view, evolutionary changes were due to the effort with which life-forms employed those body parts that were most useful under changed conditions. Thus, physiological need promoted the formation of new organs or alteration of old ones. These acquired characteristics were passed on to future generations. While various versions of this theory were common in the eighteenth century, Lamarck and the elder Darwin are significant for clearly recognizing the importance of the relationship between organisms and environment.

By the end of the eighteenth century, the philosophical and biological framework for anthropology was in place. Nineteenth-century thinkers, driven by an abundance of new data, from fossil finds in England to explorers' accounts of Africa, built on this framework. They produced new theories of biological and social evolution that were key to the development of anthropology. The insights of Charles Darwin (1809–1882) and Herbert Spencer (1820–1903) were particularly important.

Darwin held that change within species must follow natural laws like those found in the physical sciences. In *On the Origin of Species* (1988 [1859]), he outlined the theory of natural selection and proposed that it was the fundamental principle of biological change. Darwin began with the idea that more organisms were born than survived to adulthood, a widely accepted concept derived from "An Essay on the Principle of Population" by Thomas Malthus (1766–1834); then he speculated about the factors that determined which individuals survived and which did not. Given that small variations occur in the appearance or behavioral characteristics of members of any population and that these individuals must compete for food, mates, and shelter, Darwin hypothesized that these variations were instrumental in determining survival in particular environmental circumstances. Simply put, some individuals were better equipped than others to survive in their environment. Darwin called the characteristics that help them survive "adaptive." He believed that this relationship between physiology, behavior, and environment determined those who would survive, mature, reproduce, and thus pass their adaptive traits on to the next generation. Thus, environmental changes could affect the characteristics selected—or passed on—in a given species and, over a long time, alter the appearance of that species. Darwin's theory thus accounted for fossil evidence that indicated physical changes in life-forms had occurred.

Natural selection was controversial in religious circles and met with ridicule from the popular press. It was disparaged by French intellectuals (and presented in seriously flawed mistranslation when it first appeared) and was generally rejected in Germany until the twentieth century. However, in Britain and America, Darwinian evolution was readily accepted by the scientific community. In fact, Herbert Spencer had been working on a theory of human social evolutionary change several years before the publication of Darwin's work. Darwin even applied some of the concepts developed in Spencer's work in his own theory of biological evolution.

Spencer was interested in evolution as a general phenomenon, not just the evolution of specific human societies, and he applied his evolutionary approach to many fields of study. Garbarino (1977:21) calls him a "philosopher of universal evolution" because Spencer considered evolution to be one of the fundamental natural processes in the universe. His ideas had enormous impact in Britain and the United States, not only on anthropology and sociology but on literature, politics, and popular culture as well

(Carneiro 1967:xi). Spencer believed that evolution was progressive and change was from simple to more complex states—ideas that were later incorporated into a variety of anthropological theories. He believed that change was driven by a struggle for survival. Spencer is also famous for his organic analogy.

As illustrated in the selection reprinted in this book, Spencer compared human societies to biological organisms (see essay 1). He used this analogy to link biological and social evolution, implying that biological and social development from simple, undifferentiated states to complex, interrelated states followed the same processes. This suggested that social evolution could be studied in the same way that one studied biological evolution. Spencer's organic analogy was so influential that his definition of primitive societies as those societies with simple technology, undifferentiated social structure, and lack of economic specializations achieved widespread acceptance. Spencer viewed Darwin's work as supporting his own and used the organic analogy as a mechanism for applying evolution to his theory of social change. It is Spencer, not Darwin, who coined the phrase "survival of the fittest."

All humans are ethnocentric to one degree or another, and nineteenth-century Europeans and Americans were no exception. Looking with pride at their industrial advances and burgeoning economic and military power, Western societies believed they were at the pinnacle of social evolution. One consequence of Spencer's work was the popularization of a point of view called social darwinism. Social darwinists interpreted natural selection to mean that if evolution was progress and only the fittest survived, then it was the right of Western powers to dominate those who were less technologically advanced. According to this line of reasoning, the domination of one society by another proves its superiority and its advanced level of fitness. Conquest of an inferior society by a superior one was the result of the action of natural law and hence not only moral but also imperative. This was a convenient philosophy for the rapidly expanding European powers and was used to justify their imperialism, colonialism, and racism. In the United States, social darwinism was invoked as a justification for free enterprise capitalism.

It should be remembered, however, that while most of the evolutionary thinkers represented here believed their own society to be the most evolved, they were also highly critical of that society. They believed Western society was a long way from the perfection it could, in the future, obtain. It is true that Spencer argued that state welfare, education, and public health programs were contrary to the laws of nature and should be avoided because they slowed the evolutionary process that was weeding out the unfit members of society. On the other hand, he also argued against the military, the Church of England, and the perquisites of the landowning class. Despite the use of theories like his to justify colonial conquest, Spencer himself was an adamant opponent of British imperialism and criticized his nation for "picking quarrels with native races and taking possession of their lands" (quoted in Carneiro 1967:xlvi).

Two other nineteenth-century anthropologists interested in the evolution of culture as a general human phenomenon were the American Lewis Henry Morgan (1818–1881) and the Englishman Sir Edward Burnett Tylor (1832–1917). Both men believed there were universal evolutionary stages of cultural development that characterized the transition from primitive to complex societies. Because of this belief, Morgan and Tylor are known as unilineal evolutionists. Although Morgan and Tylor shared a similar evolutionary framework, their studies examined different aspects of culture. Morgan focused on the evolution of elements such as the family and subsistence patterns. Tylor's major contribution was a theory concerning the evolution of religion.

Morgan's early interest in Native American cultures, in particular patterns of marriage and descent, led to his 1871 book *Systems of Consanguinity and Affinity*, the first comparative study of kinship. But Morgan's most famous work was *Ancient Society*, published in 1877. In this book he attempted to trace the evolution of human society from primeval times to the Victorian era (which he considered the high point of human civilization). Following Turgot and other eighteenth-century writers, he divided human cultural development into three grand stages— savagery, barbarism, and civilization, with the first two stages further subdivided into lower, middle, and upper phases. Morgan accepted Spencer's idea that evolution proceeded from simple to complex and, in *Ancient Society*, outlined this progress by correlating his states of social evolution with specific developments in family structure, subsistence, and technology. For example, in Morgan's scheme, middle savagery begins with the acquisition of fish subsistence, while upper savagery is marked by the invention of the bow and arrow. For Morgan, evolutionary progress was not achieved through competition, but was propelled by the "flowering" of "germs of thought." This "flowering" was driven by the development of new subsistence strategies. The increasingly complex technologies produced after such an event were markers of evolutionary progress.

E. B. Tylor was a contemporary of Morgan. In his principal work, *Primitive Culture* (1871), Tylor outlined two ideas for which he is remembered today. First, he argued that one could reconstruct earlier stages of cultural evolution by studying "survivals." Tylor believed that virtually everything in contemporary society that did not have a function he understood was a survival from a previous stage of cultural evolution. Therefore, one could learn something about the past through the study of these cultural leftovers. His second idea concerns the evolution of religion, Tylor's special interest and the subject of the second volume of *Primitive Culture*. He postulated that the most basic concept underlying the invention of religion was animism. He outlined a developmental sequence for religion that began with animism, evolved into polytheism, and finally progressed into what he viewed as the highest form of religious belief, enlightened monotheism.

Both Morgan and Tylor believed in the fundamental similarity of human thought around the world: a concept called the psychic unity of humankind. This belief was the foundation for their unilineal evolutionary views and supported their contention that societies progressed through parallel (but independent) evolutionary stages.

The unilineal evolutionary perspective of the late nineteenth century revolves around several related themes. First, it was generally supposed that all societies evolved through the same stages and were progressing toward civilization and that Victorian society represented civilization in its highest currently extant form. Second, the whole perspective was rooted in the comparative method, which was based on the assumption that contemporary "primitive" cultures were like "living fossils," similar to early stages of current advanced cultures. As such, they were clues to cultural evolutionary development. One could study the evolutionary history of Western society by examining contemporary primitive societies. The validity of this comparative method rested on an acceptance of the concept of psychic unity. Simple and complex societies were comparable because human minds were believed to develop along the same lines. If the human mind worked the same way in all cultures, then it was assumed that unrelated societies would develop in a parallel fashion. Beliefs in the comparative method, psychic unity, parallel evolution, and progress were woven together to support the unilineal view of social evolution.

Karl Marx (1818–1883) and his frequent co-author Friedrich Engels (1820–1895), as well as Sigmund Freud (1856–1939), are far better known for their contributions to other disciplines than for their studies in anthropology. Marx and Engels were interested in economic and political theory, and Freud was a physician who attempted to unite psychology and anthropology through an all-embracing theory he called psychoanalysis. Nevertheless, their theories were critical to anthropology and have been the subject of much debate by anthropologists.

Marx's theory of social evolution was derived from philosopher Georg Wilhelm Friedrich Hegel's (1770–1831) theory of dialectical change and Marx's own understanding of evolutionary theory. Whereas scholars such as Locke and Tylor believed that cultural institutions were the product of rational thought, Marx thought that all thinking occurred within institutions. Thus, rational thought was a product of cultural institutions rather than their cause. Marx, a materialist philosopher, gave primacy to the analysis of the conditions of production within society.

Much of the work of Marx and Engels examined the conflict generated by the increasing wealth of the capitalists (bourgeoisie) at the expense of the working class (proletariat), who only sunk deeper into poverty. Marx and Engels viewed social change as an evolutionary process marked by revolution in which new levels of social, political, and economic development were achieved through class struggle. They viewed history as a sequence of evolutionary stages, each marked by a unique mode of production. Just as unilineal evolutionary theorists traced the social evolution of humans from savagery to civilization, Marx and Engels saw the history of Europe in terms of the transition from feudalism to capitalism to communism—which they believed was the next inevitable step in this process.

In their later work, Marx and Engels were deeply influenced by the work of Lewis Henry Morgan. They believed Morgan's correlation of evolutionary stages of human culture with material achievements and technology validated their evolutionary theory. Although Marx despised Spencer (whom he viewed as an apologist for capitalism), both men focused on the notion of conflict as the mechanism for social evolution.

Marx's work drew little attention in early-twentieth-century anthropology. Although some social thinkers such as Durkheim were political socialists, until the late 1920s Marx had relatively little effect on ethnographic analysis outside the Soviet Union. However, since that time, anthropologists have come to depend increasingly on his ideas. Many contemporary theories in both cultural anthropology and archaeology have come to rely on Marxist insights. This is particularly true of cultural ecologists and neomaterialist, feminist, and postmodern thinkers discussed in Parts Three and Four of this book. Today, a background in Marxist thought is basic to reading culture theory.

Sigmund Freud was an Austrian physician and neurologist who founded the field of psychoanalysis. Psychoanalytic theory, with its emphasis on unconscious psychological processes and psychological defense mechanisms such as repression, projection, and sublimation, has captured the popular imagination and become an important part of anthropological thought in this century. Freud postulated that certain psychological processes and responses were innate and universal. For example, one famous aspect of his work was his "anatomy of the mind." He proposed that

the mind consisted of "mental organs" (id, ego, and superego) that struggled for control over behavior (Bock 1988:24). Freud also proposed that all humans evolve through a universal series of psychosexual phases based in human biology: the oral, anal, genital, latency, and genital primacy stages.

Freud is best known for his study and treatment of neurosis through psychoanalysis and his work on dreams. This latter is summarized in his first book *On Dreams* (orig. 1900). Here, Freud challenged the popular European view that dreams were insignificant, calling them the "royal road to the unconscious" and outlining his method for examining their symbolic and unconscious meanings.

Freud was also fascinated by history and anthropology and familiar with the anthropological theory of the nineteenth century. Starting about 1910 on a quest that would occupy him for the rest of his life, Freud wrote a series of books and articles attempting to demonstrate how psychoanalysis could explain the origins of cultural institutions. Two of these most famous works are *Totem and Taboo* (1950 [1913]) and *Civilization and Its Discontents* (1961a [1930]). Freud believed that he could analyze cultural institutions in a way that was analogous to his method of analyzing the neurotic symptoms of his patients. In fact, the subtitle of *Totem and Taboo* is *Some Points of Agreement between the Mental Lives of Savages and Neurotics*.

Although very few people today would describe themselves as Freudian anthropologists, Freud's influence on the discipline was profound. His evolutionary ideas, particularly the notion that adults in primitive tribes were similar to children in civilized society, were widely popularized. The antievolutionary ideas of mainstream American anthropology of the early twentieth century were designed, in part, to counter these notions.

Though anthropologists rejected Freud's evolutionism, they were drawn to his ideas about the importance of early childhood and the significance of sexual symbolism. From the 1930s to the 1950s, many American anthropologists focused attention on the importance of weaning and toilet training in the development of adult personalities and cultural institutions. Symbolic and interpretive anthropologists of the 1960s, 1970s, and 1980s were attracted to the Freudian notion that many cultural ideas and symbols reflected unconscious impulses or deep-seated sexual tensions (see, for example, Obeyesekere 1981).

1. The Social Organism

Herbert Spencer (1820–1903)

SIR JAMES MACINTOSH[1] GOT GREAT CREDIT for the saying, that "constitutions are not made, but grow." In our day the most significant thing about this saying is, that it was ever thought so significant. As from the surprise displayed by a man at some familiar fact you may judge of his general culture: so from the admiration which an age accords a new thought, its average degree of enlightenment may be safely inferred. That this apothegm of Macintosh should have been quoted and requoted as it has, shows how profound has been the ignorance of social science—how a small ray of truth has seemed brilliant, as a distant rushlight looks like a star in the surrounding darkness.

Such a conception could not indeed fail to be startling when let fall in the midst of a system of thought to which it was utterly alien. Universally in Macintosh's day, as by an immense majority in our own day, all things were explained on the hypothesis of manufacture, rather than that of growth. It was held that the planets were severally projected round the sun from the Creator's hand, with exactly the velocity required to balance the sun's attraction. The formation of the

The Westminster Review (1860)

earth, the separation of the sea from land, the production of animals, were mechanical works from which God rested as a laborer rests. Man was supposed to be molded after a manner somewhat akin to that in which a modeler makes a clay figure. And of course, in harmony with such ideas, societies were tacitly assumed to be arranged thus or thus by direct interposition of Providence; or by the regulations of law-makers; or by both.[2]

Yet that societies are not artificially put together, is a truth so manifest, that it seems wonderful men should have ever overlooked it. Perhaps nothing more clearly shows the small value of historical studies as they have been commonly pursued. You need but to look at the changes going on around, or observe social organization in its leading peculiarities, to see that these are neither supernatural, nor are determined by the wills of individual men, as by implication historians commonly teach; but are consequent on <u>general natural causes</u>. The one case of the division of labor suffices to show this. It has not been by the command of any ruler that some men have become manufacturers, while others have remained cultivators of the soil. In Lancashire millions have devoted themselves

---

[1] Sir James Macintosh (1765–1832) was a British philosopher and politician whose works include "Discourse on the Study of the Law of Nature and Nations" (1799). He was a friend of Thomas Malthus.

[2] Spencer was a grand proponent of science in an age when the worldview of most of his countrymen was primarily religious. An article he wrote in 1859 asked in the title "What Knowledge Is of Most Worth?"; his emphatic answer was scientific knowledge. Spencer begins this essay by presenting—and then deflating—the popular religious doctrine of creationism. Notice the sarcasm with which he describes how humans were supposed to have been created. This style of writing is typical of Spencer, who can be both obnoxious and smug. Like many other nineteenth-century evolutionary thinkers, Spencer was anticlerical and deeply skeptical of religion.

to the making of cotton fabrics; in Yorkshire, perhaps another million live by producing woollens; and the pottery of Staffordshire, the cutlery of Sheffield, the hardware of Birmingham, severally occupy their hundreds of thousands. These are large facts in the structure of English society; but we can ascribe them neither to miracle, nor to legislation. It is not by "the hero as king," any more than by "collective wisdom," that men have been segregated into producers, wholesale distributors, and retail distributors. The whole of our industrial organization, from its most conspicuous features down to its minutest details, has become what it is, not only without legislative guidance, but, to a considerable extent, in spite of legislative hindrances. It has arisen under the pressure of human wants and activities. While each citizen has been pursuing his individual welfare, and none taking thought about division of labor, or indeed conscious of the need for it, division of labor has yet been ever becoming more complete. It has been doing this slowly and silently; scarcely any having observed it until quite modern times. By steps so small, that year after year the industrial arrangements have seemed to men just what they were before — by changes as insensible as those through which a seed passes into a tree; society has become the complex body of mutually dependent workers which we now see. And this economic organization, mark, is the all-essential organization. Through the combination thus spontaneously

evolved it is, that every citizen is supplied with daily necessaries, at the same time that he yields some product or aid to others. That we are severally alive to-day, we owe to the regular working of this combination during the past week; and could it be suddenly abolished, a great proportion of us would be dead before another week was ended. If these most conspicuous and vital arrangements of our social structure have arisen without the devising of any one, but through the individual efforts of citizens severally to satisfy their own wants, we may be tolerably certain that all the other less important social arrangements have similarly arisen.[3]

"But surely," it will be said, "the social changes directly produced by law cannot be classed as spontaneous growths. When parliaments or kings dictate this or that thing to be done, and appoint officials to do it, the process is clearly artificial; and society to this extent becomes a manufacture rather than a growth." No, not even these changes are exceptions, if they be real and permanent changes. The true sources of such changes lie deeper than the acts of legislators. To take first the simplest instance: — we all know that the enactments of representative governments ultimately depend on the national will: they may for a time be out of harmony with it, but eventually they have to conform to it. And to say that the national will is that which finally determines them, is to say that they result from the average of individual desires; or in other words — from the average of

---

[3] Here Spencer claims that societies were not supernaturally manufactured, but evolved through a natural process of growth, which he illustrates with examples from the social changes in English society caused by industrialization. Spencer's thinking reflected both evolutionism and the work of economist Adam Smith (1723–1790). Smith held that through pursuit of self-interest, individuals would be guided, as though by an invisible hand, to activities leading to the betterment of society. Spencer presents essentially the same idea here. There is also an evolutionary undercurrent. Like Darwin, Spencer conceived of evolution as operating through the accumulation of minute changes over long periods of time. For Spencer, social evolution was driven by competition among people, through which the best suited to survive were selected. Though this process may have meant misery for some, it led to progress for the society. Spencer believed that the end result of social evolution would be the elimination of social problems and the perfection of society. Following this line of thought, he coined the phrase "survival of the fittest." His ideas, popularized largely by others as social darwinism, were often used to justify the American and English class systems and colonial political system. However, it is important to note that Spencer himself was deeply critical of both imperialism and the landed aristocracy. In America, William Graham Sumner (1840–1910) was one of Spencer's most prominent followers and among the best known promoters of social darwinism. In an essay defending the concentration of wealth, he wrote: "No man can acquire a million without helping a million men to increase their little fortunes. . . . The millionaires are a product of natural selection. . . . They may fairly be regarded as the naturally selected agents of society for certain work" (1963 [1914]:156–157).

individual natures. A law so initiated, therefore, really grows out of the popular character.[4] In the case of a Government representing but a limited class, the same thing still holds, though not so manifestly. For the very existence of a supreme class monopolizing all power, is itself due to certain sentiments in the commonalty. But for the feeling of loyalty on the part of retainers, a feudal system could not exist. We see in the protest of the Highlanders against the abolition of heritable jurisdictions, that they preferred that kind of local rule. And if thus to the popular nature must be ascribed the growth of an irresponsible ruling class; then to the popular nature must be ascribed the social arrangements which that class creates in the pursuit of its own ends. Even where the Government is despotic, the doctrine still holds.[5] It is not simply that the existence of such a form of government is consequent on the character of the people, and that, as we have abundant proof, other forms suddenly created will not act, but rapidly retrograde to the old form; but it is that such regulations as a despot makes, if really operative, are so because of their fitness to the social state. Not only are his acts very much swayed by general opinion — by precedent, by the feeling of his nobles, his priesthood, his army — and are so in part results of the national character; but when they are out of harmony with the national character, they are soon practically abrogated. The utter failure of Cromwell permanently to establish a new social condition, and the rapid revival of suppressed institutions and practices after his death, show how powerless is a monarch to change the type of the society he governs. He may disturb, he may retard, or he may aid the natural process of organization; but the general course of this process is beyond his control.

Thus that which is so obviously true of the industrial structure of society, is true of its whole structure. The fact that constitutions are not made, but grow, is simply a fragment of the much larger fact, that under all its aspects and through all its ramifications, society is a growth and not a manufacture.

A dim perception that there exists some analogy between the body politic and a living individual body, was early reached, and from time to time re-appeared in literature. But this perception was necessarily vague and more or less fanciful. In the absence of physiological science, and especially of those comprehensive generalizations which it has but recently reached, it was impossible to discern the real parallelisms.

[It is a law of nature, in Spencer's view, that societies change from simple to complex. The purposes of his article are to outline this process of change and to demonstrate the similarities to the corresponding process in biological organisms. In an 850-word passage eliminated from this edition, Spencer discusses analogies similar to his own made by Plato and Thomas Hobbes. Plato, in The Republic, *compares society to the human*

---

[4] Spencer here suggests that there is some palpable force in a society that conditions its members to act in certain ways. Even actions that appear to be extremely personal are ultimately the result of this social force. This suggestion provides a portion of the foundation for Émile Durkheim's idea of collective consciousness (see essay 7) and A. L. Kroeber's of the superorganic (see essay 11). In fact, Spencer is generally considered the first person to use the term superorganic. Notice that he says that actions by rulers or other individuals may disturb evolution's workings, but that the general process is natural and beyond human control.

[5] Believing that social evolution followed natural laws, Spencer writes that rulers rule because it is a reflection of the "national will." Social inequality was ordained by nature in Spencer's view, and movements opposing this inequality were therefore doomed to failure. Spencer cites Oliver Cromwell's revolution against the English Crown, which fell apart after the death of its leader, but he may have had the more recent French revolutions of the 1780s and 1840s in mind. These revolutions and the violence that accompanied them shocked and frightened the English upper classes, who interpreted the mass riots as evidence of the bestiality of the working class. The repeated restoration of monarchy and empire in France was surely a comforting reassurance that the upper class was indeed superior and that the social evolutionary scheme of things had balanced out. As Spencer writes, "other forms suddenly created will not act, but rapidly retrograde to the old form."

psyche. Hobbes, in Leviathan, *compares it to the human body. Spencer finds that both of these analogies result in inconsistencies. He also faults Plato and Hobbes for suggesting that society was created by man and hence mechanical rather than grown as a human body or mind and hence organic.]*

Notwithstanding errors, however, these speculations have considerable significance. That such analogies, however crudely conceived, should have arrested the attention, not only of Plato and Hobbes, but of many others, is a reason for suspecting that *some* analogy exists. The untenableness of the particular comparisons above instanced is no ground for denying an essential parallelism; for early ideas are usually but vague adumbrations[6] of the truth. Lacking the great generalizations of biology, it was, as we have said, impossible to trace out the real relations of social organizations to organizations of another order. We propose here to show what are the analogies which modern science discloses to us.

Let us set out by succinctly stating the points of similarity and the points of difference. Societies agree with individual organisms in three conspicuous peculiarities:—

1. That commencing as small aggregations they insensibly augment in mass; some of them reaching eventually perhaps a hundred thousand times what they originally were.

2. That while at first so simple in structure as to be almost considered structureless, they assume, in the course of their growth, a continually increasing complexity of structure.

3. That though in their early undeveloped state there exists in them scarcely any mutual dependence of parts, these parts gradually acquire a mutual dependence, which becomes at last so great, that the activity and life of each part is made possible only by the activity and life of the rest.[7]

These three parallelisms will appear the more significant the more we contemplate them. Observe that, while they are points in which societies agree with individual organisms, they are points in which all individual organisms agree with each other, and disagree with everything else. In the course of its existence, every plant and animal increases in mass, which, with the exception of crystals, can be said of no inorganic objects. The orderly progress from simplicity to complexity displayed by societies in common with every living body whatever, is a characteristic which substantially distinguishes living bodies from the inanimate bodies amid which they move. And that functional dependence of parts, which is scarcely more manifest in animals or plants than in societies, has no counterpart elsewhere. Moreover, it should be remarked, not only that societies and organisms are alike in these peculiarities, in which they are unlike all other things; but, further, that the highest societies, like the highest organisms, exhibit them in the greatest degree. Looking at the facts in their ensemble, we may observe that the lowest types of animals do not increase to anything like the size of the higher ones; and similarly we see that aboriginal societies are comparatively limited in their growth. In complexity, our large civilized nations as much exceed the primitive savage ones, as a vertebrate animal does a zoophyte. And while in simple communities, as in simple creatures, the mutual dependence of parts is so slight, that subdivision or mutilation causes but little inconvenience; in complex communities as in complex

---

[6] *Adumbrations:* faint shadows or sketches.

[7] This paragraph contains the fundamental ideas upon which Spencer builds his evolutionary theory. He writes that societies are like organisms in three ways: (1) they grow from small groups to large aggregations; (2) they grow from simple to complex structures; and (3) they grow from a collection of independent units to an organism composed of interdependent parts. The second and third points are particularly important to his theory and were incorporated into most of the evolutionary theories of the nineteenth and twentieth centuries. Durkheim, for example, used the idea of directional movement from simplicity to complexity and relational movement from independence to interdependence in his formulation of the differences between mechanical and organic solidarity (see essay 7).

creatures, you cannot remove or injure any considerable organ without producing great disturbance or death of the rest.[8]

On the other hand, the leading differences between societies and individual organisms are these: —

1. That they have no specific external forms. This, however, is a point of contrast which loses much of its importance, when we remember that throughout the entire vegetal kingdom, as well as in some lower divisions of the animal kingdom, the forms are very indefinite, and are manifestly in part determined by surrounding physical circumstances, as the forms of societies are. If, too, it should eventually be shown, as we believe it will, that the form of every species of organism has resulted from the average play of the external forces to which it has been subject during its evolution as a species; then, that the external forms of societies should depend, as they do, on surrounding conditions, will be a further point of community.[9]

2. That whereas the living tissue where of an individual organism consists, forms one continuous mass, the living elements which make up a society, do not form a continuous mass, but are more or less widely dispersed over some portion of the earth's surface. This, which at first sight appears to be a fundamental distinction, is one which yet to a great extent disappears when we contemplate all the facts.

[In a 400-word passage, Spencer argues that human society is in this respect similar to several primitive life forms. He further suggests, though not in these terms, that the environment in which people live must be considered part of the social organism and that, if this is taken into account, societies do form a continuous mass.]

3. That while the ultimate living elements of an individual organism are mostly fixed in their relative positions, those of the social organism are capable of moving from place to place, seems a marked point of disagreement. But here, too, the disagreement is much less than would be supposed. For while citizens are locomotive in their private capacities, they are fixed in their public capacities. As farmers, manufacturers, or traders, men carry on their businesses at the same spots, often throughout their whole lives; and if they go away for a time, they leave behind others to discharge their functions in their absence. Not only does each great center of production, each manufacturing town or district, continue always in the same place; but many of the firms in such town or district are for generations carried on either by the descendants or successors of those who founded them. Just as in a living body, the individual cells that make up some important organ, severally perform their functions for a time and then disappear, leaving others to supply their vacant places; so in each part of a society, while the organ remains, the persons who compose it change. Thus, in social life, as in the life of an animal, the units as well as the larger agencies composed of them, are in the main stationary as respects the places where they discharge their duties and obtain their sustenance. So that the power of individual locomotion does not practically affect the analogy.[10]

4. That while in the body of an animal only a special tissue is endowed with feeling, in a society all the members are endowed with feeling, is

---

[8] Here you see illustrated Spencer's belief that social evolution was progressive. Those societies that are large, complex, and integrated are more evolved than those that are not. Industrialized Europe was, in his view, the best society that evolution had thus far created.

[9] Spencer says that the forms of society are, in part, determined by the surrounding physical circumstances. He is using the general evolutionary concept of the influence of environment on selection here, but his application of the idea to human societies provided a grounding that Julian Steward and the cultural ecologists used almost a century later.

[10] Spencer writes that social institutions have lives separate from and beyond the lives of the individuals who compose them. He says, "so in each part of a society, while the organ remains, the persons who compose it change." This is an important insight for both anthropology and sociology in the twentieth century, variously echoed in Max Weber's work on bureaucracy, Kroeber's on the superorganic, and Radcliffe-Brown's work on social structure.

the last and perhaps the most important distinction. Even this distinction, however, is by no means a complete one. For in some lower divisions of the animal kingdom, characterized by the absence of a nervous system, such sensitiveness as exists is possessed by all parts. It is only in the more organized forms that feeling is monopolized by one particular class of vital elements. Moreover, we must not forget that societies too, are not without a certain differentiation of this kind. Though the units of a community are all sensitive, yet they are so in unequal degrees. The classes engaged in agriculture and laborious occupations in general, are far less susceptible, intellectually and emotionally, than the rest; and especially less so than the classes of highest mental culture. Still we have here a tolerably decided contrast between bodies politic and individual bodies. And it is one which we should keep constantly in view. For it reminds us that while in individual bodies the welfare of all other parts is rightly subservient to the welfare of the nervous system, whose pleasurable or painful activities make up the good or evil of life; in bodies politic the same thing does not hold good, or holds good to but a very slight extent. It is well that the lives of all parts of an animal should be merged in the life of the whole, because the whole has a corporate consciousness capable of happiness or misery. But it is not so with a society; since its living units do not and cannot lose individual consciousness; and since the community as a whole has no general or corporate consciousness distinct from those of its components. And this is an everlasting reason why the welfare of its citizens cannot rightly be sacrificed to some supposed benefit of the State; but why, on the other hand, the State must be regarded as existing solely for the benefit of citizens. The corporate life must here be subservient to the life of the parts, in-stead of the life of the parts being subservient to the corporate life.[11]

Such, then, are the points of analogy and the points of difference. May we not say that the points of difference serve but to bring into clearer light the points of analogy? While comparison makes definite the obvious contrast between organisms commonly so called, and the social organism, it shows that even these contrasts are not nearly so decided as was to be expected. The indefiniteness of form, the discontinuity of the parts, the mobility of the parts, and the universal sensitiveness, are not only peculiarities of the social organism which have to be stated with considerable qualifications; but they are peculiarities to which the inferior classes of animals present approximations. Thus we find but little to conflict with the all important analogies. That societies slowly augment in mass; that they progress in complexity of structure; that at the same time their parts become more mutually dependent; and further, that the extent to which they display these peculiarities is proportionate to their vital activity; are traits that societies have in common with all organic bodies. And these traits in which they agree with all organic bodies and disagree with all other things — these traits which in truth constitute the very essence of organization, entirely subordinate the minor distinctions: such distinctions being scarcely greater than those which separate one half of the organic kingdom from the other. The *principles* of organization are the same; and the differences are simply differences of application.

Thus a general survey of the facts seems quite to justify the comparison of a society to a living body. We shall find that the parallelism becomes the more marked the more closely it is traced. Let us proceed to consider it in detail.

---

[11] In this paragraph Spencer clearly expresses his conviction that some classes are superior to others. Much of the negative twentieth-century view of Spencer has focused on statements like this. Because of them, Spencer is sometimes considered the high priest of racism and ethnocentrism, but this criticism may be misleading. Note that, at the end of the paragraph, Spencer tells us that the state exists solely for the benefit of its citizens. Spencer was a self-taught man and a member of the rising middle class. He did not attend a prestigious university and as a result was always, to some extent, an intellectual outsider. The position he presents here pits the rising industrialists against the legal privileges of the landowning aristocracy. Spencer sought to limit the role of the state and believed that a laissez-faire position would best allow for the progress of society. In some ways, his position was fairly close to modern libertarianism.

The lowest forms of animal and vegetable life—*Protozoa* and *Protophyta*—are chiefly inhabitants of the water.[12] They are minute bodies, most of which are made individually visible only by the microscope. All of them are extremely simple in structure; and some of them, as the *Amoeba* and *Actinophris,* almost structureless. Multiplying, as they do, by the spontaneous division of their bodies, they produce halves, which may either become quite separate and move away in different directions, or may continue attached. And by the repetition of this process of fission, aggregations of various sizes and kinds are formed. Thus among the *Protophyta* we have some classes, as the *Diatomacea* and the yeast-plant, in which the individuals may be either separate, or attached in groups of two, three, four or more; other classes in which a considerable number of individual cells are united into a thread (*Conferva, Monilia*); others in which they form a network (*Hydrodictyon*); others in which they form plates (*Ulva*); and others in which they form masses (*Laminaria, Agaricus*): all which vegetal forms, having no distinction of root, stem or leaf, are called *Thallogens.* Among the *Protozoa* we find parallel facts.[13] Immense numbers of *Amoeba*-like creatures massed together in a framework of horny fibers, are found in the extensive family of the sponges. In the *Foraminifera* we see smaller groups of such creatures arranged into more definite shapes. Not only do these almost structureless *Protozoa* unite into regular or irregular aggregations of various sizes; but among some of the more organized ones, as the *Vorticellae,* there are also produced clusters of individuals, proceeding from a common stock. But these little societies of monads, or cells, or whatever else we may call them, are societies in the lowest sense: there is no subordination of parts among them— no organization. Each of the component units lives by and for itself, neither giving nor receiving aid; there is no mutual dependence, save that consequent upon mere mechanical union.

Now do we not here clearly discern analogies to the first stages of human societies? Among the lowest races, as the Bushmen, we find but incipient aggregations: sometimes single families, sometimes two or three families wandering about together. The number of associated units is small and variable, and their union inconstant. No division of labor exists except between the sexes; and the only kind of mutual aid is that of joint attack or defence. We have nothing beyond an undifferentiated group of individuals forming the germ of a society; just as in the groups of similar cells above described, we have only the initial stage of animal and vegetal organization.

[In a 1,475-word passage removed from this edition, Spencer elaborates on his analogy. Just as more advanced plants and animals show some specialization of function, more advanced societies show evidence of social structure. Beyond sexual division of labor, government is the first structure to emerge. However, as in lower plants, specialization remains imprecise. Cells can

---

[12] In this paragraph and below, Spencer makes a highly detailed argument for the analogy between the evolution of biological organisms and that of society. The ideas of simple and complex societies, social structures, and social functions explored here imply a research program. That is, the goal of anthropology (or sociology) should be to identify social "organs" and describe their functioning. Contemporaneously with this essay, Spencer issued a prospectus for a future work, *Principles of Sociology,* in which he proposed to derive empirical generalizations from the comparative study of society (Carneiro 1967). This project was never fully realized, but Spencer's research agenda was central to the development of social anthropology in this century and influenced such thinkers as A. R. Radcliffe-Brown, Julian Steward, and most of all, George Peter Murdock. His ideas continue to be important today.

[13] To modern readers Spencer's writing style may seem highly repetitive. However, he was writing for an audience that was largely unfamiliar with the ideas he was presenting. Further, his readers had time to read and an aesthetic taste for copious examples. Gould (1994) has pointed out that, while modern American museums concentrate on the display of one or a few specimens with elaborate explanation, Victorian museums attempted to overwhelm the senses through the display of the enormous variety of nature but had relatively little explanation. Here Spencer, a model Victorian, does the same thing with words. While we have removed about 40 percent of Spencer's original 14,250-word essay, we have tried to leave enough of what, by modern standards, is excess verbiage for you to get a feel for this sort of writing.

*change function and a society's leaders may also
do other jobs. The next phase is the spread of similar biological or social units across the landscape.
Physical barriers may cause such social units to
coalesce into nations. Spencer argues that just
as some individuals among a large aggregate of
hydra will develop special functions, some communities within a large society will develop specific functions.]*

The general doctrine of the progressive division of labor, to which we are here introduced, is
more or less familiar to all readers. And further,
the analogy between the economical division of
labor and the "physiological division of labor" is
so striking, as long since to have drawn the attention of scientific naturalists: so striking, indeed, that the expression "physiological division
of labor," has been suggested by it. It is not needful, therefore, that we should treat this part of our
subject in great detail. We shall content ourselves
with noting a few general and significant facts not
manifest on a first inspection.

Throughout the whole animal kingdom, from
the *Coelenterata* upwards, the first stage of evolution is the same.[14] Equally in the germ of a
polype and in the human ovum, the aggregated
mass of cells out of which the creature is to arise,

gives origin to a peripheral layer of cells, slightly
differing from the rest which they include; and
this layer subsequently divides into two—the
inner one lying in contact with the included yolk
being commonly called the mucous layer, and the
outer exposed to surrounding agencies being
called the serous layer: or in the terms used by Professor Huxley,[15] in describing the development of
the *Hydrozoa*—the endoderm and the ectoderm.
This primary division marks out the fundamental
contrast of parts in the future organism. Out of
the mucous layer or endoderm is developed the
apparatus of nutrition; while out of the serous
layer, or ectoderm, is developed the apparatus of
external action. From the one arise the organs by
which food is prepared and absorbed, oxygen
imbibed, and blood purified; while out of the other
arise the nervous, muscular, and osseous[16] systems, by whose combined actions the movements
of the body as a whole are effected. Though this
is not a rigorously correct distinction, seeing that
some organs involve both of these primitive mem-
branes, yet the highest authorities agree in stating
it as a broad general one. Well, in the evolution of
a society we see a primary differentiation of analogous kind, which similarly underlies the whole
future structure.[17] As already pointed out, the
only contrast of parts which is visible in primitive

---

[14] The vocabulary Spencer uses when describing biology is quite technical, especially considering that this essay appeared
in a general intellectual journal rather than one specifically devoted to biology. The vocabulary he uses when referring to social formations, on the other hand, is quite simple. The effect of combining the technical language of biology with the rather
simple vocabulary of society is to make Spencer's comments on society seem much more scientifically compelling than they
actually are. Of course, in a modern sense, Spencer's argument is simply an argument by analogy and is not scientific at all.
It is neither an attempt to explore and describe the range of human social organization nor a set of conclusions based on
controlled experimentation.

[15] Thomas Henry Huxley (1825–1895) was a prominent biologist famous for his defense of Darwin and the theory of natural selection; his strong advocacy of Darwin's theory earned him the nickname "Darwin's bulldog."

[16] *Osseous:* bony; the osseous system refers to the skeleton.

[17] Here Spencer suggests that just as the first stages of embryonic development are universal for all members of the animal kingdom, so too all societies begin and develop through identical early stages. A key source of this analogy is his
reading of the work of the German-Russian embryologist Karl Ernst Von Baer (1792–1876). Von Baer outlined the parallel development of embryological forms but insisted that this did not imply repetition of adult stages. However, the analogy connecting different stages of the development of human society to the evolution of biological organisms was used
by Spencer and was common in nineteenth- and early twentieth-century anthropology. One prominent variation on this
theme derived from the work of German biologist Ernst Heinrich Haeckel (1834–1919). Haeckel claimed that ontogeny recapitulates phylogeny; that is, the growth of individuals repeats the evolutionary history of their phylum. When applied
to the evolution of society, this meant that the growth of individuals within advanced societies mirrored the stages through

societies, is that between the government and the governed. In the least organized tribes, the council of chiefs may be a body of men distinguished simply by greater courage or experience. In more organized tribes, the chief-class is definitely separated from the lower class, and often regarded as different in nature—sometimes as god-descended. And later we find these two becoming respectively freemen and slaves, or nobles and serfs. A glance at their respective functions makes it obvious that the great divisions thus early formed, stand to each other in a relation similar to that in which the primary divisions of the embryo stand to each other. For from its first appearance, the class of chiefs is that by which the external actions of the society are controlled: alike in war, in negotiation, and in migration. As we advance, we see that while the upper class grows distinct from the lower, and at the same time becomes more and more exclusively regulative and defensive in its functions, alike as kings and subordinate rulers, as priests, and as military leaders; the inferior class becomes more and more exclusively occupied in providing the necessaries of life for the community at large. From the soil, with which it comes in most direct contact, the mass of the people takes up and prepares for use the food and such rude articles of manufacture as are known; while the overlying mass of superior men, supplied with the necessaries of life by those below them, deals with circumstances external to the community—circumstances with which, by position, it is more immediately concerned. Ceasing by-and-by to have any knowledge of, or power over, the concerns of the society as a whole, the serf class becomes devoted to the processes of alimentation; while the noble class, ceasing to take any part in the process of alimentation, becomes devoted to the co-ordination and movements of the entire body politic.

Equally remarkable is a further analogy of like kind. After there has taken place in the embryo the separation of the mucous and serous layers, there presently arises between the two, a third,

known to physiologists as the vascular layer—a layer out of which is developed the system of blood-vessels. The mucous layer absorbs nutriment from the mass of yolk it encloses; this nutriment has to be transferred to the overlying serous layer, out of which the nervo-muscular system is being developed; and between the two arises the system of vessels by which the transfer is effected—a system of vessels which continues ever after to be the transferrer of nutriment from the places where it is absorbed and prepared, to the places where it is needed for growth and repair. Well, may we not clearly trace a parallel step in social progress? Between the governing and the governed there at first exists no intermediate class; and even in some societies that have reached a considerable size, there are scarcely any but the nobles and their kindred on the one hand, and the serfs on the other: the social structure being such, that the transfer of commodities takes place directly from slaves to their masters. But in societies of a higher type, there grows up between these two primitive classes, another—the trading or middle class. Equally at first as now, we may see that, speaking generally, this middle class is the analogue of the middle layer in the embryo. For all traders are essentially distributors. Whether they be wholesale dealers, who collect into large masses the commodities of various producers; or whether they be retailers, who divide out to those who want them the masses of commodities thus collected together; all mercantile men are agents of transfer from the places where things are produced to the places where they are consumed. Thus the distributing apparatus of a society answers to the distributing apparatus in a living body, not only in its functions, but in its intermediate origin and subsequent position, and in the time of its appearance.

Without enumerating the minor differentiations which these three great classes afterwards undergo, we will merely note that throughout, they follow the same general law with the differentiations of an individual organism. In a society,

---

which human social evolution had passed. Someone believing this would conclude that adults in primitive societies were very similar to children in advanced societies. Spencer had frequent recourse to "the child/savage equation" (Stocking 1987:22). Another good example of this sort of thinking is found in the Sigmund Freud essay in this volume (essay 5).

as in a rudimentary animal, we have seen that the most general and broadly contrasted divisions are the first to make their appearance; and of the subdivisions it continues true in both cases, that they arise in the order of their generality.[18]

[In a 875-word passage, Spencer argues that both societies and organisms develop in the direction of increased specialization of function. He compares the development of states to that of segmented worms. Among these, he says, lower forms are composed of many identical segments, while higher forms have organs that transcend segments. Similarly, early states are composed of many similar independent fiefdoms, but larger states have structures that completely transcend them.]

If, after contemplating these analogies of structure, we inquire whether there are any such analogies between causes and processes of organic growth, the answer is—yes. The causes which lead to the increase of bulk in any part of the body politic, are strictly analogous to those which lead to increase of bulk in any part of an individual body. In both cases the antecedent is greater functional activity consequent on greater demand. Each limb, viscus, gland, or other member of an animal, is developed by exercise—by actively discharging the duties which the body at large requires of it; and similarly, any class of laborers or artisans, any manufacturing center, or any official agency, begins to enlarge when the community devolves upon it an increase of work.[19] Moreover, in each case growth has its

conditions and its limits. That any organ in a living being may grow by exercise, there needs a due supply of blood: all action implies waste; blood brings the materials for repair; and before there can be growth, the quantity of blood supplied must be more than that requisite for repair only. So is it in a society. If to some district which elaborates for the community particular commodities—say the woollens of Yorkshire—there comes an augmented demand; and if in fulfillment of this demand a certain expenditure and wear of the manufacturing organization are incurred; and if in payment for the extra supply of woollens sent away, there comes back only such quantity of commodities as replaces the expenditure and makes good the waste of life and machinery; there can clearly be no growth. That there may be growth, the commodities obtained in return must be somewhat more than is required for these ends; and just in proportion as the excess is great will the growth be rapid. Whence it is manifest that what in commercial affairs we call *profit*, answers to the excess of nutrition over waste in a living body. To which let us add, that in both cases, where the functional activity is great and the nutrition defective, there results not growth but decay. If in an animal any organ is worked so hard that the channels which bring blood cannot furnish enough for repair, the organ dwindles; and if in the body-politic some part has been stimulated into great productivity, and cannot afterwards get paid for all its produce, certain of its members become bankrupt and it decreases in size.

---

[18] Here and below Spencer reiterates a basic principle of evolution as he understood it: evolution invariably proceeds from the simple to the complex, or, in his terminology, from the general to the specialized. This understanding of evolution was shared by most nineteenth-century thinkers and a great many in this century. Today, however, it is hotly contested. Consider, for example, two current popular writers on evolution. E. O. Wilson argues that Spencer was right — the history of biological evolution is essentially one of increasing complexity of organisms and increasing variety of species. Stephen Jay Gould, on the other hand, argues that evolution does not necessarily move in this direction and that the era of life's greatest variety was the Cambrian, some 500 million years ago.

[19] Note that the description of the evolution of both organisms and society presented here is Lamarckian rather than Darwinian. Spencer says that organs that are used more grow more. Despite the fact that his use of the phrase "survival of the fittest" and his belief in the virtues of competition tie Spencer to Darwin, his version of evolution was formulated independently of Darwin's and was not based on natural selection. Rather, he believed in the inheritance of acquired characteristics. For example, in 1855, he wrote as follows about the personality traits of members of different societies: "there can be no question that these varieties of disposition, which have a more or less evident relation to the habits of life, have been gradually induced and established in successive generations *and have become* organic" (quoted in Stocking 1987:141, emphasis added).

One more parallelism to be here noted is, that the different parts of the social organism, like the different parts of an individual organism, compete for nutriment; and obtain more or less of it according as they are discharging more or less duty. If a man's brain be suddenly very much excited, it will abstract blood from his viscera and stop digestion; or, digestion actively going on will so affect the circulation through the brain as to cause drowsiness; or great muscular exertion will determine such a quantity of blood to the limbs as to arrest digestion or cerebral action, as the case may be. And in like manner in a society, it frequently happens that great activity in some one direction causes partial arrests of activity elsewhere, by abstracting capital, that is, commodities: as instance the way in which the sudden development of our railway system hampered commercial operations; or the way in which the raising of a large military force temporarily stops the growth of leading industries.

The last few paragraphs naturally introduce the next division of our subject. Almost unawares we have come upon the analogy which exists between the blood of a living body and the circulating mass of commodities in the body-politic. We have now to trace out this analogy from its simplest to its most complex manifestations.

[In a 2,200-word passage, Spencer compares certain aspects of society to the blood and circulatory system of organisms. Lower animals have no blood or circulatory system; every cell feeds for itself. Similarly, he claims that in primitive tribes there is no system of exchange, and every family fends for itself. Somewhat more complex organisms have extremely simple digestive tracts; likewise, somewhat more complex societies have some trade in agricultural commodities along simple paths. As specialization proceeds in an organism, blood and a circulatory system are required to nourish the now specialized organs. As societies become more complex, the demands for circulation of products between laboring groups similarly increases. Spencer notes that the circulatory material (either blood for organisms or products for societies) increases not only in quantity but in complexity as well. This, of course, fits nicely with his understanding of evolution. As animals evolve,

they develop what Spencer calls "blood discs" (corpuscles) to facilitate nutrition. In societies money plays a similar role, elaborated in a sequence of analogies. Like blood cells, money itself is not consumed. Blood cells are found in greatest abundance in large organs, and money in greatest abundance in large cities. Blood in lower animals has no corpuscles, and lower societies have no money. Just as lower animals have minimally organized circulatory systems, countries where civilization is beginning have only rudimentary trails (the paths needed for the exchange of goods) through their countryside. More advanced animals have blood vessels, and more advanced societies have fenced and gravelled roads. In the highest organisms and societies, there are major blood vessels and capillaries or large main roads and small minor ones. The development of railroads that have a track for each direction is analogous to veins and arteries in a body. The analogy between society and organisms includes not only the circulatory system but also the pattern of motion of nutrients through it. In low creatures, the movement is a slow reciprocating motion. Similarly in lower societies there is movement now toward this fair or market, now toward that. In more advanced societies and animals there are "constant currents in definite directions." Moreover, as organisms evolve, they develop hearts that pump blood through the circulatory system, and societies develop large commercial centers. Blood flows more rapidly the closer it is to the heart, and trains move more rapidly and frequently the closer they are to commercial centers.]

Thus, then, we find between the distributing system in living bodies and in the body-politic, wonderfully close parallelisms. In the lowest forms of both there exists neither prepared nutriment nor a distributing apparatus; and in both, these, arising as necessary accompaniments of the differentiation of parts, approach perfection as this differentiation approaches completeness. In animals, as in societies, the distributing agencies begin to show themselves at the same relative period, and in the same relative position. In the one, as in the other, the nutritive materials circulated are at first crude and simple, gradually becoming better elaborated and more heterogeneous, and have eventually added to them a new element facilitating the nutritive processes. The channels of communication pass through similar phases of development which bring them to analogous forms. And the direction, rhythm, and rate of the circulation, progress by like steps to final conditions.[20]

We come at length to the nervous system. Having noticed the primary differentiation of societies into the governing and governed classes, and observed its analogy to the differentiation of the two primary tissues which respectively develop into the organs of alimentation and those of external action; having noticed some of the leading analogies between the development of industrial organization and that of the alimentary apparatus; and having above more fully traced the analogies between the distributing systems, social and individual; we have now to compare the appliances by which a society, as a whole, is regulated, with those by which the movements of an organism are regulated. We shall find here parallelisms equally striking with those already detailed.

The class out of which governmental organization originates is, as we have said, analogous, by origin and position, to the ectoderm of the lowest animals and of embryonic forms. And as this primitive membrane, out of which the nervo-muscular system is evolved, must, even in the first stage of its differentiation, be slightly distinguished from the rest by that greater impressibility and contractility[21] characterizing the organ to which it gives rise; so, in that superior class which is eventually transformed into the nervo-muscular system of a society (its legislative and defense appliances), does there exist in the beginning a larger endowment of the capacities re-

quired for these higher social functions. Always, in rude assemblages of men, there is a tendency for the strongest, most courageous, and most sagacious to become rulers and leaders; and in a tribe of some standing, this results in the establishment of a ruling class characterized on the average by those mental and bodily qualities which fit them for deliberation and vigorous combined action. Very significant, too, is the fact that those units of a society, who from the beginning discharge the directive and executive functions, are those in whom the directive and executive organs predominate: in other words, that what by analogy we call the nervo-muscular apparatus of a society begins to grow out of those units whose nervo-muscular systems are most developed. For the chiefs who, as individuals, or as a class, first separate themselves from the mass of a tribe, and begin to exercise control over their respective dependents and over the society as a whole, are men who have the greatest bodily vigor, the greatest bravery, or the greatest cunning—more powerful limbs, or more powerful brains, or both; while those to whom the industrious processes are chiefly left—in the smallest tribes the women, and in larger ones the least masculine men—are of less nervo-muscular power. Thus that greater impressibility and contractility which in the rudest animal forms characterize the units of the ectoderm, characterize also the units of the primitive social ectoderm; since impressibility and contractility are the respective roots of intelligence and strength.[22]

Again, in the unmodified ectoderm, as we see it in the Hydra, the units are all endowed both with impressibility and contractility; but as we as-

---

[20] Spencer, like most nineteenth-century evolutionists, saw both biological and social evolution leading to more and more perfect societies. In the twentieth century, this view finds an echo in the work of Leslie White (see essay 19), but few current evolutionists share it.

[21] Spencer uses the words *impressibility* and *contractility* to refer to the ability of the ectoderm, or outer cell layer, in a very simple animal or an embryo to remember (or learn) and to move.

[22] The evolution from simple to complex that Spencer finds across both animal species and societies is repeated within a single complex society. Rural people and the urban underclass are more primitive, while the urban elites are more advanced. Rural people and the poor may be compared to people living in less complex societies. Evolution is Spencer's overriding metaphor, and he has nested it within several different levels of society in this article. Additionally, note that in Spencer's view men are superior to women. Men do the brain work while women are left with the "industrial processes." While in his early work Spencer had suggested radical female equality, he later reversed this position and suggested that the needs of reproduction arrested the mental evolution of females at an early age (Stocking 1987:205).

cend to higher types of organization, the ectoderm differentiates into classes of units which divide those two functions between them: some, becoming exclusively impressible, cease to be contractile; while some, becoming exclusively contractile, cease to be impressible. Similarly with societies. In an aboriginal tribe the directive and executive functions are more or less equally diffused throughout the whole governing class. Each minor chief not only commands those under him, but, if need be, himself coerces them into obedience. The council of chiefs itself carries out on the battle-field its own decisions. The head chief not only makes laws, but administers justice with his own hands. But in larger and more settled communities, the directive and executive agencies begin to grow distinct from each other. As fast as his duties accumulate, the head chief, or king, confines himself more and more to directing public affairs, and leaves the execution of his will to others: he deputes others to enforce submission, to inflict punishments, or to carry out minor acts of offense and defence; and only on occasions when perhaps the safety of the society and his own supremacy are at stake, does he begin to act as well as direct. As this differentiation establishes itself, we see that the characteristics of the ruler begin to change. No longer, as in an aboriginal tribe, the strongest and most daring man, the tendency is for him to become the man of greatest cunning, foresight, and skill in the management of others; for in societies that have advanced beyond the first stage, it is chiefly such qualities that insure success in obtaining supreme power, and holding it against internal and external enemies. That is to say, that individual of the governing class who comes to be the chief directing agent, and so plays the same part that a rudimentary nervous center does in an unfolding organism, is usually one endowed with some superiorities of nervous organization.

When, advancing a stage, we contemplate communities somewhat larger and more complex, in which there have arisen, perhaps, a separate military class, a priesthood, and dispersed masses of population requiring local control, there necessarily grow up subordinate governing agents; who, as their duties accumulate, severally become more directive and less executive in their characters. And when, as commonly happens, the

king begins to collect round himself a number of advisors who aid him by communicating information, preparing subjects for his judgement, and issuing his orders; we may say that the form of organization is comparable to one very general among inferior types of animals, in which there exists a chief ganglion with a few dispersed minor ganglia under its control.

The analogies between the evolution of governmental structure in a society, and the evolution of governmental structures in living bodies, are, however, more strikingly displayed during the formation of nations by the coalescence of small communities — a process already shown to be in several respects parallel to the development of those creatures that primarily consist of many like segments. Among the other points of community between the successive rings which make up the body in the lower *Articulata*, is the possession of similar pairs of ganglia. These pairs of ganglia, though united together by nerves, are very incompletely dependent on any general controlling power. Hence it results, that when the body is cut in two, the hinder part continues to move forward under the propulsion of its numerous legs; and that when the chain of ganglia has been divided without severing the body, the hinder limbs may be seen trying to propel the body in one direction, while the fore limbs are trying to propel it in another. Among the higher *Articulata*, however, a number of the anterior pairs of ganglia, besides growing severally much larger, unite into one mass; and this great cephalic ganglion, becoming the coordinator of all the creature's movements, there no longer exists much local independence. Now may we not in the growth of a consolidated kingdom out of petty sovereignties or baronies, observe analogous changes. Like the chiefs and primitive rulers above described, feudal lords, exercising supreme power over their respective groups of retainers, discharge functions analogous to those rudimentary nervous centers; and we know that at first they, like their prototypes, were distinguished by superiority of directive and executive organization. Among these local governing centers, we see in early feudal times very little subordination. They are in frequent antagonism; they are individually restrained chiefly by the influence of large parties in their own class; and are but imperfectly and irregularly subject to that most powerful member of their order who has gained the position of head suzerain or king. Gradually, however, as the growth and organization of the society progresses, we find these local directive centers falling more and more under the control of a chief directive center. Closer commercial and distributive union between the several segments, is accompanied by closer governmental union; and these minor rulers end in being little more than agents who superintend the execution of the commands of the supreme ruler; just as the local ganglia, above described, eventually become agents which enforce in their respective segments the orders of the cephalic ganglion. Note now a further step in which the parallelism equally holds. We remarked above, when speaking of the rise of aboriginal kings, that in proportion as their territories and duties became greater, they were obliged not only to perform their executive functions by deputy, but also to gather round themselves advisers to aid them in their directive functions; and that thus, in place of a solitary governing unit, there grew up a group of governing units, comparable to a ganglion consisting of many cells. Let us here further remark, that the advisers and chief officers who thus form the rudiment of a ministry, tend from the beginning to exercise a certain control over the ruler. By the information they give and the opinions they express, they sway his judgement and affect his commands. To this extent he therefore becomes a channel through which are communicated the directions originating with them; and in course of time, when the advice of ministers becomes the acknowledged source of a king's actions, we see that he assumes very much the character of an automatic center reflecting the impressions made upon him from without.[23]

Beyond this complication in the governmental structure, many societies do not progress; but in some a much further development takes place. Our own case best illustrates this further development, and its further analogies. To kings and their ministries have been added in course of time other great directive centers, exercising a control which, at first small, has been gradually becoming predominant; as with the great governing ganglia that especially distinguish the highest class of living beings. Strange as the assertion will be thought, our Houses of Parliament discharge in the social economy, functions that are in sundry respects comparable to those discharged by the great cerebral masses in a vertebrate animal.[24] As it is in the nature of a single ganglion to be affected only by special stimuli from particular parts of the body; so it is in the nature of a single ruler to be swayed in his acts by exclusive personal or class interests. As it is in the nature of an aggregation of ganglia, closely connected with the primary one, to convey to it a greater variety of influences from more numerous organs, and thus to make its acts conform to more numerous requirements; so it is in the nature of a king surrounded by subsidiary controlling powers to adapt his rule to a greater number of public exigencies. And as it is in the nature of those great and latest developed ganglia which distinguish the highest creatures, to interpret and combine the more numerous and more complex impressions conveyed to them from all parts of the system, and to regulate the actions in such a way as duly to regard them all; so it is in the nature of those great and latest developed legislative bodies which distinguished the most advanced societies, to interpret and combine the wishes and com-

---

[23] It is important to remember the historical context within which Spencer wrote. He was writing in Britain's great period of empire building. His discussion refers to the development of British parliamentary government, and readers applied his ideas to the expansion of the British Empire.

[24] Here Spencer claims that the best case to illustrate the highest stages of social evolution is his own society and defends the intricacies of the British parliamentary system. He suggests that one purpose of government is to serve those who could be disenfranchised, but he also writes that Parliament balances out various interests and "concedes to each class as much as consists with the good of the rest." Spencer was strongly influenced by Jeremy Bentham (1748–1832) and John Stuart Mill (1806–1873), two English philosophers who championed Utilitarianism, the key tenet of which was the achievement of the greatest good for the greatest number. Since Spencer and others of his era believed that the greatest good was created through industry and that capitalists were indispensable to industry, in practice, Utilitarian ideas bolstered Victorian support for wealthy capitalists.

plaints of all classes and localities, and to regulate public affairs as much as possible in harmony with the general wants. It is the function of the cerebrum to coordinate the countless heterogeneous considerations which affect the present and future welfare of the individual as a whole; and it is the function of the House of Commons to coordinate the countless heterogeneous considerations which affect the immediate and remote welfare of the entire community. We may describe the office of the brain as that of *averaging* the interests of life, physical, intellectual, moral, social; and a good brain is one in which the desires answering to these respective interests are so balanced, that the conduct they jointly dictate, sacrifices none of them. Similarly, we may describe the office of a Parliament as that of *averaging* the interests of the various classes in a community; and a good parliament is one in which the parties answering to these respective interests are so balanced, that their united legislation concedes to each class as much as consists with the good of the rest.[25] Besides being comparable in their duties, these great directive centers, social and individual, are also comparable in the processes by which their duties are discharged. It is now a well-understood fact in Psychology, that the cerebrum is not occupied with direct impressions from without, but with the ideas of such impressions: instead of the actual sensations produced in the body, and directly appreciated by the sensory ganglia or primitive nervous centers, the cerebrum receives only the representations of these sensations; and its consciousness is called *representative* consciousness, to distinguish it from the original or *presentative* consciousness. Is it not significant that we have hit upon the same word to distinguish the function of our House of Commons?[26] We call it a representative body, because the interests with which it deals—the pains and pleasures about which it consults—are not directly presented to it, but represented to it by its various members; and a debate is a conflict of representations of the evils or benefits likely to follow from a proposed course—a description which applies with equal truth to a debate in the individual consciousness. Further it should be remarked, that in both cases, these great governing masses take no part in the executive functions. As, after a conflict of motives in the cerebrum, those which finally predominate act on the subjacent ganglia, and through their instrumentality determine the bodily actions; so the parties who, after a parliamentary struggle, finally gain the victory, do not themselves carry out their desires, but get them carried out by the executive divisions of the Government. The fulfillment of all legislative decisions continues still to devolve upon the original directive centers—the impulse passing from the Parliament to the Ministers, and from the Ministers to the King, in whose name everything is done; just as those smaller first developed ganglia, which in the lowest vertebrata are the chief controlling agents, are still in a man's brain, the agents through which the dictates of the cerebrum are worked out. And yet once more, observe that in both cases these original centers become more and more automatic. In the individual they have now little function beyond that of executing the determinations of the larger centers. In the State we see that the monarch has long been lapsing into a mere passive agent of Parliament; and that now ministries are rapidly falling into the same position. Nay, between the two cases there is a parallelism, even in respect of the exceptions to this automatic action. For in the individual it happens that under circumstances of sudden alarm, as from a loud sound close at hand, an unexpected object starting up in front, or a slip from insecure footing,

---

[25] Do you notice that throughout the essay Spencer has been comparing simple life forms like yeast and hydra to primitive societies, but in this paragraph, when discussing the English system of government, his comparison is with the brain?

[26] The defense of representative government and executive action in the second half of this paragraph must be read in the context of its time. Recall that Karl Marx's *Communist Manifesto* had been published in 1848, a year in which a series of unsuccessful revolutions had swept through Europe. One of the demands of the communists and other revolutionaries was the abolition of both representative government and monarchies. By his argument, Spencer suggested that the superiority of British parliamentary government (and to some extent the governments of other European nations) was established in natural law.

the danger is guarded against by some quick involuntary jump, or adjustment of the limbs, that takes place before there is time to consider the impending evil, and take deliberate measures to avoid it: the rationale of which is, that these violent impressions produced on the senses are reflected from the sensory ganglia to the spinal cord and muscles, without, as in ordinary cases, first passing through the cerebrum. In like manner on national emergencies calling for prompt action, the king and ministry, not having time to lay the matter before the great deliberative bodies, themselves issue commands for the requisite movements or precautions: the primitive, and now almost automatic directive centers resume for a moment their original uncontrolled power. And then, strangest of all, observe that in either case there is an after-process of approval or condemnation. The individual, on recovering from his automatic start, at once contemplates the cause of his fright; and, according to the case, concludes that it was well he moved as he did, or condemns himself for his groundless alarm. In like manner the deliberative powers in the State, discuss, as soon as may be, the unauthorized acts of the executive powers; and, deciding that the reasons were or were not sufficient, grant or withhold a bill of indemnity.

Thus far in comparing the governmental organization of the body-politic with that of an individual body, we have considered only the respective co-ordinating centers. We have yet to consider the channels through which these co-ordinating centers receive information and convey commands. In the simplest societies, as in the simplest organisms, there is no "internuncial apparatus," as Hunter styled the nervous system. Consequently, impressions can be but slowly propagated from unit to unit throughout the whole mass. The same progress, however, which in animal organization shows itself in the establishment of ganglia or directive centers, shows itself also in the establishment of nerve-threads, through which the ganglia receive and convey impressions, and so control remote organs. And in societies the like eventually takes place. After a long period during which the directive centers communicate with the various parts of the society through other means, there at length comes into existence an "internuncial apparatus" analogous to that found in individual bodies. The comparison of telegraph wires to nerves is familiar to all. It applies, however, to an extent not commonly supposed. We do not refer to the near alliance between the subtle forces employed in the two cases; though it is now held that the nerve-force, if not literally electric, is still a special form of electric action, related to the ordinary form much as magnetism is. But we refer to the structural arrangements of our telegraph system. Note first the fact that throughout the vertebrate sub-kingdom, we find the great nerve-bundles diverging from the vertebrate axis, side by side with the great arteries; and similarly we see that our groups of telegraph-wires are carried along the sides of our railways. But the most striking parallelism is this, — that into each great bundle of nerves as it leaves the axis of the body along with an artery, there enters a branch of the sympathetic nerve, which branch, accompanying the artery throughout its ramifications, has the function of regulating its diameter and otherwise controlling the flow of blood through it according to the local requirements. In like manner we find that in the group of telegraph wires running alongside each railway, there is one for the purpose of regulating the traffic — for retarding or expediting the flow of passengers and commodities as the local conditions demand. Probably when our now rudimentary telegraph system is fully developed, other analogies will be traceable.[27]

Such, then, is a general outline of the evidence which justifies in detail the comparison of

---

[27] For the modern reader one of the most striking things about Spencer is the extraordinary degree of analogical detail he claims. Today, some of his suggestions can sound comic. In another essay ("The Evolution of Society") he compares the transition from guild to factory-based production to processes within the human liver. Here he suggests that like the human nervous system, the telegraph, one of the most spectacular technological achievements of his day, appeared as the result of natural law. Spencer had, incidentally, begun his career as a civil engineer working for the London and Birmingham Railway. One wonders what he might have made of microwave transmission and satellite dishes.

a society to a living organism. The general peculiarities that societies gradually increase in mass, that they become little by little more complex, and that at the same time their parts grow more mutually dependent—these broad peculiarities which societies display in common with all living bodies, and in which they and living bodies differ from everything else; we find to involve minor analogies far closer than might have been expected. To these we would gladly have added others. We had hoped to say something respecting the different types of social organization, and something also on social metamorphoses; but we have reached our assigned limits.

2. The Science of Culture

Sir Edward Burnett Tylor (1832–1917)

CULTURE OR CIVILIZATION, TAKEN IN ITS WIDE ethnographic sense, is that complex whole which includes knowledge, belief, art, morals, law, custom, and any other capabilities and habits acquired by man as a member of society. The condition of culture among the various societies of mankind, in so far as it is capable of being investigated on general principles, is a subject apt for the study of laws of human thought and action.[1] On the one hand, the uniformity which so largely pervades civilization may be ascribed, in great measure, to the uniform action of uniform causes; while on the other hand its various grades may be regarded as stages of development or evolution each the outcome of previous history, and about to do its proper part in shaping the history of the future. To the investigation of these two great principles in several departments of ethnography, with especial consideration of the civilization of

From *Primitive Culture* (1871)

the lower tribes as related to the civilization of the higher nations, the present volumes are devoted.

Our modern investigators in the sciences of inorganic nature are foremost to recognize, both within and without their special fields of work, unity of nature, the fixity of its laws, the definite sequence of cause and effect through which every fact depends on what has gone before it, and acts upon what is to come after it. They grasp firmly the Pythagorean doctrine of pervading order in the universal Kosmos. They affirm, with Aristotle, that nature is not full of incoherent episodes, like a bad tragedy. They agree with Leibnitz in what he calls "my axiom, that nature never acts by leaps (La nature n'agit jamais par saut),"[2] as well as in his "great principle, commonly little employed, that nothing happens without its sufficient reason." Nor, again, in studying the structure and habits of plants and animals, or in investigating the lower functions even of man, are these leading ideas unacknowledged. But when we come to

---

[1] Throughout this essay, Tylor reaffirms his faith in the possibility of a science of human society analogous to the physical sciences. In this he is very much like the other thinkers of his era, particularly Herbert Spencer. The opening sentence of this essay is one of the most frequently quoted definitions of culture in anthropology. Despite this, Tylor's understanding of the meaning of culture is clearly very different from that of most modern anthropologists. While most anthropologists today believe that there are a great many different cultures, Tylor believed that "Culture" was, ultimately, a single body of information of which different human groups had greater or lesser amounts. This understanding was based on his belief in the psychic unity of humankind, here referred to as "the uniform action of uniform causes."

[2] *La nature n'agit jamais par saut:* a French phrase meaning "nature never acts by leaps." Darwin also used this phrase in an 1858 essay on variation in species (in Latin rather than French) to express the gradualism of his evolutionary theory. Tylor frequently uses foreign phrases in this essay. They almost always repeat the sentence that precedes them.

talk of the higher processes of human feeling and action, of thought and language, knowledge and art, a change appears in the prevalent tone of opinion. The world at large is scarcely prepared to accept the general study of human life as a branch of natural science, and to carry out, in a large sense, the poet's injunction to "Account for moral as for natural things." To many educated minds there seems something presumptuous and repulsive in the view that the history of mankind is part and parcel of the history of nature, that our thoughts, wills, and actions accord with laws as definite as those which govern the motion of waves, the combination of acids and bases, and the growth of plants and animals.

The main reasons of this state of the popular judgment are not far to seek. There are many who would willingly accept a science of history if placed before them with substantial definiteness of principle and evidence, but who not unreasonably reject the systems offered to them, as falling too far short of a scientific standard. Through resistance such as this, real knowledge always sooner or later makes its way, while the habit of opposition to novelty does such excellent service against the invasions of speculative dogmatism, that we may sometimes even wish it were stronger than it is. But other obstacles to the investigation of laws of human nature arise from considerations of metaphysics and theology. The popular notion of free human will involves not only freedom to act in accordance with motive, but also a power of breaking loose from continuity and acting without cause,—a combination which may be roughly illustrated by the simile of a balance sometimes acting in the usual way, but also possessed of the faculty of turning by itself without or against its weights. This view of an anomalous action of the will, which it need hardly be said is incompatible with scientific ar-

gument, subsists as an opinion patent or latent in men's minds, and strongly affecting their theoretic views of history, though it is not, as a rule, brought prominently forward in systematic reasoning. Indeed the definition of human will, as strictly according with motive, is the only possible scientific basis in such enquiries. Happily, it is not needful to add here yet another to the list of dissertations on supernatural intervention and natural causation, on liberty, predestination, and accountability. We may hasten to escape from the regions of transcendental philosophy and theology, to start on a more hopeful journey over more practicable ground. None will deny that, as each man knows by the evidence of his own consciousness, definite and natural cause does, to a great extent, determine human action. Then, keeping aside from considerations of extra-natural interference and causeless spontaneity, let us take this admitted existence of natural cause and effect as our standing ground, and travel on it so far as it will bear us. It is on this same basis that physical science pursues, with ever-increasing success, its quest of laws of nature. Nor need this restriction hamper the scientific study of human life, in which the real difficulties are the practical ones of enormous complexity of evidence, and imperfection of methods of observation.[3]

Now it appears that this view of human will and conduct, as subject to definite law, is indeed recognized and acted upon by the very people who oppose it when stated in the abstract as a general principle, and who then complain that it annihilates man's free will, destroys his sense of personal responsibility, and degrades him to a soul-less machine. He who will say these things will nevertheless pass much of his own life in studying the motives which lead to human action, seeking to attain his wishes through them, framing in his mind theories of personal character,

---

[3] In this passage, Tylor rejects both religious explanations of social phenomena and objections to social science based on the supposition of human free will. Tylor was stridently anticlerical. He saw human history as proceeding toward increasing rationality. His own religious background is significant in this context. Tylor was from a Quaker family and was highly influenced by Quaker theology. Quakers (members of the Society of Friends) do not believe in the clergy; instead, they believe that God speaks through each individual. This background had important implications for Tylor's work. Since Quakers believed in the essential unity of humankind, they emphasized a degree of tolerance and humanitarianism frequently absent in this era. The Quaker belief in a single spiritual destiny of humankind is reflected in Tylor's understanding of human social evolution.

reckoning what are likely to be the effects of new combinations, and giving to his reasoning the crowning character of true scientific enquiry, by taking it for granted that in so far as his calculation turns out wrong, either his evidence must have been false or incomplete, or his judgment upon it unsound. Such a one will sum up the experience of years spent in complex relations with society, by declaring his persuasion that there is a reason for everything in life, and that where events look unaccountable, the rule is to wait and watch in hope that the key to the problem may some day be found. This man's observation may have been as narrow as his inferences are crude and prejudiced, but nevertheless he has been an inductive philosopher "more than forty years without knowing it." He has practically acknowledged definite laws of human thought and action, and has simply thrown out of account in his own studies of life the whole fabric of motiveless will and uncaused spontaneity.[4] It is assumed here that they should be just so thrown out of account in wider studies, and that the true philosophy of history lies in extending and improving the methods of the plain people who form their judgments upon facts, and check them upon new facts.[5] Whether the doctrine be wholly or but partly true, it accepts the very condition under which we search for new knowledge in the lessons of experience, and in a word the whole course of our rational life is based upon it.

"One event is always the son of another, and we must never forget the parentage," was a remark made by a Bechuana chief to Casalis the African missionary. Thus at all times historians, so far as they have aimed at being more than mere chroniclers, have done their best to show not merely succession, but connection, among the events upon their record. Moreover, they have striven to elicit general principles of human action, and by these to explain particular events, stating expressly or taking tacitly for granted the existence of a philosophy of history.[6] Should any one deny the possibility of thus establishing historical laws the answer is ready with which Boswell in such a case turned on Johnson:[7] "Then, sir, you would reduce all history to no better than almanack." That nevertheless the labors of so many eminent thinkers should have as yet brought history only to the threshold of science need cause no wonder to those who consider the bewildering complexity of the problems which come before the general historian. The evidence from which he is to draw his conclusions is at once so multifarious and so doubtful that a full and distinct view of its bearing on a particular question is hardly to be attained, and thus the temptation becomes all but irresistible to garble it in support of some rough and ready theory of the course of events. The philosophy of history at large, explaining the past and predicting the future phenomena of man's life in the world by reference to general laws, is in fact a subject with which, in the present state of knowledge, even genius aided by wide research seems but hardly able to cope. Yet there are departments of it which, though difficult enough, seem comparatively accessible. If the field of inquiry be narrowed from History as a whole to that branch of

---

[4] In this passage Tylor continues his attack on those he considers the enemies of the application of scientific method to social science. His key method is really a call for introspection, which has some roots in the Quaker call to introspective prayer.

[5] Notice that Tylor here refers to his work as creating a philosophy of history. Tylor's anthropology involved re-creating the history of humankind's evolution to civilization. Many later anthropologists rejected such historical re-creation as unscientific or impossible.

[6] In this passage Tylor argues that the success of a philosophy of history depends on restricting the subject matter: by focusing on Culture, the historian may ignore specific events in favor of general developmental trends. Because Tylor understood culture as a unitary phenomenon that characterized peoples to one degree or another, the project was practical. For Tylor, describing Culture as an evolutionary phenomenon implied tracing the history of its development. Simple societies could be understood as living history or living fossils. In this century, American followers of Franz Boas, reacting to the evolutionary perspective, also understood the study of culture as the study of history, but for different reasons.

[7] Dr. Samuel Johnson (1709–1784), considered by many to be the greatest eighteenth-century English author, is mentioned several times in this essay. James Boswell (1740–1795) was his biographer and frequent companion.

it which is here called Culture, the history, not of tribes or nations, but of the condition of knowledge, religion, art, custom, and the like among them, the task of investigation proves to lie within far more moderate compass. We suffer still from the same kind of difficulties which beset the wider argument, but they are much diminished. The evidence is no longer so wildly heterogeneous, but may be more simply classified and compared, while the power of getting rid of extraneous matter, and treating each issue on its own proper set of facts, makes close reasoning on the whole more available than in general history. This may appear from a brief preliminary examination of the problem, how the phenomena of Culture may be classified and arranged, stage by stage, in a probable order of evolution.

Surveyed in a broad view, the character and habit of mankind at once display that similarity and consistency of phenomena which led the Italian proverb-maker to declare that "all the world is one country" "tutto il mondo e paese." To general likeness in human nature on the one hand, and to general likeness in the circumstances of life on the other, this similarity and consistency may no doubt be traced, and they may be studied with especial fitness in comparing races near the same grade of civilization. Little respect need be had in such comparisons for date in history or for place on the map; the ancient Swiss lake-dweller may be set beside the medieval Aztec, and the Ojibwa of North America beside the Zulu of South Africa. As Dr. Johnson contemptuously said when he had read about Patagonians and South Sea Islanders in Hawkesworth's Voyages, "one set of savages is like another." How true a generalization this really is, any Ethnological Museum may show. Examine for instance the edged and pointed instruments in such a collection; the inventory includes hatchet, adze, chisel, knife, saw, scraper, awl, needle, spear and arrow-head, and of these most or all belong with only differences of detail to races the most various.[8] So it is with savage occupations; the wood-chopping, fishing with net and line, shooting and spearing game, fire-making, cooking, twisting cord and plaiting baskets, repeat themselves with wonderful uniformity in the museum shelves which illustrate the life of the lower races from Kamchatka to Tierra del Fuego, and from Dahome to Hawaii. Even when it comes to comparing barbarous hordes with civilized nations, the consideration thrusts itself upon our minds, how far item after item of the life of the lower races passes into analogous proceedings of the higher, in forms not too far changed to be recognized, and sometimes hardly changed at all. Look at the modern European peasant using his hatchet and his hoe, see his food boiling or roasting over the log-fire, observe the exact place which beer holds in his calculation of happiness, hear his tale of the ghost in the nearest haunted house, and of the farmer's niece who was bewitched with knots in her inside till she fell into fits and died. If we choose out in this way things which have altered little in a long course of centuries, we may draw a picture where there shall be scarce a hand's breadth difference between an English ploughman and a negro of Central Africa. These pages will be so crowded with evidence of such correspondence among mankind, that there is no need to dwell upon its details here, but it may be used at once to override a problem which would complicate the argument, namely, the question of race. For the present purpose it appears both possible and desirable to eliminate considerations of hereditary varieties or races of man, and to treat mankind as homogeneous in nature, though placed in different grades of civilization.[9] The de-

---

[8] When Tylor speaks here about placing ethnographic materials next to each other on display, he may be considering an actual rather than a theoretical example. His observations are probably based on the Crystal Palace exhibition of 1851. Tylor was heavily influenced by Henry Christi, a Quaker ethnologist and archaeologist who was a juror at the Crystal Palace. Part of this exhibition brought artifacts from all the British Empire together and arranged them in presumed order of technical sophistication. This is what Tylor describes. The argument he makes here is a cornerstone of the comparative method in anthropology. Anthropologists of Tylor's day believed that by comparing societies around the world, a chronology of human social development could be created.

[9] Tylor here appears to reject racist explanations of cultural differences. Tylor's Quaker theology committed him to the notion of monogenesis — the belief that all human races belonged to the same species and shared the same evolutionary ori-

tails of the enquiry will, I think, prove that stages of culture may be compared without taking into account how far tribes who use the same implement, follow the same custom, or believe the same myth may differ in their bodily configuration and the color of their skin and hair.

A first step in the study of civilization is to dissect it into details, and to classify these in their proper groups. Thus, in examining weapons, they are to be classed under spear, club, sling, bow and arrow, and so forth; among textile arts are to be ranged matting, netting, and several grades of making and weaving threads; myths are divided under such headings as myths of sunrise and sunset, eclipse-myths, earthquake-myths, local myths which account for the names of places by some fanciful tale, eponymic myths which account for the parentage of a tribe by turning its name into the name of an imaginary ancestor; under rites and ceremonies occur such practices as the various kinds of sacrifice to the ghosts of the dead and to other spiritual beings, the turning to the east to worship, the purification of ceremonial or moral uncleanness by means of water or fire. Such are a few miscellaneous examples from a list of hundreds, and the ethnographer's business is to classify such details with a view to making out their distribution in geography and history, and the relations which exist among them. What this task is like may be almost perfectly illustrated by comparing these details of culture with the species of plants and animals as studied by the naturalist. To the ethnographer, the bow and arrow is a species, the habit of flattening children's skulls is a species, the practice of reckoning numbers by tens is a species. The geographical distribution of these things, and their transmission from region to region, have to be studied as the naturalist studies the geography of his botanical and zoological species. Just as certain plants and animals are peculiar to certain districts, so it is with such instruments as the Australian boomerang, the Polynesian stick-and-groove for firemaking, the tiny bow and arrow used as a lancet or phleme by tribes about the Isthmus of Panama, and in like manner with many an art, myth, or custom found isolated in a particular field. Just as the catalogue of all the species of plants and animals of a district represents its Flora and Fauna, so the list of all the items of the general life of a people represents that whole which we call its culture. And just as distant regions so often produce vegetables and animals which are analogous, though by no means identical, so it is with the details of the civilization of their inhabitants.[10] How good a working analogy there really is between the diffusion of plants and animals and the diffusion of civilization comes well into view when we notice how far the same causes have produced both at once. In district after district, the same causes which have introduced the cultivated plants and domesticated animals of civilization, have brought in with them a corresponding art and knowledge. The course of events which carried horses and wheat to America carried with them the use of the gun and the iron hatchet, while in return the old world received not only maize, potatoes, and turkeys, but the habit of smoking and the sailor's hammock.[11]

gins. He wrote: "the facts collected seem to favor the view that the wide differences in the civilization and mental state of the various races of mankind are rather differences of development than of origin, rather of degree than kind" (quoted in Stocking 1987:159). This notion was contested by the Americans Samuel G. Morton (1799–1851) and Louis Agassiz (1807–1873), key promoters of a theory called polygenesis. This theory argued that human races represented different and unequal species and was used as a "scientific" justification for slavery. Although to modern readers some of Tylor's writing has a decidedly racist cast, he was a liberal by the standards of his day.

[10] Tylor, like Spencer, draws an analogy between cultural and biological evolution. In Tylor's view, the ethnographer's job is to catalog all the practices of humankind and then arrange them into evolutionary and hierarchical order, producing something analogous to the Linnaean classification of plants and animals. We will see this analogy again in other theories found in this book.

[11] Unlike modern anthropologists, who tend to see field research as inseparable from the practice of anthropology, Tylor did not believe that it was necessary for anthropologists to be involved in data collection. It was their primary job to compile, organize, and classify data. Despite this view, Tylor did have some field experience. During a year he spent in North America in 1856, he traveled for four months by horseback in Mexico with his friend Christi. He published an account of this trip (*Anahuac: Or Mexico and the Mexicans, Ancient and Modern*) in 1861.

It is a matter worthy of consideration that the accounts of similar phenomena of culture, recurring in different parts of the world, actually supply incidental proof of their own authenticity.[12] Some years since, a question which brings out this point was put to me by a great historian "How can a statement as to customs, myths, beliefs, &c., of a savage tribe be treated as evidence where it depends on the testimony of some traveller or missionary, who may be a superficial observer, more or less ignorant of the native language, a careless retailer of unsifted talk, a man prejudiced or even wilfully deceitful?" This question is, indeed, one which every ethnographer ought to keep clearly and constantly before his mind. Of course he is bound to use his best judgment as to the trustworthiness of all authors he quotes, and if possible to obtain several accounts to certify each point in each locality. But it is over and above these measures of precaution that the test of recurrence comes in. If two independent visitors to different countries, say a medieval Mohammedan in Tartary and a modern Englishman in Dahome, or a Jesuit missionary in Brazil and a Wesleyan in the Fiji Islands, agree in describing some analogous art or rite or myth among the people they have visited, it becomes difficult or impossible to set down such correspondence to accident or willful fraud. A story by a bushranger in Australia may, perhaps, be objected to as a mistake or an invention, but did a Methodist minister in Guinea conspire with him to cheat the public by telling the same story there? The possibility of intentional or unintentional mystification is often barred by such a state of things as that a similar statement is made in two remote lands, by two witnesses, of whom A lived a century before B, and B appears never to have heard of A. How distant are the countries, how wide apart the dates, how different the creeds and characters of the observers, in the catalogue of facts of civilization, needs no farther showing to any one who will even glance at the foot-notes of the present work. And the more odd the statement, the less likely that several people in several places should have made it wrongly. This being so, it seems reasonable to judge that the statements are in the main truly given, and that their close and regular coincidence is due to the cropping up of similar facts in various districts of culture. Now the most important facts of ethnography are vouched for in this way. Experience leads the student after a while to expect and find that the phenomena of culture, as resulting from widely-acting similar causes, should recur again and again in the world. He even mistrusts isolated statements to which he knows of no parallel elsewhere, and waits for their genuineness to be shown by corresponding accounts from the other side of the earth, or the other end of history. So strong, indeed, is this means of authentication that the ethnographer in his library may sometimes presume to decide, not only whether a particular explorer is a shrewd and honest observer, but also whether what he reports is conformable to the general rules of civilization. "Non quis, sed quid."[13]

To turn from the distribution of culture in different countries, to its diffusion within these countries. The quality of mankind which tends most to make the systematic study of civilization possible is that remarkable tacit consensus or agreement which so far induces whole populations to unite in the use of the same language, to follow the same religion and customary law, to settle down to the same general level of art and knowledge. It is this state of things which makes it so far possible to ignore exceptional facts and to describe nations by a sort of general average. It is this state of things which makes it so far possible to represent immense masses of details by a few typical facts, while, these once settled, new

---

[12] The argument here is tautological. Above, Tylor maintains that the repeated occurrence of cultural traits in widely disparate locations is evidence of the psychic unity of mankind. Here he contends that he can verify or refute claims about the existence of cultural traits by reference to the theory of psychic unity. If a traveler asserted that he found traits different from others around the world, then his claims must be false. The use of this sort of reasoning was one factor that led Franz Boas and his followers to attack the work of Tylor and other evolutionists as unscientific.

[13] *Non quis, sed quid:* a Latin phrase meaning "not who, but what." It is not who made the report that is important, but rather what they reported.

cases recorded by new observers simply fall into their places to prove the soundness of the classification. There is found to be such regularity in the composition of societies of men that we can drop individual differences out of sight, and thus can generalize on the arts and opinions of whole nations, just as, when looking down upon an army from a hill, we forget the individual soldier, whom, in fact, we can scarce distinguish in the mass, while we see each regiment as an organized body, spreading or concentrating, moving in advance or in retreat. In some branches of the study of social laws it is now possible to call in the aid of statistics, and to set apart special actions of large mixed communities of men by means of taxgatherers' schedules, or the tables of the insurance-office. Among modern arguments on the laws of human action, none have had a deeper effect than generalizations such as those of M. Quetelet,[14] on the regularity, not only of such matters as average stature and the annual rates of birth and death, but the recurrence, year after year, of such obscure and seemingly incalculable products of national life as the numbers of murders and suicides, and the proportion of the very weapons of crime. Other striking cases are the annual regularity of persons killed accidentally in the London streets, and of undirected letters dropped into post-office letterboxes. But in examining the culture of the lower races, far from having at command the measured arithmetical facts of modern statistics, we may have to judge of the condition of tribes from the imperfect accounts supplied by travellers or missionaries, or even to reason upon relics of prehistoric races of whose very names and languages we are hopelessly ignorant. Now these may seem at the first glance sadly indefinite and unpromising materials for a scientific enquiry. But in fact they are neither indefinite nor unpromising, but give evidence that is good and definite, so far as it goes. They are data which, for the distinct way in which they severally denote the condition of the tribe they belong to, will actually bear comparison with the statistician's returns. The fact is that a stone arrow-head, a carved club, an idol, a grave-mound where slaves and property have been buried for the use of the dead, an account of a sorcerer's rites in making rain, a table of numerals, the conjugation of a verb, are things which each express the state of a people as to one particular point of culture, as truly as the tabulated numbers of deaths by poison, and of chests of tea imported, express in a different way other partial results of the general life of a whole community.

That a whole nation should have a special dress, special tools and weapons, special laws of marriage and property, special moral and religious doctrines is a remarkable fact, which we notice so little because we have lived all our lives in the midst of it. It is with such general qualities of organized bodies of men that ethnography has especially to deal. Yet, while generalizing on the culture of a tribe or nation, and setting aside the peculiarities of the individuals composing it as unimportant to the main result, we must be careful not to forget what makes up this main result. There are people so intent on the separate life of individuals that they cannot grasp a notion of the action of a community as a whole — such an observer, incapable of a wide view of society, is aptly described in the saying that he "cannot see the forest for the trees." But, on the other hand, the philosopher may be so intent upon his general laws of society as to neglect the individual actors of whom that society is made up, and of him it may be said that he cannot see the trees for the forest. We know how arts, customs, and ideas are shaped among ourselves by the combined actions of many individuals, of which actions both motive

---

[14] Adolphe J. Quetelet (1796–1874) was a mathematician who showed that the behavior of large groups of people could be predicted through the analysis of statistics. Quetelet called his theory "social physics," implying that he had created a science of society similar to physics. In Tylor's time, statistics was a relatively recent and influential discovery. By providing a way to match numbers with social phenomena, statistics seemed to be a method by which natural laws determining human behavior could be ascertained. Here, Tylor tries to show that ethnographic data are comparable to demographic data and can be considered equally valid. This proposition, if accepted, would provide further evidence that a valid science of culture was possible.

and effect often come quite distinctly within our view. The history of an invention, an opinion, a ceremony, is a history of suggestion and modification, encouragement and opposition, personal gain and party prejudice, and the individuals concerned act each according to his own motives, as determined by his character and circumstances. Thus sometimes we watch individuals acting for their own ends with little thought of their effect on society at large, and sometimes we have to study movements of national life as a whole, where the individuals co-operating in them are utterly beyond our observation. But seeing that collective social action is the mere resultant of many individual actions, it is clear that these two methods of enquiry, if rightly followed, must be absolutely consistent.

In studying both the recurrence of special habits or ideas in several districts and their prevalence within each district, there come before us ever reiterated proofs of regular causation producing the phenomena of human life, and of laws of maintenance and diffusion according to which these phenomena settle into permanent standard conditions of society, at definite stages of culture.[15] But, while giving full importance to the evidence bearing on these standard conditions of society, let us be careful to avoid a pitfall which may entrap the unwary student. Of course the opinions and habits belonging in common to masses of mankind are to a great extent the results of sound judgment and practical wisdom. But to a great extent it is not so. That many numerous societies of men should have believed in the influence of the evil eye and the existence of a firmament, should have sacrificed slaves and goods to the ghosts of the departed, should have handed down traditions of giants slaying monsters and men turning into beasts — all this is ground for holding that such ideas were indeed

produced in men's minds by efficient causes, but it is not ground for holding that the rites in question are profitable, the beliefs sound, and the history authentic. This may seem at the first glance a truism, but, in fact, it is the denial of a fallacy which deeply affects the minds of all but a small critical minority of mankind. Popularly, what everybody says must be true, what everybody does must be right — "Quod ubique, quod semper, quod ab omnibus creditum est, hoc est vere proprieque Catholicum" — and so forth. There are various topics, especially in history, law, philosophy, and theology, where even the educated people we live among can hardly be brought to see that the cause why men do hold an opinion, or practice a custom, is by no means necessarily a reason why they ought to do so. Now collections of ethnographic evidence, bringing so prominently into view the agreement of immense multitudes of men as to certain traditions, beliefs, and usages, are peculiarly liable to be thus improperly used in direct defence of these institutions themselves, even old barbaric nations being polled to maintain their opinions against what are called modern ideas. As it has more than once happened to myself to find my collections of traditions and beliefs thus set up to prove their own objective truth, without proper examination of the grounds on which they were actually received, I take this occasion of remarking that the same line of argument will serve equally well to demonstrate, by the strong and wide consent of nations, that the earth is flat, and nightmare the visit of a demon.

It being shown that the details of Culture are capable of being classified in a great number of ethnographic groups of arts, beliefs, customs, and the rest, the consideration comes next how far the facts arranged in these groups are produced by evolution from one another.[16] It need hardly be pointed out that the groups in question,

---

[15] Tylor's goal in *Primitive Culture* was to scientifically examine the development of religion and expose laws underlying its evolution. He aimed to show that the history of religion is characterized by increasing rationality. The path of his argument led him to explain the rationality of many "primitive" practices. Here he distinguishes between explaining such practices and defending them; it was important to him that his work was perceived as an explanation of religion rather than a defense of particular beliefs.

[16] Tylor was evolutionary and progressivist. He refers in the opening of this passage to the debate between biological evolutionists and creationists, still raging in 1871 when this piece was first published. For Tylor, the proposition that societies evolved from the most simple to most complex was self-evident. He wrote, "the educated world of Europe and America

though held together each by a common character, are by no means accurately defined. To take up again the natural history illustration, it may be said that they are species which tend to run widely into varieties. And when it comes to the question what relations some of these groups bear to others, it is plain that the student of the habits of mankind has a great advantage over the student of the species of plants and animals. Among naturalists it is an open question whether a theory of development from species to species is a record of transitions which actually took place or a mere ideal scheme serviceable in the classification of species whose origin was really independent. But among ethnographers there is no such question as to the possibility of species of implements or habits or beliefs being developed one out of another, for development in culture is recognized by our most familiar knowledge. Mechanical invention supplies apt examples of the kind of development which affects civilization at large. In the history of fire-arms, the clumsy wheellock, in which a notched steel wheel was turned by a handle against the flint till a spark caught the priming, led to the invention of the more serviceable flintlock, of which a few still hang in the kitchens of our farm-houses, for the boys to shoot small birds with at Christmas; the flintlock in time passed by an obvious modification into the percussion-lock, which is just now changing its old-fashioned arrangement to be adapted from muzzle-loading to breechloading. The medieval astrolabe passed into the quadrant, now discarded in its turn by the seaman, who uses the more delicate sextant, and so it is through the history of one art and instrument after another. Such examples of progression are known to us as direct history, but so thoroughly is this notion of development at home in our minds, that by means of it we reconstruct lost history without scruple, trusting to general knowledge of the principles of human thought and action as a guide in putting the facts in their proper order. Whether chronicle speaks or is silent on the point, no one comparing a longbow and a cross-bow would doubt that the cross-bow was a development arising from the simpler instrument. So among the fire-drills for igniting by friction, it seems clear on the face of the matter that the drill worked by a cord or bow is a later improvement on the clumsier primitive instrument twirled between the hands. That instructive class of specimens which antiquaries sometimes discover, bronze celts modelled on the heavy type of the stone hatchet, are scarcely explicable except as first steps in the transition from the Stone Age to the Bronze Age, to be followed soon by the next stage of progress, in which it is discovered that the new material is suited to a handier and less wasteful pattern. And thus, in the other branches of our history, there will come again and again into view series of facts which may be consistently arranged as having followed one another in a particular order of development, but which will hardly bear being turned round and made to follow in reversed order.[17] Such for instance are the facts I have here brought forward in a chapter on the Art of Counting, which tend to prove that as to this point of culture at least, savage tribes reached their position by learning and not unlearning, by elevation from a lower rather than by degradation from a higher state.

Among evidence aiding us to trace the courses which the civilization of the world has actually followed, is that great class of facts to denote which I have found it convenient to introduce the

---

practically settles a standard by simply placing its own nations at one end of the social series and savage tribes at the other, arranging the rest of mankind between these limits according as they correspond more closely to savage or cultured life" (quoted in Stocking 1987:162). For Tylor, the force driving this evolution was the natural development of increasingly rational thinking. While Tylor's thinking is evolutionary, he downplayed the importance of Darwinian evolution. In the preface to the 1873 edition of *Primitive Culture,* he explained the absence of references to Darwin and Spencer in the work by claiming that his work came "scarcely into contact of detail with the previous works of these eminent philosophers." However, the close connection between the work of Darwin and that of Tylor is shown by Darwin's extensive referencing of Tylor in *The Descent of Man* (1871).

[17]A popular theory in Tylor's time held that some peoples were primitive because they had degenerated from an earlier state. Tylor rejected this idea and discusses it further on in this essay.

term "survivals."[18] These are processes, customs, opinions, and so forth, which have been carried on by force of habit into a new state of society different from that in which they had their original home, and they thus remain as proofs and examples of an older condition of culture out of which a newer has been evolved. Thus, I know an old Somersetshire woman whose handloom dates from the time before the introduction of the "flying shuttle," which new-fangled appliance she has never even learnt to use, and I have seen her throw her shuttle from hand to hand in true classic fashion; this old woman is not a century behind her times, but she is a case of survival.[19] Such examples often lead us back to the habits of hundreds and even thousands of years ago. The ordeal of the Key and Bible, still in use, is a survival; the Midsummer bonfire is a survival; the Breton peasants' All Souls' supper for the spirits of the dead is a survival. The simple keeping up of ancient habits is only one part of the transition from old into new and changing times. The serious business of ancient society may be seen to sink into the sport of later generations, and its serious belief to linger on in nursery folk-lore, while superseded habits of old-world life may be modified into new-world forms still powerful for good and evil. Sometimes old thoughts and practices will burst out afresh, to the amazement of a world that thought them long since dead or dying; here survival passes into revival, as has lately happened in so remarkable a way in the history of modern spiritualism, a subject full of instruction from the ethnographer's point of view.[20] The study of the

principles of survival has, indeed, no small practical importance, for most of what we call superstition is included within survival, and in this way lies open to the attack of its deadliest enemy, a reasonable explanation. Insignificant, moreover, as multitudes of the facts of survival are in themselves, their study is so effective for tracing the course of the historical development through which alone it is possible to understand their meaning, that it becomes a vital point of ethnographic research to gain the clearest possible insight into their nature. This importance must justify the detail here devoted to an examination of survival, on the evidence of such games, popular sayings, customs, superstitions, and the like, as may serve well to bring into view the manner of its operation.

Progress, degradation, survival, revival, modification are all modes of the connexion that binds together the complex network of civilization.[21] It needs but a glance into the trivial details of our own daily life to set us thinking how far we are really its originators, and how far but the transmitters and modifiers of the results of long past ages. Looking round the rooms we live in, we may try here how far he who only knows his own time can be capable of rightly comprehending even that. Here is the "honeysuckle" of Assyria, there the fleur-de-lis of Anjou, a cornice with a Greek border runs round the ceiling, the style of Louis XIV and its parent the Renaissance share the looking-glass between them. Transformed, shifted, or mutilated, such elements of art still carry their history plainly stamped upon them; and if the history yet

---

[18] Though other thinkers such as Henry Sumner Maine (see footnote 26) also used the idea of survivals, it is considered one of Tylor's key contributions to anthropology. To him, almost any practice that seemed illogical or smacked of superstition was an example of the survival of the traits and beliefs of an earlier social form. Studying survivals was crucial since through them—and with the theory of psychic unity—a researcher could trace the course of cultural evolution.

[19] Notice Tylor's frequent references to the customs of English peasantry in this passage. For Tylor and other evolutionists, European peasantry represented a crucial intermediate step between civilization and savagery.

[20] Tylor wrote in an era when the occult was becoming a popular middle-class pastime. He himself had seen and written on psychic phenomena. While he did not believe in them, he did admit to being very impressed by the demonstrations he witnessed and unable to offer rational explanations of them (Stocking 1987:191).

[21] Here Tylor gives numerous examples of survivals. Tylor's great strength is his ability as a cultural historian; he was a master of the many details of cultural life. This passage also affirms his faith that laws of culture, similar in nature to the cause-and-effect principles of Newtonian physics, could be found. Virtually every paragraph of this essay stresses the ability of rational thinking men to divine cause-and-effect relationships.

farther behind is less easy to read, we are not to say that because we cannot clearly discern it there is therefore no history there. It is thus even with the fashion of the clothes men wear. The ridiculous little tails of the German postilion's[22] coat show themselves how they came to dwindle to such absurd rudiments; but the English clergyman's bands no longer so convey their history to the eye, and look unaccountable enough till one has seen the intermediate stages through which they came down from the more serviceable wide collars, such as Milton wears in his portrait, and which gave their name to the "band-box" they used to be kept in. In fact, the books of costume, showing how one garment grew or shrank by gradual stages and passed into another, illustrate with much force and clearness the nature of the change and growth, revival and decay, which go on from year to year in more important matters of life. In books, again, we see each writer not for and by himself, but occupying his proper place in history; we look through each philosopher, mathematician, chemist, poet, into the background of his education—through Leibnitz into Descartes, through Dalton into Priestley, through Milton into Homer. The study of language has, perhaps, done more than any other in removing from our view of human thought and action the ideas of chance and arbitrary invention, and in substituting for them a theory of development by the co-operation of individual men, through processes ever reasonable and intelligible where the facts are fully known.[23] Rudimentary as the science of culture still is, the symptoms are becoming very strong that even what seem its most spontaneous and motiveless phenomena will, nevertheless, be shown to come within the range of distinct cause and effect as certainly as the facts of mechanics. What would be popularly thought more indefinite and uncontrolled than the products of the imagination in myths and fables? Yet any systematic investigation of mythology, on the basis of a wide collection of evidence, will show plainly enough in such efforts of fancy at once a development from stage to stage, and a production of uniformity of result from uniformity of cause. Here, as elsewhere, causeless spontaneity is seen to recede farther and farther into shelter within the dark precincts of ignorance; like chance, that still holds its place among the vulgar as a real cause of events otherwise unaccountable, while to educated men it has long consciously meant nothing but this ignorance itself. It is only when men fail to see the line of connexion in events that they are prone to fall upon the notions of arbitrary impulses, causeless freaks, chance and nonsense, and indefinite unaccountability. If childish games, purposeless customs, absurd superstitions are set down as spontaneous because no one can say exactly how they came to be, the assertion may remind us of the like effect that the eccentric habits of the wild rice-plant had on the philosophy of a Red Indian tribe, otherwise disposed to see in the harmony of nature the effects of one controlling personal will. The Great Spirit, said these Sioux theologians, made all things except the wild rice; but the wild rice came by chance.

"Man," said Wilhelm von Humboldt,[24] "ever connects on from what lies at hand (der Mensch Knüpft immer an Vorhandenes an)." The notion of the continuity of civilization contained in this maxim is no barren philosophic principle, but is

---

[22] *Postilion:* a person who rides the horse on the left of the leading pair when four or more horses are used to draw a carriage, or simply the horse on the left when only one pair is used.

[23] Tylor had an early interest in linguistics and was particularly influenced by Friedrich Max Müller (1823–1900), who used the study of Sanskrit writings to discover the histories of Indo-European languages. Müller identified speakers of Indo-European languages as descendants of an ancient Aryan race. He is generally remembered as a humanist and, late in life, clearly opposed those who used the term Aryan as a racial category, but Stocking (1987:59) notes that "many of his more rhapsodic passages are . . . resonant of Aryanist racial ideology," and some of his work was later used in Nazi Germany to construct an intellectual pedigree for that regime's racist philosophy.

[24] Wilhelm von Humboldt (1767–1835) was a German diplomat, a humanist, and the founder of the University of Berlin. Humboldt's enduring legacy was his work in language. His appreciation of linguistic differences foreshadowed the work of Edward Sapir (1884–1939) and Benjamin L. Whorf (1897–1941) in this century. In 1820 he wrote: "The differences between languages are not those of sounds and signs but those of differing world view" (1963:246).

at once made practical by the consideration that they who wish to understand their own lives ought to know the stages through which their opinions and habits have become what they are. Auguste Comte[25] scarcely overstated the necessity of this study of development, when he declared at the beginning of his "Positive Philosophy" that "no conception can be understood except through its history" and his phrase will bear extension to culture at large. To expect to look modern life in the face and comprehend it by mere inspection is a philosophy whose weakness can easily be tested. Imagine any one explaining the trivial saying, "a little bird told me" without knowing of the old belief in the language of birds and beasts, to which Dr. Dasent, in the introduction to the Norse Tales, so reasonably traces its origin. To ingenious attempts at explaining by the light of reason things which want the light of history to show their meaning, much of the learned nonsense of the world has indeed been due. Sir H. S. Maine,[26] in his "Ancient Law," gives a perfect instance. In all the literature which enshrines the pretended philosophy of law, he remarks, there is nothing more curious than the pages of elaborate sophistry in which Blackstone attempts to explain and justify that extraordinary rule of English law, only recently repealed, which prohibited sons of the same father by different mothers from succeeding to one another's land. To Sir H. S. Maine, knowing the facts of the case, it was easy to explain its real origin from the "Customs of Normandy" where according to the system of agnation, or kinship on the male side, brothers by the same mother but by different fathers were of course no relations at all to one another. But when this rule "was transplanted to England, the English judges, who had no clue to its principle, interpreted it as a general prohibition against the succession of the half-blood, and extended it to consanguineous brothers, that is to sons of the same father by different wives." Then, ages after, Blackstone sought in this blunder the perfection of reason, and found it in the argument that kinship through both parents ought to prevail over even a nearer degree of kinship through but one parent.[a] Such are the risks that philosophers run in detaching any phenomenon of civilization from its hold on past events, and treating it as an isolated fact, to be simply disposed of by a guess at some plausible explanation.

In carrying on the great task of rational ethnography, the investigation of the causes which have produced the phenomena of culture, and the laws to which they are subordinate, it is desirable to work out as systematically as possible a scheme of evolution of this culture along its many lines.[27] In the following chapter [of *Primitive Culture*], on the Development of Culture, an attempt is made to sketch a theoretical course of civilization among mankind, such as appears on the whole most accordant with the evidence. By comparing the various stages of civilization among races known to history, with the aid of archaeological inference from the remains of pre-historic tribes, it seems possible to judge in a rough way of an early general condition of man, which from our point of view is to be regarded as a primitive condition, whatever yet earlier state may in reality have lain behind it. This hypothetical primitive condition corresponds in a considerable degree to that of modern savage tribes, who, in spite of their difference and distance, have in common certain elements of civilization, which seem remains of an

---

[25] Auguste Comte (1798–1857) was one of the architects of the philosophical school of positivism. Comte and other positivists denied the possibility of metaphysical knowledge and asserted that social phenomena were subject to general laws that could be discovered using the scientific method. He proposed a science of society and is often considered a founder of sociology. Comte had a profound influence on the social scientists of Tylor's generation and was a particularly powerful influence on Émile Durkheim and his followers in the early years of this century.

[26] Sir Henry Sumner Maine (1822–1888) was a legal historian and cultural evolutionist whose *Ancient Law* (1863) informed many of the anthropological discussions of Tylor's day. This passage shows an example of Maine's use of survivals.

[27] These passages contain numerous examples of the use of comparative method, which is held together, of course, by the belief in the psychic unity of humankind. If the presumption of psychic unity was incorrect, there would be no reason for societies to have followed the same stages of cultural evolution.

early state of the human race at large. If this hypothesis be true, then, notwithstanding the continual interference of degeneration, the main tendency of culture from primeval up to modern times has been from savagery towards civilization.[28] On the problem of this relation of savage to civilized life, almost every one of the thousands of facts discussed in the succeeding chapters has its direct bearing. Survival in Culture, placing all along the course of advancing civilization waymarks full of meaning to those who can decipher their signs, even now sets up in our midst primeval monuments of barbaric thought and life. Its investigation tells strongly in favor of the view that the European may find among the Greenlanders or Maoris many a trait for reconstructing the picture of his own primitive ancestors. Next comes the problem of the Origin of Language. Obscure as many parts of this problem still remain, its clearer positions lie open to the investigation whether speech took its origin among mankind in the savage state, and the result of the enquiry is that, consistently with all known evidence, this may have been the case. From examination of the Art of Counting a far more definite consequence is shown. It may be confidently asserted that not only is this important art found in a rudimentary state among savage tribes, but that satisfactory evidence proves numeration to have been developed by a rational invention from this low stage up to that in which we ourselves possess it. The examination of Mythology contained in the first volume is for the most part made from a special point of view, on evidence collected for a special purpose, that of tracing the relation between the myths of savage tribes and their analogues among more civilized nations. The issue of such enquiry goes far

to prove that the earliest myth-maker arose and flourished among savage hordes, setting on foot an art which his more cultured successors would carry on, till its results came to be fossilized in superstition, mistaken for history, shaped and draped in poetry, or cast aside as lying folly.

Nowhere, perhaps, are broad views of historical development more needed than in the study of religion.[29] Notwithstanding all that has been written to make the world acquainted with the lower theologies, the popular ideas of their place in history and their relation to the faiths of higher nations are still of the mediæval type. It is wonderful to contrast some missionary journals with Max Muller's Essays, and to set the unappreciating hatred and ridicule that is lavished by narrow hostile zeal on Brahmanism, Buddhism, Zoroastrism, beside the catholic sympathy with which deep and wide knowledge can survey those ancient and noble phases of man's religious consciousness; nor, because the religions of savage tribes may be rude and primitive compared with the great Asiatic systems, do they lie too low for interest and even for respect. The question really lies between understanding and misunderstanding them. Few who will give their minds to master the general principles of savage religion will ever again think it ridiculous, or the knowledge of it superfluous to the rest of mankind. Far from its beliefs and practices being a rubbish-heap of miscellaneous folly, they are consistent and logical in so high a degree as to begin, as soon as even roughly classified, to display the principles of their formation and development; and these principles prove to be essentially rational, though working in a mental condition of intense and inveterate ignorance. It is with a sense of attempting an investigation

---

[28] Degenerationism was a popular idea of the eighteenth and early nineteenth centuries that is explained on page 5. While Tylor felt that degeneration of particular societies was possible, he held that the general path of human society was progress, not degeneration.

[29] This and the following paragraphs introduce much of the rest of *Primitive Culture,* which is devoted to an analysis of religion. Many of Tylor's contemporaries suggested that since primitive religion was illogical and irrational, it did not lend itself to scientific study. These included Lewis Henry Morgan, who, though he did write on Iroquois beliefs, considered all primitive religion "to some extent unintelligible" (see essay 3). Tylor, on the other hand, asserted that, properly understood, primitive religious beliefs had rational bases. He further insisted that the development of religion, like most everything else, followed progressive, evolutionary laws. In much of the book that follows, Tylor traced what he believed was the evolution of religion from animism (a term he coined) to "enlightened Christianity."

which bears very closely on the current theology of our own day, that I have set myself to examine systematically, among the lower races, the development of Animism; that is to say, the doctrine of souls and other spiritual beings in general. More than half of the present work is occupied with a mass of evidence from all regions of the world, displaying the nature and meaning of this great element of the Philosophy of Religion, and tracing its transmission, expansion, restriction, modification, along the course of history into the midst of our own modern thought. Nor are the questions of small practical moment which have to be raised in a similar attempt to trace the development of certain prominent Rites and Ceremonies—customs so full of instruction as to the inmost powers of religion, whose outward expression and practical result they are.

In these investigations, however, made rather from an ethnographic than a theological point of view, there has seemed little need of entering into direct controversial argument, which indeed I have taken pains to avoid as far as possible.[30] The connexion which runs through religion, from its rudest forms up to the status of an enlightened Christianity, may be conveniently treated of with little recourse to dogmatic theology. The rites of sacrifice and purification may be studied in their stages of development without entering into questions of their authority and value, nor does an examination of the successive phases of the world's belief in a future life demand a discussion of the arguments adduced for or against the doctrine itself. The ethnographic results may then be left as materials for professed theologians, and it will not perhaps be long before evidence so fraught with meaning shall take its legitimate place. To fall back once again on the analogy of natural history, the time may soon come when it will be thought as unreasonable for a scientific student of theology not to have a competent acquaintance with

the principles of the religions of the lower races, as for a physiologist to look with the contempt of fifty years ago on evidence derived from the lower forms of life, deeming the structure of mere invertebrate creatures matter unworthy of his philosophic study.

Not merely as a matter of curious research, but as an important practical guide to the understanding of the present and the shaping of the future, the investigation into the origin and early development of civilization must be pushed on zealously. Every possible avenue of knowledge must be explored, every door tried to see if it is open. No kind of evidence need be left untouched on the score of remoteness or complexity, of minuteness or triviality. The tendency of modern enquiry is more and more toward the conclusion that if law is anywhere, it is everywhere. To despair of what a conscientious collection and study of facts may lead to, and to declare any problem insoluble because difficult and far off, is distinctly to be on the wrong side in science; and he who will choose a hopeless task may set himself to discover the limits of discovery. One remembers Comte starting in his account of astronomy with a remark on the necessary limitation of our knowledge of the stars: we conceive, he tells us, the possibility of determining their form, distance, size, and movement, whilst we should never by any method be able to study their chemical composition, their mineralogical structure, &c. Had the philosopher lived to see the application of spectrum analysis to this very problem his proclamation of the dispiriting doctrine of necessary ignorance would perhaps have been recanted in favor of a more hopeful view. And it seems to be with the philosophy of remote human life somewhat as with the study of the nature of the celestial bodies. The processes to be made out in the early stages of our mental evolution lie distant from us in time as the stars lie distant from

---

[30] Tylor is careful to distinguish his ethnographic work from a theological defense of or attack on particular beliefs. However, notice the passage here about his evidence taking its legitimate place. Tylor believed that rational, scientific knowledge had historically displaced religious belief. While Tylor was certainly no atheist, he implies that many of the religious practices of his own day are survivals of early humans' misunderstanding of the world. Note the anticlerical undercurrents in these passages. Tylor obliquely implies that Christianity itself was a survival and would not survive rational examination.

us in space, but the laws of the universe are not limited with the direct observation of our senses. There is vast material to be used in our enquiry; many workers are now busied in bringing this material into shape, though little may have yet been done in proportion to what remains to do; and already it seems not too much to say that the vague outlines of a philosophy of primaeval history are beginning to come within our view.[31]

Notes

a. Blackstone, "Commentaries," "As every man's own blood is compounded of the bloods of his respective ancestors, he only is properly of the whole or entire blood with another, who hath (so far as the distance of degrees will permit), all the same ingredients in the composition of his blood that the other hath," etc.

---

[31] While Tylor had an important influence on both his generation and future generations of anthropologists, his attempt to establish anthropology as a university discipline was largely frustrated. Backed by wealthy and influential friends, he held university positions at Oxford from 1884 until his death and received a knighthood in 1912, but a permanent position in anthropology was not established at Oxford during his lifetime. Many American anthropologists, particularly Boas and his students, rejected Tylor's work. However, some, including Leslie White and his students, looked to Tylor for inspiration. Notice the similarity between this paragraph and the last paragraph of White's "Energy and the Evolution of Culture" (essay 19), written more than seventy years later.

3. Ethnical Periods

Lewis Henry Morgan (1818–1881)

THE LATEST INVESTIGATIONS RESPECTING THE early condition of the human race are tending to the conclusion that mankind commenced their career at the bottom of the scale and worked their way up from savagery to civilization through the slow accumulations of experimental knowledge.[1]

As it is undeniable that portions of the human family have existed in a state of savagery, other portions in a state of barbarism, and still other portions in a state of civilization, it seems equally so that these three distinct conditions are connected with each other in a natural as well as necessary sequence of progress. Moreover, that this sequence has been historically true of the entire human family, up to the status attained by each branch respectively, is rendered probable by the conditions under which all progress occurs, and by the known advancement of several branches of the family through two or more of these conditions.

An attempt will be made in the following pages to bring forward additional evidence of the rudeness of the early condition of mankind, of the gradual evolution of their mental and moral powers through experience, and of their protracted struggle with opposing obstacles while winning their way to civilization. It will be drawn, in part, from the great sequence of inventions and discoveries which stretches along the entire pathway of

From *Ancient Society* (1877)

---

[1] In this first paragraph, Morgan shows that he, like other nineteenth-century anthropologists, viewed cultural evolution as progressive. His statement that humans worked their way up "to civilization through the slow accumulations of experimental knowledge" sounds very much as though he had Charles Darwin's theory of evolution by natural selection on his mind when he wrote this chapter.

human progress; but chiefly from domestic institutions, which express the growth of certain ideas and passions.[2]

As we re-ascend along the several lines of progress toward the primitive ages of mankind, and eliminate one after the other, in the order in which they appeared, inventions and discoveries on the one hand, and institutions on the other, we are enabled to perceive that the former stand to each other in progressive, and the latter in unfolding relations. While the former class have had a connection, more or less direct, the latter have been developed from a few primary germs of thought. Modern institutions plant their roots in the period of barbarism, into which their germs were transmitted from the previous period of savagery. They have had a lineal descent through the ages, with the streams of the blood, as well as a logical development.[3]

Two independent lines of investigations thus invite our attention. The one leads through inventions and discoveries, and the other through primary institutions. With the knowledge gained

therefrom, we may hope to indicate the principal stages of human development. The proofs to be adduced will be drawn chiefly from domestic institutions; the references to achievements more strictly intellectual being general as well as subordinate.[4]

The facts indicate the gradual formation and subsequent development of certain ideas, passions, and aspirations. Those which hold the most prominent positions may be generalized as growths of the particular ideas with which they severally stand connected. Apart from inventions and discoveries they are the following:

I. *Subsistence,* V. *Religion,*

II. *Government,* VI. *House Life and*

III. *Language,* 　　*Architecture,*

IV. *The Family,* VII. *Property.*

First. Subsistence has been increased and perfected by a series of successive arts, introduced at long intervals of time, and connected more or less directly with inventions and discoveries.[5]

---

[2] A common belief among social scientists of Morgan's day was that cultural evolution referred not only to technological progress but also to moral development. Notice that Morgan speaks of "winning" civilization. The influence of Darwin's concept of evolution as a battle for survival is evident in Morgan's characterization of cultural evolution as a "protracted struggle."

[3] Morgan's comment on the lineal descent of institutions through the ages refers to two different aspects of his thought. Morgan was well acquainted with *The Geological Evidence for the Antiquity of Man* by Sir Charles Lyell (1797–1875) (Tooker 1992). Thus, he was versed in the latest geological evidence demonstrating that the earth and human beings were ancient far beyond biblical projections, and he was able to incorporate this time scale in his evolutionary theory. Second, Morgan's reference to "germs of thought" refers to his belief that there were universal ideas, which like seeds, would germinate and blossom in the proper environment. Because Morgan, like Tylor, accepted this concept of the psychic unity of humankind, he believed that unilineal evolution was "natural and necessary."

[4] Morgan was interested in the evolution of culture as a pan-human event but divides the evidence used in his analysis. He proposed to trace the development of "inventions and discoveries" but considered them subordinate to the development of "primary institutions," such as subsistence, government, language, and property, that were transmitted by germs of thought. Morgan believed that inventions and discoveries were correlated with stages of cultural evolution but developed by different processes. He wrote that inventions and discoveries had a direct, progressive relationship and were connected to developments in subsistence. However, the primary institutions have "unfolding relations." They were seeded as germs of thought in the period of Savagery, germinated in the period of Barbarism, and flowered in Civilization. Although Morgan lists seven of these institutions, the one on which he placed the greatest importance was subsistence. In Morgan's view, it was developments in subsistence that lay behind evolutionary progress.

[5] The keys to cultural evolution, according to Morgan, were techniques of food production, which distinguished humans from other animals. As a result, he devoted a chapter of *Ancient Society* to outlining the development of different types of subsistence and their role in cultural evolution. Morgan speculated that human beings first subsisted by gathering wild vegetable foods, which meant that people were originally found in tropical climates. His conjecture is surprisingly accurate: modern paleontological research indicates that early human ancestors were foragers on the savannas of Africa. The

Second. The germ of government must be sought in the organization into gentes[6] in the Status of savagery; and followed down, through the advancing forms of this institution, to the establishment of political society.

Third. Human speech seems to have been developed from the rudest and simplest forms of expression. Gesture or sign language, as intimated by Lucretius,[a] must have preceded articulate language, as thought preceded speech. The monosyllabical preceded the syllabical, as the latter did that of concrete words. Human intelligence, unconscious of design, evolved articulate language by utilizing the vocal sounds. This great subject, a department of knowledge by itself, does not fall within the scope of the present investigation.[7]

Fourth. With respect to the family, the stages of its growth are embodied in systems of consanguinity and affinity, and in usages relating to marriage, by means of which, collectively, the family can be definitely traced through several successive forms.

Fifth. The growth of religious ideas is environed with such intrinsic difficulties that it may never receive a perfectly satisfactory exposition. Religion deals so largely with the imaginative and emotional nature, and consequently with such uncertain elements of knowledge, that all primitive religions are grotesque and to some extent unintelligible. This subject also falls without the plan of this work excepting as it may prompt incidental suggestions.[8]

Sixth. House architecture, which connects itself with the form of the family and the plan of domestic life, affords a tolerably complete illustration of progress from savagery to civilization. Its growth can be traced from the hut of the savage, through the communal houses of the barbarians, to the house of the single family of civilized nations, with all the successive links by which one extreme is connected with the other. This subject will be noticed incidentally.

Lastly. The idea of property was slowly formed in the human mind, remaining nascent and feeble through immense periods of time. Springing into life in savagery, it required all the experience of this period of barbarism to develop the germ, and to prepare the human brain for the acceptance of its controlling influence. Its dominance as a passion over all other passions marks the commencement of civilization. It not only led mankind to overcome the obstacles which delayed civilization, but to establish political society on the basis of territory and of property. A critical knowledge of the evolution of the idea of property would embody, in some respects, the most remarkable portion of the mental history of mankind.[9]

---

primary place of subsistence in Morgan's work was adopted later by cultural ecological thinkers such as Julian Steward (essay 18), as well as many contemporary materialists.

[6] *Gentes:* Latin for a patrilineal clan.

[7] As indicated by his reference to the Roman poet and philosopher Lucretius (96?–55 B.C.E.), Morgan subscribed to the popular idea that evolution proceeded from simple to more complex forms. This idea is expressed here in the comment that gestural forms of communication are more primitive than speech. Morgan believed that forms of communication could be ranked and that primitive people spoke primitive languages. This notion survives today in ideas about the linguistic poverty of the poor or the inferiority of nonstandard forms of English. In fact, forms of communication such as American Sign Language are just as complex and expressive as spoken language. Edward Sapir, a student of Boas, attacked the idea of simple and complex languages when he developed the notion of linguistic relativism. For Boasians, all languages were equally evolved.

[8] The idea that religion was not fit for scientific study because it was "imaginative and emotional," was common among nineteenth-century anthropologists. However, it was specifically rejected by E. B. Tylor, who attempted to trace the evolutionary history of religion in his book *Primitive Culture* (see essay 2).

[9] Morgan's assertion that the concept of property led to the beginning of civilization as well as the establishment of political organizations may have had its origin in the work of John Locke, but it dovetails nicely with Marxist concerns. One can see why Karl Marx and Friedrich Engels were so interested in Morgan's work. Marx read and extensively annotated

It will be my object to present some evidence of human progress along these several lines, and through successive ethnical periods, as it is revealed by inventions and discoveries, and by the growth of the ideas of government, of the family, and of property.

It may be here premised that all forms of government are reducible to two general plans, using the word plan in its scientific sense. In their bases the two are fundamentally distinct. The first, in the order of time, is founded upon persons, and upon relations purely personal, and may be distinguished as a society (*societas*). The gens is the unit of this organization; giving as the successive stages of integration, in the archaic period, the gens, the phratry, the tribe, and the confederacy of tribes, which constituted a people or nation (*populus*).[10] At a later period a coalescence of tribes in the same area into a nation took the place of a confederacy of tribes occupying independent areas. Such, through prolonged ages, after the gens appeared, was the substantially universal organization of ancient society; and it remained among the Greeks and Romans after civilization supervened. The second is founded upon territory and upon property, and may be distinguished as a state (*civitas*). The township or ward, circumscribed by metes and bounds, with the property it contains, is the basis or unit of the latter, and political society is the result. Political society is organized upon territorial areas, and

deals with property as well as with persons through territorial relations. The successive stages of integration are the township or ward, which is the unit of organization; the county or province, which is an aggregation of townships or wards; and the national domain or territory, which is an aggregation of counties or provinces; the people of each of which are organized into a body politic. It taxed the Greeks and Romans to the extent of their capacities, after they had gained civilization, to invent the deme or township and the city ward; and thus inaugurate the second great plan of government, which remains among civilized nations to the present hour. In ancient society this territorial plan was unknown. When it came in it fixed the boundary line between ancient and modern society, as the distinction will be recognized in these pages.

It may be further observed that the domestic institutions of the barbarous, and even of the savage ancestors of mankind, are still exemplified in portions of the human family with such completeness that, with the exception of the strictly primitive period, the several stages of this progress are tolerably well preserved. They are seen in the organization of society upon the basis of sex, then upon the basis of kin, and finally upon the basis of territory;[11] through the successive forms of marriage and of the family, with the systems of consanguinity thereby created; through house life and architecture; and through progress in usages

---

Ancient Society but died before he was able to publish anything about it. Thus, it was Engels who had the task of integrating Morgan into Marxist theory. Engels believed that, in *Ancient Society,* Morgan had developed a materialist conception of history. Further Engels claimed that Morgan's comparisons of different societies had led him to the same conclusions as Marx (Resek 1960:161). In 1884, Engels, working from Marx's annotations, published *The Origin of the Family, Private Property and the State,* which he subtitled *In the Light of the Researches of Lewis Henry Morgan.* There, he claimed Morgan had proven Marx's theory by demonstrating that private property and the state were only passing phases in the continuing evolution of human society. Although Engels believed *Ancient Society* confirmed the truth of Marxist analysis, Morgan was not a Marxist. His ideas of psychic unity and unilineal evolution are very different from Marx's notions that human nature is contingent and created through labor (see pages 55–56).

[10] *Gens* and *gentes* are synonymous terms for patrilineal clans. A *phratry* is a unilineal descent group composed of related clans. Morgan postulated that there were two basic forms of government: those based on kinship and those based on property. He believed that the modern state was founded upon notions of territory and property rather than kinship.

[11] When Morgan mentions the preservation of earlier stages that can be seen in the organization of society on the basis of sex, then kin, he is referring to the work of Johann J. Bachofen. Bachofen (1815–1887) was a lawyer and a scholar in classical mythology. He and Morgan were intimately familiar with each other's work. Morgan's descriptions of the matrilineal Iroquois in his book *The League of the Iroquois* (1851) provided Bachofen with ethnographic data to support the the-

with respect to the ownership and inheritance of property.[12]

The theory of human degradation to explain the existence of savages and of barbarians is no longer tenable. It came in as a corollary from the Mosaic cosmogony, and was acquiesced in from a supposed necessity which no longer exists. As a theory, it is not only incapable of explaining the existence of savages, but it is without support in the facts of human experience.[13]

The remote ancestors of the Aryan nations presumptively passed through an experience similar to that of existing barbarous and savage tribes. Though the experience of these nations embodies all the information necessary to illustrate the periods of civilization, both ancient and modern, together with a part of that in the Later period of barbarism, their anterior experience must be deduced, in the main, from the traceable connection between the elements of their existing institutions and inventions, and similar elements still preserved in those of savage and barbarous tribes.[14]

It may be remarked finally that the experience of mankind has run in nearly uniform channels; that human necessities in similar conditions have been substantially the same; and that the operations of the mental principle have been uniform in virtue of the specific identity of the brain of all the races of mankind. This, however, is but a part of the explanation of uniformity in results. The germs of the principal institutions and arts of life were developed while man was still a savage. To a very great extent the experience of the subsequent periods of barbarism and of civilization have been expended in the further development of these original conceptions. Wherever a connection can be traced on different continents between a present institution and a common germ, the derivation of the people themselves from a common original stock is implied.[15]

The discussion of these several classes of facts will be facilitated by the establishment of a certain number of Ethnical Periods; each representing a distinct condition of society, and distin-

---

ory he outlined in his major work *Das Mutterrecht,* or *Mother Right* (1861). In *Mother Right* (1861) Bachofen proposed that in its earliest state, society was organized and controlled by women. Only later did men assert themselves to form patriarchal, patrilineal societies. Following Bachofen's scheme, Morgan assumed that matrilineal societies such as the Iroquois were representative of an earlier stage of political evolution.

[12] Morgan considered primitive societies to be living fossils and assumed that they resembled earlier stages in the development of Western society. Because simple societies, such as foraging bands, are structured by kinship ties, Morgan assumed that similar structures characterized the earliest stages of political evolution in the "archaic" (pre-savagery) period.

[13] The "theory of degradation" or degenerationism was based on the Old Testament book of Genesis (Morgan's "Mosaic cosmogony"). The theory is explained on page 5. A leading degenerationist, W. Cooke Taylor outlined this view in *Natural History of Society* (1840). He "insisted upon a literal sequence of fall, flood, Babel, and diaspora. Some groups thereafter degenerated in savagery, but others, aided by God, progressed towards new heights of civilization" (Harris 1968:58). The "supposed necessity" Morgan mentions here refers to the view that there had been a relatively brief period of time since creation. He is saying that Lyell's work in geology has discredited degenerationism, making a biblical explanation of civilization unnecessary.

[14] Although he does not make it explicit, Morgan is referring to E. B. Tylor's concept of survivals in this paragraph. For more on survivals, refer to essay 2.

[15] The "uniform mental principle" Morgan mentions here reflects his belief in the psychic unity of humankind. Like Tylor before him, Morgan argued that unilineal evolution occurred because human thinking follows a universal course of development. But as the second half of this paragraph shows, Morgan was aware that cross-cultural similarities may imply people share a common origin, or that ideas can spread through diffusion. The concept of diffusion was popularized, at the turn of this century, by the German anthropogeographer Friedrich Ratzel (1844–1904) and his student Leo Froebenius (1873–1938). It was carried to an extreme in the first decades of the twentieth century by such radical diffusionists as the Englishmen Grafton Elliot Smith (1871–1937) and W. J. Perry (1887–1949), who proposed that all world culture had begun in Egypt and diffused from that source (Smith 1928). Additionally, when Morgan wrote that "human necessities in similar conditions have been substantially the same," he anticipated the concept of cultural types outlined in Julian Steward's theory of multilinear evolution sixty years later (see essay 18).

guishable by a mode of life peculiar to itself. The terms "Age of *Stone*," "of *Bronze*," and "of *Iron*," introduced by Danish archaeologists, have been extremely useful for certain purposes, and will remain so for the classification of objects of ancient art; but the progress of knowledge has rendered other and different subdivisions necessary. Stone implements were not entirely laid aside with the introduction of tools of iron, nor of those of bronze. The invention of the process of smelting iron ore created an ethnical epoch, yet we could scarcely date another from the production of bronze. Moreover, since the period of stone implements overlaps those of bronze and of iron, and since that of bronze also overlaps that of iron, they are not capable of a circumscription that would leave each independent and distinct.[16]

It is probable that the successive arts of subsistence which arose at long intervals will ultimately, from the great influence they must have exercised upon the condition of mankind, afford the most satisfactory bases for these divisions. But investigation has not been carried far enough in this direction to yield the necessary information. With our present knowledge the main result can be attained by selecting such other inventions or discoveries as will afford sufficient tests of progress to characterize the commencement of successive ethnical periods. Even though accepted as provisional, these periods will be found convenient and useful. Each of those about to be proposed will be found to cover a distinct culture, and to represent a particular mode of life.[17]

The period of savagery, of the early part of which very little is known, may be divided, provisionally, into three subperiods. These may be named respectively the *Older*, the *Middle*, and the *Later* period of savagery; and the condition of society in each, respectively, may be distinguished as the *Lower*, the *Middle*, and the *Upper Status* of savagery.

In like manner, the period of barbarism divides naturally into three sub-periods, which will be called, respectively, the *Older*, the *Middle*, and the *Later* period of barbarism; and the condition of society in each, respectively, will be distinguished as the *Lower*, the *Middle*, and the *Upper Status* of barbarism.

It is difficult, if not impossible, to find such tests of progress to mark the commencement of these several periods as will be found absolute in their application, and without exceptions upon all the continents. Neither is it necessary, for the purpose in hand, that exceptions should not exist. It will be sufficient if the principal tribes of mankind can be classified, according to the degree of their relative progress, into conditions which can be recognized as distinct.

I. Lower Status of Savagery[18]

This period commenced with the infancy of the human race, and may be said to have ended with the acquisition of a fish subsistence and of a knowledge of the use of fire. Mankind were then living in their original restricted habitat, and subsisting upon fruits and nuts. The commencement of articulate speech belongs to this period. No exemplification of tribes of mankind in this condition remained to the historical period.

---

[16] The terms Stone, Bronze, and Iron Ages were introduced by the first curator of the Danish National Museum, Christian J. Thomesen, in order to chronologically rank European artifacts in an 1807 exhibit. This "three-age system," as it came to be known, was soon widely used throughout Europe (Fagan 1989:34).

[17] Morgan's goal was to outline the stages of cultural evolution. He proposed that the transition between stages could be marked by the acquisition of certain kin patterns and modes of subsistence and the development of certain technological innovations. Half a century later, this insight would be essential in the work of the neoevolutionists Julian Steward and Leslie White, who examined cultural evolution in relation to subsistence and technology (essays 18 and 19). In the next several paragraphs Morgan outlines his design for separating one stage of cultural evolution from another.

[18] Here Morgan begins to outline the factors upon which he distinguishes the stages of cultural evolution. Much of the criticism of his theory was based on the fact that Morgan's system created illogical groupings, lumping together societies that we now consider to have vastly different levels of social organization. This critique was first pointed out by Franz Boas in the early part of this century (see footnote 21).

II. Middle Status of Savagery

It commenced with the acquisition of a fish subsistence and a knowledge of the use of fire, and ended with the invention of the bow and arrow. Mankind, while in this condition, spread from their original habitat over the greater portion of the earth's surface. Among tribes still existing it will leave in the Middle Status of savagery, for example, the Australians and the greater part of the Polynesians when discovered. It will be sufficient to give one or more exemplifications of each status.

III. Upper Status of Savagery

It commenced with the invention of the bow and arrow, and ended with the invention of the art of pottery. It leaves in the Upper Status of Savagery the Athapascan tribes of the Hudson's Bay Territory, the tribes of the valley of the Columbia, and certain coast tribes of North and South America; but with relation to the time of their discovery. This closes the period of Savagery.

IV. Lower Status of Barbarism

The invention or practice of the art of pottery, all things considered, is probably the most effective and conclusive test that can be selected to fix a boundary line, necessarily arbitrary, between savagery and barbarism. The distinctness of the two conditions has long been recognized, but no criterion of progress out of the former into the latter has hitherto been brought forward. All such tribes, then, as never attained to the art of pottery will be classed as savages, and those possessing this art but who never attained a phonetic alphabet and the use of writing will be classed as barbarians.

The first sub-period of barbarism commenced with the manufacture of pottery, whether by original invention or adoption. In finding its termination, and the commencement of the Middle Status, a difficulty is encountered in the unequal endowments of the two hemispheres, which began to be influential upon human affairs after the period of savagery had passed. It may be met, however, by the adoption of equivalents. In the Eastern hemisphere, the domestication of animals, and the Western, the cultivation of maize and plants by irrigation, together with the use of adobe-brick and stone in house building have been selected as sufficient evidence of progress to work a transition out of the Lower and into the Middle Status of barbarism. It leaves, for example, in the Lower Status, the Indian tribes of the United States east of the Missouri River, and such tribes of Europe and Asia as practiced the art of pottery, but were without domestic animals.

V. Middle Status of Barbarism

It commenced with the domestication of animals in the Eastern hemisphere, and in the Western with cultivation by irrigation and with the use of abode-brick and stone in architecture, as shown. Its termination may be fixed with the invention of the process of smelting iron ore. This places in the Middle Status, for example, the Village Indians of New Mexico, Mexico, Central America and Peru, and such tribes in the Eastern hemisphere as possessed domestic animals but were without a knowledge of iron. The ancient Britons, although familiar with the use of iron, fairly belong in this connection. The vicinity of more advanced continental tribes had advanced the arts of life among them far beyond the state of development of their domestic institutions.[19]

VI. Upper Status of Barbarism

It commenced with the manufacture of iron, and ended with the invention of a phonetic alphabet, and the use of writing in literary composition. Here civilization begins. This leaves in the Upper Status, for example, the Grecian tribes of the Homeric age, the Italian tribes shortly before the founding of Rome, and the Germanic tribes of the time of Caesar.

---

[19] A society's evolutionary stage was gauged by its technology, subsistence pattern, and kin and family structure together. Consequently, although groups such as the ancient Britons had acquired technological achievements of more advanced societies, such as the use of iron (diagnostic of Upper Barbarism), Morgan believes that the development of their domestic institutions places them squarely in the stage of Middle Barbarism.

VII. Status of Civilization

It commenced, as stated, with the use of a phonetic alphabet and the production of literary records, and divides into *Ancient* and *Modern*. As an equivalent, hieroglyphical writing upon stone may be admitted.

RECAPITULATION

Periods.	Conditions.
I. *Older Period of Savagery,*	I. *Lower Status of Savagery,*
II. *Middle Period of Savagery,*	II. *Middle Status of Savagery,*
III. *Later Period of Savagery,*	III. *Upper Status of Savagery,*
IV. *Older Period of Barbarism,*	IV. *Lower Status of Barbarism,*
V. *Middle Period of Barbarism,*	V. *Middle Status of Barbarism,*
VI. *Later Period of Barbarism,*	VI. *Upper Status of Barbarism,*

VII. *Status of Civilization.*

I. *Lower Status of Savagery,*	From the Infancy of the Human Race to the commencement of the next Period.
II. *Middle Status of Savagery,*	From the acquisition of a fish subsistence and a knowledge of the use of fire, to etc.
III. *Upper Status of Savagery,*	From the Invention of the Bow and Arrow, to etc.
IV. *Lower Status of Barbarism,*	From the Invention of the Art of Pottery, to etc.
V. *Middle Status of Barbarism,*	From the Domestication of animals on the Eastern hemisphere, and in the Western from the cultivation of maize and plants by Irrigation, with the use of adobe-brick and stone, to etc.
VI. *Upper Status of Barbarism,*	From the Invention of the process of Smelting Iron Ore, with the use of iron tools, to etc.
VII. *Status of Civilization,*	From the Invention of a Phonetic Alphabet, with the use of writing, to the present time.

Each of these periods has a distinct culture and exhibits a mode of life more or less special and peculiar to itself. This specialization of ethnical periods renders it possible to treat a particular society according to its condition of relative advancement, and to make it a subject of independent study and discussion. It does not affect the main result that different tribes and nations on the same continent, and even of the same linguistic family, are in different conditions at the same time, since for our purpose the *condition* of each is the material fact, the *time* being immaterial.

Since the use of pottery is less significant than that of domestic animals, of iron, or of a phonetic alphabet, employed to mark the commencement of subsequent ethnical periods, the reasons for its adoption should be stated. The manufacture of pottery presupposes village life, and considerable progress in the simple arts.[b] Flint and stone implements are older than pottery, remains of the former having been found in ancient repositories in numerous instances unaccompanied by the latter. A succession of inventions of greater need and adapted to a lower condition must have occurred before the want of pottery would be felt. The commencement of village life, with some degree of control over subsistence, wooden vessels and utensils, finger weaving with filaments of bark, basket making, and the bow and arrow make their appearance before the art of pottery. The Village Indians who were in the Middle Status of barbarism, such as the Zuñians, the Aztecs and the Cholulans, manufactured pottery in large quantities and in many forms of considerable excellence; the partially Village Indians of the United States, who were in the Lower Status of barbarism, such as the Iroquois, the Choctas, and the Cherokees, made it in smaller quantities and in a limited number of forms; but the non-horticultural Indians, who were in the Status of savagery, such as the Athapascans, the tribes of California and of the valley of the Columbia, were ignorant of its use.[c] In Lubbock's *Pre-Historic Times,* in Tylor's *Early History of Mankind,* and in Peschel's *Races of Man,* the particulars respecting this art, and the extent of its distribution, have been collected with remarkable breadth of research. It was unknown in Polynesia (with the exception of the Islands of the Tongans and Fijians), in Australia, in California, and in the Hudson's Bay Territory. Mr. Tylor remarks that "the art of weaving was unknown in most of the Islands away from Asia," and that "in most of the South Sea Islands there was no knowledge of pottery."[d] The Rev. Lorimer Fison, an English missionary residing in Australia, informed the author in answer to inquiries, that "the Australians had no woven fabrics, no pottery, and were ignorant of the bow and arrow."[20] This last fact was also true in general of the Polynesians.[21] The introduction of the ceramic art produced a new epoch in human progress in the direction of an improved living and increased domestic conveniences. While flint and stone implements—which came in earlier and required long periods of time to develop all their uses—gave the canoe, wooden vessels and utensils, and ultimately timber and plank in house architecture,[e] pottery gave a durable vessel for boiling food, which before that had been rudely accomplished in baskets coated with clay, and in ground cavities lined with skin, the boiling being effected with heated stones.[f]

Whether the pottery of the aborigines was hardened by fire or cured by the simple process of drying, has been made a question. Prof E. T. Cox, of Indianapolis, has shown by comparing the analyses of ancient pottery and hydraulic cements, "that so far as chemical constituents are concerned it (the pottery) agrees very well with the composition of hydraulic stones." He remarks further, that "all the pottery belonging to the mound-builders' age, which I have seen, is composed of alluvial clay and sand, or a mixture of the former with pulverized freshwater shells. A paste made of such a mixture possesses in a high degree the properties of hydraulic Puzzuolani and Portland cement, so that vessels formed of it hardened without being burned, as is customary with modern pottery. The fragments of shells served the purpose of gravel or fragments of stone as at present used in connection with hydraulic lime for the manufacture of artificial stone."[g] The composition of Indian pottery in analogy with that of hydraulic cement suggests the difficulties in the way of inventing the art, and tends also to explain the lateness of its introduction in the course of human experience. Notwithstanding the ingenious suggestion of Prof. Cox, it is probable that pottery was hardened by artificial heat. In some cases the fact is directly attested. Thus Adair, speaking of the Gulf Tribes, remarks that "they make earthen pots

---

[20] Morgan cites Lubbock and Fison, whose work was an important influence on his own. John Lubbock (1834–1913), also known as Lord Avebury, was an amateur ethnologist and natural historian. A prosperous banker and liberal member of Parliament, Lubbock also served as president of the Royal Anthropological Institute and Ethnological Society of London. His boyhood home was near that of Darwin, and Lubbock became close friends with Darwin and a staunch defender of the *Origin of Species.* Lubbock developed an evolutionary theory of human society based on his study of European and North American archaeology. He proposed a natural progression of social evolution from the primitive to the civilized, and he coined the terms *paleolithic* and *neolithic.* He published his ideas in *Prehistoric Times* (1865) and *The Origin of Civilization* (1871).

Lorimer Fison (1832–1907) was a missionary, journalist, and anthropologist. Morgan's studies of kinship were based on extensive questionnaires sent to European travelers and missionaries throughout the world. While in Fiji in 1869, Fison received one of these questionnaires. It drew his interest to anthropology and he became an ardent follower of Morgan, with whom he corresponded extensively. Fison's research into Australian aboriginal kinship systems, based on interviews with European settlers, provided important data for E. B. Tylor, J. G. Frazer, and Émile Durkheim as well as Morgan.

[21] Morgan's critics cited his placement of the Polynesians in Middle Savagery together with Australian Aborigines as an example of an illogical grouping created by his theory. Aboriginal society was organized by family-based foraging bands. Polynesian society, though without pottery or the technological innovations Morgan mentions here, was composed of highly stratified chiefdoms and was far more complex.

of very different sizes, so as to contain from two to ten gallons, large pitchers to carry water, bowls, dishes, platters, basins, and a prodigious number of other vessels of such antiquated forms as would be tedious to describe, and impossible to name. Their method of glazing them is, they place them over a large fire of smoky pitch-pine, which makes them smooth, black and firm."[h]

Another advantage of fixing definite ethnical periods is the direction of special investigation to those tribes and nations which afford the best exemplification of each status, with the view of making each both standard and illustrative. Some tribes and families have been left in geographical isolation to work out the problems of progress by original mental effort; and have, consequently, retained their arts and institutions pure and homogeneous; while those of other tribes and nations have been adulterated through external influence. Thus, while Africa was and is an ethnical chaos of savagery and barbarism, Australia and Polynesia were in savagery, pure and simple, with the arts and institutions belonging to that condition.[22] In like manner, the Indian family of America, unlike any other existing family, exemplified the condition of mankind in three successive ethnical periods. In the undisturbed possession of a great continent, of common descent, and with homogeneous institutions, they illustrated, when discovered, each of these conditions, and especially those of the Lower and of the Middle Status of barbarism, more elaborately and completely than any other portion of mankind. The far northern Indians and some of the coast tribes of North and South America were in the Upper Status of savagery, the partially Village Indians east of the Mississippi were in the Lower Status of barbarism, and the Village Indians of North and South Amer-

ica were in the Middle Status. Such an opportunity to recover full and minute information of the course of human experience and progress in developing their arts and institutions through these successive conditions has not been offered within the historical period. It must be added that it has been indifferently improved. Our greatest deficiencies relate to the last period named.[23]

Differences in the culture of the same period in the Eastern and Western hemispheres undoubtedly existed in consequence of the unequal endowments of the continents; but the condition of society in the corresponding status must have been, in the main, substantially similar.

The ancestors of the Grecian, Roman, and German tribes passed through the stages we have indicated, in the midst of the last of which the light of history fell upon them. Their differentiation from the undistinguishable mass of barbarians did not occur, probably, earlier than the commencement of the Middle Period of barbarism. The experience of these tribes has been lost, with the exception of so much as is represented by the institutions, inventions and discoveries which they had brought with them, and possessed when they first came under historical observation. The Grecian and Latin tribes of the Homeric and Romulian periods afford the highest exemplification of the Upper Status of barbarism.[24] Their institutions were likewise pure and homogeneous, and their experience stands directly connected with the final achievement of civilization.

Commencing, then, with the Australians and Polynesians, following with the American Indian tribes, and concluding with the Roman and Grecian who afford the highest exemplifications respectively of the six great stages of human progress, the sum of their united experiences may be sup-

---

[22] Morgan believed that diffusion confused the evolutionary process. Although he believed all groups evolved along the same path, he did not claim all people were equal. Morgan contended that different races evolved at different speeds. Thus, he talks about "ethnical chaos" because, in his view, diffusion meant that some groups were exposed to other cultures that were far beyond the simpler group's evolutionary development or capabilities.

[23] Morgan had a lifelong interest in Native American culture. He studied the linguistics and kinship systems of Native Americans and as a lawyer was active in the defense of Native American land rights. The recording of Native American culture concerned Morgan, who raises the issue in this paragraph. The fear that these cultures were disappearing motivated Franz Boas and his students to work in Native American societies in the early years of the twentieth century.

[24] The Homeric and Romulian periods refers to the times of Homer, the Greek poet of the eighth century B.C.E., and Romulus, mythological founder of Rome in 753 B.C.E.

posed fairly to represent that of the human family from the Middle Status of savagery to the end of ancient civilization. Consequently, the Aryan nations will find the type of the condition of their remote ancestors, when in savagery, in that of the Australians and Polynesians; when in the Lower Status of barbarism in that of the partially Village Indians of America; and when in the Middle Status in that of the Village Indians, with which their own experience in the Upper Status directly connects. So essentially identical are the arts, institutions and mode of life in the same status upon all the continents, that the archaic form of the principal domestic institutions of the Greeks and Romans must even now be sought in the corresponding institution of the American aborigines,

as will be shown in the course of this volume. This fact forms a part of the accumulating evidence tending to show that the principal institutions of mankind have been developed from a few primary germs of thought; and that the course and manner of their development was predetermined, as well as restricted within narrow limits of divergence, by the natural logic of the human mind and the necessary limitations of its powers.[25] Progress has been found to be substantially the same in kind in tribes and nations inhabiting different and even disconnected continents, while in the same status, with deviations from uniformity in particular instances produced by special causes. The argument when extended tends to establish the unity of origin of mankind.[26]

---

[25] One consequence of Morgan's belief that human thought was restricted along certain paths is his contention that all humans had the potential to be equal, even though this equality had not been achieved by all groups. This may explain Morgan's interest in the Iroquois and his relatively enlightened attitude toward Native Americans. Do not mistake this attitude for a belief in racial equality, however. Morgan, like most social scientists of his day, believed Caucasians were superior to other ethnic groups. Despite his respect for Native Americans, he did not consider them equal to people of northern European descent (those he calls "Aryans"). You will note that he consistently identifies the Greek, Roman, and Aryan peoples as evolving first and fastest, consigning the great African and Mesoamerican civilizations to earlier stages in his evolutionary scheme. This notion of Aryan superiority was popularized and given a "scientific" veneer by the German biologist Ernst Heinrich Haeckel, most famous for his statement of recapitulation theory, which found political expression during Adolph Hitler's rise to power in Nazi Germany. Applying the theory to ethnic groups, Haeckel argued that the "lower races" were like Caucasians during infancy. This idea is also reflected in Freud and his followers' views of people in primitive societies (see essay 5).

In another section of *Ancient Society* Morgan speaks of the inferior brain size of Native Americans and the "preeminent endowment" of the Aryan and Semitic families. This statement is racist, but Morgan was reflecting the scientific opinion of his time, which held that brain size was related to intelligence. Morgan must have been aware of the work of Dr. Samuel G. Morton, who measured the interior capacity of skull samples from different ethnic groups. In his most famous works—*Crania Americana* (1839) and *Crania Aegyptica* (1844)—Morton claimed that whites had bigger brains than any other group, from which he concluded that they were intellectually and morally superior to those other groups. Morton's data (although not his conclusions) stood unquestioned until 1981 when Harvard biologist Stephen Jay Gould published an analysis of that data. Gould discovered that Morton had committed gross errors in sampling when he chose his selection of skulls for measurement and had incorrectly analyzed his own data. When the sampling errors were corrected and the data reanalyzed, Gould found no significant differences between the skull volumes of different ethnic groups in Morton's collection.

[26] Here Morgan outlines his grand vision of cultural evolution; Australians and Polynesians in savagery, various Native American groups in different stages of barbarism depending on their types of subsistence, and the Greeks and Romans as the first examples of civilization. He supported his theory through the use of the nineteenth-century doctrine of the comparative method and psychic unity. The comparative method proposed that contemporary primitive societies were like living fossils; for example, see Morgan's assertion that the principal institutions of the Greeks and Romans can be seen in archaic form in Native American societies. A clear expression of psychic unity is also found in this paragraph. Morgan states that human development is predetermined by the "natural logic of the human mind," which was based on universal "germs of thought." This doctrine of psychic unity justified the uncritical use of the comparative method, which formed the basis for the belief in unilineal theories of cultural evolution. The logic used in this argument is thus circular: Why are there universals of cultural evolution? Because of the psychic unity of humankind. How do we know psychic unity is a valid concept? Because we see common patterns of cultural development.

In studying the condition of tribes and nations in these several ethnical periods we are dealing, substantially, with the ancient history and condition of our own remote ancestors.

Notes

a. Et pueros commendarunt mulierbreque saeclum
    Vocibus, et gestu, cum balbe significarent,
    Imbecillorum esse aequum miserier omnium.
    　　　　　　　—*De Rerum Natura*, lib. v, 1020.

b. Mr. Edwin B. Tylor observes that Goquet "first propounded, in the last century, the notion that the way in which pottery came to be made, was that people daubed such combustible vessels as these with clay to protect them from fire, till they found that clay alone would answer the purpose, and thus the art of pottery came into the world."—*Early History of Mankind*, p. 237. Goquet relates of Capt. Gonneville who visited the southeast coast of South America in 1503, that he found "their household utensils of wood, even their boiling pots, but plastered with a kind of clay, a good finger thick, which prevented the fire from burning them."—Ib. 273.

c. Pottery has been found in aboriginal mounds in Oregon within a few years past.—Foster's *Pre-Historic Races of the United States*, I, 152. The first vessels of pottery among the Aborigines of the United States seem to have been made in baskets of rushes or willows used as moulds which were burned off after the vessel hardened.—Jones's *Antiquities of Southern Indians*, p. 461. Prof. Rau's article on *Pottery. Smithsonian Report*, 1866, p. 352.

d. *Early History of Mankind*, p. 181; *Pre-Historic Times*, pp. 437, 441, 462, 477, 533, 542.

e. Lewis and Clarke (1805) found plank in use in houses among the tribes of the Columbia River.—*Travels*, Longman's Ed., 1814, p. 503. Mr. John Keast Lord found "cedar plank chipped from the solid tree with chisels and hatchets made of stone," in Indian houses on Vancouver's Island.—*Naturalist in British Columbia*, I, 169.

f. Tylor's *Early History of Mankind*, p. 265, *et seq.*

g. *Geological Survey of Indiana*, 1873, p. 119. He gives the following analysis:

Ancient Pottery, "Bone Bank," Posey Co., Indiana.

Moisture at 212°F.,	1.00	Alumina,	5.00
Silica,	36.00	Peroxide of iron,	5.50
Carbonate of lime,	25.50	Sulphuric acid,	.20
Carbonate of magnesia,	3.02	Organic matter (alkalies and loess),	23.60
			100.00

h. *History of the American Indians*, Lond. ed., 1775, p. 424. The Iroquois affirm that in ancient times their forefathers cured their pottery before a fire.

4. Feuerbach: Opposition of the Materialist and Idealist Outlook

Karl Marx (1818–1883) and Friedrich Engels (1820–1895)

THE ILLUSIONS OF GERMAN IDEOLOGY

AS WE HEAR FROM GERMAN IDEOLOGISTS, Germany has in the last few years gone through an unparalleled revolution.[1] The decomposition of the Hegelian philosophy, which began with Strauss, has developed into a universal ferment into which all the "powers of the past" are swept. In the general chaos mighty empires have arisen only to meet with immediate doom, heroes have emerged momentarily only to be hurled back into obscurity by bolder and stronger rivals. It was a revolution beside which the French Revolution was child's play, a world struggle beside which the struggles of the Diadochi [successors of Alexander the Great] appear insignificant. Principles ousted one another, heroes of the mind overthrew each other with unheard-of rapidity, and in the three years 1842–45 more of the past was swept away in Germany than at other times in three centuries.

All this is supposed to have taken place in the realm of pure thought.

Certainly it is an interesting event we are dealing with: the putrescence of the absolute spirit. When the last spark of its life had failed, the various components of this *caput mortuum*[2] began to decompose, entered into new combina-

From *The German Ideology* (1845–1846)

tions and formed new substances. The industrialists of philosophy, who till then had lived on the exploitation of the absolute spirit, now seized upon the new combinations. Each with all possible zeal set about retailing his apportioned share. This naturally gave rise to competition, which, to start with, was carried on in moderately staid bourgeois fashion. Later when the German market was glutted, and the commodity in spite of all efforts found no response in the world market, the business was spoiled in the usual German manner by fabricated and fictitious production, deterioration in quality, adulteration of the raw materials, falsification of labels, fictitious purchases, bill-jobbing and a credit system devoid of any real basis. The competition turned into a bitter struggle, which is now being extolled and interpreted to us as a revolution of world significance, the begetter of the most prodigious results and achievements.

If we wish to rate at its true value this philosophic charlatanry, which awakens even in the breast of the honest German citizen a glow of national pride, if we wish to bring out clearly the pettiness, the parochial narrowness of this whole Young-Hegelian movement and in particular the tragicomic contrast between the illusions of these heroes about their achievements and the actual achievements themselves, we must look at the whole spectacle from a standpoint beyond the frontiers of Germany.

---

[1] Marx and Engels, living in exile in Belgium, collaborated on *The German Ideology* in 1845 and 1846. They sent the manuscript to Germany for publication, but political crises prevented it from appearing. Marx later remarked that it had been abandoned to "the gnawing criticism of the mice." At the time *The German Ideology* was written, Marx and Engels were developing a thoroughly materialist worldview, which separated them from other German philosophers. This work is the first relatively complete statement of this worldview, although the materialist position it presents is foreshadowed in works like "On the Jewish Question" (1963, orig. 1844) and "The Holy Family" (1975, orig. 1845). The complete version of *The German Ideology* was not available until the 1930s. Thus, while European and American theorists of the early twentieth century were profoundly affected by Marx, they did not have this particular work.

[2] *Caput mortuum:* Latin for the head of death.

German criticism has, right up to its latest efforts, never quitted the realm of philosophy. Far from examining its general philosophic premises, the whole body of its inquiries has actually sprung from the soil of a definite philosophical system, that of Hegel.[3] Not only in their answers but in their very questions there was a mystification. This dependence on Hegel is the reason why not one of these modern critics has even attempted a comprehensive criticism of the Hegelian system, however much each professes to have advanced beyond Hegel. Their polemics against Hegel and against one another are confined to this — each extracts one side of the Hegelian system and turns this against the whole system as well as against the sides extracted by the others. To begin with they extracted pure unfalsified Hegelian categories such as "substance" and "self-consciousness," later they desecrated these categories with more secular names such as "species," "the Unique," "Man," etc.

The entire body of German philosophical criticism from Strauss to Stirner is confined to criticism of *religious* conceptions. The critics started from real religion and actual theology. What religious consciousness and a religious conception really meant was determined variously as they went along. Their advance consisted in subsuming the allegedly dominant metaphysical, political, juridical, moral and other conceptions under the class of religious or theological conceptions; and similarly in pronouncing political, juridical, moral consciousness as religious or theological, and the political, juridical, moral man — "*man*" in the last resort — as religious. The dominance of religion was taken for granted. Gradually every dominant relationship was pronounced a religious relationship and transformed into a cult, a cult of law, a cult of the State, etc. On all sides it was only a question of dogmas and belief in dogmas. The world sanctified to an ever-increasing extent till at last our venerable Saint Max was able to canonize it *en bloc* and thus dispose of it once for all.[4]

The Old Hegelians had *comprehended* everything as soon as it was reduced to an Hegelian category. The Young Hegelians *criticized* everything by attributing to it religious conceptions or by pronouncing it a theological matter. The Young Hegelians are in agreement with the Old Hegelians in their belief in the rule of religion, of concepts, of a universal principle in the existing world. Only, the one party attacks this dominion as usurpation, while the other extols it as legitimate.

Since the Young Hegelians consider conceptions, thoughts, ideas, in fact all the products of consciousness, to which they attribute an independent existence, as the real chains of men (just

---

[3] Marx, like all German philosophers of the nineteenth century, was profoundly influenced by the work of Georg Wilhelm Friedrich Hegel. Hegel was, among other things, concerned with the relationship of individuals to the state. He saw this as a spiritual process of historical development, fueled by dialectical contradiction and culminating in absolute freedom. He believed this freedom was possible under the Prussian monarchy (which, incidentally, employed him). After Hegel's death, his followers split into two camps: the Right Hegelians and the Young Hegelians. The Right Hegelians stayed very close to Hegel's teaching. The Young Hegelians, with whom Marx associated as a young man, held on to Hegel's ideas of historical progress through contradiction, but rejected the notion that freedom was possible under existing forms of the state. They supported political programs varying from liberal democracy to anarchism.

[4] Much of *The German Ideology* is a critique of the Young Hegelians from the left. Marx and Engels open with a biting sarcastic attack on them. David Friedrich Strauss (1808–1874) was an early Young Hegelian. His *Life of Jesus* (1892) held that the gospels were not literally true, but myths about early Christians. The anarchist Max Stirner (1806–1856, born Kaspar Schmidt), ridiculed here as Saint Max, bears the brunt of Marx and Engels' attack. Stirner's influential book, *The Ego and Its Own* (1918), had been published in 1844. In it, Stirner attacks Marx and Engels and calls for a thoroughly idealistic approach to changing the state — he argues that we can change society by changing our ideas about it. For Stirner, oppression and alienation are created through ideas that people accept as holy or sacred (hence Marx and Engels' epithets "holy" and "Saint"); freedom, on the other hand, originates through the ego's creation of its own ideas. Thus people can think their way into a new society, freeing themselves from the oppressive state. For Marx and Engels, this was anathema. They believed that freedom from oppression could only be achieved through changes in the material bases of society.

as the Old Hegelians declared them the true bonds of human society) it is evident that the Young Hegelians have to fight only against these illusions of consciousness.[5] Since, according to their fantasy, the relationships of men, all their doings, their chains and their limitations are products of their consciousness, the Young Hegelians logically put to men the moral postulate of exchanging their present consciousness for human, critical or egoistic consciousness, and thus of removing their limitations. This demand to change consciousness amounts to a demand to interpret reality in another way, i.e. to recognize it by means of another interpretation. The Young-Hegelian ideologists, in spite of their allegedly "world-shattering" statements, are the staunchest conservatives. The most recent of them have found the correct expression for their activity when they declare they are only fighting against *"phrases"*. They forget, however, that to these phrases they themselves are only opposing other phrases, and that they are in no way combating the real existing world when they are merely combating the phrases of this world. The only results which this philosophic criticism could achieve were a few (and at that thoroughly one-sided) elucidations of Christianity from the point of view of religious history;—all the rest of their assertions are only further embellishments of their claim to have furnished, in these unimportant elucidations, discoveries of universal importance.

It has not occurred to any one of these philosophers to inquire into the connection of German philosophy with German reality, the relation of their criticism to their own material surroundings.

FIRST PREMISES OF MATERIALIST METHOD

The premises from which we begin are not arbitrary ones, not dogmas, but real premises from which abstraction can only be made in the imagination.[6] They are the real individuals, their activity and the material conditions under which they live, both those which they find already existing and those produced by their activity. These premises can thus be verified in a purely empirical way.

The first premise of all human history is, of course, the existence of living human individuals. Thus the first fact to be established is the physical organization of these individuals and their consequent relation to the rest of nature. Of course, we cannot here go either into the actual physical nature of man, or into the natural conditions in which man finds himself—geological, oreohydrographical, climatic and so on. The writing of history must always set out from these natural bases and their modification in the course of history through the action of men.

Men can be distinguished from animals by consciousness, by religion or anything else you like. They themselves begin to distinguish themselves from animals as soon as they begin to *produce* their means of subsistence, a step which is conditioned by their physical organization. By producing their means of subsistence men are indirectly producing their actual material life.[7]

The way in which men produce their means of subsistence depends first of all on the nature of the actual means of subsistence they find in existence

---

[5] Much of the controversy over Hegelian philosophy concerned the place of religion within it, but religion was largely a surrogate for discussing politics and the state, taboo subjects for debate within Germany. Marx and Engels were living in Belgium at this time and so could speak a bit more openly about German politics.

[6] For Hegel, and most of the Right and Young Hegelians, the world was conditioned by ideas, and history was about the progress of the human spirit. For Marx, human society was based in particular material conditions, and history was driven by conflicts at the core of society. This is the root of Marx and Engels' disagreements with Hegelians. Here and in following paragraphs they lay out a materialist understanding of the world, beginning with real people and the conditions under which they live.

[7] The argument in this paragraph is basic to the Marx-Engels view: the thing that fundamentally distinguishes humans from animals is the manner in which they produce their livelihood, that is, labor. Other characteristics unique to humans are derived from labor.

and have to reproduce. This mode of production must not be considered simply as being the production of the physical existence of the individuals. Rather it is a definite form of activity of these individuals, a definite form of expressing their life, a definite *mode of life* on their part. As individuals express their life, so they are. What they are, therefore, coincides with their production, both with *what* they produce and with *how* they produce. The nature of individuals thus depends on the material conditions determining their production.[8]

This production only makes its appearance with the *increase of population*. In its turn this presupposes the *intercourse* of individuals with one another. The form of this intercourse is again determined by production.

The relations of different nations among themselves depend upon the extent to which each has developed its productive forces, the division of labour and internal intercourse. This statement is generally recognized. But not only the relation of one nation to others, but also the whole internal structure of the nation itself depends on the stage of development reached by its production and its internal and external intercourse. How far the productive forces of a nation are developed is shown most manifestly by the degree to which the division of labour has been carried. Each new productive force, insofar as it is not merely a quantitative extension of productive forces already known (for instance the bringing into cultivation of fresh land), causes a further development of the division of labour.[9]

The division of labour inside a nation leads at first to the separation of industrial and commercial from agricultural labour, and hence to the separation of *town* and *country* and to the conflict of their interests.[10] Its further development leads to the separation of commercial from industrial labour. At the same time through the division of labour inside these various branches there develop various divisions among the individuals co-operating in definite kinds of labour. The relative position of these individual groups is determined by the methods employed in agriculture, industry and commerce (patriarchalism, slavery, estates, classes). These same conditions are to be seen (given a more developed intercourse) in the relations of different nations to one another.

The various stages of development in the division of labour are just so many different forms of ownership, i.e. the existing stage in the division of labour determines also the relations of individuals to one another with reference to the material, instrument, and product of labour.[11]

The first form of ownership is tribal ownership. It corresponds to the undeveloped stage of production, at which a people lives by hunting and fishing, by the rearing of beasts or, in the highest stage, agriculture. In the latter case it presupposes a great mass of uncultivated stretches of land. The division of labour is at this stage still very elementary and is confined to a further ex-

---

[8] Here Marx and Engels pursue the importance of labor further: production is more than simply feeding oneself; through labor people create their society. Since human nature is determined by the social conditions under which people live, humans, through labor, create their own nature.

[9] Like the Hegelians, Marx and Engels believed that history had a beginning and an end. It followed a specific, scientifically knowable path. For Marx, this path was tied to modes of production and the necessary forms of property associated with each of them. These follow each other in a historically specific order. Changes in human consciousness are part of this historical progression. There can be no experience of transcendental human nature before the end of history and the emergence of a communist society.

[10] This is a critical passage. The developments Marx and Engels outline here are reminiscent of both Adam Smith's work on the division of labor and Herbert Spencer's ideas about the organic growth of societies, but with a key difference. Smith and Spencer saw the division of labor as leading to the achievement of the greatest good for the greatest number. Marx and Engels focus instead on the conflicts and oppression it generates. For them, these conflicts are critical to social development.

[11] The interplay between technology and the social relationships through which technology is put to work is central to Marx and Engels' theory. The idea of ownership is key to this. In these paragraphs, the authors describe history as a progression of different forms of ownership and, hence, different modes of production.

tension of the natural division of labour existing in the family. The social structure is, therefore, limited to an extension of the family; patriarchal family chieftains, below them the members of the tribe, finally slaves. The slavery latent in the family only develops gradually with the increase of population, the growth of wants, and with the extension of external relations, both of war and of barter.[12]

The second form is the ancient communal and State ownership which proceeds especially from the union of several tribes into a *city* by agreement or by conquest, and which is still accompanied by slavery. Beside communal ownership we already find movable, and later also immovable, private property developing, but as an abnormal form subordinate to communal ownership. The citizens hold power over their labouring slaves only in their community, and on this account alone, therefore, they are bound to the form of communal ownership. It is the communal private property which compels the active citizens to remain in this spontaneously derived form of association over against their slaves. For this reason the whole structure of society based on this communal ownership, and with it the power of the people, decays in the same measure as, in particular, immovable private property evolves. The division of labour is already more developed. We already find the antagonism of town and country; later the antagonism between those states which represent town interests and those which represent country interests, and inside the towns themselves the antagonism between industry and maritime commerce. The class relation between citizens and slaves is now completely developed.[13]

With the development of private property, we find here for the first time the same conditions which we shall find again, only on a more extensive scale, with modern private property. On the one hand, the concentration of private property, which began very early in Rome (as the Licinian agrarian law[14] proves) and proceeded very rapidly from the time of the civil wars and especially under the Emperors; on the other hand, coupled with this, the transformation of the plebeian small peasantry into a proletariat, which, however, owing to its intermediate position between propertied citizens and slaves, never achieved an independent development.

The third form of ownership is feudal or estate property. If antiquity started out from the *town* and its little territory, the Middle Ages started out from the *country*. This different starting-point was determined by the sparseness of the population at that time, which was scattered over a large area and which received no large increase from the conquerors. In contrast to Greece and Rome, feudal development at the outset, therefore, extends over a much wider territory, prepared by the Roman conquests and the spread of agriculture at first associated with it. The last centuries of the declining Roman Empire and its conquest by the barbarians destroyed a number of productive forces; agriculture had declined, industry had decayed for want of a market, trade had died out or been violently suspended, the rural and urban population had decreased. From these conditions and the mode of organization of the conquest determined by them, feudal property developed under the influence of the Germanic military constitution. Like tribal and communal ownership, it is based again on a community; but the directly producing class standing over against it is not, as in the case of the ancient community,

---

[12] Marx and Engels have stated that humans produce their own nature through labor. However, in this passage they ground their analysis in a claim about the "natural division of labour existing in the family." These assertions seem to contradict each other. Note that Marx and Engels envision the "natural" family as consisting of a patriarch who controls the members of his tribe. While a powerful male head of the household was a feature of European society of their time, it is hardly a universal aspect of primitive societies. Additionally, Marx and Engels cite no evidence to support their understanding of the family. They were aware of this problem, but almost thirty years would pass before the publication of Morgan's *Ancient Society* in 1877, which they believed resolved this issue.

[13] One of Marx and Engels' critical ideas is that history is driven by dialectical conflict. Notice the emphasis on conflict and antagonism in this outline of history. This paragraph describes the conflict between the communal action required to control slaves and private ownership of immovable property such as land.

[14] The Licinian law (367 B.C.E.) limited the amount of common land a Roman citizen could hold to about 300 acres.

the slaves, but the enserfed small peasantry. As soon as feudalism is fully developed, there also arises antagonism to the towns. The hierarchical structure of landownership, and the armed bodies of retainers associated with it, gave the nobility power over the serfs. This feudal organization was, just as much as the ancient communal ownership, an association against a subjected producing class; but the form of association and the relation to the direct producers were different because of the different conditions of production.[15]

This feudal system of landownership had its counterpart in the *towns* in the shape of corporative property, the feudal organization of trades. Here property consisted chiefly in the labour of each individual person. The necessity for association against the organized robber nobility, the need for communal covered markets in an age when the industrialist was at the same time a merchant, the growing competition of the escaped serfs swarming into the rising towns, the feudal structure of the whole country: these combined to bring about the *guilds*. The gradually accumulated small capital of individual craftsmen and their stable numbers, as against the growing population, evolved the relation of journeyman and apprentice, which brought into being in the towns a hierarchy similar to that in the country.[16]

Thus the chief form of property during the feudal epoch consisted on the one hand of landed property with serf labour chained to it, and on the other of the labour of the individual with small capital commanding the labour of journeymen.

The organization of both was determined by the restricted conditions of production—the small-scale and primitive cultivation of the land, and the craft type of industry.[17] There was little division of labour in the heyday of feudalism. Each country bore in itself the antithesis of town and country; the division into estates was certainly strongly marked; but apart from the differentiation of princes, nobility, clergy and peasants in the country, and masters, journeymen, apprentices and soon also the rabble of casual labourers in the towns, no division of importance took place. In agriculture it was rendered difficult by the strip-system, beside which the cottage industry of the peasants themselves emerged. In industry there was no division of labour at all in the individual trades themselves, and very little between them. The separation of industry and commerce was found already in existence in older towns; in the newer it only developed later, when the towns entered into mutual relations.

The grouping of larger territories into feudal kingdoms was a necessity for the landed nobility as for the towns. The organization of the ruling class, the nobility, had, therefore, everywhere a monarch at its head.

The fact is, therefore, that definite individuals who are productively active in a definite way enter into these definite social and political relations.[18] Empirical observation must in each separate instance bring out empirically, and without any mystification and speculation, the connection of the social and political structure with produc-

---

[15] In Marx and Engels' view, feudal ownership derived from the material conditions of the end of the Roman empire, in particular the collapse of the Roman economy. Both feudalism and the ancient society that preceded it involved the oppression of those who produced. The differences between these societies resulted from their use of different types of production technology. Once again social form is vitally influenced by production.

[16] Guilds are created as a result of purely material processes. They recapitulate, in the town, the social organization of the countryside. Notice that Marx and Engels understood property as including both material goods and labor. The idea of labor as a commodity that can be bought and sold is crucial to their later analysis of capitalism.

[17] Marx and Engels give priority to the conditions of production in determining society. It is, however, important to distinguish this from ecological determinism. The processes that Marx and Engels list as restricting production are all created by human agency rather than ecological necessity. Production is a human activity.

[18] The next several paragraphs contain a very direct statement of Marx's materialist philosophy. The emphasis is on observable relations and processes. Notice that Marx and Engels make no effort here to document the relationships among social and political structure and production. Much of Marx's later work was devoted to this task of documentation, particularly *Das Kapital,* the first volume of which appeared in 1867.

tion. The social structure and the State are continually evolving out of the life-process of definite individuals, but of individuals, not as they may appear in their own or other people's imagination, but as they *really* are; i.e. as they operate, produce materially, and hence as they work under definite material limits, presuppositions and conditions independent of their will.

The production of ideas, of conceptions, of consciousness, is at first directly interwoven with the material activity and the material intercourse of men, the language of real life. Conceiving, thinking, the mental intercourse of men, appear at this stage as the direct efflux of their material behaviour. The same applies to mental production as expressed in the language of politics, laws, morality, religion, metaphysics, etc. of a people. Men are the producers of their conceptions, ideas, etc. — real, active men, as they are conditioned by a definite development of their productive forces and of the intercourse corresponding to these, up to its furthest forms. Consciousness can never be anything else than conscious existence, and the existence of men is their actual life-process. If in all ideology men and their circumstances appear upside-down as in a *camera obscura*, this phenomenon arises just as much from their historical life-process as the inversion of objects on the retina does from their physical life-process.[19]

In direct contrast to German philosophy which descends from heaven to earth, here we ascend from earth to heaven.[20] That is to say, we do not set out from what men say, imagine, conceive, nor from men as narrated, thought of, imagined, conceived, in order to arrive at men in the flesh. We set out from real, active men, and on the basis of their real life-process we demonstrate the development of the ideological reflexes and echoes of this life-process. The phantoms formed in the human brain are also, necessarily, sublimates of their material life-process, which is empirically verifiable and bound to material premises. Morality, religion, metaphysics, all the rest of ideology and their corresponding forms of consciousness, thus no longer retain the semblance of independence. They have no history, no development; but men, developing their material production and their material intercourse, alter, along with this their real existence, their thinking and the products of their thinking. Life is not determined by consciousness, but consciousness by life. In the first method of approach the starting-point is consciousness taken as the living individual; in the second method, which conforms to real life, it is the real living individuals themselves, and consciousness is considered solely as *their* consciousness.

This method of approach is not devoid of premises.[21] It starts out from the real premises and does not abandon them for a moment. Its premises are men, not in any fantastic isolation and rigidity, but in their actual, empirically perceptible process of development under definite conditions. As soon as this active life-process is described, history ceases to be a collection of dead facts as it is with the empiricists (themselves still abstract), or an imagined activity of imagined subjects, as with the idealists.

Where speculation ends — in real life — there real, positive science begins: the representation of the practical activity, of the practical process of

---

[19] To Marx and Engels, ideas, the currency of the Young Hegelians, cannot by themselves have explanatory value. They claim that human thinking is conditioned by the social relations under which people live, which can only be understood with reference to material processes. For example, the fact that ideas in nineteenth-century Germany seemed to have power of their own cannot be understood apart from the social relations of that era.

[20] In this critical passage, Marx and Engels explain their reversal of Hegelian philosophy. Where Hegelian philosophy gave the driving force of history to the realm of pure thought, Marx and Engels assigned it to the material processes of production. In his critical 1974 article "Marxism, Structuralism, and Vulgar Materialism," Jonathan Friedman stresses the importance of understanding this passage. He points out that Marx and Engels are not promoting simple materialist determinism (which, following Marx, he calls vulgar materialism) but dialectical materialism, a process of change driven by opposition and contradiction.

[21] One such premise is outlined here: humans, by altering the material conditions of their lives, alter their consciousness.

development of men.[22] Empty talk about consciousness ceases, and real knowledge has to take its place. When reality is depicted, philosophy as an independent branch of knowledge loses its medium of existence. At the best its place can only be taken by a summing-up of the most general results, abstractions which arise from the observation of the historical development of men. Viewed apart from real history, these abstractions have in themselves no value whatsoever. They can only serve to facilitate the arrangement of historical material, to indicate the sequence of its separate strata. But they by no means afford a recipe or schema, as does philosophy, for neatly trimming the epochs of history. On the contrary, our difficulties begin only when we set about the observation and the arrangement—the real depiction—of our historical material, whether of a past epoch or of the present. The removal of these difficulties is governed by premises which it is quite impossible to state here, but which only the study of the actual life-process and the activity of the individuals of each epoch will make evident. We shall select here some of these abstractions, which we use in contradistinction to the ideologists, and shall illustrate them by historical example.

HISTORY: FUNDAMENTAL CONDITIONS

Since we are dealing with the Germans, who are devoid of premises, we must begin by stating the first premise of all human existence and, therefore, of all history, the premise, namely, that men must be in a position to live in order to be able to "make history." But life involves before everything else eating and drinking, a habitation, clothing and many other things. The first historical act is thus the production of the means to satisfy these needs, the production of material life itself. And indeed this is an historical act, a fundamental condition of all history, which today, as thousands of years ago, must daily and hourly be fulfilled merely in order to sustain human life. Even when the sensuous world is reduced to a minimum, to a stick as with Saint Bruno, it presupposes the action of producing the stick.[23] Therefore in any interpretation of history one has first of all to observe this fundamental fact in all its significance and all its implications and to accord it its due importance. It is well known that the Germans have never done this, and they have never, therefore, had an *earthly* basis for history and consequently never an historian. The French and the English, even if they have conceived the relation of this fact with so-called history only in an extremely one-sided fashion, particularly as long as they remained in the toils of political ideology, have nevertheless made the first attempts to give the writing of history a materialistic basis by being the first to write histories of civil society, of commerce and industry.[24]

The second point is that the satisfaction of the first need (the action of satisfying, and the instrument of satisfaction which has been acquired) leads to new needs; and this production of new needs is the first historical act. Here we recognize

---

[22] Notice the emphasis throughout this portion of the text on empiricism and science. Marx and Engels considered their theory to be scientific in the same sense as the physical sciences. They believed that philosophy, in the future, would be replaced by science. Marx devoted much of his later life to writing *Das Kapital,* in which he attempted to use his materialist perspective to explain specific historical developments.

[23] Marx and Engels open this section with yet another biting satirical attack on the Young Hegelians, particularly Bruno Bauer (their "Saint Bruno"). Bauer, one of Marx's colleagues in Berlin in the early 1840s, wrote the three-volume *Critique of the Evangelical Gospels* (1841–1842). Marx and Engels' style is important. Their mixture of name calling, satirical intellectual humor, polemic, and hyperbole set the tone for much of later writing by Marxists. Their indulgence in these tactics marginalized Marxists within academic discourse. This hyperbole may have been useful for political propaganda, but it made their work easy for others to dismiss.

[24] Marx and Engels claim Germans never had historians because they have relied on spiritual rather than material explanations. History is created by people producing the material goods of subsistence and (in the next paragraph) by the social production of new needs.

immediately the spiritual ancestry of the great historical wisdom of the Germans who, when they run out of positive material and when they can serve up neither theological nor political nor literary rubbish, assert that this is not history at all, but the "prehistoric era." They do not, however, enlighten us as to how we proceed from this non-sensical "prehistory" to history proper; although, on the other hand, in their historical speculation they seize upon this "prehistory" with especial eagerness because they imagine themselves safe there from interference on the part of "crude facts," and, at the same time, because there they can give full rein to their speculative impulse and set up and knock down hypotheses by the thousand.

The third circumstance which, from the very outset, enters into historical development, is that men, who daily remake their own life, begin to make other men, to propagate their kind: the relation between man and woman, parents and children, the *family*.[25] The family, which to begin with is the only social relationship, becomes later, when increased needs create new social relations and the increased population new needs, a subordinate one (excepting Germany), and must then be treated and analyzed according to the existing empirical data, not according to "the concept of the family," as is the custom in Germany.[a] These three aspects of social activity are not of course to be taken as three different stages, but just as three aspects or, to make it clear to the Germans, three "moments," which have existed simultaneously since the dawn of history and the first men, and which still assert themselves in history today.

The production of life, both of one's own in labour and of fresh life in procreation, now appears as a double relationship: on the one hand as a natural, on the other as a social relationship.[26] By social we understand the co-operation of several individuals, no matter under what conditions, in what manner and to what end. It follows from this that a certain mode of production, or industrial stage, is always combined with a certain mode of co-operation, or social stage, and this mode of co-operation is itself a "productive force." Further, that the multitude of productive forces accessible to men determines the nature of society, hence, that the "history of humanity" must always be studied and treated in relation to the history of industry and exchange. But it is also clear how in Germany it is impossible to write this sort of history, because the Germans lack not only the necessary power of comprehension and the material but also the "evidence of their senses," for across the Rhine you cannot have any experience of these things since history has stopped happening.[27] Thus it is quite obvious from the start that there exists a materialistic connection of men with one another, which is determined by their needs and their mode of production, and which is as old as men themselves. This connection is ever taking on new forms, and thus presents a "history" independently of the existence of any political or religious nonsense which in addition may hold men together.[28]

Only now, after having considered four moments, four aspects of the primary historical relationships, do we find that man also possesses "consciousness," but, even so, not inherent, not "pure" consciousness. From the start the "spirit" is afflicted with the curse of being "burdened" with matter, which here makes its appearance in the form of agitated layers of air, sounds, in short, of

---

[25] Here Marx and Engels turn from production to the reproduction of society. They understood reproduction as including both the biological process of human reproduction and the reproduction of social forms through time. Just as people must produce to live, societies must reproduce themselves to survive.

[26] Social forms are created by the interaction of the way in which people produce and the way in which they arrange themselves to reproduce their society. Of these, however, production is more important.

[27] In the "across the Rhine" passage, Marx and Engels attack the Hegelians who believed that history had achieved its culmination with the Prussian monarchy.

[28] A key Marxist doctrine – one later adopted by structural anthropologists – is that the real forces that drive society are hidden from view. For Marxists, specific forms of religion or politics are merely the surface appearances of the deeper forces of production and reproduction. These forces are visible only through Marxist analysis.

language. Language is as old as consciousness, language *is* practical consciousness that exists also for other men, and for that reason alone it really exists for me personally as well; language, like consciousness, only arises from the need, the necessity, of intercourse with other men. Where there exists a relationship, it exists for me: the animal does not enter into *"relations"* with anything, it does not enter into any relation at all. For the animal, its relation to others does not exist as a relation. Consciousness is, therefore, from the very beginning a social product, and remains so as long as men exist at all.[29] Consciousness is at first, of course, merely consciousness concerning the *immediate* sensuous environment and consciousness of the limited connection with other persons and things outside the individual who is growing self-conscious. At the same time it is consciousness of nature, which first appears to men as a completely alien, all-powerful and unassailable force, with which men's relations are purely animal and by which they are overawed like beasts; it is thus a purely animal consciousness of nature (natural religion) just because nature is as yet hardly modified historically. (We see here immediately: this natural religion or this particular relation of men to nature is determined by the form of society and vice versa. Here, as everywhere, the identity of nature and man appears in such a way that the restricted relation of men to nature determines their restricted relation to one another, and their restricted relation to one another determines men's restricted relation to nature.) On the other hand, man's consciousness of the necessity of associating with the individuals around him is the beginning of the consciousness that he is living in society at all.[30] This beginning is as animal as social life itself at this stage. It is mere herd-consciousness, and at this point man is only distinguished from sheep by the fact that with him consciousness takes the place of instinct or that his instinct is a conscious one. This sheep-like or tribal consciousness receives its further development and extension through increased productivity, the increase of needs, and, what is fundamental to both of these, the increase of population. With these there develops the division of labour, which was originally nothing but the division of labour in the sexual act, then that division of labour which develops spontaneously or "naturally" by virtue of natural predisposition (e.g. physical strength), needs, accidents, etc. etc. Division of labour only becomes truly such from the moment when a division of material and mental labour appears. (The first form of ideologists, *priests,* is concurrent.) From this moment onwards consciousness *can* really flatter itself that it is something other than consciousness of existing practice, that it *really* represents something without representing something real; from now on consciousness is in a position to emancipate itself from the world and to proceed to the formation of "pure" theory, theology, philosophy, ethics, etc. But even if this theory, theology, philosophy, ethics, etc. comes into contradiction with the existing relations, this can only occur because existing social relations have come into contradiction with existing forces of production; this, moreover, can also occur in a particular national sphere of relations through the appearance of the contradiction, not within the national orbit, but between this national consciousness and the practice of other nations, i.e. between the national and the general consciousness of a nation (as we see it now in Germany).

---

[29] Most other nineteenth-century anthropological writers, perhaps taking their cue from Locke, think of the human mind as evolving through some universal unfolding of natural law. Marx, on the other hand, saw the mind as conditioned by social institutions and claimed there was no such thing as human thought apart from the institutions within which humans do their thinking. However, he did not extend this idea to his own work, maintaining his belief in the truth-generating capacities of science.

[30] Particular forms of consciousness arise from specific social arrangements, not vice versa. Cultural ecologists and cultural materialists of the mid and late twentieth century will use this key insight (see essays 18 to 24). According to Marx and Engels, the development of consciousness that is distinctly human is dependent on increased population and division of labor. The implication is that the most "primitive" human groups have consciousness that is virtually indistinguishable from that of animals.

Moreover, it is quite immaterial what consciousness starts to do on its own: out of all such muck we get only the one inference that these three moments, the forces of production, the state of society, and consciousness, can and must come into contradiction with one another, because the *division of labour* implies the possibility, nay the fact that intellectual and material activity—enjoyment and labour, production and consumption—devolve on different individuals, and that the only possibility of their not coming into contradiction lies in the negation in its turn of the division of labour.[31] It is self-evident, moreover, that "specters," "bonds," "the higher being," "concept," "scruple," are merely the idealistic, spiritual expression, the conception apparently of the isolated individual, the image of very empirical fetters and limitations, within which the mode of production of life and the form of intercourse coupled with it move.

PRIVATE PROPERTY AND COMMUNISM

With the division of labour, in which all these contradictions are implicit, and which in its turn is based on the natural division of labour in the family and the separation of society into individual families opposed to one another, is given simultaneously the *distribution,* and indeed the *unequal* distribution, both quantitative and qualitative, of labour and its products, hence property: the nucleus, the first form, of which lies in the family, where wife and children are the slaves of the husband.[32] This latent slavery in the family, though still very crude, is the first property, but even at this early stage it corresponds per-

fectly to the definition of modern economists who call it the power of disposing of the labour-power of others. Division of labour and private property are, moreover, identical expressions: in the one the same thing is affirmed with reference to activity as is affirmed in the other with reference to the product of the activity.

Further, the division of labour implies the contradiction between the interest of the separate individual or the individual family and the communal interest of all individuals who have intercourse with one another. And indeed, this communal interest does not exist merely in the imagination, as the "general interest," but first of all in reality, as the mutual interdependence of the individuals among whom the labour is divided. And finally, the division of labour offers us the first example of how, as long as man remains in natural society, that is, as long as a cleavage exists between the particular and the common interest, as long, therefore, as activity is not voluntarily, but naturally, divided, man's own deed becomes an alien power opposed to him, which enslaves him instead of being controlled by him.[33] For as soon as the distribution of labour comes into being, each man has a particular, exclusive sphere of activity, which is forced upon him and from which he cannot escape. He is a hunter, a fisherman, a shepherd, or a critical critic, and must remain so if he does not want to lose his means of livelihood; while in communist society, where nobody has one exclusive sphere of activity but each can become accomplished in any branch he wishes, society regulates the general production and thus makes it possible for me to do one thing today and another tomorrow, to hunt in the morning, fish in the afternoon, rear

---

[31] With the appearance of human society and division of labor, comes dialectical conflict. For Marx and Engels, this is the fundamental driving force of history.

[32] Notice the concern with gender and the subjugation of women and children present in this paragraph. Because it was a good tool for analyzing relations of inequality between genders, Marxism proved appealing to many feminist scholars. See Eleanor Leacock's essay (33) in this volume for an example of Marxist-feminist scholarship.

[33] Division of labor makes society possible, but it also destroys freedom and creates alienation. Alienation or estrangement, a key Marxist concept, refers to the separation of the individual from either the preconditions or the products of labor, or, in this case, from life's necessities. Alienation was understood by Marx and Engels as antithetical to freedom. Specialization in one activity creates alienation in all others. They believed utopian communist society would end contradiction between the individual and the forces of production and hence, end alienation.

cattle in the evening, criticize after dinner, just as I have a mind, without ever becoming hunter, fisherman, shepherd or critic. This fixation of social activity, this consolidation of what we ourselves produce into an objective power above us, growing out of our control, thwarting our expectations, bringing to naught our calculations, is one of the chief factors in historical development up till now.[34]

(And out of this very contradiction between the interest of the individual and that of the community the latter takes an independent form as the *State*, divorced from the real interests of individual and community, and at the same time as an illusory communal life, always based, however, on the real ties existing in every family and tribal conglomeration—such as flesh and blood, language, division of labour on a larger scale, and other interests—and especially, as we shall enlarge upon later, on the classes, already determined by the division of labour, which in every such mass of men separate out, and of which one dominates all the others.[35] It follows from this that all struggles within the State, the struggle between democracy, aristocracy, and monarchy, the struggle for the franchise, etc. etc. are merely the illusory forms in which the real struggles of the different classes are fought out among one another. Of this the German theoreticians have not the faintest inkling, although they have received a sufficient introduction to the subject in the *Deutsch-Französische Jahrbücher* and *Die Heilige Familie*.[36] Further, it follows that every class which is struggling for mastery, even when its

domination, as is the case with the proletariat, postulates the abolition of the old form of society in its entirety and of domination itself, must first conquer for itself political power in order to represent its interest in turn as the general interest, which immediately it is forced to do. Just because individuals seek *only* their particular interest, which for them does not coincide with their communal interest, the latter will be imposed on them as an interest "alien" to them, and "independent" of them, as in its turn a particular, peculiar "general" interest; or they themselves must remain within this discord, as in democracy. On the other hand, too, the *practical* struggle of these particular interests, which constantly *really* run counter to the communal and illusory communal interests, makes *practical* intervention and control necessary through the illusory "general" interest in the form of the State.)

The social power, i.e. the multiplied productive force, which arises through the co-operation of different individuals as it is determined by the division of labour, appears to these individuals, since their cooperation is not voluntary but has come about naturally, not as their own united power, but as an alien force existing outside them, of the origin and goal of which they are ignorant, which they thus cannot control, which on the contrary passes through a peculiar series of phases and stages independent of the will and the action of man, nay even being the prime governor of these.[37]

How otherwise could for instance property have had a history at all, have taken on different

---

[34] Marx and Engels claim that alienation is rooted in specialization and here envision a society in which people do not specialize in a single job. But can one be an engineer one day and a doctor the next? Marx and Engels' view of a society without alienation is utopian, but if specialization is an inevitable part of industrial society, their vision cannot be achieved.

[35] This paragraph is a marginal note to the paragraph above it in the original manuscript. Several important Marxist principles are laid out in it. First, all of history is ultimately the history of class struggle (the famous opening of the *Manifesto*, written two years later). Second, this class struggle is the hidden, underlying dynamic driving political and economic history. Third, the state is an instrument of control and oppression. However, seizing control of the state is a necessary step in changing society.

[36] *Deutsch-Französische Jahrbücher* (The German-French Annals, 1844) was a radical periodical edited by Marx and his friend Arnold Ruge. Only one issue of it appeared. *Die Heilige Familie (The Holy Family*, 1845) was Marx and Engels' first collaboration. It was a mocking, satirical attack on Bruno Bauer and other Young Hegelians.

[37] Marx and Engels argue here that even though people compose society, they are alienated from it. It seems as something external to them, when in fact, through their production, they create it. Communism will allow the people to break through this form of otherness.

forms, and landed property, for example, according to the different premises given, have proceeded in France from parcellation to centralization in the hands of a few, in England from centralization in the hands of a few to parcellation, as is actually the case today?[38] Or how does it happen that trade, which after all is nothing more than the exchange of products of various individuals and countries, rules the whole world through the relation of supply and demand—a relation which, as an English economist[39] says, hovers over the earth like the fate of the ancients, and with invisible hand allots fortune and misfortune to men, sets up empires and overthrows empires, causes nations to rise and to disappear—while with the abolition of the basis of private property, with the communistic regulation of production (and, implicit in this, the destruction of the alien relation between men and what they themselves produce), the power of the relation of supply and demand is dissolved into nothing, and men get exchange, production, the mode of their mutual relation, under their own control again?

In history up to the present it is certainly an empirical fact that separate individuals have, with the broadening of their activity into world-historical activity, become more and more enslaved under a power alien to them (a pressure which they have conceived of as a dirty trick on the part of the so-called universal spirit, etc.), a power which has become more and more enormous and, in the last instance, turns out to be the *world market*. But it is just as empirically established that, by the overthrow of the existing state of society by the communist revolution (of which more below)

and the abolition of private property which is identical with it, this power, which so baffles the German theoreticians, will be dissolved; and that then the liberation of each single individual will be accomplished in the measure in which history becomes transformed into world history. From the above it is clear that the real intellectual wealth of the individual depends entirely on the wealth of his real connections. Only then will the separate individuals be liberated from the various national and local barriers, be brought into practical connection with the material and intellectual production of the whole world and be put in a position to acquire the capacity to enjoy this all-sided production of the whole earth (the creations of man). *All-round* dependence, this natural form of the *world-historical* co-operation of individuals, will be transformed by this communist revolution into the control and conscious mastery of these powers, which, born of the action of men on one another, have till now overawed and governed men as powers completely alien to them. Now this view can be expressed again in speculative-idealistic, i.e. fantastic, terms as "self-generation of the species" ("society as the subject"), and thereby the consecutive series of interrelated individuals connected with each other can be conceived as a single individual, which accomplishes the mystery of generating itself. It is clear here that individuals certainly make *one another*, physically and mentally, but do not make themselves.[40]

This "alienation" (to use a term which will be comprehensible to the philosophers) can, of course, only be abolished given two *practical* premises. For it to become an "intolerable" power,

---

[38] Marx and Engels are very Hegelian in their approach to alienation. Hegel's philosophy dealt with the spirit's alienation from the world, and he viewed history as the process of dissolving this alienation. Marx and Engels here see a human structure—trade and the division of labor—as creating alienation, and communism as providing a way to break through the otherness thus engendered.

[39] Adam Smith.

[40] As Hegelians, Marx and Engels saw world history as following an inevitable path. Individual societies may have their own histories, but the destiny of the world was fixed, with communism the ultimate end of this path. Marx and Engels believed that communist revolution must be a worldwide event and that it must happen first in highly industrialized societies. Anything that increased worldwide productivity and industrialization would favor its appearance, hence their seemingly contradictory embrace of British colonialism.

At the time of *The German Ideology*, the authors believed that the preconditions for revolution had been met, and a communist society was imminent. They altered this belief after the failure of the European revolutions of 1848–1849, which convinced them that the changes they were witness to in Europe were the birth pangs of capitalism rather than its death throes. While they still believed that dialectical contradictions led history inevitably toward communist society, they i.e. a power against which men make a revolution, it must necessarily have rendered the great mass of humanity "propertyless," and produced, at the same time, the contradiction of an existing world of wealth and culture, both of which conditions presuppose a great increase in productive power, a high degree of its development. And, on the other hand, this development of productive forces (which itself implies the actual empirical existence of men in their *world-historical,* instead of local, being) is an absolutely necessary practical premise because without it *want* is merely made general, and with *destitution* the struggle for necessities and all the old filthy business would necessarily be reproduced; and furthermore, because only with this universal development of productive forces is a *universal* intercourse between men established, which produces in all nations simultaneously the phenomenon of the "propertyless" mass (universal competition), makes each nation dependent on the revolutions of the others, and finally has put *world-historical,* empirically universal individuals in place of local ones. Without this, (1) communism could only exist as a local event; (2) the *forces* of intercourse themselves could not have developed as *universal,* hence intolerable powers: they would have remained home-bred conditions surrounded by superstition; and (3) each extension of intercourse would abolish local communism. Empirically, communism is only possible as the act of the dominant peoples "all at once" and simultaneously, which presupposes the universal development of productive forces and the world intercourse bound up with communism. Moreover, the mass of *propertyless* workers — the utterly precarious position of labour-power on a mass scale cut off from capital or from even a limited satisfaction and, therefore, no longer merely temporarily deprived of work itself as a secure

source of life — presupposes the *world market* through competition. The proletariat can thus only exist *world-historically,* just as communism, its activity, can only have a "world-historical" existence. World historical existence of individuals means, existence of individuals which is directly linked up with world history.

Communism is for us not a *state of affairs* which is to be established, an *ideal* to which reality [will] have to adjust itself. We call communism the *real* movement which abolishes the present state of things. The conditions of this movement result from the premises now in existence.[41]

Notes

a. The building of houses. With savages each family has as a matter of course its own cave or hut like the separate family tent of the nomads. This separate domestic economy is made only the more necessary by the further development of private property. With the agricultural peoples a communal domestic economy is just as impossible as a communal cultivation of the soil. A great advance was the building of towns. In all previous periods, however, the abolition of individual economy, which is inseparable from the abolition of private property, was impossible for the simple reason that the material conditions governing it were not present. The setting-up of a communal domestic economy presupposes the development of machinery, of the use of natural forces and of many other productive forces — e.g., of water-supplies, of gas-lighting, steam-heating, etc., the removal [of the antagonism] of town and country. Without these conditions a communal economy would not in itself form a new productive force; lacking any material basis and resting on a purely theoretical foundation, it would be a mere freak and would end in nothing more than a monastic economy — What was possible can be seen in the towns brought about by condensation and the erection of communal buildings for various definite purposes (prisons, barracks, etc.). That the abolition of individual economy is inseparable from the abolition of the family is self-evident.

---

now saw this society as still distant. Much greater industrialization and internationalization of the economy would be needed. (This assumption set a conundrum for Marxists after the Russian Revolution: how could the communist revolution have occurred in one of Europe's most technologically backward societies?)

[41] While Marx and Engels believed that the communist revolution would be distant, they also believed that people could speed its arrival. Humans, through production, created their own society. Therefore, they and their followers hoped to use their understanding of the links between material production and the production of consciousness to take actions that would hasten the course of history.

5. The Return of Totemism in Childhood

Sigmund Freud (1856–1939)

THERE ARE NO GROUNDS FOR FEARING THAT psychoanalysis, which first discovered that psychical acts and structures are invariably overdetermined,* will be tempted to trace the origin of anything so complicated as religion to a single source.[1] If psycho-analysis is compelled—and is, indeed, in duty bound—to lay all the emphasis upon one particular source, that does not mean it is claiming either that that source is the only one or that it occupies first place among the numerous contributory factors. Only when we can synthesize the findings in the different fields of research will it become possible to arrive at the

From *Totem and Taboo* (1913)

relative importance of the part played in the genesis of religion by the mechanism discussed in these pages. Such a task lies beyond the means as well as beyond the purposes of a psycho-analyst.[2]

(1)

In the first of this series of essays we became acquainted with the concept of totemism.[3] We heard that totemism is a system which takes the place of a religion among certain primitive peoples of Australia, America and Africa, and provides the basis of their social organization. As we have heard, it was a Scotsman, McLennan,[4] who

---

[1] "The Return of Totemism in Childhood" is from Freud's 1913 book *Totem and Taboo.* This essay was originally one of a set published in the psychoanalytic journal *Imago,* under the title "On Some Points of Agreement Between the Mental Lives of Savages and Neurotics." Freud's original essay contains over seventy footnotes. Space limitations prevent us from reproducing them here, but asterisks have been included to give the reader an idea of the volume of notes Freud wrote.

In formulating psychoanalysis, Freud placed great importance on anthropological data. He sought to unite the social sciences under the rubric of psychoanalysis and believed ethnographic data validated his theory. In the preface to *Totem and Taboo,* Freud wrote: "They [the essays] seek to bridge the gap between students of such subjects as social anthropology, philology and folklore on the one hand, and psycho-analysis on the other" (1950:x).

[2] Freud's comments on the origin of religion are a reference to the great variety of competing theories concerned with the question of how religion developed. Although this issue is largely ignored today, scholars of the late nineteenth and early twentieth centuries devoted much time and thought to the subject, and Freud was well versed in their writings. In *Comparative Mythology* (1856), Max Müller proposed that religion sprang from spontaneous reactions of awe and fear evoked by natural phenomena, especially the sun. Another view on the subject was outlined by E. B. Tylor, in *Primitive Culture* (see essay 2), who proposed that animism was the fundamental concept upon which religion was based.

Freud also was influenced by Émile Durkheim's *Elementary Forms of the Religious Life* (orig. 1912), which he cites in a section of the essay omitted from this volume. In this book, Durkheim outlined a sociological theory of the origins of religion, proposing that a central facet of religion was the distinction people made between sacred and profane. He understood religion as a set of beliefs and practices dealing with the sacred sphere of life. Durkheim stressed that the origins of religion could be found in social interaction. Like Freud, he focused on totems and their use by Australian aboriginal groups, whom he believed to be the most primitive people on earth and thus representative of earlier stages of human cultural evolution. According to Durkheim, the totem represented the deity as well as the group itself. Thus, the clan and its gods were identical, and the worship of totem figures linked religion and society together. Group rituals served to promote solidarity among members and reinforce their common beliefs.

[3] The nature and symbolic expression of totems has been the subject of numerous studies since Freud's day. The term *totem,* as Freud is using it, refers to an animal from which a kin group such as a lineage claims descent.

[4] John Ferguson McLennan (1827–1881) was a key spokesman for sociocultural evolutionism. In *Primitive Marriage* (1865), his best known work, he outlined the evolution of marriage. In the nineteenth century *Primitive Marriage* was frequently reprinted as part of *Studies in Ancient History.* In this and other works, his approach was based on the comparative method and the doctrine of survivals. Among other things, he coined the term *exogamy.*

in 1869 first drew general attention to the phenomena of totemism (which had hitherto been regarded as mere curiosities) by giving voice to a suspicion that a large number of customs and usages current in various societies ancient and modern were to be explained as remnants of a totemic age. Since that date science has fully accepted his estimate of totemism. Let me quote, as one of the most recent statements on the subject, a passage from Wundt's[5] *Elemente der Volkerpsychologie* (1912, 139): "In the light of all these facts, the conclusion appears highly probable that at some time totemic culture everywhere paved the way for a more advanced civilization, and, thus, that it represents a transitional stage between the age of primitive men and the era of heroes and gods." [English translation, 139.]

[*Freud begins this article with an extensive discussion of totemism, starting with a twelve-point description of totemism by Salomon Reinach written in 1900. Reinach (1858–1932) was an eminent French art historian. Author of over seventy books and 5,000 articles, his most popular works were a history of art called* Apollo, *and* Orpheus, *a general history of religion. Because Freud finds fault with Reinach's characterization of totemism and adopts Frazer's definition, which he outlines later, we have omitted the 419-word discussion of Reinach's work, which contains one footnote.*]

To obtain a correct picture of the nature of totemism we must turn to another author, who has devoted a four-volume work to the subject, which combines the fullest collection of the relevant observations with the most detailed discussion of the problems they raise. We shall remain indebted to J. G. Frazer,[6] the author of *Totemism and Exogamy* (1910), both for enjoyment and instruction, even if psycho-analytic research may lead to conclusions which differ widely from his.*

"A totem", wrote Frazer in his first essay on the subject,* "is a class of material objects which a savage regards with superstitious respect, believing that there exists between him and every member of the class an intimate and altogether special relation. . . . The connection between a man and his totem is mutually beneficent; the totem protects the man, and the man shows his respect for the totem in various ways, by not killing it if it be an animal, and not cutting or gathering it if it be a plant. As distinguished from a fetish, a totem is never an isolated individual, but always a class of objects, generally a species of animals or of plants, more rarely a class of inanimate natural objects, very rarely a class of artificial objects. . . .

"Totems are of at least three kinds: (1) the clan totem, common to a whole clan, and passing by inheritance from generation to generation; (2) the sex totem, common either to all the males or to all the females of a tribe, to the exclusion in either case of the other sex; (3) the individual totem, belonging to a single individual and not passing to his descendants. . . ."

The last two kinds of totem do not compare in significance with the clan totem. Unless we are

---

[5] Wilhelm Wundt (1832–1920) is regarded as the founder of experimental psychology. He obtained his doctorate of medicine from the University of Heidelberg in 1856 and spent almost fifty years at the University of Leipzig, where he held a chair in philosophy. Freud cites Wundt's 1912 book *Elements of Folk Psychology,* but Wundt is best known for his *Principles of Physiological Psychology,* which established psychology's claim as an independent science. Wundt was a leading intellectual in his day and influenced many European scholars. Durkheim, for example, spent a year in Germany studying Wundt's philosophy.

[6] Sir James Frazer (1854–1941) was one of the most eminent English anthropologists of the late nineteenth century. His thirteen-volume study of ritual and folklore, *The Golden Bough* (1911–1915, orig. 1890), was enormously influential, and Freud cites him several times in this essay. Frazer believed that humans passed through three stages of intellectual development: from magic to religion to science. He correlated these stages with the evolutionary increase in human analytical powers. In Frazer's view, religion was a break with earlier magical beliefs. When people realized that magic did not work, they turned to a belief in higher powers; thus, religion was born (Malefijt 1989:54). Frazer believed that scientific thinking would replace religious belief. This view ties in nicely with Freud's theory of psychosexual development and his belief that primitive peoples were in a stage of psychic childhood similar to that of his neurotic patients.

quite mistaken, they are late developments and of little importance for the essential nature of the totem.

"The clan totem is reverenced by a body of men and women who call themselves by the name of the totem, believe themselves to be of one blood, descendants of a common ancestor, and are bound together by common obligations to each other and by a common faith in the totem. Totemism is thus both a religious and a social system. In its religious aspect it consists of the relations of mutual respect and protection between a man and his totem; in its social aspect it consists of the relations of the clansmen to each other and to men of other clans.[7] In the later history of totemism these two sides, the religious and the social, tend to part company; the social system sometimes survives the religious; and, on the other hand, religion sometimes bears traces of totemism in countries where the social system based on totemism has disappeared. How in the origin of totemism these two sides were related to each other it is, in our ignorance of that origin, impossible to say with certainty. But on the whole the evidence points strongly to the conclusion that the two sides were originally inseparable; that, in other words, the farther we go back, the more we should find that the clansman regards himself and his totem as beings of the same species, and the less he distinguishes between conduct towards his totem and towards his fellow-clansmen."

In giving particulars of totemism as a religious system, Frazer begins by stating that the members of a totem clan call themselves by the name of their totem, and commonly believe themselves to be actually descended from it.* It follows from this belief that they will not hunt the totem animal or kill or eat it and, if it is something other than an animal, they refrain from making use of it in other ways. The rules against killing or eating the totem are not the only taboos; sometimes they are forbidden to touch it, or even to look at it; in a number of cases the totem may not be spo-

ken of by its proper name. Any violation of the taboos that protect the totem are automatically punished by severe illness or death.*

Specimens of the totem animal are occasionally reared by the clan and cared for in captivity.* A totem animal that is found dead is mourned for and buried like a dead clansman. If it is necessary to kill a totem animal, this is done according to a prescribed ritual of apologies and ceremonies of expiation.

The clan expects to receive protection and care from its totem. If it is a dangerous animal (such as a beast of prey or a venomous snake) there is a presumption that it will do no harm to its clansmen; and if that expectation is not fulfilled the injured man is expelled from the clan. Oaths, in Frazer's opinion, were originally ordeals; thus, many tests of descent and legitimacy were submitted for decision to the totem. The totem gives help in sickness and delivers omens and warnings to its clan. The appearance of the totem in or about a house is often regarded as an omen of death; the totem has come to fetch his kinsman.*

In particular important circumstances the clansman seeks to emphasize his kinship with the totem by making himself resemble it externally, by dressing in the skin of the animal, by incising a picture of the totem upon his own body, and so on. This identification with the totem is carried into effect in actions and words on the ceremonial occasions of birth, initiation and burial. Various magical and religious purposes are served by dances in which all the clansmen disguise themselves as their totem and imitate its behavior. Lastly, there are ceremonies in which the totem animal is ceremoniously killed.*

The social aspect of totemism is principally expressed in a severely enforced injunction and a sweeping restriction.

The members of a totem clan are brothers and sisters and are bound to help and protect one another. If a member of a clan is killed by someone outside it, the whole clan of the aggressor is

---

[7] Frazer's realization that totemism is both a religious and a social phenomenon and his identification of totemism as one of the central organizing elements in primitive societies help us to understand why Freud focused on totemism for his psychoanalytic analysis of culture.

responsible for the deed and the whole clan of the murdered man is at one in demanding satisfaction for the blood that has been shed. The totem bond is stronger than that of the family in our sense. The two do not coincide, since the totem is as a rule inherited through the female line, and it is possible that paternal descent may originally have been left entirely out of account.

The corresponding taboo restriction prohibits members of the same totem clan from marrying or having sexual intercourse with each other. Here we have the notorious and mysterious correlate of totemism — exogamy.[8] I have devoted the whole of the first essay in the present volume to that subject, so that here I need only repeat that it originates from the intensification among savages of the horror of incest, that it would be fully explained as an assurance against incest under conditions of group marriage, and that it is primarily aimed at restraining the *younger* generation from incest and that only as a later development does it interfere with the older generation.[9]

To Frazer's account of totemism — one of the earliest in the literature of the subject — I will add a few extracts from one of the most recent ones. In his *Elemente der Volkerpsychologie*, Wundt (1912, 116 ff.) writes as follows: "The totem animal is also usually regarded as the ancestral animal of the group in question. 'Totem' is, on the one hand, a group name, and, on the other, a name indicative of ancestry. In the latter connection it has also a mythological significance. These various ideas, however, interplay in numerous ways. Some of the meanings may recede, so that totems have frequently become a mere nomenclature of tribal divisions, while at other times the idea of ancestry, or, perhaps also, the cult significance, predominates. . . ." The concept of the totem has a decisive influence upon

tribal division and tribal organization, which are subject to certain norms of custom. "These norms, and their fixed place in the beliefs and feelings of the tribal members, are connected with the fact that originally, at all events, the totem animal was regarded, for the most part, as having not merely given its name to a group of tribal members but as having actually been its forefather. . . . Bound up with this is the further fact that these animal ancestors possessed a cult. . . . Aside from specific ceremonies and ceremonial festivals, this animal cult originally found expression primarily in the relations maintained towards the totem animal. It was not merely a particular animal that was to a certain extent held sacred, but every representative of the species. The totem members were forbidden to eat the flesh of the totem animal, or were allowed to do so only under specific conditions. A significant counter-phenomenon, not irreconcilable with this, is the fact that on certain occasions the eating of the totem flesh constituted a sort of ceremony. . . ."

". . . The most important social aspect of this totemic tribal organization, however, consists in the fact that it involved certain norms of custom regulating the intercourse of the separate groups with one another. Of these norms, those governing marriage relations were of first importance. The tribal organization of this period was bound up with an important institution, *exogamy*, which originated in the totemic age." [English translation, 116 f.]

If we seek to penetrate to the original nature of totemism, without regard to subsequent accretions or attentuations, we find that its essential characteristics are these: Originally, all totems were animals, and were regarded as the ancestors of the different clans. Totems were inherited only through the female line. There was a prohibition

---

[8] Exogamy dictates that one must choose a spouse from outside of one's own group.

[9] Freud proposes that totemic exogamy (marriage outside the totemic group) originated as an assurance against incest under "conditions of group marriage" but doesn't cite any source for his contention that group marriage was common among primitive peoples. This comment possibly refers to Lewis Henry Morgan's consanguine and punaluan stages of family evolution. In Part III of *Ancient Society*, Morgan discussed the evolution of family types. The consanguine system, the first form of family according to Morgan, was based on the intermarriage of brothers and sisters. The second stage of family evolution was the punaluan system, which was based on the intermarriage of brothers to each other's wives and sisters to each other's husbands. In Morgan's scheme, these two forms of family belonged to the period of savagery.

against killing the totem (or which, under primitive conditions, is the same thing—against eating it). Members of a totem clan were forbidden to practice sexual intercourse with one another.*

We shall now, perhaps, be struck by the fact that in Reinach's *Code du totémisme* one of the two principal taboos, that of exogamy, is not mentioned at all, while the belief upon which the second one is founded, namely descent from the totem animal, is only referred to in passing. My reason, however, for selecting the account given by Reinach (a writer, incidentally, who has made very valuable contributions to the subject) was to prepare us for the differences of opinion between the authorities—differences into which we must now enter.

(2)

The more incontestable became the conclusion that totemism constitutes a regular phase in all cultures, the more urgent became the need for arriving at an understanding of it and for throwing light upon the puzzle of its essential nature.[10] Everything connected with totemism seems to be puzzling: the decisive problems concern the origin of the idea of descent from the totem and the reasons for exogamy (or rather for the taboo upon incest of which exogamy is the expression), as well as the relation between these two institutions, totemic organization and prohibition of incest. Any satisfactory explanation should be at once an historical and a psychological one. It should tell us under what conditions this peculiar institution developed and to what psychical needs in men it has given expression.

My readers will, I am sure, be astonished to hear of the variety of angles from which attempts have been made to answer these questions, and

of the wide divergences of opinion upon them put forward by the experts. Almost any generalization that could be made on the subject of totemism and exogamy seems open to question. Even the account that I have just given, derived from the book published by Frazer in 1887, is open to the criticism that it expresses the present writer's arbitrary preferences; and indeed it would be contested today by Frazer himself, who has repeatedly changed his opinions on the subject.*

It is plausible to suppose that an understanding of the essential nature of totemism and exogamy would best be arrived at, if it were possible to come nearer to the origins of the two institutions. But in this connection we must bear in mind Andrew Lang's[11] warning that even primitive peoples have not retained the original forms of those institutions nor the conditions which gave rise to them; so that we have nothing whatever but hypotheses to fall back upon as a substitute for the observations which we are without.* Some of the attempted explanations seem, in the judgment of a psychologist, inadequate at the very outset: they are too rational and take no account of the emotional character of the matters to be explained. Others are based on assumptions which are unconfirmed by observation. Yet others rely upon material which would be better interpreted in another way. There is generally little difficulty in refuting the various views put forward: the authorities are as usual more effective in their criticisms of one another's work than in their own productions. The conclusion upon most of the points raised must be a non liquet.[12] It is not surprising, therefore, that in the most recent literature on the subject (which is for the most part passed over in the present work) an unmistakable tendency emerges to reject any general solution of totemic problems as impracticable. (See, for

---

[10] In this paragraph, Freud establishes the importance of totemism to his theory. It is "urgent" to understand totemism because he believes it is universal, a "regular phase in all cultures," and because it is an element of kinship and sexuality. Thus, he ties totemism to his theory of human psychology.

[11] Andrew Lang (1844–1912) was a student of Tylor as well as a leading critic of Tylor's theory of animism. Lang considered it unlikely that animism led to beliefs about deities; he proposed that monotheism preceded animism, pointing out that many simple societies had conceptions of a supreme deity. Thus animism might have been a corruption of this original belief.

[12] *Non liquet:* Latin for not apparent or not clear.

instance, Goldenweiser, 1910.)[13] In the discussion of these conflicting hypotheses which follows, I have ventured to disregard their chronological sequence.

[*We have chosen to skip Freud's 5,472-word discussion (with 25 footnotes) of the various theories on the origins of totemism and exogamy. In this section Freud divides the theories on the origins of totemism into three groups — the nominalist, sociological, and psychological — and explains why he feels each is inadequate. The principal theorists he mentions and refutes are Max Müller, Herbert Spencer, Andrew Lang, Émile Durkheim, James Frazer, and Franz Boas.*

In the next section Freud discusses various theories concerning the origin of exogamy in relation to totemism. Some of the theorists he critiques are Frazer, Durkheim, Westermarck, and, finally, Charles Darwin, which is where we return to Freud's text.]

I must, however, mention one other attempt at solving it. It is of a kind quite different from any that we have so far considered, and might be described as "historical."

This attempt is based upon an hypothesis of Charles Darwin's upon the social state of primitive men. Darwin deduced from the habits of the higher apes that men, too, originally lived in comparatively small groups or hordes* within which the jealousy of the oldest and strongest male prevented sexual promiscuity. "We may indeed conclude from what we know of the jealousy of all male quadrupeds, armed, as many of them are, with special weapons for battling with their rivals, that promiscuous intercourse in a state of nature is extremely improbable. . . . Therefore, if we look far enough back in the stream of time, . . . judging from the social habits of man as he now exists . . . the most probable view is that primeval man aboriginally lived in small communities, each with as many wives as he could support and obtain, whom he would have jealously guarded against all other men. Or he may have lived with several wives by himself, like the Gorilla; for all the natives 'agree that but one adult male is seen in a band; when the young male grows up, a contest takes place for mastery, and the strongest, by killing and driving out the others, establishes himself as the head of the community.' (Dr. Savage, in *Boston Journal of Nat. Hist.*, vol. v, 1845–7, p. 423.) 'The younger males, being thus expelled and wandering about, would, when at last successful in finding a partner, prevent too close interbreeding within the limits of the same family.'" (Darwin, 1871, 2, 362 f.)[14]

Atkinson (1903) seems to have been the first to realize that the practical consequence of the conditions obtaining in Darwin's primal horde must be exogamy for the young males. Each of them might, after being driven out, establish a similar horde, in which the same prohibition upon sexual intercourse would rule owing to its leader's jealousy. In course of time this would produce what grew into a conscious law: "No sexual relations between those who share a common home." After the establishment of totemism this regulation would assume another form and would run: "No sexual relations within the totem."

---

[13] Alexander Goldenweiser (1880–1940) was a student of Boas. The work Freud refers to is an article in the *Journal of American Folklore* called "Totemism: An Analytical Study." Reading Durkheim, Frazer, and Freud, one gets the impression that totemism was based on a concrete collection of elements. Goldenweiser argued that many of the factors assumed to be associated in totemism could actually be combined in different ways or were sometimes nonexistent.

[14] It was common for nineteenth- and early-twentieth-century theorists to believe that primitive societies such as the Australian Aborigines were models of earlier stages of human cultural evolution. Charles Darwin took this analogy one step further by suggesting that the behavior of primate bands can be used as a model for the behavior of early humans. Pay particular attention to Freud's use of Darwin's idea in his description of the earliest state of human society, primal patricide, and the origins of totemism (pages 76–80). Freud believed that the psychological structure of human beings was based on biological factors. Thus, Darwin's evolutionary explanation of exogamy would have been attractive to him. By the way, although both analogies are common, they are false. Just as the Australian Aborigines have a developmental history as long as Western society and thus are not necessarily a model for the earliest forms of human society, so too the higher primates are the products of an evolutionary history as long as that of human beings. They do not necessarily provide an accurate model for the behavior of early humans.

Andrew Lang (1905, 114 and 143) accepted this explanation of exogamy. In the same volume, however, he supports the other theory (held by Durkheim), according to which exogamy was a resultant of the totemic laws. [Cf. p. 120.] It is a little difficult to bring these two points of view into harmony: according to the first theory exogamy would have originated before totemism, while according to the second it would have been derived from it.*

(3)

Into this obscurity one single ray of light is thrown by psycho-analytic observation.

There is a great deal of resemblance between the relations of children and of primitive men towards animals.[15] Children show no trace of the arrogance which urges adult civilized men to draw a hard-and-fast line between their own nature and that of all other animals. Children have no scruples over allowing animals to rank as their full equals. Uninhibited as they are in the avowal of their bodily needs, they no doubt feel themselves more akin to animals than to their elders, who may well be a puzzle to them.

Not infrequently, however, a strange rift occurs in the excellent relations between children and animals. A child will suddenly begin to be frightened of some particular species of animal and to avoid touching or seeing any individual of that species. The clinical picture of an animal phobia emerges — a very common, and perhaps the earliest, form of psycho-neurotic illness occurring in childhood. As a rule the phobia is attached to animals in which the child has hitherto shown a specially lively interest and it has nothing to do with any particular individual animal. There is no large choice of animals that may become objects of a phobia in the case of children living in towns: horses, dogs, cats, less often birds, and with striking frequency very small creatures such as beetles and butterflies. The senseless and immoderate fear shown in these phobias is sometimes attached to animals only known to the child from picture books and fairy tales. On a few rare occasions it is possible to discover what has led to an unusual choice of this kind; and I have to thank Karl Abraham for telling me of a case in which the child himself explained that his fear of wasps was due to their colour and stripes reminding him of tigers, which from all accounts were beasts to be feared.*

No detailed analytic examination has yet been made of children's animal phobias, though they would greatly repay study. This neglect has no doubt been due to the difficulty of analyzing children of such a tender age. It cannot therefore be claimed that we know the general meaning of these disorders and I myself am of the opinion that this may not turn out to be of a uniform nature. But a few cases of phobias of this kind directed towards the larger animals have proved accessible to analysis and have thus yielded their secret to the investigator. It was the same in every case: where the children concerned were boys, their fear related at bottom to their father and had merely been displaced on to the animal.[16]

Everyone with psycho-analytic experience will no doubt have come across cases of the sort and have derived the same impression from them. Yet I can quote only a few detailed publications on the subject. This paucity of literature is an accidental circumstance and it must not be supposed

---

[15] Freud proposed that individuals evolve through five psychosexual phases beginning with the oral stage and ending with genital primacy. Similarly, he believed that societies evolved through corresponding stages of development. Thus, the thought processes of adults in "primitive" societies were similar to those of children in "civilized" societies. This argument is a rephrasing of the German biologist Ernst Heinrich Haeckel's recapitulation theory. Based on studies of fetal development, Haeckel proposed that embryonic development repeats the evolutionary history of a species or phylum (ontogeny recapitulates phylogeny). Although recapitulation theory was discredited in his lifetime, Freud believed in it and incorporated it into his theory of psychological development. Note also that along this same line of thought, Freud makes an assertion about the relationships of children and primitive humans toward animals. This point introduces his discussion of animal phobias.

[16] Freud has not taken a detour away from totemism into phobias; rather, he is carefully constructing an argument. After beginning this essay with an outline of the characteristics of totemism, now he is explaining animal phobias in terms of

that our conclusions are based on a few scattered observations. I may mention, for instance, a writer who has studied the neuroses of childhood with great understanding—Dr. M. Wulff, of Odessa.* In the course of a case-history of a nine-year-old boy he reports that at the age of four the patient had suffered from a dog-phobia. "When he saw a dog running past in the street, he would weep and call out: 'Dear doggie, don't bite me! I'll be good!' By 'being good' he meant 'not playing on the fiddle'"—not masturbating. (Wulff, 1912, 15.) "The boy's dog-phobia," the author explains, "was in reality his fear of his father displaced on to dogs; for his curious exclamation 'Doggie, I'll be good!'—that is, 'I won't masturbate'—was directed to his father, who had forbidden him to masturbate." Wulff adds a footnote which is in complete agreement with my views and at the same time bears witness to the frequent occurrence of such experiences: "Phobias of this type (phobias of horses, dogs, cats, fowls and other domestic animals) are, in my opinion, at least as common in childhood as *pavor nocturnus*;[17] and in analysis they almost invariably turn out to be a displacement on to the animals of the child's fear of one of his parents. I should not be prepared to maintain that the same mechanism applies to the widespread phobias of rats and mice." [Ibid., 16.]

I recently published (1909a) an "Analysis of a Phobia in a Five-Year-Old Boy," the material of which was supplied to me by the little patient's father. The boy had a phobia of horses, and as a result he refused to go out in the street. He expressed a fear that the horse would come into the room and bite him; and it turned out that this must be the punishment for a wish that the horse might fall down (that is, die). After the boy's fear of his father had been removed by reassurances, it became evident that he was struggling against wishes which had as their subject the idea of his father being absent (going away on a journey, dying). He regarded his father (as he made all too clear) as a competitor for the favours of his mother, towards whom the obscure foreshadowings of his budding sexual wishes were aimed. Thus he was situated in the typical attitude of a male child towards his parents to which we have given the name of the "Oedipus complex" and which we regard in general as the nuclear complex of the neuroses. The new fact that we have learnt from the analysis of "little Hans"—a fact with an important bearing upon totemism—is that in such circumstances children displace some of their feelings from their father on to an animal.[18]

Analysis is able to trace the associative paths along which this displacement passes—both the fortuitous paths and those with a significant content. Analysis also enables us to discover the *motives* for the displacement. The hatred of his father that arises in a boy from rivalry for his mother is not able to achieve uninhibited sway over his mind; it has to contend against his old-established

---

children's fear of their fathers. His end goal is to link anthropology and psychology using the Oedipal complex, which played a crucial role in Freud's thinking and was an integral part of his theory of psychosexual development. The concept was named after the Greek myth of Oedipus, who unknowingly killed his father and married his mother. Freud believed that there was a stage of psychosexual development during which young boys feared and hated their fathers because these men were rivals for the love and affection of their mothers. In this essay he speculates that children's Oedipal fears are expressed through animal phobias and that the phobias and associated taboos are similar to the obsessive-compulsive behaviors of neurotic patients.

[17] *Pavor nocturnus:* Latin for nightmares or night terrors.

[18] In this discussion of phobias, Freud is preparing to link the anthropological data on totemism with information from psychoanalysis. Cases of animal phobias, he says, are based on fear that little boys displace from their fathers onto animals (because of the Oedipal complex). Freud reasoned that if the thought of primitive humans is similar to that of civilized children, then the insights derived from his psychoanalysis of children should be applicable to the analysis of primitive societies. Note also the unsubstantiated leaps of faith Freud makes in this paragraph. He begins the passage by saying he got his information in this case from the boy's father, but later relates that the boy "regarded his father (as he made all too clear) as a competitor for the favors of his mother." If Freud only spoke to the boy's father, perhaps the father was projecting his own jealousy, for the time his wife spent with their child, onto his son. Assuming Freud accurately recorded the particulars of the case, how are we to separate the son's wishes from the father's fears? Isn't psychoanalysis wonderful?

affection and admiration for the very same person. The child finds relief from the conflict arising out of this double-sided, this ambivalent emotional attitude towards his father by displacing his hostile and fearful feelings on to a *substitute* for his father. The displacement cannot, however, bring the conflict to an end, it cannot effect a clear-cut severance between the affectionate and the hostile feelings. On the contrary, the conflict is resumed in relation to the object on to which the displacement has been made; the ambivalence is extended to *it*. There could be no doubt that little Hans was not only *frightened* of horses; he also approached them with admiration and interest. As soon as his anxiety began to diminish, he identified himself with the dreaded creature: he began to jump about like a horse and in his turn bit his father.* At another stage in the resolution of his phobia he did not hesitate to identify his parents with some other large animals.*

It may fairly be said that in these children's phobias some of the features of totemism reappear, but reversed into their negative. We are, however, indebted to Ferenczi[19] (1913*a*) for an interesting history of a single case which can only be described as an instance of *positive* totemism in a child. It is true that in the case of little Árpád (the subject of Ferenczi's report) his totemic interests did not arise in direct relation with his Oedipus complex but on the basis of its narcissistic precondition, the fear of castration. But any attentive reader of the story of little Hans will find abundant evidence that he, too, admired his father as possessing a big penis and feared him as threatening his own. The same part is played by the father alike in the Oedipus and the castration complexes — the part of a dreaded enemy to the sexual interests of childhood. The punishment which he threatens is castration, or its substitute, blinding.*

When little Árpád was two and a half years old, he had once, while he was on a summer hol-iday, tried to micturate[20] into the fowl-house and a fowl had bitten or snapped at his penis. A year later, when he was back in the same place, he himself turned into a fowl; his one interest was in the fowl-house and in what went on there and he abandoned human speech in favour of cackling and crowing. At the time at which the observation was made (when he was five years old) he had recovered his speech, but his interests and his talk were entirely concerned with chickens and other kinds of poultry. They were his only toys and he only sang songs that had some mention of fowls in them. His attitude towards his totem animal was superlatively ambivalent: he showed both hatred and love to an extravagant degree. His favourite game was playing slaughtering fowls. "The slaughtering of poultry was a regular festival for him. He would dance round the animals' bodies for hours at a time in a state of intense excitement."* But afterwards he would kiss and stroke the slaughtered animal or would clean and caress the toy fowls that he had himself ill-treated.

Little Árpád himself saw to it that the meaning of his strange behaviour should not remain hidden. From time to time he translated his wishes from the totemic language into that of everyday life. "My father's the cock," he said on one occasion, and another time: "Now I'm small, now I'm a chicken. When I get bigger I'll be a fowl. When I'm bigger still I'll be a cock." On another occasion he suddenly said he would like to eat some "fricassee of mother" (on the analogy of fricassee of chicken). [Ibid., 249.] He was very generous in threatening other people with castration, just as he himself had been threatened with it for his masturbatory activities.

There was no doubt, according to Ferenczi, as to the sources of Árpád's interest in events in the poultry-yard: "the continual sexual activity between the cock and hens, the laying of eggs and

---

[19] Sandor Ferenczi (1873–1933) was a member of Freud's inner circle of colleagues. A physician by training, he was the founder of the Hungarian psychoanalytic society and held the first professorship in psychoanalysis at the University of Budapest. He is remembered, in part, for inventing a form of privation therapy. When patients resisted treatment, Ferenczi ordered them to abstain from eating, defecation, or sex in order to break through their defenses and to provide the energy needed for therapy.

[20] *Micturate:* to urinate.

the hatching out of the young brood gratified his sexual curiosity, the real object of which was *human* family-life." [Ibid., 250.] He showed that he had formed his own choice of sexual objects on the model of life in the hen-run, for he said one day to the neighbour's wife: "I'll marry you and your sister and my three cousins and the cook; no, not the cook, I'll marry my mother instead." [Ibid, 252.][21]

Later on we shall be able to assess the worth of this observation more completely. At the moment I will only emphasize two features in it which offer valuable points of agreement with totemism: the boy's complete identification with his totem animal* and his ambivalent emotional attitude to it. These observations justify us, in my opinion, in substituting the father for the totem animal in the formula for totemism (in the case of males). It will be observed that there is nothing new or particularly daring in this step forward. Indeed, primitive men say the very same thing themselves, and, where the totemic system is still in force to-day, they describe the totem as their common ancestor and primal father. All we have done is to take at its literal value an expression used by these people, of which the anthropologists have been able to make very little and which they have therefore been glad to keep in the background. Psychoanalysis, on the contrary, leads us to put special stress upon this same point and to take it as the starting-point of our attempt at explaining totemism.*

The first consequence of our substitution is most remarkable. If the totem animal is the father, then the two principal ordinances of totemism, the two taboo prohibitions which constitute its core — not to kill the totem and not to have sexual relations with a woman of the same totem — coincide in their content with the two crimes of Oedipus, who killed his father and married his mother, as well as with the two primal wishes of children, the insufficient repression or the reawakening of which forms the nucleus of perhaps

every psychoneurosis. If this equation is anything more than a misleading trick of chance, it must enable us to throw a light upon the origin of totemism in the inconceivably remote past. In other words, it would enable us to make it probable that the totemic system — like little Hans' animal phobia and little Árpád's poultry perversion — was a product of the conditions involved in the Oedipus complex. In order to pursue this possibility, we shall have, in the following pages, to study a feature of the totemic system (or, as we might say, of the totemic religion) which I have hitherto scarcely found an opportunity of mentioning.

[We have chosen to skip section 4 of Freud's article (2,866 words and 10 footnotes), which is concerned primarily with a discussion of a custom called the "totem meal" formulated by William Robertson Smith (1846–1894). Basically, Robertson Smith described a ceremonial feast in which the members of a totem would kill and eat their totem animal as a symbol of their fellowship and relationship to one another and their god. Freud writes "The sacrifice was a sacrament and the sacrificial animal was itself a member of the clan. It was in fact the ancient totem animal, the primitive god himself, by the killing and consuming of which the clansmen renewed and assured their likeness to the god."]

(5)

Let us call up the spectacle of a totem meal of the kind we have been discussing, amplified by a few probable features which we have not yet been able to consider. The clan is celebrating the ceremonial occasion by the cruel slaughter of its totem animal and is devouring it raw — blood, flesh and bones, the clansmen are there, dressed in the likeness of the totem and imitating it in sound and movement, as though they are seeking to stress their identity with it. Each man is con-

---

[21] After being bitten by a chicken, little Árpád formed a totemlike obsession with chickens, which he substituted for his interest in human sexuality. According to Freud, Árpád's statements that he would like to eat "fricassee of mother" and that, when grown, he would marry his mother, show how he substituted the totem animal (a cock) for his father. Here, in the case of little Árpád, Freud provides the psychoanalytic link between neurosis and totemism.

scious that he is performing an act forbidden to the individual and justifiable only through the participation of the whole clan; nor may anyone absent himself from the killing and the meal. When the deed is done, the slaughtered animal is lamented and bewailed. The mourning is obligatory, imposed by dread of a threatened retribution. As Robertson Smith (1894, 412) remarks of an analogous occasion, its chief purpose is to disclaim responsibility for the killing.

But the mourning is followed by demonstrations of festive rejoicing: every instinct is unfettered and there is license for every kind of gratification. Here we have easy access to an understanding of the nature of festivals in general. A festival is a permitted, or rather an obligatory, excess, a solemn breach of a prohibition. It is not that men commit the excesses because they are feeling happy as a result of some injunction they have received. It is rather that excess is of the essence of a festival; the festive feeling is produced by the liberty to do what is as a rule prohibited.

What are we to make, though, of the prelude to this festive joy—the mourning over the death of the animal? If the clansmen rejoice over the killing of the totem—a normally forbidden act—why do they mourn over it as well?

As we have seen, the clansmen acquire sanctity by consuming the totem: they reinforce their identification with it and with one another. Their festive feelings and all that follows from them might well be explained by the fact that they have taken into themselves the sacred life of which the substance of the totem is the vehicle.

Psycho-analysis has revealed that the totem animal is in reality a substitute for the father; and this tallies with the contradictory fact that, though the killing of the animal is as a rule forbidden, yet its killing becomes a festive occasion—the fact

that it is killed and yet mourned. The ambivalent emotional attitude, which to this day characterizes the father-complex in our children and which often persists into adult life, seems to extend to the totem animal in its capacity as substitute for the father.

If, now, we bring together the psycho-analytic translation of the totem with the fact of the totem meal and with Darwin's theories of the earliest state of human society, the possibility of a deeper understanding emerges—a glimpse of a hypothesis which may seem fantastic but which offers the advantage of establishing an unsuspected correlation between groups of phenomena that have hitherto been disconnected.

There is, of course, no place for the beginnings of totemism in Darwin's primal horde. All that we find there is a violent and jealous father who keeps all the females for himself and drives away his sons as they grow up. This earliest state of society has never been an object of observation. The most primitive kind of organization that we actually come across—and one that is in force to this day in certain tribes—consists of bands of males; these bands are composed of members with equal rights and are subject to the restrictions of the totemic system, including inheritance through the mother. Can this form of organization have developed out of the other one? and if so along what lines?[22]

If we call the celebration of the totem meal to our help, we shall be able to find an answer. One day* the brothers who had been driven out came together, killed and devoured their father and so made an end of the patriarchal horde. United, they had the courage to do and succeeded in doing what would have been impossible for them individually. (Some cultural advance, perhaps, command over some new weapon, had given them a sense of superior strength.) Cannibal savages as

---

[22] Freud was widely criticized for the hypothesis he proposed in this work and for his discussion of the origins of totemism. But given his statement in this paragraph, "This earliest state of society has never been an object of observation," we can clearly see that he was proposing a hypothetical construct based on his own psychoanalytic background and his reading of the scientific literature available in his time. For example, Freud cites *Primal Law,* a 1903 book by J. J. Atkinson. In this work Atkinson concluded that the conditions in Darwin's primal horde must have necessitated exogamy for young males, and that this ultimately led to totem exogamous marriage. Also, note that Freud's contention that the earliest state of society had never been observed fits nicely with Morgan's statement that there were no examples of lower savagery in existence (see essay 3).

they were, it goes without saying that they devoured their victim as well as killing him. The
violent primal father had doubtless been the
feared and envied model of each one of the company of brothers: and in the act of devouring
him they accomplished their identification with
him, and each one of them acquired a portion of
his strength. The totem meal, which is perhaps
mankind's earliest festival, would thus be a repetition and a commemoration of this memorable
and criminal deed, which was the beginning of so
many things — of social organization, of moral restrictions and of religion.*[23]

In order that these latter consequences may
seem plausible, leaving their premises on one
side, we need only suppose that the tumultuous
mob of brothers were filled with the same contradictory feelings which we can see at work in
the ambivalent father-complexes of our children
and of our neurotic patients. They hated their father, who presented such a formidable obstacle to
their craving for power and their sexual desires;
but they loved and admired him too. After they
had got rid of him, had satisfied their hatred and
had put into effect their wish to identify themselves with him, the affection which had all this
time been pushed under was bound to make itself
felt.* It did so in the form of remorse. A sense of
guilt made its appearance, which in this instance
coincided with the remorse felt by the whole
group. The dead father became stronger than the
living one had been — for events took the course
we so often see them follow in human affairs to
this day. What had up to then been prevented by
his actual existence was thenceforward prohibited by the sons themselves, in accordance with
the psychological procedure so familiar to us in
psycho-analysis under the name of "deferred obedience." They revoked their deed by forbidding

the killing of the totem, the substitute for their father; and they renounced its fruits by resigning
their claim to the women who had now been set
free. They thus created out of their filial sense of
guilt the two fundamental taboos of totemism,
which for that very reason inevitably corresponded
to the two repressed wishes of the Oedipus complex. Whoever contravened those taboos became
guilty of the only two crimes[24] with which primitive society concerned itself.*

The two taboos of totemism with which
human morality has its beginning, are not on a par
psychologically. The first of them, the law protecting the totem animal, is founded wholly on
emotional motives: the father had actually been
eliminated, and in no real sense could the deed be
undone. But the second rule, the prohibition of
incest, has a powerful practical basis as well. Sexual desires do not unite men but divide them.
Though the brothers had banded together in order
to overcome their father, they were all one another's rivals in regard to the women. Each of
them would have wished, like his father, to have
all the women to himself. The new organization
would have collapsed in a struggle of all against
all, for none of them was of such overmastering
strength as to be able to take on his father's part
with success. Thus the brothers had no alternative, if they were to live together, but — not,
perhaps, until they had passed through many dangerous crises — to institute the law against incest,
by which they all alike renounced the women
whom they desired and who had been their chief
motive for despatching their father. In this way
they rescued the organization which had made
them strong — and which may have been based on
homosexual feelings and acts, originating perhaps
during the period of their expulsion from the
horde. Here, too, may perhaps have been the germ

---

[23] The central element of Freud's theory is described in this and the following paragraph: totemism, a fundamental building block of culture, was created through the act of primal patricide. Although Freud constructed an ingenious argument,
this theory is pure fancy. Comments such as "it goes without saying that they devoured their victim as well as killing him"
are treated as statements of fact, but no supporting evidence is offered. Mainstream American anthropology accepted
some of Freud's ideas but absolutely rejected this primal family theory. In fact, Franz Boas frequently criticized Freud directly (see essay 10).

[24] Those two crimes are murder and incest according to a footnote in the original manuscript.

of the institution of matriarchy, described by Bachofen[25] [1861], which was in turn replaced by the patriarchal organization of the family.

On the other hand, the claim of totemism to be regarded as a first attempt at a religion is based on the first of these two taboos—that upon taking the life of the totem animal. The animal struck the sons as a natural and obvious substitute for their father; but the treatment of it which they found imposed on themselves expressed more than the need to exhibit their remorse. They could attempt, in their relation to this surrogate father, to allay their burning sense of guilt, to bring about a kind of reconciliation with their father. The totemic system was, as it were, a covenant with their father, in which he promised them everything that a childish imagination may expect from a father—protection, care and indulgence—while on their side they undertook to respect his life, that is to say, not to repeat the deed which had brought destruction on their real father. Totemism, moreover, contained an attempt at self justification: "If our father had treated us in the way the totem does, we should never have felt tempted to kill him." In this fashion totemism helped to smooth things over and to make it possible to forget the event to which it owed its origin.[26]

Features were thus brought into existence which continued thenceforward to have a determining influence on the nature of religion. Totemic religion arose from the filial sense of guilt, in an attempt to allay that feeling and to appease the father by deferred obedience to him. All later religions are seen to be attempts at solving the same problem. They vary according to the stage of civilization at which they arise and according to the methods which they adopt; but all have the same end in view and are reactions to the same great event with which civilization began and which, since it occurred, has not allowed mankind a moment's rest.

There is another feature which was already present in totemism and which has been preserved unaltered in religion. The tension of ambivalence was evidently too great for any contrivance to be able to counteract it; or it is possible that psychological conditions in general are unfavourable to getting rid of these antithetical emotions. However that may be, we find that the ambivalence implicit in the father-complex persists in totemism and in religions generally. Totemic religion not only comprised expressions of remorse and attempts at atonement, it also served as a remembrance of the triumph over the father. Satisfaction over that triumph led to the institution of the memorial festival of the totem meal, in which the restrictions of deferred obedience no longer held. Thus it became a duty to repeat the crime of parricide again and again in the sacrifice of the totem animal, whenever, as a result of the changing conditions of life, the cherished fruit of the crime—appropriation of the paternal attributes—threatened to disappear. We shall not be surprised to find that the element of filial rebelliousness also emerges, in the *later* products of religion, often in the strangest disguises and transformations.

Hitherto we have followed the developments of the *affectionate* current of feeling towards the father, transformed into remorse, as we find them in religion and in moral ordinances (which are not sharply distinguished in totemism). But we must not overlook the fact that it was in the main with the impulses that led to parricide that the victory lay. For a long time afterwards, the social fraternal feelings, which were the basis of the whole transformation, continued to exercise a

---

[25] Johan Jakob Bachofen (1815–1887) is best known for his 1861 book *Das Mutterecht (Mother Right)*, in which he hypothesized that the European-style patriarchal family had evolved from an earlier matriarchal system. Freud here proposes that the breakup of the primal horde, caused by the sons' common desire for the same women, led to the formation of Bachofen's matriarchal society. Freud's statement that sexual desire divides men and is a part of the "struggle of all against all" is Darwinian. Similarly, Freud's primal family story is derived from Darwin, who proposed that rules of exogamy were a result of senior male dominance of primal family groups.

[26] Note Freud's reliance on words like *natural* and *obvious*, which cover for the absence of data to support his theory.

profound influence on the development of society. They found expression in the sanctification of the blood tie, in the emphasis upon the solidarity of all life within the same clan. In thus guaranteeing one another's lives, the brothers were declaring that no one of them must be treated by another as their father was treated by them all jointly. They were precluding the possibility of a repetition of their father's fate. To the religiously based prohibition against killing the totem was now added the socially based prohibition against fratricide. It was not until long afterwards that the prohibition ceased to be limited to members of the clan and assumed the simple form: "Thou shalt do no murder." The patriarchal horde was replaced in the first instance by the fraternal clan, whose existence was assured by the blood tie. Society was now based on complicity in the common crime; religion was based on the sense of guilt and the remorse attaching to it; while morality was based partly on the exigencies of this society and partly on the penance demanded by the sense of guilt.

Thus psycho-analysis, in contradiction to the more recent views of the totemic system but in agreement with the earlier ones, requires us to assume that totemism and exogamy were intimately connected and had a simultaneous origin.

[We have skipped section 6 of Freud's article, which is a 3,260-word (and 7-footnote) discussion of the relationship between totemic sacrifice, the father-son relationship, and Christianity. The principal point of the section is that the concept of God, like the totem ancestor, is formed in the likeness of one's father. Psychoanalysis shows us, Freud says, that "at bottom God is nothing other than an exalted father." Thus for Freud, his primal family story accounted for rules of marriage and kinship, the incest taboo, totemism and ultimately, religion.]

(7)

An event such as the elimination of the primal father by the company of his sons must inevitably have left ineradicable traces in the history of humanity; and the less it itself was recollected, the more numerous must have been the substitutes to which it gave rise.* I shall resist the tempta-

tion of pointing out these traces in mythology, where they are not hard to find, and shall turn in another direction and take up a suggestion made by Salomon Reinach in a most instructive essay on the death of Orpheus.*

[We have skipped Freud's 483-word discussion (with 1 footnote) of the Greek myth of Orpheus, in which Freud finds evidence for his primal family story. Freud believed that the psychological processes proposed in his theory were universal. He cites accounts from different time periods and different cultures, such as Australian aboriginal practices, Greek tragedy, and the Passion of Christ, to support this contention. However, he leans most heavily on examples from Western culture and history.]

At the conclusion, then, of this exceedingly condensed inquiry, I should like to insist that its outcome shows that the beginnings of religion, morals, society and art converge in the Oedipus complex. This is in complete agreement with the psycho-analytic finding that the same complex constitutes the nucleus of all neuroses, so far as our present knowledge goes. It seems to me a most surprising discovery that the problems of social psychology, too, should prove soluble on the basis of one single concrete point — man's relation to his father. It is even possible that yet another psychological problem belongs in this same connection. I have often had occasion to point out that emotional ambivalence in the proper sense of the term — that is, the simultaneous existence of love and hate towards the same object — lies at the root of many important cultural institutions. We know nothing of the origin of this ambivalence. One possible assumption is that it is a fundamental phenomenon of our emotional life. But it seems to me quite worth considering another possibility, namely that originally it formed no part of our emotional life but was acquired by the human race in connection with their father-complex,* precisely where the psychoanalytic examination of modern individuals still finds it revealed at its strongest.*

[We have omitted Freud's 620-word discussion of what he calls "the uncertainties of my premises." In the omitted material Freud outlines the diffi-

culties with his theory. First is his assumption of a collective mind that functions in the same manner as the mind of an individual. Freud believes that this collective mind must exist in order for the guilt resulting from the primal patricide described in this essay to have persisted for thousands of years and in generations "which can have no knowledge of that action." Having raised this question, Freud turns to a discussion of social psychology and explains that all of social psychology makes the same assumption of a collective mind. Indeed, in Freud's view, social psychology could not exist without it. However, he says that social psychology has shown little interest in explaining the "continuity in the mental life of successive generations".]

Another difficulty might actually be brought forward from psycho-analytic quarters. The earliest moral precepts and restrictions in primitive society have been explained by us as reactions to a deed which gave those who performed it the concept of 'crime.' They felt remorse for the deed and decided that it should never be repeated and that its performance should bring no advantage. This creative sense of guilt still persists among us. We find it operating in a social manner in neurotics, and producing new moral precepts and persistent restrictions, as an atonement for crimes that have been committed and as a precaution against the committing of new ones.* If, however, we inquire among these neurotics to discover what were the deeds which provoked these reactions, we shall be disappointed. We find no deeds, but only impulses and emotions, set upon evil ends but held back from their achievement. What lie behind the sense of guilt of neurotics are always *psychical* realities and never *factual* ones. What characterizes neurotics is the fact that they prefer psychical to factual reality and react just as seriously to thoughts as normal persons do to realities.

May not the same have been true of primitive men? We are justified in believing that, as one of the phenomena of their narcissistic organization, they overvalued their psychical acts to an extraordinary degree.* Accordingly the mere hostile *impulse* against the father, the mere existence of a wishful *phantasy* of killing and devouring him, would have been enough to produce the moral reaction that created totemism and taboo. In this way we should avoid the necessity for deriving the origin of our cultural legacy, of which we justly feel so proud, from a hideous crime, revolting to all our feelings. No damage would thus be done to the causal chain stretching from the beginning to the present day, for psychical reality would be strong enough to bear the weight of these consequences. To this it may be objected that an alteration in the form of society from a patriarchal horde to a fraternal clan did actually take place. This is a powerful argument, but not a conclusive one. The alteration might have been effected in a less violent fashion and none the less have been capable of determining the appearance of the moral reaction. So long as the pressure exercised by the primal father could be felt, the hostile feelings towards him were justified and remorse on their account would have to await a later day. And if it is further argued that everything derived from the ambivalent relation to the father — taboo and the sacrificial ordinance — is characterized by the deepest seriousness and the most complete reality, this further objection carries just as little weight. For the ceremonials and inhibitions of obsessional neurotics show these same characteristics and are nevertheless derived only from psychical reality — from intentions and not from their execution. We must avoid transplanting a contempt for what is merely thought or wished from our commonplace world, with its wealth of material values, into the world of primitive men and neurotics, of which the wealth lies only within themselves.[27]

Here we are faced by a decision which is indeed no easy one. First, however, it must be confessed that the distinction, which may seem

---

[27] Here Freud equivocates on his claim that the Oedipal family actually existed, using a nice rhetorical device. Throughout the article he presents a strong case that in the primal family patricide and cannibalism were real events — and that he is presenting historical fact. Here he says that even if these events did not actually happen, even if it was all a hostile fantasy, the guilt and shame would still have produced the same moral reaction.

fundamental to other people, does not in our judgment affect the heart of the matter. If wishes and impulses have the full value of facts for primitive men, it is our business to give their attitude our understanding attention instead of correcting it in accordance with our own standards. Let us, then, examine more closely the case of neurosis-comparison which led us into our present uncertainty. It is not accurate to say that obsessional neurotics, weighed down under the burden of an excessive morality, are defending themselves only against *psychical* reality and are punishing themselves for impulses which were merely *felt*. *Historical* reality has a share in the matter as well. In their childhood they had these evil impulses pure and simple, and turned them into acts so far as the impotence of childhood allowed. Each of these excessively virtuous individuals passed through an evil period in his infancy—a phase of perversion which was the forerunner and precondition of the later period of excessive morality. The analogy between primitive men and neurotics will therefore be far more fully established if we suppose that in the former instance, too, psychical reality—as to the form taken by which we are in no doubt—coincided at the beginning with factual reality: that primitive men actually *did* what all the evidence shows that they intended to do.

Nor must we let ourselves be influenced too far in our judgment of primitive men by the analogy of neurotics.[28] There are distinctions, too, which must be borne in mind. It is no doubt true that the sharp contrast that *we* make between thinking and doing is absent in both of them. But neurotics are above all *inhibited* in their actions: with them the thought is a complete substitute for the deed. Primitive men, on the other hand,

are *uninhibited*: thought passes directly into action. With them it is rather the deed that is a substitute for the thought. And that is why, without laying claim to any finality of judgment, I think that in the case before us it may safely be assumed that "in the beginning was the Deed."*

References

Abraham, K. (1914). "Über Einschränkungen und Umwandlungen der Schaulust bei den Psychoneurotikern" *Jb. Psychoanal.*, 6, 25. [English translation: "Restrictions and Transformations of Scopophilia in Psycho-Neurotics."]

Atkinson, J. J. (1903). *Primal Law*, London. (Included in Lang, A., *Social Origins*.)

Darwin, C. (1871). *The Descent of Man* (2 vols.), London.

Eder, M. D. (1913). "Augenträume," *Int. Z. Psychoanal.*, 1, 157.

Ferenczi, S. (1913a). "Ein kleiner Hahnemann," *Int. Z. Psychoanal.*, 1, 240. [English translation: "A Little Chanticleer," *Contributions to Psycho-Analysis.*]

———. (1913b). "Zur Augensymbolik," *Int. Z. Psychoanal.*, 1, 161. [English translation: "On Eye Symbolism," *Contributions to Pyscho-Analysis.*]

Frazer, J. G. (1887). "Totemism," Edinburgh (Reprinted in *Totemism and Exogamy* [4 vols.], London [1910].)

———. "The Origin of Totemism," (1899). *Fortnightly Review.* (Reprinted in Frazer, 1910, 1, 101.)

Freud, S. (1909a). "Analyse der Phobie eines fünfjährigen Knaben," *Gesammelte Schriften*, 8, 127; *GesammelteWerke*, 7, 243. [English translation: "Analysis of a Phobia in a Five-Year-Old Boy," *Collected Papers.*]

Goldenweiser, A. (1910). "Totemism, an Analytical Study," *J. Am. Folk-Lore*, 23, 179.

Lang, A. (1905). *The Secret of the Totem*, London.

———. (1911). "Lord Avebury on Marriage, Totemism, and Religion," *Folk-Lore*, 22, 402.

---

[28] Implicit in the last several paragraphs of the article is Freud's belief that the psychic reality of modern people (in particular the Oedipal complex) is due to the actions of a prehistoric group who killed and ate their father. His linking of the Oedipal conflict with totemic beliefs in primitive societies is a psychological version of recapitulation theory: he believed that we repeat the actions of our primal ancestors in our own individual psychological development. Just as Freud's proposed "primal horde" killed and ate their father out of hatred based in their desire for sex with their mother, so we too (according to Freud) psychologically repeat the actions of these ancestors through the Oedipal complex. This theory also accounts for the origin of religion. Freud wrote extensively on the origins of Judeo-Christian religious tradition in his 1939 work *Moses and Monotheism*. There he also invoked the Oedipal complex and argued that a belief in God is based on a psychological model of our fathers.

McLennan, J. F. (1869–70). "The Worship of Animals and Plants," *Fortnightly Rev.*, N.S. 6, 407 and 562; N.S. 7, 194. (Reprinted in same author's *Studies in Ancient History; Second Series,* London, 1896.)

Rank, O. (1913). "Eine noch nicht beschriebene Form des Ödipus-Traumes," *Int. Z. Psychoanal.*, 1, 151.

Schriftenitler, R. (1913). "Zur Augensymbolik," *Int. Z. Psychoanal.*, 1, 159.

Smith, W. Robertson (1894). *Lectures on the Religion of the Semites,* new [2nd] ed., London. (1st ed., 1889)

Wundt, W. (1912). *Elemente der Völkerpsychologie.* Leipzig.

The Foundations of Sociological Thought

Like anthropology, sociology is based on the work of philosophers and scientists of the nineteenth century, and the two disciplines share many ideas. Indeed, at the turn of the twentieth century, a clear distinction between anthropology and sociology had not yet been formed. The theories of the early sociological thinkers are worth exploring because they exerted a profound effect on anthropology that continues to be felt today. In fact, all of the theoreticians discussed here adopted a cross-cultural approach in their work.

One individual central in the creation of modern sociology is Émile Durkheim (1858–1917). He is responsible for formulating some of the basic concepts of the discipline and for training the first generation of French sociologists at the beginning of the twentieth century. Durkheim's theory of sociology centered on the question of social cohesion (the term he used was *social solidarity*): he wished to understand what held societies together. He concluded that social solidarity was primarily the result of a force arising from participation in a shared system of beliefs and values, which molded and controlled individual behavior. Durkheim called this system *l'âme collective,* a phrase usually translated into English as "the collective conscience." However, the French word *âme* can also be translated as "soul," "spirit," "sentiment," or "sensibility," and Durkheim intended all of these meanings. He believed that the collective conscience originated in the communal interactions and experiences of members of a society. Because people were born and raised within this shared context of the collective conscience, it determined their values, their beliefs (which he called *collective representations*), and their behaviors. Ultimately, it made life possible and meaningful. For the most part,

social cohesion was maintained because everyone in a society shared its set of collective representations. As you can see, Durkheim's collective conscience foreshadowed the modern concept of culture, although he was not familiar with the term and did not use it in his work.

Durkheim believed that the collective conscience was a psychological entity that, although carried by members of a society, superseded individual existence and could not be explained in terms of individual behavior. In other words, the collective conscience had a *superorganic* existence. Given that it was not a material thing, how could the collective conscience be scientifically studied? Durkheim proposed that the appropriate units of analysis were *social facts* — the social and behavioral rules that exist before an individual is born into a society and which that person learns and observes as a member of that society. They can be recognized by their pervasiveness within a society (they are not individualistic) and by their coercive quality. People feel obligated to observe their constraints. Durkheim believed social facts could be studied independently of individual actions.

Like the other theorists of his day, Durkheim supposed technologically primitive peoples to be examples of earlier stages of cultural evolution. He studied primitive societies, in particular the Australian Aborigines, attempting to determine the form and nature of the collective conscience in these societies. In his analysis, he applied the concepts of mechanical and organic solidarity he had developed in his earlier work, *The Division of Labor in Society,* published in 1893. Primitive societies were held together by what Durkheim called *mechanical solidarity.* He believed that in such societies, there were no individuals in the modern sense. Rather, "collective conscience completely envelopes [individual] conscience and coincides with it at every point" (1933:43). Because of this, such societies lack internal differentiation; their parts are interchangeable. Therefore, segments can break away without disrupting the functioning of the entire society. In these societies, kinship forms the primary bond between people. Industrialized societies, on the other hand, are held together by *organic solidarity* — a pattern in which collective conscience is at least partially differentiated from individual conscience. One result is occupational specialization — people need each other to function. In this type of society, the primary ties between individuals come from economic and occupational interdependence and cooperation rather than from kinship. Durkheim believed that individual freedom, and ultimately happiness, were maximized under organic solidarity.

The influence of nineteenth-century evolutionary thought can be clearly seen in Durkheim's study of primitive societies. He believed that societies evolved from mechanical to organic solidarity, that is, from simple undifferentiated groups into more advanced differentiated societies. In this respect, his work develops some of the implications of Herbert Spencer's organic analogy (see essay 1). Unlike Spencer, Charles Darwin, and Karl Marx, who wrote in terms of the human struggle for survival, Durkheim focused on the solidarity within a society. Though he certainly did not view complex societies as free from conflict (some of his best-known work is on suicide), Durkheim believed that social differentiation and specialization led to increased social cohesion. Strife in modern society resulted from the current incomplete elaboration of organic solidarity, and ultimately, it would greatly diminish.

Durkheim postulated that all people understood the world through socially created systems of classification. Believing that these were essentially dualistic in nature, Durkheim wrote, in *The Elementary Forms of the Religious Life* (1965 [1912]), that people separated their world into "sacred" and "profane" spheres. His emphasis on systems of classification and binary opposition would have enormous effect on later theories, in particular, French structuralism, ethnoscience,

and cognitive anthropology.

Durkheim adopted what anthropologists in later decades termed a "functionalist" approach to the analysis of society. His analysis of social institutions and beliefs was often couched in terms of their contribution to promoting and maintaining social solidarity. This aspect of his work is central to the work of many of Durkheim's students, and it forms the basis of the British functionalist and structural-functionalist schools of anthropological thought exemplified by Bronislaw Malinowski and A. R. Radcliffe-Brown (see essays 13 and 14).

Around the turn of the twentieth century, Durkheim's work attracted an influential group of scholars, some of whom were his relatives. Together, between 1898 and 1912, they published a journal called *L'Année Sociologique*. As a result, they are collectively known as the *L'Année Sociologique* school. Unhappily, World War I exacted a heavy toll on Durkheim and his students. Virtually all of his followers, including his son, were killed in the trenches of the western front, and Durkheim himself died before the war ended.

Durkheim's nephew Marcel Mauss (1872–1950) was one of the few members of the *L'Année Sociologique* school to survive the war, and he was considered one of the school's leading thinkers. In the wake of the disaster that had befallen his friends and colleagues, however, he neglected his own work to concentrate on publishing the work of his mentor, Durkheim, and his deceased colleagues. One exception to this was his publication in 1924 of *The Gift*, a portion of which is reprinted here. In this essay, Mauss shows that gift-giving in primitive societies is often a part of political and social obligations and reflects or expresses the society's underlying social structure.

The last contributor to this section is the German sociologist Max Weber (1864–1920). Although best known for his work in sociology, Weber was trained in law and in history and held academic posts in economics. Unlike Durkheim, Weber was concerned with the action of individuals as well as social groups. According to Weber, the ultimate base of social action is individual behavior a person undertakes in relation to others; that behavior is best judged by whether the action is rational or not. While Weber was relatively poorly versed in the ethnography of "primitive" societies, he was extremely interested in Asia and wrote extensively on religion in China and India.

Much of Weber's work was influenced by Marx, and he attempted to develop Marx's thoughts on social class. Like Marx, he believed that social class was related to property ownership and control of the means of production. Unlike Marx, he believed that classes, in and of themselves, could not act and that status (or honor) and party could also cut across class lines. In his essay "Class, Status, Party," Weber develops this theory of class stratification, status, parties (groups that exist to pursue power), and the role of the individual in society.

Another critical feature that differentiates Weber's work from Marx's is the prominent role he gave to individual action and ideology. Both Marx and Weber saw these as ultimately grounded in systems of production, but in Weber's work, individuals and ideologies take on the capacity for action and culture change that is much less evident in Marx.

One of Weber's best-known explanations of the role of ideology is *The Protestant Ethic and the Spirit of Capitalism* (1958 [1904–1905]). Like Marx, Weber analyzed the rise of capitalism, and like Marx, he saw the roots of capitalism in fundamental changes in relations of production, such as the displacement of peasants. However, unlike Marx, he found these material causes insufficient to explain the emergence and success of capitalism. Instead, he proposed that these changes, coupled with a new Calvinist ethic that emphasized moral accountability and self-discipline, explain capitalism's rise. It is critical to Weber's point that Calvinism did not emerge from capitalism. It was aimed at assuring personal salvation, not profits. However, coinciding with changes in relations of production, it greatly favored the emergence of a powerful capitalist bourgeoisie.

Weber believed that individuals could profoundly affect their societies. Prophets could emerge who could change the way people around them thought. He called the ability of an individual to influence others "charisma" and developed this notion in *Collected Essays in the Sociology of Religion* (1993 [1920]). There, he defined charisma as an "extraordinary power"—a sort of spiritual power possessed by an individual. Weber did not explain the source of charisma. He said that it simply exists naturally in some people. In others, it is a germ that must be awakened. The power of charisma enables certain individuals to lead their societies and change the thinking of those around them. The notion of charisma gives the individual a place in Weber's work that is lacking in Marx's theory.

Weber's influence on later anthropological work is subtle, but significant. His emphasis on individual, rational social action was incorporated into Bronislaw Malinowski's theory of psychological functionalism. His work on forms of authority influenced many anthropological thinkers (see Morton Fried, essay 21) as did his analysis of the Protestant ethic and capitalism (see Julian Steward, essay 18, and Clifford Geertz, essay 37). Weber's work on religion influenced Roy Rappaport (1994:167) as well as Anthony F. C. Wallace, Peter Worsley, and Jean and John Comaroff (Erikson 1998:112).

Many symbolic, interpretive, and postmodern anthropologists were influenced by Weber's notion of *verstehen,* usually translated as "understanding." Weber used the term to mean the empathetic identification with those you are observing in order to better understand their motives and the meaning of their behavior. In particular, the essays in this volume by Clifford Geertz and Renato Rosaldo (essays 37 and 38) illustrate how this principle has been used by anthropologists.

6. What Is a Social Fact?

Émile Durkheim (1858–1917)

BEFORE INQUIRING INTO THE METHOD SUITED to the study of social facts, it is important to know which facts are commonly called "social." This information is all the more necessary since the designation "social" is used with little precision. It is currently employed for practically all phenomena generally diffused within society, however small their social interest. But on that basis, there are, as it were, no human events that may not be called social. Each individual drinks, sleeps, eats, reasons; and it is to society's interest that these functions be exercised in an orderly manner. If, then, all these facts are counted as "social" facts, sociology would have no subject matter exclusively its own, and its domain would be confused with that of biology and psychology.[1]

But in reality there is in every society a certain group of phenomena which may be differentiated from those studied by the other natural sciences. When I fulfill my obligations as brother, husband, or citizen, when I execute my contracts, I perform duties which are defined, externally to myself and my acts, in law and in custom. Even if they conform to my own sentiments and I feel their reality subjectively, such reality is still objective, for I did not create them; I merely inherited them through my education. How many times it happens, moreover, that we are ignorant of the details of the obligations incumbent upon us, and that in

order to acquaint ourselves with them we must consult the law and its authorized interpreters! Similarly, the church-member finds the beliefs and practices of his religious life ready-made at birth; their existence prior to his own implies their existence outside of himself. The system of signs I use to express my thought, the system of currency I employ to pay my debts, the instruments of credit I utilize in my commercial relations, the practices followed in my profession, etc., function independently of my own use of them. And these statements can be repeated for each member of society. Here, then, are ways of acting, thinking, and feeling that present the noteworthy property of existing outside the individual consciousness.

These types of conduct or thought are not only external to the individual but are, moreover, endowed with coercive power, by virtue of which they impose themselves upon him, independent of his individual will. Of course, when I fully consent and conform to them, this constraint is felt only slightly, if at all, and is therefore unnecessary. But it is, nonetheless, an intrinsic characteristic of these facts, the proof thereof being that it asserts itself as soon as I attempt to resist it. If I attempt to violate the law, it reacts against me so as to prevent my act before its accomplishment, or to nullify my violation by restoring the damage, if it is accomplished and reparable, or to make me expiate it if it cannot be compensated for otherwise.[2]

From *Rules of the Sociological Method* (1895)

---

[1] Durkheim's goal in writing this essay was to show that sociology could be a field of study distinct from other sciences. He wrote at a time when the divisions between anthropology, sociology, and psychology, as we know them today, did not exist. Durkheim was concerned to establish what he considered a new and independent science, which required having something in particular to study, a subject matter that could distinguish it from other sciences. That subject matter, Durkheim proposed, was social facts. As a follower of the French positivist Auguste Comte (1798–1857), Durkheim was vitally concerned with establishing the reality of social facts. Comte insisted that philosophy (and social science) be based on precise, observable facts subject to general laws. If the existence of such facts could not be demonstrated, sociology had no place in science.

[2] Durkheim argues that social facts are real because their effects can be felt. People are compelled to live according to the rules of their society and violate them at their peril. Fertile ground for discovering examples of social facts can be

In the case of purely moral maxims; the public conscience exercises a check on every act which offends it by means of the surveillance it exercises over the conduct of citizens, and the appropriate penalties at its disposal. In many cases the constraint is less violent, but nevertheless it always exists. If I do not submit to the conventions of society, if in my dress I do not conform to the customs observed in my country and in my class, the ridicule I provoke, the social isolation in which I am kept, produce, although in an attenuated form, the same effects as a punishment in the strict sense of the word. The constraint is nonetheless efficacious for being indirect. I am not obliged to speak French with my fellow-countrymen nor to use the legal currency, but I cannot possibly do otherwise. If I tried to escape this necessity, my attempt would fail miserably. As an industrialist, I am free to apply the technical methods of former centuries; but by doing so, I should invite certain ruin. Even when I free myself from these rules and violate them successfully, I am always compelled to struggle with them. When finally overcome, they make their constraining power sufficiently felt by the resistance they offer. The enterprises of all innovators, including successful ones, come up against resistance of this kind.[3]

Here, then, is a category of facts with very distinctive characteristics: it consists of ways of acting, thinking, and feeling, external to the individual, and endowed with a power of coercion, by reason of which they control him. These ways of thinking could not be confused with biological phenomena, since they consist of representations and of actions; nor with psychological phenomena, which exist only in the individual consciousness and through it. They constitute, thus, a new variety of phenomena; and it is to them exclusively that the term "social" ought to be applied. And this term fits them quite well, for it is clear that, since their source is not in the individual, their substratum can be no other than society, either the political society as a whole or some one of the partial groups it includes, such as religious denominations, political, literary, and occupational associations, etc. On the other hand, this term "social" applies to them exclusively, for it has a distinct meaning only if it designates exclusively the phenomena which are not included in any of the categories of facts that have already been established and classified. These ways of thinking and acting therefore constitute the proper domain of sociology. It is true that, when we define them with this word "constraint," we risk shocking the zealous partisans of absolute individualism. For those who profess the complete autonomy of the individual, man's dignity is diminished whenever he is made to feel that he is not completely self-determinant. It is generally accepted today, however, that most of our ideas and our tendencies are not developed by ourselves but come to us from without. How can they become a part of us except by imposing themselves upon us? This is the whole meaning of our definition. And it is generally accepted, moreover, that social constraint is not necessarily incompatible with the individual personality.[a]

Since the examples that we have just cited (legal and moral regulations, religious faiths, financial systems, etc.) all consist of established beliefs and practices, one might be led to believe that social facts exist only where there is some social organization. But there are other facts without such crystallized form which have the same

---

found in a society's general rules of behavior, such as the informal rules about what is appropriate to eat and how to eat. Most readers of this book probably have an aversion to eating insects—not because there is a law against eating them, but because of informal rules that shape behavior. Even thinking about eating insects probably disgusts most Americans, which is how the effects of the social fact can be observed.

[3] Although Durkheim refers to social facts as "laws" and speaks of "executing contracts," he is not just thinking of laws in the legal sense. He was referring to the general rules of behavior that people unconsciously follow; rules we internalize through growing up in a society—what he calls "moral maxims." He argues that public opinion also controls people's conduct, in particular, through mechanisms such as shaming, ridicule, and ostracism. For instance, it is not illegal to pick your nose in public, but it does violate an informal rule of behavior. Taking this action provokes reactions of disgust from onlookers, and the offender would feel embarrassed or ashamed and probably not repeat the action.

objectivity and the same ascendancy over the individual. These are called "social currents." Thus the great movements of enthusiasm, indignation, and pity in a crowd do not originate in any one of the particular individual consciousnesses. They come to each one of us from without and can carry us away in spite of ourselves. Of course, it may happen that, in abandoning myself to them unreservedly, I do not feel the pressure they exert upon me. But it is revealed as soon as I try to resist them. Let an individual attempt to oppose one of these collective manifestations and the emotions that he denies will turn against him. Now, if this power of external coercion asserts itself so clearly in cases of resistance, it must exist also in the first-mentioned cases, although we are unconscious of it. We are then victims of the illusion of having ourselves created that which actually forced itself from without. If the complacency with which we permit ourselves to be carried along conceals the pressure undergone, nevertheless it does not abolish it. Thus, air is no less heavy because we do not detect its weight. So, even if we ourselves have spontaneously contributed to the production of the common emotion, the impression we have received differs markedly from that which we would have experienced if we had been alone. Also, once the crowd has dispersed, that is, once these social influences have ceased to act upon us and we are alone again, the emotions which have passed through the mind appear strange to us, and we no longer recognize them as ours. We realize that these feelings have been impressed upon us to a much greater extent than they were created by us. It may even happen that they horrify us, so much were they contrary to our nature. Thus, a group of individuals, most of whom are perfectly inoffensive, may, when gathered in a crowd, be drawn into acts of atrocity. And what we say of these transitory outbursts applies similarly to those more permanent currents of opinion on religious, political, literary, or artistic matters which are constantly being formed around us, whether in society as a whole or in more limited circles.[4]

To confirm this definition of the social fact by a characteristic illustration from common experience, one need only observe the manner in which children are brought up. Considering the facts as they are and as they have always been, it becomes immediately evident that all education is a continuous effort to impose on the child ways of seeing, feeling, and acting which he could not have arrived at spontaneously. From the very first hours of his life, we compel him to eat, drink, and sleep at regular hours; we constrain him to cleanliness, calmness, and obedience; later we exert pressure upon him in order that he may learn proper consideration for others, respect for customs and conventions, the need for work, etc. If, in time, this constraint ceases to be felt, it is because it gradually gives rise to habits and to internal tendencies that render constraint unnecessary; but nevertheless it is not abolished, for it is still the source from which these habits were derived. It is true that, according to Spencer, a rational education ought to reject such methods, allowing the child to act in complete liberty; but as this pedagogic theory has never been applied by any known people, it must be accepted only as an expression of personal opinion, not as a fact which can contradict the aforementioned observations. What makes these facts particularly instructive is that the aim of education is, precisely,

---

[4] Durkheim differentiates social facts, which are enduring, from transitory social currents. Social currents, such as the momentary emotions sweeping a crowd, give a taste of the power of social facts. As members of a crowd, we are clearly capable of emotions (and actions) beyond our own capabilities or desires.

Issues of crowd behavior were very much on the minds of writers of this era (see footnote 1, page 141, for another example). The unsuccessful European revolutions of 1848 and the Paris Commune of 1871 had included striking displays of mob and government violence. In 1894, a year before the publication of this essay, Alfred Dreyfus (1859–1935), the only Jewish officer in the French Army's General Staff, was wrongly convicted of spying for the Germans. The affair inflamed mob passions against Jews, socialists, and other minorities. The proto-fascist politician and author, Maurice Barrès (1862–1923) called for a leader who would be an embodiment of the collective will of the masses. Durkheim, as a secular, Jewish socialist, must have been deeply impressed and concerned.

the socialization of the human being; the process of education, therefore, gives us in a nutshell the historical fashion in which the social being is constituted. This unremitting pressure to which the child is subjected is the very pressure of the social milieu which tends to fashion him in its own image, and of which parents and teachers are merely the representatives and intermediaries.[5]

It follows that sociological phenomena cannot be defined by their universality. A thought which we find in every individual consciousness, a movement repeated by all individual manifestations, is not thereby a social fact. If sociologists have been satisfied with defining them by this characteristic, it is because they confused them with what one might call their reincarnation in the individual. It is, however, the collective aspects of the beliefs, tendencies, and practices of a group that characterize truly social phenomena. As for the forms that the collective states assume when refracted in the individual, these are things of another sort. This duality is clearly demonstrated by the fact that these two orders of phenomena are frequently found dissociated from one another. Indeed, certain of these social manners of acting and thinking acquire, by reason of their repetition, a certain rigidity which on its own account crystallizes them, so to speak, and isolates them from the particular events which reflect them. They thus acquire a body, a tangible form, and constitute a reality in their own right, quite distinct from the individual facts which produce it. Collective habits are inherent not only in the successive acts which they determine but, by

a privilege of which we find no example in the biological realm, they are given permanent expression in a formula which is repeated from mouth to mouth, transmitted by education, and fixed even in writing. Such is the origin and nature of legal and moral rules, popular aphorisms and proverbs, articles of faith wherein religious or political groups condense their beliefs, standards of taste established by literary schools, etc. None of these can be found entirely reproduced in the applications made of them by individuals, since they can exist even without being actually applied.[6]

No doubt, this dissociation does not always manifest itself with equal distinctness, but its obvious existence in the important and numerous cases just cited is sufficient to prove that the social fact is a thing distinct from its individual manifestations. Moreover, even when this dissociation is not immediately apparent, it may often be disclosed by certain devices of method. Such dissociation is indispensable if one wishes to separate social facts from their alloys in order to observe them in a state of purity. Currents of opinion, with an intensity varying according to the time and place, impel certain groups either to more marriages, for example, or to more suicides, or to a higher or lower birthrate, etc. These currents are plainly social facts. At first sight they seem inseparable from the forms they take in individual cases. But statistics furnish us with the means of isolating them. They are, in fact, represented with considerable exactness by the rates of births, marriages, and suicides, that is, by the number obtained by dividing the average annual

---

[5] Modern anthropologists call this process *enculturation* and believe that it is largely unconscious. In other words, we think and act the way we do largely because of the unconscious internalization of cultural constraints imposed on us during childhood, not because of conscious, rational choice. Durkheim's citation of Herbert Spencer here is strange because the name that would come to the mind of any French intellectual reading this passage is Jean-Jacques Rousseau (1712–1778), whose 1762 book *Emile* proposed a similar theory of "natural" education. So why does Durkheim, writing in French, cite Spencer, an Englishman, and not Rousseau, who was French? Probably because he considered Spencer a scientist and Rousseau a philosopher and wished to emphasize the scientific nature of his work.

[6] Since they are beyond the individual, social facts must have an existence apart from their individual manifestations. Indeed, individual behavior can only approximate the rules of behavior. Durkheim was familiar with Platonic philosophy and his argument parallels that perspective. Plato, in his *Republic,* proposed that objects on earth are imperfect representations of ideal forms existing beyond human consciousness; Durkheim suggests that actual behavior is the imperfect representation of crystallized social facts existing beyond individual awareness. A problem with this view is that a social fact must somehow be teased out of a myriad of individual manifestations, none of which accurately reflects it. Will all observers find the same social facts?

total of marriages, births, suicides, by the number of persons whose ages lie within the range in which marriages, births, and suicides occur.[b] Since each of these figures contains all the individual cases indiscriminately, the individual circumstances which may have had a share in the production of the phenomenon are neutralized and, consequently, do not contribute to its determination. The average, then, expresses a certain state of the group mind (*l'âme collective*).[7]

Such are social phenomena, when disentangled from all foreign matter. As for their individual manifestations, these are indeed, to a certain extent, social, since they partly reproduce a social model. Each of them also depends, and to a large extent, on the organopsychological constitution of the individual and on the particular circumstances in which he is placed. Thus they are not sociological phenomena in the strict sense of the word. They belong to two realms at once; one could call them sociopsychological. They interest the sociologist without constituting the immediate subject matter of sociology. There exist in the interior of organisms similar phenomena, compound in their nature, which form in their turn the subject matter of the "hybrid sciences," such as physiological chemistry, for example.

The objection may be raised that a phenomenon is collective only if it is common to all members of society, or at least to most of them — in other words, if it is truly general. This may be true; but it is general because it is collective (that is, more or less obligatory), and certainly not collective because general. It is a group condition repeated in the individual because imposed on him. It is to be found in each part because it exists in the whole, rather than in the whole because it exists in the parts.[8] This becomes conspicuously evident in those beliefs and practices which are transmitted to us ready-made by previous generations; we receive and adopt them because, being both collective and ancient, they are invested with a particular authority that education has taught us to recognize and respect. It is, of course, true that a vast portion of our social culture is transmitted to us in this way; but even when the social fact is due in part to our direct collaboration, its nature is not different. A collective emotion which bursts forth suddenly and violently in a crowd does not express merely what all the individual sentiments had in common; it is something entirely different, as we have shown. It results from their being together, a product of the actions and reactions which take place between individual consciousnesses; and if each individual consciousness echoes the collective sentiment, it is by virtue of the special energy resident in its collective origin. If all hearts beat in unison, this is not the result of a spontaneous and pre-established harmony but rather because an identical force propels them in the same direction. Each is carried along by all.[9]

We thus arrive at the point where we can formulate and delimit in a precise way the domain

---

[7] The use of statistics to predict behavior was of relatively recent origin when Durkheim wrote this article. The astronomer-turned-statistician Adolphe J. Quetelet published two volumes, *On Man and the Development of His Faculties* (1835) and *Of the Social System and the Laws Which Rule It* (1848), in which probability theory was first applied to population characteristics (Tylor also refers to Quetelet in essay 2). Because the behavioral characteristics of a population are predictable through statistical analysis, Durkheim saw statistics as a scientific method for identifying social facts. In this paragraph he mentions their use in analyzing suicide rates. One of Durkheim's most influential works was *Suicide: A Study in Sociology* (1897), which appeared two years after this essay and makes extensive use of statistics.

[8] Although the wording may be confusing, Durkheim makes an important point at the outset of this paragraph. He thought that a belief or behavior held in common by members of a society was prevalent *because* it was a collective phenomenon. Everyone shares social facts because they are collective; they are not collective simply because everyone shares them. Social facts precede individuals and are imposed upon them.

[9] In this paragraph, Durkheim returns once again to the problem of the crowd. He suggests that by virtue of coming together, people create a "special energy," which in *The Elementary Forms of the Religious Life* (1965 [1912]), he called "l'âme collective". The use of the term "energy" is important. Durkheim wished to show that sociology was a science and borrowed some of the vocabulary of physics to make his point. Just as the physicists of his day were concerned with the discovery of laws of energy, Durkheim wanted to uncover the laws underlying the behavior of this "social energy."

of sociology.[10] It comprises only a limited group of phenomena. A social fact is to be recognized by the power of external coercion which it exercises or is capable of exercising over individuals, and the presence of this power may be recognized in its turn either by the existence of some specific sanction or by the resistance offered against every individual effort that tends to violate it. One can, however, define it also by its diffusion within the group, provided that, in conformity with our previous remarks, one takes care to add as a second and essential characteristic that its own existence is independent of the individual forms it assumes in its diffusion. This last criterion is perhaps, in certain cases, easier to apply than the preceding one. In fact, the constraint is easy to ascertain when it expresses itself externally by some direct reaction of society, as is the case in law, morals, beliefs, customs, and even fashions.[11] But when it is only indirect, like the constraint which an economic organization exercises, it cannot always be so easily detected. Generality combined with externality may, then, be easier to establish. Moreover, this second definition is but another form of the first; for if a mode of behavior whose existence is external to individual consciousnesses becomes general, this can only be brought about by its being imposed upon them.[c]

But these several phenomena present the same characteristic by which we defined the others. These "ways of existing" are imposed on the individual precisely in the same fashion as the "ways of acting" of which we have spoken. Indeed, when we wish to know how a society is divided politically, of what these divisions themselves are composed, and how complete is the fusion existing between them, we shall not achieve our purpose by physical inspection and by geographical observations; for these phenomena are social, even when they have some basis in physical nature. It is only by a study of public law that a comprehension of this organization is possible, for it is this law that determines the organization, as it equally determines our domestic and civil relations. This political organization is, then, no less obligatory than the social facts mentioned above. If the population crowds into our cities instead of scattering into the country, this is due to a trend of public opinion, a collective drive that imposes this concentration upon the individuals. We can no more choose the style of our houses than of our clothing—at least, both are equally obligatory. The channels of communication prescribe the direction of internal migrations and commerce, etc., and even their extent.[12] Consequently, at the very most, it should be necessary to add to the list of phenomena which we have enumerated as presenting the distinctive criterion of a social fact only one additional category, "ways of existing"; and as this enumeration was not meant to be rigorously exhaustive, the addition would not be absolutely necessary.

Such an addition is perhaps not necessary, for these "ways of existing" are only crystallized "ways of acting." The political structure of a society is merely the way in which its component segments

---

[10] In this paragraph, Durkheim summarizes the characteristics of social facts: they are external to individuals and coercive. Sometimes social facts are enshrined in law or can be recognized by the negative reaction of others when a principle is violated. Frequently they can be determined by the statistical analysis of a population's behavior.

[11] Durkheim says that the constraint exercised by social facts is easily recognized when expressed "externally by some direct reaction of society, as is the case in law, morals, beliefs, customs and even fashions." Compare this statement to Tylor's famous definition of culture, which opens *Primitive Culture* (1871; see essay 2): "Culture or civilization, taken in its wide ethnographic sense, is that complex whole which includes knowledge, belief, art, morals, law, custom, and any other capabilities and habits acquired by man as a member of society." Although not cited, it appears Durkheim's formulation was influenced by Tylor's definition. He may well have conceived of society as a collection of social facts.

[12] Durkheim contends in this paragraph that social movements, such as the change from rural to predominantly urban lifestyles, are driven by collective opinion, revealing himself as a strict idealist. Unlike Marxists, cultural ecologists, and cultural materialists, he attributes social changes to changes in ideas and opinions rather than changes in material structures such as the development of industrial capitalism.

have become accustomed to live with one another. If their relations are traditionally intimate, the segments tend to fuse with one another, or, in the contrary case, to retain their identity. The type of habitation imposed upon us is merely the way in which our contemporaries and our ancestors have been accustomed to construct their houses. The methods of communication are merely the channels which the regular currents of commerce and migrations have dug, by flowing in the same direction. To be sure, if the phenomena of a structural character alone presented this permanence, one might believe that they constituted a distinct species. A legal regulation is an arrangement no less permanent than a type of architecture, and yet the regulation is a "physiological" fact. A simple moral maxim is assuredly somewhat more malleable, but it is much more rigid than a simple professional custom or a fashion. There is thus a whole series of degrees without a break in continuity between the facts of the most articulated structure and those free currents of social life which are not yet definitely molded. The differences between them are, therefore, only differences in the degree of consolidation they present. Both are simply life, more or less crystallized.[13] No doubt, it may be of some advantage to reserve the term "morphological" for those social facts which concern the social substratum, but only on condition of not overlooking the fact that they are of the same nature as the others. Our definition will then include the whole relevant range of facts if we say: *A social fact is every way of acting, fixed or not, capable of exercising on the individual an external constraint; or again, every way of acting which is general throughout a given society, while at the same time existing in its own right independent of its individual manifestations.*[d]

Notes

a. We do not intend to imply, however, that all constraint is normal. We shall return to this point later.

b. Suicides do not occur at every age, and they take place with varying intensity at the different ages in which they occur.

c. It will be seen how this definition of the social fact diverges from that which forms the basis of the ingenious system of M. Tarde. First of all, we wish to state that our researches have nowhere led us to observe that preponderant influence in the genesis of collective facts which M. Tarde attributes to imitation. Moreover, from the preceding definition, which is not a theory but simply a résumé of the immediate data of observation, it seems indeed to follow, not only that imitation does not always express the essential and characteristic features of the social fact, but even that it never expresses them. No doubt, every social fact is imitated; it has, as we have just shown, a tendency to become general, but that is because it is social, i.e., obligatory. Its power of expansion is not the cause but the consequence of its sociological character. If, further, only social facts produced this consequence, imitation could perhaps serve, if not to explain them, at least to define them. But an individual condition which produces a whole series of effects remains individual nevertheless. Moreover, one may ask whether the word "imitation" is indeed fitted to designate an effect due to a coercive influence. Thus, by this single expression, very different phenomena, which ought to be distinguished, are confused.

d. This close connection between life and structure, organ and function, may be easily proved in sociology because between these two extreme terms there exists a whole series of immediately observable intermediate stages which show the bond between them. Biology is not in the same favorable position. But we may well believe that the inductions on this subject made by sociology are applicable to biology and that, in organisms as well as in societies, only differences in degree exist between these two orders of facts.

---

[13] It is easy to see the coercive element in illegal or immoral acts, where violation of a rule results (at least theoretically) in punishment. However, coercion is also present in ways of behaving that are outside of the individual and general throughout society, such as participation in the capitalist economic system or living in a certain type of house. Durkheim calls these phenomena "ways of existing." He further suggests that ways of existing and acting are variable in degree of fixity. There is, for example, a continuum of rigidity between custom and law, but both are still included in Durkheim's famous definition of social facts presented at the end of the paragraph.

7. The Cosmological System of Totemism and the Idea of Class

Émile Durkheim (1858–1917)

WE ARE BEGINNING TO SEE THAT TOTEMISM IS a much more complex religion than it first appeared to be. We have already distinguished three classes of things which it recognizes as sacred, in varying degrees: the totemic emblem, the animal or plant whose appearance this emblem reproduces, and the members of the clan.[1] However, this list is not yet complete. In fact, a religion is not merely a collection of fragmentary beliefs in regard to special objects like those we have just been discussing. To a greater or less extent, all known religions have been systems of ideas which tend to embrace the universality of things, and to give us a complete representation of the world. If totemism is to be considered as a religion comparable to the others, it too should offer us a conception of the universe. As a matter of fact, it does satisfy this condition.

1

The fact that this aspect of totemism has generally been neglected is due to the too narrow notion of the clan which has been prevalent. Ordinarily it is regarded as a mere group of human beings. Being a simple subdivision of the tribe, it seems that like this, it is made up of nothing but men. But in rea-

From *The Elementary Forms of the Religious Life* (1912)

soning thus, we substitute our European ideas for those which the primitive has of man and of society. For the Australian, things themselves, everything which is in the universe, are a part of the tribe; they are constituent elements of it and, so to speak, regular members of it; just like men, they have a determined place in the general scheme of organization of the society. "The South Australian savage," says Fison, "looks upon the universe as the Great Tribe, to one of whose divisions he himself belongs — and all things, animate and inanimate, which belong to his class are parts of the body corporate whereof he himself is a part."[a] As a consequence of this principle, whenever the tribe is divided into two phratries,[2] all known things are distributed between them. "All nature," says Palmer, in speaking of the Bellinger River tribe, "is also divided into class [phratry] names. . . . The sun and moon and stars are said . . . to belong to classes [phratries] just as the blacks themselves."[b] The Port Mackay tribe in Queensland has two phratries with the names Yungaroo and Wootaroo, as do the neighboring tribes. Now as Bridgmann says, "all things, animate and inanimate, are divided by these tribes into two classes, named Yungaroo and Wootaroo."[c] Nor does the classification stop here. The men of each phratry are distributed among a certain number of clans; likewise, the things attributed to each phratry are in their turn distrib-

---

[1] Durkheim was concerned with the mechanisms that held societies together. He believed that social cohesion was maintained because people in a society shared the same values and beliefs and reinforced those beliefs through rituals or communal action. For example, cohesion in simple societies was achieved through totemic beliefs (modeled on their own social relationships) and religious rituals (which reinforced those beliefs through communal action).

Sigmund Freud, in *Totem and Taboo* (1950 [1913]), used totems to establish a link between psychoanalysis and anthropology and used psychoanalytic concepts to explain anthropological data (see essay 5). Durkheim, on the other hand, discussed how totemic beliefs structure society, contribute to social solidarity, and ultimately represent society. According to him, because totems are the fundamental form of kinship division, and these divisions compose the basic structure of society, the worship of totem ancestors represents the worship of society itself.

[2] Lorimer Fison (1832–1907) was a missionary, journalist, and anthropologist. He was a follower of Lewis Henry Morgan, and they corresponded extensively. Fison's research into Australian Aboriginal kinship systems, based on interviews with European settlers, provided important data for Morgan, Tylor, and James George Frazer, as well as Durkheim.

A *phratry* is a unilineal descent group composed of two or more clans.

uted among the clans of which the phratry is composed. A certain tree, for example, will be assigned to the Kangaroo clan, and to it alone; then, just like the human members of the clan, it will have the Kangaroo as totem; another will belong to the Snake-clan; clouds will be placed under one totem, the sun under another, etc. All known things will thus be arranged in a sort of tableau or systematic classification embracing the whole of nature.

We have given a certain number of these classifications elsewhere,[d] at present we shall confine ourselves to repeating a few of these as examples. One of the best known of these is the one found in the Mount Gambier tribe. This tribe includes two phratries, named respectively the Kumite and the Kroki; each of these, in its turn, is subdivided into five clans. Now "everything in nature belongs to one or another of these ten clans";[e] Fison and Howitt say that they are all "included" within it. In fact, they are classified under these ten totems just like species in their respective classes. This is well shown by the following table based on information gathered by Curr and by Fison and Howitt.[f]

Phratries	Clans	Things Classed in Each Clan
Kumite	Fish-hawk	Smoke, honey-suckle, certain trees, etc.
	Pelican	Blackwood-trees, dogs, fire, frost, etc.
	Crow	Rain, thunder, lightning, clouds, hail, winter, etc.
	Black cockatoo	The stars, the moon, etc.
	A non-poisonous snake	Fish, seal, eel, the stringybark-tree, etc.
Kroki	Tea-tree	Duck, crayfish, owls, etc.
	An edible root	Bustard, quail, a small kangaroo, etc.
	A white crestless cockatoo	Kangaroo, the summer, the sun, wind, the autumn, etc.
	Details are lacking for the fourth and fifth Kroki clans.	

[The next several paragraphs of Durkheim's article (about 280 words) are given to describing examples of totems in a variety of Australian aboriginal tribes. His basic point is that the Australian Aborigines subdivide themselves and all the objects in their world into related totems. The passage includes 4 footnotes.]

If we remember that there are many other clans (Howitt names twelve and Mathews fourteen and adds that his list is incomplete[g]), we will understand how all the things in which the native takes an interest find a natural place in these classifications.

Similar arrangements have been observed in the most diverse parts of the Australian continent; in South Australia, in Victoria, and in New South Wales (among the Euahlayi[h]); very clear traces of it are found in the central tribes.[i] In Queensland, where the clans seem to have disappeared and where the matrimonial classes are the only subdivisions of the phratry, things are divided up among these classes. Thus the Wakelbura are divided into two phratries, Mallera and Wutaru; the classes of the first are called Kurgilla and Banbe, those of the second, Wungo and Obu. Now to the Banbe belong the opossum, the kangaroo, the dog, honey of little bees, etc.; to the Wungo are attributed the emu, the bandicoot, the black duck, the black snake, the brown snake; to the Obu, the carpet snake, the honey of stinging bees, etc.; to the Kurgilla, the porcupine, the turkey of the plains, water, rain, fire, thunder, etc.[j]

This same organization is found among the Indians of North America. The Zuni have a system of classification which, in its essential lines, is in all points comparable to the one we have just described. That of the Omaha rests on the same principles as that of the Wotjobaluk.[k] An echo of these same ideas survives even into the more advanced societies. Among the Haida, all the gods and mythical beings who are placed in charge of the different phenomena of nature are classified in one or the other of the two phratries which make up the tribe just like men; some are Eagles, the others, Crows.[l] Now the gods of things are only another aspect of the things which they govern.[m] This mythological classification is therefore merely another form of the preceding one. So we may rest assured that this way of conceiving the world is independent of all ethnic or geographic particularities; and at the same time it is clearly seen to be closely united to the whole system of totemic beliefs.[3]

2

In the paper to which we have already made allusion several times, we have shown what light these facts throw upon the way in which the idea of kind or class was formed in humanity.[4] In fact, these systematic classifications are the first we meet with in history, and we have just seen that they are modeled upon the social organization, or rather that they have taken the forms of society as their framework. It is the phratries which have served as classes, and the clans as species. It is because men were organized that they have been able to organize things, for in classifying these latter, they limited themselves to giving them places in the groups they formed themselves.[5] And if these different classes of things are not merely put next to each other, but are arranged according to a unified plan, it is because the social

groups with which they commingle themselves are unified and, through their union, form an organic whole, the tribe. The unity of these first logical systems merely reproduces the unity of the society. Thus we have an occasion for verifying the proposition which we laid down at the commencement of this work, and for assuring ourselves that the fundamental notions of the intellect, the essential categories of thought, may be the product of social factors.[6] The above-mentioned facts show clearly that this is the case with the very notion of category itself.

However, it is not our intention to deny that the individual intellect has of itself the power of perceiving resemblances between the different objects of which it is conscious. Quite on the contrary, it is clear that even the most primitive and simple classifications presuppose this faculty. The Australian does not place things in the same clan or in different clans at random. For him as for us, similar images attract one another, while opposed ones repel one another, and it is on the basis of these feelings of affinity or of repulsion that he classifies the corresponding things in one place or another.

---

[3] Durkheim was concerned with documenting the universality of his theory through the use of cross-cultural ethnographic data. He cites a wide variety of examples from different parts of the world and concludes that totemism exists "independent of ethnic and geographic particularities." This issue is important because he believed totemism was one of the fundamental elements of primitive social organization. Writing at the same time as Durkheim, Franz Boas challenged the use of cross-cultural comparison (see essay 10). Boas believed that every society was the product of its own historical development. To understand a society, one needed to study the environmental and historical circumstances under which it developed.

[4] Although Durkheim does not specify what paper he is referring to in this passage, it is probably the article *"De quelques formes primitives de classification"* ("Primitive Forms of Classification"), co-authored with Mauss, which appeared in *L'Année Sociologique* in 1903.

[5] Durkheim asserted that totemic classification of the objects in the world was based on the social classification of people. Thus, totemic classification was derived from a model of social structure. Compare the very different treatment Freud accorded to totemism in *Totem and Taboo* (1950 [1913]), essay 5, in which totemism originated in the memorialization of the primal father who was killed and eaten by his sons. Thus, in Freud's view, social classification was derived from totemism.

[6] In this paragraph Durkheim writes that "the fundamental notions of the intellect" and "the essential categories of thought" are the products of social factors, not individual invention. In the introduction to his book Durkheim wrote

> Collective representations are the result of an immense co-operation, which stretches out not only into space but into time as well; to make them, a multitude of minds have associated, united and combined their ideas and sentiments; for them, long generations have accumulated their experience and knowledge. A special intellectual activity is therefore concentrated in them which is infinitely richer and complexer than that of the individual. (1965:29)

In the final sentence of this paragraph in the essay, Durkheim notes that the very notion of a category of classification is itself a social construction. This is one of the critical insights upon which ethnoscience and cognitive anthropology were constructed in the 1950s and 1960s (see essays 28 and 29). Durkheim reiterates his belief that society is the model from which categories of classification are derived and that these shared models are the foundation of social solidarity. He writes that the unity of categories reproduces the unity of society.

There are also cases where we are able to perceive the reasons which inspired this. The two phratries were very probably the original and fundamental bases for these classifications, which were consequently bifurcate at first. Now, when a classification is reduced to two classes, these are almost necessarily conceived as antitheses; they are used primarily as a means of clearly separating things between which there is a very marked contrast. Some are set at the right, the others at the left.[7] As a matter of fact this is the character of the Australian classifications. If the white cockatoo is in one phratry, the black one is in the other; if the sun is on one side, the moon and the stars of night are on the opposite side.[n] Very frequently the beings which serve as the totems of the two phratries have contrary colours.[o] These oppositions are even met with outside of Australia. Where one of the phratries is disposed to peace, the other is disposed to war,[p] if one has water as its totem, the other has earth.[q] This is undoubtedly the explanation of why the two phratries have frequently been thought of as naturally antagonistic to one another. They say that there is a sort of rivalry or even a constitutional hostility between them.[r] This opposition of things has extended itself to persons; the logical contrast has begotten a sort of social conflict.[s]

It is also to be observed that within each phratry, those things have been placed in a single clan which seem to have the greatest affinity with that serving as totem. For example, the moon has been placed with the black cockatoo, but the sun, together with the atmosphere and the wind, with the white cockatoo. Or again, to a totemic animal has been united all that serves him as food,[t] as well as the animals with which he has the closest connection.[u] Of course, we cannot always understand the obscure psychology which has caused many of these connections and distinctions, but the preceding examples are enough to show that a certain intuition of the resemblances and differences presented by things has played an important part in the genesis of these classifications.

But the feeling of resemblances is one thing and the idea of class is another. The class is the external framework of which objects perceived to be similar form, in part, the contents. Now the contents cannot furnish the frame into which they fit. They are made up of *vague and fluctuating* images, due to the superimposition and partial fusion of a *determined number of individual images,* which are found to have common elements; the framework, on the contrary, is a *definite form,* with fixed outlines, but which may be applied to an *undetermined number of things,* perceived or not, actual or possible. In fact, every class has possibilities of extension which go far beyond the circle of objects which we know, either from direct experience or from resemblance. This is why every school of thinkers has refused, and not with good reason, to identify the idea of class with that of a generic image. The generic image is only the indistinctly-bounded residual representation left in us by similar representations, when they are present in consciousness simultaneously; the class is a logical symbol by means of which we think distinctly of these similarities and of other analogous ones. Moreover, the best proof of the distance separating these two notions is that an animal is able to form generic images though ignorant of the art of thinking in classes and species.[8]

---

[7] Durkheim's belief that human systems of classification were dualistic is expressed in this paragraph. One of the first studies suggesting the dualistic nature of human thought was the 1909 article "The Pre-eminence of the Right Hand: A Study in Religious Polarity" by Durkheim's student Robert Hertz (1881–1915). In this essay he examined the values placed on right- and left-handedness and analyzed the social function of these beliefs in society. Hertz said that the valuation of right- over left-handedness was a social fact that reflected the fundamental religious dichotomy between sacred and profane. Durkheim draws from Hertz's article in the next few paragraphs. Durkheim's ideas on dual classification form one of the principal assumptions underlying French structuralism as practiced by Claude Lévi-Strauss (see essays 25–27).

[8] In this section, Durkheim is discussing how humans classify things into groups. He begins by talking about the classification of people and objects into totems. He says the contents of a class do not construct the boundaries of that class but that the class framework is external: humans impose these class boundaries on the objects in the world. The obvious question, then, is what are the origins of these classes? In the next paragraph he tries to answer this question. Durkheim

The idea of class is an instrument of thought which has obviously been constructed by men. But in constructing it, we have at least had need of a model; for how could this idea ever have been born, if there had been nothing either in us or around us which was capable of suggesting it to us? To reply that it was given to us *a priori*[9] is not to reply at all; this lazy man's solution is, as has been said, the death of analysis. But it is hard to see where we could have found this indispensable model except in the spectacle of the collective life. In fact, a class is not an ideal, but a clearly defined group of things between which internal relationships exist, similar to those of kindred. Now the only groups of this sort known from experience are those formed by men in associating themselves. Material things may be able to form collections of units, or heaps, or mechanical assemblages with no internal unity, but not groups in the sense we have given the word. A heap of sand or a pile of rock is in no way comparable to that variety of definite and organized society which forms a class. In all probability, we would never have thought of uniting the beings of the universe into homogeneous groups, called classes, if we had not had the example of human societies before our eyes, if we had not even commenced by making things themselves members of men's society, and also if human groups and logical groups had not been confused at first.[v]

It is also to be borne in mind that a classification is a system whose parts are arranged according to a hierarchy. There are dominating members and others which are subordinate to the first; species and their distinctive properties depend upon classes and the attributes which characterize them; again, the different species of a single class are conceived as all placed on the same level in regard to each other. Does someone prefer to regard them from the point of view of the understanding? Then he represents things to himself in an inverse order: he puts at the top the species that are the most particularized and the richest in reality, while the types that are most general and the poorest in qualities are at the bottom. Nevertheless, all are represented in a hierarchic form. And we must be careful not to believe that the expression has only a metaphorical sense here: there are really relations of subordination and coordination, the establishment of which is the object of all classification, and men would never have thought of arranging their knowledge in this way if they had not known beforehand what a hierarchy was. But neither the spectacle of physical nature nor the mechanism of mental associations could furnish them with this knowledge. The hierarchy is exclusively a social affair. It is only in society that there are superiors, inferiors and equals. Consequently, even if the facts were not enough to prove it, the mere analysis of these ideas would reveal their origin. We have taken them from society, and projected them into our conceptions of the world. It is society that has furnished the outlines which logical thought has filled in.[10]

3

But these primitive classifications have a no less direct interest for the origins of religious thought.

---

carefully distinguishes between generic images and ideas of class. The generic image is based on a vague feeling of affinity, whereas a class is a fixed framework in which an indefinite number of objects can be categorized. This idea is critical in the development of ethnoscience and is implicit in the concept of domains (see essays 28 and 29). In the final statement in this paragraph, Durkheim says the best proof of the distinction between generic images and classes is that an animal is able to form generic images but not think in classes! We find this intriguing. This statement is probably based on the experimental psychology of Durkheim's time, but as he provides no citation, we do not really know what he was referring to.

[9] *A priori:* Latin for without or before examination.

[10] Durkheim emphasized the idea that systems of classification reflect the social categories a group imposes on its members. There is an additional level at which imposition may be at work in this essay — one of which Durkheim was unaware. Is it possible that Durkheim is projecting his own Eurocentric vision of a hierarchical world onto the Australian Aboriginal worldview? His statement that the object of all classification is to rank elements in relations of subordination or domination may tell us more about the society in which Durkheim lived than Aboriginal society.

They imply that all the things thus classed in a single clan or a single phratry are closely related both to each other and to the thing serving as the totem of this clan or phratry. When an Australian of the Port Mackay tribe says that the sun, snakes, etc., are of the Yungaroo phratry, he does not mean merely to apply a common, but none the less a purely conventional, nomenclature to these different things; the word has an objective signification for him. He believes that "alligators really *are* Yungaroo and that kangaroos are Wootaroo. The sun *is* Yungaroo, the moon Wootaroo, and so on for the constellations, trees, plants, etc."[w] An internal bond attaches them to the group in which they are placed; they are regular members of it. It is said that they belong to the group,[x] just exactly as the individual men make a part of it; consequently, the same sort of a relation unites them to these latter. Men regard the things in their clan as their relatives or associates; they call them their friends and think that they are made out of the same flesh as themselves.[y] Therefore, between the two there are elective affinities and quite special relations of agreement. Things and people have a common name, and in a certain way they naturally understand each other and harmonize with one another. For example, when a Wakelbura of the Mallera phratry is buried, the scaffold upon which the body is exposed "must be made of the wood of some tree belonging to the Mallera phratry."[z] The same is true for the branches that cover the corpse. If the deceased is of the Banbe class, a Banbe tree must be used. In this same tribe, a magician can use in his art only those things which belong to his own phratry;[aa] since the others are strangers to him, he does not know how to make them obey him. Thus a bond of mystic sympathy unites each individual to those beings, whether living or not, which are associated with him; the result of this is a belief in the possibility of deducing what he will do or what he has done from what they are doing. Among these same Wakelbura, when a man dreams that he has killed an animal belonging to a certain social division, he expects to meet a man of this same division the next day.[bb] Inversely, the things attributed to a clan or phratry cannot be used against the members of this clan or phratry. Among the Wotjobaluk, each phratry has its own special trees. Now in hunting an animal of the Gurogity phratry, only arms whose wood is taken from trees of the other phratry may be used, and *vice versa;* otherwise the hunter is sure to miss his aim.[cc] The native is convinced that the arrow would turn of itself and refuse, so to speak, to hit a kindred and friendly animal.[11]

Thus the men of the clan and the things which are classified in it form by their union a solid system, all of whose parts are united and vibrate sympathetically. This organization, which at first may have appeared to us as purely logical, is at the same time moral. A single principle animates it and makes its unity: this is the totem. Just as a man who belongs to the Crow clan has

---

[11] Although Durkheim makes no specific citations, his comments closely follow an earlier work by his fellow French scientist Lucien Levy-Bruhl (1857–1939), who is best known for his discussion of primitive mentality. In an article published in 1910, "Fonctions mentales dans les sociétés inférieures" (published in translation in 1966 as *How Natives Think*), Levy-Bruhl used information on the Bororo of central Brazil to support his theory that thought in primitive societies was less advanced than that in civilized societies. He writes

> The Bororo . . . boast that they are red araras (parakeets). This does not merely signify that after their death they become araras, nor that araras are metamorphosed Bororos, and must be treated as such. . . . It is not a name they give themselves, nor a relationship that they claim. What they desire to express by it is actual identity. . . . All communities which are totemic in form admit of collective representations of this kind, implying similar identity of the individual members of a totemic group and their totem. (quoted in Crocker 1977:165)

Although Durkheim and Levy-Bruhl discuss the features of totemic classification for different purposes, the work of both men influenced the later thoughts of the French structuralist Claude Lévi-Strauss. Levy-Bruhl says the Bororo think they are parrots to prove his point that primitive people have a primitive mentality; Durkheim believes the Bororo say they are parrots as a way of understanding and classifying their world. Building a theory based on the work of both men, Lévi-Strauss argued that the Bororo think they are parrots because the human brain is organized in such a way that classifying the world in this fashion is naturally appealing.

within him something of this animal, so the rain, since it is of the same clan and belongs to the same totem, is also necessarily considered as being "the same thing as a crow"; for the same reason, the moon is a black cockatoo, the sun a white cockatoo, every black-nut tree a pelican, etc. All the beings arranged in a single clan, whether men, animals, plants or inanimate objects, are merely forms of the totemic being. This is the meaning of the formula which we have just cited and this is what makes the two really of the same species: all are really of the same flesh in the sense that all partake of the nature of the totemic animal. Also, the qualifiers given them are those given to the totem.^{dd} The Wotjobaluk give the name *Mir* both to the totem and to the things classed with it.^{ee} It is true that among the Arunta, where visible traces of classification still exist, as we shall see, different words designate the totem and the other beings placed with it; however, the name given to these latter bears witness to the close relations which unite them to the totemic animal. It is said that they are its *intimates,* its *associates,* its *friends;* it is believed that they are inseparable from it.^{ff} So there is a feeling that these are very closely related things.[12]

But we also know that the totemic animal is a sacred being. All the things that are classified in the clan of which it is the emblem have this same character, because in one sense, they are animals of the same species, just as the man is. They, too, are sacred, and the classifications which locate them in relation to the other things of the universe, by that very act give them a place in the religious world. For this reason, the animals or plants among these may not be eaten freely by the human members of the clan. Thus in the Mount Gambier tribe, the men whose totem is a certain non-poisonous snake must not merely refrain

from eating the flesh of this snake; that of seals, eels, etc., is also forbidden to them.^{gg} If, driven by necessity, they do eat some of it, they must at least attenuate the sacrilege by expiatory rites, just as if they had eaten the totem itself.^{hh} Among the Euahlayi, where it is permitted to use the totem, but not to abuse it, the same rule is applied to the other members of the clan.ⁱⁱ Among the Arunta, the interdictions protecting the totemic animal extend over the associated animals;^{jj} and in any case, particular attention must be given to these latter.^{kk} The sentiments inspired by the two are identical.^{ll}

[In an 870-word section (with 15 footnotes) Durkheim discusses the process by which new totems are formed. He says that as clans undergo division or as already existing subdivisions within a clan become more pronounced, subtotems are formed. When a subclan splits completely from its parent clan, the subtotem becomes a new totem. This discussion is followed by a number of ethnographic examples.]

So the field of religious things extends well beyond the limits within which it seemed to be confined at first. It embraces not only the totemic animals and the human members of the clan; but since no known thing exists that is not classified in a clan and under a totem, there is likewise nothing which does not receive to some degree something of a religious character. When, in the religions which later come into being, the gods properly so-called appear, each of them will be set over a special category of natural phenomena, this one over the sea, that one over the air, another over the harvest or over fruits, etc., and each of these provinces of nature will be believed to draw what life there is in it from the god upon whom it depends. This division of nature among

---

[12] In the first sentence of this paragraph, Durkheim writes that the men of a clan and all the things classified with it form a system whose parts "are united and vibrate sympathetically." This is very close to the concept of mechanical solidarity, which Durkheim used to refer to social cohesion based on kinship. Durkheim appears to say that the concept of totemism is the central unifying symbol of a society with mechanical solidarity. In large, industrial societies, however, different social groups may have different sets of rules—the collective conscience is no longer the sole regulator of action. Social cohesion in this situation is maintained through professional and social ties created by the interdependence of classes, professions, and services necessary to maintain a complex society. Durkheim called this form of cohesion organic solidarity.

the different divinities constitutes the conception which these religions give us of the universe. Now so long as humanity has not passed the phase of totemism, the different totems of the tribe fulfill exactly the same functions that will later fall upon the divine personalities. In the Mount Gambier tribe, which we have taken as our principal example, there are ten clans; consequently the entire world is divided into ten classes, or rather into ten families, each of which has a special totem as its basis. It is from this basis that the things classed in the clan get all their reality, for they are thought of as variant forms of the totemic being; to return to our example, the rain, thunder, lightning, clouds, hail and winter are regarded as different sorts of crows. When brought together, these ten families of things make up a complete and systematic representation of the world; and this representation is religious, for religious notions furnish its basis. Far from being limited to one or two categories of beings, the domain of totemic religion extends to the final limits of the known universe. Just like the Greek religion, it puts the divine everywhere; the celebrated formula παντα πληρη θεων (everything is full of the gods), might equally well serve it as motto.[13]

However, if totemism is to be represented thus, the notion of it which has long been held must be modified on one essential point. Until the discoveries of recent years, it was made to consist entirely in the cult of one particular totem, and it was defined as the religion of the clan. From this point of view, each tribe seemed to have as many totemic religions, each independent of the others, as it had different clans. This conception was also in harmony with the idea currently held of the clan; in fact, this was regarded as an autonomous society,[mm] more or less closed to other similar societies, or having only external and superficial relations with these latter. But the reality is more complex. Undoubtedly, the cult of each totem has its home in the corresponding clan; it is there, and only there, that it is celebrated; it is members of the clan who have charge

of it; it is through them that it is transmitted from one generation to another, along with the beliefs which are its basis. But it is also true that the different totemic cults thus practised within a single tribe do not have a parallel development, though remaining ignorant of each other, as if each of them constituted a complete and self-sufficing religion. On the contrary, they mutually imply each other; they are only the parts of a single whole, the elements of a single religion. The men of one clan never regard the beliefs of neighboring clans with that indifference, skepticism or hostility which one religion ordinarily inspires for another which is foreign to it; they partake of these beliefs themselves. The Crow people are also convinced that the Snake people have a mythical serpent as ancestor, and that they owe special virtues and marvelous powers to this origin. And have we not seen that at least in certain conditions, a man may eat a totem that is not his own only after he has observed certain ritual formalities? Especially, he must demand the permission of the men of this totem, if any are present. So for him also, this food is not entirely profane; he also admits that there are intimate affinities between the members of a clan of which he is not a member and the animal whose name they bear. Also, this community of belief is sometimes shown in the cult. If in theory the rites concerning a totem can be performed only by the men of this totem, nevertheless representatives of different clans frequently assist at them. It sometimes happens that their part is not simply that of spectators; it is true that they do not officiate, but they decorate the officiants and prepare the service. They themselves have an interest in its being celebrated; therefore, in certain tribes, it is they who invite the qualified clan to proceed with the ceremonies.[nn] There is even a whole cycle of rites which must take place in the presence of the assembled tribe: these are the totemic ceremonies of initiation.[oo]

Finally, the totemic organization, such as we have just described it, must obviously be the result of some sort of an indistinct understanding

---

[13] This is a crucial paragraph. Durkheim says that the original form of religion was totemism, which is modeled on human society and integrates all humans, animals, and objects into one system of religious classification. As the gods of later religions replace the roles held by totems in simpler societies, the gods, too, are modeled after human society.

between all the members of the tribe. It is impossible that each clan should have made its beliefs in an absolutely independent manner; it is absolutely necessary that the cults of the different totems should be in some way adjusted to each other, since they complete one another exactly. In fact, we have seen that normally a single totem is not repeated twice in the same tribe, and that the whole universe is divided up among the totems thus constituted in such a way that the same object is not found in two different clans. So methodical a division could never have been made without an agreement, tacit or planned, in which the whole tribe participated.[14] So the group of beliefs which thus arise are partially (but only partially) a tribal affair.[pp]

To sum up, then, in order to form an adequate idea of totemism, we must not confine ourselves within the limits of the clan, but must consider the tribe as a whole. It is true that the particular cult of each clan enjoys a very great autonomy; we can now see that it is within the clan that the active ferment of the religious life takes place. But it is also true that these cults fit into each other and the totemic religion is a complex system formed by their union, just as Greek polytheism was made by the union of all the particular cults addressed to the different divinities. We have just shown that, thus understood, totemism also has its cosmology.[15]

Notes

a. *Kamilaroi and Kurnai*, p. 170.

b. *Notes on Some Australian Tribes, J.A.I.,* XIII, p. 300.

c. In Curr, *Australian Race,* III, p. 45; Brough Smyth, *The Aborgines of Victoria,* I, p. 91; Fison and Howitt, *Kamilaroi and Kurnai,* p. 168.

d. Durkheim and Mauss, *De quelques formes primitives de classification,* in Année Sociol., VI, pp. 1 ff.

e. Curr, III, p. 461.

f. Curr and Fison were both informed by the same person, D. S. Stewart.

g. The tables of Mathews and Howitt disagree on many important points. It even seems that clans attributed by Howitt to the Kroki phratry are given to the Gamutch phratry by Mathews, and inversely. This proves the great difficulties that these observations present. But these differences are without interest for our present question.

h. Mrs. Langloh Parker, *The Euahlayi Tribe,* pp. 12 ff.

i. The facts will be found below.

j. Carr, III, p. 27. Cf. Howitt, *Nat. Tr.,* p. 112. We are merely mentioning the most characteristic facts. For details, one may refer to the memoir already mentioned on *Les classifications primitives.*

k. *Ibid.,* pp. 34 ff.

l. Swanton, *The Haida,* pp. 13–14, 17, 22.

m. This is especially clear among the Haida. Swanton says that with them every animal has two aspects. First, it is an ordinary animal to be hunted and eaten; but it is also a supernatural being in the animal's form, upon which men depend. The mythical beings corresponding to cosmic phenomena have the same ambiguity (Swanton, *ibid.,* 16, 14, 25).

n. See above, p. 166. This is the case among the Gournditch-mara (Howitt, *Nat. Tr.,* p. 124), in the tribes studied by Cameron near the Dead Lake, and among the Wotjobaluk (*ibid.,* pp. 125, 250).

o. J. Mathews, *Two Representative Tribes,* p. 139; Thomas, *Kinship and Marriage,* pp. 53 f.

p. Among the Osage, for example, see Dorsey, *Siouan Sociology,* in XVth Rep., pp. 233 ff.

q. At Mabuiag, an island in Torrès' Strait (Haddon, *Head Hunters,* p. 132), the same opposition is found between the two phratries of the Arunta: one

---

[14] Durkheim presents an extremely interesting idea here. He says that the universe is divided among the totems, with each totem having a set of elements identified as part of its totemic classification. As the same object is not found in two different totems, the systems complement each other. Thus, when all the clans assemble, an observer is presented with a complete model of the aboriginal universe.

[15] Durkheim focused on totems because he believed them to be the most elementary form of religion and therefore simple to analyze and understand. However, he did not believe that totemic religions were different in kind from the religions of complex societies. His argument was revolutionary in that he asserted that all religions, including Christianity, were based on fundamentally similar patterns. Furthermore, Durkheim believed that all religions were fundamentally equal. In the introduction to *The Elementary Forms of the Religious Life* he wrote, "In reality, then, there are no religions which are false. All are true in their own fashion; all answer, though in different ways, to the given conditions of human existence. . . . They respond to the same needs, they play the same role, they depend upon the same causes" (1965:15).

includes the men of a water totem, the other those of earth (Strehlow, I, p. 6).

r. Among the Iroquois there is a sort of tournament between the two phratries (Morgan, *Ancient Society*, p. 94). Among the Haida, says Swanton, the members of the two phratries of the Eagle and the Crow "are frequently considered as avowed enemies. Husband and wife (who must be of different phratries) do not hesitate to betray each other" (*The Haida*, p. 62). In Australia this hostility is carried into the myths. The two animals serving the phratries as totems are frequently represented as in a perpetual war against each other (see J. Mathews, *Eaglehawk and Crow, a Study of Australian Aborigines*, pp. 14 ff). In games, each phratry is the natural rival of the other (Howitt, *Nat. Tr.*, p. 770).

s. So Thomas has wrongly urged against our theory of the origin of the phratries its inability to explain their opposition (*Kinship and Marriage*, p. 69). We do not believe that it is necessary to connect this opposition to that of the profane and the sacred (see Hertz, *La prééminence de la main droite*, in the *Revue Philosophique*, Dec., 1909, p. 559). The things of one phratry are not profane for the other; both are a part of the same religious system (see below, p. 181).

t. For example, the clan of the Tea-tree includes the grasses, and consequently herbivorous animals (see *Kamilaroi and Kurnai*, p. 169). This is undoubtedly the explanation of a particularity of the totemic emblems of North America pointed out by Boas. "Among the Tlinkit," he says, "and all the other tribes of the coast, the emblem of a group includes the animals serving as food to the one whose name the group bears" (*Fifth Rep. of the Committee, etc. British Association for the Advancement of Science*, p. 25).

u. Thus, among the Arunta, frogs are connected with the totem of the gumtree, because they are frequently found in the cavities of this tree; water is related to the water-hen; with the kangaroo is associated a sort of parrot frequently seen flying about this animal (Spencer and Gillen, *Nat. Tr.*, pp. 146–147, 448).

v. One of the signs of this primitive lack of distinction is that territorial bases are sometimes assigned to the classes just as to the social divisions with which they were at first confounded. Thus, among the Watjobaluk in Australia and the Zuñi in America, things are ideally distributed among the different regions of space, just as the clans are. Now this regional distribution of things and that of the clans coincide (see *De quelques formes primitives de classification*, pp. 34 ff.). Classifications keep some-

thing of this special character even among relatively advanced peoples, as for example, in China (ibid., pp. 55 ff.).

w. Bridgmann, in Brough Smyth, *The Aborigines of Victoria*, I, p. 91.

x. Fison and Howitt, *Kamilaroi and Kurnai*, p. 168; Howitt, *Further Notes on the Australian Class Systems*, *J.A.I.*, XVIII, p. 60.

y. Curr, III, p. 461. This is about the Mount Gambier tribe.

z. Howitt, *On Some Australian Beliefs*, *J.A.I.*, XIII, p. 191, n. 1.

aa. Howitt, *Notes on Australian Message Sticks*, *J.A.I.*, XVIII, p. 326; *Further Notes*, *J.A.I.*, XVIII, p. 61, n. 3.

bb. Curr, III, p. 28.

cc. Mathews, *Ethnological Notes on the Aboriginal Tribes of N.S. Wales and Victoria*, in *Journ. and Proceed. of the Royal Soc. of N.S. Wales*, XXXVIII, p. 294.

dd. Cf. Curr, III, p. 461; and Howitt, *Nat. Tr.*, p. 146. The expressions *Tooman* and *Wingo* are applied to the one and the other.

ee. Howitt, *Nat. Tr.*, p. 123.

ff. Spencer and Gillen, *Nat. Tr.*, pp. 447 ff.; cf. Strehlow, III, pp. xii ff.

gg. Fison and Howitt, *Kamilaroi and Kurnai*, p. 169.

hh. Turr, III, p. 462.

ii. Mrs. Parker, *The Euahlayi Tribe*, p. 20.

jj. Spencer and Gillen, *Nor. Tr.*, p. 151; *Nat. Tr.*, p. 447; Strehlow, III, p. xii.

kk. Spencer and Gillen, *Nat. Tr.*, p. 449.

ll. However, there are certain tribes in Queensland where the things thus attributed to a social group are not forbidden for the members of the group: this is notably the case with the Wakelbura. It is to be remembered that in this society, it is the matrimonial classes that serve as the framework of the classification (see above, p. 169). Not only are the men of one class allowed to eat the animals attributed to this class, but *they may eat no others*. All other food is forbidden them (Howitt, *Nat. Tr.*, p. 113; Curr, III, p. 27).

But we must not conclude from this that these animals are considered profane. In fact, it should be noticed that the individual not only has the privilege of eating them, but that he is compelled to do so, for he cannot nourish himself otherwise. Now the imperative nature of this rule is a sure sign that we are in the presence of things having a religious nature, only this has given rise to a positive obligation rather than the negative one known as an interdiction. Perhaps it is not quite impossible to see how this deviation came about. We have seen above (p. 163) that every individual is thought to have a sort of property-right over his totem and consequently over the things dependent upon it. Perhaps, under the influence of special circumstances, this aspect of the totemic relation was developed, and they naturally came to believe that only the members of the clan had the right of disposing of their totem and all that is connected with it, and that others, on the contrary, did not have the right of touching it. Under these circumstances, a tribe could nourish itself only on the food attributed to it.

mm. Thus it comes about that the clan has frequently been confounded with the tribe. This confusion, which frequently introduces trouble into the writings of ethnologists, has been made especially by Curr (I, pp. 61 ff.).

nn. This is the case especially among the Warramunga (*Nor. Tr.*, p. 298).

oo. See, for example, Spencer and Gillen, *Nat. Tr.*, p. 380 and *passim*.

pp. One might even ask if tribal totems do not exist sometimes. Thus, among the Arunta, there is an animal, the wild cat, which serves as totem to a particular clan, but which is forbidden for the whole tribe; even the people of other clans can eat it only very moderately (*Nat. Tr.*, p. 168). But we believe that it would be an abuse to speak of a tribal totem in this case, for it does not follow from the fact that the free consumption of an animal is forbidden that this is a totem. Other causes can also give rise to an interdiction. The religious unity of the tribe is undoubtedly real, but this is affirmed with the aid of other symbols. We shall show what these are below (Bk. II, ch. ix).

8. Excerpts from *The Gift*

Marcel Mauss (1872–1950)

[Our reprint of Mauss' work opens with section three of Chapter 2. In sections one and two of that chapter, comprising about 5,000 words, Mauss describes the rules of generosity on the Andaman Islands and the Kula trade in Melanesia, as well as other associated exchange practices. These exchanges, he believes, are the material expressions of Émile Durkheim's social facts. They are used to forge and maintain alliances, and they replicate the divisions between the people involved in them. The interdependence of the exchange network increases social solidarity. He continues here with a discussion of potlatch among Native Americans.]

From Chapters 2 and 4 of *The Gift* (1924)

3. Honour and Credit (North-West America)

From these observations on Melanesian and Polynesian peoples our picture of gift economy is already beginning to take shape.[1] Material and moral life, as exemplified in gift exchange, functions there in a manner at once interested and obligatory. Furthermore, the obligation is expressed in myth and imagery, symbolically and collectively; it takes the form of interest in the objects exchanged; the objects are never completely separated from the men who exchange them; the communion and alliance they establish are well-nigh indissoluble. The lasting influence of the objects exchanged is a direct expression of the manner in which sub-groups within segmentary societies of

---

[1] The parts of Mauss' essay reproduced here contain over one hundred notes. Space limitations prevent us from reproducing them here, but asterisks have been included to give the reader an idea of the volume of notes Mauss wrote. The intrepid reader can look them up in a complete version of *The Gift*.

an archaic type are constantly embroiled with and feel themselves in debt to each other.

Indian societies of the American North-West have the same institutions, but in a more radical and accentuated form.[2] Barter is unknown there. Even now after long contact with Europeans it does not appear that any of the considerable and continual transfers of wealth take place otherwise than through the formality of the potlatch.* We now describe this institution as we see it.

First, however, we give a short account of these societies.[3] The tribes in question inhabit the North-West American coast — the Tlingit and Haida of Alaska,* and the Tsimshian and Kwakiutl of British Columbia.* They live on the sea or on the rivers and depend more on fishing than on hunting for their livelihood; but in contrast to the Melanesians and Polynesians they do not practice agriculture. Yet they are very wealthy, and even at the present day their fishing, hunting and trapping activities yield surpluses which are considerable even when reckoned on the European scale. They have the most substantial houses of all the American tribes, and a highly evolved cedar industry. Their canoes are good; and although they seldom venture out on to the open sea they are skillful in navigating around their islands and in coastal waters. They have a high standard of material culture. In particular, even back in the eighteenth century, they collected, smelted, molded and beat local copper from Tsimshian and Tlingit country. Some of the copper in the form of decorated shields they used as a kind of currency. Almost certainly another form of currency was the beautifully embellished Chilkat blanket-work still used ornamentally, some of it being of considerable value.* The peoples are excellent carvers and craftsmen. Their pipes, clubs and sticks are the pride of our ethnological collections. Within broad limits this civilization is remarkably uniform. It is clear that the societies have been in contact with each other from very early days, although their languages suggest that they belong to at least three families of peoples.*

Their winter life, even with the southern tribes, is very different from their summer life. The tribes have a two-fold structure: at the end of spring they disperse and go hunting, collect berries from the hillsides and fish the rivers for salmon; while in winter they concentrate in what are known as towns. During this period of concentration they are in a perpetual state of effervescence.[4] The social life becomes intense in the extreme, even more so than in the concentrations of tribes that manage to form in the summer. This life consists of continual movement. There are constant visits of whole tribes to others, of clans to clans and families to families. There is feast upon feast, some of long duration. On the occasion of a marriage, on various ritual occasions, and on social advancement, there is reckless consumption of everything which has been amassed with great industry from some of the richest coasts of the world during the course of summer and autumn. Even private life passes in this manner; clansmen are invited when a seal is killed or a box of roots or berries opened; you invite everyone when a whale runs aground.

---

[2] Mauss implies here that the purpose of these practices cannot be explained simply by economics. If their root purposes were economic, they would have disappeared with European contact.

[3] The next several paragraphs provide a broad ethnographic description of the potlatch customs of several Northwest Native American groups, much of which is drawn from Franz Boas' work. Mauss' description is a catalogue of material culture, but his real interests lie in examining patterns of social interaction.

[4] For Durkheim and his followers, members of the *L'Année Sociologique* school, the idea of periods of "effervescence" was critical in the binary separation of sacred and profane. For example, discussing the Australian Aborigines in *The Elementary Forms of the Religious Life,* Durkheim wrote that sacred times, when people assemble, were marked by "a sort of electricity . . . which transports them to exaltation. Every sentiment expressed finds a place without resistance in all the minds . . . each re-echoes the others, and is re-echoed by the others. . . . How could such experiences as these . . . fail to leave [an individual convinced] that there really exist two heterogeneous and mutually incomparable worlds?" (1965:245–50).

Social organization, too, is fairly constant throughout the area though it ranges from the matrilineal phratry (Tlingit and Haida) to the modified matrilineal clan of the Kwakiutl; but the general characters of the social organization and particularly of totemism are repeated in all the tribes. They have associations like those of the Banks Islanders of Melanesia, wrongly called "secret societies," which are often inter-tribal; and men's and women's societies among the Kwakiutl cut across tribal organization. A part of the gifts and counterprestations[5] which we shall discuss goes, as in Melanesia,* to pay one's way into the successive steps* of the associations. Clan and association ritual follows the marriage of chiefs, the sale of coppers, initiations, shamanistic seances and funeral ceremonies, the latter being more particularly pronounced among the Tlingit and Haida. These are all accomplished in the course of an indefinitely prolonged series of potlatches. Potlatches are given in all directions, corresponding to other potlatches to which they are the response. As in Melanesia the process is one of constant give-and-take.

The potlatch, so unique as a phenomenon, yet so typical of these tribes, is really nothing other than gift-exchange.[6] The only differences are in the violence, rivalry and antagonism aroused, in a lack of jural[7] concepts, and in a simpler structure. It is less refined than in Melanesia, especially as regards the northern tribes, the Tlingit and the Haida,* but the collective nature of the contract is more pronounced than in Melanesia and Polynesia.* Despite appearances, the institutions here are nearer to what we call simple total prestations. Thus the legal and economic concepts attached to them have less clarity and conscious precision. Nevertheless, in action the principles emerge formally and clearly.

There are two traits more in evidence here than in the Melanesian potlatch or in the more evolved and discrete institutions of Polynesia: the themes of credit and honour.*

As we have seen, when gifts circulate in Melanesia and Polynesia the return is assured by the virtue of the things passed on, which are their own guarantees. In any society it is in the nature of the gift in the end to being its own reward. By definition, a common meal, a distribution of *kava*,[8] or a charm worn, cannot be repaid at once. Time has to pass before a counterprestation can be made. Thus the notion of time is logically implied when one pays a visit, contracts a marriage or an alliance, makes a treaty, goes to organized games, fights or feasts of others, renders ritual and honorific service and "shows respect," to use the Tlingit term.* All these are things exchanged side by side with other material objects, and they are the more numerous as the society is wealthier.

On this point, legal and economic theory is greatly at fault.[9] Imbued with modern ideas, current theory tends towards *a priori* notions of evolution,* and claims to follow a so-called necessary logic; in fact, however, it remains based on

---

[5] Mauss' work deals with a class of phenomena he calls *prestations,* which are a type of gift exchange between groups. They appear "disinterested and spontaneous" but are, in reality, neither. Rather, they are obligatory and enacted under a highly specific system of reciprocity.

[6] Mauss followed Durkheim's idea of social evolution from mechanical to organic solidarity. Simple societies, such as those he is describing, are characterized by mechanical solidarity, which means that their social institutions are not separated, as in complex society. Instead, a few phenomena – called *total social phenomena* – simultaneously express a great many institutions. Potlatch exchange, as Mauss details below, is such a phenomenon.

[7] *Jural:* legal.

[8] *Kava:* a Polynesian ritual beverage consumed to produce a euphoric state. Made from the roots of the Kava plant, which is *Piper methysticum.*

[9] Here Mauss takes aim at simple linear evolutionary schemes. Durkheim and Mauss were hostile to Darwinian models of social evolution, which stressed conflict and competition. In Durkheim's model, social evolution is driven by the need to achieve social solidarity at greater levels of population density and complexity.

old traditions. Nothing could be more dangerous than what Simiand[10] called this "unconscious sociology." For instance, Cuq could still say in 1910: "In primitive societies barter alone is found; in those more advanced, direct sale is practiced. Sale on credit characterizes a higher stage of civilization; it appears first in an indirect manner, a combination of sale and loan."* In fact the origin of credit is different. It is to be found in a range of customs neglected by lawyers and economists as uninteresting: namely the gift, which is a complex phenomenon especially in its ancient form of total prestation which we are studying here. Now a gift necessarily implies the notion of credit. Economic evolution has not gone from barter to sale and from cash to credit. Barter arose from the system of gifts given and received on credit, simplified by drawing together the moments of time which had previously been distinct. Likewise purchase and sale—both direct sale and credit sale—and the loan, derive from the same source. There is nothing to suggest that any economic system which has passed through the phase we are describing was ignorant of the idea of credit, of which all archaic societies around us are aware. This is a simple and realistic manner of dealing with the problem, which Davy[11] has already studied, of the "two moments of time" which the contract unites.*

No less important is the role which honour plays in the transactions of the Indians. Nowhere else is the prestige of an individual as closely bound up with expenditure, and with the duty of returning with interest gifts received in such a way that the creditor becomes the debtor. Consumption and destruction are virtually unlimited. In some potlatch systems one is constrained to expend everything one possesses and to keep nothing.* The rich man who shows his wealth by spending recklessly is the man who wins prestige.[12] The principles of rivalry and antagonism are basic. Political and individual status in associations and clans, and rank of every kind, are determined by the war of property, as well as by armed hostilities, by chance, inheritance, alliance or marriage.* But everything is conceived as if it were a war of wealth.* Marriage of one's children and one's position at gatherings are determined solely in the course of the potlatch given and returned. Position is also lost as in war, gambling,* hunting and wrestling.* Sometimes there is no question of receiving return; one destroys simply in order to give the appearance that one has no desire to receive anything back.* Whole cases of candlefish or whale oil,* houses, and blankets by the thousand are burnt; the most valuable coppers are broken and thrown into the sea to level and crush a rival. Progress up the social ladder is made in this way not only for oneself but also for one's family. Thus in a system of this kind much wealth is continually being consumed and transferred. Such transfers may if desired be called exchange or even commerce or sale;* but it is an aristocratic type of commerce characterized by etiquette and generosity; moreover, when it is carried out in a different spirit, for immediate gain, it is viewed with the greatest disdain.*

We see, then, that the notion of honour, strong in Polynesia, and present in Melanesia, is exceptionally marked here. On this point the classical writings made a poor estimate of the motives which animate men and of all that we owe to societies that preceded our own. Even as informed a scholar as Huvelin felt obliged to deduce the notion of honour—which is reputedly *without* efficacy—from the notion of magical efficacy.* The truth is more complex. The notion of honor is no more foreign to these civilizations than the notion

---

[10] François Simiand (1873–1935) was a French economic historian. A student of Durkheim and a socialist, he was critical of scholars of his day and suggested that history could not be studied apart from social and economic structures.

[11] Georges Davy (1883–1955) was a member of the *L'Année Sociologique* school and a specialist in the sociology of law. He made extensive use of Mauss' analysis of the potlatch in describing the transition from statute to contractual law.

[12] For Mauss, neither psychology nor economics could explain the vast destruction of property caused by the potlatch or the seemingly illogical behavior of its participants. Instead, he believed that potlatch was about the status of groups, their maintenance of internal cohesion, and their relations with each other.

of magic.* Polynesian *mana* itself symbolizes not only the magical power of the person but also his honour, and one of the best translations of the word is "authority" or "wealth."* The Tlingit or Haida potlatch consists in considering mutual services as honours.* Even in really primitive societies like the Australian, the "point of honor" is as ticklish as it is in ours; and it may be satisfied by prestations, offerings of food, by precedence or ritual, as well as by gifts.* Men could pledge their honor long before they could sign their names.[13]

The North-West American potlatch has been studied enough as to the form of the contract. But we must find a place for the researches of Davy and Adam in the wider framework of our subject. For the potlatch is more than a legal phenomenon; it is one of those phenomena we propose to call "total." It is religious, mythological and shamanistic because the chiefs taking part are incarnations of gods and ancestors, whose names they bear, whose dances they dance and whose spirits possess them.* It is economic; and one has to assess the value, importance, causes and effects of transactions which are enormous even when reckoned by European standards. The potlatch is also a phenomenon of social morphology; the reunion of tribes, clans, families and nations produces great excitement. People fraternize but at the same time remain strangers; community of interest and opposition are revealed constantly in a great whirl of business.* Finally, from the jural point of view, we have already noted the contractual forms and what we might call the human element of the contract, and the legal status of the contracting parties—as clans or families or with reference to rank or marital condition; and to this we now add that the material objects of the contracts have a virtue of their own which causes them to be given and compels the making of counter-gifts.

It would have been useful, if space had been available, to distinguish four forms of American potlatch: first, potlatch where the phratries and chiefs' families alone take part (Tlingit); second, potlatches in which phratries, clans, families and chiefs take more or less similar roles (Haida); third, potlatch with chiefs and their clans confronting each other (Tsimshian); and fourth, potlatch of chiefs and fraternities (Kwakiutl). But this would prolong our argument, and in any case three of the four forms (with the exception of the Tsimshian) have already been comparatively described by Davy.* But as far as our study is concerned all the forms are more or less identical as regards the elements of the gift, the obligation to receive and the obligation to make a return.

4. The Three Obligations: Giving, Receiving, Repaying[14]

THE OBLIGATION TO GIVE

This is the essence of potlatch. A chief must give a potlatch for himself, his son, his son-in-law or daughter* and for the dead.* He can keep his authority in his tribe, village and family, and maintain his position with the chiefs inside and outside his nation,* only if he can prove that he is favorably regarded by the spirits, that he possesses fortune* and that he is possessed by it.* The only way to demonstrate his fortune is by expending it to the humiliation of others, by putting them "in the shadow of his name."* Kwakiutl and Haida noblemen have the same notion of "face"

---

[13] Here, and in other passages, Mauss attacks simplistic understandings of primitive people as morally inferior to Europeans. Though optimistic about the future of civilization, he was highly critical of his own society and, to some degree, romanticized the primitive. In the conclusion to *The Gift,* he wrote, "Hence, we should return to the old and elemental. Once again we shall discover . . . the joy of giving in public, the delight in generous artistic expenditure, the pleasure of hospitality in the public or private feast. . . . We can visualize a society in which these principles obtain. . . . For honour, disinterestedness and corporate solidarity are not vain words, nor do they deny the necessity for work" (1967:67).

[14] In this section, Mauss describes what he believes is a fundamental pattern underlying prestations. Since prestations are total social phenomena, this same pattern must also underlie other aspects of society. This insight was of crucial importance in the development of Lévi-Strauss' French structural anthropology (see essay 25). Lévi-Strauss said, on reading *The Gift,* that his mind was "overcome by the certainty as yet undefinable of assisting in a decisive event in the evolution of science" (quoted in Harris 1968:484).

as the Chinese mandarin or officer.* It is said of one of the great mythical chiefs who gave no feast that he had a "rotten face."* The expression is more apt than it is even in China; for to lose one's face is to lose one's spirit, which is truly the "face," the dancing mask, the right to incarnate a spirit and wear an emblem or totem. It is the veritable *persona* which is at stake, and it can be lost in the potlatch* just as it can be lost in the game of gift-giving,* in war,* or through some error in ritual.* In all these societies one is anxious to give; there is no occasion of importance (even outside the solemn winter gatherings) when one is *not* obliged to invite friends to share the produce of the chase or the forest which the gods or totems have sent;* to redistribute everything received at a potlatch; or to recognize services* from chiefs, vassals or relatives* by means of gifts. Failing these obligations — at least for the nobles — etiquette is violated and rank is lost.*

The obligation to invite is particularly evident between clans or between tribes. It makes sense only if the invitation is given to people other than members of the family, clan or phratry.* Everyone who can, will or does attend the potlatch must be invited.* Neglect has fateful results.* An important Tsimshian myth* shows the state of mind in which the central theme of much European folklore originated: the myth of the bad fairy neglected at a baptism or marriage.[13] Here the institutional fabric in which it is sewn appears clearly, and we realize the kind of civilization in which it functioned. A princess of one of the Tsimshian villages conceives in the "Country of the Otters" and gives birth miraculously to "Little Otter." She returns with her child to the village of her father, the chief. Little Otter catches halibut with which her father feeds all the tribal chiefs. He introduces Little Otter to everyone and requests them not to kill him if they find him fishing in his animal form: "Here is my grandson who

has brought for you this food with which I serve you, my guests." Thus the grandfather grows rich with all manner of wealth brought to him by the chiefs when they come in the winter hunger to eat whale and seal and the fresh fish caught by Little Otter. But one chief is not invited. And one day when the crew of a canoe of the neglected tribe meets Little Otter at sea the bowman kills him and takes the seal. The grandfather and all the tribes search high and low for Little Otter until they hear about the neglected tribe. The latter offers its excuses; it has never heard of Little Otter. The princess dies of grief; the involuntarily guilty chief brings the grandfather all sorts of gifts in expiation. The myth ends: "That is why the people have great feasts when a chief's son is born and gets a name; for none may be ignorant of him."* The potlatch — the distribution of goods — is the fundamental act of public recognition in all spheres, military, legal, economic and religious. The chief or his son is recognized and acknowledged by the people.

Sometimes the ritual in the feasts of the Kwakiutl and other tribes in the same group expresses this obligation to invite.* Part of the ceremonial opens with the "ceremony of the dogs." These are represented by masked men who come out of one house and force their way into another. They commemorate the occasion on which the people of the three other tribes of Kwakiutl proper neglected to invite the clan which ranked highest among them, the Guetela who, having no desire to remain outsiders, entered the dancing house and destroyed everything.*

THE OBLIGATION TO RECEIVE

This is no less constraining.[16] One does not have the right to refuse a gift or a potlatch.* To do so would show fear of having to reply, and of being abased in default. One would "lose the weight" of

---

[15] The comparison of the Tsimshian myth to European folklore here presupposes an evolutionary framework. Mauss, like many other social thinkers, saw primitive cultures as living fossils. Given this premise, it followed that current Tsimshian myths were equivalent to ancient European folktales.

[16] Notice that, while Mauss has said that prestations do sometimes serve an economic role, his discussion of potlatch is not economic. Instead, the potlatch is seen as symbolic of social relations between groups, which is why he can say that the obligation to receive is "no less constraining" than the obligation to give.

one's name by admitting defeat in advance.* In certain circumstances, however, a refusal can be an assertion of victory and invincibility.* It appears at least with the Kwakiutl that a recognized position in the hierarchy, or a victory through previous potlatches, allows one to refuse an invitation or even a gift without war ensuing. If this is so, then a potlatch must be carried out by the man who refuses to accept the invitation. More particularly, he has to contribute to the "fat festival" in which a ritual of refusal may be observed.* The chief who considers himself superior refuses the spoonful of fat offered him: he fetches his copper and returns with it to "extinguish the fire" (of the fat). A series of formalities follow which mark the challenge and oblige the chief who has refused to give another potlatch or fat festival.* In principle, however, gifts are always accepted and praised.* You must speak your appreciation of food prepared for you.* But you accept a challenge at the same time.* You receive a gift "on the back." You accept the food and you do so because you mean to take up the challenge and prove that you are not unworthy.* When chiefs confront each other in this manner they may find themselves in odd situations and probably they experience them as such. In like manner in ancient Gaul and Germany, as well as nowadays in gatherings of French farmers and students, one is pledged to swallow quantities of liquid to "do honor" in grotesque fashion to the host. The obligation stands even although one is only heir to the man who bears the challenge.* Failure to give or receive,* like failure to make return gifts, means a loss of dignity.*

THE OBLIGATION TO REPAY

Outside pure destruction the obligation to repay is the essence of potlatch.* Destruction is very often sacrificial, directed towards the spirits, and apparently does not require a return unconditionally, especially when it is the work of a superior clan chief or of the chief of a clan already recognized as superior.* But normally the potlatch must be returned with interest like all other gifts. The interest is generally between 30 and 100 per cent. a year. If a subject receives a blanket from his chief for a service rendered he will return two on the occasion of a marriage in the chief's family or on the initiation of the chief's son. But then the chief in his turn redistributes to him whatever he gets from the next potlatch at which rival clans repay the chief's generosity.

The obligation of worthy return is imperative.* Face is lost for ever if it is not made or if equivalent value is not destroyed.*

The sanction for the obligation to repay is enslavement for debt. This is so at least for the Kwakiutl, Haida and Tsimshian. It is an institution comparable in nature and function to the Roman *nexum*.[17] The person who cannot return a loan or potlatch loses his rank and even his status of a free man. If among the Kwakiutl a man of poor credit has to borrow he is said to "sell a slave." We need not stress the similarity of this expression with the Roman one.* The Haida say, as if they had invented the Latin phrase independently, that a girl's mother who gives a betrothal payment to the mother of a young chief "puts a thread on him."

Just as the Trobriand *kula* is an extreme case of gift exchange, so the potlatch in North-West America is the monster child of the gift system. In societies of phratries, amongst the Tlingit and Haida, we find important traces of a former total prestation (which is characteristic of the Athabascans, a related group). Presents are exchanged on any pretext for any service, and everything is returned sooner or later for redistribution.* The Tsimshian have almost the same rules.* Among the Kwakiutl these rules, in many cases, function outside the potlatch.* We shall not press this obvious point; old authors described the potlatch in such a way as to make it doubtful whether it was or was not a distinct institution.* We may recall that with the Chinook, one of the least known tribes but one which would repay study, the word "potlatch" means "gift."*

---

[17] The nexum was a system of contracting a loan in ancient Rome in which the loan was made in the presence of five witnesses. Debtors could be held in bondage for failure to repay.

5. The Power in Objects of Exchange

Our analysis can be carried farther to show that in the things exchanged at a potlatch there is a certain power which forces them to circulate, to be given away and repaid.

To begin with, the Kwakiutl and Tsimshian, and perhaps others, make the same distinction between the various types of property as do the Romans, Trobrianders and Samoans. They have the ordinary articles of consumption and distribution and perhaps also of sale (I have found no trace of barter). They have also the valuable family property—talismans, decorated coppers, skin blankets and embroidered fabrics.* This class of articles is transmitted with that solemnity with which women are given in marriage, privileges are endowed on sons-in-law, and names and status are given to children and daughters' husbands.* It is wrong to speak here of alienation, for these things are loaned rather than sold and ceded.[18] Basically they are *sacra*[19] which the family parts with, if at all, only with reluctance.

Closer observation reveals similar distinctions among the Haida. This tribe has in fact sacralized, in the manner of Antiquity, the notions of property and wealth.[20] By a religious and mythological effort of a type rare enough in the Americas they have managed to reify an abstraction: the "Property Woman," of whom we possess myths and a description.* She is nothing less than the mother, the founding goddess of the dominant phratry, the Eagles. But oddly enough—a fact which recalls the Asiatic world and Antiquity—she appears identical with the "queen," the principal piece in the game of tip-cat, the piece that wins everything and whose name the Property Woman bears. This goddess is found in Tlingit* country and her myth, if not her cult, among the Tsimshian* and Kwakiutl.*

Together these precious family articles constitute what one might call the magical legacy of the people; they are conceived as such by their owner, by the initiate he gives them to, by the ancestor who endowed the clan with them, and by the founding hero of the clan to whom the spirits gave them.* In any case in all these clans they are spiritual in origin and nature.* Further, they are kept in a large ornate box which itself is endowed with a powerful personality, which speaks, is in communion with the owner, contains his soul, and so on.*

Each of these precious objects and tokens of wealth has, as amongst the Trobrianders, its name,* quality and power.* The large *abalone* shells,* the shields covered with them, the decorated blankets with faces, eyes, and animal and human figures embroidered and woven into them, are all personalities.* The houses and decorated beams are themselves beings.* Everything speaks—roof, fire, carvings and paintings; for the magical house is built not only by the chief and his people and those of the opposing phratry but also by the gods and ancestors; spirits and young initiates are welcomed and cast out by the house in person.*

Each of these precious things has, moreover, a productive capacity within it.* Each, as well as being a sign and surety of life, is also a sign and surety of wealth, a magico-religious guarantee of rank and prosperity.* Ceremonial dishes and spoons decorated and carved with the clan totem or sign of rank, are animate things.* They are replicas of the never ending supply of tools, the creators of food, which the spirits gave to the ancestors. They are supposedly miraculous. Objects are confounded with the spirits who made them,

---

[18] Mauss' comment on alienation illustrates his insistence that the transactions he describes are not economic—that is, they are not driven by the desire to maximize material profit or minimize loss. Therefore, he believed that the term alienation (frequently used by Marxist economists) was not appropriate.

[19] *Sacra:* Latin for objects of devotion.

[20] Durkheim and his followers divided the cultural world into the sacred and profane. Here, Mauss demonstrates the sacred nature of gift-giving. Twenty years later, Lévi-Strauss and his followers emphasized the binary division of sacred and profane employed by *L'Année Sociologique* thinkers along with the use of binary opposition by structural linguists (see essays 25–27).

and eating utensils with food. Thus Kwakiutl dishes and Haida spoons are essential goods with a strict circulation and are carefully shared out between the families and clans of the chiefs.

6. Money of Renown (Renommiergeld)*

Decorated coppers* are the most important articles in the potlatch, and beliefs and a cult are attached to them. With all these tribes copper, a living being, is the object of cult and myth.* Copper, with the Haida and Kwakiutl at least, is identified with salmon, itself an object of cult.* But in addition to this mythical element each copper is by itself an object of individual belief.* Each principal copper of the families of clan chiefs has its name and individuality;* it has also its own value,* in the full magical and economic sense of the word which is regulated by the vicissitudes of the potlatches through which it passes and even by its partial or complete destruction.*

Coppers have also a virtue which attracts other coppers to them, as wealth attracts wealth and as dignity attracts honours, spirit-possession and good alliances.* In this way they live their own lives and attract other coppers.* One of the Kwakiutl coppers is called "Bringer of Coppers" and the formula describes how the coppers gather around it, while the name of its owner is "Copper-Flowing-Towards-Me."* With the Haida and Tlingit, coppers are a "fortress" for the princess who owns them; elsewhere a chief who owns them is rendered invincible.* They are the "flat divine objects" of the house.* Often the myth identifies together the spirits who gave the coppers, the owners and the coppers themselves.* It is impossible to discern what makes the power of the one out of the spirit and the wealth of the other; a copper talks and grunts, demanding to be given away or destroyed;* it is covered with blankets to keep it warm just as a chief is smothered in the blankets he is to distribute.*

From another angle we see the transmission of wealth and good fortune.* The spirits and minor spirits of an initiate allow him to own coppers and talismans which then enable him to acquire other coppers, greater wealth, higher rank and more spirits (all of these being equivalents). If we consider the coppers with other forms of wealth which are the object of hoarding and potlatch—masks, talismans and so on—we find they are all confounded in their uses and effects.* Through them rank is obtained; because a man obtains wealth he obtains a spirit which in turn possesses him, enabling him to overcome obstacles heroically. Then later the hero is paid for his shamanistic services, ritual dances and trances. Everything is tied together; things have personality, and personalities are in some manner the permanent possession of the clan. Titles, talismans, coppers and spirits of chiefs are homonyms and synonyms, having the same nature and function.* The circulation of goods follows that of men, women and children, of festival ritual, ceremonies and dances, jokes and injuries. Basically they are the same. If things are given and returned it is precisely because one gives and returns "respects" and "courtesies." But in addition, in giving them, a man gives himself, and he does so because he owes himself—himself and his possessions—to others.[21]

7. Primary Conclusion

From our study of four important groups of people we find the following: first, in two or three of the groups, we find the potlatch, its leading motive and its typical form. In all groups we see the archaic form of exchange—the gift and the return gift. Moreover, in these societies we note the circulation of objects side by side with the circulation of persons and rights. We might stop at this point. The amount, distribution and importance of our data authorize us to conceive of a regime embracing a large part of humanity over a long transitional phase, and persisting to this day among peoples

---

[21] In this paragraph, Mauss claims that the goods given in potlatch are, in essence, indistinguishable from the people giving them. The goods have personalities and are members of households. Giving them is then spiritually the same as the movement of people from household to household. Later, in his first major work, *Les Structures Elémentaires de la Parenté* (1949) (*The Elementary Structures of Kinship*), Lévi-Strauss expanded this line of argument by analyzing the exchange of women between groups as a fundamental social phenomenon.

other than those described. We may then consider that the spirit of gift exchange is characteristic of societies which have passed the phase of "total prestation" (between clan and clan, family and family) but have not yet reached the stage of pure individual contract, the money market, sale proper, fixed price, and weighed and coined money.[22]

[The Gift, in its entirety, is a reasonably short essay (only about 80 pages plus extensive notes in the Norton Library edition). The passage you have just read is the conclusion of Chapter 2. Chapter 3 is titled "Survivals in Early Literature" and discusses written evidence for Mauss's theory of gift-giving from ancient Roman law, ancient Hindu legal documents, early Germanic society, and, very briefly, Chinese law. Chapter 4 is titled "Conclusions." The first two sections, which we have excluded here, are moral conclusions and political and economic conclusions. They consist of about 4,750 words and 23 footnotes. We rejoin the text with the sociological and ethical conclusions with which Mauss ends his essay.]

3. Sociological and Ethical Conclusions

We may be permitted another note about the method we have used. We do not set this work up as a model; it simply proffers one or two suggestions. It is incomplete: the analysis could be pushed farther.* We are really posing questions for historians and anthropologists and offering possible lines of research for them rather than resolving a problem and laying down definite answers. It is enough for us to be sure for the moment that we have given sufficient data for such an end.

This being the case, we would point out that there is a heuristic element in our manner of treatment.[23] The facts we have studied are all "total" social phenomena. The word "general" may be preferred although we like it less. Some

of the facts presented concern the whole of society and its institutions (as with potlatch, opposing clans, tribes on visit, etc.); others, in which exchanges and contracts are the concern of individuals embrace a large number of institutions.

These phenomena are at once legal, economic, religious, aesthetic, morphological and so on. They are legal in that they concern individual and collective rights, organized and diffuse morality; they may be entirely obligatory, or subject simply to praise or disapproval. They are at once political and domestic, being of interest both to classes and to clans and families. They are religious; they concern true religion, animism, magic and diffuse religious mentality. They are economic, for the notions of value, utility, interest, luxury, wealth, acquisition, accumulation, consumption and liberal and sumptuous expenditure are all present, although not perhaps in their modern senses. Moreover, these institutions have an important aesthetic side which we have left unstudied; but the dances performed, the songs and shows, the dramatic representations given between camps or partners, the objects made, used, decorated, polished, amassed and transmitted with affection, received with joy, given away in triumph, the feasts in which everyone participates—all these, the food, objects and services, are the source of aesthetic emotions as well as emotions aroused by interest.* This is true not only of Melanesia but also, and particularly, of the potlatch of North-West America and still more true of the market-festival of the Indo-European world. Lastly, our phenomena are clearly morphological. Everything that happens in the course of gatherings, fairs and markets or in the feasts that replace them, presupposes groups whose duration exceeds the season of social concentration, like the winter potlatch of the Kwakiutl or the few weeks of the Melanesian maritime expeditions. Moreover, in order that these meetings may be carried out in peace, there must be roads or water for transport

---

[22] This conclusion points once again to the evolutionary nature of Mauss' thinking.

[23] In this paragraph and below, Mauss provides a comprehensive definition of total social phenomena, suggesting that the investigation of such phenomena provides an outstanding pathway for developing an understanding of society in general. Mauss claims that total social phenomena are morphological. That is, they reveal the underlying structure of the groups practicing them.

and tribal, inter-tribal or international alliances—*commercium* and *connubium*.*[24]

We are dealing then with something more than a set of themes, more than institutional elements, more than institutions, more even than systems of institutions divisible into legal, economic, religious and other parts. We are concerned with "wholes," with systems in their entirety. We have not described them as if they were fixed, in a static or skeletal condition, and still less have we dissected them into the rules and myths and values and so on of which they are composed. It is only by considering them as wholes that we have been able to see their essence, their operation and their living aspect, and to catch the fleeting moment when the society and its members take emotional stock of themselves and their situation as regards others. Only by making such concrete observation of social life is it possible to come upon facts such as those which our study is beginning to reveal. Nothing in our opinion is more urgent or promising than research into "total" social phenomena.[25]

The advantage is twofold. Firstly there is an advantage in generality, for facts of widespread occurrence are more likely to be universal than local institutions or themes, which are invariably tinged with local color. But particularly the advantage is in realism. We see social facts in the round, as they really are. In society there are not merely ideas and rules, but also men and groups and their behaviours. We see them in motion as an engineer sees masses and systems, or as we observe octopuses and anemones in the sea. We see groups of men, and active forces, submerged in their environments and sentiments.[26]

Historians believe and justly resent the fact that sociologists make too many abstractions and separate unduly the various elements of society.[27] We should follow their precepts and observe what is given. The tangible fact is Rome or Athens or the average Frenchman or the Melanesian of some island, and not prayer or law as such. Whereas formerly sociologists were obliged to analyze and abstract rather too much, they should now force themselves to reconstitute the whole. This is the way to reach incontestable facts. They will also find a way of satisfying psychologists who have a pronounced viewpoint, and particularly psycho-pathologists, since there is no doubt that the object of their study is concrete. They all observe, or at least ought to, minds as wholes and not minds divided into faculties. We should follow suit. The study of the concrete, which is the study of the whole, is made more readily, is more interesting and furnishes more explanations in the sphere of sociology than the study of the abstract. For we observe complete and complex beings. We too describe them in their organisms and *psychai* as well as in their behavior as groups, with the attendant psychoses: sentiments, ideas and desires of the crowd, of organized societies and their sub-groups. We see bodies and their reactions, and their ideas and sentiments as interpretations or as motive forces. The aim and principle of sociology is to observe and understand the whole group in its total behavior.

It is not possible here—it would have meant extending a restricted study unduly—to seek the morphological implications of our facts. It may be

---

[24] *Commercium and connubium:* Latin for commerce and intermarriage.

[25] Here Mauss seems to emphasize the holism that was part of American anthropology of his era, particularly Boas' thought. Mauss cites Boas' work many times in the present article. However, the application of holism to total social phenomena is distinctly his own. Boas and his followers did not believe that total social phenomena existed; they tended to believe that the different aspects of culture were of equal importance.

[26] Mauss relies on Durkheim's idea of a social fact. For Durkheim, sociology was the analysis of social facts. He defines these as "every way of acting, fixed or not, capable of exercising on the individual an external constraint; or again, every way of acting which is general throughout a given society, while at the same time existing in its own right independent of its individual manifestations" (see essay 6).

[27] At the turn of the century, academic disciplines were not divided the same way they are today. One of Durkheim's concerns, here echoed by Mauss, was to show that sociology is a discipline with its own area of study and is distinct from history or psychology. The concern of modern anthropologists is frequently the reverse. Recent theorists such as Renato Rosaldo have explored how history and psychology provide fundamental insights into anthropology (see essay 38).

worth while, however, to indicate the method one might follow in such a piece of research.

All the societies we have described above with the exception of our European societies are segmentary. Even the Indo-Europeans, the Romans before the Twelve Tables, the Germanic societies up to the *Edda*, and Irish society to the time of its chief literature, were still societies based on the clan or on great families more or less undivided internally and isolated from each other externally. All these were far removed from the degree of unification with which historians have credited them or which is ours today. Within these groups the individuals, even the most influential, were less serious, avaricious and selfish than we are; externally at least they were and are generous and more ready to give. In tribal feasts, in ceremonies of rival clans, allied families or those that assist at each other's initiation, groups visit each other; and with the development of the law of hospitality in more advanced societies, the rules of friendship and the contract are present — along with the gods — to ensure the peace of markets and villages; at these times men meet in a curious frame of mind with exaggerated fear and an equally exaggerated generosity which appear stupid in no one's eyes but our own. In these primitive and archaic societies there is no middle path. There is either complete trust or mistrust. One lays down one's arms, renounces magic and gives everything away, from casual hospitality to one's daughter or one's property. It is in such conditions that men, despite themselves, learnt to renounce what was theirs and made contracts to give and repay.

But then they had no choice in the matter. When two groups of men meet they may move away or in case of mistrust or defiance they may resort to arms; or else they can come to terms. Business has always been done with foreigners, although these might have been allies. The people of Kiriwina said to Malinowski:[28] "The Dobu man is not good as we are. He is fierce, he is a man-eater. When we come to Dobu, we fear him, he might kill us! But see! I spit the charmed ginger root and their mind turns. They lay down their spears, they receive us well."* Nothing better expresses how close together lie festival and warfare.

Thurnwald describes with reference to another Melanesian tribe, with genealogical material, an actual event which shows just as clearly how these people pass in a group quite suddenly from a feast to a battle.* Buleau, a chief, had invited Bobal, another chief, and his people to a feast which was probably to be the first of a long series. Dances were performed all night long. By morning everyone was excited by the sleepless night of song and dance. On a remark made by Buleau one of Bobal's men killed him; and the troop of men massacred and pillaged and ran off with the women of the village. "Buleau and Bobal were more friends than rivals" they said to Thurnwald. We all have experience of events like this.

It is by opposing reason to emotion and setting up the will for peace against rash follies of this kind that peoples succeed in substituting alliance, gift and commerce for war, isolation and stagnation.

The research proposed would have some conclusion of this kind.[29] Societies have progressed

---

[28] Mauss refers to anthropologist Bronislaw Malinowski, best known for his work in the Trobriand Islands. We present an extract from Malinowski's *Argonauts of the Western Pacific* (1922) in essay 13. Richard Thurnwald (1869–1954), mentioned in the next paragraph, led research expeditions to the South Pacific in the early twentieth century. He was the founder of the journal *Sociologus* and a key voice in midcentury German anthropology.

[29] According to Durkheim's ideas about evolution, primitive mechanistic solidarity gives way to modern organic solidarity. In this scheme, there is constant progress toward interdependence, and society reaches ever higher levels of integration. Rather than segments of society being opposed to each other in class warfare, as Marxist analysts claim, or engaged in a Malthusian struggle for survival, as Spencerians believed, every part of society should be seen as working for the peace and benefit of the whole.

Although Durkheim believed that social evolution would be characterized by a progression of ever better social forms, Mauss' life was tragic. His mentor Durkheim died in 1917. Few of the members of *L'Année Sociologique*, many of whom were his close friends, survived World War I. When *The Gift* was published, in 1925, conditions in Europe were far from stable. These concluding paragraphs to *The Gift* must be read in this context. They are, at the same time, an affirmation of Durkheim's belief in progress and a plea for peace and harmony in the aftermath of war.

in the measure in which they, their sub-groups and their members, have been able to stabilize their contracts and to give, receive and repay. In order to trade, man must first lay down his spear. When that is done he can succeed in exchanging goods and persons not only between clan and clan but between tribe and tribe and nation and nation, and above all between individuals. It is only then that people can create, can satisfy their interests mutually and define them without recourse to arms. It is in this way that the clan, the tribe and nation have learnt—just as in the future the classes and nations and individuals will learn—how to oppose one another without slaughter and to give without sacrificing themselves to others. That is one of the secrets of their wisdom and solidarity.

There is no other course feasible. The *Chronicles of Arthur** relate how King Arthur, with the help of a Cornish carpenter, invented the marvel of his court, the miraculous Round Table at which his knights would never come to blows. Formerly because of jealousy, skirmishes, duels and murders had set blood flowing in the most sumptuous of feasts. The carpenter says to Arthur: "I will make thee a fine table, where sixteen hundred may sit at once, and from which none need be excluded . . . And no knight will be able to raise combat, for there the highly placed will be on the same level as the lowly." There was no "head of the table" and hence no more quarrels. Wherever Arthur took his table, contented and invincible remained his noble company. And this today is the way of the nations that are strong, rich, good and happy. Peoples, classes, families and individuals may become rich, but they will not achieve happiness until they can sit down like the knights around their common riches. There is no need to seek far for goodness and happiness. It is to be found in the imposed peace, in the rhythm of communal and private labor, in wealth amassed and redistributed, in the mutual respect and reciprocal generosity that education can impart.

Thus we see how it is possible under certain circumstances to study total human behavior; and how that concrete study leads not only to a science of manners, a partial social science, but even to ethical conclusions—"civility," or "civics" as we say today. Through studies of this sort we can find, measure and assess the various determinants, aesthetic, moral, religious and economic, and the material and demographic factors, whose sum is the basis of society and constitutes the common life, and whose conscious direction is the supreme art—politics in the Socratic sense of the word.

9. Class, Status, Party

Max Weber (1864–1920)

1: Economically Determined Power and the Social Order[a]

LAW EXISTS WHEN THERE IS A PROBABILITY THAT an order will be upheld by a specific staff of men who will use physical or psychical compulsion with the intention of obtaining conformity with the order, or of inflicting sanctions for infringement of it. The structure of every legal order directly influences the distribution of power, economic or otherwise, within its respective community. This is true of all legal orders and not only that of the state. In general, we understand by "power" the chance of a man or of a number of men to realize their own will in a communal action even against the resistance of others who are participating in the action.[1]

"Economically conditioned" power is not, of course, identical with "power" as such. On the contrary, the emergence of economic power may be the consequence of power existing on other grounds. Man does not strive for power only in order to enrich himself economically. Power, including economic power, may be valued "for its own sake." Very frequently the striving for power

From *Economy and Society* (1922)

is also conditioned by the social "honor" it entails. Not all power, however, entails social honor: The typical American Boss, as well as the typical big speculator, deliberately relinquishes social honor. Quite generally, "mere economic" power, and especially "naked" money power, is by no means a recognized basis of social honor. Nor is power the only basis of social honor. Indeed, social honor, or prestige, may even be the basis of political or economic power, and very frequently has been. Power, as well as honor, may be guaranteed by the legal order, but, at least normally, it is not their primary source. The legal order is rather an additional factor that enhances the chance to hold power or honor; but it cannot always secure them.[2]

The way in which social honor is distributed in a community between typical groups participating in this distribution we may call the "social order." The social order and the economic order are, of course, similarly related to the "legal order." However, the social and the economic order are not identical. The economic order is for us merely the way in which economic goods and services are distributed and used. The social order is of course conditioned by the economic order to a high degree, and in turn it reacts upon it.[3]

---

[1] This essay was part of Weber's massive posthumous work, *Wirtschaft und Gesellschaft* (*Economy and Society*). Probably written between 1915 and 1920, it was first published in 1922. *Wirtschaft und Gesellschaft* was one volume of an extensive series of studies in the social sciences that Weber organized for the German publishing house Siebeck. Much of Weber's work was written in response to Karl Marx (see essay 4), and the relationship between the two is complex. The first section of the essay sets Weber's argument. In contrast to Marx, Weber insists that individual identity is not subsumed by class identity. Status and party may, and frequently do, cut across class membership. In this essay, he presents and discusses each of these forms of identity.

[2] Social thinkers and political activists (and Weber was both) in the Germany of Weber's time were extreme conservatives (generally members of the landowning upper class) or radicals who often espoused Marxist ideals (generally those identified with industrial workers). Weber—from a family whose wealth was based in textile manufacturing—identified with neither the conservative landowners nor the radical workers, but was a political liberal trying to sit midway between the two.

[3] Weber felt that Marx's methods of analysis produced valuable insights. However, he believed that they leaned too heavily on economics and dialectical conflict between forces of production and relations of production as the motor driving social evolution. Weber incorporated much Marxist thought into his theories, yet he was not a Marxist and did not believe in a communist utopia. In the days of the cold war, this might have been a factor in his appeal to American sociologists and anthropologists.

Now: "classes," "status groups," and "parties" are phenomena of the distribution of power within a community.

2: Determination of Class-Situation by Market-Situation

In our terminology, "classes" are not communities; they merely represent possible, and frequent, bases for communal action. We may speak of a "class" when (1) a number of people have in common a specific causal component of their life chances, in so far as (2) this component is represented exclusively by economic interests in the possession of goods and opportunities for income, and (3) is represented under the conditions of the commodity or labor markets.[4] [These points refer to "class situation," which we may express more briefly as the typical chance for a supply of goods, external living conditions, and personal life experiences, in so far as this chance is determined by the amount and kind of power, or lack of such, to dispose of goods or skills for the sake of income in a given economic order. The term "class" refers to any group of people that is found in the same class situation.]

It is the most elemental economic fact that the way in which the disposition over material property is distributed among a plurality of people, meeting competitively in the market for the purpose of exchange, in itself creates specific life chances. According to the law of marginal utility this mode of distribution excludes the non-owners from competing for highly valued goods; it favors the owners and, in fact, gives to them a monopoly to acquire such goods. Other things being equal, this mode of distribution monopolizes the opportunities for profitable deals for all those who, provided with goods, do not necessarily have to exchange them. It increases, at least generally, their power in price wars with those who, being propertyless, have nothing to offer but their services in native form or goods in a form constituted through their own labor, and who above all are compelled to get rid of these products in order barely to subsist. This mode of distribution gives to the propertied a monopoly on the possibility of transferring property from the sphere of use as a "fortune," to the sphere of "capital goods"; that is, it gives them the entrepreneurial function and all chances to share directly or indirectly in returns on capital. All this holds true within the area in which pure market conditions prevail. "Property" and "lack of property" are, therefore, the basic categories of all class situations. It does not matter whether these two categories become effective in price wars or in competitive struggles.

Within these categories, however, class situations are further differentiated: on the one hand, according to the kind of property that is usable for returns; and, on the other hand, according to the kind of services that can be offered in the market. Ownership of domestic buildings; productive establishments; warehouses; stores; agriculturally usable land, large and small holdings—quantitative differences with possibly qualitative consequences—; ownership of mines; cattle; men (slaves); disposition over mobile instruments of

---

[4] Weber's definition of class overlapped Marx's, yet differed from it. For Marx, class signified a specific relationship to the means of production. In a class society, one class has ownership or control of the means of production, and another is employed producing surplus for that owner class. Further, classes are born in the struggle for control of the means of production. For Marx, understanding the role of class was key to the analysis of society; all other identifications were secondary. While Weber focused on ownership of property as the constitutive element of class, he downplayed other elements of Marx's analysis. In particular, Weber suggested that class does not necessarily have analytic primacy—other elements of identity may be of equal or greater importance. Moreover, Weber gave conflict less of a role in generating and maintaining class relationships than Marx did. For Marx, this conflict was critical since it drove history (recall *The Communist Manifesto* (1972 [1848]:241): "The history of all hitherto existing society is the history of class struggles"). For Weber, other forces are of much greater importance in social change. For example, Weber saw social evolution as a generalized process toward increased rationalization and bureaucratization that necessarily entailed the destruction of individual liberties. He believed that charisma acted in opposition to this force. Through strength of personality, the charismatic individual was able to break the bonds of routine and radically redirect society.

production, or capital goods of all sorts, especially money or objects that can be exchanged for money easily and at any time; disposition over products of one's own labor or of others' labor differing according to their various distances from consumability; disposition over transferable monopolies of any kind—all these distinctions differentiate the class situations of the propertied just as does the "meaning" which they can and do give to the utilization of property, especially to property which has money equivalence. Accordingly, the propertied, for instance, may belong to the class of rentiers or to the class of entrepreneurs.

Those who have no property but who offer services are differentiated just as much according to their kinds of services as according to the way in which they make use of these services, in a continuous or discontinuous relation to a recipient. But always this is the generic connotation of the concept of class: that the kind of chance in the *market* is the decisive moment which presents a common condition for the individual's fate. "Class situation" is, in this sense, ultimately "market situation." The effect of naked possession *per se* which among cattle breeders gives the non-owning slave or serf into the power of the cattle owner, is only a forerunner of real "class" formation. However, in the cattle loan and in the naked severity of the law of debts in such communities, for the first time mere "possession" as such emerges as decisive for the fate of the individual. This is very much in contrast to the agricultural communities based on labor. The creditor-debtor relation becomes the basis of "class situations" only in those cities where a "credit market," however primitive, with rates of interest increasing according to the extent of dearth and a factual monopolization of credits, is developed by a plutocracy. Therewith "class struggles" begin.

Those men whose fate is not determined by the chance of using goods or services for themselves on the market, e.g, slaves, are not, however, a "class" in the technical sense of the term. They are, rather, a "status group."

3: Communal Action Flowing from Class Interest

According to our terminology, the factor that creates "class" is unambiguously economic interest, and indeed, only those interests involved in the existence of the "market." Nevertheless, the concept of "class-interest" is an ambiguous one: even as an empirical concept it is ambiguous as soon as one understands by it something other than the factual direction of interests following with a certain probability from the class situation for a certain "average" of those people subjected to the class situation. The class situation and other circumstances remaining the same, the direction in which the individual worker, for instance, is likely to pursue his interests may vary widely, according to whether he is constitutionally qualified for the task at hand to a high, to an average, or to a low degree. In the same way, the direction of interests may vary according to whether or not a *communal* action of a larger or smaller portion of those commonly affected by the "class situation," or even an association among them, e.g., a "trade union," has grown out of the class situation from which the individual may or may not expect promising results. [Communal action refers to that action which is oriented to the feeling of the actors that they belong together. Societal action, on the other hand, is oriented to a rationally motivated adjustment of interests.] The rise of societal or even of communal action from a common class situation is by no means a universal phenomenon.[5]

The class situation may be restricted in its effects to the generation of essentially *similar* reactions, that is to say, within our terminology, of "mass actions." However, it may not have even this

---

[5] Underlying Weber's analysis is a concern for the issues of action and abstraction. For Weber, a class was an abstraction and therefore, in and of itself, could perform no action; thus the actions that flow from class interest were problematic. In order to act, any group must be organized. In this passage, Weber shows that the actions of classes must be mediated by individuals. However, individual variation within a class may be so great that it prevents the emergence of any generalized class consciousness or class struggle. Parties and status groups, discussed below, play key roles in organizing classes.

result. Furthermore, often merely an amorphous communal action emerges. For example, the "murmuring" of the workers known in ancient oriental ethics: the moral disapproval of the work-master's conduct, which in its practical significance was probably equivalent to an increasingly typical phenomenon of precisely the latest industrial development, namely, the "slow down" (the deliberate limiting of work effort) of laborers by virtue of tacit agreement. The degree in which "communal action" and possibly "societal action," emerges from the "mass actions" of the members of a class is linked to general cultural conditions, especially to those of an intellectual sort. It is also linked to the extent of the contrasts that have already evolved, and is especially linked to the *transparency* of the connections between the causes and the consequences of the "class situation." For however different life chances may be, this fact in itself, according to all experience, by no means gives birth to "class action" (communal action by the members of a class). The fact of being conditioned and the results of the class situation must be distinctly recognizable.[6] For only then the contrast of life chances can be felt not as an absolutely given fact to be accepted, but as a resultant from either (1) the given distribution of property, or (2) the structure of the concrete economic order. It is only then that people may react against the class structure not only through acts of an intermittent and irrational protest, but in the form of rational association. There have been "class situations" of the first category (1), of a specifically naked and transparent sort, in the urban centers of Antiquity and during the Middle Ages; especially then, when

great fortunes were accumulated by factually monopolized trading in industrial products of these localities or in foodstuffs.[7] Furthermore, under certain circumstances, in the rural economy of the most diverse periods, when agriculture was increasingly exploited in a profit-making manner. The most important historical example of the second category (2) is the class situation of the modern "proletariat."

4: Types of Class Struggle

Thus every class may be the carrier of any one of the possibly innumerable forms of "class action," but this is not necessarily so. In any case, a class does not in itself constitute a community. To treat "class" conceptually as having the same value as "community" leads to distortion. That men in the same class situation regularly react in mass actions to such tangible situations as economic ones in the direction of those interests that are most adequate to their average number is an important and after all simple fact for the understanding of historical events. Above all, this fact must not lead to that kind of pseudo-scientific operation with the concepts of "class" and "class interests" so frequently found these days and which has found its most classic expression in the statement of a talented author, that the individual may be in error concerning his interests but that the "class" is "infallible" about its interests.[8] Yet, if classes as such are not communities, nevertheless class situations emerge only on the basis of communalization. The communal action that brings forth class situations, however, is not basi-

---

[6] Like the Marxists, Weber saw ideology as frequently masking the true nature of relations among people. Society could be understood by debunking the myths and ideological assertions that often cover economically or politically motivated action. Here he suggests that in order for class action to take place, class consciousness must already exist. However, various ideological structures may prevent classes from becoming aware of the true nature of their oppression and hence prevent the formation of class consciousness.

[7] Although Weber wrote on India and China, by far his primary interest was European history and society, and most of his analysis was driven by his understanding of these. His original scholarly interest was in history, and he wrote his doctoral thesis on trading companies during the Middle Ages. He later wrote essays on the social structure of ancient society. He refers frequently to both the European Middle Ages and to ancient Greece and Rome throughout his writing.

[8] The talented author Weber refers to in this passage is, of course, Marx. The point here is to highlight his disagreement with the Marxists. Marxism is a theory of class and group action in which the individual plays little role. For Weber, on the other hand, individuals and their relationships to social groups were of great importance. For Marxists, conflict be-

cally action between members of the identical class; it is an action between members of different classes. Communal actions that directly determine the class situation of the worker and the entrepreneur are: the labor market, the commodities market, and the capitalistic enterprise. But, in its turn, the existence of a capitalistic enterprise presupposes that a very specific communal action exists and that it is specifically structured to protect the possession of goods *per se* and especially the power of individuals to dispose, in principle freely, over the means of production. The existence of a capitalistic enterprise is preconditioned by a specific kind of "legal order." Each kind of class situation, and above all when it rests upon the power of property *per se,* will become most clearly efficacious when all other determinants of reciprocal relations are, as far as possible, eliminated in their significance. It is in this way that the utilization of the power of property in the market obtains its most sovereign importance.

Now "status groups" hinder the strict carrying through of the sheer market principle. In the present context they are of interest to us only from this one point of view. Before we briefly consider them, note that not much of a general nature can be said about the more specific kinds of antagonism between "classes" (in our meaning of the term). The great shift, which has been going on continuously in the past, and up to our times, may be summarized, although at the cost of some precision: the struggle in which class situations are effective has progressively shifted from consumption credit toward, first, competitive struggles in the commodity market and, then, toward price wars on the labor market. The "class struggles" of antiquity—to the extent that they were genuine class struggles and not struggles between status groups—were initially carried on by indebted peasants, and perhaps also by artisans threatened by debt bondage and struggling against urban creditors. For debt bondage is the normal result of the differentiation of wealth in commercial cities, especially in seaport cities. A similar situation has existed among cattle breeders. Debt relationships as such produced class action up to the time of Cataline.[9] Along with this, and with an increase in provision of grain for the city by transporting it from the outside, the struggle over the means of sustenance emerged. It centered in the first place around the provision of bread and the determination of the price of bread. It lasted throughout antiquity and the entire Middle Ages. The propertyless as such flocked together against those who actually and supposedly were interested in the dearth of bread. This fight spread until it involved all those commodities essential to the way of life and to handicraft production. There were only incipient discussions of wage disputes in antiquity and in the Middle Ages. But they have been slowly increasing up into modern times. In the earlier periods they were completely secondary to slave rebellions as well as to fights in the commodity market.[10]

The propertyless of antiquity and of the Middle Ages protested against monopolies, preemption, forestalling, and the withholding of goods from the market in order to raise prices. Today the central issue is the determination of the price of labor.

---

tween social groups was the key force that drives history. Weber suggests that such conflict can only exist when classes and groups are organized under quite specific conditions. A class, in the example here, cannot be infallible about its interests because a class is an abstraction and cannot have interests outside of a very particular context. In this passage he illustrates some of the conditions under which class interests and struggle are likely to exist or historically did exist.

[9] Cataline: Lucius Sergius Catilina (108–62 B.C.E.) was a soldier and politician in the Roman Republic.

[10] In this passage Weber presents a very rough outline of the history of European class struggles. Weber viewed sociology as the background information necessary to do history. The goal of his sociology was to propose general principles, but he believed that the actual unfolding of history was predicated on individual action and thus beyond any law. He wrote that "The reduction of empirical reality . . . to 'laws' is meaningless" and that "A systematic science of culture . . . would be senseless in itself" (quoted in Ritzer 1992:114). Franz Boas was probably quite familiar with Weber's work and had a similar understanding of the role of the individual. He, too, was suspicious of any attempt to make anthropology a science of culture based in the discovery of natural laws.

This transition is represented by the fight for access to the market and for the determination of the price of products. Such fights went on between merchants and workers in the putting-out system of domestic handicraft during the transition to modern times. Since it is quite a general phenomenon we must mention here that the class antagonisms that are conditioned through the market situation are usually most bitter between those who actually and directly participate as opponents in price wars. It is not the rentier, the share-holder, and the banker who suffer the ill will of the worker, but almost exclusively the manufacturer and the business executives who are the direct opponents of workers in price wars. This is so in spite of the fact that it is precisely the cash boxes of the rentier, the share-holder, and the banker into which the more or less "unearned" gains flow, rather than into the pockets of the manufacturers or of the business executives.[11] This simple state of affairs has very frequently been decisive for the role the class situation has played in the formation of political parties. For example, it has made possible the varieties of patriarchal socialism and the frequent attempts — formerly, at least — of threatened status groups to form alliances with the proletariat against the "bourgeoisie."

5: Status Honor

In contrast to classes, *status groups* are normally communities.[12] They are, however, often of an amorphous kind. In contrast to the purely economically determined "class situation" we wish to designate as "status situation" every typical component of the life fate of men that is determined by a specific, positive or negative, social estimation of *honor*. This honor may be connected with any quality shared by a plurality, and, of course, it can be knit to a class situation: class distinctions are linked in the most varied ways with status distinctions. Property as such is not always recognized as a status qualification, but in the long run it is, and with extraordinary regularity. In the subsistence economy of the organized neighborhood, very often the richest man is simply the chieftain. However, this often means only an honorific preference. For example, in the so-called pure modern "democracy," that is, one devoid of any expressly ordered status privileges for individuals, it may be that only the families coming under approximately the same tax class dance with one another. This example is reported of certain smaller Swiss cities. But status honor need not necessarily be linked with a "class situation." On the contrary, it normally stands in sharp opposition to the pretensions of sheer property.

Both propertied and propertyless people can belong to the same status group, and frequently they do with very tangible consequences. This "equality" of social esteem may, however, in the long run become quite precarious. The "equality" of status among the American "gentlemen," for instance, is expressed by the fact that outside the subordination determined by the different functions of "business," it would be considered strictly repugnant — wherever the old tradition still prevails — if even the richest "chief," while playing billiards or cards in his club in the evening, would not treat his "clerk" as in every sense fully his equal in birthright. It would be repugnant if the American "chief" would bestow upon his "clerk" the condescending "benevolence" marking a dis-

---

[11] Here Weber points out that class struggles are often misdirected, a significant critique of the Marxist view. If class struggles were truly between classes, owners such as rentiers, shareholders, and bankers should suffer the wrath of the working class as much as manufacturers and business executives. Weber claims, however, that they do not because they are less likely to be in direct contact with the workers.

[12] Above, Weber has described the operation of class within society. Here and below, he adds what he considers two other forces that cut across class identification and compete with it for prominence in social action: status and party. For Weber, class, status, and party are overlapping identifications. None of them has universal analytic priority, but rather identification with one or the other is dependent on circumstances. This idea of overlapping identities anticipates much of current interpretive and postmodern anthropology.

tinction of "position," which the German chief can never dissever from his attitude. This is one of the most important reasons why in America the German "clubby-ness" has never been able to attain the attraction that the American clubs have.[13]

6: Guarantees of Status Stratification

In content, status honor is normally expressed by the fact that above all else a specific *style of life* can be expected from all those who wish to belong to the circle. Linked with this expectation are restrictions on "social" intercourse (that is, intercourse which is not subservient to economic or any other of business's "functional" purposes). These restrictions may confine normal marriages to within the status circle and may lead to complete endogamous closure. As soon as there is not a mere individual and socially irrelevant imitation of another style of life, but an agreed-upon communal action of this closing character, the "status" development is under way.

In its characteristic form, stratification by "status groups" on the basis of conventional styles of life evolves at the present time in the United States out of the traditional democracy.[14] For example, only the resident of a certain street ("the street") is considered as belonging to "society," is qualified for social intercourse, and is visited and invited. Above all, this differentiation evolves in such a way as to make for strict submission to the fashion that is dominant at a given time in society. This submission to fashion also exists among men in America to a degree unknown in Germany. Such submission is considered to be an indication of the fact that a given man *pretends* to qualify as a gentleman. This submission decides, at least *prima facie*,[15] that he will be treated as such. And this recognition becomes just as important for his employment chances in "swank" establishments, and above all, for social intercourse and marriage with "esteemed" families, as the qualification for dueling among Germans in the Kaiser's day. As for the rest: certain families resident for a long time, and, of course, correspondingly wealthy, e.g., "F.F.V., i.e. First Families of Virginia," or the actual or alleged descendants of the "Indian Princess" Pocahontas, of the Pilgrim fathers, or of the Knickerbockers,[16] the members of almost inaccessible sects and all sorts of circles setting themselves apart by means of any other characteristics and badges . . . all these elements usurp "status" honor. The development of status is essentially a question of stratification resting upon usurpation. Such usurpation is the normal origin of almost all status honor. But the road from this purely conventional situation to legal privilege, positive or negative, is easily traveled as soon as a certain stratification of the social order has in fact been "lived in" and has achieved stability by virtue of a stable distribution of economic power.

7: "Ethnic" Segregation and "Caste"

Where the consequences have been realized to their full extent, the status group evolves into a

---

[13] Weber's 1904 visit to America made a profound and lasting impression on him. Though greatly disturbed by the position of African Americans and immigrants, in many respects he viewed America as, for better and worse, the model of a new society. He felt that in America, rationalization and bureaucratization had proceeded to the greatest extent. The example of boss and worker treating each other as equals may appear fanciful to the modern reader, but for Weber, it illustrated the compartmentalization and bureaucratization of American life.

[14] While Weber recognized a link between economic position and status, he also believed that there were many other ways to acquire status. The examples he uses here are drawn from American society but reflect the extremely status-conscious German society. Weber himself came from a family of factory owners. He had trained in law at Heidelberg and been a member of his father's prestigious dueling fraternity. He had scars from the dueling he refers to in this passage. After his studies and a year of military training, he was commissioned as an officer in the German army.

[15] *Prima facie:* Latin for at first sight.

[16] *Knickerbockers* refers to the descendants of the Dutch settlers of New York.

closed "caste."[17] Status distinctions are then guaranteed not merely by conventions and laws, but also by *rituals*. This occurs in such a way that every physical contact with a member of any caste that is considered to be "lower" by the members of a "higher" caste is considered as making for a ritualistic impurity and to be a stigma which must be expiated by a religious act. Individual castes develop quite distinct cults and gods.

In general, however, the status structure reaches such extreme consequences only where there are underlying differences which are held to be "ethnic." The "caste" is, indeed, the normal form in which ethnic communities usually live side by side in a "societalized" manner. These ethnic communities believe in blood relationship and exclude exogamous marriage and social intercourse. Such a caste situation is part of the phenomenon of "pariah" peoples and is found all over the world. These people form communities, acquire specific occupational traditions of handicrafts or of other arts, and cultivate a belief in their ethnic community. They live in a "diaspora" strictly segregated from all personal intercourse, except that of an unavoidable sort, and their situation is legally precarious. Yet, by virtue of their economic indispensability, they are tolerated, indeed, frequently privileged, and they live in interspersed political communities. The Jews are the most impressive historical example.

A "status" segregation grown into a "caste" differs in its structure from a mere "ethnic" segregation: the caste structure transforms the horizontal and unconnected coexistences of ethnically segregated groups into a vertical social system of super- and subordination. Correctly formulated: a comprehensive societalization integrates the ethnically divided communities into specific political and communal action.[18] In their consequences they differ precisely in this way: ethnic coexistences condition a mutual repulsion and disdain but allow each ethnic community to consider its own honor as the highest one; the caste structure brings about a social subordination and an acknowledgment of "more honor" in favor of the privileged caste and status groups. This is due to the fact that in the caste structure ethnic distinctions as such have become "functional" distinctions within the political societalization (warriors, priests, artisans that are politically important for war and for building, and so on). But even pariah people who are most despised are usually apt to continue cultivating in some manner that which is equally peculiar to ethnic and to status communities: the belief in their own specific "honor." This is the case with the Jews.

Only with the negatively privileged status groups does the "sense of dignity" take a specific deviation. A sense of dignity is the precipitation in individuals of social honor and of conventional demands which a positively privileged status group raises for the deportment of its members. The sense of dignity that characterizes positively privileged status groups is naturally related to their "being" which does not transcend itself, that is, it is to their "beauty and excellence" (καλο-κάγαθια). Their kingdom is "of this world." They live for the present and by exploiting their great past. The sense of dignity of the negatively privileged strata naturally refers to a future lying beyond the

---

[17] Weber developed his notions of caste more fully in his work on the Indian caste system, but he clearly believed the term *caste* applied to a wide variety of social systems. He spends a good deal of time discussing caste here because he sees it as an extreme manifestation of status differences. One of Weber's contributions to sociology is the idea of the ideal type, a "one-sided accentuation of one or more points of view" (quoted in Ritzer 1992). Weber uses *ideal* in the sense of the most extreme logical possibility rather than in the sense of best. He looked for, or logically constructed, extreme examples to gain insight into more typical social forms. Although the use of ideal types provides clear examples amenable to analysis, it may also obscure the complexity of social life.

[18] Notice Weber's use of the words *society* and *societalization.* He theorized that there were three basic types of social structure: the community, the association, and the society (Gerth and Mills 1946:57). To some degree, he understood history as a progression from community to society, with society marked by increased rationalization and bureaucratization. In Weber's usage, society is what modern anthropologists might refer to as state-level society. For Weber, when a group became societalized, it also became bureaucratized.

present, whether it is of this life or of another. In other words, it must be nurtured by the belief in a providential "mission" and by a belief in a specific honor before God. The "chosen people's" dignity is nurtured by a belief either that in the beyond "the last will be the first," or that in this life a Messiah will appear to bring forth into the light of the world which has cast them out the hidden honor of the pariah people. This simple state of affairs, and not the "resentment" which is so strongly emphasized in Nietzsche's much admired construction in the *Genealogy of Morals,* is the source of the religiosity cultivated by pariah status groups. In passing, we may note that resentment may be accurately applied only to a limited extent; for one of Nietzsche's main examples, Buddhism, it is not at all applicable.[19]

Incidentally, the development of status groups from ethnic segregations is by no means the normal phenomenon. On the contrary, since objective "racial differences" are by no means basic to every subjective sentiment of an ethnic community, the ultimately racial foundation of status structure is rightly and absolutely a question of the concrete individual case.[20] Very frequently a status group is instrumental in the production of a thoroughbred anthropological type. Certainly a status group is to a high degree effective in producing extreme types, for they select personally qualified individuals (e.g., the Knighthood selects those who are fit for warfare, physically and psychically). But selection is far from being the only,

or the predominant, way in which status groups are formed: Political membership or class situation has at all times been at least as frequently decisive. And today the class situation is by far the predominant factor, for of course the possibility of a style of life expected for members of a status group is usually conditioned economically.

8: Status Privileges

For all practical purposes, stratification by status goes hand in hand with a monopolization of ideal and material goods or opportunities, in a manner we have come to know as typical.[21] Besides the specific status honor, which always rests upon distance and exclusiveness, we find all sorts of material monopolies. Such honorific preferences may consist of the privilege of wearing special costumes, of eating special dishes taboo to others, of carrying arms—which is most obvious in its consequences—the right to pursue certain non-professional dilettante artistic practices, e.g. to play certain musical instruments. Of course, material monopolies provide the most effective motives for the exclusiveness of a status group; although, in themselves, they are rarely sufficient, almost always they come into play to some extent. Within a status circle there is the question of intermarriage: the interest of the families in the monopolization of potential bridegrooms is at least of equal importance and is parallel to the

---

[19] The work of Friedrich Wilhelm Nietzsche (1844–1900) was extremely influential for German social thinkers of the late nineteenth century. He was concerned, among other things, with the benefit that people gained from holding certain types of ideas. Simply put, his resentment theory (from *On the Genealogy of Morals* (1956 [1887]) states that, because they cannot bear the psychological burden of low position, oppressed people turn the characteristics of their subjugation into sources of honor. Thus, Nietzsche believed that ascetic Christian morality reflected the resentment of early Christians who were often slaves (Gerth and Mills 1946:62). While Weber is concerned with individual psychology, he understands the attribution of elevated moral status to oppressed peoples as a group function—one that maintains the status differentials of the caste system—rather than as an individual psychological coping mechanism. Weber probably considered resentment theory inapplicable to Buddhism because that religion's founder, the Indian prince Siddhartha Gautama (563?–483? B.C.E.), was a man of high status.

[20] Note that Weber argues that caste groups may be separated by perceived racial distinctions but are not *created* by these. Rather, differential status may, in time, create distinctions that are then *perceived* as racial. This is a fairly radical point.

[21] Weber suggests that while economic privileges are frequently one important aspect of status, they are rarely sufficient to explain stratification. Other, less material privileges may well be more important.

interest in the monopolization of daughters. The daughters of the circle must be provided for. With an increased enclosure of the status group, the conventional preferential opportunities for special employment grow into a legal monopoly of special offices for the members. Certain goods become objects for monopolization by status groups. In the typical fashion these include "entailed estates" and frequently also the possessions of serfs or bondsmen and, finally, special trades. This monopolization occurs positively when the status group is exclusively entitled to own and to manage them; and negatively when, in order to maintain its specific way of life, the status group must *not* own and manage them.

The decisive role of a "style of life" in status "honor" means that status groups are the specific bearers of all "conventions."[22] In whatever way it may be manifest, all "stylization" of life either originates in status groups or is at least conserved by them. Even if the principles of status conventions differ greatly, they reveal certain typical traits, especially among those strata which are most privileged. Quite generally, among privileged status groups there is a status disqualification that operates against the performance of common physical labor. This disqualification is now "setting in" in America against the old tradition of esteem for labor. Very frequently every rational economic pursuit, and especially "entrepreneurial activity," is looked upon as a disqualification of status. Artistic and literary activity is also considered as degrading work as soon as it is exploited for income, or at least when it is connected with hard physical exertion. An example is the sculptor working like a mason in his dusty smock as over against the painter in his salon-like "studio" and those forms of musical practice that are acceptable to the status group.

9: Economic Conditions and Effects of Status Stratification

The frequent disqualification of the gainfully employed as such is a direct result of the principle of status stratification peculiar to the social order, and of course, of this principle's opposition to a distribution of power which is regulated exclusively through the market. These two factors operate along with various individual ones, which will be touched upon below.

We have seen above that the market and its processes "knows no personal distinctions": "functional" interests dominate it. It knows nothing of "honor." The status order means precisely the reverse, viz.: stratification in terms of "honor" and of styles of life peculiar to status groups as such. If mere economic acquisition and naked economic power still bearing the stigma of its extra-status origin could bestow upon anyone who has won it the same honor as those who are interested in status by virtue of style of life claim for themselves, the status order would be threatened at its very root. This is the more so as, given equality of status honor, property *per se* represents an addition even if it is not overtly acknowledged to be such. Yet if such economic acquisition and power gave the agent any honor at all, his wealth would result in his attaining more honor than those who successfully claim honor by virtue of style of life. Therefore all groups having interests in the status order react with special sharpness precisely against the pretensions of purely economic acquisition. In most cases they react the more vigorously the more they feel themselves threatened.[23] Calderon's respectful treatment of the peasant, for instance, as opposed to Shakespeare's simultaneous and ostensible disdain of the *canaille* illustrates the dif-

---

[22] In his emphasis on consumption as a marker of status, Weber may have been strongly influenced by the economic and social theorist Thorstein Veblen (1857–1929). Veblen's *The Theory of the Leisure Class* (1912 [1899]) suggested that there was a conflict between making goods and making money: monied classes increasingly freed themselves from any involvement in labor. Weber expands upon this topic in the section below.

[23] To a modern American reader, this passage may sound terribly anachronistic. For most of us, enormous wealth is likely to confer status almost instantly. In Weber's nineteenth-century world, quick wealth was often considered to be tainted, and the old rich had little respect for those who acquired their money more recently. To Weber — member of a dueling society, officer, and nationalist — honor and the acquisition of status played a role that is, for most of us today, quite alien.

ferent way in which a firmly structured status order reacts as compared with a status order that has become economically precarious.[24] This is an example of a state of affairs that recurs everywhere. Precisely because of the rigorous reactions against the claims of property *per se* the "parvenu"[25] is never accepted, personally and without reservation, by the privileged status groups, no matter how completely his style of life has been adjusted to theirs. They will only accept his descendants who have been educated in the conventions of their status group and who have never besmirched its honor by their own economic labor.

As to the general *effect* of the status order, only one consequence can be stated, but it is a very important one: the hindrance of the free development of the market occurs first for those goods which status groups directly withheld from free exchange by monopolization.[26] This monopolization may be effected either legally or conventionally. For example, in many Hellenic cities during the epoch of status groups, and also originally in Rome, the inherited estate (as is shown by the old formula for indiction against spendthrifts) was monopolized just as were the estates of knights, peasants, priests, and especially the clientele of the craft and merchant guilds. The market is restricted, and the power of naked property *per se* which gives its stamp to "class formation," is pushed into the background. The results of this process can be most varied. Of course, they do not necessarily weaken the contrasts in the economic situation. Frequently they strengthen these contrasts, and in any case, where stratification by status permeates a community as strongly as was the case in all political communities of antiquity and of the Middle Ages, one can never speak of a genuinely free market competition as we understand it today. There are wider effects than this direct exclusion of special

goods from the market. From the contrariety between the status order and the purely economic order mentioned above, it follows that in most instances the notion of honor peculiar to status absolutely abhors that which is essential to the market: higgling. Honor abhors higgling among peers and occasionally it taboos higgling for the members of a status group in general. Therefore, everywhere some status groups, and usually the most influential, consider almost any kind of overt participation in economic acquisition as absolutely stigmatizing.

With some over-simplification, one might thus say that "classes" are stratified according to their relations to the production and acquisition of goods; whereas "status groups" are stratified according to the principles of their *consumption* of goods as represented by special "styles of life."

An "occupational group" is also a status group. For normally, it successfully claims social honor only by virtue of the special style of life which may be determined by it. The differences between classes and status groups frequently overlap. It is precisely those status communities most strictly segregated in terms of honor (viz. the Indian castes) who today show, although within very rigid limits, a relatively high degree of indifference to pecuniary income. However, the Brahmins seek such income in many different ways.

As to the general economic conditions making for the predominance of stratification by "status," only very little can be said.[27] When the bases of the acquisition and distribution of goods are relatively stable, stratification by status is favored. Every technological repercussion and economic transformation threatens stratification by status and pushes the class situation into the foreground. Epochs and countries in which the naked class situation is of predominant significance are regularly the periods of technical and economic transformations. And every slowing down of the

---

[24] *Calderon* refers to Spanish playwright Pedro Calderon de la Barca (1600–1681). A *canaille* is a mob.

[25] *Parvenu:* people with manners that ill-fit their newfound wealth.

[26] In this paragraph, Weber provides a concise summary of his understanding of class and status.

[27] Compare the conception of change here with Marx's understanding of change caused by conflict between classes. In both cases, conflict between ideological superstructure and technological base play crucial roles.

shifting of economic stratifications leads, in due course, to the growth of status structures and makes for a resuscitation of the important role of social honor.

10: Parties

Whereas the genuine place of "classes" is within the economic order, the place of "status groups" is within the social order, that is, within the sphere of the distribution of "honor." From within these spheres, classes and status groups influence one another and they influence the legal order and are in turn influenced by it. But "parties" live in a house of "power."

Their action is oriented toward the acquisition of social "power," that is to say, toward influencing a communal action no matter what its content may be. In principle, parties may exist in a social "club" as well as in a "state." As over against the actions of classes and status groups, for which this is not necessarily the case, the communal actions of "parties" always mean a societalization. For party actions are always directed toward a goal which is striven for in planned manner. This goal may be a "cause" (the party may aim at realizing a program for ideal or material purposes), or the goal may be "personal" (sinecures, power, and from these, honor for the leader and the followers of the party). Usually the party action aims at all these simultaneously. Parties are, therefore, only possible within communities that are societalized, that is, which have some rational order and a staff of persons available who are ready to enforce it. For parties aim precisely at influencing this staff, and if possible, to recruit it from party followers.[28]

In any individual case, parties may represent interests determined through "class situation" or "status situation," and they may recruit their following respectively from one or the other. But they need be neither purely "class" nor purely "status" parties. In most cases they are partly class parties and partly status parties, but sometimes they are neither.[29] They may represent ephemeral or enduring structures. Their means of attaining power may be quite varied, ranging from naked violence of any sort to canvassing for votes with coarse or subtle means: money, social influence, the force of speech, suggestion, clumsy hoax, and so on to the rougher or more artful tactics of obstruction in parliamentary bodies.

The sociological structure of parties differs in a basic way according to the kind of communal action which they struggle to influence. Parties also differ according to whether or not the community is stratified by status or by classes. Above all else, they vary according to the structure of domination within the community. For their leaders normally deal with the conquest of a community. They are, in the general concept which is maintained here, not only products of specially modern forms of domination. We shall also designate as parties the ancient and medieval "parties," despite the fact that their structure differs basically from the structure of modern parties. By virtue of these structural differences of domination it is impossible to say anything about the structure of parties without discussing the structural forms of social domination *per se*. Parties, which are always structures struggling for domination, are very frequently organized in a very strict "authoritarian" fashion.

Concerning "classes," "status groups," and "parties," it must be said in general that they necessarily presuppose a comprehensive societalization, and especially a political framework of communal action, within which they operate. This does not mean that parties would be confined by the frontiers of any individual political

---

[28] Weber understood parties very broadly as any group committed to using power to achieve a certain goal. Thus, his understanding of party was not limited to official state political parties. For Weber, two things separated parties from classes and status groups: they existed to pursue power, and they strove to achieve a specific goal or cause. These gave them much more definite shape than Weber perceives in either class or status groups.

[29] Just as class and status sometimes coincide, party may as well. However, such overlapping cannot be assumed. Class, status, and party are often different and contradictory institutions.

community. On the contrary, at all times it has been the order of the day that the societalization (even when it aims at the use of military force in common) reaches beyond the frontier of politics.[30] This has been the case in the solidarity of interests among the oligarchs and among the democrats in Hellas, among the Guelfs and among Ghibellines in the Middle Ages, and within the Calvinist party during the period of religious struggles.[31] It has been the case up to the solidarity of the landlords (international congress of agrarian landlords), and has continued among princes (holy alliance, Karlsbad decrees), socialist workers, conservatives (the longing of Prussian conservatives for Russian intervention in 1850).

But their aim is not necessarily the establishment of new international political, i.e. *territorial,* dominion. In the main they aim to influence the existing dominion.

[The posthumously published text breaks off here. We omit an incomplete sketch of types of "warrior estates."]

Note

a. *Wirtschaft und Gesellschaft,* part III, chap. 4, pp. 631–40. The first sentence in paragraph one and the several definitions in this chapter which are in brackets do not appear in the original text. They have been taken from other contexts of *Wirtschaft und Gesellschaft.*

---

[30] Weber's description of parties reaching across political communities must be considered in the context of the debate between Weber and the Marxists. Communist parties of Weber's era were aimed precisely at political action across international boundaries. Unlike the Marxists, Weber does not view these parties as historically unique and is equivocal about their chances for success.

[31] Hellas refers to classical Greece. The Guelfs and the Ghibellines were the major political factions of twelfth- and thirteenth-century Italy. The Guelfs defeated the Ghibellines in 1268.

Historical Particularism

There was a great deal of ethnographic writing in late nineteenth-century America. The Bureau of American Ethnology had been founded under John Wesley Powell (1834–1902; better known as the explorer of the Grand Canyon) in 1879. America had already produced Lewis Henry Morgan, a great anthropological theorist (see essay 3). Early anthropologists such as Alice Fletcher (1838–1923), Otis Mason (1838–1908), James Mooney (1861–1921), and Frank Cushing (1857–1900) were actively pursuing ethnographic investigations. Despite this ferment, it was not until the turn of the century that anthropology coalesced as an academic discipline in America. When it did, the ideas of a single individual, Franz Boas (1858–1942), had enormous impact. The method of research he pioneered, later labeled *historical particularism,* is widely considered the first American-born school of anthropological thought, and Boas himself is often deemed the father of American anthropology.

Boas was born to a secular and intellectual German Jewish family. His father was a merchant with liberal political views and his mother was a radical freethinker, the founder of a kindergarten devoted to the "consciousness of mutual interdependence" in children (Frank 1997:733). Boas described his home as a place in which "the ideals of the revolution of 1848 were a living force" (1974 [1938]:41). His background emphasized the freedom, dignity, and fundamental equality of all peoples. He remained deeply devoted to these ideas throughout his life.

Boas' education emphasized the physical sciences of his day. After graduating from Gymnasium in 1877, he went first to the University of Heidelberg, then to Bonn, and finally to Kiel where

he received his Ph.D. His examination subjects were geography, physics, and philosophy, and his dissertation was called *"Contribution to the Understanding of the Color of Water."* Although his studies emphasized quantitative data, he later wrote that these studies caused him to realize that "there are domains of our experience in which the concepts of quantity . . . are not applicable" (1974 [1938]:42).

As a Jewish liberal, Boas had few opportunities for academic employment in late nineteenth-century Germany and, by 1882, had already begun contemplating emigration to the United States. However, in 1883, he seized an opportunity to do research on migration patterns and sea water among the Eskimo on Baffin Island. Boas spent fifteen months in "the sublime loneliness of the arctic" (quoted in Stocking 1974:22), and the experience changed him from a geographer to an ethnographer. His experiences of the Eskimo convinced him that the liberal and humanistic values of his childhood could be applied to the study of human society. In an oft-quoted passage from his diary, Boas wrote

> As a thinking person, for me the most important result of this trip lies in the strengthening of my point of view that the idea of a "cultured" individual is merely relative and that a person's worth should be judged by his *Herzensbildung* [roughly, "education of the heart"]. This quality is present or absent here among the Eskimo, just as among us. (quoted in Langness 1987:530)

After spending the winter of 1884–1885 in New York, Boas returned to Germany in 1885 to take positions at the Berlin Ethnological Museum (the *Museum für Volkenkunde*) and the University of Berlin. However, he soon left Germany once more, this time to visit the Kwakiutl and other tribes on northern Vancouver Island in Canada—groups he was to study for the rest of his life. In 1886, after a brief return to Germany, he decided to emigrate to the United States.

His first position in America was at Clark University, but he quarreled with the administration and left that position for a job with the World's Columbian Exposition, a fair held in Chicago in 1893 to celebrate the 400th anniversary of Columbus' arrival in America. The Field Museum of Anthropology grew out of this exhibition, and Boas briefly became the curator of anthropology there. Once again, he left after quarreling with the museum's administration, and in 1896 he moved to Columbia University as a lecturer in physical anthropology. In 1899 he became a professor of anthropology and spent the rest of his career at Columbia. He retired in 1936 but remained active in anthropology until his death six years later.

Boas began his career at a time when anthropology was not recognized as a science, or even a field of university study. With his training in the physical sciences, he brought a rigorous approach to ethnographic fieldwork. He repudiated the social darwinism and evolutionary speculation that had marked anthropology up to this time. Boas' emphasis on the careful collection of ethnographic data and his rejection of the comparative method in favor of ethnographic field experience were, in part, a reaction to the uncritical use of the comparative method by the unilineal evolutionists of his day.

Boas supported biological evolution, but he maintained that the sweeping generalizations of the unilineal social evolutionists were not scientifically valid. He based much of his attack on the distinction between convergent and parallel evolution. Evolutionists assumed that similar cultural traits were the result of parallel development driven by universal evolutionary law. Boas showed that it was possible for the same characteristics to come about through different processes. In "The Limitations of the Comparative Method in Anthropology" (1896), Boas demonstrated that cultures may have similar traits for a variety of

reasons, including diffusion and trade. Corresponding environments or historical accident may produce similar cultural traits independent of any universal evolutionary process. Thus, the existence of such traits could not be used as evidence for universal stages of cultural evolution.

Boas believed that to explain cultural customs, one must examine them from three fundamental perspectives: environmental conditions, psychological factors, and historical connections. Of these, history was the most important. He felt that societies were created by their own historical circumstances. Thus, the best explanations of cultural phenomena were to be found by studying the historical development of the societies in which they occurred. This focus on the specific histories of individual societies gave the school of thought associated with him its name—historical particularism—although Boas never used this label. The term was coined by Marvin Harris in the 1960s.

Historical particularists adopted a holistic approach that included studying prehistory, linguistics, and physical anthropology. It was this version of holism that was instituted in American university departments. The hallmark of historical particularism became the intensive study of specific cultures through long periods of fieldwork. Boas argued that it was only through living with a people and learning their language that one could develop an accurate understanding of a culture. He and his students were driven by the belief that "primitive" societies such as those of Native Americans were rapidly disappearing. The situation of Native Americans, decimated and forced into reservations, gave a sense of urgency to American anthropologists. Boas and his students felt the immediate need to retrieve a vanished past from the memories of those old enough to recall it, and this conditioned much of the theory and method in American, as opposed to British, anthropology.

Boas also pioneered the concept of cultural relativism in anthropology. Whereas cultural evolutionists argued that technologically simple societies were inferior to Western civilization, Boas countered that societies were unique entities that could not be compared. Cultural traits of a society were the result of the historical and environmental evolution of that society and could only be understood within that context. Consequently, terms such as *primitive, inferior,* and *superior* did not have cross-cultural validity.

Because Boas discredited the unilineal evolutionary schemes popular in his day and insisted that societies were the result of their particular histories and could not be compared, he is often perceived as antitheoretical. Boas recognized the need for new theoretical perspectives but believed that more general theories of human behavior would arise spontaneously once enough data had been collected. He was uninterested in theory building, and the central tenet of historical particularism—that cultures are primarily the result of their unique histories—is inimical to any general theory of culture.

Though he did not leave a coherent theory, Boas had a profound effect on the development of anthropology. He almost single-handedly trained the first generation of American anthropologists and directed their initial field studies. Individuals such as Alfred Louis Kroeber (1876–1960), Robert Lowie (1883–1957), Edward Sapir (1884–1939), Margaret Mead (1901–1978), Melville Herskovits (1895–1963), Paul Radin (1883–1959), Ruth Fulton Benedict (1887–1948), Clark Wissler (1870–1947), Ashley Montagu (1905–), and many others were his students. Several of these researchers' works appear or are mentioned later in this text.

Although Boas and his students dominated American anthropology from about 1911 until after World War II (Stocking 1992:117), they were not unopposed. In the late nineteenth century, anthropology in America was controlled by scholars from Harvard (sometimes called the Maya Group, after their interest in Mayan studies) and the Smithsonian (called the Washington Group). Academics from these institutions, drawn largely from old WASP families, subscribed to programs of evolutionary anthropology. Many were devoted to race-science attempts to prove the superiority of Northern Europeans. These anthropologists objected to Boas and his students, most of whom were either immigrants themselves or the sons and daughters of immigrants, and many of whom were Jewish. They opposed Boas' notions of cultural relativism and racial equality.

Boas' most virulent enemies were members of the anthropology division of the National Research Council (an organization founded to promote U.S. aims in World War I) and the Galton Society. Both organizations were interested in racial science and eugenics. Key members of both organizations included Charles B. Davenport (1866–1944), Madison Grant (1865–1937), and Ales Hrdlicka (1869–1943) (Stocking 1968:289).

Issues of cultural relativism, racism, eugenics, and opposition to immigrants were exacerbated by Boas' pacifism and opposition to World War I. In 1919, Boas wrote a letter to *The Nation* castigating unnamed anthropologists for working as spies for the American government. He wrote that such actions undermined belief in the "truthfulness of science" and "raised a new barrier" against international scientific cooperation (quoted in Stocking 1968:274). Additionally, he called President Woodrow Wilson a hypocrite. The letter brought a series of old grievances and resentments against Boas to the surface at the American Anthropological Association meeting, which took place ten days after its publication. The Harvard and Smithsonian anthropologists moved successfully to have Boas censured by the association, stripped of membership in its governing council, and pressured to resign from the National Research Council (Stocking 1968:273). Despite this momentary victory, Boas' enemies could not change the fact that he and his students already controlled key positions in anthropology departments around the country and were the most important group of scholars shaping American anthropology.

Next to Boas, the most influential figure in American anthropology during the first half of the twentieth century was A. L. Kroeber, the first of Boas' students to receive a doctorate in anthropology at Columbia University. Throughout his life Kroeber maintained the Boasian historical perspective in his work, but he split from Boas over two crucial issues. First, Kroeber rejected Boas' presumption that anthropology was ultimately a discipline devoted to the study of humankind's origins. Their second disagreement seems to us more important. Boas believed that individuals played a significant role in a culture's development and change; Kroeber argued that this was not the case. In 1917, Kroeber published "The Superorganic," in which he adopted a view of culture very close to that expressed by the French sociologist Émile Durkheim (see essays 6 and 7). Kroeber argued that although culture came from and was carried by human beings, it could not be reduced to individual psychology. He maintained that culture was a pattern that transcended and controlled individuals. This idea is very similar to Durkheim's "collective conscience." Culture played a powerful determining role in individual human behavior. Individual accomplishment resulted from historical trends within society rather than anything important about the individual. "For example, Bach, born in a tribal society, could not have written a single sonata" (Garbarino 1977:53).

To illustrate his theory, Kroeber spent much of his career demonstrating how patterns of art, fashion, and technology came and went independently of individual artists, designers, and inventors. The essay we have selected for this volume is one of Kroeber's most famous examples of this type of work. In it he argues that basic features of women's clothing appear and then go out of fashion with predictable regularity and that the pattern is independent of any individual designer.

Kroeber also pursued the Boasian notion of studying cultures in relation to their environmental surroundings. In his study *Cultural and Natural Areas of Native North America* (1939), he mapped geographical, climatological, and vegetation distribution in relation to Native American cultures. This work was influential among his students, particularly Julian Steward, who went on to develop the cultural ecological approach to the analysis of culture.

While Kroeber believed that the individual was unimportant in cultural analysis, other students of Boas saw individuals as of paramount importance to anthropology. Paul Radin, especially, typified this approach, and the selection from his work printed here demonstrates his focus on the relationship between specific men and women and their own culture. His book *Crashing Thunder: The Autobiography of a Winnebago Indian* (1926) is a good example of this—an ethnography in the form of a single individual's life history. Like Boas, Radin believed that it was only through long-term intensive study, including the mastery of language, that an anthropologist could fully comprehend another culture. Following this principle, Radin studied Winnebago society for fifty years, producing a comprehensive record of the culture. Curiously, Radin's focus on the individual distanced him from Boas' own conviction that anthropology was a natural science. His emphasis on life histories moved anthropology in the direction of biography and literature.

Although anthropologists today rarely identify themselves as historical particularists, it is almost impossible to overestimate the influence of Boas and historical particularism on mainstream American anthropology. The effects of Boas' critical insights are seen most clearly in the work of his students in the first half of this century, but clear echoes of Boasian thought are present in ethnoscience and cognitive anthropology as well as in the symbolic and postmodern approaches to the study of culture.

10. The Methods of Ethnology

Franz Boas (1858–1942)

DURING THE LAST TEN YEARS THE METHODS of inquiry into the historical development of civilization have undergone remarkable changes. During the second half of the last century evolutionary thought held almost complete sway and investigators like Spencer, Morgan, Tylor, Lubbock, to mention only a few, were under the spell of the idea of a general, uniform evolution of culture in which all parts of mankind participated. The newer development goes back in part to the influence of Ratzel, whose geographical training impressed him with the importance of diffusion and migration. The problem of diffusion was taken up in detail particularly in America, but was applied in a much wider sense by Foy and Graebner, and finally seized upon in a still wider application by Elliot Smith and Rivers, so that at the present time, at least among certain groups of investigators in England and also in Germany, ethnological research is based on the concept of migration and dissemination rather than upon that of evolution.[1]

A critical study of these two directions of inquiry shows that each is founded on the application of one fundamental hypothesis.[2] The evolutionary point of view presupposes that the course of historical changes in the cultural life of mankind follows definite laws which are applicable everywhere, and which bring it about that cultural development is, in its main lines, the same among all races and all peoples. This idea is clearly expressed by Tylor in the introductory pages of his classic work "Primitive Culture." As soon as we admit that the hypothesis of a uniform evolution has to be proved before it can be accepted, the whole structure loses its foundation. It is true that there are indications of parallelism of development in different parts of the world, and that similar customs are found in the most diverse and widely separated parts of the globe. The occurrence of these similarities, which are distributed so irregularly that they cannot readily be explained on the basis of diffusion, is one of the foundations of the evolutionary hypothesis, as it was the foundation of Bastian's[3] psychologizing treatment of cultural phenomena. On the other hand, it may be recognized that the hypothesis implies the thought that our modern Western European civilization represents the highest cultural development towards which all other more primitive cultural types tend, and that, therefore,

(1920)

---

[1] In this essay, Boas attacks evolutionary theorists such as those represented in this volume. He also attacks diffusionists, whom we have discussed in notes only (see essay 3, footnote 15, for example). He mentions some particularly eminent diffusionists here. Fritz Graebner (1877–1934) and Friedrich Ratzel (1844–1904) were founders of the German *Kulturkreis* ("culture circle") school of diffusionism. *Kulturkreis* members were tightly linked to the Catholic church, and in much of their work they attempted to make newly available ethnographic data correspond with prevailing biblical interpretation (Harris 1968:379). In Cologne, Graebner worked as assistant to museum director Willy Foy (1873–1929). Graebner and Foy collaborated on Graebner's book *Die Methode der Ethnologie* (1911), which Boas brutally critiqued in an essay in *Science* that same year. Grafton Elliot Smith (1871–1937) and William Halse Rivers Rivers (that's right, Rivers Rivers) (1864–1922) were radical English diffusionists who believed that all civilization had diffused from Egypt. They are discussed in greater detail in the notes to essays in the next section.

[2] Boas' attack on the evolutionists rested on what he considered a logical flaw in their argument. According to him, their argument assumes what it is trying to prove: that historical changes in human culture follow general laws. Boas supported the Darwinian model of biological evolution but was hostile to its application to social evolution.

[3] Adolf Bastian (1826–1905) was a German theorist of psychic unity who believed that a few fundamental ideas, common to humankind, were the building blocks of culture. Bastian was acquainted with Boas in Berlin in the early 1880s.

retrospectively, we construct an orthogenetic[4] development towards our own modern civilization. It is clear that if we admit that there may be different ultimate and coexisting types of civilization, the hypothesis of one single general line of development cannot be maintained.

Opposed to these assumptions is the modern tendency to deny the existence of a general evolutionary scheme which would represent the history of the cultural development the world over.[5] The hypothesis that there are inner causes which bring about similarities of development in remote parts of the globe is rejected and in its place it is assumed that identity of development in two different parts of the globe must always be due to migration and diffusion. On this basis historical contact is demanded for enormously large areas. The theory demands a high degree of stability of cultural traits such as is apparently observed in many primitive tribes, and it is furthermore based on the supposed correlation between a number of diverse and mutually independent cultural traits which reappear in the same combinations in distant parts of the world. In this sense, modern investigation takes up anew Gerland's theory of the persistence of a number of cultural traits which were developed in one center and carried by man in his migrations from continent to continent.

It seems to me that if the hypothetical foundations of these two extreme forms of ethnological research are broadly stated as I have tried to do here, it is at once clear that the correctness of the assumptions has not been demonstrated, but that arbitrarily the one or the other has been selected for the purpose of obtaining a consistent picture of cultural development.[6] These methods are essentially forms of classification of the static phenomena of culture according to two distinct principles, and interpretations of these classifications as of historical significance, without, however, any attempt to prove that this interpretation is justifiable. To give an example: It is observed that in most parts of the world there are resemblances between decorative forms that are representative and others that are more or less geometrical. According to the evolutionary point of view, their development is explained in the following manner: the decorative forms are arranged in such order that the most representative forms are placed at the beginning. The other forms are so placed that they show a gradual transition from representative forms to purely conventional geometric forms. This order is then interpreted as meaning that geometric designs originated from representative designs which gradually degenerated. This method has been pursued, for instance, by Putnam, Stolpe, Balfour, and Haddon, and by Verworn and, in his earlier writings, by von den Steinen. While I do not mean to deny that this development may have occurred, it would be rash to generalize and to claim that in every case the classification which has been made according to a definite principle represents an historical development. The order might as well be reversed and we might begin with a simple geometric element which, by the addition of new traits, might be developed into a representative design, and we might claim that this order represents an historical sequence. Both of these possibilities were considered by Holmes[7] as early as 1885. Neither

---

[4] *Orthogenetic:* evolution along definite, predetermined lines.

[5] Above, Boas has focused his assault on cultural evolutionists. Here he turns his attack to the diffusionists.

[6] This paragraph is typical of Boas' method of attack: he does not attack particular examples, but looks for flaws in methodology. Trained in physics, mathematics, and geography, Boas brought a striving for meticulous scientific methodology to anthropology. Essentially, he faults his opponents for sloppy thinking. Writing in this way, he seems to imply that a rigorously scientific presentation of the data might allow the construction of an evolutionary model of human society. In fact Boas staunchly opposed evolutionary explanations. He believed profoundly in human equality and viewed social evolutionary theories as undermining this position. Thus, while Boas couches his arguments against social evolution in methodological terms, his ultimate reasons for making such arguments are deeply held moral convictions.

[7] Notice Boas' passing reference to William Henry Holmes (1846–1933), who was John Wesley Powell's successor at the Bureau of American Ethnology. In 1919, the year before this essay was published, Holmes led the American Anthropological Association's successful effort to censure Boas.

the one nor the other theory can be established without actual historical proof.

The opposite attitude, namely, origin through diffusion, is exhibited in Heinrich Schurtz's attempt to connect the decorative art of Northwest America with that of Melanesia. The simple fact that in these areas elements occur that may be interpreted as eyes, induced him to assume that both have a common origin, without allowing for the possibility that the pattern in the two areas — each of which shows highly distinctive characteristics — may have developed from independent sources. In this attempt Schurtz followed Ratzel, who had already tried to establish connections between Melanesia and Northwest America on the basis of other cultural features.

While ethnographical research based on these two fundamental hypotheses seems to characterize the general tendency of European thought, a different method is at present pursued by the majority of American anthropologists. The difference between the two directions of study may perhaps best be summarized by the statement that American scholars are primarily interested in the dynamic phenomena of cultural change, and try to elucidate cultural history by the application of the results of their studies; and that they relegate the solution of the ultimate question of the relative importance of parallelism of cultural development in distant areas, as against worldwide diffusion, and stability of cultural traits over long periods to a future time when the actual conditions of cultural change are better known.[8] The American ethnological methods are analogous to those of European, particularly of Scandinavian,

archaeology, and of the researches into the prehistoric period of the eastern Mediterranean area.

It may seem to the distant observer that American students are engaged in a mass of detailed investigations without much bearing upon the solution of the ultimate problems of a philosophic history of human civilization. I think this interpretation of the American attitude would be unjust because the ultimate questions are as near to our hearts as they are to those of other scholars, only we do not hope to be able to solve an intricate historical problem by a formula.[9]

First of all, the whole problem of cultural history appears to us as an historical problem. In order to understand history it is necessary to know not only how things are, but how they have come to be. In the domain of ethnology, where, for most parts of the world, no historical facts are available except those that may be revealed by archaeological study, all evidence of change can be inferred only by indirect methods. Their character is represented in the researches of students of comparative philology.[10] The method is based on the comparison of static phenomena combined with the study of their distribution. What can be done by this method is well illustrated by Dr. Lowie's[11] investigations of the military societies of the Plains Indians, or by the modern investigation of American mythology. It is, of course, true that we can never hope to obtain incontrovertible data relating to the chronological sequence of events, but certain general broad outlines can be ascertained with a high degree of probability, even of certainty.

As soon as these methods are applied, primitive society loses the appearance of absolute sta-

---

[8] When Boas speaks here of American anthropologists, he is really referring to himself and the many students he trained. The particular issue of cultural change with which they were concerned was the acculturation and disappearance of Native American groups. Despite Boas' claim that American anthropologists analyze culture change, he and his followers were often faulted for producing an essentially static anthropology unable to deal effectively with change.

[9] Boas was concerned with methodology rather than theory. European anthropologists often accused Boas and his students of producing an atheoretical anthropology concerned only with the collection of data. In the following paragraphs, he attempts to answer this charge.

[10] *Philology:* the study of written records, their authenticity and original form, and the determination of their meaning.

[11] Robert Lowie (1883 – 1957), a student of Boas and, later, professor of anthropology at Berkeley, was an influential voice in American anthropology in the 1930s and 1940s. Boas' reference here is to Lowie's 1913 article "Military Societies of the Crow Indians."

bility which is conveyed to the student who sees a certain people only at a certain given time. All cultural forms rather appear in a constant state of flux and subject to fundamental modifications.

It is intelligible why in our studies the problem of dissemination should take a prominent position. It is much easier to prove dissemination than to follow up developments due to inner forces, and the data for such a study are obtained with much greater difficulty. They may, however, be observed in every phenomenon of acculturation in which foreign elements are remodeled according to the patterns prevalent in their new environment, and they may be found in the peculiar local developments of widely spread ideas and activities. The reason why the study of inner development has not been taken up energetically is not due to the fact that from a theoretical point of view it is unimportant, it is rather due to the inherent methodological difficulties.[12] It may perhaps be recognized that in recent years attention is being drawn to this problem as is manifested by the investigations on the processes of acculturation and of the interdependence of cultural activities which are attracting the attention of many investigators.

The further pursuit of these inquiries emphasizes the importance of a feature which is common to all historic phenomena. While in natural sciences we are accustomed to consider a given number of causes and to study their effects, in historical happenings we are compelled to consider every phenomenon not only as effect but also as cause.[13] This is true even in the particular application of the laws of physical nature, as, for instance, in the study of astronomy in which the position of certain heavenly bodies at a given mo-

ment may be considered as the effect of gravitation, while, at the same time, their particular arrangement in space determines future changes. This relation appears much more clearly in the history of human civilization. To give an example: a surplus of food supply is liable to bring about an increase of population and an increase of leisure, which gives opportunity for occupations that are not absolutely necessary for the needs of every day life. In turn the increase of population and of leisure, which may be applied to new inventions, gives rise to a greater food supply and to a further increase in the amount of leisure, so that a cumulative effect results.

Similar considerations may be made in regard to the important problem of the relation of the individual to society, a problem that has to be considered whenever we study the dynamic conditions of change.[14] The activities of the individual are determined to a great extent by his social environment, but in turn his own activities influence the society in which he lives, and may bring about modifications in its form. Obviously, this problem is one of the most important ones to be taken up in a study of cultural changes. It is also beginning to attract the attention of students who are no longer satisfied with the systematic enumeration of standardized beliefs and customs of a tribe, but who begin to be interested in the question of the way in which the individual reacts to his whole social environment, and to the differences of opinion and of mode of action that occur in primitive society and which are the causes of far-reaching changes.

In short then, the method which we try to develop is based on a study of the dynamic changes in society that may be observed at the present

---

[12] Note that Boas does not claim his opponents' conclusions are necessarily wrong, simply that they are not supported by competent research.

[13] Boas here defines the position that came to be called historical particularism: rather than operating under the constraints of some universal law, cultures are *sui generis* (that is, they create themselves). Thus, cultures can only be understood with reference to their particular historical development.

[14] Notice Boas' focus on the effects of an individual on society. During his life, Boas moved from a position that gave individuals little importance to one that gave them much more. The issue split Boas' followers. Kroeber argued that individuals had little importance (see essay 11); Radin contended that anthropology should concentrate on individual life histories (see essay 12).

time. We refrain from the attempt to solve the fundamental problem of the general development of civilization until we have been able to unravel the processes that are going on under our eyes.[15]

Certain general conclusions may be drawn from this study even now. First of all, the history of human civilization does not appear to us as determined entirely by psychological necessity that leads to a uniform evolution the world over. We rather see that each cultural group has its own unique history, dependent partly upon the peculiar inner development of the social group, and partly upon the foreign influences to which it has been subjected. There have been processes of gradual differentiation as well as processes of leveling down differences between neighboring cultural centers, but it would be quite impossible to understand, on the basis of a single evolutionary scheme, what happened to any particular people. An example of the contrast between the two points of view is clearly indicated by a comparison of the treatment of Zuñi civilization by Frank Hamilton Cushing[16] on the one hand, on the other by modern students, particularly by Elsie Clews Parsons, A. L. Kroeber and Leslie Spier.[17] Cushing believed that it was possible to explain Zuñi culture entirely on the basis of the reaction of the Zuñi mind to its geographical environment, and that the whole of Zuñi culture could be explained as the development which followed necessarily from the position in which the people were placed. Cushing's keen insight into the Indian mind and his thorough knowledge of the most intimate life of the people gave great plausibility to his interpretations. On the other hand, Dr. Parsons' studies prove conclusively the deep influence which Spanish ideas have had on Zuñi culture, and, together with Professor Kroeber's investigations, give us one of the best examples of acculturation that have come to our notice. The psychological explanation is entirely misleading, notwithstanding its plausibility; and the historical study shows us an entirely different picture, in which the unique combination of ancient traits (which in themselves are undoubtedly complex) and of European influences has brought about the present condition.

Studies of the dynamics of primitive life also show that an assumption of long continued stability such as is demanded by Elliot Smith[18] is without any foundation in fact. Wherever primitive conditions have been studied in detail, they can be proved to be in a state of flux, and it would seem that there is a close parallelism between the history of language and the history of general cultural development. Periods of stability are followed by periods of rapid change. It is exceedingly improbable that any customs of primitive people should be preserved unchanged for thousands of years. Furthermore, the phenomena of acculturation prove that a transfer of customs from one region into another without concomitant changes due to acculturation is very rare. It is, therefore, very unlikely that ancient Mediterranean customs could be found at the present time practically unchanged in different parts of the globe, as Elliot Smith's theory demands.

---

[15] In other words, Boas' approach was to be purely inductive. Theoretical claims, he believed, could not be supported without the collection of large amounts of data. He is generally understood to have believed that the attempt to formulate a general theory was not wrong, just extremely premature. However, Boas insisted that cultures could only be understood with respect to their unique historical development. Building theory, on the other hand, necessarily involves comparison and generalization. Thus, it seems unlikely that Boasian-style anthropology could ever generate broad theoretical propositions. Harris has noted that Boas "could never . . . feel at ease in the presence of a generalization" (1968:260).

[16] Frank Hamilton Cushing (1857–1900) spent five years with the Zuñi people (1879–1884) and was initiated into their Bow Priest Society. He wrote extensively on Zuñi religion and technology. Here, Boas critiques Cushing's work as ahistorical.

[17] Kroeber and Leslie Spier (1893–1961) were trained by Boas. Elsie Clew Parsons (1875–1941) worked extensively with him (one of his monographs is dedicated to her).

[18] As mentioned above, the diffusionist Grafton Elliot Smith had theorized that all complex cultural traits diffused from Egypt. The radical diffusionists believed that humans were not inherently inventive, and as a result, societies remained static for long periods. Boas disagreed with this contention.

While on the whole the unique historical character of cultural growth in each area stands out as a salient element in the history of cultural development, we may recognize at the same time that certain typical parallelisms do occur. We are, however, not so much inclined to look for these similarities in detailed customs but rather in certain dynamic conditions which are due to social or psychological causes that are liable to lead to similar results. The example of the relation between food supply and population to which I referred before may serve as an example. Another type of example is presented in those cases in which a certain problem confronting man may be solved by a limited number of methods only. When we find, for instance, marriage as a universal institution, it may be recognized that marriage is possible only between a number of men and a number of women; a number of men and one woman; a number of women and one man; or one man and one woman. As a matter of fact, all these forms are found the world over and it is, therefore, not surprising that analogous forms should have been adopted quite independently in different parts of the world, and, considering both the general economic conditions of mankind and the character of sexual instinct in the higher animals, it also does not seem surprising that group marriage and polyandrous marriages should be comparatively speaking rare. Similar considerations may also be made in regard to the philosophical views held by mankind. In short, if we look for laws, the laws relate to the effects of physiological, psychological, and social conditions, not to sequences of cultural achievement.[19]

In some cases a regular sequence of these may accompany the development of the psychological or social status. This is illustrated by the sequence of industrial inventions in the Old World and in America, which I consider as independent. A period of food gathering and of the use of stone was followed by the invention of agriculture, of pottery and finally of the use of metals. Obviously, this order is based on the increased amount of time given by mankind to the use of natural products, of tools and utensils, and to the variations that developed with it. Although in this case parallelism seems to exist on the two continents, it would be futile to try to follow out the order in detail. As a matter of fact, it does not apply to other inventions. The domestication of animals, which, in the Old World must have been an early achievement, was very late in the New World, where domesticated animals, except the dog, hardly existed at all at the time of discovery. A slight beginning had been made in Peru with the domestication of the llama, and birds were kept in various parts of the continent.[20]

A similar consideration may be made in regard to the development of rationalism. It seems to be one of the fundamental characteristics of the development of mankind that activities which have developed unconsciously are gradually made the subject of reasoning.[21] We may observe this process everywhere. It appears, perhaps, most clearly in the history of science which has gradually extended the scope of its inquiry over an ever-widening field and which has raised into consciousness human activities that are automatically performed in the life of the individual and of society.

I have not heretofore referred to another aspect of modern ethnology which is connected with the growth of psycho-analysis. Sigmund Freud has attempted to show that primitive

---

[19] Equifinality is a key aspect of Boas' theoretical position. He argues that the presence of similar traits in many societies is not necessarily evidence either for psychic unity or large-scale diffusion. They may be the result of convergent evolution and independent invention. Note also a key point in this passage: Boas says that one reason for the development of similar institutions is that logically, certain things can only be done in a limited number of ways. Thus, in his example here, one reason for similarities in marriage patterns is the low number of ways it is possible to construct an institution such as marriage.

[20] This paragraph is an attack on Morgan (see essay 3), who used the presence of specific technologies or items of material culture to mark eras in his scheme of cultural evolution.

[21] It is curious that, having attacked the principle of psychic unity, Boas here relies on a statement about the universal nature of humankind.

thought is in many respects analogous to those forms of individual psychic activity which he has explored by his psycho-analytical methods. In many respects his attempts are similar to the interpretation of mythology by symbolists like Stucken. Rivers has taken hold of Freud's suggestion as well as of the interpretations of Graebner and Elliot Smith, and we find, therefore, in his new writings a peculiar disconnected application of a psychologizing attitude and the application of the theory of ancient transmission.[22]

While I believe some of the ideas underlying Freud's psycho-analytic studies may be fruitfully applied to ethnological problems, it does not seem to me that the one-sided exploitation of this method will advance our understanding of the development of human society. It is certainly true that the influence of impressions received during the first few years of life has been entirely underestimated and that the social behavior of man depends to a great extent upon the earliest habits which are established before the time when connected memory begins, and that many so-called racial or hereditary traits are to be considered rather as a result of early exposure to a certain form of social conditions. Most of these habits do not rise into consciousness and are, therefore, broken with difficulty only. Much of the difference in the behavior of adult male and female may go back to this cause. If, however, we try to apply the whole theory of the influence of suppressed desires to the activities of man living under different social forms, I think we extend beyond their legitimate limits the inferences that may be drawn from the observation of normal and abnormal individual psychology. Many other factors are of greater importance. To give an example: The phenomena of language show clearly

that conditions quite different from those to which psycho-analysts direct their attention determine the mental behavior of man.[23] The general concepts underlying language are entirely unknown to most people. They do not rise into consciousness until the scientific study of grammar begins. Nevertheless, the categories of language compel us to see the world arranged in certain definite conceptual groups which, on account of our lack of knowledge of linguistic processes, are taken as objective categories and which, therefore, impose themselves upon the form of our thoughts. It is not known what the origin of these categories may be, but it seems quite certain that they have nothing to do with the phenomena which are the subject of psycho-analytic study.

The applicability of the psycho-analytic theory of symbolism is also open to the greatest doubt. We should remember that symbolic interpretation has occupied a prominent position in the philosophy of all times. It is present not only in primitive life, but the history of philosophy and of theology abounds in examples of a high development of symbolism, the type of which depends upon the general mental attitude of the philosopher who develops it. The theologians who interpreted the Bible on the basis of religious symbolism were no less certain of the correctness of their views, than the psycho-analysts are of their interpretations of thought and conduct based on sexual symbolism. The results of a symbolic interpretation depend primarily upon the subjective attitude of the investigator who arranges phenomena according to his leading concept. In order to prove the applicability of the symbolism of psycho-analysis, it would be necessary to show that a symbolic interpretation from

---

[22] Freud's psychoanalytic theory was extremely popular in the 1920s. While Boas and his students were profoundly affected by portions of Freud's work, they entirely rejected his treatment of the origins and development of society (see essay 5). However, for many of Boas' students, some of Freud's other insights were critical. Margaret Mead and Ruth Benedict developed their views on culture and personality partially in reaction to Freud's ideas. Others, such as Cora Du Bois (1903–1991) and Abram Kardiner (1891–1981), attempted to apply Freudian psychology to anthropology (see the section "Culture and Personality" in this volume).

[23] Linguistics was a particular interest of Boas and his students. In this paragraph, Boas refers to the idea that language determines the categories we use to think. This line of reasoning was pursued by Boas' student, Edward Sapir (1884–1939) and Sapir's student and colleague, Benjamin Lee Whorf (1897–1941). Today, it is known as the Sapir-Whorf hypothesis.

other entirely different points of view would not be equally plausible, and that explanations that leave out symbolic significance or reduce it to a minimum would not be adequate.[24]

While, therefore, we may welcome the application of every advance in the method of psychological investigation, we cannot accept as an advance in ethnological method the crude transfer of a novel, one-sided method of psychological investigation of the individual to social phenomena the origin of which can be shown to be historically determined and to be subject to influences that are not at all comparable to those that control the psychology of the individual.[25]

---

[24] Boas' assault on psychoanalysis is similar to his attack on evolutionists and diffusionists: he faults it on methodological grounds. All of Boas' criticisms are intended to reinforce his call for an inductive methodology in anthropology. He insisted that it was only through the meticulous collection of empirical data that anthropologists could hope to understand cultures.

[25] The particular attacks Boas makes in this essay are repeated frequently in anthropology. For example, Boas' criticism of psychology as dependent on "[the] subjective attitude of the investigator who arranges phenomena according to his leading concept" is repeated almost word for word by ethnoscientists and cognitive anthropologists in the 1950s and 1960s in their critique of other forms of anthropology (see essays 28 and 29) and in slightly different form by postmodernists as well (see essays 38 and 39).

11. On the Principle of Order in Civilization as Exemplified by Changes of Fashion

A. L. Kroeber (1876–1960)

THE IDEA HAS NO DOUBT OFTEN BEEN HELD which the talented dogmatist Le Bon voiced in the assertion that most social phenomena are expressible by nearly similar and presumably simple geometrical curves.[a] The rise and fall of national arts and of national fortunes certainly seem to bear out such a conception, even though definite proof has apparently never been attempted. His-

(1919)

torians frequently allude to the development and degeneration of a state, or of some aspect of its civilization, as if such symmetrical growths and declines were familiar and normally recurring events; but they beware rather consistently from formulating the assumption into a principle, or proclaiming it as an abstract and accurate law.[1]

If one considers the story of the Elizabethan drama from its stiffly archaic inceptions through the awakening in Greene and Marlowe, the

---

[1] Although individual humans were the carriers of culture, Kroeber believed that the individual had little if any effect on culture. He maintained that culture had an existence outside of us and compelled us to conform to patterns that could be statistically demonstrated. Because of this, he referred to culture as *superorganic*. Once the existence of these patterns was demonstrated, Kroeber believed they could be studied and the basic theoretical principles governing culture change outlined. Kroeber wrote this essay to illustrate the superorganic nature of culture. Here he uses changes in fashion to show that cyclical patterns of change have occurred beyond the influence or understanding of any given individual.

Gustave Le Bon (1841–1931) is best known for his book *The Crowd* (1895), a study in mass psychology, in which he attempted to explain the dynamics of crowd behavior. Le Bon promoted ideas of national character and the superiority of the Anglo-Saxon race. In his belief, children, the insane, primitives, degenerates, and socialists were inferior beings.

Shakespearian glory, the slackening to the level of Fletcher, Webster, Ford, and Massinger, to the close of the playhouses by the civil war, the picture of all even-sided curve rises in the mind.[2] The masterpieces of the greatest member of the school fall in the first decade of the seventeenth century. His more prolix and less intense tragedies and comedies, and the plays of contemporaries nearest him in achievement, precede and follow by a few years. Each quinquennium more distant from the culmination is marked by greater crudity in recession, more extended laxity in progression of time; and the total duration before and after the acme is substantially equal.[b]

If such a surge stood unique, it would be meaningless. But it is so often repeated in the history of aesthetics, that something of a generic principle must be involved. The classic French drama, that of Spain, of ancient Athens; the briefly great literatures of Rome, Portugal, and Germany; the so-called romantic poetry of England—even the minor stirring known as American literature; Italian art of the Renaissance; the Dutch and Flemish schools of painting; Greek sculpture—and, we might add, philosophy—each of these isolable movements has been traced through a similar course of origin, growth, climax, decline, and either death or petrifaction, analogous to the life stories of organisms.[3]

While however we are obviously hovering above a latent principle embodied in these phenomena, its expression in exact form, capable of successful application in the resolution of other events of human history, is difficult; chiefly because the variability of the phenomena is qualitative, whereas a workable law or deterministic principle must be quantitative in its nature. It would indeed be possible to assemble comparative ratings of the degrees of achievement attained by each participant in any of these movements, to convert these ratings into numbers, and to trust to the averaging of opinions to efface, to a greater or less extent, the subjectivity of the individual judgments used. But such a procedure is too loose to promise much real advance of understanding. After all, it would rest on a series or composite photographs of verdicts as to qualities, and not on verifiable measurements.

The field of political history is also rich in data that point in the same direction. As a boy it seemed to me possible to express numerically the relative strength and prestige of the several Greek city states at intervals of equal duration, and thus to outline sharply the varying course of Hellenic history; and I remember computations actually entered in the attempt, which has very likely been made at one time or another by others. Everyone will recall in this connection the comment on the fall of Rome under Romulus Augustulus, whose name combined that of the founder and that of the exponent of the greatest success of the eternal city; and how, as at the laying of the walls first six and then twelve vultures flew overhead, the state grew, and then declined, for a total existence

---

[2] Although his essay focuses on cyclical changes in fashion, Kroeber believed that this pattern, which could be statistically illustrated by a curve, applied to all manner of cultural phenomena. Kroeber had earned a masters degree in literature at Columbia and was already teaching when he began to study anthropology with Franz Boas. His discussion of the florescence and decay of the Elizabethan theater demonstrates this background in literature. He later discusses the rise and fall of civilizations.

[3] Kroeber had a lifelong interest in the arts that he integrated into his anthropological work, beginning with his 1901 doctoral dissertation "Decorative Symbols of the Arapaho." In *Cultural and Natural Areas of Native North America* (1939), he outlined the difference between value culture and reality culture. Reality culture consisted of traits concerned with aspects of culture such as subsistence and economics. Value culture, Kroeber's main interest, dealt with the arts, literature, and fashion. Despite Kroeber's emphasis, his student Julian Steward focused on aspects of reality culture and explored the relationship between culture and environment (see essay 18).

Since he was trained by Boas, one expects Kroeber to be a relativist, but he clearly ranks the different schools of art and literature in this discussion in a way that modern anthropologists would be reluctant to do. We believe an evolutionary perspective is implicit in his writing and that when he mentions the growth, climax, and decline in styles of art or literature, he is making a value judgment about the artistic quality of the material. If so, what does it say about Kroeber's relativism?

of an equal number of centuries. The anecdote is a play of symbolic fancy primarily, or perhaps a mnemonic device; but it also appeals dimly to a sense of historic necessity, of rhythmic inevitability, such as the later middle ages were fond of dwelling on in allusions to the wheel of fortune which revolved for nations as well as persons.

There is no need of citing at length similar cyclical growths familiar from more modern times: the rise and flourishing and decay of Venice, Florence, Poland, Portugal, Spain, and Holland.[c] There are even cases of repetition, as of the acmes reached by France under Louis XIV, Napoleon I, and Napoleon III—the three crests themselves constituting an ascending and descending climax of a higher order. Lane-Poole, in his diagrammatic representations of the history of the Mohammedan chalifates and kingdoms, although operating solely with the elements of geography and time, gives several figures that approach closely to a polygon of frequency or normal curve such as the statistical sciences employ.[d]

Political fortunes have this advantage over the fluctuations of the arts: they are readily expressible, and with substantial accuracy, in such quantitative terms as square miles of territory or drachmas or pounds of tribute and revenue. On the other hand, they suffer, as a medium for analysis, through their complexity. Any one of a number of factors, or any combination of them, may make or unmake a nation: a change of political institutions, a military invention, an economic alteration, a new demand or utilization of natural resources, a wave of religious fervor. The resultant of these variables being a composite, would in many cases show little regularity. Then, too, where a concentrated political organization

has been achieved, opportunities are put in the hand of an occasional genius, or even of the man of unusual talent, for much more spectacular accomplishment, perhaps, than in the fields of artistic and intellectual endeavor. An Aristotle or Goethe needs predecessors, a Genghis Khan or Napoleon only a constellation.[4]

The fields of religion and society are not so open to these objections, but suffer from lack of statistics. Census data are less common, except in the most recent years, than records of territories and dynasties. In the matter of religion, also, they necessarily relate chiefly to its organizational aspects, which, being crystallizations, do not keep pace with inward movements, and change by distorting jerks instead of fluidly.[5]

Manufactured objects offer an approach which no other class of civilizational data presents: they can be accurately and easily measured. Yet often there are difficulties in this domain also. The series of articles preserved from the past are often insufficiently large, or from interrupted periods, or of uncertain date. Then, utilitarian pieces can not modify freely. Their purpose is likely to impose definite and narrow limits on their variability of form. A new material, or an added invention, may bring about a modification as sudden as it is radical; after which a new era of comparative stability ensues. Material objects whose chief end is ornament—jewelry, for instance—are much more free from the last mentioned defect. Still more promising are decorative or semi-decorative things of which satisfactory illustrations are available in numbers, in place of the concrete specimens themselves: articles of dress, for instance, as represented in fashion magazines. Such journals have existed for

---

[4] This is an interesting paragraph for it shows the influence of Boas on Kroeber's thought, but it seems to contradict the main premise of this essay. Kroeber writes that in the appropriate situation individuals can achieve great political accomplishments by themselves, whereas artists and scientists build on the work of those that precede them. This coincides nicely with Boas' view that individuals can have an effect on their culture, but it contradicts Kroeber's main argument: that culture is superorganic.

[5] In this and the preceding paragraphs, Kroeber is setting the stage for his choice of fashion as the subject for measurement in his study. One can see the rise and fall of art he says, but it is difficult to scientifically measure because artistic judgment is subjective. Political history is rich in examples of the cyclical rise and fall of civilizations he tells us, but political power has too many complex factors to make a good example. Religion and society are poor examples because they are not easily quantified. So what phenomenon can be measured and analyzed to show the cyclical change of culture? Manufactured goods!

over a century; they are exactly dated; and they bring together in each volume a considerable number of examples to which rule or calipers can be applied without hindrance. That the actual wear of average men and women lags somewhat ineffectually behind the incisive styles of models or pictures, is immaterial. A knowledge of the course followed by ideals of dress is quite as valuable, as a contribution to the understanding of civilization, as knowledge of real dress; and this both *per se* and as an exemplification of the processes involved.[6]

FASHIONS IN DRESS

Twenty years ago the project of inquiring into the principles that guide fashion arose in my mind, and I went so far as to turn the leaves of volume after volume of a Parisian journal devoted to dress. But the difficulties were discouraging. Pivotal points seemed hard to find in the eternal flux. One might measure collars or sleeves or ruffles for some years, and then collars and sleeves and ruffles disappeared. One lady in a plate was seated, another erect, a third in profile, the fourth elevated her arms. If one took as a base the total length of the figure, coiffures fell and rose by inches from time to time, or were entirely concealed by hats or nets. I abandoned the plan as infeasible.

In 1918 I renewed the endeavor, this time with less ambitious scope and greater readiness to seize on any opening. I decided to attempt only eight measurements, four of length and four of width, all referring to the figure or dress as a whole, and to disregard all superficial parts or trimmings. Strict comparability of data being essential, it was necessary to confine observations to clothing of a single type. Women's full evening toilette was selected. This has served the same

definite occasions for more than a century; does not therefore vary in purpose as does day dress, nor seasonally like street clothing. The material always remains silk, and there have been no totally new fundamental concepts introduced, such as the shirtwaist and tailored suit. The variations are therefore purely stylistic. And while this range promised to be perhaps somewhat narrower than those of certain other types of women's wear, this was of little moment. If any principle could be determined, it would apply *a fortiori*[7] to the more changeable kinds of clothing.

MEASUREMENTS

The measurements made were the following:

1. Total length of figure from the center of the mouth to the tip of the toe. If the shoe was covered, the lowest point of the skirt edge was chosen. The selection of the mouth obviated all difficulties arising from alteration of hairdress.

2. Distance from the mouth to the bottom of the skirt. This equals the last measurement less the height of the skirt from the ground.

3. Distance from the mouth to the minimum diameter across the waist. This serves as some sort of indication of the length of the waist or corsage, that is, of the upper part of the figure. The true waist line of the dress has been disregarded. It would have been much more significant stylistically and probably shown more decided variations; but there are periods when it vanishes. When the waist line is visible and below the minimum diameter of the waist, the distance between the two was also noted.

---

[6] Kroeber's choice of subject material, elite fashions, is interesting. One probable reason for this choice is that research material (fashion magazines) was easily available in local libraries. At the same time, he dismisses the actual clothing of "average men and women" as "immaterial" and seems to ignore the fact that the styles that appear in high fashion magazines are rarely worn by the majority of the population. If one is discussing cultural trends, are his omissions significant? Further, Kroeber generalizes about constant trends in human culture on the basis of an isolated phenomenon observed over a relatively short duration. Some critics argue that these are basic problems that affect all of American anthropology in this century. Whether or not that is the case, they clearly raise important questions about the validity of Kroeber's study.

[7] *A fortiori:* Latin for all the more.

4. Depth or length of decolletage, measured from the mouth to the middle of the corsage edge in front.

5. Diameter of the skirt at its hem or base.

6. Maximum diameter of the skirt at any point above the base. In some cases this exceeds the diameter at the bottom. Ordinarily it is smaller, but in some instances nevertheless definitely visible: that is, the skirt swells, constricts, and flares again. This diameter did not prove a generally useful measurement. Whenever it could be taken, the distance from its middle to the mouth was also recorded as a supplementary datum.

7. Minimum diameter in the region of the waist.

8. Width of shoulders, or more accurately, width of the decolletage across the shoulders. In the earlier years of the period covered, the upper edge of the dress frequently passes below the point of the shoulder, across the uppermost part of the arm, as a bertha or slight sleeve. In such cases the measurement was recorded. Of recent years, the corsage often really ends under the arms, being held up in appearance by straps over the shoulders. Here it seemed best to measure the distance between the straps. When however the strap is pushed off the shoulder to fall loosely down the arm, or is wholly wanting, the present measurement had to be omitted.

Ten figures were measured for each calendar year, the first ten suitable for measurement being taken from each volume, so as to ensure random instead of subjective selection. Fashion journals of the middle of the nineteenth century contain fewer illustrations than recent ones. It sometimes happened therefore that only seven or eight toilettes were represented in the numbers from the first of January until summer, when full dress styles suspend seasonally. In such cases the rear end of the volume of the preceding year was drawn upon to supplement the deficiency. An entry like 1857 is thus normally based on plates issued from January to March or April or May of that year, but occasionally would begin in December or even November of 1856. Even at that, insufficiency of material or oversight has resulted in a few years being represented by only nine sets of measurements. Unfortunately also, there is scarcely a year for which ten illustrations could be found in each of which all eight measurements were recordable. A gown may be shown very completely in full face except for one corner of the skirt, which is hidden behind the chair of a seated companion. The basal skirt width can often be pretty well guessed in such cases, and an estimate was generally made; but only actual measurements have been included in the averages discussed. If in the taking of the observations such a deficient figure had been passed over, the next picture might have indeed exhibited the desired skirt width, but failed to show two or three other features; and too firm an insistence on all eight traits would often have yielded only three or four instead of ten measurable illustrations in a year. For instance, there are periods when it was overwhelmingly fashionable to hold the forearm horizontal, or to bring out the convexity of the bust by drawing it in semi-profile. In such years waist diameters are mostly obscured by the arm, and full shoulder widths very hard to get. The consequence of all these little circumstances is that the majority of the eight features observed are represented, year by year, by less than ten measurements, sometimes only by four or five. On the whole, preference was given to observations of the entire figure length, which was to be used as a norm for computations; and to the two next greatest measures, skirt length and width. For these, then, the series of data are fullest.[8]

It must be admitted that ten measures is not a very large maximum from which to derive

---

[8] Kroeber's discussion of his methodology leaves numerous questions unanswered. For example, how many different designers were represented in his sample? How did he extrapolate real-life measurements from pictures in magazines? To what extent were the pictures, often drawings rather than photographs, accurate reproductions of the clothing they depicted? Kroeber has described an elaborate but fundamentally flawed research procedure. He dismisses any notion that the problems in his plan may have seriously compromised his results.

reasonably true averages in so variable a thing as fashionable dress, where each design strives almost as keenly after distinctiveness as after conformity to the prevailing style. I was conscious of this slenderness of basis. But the measurements as well as the reductions to percentages and averages are time-consuming; and for a preliminary investigation it seemed wiser to obtain a comparatively long series of small groups of measurements than to operate with measurement groups of a size more reliable for averages but covering fewer years. Ten cases from each of seventy-five years would give a better surveying perspective than twenty-five cases continued for thirty years; in addition to which the ten or approximately ten illustrations were rather readily obtainable, whereas it would have been bibliographically exacting to find twenty-five for most of the earlier years.

The outcome vindicated the hazard. The smallness of the series is unquestionably the cause of many of the fluctuating irregularities that appear in the chronologically arranged results.[9] But in the case of every dimension the irregularities are not so great as to prevent recognition of the underlying drifts and tendencies; whereas the period of these tendencies is mostly so long that they would have been very imperfectly determinable, and often not at all, within a compass of only thirty years. In fact it would have been desirable if the range of investigation could have been extended from 75 years to 125. The net result of a larger series of cases would therefore have been a probable smoothing and increased regularity of the plotted curves expressive of the course of

fashion; and some segregation of the present irregularities into historically true ones and others that represent only statistical inadequacy. But presumably nothing more would have eventuated from the increase of data.[10]

I may here express my conviction that any farther quantitative investigations that may be undertaken as to the course of stylistic changes should be planned to cover if possible a period of from one to two centuries, whether they concern fashions of dress or of jewelry, silverware, or furniture.

[We have omitted a section of Kroeber's article called "The Data Obtained." This is a detailed 3,000-word description, with one footnote, of the fashion changes in skirt width and length, the diameter and length of waists, and the height and width of decolletage, over a period of about seventy years. Kroeber's essay continues with his discussion of the periodic rhythms he observes in his data.][11]

COMPARISON OF THE SEVERAL RHYTHMS

We have, I think, now found reasonable evidence of an underlying pulsation in the width of civilized women's skirts, which is symmetrical and extends in its up and down beat over a full century; of an analogous rhythm in skirt length, but with a period of only about a third the duration; some indication that the position of the waist line may completely alter, also following a "normal" curve,

---

[9] Kroeber was concerned with documenting cultural cycles over long periods. Consequently, he believed that the irregularities in his data were due to the limited sample size of his measurements. One could equally assume that long-term cultural cycles do not exist and cite Kroeber's "irregularities" as evidence that his original assumption was false.

[10] Unlike the ethnographic writing of his day, this essay with its introduction, methodology, data, and conclusion sections, copied a scientific style. Further, Kroeber's use of statistical analysis separated his study from earlier work. It is true that Émile Durkheim (see essays 6 and 7) used statistical analysis extensively in his study of suicide, but the use of statistics as a method of ethnographic research was in its infancy.

[11] Kroeber repeatedly uses words such as *period* and *duration*. In the section we have eliminated he speaks of wavelength as well. The invention of radio is part of the social context in which Kroeber wrote, and this clearly shaped his choice of metaphor. Radio was invented in the late nineteenth century, but human speech was not transmitted until 1906. In 1918, just a year before this article was published, Edwin Armstrong perfected the superheterodyne circuit. This invention, a key technological achievement of its age, made the mass-marketing of radio possible. The equivalent today would be the development of the silicon chip.

in a seventy-year period; and a possibility that the width of shoulder exposure varies in the same manner, but with the longest rhythm of all, since the continuity of tendency in one direction for seventy years establishes a periodicity of about a century and a half, if the change in this feature of dress follows a symmetrically recurrent plan.[12]

There is something impressive in the largeness of these lapses of time. We are all in the habit of talking glibly of how this year's fashion upsets that of last year. Details, trimmings, pleats and ruffles, perhaps colors and materials, all the conspicuous externalities of dress, do undoubtedly alter rapidly; and it is in the very nature of fashion to bring these to the fore. They are driven into our attention, and soon leave a blurred but overwhelming impression of incalculably chaotic fluctuations, of reversals that are at once bewildering and meaningless, of a sort of lightning-like prestidigitation to which we bow in dumb recognition of its uncontrollability. But underneath this glittering maze, the major proportions of dress change with a slow majesty, in periods often exceeding the duration of human life, and at least sometimes with the even regularity of the swing of an enormous pendulum. The child whose braids hang down her back may be reasonably sure that in the years when her daughters are being born she will wear longer dresses than her mother now goes about in; and that her skirts promise to be wider each successive decade until she is a grandmother. There is something in these phenomena, for all their reputed arbitrariness, that resembles

what we call law: a scheme, an order on a scale not without a certain grandeur. Not that the fashion of a future date can be written now. Every style is a component of far too many elements, and in part uniquely entering elements, to make true prediction possible. But it does seem that some forecast can be made for any one basic element whose history has been sufficiently investigated; and that, when the event arrives, if the anticipation be proved to have been more or less erroneous, the source of the aberration may be clear, and the disturbingly injected forces stand revealed as subject to an order of their own.[13]

It is not to be expected that the development and decline of every trait of dress or civilization should follow a normal curve, that is, a symmetrical course. For an element of civilization wholly unrelated to all others, such symmetry could perhaps be anticipated. But completely integral elements are an idea rather than a fact. There must always be some interaction with other factors in the same and cognate phases of culture, and occasional interferences from more remote domains. A certain proportion of features should therefore follow irregular courses, or asymmetrical curves; and in this class it seems that diameter of the waist and depth of decolletage should be placed.[e]

Secondary tremors ruffling the evenness of the great pulsations are at first sight disturbing to the concept of orderliness, but on analysis confirmatory, in that they reveal an increase of the intricacy of the operative forces without diminishing their regularity. In this manner the long

---

[12] We have omitted the charts and tables in which Kroeber presents his measurements. However, the types of information collected and tabular presentation of raw data illustrate what was considered scientific anthropology in Kroeber's day. Boas' training in the physical sciences, and the resulting emphasis he placed on anthropology as a science, led many of his students to stress the collection of quantifiable data. Data were commonly gathered in the form of trait lists, where the presence or absence of hundreds of cultural traits such as tattooing, clothing materials, styles of house construction, and so on, could be checked off. These lists could then be tabulated, charted, graphed and statistically analyzed, as Kroeber did in this article. Although no one today is walking around with one of Kroeber's trait lists, this emphasis on the collection of quantifiable information is still an important focus of many schools of anthropological thought. It forms one of the lines between those who consider anthropology a science and those who believe anthropology is more an interpretive art.

[13] Kroeber believed that anthropology was essentially history, but also scientific in that one could discover the laws that governed culture change. This conviction is expressed here in his contention that changes of fashion are predictable if one has enough data. Note too that Kroeber's emphasis is on time periods that exceed the human life span. The implication is that humans are not important in these cycles of change. However, Kroeber has analyzed only seventy-five years of fashion. How would he have accounted for Nehru jackets, bell-bottoms, and other popular styles of the 1960s? Would his patterns have predicted current fashions?

range curves for width of skirt and shoulders, each bearing about three superimposed but symmetrical minor crests, add substance to the generic conclusions reached.

Finally, while it would make for the greater simplicity of historical causality if it were found that acmes of fashion came in recurrences of equal periodicity, such regularity can hardly be expected. There is no conceivable reason why there should be anything inherent in the nature of dress tending toward a change from full to narrow and back to full skirts in a century. All historical phenomena are necessarily unique in some degree, in the field of nature as well as of human activity; and a similar rhythm of fashion might well extend over a thousand, a hundred, or ten years in different eras or among separate nations. Again, therefore, there is if not support for the idea of "law," at least no disconcertion in the fact that the past quarter century on the whole evinces distinctly more rapid and extreme variations of fashion than the half century preceding. This is the case for every feature examined except shoulder width.[14]

CONCLUSIONS AS TO CHANGE IN CIVILIZATION

The fact of regularity in social change is the primary inference from our phenomena. The amplitude of the periodicities is of hardly less importance. Their very magnitude dwarfs the influence which any individual can possibly have exerted in an alteration of costume. Were each rhythm confined to a few years, it might be thought that a mind, a particular genius, was its motivating impulse; and the claim would certainly be asserted by those who like to see history as only a vast complex of biographies. But when a swing of fashion requires a century for its satisfaction, a minimum of at least several personalities is involved. No matter how isolating one's point of view, how resistant to a social or super-individual interpretation, how much inclined to explain the general from the particular and to derive the fashions of a world from the one focus of Paris, the fact remains that a succession of human beings have contributed successively to the same end. Once the existence of tendencies or forces transcending the limits of organically inherited personality is thus admitted, the entire field of the history of civilization becomes disputable ground for the two conflicting interpretations. If the major swing of skirt proportions during the nineteenth century is the product, wholly or partly, of super-individual causes, it becomes a valid speculation whether the smaller developments are not also due to similar mechanisms. The re-introduction of the train in 1863, the invention of the Grecian bend in 1872, may now be looked upon as the product of the dress styles that preceded them, or of other cultural factors affecting style, more justifiably than they can be attributed to the talent of a specially gifted mind and hand. The wedge has entered.[15]

It is also evident how little even the intensest individual faculty can have added to the outcome of the greater revolutions, how little hastened

---

[14] Kroeber states that he found patterns within patterns in his data, that some of the data's distribution through time was asymmetrical, and even that the cycles of change might extend for widely different periods of time in different countries or eras. This brings up an interesting philosophical question that is argued among theorists in the sciences today: do the patterns that are discovered actually exist, or do we impose patterns on the data as our way of understanding them? This question has become particularly significant to anthropologists who follow the postmodernist school of thought.

[15] The popular notion of history in Kroeber's day was the "great man" theory of history, in which history is composed of the actions of individuals who determine or change the course of events around them. (Consider his comment about Napoleon and Genghis Khan earlier in this essay.) Kroeber argued against this theory of history in favor of the view that events run in patterns beyond an individual's awareness and control. He saw his study as the "wedge" that called the popular view of history into question. He then makes the analogy of culture as a tide within which humans float. Those who fight the tide, whose genius is too far out of step with their time, are condemned to futility; those who succeed do so within a certain cultural and historical context. For example, if Albert Einstein had been born an Australian Aborigine in the sixteenth century, he might well have been recognized as an intelligent individual, but he would not have formulated the theory of relativity. Einstein's genius was recognized and fulfilled because of the cultural context in which he lived and

their momentum. When a tide sets one way for fifty years, men float with it, or thread their course across it; those who breast the vast stream condemn themselves in advance to futility of accomplishment. A designer born with an inextinguishable talent for emphasizing what we may call the horizontal as opposed to the vertical lines of the figure, and maturing twenty-five years ago, might have possessed ten times the genius of a Poiret or Worth:[16] he would yet have been compelled to curb it into the channels which they followed, or waste it on unworn and unregarded creations. What it is that causes fashions to drive so long and with ever increasing insistence toward the consummation of their ends, we do not know; but it is clear that the forces are social, and not the fortuitous appearance of personalities gifted with this taste or that faculty. Again the principle of civilizational determinism scores as against individualistic randomness.

It would be extravagant to infer that these conclusions deny the validity of superior minds, or even that they tend to minimize the differences between genius and competent individuals and incompetent ones, and that the gulf between their extremes is vast. The existence of varying degrees of intellectual quality does not touch, one way or the other, the finding that there operate super-individual principles which determine the course of social events. The content of history as a sum and in its parts, so far as these have civilizational meaning, is the product of such principles. Whether individual X or individual Y is to have the larger share in bringing one particular product of his culture to fruition, depends on their respective native endowments, plus a greater or less modification by their educations, personal environments, and settings of circumstance. For the career of X, it is obviously of the greatest importance that his heredity and opportunities be more favorable than those of other individuals. On the contrary, given this advantage, it will very little affect his success in life whether his society be moving from polytheism to monotheism, from monarchy to democracy or democracy to tyranny, from bronze to iron, from the wearing of wide skirts to narrow, or the reverse.

Conversely, so far as these social changes are concerned, it can well be argued on theoretical grounds that the greater or less innate capacity of this or that individual, or of any limited number of individuals, is of negligible consequence. That this factor is actually negligible from the aspect of civilization, the analysis of the data here presented, goes to show. In short, monotheism arises, an iron technique is discovered, institutions change, or dresses become full at a given period and place—subsequent to other cultural events and as the result of them, in other words—because, they must.[17]

---

worked. Culture, not individual achievement, is the driving force behind cultural change in Kroeber's eyes. This is in direct contrast to Boas' view of history and was a lifelong source of conflict between the two.

Kroeber's mentor Boas was a political activist. For example, he was an outspoken opponent of racism (Hyatt 1990). Kroeber was more conservative. His doctrine of cultural inevitability has a nineteenth-century flavor to it. About Kroeber, Eric Wolf wrote, "One can find throughout his writings a strong sense of distaste for anything that had to do with politics, with involvement in nonscience, and I think also with sociology—all those enterprises that had to do, he thought, with trying to improve the world" (1981:48–49).

The *Grecian bend* referred to is a posture where the torso is thrust forward and the buttocks backward. This posture was emphasized in late nineteenth-century women's fashions by the use of a bustle, which was attached to the back of a skirt.

[16] Paul Poiret (1879–1944) and Charles Frederick Worth (1825–1895) were important turn-of-the-century fashion designers. Both worked in Paris. Worth is credited with originating the fashion show; Poiret declared that corsets were outmoded and made high-waisted gowns popular.

[17] Kroeber staked out an extreme position. He says that culture is *sui generis,* that cultural events happen "because, they must." If this position sounds particularly fatalistic, keep in mind that Kroeber had suffered through a series of personal tragedies in the years before the publication of this essay. His first wife died in 1913, followed soon after by Ishi, Kroeber's Yana Indian friend, in 1916. It was also a depressing time in the United States as a whole. The essay was written during the time of the great influenza epidemic that broke out at the end of World War I. Between September 1918 and June 1919 about 675,000 Americans died (Crosby 1989:206).

Historians may have been chary of asserting such a principle; but the greatest minds among them have time and again accepted it implicitly, though vaguely. This is as true of Thucydides as of Gibbon, and explains why Herodotus was as much interested in ethnology as in anecdotes, and Tacitus could place a Germania beside his Annals.[18]

Among the commonality of men, such a recognition has not obtained, and does not now hold. What above all they are interested in, is their own lives and fortunes, their own feelings and acts, their competitions with other individuals and personal relations to them. Therefore, when they listen to history, or tell it, they look for what history can reflect that is similar; and what it offers of psychology and morality in its biographies, or those of its parts which can be distorted into dramatic crises or romantic tales, they seize with avidity.

The satisfaction of these interests has its justifiable function; only it prevents instead of cultivating an understanding of the workings of civilization. The individualistic view of historical phenomena is in its nature subjective, and its treatment must always remain subjective. To find "law" in the infinite intricacy of millions of interplaying personalities is hopeless. We can not even begin to get the facts as they happened. A geologist could as usefully set himself the task of explaining the size and shape of each pebble in a gravel bed. We are but such stones. Being human, we cannot however divest ourselves of inquisitiveness about other human beings as human beings, nor of inquisitiveness into their morality and psychology and of the desire for an aesthetic representation of their actions. Only, the pursuit of such impulses does not lead to knowledge that is scientifically applicable; nor to a comprehension of what lies beyond ourselves as individuals; of that which touches and permeates our lives at all moments, which is the material on which our energies are released, which could not be if we did not exist, but which yet endures before and after, and grows and changes into forms that are not of our making but of its own definite unfolding. Our minds instinctively resist the first shock of the recognition of a thing so intimately woven into us and yet so far above and so utterly uncontrollable by our wills. We feel driven to deny its reality, to deny even the validity of dealing with it as an entity; just as men at large have long and bitterly resented admitting the existence of purely automatic forces and system in the realm that underlies and carries and makes possible the existence of our personalities: the realm of nature. The center of our interests must always be personal. Yet this pivoting has not prevented an increasing realization of objectivity; nor will it prevent the realization that objectivity is to be found on levels beyond us in both directions, instead on one only. The superorganic or superpsychic or superindividual that we call civilization appears to have an existence, an order, and a causality as objective and as determinable as those of the subpsychic or inorganic. At any rate, no insistence on the subjective aspects of personality can refute this objectivity, not hinder its ultimate recognition; just as no advance in objective understanding has ever cramped the activity of personality.[19]

BERKELEY, CALIFORNIA.

---

[18] In a bit of intellectual hubris, Kroeber claims that both ancient and modern scholars implicitly supported his theory, but he provides no evidence that this is actually the case.

[19] The final paragraph in this article is a criticism of the work of anthropologists such as Boas and Paul Radin (essay 12) and a strong endorsement of Kroeber's superorganic theory of culture. Kroeber compares studying individuals in anthropology to attempting to understand geology by explaining the size and shape of each pebble in a bed of gravel. He says the pursuit of individual biographical data does not yield scientific data, or knowledge of what lies beyond people as individuals—that is, culture.

Note the teleological nature of this closing paragraph. Kroeber says we resist accepting that we are driven along by cultural forces rather than our individual wills, but that this resistance cannot refute the truth of his position, which he claims is a fact of nature. Underneath it all, Kroeber, we believe, was an evolutionist in the style of Herbert Spencer (see essay 1). Although Kroeber utterly rejected the natural selection model of social evolution, he did believe in the inexorable progress of science and rationality and believed the evolution of culture was analogous to the lives of organisms. This belief in progress is embedded deeply in his writing.

Notes

a. *The Psychology of Peoples,* London, 1898 (New York, 1912), page 12, footnote.

b. *Ralph Roister Doister,* published 1566; *Gammer Gurton's Needle,* 1575; Lyly wrote 1580–93; Greene died 1592, Kyd 1594, Peele 1598; blank verse in *Tamburlaine,* 1587; Shakespeare's first period, 1589–94; Marlowe died 1593; Shakespeare's second period, 1594–1601; third period—"Hamlet," "Othello," "Lear," "Macbeth"—1601–08; Jonson wrote chiefly 1598–1614; Shakespeare's fourth period, 1608–1613; Webster's best plays, 1612, 1616; Beaumont died 1616; Fletcher died 1625; Ford's best plays, 1629–34; Massinger, first play 1620, died 1639; closing of the playhouses, 1642.

c. Compare Quetelet's bold attempt in *Du Systéme Social,* 1848, to determine a normal duration of empires and cities.

d. S. Lane-Poole, *The Mohammedan Dynasties,* 1894. See especially "Growth" and "Decline of the Ottoman Empire," pages 190, 191; also "Mogul Emperors" on diagram facing page xx.

e. Clark Wissler, *American Anthropologist,* N.S., vol XVIII, pp. 190–197, 1916, points out that the distribution of sherds of certain decorative styles in the successive levels of the refuse heap at the ancient New Mexican pueblo of San Cristobal, as excavated and reported on by N. C. Nelson, follows typical curves, these curves each representing "the rise and decline of a cultural trait." Each foot of debris may be taken as representing an approximately equal duration of deposition, as indicated by the fairly steady numbers of sherds of all types found at each depth. The figures are, for black-on-white painted ware, 103, 107, 118, 40, 8, 2, 6, 10, 2, 2; and for black or brown glazed yellow ware, 0, 3, 45, 91, 192, 128, 52, 68, 64, 24. The latter series may be skew.

12. Right and Wrong

Paul Radin (1883–1959)

ON NO SUBJECT CONNECTED WITH PRIMITIVE people does so much confusion exist in the mind of the general public and have so many ill-considered statements been made as on the nature of their behavior to one another.[1] The prevalent view to-day among laymen is that they are at all times the plaything of their passions, and that self-control and poise are utterly alien to their character, if not, indeed, quite beyond their reach. We have seen in fact that even so open-minded and sympathetic a scholar as Jung apparently still accepts this view (c.f. 39). That an example like the one used by Jung should in all

From *Primitive Man as Philosopher* (1927)

good faith be given as representative of the normal or even the abnormal reaction of a primitive man to a given emotional situation, shows the depth of ignorance that still exists on this subject. Now quite apart from the manifest absurdity involved in the belief that any parent in a primitive group would wreak his rage at his lack of success in hunting, in this murderous fashion upon the first object that came within his reach, even if it be his innocent and beloved child, there are a hundred and one reasons that would have deterred him, even had he been the uncontrolled animal the illustration assumes him to have been. However, let that pass. The illustration has its uses, for it permits the contrast between the generally accepted belief and the true nature of the

---

[1] One of Franz Boas' most important principles was cultural relativism, and among his students, Radin was one of its most vociferous supporters. For Radin, the intrinsic sophistication, wisdom, and value of culture was evident from the details of the lives of his informants. Radin's anthropology focused on extensive fieldwork among the Winnebago Indians, and his association with them lasted fifty years. He spoke excellent Winnebago and was widely considered one of the best fieldworkers among Boas' students.

facts to emerge all the more definitely. Actually the situation is quite different.[2]

Briefly stated, the underlying idea of conduct among most primitive tribes is self-discipline, self-control and a resolute endeavor to observe a proper measure of proportion in all things. I am well aware that in some tribes this is more definitely expressed than in others and that not infrequently certain excrescences[3] in their ceremonial life seem to contradict this assertion. Yet I think most field ethnologists would agree with me. Since in the face of so formidable a body of opinion apparently to the contrary, incontrovertible evidence will be demanded of me to substantiate so broad and explicit a statement, I shall confine myself in my presentation of the facts to a tribe which I know personally and where the material which I use can be definitely controlled. The data upon which I rely come from the Winnebago Indians of Wisconsin and Nebraska and are to be found in two monographs published by me. Only statements made by the Winnebago themselves in accounts either actually written by themselves or contained in verbatim descriptions of the rituals obtained in the original Winnebago are used in order to obviate all inaccuracy.

I can think of no better method of introducing the subject than by quoting appropriate passages from the Winnebago texts secured[4] and then discussing them in the light of the knowledge they throw upon the system of ethics enunciated and, more specifically, upon the type of self-control implied. For facility of reference I shall number these passages:[a]

1. It is always good to be good.

2. What does life consist of but love?

3. Of what value is it to kill?

4. You ought to be of some help to your fellow men.

5. Do not abuse your wife; women are sacred.

6. If you cast off your dress for many people, they will be benefitted by your deed.

7. For the good you do every one will love you.

8. Never do any wrong to children.

9. It is not good to gamble.

10. If you see a helpless old man, help him if you have anything at all.

11. If you have a home of your own, see to it that whoever enters it obtains something to eat. Such food will be a source of death to you if withheld.

12. When you are recounting your war deeds on behalf of the departed soul, do not try to add to your honor by claiming more for yourself than you have actually accomplished. If you tell a falsehood

---

[2] Carl Gustave Jung (1875–1961) was a Swiss psychologist and early follower of Freud who broke with him over the role of sexuality in the development of neuroses. For anthropologists, among Jung's most important ideas are his concepts of the collective unconscious and archetypes. The reference to Jung in this paragraph concerns an example of what Jung called "primitive mentality" that Radin took from Jung's *Psychological Types* (1971 [1923]). Jung had written an account of a Bushman who, enraged at having caught nothing while fishing, strangled his young son who ran out to greet him and then mourned for the boy with "the same abandon and lack of comprehension as had before made him strangle him" (Radin 1957:39).

Radin wished to show that "primitive" thinking was similar to that of modern, "civilized" people – that it is sophisticated, profound, and self-aware. This was central to his life's work. In claiming that primitive peoples can be philosophers, as he does in the title of the book from which this extract is taken, he is attacking cultural evolutionism, particularly the idea that ontogeny recapitulates phylogeny. This idea, perhaps most forcefully stated by Freud, suggests that primitive people are childlike and hence lack self-discipline and self-control.

[3] *Excrescences:* normal or abnormal growths or appendages such as horns or bunions. Radin uses the term to refer to Native American practices such as ecstatic trances.

[4] Radin's method was to try to stay very close to "pure" ethnographic material. In many of his works, translated folklore or ethnographic observations are presented with little or no commentary. Some good examples are "Description of a Winnebago Funeral" (1911) and "Ojibwa Ethnological Chit Chat" (1924).

then and exaggerate your achievements you will die beforehand. The telling of truth is sacred. Tell less than you did. The old men say it is wiser.

13. Be on friendly terms with every one and then every one will love you.

14. Marry only one person at a time.

15. Do not be haughty with your husband. Kindness will be returned to you and he will treat you in the same way in which you treat him.

16. Do not imagine that you are taking your children's part if you just speak about loving them. Let them see it for themselves.

17. Do not show your love for other people so that people notice it. Love them but let your love be different from that for your own.

18. As you travel along life's road, never harm any one or cause any one to feel sad. On the contrary, if at any time you can make a person feel happy, do so. If at any time you meet a woman away from your village and you are both alone and no one can see you, do not frighten her or harm her.

19. If you meet any one on the road, even if it is only a child, speak a cheering word before you pass on.

20. If your husband's people ever ask their own children for something when you are present, assume that they had asked it of you. If there is anything to be done, do not wait till you are asked to do it but do it immediately.

21. Never think a home is yours until you have made one for yourself.

22. If you have put people in charge of your household, do not nevertheless act as though the home were still yours.

23. When visiting your husband's people, do not act as if you were far above them.

Obviously we are here in the presence of a fairly well elaborated system of conduct. To those who consistently deny to primitive man any true capacity for abstract thinking or objective formulation of an ethical code—and their number is very large both among scholars and laymen—the injunctions given above would probably be interpreted as having a definitely concrete significance. That is, they are not to be regarded as attempts at generalization in any true sense of the word but merely as inherently wise saws and precepts of a practical and personal application. Now there is sufficient justification for such a view to warrant our discussing it before we proceed any further.[5]

A number of the precepts given avowedly allow a concrete practical and personal application. In 5, for example, we are told, "If you abuse your wife you will die in a short time. Our grandmother Earth is a woman and in abusing your wife you will be abusing her. Since it is she who takes care of us, by your actions you will be practically killing yourself." To precept 10 is added the following: "If you happen to possess a home, take him (the old man) there and feed him for he may suddenly make uncomplimentary remarks about you. You will be strengthened thereby."

We thus do indeed seem to obtain the impression that a Winnebago in being good to a helpless old man is guided by motives secondary to those implied in the precept as quoted. And what follows would seem to strip our apparently generous precept of whatever further altruistic value still attaches to it, for there it is stated that perhaps the old man is carrying under his arm a box of medicines that he cherishes very much and which he will offer to you. Similarly in precept 11 we find, "If you are stingy about giving food someone may kill you." Indeed, I think we shall have to admit that in the majority of cases none of the Winnebago virtues or actions are extolled for their own sake, and that in every instance they have reference to and derive their validity from whatever relation they possess to the preponderatingly practical needs of human intercourse. "Don't be a fool," precept 5 seems to imply "and

---

[5] Childish, and hence primitive, thinking was supposed to be tied to specific, immediate stimulus; primitives were supposed to be incapable of abstraction. Therefore, Radin wants to show that the points he has outlined are general and abstract.

don't treat your wife badly, because if you do, you'll run the risk of having the woman's protecting deity, the Earth, punish you." I should not even be surprised if, in concrete instances, the moral was further emphasized by giving examples of how men were punished who had abused their wives. We are fairly obviously told to be guided by the practical side of the question, i.e., take no risks and get the most out of every good action you perform.

Now all this sounds extremely cynical and practical. But we must be fair and not too hasty in drawing our inferences. First of all it should be asked if the Winnebago in actual practice give the impression of always being guided by egotistical and ulterior motives, and second it should be borne in mind that if we can really prove that the ideal of human conduct is on a high plane, we need not concern ourselves needlessly with the apparent nature of the motives prompting individual acts. As a matter of fact primitive people are much less guided by consciously selfish and ulterior motives than we are, not because of any innate superiority over ourselves in this regard but because of the conditions under which they live.[6] But, quite apart from this consideration, ought we in fact to lay undue stress on illustrations following what is clearly a general principle? Are we not after all, in our illustrations, merely dealing with a statement of what happens when some general principle of the ethical code is transgressed, and not primarily with an explanation of the principle? I do not feel, therefore, that even those instances which seem superficially to corroborate the prevalent assumption of primitive man's inability to formulate an abstract ethical creed, actually bear out, when more carefully examined, the contention of its advocates.

Now the question of the capacity of the Winnebago to formulate an ethical code in a fairly abstract fashion is of fundamental importance for the thesis of this chapter and that is why I am laying so much stress on it; for if it were not true our precepts would have to be regarded in the nature of mere proverbs and practical folk wisdom, as nothing higher indeed than crystallized maxims of conduct.

There are, however, in our list certain precepts where the abstract formulation is undeniable, where, in fact, reference to the particular context in which the precepts occur not only shows no secondary concrete significance, but, on the contrary, a reinforcement of their abstract and general connotation. In precept 1 the full statement is this: "If you hear of a person traveling through your country and you want to see him, prepare your table and send for him. In this manner you will do good and it is always good to do good, it is said." Similarly in precept 2. Here it is in the course of a speech delivered at a ceremony that the phrase occurs: "what does life consist of but love?" "All the members of the clan have given me counsel," the speaker says, "and all the women and children have pleaded in my behalf with the spirits. What love that was! And of what does life consist but of love?"

Here we have no concrete practical implications. The statements are meant to be taken as general propositions. They are very remarkable enunciations and we may legitimately draw from their existence the inference that even in so-called "primitive" tribes, certain individuals have apparently felt within themselves the same moral truths that are regarded as the glory of our great moralists, and that they have formulated these truths in general terms.

So much for the actual formulation. What, however, does this Winnebago creed tell us about the idea of conduct itself? Does it teach us that love and forbearance are to be practiced for their own sake and is the love of which they speak identical with or even comparable to our idea of love?

When a Western European speaks of love, forbearance, remorse, sorrow, etc., he generally understands by these terms some quality belonging to an individual and for the possession of which

---

[6] Note Radin's point that the conditions under which people live, rather than any innate fundamental differences, determine their understanding of the world. This is basic to Boasian cultural relativism. Boas used his experience on Baffin Island to support his deeply held belief in human equality. Radin used his long experience with the Winnebago to similar ends.

he is to be honored and praised.[7] We do not ask whether the love or the virtue in question is of an intelligent nature, whether it does harm or good, or whether we have any right to it. Who among us would speak of an individual not being entitled to his remorse or sorrow? We assume that the mere expression of remorse and sorrow is somehow ethically praiseworthy. If we see a man of manifestly weak character but of a loving disposition, even if his actions are inconsistent with a true love for his fellow men, insist that he loves them, while we may condemn him, we are inclined to overlook much in recognition of his enunciation of the principle that love of mankind is the highest ideal of life. In much the same way do we look upon any manifestation of sincere remorse or sorrow. We simply regard love, remorse, sorrow, etc., as inalienable rights of man, quite independent of any right, as it were, he may possess to express them. In other words, the Western European ethics is frankly egocentric and concerned primarily with self-expression. The object toward which love, remorse, repentance, sorrow, is directed is secondary. Christian theology has elevated them all to the rank of virtues as such, and enjoins their observance upon us because they are manifestations of God's, if not of man's way.

Among primitive people this is emphatically not true. Ethics there is based upon behavior. No mere enunciation of an ideal of love, no matter how often and sincerely repeated, would gain an individual either admiration, sympathy, or respect. Every ethical precept must be submitted to the touchstone of conduct. The Winnebago moralist would insist that we have no right to preach an ideal of love or to claim that we love, unless we have lived up to its practical implications. That is the fundamental basis of all primitive education and is unusually well expressed among the Winnebago. "When you are bringing up children," runs the injunction to a young mother, "do not imagine that you are taking their part if you merely speak of loving them. Let them see it for themselves; let them know what love is by seeing you give away things to the poor. Then they will see your good deeds and then they will know whether you have been telling the truth or not." An exactly similar attitude is taken toward remorse. "If you have always loved a person, then when he dies you will have the right to feel sorrow." No amount of money spent upon the funeral of a person with whom you had been quarreling will make amends.

But it is not merely love, remorse, etc., to which you have no right as such. You have equally no right to the glory attendant upon joining a war party unless it is done in the right spirit. In the document from which most of our statements have been taken—the autobiography of a Winnebago Indian[8]—a man is represented as being about to embark on a war party because his wife has run away from him. "Such a man," the author insists, "is simply throwing away his life. If you want to go on the warpath, do not go because your wife has been taken away from you but because you feel courageous enough to go."

In consonance with such an attitude is the differentiation in the degree of love insisted upon. Love everybody, it is demanded, but do not love them all equally. Above all do not love your neighbor as you love those of your own blood. "Only if you are wicked," the injunction says, "will you love other people's children more than your own." The injunction certainly says that we must love everybody but this must be humanly understood, and humanly understood you cannot, of course,

---

[7] In this paragraph and below, Radin turns the tables on Jung's argument. He suggests (at least implicitly) that as regards questions of morality, so-called "primitive thinking" is, in fact, more sophisticated than our own. There is a subtext here. Radin, from a particularly rationalistic Jewish background and son of a rabbi, critiques Christian theology.

[8] The document referred to here is *Crashing Thunder: The Autobiography of an American Indian*. Originally published in 1926, this autobiography of Radin's key informant has been frequently reprinted and remains popular both among anthropologists and the general public. Radin's interest in autobiography was guided by his belief that the individual was of paramount importance and that an individual in a primitive society had a total understanding of his or her culture. Thus, a thorough understanding of an individual gave the anthropologist complete understanding of the culture to which that person belonged.

love everyone alike. The Winnebago would contend that such a statement would be untrue and that any attempt to put it into practice must manifestly lead to insincerity. It would, moreover, be definitely unjust in that it might make for the neglect of those whom primarily you ought to love most. Here the difference between the attitude of primitive man and that of Western Europe is most clearly brought out. According to primitive standards you deserve neither credit nor discredit, neither praise nor condemnation, for giving expression to a normal human emotion. It is the manner in which, in your relations to the other members of the tribe, you *distribute* this emotion and the degree to which it is felt by others to be sincere, that calls forth respect and admiration.[9] It is wicked to love other people's children as much as your own; it is wicked to love your wife to the detriment of your family and yourself; it is wicked to love your enemy while he is your enemy. An excellent illustration of this conviction—that it is fundamentally wicked and unintelligent to make the expression of even a socially commendable emotion like love an end in itself—is contained in the following passage taken from the autobiography quoted above:

> When you get married do not make an idol of the woman you marry; do not worship her. If you worship a woman she will insist upon greater and greater worship as time goes on. It may be that when you get married you will listen to the voice of your wife and you will refuse to go on the warpath. Why should you thus run the risk of being ridiculed? After a while you will not be allowed to go to a feast. In time even your sisters will not think anything of you. (You will become jealous) and after your jealousy has developed to its highest pitch your wife will run away. You have let her know by your actions that you worship a woman and one alone. As a result she will run away from you. If you think that a woman (your wife) is

the only person you ought to love, you have humbled yourself. You have made the woman suffer and have made her feel unhappy. You will be known as a bad man and no one will want to marry you again. (Perhaps afterwards) when people go on the warpath you will join them because you feel unhappy at your wife's desertion. You will then, however, simply be throwing away your life.

A complete insight is afforded by this example into every phase of Winnebago ethics. You are to love your wife, for instance, but it is to be kept within personally and socially justifiable limits. If not, the whole adjustment of an individual to his environment is disturbed and injustice is eventually done to every one concerned—to his family, to his wife, and to himself. Marked exaggeration and disproportion would, from a practical point of view, be unthinkable in a primitive community. The result, in the hypothetical case we discussed above, is clear; loss of life and suicide, and possibly even the dragging of innocent people into your calamity—those, for instance, who are going on a warpath properly prepared spiritually.

The psychology expressed here is unimpeachable. To have analyzed the situation so completely and so profoundly and to have made this analysis the basis of social behavior is not a slight achievement, and this achievement is to be evaluated all the more highly because the Winnebago was predominantly a warrior culture. The objectivity displayed is altogether unusual, the husband's, the wife's, the tribal viewpoints, all are presented fairly and clearly.[10]

Notes

a. All these passages, with the exception of 3, 18, 19, and 20, come from *Crashing Thunder: The Autobiography of an American Indian*, edited by Paul Radin; 3 comes from the myth given on page 79 of *Primitive Man as Philosopher*, and the others from the *37th report of the Bureau of American Ethnology*.

---

[9] It is interesting that Radin stressed the logical, rational element of Winnebago thinking. These are elements that Radin's contemporaries saw in his personality.

[10] Radin was not openly political. However, he was an eloquent spokesman for native and minority people and frequently published articles in the popular press. In this, he carried on Boas' commitment to moral engagement in the social sciences.

Functionalism

*I*n the first thirty years of the twentieth century, Franz Boas and his students were clearly the dominant anthropological thinkers in America, and the evolutionary model was temporarily abandoned. Boasians used intensive fieldwork and data collection to investigate the origins of cultural phenomena from a historical rather than an evolutionary perspective. In Britain, on the other hand, the reaction to cultural evolution did not occur with the same force. With no single figure comparable to Boas, British anthropologists were divided in two camps: the diffusionists and the functionalists. It is the latter group that concerns us here.

In the 1880s and 1890s, a new group of anthropological thinkers, led by Alfred Cort Haddon (1855–1940) emerged in Britain. Haddon was deeply influenced by Tylor, Frazer, and Spencer, but was trained in anatomy and zoology. In the 1880s, he held a position at the Royal College of Science in Dublin. In 1888, dissatisfied with life in Dublin, Haddon journeyed to the Torres Straits, between New Guinea and Australia, in the hopes that an important expedition might get him a better job (Stocking 1992:21). Haddon went to the Torres Straits primarily to study coral reefs, but once there, he became fascinated by the tales of the old men, and by the time he returned he was committed to anthropology.

Even though he went to study biology, Haddon brought several works of anthropology along on his trip, including *Notes and Queries on Anthropology for the Use of Travelers and Residents in Uncivilized Lands*. *Notes and Queries* was a book-length questionnaire designed to help untrained observers collect information of use to anthropologists. The original version appeared in 1874 and was periodically updated until the 1950s. *Notes and Queries* was a collaborative work by many anthropologists, but Tylor was the primary author of the nineteenth-century editions. Haddon used *Notes and Queries* to collect and organize data.

Once back in England, Haddon moved to Cambridge University, where he became the first lecturer in physical anthropology. He published some of the data he had collected in the Torres Straits but soon became convinced that another expedition was essential. He hoped to make a comprehensive study of native body types, psychology, language, and material culture. To this end, he enlisted an interdisciplinary team of scholars, including the physician Charles Seligman (1873–1940), the experimental psychologist W. H. R. (William Halse Rivers) Rivers (1864–1922), and his student, William McDougall (1871–1938). Other members of the team were specialists in photography and language.

The Torres Straits expedition was a defining moment in the development of anthropology in Britain. Haddon and his colleagues set a high standard for anthropological fieldwork, and after their return to England, they published extensive accounts of their research. Haddon, Rivers, and Seligman went on to hold university positions, Haddon and Rivers at Cambridge and Seligman at the London School of Economics. In these positions, they were critical in the training of the key thinkers of British functionalist anthropology. McDougall became one of the founders of experimental psychology in the United States.

Although Haddon and his colleagues were profoundly affected by Spencer and Tylor, the focus of their research was different. They were less interested in determining the course of human social evolution than in describing the material, social, physiological, and psychological characteristics of different people. Their students absorbed this emphasis on fieldwork and description but also attempted to carry out the research agenda implied in Spencer's "The Social Organism" (see essay 1). If, as Spencer claimed, society is like an organism, anthropologists should be able to describe the different organs that compose the organism, determine what each part does, and show the ways in which each is related to the others. Thus, functionalists attempted to describe the various institutions that made up society, explain what they do, and show their contribution to the overall maintenance of society.

Functionalism in anthropology is generally divided into two schools of thought, each associated with a key personality. Psychological functionalism is linked to Bronislaw Malinowski (1884–1942). For the psychological functionalist, cultural institutions function to meet the basic physical and psychological needs of people in a society. Like Boas, Malinowski's method was based on extensive in-depth fieldwork that supported his theoretical position.

The second school, structural functionalism, is associated with A. R. Radcliffe-Brown (1881–1955). Structural functionalists, who drew heavily on Durkheim's work, sought to understand how cultural institutions maintained the equilibrium and cohesion of a society. Like Durkheim, the structural functionalists were interested in studying the underlying structure of societies. Radcliffe-Brown and his students searched for social laws that could be derived from the comparative study of different cultures.

Bronislaw Malinowski was trained in the physical sciences and received a Ph.D. in physics and mathematics. Despite this training, Malinowski was captivated by Sir James Frazer's book *The Golden Bough,* and in 1910 he enrolled in the London School of Economics (LSE), where he studied anthropology under Charles Seligman. At the outbreak of World War I, Malinowski was traveling in the British-controlled South Pacific. He had intended that the trip, undertaken for ethnographic research, be relatively brief. However, Malinowski was from Krakow, in a part of Polish Galicia that had been controlled by Austria since 1849. Thus, he was an enemy national, and the British forbade his return to Europe. They did

permit him to stay in the Trobriand Islands from 1915 to 1918, and he conducted ethnographic research there for almost two years. Malinowski's intensive day-to-day contact with his informants and his familiarity with the local language set a high standard for modern ethnographic fieldwork. After the war, Malinowski returned to England and accepted a teaching position at the LSE, where he spent most of his career, training many of the finest English anthropologists of his era.

Malinowski shared Radcliffe-Brown's sense of society as a system of interrelated features but took his theory of functionalism in a very different direction. He was concerned with how individuals pursued their own ends within the constraints of their culture. Malinowski believed that culture existed to satisfy seven basic human needs: nutrition, reproduction, bodily comforts, safety, relaxation, movement, and growth (1939). He wished to demonstrate how various cultural beliefs and practices contributed to the smooth functioning of society while providing individual biological or psychological benefits. For example, in his 1925 essay "Magic, Science, and Religion," Malinowski discussed the nature of thought in primitive societies and demonstrated the psychological functions served by supernatural beliefs such as magic. By basing his theory on physiological and biopsychological needs, Malinowski gave his theory of culture a universal character. Because these needs were satisfied through cultural institutions, he was able to identify particular cultural and societal formations set up to fulfill them (Applebaum 1987:112). Malinowski was famous for his ethnographic reporting, and he was skilled at weaving theoretical ideas into his ethnographic discussions. Our selection, in essay 13, reflects this talent and illustrates Malinowski's skill as an ethnographer.

A. R. Radcliffe-Brown studied anthropology at Cambridge under Haddon and Rivers. Unlike Malinowski, he was heavily influenced by the work of Durkheim. Although he did fieldwork in the Andaman Islands and Australia, Radcliffe-Brown was more interested in deriving social laws governing behavior from the comparative study of different cultures than in intensive fieldwork in one culture. Durkheim's influence is evident in Radcliffe-Brown's attempts to illustrate how cultural systems function to maintain a society's equilibrium. For example, in his famous 1940 article "On Joking Relationships," Radcliffe-Brown demonstrated how hostility can be expressed in a nonthreatening manner through ritualized disrespect between kinsmen without jeopardizing the social structure. Like Durkheim, Radcliffe-Brown insisted that anthropology was a science. In his view, anthropologists should concern themselves with the search for universal laws of human behavior equivalent to the laws of the natural sciences.

Although he used the term *culture* in his early work, Radcliffe-Brown rejected the concept later in his career. He believed that culture was an abstract concept and that—because the values and norms of a society could not be observed—a science of culture was impossible (Garbarino 1977:58). Radcliffe-Brown preferred to limit his research to social structures, the principles that organize persons in a society (such as kinship), or the actual roles and relationships that can be observed firsthand. To illustrate this perspective, Radcliffe-Brown used Spencer's organic analogy (and acknowledged his debt to Spencer). He wrote

> An animal organism is an agglomeration of cells and interstitial fluids arranged in relation to one another not as an aggregate but as an integrated living whole. The system of relations by which these units are related is the organic structure. As the terms are here used the organism is not itself the structure; it is a collection of units (cells or molecules) arranged in a structure, i.e. in a set of relations; the organism has a structure. The structure is thus to be defined as a set of relations between entities. Over a period its constituent cells do not remain the same. But the structural arrangement of the constituent units does remain similar. (Radcliffe-Brown 1965 [1940]: 178–179)

Applying this analogy to anthropological data, Radcliffe-Brown argued that it is more useful to study kinship systems than to study the individuals in a society because people die, but the kin structure remains the same from generation to generation. In Radcliffe-Brown's view, Malinowski's focus on individuals led nowhere. To use a cliché, Radcliffe-Brown thought that Malinowski did not see the forest for the trees.

We have chosen two articles to represent structural functionalism. Essay 14 clearly illustrates Radcliffe-Brown's focus on social structure rather than individual behavior. It underscores his belief that functionalist studies are scientific and that universal laws of human behavior could be formulated through cross-cultural comparisons. Our second selection (essay 15) is by E. E. Evans-Pritchard (1902–1973). Evans-Pritchard was a student of Malinowski's, but his work was most profoundly affected by Radcliffe-Brown, whom he met at Oxford in 1935. The extract we present here concerns the structure of kinship among the Nuer, an East African society of cattle herders, and how this structure regulates warfare and the distribution of resources.

For American anthropology students, one curious and striking aspect of British anthropology is the prevalence of people with hyphenated last names. In Britain, such names generally signify upper- or upper-middle-class origins. When functionalism developed, however, anthropology was not a profession for gentlemen. In the early years of the century, anthropology languished at Oxford and Cambridge, the most prestigious universities. Cambridge anthropologists A. C. Haddon and W. H. R. Rivers were considered ungentlemanly by other members of the faculty (Leach 1984:5). However, anthropology prospered at the London School of Economics, an institution founded by members of the socialist Fabian society. In the 1920s, the LSE was a low-status institution, but there the people who became the leaders of British social anthropology attended Malinowski's seminars. These included Evans-Pritchard, Isaac Schapera (1905–?), Audrey Richards (1899–1984), Raymond Firth (1901–), Meyer Fortes (1906–1983), Lucy Mair (1901–1986), and S. F. Nadel (1903–1956). While Malinowski built the anthropology program at the LSE, at Cambridge his books *Sex and Repression in Savage Society* (1955 [1927]) and *The Sexual Life of Savages in Northwestern Melanesia* (1929b) were kept in a special section of the library and could only be read with permission of a senior college official (Leach 1984:8). Given anthropology's social position, it is interesting to note that while Radcliffe-Brown liked to portray himself as an English country gentleman, he was born Alfred Reginald Brown and started his education at the Royal Commercial Travellers School. He changed his name to Radcliffe-Brown in 1926 when he moved from Cape Town to Sydney (Leach 1984:21).

We stated in the first section of this book that scientific theories are a product of the social and cultural context in which they are conceived. Functionalism was conceived and practiced largely by European anthropologists in territories that were European colonial possessions such as the Trobriand Islands, Australia, India, and East Africa. Given this context, it is surely no accident that these thinkers studied the function of cultural institutions in relation to the maintenance of social order and the smooth working of society. This focus was precisely the aspect of non-Western societies in which colonial governments were most interested.

The nature of the relationship between anthropology and colonialism is highly equivocal. It is certainly true that British anthropologists often thought about their usefulness to colonial administrations. From the turn of the twentieth century until World War II, anthropologists tried to sell their expertise to governments. But governments, with few exceptions, were not particularly interested in listening to anthropologists. Haddon campaigned persistently (but unsuccessfully) for an "imperial bureau of ethnology" designed to help the state deal with "conflicts derived from racial and cultural variation that arose both in the colonies and at home" (Kuklick 1991:44). Radcliffe-Brown held positions in Cape Town and in Sydney in which he was responsible for training officials to govern indigenous peoples. However, he too met with limited success (Kuklick 1991:48). The critical funding agency for anthropological research in this era was not the government but the Laura Spelman Rockefeller Memorial, a privately controlled charitable trust located in the United States and interested in issues of social welfare (Goody 1995:14). There were other sources of funds, and some anthropologists even staged their own fund raisers. French ethnographer Marcel Griaule (1898–1956) put on circuses to raise money to fund his research (Goody 1995:17).

After World War II, Britain was particularly eager to employ anthropologists as colonial advisors, but by that time, anthropologists were no longer interested in working for governments. Colonial officials were exasperated by their inability to find anthropological advisors (Kuklick 1991:14).

One other observation about functionalism is warranted: the functionalists were typically only marginally interested in history. While American anthropology at this time was based largely on reconstruction of cultures from interviews with informants, British anthropologists were able to directly observe native societies in action (or thought they were). Under these circumstances, they believed that issues of the functioning of the current system were of primary importance. They asserted that historical reconstruction did little to clarify the current functioning of social institutions—indeed, they were deeply skeptical of historical reconstructions. Many functionalists held that since most of the societies they studied lacked writing, such reconstructions could be little more than fictions. As a result, they examined societies as if they were timeless and thus were able to account for social change.

Functionalism lost its place of theoretical prominence after World War II. Because of the massive social, cultural, and political transformations that resulted from the war, interest in functionalism declined, to be replaced by concern with theories of cultural change. Despite this, the work of Malinowski, Radcliffe-Brown, and their students Fortes, Max Gluckman (1911–1965), Schapera, Richards, and others continues to be widely read and to provide inspiration for modern anthropologists. Many of Malinowski's works, for example, are still in print today, over half a century after their original publication. Although few people would refer to themselves as structural-functional anthropologists today, and there are virtually no explicitly functional theoretical papers being published, key functionalist concepts are still implicit in a great deal of anthropology. Functionalism continues to be a powerful idea, and most anthropologists are probably more functionalist than is generally acknowledged.

13. The Essentials of the Kula

Bronislaw Malinowski (1884–1942)

I

Having thus described the scene, and the actors, let us now proceed to the performance.[1] The Kula is a form of exchange, of extensive, inter-tribal character; it is carried on by communities inhabiting a wide ring of islands, which form a closed circuit. This circuit can be seen on Map V, where it is represented by the lines joining a number of islands to the North and East of the East end of New Guinea. Along this route, articles of two kinds, and these two kinds only, are constantly travelling in opposite directions. In the direction of the hands of a clock, moves constantly one of these kinds — long necklaces of red shell, called *soulava*. . . . In the opposite direction moves the other kind — bracelets of white shell called *mwali*. . . . Each of these articles, as it travels in its own direction on the closed circuit, meets on its way articles of the other class, and is constantly being exchanged for them. Every movement of the Kula articles, every detail of the transactions is fixed and regulated by a set of traditional rules and conventions, and some acts of the Kula are accompanied by an elaborate magical ritual and public ceremonies.

From *Argonauts of the Western Pacific* (1922)

On every island and in every village, a more or less limited number of men take part in the Kula — that is to say, receive the goods, hold them for a short time, and then pass them on. Therefore every man who is in the Kula, periodically though not regularly, receives one or several *mwali* (arm-shells), or a *soulava* (necklace of red shell discs), and then has to hand it on to one of his partners, from whom he receives the opposite commodity in exchange. Thus no man ever keeps any of the articles for any length of time in his possession. One transaction action does not finish the Kula relationship, the rule being "once in the Kula, always in the Kula," and a partnership between two men is a permanent and lifelong affair. Again, any given mwali or soulava may always be found travelling and changing hands, and there is no question of its ever settling down, so that the principle "once in a Kula, always in a Kula" applies also to the valuables themselves.

The ceremonial exchange of the two articles is the main, the fundamental aspect of the Kula. But associated with it, and done under its cover, we find a great number of secondary activities and features.[2] Thus, side by side with the ritual exchange of arm-shells and necklaces, the natives carry on ordinary trade, bartering from one island to another a great number of utilities, often unprocurable in the district to which they are

---

[1] "The Essentials of the Kula" is the third chapter of Malinowski's 1922 monograph *Argonauts of the Western Pacific*. In the introduction and first two chapters of this work, Malinowski discusses his research methods, the geography of the region, and the different "races" of people who inhabit it, as well as their notions of magic, sorcery, and power. Here, he begins his discussion of the Kula, perhaps the thing for which this book is best remembered. Malinowski stands out as an ethnographer for his skill at weaving theoretical arguments into his ethnographic descriptions. In this chapter alone, one can find elements of Spencer, Durkheim, Freud, and Malinowski's own functional views as well as an argument about the economic nature of primitive societies.

[2] Malinowski's theory is referred to today as psychological functionalism. He believed there were seven universal biological and psychological needs and that cultural institutions existed to satisfy those needs. According to Malinowski, these basic needs were converted to cultural behavior through the use of symbols, which also served to mold individual behavior to group standards. The role of functionalism, in Malinowski's view, was to demonstrate how social institutions operated to fill these needs. The Kula served a psychological function in that individuals were able to achieve prestige through their participation. By setting up a network of trading partners and allies throughout the islands, it also provided an increased level of physical security for the participants.

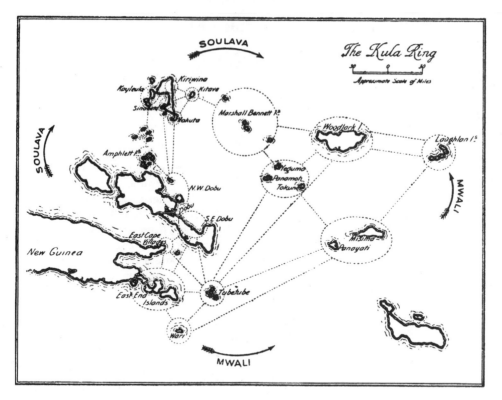

Map V. The Kula ring

imported, and indispensable there. Further, there are other activities, preliminary to the Kula, or associated with it, such as the building of sea-going canoes for the expeditions, certain big forms of mortuary ceremonies, and preparatory taboos.

The Kula is thus an extremely big and complex institution, both in its geographical extent, and in the manifoldness of its component pursuits. It welds together a considerable number of tribes, and it embraces a vast complex of activities, interconnected, and playing into one another, so as to form one organic whole.[3]

Yet it must be remembered that what appears to us an extensive, complicated, and yet well ordered institution is the outcome of ever so many doings and pursuits, carried on by savages, who have no laws or aims or characters definitely laid down.[4] They have no knowledge of the *total outline* of any of their social structure. They know their own motives, know the purpose of individual actions and the rules which apply to them, but how, out of these, the whole collective institution shapes, this is beyond their mental range. Not even the most intelligent native has any clear idea

---

[3] Malinowski takes pains throughout this chapter to emphasize the size and complexity of the Kula. His understanding of it was conditioned by Spencer's notion of the social organism as a complex system of interrelated parts.

[4] Notice Malinowski's characterization of the Trobriand Islanders in this and the next paragraph as aware of their individual actions and motives but unable to see their entire system. It takes an outsider, the ethnographer according to Malinowski, to conduct an objective analysis of a society and its institutions — a point that Victor Turner echoed half a century later (see essay 36). Malinowski is not denigrating the intelligence of the Trobriand Islanders here, for he believed

of the Kula as a big, organized social construction, still less of its sociological function and implications. If you were to ask him what the Kula is, he would answer by giving a few details, most likely by giving his personal experiences and subjective views on the Kula, but nothing approaching the definition just given here. Not even a partial coherent account could be obtained. For the integral picture does not exist in his mind; he is in it, and cannot see the whole from the outside.

The integration of all the details observed, the achievement of a sociological synthesis of all the various, relevant symptoms, is the task of the Ethnographer. First of all, he has to find out that certain activities, which at first sight might appear incoherent and not correlated, have a meaning. He then has to find out what is constant and relevant in these activities and what accidental and inessential, that is, to find out the laws and rules of all the transactions. Again, the Ethnographer has to *construct* the picture of the big institution, very much as the physicist constructs his theory from the experimental data, which always have been within reach of everybody but which needed a consistent interpretation. I have touched on this point of method in the Introduction (Divisions V and VI), but I have repeated it here, as it is necessary to grasp it clearly in order not to lose the right perspective of conditions as they really exist among the natives.

II

In giving the above abstract and concise definition, I had to reverse the order of research, as this is done in ethnographic field-work, where the most generalised inferences are obtained as the result of long inquiries and laborious inductions. The general definition of the Kula will serve as a sort of plan or diagram in our further concrete and detailed descriptions. And this is the more necessary as the Kula is concerned with the exchange of wealth and utilities, and therefore it is an economic institution, and there is no other aspect of primitive life where our knowledge is more scanty and our understanding more superficial than in Economics. Hence misconception is rampant, and it is necessary to clear the ground when approaching any economic subject.

Thus in the Introduction we called the Kula a "form of trade," and we ranged it alongside other systems of barter. This is quite correct, if we give the word "trade" a sufficiently wide interpretation, and mean by it any exchange of goods. But the word "trade" is used in current Ethnography and economic literature with so many different implications that a whole lot of misleading, preconceived ideas have to be brushed aside in order to grasp the facts correctly. Thus the *a priori* current notion of primitive trade would be that of an exchange of indispensable or useful articles, done without much ceremony or regulation, under stress of dearth or need, in spasmodic, irregular intervals — and this done either by direct barter, everyone looking out sharply not to be done out of his due, or, if the savages were too timid and distrustful to face one another, by some customary arrangement, securing by means of heavy penalties compliance in the obligations incurred or imposed.[a5] Waiving for the present the question how far this conception is valid or not in general — in my opinion it is quite misleading — we

---

the same principle to be true for people in Western societies. The point that a person cannot objectively analyze the system in which he or she participates is a central tenet of psychoanalytic thought. A selection of Freud's work was made available to Malinowski in the field by his professor Charles G. Seligman (1873–1940), and Malinowski's opinion on the issue may have been influenced by Freud's writings. Seligman, a medical doctor, was a member of the Torres Straits expedition and wrote the groundbreaking *The Melanesians of British New Guinea* (1910), which set the stage for Malinowski's research. Seligman found Freud useful in his work with victims of shell shock during World War I. Malinowski, on the other hand, became a key critic of Freud and used data from the Trobriands to attack Freud's Oedipal theory in *Sex and Repression in Savage Society* (1955 [1927]). Note also the analogy Malinowski makes between ethnography and the physical sciences.

[5] In his first footnote, Malinowski references the German economist Carl Bücher (1847–1930), whose *Industrial Evolution,* first published in Germany in 1893, was enormously influential in Europe, and by 1901 had been translated into English, French, and Russian. Bücher developed a three-stage view of economic evolution, proposing that households led to towns,

have to realise clearly that the Kula contradicts in almost every point the above definition of "savage trade." It shows us primitive exchange in an entirely different light.

The Kula is not a surreptitious and precarious form of exchange. It is, quite on the contrary, rooted in myth, backed by traditional law, and surrounded with magical rites. All its main transactions are public and ceremonial, and carried out according to definite rules. It is not done on the spur of the moment, but happens periodically, at dates settled in advance, and it is carried on along definite trade routes, which must lead to fixed trysting places. Sociologically, though transacted between tribes differing in language, culture, and probably even in race, it is based on a fixed and permanent status, on a partnership which binds into couples some thousands of individuals. This partnership is a lifelong relationship, it implies various mutual duties and privileges, and constitutes a type of inter-tribal relationship on an enormous scale. As to the economic mechanism of the transactions, this is based on a specific form of credit, which implies a high degree of mutual trust and commercial honour—and this refers also to the subsidiary,

minor trade, which accompanies the Kula proper. Finally, the Kula is not done under stress of any need, since its main aim is to exchange articles which are of no practical use.

From the concise definition of Kula given at the beginning of this chapter, we see that in its final essence, divested of all trappings and accessories, it is a very simple affair, which at first sight might even appear tame and unromantic. After all it only consists of an exchange, interminably repeated, of two articles intended for ornamentation, but not even used for that to any extent. Yet this simple action—this passing from hand to hand of two meaningless and quite useless objects—has somehow succeeded in becoming the foundation of a big inter-tribal institution, in being associated with ever so many other activities. Myth, magic and tradition have built up around it definite ritual and ceremonial forms, have given it a halo of romance and value in the minds of the natives, have indeed created a passion in their hearts for this simple exchange.[6]

The definition of the Kula must now be amplified, and we must describe one after the other its fundamental characteristics and main rules, so that it may be clearly grasped by what mechanism

---

which led to national economies. The factor that differentiated these stages was the role of exchange. He believed that contemporary primitive societies represented a pre-economic stage of society (Firth 1964:210). Bücher writes that "primitive man lives only for the present . . . shuns all regular work . . . has not the conception of duty, not of a vocation as a moral function in life" (1968 [1901]:82). These views influenced the work of scholars such as Max Weber (see essay 9) and Marcel Mauss (see essay 8). Malinowski—though sympathetic to Bücher's attempts to understand primitive economy— wrote *Argonauts* as a reaction to this view of primitive humans, using the Kula as a counterexample. Later in *Argonauts* he wrote, "Now I hope that whatever the meaning of the Kula might be for Ethnology, for the general science of culture, the meaning of the Kula will consist in being instrumental to dispel such crude, rationalistic conceptions of primitive mankind, and to induce both the speculator and the observer to deepen the analysis of economic facts" (1922:516).

[6] Malinowski believed that technologically primitive peoples were fully rational and just as intelligent as "civilized" people, but the point of the economic discussion in *Argonauts* is to critique the concept of "economic man." This is the notion that human beings rationally deploy limited resources to competing ends in such a way as to increase their personal benefit. This idea lies behind Adam Smith's *Wealth of Nations* (1976 [1776]) and most of Western economics. Malinowski's attack at its most vitriolic is found on page 60 of *Argonauts,* where he writes, "Another notion which must be exploded, once and forever, is that of the Primitive Economic Man of some current economic textbooks. This fanciful, dummy creature, who has been very tenacious of existence in popular and semi-popular economic literature and whose shadow haunts even the minds of competent anthropologists, blighting their outlook with a preconceived idea, is an imaginary, primitive man, or savage, prompted in all his actions by a rationalistic concept of self-interest, and achieving his aims directly with the minimum of effort." Malinowski wanted "rational man" but not "economic man," and he needed to show that it was possible to have one without the other. In large part, this is the goal of the Kula discussion. To Malinowski, the Kula is a highly elaborate and rational system of exchange that has an economically irrational end: the distribution of goods that have no utilitarian value. Much of later substantivist economics treated Malinowski's attack as virtually a founding document of their form of analysis. On the other hand, Firth says Malinowski's attack was essentially against a straw man (1964:217).

the mere exchange of two articles results in an institution so vast, complex, and deeply rooted.

III

First of all, a few words must be said about the two principal objects of exchange, the arm-shells (*mwali*) and the necklaces (*soulava*). The arm-shells are obtained by breaking off the top and the narrow end of a big, cone-shaped shell (*Conus millepunctatus*) and then polishing up the remaining ring. These bracelets are highly coveted by all the Papuo-Melanesians of New Guinea, and they spread even into the pure Papuan district of the Gulf.[b] The manner of wearing the arm-shells is illustrated by Plate XVII, where the men have put them on on purpose to be photographed.[7]

The use of the small discs of red spondylus shell out of which the *soulava* are made, is also of very wide diffusion. There is a manufacturing centre of them in one of the villages in Port Moresby, and also in several places in Eastern New Guinea, notably in Rossell Island, and in the Trobriands. I have said "use" on purpose here, because these small beads, each of them a flat, round disc with a hole in the centre, coloured anything from muddy brown to carmine red, are employed in various ways for ornamentation. They are most generally used as part of earrings, made of rings of turtle shell, which are attached to the ear lobe, and from which hang a cluster of the shell discs. These earrings are very much worn, and, especially among the Massim, you see them on the ears of every second man or woman, while others are satisfied with turtle shell alone, unornamented with the shell discs. Another everyday ornament, frequently met with and worn, especially by young girls and boys, consists of a short necklace, just encircling the neck, made of the red spondylus discs, with one or more cowrie shell pendants. These shell discs can be, and often are, used in the make-up of the various classes of the more elaborate ornaments, worn on festive occasions only. Here however, we are more especially concerned with the very long

necklaces, measuring from two to five metres, made of spondylus discs, of which there are two main varieties, one, much the finer, with a big shell pendant, the other made of bigger discs, and with a few cowrie shells or black banana seeds in the centre. . . .

The arm-shells on the one hand, and the long spondylus shell strings on the other, the two main Kula articles, are primarily ornaments. As such, they are used with the most elaborate dancing dress only, and on very festive occasions such as big ceremonial dances, great feasts, and big gatherings, where several villages are represented. . . . Never could they be used as everyday ornaments, nor on occasions of minor importance such as a small dance in the village, a harvest gathering, a love-making expedition, when facial painting, floral decoration and smaller though not quite everyday ornaments are worn. . . . But even though usable and sometimes used, this is not the main function of these articles. Thus, a chief may have several shell strings in his possession, and a few arm-shells. Supposing that a big dance is held in his or in a neighbouring village, he will not put on his ornaments himself if he goes to assist at it, unless he intends to dance and decorate himself, but any of his relatives, his children or his friends and even vassals, can have the use of them for the asking. If you go to a feast or a dance where there are a number of men wearing such ornaments, and ask anyone of them at random to whom it belongs, the chances are that more than half of them will answer that they themselves are not the owners, but that they had the articles lent to them. These objects are not owned in order to be used; the privilege of decorating oneself with them is not the real aim of possession.

Indeed—and this is more significant—by far the greater number of the arm-shells, easily ninety per cent, are of too small a size to be worn even by young boys and girls. A few are so big and valuable that they would not be worn at all, except once in a decade by a very important man on a very festive day. Though all the shell-strings can be worn, some of them are again considered too valuable, and are

---

[7] Unusually for the period in which this was written, Malinowski tells the reader about the conditions under which the photograph (not included in this volume) was taken. This is a level of ethnographic reporting that did not become common until the 1970s and 1980s. Ellipses throughout this section indicate the deletion of other references to photographs.

cumbersome for frequent use, and would be worn on very exceptional occasions only.

This negative description leaves us with the questions: why, then, are these objects valued, what purpose do they serve? The full answer to this question will emerge out of the whole story contained in the following chapters, but an approximate idea must be given at once. As it is always better to approach the unknown through the known, let us consider for a moment whether among ourselves we have not some type of objects which play a similar role and which are used and possessed in the same manner. When, after a six years' absence in the South Seas and Australia, I returned to Europe and did my first bit of sight-seeing in Edinburgh Castle, I was shown the Crown Jewels. The keeper told many stories of how they were worn by this or that king or queen on such and such occasion, of how some of them had been taken over to London, to the great and just indignation of the whole Scottish nation, how they were restored, and how now everyone can be pleased, since they are safe under lock and key, and no one can touch them. As I was looking at them and thinking how ugly, useless, ungainly, even tawdry they were, I had the feeling that something similar had been told to me of late, and that I had seen many other objects of this sort, which made a similar impression on me.[8]

And then arose before me the vision of a native village on coral soil, and a small, rickety platform temporarily erected under a pandanus thatch, surrounded by a number of brown, naked men, and one of them showing me long, thin red strings, and big, white, worn-out objects, clumsy to sight and greasy to touch. With reverence he

also would name them, and tell their history, and by whom and when they were worn, and how they changed hands, and how their temporary possession was a great sign of the importance and glory of the village. The analogy between the European and the Trobriand *vaygu'a* (valuables) must be delimited with more precision. The Crown Jewels, in fact, any heirlooms too valuable and too cumbersome to be worn, represent the same type as *vaygu'a* in that they are merely possessed for the sake of possession itself, and the ownership of them with the ensuing renown is the main source of their value. Also both heirlooms and *vaygu'a* are cherished because of the historical sentiment which surrounds them. However, ugly, useless, and — according to current standards — valueless an object may be, if it has figured in historical scenes and passed through the hands of historic persons, and is therefore an unfailing vehicle of important sentimental associations, it cannot but be precious to us. This historic sentimentalism, which indeed has a large share in our general interest in studies of past events, exists also in the South Seas. Every really good Kula article has its individual name, round each there is a sort of history and romance in the traditions of the natives. Crown Jewels or heirlooms are insignia of rank and symbols of wealth respectively, and in olden days with us, and in New Guinea up till a few years ago, both rank and wealth went together. The main point of difference is that the Kula goods are only in possession for a time, whereas the European treasure must be permanently owned in order to have full value.[9]

Taking a broader, ethnological view of the question, we may class the Kula valuables among

---

[8] Malinowski is considered one of the great ethnographers in anthropological history in part because of his gift for ethnographic reportage. He believed it was important to understand how natives perceived their world and passed this understanding on to his readers by comparisons such as that presented here between *vaygu'a* and the Crown Jewels of Scotland. Like the jewels, *vaygu'a* do not have a practical utility; rather their value is symbolic, derived from their age and history. In making this comparison, Malinowski uses a nontechnical example easily accessible to a popular audience. *Argonauts,* like many of Malinowski's other works, was designed to be read by educated laypersons as well as professional anthropologists.

[9] In the passage above, Malinowski tries to give us a native's perspective when he explains what the Kula items mean to their recipients. Malinowski's writing style gave him a reputation as a man with great personal empathy for the people he studied. Admirers of Malinowski were greatly disillusioned when his diaries were published in 1967 (*A Diary in the Strict Sense of the Term*). The diaries showed that Malinowski was intensely unhappy and lonely much of the time, was constantly preoccupied with his health, and often spoke of the Trobriand Islanders in racist terms. In other words, he reacted like most people of his era (and perhaps our own) when forced into unfamiliar circumstances for a long period of time.

the many "ceremonial" objects of wealth; enormous, carved and decorated weapons, stone implements, articles of domestic and industrial nature, too well decorated and too clumsy for use. Such things are usually called "ceremonial," but this word seems to cover a great number of meanings and much that has no meaning at all. In fact, very often, especially on museum labels, an article is called "ceremonial" simply because nothing is known about its uses and general nature. Speaking only about museum exhibits from New Guinea, I can say that many so-called ceremonial objects are nothing but simply overgrown objects of use, which preciousness of material and amount of labour expended have transformed into reservoirs of condensed economic value. Again, others are used on festive occasions, but play no part whatever in rites and ceremonies, and serve for decoration only, and these might be called *objects of parade* (compare Chap VI, Div. I). Finally, a number of these articles function actually as instruments of a magical or religious rite, and belong to the intrinsic apparatus of a ceremony. Such and such only could be correctly called *ceremonial*. During the *So'i* feasts among the Southern Massim, women carrying polished axe blades in fine carved handles, accompany with a rhythmic step to the beat of drums, the entry of the pigs and mango saplings into the village. . . . As this is part of the ceremony and the axes are an indispensable accessory, their use in this case can be legitimately called "ceremonial." Again, in certain magical ceremonies in the Trobriands, the *towosi* (garden magician) has to carry a mounted axe blade on his shoulders, and with it he delivers a ritual blow at a *kamkokola* structure. . . .

The *vaygu'a*—the Kula valuables—in one of their aspects are overgrown objects of use. They are also, however, *ceremonial* objects in the narrow and correct sense of the word. This will become clear after perusal of the following pages, and to this point we shall return in the last chapter.

It must be kept in mind that here we are trying to obtain a clear and vivid idea of what the Kula valuables are to the natives, and not to give a detailed and circumstantial description of them, nor to define them with precision. The comparison with the European heirlooms or Crown Jewels was given in order to show that this type of ownership is not entirely a fantastic South Sea custom, untranslatable into our ideas. For—and this is a point I want to stress—the comparison I have made is not based on purely external, superficial similarity. The psychological and sociological forces at work are the same, it is really the same mental attitude which makes us value our heirlooms, and makes the natives in New Guinea value their *vaygu'a*.

IV

The exchange of these two classes of *vaygu'a*, of the arm-shells and the necklaces, constitutes the main act of the Kula. This exchange is not done freely, right and left, as opportunity offers, and where the whim leads. It is subject indeed to strict limitations and regulations. One of these refers to the sociology of the exchange, and entails that Kula transactions can be done only between partners. A man who is in the Kula—for not everyone within its district is entitled to carry it on—has only a limited number of people with whom he deals. This partnership is entered upon in a definite manner, under fulfillment of certain formalities, and it constitutes a life-long relationship. The number of partners a man has varies with his rank and importance. A commoner in the Trobriands would have a few partners only, whereas a chief would number hundreds of them. There is no special social mechanism to limit the partnership of some people and extend that of the others, but a man would naturally know to what number of partners he was entitled by his rank and position. And there would be always the example of his immediate ancestors to guide him. In other tribes, where the distinction of rank is not so pronounced, an old man of standing, or a headman of a hamlet or village would also have hundreds of Kula associates, whereas a man of minor importance would have but few.

Two Kula partners have to *kula* with one another, and exchange other gifts incidentally; they behave as friends, and have a number of mutual duties and obligations, which vary with the distance between their villages and with their reciprocal status. An average man has a few partners near by, as a rule his relations-in-law or his friends, and with these partners, he is generally on very friendly terms. The Kula partnership is one of the special bonds which unite two men into one of the standing relations of mutual exchange of gifts and services so characteristic of these natives. Again, the average man will have one or two chiefs in his or in the neighbouring districts with whom he *kulas*. In such a case, he would be bound to assist and serve them in various ways, and to offer them the pick of his *vaygu'a* when he gets a fresh supply. On the other hand he would expect them to be specially liberal to him.

The overseas partner is, on the other hand, a host, patron and ally in a land of danger and insecurity. Nowadays, though the feeling of danger still persists, and natives never feel safe and comfortable in a strange district, this danger is rather felt as a magical one, and it is more the fear of foreign sorcery that besets them. In olden days, more tangible dangers were apprehended, and the partner was the main guarantee of safety. He also provides with food, gives presents, and his house, though never used to sleep in, is the place in which to foregather while in the village. Thus the Kula partnership provides every man within its ring with a few friends near at hand, and with some friendly allies in the far-away, dangerous, foreign districts. These are the only people with whom he can *kula,* but, of course, amongst all his partners, he is free to choose to which one he will offer which object.

Let us now try to cast a broad glance at the cumulative effects of the rules of partnership. We see that all around the ring of Kula there is a network of relationships, and that naturally the whole forms one interwoven fabric. Men living at hundreds of miles' sailing distance from one another are bound together by direct or intermediate partnership, exchange with each other, know of each other, and on certain occasions meet in a large inter-tribal gathering. . . . Objects given by one, in time reach some very distant indirect partner or other, and not only Kula objects, but various articles of domestic use and minor gifts. It is easy to see that in the long run, not only objects of material culture, but also customs, songs, art motives and general cultural influences travel along the Kula route. It is a vast, inter-tribal net of relationships, a big institution, consisting of thousands of men, — all bound together by one common passion for Kula exchange, and secondarily, by many minor ties and interests.[10]

Returning again to the personal aspect of the Kula, let us take a concrete example, that of *an average man* who lives, let us assume, in the village of Sinaketa, an important Kula centre in the Southern Trobriands. He has a few partners, near and far, but they again fall into categories, those who give him arm-shells, and those who give him necklaces. For it is naturally an invariable rule of the Kula that arm-shells and necklaces are never received from the same man, since they must travel in different directions. If one partner gives the arm-shells, and I return to him a necklace, all future operations have to be of the same type. More than that, the nature of the operation between me, the man of Sinaketa, and my partner, is determined by our relative positions with regard to the points of the compass. Thus I, in Sinaketa, would receive from the North and East only arm-shells; from the South and West, necklaces are given to me. If I have a near partner next door to me, if his abode is North or East of mine, he will always be giving me arm-shells and receiving necklaces from me. If, at a later time, he were to shift his residence within the village, the old relationship would obtain, but if he became a member of another village community on the other side of me the relationship would be reversed. The partners in villages to the North of Sinaketa, in the district of Luba, Kulumata, or Kiriwina all supply me with arm-shells. These I hand over to my partners in the South, and receive from them necklaces. The South in this case means the southern districts of Boyowa, as well as the Amphletts and Dobu.

Thus every man has to obey definite rules as to the geographical direction of his transactions. At any point in the Kula ring, if we imagine him turned towards the centre of the circle, he receives the arm-shells with his left hand, and the

---

[10] Following Spencer's organic analogy, functionalists tended to see societies as collections of interrelated parts that worked together to promote the society's smooth functioning and equilibrium. Malinowski's emphasis on the Kula as a mechanism for establishing ties between people on different islands is apparent in the previous few paragraphs. He characterizes the Kula as a "vast, inter-tribal net of relationships."

necklaces with his right, and then hands them both on. In other words, he constantly passes the arm-shells from left to right, and the necklaces from right to left.

Applying this rule of personal conduct to the whole Kula ring, we can see at once what the aggregate result is. The sum total of exchanges will not result in an aimless shifting of the two classes of article, in a fortuitous come and go of the arm-shells and necklaces. Two continuous streams will constantly flow on, the one of necklaces following the hands of a clock, and the other, composed of the arm-shells, in the opposite direction. We see thus that it is quite correct to speak of the *circular* exchange of the Kula, of a ring or circuit of moving articles (comp. Map V). On this ring, all the villages are placed in a definitely fixed position with regard to one another, so that one is always on either the arm-shell or on the necklace side of the other.

Now we pass to another rule of the Kula, of the greatest importance. As just explained "the arm-shells and shellstrings always travel in their own respective directions on the ring, and they are never, under any circumstances, traded back in the wrong direction. Also, they never stop. It seems almost incredible at first, but it is the fact, nevertheless, that no one ever keeps any of the Kula valuables for any length of time. Indeed, in the whole of the Trobriands there are perhaps only one or two specially fine armshells and shell necklaces permanently owned as heirlooms, and these are set apart as a special class, and are once and for all out of the Kula. 'Ownership,' therefore, in Kula, is quite a special economic relation. A man who is in the Kula never keeps any article for longer than, say, a year or two. Even this exposes him to the reproach of being niggardly, and certain districts have the bad reputation of being 'slow' and 'hard' in the Kula. On the other hand, each man has an enormous number of articles

passing through his hands during his life time, of which he enjoys a temporary possession, and which he keeps in trust for a time. This possession hardly ever makes him use the articles, and he remains under the obligation soon again to hand them on to one of his partners. But the temporary ownership allows him to draw a great deal of renown, to exhibit his article, to tell how he obtained it, and to plan to whom he is going to give it. And all this forms one of the favourite subjects of tribal conversation and gossip, in which the feats and the glory in Kula of chiefs or commoners are constantly discussed and rediscussed."[c] Thus every article moves in one direction only, never comes back, never permanently stops, and takes as a rule some two to ten years to make the round.[11]

This feature of the Kula is perhaps its most remarkable one, since it creates a new type of ownership, and places the two Kula articles in a class of their own. Here we can return to the comparison drawn between the *vaygu'a* (Kiriwinian valuables) and the European heirlooms. This comparison broke down on one point: in the European objects of this class, permanent ownership, lasting association with the hereditary dignity or rank or with a family, is one of its main features.

In this the Kula articles differ from heirlooms, but resemble another type of valued object, that is, trophies, gauges of superiority, sporting cups, objects which are kept for a time only by the winning party, whether a group or an individual. Though held only in trust, only for a period, though never used in any utilitarian way, yet the holders get from them a special type of pleasure by the mere fact of owning them, of being entitled to them. Here again, it is not only a superficial, external resemblance, but very much the same mental attitude, favoured by similar social arrangements. The resemblance goes so far that

---

[11] Malinowski was concerned with differentiating his brand of functionalism from that of A. R. Radcliffe-Brown (see essay 14). Malinowski's theory was derived from his personal experiences in the field and was concerned with behavior within a cultural context, whereas Radcliffe-Brown studied social structure as an abstract representation that he believed existed independent of human beings. One of the most important differences between the two theorists was that Malinowski believed in the importance of individuals within a culture. Here he speaks of the Kula as many individual transactions taking place simultaneously. Radcliffe-Brown, on the other hand, believed that the study of culture as individual human behavior was impossible.

in the Kula there exists also the element of pride in merit, an element which forms the main ingredient in the pleasure felt by a man or group holding a trophy. Success in Kula is ascribed to special, personal power, due mainly to magic, and men are very proud of it. Again, the whole community glories in a specially fine Kula trophy, obtained by one of its members.

All the rules so far enumerated—looking at them from the individual point of view—limit the social range and the direction of the transactions as well as the duration of ownership of the articles. Looking at them from the point of view of their integral effect, they shape the general outline of the Kula, give it the character of the double-closed circuit. Now a few words must be said about the nature of each individual transaction, in so far as its *commercial technicalities* are concerned. Here very definite rules also obtain.

V

The main principle underlying the regulations of actual exchange is that the Kula consists in the bestowing of a ceremonial gift, which has to be repaid by an equivalent counter-gift, after a lapse of time, be it a few hours or even minutes, though sometimes as much as a year or more may elapse between payments.[d] But it can never be exchanged from hand to hand with the equivalence between the two objects discussed, bargained about and computed. The decorum of the Kula transaction is strictly kept, and highly valued. The natives sharply distinguish it from barter, which they practise extensively, of which they have a clear idea, and for which they have a settled term—in Kiriwinian: *gimwali*. Often, when criticising an incorrect, too hasty, or indecorous procedure of Kula, they will say: "He conducts his Kula as if it were *gimwali*."

The second very important principle is that the equivalence of the counter-gift is left to the giver, and cannot be enforced by any kind of coercion. A partner who has received a Kula gift is expected to give back fair and full value, that is, to give as good an arm-shell as the necklace he receives, or vice versa. Again, a very fine article must be replaced by one of equivalent value, and not by several minor ones, though intermediate gifts may be given to mark time before the real repayment takes place.[12]

If the article given as counter-gift is not equivalent, the recipient will be disappointed and angry, but he has no direct means of redress, no means of coercing his partner, or of putting an end to the whole transaction. What then are the forces at work which keep the partners to the terms of the bargain? Here we come up against a very important feature of the native's mental attitude towards wealth and value. The great misconception of attributing to the savage a pure economic nature, might lead us to reason incorrectly thus: "The passion of acquiring, the loathing to lose or give away, is the fundamental and most primitive element in man's attitude to wealth. In primitive man, this primitive characteristic will appear in its simplest and purest form. *Grab and never let go* will be the guiding principle of his life."[e] The fundamental error in this reasoning is that it assumes that "primitive man," as represented by the present-day savage, lives, at least in economic matters, untrammeled by conventions and social restrictions. Quite the reverse is the case. Although, like every human being, the Kula native loves to possess and therefore desires to acquire and dreads to lose, the social code of rules, with regard to give and take by far overrides his natural acquisitive tendency.[13]

This social code, such as we find it among the natives of the Kula is, however, far from weakening the natural desirability of possession; on the

---

[12] Malinowski's Kula description is considered one of the seminal works in the development of economic anthropology and had a major impact on scholars of his day. Mauss, for example, believed the Kula was similar to the potlatch, and he frequently references *Argonauts of the Western Pacific* in *The Gift,* which was published three years after *Argonauts.* The first two principles of the Kula outlined at the start of this section are fundamental elements of prestation adopted and discussed by Mauss in his work (see essay 8).

[13] Structural functionalists such as Radcliffe-Brown trace their intellectual descent directly from Durkheim. Malinowski was a bitter rival of Radcliffe-Brown, but he too was influenced by the French sociologist. In one article Malinowski called so-

contrary, it lays down that to possess is to be great, and that wealth is the indispensable appanage of social rank and attribute of personal virtue. But the important point is that with them to possess is to give—and here the natives differ from us notably. A man who owns a thing is naturally expected to share it, to distribute it, to be its trustee and dispenser. And the higher the rank the greater the obligation. A chief will naturally be expected to give food to any stranger, visitor, even loiterer from another end of the village. He will be expected to share any of the betel-nut or tobacco he has about him. So that a man of rank will have to hide away any surplus of these articles which he wants to preserve for his further use. In the Eastern end of New Guinea a type of large basket, with three layers, manufactured in the Trobriands, was specially popular among people of consequence, because one could hide away one's small treasures in the lower compartments. Thus the main symptom of being powerful is to be wealthy, and of wealth is to be generous. Meanness, indeed, is the most despised vice, and the only thing about which the natives have strong moral views, while generosity is the essence of goodness.

This moral injunction and ensuing habit of generosity, superficially observed and misinterpreted, is responsible for another wide-spread misconception, that of the *primitive communism of savages*. This, quite as much as the diametrically opposed figment of the acquisitive and ruthlessly tenacious native, is definitely erroneous, and this will be seen with sufficient clearness in the following chapters.[14]

Thus the fundamental principle of the natives' moral code in this matter makes a man do his fair share in Kula transaction and the more important he is, the more will he desire to shine by his generosity. *Noblesse oblige*[15] is in reality the social norm regulating their conduct. This does not mean that people are always satisfied, and that there are no squabbles about the transactions, no resentments and even feuds. It is obvious that, however much a man may want to give a good equivalent for the object received, he may not be able to do so. And then, as there is always a keen competition to be the most generous giver, a man who has received less than he gave will not keep his grievance to himself, but will brag about his own generosity and compare it to his partner's meanness; the other resents it, and the quarrel is ready to break out. But it is very important to realise that there is no actual haggling, no tendency to do a man out of his share. The giver is quite as keen as the receiver that the gift should be generous, though for different reasons. Then, of course, there is the important consideration that a man who is fair and generous in the Kula will attract a larger stream to himself than a mean one.[16]

The two main principles, namely, first that the Kula is a gift repaid after an interval of time by a counter-gift, and not a bartering; and second, that the equivalent rests with the giver, and cannot be enforced, nor can there be any haggling or going back on the exchange—these underlie all the transactions. A concrete outline of how they are carried on, will give a sufficient preliminary idea.

---

cial structure a "vast conditioning apparatus" (Malinowski 1939), and here he says it overrides a person's natural acquisitiveness. In some respects these comments seem to echo Durkheim's definition of a social fact (essay 6), but there are critical differences. Durkheim emphasized the independent nature of the collective conscience, which he believed had an existence apart from any individual and operated by its own laws. Malinowski, on the other hand, believed that culture existed to serve human needs and that, ultimately, these needs were individual physiological and psychological requirements.

[14] Malinowski was writing just a few years after the Russian Revolution, when communist rhetoric was fashionable in Europe and the United States. This comment on primitive communism is a critique of the Marxist five-stage theory of history—Marx had suggested that European society had evolved through stages of primitive communism, ancient slave societies, feudalism, and capitalism. He believed that this evolution would end with the stage of socialism-communism. Many Marxists believed these stages could be found in all societies.

[15] *Noblesse oblige:* benevolent and honorable behavior, originally thought to be an obligation of persons of high rank.

[16] Notice how Malinowski acknowledges the presence of conflict but minimizes its effect. For him, conflict exists but does not drive the system; rather, it is an aberration in what is generally a smoothly functioning organism.

"Let us suppose that I, a Sinaketa man, am in possession of a pair of big arm-shells. An overseas expedition from Dobu in the d'Entrecasteaux Archipelago, arrives at my village. Blowing a conch shell, I take my arm-shell pair and I offer it to my overseas partner, with some words as 'This is a *vaga* (opening gift)—in due time, thou returnest to me a big *soulava* (necklace) for it!' Next year, when I visit my partner's village, he either is in possession of an equivalent necklace, and this he gives to me as *yotile* (return gift), or he has not a necklace good enough to repay my last gift. In this case he will give me a small necklace—avowedly not equivalent to my gift—and he will give it to me as *basi* (intermediary gift). This means that the main gift has to be repaid on a future occasion, and the *basi* is given in token of good faith—but it, in turn, must be repaid by me in the meantime by a gift of small arm-shells. The final gift, which will be given to me to clinch the whole transaction, would then be called *kudu* (clinching gift) in contrast to *basi*" (loc. cit., p. 99).

Although haggling and bargaining are completely ruled out of the Kula, there are customary and regulated ways of bidding for a piece of *vaygu'a* known to be in the possession of one's partner. This is done by the offer of what we shall call solicitary gifts, of which there are several types. "If I, an inhabitant of Sinaketa, happen to be in possession of a pair of arm-shells more than usually good, the fame of it spreads, for it must be remembered that each one of the first-class arm-shells and necklaces has a personal name and a history of its own, and as they circulate around the big ring of the Kula, they are all well known, and their appearance in a given district always creates a sensation. Now, all my partners—whether from overseas or from within the district—compete for the favour of receiving this particular article of mine, and those who are specially keen try to obtain it by giving me *pokala* (offerings) and *kaributu* (solicitary gifts). The former (*pokala*) consist as a rule of pigs, especially fine bananas, and yams or taro; the latter (*kaributu*) are of greater value: the valuable, large axe blades (called *beku*), or lime spoons of whale bone are given" (loc. cit., p. 100). The further complication in the repayment of these solicitary gifts and a few more technicalities and technical expres-sions connected herewith will be given later on in Chapter IV.

VI

I have enumerated the main rules of the Kula in a manner sufficient for a preliminary definition, and now a few words must be said about the associated activities and secondary aspects of the Kula. If we realise that at times the exchange has to take place between districts divided by dangerous seas, over which a great number of people have to travel by sail, and do so keeping to appointed dates, it becomes clear at once that considerable preparations are necessary to carry out the expedition. Many preliminary activities are intimately associated with the Kula. Such are, particularly, the building of canoes, preparation of the outfit, the provisioning of the expedition, the fixing of dates and social organisation of the enterprise. All these are subsidiary to the Kula, and as they are carried on in pursuit of it, and form one connected series, a description of the Kula must embrace an account of these preliminary activities. The detailed account of canoe-building, of the ceremonial attached to it, of the incidental magical rites, of the launching and trial run, of the associated customs which aim at preparing the outfit—all this will be described in detail in the next few chapters.

Another important pursuit inextricably bound up with the Kula, is that of the *secondary trade*. Voyaging to far-off countries, endowed with natural resources unknown in their own homes, the Kula sailors return each time richly laden with these, the spoils of their enterprise. Again, in order to be able to offer presents to his partner, every outward bound canoe carries a cargo of such things as are known to be most desirable in the overseas district. Some of this is given away in presents to the partners, but a good deal is carried in order to pay for the objects desired at home. In certain cases, the visiting natives exploit on their own account during the journey some of the natural resources overseas. For example, the Sinaketans dive for the spondylus in Sanaroa Lagoon, and the Dobuans fish in the Trobriands on a beach on the southern end of the island. The second trade is complicated still more by the fact that such big Kula centres as, for instance, Sinaketa, are not efficient in any of the industries of special value to the Dobuans. Thus, Sinaketans have to procure the necessary store of goods from the inland villages of Kuboma, and this they do on minor trading expeditions preliminary to the Kula. Like the canoe-building, the secondary trading will be described in detail later on, and has only to be mentioned here.[17]

Here, however, these subsidiary and associated activities must be put in proper relation with regard to one another and to the main transaction. Both the canoe-building and the ordinary trade have been spoken of as secondary or subsidiary to the Kula proper. This requires a comment. I do not, by thus subordinating the two things in importance to the Kula mean to express a philosophical reflection or a personal opinion as to the relative value of these pursuits from the point of view of some social teleology. Indeed, it is clear that if we look at the acts from the outside, as comparative sociologists and gauge their real utility, trade and canoe-building will appear to us as the really important achievements, whereas we shall regard the Kula only as an indirect stimulus, impelling the natives to sail and to trade. Here, however, I am not dealing in sociological, but in pure ethnographical description and any sociological analysis I have given is only what has been absolutely indispensable to clear way misconceptions and to define terms.[f18]

By ranging the Kula as the primary and chief activity, and the rest as secondary ones, I mean

that this precedence is implied in the institutions themselves. By studying the behaviour of the natives and all the customs in question, we see that the Kula is in all respects the main aim: the dates are fixed, the preliminaries settled, the expeditions arranged, the social organisation determined, not with regard to trade, but with regard to Kula. On an expedition, the big ceremonial feast, held at the start, refers to the Kula; the final ceremony of reckoning and counting the spoil refers to Kula, not to the objects of trade obtained. Finally, the magic, which is one of the main factors of all the procedure, refers only to the Kula, and this applies even to a part of the magic carried out over the canoe. Some rites in the whole cycle are done for the sake of the canoe itself, and others for the sake of Kula. The construction of the canoes is always carried on directly in connection with a Kula expedition. All this, of course, will become really clear and convincing only after the detailed account is given. But it was necessary at this point to set the right perspective in the relation between the main Kula and the trade.

Of course not only many of the surrounding tribes who know nothing of the Kula do build canoes and sail far and daringly on trading expeditions, but even within the Kula ring, in the Trobriands for instance, there are several villages who do not *kula,* yet have canoes and carry on energetic overseas trade. But where the Kula is practiced, it governs all the other allied activities, and canoe-building and trade are made subsidiary to it. And this is expressed both by the nature of

---

[17] Later theorists were critical of Malinowski's comments on the nature of primitive economies. Malinowski insisted that the Kula was a rational system directed toward nonrational ends, that is, the exchange of items with only symbolic value. Because of this he gives little weight to the fact that the offerings given to induce a partner to part with good *vaygu'a* are utilitarian items such as pigs, bananas, yams, and axe blades. Although this secondary trade is repeatedly mentioned, Malinowski does not analyze it to see if participants gain an economic benefit. Critics suggest that in insisting that his perspective on the Kula is the right one, Malinowski ignores the data that disprove his theory.

[18] Malinowski's footnote is important because it is directed at the diffusionists and the Boasians whose ideas were popular at this time. Participant observation and the integration of culture were central aspects of the work of Franz Boas (see essay 10), and Malinowski's work consistently incorporates these ideas. However, Boas and Malinowski disagreed on the importance of history. Boas believed that the current state of a culture could only be understood through the study of its history. Malinowski vehemently disagreed. In this note, Malinowski says that reconstructing history is an "unpardonable sin" and that he is unconcerned with searching for origins of institutions, preferring to spend his time working out the interrelations of elements within a society. Similarly, Malinowski dismissed popular diffusionists such as W. H. R. Rivers and Grafton Elliot Smith (1871–1937), who were trying to prove that all culture began in ancient Egypt and diffused from there.

the institutions and the working of all the arrangements on the one hand, and by the behaviour and explicit statements of the natives on the other.

The Kula—it becomes, I hope, more and more clear—is a big, complicated institution, insignificant though its nucleus might appear. To the natives, it represents one of the most vital interests in life, and as such it has a ceremonial character and is surrounded by magic. We can well imagine that articles of wealth might pass from hand to hand without ceremony or ritual, but in the Kula they never do. Even when at times only small parties in one or two canoes sail overseas and bring back *vaygu'a,* certain taboos are observed, and a customary course is taken in departing, in sailing, and in arriving; even the smallest expedition in one canoe is a tribal event of some importance, known and spoken of over the whole district. But the characteristic expedition is one in which a considerable number of canoes take part, organised in a certain manner, and forming one body. Feasts, distributions of food and other public ceremonies are held, there is one leader and master of the expedition, and various rules are adhered to, in addition to the ordinary Kula taboos and observances.

The ceremonial nature of the Kula is strictly bound up with another of its aspects—magic. "The belief in the efficiency of magic dominates the Kula, as it does ever so many other tribal activities of the natives. Magical rites must be performed over the sea-going canoe when it is built, in order to make it swift, steady and safe; also magic is done over a canoe to make it lucky in the Kula. Another system of magical rites is done in order to avert the dangers of sailing. The third system of magic connected with overseas expeditions is the *mwasila* or the Kula magic proper. This system consists in numerous rites and spells, all of which act directly on the mind (*nanola*) of one's

partner, and make him soft, unsteady in mind, and eager to give Kula gifts" (loc. cit., p. 100).[19]

It is clear that an institution so closely associated with magical and ceremonial elements, as is the Kula, not only rests on a firm, traditional foundation, but also has its large store of legend. "There is a rich mythology of the Kula in which stories are told about far-off times when mythical ancestors sailed on distant and daring expeditions. Owing to their magical knowledge they were able to escape dangers to conquer their enemies, to surmount obstacles, and by their feats they established many a precedent which is now closely followed by tribal custom. But their importance for their descendants lies mainly in the fact that they handed on their magic, and this made the Kula possible for the following generations" (loc. cit., p. 100).

The Kula is also associated in certain districts, to which the Trobriands do not belong, with the mortuary feasts called *so'i.* The association is interesting and important and in Chapter XX an account of it will be given.

The big Kula expeditions are carried on by a great number of natives, a whole district together. But the geographical limits, from which the members of an expedition are recruited, are well defined. Glancing at Map V, "we see a number of circles, each of which represents a certain sociological unit which we shall call a Kula community. A Kula community consists of a village or a number of villages, who go out together on big overseas expeditions, and who act as a body in the Kula transactions, perform their magic in common, have common leaders, and have the same outer and inner social sphere, within which they exchange their valuables. The Kula consists, therefore, first of the small, internal transactions within a Kula community or contiguous communities, and secondly, of the big overseas expeditions in which the exchange of articles takes place

---

[19] Magic plays an important role in Trobriand Island society, and Malinowski discusses the subject in other chapters of *Argonauts* and in his later works *Magic, Science, and Religion* (1954 [1925]) and *Coral Gardens and Their Magic* (1935). Malinowski was reacting against the theory of one of his mentors, Sir James Frazer. Frazer, a popular theorist of anthropology and religion, argued that people in primitive societies had magical beliefs and other superstitions because they had some form of primitive mentality and were incapable of scientific thought. Concerned with presenting people in simple societies as rational, Malinowski was careful to distinguish the contexts in which magic was used. He argued that the Trobrianders were just as intelligent as anyone else and used magic in circumstances that were beyond rational control. Thus, magic had a psychological function: to reassure individuals in unpredictable situations.

between two communities divided by the sea. In the first, there is a chronic, permanent trickling of articles from one village to another, and even within the village. In the second, a whole lot of valuables, amounting to over a thousand articles at a time, are exchanged in one enormous transaction, or, more correctly, in ever so many transactions taking place simultaneously" (loc. cit., p. 101).[20] "The Kula trade consists of a series of such periodical overseas expeditions, which link together the various island groups, and annually bring over big quantities of *vaygu'a* and of subsidiary trade from one district to another. The trade is used and used up, but the *vaygu'a* — the arm-shells and necklets — go round and round the ring" (loc. cit., p. 105).

In this chapter, a short, summary definition of the Kula has been given. I enumerated one after the other its most salient features, the most remarkable rules as they are laid down in native custom, belief and behaviour. This was necessary in order to give a general idea of the institution before describing its working in detail. But no abridged definition can give to the reader the full understanding of a human social institution. It is necessary for this, to explain its working concretely, to bring the reader into contact with the people, show how they proceed at each successive stage, and to describe all the actual manifestations of the general rules laid down in abstract.

As has been said above, the Kula exchange is carried on by enterprises of two sorts; first there are the big overseas expeditions, in which a more or less considerable amount of valuables are carried at one time. Then there is the inland trade in which the articles are passed from hand to hand, often changing several owners before they move a few miles.

The big overseas expeditions are by far the more spectacular part of the Kula. They also contain much more public ceremonial, magical ritual, and customary usage. They require also, of course, more of preparation and preliminary activity. I shall therefore have a good deal more to say about the overseas Kula expeditions than about the internal exchange.

As the Kula customs and beliefs have been mainly studied in Boyowa, that is, the Trobriand Islands, and from the Boyowan point of view, I shall describe, in the first place, the typical course of an overseas expedition, as it is prepared, organized, and carried out from the Trobriands. Beginning with the construction of the canoes, proceeding to the ceremonial launching and the visits of formal presentation of canoes, we shall choose then the community of Sinaketa, and follow the natives on one of their overseas trips, describing it in all details. This will serve us as a type of a Kula expedition to distant lands. It will then be indicated in what particulars such expeditions may differ in other branches of the Kula, and for this purpose I shall describe an expedition from Dobu, and one between Kiriwina and Kitava. An account of inland Kula in the Trobriands, of some associated forms of trading and of Kula in the remaining branches will complete the account.

In the next chapter I pass, therefore, to the preliminary stages of the Kula, in the Trobriands, beginning with a description of the canoes.

Notes

a. By "current view," I mean such as is to be found in textbooks and in passing remarks, scattered through economic and ethnological literature. As a matter of fact, Economics is a subject very seldom touched upon either in theoretical works or Ethnology, or in accounts of field-work. I have enlarged on this deficiency in the article on "Primitive Economics," published in the *Economic Journal*, March, 1921.

The best analysis of the problem of savage economy is to be found, in spite of its many shortcomings, in K. Bücher's "Industrial Evolution," English translation, 1901. On primitive trade, however, his views are inadequate. In accordance with his general view that savages have no national economy, he maintains that any spread of goods among natives is achieved by non-economic means, such as robbery, tributes and gifts. The information contained in the present volume is incompatible with Bücher's views, nor could he have maintained them had he been

---

[20] The above paragraphs demonstrate Malinowski's belief that culture was a system of interrelated parts. One cannot study the Kula alone, because it is interconnected with other aspects of Trobriand life such as canoe-building, magic, and family structure. Spencer's organic analogy can be seen behind Malinowski's model of the Kula. The Kula is a system in a physical sense; it can be diagrammed like the circulatory system of the body.

acquainted with Barton's description of the Hiri (contained in Seligman's "Melanesians").

A summary of the research done on Primitive Economics, showing, incidentally, how little real, sound work has been accomplished, will be found in Pater W. Kopper's "Die Ethnologische Wirtschaftsforschung" in *Anthropos*, X–XI, 1915–16, pp. 611–651, and 971–1079. The article is very useful, where the author summarises the views of others.

b. Professor C. G. Seligman, op. cit., p. 93, states that arm-shells, *toea*, as they are called by the Motu, are traded from the Port Moresby district westward to the Gulf of Papua. Among the Motu and Koita, near Port Moresby, they are highly valued, and nowadays attain very high prices, up to £30, much more than is paid for the same article among the Massim.

c. This and the following quotations are from the Author's preliminary article on the Kula in *Man*, July, 1920. Article number 51, p. 100.

d. In order not to be guilty of inconsistency in using loosely the word "ceremonial" I shall define it briefly. I shall call an action ceremonial, if it is (1) public; (2) carried on under observance of definite formalities; (3) if it has sociological, religious, or magical import, and it carries with it obligations.

e. This is not a fanciful construction of what an erroneous opinion might be, for I could give actual examples proving that such opinions have been set forth, but as I am not giving here a criticism of existing theories of Primitive Economics, I do not want to overload this chapter with quotations.

f. It is hardly necessary perhaps to make it quite clear that all questions of origins of development or history of the institutions have been rigorously ruled out of this work. The mixing up of speculative or hypothetical views with an account of facts is, in my opinion an unpardonable sin against ethnographic method.

14. The Mother's Brother in South Africa[a]

A. R. Radcliffe-Brown (1881–1955)

AMONGST PRIMITIVE PEOPLES IN MANY PARTS of the world a good deal of importance is attached to the relationship of mother's brother and sister's son.[1] In some instances, the sister's son has certain special rights over the property of his mother's brother. At one time it was usual to regard these customs as being connected with matriarchal institutions, and it was held that their presence in a patrilineal people could be regarded as evidence

(1924)

that that people had at some time in the past been matrilineal.[2] This view is still held by a few anthropologists and has been adopted by Mr. Junod in his book on the BaThonga people of Portuguese East Africa. Referring to the customs relating to the behavior of the mother's brother and the sister's son to one another, he says: "Now, having enquired with special care into this most curious feature of the Thonga system, I come to the conclusion that the only possible explanation is that, in former and very remote times, our tribe has passed through the matriarchal stage."

---

[1] This essay is one of Radcliffe-Brown's earliest statements of functionalism and has several features of his later work. It tries to treat anthropological investigations as scientific and to show general laws of social organization.

[2] The idea that some social customs were survivals of an early matrilineal and matriarchal stage of society was a common part of nineteenth-century evolutionism. Morgan (see essay 3) proposed an evolutionary scheme for the family that began with the matrilineal clan and proceeded to the nuclear family. Johann Jakob Bachofen argued that societies moved from concubinage ("hetairism") to matriarchy and then to patriarchy. Bachofen's and Morgan's ideas on the evolution of the family have been rejected by modern anthropology but remain part of popular culture, appearing in the work of a few feminist writers and in Robert Graves' (1895–1985) influential *The White Goddess* (1948).

(Junod, *The Life of a South African Tribe*, 1913, Vol. I, p. 253.)[3]

It is with this theory that I wish to deal in this paper; but I do not propose to repeat or add to the objections that have been raised against it by various critics in recent years. Purely negative criticism does not advance a science. The only satisfactory way of getting rid of an unsatisfactory hypothesis is to find a better one. I propose, therefore, to put before you an alternative hypothesis, and if I am successful, not in proving my hypothesis, but in showing that it does give a possible explanation of the facts, I shall at least have refuted the view of Mr. Junod that the explanation he accepts is the "only possible" one.

For many African tribes we have almost no information about customs of this kind. Not that the customs do not exist, or are not important to the natives themselves, but because the systematic and scientific study of the natives of this country has as yet hardly begun. I shall, therefore, have to refer chiefly to the customs of the BaThonga as recorded by Mr. Junod. These are to be found in the first volume of the work quoted above (pp. 225 *et seq.*, and pp. 253 *et seq.*). Some of the more important of them may be summarized as follows:

1. The uterine nephew[4] all through his career is the object of special care on the part of his uncle.
2. When the nephew is sick the mother's brother sacrifices on his behalf.
3. The nephew is permitted to take many liberties with his mother's brother; for example, he may go to his uncle's home and eat up the food that has been prepared for the latter's meal.
4. The nephew claims some of the property of his mother's brother when the latter dies, and may sometimes claim one of the widows.
5. When the mother's brother offers a sacrifice to his ancestors the sister's son steals and consumes the portion of meat or beer offered to the gods.

It must not be supposed that these customs are peculiar to the BaThonga.[5] There is evidence that similar customs may be found amongst other African tribes, and we know of the existence of similar customs amongst other peoples in various parts of the world. In South Africa itself customs of this kind have been found by Mrs. Hoernle[6] amongst the Nama Hottentots. The sister's son may behave with great freedom towards his mother's brother, and may take any particularly fine beast from his herd of cattle, or any particularly fine object that he may possess. On the contrary, the mother's brother may take from his nephew's herd any beast that is deformed or decrepit, and may take any old and worn-out object he may possess.

What is particularly interesting to me is that in the part of Polynesia that I know best, that is, in the Friendly Islands (Tonga) and in Fiji, we find customs that show a very close resemblance

---

[3] Henri Junod (1863–1934) was a missionary who lived among the BaThonga and wrote a detailed description of them that relied on historical reconstruction to explain BaThonga kinship behavior. Radcliffe-Brown proposes to offer an explanation that does not rely on history. British functionalist thinkers believed that it was impossible to accurately reconstruct the history of preliterate societies and so restricted their analysis to the structure of current societies.

[4] A uterine nephew is a sister's son.

[5] At the time he wrote this essay, Radcliffe-Brown lived in South Africa. Much of his life was spent as an academic nomad. He worked in South Africa, Australia, the United States (where he held a chair at the University of Chicago), and several other nations.

[6] Agnes Winnifred Hoernle (1885–1960) was a South African anthropologist who trained at Cambridge with Haddon and Rivers and studied with Durkheim at the Sorbonne. She was a close friend of Radcliffe-Brown during his tenure at the University of Cape Town (1921–1926) and became a powerful spokesperson for his ideas. Her students included Max Gluckman (1911–1975) and Hilda Kuper (1911–1992). Beginning in 1912, she conducted extensive fieldwork among the Nama. Radcliffe-Brown is most likely referencing a draft of her article "The Social Organization of the Nama Hottentots of Southwest Africa" (1925) published the year after his essay.

to those of the BaThonga.[7] There, also, the sister's son is permitted to take many liberties with his mother's brother, and to take any of his uncle's possessions that he may desire. And there also we find the custom that, when the uncle makes a sacrifice, the sister's son takes away the portion offered to the gods, and may eat it. I shall, therefore, make occasional references to the Tongan customs in the course of this paper.

These three peoples, the BaThonga, the Nama, and the Tongans, have patrilineal or patriarchal institutions; that is, the children belong to the social group of the father, not to that of the mother; and property is inherited in the male line, passing normally from a father to his son. The view that I am opposing is that the customs relating to the mother's brother can only be explained by supposing that, at some past time, these peoples had matrilineal institutions, such as are found today amongst other primitive peoples, with whom the children belong to the social group of the mother, and property is inherited in the female line, passing from a man to his brother and to his sister's sons.

It is a mistake to suppose that we can understand the institutions of society by studying them in isolation without regard to other institutions with which they coexist and with which they may be correlated, and I wish to call attention to a correlation that seems to exist between customs relating to the mother's brother and customs relating to the father's sister.[8] So far as present information goes, where we find the mother's brother important we also find that the father's sister is equally important, though in a different way. The custom of allowing the sister's son to take liberties with his mother's brother seems to be generally accompanied with an obligation of particular respect and obedience to the father's sister. Mr. Junod says little about the father's sister amongst the BaThonga.

Speaking of a man's behavior to this relative (his *rarana*) he says simply: "He shows her great respect. However, she is not in any way a mother (*mamana*)" (op. cit., p. 223). About the Nama Hottentots we have better information, and there the father's sister is the object of the very greatest respect on the part of her brother's child. In Tonga this custom is very clearly defined. A man's father's sister is the one relative above all others whom he must respect and obey. If she selects a wife for him he must marry her without even venturing to demur or to voice any objection; and so throughout his life. His father's sister is sacred to him; her word is his law; and one of the greatest offenses of which he could be guilty would be to show himself lacking in respect to her.

Now this correlation (which is not confined, of course, to the three instances I have mentioned, but seems, as I have said, to be general) must be taken into account in any explanation of the customs relating to the mother's brother, for the correlated customs are, if I am right, not independent institutions, but part of one system; and no explanation of one part of the system is satisfactory unless it fits in with an analysis of the system as a whole.

In most primitive societies the social relations of individuals are very largely regulated on the basis of kinship. This is brought about by the formation of fixed and more or less definite patterns of behavior for each of the recognized kinds of relationship. There is a special pattern of behavior, for example, for a son towards his father, and another for a younger brother towards his elder brother. The particular patterns vary from one society to another; but there are certain fundamental principles or tendencies which appear in all societies, or in all those of a certain type. It is these general tendencies that it is the special task of social anthropology to discover and explain.[9]

---

[7] During World War I, Radcliffe-Brown was the director for education on Tonga, then a British colony. Earlier, he had done fieldwork on the Andaman Islands in the Sea of Bengal (between India and Malaysia).

[8] Radcliffe-Brown used the organic analogy developed by Spencer (see essay 1). He understood a society as composed of many interrelated, smoothly functioning parts and insisted that aspects of society could not be studied in isolation. Consistent with this analogy, he viewed the proper function of social institutions as the smooth maintenance of society. As with an organism, when society is healthy, everything functions well together.

[9] Unlike the Boasians, functionalists like Radcliffe-Brown were concerned with the discovery of scientific laws that would be valid for all societies.

Once we start tracing out relationship to any considerable distance the number of different kinds of relatives that it is logically possible to distinguish is very large.[10] This difficulty is avoided in primitive society by a system of classification, by which relatives of what might logically be held to be of different kinds are classified into a limited number of kinds. The principle of classification that is most commonly adopted in primitive society may be stated as that of the equivalence of brothers. In other words if I stand in a particular relation to one man I regard myself as standing in the same general kind of relation to his brother; and similarly with a woman and her sister. In this way the father's brother comes to be regarded as a sort of father, and his sons are, therefore, relatives of the same kind as brothers. Similarly, the mother's sister is regarded as another mother, and her children are therefore brothers and sisters. The system is the one to be found amongst the Bantu tribes of South Africa, and amongst the Nama Hottentots, and also in the Friendly Islands. By means of this principle primitive societies are able to arrive at definite patterns of behavior towards uncles and aunts and cousins of certain kinds. A man's behavior towards his father's brother must be of the same general kind as his behavior towards his own father and he must behave to his mother's sister according to the same pattern as towards his mother. The children of his father's brother or of the mother's sister must be treated in very much the same way as brothers and sisters.[11]

This principle, however, does not give us immediately any pattern for either the mother's brother or the father's sister. It would be possible, of course, to treat the former as being like a father and the latter as similar to a mother, and this course does seem to have been adopted in a few societies. A tendency in this direction is found in some parts of Africa and in some parts of Polynesia. But it is characteristic of societies in which the classificatory system of kinship is either not fully developed or has been partly effaced.[12]

Where the classificatory system of kinship reaches a high degree of development or elaboration another tendency makes its appearance: the tendency to develop patterns for the mother's brother and the father's sister by regarding the former as a sort of male mother and the latter as a sort of female father. This tendency sometimes makes its appearance in language. Thus, in South Africa the common term for the mother's brother is *malume* or *umalume*, which is a compound formed from the stem for "mother"—*ma*—and a suffix meaning "male." Amongst the BaThonga the father's sister is called *rarana*, a term which Mr. Junod explains as meaning "female father." In some South African languages there is no special term for the father's sister; thus in Xosa, she is denoted by a descriptive term *udade bo bawo*, literally "father's sister." In Zulu she may be referred to by a similar descriptive term or she may be spoken of simply as *ubaba*, "father," just like the father's brothers. In the Friendly Islands the mother's brother may be denoted by a special term *tuasina*, or he may be called *fa'e tangata*, literally "male mother."[13] This similarity between South Africa and Polynesia cannot, I think, be regarded as accidental; yet there is no possible connection between the Polynesian languages and the Bantu languages, and I find it very difficult to conceive that

---

[10] Radcliffe-Brown was profoundly influenced by his reading of Durkheim. In this passage, he relies on some of the insights of Durkheim and Mauss' work on classification (see essays 6–8).

[11] Notice Radcliffe-Brown's use of the idea of logic in this passage. For the functionalists, social systems were eminently rational, logical, and explicable.

[12] In mentioning systems not fully developed or partly effaced, Radcliffe-Brown reflects a view that kinship systems come in ideal types, though societies may, for various reasons, deviate from them.

[13] In relying here on native terms, Radcliffe-Brown is using the same type of data Morgan and Junod used to suggest an earlier matrilineal phase for these societies. However, Radcliffe-Brown is using it to suggest a cross-cultural law of social relationships.

the two regions have adopted the custom of calling the mother's brother by a term meaning "male mother" either from one another or from one common source.[14]

Now let us see if we can deduce what ought to be the patterns of behavior towards the mother's brother and the father's sister in a patrilineal society on the basis of the principle or tendency which I have suggested is present.[15] To do this we must first know the patterns for the father and the mother respectively, and I think that it will, perhaps, be more reassuring if I go for the definition of these to Mr. Junod's work, as his observations will certainly not have been influenced by the hypothesis that I am trying to prove.[16]

The relationship of father, he says, "implies respect and even fear. The father, though he does not take much trouble with his children, is, however, their instructor, the one who scolds and punishes. So do also the father's brothers" (op. cit., p. 222). Of a man's own mother he says: "She is his true *mamana,* and this relation is very deep and tender, combining respect with love. Love, however, generally exceeds respect" (op. cit., p. 224). Of the mother's relation to her children we read that "She is generally weak with them and is often accused by the father of spoiling them."

There is some danger in condensed formulæ, but I think we shall not be far wrong in saying that in a strongly patriarchal society, such as we find in South Africa, the father is the one who must be respected and obeyed, and the mother is the one from whom may be expected tenderness and indulgence. I could show you, if it were necessary, that the same thing is true of the family life of the Friendly Islanders.

If, now, we apply the principle that I have suggested is at work in these peoples it will follow that the father's sister is one who must be obeyed and treated with respect, while from the mother's brother indulgence and care may be looked for. But the matter is complicated by another factor. If we consider the relation of a nephew to his uncle and aunt, the question of sex comes in. In primitive societies there is a marked difference in the behavior of a man towards other men and that towards women. Risking once more a formula, we may say that any considerable degree of familiarity is generally only permitted in such a society as the BaThonga between persons of the same sex. A man must treat his female relatives with greater respect than his male relatives. Consequently the nephew must treat his father's sister with even greater respect than he does his own father. (In just the same way, owing to the principle of respect for age or seniority, a man must treat his father's elder brother with more respect than his own father.) Inversely, a man may treat his mother's brother, who is of his own sex, with a degree of familiarity that would not be possible with any woman, even his own mother. The influence of sex on the behavior of kindred is best seen in the relations of brother and sister. In the Friendly Islands and amongst the Nama a man must pay great respect to his sister, particularly his eldest sister, and may never indulge in any familiarities with her. The same thing is true, I believe, of the South African Bantu. In many primitive societies the father's sister and the elder sisters are the objects of the same general kind of behavior, and in some of these the two kinds of relatives are classified together and denoted by the same name.[17]

---

[14] Notice that diffusionism is mentioned here but given little attention or importance. While extreme diffusionists such as Elliot Smith and Rivers (one of Radcliffe-Brown's teachers) were very active at this time, Radcliffe-Brown had no interest in their theories. Like the evolutionists, diffusionists were vitally concerned with historical relations between societies. Radcliffe-Brown was not.

[15] Radcliffe-Brown was guided in part by his teacher Rivers. Rivers, a medical doctor who had joined the 1898 Torres Straits expedition, devised what he called the "genealogical method," suggesting that a truly scientific anthropology could be achieved through the systematic study of kinship (Rivers 1910). Though his reputation was diminished by his association with Elliot Smith and diffusionism, he played a critically important role in early British social anthropology.

[16] Note the use of "hypothesis" and "prove" and "formula." Radcliffe-Brown is writing in a scientific idiom, using the language of science to lay claim to the accuracy and precision associated with the hard sciences.

[17] Radcliffe-Brown's work, like most anthropology until the recent past, is written entirely from a male perspective. This passage is a good example. We hear nothing about relations between nieces and others. Males are the focus of attention,

We have deduced from our assumed principle a certain pattern of behavior for the father's sister and for the mother's brother. Now these patterns are exactly what we find amongst the BaThonga, amongst the Hottentots, and in the Friendly Islands.[18] The father's sister is above all relatives the one to be respected and obeyed. The mother's brother is the one relative above all from whom we may expect indulgence, with whom we may be familiar and take liberties. Here, then, is an alternative "possible explanation" of the customs relating to the mother's brother, and it has this advantage over Mr. Junod's theory that it also explains the correlated customs relating to the father's sister. This brings us, however, not to the end but to the beginning of our enquiry. It is easy enough to invent hypotheses. The important and difficult work begins when we set out to verify them. It will be impossible for me, in the short time available, to make any attempt to verify the hypothesis I have put before you. All I can do is to point out certain lines of study which will, I believe, provide that verification.

The first and most obvious thing to do is to study in detail the behavior of the sister's son and the mother's brother to one another in matriarchal societies. Unfortunately, there is practically no information on this subject relating to Africa, and very little for any other part of the world. Moreover, there are certain false ideas connected with this distinction of societies into matriarchal and patriarchal that it is necessary to remove before we attempt to go further.

In all societies, primitive or advanced, kinship is necessarily bilateral. The individual is related to certain persons through his father and to others through his mother, and the kinship system of the society lays down what shall be the character of his dealings with his paternal relatives and his maternal relatives respectively. But society tends to divide into segments (local groups, lineages,

clans, etc.), and when the hereditary principle is accepted, as it most frequently is, as the means of determining the membership of a segment, then it is necessary to choose between maternal or paternal descent. When a society is divided into groups with a rule that the children belong to the group of the father we have patrilineal descent, while if the children always belong to the group of the mother the descent is matrilineal.

There is, unfortunately, a great deal of looseness in the use of the terms matriarchal and patriarchal, and for that reason many anthropologists refuse to use them. If we are to use them at all, we must first give exact definitions. A society may be called patriarchal when descent is patrilineal (i.e. the children belong to the group of the father), marriage is patrilocal (i.e. the wife removes to the local group of the husband), inheritance (of property) and succession (to rank) are in the male line, and the family is patripotestal (i.e. the authority over the members of the family is in the hands of the father or his relatives). On the other hand, a society can be called matriarchal when descent, inheritance and succession are in the female line, marriage is matrilocal (the husband removing to the home of his wife), and when the authority over the children is wielded by the mother's relatives.

If this definition of these opposing terms is accepted, it is at once obvious that a great number of primitive societies are neither matriarchal nor patriarchal, though some may incline more to the one side, and others more to the other. Thus, if we examine the tribes of Eastern Australia, which are sometimes spoken of as matriarchal, we find that marriage is patrilocal, so that membership of the local group is inherited in the male line, the authority over the children is chiefly in the hands of the father and his brothers, property (what there is of it) is mostly inherited in the male line, while, as rank is not recognized, there is no question of

---

the actors; females are passive, "the objects of . . . behavior." How does a woman behave toward her mother's brother? Radcliffe-Brown does not raise the issue, let alone answer it. The male perspective was largely unchallenged in anthropology until the 1970s.

[18] Radcliffe-Brown speaks here in scientific language but then announces that he will rely on anecdotal evidence. He makes claims such as "I think I could show you quite conclusively" but declines to offer the proof to which he alludes. The critics of British functionalism claimed that while functionalism had scientific pretenses and used scientific language, in actuality it produced very little data or theory that was scientifically valid.

succession. The only matrilineal institution is the descent of the totemic group, which is through the mother, so that these tribes, so far from being matriarchal, incline rather to the patriarchal side. Kinship amongst them is thoroughly bilateral, but for most purposes kinship through the father is of more importance than kinship through the mother. There is some evidence, for example, that the obligation to avenge a death falls upon the relatives in the male line rather than upon those in the female line.

We find an interesting instance of this bilateralism, if it may be so called, in South Africa, in the OvaHerero tribe. The facts are not quite certain, but it would seem that this tribe is subdivided into two sets of segments crossing one another. For one set (the *omaanda*) descent is matrilineal, while for the other (*otuzo*) it is patrilineal. A child belongs to the *eanda* of its mother and inherits cattle from its mother's brothers, but belongs to the *oruzo* of its father and inherits his ancestral spirits. Authority over the children would seem to be in the hands of the father and his brothers and sisters.

It is now clear, I hope, that the distinction between matriarchal and patriarchal societies is not an absolute but a relative one. Even in the most strongly patriarchal society some social importance is attached to kinship through the mother; and similarly in the most strongly matriarchal society the father and his kindred are always of some importance in the life of the individual.

In Africa we have in the south-east a group of tribes that incline strongly to patriarchy, so much so, in fact, that we may perhaps justifiably speak of them as patriarchal. Descent of the social group, inheritance of property, succession to chieftainship, are all in the male line; marriage is patrilocal, and authority in the family is strongly patripotestal. In the north of Africa, in Kenya and the surrounding countries, there is another group of strongly patriarchal peoples, some of them Bantu-speaking, while others are Nilotic or Hamitic. Between these two patriarchal regions there is a band of peoples stretching apparently right across Africa from east to west, on the level of Nyasaland and Northern Rhodesia, in which the tendency is towards matriarchal institutions. Descent of the social group, inheritance of property, and succession to the kingship or chieftainship are in the female line. In some of the tribes marriage seems to be matrilocal, at any rate temporarily if not permanently, i.e. a man on marriage has to go and live with his wife's people.

It is about these people and their customs that we urgently need information if we are to understand such matters as the subject of this paper. Of one tribe of this region we have a fairly full description in the work of Smith and Dale (*The Ila-speaking People of Northern Rhodesia*, 1920). Unfortunately, on the very points with which I am now dealing the information is scanty and certainly very incomplete. There are, however, two points I wish to bring out. The first concerns the behavior of the mother's brother to his sister's son. We are told that "the mother's brother is a personage of vast importance; having the power even of life and death over his nephews and nieces, which no other relations, not even the parents, have; he is to be held in honor even above the father. This is *avunculi potestas*, which among the Balla is greater than *patria potestas*.[19] In speaking of the mother's brother, it is customary to use an honorific title given to people who are respected very highly" (op. cit., Vol. I, p. 230). This kind of relation between the mother's brother and the sister's son is obviously what we might expect in a strongly matriarchal society. But how then, on Mr. Junod's theory, can we explain the change which must have taken place from this sort of relation to that which now exists among the BaThonga?[20]

This brings me to another point which it will not be possible to discuss in detail but which has an important bearing on the argument. We have been considering the relation of the sister's son to his mother's brother; but if we are to reach a really final explanation, we must study also the behavior of a man to his other relatives on the

---

[19] *Avunculi potestas:* Latin for uncle's power. *Patria potestas:* Latin for father's power.

[20] Thus, Radcliffe-Brown asks: if we follow Junod's theory that the BaThonga were matriarchal in the past, how did relations between mother's brother and sister's son change from extreme respect to extreme familiarity?

mother's side, and to his mother's group as a whole. Now in the Friendly Islands the peculiar relation between a sister's son and a mother's brother exists also between a daughter's son and his mother's father. The daughter's son must be honoured by his grandfather. He is "a chief" to him. He may take his grandfather's property, and he may take away the offering that his grandfather makes to the gods at a kava ceremony. The mother's father and the mother's brother are the objects of very similar behavior patterns, of which the outstanding feature is the indulgence on the one side and the liberty permitted on the other. Now there is evidence of the same thing amongst the BaThonga, but again we lack the full information that we need. Mr. Junod writes that a grandfather "is more lenient to his grandson by his daughter than his grandson by his son" (op. cit., p. 227). In this connection the custom of calling the mother's brother *kokwana* (grandfather) is significant.[21]

Now here is something that it seems impossible to explain on Mr. Junod's theory. In a strongly matriarchal society the mother's father does not belong to the same group as his grandchild and is not a person from whom property can be inherited or who can exercise authority. Any explanation of the liberties permitted towards the mother's brother cannot be satisfactory unless it also explains the similar liberties towards the mother's father which are found in Polynesia, and apparently to some extent in South Africa. This Mr. Junod's theory clearly does not do, and cannot do.[22]

But on the hypothesis that I have put forward the matter is fairly simple. In primitive society there is a strongly marked tendency to merge the individual in the group to which he or she belongs. The result of this in relation to kinship is a tendency to extend to all the members of a group a certain type of behavior which has its origin in a relationship to one particular member of the group. Thus the tendency in the BaThonga tribe would seem to be to extend to all the members of the mother's group (family or lineage) a certain pattern of behavior which is derived from the special pattern that appears in the behavior of a son towards his mother. Since it is from his mother that he expects care and indulgence he looks for the same sort of treatment from the people of his mother's group, i.e. from all his maternal kin. On the other hand it is to his paternal kin that he owes obedience and respect. The patterns that thus arise in relation to the father and the mother are generalized and extended to the kindred on the one side and on the other. If I had time I think I could show you quite conclusively that this is really the principle that governs the relations between an individual and his mother's kindred in the patriarchal tribes of South Africa. I must leave the demonstration, however, to another occasion. I can do no more now than illustrate my statement.

The custom, often miscalled bride-purchase and generally known in South Africa as *lobola,* is, as Mr. Junod has well shown, a payment made in compensation to a girl's family for her loss when she is taken away in marriage. Now, since in the patriarchal tribes of South Africa a woman belongs to her father's people, the compensation has to be paid to them. But you will find that in many of the tribes a certain portion of the "marriage payment" is handed over to the mother's brother of the girl for whom it is paid. Thus, amongst the BaPedi, out of the *lenyalo* cattle one head (called *hloho*) is handed to the mother's brother of the girl. Amongst the BaSotho a portion of the cattle received for a girl on her marriage may

---

[21] Notice Radcliffe-Brown's analysis through these passages: he discusses structural relations between positions in social hierarchies. Individuals are merely placeholders in the structures; the structures themselves are social facts, parts of the collective conscious (which he derives from Durkheim and the *L'Année Sociologique* school). Contrast this with Malinowski's work (essay 13). While Malinowski focused on the biological and psychological needs of individuals, Radcliffe-Brown focused almost exclusively on impersonal positions within the social structure.

[22] Radcliffe-Brown constructs his arguments based almost exclusively on his reading of the ethnographic reports of others. His own fieldwork is rarely mentioned. He had done fieldwork among the Andaman Islanders and among the Kariera in Australia, but he is not known for his ethnographic talents and had little interest in writing ethnography. He did not publish *The Andaman Islanders,* his account of his 1906–1908 fieldwork, until 1922. It is not widely read today.

sometimes be taken by her mother's brother, this being known as *ditsoa*. Now the natives state that the *ditsoa* cattle received by the mother's brother are really held by him on behalf of his sister's children. If one of his sister's sons or daughters is ill he may be required to offer a sacrifice to his ancestral spirits, and he then takes a beast from the *ditsoa* herd. Also, when the sister's son wishes to obtain a wife, he may go to his mother's brother to help him to find the necessary cattle and his uncle may give him some of the *ditsoa* cattle received at the marriage of his sister, or may even give him cattle from his own herd, trusting to being repaid from the *ditsoa* cattle to be received in the future from the marriage of a niece. I believe that the Native Appeal Court has decided that the payment of *ditsoa* to the mother's brother is a voluntary matter and cannot be regarded as a legal obligation, and with that judgment I am in agreement.[23] I quote this custom because it illustrates the sort of interest that the mother's brother is expected to take in his sister's son, in helping him and looking after his welfare. It brings us back to the question as to why the mother's brother may be asked to offer sacrifices when his nephew is sick.

In south-east Africa ancestor worship is patrilineal, i.e. a man worships and takes part in sacrifices to the spirits of his deceased relatives in the male line. Mr. Junod's statements about the BaThonga are not entirely clear. In one place he says that each family has two sets of gods, those on the father's side and those on the mother's; they are equal in dignity and both can be invoked (op. cit., II, p. 349, and I, p. 256, note). But in another place it is stated that if an offering has to be made to the gods of the mother's family this must be through the maternal relatives, the *malume* (op. cit., II, p. 367). Other passages confirm this and show us that ancestral spirits can only be directly approached in any ritual by their descendants in the male line.

The natives of the Transkei are very definite in their statements to me that a person's maternal gods, the patrilineal ancestors of his mother, will never inflict supernatural punishment upon him by making him sick. (I am not quite so sure about the Sotho tribes, but I think that they probably have similar views.) On the other hand a married woman can receive protection from the ancestral spirits of her patrilineal lineage, and so can her young children as long as they are attached to her. For children are only fully incorporated in their father's lineage when they reach adolescence. So in the Transkei a woman, when she marries, should be given a cow, the *ubulunga* cow, by her father, from the herd of her lineage, which she can take to her new home. Since she may not drink the milk from her husband's herd during the early period of her married life she can be provided with milk from this beast that comes from her lineage. This cow constitutes a link between herself and her lineage, its cattle, and its gods, for cattle are the material link between the living members of the lineage and the ancestral spirits. So if she is sick she can make for herself a necklace of hairs from the tail of this cow and so put herself under the protection of her lineage gods. Moreover, if one of her infant children is sick, she can make a similar necklace which is thought to give protection to the child. When her son is grown up he should receive an *ubulunga* bull from his father's herd, and thereafter it is from the tail of this beast that he will make a protective amulet; similarly the daughter, when she marries, is detached from her mother, and may receive an *ubulunga* cow from her father.[24]

But though, according to the statements made to me, the maternal ancestors will not punish their descendant with sickness, they can be appealed to for help. When, therefore, a child is sick the parents may go to the mother's brother of the child, or to the mother's father if he is still living, and ask that a sacrifice shall be offered, and

---

[23] The Native Appeal Court decision demonstrates how information derived from functionalist ethnography (in this case kinship) could be applied by the colonial administrators who permitted and sometimes financed fieldwork.

[24] Compare Radcliffe-Brown's linking of the *ubulunga*, religion, and kin with Durkheim's treatment of totem in *The Elementary Forms of Religious Life*. Here, cattle link individuals to their lineages and to the supernatural world. In Durkheim's analysis, the same function is performed by the totem.

an appeal for help made to the child's maternal ancestors. This, at any rate, is stated as a practice in the Sotho tribes, and one of the purposes of the *ditsoa* cattle that go from the marriage payment to the mother's brother of the bride is said to be to make provision for such sacrifices if they should be needed.

This brings us to the final extension of the principle that I have suggested as the basis of the customs relating to the mother's brother. The pattern of behavior towards the mother, which is developed in the family by reason of the nature of the family group and its social life, is extended with suitable modifications to the mother's sister and to the mother's brother, then to the group of maternal kindred as a whole, and finally to the maternal gods, the ancestors of the mother's group. In the same way the pattern of behavior towards the father is extended to the father's brothers and sisters, and to the whole of the father's group (or rather to all the older members of it, the principle of age making important modifications necessary), and finally to the paternal gods.

The father and his relatives must be obeyed and respected (even worshipped, in the original sense of the word), and so therefore also must be the paternal ancestors.[25] The father punishes his children, and so may the ancestors on the father's side. On the other hand, the mother is tender and indulgent to her child, and her relatives are expected to be the same, and so also the maternal spirits.

A very important principle, which I have tried to demonstrate elsewhere (*The Andaman Islanders*, Chapter V), is that the social values current in a primitive society are maintained by being expressed in ceremonial or ritual customs.[26] The set of values that we here meet with in the relations of an individual to his kindred on the two sides must, therefore, also have their proper ritual expression. The subject is too vast to deal with at

all adequately here, but I wish to discuss one point. Amongst the BaThonga, and also in Western Polynesia (Fiji and Tonga), the sister's son (or in Tonga also the daughter's son) intervenes in the sacrificial ritual. Mr. Junod describes a ceremony of crushing down the hut of a dead man in which the *batukulu* (sister's children) play an important part. They kill and distribute the sacrificial victims and when the officiating priest makes his prayer to the spirit of the dead man it is the sister's sons who, after a time, interrupt or "cut" the prayer and bring it to an end. They then, among the BaThonga clans, seize the portions of the sacrifice that have been dedicated to the spirit of the dead man and run away with them, "stealing" them (op. cit., I, p. 162).

I would suggest that the meaning of this is that it gives a ritual expression to the special relation that exists between the sister's son and the mother's brother. When the uncle is alive the nephews have the right to go to his village and take his food. Now that he is dead they come and do this again, as part of the funeral ritual, and as it were for the last time, i.e. they come and steal portions of meat and beer that are put aside as the portion of the deceased man.

The same sort of explanation will be found to hold, I think, of the part played in sacrificial and other ritual by the sister's son both amongst the Bantu of South Africa and also in Tonga and Fiji. As a man fears his father, so he fears and reverences his paternal ancestors, but he has no fear of his mother's brother, and so may act irreverently to his maternal ancestors; he is, indeed, required by custom so to act on certain occasions, thus giving ritual expression to the special social relations between a man and his maternal relatives in accordance with the general function of ritual, as I understand it.

It will, perhaps, be of help if I give you a final brief statement of the hypothesis I am advancing,

---

[25] Note here again that, like Durkheim, Radcliffe-Brown sees kinship relations reflected in religion.

[26] When Radcliffe-Brown did his fieldwork in the Andaman Islands, he intended to write a historical reconstruction. However, when he returned from the field, he read Durkheim and was profoundly influenced by him. The first half of *The Andaman Islanders* is a conventional historical account, but the second half (chapters 5 and 6) relies heavily on Radcliffe-Brown's reading of Durkheim, particularly *The Elementary Forms of Religious Life.* Compare Radcliffe-Brown's analysis here to Durkheim's analysis of the function of ceremony in essay 7.

with the assumptions involved in it and some of its important implications.

1. The characteristic of most of these societies that we call primitive is that the conduct of individuals to one another is very largely regulated on the basis of kinship, this being brought about by the formation of fixed patterns of behavior for each recognized kind of kinship relation.

2. This is sometimes associated with a segmentary organization of society, i.e. a condition in which the whole society is divided into a number of segments (lineages, clans).

3. While kinship is always and necessarily bilateral, or cognatic, the segmentary organization requires the adoption of the unilineal principle, and a choice has to be made between patrilineal and matrilineal institutions.

4. In patrilineal societies of a certain type, the special pattern of behavior between a sister's son and the mother's brother is derived from the pattern of behavior between the child and the mother, which is itself the product of the social life within the family in the narrow sense.

5. This same kind of behavior tends to be extended to all the maternal relatives, i.e. to the whole family or group to which the mother's brother belongs.[b]

6. In societies with patrilineal ancestor worship (such as the BaThonga and the Friendly Islanders) the same type of behavior may also be extended to the gods of the mother's family.

7. The special kind of behavior to the maternal relatives (living and dead) or to the maternal group and its gods and sacra, is expressed in definite ritual customs, the function of ritual here, as elsewhere, being to fix and make permanent certain types of behavior, with the obligations and sentiments involved therein.

In conclusion, may I point out that I have selected the subject of my contribution to this meeting because it is one not only of theoretical but also of practical interest.[27] For instance, there is the question as to whether the Native Appeal Court was really right in its judgment that the payment of the *ditsoa* cattle to the mother's brother of a bride is not a legal but only a moral obligation. So far as I have been able to form an opinion, I should say that the judgment was right.

The whole subject of the payments at marriage (*lobola*) is one of considerable practical importance at the present time to missionaries and magistrates, and to the natives themselves. Now the study of the exact position in which a person stands to his maternal relatives is one without which it is impossible to arrive at a completely accurate understanding of the customs of *lobola*. One of the chief functions of *lobola* is to fix the social position of the children of a marriage. If the proper payment is made by a family, then the children of the woman who comes to them in exchange for the cattle belong to that family, and its gods are their gods. The natives consider that the strongest of all social bonds is that between a child and its mother, and therefore by the extension that inevitably takes place there is a very strong bond between the child and its mother's family. The function of the *lobola* payment is not

---

[27] Note Radcliffe-Brown's concern with practical application. He had been a colonial administrator himself. Many of the functionalists saw service to the colonial administrations of their research areas as one aim of their work. Malinowski argued, in an article entitled "Practical Anthropology" (1929a), that this should be a key goal. Then (as today) access to funding was an important reason for stressing the applied aspects of anthropological research: much of the money that funded research projects came from the Colonial Social Science Research Council. In general, the functionalists did not question the basic fact of colonization or the subservient position of the colonized. Both paternalism and social evolutionism were implied in their writings. They believed that benevolent colonialism offered the native the chance of progress. On the other hand, they considered themselves friends of those they studied and argued on their behalf before colonial administrations. The same Malinowski who authored "Practical Anthropology" also wrote the preface to Jomo Kenyatta's *Facing Mount Kenya: The Traditional Life of the Gikuyu* (1979 [1938]). Kenyatta was one of Malinowski's students but is better remembered as a leader of Kenya's fight for independence and that nation's first president.

to destroy but to modify this bond, and to place the children definitely in the father's family and group for all matters concerning not only the social but also the religious life of the tribe. If no *lobola* is paid the child inevitably belongs to the mother's family, though its position is then irregular. But the woman for whom the *lobola* is paid does not become a member of the husband's family; their gods are not her gods; and that is the final test. I have said enough, I hope, to show that the proper understanding of customs relating to the mother's brother is a necessary preliminary to any final theory of *lobola*.

Notes

a. A paper read before the South African Association for the Advancement of Science, 9 July 1924, and printed in *South African Journal of Science* Vol. XXI, pp. 542–55.

b. This extension from the mother's brother to the other maternal relatives is shown in the BaThonga

tribe in the kinship terminology. The term *malume*, primarily applied to the mother's brother, is extended to the sons of those men, who are also *malume*. If my mother's brothers are dead it is their sons who will have to sacrifice on my behalf to my maternal ancestors. In the northern part of the tribe the term *malume* has gone out of use, and the mother's father, the mother's brother, and the sons of the mother's brother are all called *kokwana* (grandfather). However absurd it may seem to us to call a mother's brother's son, who may be actually younger than the speaker, by a word meaning "grandfather," the argument of this paper will enable us to see some meaning in it. The person who must sacrifice on my behalf to my maternal ancestors is first my mother's father, then, if he is dead, my mother's brother, and after the decease of the latter, his son, who may be younger than I am. There is a similarity of function for these three relationships, a single general pattern of behavior for me towards them all and this is again similar in general to that for grandfathers. The nomenclature is, therefore, appropriate.

15. The Nuer of the Southern Sudan

E. E. Evans-Pritchard (1902–1973)

I WRITE SHORTLY OF THE NUER[1] BECAUSE I have already recorded a considerable part of my observations on their political constitution and the whole is about to be published as a book.[a] They have, nevertheless, been included in this volume for the reasons that their constitution is representative of East Africa and that it provides us with an extreme political type.[2]

(1940)

I. Distribution

To discover the principles of their anarchic state we must first review briefly the oecology of the people: their means of livelihood, their distribution, and the relation of these to their surroundings.[3] The Nuer practice cattle-husbandry and agriculture. They also fish, hunt, and collect wild fruits and roots. But, unlike the other sources of their food supply, cattle have more than nutritive interest, being indeed of greater value in their

---

[1] This essay first appeared in *African Political Systems* (1940), a volume of essays edited by Meyer Fortes and Evans-Pritchard. In that same year, he published *The Nuer,* his classic account of these people. He later wrote two additional accounts of Nuer life: *Kinship and Marriage Among the Nuer* (1951a) and *Nuer Religion* (1956).

[2] The British structural-functionalists attempted to create abstract analytic descriptions of society and formulate universal principles of social organization. Notice in the opening paragraph that Evans-Pritchard thinks a description of the Nuer is useful because they are representatives of a cultural type rather than because they are a unique cultural manifestation.

[3] Evans-Pritchard opens his essay with a description of Nuer ecology. His book-length treatment of this material contains over forty pages of such description, including information on temperature, rainfall, and settlement patterns. In general,

eyes than anything else. So, although they have a mixed economy, Nuer are predominantly pastoral in sentiment.

Nuerland is more suited for stock-breeding than for agriculture: it is flat, clayey, savannah country, parched and bare during the drought and flooded and covered with high grasses during the rains.[4] Heavy rain falls and the rivers overflow their banks from June to December. There is little rain and the rivers are low from December to June. The year thus comprises two seasons of about equal duration. This seasonal dichotomy, combined with pastoral interests, profoundly affects political relations.

During the rains Nuer live in villages perched on the backs of knolls and ridges or dotted over stretches of slightly elevated ground, and engage in the cultivation of millet and maize. The country which intervenes between village and village, being more or less flooded for six months, is then unsuitable for habitation, agriculture, or grazing. Anything from five to twenty miles may separate neighbouring villages, while greater distances may divide sections of a tribe and tribe from tribe.

At the end of the rains, the people burn the grasses to provide new pasture and leave their villages to reside in small camps. When the drought becomes severe, the inmates of these intermediate camps concentrate on permanent water supplies. Although these moves are made primarily for the sake of the cattle, they also enable the Nuer to fish, which is generally impossible from village sites, and, to a lesser degree, to hunt and collect wild fruits and roots. When the rains set in again, they return to their villages, where the cattle have protection and the higher ground permits agriculture.

The distribution of the Nuer is determined by the physical conditions and mode of life we have outlined. During the rains, villages are separated, though by no means isolated, from their neighbours by flooded stretches of grassland, and local communities are therefore very distinct units. During the drought, people of different villages of the same district eventually concentrate on permanent water-supplies and share common camps. On the other hand, some families of a village may go to one camp and some to another, though the majority form a local community throughout the year.

Nuer seldom have a surplus of food and at the beginning of the rains it is often insufficient for their needs.[5] Indeed, it may be said that they are generally on the verge of want and that every few years they face more or less severe famine. In these conditions, it is understandable that there is much sharing of food in the same village, especially among members of adjacent homesteads and hamlets. Though at any time some members may have more cattle and grain than others, and these are their private possessions, people eat in one another's homesteads at feasts and at daily meals, and food is in other ways shared, to such an extent that one may speak of a common stock. Food is most abundant from the end of September to the middle of December in a normal year, and it is during these months that most ceremonies, dances, &c., take place.

The Nuer have a very simple technology. Their country lacks iron and stone and the number and variety of trees are small, and they are generally unsuited for constructive purposes other than building. This paucity of raw materials, together with a meagre food supply, contracts social ties, drawing

---

British social anthropologists recognized environment as an important factor, but emphasized social organization, which they viewed as only loosely articulated with ecology. Evans-Pritchard, however, was particularly concerned with the relationship of ecology to social organization. Because of this, he is sometimes seen as among the forerunners of modern cultural ecology.

[4] Like the historical particularists, the structural-functionalists set very high standards for fieldwork. Evans-Pritchard considered his fieldwork to have been done under extremely difficult circumstances. In the introduction to *The Nuer,* he wrote, "A man must judge his labors by the obstacles he has overcome and the hardships he has endured, and by these standards I am not ashamed of the results" (1940:9).

[5] In this and the next several paragraphs, you will notice some strong similarities to Julian Steward's essay on the patrilineal band, which first appeared in 1936 (see essay 18).

the people of village or camp closer, in a moral sense, for they are in consequence highly interdependent and their pastoral, hunting, fishing, and, to a lesser degree, their agricultural activities are of necessity joint undertakings. This is especially evident in the dry season, when the cattle of many families are tethered in a common kraal and driven as a single herd to the grazing grounds.

Thus, while in a narrow sense the economic unit is the household, the larger local communities are, directly or indirectly, cooperative groups combining to maintain existence, and corporations owning natural resources and sharing in their exploitation. In the smaller local groups the co-operative functions are more direct and evident than in the larger ones, but the collective function of obtaining for themselves the necessities of life from the same resources is in some degree common to all local communities from the household to the tribe.

These local communities are the monogamous family attached to a single hut, the household occupying a single homestead, the hamlet, the village, the camp, the district, tribal sections of varying size, the tribe, the people, and the international community the limits of which are a Nuer's social horizon.[6] We regard the family, the household, and the hamlet as domestic, rather than political, groups, and do not discuss them further in detail.

The distribution of these local communities is very largely determined by physical conditions, especially by the presence of ground which remains above flood-level in the rains, and of permanent water which survives the drought. In any village, the size of population and the arrangement of homesteads is determined by the nature of the site. When perched on an isolated knoll, homesteads are crowded together; when strung out along a ridge, they are more widely separated; and when spread over a broad stretch of higher ground, several hundred yards may intervene between one hamlet and the next. In any large village, the homesteads are grouped in clusters, or hamlets, the inmates of which are generally close kinsmen and their spouses. It is not possible to give more than a rough indication of the size of a village population, but it may be said to vary from 50 to several hundred souls. An aggregate of villages lying within a radius which allows easy inter-communication we call a "district." This is not a political group for it can only be defined in relation to each village, since the same villages may be included in more than one district; and we do not regard a local community as a political group unless the people who comprise it speak of themselves as a community by contrast with other communities of the same kind and are so regarded by outsiders. Nevertheless, a district

---

[6] Notice that the focus of Evans-Pritchard's study is the political organization of the Nuer. The maintenance of social order in societies without governments recognizable to Europeans was a key intellectual problem in the anthropology of Evans-Pritchard's day. People other than anthropologists were interested in this problem as well — Evans-Pritchard's study of the Nuer was undertaken at the request of the government of Anglo-Egyptian Sudan, which funded it. Indeed, at the time Evans-Pritchard first visited the Nuer, a Nuer revolt against the British government had just ended. Clearly the reports made by an anthropologist could be very useful in the task of establishing colonial control. The Anglo-Egyptian government of Sudan was particularly interested in a study of the Nuer political system because they intended to rule Nuerland.

British colonialism generally preferred to rule through already existing political structures rather than to create new ones. Thus, studies of indigenous political systems were particularly important. This was especially the case in Sudan, where in 1885, a rebel army led by Mohammed Ahmed (1844 – 1885), known as the Mahdi (Arabic for "the [divinely] guided one"), laid siege to Khartoum, the capital, and captured it. The British commander, General Charles "Chinese" Gordon (1833 – 1885), a popular hero in England, was killed in the attack, and the Mahdi's followers retained control of the Sudan until 1898. The incident was greatly exploited by the popular press (and, later, the movies).

The relationship between the British anthropologists of this era and colonialism is problematic. Anthropologists were anxious to receive funding from the government, so they argued that their research projects were useful in governing. Though they frequently campaigned for natives' rights, they generally believed in the legitimacy of colonial authority. These practices are certainly not unique to the structural-functionalists. Anthropologists (and other social and physical scientists) still argue the usefulness of their work in order to receive funding, a practice that continues to raise interesting moral and political questions.

tends to coincide with a tertiary tribal section and its network of social ties are what gives the section much of its cohesion. People of the same district often share common camps in the drought and they attend one another's weddings and other ceremonies. They intermarry and hence establish between themselves many affinal and cognatic relationships which, as will be seen later, crystallize round an agnatic nucleus.

Villages, the political units of Nuerland, are grouped into tribal sections. There are some very small tribes to the west of the Nile which comprise only a few adjacent villages. In the larger tribes to the west of the Nile and in all the tribes to the east of it, we find that the tribal area is divided into a number of territorial sections separated by stretches of unoccupied country, which intervene also between the nearest habitations of contiguous tribes.

As all Nuer leave their villages to camp near water, they have a second distribution in the dry season. When they camp along a river, these camps sometimes succeed one another every few miles, but when they camp around inland pools, twenty to thirty miles often separate one camp from the next. The territorial principle of Nuer political structure is deeply modified by seasonal migration. People who form separate village communities in the rains may unite in a common camp in the drought. Likewise, people of the same village may join different camps. Also, it is often necessary, in the larger tribes, for members of a village to traverse wide tracts of country, occupied by other village communities, to reach water, and their camp may lie close to yet other villages. To avoid the complete loss of their herds by rinderpest or some other misfortune, Nuer often distribute the beasts in several camps.

In western Nuerland, where the tribes are generally smaller than to the east of the Nile, there is usually plenty of water and pasturage, and it is possible, therefore, for village communities of the rains to maintain a relative isolation in the drought. But where, as in the Lou tribe, for example, scarcity of water and pasturage compels more extensive movement and greater concentration, people who are very widely distributed may have more social contact with one another than is the case in western Nuerland. The isolation

and autonomy of local communities are broken up by economic necessity and the size of the political group is thereby enlarged. This fact has to be considered in relation to the further fact that to the east of the Nile wider stretches of elevated ground allow larger local concentrations in the rains than is usual to the west of that river. Moreover, seasonal concentration offers an explanation, though by no means a full one, of the location of tribal boundaries, since they are determined not only by the distribution of villages, but also by the direction in which the people turn in their move to dry season pastures. Thus the tribes of the Zeraf Valley fall back on the Zeraf River and therefore do not share camps with the Lou tribe, and that part of the Lou tribe which moves east and north-east make their camps on the Nyanding River and on the upper reaches of the Pibor and do not share their waters and pasture with the Jikany tribes, who move to the upper reaches of the Sobat and the lower reaches of the Pibor. Furthermore, that some of the larger Nuer tribes are able to preserve a degree of tribal unity without governmental organs may in part be attributed to a seasonal migration, since, as explained above, the different local sections are forced by the severity of the latitude into mutual contact and develop some measure of forbearance and recognition of common interests.

Likewise, a tribal section is a distinct segment, not only because its villages occupy a well-demarcated portion of its territory, but also in that it has its unique dry-season pastures. The people of one section move off in one direction and the people from an adjoining section move off in a different direction. Dry-season concentrations are never tribal, but always sectional, and at no time and in no area is the population dense.

The total Nuer population is round about 300,000. I do not know the total square mileage of the country, but to the east of the Nile, where there are, on a rough estimate, some 180,000 Nuer, they are said to occupy 26,000 square miles, with the low density of about seven to the square mile. The density is probably no higher to the west of the Nile. Nowhere is there a high degree of local concentration.

Although dry-season movement produces more social interrelations between members of

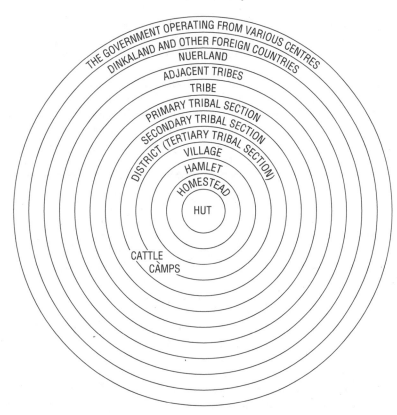

Diagram No. I

different tribal sections than the rainy season distribution might lead us to expect, these contacts are mainly individual or, when they concern groups, only smaller local communities, and not the larger tribal sections, are brought into association. This is probably one of the reasons for the lack of structural complexity and of great variation of types of social relations among the Nuer. Outside small kinship groups and village and camp communities, there are no co-operative economic combinations and there are no organized ritual associations. Except for occasional military ventures, active corporate life is restricted to small tribal segments. (See Diagram No. I.)

II. Tribal System

What is a Nuer tribe?[7] The most obvious characteristic is its territorial unity and exclusiveness, and this was even more marked before European conquest than today. The population of a tribe varies from a few hundreds among some small tribes to the west of the Nile—if these are rightly regarded as tribes, for very little research was conducted in

---

[7] Evans-Pritchard opens this section with a question that must have seemed incongruous to many of his readers. Generally, tribes (or some broadly equivalent term) have been accepted as the given units of anthropological research. Many other essays in this volume, for example, refer frequently to tribes or ethnic groups and implicitly assume that these are easily identified. Here, Evans-Pritchard shows that for the Nuer at least, the question is problematic, as tribal identity is complex and situational rather than uniformly imposed.

that area—to many thousands. Most tribes have a population of over 5,000 and the largest number between 30,000 and 40,000 souls. Each tribe is economically self-sufficient, having its own pastures, water-supplies, and fishing reservations, which its members alone have the right to exploit. It has a name which is the symbol of its distinction. The tribes' men have a sense of patriotism: they are proud to be members of their tribe and they consider it superior to other tribes. Each tribe has within it a dominant clan which furnishes a kinship framework on which the political aggregate is built up. Each also regulates independently its age-set organization.

None of the above-mentioned attributes clearly make a formal distinction between a tribe and its divisions. The simplest definition states that a tribe is the largest community which considers that disputes between its members should be settled by arbitration and that it ought to combine against other communities of the same kind and against foreigners. In these two respects there is no larger political group than the tribe and all smaller political groups are sections of it.

Within a tribe there is law: there is machinery for settling disputes and a moral obligation to conclude them sooner or later. If a man kills a fellow tribesman, it is possible to prevent, or curtail, a feud by payment of cattle. Between tribe and tribe there is no means of bringing together the parties to a dispute and compensation is neither offered nor demanded. Thus, if a man of one tribe kills a man of another tribe, retribution can only take the form of intertribal warfare. It must not be supposed that feuds within a tribe are easy to conclude. There is considerable control over retaliation within a village, but the larger the local community the more difficult settlement becomes. When two large divisions of a tribe are concerned in a feud, the chances of immediate arbitration and settlement are remote. The force of law varies with the distance in tribal structure that separates the persons concerned. Nevertheless, so long as a sense of community endures and the legal norm is formally acknowledged within a tribe, whatever may be the inconsistencies and contradictions that appear in the actual relations between tribesmen, they still consider themselves to be a united group. Then either the contradiction of feuds is felt and they are settled, the unity of the tribe being maintained thereby, or they remain so long unsettled that people give up all hope and intention of ever concluding them and finally cease to feel that they ought to be concluded, so that the tribe tends to split and two new tribes come into being.[8]

Nor must it be supposed that the political limits of the tribe are the limits of social intercourse. People move freely all over Nuerland and are unmolested if they have not incurred blood-guilt. They marry and, to a small extent, trade across tribal boundaries, and pay visits to kinsmen living outside their own tribe. Many social relations, which are not specifically political, link members of different tribes. One has only to mention that the same clans are found in different tribes and that everywhere the age-sets are coordinated. Any Nuer may leave his tribe and settle in a new tribe, of which he thereby becomes a member. In time of peace, even Dinka foreigners may visit Nuerland unharmed. Moreover, we must recognize that the whole Nuer people form a single community, territorially unbroken, with common culture and feeling of exclusiveness. Their common language and values permit ready inter-communication. Indeed, we might speak of the Nuer as a nation, though only in a cultural sense, for there is no common political organization or central administration.[9]

---

[8] Evans-Pritchard was a student of Bronislaw Malinowski (see essay 13), but wrote as much in reaction to Malinowski as in emulation of him. He met A. R. Radcliffe-Brown while at Oxford in 1935 and was deeply influenced by him when he wrote this essay. While Malinowski's work was based on ethnographic description, Radcliffe-Brown's concentrated on abstract, analytical models of society (see essay 14). Here and in his books on the Nuer, Evans-Pritchard presents a technical analysis of Nuer social structure. Like Radcliffe-Brown, he hoped to create a precise, scientific social anthropology. However, you will note below that some substantial similarities between Evans-Pritchard and Malinowski remain.

[9] Like Radcliffe-Brown, Evans-Pritchard owes a profound debt to Durkheim and his followers, particularly Marcel Mauss. The idea of social fact is implicit in their goal of delineating social structures. Many of the theoretical issues in *The Nuer,*

Besides being the largest group in which legal obligation is acknowledged, a tribe is also the largest group which habitually combines for offence and defence. The younger men of the tribe went, till recently, on joint raiding expeditions against the Dinka and waged war against other Nuer tribes. Raids on the Dinka were very frequent; war between tribes less so. In theory, if two sections of different tribes were engaged in hostilities, each could rely on the support of the other sections of the same tribe, but in practice they did not always join in. Contiguous tribes sometimes combined against foreigners, especially against the Dinka, though there was no moral obligation to do so, the alliance was of short duration, and the allies conducted their operations independently, even when in collaboration.

At the present time, Nuer are to the west and south bordered by Dinka, who appear to have very much the same kind of political system as their own, i.e. they comprise a congeries of tribes without centralized government. From the earliest times the Nuer have been fighting the Dinka and have been generally on the offensive. We know that during the first half of the last century waves of Nuer broke from their homeland to the west of the Nile on to the Dinka lands to the east of that river and that they conquered and absorbed the inhabitants in most of what is now eastern Nuerland (the Nuer distinguish between *Nath cieng,* the "homeland," or western Nuer, and *Nath doar,* the "migrated," or eastern Nuer). Fighting between the two peoples has continued till the present time but there does not appear, if maps made by early travellers are to be trusted, to have been much change of territory during the last fifty years. This eastwards migration is a fact that has to be taken into account, with those related earlier, if we wish to know why the eastern tribes are larger, territorially and numerically, than the western tribes, for it may be assumed that the struggle of conquest and settlement, and absorption of Dinka on an unprecedented scale, had some effect on the migrating hordes.

To the north, the Nuer are in varying degrees of contact with Arabs, the peoples of the Nuba Hills, the powerful Shilluk kingdom, and certain small communities in Darfung (Burun and Koma); while to the east and south-east they are bordered by the Galla of Ethiopia, the Anuak, and the Beir. Wherever the Nuer have direct relations with these peoples, they are hostile in character.

Arab slave-raiders from the Northern Sudan intruded here and there into the more accessible portions of Nuerland in the second half of the nineteenth century, but nowhere did they gain the upper hand or, indeed, make a marked impression on the Nuer, who opposed them as strongly as they resisted later the Egyptian Government, which undertook no serious operations against them. The Nuer likewise treated British rule with open disrespect till, as a result of lengthy military operations between 1928 and 1930, their opposition was broken and they were brought under effective administration. With the exception of this last episode in their history, the Nuer may be said to have reached in their foreign relations a state of equilibrium and of mutual

---

especially the nesting of segmentary lineages described here, derive from Durkheim's *The Division of Labor in Society* (originally published in 1893, but not available in English until 1933). However, this passage and the one below, like many others in *The Nuer,* expose critical tensions within the work.

As a structural-functionalist, Evans-Pritchard's goal was to analyze the operation of the social structure, which was generally understood to exist independently of both history and individual actions. His analysis frequently included the recounting of recent historical events, which he used as specific illustrations of principles of social organization that he believed transcended them. This clearly reflects the influence of Durkheimian sociology, particularly his search for social facts and collective conscience. The tension comes from Evans-Pritchard's frequent acknowledgment that the historical narration on which his analysis of social structure depends does not quite fit the structural patterns it should. The social facts that he should be able to abstract in clear terms are elusive. Variations depend on individual and historical circumstances, and these seem beyond the reach of social analysis. Issues of this nature eventually led Evans-Pritchard to reject both Radcliffe-Brown's theories and any possibility of a science of anthropology. Toward the end of his life, he viewed anthropology as more similar to history than to social science. He wrote in 1951, "Social anthropology is best regarded as an art and not as a social science" (1951b:85).

Map of Dinka, Nuer, Shilluk, Anuak

hostility which was expressed from time to time in fighting.[10]

A tribe is divided into territorial segments which regard themselves as separate communities. We refer to the divisions of a tribe as primary, secondary, and tertiary tribal sections. Primary sections are segments of a tribe, secondary sections are segments of a primary section, and tertiary sections are segments of a secondary section. A tertiary section is divided into villages and villages into domestic groups. A member of Z2 tertiary division of tribe B sees himself as a member of Z2 community in relation to Z1, but he regards himself as a member of Y2 and not of Z in relation to Y1. Likewise, he regards himself as a member of Y, and not of Y2, in relation to X. He regards himself as a member of tribe B, and not of its primary section Y, in relation to tribe A. Thus, on a structural plane, there is always contradiction in the definition of a political group, for a man is a member of it in virtue of his non-membership of other groups of the same type which he stands outside of, and he is likewise not a member of the same community in virtue of his membership of a segment of it which stands in opposition to its other segments. Hence a man counts as a member of a political group in one situation and not as a member of it in a different situation, e.g. he is a member of a tribe in relation to other tribes and he is not a member of it

---

[10] Notice the use of *equilibrium* here. Structural-functionalists generally conceived of societies as functioning normally at some sort of equilibrium. This is consistent with the organic analogy. When stability is disturbed, as with the historical events mentioned here, the ensuing social process returns the society to a state of balance (but, as Evans-Pritchard shows, not necessarily harmony).

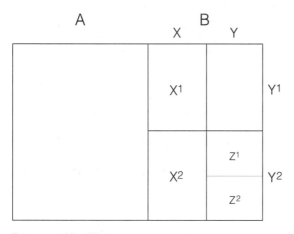

Diagram No. II

in so far as his segment of the tribe is opposed to other segments.[11] In studying the Nuer political constitution, it is therefore essential that we view it together with those of their enemies as a single political system, for the outstanding structural characteristic of Nuer political groups is their relativity. A tribal segment is a political group in relation to other segments of the same kind, and they jointly form a tribe only in relation to other Nuer tribes and to adjacent foreign tribes which form part of their political system, and without these relations very little meaning can be attached to the concepts of "tribe" and "tribal segment." That the distinction and individuality of a political group is in relation to groups of the same kind is a generalization that embraces all Nuer local communities, from the largest to the smallest.[12]

The relation between tribes and between segments of a tribe which gives them political unity and distinction is one of opposition. Between tribes, or federations of tribes, and foreign peoples this opposition is expressed, on the Nuer side at any rate, by contempt and persistent raiding, often carried out in a reckless and brutal manner. Between Nuer tribes, opposition is expressed by actual warfare or by acceptance that a dispute cannot, and ought not, to be settled in any other way. In intertribal warfare, however, women and children are neither speared nor enslaved. Between segments of the same tribe, opposition is expressed by the institution of the feud. A fight between persons of the same village or camp is as far as possible restricted to duelling with clubs. The hostility and mode of expression in these different relations varies in degree and in the form it takes.[13]

Feuds frequently break out between sections of the same tribe and they are often of long duration. They are more difficult to settle the larger the sections involved. Within a village feuds are easily settled and within a tertiary tribal section they are concluded sooner or later, but when still

---

[11] In this passage, Evans-Pritchard emphasizes contradiction and the relative nature of social identification. Some have seen elements of French structuralist thinking in this focus on structure and opposition (see essay 25). More recently, postmodernist thinkers such as Renato Rosaldo (essay 38) have used similar segmentary models to draw attention to the fragmentary and situational nature of personal and group identity.

[12] The Nuer *cieng* means "home," but Evans-Pritchard points out that its use is situational. The size of the area an individual considers home depends on the specific circumstances of the question. By way of explanation Evans-Pritchard notes, "If one meets an Englishman in Germany and asks him where his home is, he may reply that it is England. If one meets the same man in London and asks him the same question, he will tell one that his home is in Oxfordshire" (1940:136). Evans-Pritchard's use of a British example made his ideas more comprehensible to his readers but also illustrated the fact that, while analyzing the Nuer, he believes he is uncovering social facts of far more general significance. Malinowski used the same technique when he compared kula valuables to the Crown Jewels (see essay 13).

[13] The emphasis in this passage on relations between tribal segments illustrates the close connection of Evans-Pritchard's thought with French sociology and anthropology. Compare Evans-Pritchard's understanding of segments that are defined by their relations with Durkheim's descriptions of the relationships between different totem sections (essay 7). This same type of relational argument occurs later in French structural anthropology, particularly in the analysis of myth (see essays 25, 26, and 27). Because British social anthropology is rooted in fieldwork and concrete description, it is hard to see it as a forerunner of French structuralism, a school that depends more overtly on interpretive virtuosity. However, structuralism proved very attractive to many British social anthropologists.

larger groups are involved they may never be settled, especially if many persons on either side have been killed in a big fight.

A tribal section has most of the attributes of a tribe: name, sense of patriotism, a dominant lineage, territorial distinction, economic resources, and so forth. Each is a tribe in miniature, and they differ from tribes only in size, in degree of integration, and in that they unite for war and acknowledge a common principle of justice.

The strength of the sentiment associated with local groups is roughly relative to their size. Feeling of unity in a tribe is weaker than feeling of unity within its sections. The smaller the local group, the more the contacts its members have with one another and the more these contacts are co-operative and necessary for the maintenance of the life of the group. In a big group, like the tribe, contacts are infrequent, short, and of limited type. Also the smaller the group the closer and the more varied the relationships between its members, residential relations being only one strand in a network of agnatic, cognatic, and affinal relationships. Relationships by blood and marriage become fewer and more distant the wider the group.

It is evident that when we speak of a Nuer tribe we are using a relative term, for it is not always easy to say, on the criteria we have used, whether we are dealing with a tribe with two primary segments or with two tribes. The tribal system as defined by sociological analysis can, therefore, only be said to approximate to any simple diagrammatic presentation. A tribe is an exemplification of a segmentary tendency which is characteristic of the political structure as a whole. The reason why we speak of Nuer political groups, and of the tribe in particular, as relative groups and state that they are not easily described in terms of political morphology, is that political relations are dynamic. They are always changing in one direction or another. The most evident movement is towards fission. The tendency of tribes and tribal sections towards fission and internal opposition between their parts is balanced by a tendency in the direction of fusion, of the combination or amalgamation of groups. This tendency towards fusion is inherent in the segmentary character of Nuer political structure, for, although any group tends to split into opposed parts, these parts tend to fuse in relation to other groups. Hence fission and fusion are two aspects of the same segmentary principle and the Nuer tribe and its divisions are to be understood as a relation between these two contradictory, yet complementary, tendencies. Physical environment, way of livelihood, mode of distribution, poor communications, simple economy, &c., to some extent explain the incidence of political cleavage, but the tendency towards segmentation seems to be inherent in political structure itself.

III. Lineage System

Tribal unity cannot be accounted for by any of the facts we have so far mentioned, taken alone or in the aggregate, but only by reference to the lineage system.[14] The Nuer clan is not an undifferentiated group of persons who recognize their common kinship, as are many African clans, but is highly segmented. The segments are genealogical structures, and we therefore refer to them as lineages and to the clan as an exogamous system of lineages which trace their descent to a common ancestor. The defining characteristic of a lineage is that the relationship of any member of it to other members can be exactly stated in genealogical terms. His relationship to members of other lineages of the same clan is, therefore, also known, since lineages are genealogically related. Thus, in the diagram below, A is a clan which is segmented into maximal lineages B and C and these again bifurcate into major lineages D, E, F, and G. In the same manner, minor lineages H, I, J, and K are segments of major lineages E and F; and L, M, N, and O are minimal lineages which are segments of minor lineages H and J. The whole clan is a genealogical structure, i.e. the letters represent persons to whom the clan and its

---

[14] Notice the influence of both Spencer and Radcliffe-Brown on Evans-Pritchard's work here. He understands Nuer society as a series of systems functioning in an integrated manner to create an operating society. The lineage system described here is much the same as the political system outlined above and is presented in a similar way. That is, precise descriptions and drawings lay out a model of the way the system should work.

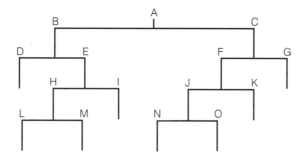

Diagram No. III

segments trace their descent, and from whom they often take their names. There must be at least twenty such clans in Nuerland, without taking into account many small lineages of Dinka origin.

The Nuer lineage is a group of agnates, and comprises all living persons descended, through males only, from the founder of that particular line. Logically, it also includes dead persons descended from the founder, but these dead persons are only significant in that their genealogical position explains the relationship between the living. The wider agnatic kinship is recognized the further back descent has to be traced, so that the depth of a lineage is always in proportion to its width.

The Nuer clan, being thus highly segmented, has many of the characteristics which we have found in tribal structure. Its lineages are distinct groups only in relation to each other. Thus, in the diagram, M is a group only by opposition to L, H is a group only by opposition to I, D is a group only by opposition to E, and so on. There is always fusion of collateral lineages of the same branch in relation to a collateral branch, e.g. in the diagram, L and M are no longer separate minimal lineages, but are a single minor lineage, H, in

opposition to I, and D and E are no longer separate major lineages, but are a single maximal lineage, B, in opposition to C. Hence two lineages which are equal and opposite are composite in relation to a third, so that a man is a member of a lineage in relation to a certain group and not a member of it in relation to a different group. Lineages are thus essentially relative groups, like tribal sections, and, like them, also are dynamic groups. Therefore they can only be described satisfactorily in terms of values and situations.[15]

Nuer lineages are not corporate localized communities[16] though their members often have an association with a locality and speak of the locality as though it were an exclusive agnatic group. Every Nuer village is associated with a lineage, and though the members of it often comprise a small proportion of the community, it is identified with them in such a way that we may speak of it as an aggregate of persons clustered around an agnatic nucleus. The aggregate is linguistically identified with the nucleus by the designation of the village community by the name of the lineage. It is only in reference to rules of exogamy and certain ritual activities that one needs to regard lineages as completely autonomous groups. In social life generally, they function within local communities, of all sizes from the village to the tribe, and as part of them. We cannot here discuss the ways by which residential groups become a network of kinship ties—marriage, adoption, and various fictions—but the result tends to be that a local group is a cognatic cluster round an agnatic core,[17] the rules of exogamy being the operating principle in this tendency.

Nuer clans are everywhere much dispersed, so that in any village or camp one finds representatives of diverse clans. Small lineages have

---

[15] Once again, the principles of opposition and relative position are stressed in this passage. Importantly, Evans-Pritchard emphasizes the overlap between tribal and lineage identity and the situational nature of all Nuer identity. Since the clan and political structures exist only in response to specific situations, individual decision making may have great importance. The implications of overlapping and situational identity are viewed by some postmodern anthropologists as foreshadowing their own ideas. Structural-functional thought is usually seen as denying the role of the individual, but this analysis suggests that Evans-Pritchard gives implicit importance to individual actors (Karp and Maynard 1983:488).

[16] A *corporate community* is one whose members jointly control resources.

[17] *Agnates* are people related through male relatives only; *cognates* are people related through a common ancestor of either sex. A "cognatic cluster round an agnatic core" is a group of related males plus all the people related to them through either males or females.

moved freely over Nuerland and have settled here and there and have aggregated themselves to agnatically unrelated elements in local communities. Migration and the absorption of Dinka have been circumstances favouring the dispersal and mixture of clans. Being a conquering, pastoral people and not having an ancestral cult, the Nuer have never been bound to any particular spot by necessity or sentiment.

Nevertheless, there is a straight relation between political structure and the clan system, for a clan, or a maximal lineage, is associated with each tribe, in which it occupies a dominant position among other agnatic groups. Moreover, each of its segments tends to be associated with a segment of the tribe in such a way that there is a correspondence, and often a linguistic identification, between the parts of a clan and the parts of a tribe. Thus if we compare Diagrams II and III and suppose clan A to be the dominant clan in tribe B, then maximal lineages B and C correspond to primary sections X and Y; major lineages D and E correspond to secondary section X1 and X2; major lineages F and G correspond to secondary sections Y1 and Y2; and minor lineages J and K correspond to tertiary sections Z1 and Z2.

We speak of a clan which is dominant in a tribe as the aristocratic clan, although, except on the periphery of Nuer expansion eastwards, its predominance gives prestige rather than privilege.[18] Its members are in a minority—often a very small minority—in the tribe. Not all members of the aristocratic clan live in the tribe where it is dominant, but many are also found in other tribes. Not all clans are associated with a tribe in this manner. A man is only an aristocrat in the one tribe in which his clan is dominant. If he lives in another tribe, he is not an aristocrat there.

There is consequently in every tribe some social differentiation. There are aristocrats, Nuer of other clans, and Dinka, but these strata are not classes and the second and third are properly to be regarded as categories rather than as groups. The Dinka who have been absorbed into Nuer society have been for the most part incorporated into their kinship system by adoption and marriage, and conquest has not led to the development of classes or castes. This is, perhaps, to be attributed, in part at any rate, to the fact that the Dinka, like the Nuer, are chiefly pastoralists and that in other respects their ways of life are very similar.

Without presenting all the evidence and without making every qualification, we attempt an explanation of why Nuer clans, especially the dominant clans, are segmented into lineages to a far greater degree than is usual among African peoples. In our view, they are segmented because the political structure to which they correspond is segmented in the way we have described. Social obligations among the Nuer are expressed chiefly in a kinship idiom and the interrelations of local communities within a tribe are defined in terms of agnatic relationship. Therefore, as the tribe segments the clan segments with it and the point of separation between the tribal sections becomes the point of divergence in the clan structure of the lineages associated with each section. For, as we have seen, clans and their lineages are not distinct corporate groups, but are embodied in local communities, through which they function structurally. Such being the case, it is not surprising that they take the form of the State which gives them corporate substance.

Those clans which are associated with tribes have generally greater lineage extension and depth than those which are not so associated, and the larger the tribe the more significance this association has for the Nuer. It is in the largest tribes, territorially and numerically, and those which have expanded most and assimilated most foreigners, like the Lou and Eastern Gaajak and Gaajok tribes, that we find the greatest attention paid to the distinct and dominant position of the aristocratic clans. Indeed, not only do political re-

---

[18] Generally, an aristocracy is understood by economists as a group with privileged access to resources. The presence of an aristocracy implies a society composed of classes. Though Evans-Pritchard uses the term *aristocratic,* he reports that the Nuer appear to have social differentiation with only minimal distinctions in wealth and power. While Evans-Pritchard does discuss the material basis of Nuer life, his analysis avoids the application of either capitalist or Marxist economics to Nuer tribal and lineage systems. Specific acts by individual Nuer may be motivated by desire for gain, but the system itself does not have an economic rationale. This understanding is consistent with Malinowski's perception of the role of economics in primitive communities (see essay 13).

lations affect the clan structural form, splitting it into segments along the lines of political fission, but also the clan system may be said to have a corresponding action on the political structure. In a confusion of lineages of different clan origin and in an amorphous network of cognatic links, the political structure is given consistent form, in the language of kinship, by one clan — a single system of lineages — being made to correspond to the tribe and to its structure of opposed segments. Just as a man is a member of a tribal segment opposed to other segments of the same order and yet also a member of the tribe which embraces all these segments, so also he is a member of a lineage opposed to other lineages of the same order and yet also a member of the clan which embraces all these lineages, and there is a strict correspondence between these two sets of affiliations, since the lineage is embodied in the segment and the clan in the tribe. Moreover, the distance in clan structure between two lineages of a dominant clan tends to correspond to the distance in tribal structure between the two sections with which they are associated. Thus the system of lineages of the dominant clan enables the Nuer to think of their tribe in the highly consistent form of clan structure. In each segment the network of kinship ties are given unity and coherence by their common relationship to the lineage of the dominant clan that resides there, and as these separate lineages are composite in relation to other clans so the whole tribe is built around an exclusive agnatic framework. Though the sections may tend to draw apart and to split, a common agnatic value, shared by the dominant lineages contained in them, endures.

IV. Age-set System

Another tribal institution is the age-set system,[19] which is socially more significant among the Nuer than among other Nilotic peoples of the Sudan. Nuer boys pass into the grade of manhood through a severe ordeal and a series of rites connected with it. These initiations take place whenever there are a sufficient number of boys of from about fourteen to sixteen years of age in a village or district. All the youths who have been initiated in a successive number of years belong to one age-set, and there is a four-year interval between the last batch of initiates of one set and the first batch of the next set, and during this interval no boys may be initiated. The initiation period is open for about six years, so that, with the four years of the closed period, there are about ten years between the commencement of any age-set and the commencement of the set that precedes or succeeds it. The age-sets are not organized in a cycle.

Nuer age-sets are a tribal institution in the sense that, in the larger tribes at any rate, all the sections of a tribe have the same open and closed periods and call the sets by the same names. They are also the most characteristic of all Nuer national institutions, for initiation scars are the sign of their communion and the badge of their supremacy.[20] Moreover, though each big tribe has its own age-set organization, adjacent tribes coordinate their sets in periods and nomenclature, so that the Western Nuer, the Eastern Nuer, and the Central Nuer tend to fall into three divisions in this respect. But even when a man travels from one end of Nuerland to the other, he can always, and easily, perceive the set which is equivalent to his own in each area. The age-set system, therefore, like the clan system, whilst having a tribal connotation, is not bound by lines of political cleavage.

There is usually in each tribe a man whose privilege it is to open and close initiation periods and to give each set its name. This man belongs to one of those lineages which have a special ritual relationship to cattle and are known as "Men of the Cattle." He opens and closes initiation periods in his own district, and other districts of his tribe follow suit. Once a period has been

---

[19] An *age-set,* quite common in East Africa, is a named association of people of approximately the same age. Age-set members generally form extremely close and durable bonds. Some societies have a series of names that are used repeatedly over the course of many years; this is a cyclical age-set. Evans-Pritchard notes that Nuer age-sets are not cyclical.

[20] For males, Nuer initiation into the age-set involves making a series of parallel incisions in the forehead of the novice. The resulting scars, called *gar,* are a mark of adult status.

opened, each village and district initiates its boys when it pleases. The age-sets have no corporate activities and cannot be said to have specific political functions. There are no grades of "warriors" and "elders" concerned with the administration of the country,[21] and the sets are not regiments, for a man fights with the members of his local community, irrespective of age. In the rites of initiation there is no educative or moral training. There is no leadership in the sets.

There are probably never more than six sets in existence at any time, since six sets cover about seventy-five years. As each set dies its name is remembered only for a generation or two. Each set becomes more senior as the years go on, so that a man rises from a junior to a middle, and from a middle to a senior position in his community as a member of a group. The stratification of the age-set system is thus a further exemplification of the principle of segmentation which we have seen to be a characteristic of the political and kinship systems.[22] There is further stratification within each set, but this is not of great importance, for the set sees itself, and is seen by others, as an undivided group in relation to other sets, and its divisions become merged as the set becomes more senior. A set once complete does not change its membership, but the sets are constantly changing their positions in relation to the whole system. There is also a certain relativity about these stratified sets similar to that we noted about tribal sections and clans, for, while they keep their distinction, there is often a situational fusion of two sets in relation to a third. This is especially apparent at feasts. Whether a set is regarded as junior or equal depends not only on its position in the age-set structure, but also on the status of a third set concerned in any situation, a tendency due to the connection between age-sets and generations.

The most evident action of age-sets in determining behaviour is the way duties and privileges are effected by a transition from boyhood to manhood. Also, in virtue of the position of his set in the structure, every male Nuer is in a status of seniority, equality, or juniority towards every other Nuer man. Some men are his "sons," some his "brothers," and some his "fathers."[23] Without entering here into further detail, we may say that the attitude of a man towards other men of his community is largely determined by their respective positions in the age-set system. Hence age relations, like kinship relations, are structural determinants of behaviour. The age-set system may, moreover, be regarded as a political institution, since it is, to a large extent, segmented tribally and since it divides a tribe—as far as its male members are concerned—into groups, based on age, which stand in a definite relation to each other. We do not consider, however, that it has any direct accord with the tribal structure, based on territorial segmentation, which we have recorded. The politico-territorial system and the age-set system are both consistent in themselves and to some extent overlap, but they are not interdependent.

V. Feuds and Other Disputes

The political system operates largely, we think, through the institution of the feud which is regulated by a mechanism known as the "leopard-skin chief," a title we retain, although the appellation of "chief" is misleading.[24] This person is one of

---

[21] Here Evans-Pritchard distinguishes age-sets from age-grades. Age-set membership is permanent; grades are a series of statuses, such as warriors and elders, through which individuals pass as they grow older.

[22] Evans-Pritchard notes that the structure of age-sets is in some ways similar to that of both the political and lineage systems. Thus, age-sets provide a third set of identities for individual Nuer. It is not clear that Evans-Pritchard had read Max Weber, but the notions of overlapping and parallel identities found throughout this essay bear some resemblance to the Weber essay in this volume (9).

[23] Evans-Pritchard points out that the age-set system, like the political system, follows an idiom of kinship. He is clearly influenced by Mauss, who argued that in simple societies a few phenomena express many institutions. He called these "total social phenomena" (see essay 8, footnote 6). Here, Evans-Pritchard is suggesting that for the Nuer, kinship is essentially a total social phenomenon.

[24] In this section, Evans-Pritchard attempts to provide a model of the method through which the Nuer maintain social order in the absence of centralized political institutions, a matter of important concern to both structural-functional an-

those specialists who are concerned, in a ritual capacity, with various departments of Nuer social life and of nature. Leopard-skin chiefs belong to certain lineages only, though not all members of these lineages utilize their hereditary ritual powers. In most of Nuerland, the lineages are not branches of dominant clans.

When a man has killed another, he must at once go to a chief, who cuts his arm so that the blood may flow. Until this mark of Cain has been made, the slayer may neither eat nor drink. If he fears vengeance, as is normally the case, he remains at the chief's home, for it is sanctuary. Within the next few months the chief elicits from the slayer's kin that they are prepared to pay compensation to avoid a feud and he persuades the dead man's kin that they ought to accept compensation. During this period neither party may eat or drink from the same vessels as the other and they may not, therefore, eat in the home of the same third person. The chief then collects the cattle — till recently some forty to fifty beasts — and takes them to the dead man's home, where he performs various sacrifices of cleansing and atonement. Such is the procedure of settling a feud, and before the present administration it had often to be used, for the Nuer are a turbulent people who esteem courage the highest virtue and skill in fighting the most necessary accomplishment.

In so brief a description, one may give the impression that the chief judges the case and compels acceptance of his decision. Nothing could be further from the facts. The chief is not asked to deliver a judgement: it would not occur to Nuer that one was required. He appears to force the kin of the dead man to accept compensation by his insistence, even to the point of threatening to curse them, but it is an established convention that he shall do so, in order that the bereaved relatives may retain their prestige. What seems really to have counted were the acknowledgement of community ties between the parties concerned, and hence of the moral obligation to settle the affair by the acceptance of a traditional payment, and the wish, on both sides, to avoid, for the time being at any rate, further hostilites.[25]

A feud directly affected only close agnatic kinsmen on both sides. One did not avenge oneself on cognates or on distant agnates. Nevertheless, we believe that the feud had a wider social connotation and that therein lies its political significance. We must first recognize that feuds are more easily settled the smaller the group involved. When a man kills a near kinsman or a close neighbour, the matter is quickly closed by compensation, often on a reduced scale, being soon offered and accepted, for when a homicide occurs within a village general opinion demands an early settlement, since it is obvious to every one that were vengeance allowed corporate life would be impossible. At the other end of the scale, when a homicide occurs between primary or secondary sections of a tribe, there is little chance of an early settlement and, owing to distance, vengeance is not easily achieved, so that unsettled feuds accumulate. Such homicides are generally the result of intertribal fights in which several persons are killed. This not only increases the difficulty of settlement, but continues between the sections the mutual hostility that occasioned the fight, for, not only the close agnatic kinsmen of the dead, but entire local communities are involved. Feud, as a choice between direct vengeance and acceptance of compensation, without the necessity of immediate settlement, but requiring eventual conclusion, is especially a condition that flourishes between villages of the same district. The kinsmen of the dead man are

---

thropologists and colonial administrators. Evans-Pritchard suggests that the main way social order is maintained is through the institution of the feud. To some degree, this is curious. Structural-functionalist anthropologists view society as a smoothly functioning organism; the fact that feuding is endemic in Nuer society, at first glance, seems to contradict that view. Evans-Pritchard argues that feuding – apparent disorder – does maintain that social order. The idea of the feud as a mechanism to maintain rather than disrupt social order had a powerful impact on other British social anthropologists. For example, an influential essay by Max Gluckman (1911 – 1975) is titled "The Peace and the Feud" (1967 [1956]).

[25] Notice, in this paragraph, the emphasis on the acknowledgment of social ties. The feud is the mechanism by which social ties are reinforced and reproduced. Thus, rather than being disruptive of the social order, feuds are fundamental to the formation of that order.

near enough to strike at the kinsmen of the slayer and far enough from them to permit a temporary state of hostility between the local communities to which the parties belong. For whole communities are of necessity involved, though they are not subject to the rigid taboos that a homicide imposes on close agnatic kinsmen of slayer and slain, nor are they threatened with vengeance. Nevertheless, their members are, as a rule, closely related by cognatic or affinal ties to the principals and must assist them if there is an open fight. At the same time, these communities have frequent social contacts, so that eventually the mechanism of the leopard-skin chief has to be employed to prevent their complete dislocation. The feud thus takes on a political complexion and expresses the hostility between political segments.[26]

The balanced opposition of political segments is, we believe, largely maintained by the institution of the feud which permits a state of latent hostility between local communities, but allows also their fusion in a larger group. We say that the hostility is latent because even when a feud is being prosecuted there is no uninterrupted endeavour to exact vengeance, but the kinsmen of the dead may take any opportunity that presents itself to accomplish their purpose; and, also, because even when compensation has been accepted the sore rankles and the feud may, in spite of settlement, break out again, for Nuer recognize that in sentiment a feud goes on for ever. The leopard-skin chief does not rule and judge, but acts as mediator through whom communities desirous of ending open hostility can conclude an active state of feud. The feud, including the role played in it by the chief, is thus a mechanism by which the political structure maintains itself in the form known to us.[27]

The leopard-skin chief may also act as mediator in disputes concerning ownership of cattle, and he and the elders on both sides may express their opinion on the merits of a case. But the chief does not summon the defendants, for he has neither court nor jurisdiction and, moreover, has no means of compelling compliance. All he can do is to go with the plaintiff and some elders of his community to the home of the defendant and to ask him and his kinsmen to discuss the matter. Only if both sides are willing to submit to arbitration can it be settled. Also, although the chief, after consultation with the elders, can give a verdict, this verdict is reached by general agreement and in a large measure, therefore, arises from an acknowledgement by the defendant's or plaintiff's party that the other party has justice on its side. It is, however, very seldom that a chief is asked to act as mediator, and there is no one else who has authority to intervene in disputes, which are settled by other than legal methods.

In the strict sense of the word, the Nuer have no law. There is no one with legislative or juridical functions. There are conventional payments considered due to a man who has suffered certain injuries — adultery with his wife, fornication with his daughter, theft, broken limbs, &c. — but these do not make a legal system, for there is no constituted and impartial authority who decides on the rights and wrongs of a dispute and there is no external power to enforce such a decision were it given. If a man has right on his side, and, in virtue of that, obtains the support of his kinsmen and they are prepared to use force, he has a good chance of obtaining what is due to him, if the parties live near to one another. The usual way of obtaining one's due is to go to the debtor's kraal and

---

[26] This emphasis on conflict and the reproduction of social ties, combined with other materialist elements in Evans-Pritchard's writing, may suggest that he was heavily influenced by Marx, but this is unlikely. While both structural-functionalist and *L'Année Sociologique* thinkers were frequently political socialists (Durkheim himself was a friend and supporter of the French Socialist leader Jean Jaures), they generally rejected Marxist modes of social analysis. In fact, Evans-Pritchard's notion of conflict is not at all Marxist. For Marxists, conflict was generated by differential access to resources and leads to progressive changes in society. For Evans-Pritchard, the causes of conflict were idiosyncratic (for example, murders committed for personal reasons), and conflict serves to maintain rather than alter social relations.

[27] Note that Evans-Pritchard repeatedly makes the point that the leopard-skin chief's power is not based on any control of resources but rests purely on prestige that derives ultimately from a ranking of lineages. This is consistent with his earlier noneconomic analysis of the aristocracy.

take his cattle. To resist is to run the risk of homicide and feud. It seems that whether, and how, a dispute is settled depends very largely on the relative positions of the persons concerned in the kinship and age-set systems and the distance between their communities in tribal structure. In theory, one can obtain redress from any member of one's tribe, but, in fact, there is little chance of doing so unless he is a member of one's local community and a kinsman. The force of "law" varies with the position of the parties in political structure, and thus Nuer "law" is essentially relative, like the structure itself.

During the year I spent with the Nuer, I never heard a case being conducted, either before an individual or before a council of elders, and I received the impression that it is very rare for a man to obtain redress except by force or threats of force. And if the Nuer has no law, likewise he lacks government. The leopard-skin chief is not a political authority and the "Man of the Cattle" and other ritual agents (totemic specialists, rainmakers, fetich-owners, magicians, diviners, &c.) have no political status or functions, though they may become prominent and feared in their locality. The most influential men in a village are generally the heads of joint families, especially when they are rich in cattle, of strong character, and members of the aristocratic clan. But they have no clearly defined status or function. Every Nuer, the product of a hard and equalitarian upbringing, deeply democratic, and easily roused to violence, considers himself as good as his neighbour; and families and joint families, whilst coordinating their activities with those of their fellow villagers, regulate their affairs as they please. Even in raids, there is very little organization, and leadership is restricted to the sphere of fighting and is neither institutionalized nor permanent. It is politically significant only when raids are controlled and organized by prophets. No Nuer specialists can be said to be political agents and to represent, or symbolize, the unity and exclusiveness of local groups, and, apart from the prophets, none can be said to have more than local prominence. All leaders, in this vague sense of influential persons in a locality, are adults and, except for the occasional prophetess, all are men.

Owing to the fact that Nuer prophets had been the foci of opposition to the Government, they were in disgrace, and the more influential of them under restraint or in hiding, during my visit to Nuerland, so that I was not able to make detailed observations on their behaviour.[28] Nuer are unanimous in stating that they did not arise much before the end of the last century and there is some evidence to suggest that their emergence was connected with the spread of Mahdism. However that may be, there can be no doubt that powerful prophets arose about the time of Arab intrusion into Nuerland and that at the time of British conquest they were more respected and had wider influence than any other persons. No extensive raids were undertaken without their sanction and often they led them, received part of the spoil, and to some extent supervised the division of the rest of it. Though there seems to be good evidence that the earlier prophets were no more than ritual agents, some of the later ones appear to have begun to settle disputes, at any rate in their own districts. However, their chief political importance rather lay elsewhere. For the first time a single person symbolized, even if in a mainly spiritual form, the unity of a tribe, for the prophets were essentially tribal figures, though—and this fact is also of great political significance—their influence often extended over tribal boundaries and brought about a larger degree of unity among adjacent tribes than there appears to have been hitherto. When we add that there

---

[28] Evans-Pritchard's rather long digression on prophets is interesting. Nuer prophets—individuals who were believed to be possessed by sky spirits—were instrumental in the fierce Nuer resistance to British colonialism. Remember that when Evans-Pritchard was first in Nuerland in 1930, this resistance was still going on. Evans-Pritchard does two unusual things for a structural-functional anthropologist in this passage. First, he attempts some historical reconstruction and attempts to show the origin of a cultural attribute. (Malinowski warned explicitly against both of these practices.) Second, he associates prophets with diffusion and social change, subjects that structural-functional anthropology is generally considered to deal with only poorly.

was a tendency for the spirits which possessed prophets to pass, at their deaths, into their sons, we are justified in concluding that development was taking place towards a higher degree of federation between tribes and towards the emergence of political leadership, and in explaining these changes by reference to Arab and European intrusion. Opposition between Nuer and their neighbours had always been sectional. They were now confronted by a more formidable and a common enemy. When the Government overthrew the prophets, this development was checked.

VI. Summary

We have briefly described and analyzed what we regard as Nuer political structure: the relations between territorial segments within a territorial system and the relations between that and other social systems within an entire social structure. We have examined intertribal relations, and the relations between tribal segments. It is these relations, together with the tribal and intertribal contacts with foreign peoples, that we define as the Nuer political system. In social life the political is combined with other systems, particularly the clan system and the age-set system, and we have considered what relation they bear to the political structure. We have also mentioned those ritual specialisms which have political significance. The political system has been related to environmental conditions and modes of livelihood.

The Nuer constitution is highly individualistic and libertarian. It is an acephalous state, lacking legislative, judicial, and executive organs. Nevertheless, it is far from chaotic. It has a persistent and coherent form which might be called "ordered anarchy." The absence of centralized government and of bureaucracy in the nation, in the tribe, and in tribal segments—for even in the village authority is not vested in any one—is less remarkable than the absence of any persons who represent the unity and exclusiveness of these groups.

It is not possible from a study of Nuer society alone, if it be possible at all, to explain the presence and absence of political institutions in terms of their functional relationship to other institutions.[29] At best we can say that certain social characteristics seem to be consistent. Environmental conditions, mode of livelihood, territorial distribution, and form of political segmentation appear to be consistent. So do the presence of clans with genealogical structure and a developed age-set system seem to go together with absence of political authority and of class stratification. Comparative studies alone will show whether generalizations of such a kind are true and, moreover, whether they are useful. We cannot here discuss these questions and will only say, in conclusion, that the consistency we perceive in Nuer political structure is one of process rather than of morphology. The process consists of complementary tendencies towards fission and fusion which, operating alike in all political groups by a series of inclusions and exclusions that are controlled by the changing social situation, enable us to speak of a system and to say that this system is characteristically defined by the relativity and opposition of its segments.

Notes

a. This record is printed in a series of papers in *Sudan Notes and Records* from 1933 to 1938. The research was done on four expeditions and was financed mainly by the Government of the Anglo-Egyptian Sudan and partly through a Leverhulme Fellowship. Rather than merely describe again what I have already described elsewhere, I have presented my material in a more abstract form than would be permissible were a descriptive account not accessible.

---

[29] This concluding paragraph points to two general characteristics of British structural-functional anthropology. Though Evans-Pritchard made a foray into historical reconstruction above, here he confirms that his goal has been to explicate the existing system rather than to explain its origins. Further, he suggests that the goal of anthropology should be to formulate general laws of social organization, which can only be done through cross-cultural comparison. Finally, he returns again (if indirectly) to the organic metaphor that lies at the base of much of this style of social analysis: society is a set of interdependent institutions that "go together" to make a smoothly functioning social organism.

Culture and Personality

The organic analogy of the British structural-functionalists necessarily implied a holistic view of culture. On the other hand, while Franz Boas insisted on the holistic study of culture, he lacked a compelling principle to guide his work. Although he used the rhetoric of holism, many of the historical particularists tended to treat culture as a chance association of disparate features. One way that several of Boas' students sought to circumvent this problem without challenging the bases of historical particularism was through ideas borrowed from psychoanalysis and Gestalt psychology. Gestalt psychologists examined personality as an interrelated psychological pattern rather than a collection of separate elements. This insight particularly influenced the work of Ruth Fulton Benedict (1887–1948), Margaret Mead (1901–1978), and others, who focused on the psychological concept of personality as their unifying theme.

Benedict, Mead, Abram Kardiner (1891–1981), and Cora Du Bois (1903–1991) examined the problem of how humans acquired culture and culture's relationship to individual personality. Because they focused on the interaction between individual personality and culture, they became known as founding members of the culture and personality school. Lett (1987) points out the three broad themes represented in this perspective: the relationship between culture and human nature (represented here by Mead's essay); the relationship between culture and individual personality (represented by Benedict's essay); and the relationship between culture and a society's typical personality type, which was explored by Kardiner and Du Bois.

The interest of anthropologists in Sigmund Freud's psychoanalytic theory was a major impetus behind the development of the culture and personality field. A. L. Kroeber, for example, underwent psychoanalysis and practiced as a lay analyst for a brief time. Although most anthropologists rejected Freud's forays into anthropological theory, they were interested in the effect of culture on the individual and recognized psychoanalysis as a powerful tool for probing the human psyche.

The major figures associated with founding this school all had close ties to Boas and to each other. For example, Edward Sapir was one of Boas' most gifted students. Although primarily known for his work in linguistics, Sapir was well versed in psychoanalytic literature and was good friends with Benedict, who also taught at Columbia with Boas. Their correspondence played an important role in shaping Benedict's theories. Mead was one of Benedict's first students and also studied under Boas.

Benedict came to anthropology from literature, having taught English before starting her career in anthropology. Her interest in the interplay between culture and personality was encouraged by her friend Sapir and her mentor Boas. A cultural relativist in the Boasian tradition, Benedict believed that there were no higher or lower cultures, just different lifestyles. Elaborating on this belief, Benedict wrote an article called "Anthropology and the Abnormal" (1934a), in which she argued that normal and abnormal were culturally determined, and that what was abnormal in one culture might be perfectly acceptable in another. The most comprehensive expression of Benedict's ideas was her book *Patterns of Culture* (1934b). Here, Benedict proposed that each culture had a unique pattern, called a cultural configuration, which determined the fundamental personality characteristics of its members. To illustrate this concept, Benedict selected three societies: Zuñi, Dobu, and the Kwakiutl. Relying on her own and Elsie Clew Parsons' (1874–1941) observations among the Zuñi, Reo Fortune's (1903–1979) work with the people of Dobu, and Boas' writings on the Kwakiutl, Benedict described the configuration for each society based on the dominant personality characteristics observed in those cultures. It was Benedict's contention that people were molded into their culture's dominant personality type through enculturation, what Garbarino calls a "master plan of psychological patterning" (1977:66). Thus, Zuñi peoples were identified as Apollonian, Dobuans as paranoid, and the Kwakiutl as Dionysian.

Boas' students were predisposed to look for cultural influences on personality development because of their mentor's focus on the effect of historical circumstances on cultural developments. Margaret Mead's work clearly illustrates this theme. In a series of studies, Mead focused on the influence of culture on human social development. Starting with *Coming of Age in Samoa* (1928) and continuing with *Growing Up in New Guinea* (1930) and one of her more controversial books, *Sex and Temperament in Three Primitive Societies* (1935), Mead attempted to separate the biological and cultural factors that control human behavioral and personality development. Together with Benedict's *Patterns of Culture,* Mead's trilogy firmly established the cultural configuration and national character approaches in American psychological anthropology (Hsu 1980:349).

Later in Mead's career, particularly in a 1942 study conducted with her third husband, Gregory Bateson (1904–1980), the influence of Freud showed strongly in her work. In *Balinese Character: A Photographic Analysis* (Bateson and Mead 1942), they tried to visually document how child-rearing techniques affected Balinese personality development.

Margaret Mead was also one of the most colorful figures in American anthropology. She was born in Philadelphia, the daughter of a professor at the Wharton School of the University of Pennsylvania. Like her mentor, Ruth Benedict, she had an early interest in literature. During her undergraduate career at Barnard College in New York City, she was a member of a literary group called the Ash Can Cats (Lutkehaus 1995:189).

In 1923 Mead began her graduate career at Columbia University, working with both Ruth Benedict and Franz Boas. Her relationship with her mentor Benedict was particularly intense. Mead and Benedict became lovers after the completion of her dissertation, a relationship that continued until Benedict's death in 1948 (Bateson 1984:117).

In 1925 Mead did her first fieldwork in Samoa. It was the only fieldwork she was to undertake alone, and it became the basis of her first book, *Coming of Age in Samoa* (1928). *Coming of Age* was an immediate hit, launching Mead on a long career as one of anthropology's most prolific authors. She published 39 books (15 of them collaborations) and almost 1,400 other pieces of various kinds. Many of these were brief essays designed for popular consumption. She wrote regularly for *The Nation* and *The New York Times.* For seventeen years, with her collaborator Rhoda Metraux (1914–), she wrote a monthly column for the women's magazine *Redbook.* In addition to this, she made films and appeared frequently on radio and television. By the late 1950s and 1960s, her regular appearances on television talk shows made her one of the best-known academics in American life, and certainly the best-known anthropologist. Publication in the popular press placed Mead squarely in the tradition of Franz Boas, who frequently wrote for a general rather than professional audience.

Mead's personal life was particularly tumultuous. In addition to her long affair with Benedict, she was married three times. Her first marriage to her childhood sweetheart Luther Cressman began in 1923. In 1925, he left to continue his studies in theology in Europe, and she to begin her fieldwork in Samoa. On the way back from Samoa, Mead met and fell in love with the Australian anthropologist and psychologist Reo Fortune. She divorced Cressman and married Fortune in 1928. In the late 1920s and early 1930s, Fortune and Mead continued to do fieldwork together in New Guinea. In 1932, while working on the Sepik River in New Guinea, Fortune and Mead met British anthropologist and psychologist Gregory Bateson.

From 1932 to 1935, Mead, Fortune, and Bateson worked together and occasionally lived together. During this time, Mead fell in love with Bateson. When the three returned from the field in 1935, Mead divorced Fortune, and in 1936 she married Bateson. Soon after, they left to conduct research together in Bali. Mead's only child, Mary Catherine Bateson, was born to the couple in 1939. Catherine Bateson is today a linguist and anthropologist specializing in Middle Eastern culture. Mead and Bateson divorced in 1950.

Mead's own sex life certainly affected her interests and work. The research for *Sex and Temperament in Three Primitive Societies,* the introduction of which we reprint here, was done while she, Fortune, and Bateson lived together in New Guinea. Mead's daughter later wrote

> It is not accidental that when Margaret was on the Sepik, struggling with the question of diversity in herself and in her ways of loving, she was formulating the contrasts between three New Guinea peoples who dealt very differently with maleness and femaleness, with assertion and creativity. (Bateson 1984:160)

The introduction to *Sex and Temperament* clearly shows Mead's interest in culture as a primary factor determining masculine and feminine social characteristics and behavior. The book, written for a popular rather than a professional audience, was designed to demonstrate the range of cultural diversity (McDowell 1980:278).

Although Benedict's and Mead's work had great popular appeal, both were widely criticized by anthropologists. Both assumed culture as a given and claimed that it determined personality, but neither could specify how this process occurred. If culture determined personality, where did it originate?

In the 1930s and 1940s, psychoanalyst Abram Kardiner, in collaboration with anthropologists Du Bois, Sapir, and Ralph Linton (1893–1953), among others, developed a neo-Freudian approach to the study of these questions. According to Langness (1987), Kardiner formulated his theory after reading *The Future of an Illusion* (1961 [1928]), in which Freud proposed that children's early life experiences determine their later religious beliefs. For example, children raised in a household with a strict authoritarian father conceptualize their deities as demanding, always observant, and determined to punish misbehavior. Following this line of thought, Kardiner advanced a theory that explained the mechanism by which culture determined personality.

Kardiner proposed what he called the "basic personality structure"—a collection of fundamental personality traits shared by the normal members of a society. Following Freud, he hypothesized that the foundations of personality development were set in early childhood. He argued that since child-rearing procedures such as disciplining, weaning, and toilet training (what Kardiner termed "primary institutions") are generally standardized within a society, all members of that society are subjected to the same basic influences on their personality development. Consequently, a society's primary institutions lead to the formation of its basic personality structure. Personality, in turn, influences culture through the creation of secondary institutions. These are cultural institutions, such as religion, created to satisfy the needs of personality through the psychological mechanism of projection.

Kardiner tested his theory with anthropological data supplied by his anthropologist colleagues in a series of seminars in 1936 and 1937. It soon became apparent to Kardiner that no data had been collected specifically for the sort of analysis he proposed. To resolve this issue, anthropologist Cora Du Bois traveled to the island of Alor in the Dutch East Indies to gather the appropriate types of information. Du Bois collected a variety of ethnographic and psychological data (such as Rorschach tests, life histories, and reports of dreams) from Alorese informants. After her return in 1939, Du Bois, Kardiner, and other independent analysts reviewed the data; they all reached the same fundamental conclusions concerning the basic characteristics of Alorese personality.

A weakness in Kardiner's theory was that the basic personality structure could not account for the variation in personality present in even the smallest society. To finesse this problem, Du Bois proposed the modal personality—the personality type that was statistically most common in a society (Kaplan and Manners 1972). Like Kardiner, Du Bois hypothesized that primary institutions would lead to the formation of a basic set of personality characteristics (as illustrated by her Alorese information), but there would also exist individual variation in how personalities developed and were expressed. The modal personality provided a theoretical tool for examining the interplay of personality and culture while allowing for the psychological variation that exists among the members of a society.

The outbreak of World War II provided anthropologists with opportunities to push culture and personality research still further. In the 1940s and during the Cold War, the United States became vitally interested in studying the psychology of the citizens of the nations with which it was in conflict. The culture and personality theorists responded with national character studies. Although an outgrowth of the work on modal personality, these studies were different in several ways. First, they dealt with industrial nation-states rather than primitive societies. Culture and personality theorists typically worked with small numbers of people and relied on descriptive ethnography. Because national character studies involved nations with millions of people, participant observation was inappropriate; because the nations being studied were sometimes hostile, participant observation was often impractical. To find their way around these problems, anthropologists interviewed immigrants, analyzed literature and films, and searched government records. The results were mixed.

Two of the most famous national character studies are Benedict's *Chrysanthemum and the Sword* (1946), a study of the Japanese, and Geoffrey Gorer (1905–1985) and John Rickman's

(1891–1951) *The People of Great Russia: A Psychological Study* (1949). Both followed a neo-Freudian approach, attempting to relate child-rearing practices to adult personality types. Benedict, for example, examined Japanese toilet-training practices in relation to the alleged Japanese preoccupation with obedience and order. Gorer and Rickman hypothesized that the Russian national character (supposedly a manic-depressive personality type) resulted from the practice of swaddling infants. It is easy to see how this study fit into the politics of the Cold War.

While Benedict's work has withstood the test of time somewhat better than Gorer and Rickman's, subsequent research has shown that most of the national character studies were simply inaccurate. The practice of swaddling, for example, was not widespread in Russia; thus it could not explain the Russian personality type—if such a thing existed. Such errors played a large part in the declining popularity of national character studies. By the late 1950s, most anthropologists had rejected the psychoanalytic approach to cultural analysis.

Despite this decline of scholarly acceptance, culture and personality, and national character studies in particular, remain keen areas of popular interest. Introductory books in cultural anthropology still reference Mead's and Benedict's work (see Crapo 1993 and Kottak 1994). Numerous books, such as Harrison's *Who Prospers: How Cultural Values Shape Economic and Political Success* (1992), are published detailing aspects of the cultural personality of this or that group. Usually, like Copeland's *Going International: How to Make Friends and Deal Effectively in the Global Marketplace* (1985), these are marketed as guides for businesspeople.

16. Psychological Types in the Cultures of the Southwest

Ruth Fulton Benedict (1887–1948)

THE CULTURE OF THE PUEBLO INDIANS IS strongly differentiated from that of surrounding peoples.[1] Most obviously, all aspects of their life are highly ritualized, highly formalized. No one has lived among them who has not been struck by the importance of the formal detail in rite and dance, the intricate interrelations of the ceremonial organization, the lack of concern with personal religious experience or with personal prestige or exploit. The emphasis in their all-absorbing ceremonial routine is placed where it was in the medieval Roman church of certain periods, on the formal observance, the ritualistic detail for its own sake.

This is so conspicuously true for the Southwest peoples that in descriptions of their culture we have been content to let the matter rest with this characterization. Yet in a civilization such as that of the North American Indians high ritualistic development sets no group off in any definitive fashion from the vast majority of peoples. The ritual of the sun dance, the peace pipe ceremonies, the cult groups, and age-societies of the Plains, or the winter ceremonial of the Northwest Coast bulk perhaps slightly less prominently in the total life of these people than the calendric dances and retreats of the Southwest, but it is not by any such matter of gradation that the South-

(1930)

west is set off from other American Indian cultures. There is in their cultural attitudes and choices a difference in psychological type fundamentally to be distinguished from that of surrounding regions. It goes deeper than the presence or the absence of ritualism; ritualism itself is of a fundamentally different character within this area, and without the understanding of this fundamental psychological set among the Pueblo peoples we must be baffled in our attempts to understand the cultural history of this region.[a]

It is Nietzsche who has named and described, in the course of his studies in Greek tragedy, the two psychological types which have established themselves in the region of the Southwest in the cultures of the Pueblo.[2] He has called them the Dionysian and the Apollonian. He means by his classification essentially confidence in two diametrically different ways of arriving at the values of existence.[b] The Dionysian pursues them through "the annihilation of the ordinary bounds and limits of existence"; he seeks to attain in his most valued moments escape from the boundaries imposed upon him by his five senses, to break through into another order of experience. The desire of the Dionysian, in personal experience or in ritual, is to press beyond, to reach a certain psychological state, to achieve excess. The closest analogy to the emotions he seeks is drunkenness, and he values the illuminations of frenzy. With

---

[1] Benedict did fieldwork among the Zuñi, Cochiti, and Pima throughout the mid-1920s. This paper, presented in 1928, was her first major analysis of her experiences there. In it, she develops themes later elaborated in *Patterns of Culture,* published in 1934. Perhaps because it was designed for a popular audience and written in an engaging style, *Patterns of Culture* became an enduring classic of anthropology—one still frequently read by students in introductory courses. Despite frequent criticism, Benedict's descriptions of Native American cultures and her theoretical position have had an important effect on American anthropology.

[2] Benedict derives her categories of Apollonian and Dionysian from *The Birth of Tragedy* (published in 1872), a study of the origins of Greek drama by German philosopher Friedrich Nietzsche (1844–1900). Some biographers have suggested that Benedict's intellectual preference for this classification scheme was related to her experience as a very young child, when, at her father's open-casket funeral, she experienced the contrast between her mother's open grief and her father's calm, tragic corpse (Modell 1983:1).

Blake,[3] he believes "the path of excess leads to the palace of wisdom." The Apollonian distrusts all this, if by chance he has any inkling of the occurrence of such experiences; he finds means to outlaw them from his conscious life. He "knows but one law, measure in the Hellenic sense." He keeps the middle of the road, stays within the known map, maintains his control over all disruptive psychological states. In Nietzsche's fine phrase, even in the exaltation of the dance, "he remains what he is, and retains his civic name."[c]

The Southwest Pueblos are, of course, Apollonian, and in the consistency with which they pursue the proper valuations of the Apollonian they contrast with very nearly the whole of aboriginal America. They possess in a small area, islanded in the midst of predominantly Dionysian cultures, an *ethos* distinguished by sobriety, by its distrust of excess, that minimizes to the last possible vanishing point any challenging or dangerous experiences. They have a religion of fertility without orgy, and absorption in the dance without using it to arrive at ecstasy. They have abjured torture. They indulge in no wholesale destruction of property at death. They have never made or bought intoxicating liquors in the fashion of other tribes about them, and they have never given themselves up to the use of drugs. They have even stripped sex of its mystic danger. They allow to the individual no disruptive role in their social order. Certainly in all of these traits they stand so

strikingly over against their neighbors that it is necessary to seek some explanation for the cultural resistances of the Pueblos.[4]

The most conspicuous contrast, in the Pueblos, is their outlawry of the divine frenzy and the vision. Now in North America at large the value of ecstatic experience in religion is a cornerstone of the whole religious structure. It may be induced by intoxicants and drugs; it may be self-induced—which may include such means as fasting and torture—or it may be achieved in the dance.

We may consider first the ecstasy induced by intoxicants and drugs.[5] For the neighboring Pima, who share the culture of the primitive tribes of northern Mexico, intoxication is the visible mirroring of religion, it is the symbol of its exaltation, the pattern of its mingling of clouded vision and of insight. Theory and practice are explicitly Dionysian.

> "And I was made drunk and given the sacred songs;"
> "He breathed the red liquor into me,"

are in their songs common forms of reference to the shamanistic experience. Their great ceremony is the drinking of the "tizwin," the fermented juice of the fruit of the giant cactus. The ceremony begins with all religious formality and the recitation of ritual, but its virtue lies in the intoxication itself; the desired state is that of roused excitement, and they accept even extreme violence

---

[3] The reference is to William Blake (1757–1827), an English poet, painter, and visionary. Benedict, who had studied English literature at Vassar College, was a more artful writer than most anthropologists. In addition to her anthropological works, Benedict wrote poetry under the pen name of Anne Singleton, a name that may be revealing of her personality. Her poems appeared in literary magazines, but she was unable to get a collection of them published. Thankfully for anthropology, her inability to find a publisher for her book dissuaded her from a career in poetry.

[4] Benedict speaks here of seeking explanation for Pueblo Apollonian behavior, but offers none. Benedict saw culture as personality writ large. She believed that societies were able to choose their cultures out of the full range of human variability, but she was not concerned with understanding why a society would choose one type of culture rather than another. While Benedict's work offered many examples of Pueblo Apollonian behavior, it provided no historical context—she made no attempt to explain the origins of the cultural personalities she documented. The lack of history is surprising since Franz Boas, her teacher, placed such an emphasis on historical reconstruction. Despite their Boasian backgrounds, culture and personality writers were generally ahistorical.

[5] While Benedict's anthropology is psychological, it is not Freudian. Like other Boasians, she rejected Freud's notions of cultural evolution as nonscientific and ethnocentric. She traced her intellectual descent from the German psychologist Wilhelm Dilthey (1883–1911), who believed that the goal of psychology was to understand the inner life of the mind. He also proposed the existence of different *weltanshauungen* or worldviews, which were categories much like Benedict's Apollonian and Dionysian.

more readily than a state of lethargy. Their ideal is to stave off the final insensibility indefinitely while achieving the full excitation of the intoxicant. This is of course a form of fertility and health magic and is in complete accord with the Dionysian slant of their culture.

It is much commoner, north of Mexico, to use drugs rather than intoxicants for religious ends. The peyote or mescal bean of northern Mexico has been traded up the Mississippi Valley as far as the Canadian border, and has been the occasion of serious religious movements among many tribes. It gives supernormal experiences with particularly strong affect, no erotic excitation, very often brilliant color images. The cult is best described for the Winnebago[d] where the peyote is identified with the supernatural. "It is the only holy thing I have been aware of in all my life"; "this medicine alone is holy and has rid me of all evil."[e] It was eaten everywhere with the object of attaining the trance or supernormal sensations which the drug can give. The Arapaho ate it in an all-night ceremony after which the effects of the drug prolonged themselves throughout the following day.[f] The Winnebago speak of eating it for four days and nights without sleep.

The *datura* is a more drastic poison. I have been told by the Serrano[6] and Cahuilla of boys who have died as a result of the drink, and the Luiseño tell also the same story.[g] It was used by the tribes of Southern California, and north including the Yokuts, for the initiation of boys at puberty. Among the Serrano the boys were overcome by the drug during the night and lay in a comatose condition through the next day and night, during which time they were granted visions. On the following day they ran a race.[h] Among the Luiseño it seems to have been the same, four nights of trance being spoken of as excessive.[i] The

Diegueño reckon only one night of complete stupefaction.[j] The Mohave drank *datura* in order to gain luck in gambling; they were said to be unconscious for four days,[k] during which time they received their power in a dream.

None of these alcohol- and drug-induced excitations have gained currency among the Pueblos.[7] The Pima are the nearest settled neighbors of the Zuñi to the southwest and easily accessible; tribes of the Plains with which the eastern Pueblos came in contact are the very ones in which peyote practices are important; and to the west the tribes of Southern California share certain characteristic traits of this very Pueblo culture. The absence of these traits in the Pueblos is therefore not due to the cultural isolation of impassable barriers. We know too that the period of time during which the Pueblos and their neighbors have been settled relatively near to one another is of considerable antiquity. But the Pueblos have defended themselves against the use of drugs and intoxicants to produce trance or excitement even in cases where the drugs themselves are known among them. Any Dionysian effect from them is, we may infer, repulsive to the Pueblos, and if they receive cultural recognition at all it is in a guise suited to Apollonian sobriety. They did not themselves brew any native intoxicant in the old days, nor do they now. Alone among the Indian reservations, the whiskey of the whites has never been a problem in the Southwest. When, in 1912, drinking seemed to be making some headway among the younger generation in Zuñi, it was the Pueblo elders themselves who took the matter in hand. It is not that it is a religious taboo; it is deeper than that, it is uncongenial. The peyote has been introduced only in Taos, which is in many ways marginal to Pueblo culture.

---

[6] While Benedict here mentions her own 1922 study of the Serrano, she did little fieldwork, preferring instead to draw on studies from many sources.

[7] Benedict started her career in ethnology as a student of Elsie Clew Parsons (1875–1941) at the New School for Social Research but soon went to study under Franz Boas at Columbia. After the completion of her dissertation, she remained with Boas until his retirement in 1936; she herself continued at Columbia until her death in 1948. The particularly close relationship between Boas and Benedict gave her exceptional access to the work and friendship of his other students, particularly Edward Sapir, Mead, (essay 17), and Kroeber (see essay 11). Both their work, and her conversations and correspondence with them, had a profound influence on Benedict's anthropology. Note the strong reliance on work by Boas, his students, and friends in Benedict's notes to this essay.

Datura is used in Zuñi as it was in ancient Mexico[l] in order to discover a thief, and Mrs. Stevenson[8] gives an account of the manner of its use.[m] Read in connection with her quotations on datura poisoning and the two to four day trances of the Mohave and Mission Indians, it is a classic example of the Apollonian recasting of a Dionysian technique. In Zuñi the man who is to take the drug has a small quantity put in his mouth by the officiating priest, who then retires to the next room and listens for the incriminating name from the lips of the man who has taken the *datura*. He is not supposed to be comatose at any time; he alternately sleeps and walks about the room. In the morning he is said to have no memory of the insight he has received. The chief care is to remove every trace of the drug and two common desacratizing techniques are employed: first, he is given an emetic, four times, till every vestige of the drug is supposed to be ejected; then his hair is washed in yucca suds.[9] The other Zuñi use of *datura* is even further from any connection with a Dionysian technique; members of the priestly orders go out at night to plant prayer sticks on certain occasions "to ask the birds to sing for rain," and at such times a minute quantity of the powdered root is put into the eyes, ears, and mouth of each priest. Here any connections with the physical properties of the drug are lost sight of.

Much more fundamental in North America than any use of drugs or alcohol to induce ecstasy was the cult of the self-induced vision. This was a near-universality from ocean to ocean, and everywhere it was regarded as the source of religious power. The Southwest is by no means beyond the southern limits of its distribution, but it is the one outstanding area of North America where the characteristic development of the vision is not found. This experience has several quite definite characteristics for North America: it is achieved characteristically in isolation, and it gives to the successful individual a personal manitou or guardian spirit who stands to him in a definite life-long relationship. Though west of the Rockies it is often regarded as an involuntary blessing available only for those of a particular psychological make-up, throughout the great extent of the continent it is sought by isolation and fasting, and in the central part of the continent often by self-torture. This "vision," from which supernatural power was supposed to flow, did not by any means signify only supernormal or Dionysian experiences, but it provided always a pattern within which such an experience had peculiar and institutionalized value; and in the great majority of cases it was these more extreme experiences that were believed to give the greater blessing.

The absence of this vision complex in the Southwest is one of the most striking cases of cultural resistance or of cultural reinterpretation that we know in North America. The formal elements are found there: the seeking of dangerous places, the friendship with a bird or animal, fasting, the belief in special blessings from supernatural encounters. But they are no longer instinct with the will to achieve ecstasy. There is complete reinterpretation. In the pueblos they go out at night to feared or sacred places and listen for a voice, not that they may break through to communication with the supernatural, but that they

---

[8] Matilda Stevenson (1849–1915) was a pioneering American ethnographer who did extensive fieldwork among the Zuñi between 1879 and 1915 and published several monographs on them. Stevenson, founder and first president of the Women's Anthropological Society, was one of the first ethnographers to do work that centered on women and children.

[9] Two aspects of Boasian thought exerted particularly strong influences on Benedict. The first was cultural relativism. Notice that her language describing the use of hallucinogens, an exotic and possibly offensive cultural practice, is matter-of-fact and nonjudgmental. While Apollonian culture traits might seem more desirable to upper-middle-class intellectual Americans (her primary audience), her writing here and in *Patterns of Culture* describes Apollonian and Dionysian cultures as equally attractive.

The second Boasian influence was an emphasis on holism. Boas suggested that cultures were integrated; Benedict pushed this idea further. She saw culture as having internal logical consistency and being characterized by a single dominant trend or pattern. This essay is largely an exercise in the demonstration of the holism that she saw in culture in general and among the Pueblo peoples in particular. Throughout the essay, she tries to show that all Pueblo practices, even the use of hallucinogenic drugs, fit the restrained, Apollonian worldview.

may take the omens of good luck and bad. It is regarded as a minor ordeal during which you are badly frightened, and the great taboo connected with it is that you must not look behind you on the way home no matter what seems to be following you. The objective performance is much the same as in the vision quest; in each case, they go out during the preparation for a difficult undertaking—in the Southwest often a race—and make capital of the darkness, the solitariness, the appearance of animals. But the significance is utterly different.[10]

Fasting, the technique most often used in connection with the self-induced vision, has received the same sort of reinterpretation in the Southwest. It is no longer utilized to dredge up experiences that normally lie below the level of consciousness; it is here a requirement for ceremonial cleanness. Nothing could be more unexpected to a Pueblo Indian than any theory of a connection between fasting and any sort of exaltation. Fasting is required during all retreats, before participation in a dance, in a race, etc., etc., but it is never followed by power-giving experience; it is never Dionysian. Fasting, also, like drugs and visions, has been revamped to the requirements of the Apollonian.

Torture, on the contrary, has been much more nearly excluded.[11] It is important only in the initiations and dances of certain curing societies[n] and in these cases there is no suggestion of any states of self-oblivion. It is interesting that the Pueblos have been exposed to self-torture practices, both in the aboriginal culture of the Plains, and in European-derived practices of the Mexican Penitentes.[12] The eastern Pueblos are in the very heart of the Santa Fe Penitentes country and these Mexicans attend their dances and ceremonies regularly and without hindrance. Much in their practice they have in common with the Indians: the retreats in the ceremonial house, the organization of the brotherhood (priesthood, for the Indian), the planting of crosses. But the self-lashing with cactus whips, the crucifixion on Good Friday, are alien; torture has not penetrated Pueblo life either from these practices or from those of the Plains or of California. Among the Pueblos, every man's hand has its five fingers,[13] and unless he has been tortured as a witch, he is unscarred.

No more than the Pueblos have allowed ecstasy as induced by alcohol or drugs, or under the guise of the vision, have they admitted it as induced by the dance. Perhaps no people in North America spend more time in dance than the Southwest Pueblos. But its use as the most direct technique at our command for the inducement of supernormal experience is alien to them. With the frenzy of a Nootka bear dance, of a Kwakiutl cannibal dance, of a ghost dance, of a Mexican whirling dance, their dancing has nothing in common. It is rather a technique of monotonous appeal, of unvarying statement; always, in the phrase of Nietzsche's I used before, "they remain as they are and retain their civic names." Their theory seems to be that by the reiteration of the dance they can exercise compulsion upon the forces they wish to influence.

There are several striking instances of the loss, for the Pueblos, of the Dionysian significance of specific dance behavior, the objective aspects of which they still share with their neighbors. The best is probably the dance upon the altar. For the Cora of northern Mexico the climax

---

[10] Benedict's focus here is not on the actions performed, but on how the actors interpret their actions. Boas wanted to build anthropology on a scientific, empirical model; Benedict came to see anthropology as an interpretive art, as much a humanity as a social science. At the end of her life, she wrote that anthropology stood at the boundary between science and the humanities (1948:585). This view has made her an important figure for many interpretive and postmodern anthropologists.

[11] Notice that Benedict offers no reason why the Pueblo have rejected torture. It is simply an aspect of their culture, and culture is an independent force creating itself.

[12] *Penitentes* are individuals who, at Easter, imitate the suffering of Jesus by whipping themselves and imitating his crucifixion.

[13] *Five fingers* refers to a common Plains Indian practice of chopping off a finger joint in mourning or for spiritual purposes.

of the whirling dance is reached in the dancer's ecstatic, and otherwise sacrilegious, dancing upon the ground altar itself. In his madness it is destroyed, trampled into the sand again.[o] But this is also a Pueblo pattern. Especially the Hopi at the climax of their dances in the kivas dance upon the altar destroying the ground painting. Here there is no ecstasy; it is raw material used to build up one of the common Pueblo dance patterns where two "sides" which have previously come out alternately from opposite sides, now come out together for the dance climax. In the snake dance, for instance,[p] in the first set Antelope (dancer of Antelope society) dances, squatting, the circuit of the altar, retires; Snake (dancer of Snake society) repeats. In the second set Antelope receives a vine in his mouth and dances before the initiates trailing it over their knees; retires; Snake repeats with a live rattlesnake held in the same fashion. In the final set Antelope and Snake come out together, dancing together upon the altar, still in the squatting position, and destroy the ground painting. It is a formal sequence, like a Morris dance.[14]

It is evident that ecstatic experience is not recognized in the Southwest and that the techniques associated with it in other areas are reinterpreted or refused admittance. The consequence of this is enormous: it rules out shamanism. For the shaman, the religious practitioner whose power comes from experiences of this type, is everywhere else in North America of first rate importance. Wherever the authority of religion is derived from his solitary mental aberrations and stress experiences and his instructions derived therefrom are put into practice by the tribe as a sacred privilege, that people is provided with a technique of cultural change which is limited only by the unimaginativeness of the human mind.[15] This is a sufficient limitation; so much so

that it has never been shown that cultures which operate on this basic theory are more given to innovation than those which disallow such disruptive influences. This should not blind us to the fact, however, that the setting in these two cultures for the exercise of individuality is quite different; individual initiative which would be fully allowed in the one case[q] would in the other be suspect, and these consequences are fully carried out in the Southwest. They have hardly left space for an impromptu individual act in their closely knit religious program; if they come across such an act they label the perpetrator a witch. One of the Zuñi tales I have recorded tells of the chief priest of Zuñi who made prayer sticks and went out to deposit them. It was not the time of the moon when prayer sticks must be planted by members of the curing societies, and the people said, "Why does the chief priest plant prayer sticks? He must be conjuring." As a matter of fact he was calling an earthquake for a private revenge. If this is so in the most personal of Zuñi religious acts, that of planting prayer sticks, it is doubly so of more formal activities like retreats, dances, etc. Even individual prayers of the most personal sort—those where cornmeal is scattered—must be said at sunrise, or over a dead animal, or at a particular point in a program, etc.; the times and seasons are always stipulated. No one must ever wonder why an individual was moved to pray.

Instead therefore of shamans with their disruptive influence upon communal practices and settled traditions, the Southwest has religious practitioners who become priests by rote memorizing and by membership in societies and cult groups. This membership is determined by heredity and by payment[r] for though in their own theory serious illness or an accident like snake bite or being struck by lightning are the accepted

---

[14] Critics have frequently accused Benedict of being so guided by her vision of the logical constancy of culture that she distorted her data. They point out that, Benedict's claims to the contrary, alcoholism was common on the Pueblo reservations during her fieldwork (and is so today). In this passage, Benedict suggests that a dance done with a live rattlesnake in the mouth is not an ecstatic ritual. Maybe so, but most observers would probably disagree.

[15] Benedict comments in passing on the "unimaginativeness of the human mind." Like Boas, Benedict believed that within a culture, most traits originated by diffusion rather than independent invention. However, neither agreed at all with the radical European diffusionist thinkers.

reasons for membership in certain societies, there are always alternative ways of joining even the curing societies so that no man with interest and sufficient means remains outside. In Zuñi heredity is the chief factor in membership in the priestly groups, payment in the curing societies; in neither is individual supernatural power ever claimed by any member as a result of personal illumination. Those who practice curing in Zuñi are merely those who by payment and by knowledge of ritual have reached the highest orders of the curing societies and received the personal corn fetish, the *mili*.

If the ecstasy of the Dionysian has been rejected in the Southwest with all its implications, so too has the orgy.[16] There is no doubt that the idea of fertility bulks large in the religious practices of the Southwest,[s] and with fertility rites we almost automatically couple orgy, so universally have they been associated in the world. But the Southwest has a religion of fertility founded on other associations. Haeberlin's study gives a useful summary of the type of ritual that is here considered to have this efficacy.[t] The cylinders the men carry and the amulets carried by the women in ceremonies are sex symbols and are thrown by them into springs or onto ground paintings; or in the women's dance two are dressed as male dancers and shoot arrows into a bundle of cornhusks; or a line of women with yucca rings run in competition with a line of men with kicking sticks. In Peru in a race of exactly similar import, men racing women, the men ran naked and violated every woman they overtook.[u] The pattern is self-evident and common throughout the world, but not in the Southwest. In Zuñi there are three occasions on which laxness is countenanced. One of these is in the retreat of the Tlewekwe society,

which has power over cold weather. The priestesses of the medicine bundle of this society (*te etone*) and the associated bundle (*mu etone*) during one night receive lovers, and they collect a thumb's length of turquoise from their partners to add to the decorations of their bundles. It is an isolated case in Zuñi and the society can no longer be very satisfactorily studied. The other two cases are rather a relaxation of the customary strict chaperonage of the young people, and occur at the ceremonial rabbit hunt[v] and on the nights of the scalp dance; children conceived on these nights are said to be exceptionally vigorous. Doctor Bunzel[17] writes, "These occasions on which boys and girls dance together or are out together at night provide an opportunity for sweethearts. There is no promiscuity, and they are never, never orgiastic in character. There is amiable tolerance of sexual laxity; a 'boys will be boys' attitude." It is all very far indeed from the common Dionysian sex practices for the sake of fertility.

It is not only in connection with fertility and sex that orgy is common among the peoples of America. In the region immediately surrounding the Southwest, there is on the one hand the orgy of sun dance torturing to the east and the orgy of wholesale destruction in the mourning ceremonies to the west. As I have said, torture plays a very slight role in the Southwest, orgiastic or otherwise. Mourning is made oppressive by fear of the dead, but there is no trace of abandon. Mourning here is made into the semblance of an anxiety complex; it is a completely different thing from the wild scenes of burning the dead in a bonfire of offered property and of clothes stripped from the mourner's backs that the Mohave practice[w] and that is found in such Dionysian fullness

---

[16] Throughout this essay, but particularly here and below, the examples given are quite sensational, even risqué. This is typical of much of the anthropology of Benedict's time and, in her case, there were at least two reasons for it. First, she often wrote for a popular audience, and like Freud, Mead, and Malinowski, used the lure of the discussion of forbidden topics such as sex to attract and hold her audience. Second, she was a firm believer in cultural relativism. Showing exotic cultural practices that were unacceptable to her audience in a calm and rational light helped build the case for the acceptance of all cultures as equally valid. In this connection, it should be noted that Benedict practiced what she preached. She was a bitter opponent of racism and a forceful advocate for tolerance within her own society.

[17] Like many of those that Benedict mentions, Ruth Bunzel (1898–1990) was a student of Boas and a member of Benedict's own circle. She is particularly remembered for her studies of Zuñi pottery making.

commonly in California, where among the Maidu mourners have to be forcibly restrained from throwing themselves into the flames,[x] and among the Pomo they snatch pieces of the corpse and devour them.[y]

One Dionysian ceremony of wide American distribution has established itself in the Southwest—the scalp dance.[18] This is the victory dance of the Plains, or the women's dance, and the position of honor given to women in it, the four-circle coil danced around the encampment, the close-fitting war bonnet, certain treatments of the scalp, are the same in the Southwest as on the Plains. The wilder abandons of the Plains dance are, as we should expect, omitted, but there occurs in this dance, at least in Zuñi, one of the few ritual Dionysian acts of the Southwest—the washing and biting of the scalp. For the repulsion against contact with bones or a corpse is intense among these people, so that it makes an occasion for horror out of placing a scalp between the teeth, whereas placing a snake between the teeth in the snake dance is no such matter. The woman who carries the scalp in the dance—the position of honor—must rise to this pitch and every girl is said to dread being called out for the role.

Ecstasy and orgy, therefore, which are characteristic of America at large are alien in the Southwest. Let me illustrate this fundamental Apollonian bent in the Southwest by certain specific examples of the way in which it has worked itself out in their culture.

There is considerable emphasis in North America upon the ritualistic eating of filth and it is in this category that the very slightly developed cannibalistic behavior of the Northwest Coast belongs.[19] That is, the emphasis there is never, as so often in cannibalism, upon the feast, nor on doing honor to or reviling the dead. The cannibal dance of the Kwakiutl is a typically Dionysian ritual.[z] It is not only that it is conceived as a dramatization of a condition of ecstasy which the main participant must dance to its climax before he can be restored to normal life; every ritualistic arrangement is designed—I do not mean consciously—to heighten the sense of the anti-natural act. A long period of fasting and isolation precedes the rite, the dance itself is a crouching, ecstatic pursuit of the prepared body held outstretched toward him by a woman attendant. With the required ritualistic bites the anti-natural climax is conceived to be attained, and prolonged vomiting and fasting and isolation follows.

In the filth eating of the Southwest, which is the psychological equivalent to this initiation of the Kwakiutl cannibal, the picture is entirely different. The rite is not used to attain horror, nor to dramatize a psychological climax of tension and release. Captain Bourke has recorded the Newekwe feast he attended with Cushing, at which gallon jars of urine were consumed by the members of the society. The picture is as far from that of the Kwakiutl rite as any buffoonery of our circus clowns. The atmosphere was one of coarse joviality, each man trying to outdo the others. "The dancers swallowed huge decanters, smacked their lips, and amid the roaring merriment of the spectators, remarked that it was very, very good. The clowns were now upon their mettle, each trying to surpass his neighbors in feats of nastiness."[aa]

The same comment is true not only of filth eating but of clowning in the Southwest in general.[20] I take it that the true Dionysian use of clowning is as comic relief in sacred ceremonial where the release from tension is as full of meaning as the preceding tension, and serves to accentuate it. This use of clowning seems to have been

---

[18] In this passage, Benedict seems to allow that an Apollonian society can include some Dionysian practices. However, this apparent contradiction is resolved by the fact that those who perform the Dionysian act dread participating in it.

[19] Here, as in *Patterns of Culture*, Benedict uses the Kwakiutl as her chief example of a Dionysian culture. In so doing, she relied almost entirely on the work of Boas. She had access not only to Boas' published work, but also to his notebooks and journals. More importantly, she worked closely with Boas for almost twenty years.

[20] Notice Benedict's use of the first person in this paragraph and below. Her reporting of Pueblo clowning is not couched in neutral, scientific language; rather she focuses on how things seemed to her. This articulates well with her view of anthropology as an interpretive art.

developed, for instance, in the ancient Aztec rites. Now I have never seen any clowning in the Pueblos that seemed to me remotely even to partake of this character, and I do not know of any description which would indicate its presence. Clowning can be buffoonery with no Dionysian implications, as we know well enough from the examples in our own civilization. It is this same use that is most prominent in the Southwest, but clowning is used there also for social satire, as in the take-offs of agents, churches, Indian representatives, etc., and it is common too as a substitute for the joking-relationship, which is absent here, and its license for very personal public comment.

Another striking example of the Southwest Apollonian bent is their interpretation of witch power. The Southwest has taken the European witch complex with all its broomsticks and witches' animal suits and eyes laid on a shelf, but they have fitted it into their own *Weltanschauung*. The most articulate statement that I know of a widespread attitude is still in manuscript in Doctor Parson's monograph on Isleta.[21] The difference, for Isleta, between witch power and good power is simply that good supernatural power is always removed from you as soon as you have put it to the use you intended; witch power is non-removable, it rides you for life. Their practice perfectly agrees with this; after every sacred investiture every participant in any rite is desacratized, the unwanted mysterious power is laid aside. Nothing could conceptualize more forcibly their discomfort in the face of mystery. Even the best supernatural power is uncanny.

Their lack of comprehension of suicide is, I think, another specific Apollonian trait. The Pima tell many stories of men who have killed themselves for women, and the Plains made suicide a ceremonial pattern; fundamentally their vows to assume the slit sash were suicide pledges in order to raise their rank. But the Pueblos tell the most inept stories[bb] which are obvious misunderstandings of the concept. Again and again I have tried to convey the general idea of suicide to different Pueblo Indians, either by story or by exposition. They always miss the point. Yet in their stories they have the equivalent. There are a number of Zuñi stories[cc] which tell of a man or woman whose spouse has been unfaithful—or of priests whose people have been unruly; they send messengers, often birds, to the Apache and summon them against their pueblo. When the fourth day has come—nothing ever happens in the Southwest till the fourth day—they wash themselves ceremonially and put on their finest costumes and go out to meet the enemy that they may be the first to be killed. When I have asked them about suicide no one has ever mentioned these stories, though they had perhaps been told that very day, and indeed they do not see them in that light at all. They are ritual revenge and the Dionysian gesture of throwing away one's life is not in question.

The cultural situation in the Southwest is in many ways hard to explain.[22] With no natural barriers to isolate it from surrounding peoples, it presents probably the most abrupt cultural break that we know in America. All our efforts to trace out the influences from other areas are impressive for the fragmentariness of the detail; we find bits of the weft or woof of the culture, we do not find any very significant clues to its pattern. From the point of view of the present paper this clue is to be found in a fundamental psychological set which has undoubtedly been established for centuries in the culture of this region, and which has bent to its own uses any details it imitated from surrounding peoples and has created an intricate cultural pattern to express its own preferences. It is not only that the understanding of this psychological set is necessary for a descriptive statement of this culture; without it the cultural dynamics

---

[21] Benedict draws much of her information on the Pueblos from the work of Parsons, her first teacher, who worked extensively among the Pueblos and published many books on them. Boas and Parsons were very close friends and did some of their research together.

[22] In conclusion, Benedict again declares the fundamental inexplicability of culture. In *Patterns of Culture,* she used a Digger Indian myth to explain cultural origins and differences: "God gave to every people . . . a cup of clay, and from this cup they drank their life. . . . They all dipped in the water but their cups were different" (1934b:33).

of this region are unintelligible. For the typical choices of the Apollonian have been creative in the formation of this culture, they have excluded what was displeasing, revamped what they took, and brought into being endless demonstrations of the Apollonian delight in formality, in the intricacies and elaborations of organization.

Notes

Proceedings of the Twenty-third International Congress of Americanists, September 1928 (New York, 1930), 572–81.

a. For the theoretical justification of this position in the study of culture see Benedict, Ruth, "Cultures and Psychological Types," *America Anthropologist,* N. S., in press.

b. I have not followed Nietzsche's definitions in their entirety; I have used that aspect which is pertinent to the problems of the Southwest.

c. *Birth of Tragedy,* p. 68.

d. Radin, Paul, "The Winnebago Tribe," *Thirty-seventh Annual Report Bureau of American Ethnology,* Washington, 1923, 388–426.

e. Ibid., pp. 408; 392.

f. Kroeber, A. L., "The Arapaho," *Bulletin, American Museum of Natural History,* vol. 18, New York, 1907, p. 398.

g. Kroeber, A. L., "Handbook of the Indians of California," *Bulletin 78, Bureau of American Ethnology,* Washington, 1925, p. 669.

h. Benedict, Ruth, "A Brief Sketch of Serrano Culture," *American Anthropologist,* N. S., vol. 26, pp. 366–392, 1924, p. 383.

i. Kroeber, A. L., *Handbook,* p. 669.

j. Ibid.

k. Ibid., p. 779.

l. Safford, William E., "Narcotic Daturas of the Old and New World; an Account of Their Remarkable Properties and Their Uses as Intoxicants and in Divination," *Annual Report, Smithsonian Institution for 1920,* pp. 537–567, Washington, 1922, p. 551.

m. Stevenson, Matilda C., "The Zuñi Indians, Their Mythology, Esoteric Fraternities and Ceremonies," *Twenty-third Annual Report, Bureau of American Ethnology,* Washington, 1904, p. 89.

n. Cushing, F. H., "My Experience in Zuñi," *Century Magazine,* N. S., 4, p. 31; Stevenson, M. A., *The Zuñi Indians,* p. 503. "All are filled with the spirit of good nature."

o. Preuss, K. T., *Die Nayarit-Expedition.* Leipzïg, 1912, p. 55.

p. Voth, H. R., "Oraibi Summer Snake Ceremony," *Field Columbian Museum, Publication 83.* Chicago, 1903, p. 299.

q. See Radin, Paul, *Primitive Man as Philosopher.* New York and London, 1927, pp. 257–275, for discussion of the wide limits of individualism among the Winnebago.

r. Except for the war chiefs' societies where it was necessary to have taken a scalp.

s. Haeberlin, H. K., "The Idea of Fertilization in the Culture of the Pueblo Indians," *Memoirs, American Anthropological Association,* vol. 3, no. 1, 1916.

t. Ibid., especially p. 39 ff.

u. Arriaga, P. J., *Extirpacion de la Idolotria del Peru.* Lima, 1621, p. 36 sq.

v. Information from Dr. Ruth Bunzel.

w. Kroeber, *"Handbook,"* p. 750.

x. Ibid., p. 431.

y. Ibid., p. 253.

z. Boas, Franz, "The Social Organization and Secret Societies of the Kwakiutl," *Report, United States National Museum for 1895,* Washington, 1897, p. 537 sq.

aa. Bourke, John G., *Compilation of Notes and Memoranda Bearing on the Use of Human Ordure and Human Urine in Rites of a Religious or Semireligious Character among Various Nations.* Washington, 1888, p. 9.

bb. Parsons, Elsie Clews, "A Zuñi Detective," *Man,* vol. 16, pp. 168–170, London, 1916, p. 169.

cc. Benedict, R., Mss.

17. Introduction

Margaret Mead (1901–1978)

WHEN WE STUDY THE SIMPLER SOCIETIES, WE cannot but be impressed with the many ways in which man has taken a few hints and woven them into the beautiful imaginative social fabrics that we call civilizations.[1] His natural environment provided him with a few striking periodicities and contrasts—day and night, the change of seasons, the untiring waxing and waning of the moon, the spawning of fish and the migration-times of animals and birds. His own physical nature provided other striking points—age and sex, the rhythm of birth, maturation, and senescence, the structure of blood-relationship. Differences between one animal and another, between one individual and another, differences in fierceness or in tenderness, in bravery or in cunning, in richness of imagination or plodding dullness of wit—these provided hints out of which the ideas of rank and caste, of special priesthoods, of the artist and the oracle, could be developed. Working with clues as universal and as simple as these, man made for himself a fabric of culture within which each human life was dignified by form and meaning. Man became not merely one of the beasts that mated, fought for its food, and died, but a human being, with a name, a position, and a god. Each people makes this fabric differently, selects some clues and ignores others, emphasizes a different sector of the whole arc of human potentialities. Where one culture uses as a main thread the vulnerable ego, quick to take insult or perish of shame, another selects uncompromising bravery and even, so that there may be no admitted cowards, may like the Cheyenne Indians invent a specially complicated social position for the overfearful. Each simple, homogeneous culture can give scope to only a few of the varied human endowments, disallowing or penalizing others too antithetical or too unrelated to its major emphases to find room within its walls. Having originally taken its values from the values dear to some human temperaments and alien to others, a culture embodies these values more and more firmly in its structure, in its political and religious systems, in its art and its literature; and each new generation is shaped, firmly and definitely, to the dominant trends.

Now as each culture creates distinctively the social fabric in which the human spirit can wrap itself safely and intelligibly, sorting, reweaving, and discarding threads in the historical tradition that it shares with many neighboring peoples, it may bend every individual born within it to one type of behavior, recognizing neither age, sex, nor special disposition as points for differential elaboration. Or a culture may seize upon the very obvious facts of difference in age, in sex, in strength, in beauty, or the unusual variations, such as a native propensity to see visions or dream dreams, and make these dominant cultural themes. So societies such as those of the Masai and the Zulus make a grading of all individuals by age a basic point of organization, and the Akikiyu of East Africa make a major drama out of the ceremonial

From *Sex and Temperament in Three Primitive Societies* (1935)

---

[1] Mead was influenced by Ruth Benedict in her writing style, her strong emphasis on cultural relativism, and her belief in patterns in human culture. Note the psychological emphasis placed in the first paragraph. According to Mead, social stratification developed out of personal differences between individuals. Humans select their cultures, choosing some traits and ignoring others. In the last line of this paragraph, she even paraphrases Benedict's cultural configuration concept. Although *Patterns of Culture* was published only one year before Mead's book, Mead had read an early draft of Benedict's work while conducting the field research upon which *Sex and Temperament* was based (Sanday 1980:342). Compare the opening quotation in Benedict's book—"In the beginning God gave to every people a cup of clay, and from this cup they drank their life"—to Mead's "man made for himself a fabric of culture within which each human life was dignified by form and meaning."

ousting of the older generation by the younger. The aborigines of Siberia dignified the nervously unstable individual into the shaman, whose utterances were believed to be supernaturally inspired and were a law to his more nervously stable fellow tribesmen. Such an extreme case as this, where a whole people bows down before the word of an individual whom we would classify as insane, seems clear enough to us. The Siberians have imaginatively and from the point of view of our society unjustifiably, elevated an abnormal person into a socially important one. They have built upon a human deviation that we would disallow, or if it became troublesome, imprison.[2]

If we hear that among the Mundugumor people of New Guinea children born with the umbilical cord wound around their necks are singled out as of native and indisputable right artists, we feel that here is a culture which has not merely institutionalized a kind of temperament that we regard as abnormal—as in the case of the Siberian shaman—but also a culture that has arbitrarily associated, in an artificial and imaginative way, two completely unrelated points: manner of birth and an ability to paint intricate designs upon pieces of bark. When we learn further that so firmly is this association insisted upon that only those who are so born can paint good pictures, while the man born without a strangulating cord labours humble and unarrogant, and never attains any virtuosity, we see the strength that lies in such irrelevant associations once they are firmly embedded in the culture.

Even when we encounter less glaring cases of cultural elaboration, when we read of a people in which the first-born son is regarded as different in kind from his later-born brethren, we realize that here again the human imagination has been at work, re-evaluating a simple biological fact. Although our own historical tradition hints to us that the first-born is "naturally" a little more important than the others, still when we hear that among the Maori the first-born son of a chief was so sacred that only special persons could cut his infant locks without risking death from the contact, we recognize that man has taken the accident of order of birth and raised a superstructure of rank upon it. Our critical detachment, our ability to smile over these imaginative flights of fancy—which see in the first-born or the last-born, the seventh child of the seventh child, the twin, or the infant born in a caul[3] a being specially endowed with precious or maleficent powers—remains undisturbed. But if we turn from these "self-evident" primitive constructs to points of elaboration that we share with primitive peoples, to points concerning which we are no longer spectators, but instead are deeply involved, our detachment vanishes. It is no doubt purely imaginative to attribute ability to paint to birth with the cord about the neck, or the power to write poetry to one born a twin. To choose leaders or oracles from aberrant and unusual temperaments that we brand as insane is not wholly imaginative, but at least is based on a very different premise, which selects a natural potentiality of the human race that we neither use nor honour. But the insistence upon a thousand and one innate differences between men and women, differences many of which show no more immediate relationship to the biological facts of sex than does ability to paint to manner of birth, other differences which show a congruence with sex that is neither universal nor necessary—as is the case in the association of epileptic seizure and religious gift—this indeed we do not regard as an imaginative creation of the human mind busy patterning a bare existence with meaning.[4]

This study is not concerned with whether there are or are not actual and universal differ-

---

[2] In this paragraph, Mead makes a strong statement of cultural relativism. In particular, she emphasizes Benedict's contention that what is abnormal in one culture may be celebrated in another and provides a series of ethnographic examples to illustrate this point. Along with the issue of cultural relativity, Mead introduces the major point of this work. She says that cultures choose to emphasize issues like sex, age, or beauty, or ignore them. In other words, these factors are culturally rather than biologically determined.

[3] *Caul:* an infant in a caul is born partially covered with membrane from the uterus.

[4] Mead continues her attack on biological determinism in this paragraph. She says that Westerners can accept that there is great variation in beliefs and customs between cultures but inappropriately resist the notion that almost all the differ-

ences between the sexes, either quantitative or qualitative. It is not concerned with whether women are more variable than men, which was claimed before the doctrine of evolution exalted variability, or less variable, which was claimed afterwards. It is not a treatise on the rights of women, nor an inquiry into the basis of feminism. It is, very simply, an account of how three primitive societies have grouped their social attitudes towards temperament about the very obvious facts of sex difference. I studied this problem in simple societies because here we have the drama of civilization writ small, a social microcosm alike in kind, but different in size and magnitude, from the complex social structures of peoples who, like our own, depend upon a written tradition and upon the integration of a great number of conflicting historical traditions. Among the gentle mountain-dwelling Arapesh, the fierce cannibalistic Mundugumor, and the graceful head-hunters of Tchambuli, I studied this question. Each of these tribes had, as has every human society, the point of sex-difference to use as one theme in the plot of social life, and each of these three peoples has developed that theme differently. In comparing the way in which they have dramatized sex-difference, it is possible to gain a greater insight into what elements are social constructs, originally irrelevant to the biological facts of sex-gender.[5]

Our own society makes great use of this plot. It assigns different roles to the two sexes, surrounds them from birth with an expectation of different behaviour; plays out the whole drama of courtship, marriage, and parenthood in terms of types of behaviour believed to be innate and therefore appropriate for one sex or for the other. We know dimly that these roles have changed even within our history. Studies like Mrs. Putnam's *The Lady*[a] depict woman as an infinitely malleable lay figure upon which mankind has draped ever varying period-costumes, in keeping with which she wilted or waxed imperious, flirted or fled. But all discussions have emphasized not the relative social personalities assigned to the two sexes, but rather the superficial behavior-patterns assigned to women, often not even to all women, but only to women of the upper class. A sophisticated recognition that upper-class women were puppets of a changing tradition blurred rather than clarified the issue. It left untouched the roles assigned to men, who were conceived as proceeding along a special masculine road, shaping women to their fads and whims in womanliness. All discussion of the position of women, of the character and temperament of women, the enslavement or the emancipation of women, obscures the basic issue—the recognition that the cultural plot behind human relations is the way in which the roles of the two sexes are conceived, and that the growing boy is shaped to a local and special emphasis as inexorably as is the growing girl.[6]

The Vaërtings attacked the problem in their book *The Dominant Sex*[b] with their critical imagination handicapped by European cultural tradi-

---

ences we identify between men and women are also cultural. The biological facts of man- and womanhood, she argues, cannot explain the variation in gender behavior across cultures. In this and many other works, Mead focused on child-rearing as one of the processes by which people learn their culture's patterns (McDowell 1980:283).

[5] It may be hard to conceptualize the climate in which Mead was writing, but it is useful to remember that women had only been given the right to vote fifteen years before the publication of this book. Biological theories about the place of men and women in society were still strong. Consequently, Mead is disingenuous in this passage. She is careful to claim her book is not about women's rights or feminism but simply offers an objective description of men and women in three different societies. Of course, it *is* about women's rights and feminism, and she is attacking the common theories that stated that women were inherently inferior to men, but Mead makes her argument indirectly. She demonstrates that the ways we categorize men and women as masculine and feminine are cultural, not biological. She steers the reader to this conclusion obliquely by showing how American beliefs are different from beliefs in other cultures. Notice also the whack she takes at the evolutionists and their thoughts on feminism in the second sentence. It's a good line.

[6] Contrary to Putnam, Mead argues that gender stereotyping is as inexorable for boys as it is for girls. The determination of maleness and femaleness is arbitrary. Thus, the question is not only the "enslavement or emancipation of women" but also of men. Mead may have been trying to make her argument more palatable to men.

tion.[7] They knew that in some parts of the world there had been and still were matriarchal institutions which gave to women a freedom of action, endowed women with an independence of choice that historical European culture granted only to men. By simple sleight-of-hand they reversed the European situation, and built up an interpretation of matriarchal societies that saw women as cold, proud, and dominant, men as weak and submissive. The attributes of women in Europe were foisted upon men in matriarchal communities—that was all. It was a simple picture, which really added nothing to our understanding of the problem, based as it was upon the limiting concept that if one sex is dominating in personality, the other sex must be ipso facto submissive. The root of the Vaërtings' mistake lies in our traditional insistence upon contrasts between the personality of the two sexes, in our ability to see only one variation upon the theme of the dominant male, and that the hen-pecked husband. They did conceive, however, of the possibility of a different arrangement of dominance from our traditional one, mainly because to thinking based upon patriarchal institutions the very existence of a matriarchal form of society carries with it an implication of an imaginary reversal of the temperamental position of the two sexes.

But recent studies of primitive peoples have made us more sophisticated.[c] We know that human cultures do not all fall into one side or the other of a single scale and that it is possible for one society to ignore completely an issue which two other societies have solved in contrasting ways. Because a people honour the old may mean that they hold children in slight esteem, but a people may also, like the Ba Thonga of South Africa, honour neither old people nor children or, like the Plains Indians, dignify the little child and the grandfather; or, again, like the Manus and parts of modern America, regard children as the most important group in society. In expecting simple reversals—that if an aspect of social life is not specifically sacred, it must be specifically secular; that if men are strong, women must be weak—we ignore the fact that cultures exercise far greater licence than this in selecting the possible aspects of human life which they will minimize, overemphasize, or ignore. And while every culture has in some way institutionalized the roles of men and women, it has not necessarily been in terms of contrast between the prescribed personalities of the two sexes, nor in terms of dominance or submission. With the paucity of material for elaboration, no culture has failed to seize upon the conspicuous facts of age and sex in some way, whether it be the convention of one Philippine tribe that no man can keep a secret, the Manus assumption that only men enjoy playing with babies, the Toda prescription of almost all domestic work as too sacred for women, or the Arapesh insistence that women's heads are stronger than men's. In the division of labour, in dress, in manners, in social and religious functioning—sometimes in only a few of these respects, sometimes in all—men and women are socially differentiated, and each sex, as a sex, forced to conform to the role assigned to it. In some societies, these socially defined roles are mainly expressed in dress or occupation, with no insistence upon innate temperamental differences. Women wear long hair and men wear short

---

[7] Mathilde and Mathis Vaërting published their book in 1923, resurrecting the "mother-right" school of thought that had been popular in Europe off and on since the middle of the nineteenth century. In *Das Mutterrecht* (*Mother Right,* 1861), the evolutionist Johann Jakob Bachofen popularized the idea that the earliest human civilizations were governed by women, who were eventually overthrown and subjugated by men. Since Bachofen, this theory has appeared in a number of guises. For example, in *The Witch-Cult in Western Europe* (1921), Margaret Murray (1863–1963) proposed a similar argument in relation to the witchcraft persecutions of the Renaissance. Murray argued that pre-Christian religion took the form of a fertility cult centered on the goddess Diana, who had a horned consort. According to Murray, male-dominated Christianity perverted this religion by twisting the cult's nature symbolism into devil worship and instigating the witch trials of the Renaissance. Another incarnation of this idea was expressed in Robert Graves' *The White Goddess* (1948). Mead uses this discussion of the Vaërtings' book not only to criticize their point of view, but also to condemn the tendency to view situations as dichotomous extremes (if women are dominant, then men must be submissive; if men are strong, then women must be weak).

hair, or men wear curls and women shave their heads; women wear skirts and men wear trousers, or women wear trousers and men wear skirts. Women weave and men do not, or men weave and women do not. Such simple tie-ups as these between dress or occupation and sex are easily taught to every child and make no assumptions to which a given child cannot easily conform.[8]

It is otherwise in societies that sharply differentiate the behaviour of men and of women in terms which assume a genuine difference in temperament. Among the Dakota Indians of the Plains, the importance of an ability to stand any degree of danger or hardship was frantically insisted upon as a masculine characteristic. From the time that a boy was five or six, all the conscious educational effort of the household was bent towards shaping him into an indubitable male. Every tear, every timidity, every clinging to a protective hand or desire to continue to play with younger children or with girls, was obsessively interpreted as proof that he was not going to develop into a real man. In such a society it is not surprising to find the berdache, the man who had voluntarily given up the struggle to conform to the masculine role and who wore female attire and followed the occupations of a woman. The institution of the berdache in turn served as a warning to every father; the fear that the son might become a berdache informed the parental efforts with an extra desperation, and the very pressure which helped to drive a boy to that choice was redoubled. The invert who lacks any

discernible physical basis for his inversion has long puzzled students of sex, who when they can find no observable glandular abnormality turn to theories of early conditioning or identification with a parent of opposite sex. In the course of this investigation, we shall have occasion to examine the "masculine" woman and the "feminine" man as they occur in these different tribes, to inquire whether it is always a woman of dominating nature who is conceived as masculine, or a man who is gentle, submissive, or fond of children or embroidery who is conceived as feminine.[9]

In the following chapters we shall be concerned with the patterning of sex behaviour from the standpoint of temperament, with the cultural assumptions that certain temperamental attitudes are "naturally" masculine and others "naturally" feminine. In this matter, primitive people seem to be, on the surface, more sophisticated than we are. Just as they know that the gods, the food habits, and the marriage customs of the next tribe differ from those of their own people, and do not insist that one form is true or natural while the other is false or unnatural, so they often know that the temperamental proclivities which they regard as natural for men or for women differ from the natural temperaments of the men and women among their neighbours. Nevertheless, within a narrower range and with less of a claim for the biological or divine validity of their social forms than we often advance, each tribe has certain definite attitudes towards temperament, a theory of what human beings, either men or

---

[8] Here you see a strong statement of the cultural nature of sex roles. Interestingly, Mead reversed this argument in her 1949 book *Male and Female.* There she argued that variability in sex roles was conditioned by biology, specifically, the reproductive functions and anatomical differences between men and women (Sanday 1980:340).

Additionally, she directly attacks the French sociologist Émile Durkheim in this paragraph. Durkheim had suggested that cultural dichotomies (sacred-profane, right-left, and so on) were a fundamental human method of conceptualizing the world. Here she says that the sacred-profane distinction does not exist and that seeing things in terms of dichotomies ignores all the possibilities in between.

[9] Mead uses the term "invert" to refer to *berdache* in Native American societies. Her references to the "feminine man" and "masculine woman" make it clear she is referring to homosexuality. Her mention of "early conditioning or identification with a parent of opposite sex" is a reference to the psychoanalytic explanation for homosexuality. Although Mead is specifically addressing these topics in a discussion of peoples in New Guinea, she must also have been struggling with issues of sexuality and gender roles in her personal life. Mead — a strong, outspoken woman in a field dominated by men — was intimately involved with another woman, Ruth Benedict. Furthermore, while conducting the research upon which this book was based with Reo Fortune, her second husband, she had met and become interested in Gregory Bateson, who later became her third husband.

women or both, are naturally like, a norm in terms of which to judge and condemn those individuals who deviate from it.[10]

Two of these tribes have no idea that men and women are different in temperament. They allow them different economic and religious roles, different skills, different vulnerabilities to evil magic and supernatural influences. The Arapesh believe that painting in colour is appropriate only to men, and the Mundugumor consider fishing an essentially feminine task. But any idea that temperamental traits of the order of dominance, bravery, aggressiveness, objectivity, malleability, are inalienably associated with one sex (as opposed to the other) is entirely lacking. This may seem strange to a civilization which in its sociology, its medicine, its slang, its poetry, and its obscenity accepts the socially defined differences between the sexes as having an innate basis in temperament and explains any deviation from the socially determined role as abnormality of native endowment or early maturation. It came as a surprise to me because I too had been accustomed to use in my thinking such concepts as "mixed type," to think of some men as having "feminine" temperaments, of some women as having "masculine" minds.[11] I set as my problem a study of the conditioning of the social personalities of the two sexes, in the hope that such an investigation would throw some light upon sex-differences. I shared the general belief of our society that there was a natural sex-temperament which could at the most only be distorted or diverted from normal expression. I was innocent of any suspicion that the temperaments which we regard as native to one sex might instead be mere variations of human temperament, to which the members of either or both sexes may, with more or less success in the case of different individuals, be educated to approximate.

Notes

a. E. J. S. Putnam, *The Lady*, Sturgis and Walton, 1910.

b. Mathilde and Mathis Vaërting, *The Dominant Sex*, Doran, 1923.

c. See especially Ruth Benedict, *Patterns of Culture*, Houghton Mifflin, 1934.

---

[10] Along with cultural relativism, a persistent strain in American anthropology has been to romanticize primitive peoples as being inherently wise or somehow living closer to and more in tune with nature. This theme is very strong in Mead's work. In *Coming of Age in Samoa* (1928), for example, Mead presents Samoan life as almost utopian.

[11] Once again, note Mead's style. In this last paragraph she shifts from a third-person description to a first-person confession. This is important since she ultimately bases her theory on her personal experiences in New Guinea and the authority these experiences give her as an ethnographer. By reading the book, she hopes, you will be converted as she was.

Cultural Ecology and Neoevolutionary Thought

$\mathcal{A}$ major theoretical shift occurred in American anthropology in the late 1940s and the 1950s. For the first half of the century, the principal work in American anthropology was based on the Boasian tradition or the neo-Freudian approach of the culture and personality school. Beginning in the 1930s, the antievolutionary perspective of the Boasian tradition had once again to compete with new and more sophisticated evolutionary approaches proposed by Julian Steward (1902–1972), Leslie White (1900–1975), and George Peter Murdock (1897–1985).

Steward and White developed a techno-environmental approach to cultural change, and both were influenced by Marxist thought. Steward developed an ecological approach that focused on the adaptation of individual cultures to specific environmental circumstances. White is best known for his formulation of a general evolutionary theory of culture, an approach that had been abandoned after Boas thrashed unilineal evolutionary theory at the turn of the century. Murdock was influential in resurrecting cross-cultural comparisons in anthropology. Like Steward, and Lewis Henry Morgan and E. B. Tylor before them, Murdock was interested in large-scale cross-cultural analysis. He is best known for his creation of the Human Relations Area Files, or HRAF. Harris (1968:606) credits Murdock, Steward, and White's revival of this form of analysis with the "mid-century collapse of historical particularism." Although Harris' eulogy for historical particularism was premature, these three men set the foundation for the formulation of ecological anthropology and cultural materialism, two of the most influential forms of anthropological analysis since the 1960s.

Julian Steward was a student of A. L. Kroeber and developed his evolutionary theory despite the disdain of his famous mentor. Steward devoted most of his energy to the study of the environmental adaptation of specific societies. His first research was in archaeology, but he then moved to ethnography and worked with the Shoshoni, the Pueblo, and later the Carrier Indians in British Columbia. Steward also devoted a great deal of energy to the study of parallel developmental sequences in the evolution of civilizations in the New and Old Worlds.

Steward proposed that cultures in similar environments would tend to follow the same developmental sequences and formulate similar responses to their environmental challenges. He termed those cultural features most closely associated with subsistence practices the "cultural core" (1955). Cultures that shared similar core features belonged to the same *culture type*. Having identified these culture types, he compared and sorted them into a hierarchy arranged by complexity. Steward's original ranking was family, multifamily, and state-level societies; these categories were later refined by his followers into the now familiar classifications of band, tribe, chiefdom, and state.

Steward did not believe that cultures followed a single universal sequence of development. He proposed that cultures could evolve in any number of distinct patterns depending on their environmental circumstances. Consequently, he called his theory *multilinear* evolution, to distinguish it from nineteenth-century unilineal evolutionary theories. The methodology Steward outlined for multilinear evolution involved a field of study he called *cultural ecology;* that is, the examination of the cultural adaptations formulated by human beings to meet the challenges posed by their environments. The selection of Steward's work, presented in essay 18, clearly shows how he viewed culture as an evolutionary adaptation to the environment.

Leslie White was trained in Boasian historical particularism. He was a student of Boas' student Edward Sapir at the University of Chicago but found Boasian anthropology intellectually unsatisfying. In his first teaching post at the University of Buffalo, he discovered and read the work of nineteenth-century evolutionists such as Herbert Spencer and particularly Lewis Henry Morgan. White's research led him to the conclusion that unilineal evolutionary theory was fundamentally sound, but that nineteenth-century evolutionists had worked with inadequate data. Following Spencer, White argued that evolutionary development from simple to complex, with increasing specialization of parts, was just as valid for cultures as it was in biology. The problem was developing a quantifiable, universal standard of measurement. In his 1943 article "Energy and the Evolution of Culture," White proposed that the control of energy was a key factor in cultural evolution and could serve as the standard by which to measure evolutionary progress. According to White, culture was the means by which humans adapted to nature. Greater cultural complexity and specialization were achieved by increased concentration of energy. White proposed a grand, universal law of cultural evolution: culture advances as the amount of energy harnessed per capita per year increases, or as the efficiency with which energy is utilized increases. In this article, presented in essay 19, White traces the evolution of human culture, like Morgan, using technological advances in the utilization of energy sources.

Inspired by his reading of Marx, White separated culture into three analytical levels—the technological, sociological, and ideological. Like Marx, he believed that all the institutions of society contributed to the evolution of culture. But he also believed that technology played the primary role in social evolution and that changes in technology affected a society's institutions and value systems. Like many other Americans influenced by Marx, however, White did not use Marxist dialectics in his analysis of society.

George Peter Murdock received his undergraduate and graduate degrees at Yale University and taught there for thirty-two years. He also rejected the Boasian approach to anthropology. In direct opposition to Boas' avoidance of cross-cultural generalizations, Murdock was interested in the statistical testing of cross-cultural hypotheses. Toward this end he established the Cross-Cultural Survey in 1937, which a decade later formed the basis of the HRAF, a huge bank of ethnographic data on over one thousand societies. This information is indexed according to standardized categories. Using this information, one can conduct cross-cultural quantitative analyses and test cultural hypotheses in a wide variety of societies.

In addition to creating the HRAF, Murdock is remembered for his 1949 book *Social Structure*. He believed that a universal set of principles governed the relationship between family structure, kinship, and marriage practices. In *Social Structure* Murdock attempted to determine these principles through quantitative analysis and, using the comparative data from 250 societies, was able to demonstrate the utility of the HRAF.

Murdock generally saw his work as deriving from the positivist approach of Spencer, but he recognized that Morgan's (1870) study of kinship was instrumental in shaping the quantitative-comparative approach he developed in *Social Structure*. On the opening page of his chapter on kinship, Murdock wrote "The scientific significance of kinship systems was first appreciated by Morgan in what is perhaps the most original and brilliant single achievement in the history of anthropology" (1960:61). Additionally, Morgan is one of the anthropologists to whom *Social Structure* is dedicated. The Murdock essay presented here, "Family Stability in Non-European Cultures," illustrates his preoccupation with analyzing comparative data to arrive at universal principles and demonstrates his use of tables from which statistical conclusions about the societies can be derived.

Although White, Steward, and Murdock were evolutionists, they had very different perspectives on cultural evolution. Steward's multilinear evolution is specific and relativistic; he analyzed the adaptation of each culture to its specific environment. White's evolutionary scheme is general and abandons cultural relativism. In his view, cultures can be measured by specific, absolute standards and can be ranked on a universal scale. In the 1960s Marshall Sahlins (1930–) and Elman Service (1915–1996) attempted to reconcile these two approaches. Based on yet another analogy with biological evolution, they suggested that evolution follows two paths. The first is general evolution, a grand movement from simple to complex. The second is specific evolution, the change of individual cultures in response to their particular environmental circumstances (Sahlins and Service 1960).

Murdock's cross-cultural comparisons of cultural traits in many ways paralleled Steward's theory of multilinear evolution, and his attempts to statistically demonstrate universal principles of kin relations resembled White's effort to formulate a universal theory of cultural evolution. However, Murdock focused his efforts on the evolution of aspects of social structure such as kin terminology, family structure, and marriage patterns. Steward and White dealt almost exclusively with material culture and largely ignored kinship.

No theoretical viewpoint is immune to the political context in which it develops, and cultural ecology is a particularly good example of this point. The cultural ecologists relied heavily on the insights of Marxist analysis, but given the virulently anticommunist political climate of the United States at the time, they generally did not cite Marx openly. Steward disguised the influence of Marx in his work and was thus able to avoid controversy. White did not cite Marx either, but he was openly socialist and courted controversy.

White visited the Soviet Union for eight weeks in the summer of 1929. By the time he returned, he was convinced that "the Russian Revolution was the most significant event in modern history" (Peace 1998:85). When the American Association for the Advancement of Science met in 1930, he gave an address, called "An Anthropological Appraisal of the Russian Revolution," praising the Soviet Union and predicting disaster for capitalist nations. The address received front-page attention in *The New York Times* and *Pravda* (the official state newspaper of the Soviet Union) and created a firestorm. White was pleased by the attention his views generated, but he was also worried about his position at the University of Michigan. Under attack by the Catholic church and the university administration, for many years White avoided writing anything that could be considered directly political or religious. Despite his caution, he was repeatedly humiliated by the university administration. They denied him promotion and pay raises for thirteen years (Peace 1998:89).

White was eventually widely acclaimed for his work. In the late 1950s and 1960s, he received numerous awards, two honorary degrees, and was elected president of the American Anthropological Association. His prominence allowed him to be politically active once more. In 1957, just after the Russians launched the satellite Sputnik, White said, "A cultural system that can launch earth satellites can dispense with gods entirely." The quote was carried in *The New York Times,* and clergy in Michigan, where White taught, responded by calling for his dismissal. The university refused and White later responded to the situation by asking whether God "need[ed] a protective clergyman to defend Him" (in Carneiro 1981).

Although a materialist like Steward and White, Murdock was not a Marxist and avoided political controversies. However, his research did not escape the critical appraisal of other anthropologists. One of the most telling criticisms of Murdock's work is the same as that which Boas leveled at the nineteenth-century evolutionists in his 1896 article "The Limitations of the Comparative Method in Anthropology." That is, the data upon which Murdock's analyses were based were taken out of their appropriate cultural contexts, thus invalidating the reliability of the analysis. Murdock's popularity was largely limited to American anthropologists. Many British social anthropologists considered Murdock's work to be nothing more than mere classifying of data.

18. The Patrilineal Band[a]

Julian Steward (1902–1972)

LOOSE AGGREGATES OF COMPARATIVELY INDE-
pendent families such as those of the Shoshoni occur only rarely because in most parts of the world
subsistence patterns required sufficient regularity
of co-operation and leadership to give definite
form and stability to multifamily social groups.
There are many kinds of such multifamily groups
of which the patrilineal band is but one.

The patrilineal band illustrates several concepts. First, it is a cultural type whose essential
features—patrilineality, patrilocality, exogamy,
land ownership, and lineage composition—constituted a cultural core which recurred cross-
culturally with great regularity, whereas many
details of technology, religion, and other aspects of
culture represent independent variables, the nature of which was determined by diffusion or by
unique local circumstances. Second, its cultural
core resulted from ecological adaptations which,
under the recurrent conditions of environment
and subsistence technology, could vary only within
minor limits. Third, it represents a level of sociocultural integration slightly higher than that of the
Shoshoni family; for its multifamily aggregates
found cohesion not only in kinship relations but in
co-operative hunting, in common landownership,
and to some extent in joint ceremonies.[1]

I shall analyze the cultures of these bands
as they occurred among the Bushmen of South
Africa, some of the Congo Negritos of Central
Africa, some Philippine Negritos, the Austra-

(1955)

lians, the Tasmanians, some southern California
Shoshonean-speaking groups, and the Ona of
Tierra del Fuego. Other tribes besides those covered in the present survey no doubt had the same
pattern.

The essential features of these bands are most
readily explained as the independent product of
similar patterns of adaptation of technology and
certain social forms to the environment. There are
only two other possible explanations of the patrilineal band. First, that the pattern was borrowed
from neighboring tribes. This explanation is unten-
able since their neighbors did not have the pattern.
Second, that the pattern is the heritage of some archaic culture which developed at an early period of
human history and has been preserved ever since.
Perhaps some social patterns do have great persistence, but they must meet some need. It would be
stretching credulity much too far to suppose that a
pattern which is closely adapted to a special kind of
subsistence had persisted for thousands of years
among tribes who had wandered through dozens of
unlike environments to the remotest corners of the
earth, especially when other hunting and gathering
tribes had lost these patterns and acquired types of
society appropriate to their mode of life. Moreover,
like most cultural historical theories, neither the
hypothesis of diffusion nor of archaic heritage provides an explanation of how and why the patrilineal
band developed in the first place. The cultural ecological hypothesis on the other hand is not only explanatory but it is by far the simplest and most
consistent with the facts.[2]

---

[1] Steward's preoccupation with the causes of culture is immediately evident in this first passage. Unlike the historical particularists, Steward was interested in discovering general laws of culture.

Steward divided culture into core and secondary features. He probably got the division from his professor A. L. Kroeber,
who divided culture into value and utility components – Steward's *culture core* was similar to Kroeber's *utility culture*. It
consisted of those cultural traits that Steward felt were closest to subsistence activities and economic arrangements. A key
difference between the two men is that Kroeber thought the value culture more interesting and important than the utility culture, whereas Steward focused his studies on the utility features. Collections of elements of the culture core that
regularly occur cross-culturally, such as the patrilineal band described here, he termed *culture types*.

[2] In this passage, Steward differentiates his own cultural ecological approach from that of the historical particularists,
which he claims has little explanatory power. He further distinguished himself from the nineteenth-century evolutionists

The cultural ecological explanation of the patrilineal band hinges on an identity of exploitative patterns rather than of technology or environment. Technology and environment were similar in crucial respects, but they were not identical in their totality. Cultures do not exploit their entire environments, and it is, therefore, necessary to consider only those features which bear upon the productive patterns.[3] The environments of the patrilineal bands were similar in that, first, they had limited and scattered food resources, which not only restricted population to a low density but which prevented it from assembling in large, permanent aggregates. Second, the principal food resource was game, which unlike wild seeds, may be profitably taken collectively. Third, the game occurred in small, nonmigratory bands rather than in large, migratory herds. This kind of game can support only small aggregates of people, who remain within a restricted territory. Large herds, on the other hand, support much larger aggregates who can remain together as they follow the herds. These latter aggregates were bilateral or composite bands.

Dispersed and small game herds are, therefore, a condition of patrilineal bands, but this does not mean identity of environment, for deserts, jungles, and mountains tend to limit the number of game and the distance it could wander.[4] Of the tribes examined here, the Bushmen, Australians, and southern California Shoshoneans lived in areas which had sparse game because of extreme aridity. Moreover, all were affected by the limited sources of water. In Tierra del Fuego, the habitat is one of wet plains but guanaco[5] and small rodents, the principal foods, were scattered and nonmigratory. The Congo Negritos[6] and the Philippine Negritos lived in the tropical rain forests, the former in lowlands and the latter in mountains.

Exploitative technology of these societies varied considerably in detail, but in all cases it included weapons of about equal efficiency and hunting patterns which entailed as much cooperation as circumstances permitted. The Bushmen used bows, poisoned arrows, clubs, pitfalls, poisoned springs, grass fires, dogs, and surrounds. The Congo Negritos employed bows, poisoned and nonpoisoned arrows, spears, knives, and long game nets. The Shoshoneans had bows, thrown clubs, traps, nets, surrounds, and drives. The Ona used bows, spears, clubs, slings, and spring pole nooses. Australian technology may have been less efficient in that it lacked the bow, but it included

---

such as Morgan and Tylor, who saw the existence of such bands as survivals of some preexisting social form, precisely the second possibility that Steward mentions and discounts here. Unlike other Boasians, Steward's research emphasized cross-cultural comparison, but his rejection of the idea of psychic unity separates his work from the comparative method of the nineteenth-century evolutionists.

[3] Steward's cultural ecology is often misunderstood as a sort of ecological determinism, but his emphasis was on the process of human labor within the environment. Steward was concerned with the technological process by which people exploited their environment, and his analysis focused on how different subsistence strategies necessitated different social structures. This emphasis derives from Steward's reading of Marx.

[4] Here and below, Steward focuses on the interplay between environment and technology. The idea that environment determined culture — a position known as geographical determinism — was not new. One prominent advocate was the British historian Henry Thomas Buckle (1821–1862), who believed history to be governed by laws of nature. The development of nations could be explained by the general effect of nature upon the human mind as well as the specific effects of climate, food, soil, and so on. American anthropologist Clark Wissler (1870–1947), a student of Boas, was also interested in environment and culture. His research convinced him that there was a relationship between the two. In a series of works, including *The Relation of Nature to Man in Aboriginal America* (1926), Wissler attempted to map American cultural areas based on the principal modes of food production. Steward was not a geographical determinist such as Buckle, and his formulation was more sophisticated than that of Wissler. He believed that certain types of society are extremely likely to occur under particular conditions of technology and environment.

[5] *Guanaco:* a South American ruminant, of which the llama and alpaca are domesticated varieties.

[6] *Negrito:* in Steward's day, the parlance of racial classification included the term *Negrito,* used for short, dark-skinned peoples. These included people in Africa, India, the Philippines, and the Malay Peninsula. The term is rarely used today.

clubs, spears, and the spear-thrower. The sociological effect of hunting scattered game individually or collectively was the same everywhere.

The interaction between a bow-spear-club technology and a small, nonmigratory herd food resource tended to produce the patrilineal band. This type of band was the normal result of the adaptive processes of cultural ecology, and though various factors constantly operated to destroy the ideal pattern, as will be shown, interaction of technology and environment was such as to restore it. Only a basic change in environment or technology could have eliminated the patrilineal band. The inevitability of such bands under the given conditions is shown by its persistence along with clans, moieties, and other special patterns in the different groups, and, in the case of the Congo, an interdependence of the hunting Negritos and farming Bantu tribes who inhabited the same area.

With a given population density, the size of the territory and of the band which owns it are direct variables. If the group is enlarged the territory must also be increased in order to support it. Among the ethnic groups in question, however, the population is sparse, ranging from a maximum which seldom exceeds one person per 5 square miles to one person per 50 or more square miles. This prevents indefinite enlargement of the band because there would be no means of transporting the food to the people or the people to the food. The area which the band can conveniently forage averages some 100 square miles and seldom exceeds 500 square miles, a tract roughly 20 miles to a side. Consequently, the band averages 50 individuals and seldom exceeds 100.[b] Only in regions of unusual resources—for example,

where there are herds of migratory game—does the group size surpass these figures.

We now have to consider why these bands are patrilineal. First, it is characteristic of hunters in regions of sparse population for postmarital residence to be patrilocal. This has several causes. If human beings could be conceived stripped of culture, it is not unreasonable to suppose that innate male dominance would give men a commanding position.[c] If, in addition to native dominance, however, the position of the male is strengthened by his greater economic importance, as in a hunting culture,[d] or even if women are given greater economic importance than men, it is extremely probable that postmarital residence will be patrilocal.[7]

But in these small bands patrilocal residence will produce the fact or fiction that all members of the band are patrilineally related[e] and hence matrimonially taboo. Band exogamy—that is local exogamy—is therefore required. Probably at one time or another such bands have actually consisted of relatives with traceable connection. Genealogical data on the tribes of southern California, for example, show that more often than not the band comprises a true patrilineal lineage. Because life is so precarious that increase of the total population is impossible and budding collateral lineages often become extinct, the possibility is small that several independent families which have no traceable connection will develop in any band. Such families will occur only if the band is extraordinarily large. And even in this case, the fiction of relationship may be perpetuated after the connection is forgotten if group unity is reinforced by patronymy, myths, and other factors.[f8]

---

[7] Rather than arguing that material conditions (hunting) give rise to social forms (patrilineality), Steward here relies on the supposition of biological differences between males and females to explain the origins of patrilineality. It is an uncharacteristically weak explanation, especially given the last line of this paragraph, when he asserts the adoption of patrilocality regardless of whether males or females are relatively more influential in a society.

[8] Notice that Steward's explanation is generally materialist. Cultural fictions (the name of the patrilineage for example) are necessitated by ecological conditions.

This materialist basis was influenced by Marx (see essay 4). The intellectual climate of his day prevented Steward from referencing Marx, but he had read Marx's work. Despite this, Steward cannot be considered a Marxist, nor was he as heavily influenced by Marx as was Leslie White, the other major American materialist of this era (see essay 19). Unlike Steward, White's work was concerned with establishing an overall evolutionary scheme for society and with the roles of conflict and class within society: these are typically Marxist issues. Steward's work lacks the characteristically Marxist emphasis

For these reasons, the bands of hunters who live in sparsely populated areas must ordinarily be patrilineal. But special factors may make them temporarily composite. Thus, if unrelated and hence intermarriageable families exist within a band, local exogamy and patrilocal residence with respect to the band are unnecessary. This will occur when parallel-cousin marriage is permitted or where bands have, for various reasons, become unusually large and lack any factor that would create or perpetuate a fiction of relationship between its members. Occasionally, matrilocal residence will introduce families which are not related patrilineally into a band. This will prevent strictly patrilineal inheritance of band territory and tend to weaken the fiction of relationship between band members. For these reasons, patrilineal bands at certain times or places deviate from the ideal pattern and consist of unrelated families. In this respect, they resemble composite bands, but whereas the latter normally must remain composite, patrilineal bands tend to return to their typical pattern. The factors which produce composite bands will be analyzed subsequently.

Political unity in all bands is very similar. Centralized control exists only for hunting, for rituals, and for the few other affairs that are communal. Consequently, the leader has temporary and slight authority. In patrilineal bands, he is usually the head of the lineage, which, being a status based on kinship, is usually not formally institutionalized. The shaman, however, controls many collective activities, and he is feared and respected for his supernatural power, which often gives him more influence than the other leaders. Bands which are ordinarily autonomous may temporarily unite for special occasions such as Australian and Fuegian initiation ceremonies. Although the reason for this larger unity is religious and social, food supply strictly limits the duration of multiband gatherings.

The occurrence of clans among Australians, Ojibway, and others, of moieties in Australia and in southern California, and of other social forms in no way affects the cause-and-effect relationships involved in the formation of the patrilineal band.[9] Such institutions are variables with respect to the pattern we have analyzed. Their presence or absence is to be explained by diffusion or by some special local factors and not by adaptations of technology to environment.[10]

TRIBES WITH THE PATRILINEAL BAND

In the following pages some patrilineal bands will be discussed in detail, showing reasons in each case for departures from the ideal pattern.[11]

The Bushmen[g]

A hunting and gathering culture imposed upon an arid and unproductive native environment produced a sparse population among the Bushmen. Population aggregates were necessarily small[h] and the group that co-operated in various undertakings was a politically autonomous patrilineal lineage. Although the band or lineage split seasonally into smaller units, probably family groups, it owned and communally utilized a definite territory. Some hunting required joint effort of all band members, and game was often shared by all.

The bands of the Northwestern Bushmen, including the Heikum, were ordinarily patrilineal owing to patrilocal residence and local or band

---

on conflict as a motor of evolution. He was far more interested in showing the specific interrelations among technology, environment, and society. Further, as Harris (1968) notes, while Steward's division of culture into core and secondary features sounds superficially like Marx's division of society into base and superstructure, it is quite different. Marx saw superstructure as arising from base; Steward generally saw secondary features as virtually unrelated to the core.

[9] When the members of a tribe are divided into two groups, these divisions are called *moieties.*

[10] Critics of Steward's work point out that he explained away those things that did not fit the patterns he outlined by suggesting, as he does here, that they were secondary features resulting from diffusion or the specific history of the group under study.

[11] In this section of the essay, Steward cites evidence from a wide variety of societies to support his contention that certain environmental and technological constraints lead to the formation of patrilineal bands.

exogamy. The Naron bands, however, were sometimes composite because matrilocal residence, which was practiced occasionally in order that the wife's mother might help the wife with her children, introduced families which were not related patrilineally into the same band. This weakened patrilineal inheritance of the estate and tended to obviate the necessity of band exogamy, which, however, was preferred (Schapera, 1930:81–85). The Cape, Namib, and !Okung bands also tended to be composite because, although band exogamy was preferred, matrilocal residence, for a reason which has not been revealed, was sometimes practiced. Band endogamy, moreover, was facilitated by cousin marriage, parallel or cross, which was barred among the Northwestern groups (Schapera, 1930:82–83; 102–07).[12]

Schebesta (1931) reports what appears to be an identical pattern. The Bambuti, Efe, Bac'wa, and Batwa of the Belgian Congo had exogamous, patrilocal, and generally autonomous sibs ("sippe") or families of male relatives numbering sixty to sixty-five persons each. Apparently, the "totemic clans" of these people were the same as lineages, that is, they were localized clans or sibs.

Central African Negritos

Several scattered groups of Negritos or pygmies living in the dense tropical rain forests of the Congo in equatorial Africa also belonged to the patrilineal band type. The bands were predominantly hunters, and the exploitative patterns produced the features typical of the patrilineal band despite the fact that the pygmies lived in a close dependency relationship with the Bantu Negroes.[13]

In the Ituri Forest (Putnam, 1948:322–42), a Negro village and a pygmy band jointly owned about 100 square miles of country. The Negroes were largely farmers, and the pygmies were entirely hunters, the latter supplying the former with meat in exchange for vegetable foods. The dependence of the pygmy upon the Negro might account for the cohesion of the pygmy band and for the pattern of land-tenure, but it would not account for the patrilineality and exogamy, which must be explained by the low population density, the small band size, and the predominance of hunting.

The bands ranged in size from 100 to 200 persons, 150 being the average. All families were normally related through the male line, and the band, therefore, constituted a locally exogamous and patrilocal group. The cohesion of the lineage or band was reinforced by the belief that a totemic animal was the ancestor of the band and by myths. The band contained unrelated families only when exceptional circumstances introduced a man from some other band, for example, when a man could not get along in his own band or when he had trouble with his Negro group. The patrilineal features resulted from the hunting pattern. The men spent all their time hunting for game which was normally scattered. They used nets in collective drives or else bows, spears, and knives in individual stalking. The game was varied and included turtles, rats, antelope, buffalo, and elephants. Hunting was restricted to the band's territory, the size of which must be interpreted as the optimum which can be exploited. Had the territory been substantially larger, the band would have surpassed a kin group in size and therefore ceased to be exogamous and patrilocal. However, the sparse population, the limitations upon the area which could be hunted, and the patrilocality after marriage produced localized lineages.

These bands sometimes tended to be composite for two reasons. First, it was customary at marriage for the husband's band to furnish a

---

[12] Harris (1968:667) claims that Steward's listing of factors responsible for patrilineal, complex, or matrilineal band formation are "fortuitous and quixotic." Note the reliance in this passage and later in this essay on "a reason which has not been revealed" and other such devices.

[13] The fact that hunting bands of pygmies lived in close proximity to agricultural Bantus was critical for Steward. Traditional evolutionary schemes had placed agriculture far above hunting and gathering. If diffusion alone could account for cultural traits and agriculture was superior to hunting and gathering, why had the pygmies not adopted it? Steward felt he could solve this problem using a cultural ecological approach.

woman who married a member of his wife's band. When no woman was available, the man lived with his wife's people. Second, band endogamy, that, marriage between related members of the band, though felt to be a breach of incest laws, was often practiced when other bands were remote and inaccessible (Schmidt, 1910:173).

The Negritos of Gabon in French Equatorial Africa were grouped in some 100 or 150 villages, each of which usually comprised one family "rangée sous l'authorité d'un seul chef, le père du clan, généralement de 30 a 35 individus males."[14] These seemed to be independent, patrilocal, and exogamous, and therefore true patrilineal bands. But they belonged to some kind of larger patrilineal totemic clans, which were preferably, but not always, exogamous (Trilles, 1932:20–23, 143–51, 409–18).[15]

Semang

The more or less inadequate information now available indicates that many of the Negritos of the Malay peninsula possessed the patrilineal band. Largely hunters and gatherers and more or less isolated in the sparsely settled mountain forests, the Semang groups were small, ranging, according to fragments of evidence recorded by Schebesta (1929), from individual families which were probably temporary subdivisions to groups of 50 or more persons. These seem to have been politically autonomous, landowning bands. Skeat and Blagden (1900:495–97) say that the Kedah Semang band often amounted to an enlarged family and, somewhat obscurely, that the chief was practically "the head of a family, which in this case is represented by a larger family, the tribe." It may be, however, that band territory was sometimes further subdivided among bilateral families so that each owned an area for its durian trees.

Schebesta says (1929:83, 234, 279) that "the individual groups wander within the tribal boundaries but always return to their family territory, especially at the time of the durian crop" and that the trees are owned by men as family heads. These family tracts were, perhaps, comparable to the Algonkian and Althabaskan beaver-trapping territories.

That these bands were truly patrilineal is indicated by Schebesta's statement (1929) that the unit of society was the "sib" like that of the Congo Negritos, but he does not particularize its characteristics. Elsewhere he observes that there was considerable band exogamy and patrilocal residence, although he recorded one band that was composite. One reason for the occurrence of the latter among the Kenta Semang was that durian trees were sometimes inherited matrilineally. This would, of course, favor matrilocal residence and tend to set up a composite band.

Philippine Negritos

The predominantly hunting and gathering Philippine Negritos lived in comparative isolation from the Malaysians. They were clustered in bands which Vanoverbergh (1925:430–33), says comprise "a certain group of families." These remained in the same portion of the forest and seasonally exploited different parts of an area which had a radius of not over twenty miles. Trespass on the land of neighboring bands was not forbidden but was avoided. The land was hunted communally by its owners, but cultivated trees and honey nests were privately owned. It is not recorded, however, how trees were inherited. Bands seem to have been politically autonomous, but the lack of an institutionalized band chief is implied by the somewhat vague statement that authority rested in the father of the family.

---

[14] *"rangée . . . males"*: The French comment means placed under the authority of a single leader, usually the eldest of the clan, and consisting of thirty to thirty-five men.

[15] In assembling his cases, Steward relied on historical accounts as well as then current ethnography. The use of these sources was important for him since his intellectual achievement was to explain the presence of the band in very different and widely distributed locales. Use of historical accounts was problematic, however, since it led him to use sources that were not very reliable and to discuss groups, such as the Tasmanians, which had disappeared by his era. Further, much of the information he presents here, for example, his description of the Central African Negritos, has since been shown to be invalid, or, at best, only partially correct. Does this invalidate his argument?

There is some indication that Philippine Negrito bands have recently changed from patrilineal to composite.[16] Schmidt (1910:72–73), quoting Blumentritt on the Zambales-Bataam, says that the bands are now endogamous but at the end of the eighteenth century were exogamous. Present-day endogamy is further shown by the presence of unrelated families in the same band.[i] Nevertheless, patrilocal residence is recorded, although it is not clear whether residence is patrilocal with respect to the band or the family.

There is, therefore, some doubt as to the frequency of the two types of bands and the customs concerning residence and other matters which would produce them. It appears, however, that some factor has tended to produce a change from patrilineal to composite bands during the past century. At least one important cause of composite bands today is the practice of marrying cousins. Although marriage was preferably between cross-cousins, parallel-cousins were eligible for matrimony (Vanoverberg, 1925:425–28).[17]

Australians[j]

The relatively low productivity of Australia permitted but a sparse population which averaged only 1 person per 12 square miles for the entire continent.[k] The population was grouped into relatively small, autonomous bands which Radcliffe-Brown calls hordes. Each band comprised 20 to 50 individuals and owned 100 to 150 square miles of land. The male members of the band inherited and communally hunted their tract, which was definitely bounded and protected from trespass.[l]

These bands were truly patrilineal, and they approximated male lineages. They were almost universally exogamous and patrilocal. The idea of relationship between band members was further reinforced by kinship terminology. Even those ethnic groups which had moieties, sections (formerly called "marriage classes"), and matrilineal clans and totems had not, except in a portion of western Australia, lost the patrilineal band (Radcliffe-Brown, 1931:438).

Tasmanians

Information on the Tasmanians, though incomplete, indicates the aboriginal presence of the patrilineal band. The scant population[m] was divided into autonomous bands of 30 to 40 persons each. Each band owned a tract of land on which it wandered seasonally in search of food. It protected its hunting rights against trespass, which was a common cause of war (Roth, 1899:58–59, 104–07).

The Tasmanian band must have been patrilineal, for evidence assembled by Roth indicates, although it does not prove beyond question, that the band was exogamous and marriage patrilocal.

The Ona of Tierra del Fuego

The Ona of Tierra del Fuego fall strictly into the patrilineal band pattern. The low subsistence level, based largely upon guanaco hunting, produced a population of only one individual to 4.5 or 5 square miles. This was grouped in politically independent bands of 40 to 120 persons, each owning an average of 410 square miles. Gusinde (1931) believes that the manner of life would not have supported larger aggregates. Each territory was named, band rights to it were sanctioned by myths, and hunting privileges were protected against trespass. Although each band was politically autonomous, there was no institution of chief.

The band was patrilineal because it was exogamous and patrilocal. Local exogamy was required even among the large bands in which relationship between members was not traceable, for native theory held that each band was a male lineage.

---

[16] Tracing out the ways in which culture changed was to become one of Steward's key concerns. He is known as the creator of multilinear evolutionism, which he contrasted with nineteenth-century unilineal evolution and his contemporary Leslie White's universal evolution. He argued that unlike White and his nineteenth-century predecessors, he was not interested in formulating a general, universal plan of evolution but rather with showing how particular cultures changed and developed (1955:11–19).

[17] Steward's is an uneasy evolutionism. It is perhaps best seen as a compromise between his historical-particularist training and his goal of creating an anthropology based in the discovery of causal principles. He placed societies in an essentially unilineal evolutionary scheme from family to multifamily to state civilization. He then focused on the multiple pathways that societies may take between evolutionary stages.

Tehuelche of Patagonia

The Tehuelche of Patagonia, although very incompletely known, are instructive when compared with the Ona. Also dependent largely upon herds of guanaco, their economic life appears formerly to have resembled that of the Fuegians. There is evidence that they were divided into bands, each having some degree of localization[n] and led in its travels, etc., by a patrilineal chief (Outes and Bruch, 1910:126; Beerbohn, 1881:93) who was called "father" (Musters, 1873:194). The band chief, however, acknowledged a general cacique, who, according to Musters, had very little authority. The institution of general or tribal cacique[18] may easily have developed subsequent to the arrival of the European.

The introduction of the horse about a century and a half ago completely altered ecological conditions in Patagonia. It enabled people to move widely in pursuit of guanaco herds and to transport foods considerable distances. This would, of course, have tended to eliminate band ownership of small parcels of territory, even had it existed. It also permitted enlargement of population aggregates far beyond the size of the usual lineage. Further motivation for amalgamation of formerly separate bands was provided by internecine strife, which was stimulated by competition for foods and war against the white man. The political unit consequently increased in size and had a single, although not absolute, chief. Thus, in 1871, bands numbered as many as 400 or 500 persons, although they occasionally split into smaller groups (Musters, 1873:64, 70, 96–97, 117, 188). As there is no mention of exogamy of any form, it must be assumed that these bands were composite. This is common elsewhere in bands of such size.[19]

Southern Californians

The Shoshonean-speaking Serrano, Cahuilla, and Luiseño, and some of the Yuman-speaking Diegueño of southern California were divided into patrilineal bands.[20] This region is exceptional in that abundance of acorns and other wild seeds permitted the unusually dense native population of one person per square mile. But this great density was accompanied by small territory size rather than large band size, probably because the very few and small sources of water prevented greater concentration of people. Therefore, bands averaged only fifty individuals and the territory only fifty square miles.

The other factors producing the patrilineal bands were those which operated elsewhere. Because of patrilocal residence coupled with the small size of the bands, most of them were actual patrilineal lineages so local exogamy was required. In addition, a band chief, "priest," ceremonies, ceremonial house and bundle, and myths contributed to group cohesion (Strong, 1927, 1929; Gifford, 1918, 1926, 1931; Kroeber, 1925, 1934). This strongly fortified patrilineal pattern may also have served to maintain the band at lineage size.

---

[18] *Cacique* refers to a leader in Mesoamerican Indian communities.

[19] Here Steward gives an example of the effect of technological change on social structure: the introduction of the horse led to an increase in band size. Examples linking technology and social structure were essential because they were the sort of things that would leave traces in the archaeological record, which meant that archaeological data could be used to bolster Steward's theoretical position. This connection between theory in cultural anthropology and archaeology was one of the factors leading to the emergence of the new archaeology in the 1960s. Steward had, in fact, begun his career as an archaeologist working in the Columbia River valley.

[20] Steward's most protracted fieldwork was among the Shoshoni in Utah, and here, as he describes Southern California peoples, he is closest to his own fieldwork interests. His fieldwork experiences were important for two reasons. First, working among the traditional Shoshoni, he was struck by the small group size and the extremely demanding environment they inhabited. In the deserts of the Great Basin, the powerful influences of environment and technology might have been more evident than they were in many other places. Second, Steward was known for his fieldwork technique. He was highly critical of ethnographic studies that used material collected from people no longer engaged in aboriginal lifestyles. He encouraged an ethnography based on recording actual behavior rather than one based on what people said about past behavior. It is ironic that in developing multilinear evolution, he, of necessity, had to rely on secondhand data collected under conditions that were not well known, precisely the type of information he distrusted.

The culturally similar neighboring Cupeño provide an illuminating contrast to these groups. Because the local abundance of food and water permitted greater concentration, they were able to live in two permanent towns, each numbering some 250 persons. Each village contained several lineages and had a chief. Bands were, therefore, of the composite type (Gifford, 1926:394–96; Strong, 1929:188–90, 233).

CAUSAL FORMULATION FOR PATRILINEAL BANDS

In any society there are certain cultural factors which potentially give cohesion to aggregates of several families: marriage, extension of kinship ties and corollary extensions of incest taboos, group ceremonies, myths, games, and other features. These features may be derived from cultural heritage of the group or they may be borrowed from neighboring tribes. In each group they are integrated in a total sociocultural system, but the nature of this system is not explained merely by tracing the diversified history of the features or by describing the functional interdependency of the parts. These features must be adjusted to the subsistence patterns that are established through the exploitation of a particular habitat by means of a particular technology; and the subsistence patterns are only partly explainable in terms of culture history. The use of bows and arrows, traps, hunting nets, game drives, or grass firing can generally be traced to diffusion, but the hunting patterns and the social effect of these patterns are quite unlike

in areas of sparse and scattered game and in areas of large herds of migratory game. Among societies which devote a very great portion of their time and energy to food-getting, these differences in hunting patterns will greatly affect the size, permanency, composition, and general behavior patterns of the group. The extent and degree to which subsistence patterns affect the total structure of the society and the functional integration of its various parts are questions to be answered by empirical procedure.[22]

The patrilineal band represents a social type the principal features of which are determined within exceedingly narrow limits by the cultural ecology—by the interaction of technology and environment. Other features, such as clans, moieties, age-grades, men's tribal societies, group ceremonialism, totemism, and mythology may or may not also be present. If they do form part of the cultural inventory of the band, they are integrated to the patrilineal pattern. A causal formulation of the factors producing the patrilineal band may therefore omit these various historically-derived features, for the latter are of interest only when attention is shifted to the uniqueness of each culture and they do not help explain the patrilineal features which are the subject of inquiry.

The factors which produce the patrilineal band are:[22]

1. A population density of one person or less — usually much less — per square mile, which is caused by a hunting and gathering technology in areas of scarce wild foods;

---

[21] This passage contains a critique of historical particularism and functionalism and outlines Steward's theoretical position. Staking out this position brought him into direct conflict with many other Boasians. For example, in this passage, Steward discards unique historically derived features as having no explanatory value. However, it was precisely these unique features that Kroeber and many other historical particularists were interested in documenting. They believed these showed the creative genius of humankind. Unsurprisingly, the relationship between Kroeber and Steward was not close. Kroeber considered Steward a promising but not particularly interesting student. Steward respected Kroeber but was fundamentally at odds with most of what he stood for (Wolf 1981:63).

[22] While Steward rejected much of what his professors believed, his work was not unprecedented in American anthropology. Earlier, members of the culture area school attempted to map North and South America into a series of areas of similar cultures, which, they noted, tended to overlap with ecological zones. Otis Mason (1838–1908) formulated one such version in the 1890s, but Boas and his students Kroeber and Wissler created a more definitive mapping in the teens and early twenties (see Mason 1895, Holmes 1914, Wissler 1917). The culture area theorists tended to see environment as a passive factor placing broad restrictive limits on cultural possibilities. Steward saw the combination of technology and environment as playing a far more causal role in determining social systems.

2. An environment in which the principal food is game that is nonmigratory and scattered, which makes it advantageous for men to remain in the general territory of their birth;

3. Transportation restricted to human carriers;

4. The cultural-psychological fact, which cannot be explained by local adaptation, that groups of kin who associate together intimately tend to extend incest taboos from the biological family to the extended family thus requiring group exogamy.

These four factors interact as follows: The scattered distribution of the game, the poor transportation, and the general scarcity of the population make it impossible for groups that average over 50 or 60 persons and that have a maximum of about 100 to 150 persons to associate with one another frequently enough and to carry out sufficient joint activities to maintain social cohesion. The band consists of persons who habitually exploit a certain territory over which its members can conveniently range. Customary use leads to the concept of ownership. Were individual families to wander at will, hunting the game in neighboring areas, competition would lead to conflict. Conflict would call for alliance with other families, allies being found in related families. As the men tend to remain more or less in the territory in which they have been reared and with which they are familiar, patrilineally related families would tend to band together to protect their game resources. The territory would therefore become divided among these patrilineal bands.

It is worth noting that the nature of Great Basin Shoshonean land-use precluded the banding together of patrilineal families and landownership. For two reasons, the pine nut, which was the principal food, had a very different sociological effect than game hunting. First, good crops were so abundant that there was never competition for it. Second, abundant crops occurred each year in very different localities and they brought different groups together each time.[23]

Among the patrilineal bands, the component biological families associated together sufficiently often to permit an extension of incest taboos to all members. Prohibition of marriage within the immediate biological family is universal among mankind. There are generally extensions of marriage restrictions to collateral relatives of the second or third degree, though cross-cousins may marry in certain cultures. The patrilineal bands were so small that they usually consisted of known relatives who commonly fall within the prohibited degrees of relationship, and cross-cousins — the father's sister's daughter or the mother's brother's daughter — would normally be in another band. Band exogamy is therefore required.

The several features of the patrilineal band reinforce one another. Patrilocal residence after marriage because the male wishes to remain in country he knows causes an area to be habitually occupied, utilized, and defended by patrilineally-related families. Local exogamy prevents the introduction into the band of unrelated families, so that the band becomes in fact, a patrilineal lineage.[24]

The requirement that the band be exogamous may persist after traceable kinship relations in the group are forgotten if the patrilineal complex is reinforced by other features, such as names, kinship terminology, myths, ceremonies, totems, and the like. Thus, the bands of Australia, southern California, and Tierra del Fuego conform more rigidly to the pattern because they possess such supports. Among the Bushmen and Negritos patrilineal bands may often temporarily become composite bands when special conditions exist.

A theory of the patrilineal band which sought its origin in purely cultural-historical terms would

---

[23] Steward was also influenced by his work with Carl Sauer (1889–1975), a geographer interested in anthropology and archaeology who stressed an approach to geography based on the interaction of humans and environment. Sauer was at Berkeley during Steward's time there, and he had an important impact on Kroeber and his students. Sauer, incidentally, is also infamous for his belief that Irish monks visited North America before the Vikings.

[24] Steward's approach is oriented toward technology and environment, but he frequently refers to psychology as an important factor (as here, where he discusses the male's wishes). Steward's work is contemporaneous with the culture and personality school (see essays 16 and 17), which relied heavily on psychological explanations.

be confronted by insuperable difficulties.[25] Such a theory would have to assume either that the band inherited the basic patrilineal pattern from some archaic world-wide culture or that it borrowed it from some neighboring tribes. As we have seen, primitive nonagricultural peoples in areas of seed resources, of fish, or of large game herds do not have the patrilineal band because these areas are not conducive to the exploitation of a certain restricted territory by small groups of men in the manner found among the patrilineal band peoples. It is inconceivable that this pattern could have survived the migrations of mankind over dozens of unlike environments during thousands of years. The theory of borrowing from neighbors will not stand up because the neighbors of these tribes simply do not have patrilineal bands.

A holistic or functional explanation minimizes the importance of cultural ecology by insisting that all features of the culture are equally cause and effect.[26] This simply evades the issue of causality. As we have seen, the clans, moieties, men's tribal societies, and other special features occur with only some of the patrilineal patterns and they also occur among quite different kinds of societies. There is a functional interrelationship between hunting in a restricted area, the male's continued residence in that area, patrilocality, and local exogamy. Exogamy within a localized patrilineal group causes the men to hunt scattered game in certain ways. The groups hunt what is available with devices at their command; men best remain in the territory where they were raised; their wives come to their territory after marriage; and the bands are so small that people are related and, given concepts of incest, local exogamy is practiced. It is not claimed that the cultural ecological factors explain everything about

the patrilineal band. They explain why these bands differ from other bands which have a similar technology and similar potentialities for extending incest taboos outward from the biological family.

A common explanation of the patrilineal band is that it is merely a localized clan, and diffusionists seek to trace its source to clans elsewhere. Societies which have clans may influence patrilineal bands in two ways; first, borrowed clans may crosscut the bands but fail to change their basic patterns; second, clan myths, ceremonies, and other features may be borrowed by the band and reinforce its local unity. But diffused unilateral structure and exogamy cannot explain the adjustment of male lineages to exploitative activities. In fact, the concept of the patrilineal band has greater value in explaining the clan than vice versa. If, for reasons stated here, a localized patrilineal group develops, it is in effect a localized clan. Whether it should properly be called a clan, however, would depend upon whether it is exogamous regardless of locality. Those groups which have reinforcing features, such as the southern California Shoshoneans, the Australians, and others, would be clans if exogamy continued after they were dislocated from their territories and the different bands mixed up. Evidently this has happened often in human history and clans have developed in many places. We shall subsequently show how the data of archaeology and ethnography support such an interpretation of the origin of clans among the Pueblo Indians of the Southwest.[27]

CULTURAL VARIABLES AND THE PATRILINEAL BAND

The features of the patrilineal band which must be explained by ecological factors are patrilineal-

---

[25] In this passage and later, Steward attacks the other prominent theoretical positions of his time. This paragraph dismisses historical particularism; later he takes on functionalism and diffusionism.

[26] When Steward presented the first version of this paper in 1936, British functionalism was growing increasingly important in this country. A. R. Radcliffe-Brown, then at the University of Chicago, was a loud and eloquent critic of the Boasians. This passage is aimed directly at his thinking. Radcliffe-Brown identified an ecological-adaptive aspect of social structure but assigned it no particular importance. Steward argues that because of this, Radcliffe-Brown's system describes but does not explain culture.

[27] Kroeber had done important work in tracing the diffusion of cultural traits throughout the Southwest. Additionally, radical diffusionist theories were popular in Britain and Germany when Steward wrote. Steward's point is that while diffusion of traits can be shown to exist, the traits are always modified to fit the ecological conditions of the society accepting them.

ity, patrilocality, exogamy, landownership, and informal and limited leadership.[28] Many other features however, were fairly variable in form despite this basic pattern. A substantial range of possible alternatives made diffusion a more direct explanation of their presence.

Some of the technological traits secondary to the main hunting patterns were extremely variable. Containers used in transporting, preparing, and storing food, for example, could not be elaborate, heavy, or numerous because of the nomadic life, but the materials of which they were made, their specific forms, and their decorations were quite variable. The Congo Negritos, Semang, Shoshoneans, and Ona used basketry of various weaves, shapes, and ornamentation; the Bushmen and Congo Negritos employed some pottery; the other areas utilized skins, shells, bark, or other convenient materials. Fire was made with the wooden drill by the Bushmen and Shoshoneans, with the fire saw by the Semang, and with pyrite and stone by the Ona. The Congo Negritos had no means of making fire and were forced to borrow it if their own went out. Shelters were limited by the requirement that they be quickly and easily put together of materials available. These bands used natural shelters, such as caves, when possible. Otherwise, they built mere windbreaks, brush- or skin-covered conical lodges, or dome-shaped brush houses. Similar huts are found scattered throughout the world among primitive peoples, and it would be rather profitless to speculate as to whether they diffused or not, for they are so elementary that it would require no great ingenuity to invent them. Clothing was scant and made with simple skills, but styles varied locally: string skirts or aprons, wrap-around skin skirts, breechclouts, robes, and the like, or perhaps nothing but a few smudges of paint.

Musical instruments and games were generally simple, for extensive paraphernalia was out of the question. The former were generally learned from neighboring tribes. For example, the Semang used flutes, jew's-harps, guitars, and drums borrowed from their Malay neighbors; and the Bushmen had musical bows, flutes, cocoon rattles, and drums, all probably acquired from the Bantu; while the southern California Shoshoneans used only flutes and rattles; the Australians swung bull-roarers and pounded sticks on rolled-up hides; the Ona struck sticks together; and the African Negritos thumped hollow logs.

A certain distinctiveness is evident in many features of social organization. While the formal aspects of these are attributable to diffusion, their functional significance was very similar because of their role in the total culture. Several of the bands had men's tribal societies—religious organizations into which young men were initiated during rites from which women and children were barred. The neophytes were scarified, given hunting tests, and made to observe food taboos while religion was explained to them. The Australian societies used bull-roarers in their ceremonies, whereas the Ona used masks and special huts and had rites based on the concept of death and resurrection of the initiate. Southern California Shoshoneans lacked such societies, but their group fetish bundle, ritual, and ceremonial leader had a similar function in reinforcing group cohesion. These and other social features, however, were not necessary to existence of the patrilineal band pattern, and they can hardly constitute the primary basis of cultural typology. The Semang have no men's society.

The presence in any society of the patrilineal band and the tribal society must be "explained" in different terms. The secret society is scattered throughout the world in many kinds of cultures and there is little doubt that it represents a very ancient pattern which has fitted certain psychological-cultural needs as well as a variety

---

[28] In this section, Steward explores cultural variables that he considers secondary features, those aspects of culture not closely tied to the cultural core and determined by purely cultural-historical factors such as random innovation and diffusion. While this section of the essay is fairly long (over 1,300 words), much of it is a simple cataloging of cultural traits with little or no analysis of them. This presentation reflects two factors: first, Steward's training in historical particularism (the collection and cataloging of cultural traits was precisely the sort of anthropology Kroeber urged on his followers); and second, the likelihood that Steward placed little importance on the information he presents here. From the lack of analysis and the fact that this section is only weakly articulated with the rest of the essay, it appears that Steward considered this material a collection of virtually random facts of no particular interest.

of cultural functions so well that it has persisted in spite of tremendous cultural change and that it has even diffused from one type of culture to another. The secret society can in no way be considered a cause of the patrilineal pattern or of the type of land use that underlies this pattern.[29]

There were other social features which, from the point of view of the patrilineal pattern, were secondary or variable and which were found also among tribes lacking the patrilineal band. Some of the northern Australians had matrilineal moieties, which were probably diffused from Melanesia. The combination of these with localized patrilineal, exogamous groups created a very complex organization. The uniqueness of this organization—the fact that it consisted of functionally interrelated parts—does not mean that the origin of its parts cannot be treated separately and in causal terms. The southern California Shoshoneans had moieties which cut across localized patrilineal bands, but these functioned primarily at death ceremonies.

The religious patterns of these tribes were affected by the ecological adjustments principally in a negative sense: they lacked complicated and institutionalized worship of the kinds found among more developed cultures, there being little ceremonialism dedicated to group purposes. Rites were concerned primarily with birth, puberty, sickness, death, and other crisis situations of individuals. The patterns of these crisis rites and of shamanism show certain general similarity to one another and very probably they represent in large part an ancient heritage which survived throughout the world in cultures of many kinds. That is,

these rites show a great deal of stability, their basic patterns persisting in many cultural contexts which are quite dissimilar. This fact makes it obviously quite absurd to conceive that religion could be the starting point, the primary factor, in an investigation of the origin of social forms and economic patterns. Religion was a functional part of each culture, but from the point of view of the basic social types and cultural ecological determinants its form was a relatively independent variable.[30]

The local forms and functions of the puberty rites are an illustration of the considerable range of variations that could be woven into the basic pattern of the patrilineal band.[31] We have already seen how puberty rites stressed the maturing of young men among the Northwest Bushmen, the Australians, and the Ona to the extent that the adult males constituted a secret organization. The Congo Negritos may also have had such societies; at least, it is clear that in the Ituri Forest young Pygmy men together with the sons of their Negro overlords were circumcised in groups every few years, each group becoming an age-grade society. The other tribes wholly lacked any such formal grouping of their males. Among the Semang, children of both sexes were merely inducted into the status of puberty by a simple rite at which they were painted, tattooed, scarified, and had their teeth filed. The Shoshoneans of southern California, like their nonpatrilineal neighbors, had observances for both sexes. Pubescent girls were "roasted" in a pit and required to race each day, to scratch themselves only with a stick, and to refrain from drinking cold water. Boys were

---

[29] Here and later, Steward attempts to demonstrate that the cultural features he believes are secondary have little causal significance for the cultural core: subsistence, technology, and social structure.

[30] Here Steward reaffirms his basic materialism: material conditions condition ideas, not vice versa. This passage seems to be a direct attack on Tylor, who saw the progressive rationalization of religion as one of the fundamental processes driving cultural change (see essay 2). But why would Steward attack Tylor more than a half century after the publication of *Primitive Culture* and two decades after the latter's death? It is more likely that he was thinking of Max Weber. The English translation of Weber's highly influential *The Protestant Ethic and the Spirit of Capitalism* had been published in 1930, not many years before the first appearance of Steward's essay. In this book Weber argued that Protestant theology was critical to the advent of capitalism in Europe.

[31] Steward turns the historical particularists' practice of cataloging cultural traits against them. Here, his style of writing is significant. By presenting a seemingly random listing of traits, he draws the reader to the conclusion that such a presentation, and hence the historical-particularist research program, can have little explanatory value.

Table 1. Patrilineal Bands

	Number of persons per square mile	Average size of band	Average number of square miles in band territory	Permanent residence patrilocal with respect to band	Exogamy of band, i.e., locality, required	Band politically autonomous, weak chief	References and remarks
N. W. Bushmen	?	50–60	?	X	X	X	Schapera, 1926, 1930; Dornan, 1925:85; Stow, 1905:33, 229–30; Dunn, 1931:7, 22
Congo Negritos — Bambuti, Efe, Bac'wa, Batwa	?	60–65	?	X	X	X	Schebesta, 1931; Schmidt, 1910
Negritos — Gabon	?	20–70	?	X	X	X	Trilles, 1932
Semang	½–⅛	35?	?		(X)	X	Schebesta, 1929; Skeat and Blagden, 1900
Australia — W	⅕	30	150	X	X	X	Radcliffe-Brown, 1930:688
— S	?	40–	?	X	X	X	Radcliffe-Brown, 1930:690
Victoria	1/15	50+	750	X	X	X	Radcliffe-Brown, 1930:691
Queensland	3/10	30	100	X	X	X	Radcliffe-Brown, 1930:694
Herbert R.	⅕	20–25	100	X	X	X	Radcliffe-Brown, 1930:696
Average	1/12	35	420	X	X	X	
Tasmania	⅛–1/13	30–40	350	X	X	X	Radcliffe-Brown, 1930:695; Roth, 1899
Ona	¼–⅕	40–120	410	X	X	X	Gusinde, 1931
California: Miwok, Luiseño, Serrano, Cahuilla, Cupeño	1	50	50	X	X	X	Gifford, 1926; Kroeber, 1925:883, 58; Strong, 1927, 1929; Gifford, 1926
Diegueño (N & S)	½	50?	50?	X	X	X	Gifford, 1926

drugged, lectured on tribal lore and morality, subjected to biting ants, and required to dance. Among the Semang both sexes were painted, scarified, and tattooed at adolescence.

In all these tribes, as in hundreds of others throughout the world, the shaman's chief function was to cure disease by supernatural means, generally through singing and sucking out the supposed cause of disease. He had certain other functions, however, which varied with the special local patterning of religion. Among the Bushmen, for example, he officiated at puberty ceremonies, and among the Semang he mediated between mankind and the thunder god.

Death observances were matters of private ritual among most of these bands, but the Shoshoneans of southern California developed them into a ceremony which greatly strengthened group cohesion. An annual mourning ceremony was held under the direction of a special ceremonial leader, while images of the deceased were burned and myths were recited to commemorate the dying god. This ceremony seems to have contributed greatly to the cohesion of Shoshonean bands, and it may partly explain why the bands continued to regard themselves as kin groups and to practice exogamy after they became dislocated from their territories, scattered, and lost genealogical knowledge of their relationship to one another.[32]

Notes

a. This is an adaptation and expansion of the article, "The Economic and Social Basis of Primitive Bands," in *Essays in Honor of A. L. Kroeber* (University of California Press, 1936), pp. 331–50.

b. Wilhelm Koppers observes that 15 to 20 individuals is common and about 100 the probable limit. See Wilhelm Koppers, *Die Anfänge des menschlichen Gemeinschaftslebens* (Vienna, 1921), p. 72.

c. Bingham observed gorillas in a state of nature in groups of eight to twenty-two individuals, each group under a dominant male; chimpanzees are said to be similar; and it is probable that the males among the baboons observed in nature by Zuckerman had a comparable dominance. See Harold C. Bingham, *Gorillas in a Native Habitat.* Report Joint Expedition of 1929–1932 by Yale University and Carnegie Institution of Washington for Psychobiological Study of Mountain Gorillas (*Gorilla berengei*) in Parc National Albert, Belgian Congo Africa (1932). Also see S. Zuckerman, *The Social Life of Monkeys and Apes* (New York: Harcourt, Brace and Company, 1932).

d. E.g., the extraordinarily low status of women in the arduous hunting area of northern Canada. Radcliffe-Brown has observed that Australian hunters would be much less successful in territory which was not known to them from childhood.

e. Relationship is seldom traced beyond three generations among these people.

f. I make no effort to solve the very difficult problem of why there are incest laws at all. Marriage with relatives to the third generation, i.e., cousins, is taboo in most of these cases, although cross-cousin and even parallel-cousin marriage is permitted among several.

g. This section is based on I. Schapera, "A Preliminary Consideration of the Relationship between the Hottentots and the Bushmen," *South African Journal of Science*, XXIII (1926), 833–66; I. Schapera, *The Khoisan Peoples of South Africa* (London, 1930); S. S. Dornan, *Pygmies and Bushmen of the Kalahari* (London, 1925); E. J. Dunn, *The Bushman* (London, 1931); George W. Stow, *The Native Races of South Africa* (New York, 1905); S. Passarge, *Die Buschmanner der Kalahari* (Berlin, 1907).

h. Schapera, *The Khoisan Peoples of South Africa*, pp. 67–81, has gleaned a few figures on band size from various sources: Cape Bushmen, who were seriously affected by foreign contacts, 100 to 150, according to one estimate, and 3 to 4 families each, according to a more recent figure; Heichware, 20; Kalahari, 30; !Okung, not exceeding 30; Northwestern Bushmen, ranging from 20 to 150 and probably averaging 50 to 60 each.

i. Morice Vanoverbergh, "Negritos of Northern Luzon," *Anthropos*, XXV (1930), 538–39, found that some bands contained related males and also that related males occurred in different bands.

j. This material is largely from A. R. Radcliffe-Brown, "Former Numbers and Distribution of the Australian Aborigines," *Official Yearbook of the Commonwealth of Australia*, No. 23 (1930), pp. 671–96, and Radcliffe-Brown, "The Social Organization of Australian Tribes, I–III," *Oceania* I (1930, 1931) 34–63, 204–46, 426–56 (especially pp. 436–39, 455).

k. Radcliffe-Brown, *Official Yearbook of the Commonwealth of Australia*, No. 23 (1930), p. 696. The population range was 1 person per 2 square miles in the most fertile section to 1 per 38 square miles in the more arid regions.

l. D. Sutherland Davidson, "The Family Hunting Territory in Australia," *American Anthropologist*, n.s., XXX (1928), 614–32. Davidson has collected evidence that in some localities the landowning group was the bilateral family. It is the opinion of Radcliffe-Brown, *Oceania*, I (1931), 438, however, that "the particularism of the family whereby it might tend to become an isolated unit is neutralized by the horde [i.e., band] solidarity."

m. Radcliffe-Brown, *Official Yearbook of the Commonwealth of Australia*, No. 23 (1930), p. 695, gives the

---

[32] Steward's work had a profound effect on the anthropologists of his day. Although his career, unlike that of Boas or White, was characterized by many short stays at different universities, he was a charismatic professor and attracted an important following. Among the students of Steward who later became prominent anthropologists were Stanley Diamond (1922–1991), Morton H. Fried (1923–1986) (see essay 21), Sidney Mintz (1922–), Elman Service (1915–1996), Elliott Skinner (1924–), and Eric Wolf (1923–1999).

aboriginal total as probably 2,000 or 3,000, which is one person to 8 or 13 square miles.

n. Antonio Serrano, *Los Primitivos Habitantes del Territorio Argentina* (Buenos Aires, 1930), p. 157. Nuñoz, quoted by Serrano, says that among the Northern Tehuelche the head chief owned the land and that the lesser chiefs could not change their land without giving notice to him.

References

Beerbohn, Julius
1881. *Wanderings in Patagonia or Life Among the Ostrich-Hunters.* London.

Gifford, E. W.
1918. "Clans and Moieties in Southern California," *University of California Publications in American Archaeology and Ethnology,* XIV, 155–219.
1926. "Miwok Lineages and the Political Unit in Aboriginal California," *American Anthropologist,* n.s., XXVIII, 389–401.
1931. "The Kamia of the Imperial Valley," *Bureau of American Ethnology Bulletin 97.*

Gusinde, Martin
1931. "Die Feuerland Indianer. Bande I. Die Selk'nam. Verlag der Internationalen Zeitschrift," *Anthropos,* pp. 302–06.

Kroeber, A. L.
1925. "Handbook of the Indians of California," *Bureau of American Ethnology Bulletin 78.*
1934. "Native American Population," *American Anthropologist,* n.s., XXXVI, No. 1, pp. 1–25.

Musters, George C.
1873. *At Home with the Patagonians. A Year's Wandering over Untrodden Ground from the Straits of Magellan to the Rio Negro.* London.

Outes, Felix, F., and Carlos Bruch
1910. *Los Aborigines de la Republica Argentina.* Buenos Aires.

Putnam, Patrick
1948. "The Pygmies of the Ituri Forest," in Carleton S. Coon, *A General Reader in Anthropology.* New York: H. Holt and Company, pp. 322–342.

Radcliffe-Brown, A. R.
1931. "The Social Organization of Australian Tribes, III," *Oceania,* I, 426–56.

Roth, H. Ling
1899. *The Aborigines of Tasmania.* Halifax (England): F. King and Sons.

Schapera, I.
1926. "A Preliminary Consideration of the Relationship between the Hottentots and the Bushmen." *South African Journal of Science,* XXIII, 833–66.

Schebesta, Paul
1929. *Among the Forest Dwarfs of Malaya.* London.
1931. "Erste Mitteilungen uber die Ergebnisse meiner Forschungsreise bei den Pygmaen in Belgische-Kongo," *Anthropos,* XXVI, 1–17.

Schmidt, P. W.
1910. "Die Stellung der Pygmaenvolker in der Entwicklungsgeschichte des Menshen," *Studien u. Forschungen zur Menschen-u. Volkerkunde.* Stuttgart.

Skeat, W. W., and C. O. Blagden
1900. *Pagan Races of the Malay Peninsula.* London and New York: The Macmillan Company.

Strong, W. D.
1927. "An Analysis of Southwestern Society," *American Anthropologist,* n.s., XXIX, 1–61.
1929. "Aboriginal Society in Southern California," *University of California Publications in American Archaeology and Ethnology,* XXVI, 1–358.

Trilles, R. P.
1932. "Les Pygmees de la Foret Equatorial," *Anthropos,* 1–530.

Vanoverbergh, Morice
1925. "Negritos of Northern Luzon," *Anthropos,* XX, 148–99, 399–443.

19. Energy and the Evolution of Culture

Leslie White (1900–1975)

EVERYTHING IN THE UNIVERSE MAY BE DEscribed in terms of energy.[a] Galaxies, stars, molecules and atoms may be regarded as organizations of energy. Living organisms may be looked upon as engines which operate by means of energy derived directly or indirectly from the sun. The civilizations, or cultures of mankind, also, may be regarded as a form of organization of energy.

(1943)

Culture is an organization of phenomena—material objects, bodily acts, ideas, and sentiments—which consists of or is dependent upon the use of symbols. Man, being the only animal capable of symbol-behavior, is the only creature to possess culture.[b] Culture is a kind of behavior. And behavior, whether of man, mule, plant, comet or molecule, may be treated as a manifestation of energy. Thus we see, on all levels of reality,[c] that phenomena lend themselves to description and interpretation in terms of energy. Cultural anthropology is that branch of natural science[d] which deals with matter-and-motion, i.e., energy, phenomena in cultural form, as biology deals with them in cellular, and physics in atomic, form.[1]

The purpose of culture is to serve the needs of man. These needs are of two kinds: (1) those which can be served or satisfied by drawing upon resources within the human organism alone. Singing, dancing, myth-making, forming clubs or associations for the sake of companionship, etc., illustrate this kind of needs and ways of satisfying them. (2) The second class of needs can be satisfied only by drawing upon the resources of the external world, outside the human organism. Man must get his food from the external world. The tools, weapons, and other materials with which man provides himself with food, shelter from the elements, protection from his enemies, must likewise come from the external world. The satisfaction of spiritual and aesthetic needs through singing, dancing, myth-making, etc., is possible, however, only if man's bodily needs for food, shelter, and defense are met. Thus the whole cultural structure depends upon the material, mechanical

means with which man articulates himself with the earth. Furthermore, the satisfaction of human needs from "inner resources" may be regarded as a constant,[e] the satisfaction of needs from the outer resources a variable. Therefore, in our discussion of cultural development we may omit consideration of the constant factor and deal only with the variable—the material, mechanical means with which man exploits the resources of nature.

The articulation-of-man-with-the-earth process may be analyzed and resolved into the following five factors: (1) the human organism, (2) the habitat, (3) the amount of energy controlled and expended by man, (4) the ways and means in which energy is expended, and (5) the human-need-serving product which accrues from the expenditure of energy. This is but another way of saying that human beings, like all other living creatures, exploit the resources of their habitat, in one way or another in order to sustain life and to perpetuate their kind.

Of the above factors, we may regard the organic factor as a constant. Although peoples obviously differ from each other physically, we are not able to attribute differences in culture to differences in physique (or "mentality"). In our study of culture, therefore, we may regard human race as of uniform quality, i.e., as a constant, and, hence, we eliminate it from our study.[2]

No two habitats are alike; every habitat varies in time. Yet, in a study of culture as a whole,[f] we may regard the factor of habitat as a constant: we simply reduce the need-serving, welfare-promoting resources of particular habitats to an average. (In a consideration of particular manifestations of

---

[1] This arresting opening passage reveals several aspects of White's thinking at this stage of his career. Because he saw anthropology as a branch of natural science, he believed that the research methods used in the sciences, when applied to anthropology, would reveal the laws of culture. Later in this essay, White provides a materialist and functionalist basis for the analysis of culture. His "functions and needs" approach is reminiscent of Bronislaw Malinowski, whom he admired (see essay 13), and Herbert Spencer (see essay 1). However, his emphasis on "material, mechanical means" reflects his grounding in Karl Marx (see essay 4).

    White was trained in the Boasian tradition. He studied at the New School for Social Research under Alexander Goldenweiser (1880–1940), a student of Franz Boas and the mentor of Ruth Benedict. At Chicago, where he received his Ph.D., he worked with Edward Sapir, another of Boas' students. However, his theoretical work diverged sharply from that of the Boasians.

[2] As a teenager, White was interested in astronomy and intended to become a physicist. His style of writing and of argument reflect this background. White argues in a scientific idiom—defining and eliminating or analyzing variables and describing laws. Like other Boasians, he discounts the effects of race.

culture we would of course have to deal with their respective particular habitats.) Since we may regard habitat as a constant, we exclude it, along with the human organism, from our study of the development of culture.[3]

This leaves us, then, three factors to be considered in any cultural situation: (1) the amount of energy per capita per unit of time harnessed and put to work within the culture, (2) the technological means with which this energy is expended, and (3) the human-need-serving product that accrues from the expenditure of energy.[4] We may express the relationship between these factors in the following simple formula: $E \times T = P$ in which E represents the amount of energy expended per capita per unit of time, T the technological means of its expenditure, and P the magnitude of the product per unit of time. This may be illustrated concretely with the following simple example: A man cuts wood with an axe. Assuming the quality of the wood and the skill of the workman to be constant, the amount of wood cut in a given period of time, say an hour, depends, on the one hand upon the amount of energy the man expends during this time: the more energy expended, the more wood cut. On the other hand, the amount of wood cut in an hour depends upon the kind of axe used. Other things being equal, the amount of wood cut varies with the quality of the axe: the better the axe the more wood cut. Our workman can cut more wood with an iron, or steel, axe than with a stone axe.

The efficiency with which human energy is expended mechanically depends upon the bodily skills of the persons involved, and upon the nature of the tools employed. In the following discussion we shall deal with skill in terms of averages.[5] It is obvious, of course, that, other things being equal, the product of the expenditure of human energy varies directly as the skill employed in the expenditure of this energy. But we may reduce all particular skills, in any given situation, to an average which, being constant, may be eliminated from our consideration of culture growth. Hereafter, then, when we concern ourselves with the efficiency with which human energy is expended mechanically, we shall be dealing with the efficiency of tools only.

With reference to tools, man can increase the efficiency of the expenditure of his bodily energy in two ways: by improving a tool, or by substituting a better tool for an inferior one. But with regard to any given kind of tool, it must be noted that there is a point beyond which it cannot be improved. The efficiency of various tools of a certain kind varies; some bows are better than others. A bow, or any other implement, may vary in efficiency between 0 per cent and 100 per cent. But there is a maximum, theoretically as well as actually, which cannot be exceeded. Thus, the efficiency of a canoe paddle can be raised or lowered by altering its length, breadth, thickness, shape, etc. Certain proportions or dimensions would render it useless, in which case its efficiency would be 0 per cent. But, in the direction of improvement, a point is reached, ideally as well as practically, when no further progress can be made—any further change would be a detriment. Its efficiency is now at its maximum (100 per cent). So it is with a canoe, arrow, axe, dynamo, locomotive, or any other tool or machine.

We are now ready for some generalizations about cultural development.[6] Let us return to our formula, but this time let us write it $E \times F = P$,

---

[3] While White was concerned with the relationship between humans and nature, he did not share Steward's interest in the effects of specific environments on culture (see essay 18).

[4] The concerns upon which White focuses in this essay, especially technology, reflect the influence of Marx on his works. White visited the Soviet Union in 1929 and, while there, was inspired by his reading of Marx and Engels. He later corresponded briefly with the communist Leon Trotsky (Beardsley 1976:619). He told one of his students that he had profitably read the last chapter of Marx's work *Capital* sixteen times (Carneiro 1981).

[5] Here and later, White refers to numbers and writes equations, suggesting that he is measuring attributes that can be quantified, perhaps with relative ease. However, White and his followers had great trouble actually providing agreed-on, concrete, quantitative measures of the variables they discussed. As a result, critics considered their work pseudoscientific.

[6] In this passage, White writes of degrees of cultural development. This places him in direct opposition to most Boasians, who held that comparing cultures in this manner was impossible and came dangerously close to ethnocentrism.

in which E and P have the same values as before — E, the amount of energy expended; P the product produced — while F stands for the efficiency of the mechanical means with which the energy is expended. Since culture is a mechanism for serving human needs, cultural development may be measured by the extent to which, and the efficiency with which, need-serving goods or services are provided. P, in our formula, may thus stand for the total amount of goods or services produced in any given cultural situation. Hence P represents the status of culture, or, more accurately, the degree of cultural development. If, then, F, the efficiency with which human energy is expended, remains constant, then P, the degree of cultural development, will vary as E, the amount of energy expended per capita per year[g] varies:

$$\frac{E_1 \times F}{E_2 \times F} = \frac{P_1}{P_2}$$

Thus we obtain the first important law of cultural development: *Other things being equal, the degree of cultural development varies directly as the amount of energy per capita per year harnessed and put to work.*[7]

Secondly, if the amount of energy expended per capita unit of time remains constant, then P varies as F:

$$\frac{E \times F_1}{E \times F_2} = \frac{P_1}{P_2}$$

and we get the second law of cultural development: *Other things being equal, the degree of cultural development varies directly as the efficiency of the technological means with which the harnessed energy is put to work.*

It is obvious, of course, that E and F may vary simultaneously, and in the same or in opposite directions. If E and F increase simultaneously P will increase faster, naturally, than if only one increased while the other remained unchanged. If E and F decrease simultaneously P will decrease more rapidly than if only one decreased while the other remained constant. If E increases while F decreases, or vice versa, then P will vary or remain unchanged, depending upon the magnitude of the changes of these two factors and upon the proportion of one magnitude to other. If an increase in E is balanced by a decrease in F, or vice versa, then P will remain unchanged. But should E increase faster than F decrease or vice versa, then P would increase; if E decreases faster than F increases, or vice versa, then P would decrease.

We have, in the above generalizations *the* law of cultural evolution: *culture develops when the amount of energy harnessed by man per capita per year is increased; or as the efficiency of the technological means of putting this energy to work is increased; or, as both factors are simultaneously increased.*

All living beings struggle to live, to perpetuate their respective kinds.[8] In the human species the struggle for survival assumes the cultural form. The human struggle for existence expresses itself in a never-ending attempt to make of culture a more effective instrument with which to provide security of life and survival of the species. And one of the ways of making culture a more powerful instrument is to harness and to put to work within it more energy per capita per year. Thus, wind, and water and fire are harnessed; animals are domesticated, plants cultivated; steam engines are built. The other way of improving culture as an instrument of adjustment and control is to invent new and better tools and improve old ones. Thus energy for culture-living and culture-building is augmented in quantity, is expended more efficiently, and culture advances.

---

[7] Here and later, White offers several laws of culture. These occasioned a dispute between White and Steward. Steward's critique was that White's laws were so general as to be virtually self-evident and told nothing about the specifics of change within a culture. White responded that this, while true, was the fundamental nature of universal laws. Supporting White's defense of his laws, Harris (1968:649) asks, "Does the law of gravitation tell us nothing about particulars? When one predicts a particular eclipse on a particular planet . . . has this no relation to the general law?"

[8] White's emphasis on struggle reflects his reading of both Darwin and Marx. Compare his statement here to Marx's famous dictum that all history is the history of class struggle. In Marx, social classes struggle for control of the means of production. For White, the struggle is for increased control of energy and increased efficiency of energy usage.

Thus we know, not only *how* culture evolves, but *why*, as well. The urge, inherent in all living species, to live, to make life more secure, more rich, more full, to insure the perpetuation of the species, seizes upon, when it does not produce, better[h] (i.e., more effective) means of living and surviving. In the case of man, the biological urge to live, the power to invent and to discover, the ability to select and use the better of two tools or ways of doing something—these are the factors of cultural evolution.[9] Darwin could tell us the consequences of variations, but he could not tell us how these variations were produced. We know the motive force as well as the means of cultural evolution. The culturologist[10] knows more about cultural evolution than the biologist, even today, knows about biological evolution.[i]

A word about man's motives with regard to cultural development. We do not say that man deliberately set about to improve his culture. It may well have been, as Morgan[j] suggested, decades before Lowie[k] emphasized the same point, that animals were first domesticated through whim or caprice rather than for practical, utilitarian reasons. Perhaps agriculture came about through accident. Hero's steam engine was a plaything. Gunpowder was first used to make pretty fireworks. The compass began as a toy. More than this, we know that peoples often resolutely oppose technological advances with a passionate devotion to the past and to the gods of their fathers. But all of this does not alter the fact that domesticated animals and cultivated plants have been used to make life more secure. Whatever may have been the intentions and motives (if any) of the inventors or discoverers of the bow and arrow, the wheel, the furnace and forge, the steam engine, the microscope, etc., the fact remains that these things have been seized upon by mankind and employed to make life more secure, comfortable, pleasant, and permanent. So we may disregard the psychological circumstances under which new cultural devices were brought into being. What is significant to the cultural evolutionist is that inventions and discoveries have been made, new tools invented, better ways of doing things found, and that these improved tools and techniques are kept and used until they are in turn replaced.

So much for the laws, or generalizations derived from our basic formula. Let us turn now to concrete facts and see how the history of culture is illuminated and made intelligible by these laws.

In the beginning of culture history, man had only the energy of his own body under his control and at his disposal for culture-living and culture-building. And for a very long period of time this was almost the only source of energy available to him. Wind, water, and fire were but rarely used as forms of energy. Thus we see that, in the first stage of cultural development, the only source of energy under man's control and at his disposal for culture-building was, except for the insignificant and limited use of wind, water and fire, his own body.

The amount of energy that could be derived from this source was very small. The amount of energy at the disposal of a community of 50, 100, 300 persons would be 50, 100, or 300 times the energy of the average member of the community, which,

---

[9] Much of American anthropology has denied the existence of any but the most rudimentary human instincts. White goes against this trend. Here he relies on the existence of a biologically based drive to use culture to make life "more rich, more full."

[10] As this essay shows, White was much given to inventing new words and phrases. He called his work *culturology* rather than anthropology and proposed that culturology was a science and that it treated cultural phenomena as obeying their own laws, distinct from human biology or individual psychology. In this, he was clearly influenced by Kroeber's idea of the superorganic (see essay 11) and Durkheim's notion of the collective conscience (see essays 6 and 7). White once wrote that great men were no more personally effective in shaping the general course of culture than a "sack of sawdust" (1949:279).

White's insistence that culture follows its own path independent of individual humans, however, seems to contradict his notion that culture exists to make life more secure for humans. At the end of his life, he confronted this problem. White's emphasis on the notion of culture as a system and evidence that culture was often maladaptive led him to reject the idea that culture exists to serve people's needs. In his last work he wrote, "We no longer think of culture as designed to serve the needs of man; culture goes its own way in accordance with laws of its own. Man lives within the embrace of cultural systems, and enjoys or suffers whatever they mete out to him" (1975:159).

when infants, the sick, the old and feeble are considered, would be considerably less than one "man-power" per capita. Since one "man-power" is about one-tenth of one horsepower, we see that the amount of energy per capita in the earliest stage of cultural development was very small indeed—perhaps 1/20th horsepower per person.

Since the amount of energy available for culture building in this stage was finite and limited, the extent to which culture could develop was limited. As we have seen, when the energy factor is a constant, cultural progress is made possible only by improvements in the means with which the energy is expended, namely, the technology. Thus, in the human-energy stage of cultural development progress is achieved only by inventing new tools—the bow and arrow, harpoon, needle, etc., by improving old ones—new techniques of chipping flint implements, for example. But when man has achieved maximum efficiency in the expenditure of energy, and when he has reached the limits of his finite bodily energy resources, then his culture can develop no further. Unless he can harness additional quantities of energy—by tapping new sources—cultural development will come to an end. Man would have remained on the level of savagery[1] indefinitely if he had not learned to augment the amount of energy under his control and at his disposal for culture-building by harnessing new sources of energy. This was first accomplished by the domestication of animals and by the cultivation of plants.[11]

Man added greatly to the amount of energy under his control and at his disposal for culture-building when he domesticated animals and brought plants under cultivation.[12] To be sure, man nourished himself with meat and grain and clothed himself with hides and fibers long before animal husbandry and agriculture came into being. But there is a vast difference between merely exploiting the resources of nature and harnessing the forces of nature. In a wild food economy, a person, under given environmental conditions, expends a certain amount of energy (we will assume it is an average person so that the question of skill may be ignored) and in return he will secure, on the average, so much meat, fish, or plant food. But the food which he secures is itself a form and a magnitude of energy. Thus the hunter or wild plant-food gatherer changes one magnitude of energy for another: m units of labor for n calories of food. The ratio between the magnitude of energy obtained in the form of food and the magnitude expended in hunting and gathering may vary. The amount obtained may be greater than, less than (in which case the hunter-gatherer would eventually perish), or equal to, the amount expended. But although the ratio may vary from one situation to another, it is in any particular instance fixed: that is, the magnitude of energy-value of the game taken or plant-food gathered remains constant between the time that it is obtained and the time of its consumption. (At least it does not increase, it may in some instances decrease through natural deterioration.)

In a wild food economy, an animal or a plant is of value to man only after it has ceased to be an animal or a plant, i.e., a living organism. The hunter kills his game, the gatherer digs his roots and bulbs, plucks the fruit and seeds. It is differ-

---

[11] White's description of the relationship between technology and culture was heavily influenced by Marx's idea of a mode of production. Marxists understand different societies as being determined by particular combinations of relations of production and forces of production (see essays 4, 22, and 33). White's analysis is similar but perhaps less complex. He sees different types of society as fundamentally conditioned by the different types of technology they use.

[12] The evolutionary perspective of the nineteenth century had been largely abandoned by American cultural anthropologists, but after World War I it was rehabilitated by archaeologists and European anthropologists. While they explicitly rejected the ethnocentric and racist formulations of nineteenth-century evolutionary theory, they retained and elaborated its basic elements. White saw little resemblance between his work and that of V. Gordon Childe (1892–1957), but this passage, and much of White's analysis later, shows that influence (Service 1976:613). Childe was an Australian-born archaeologist and culture theorist who lived and worked largely in Great Britain. Openly Marxist, he is remembered for, among other things, coining the term *Neolithic Revolution*. He and others conducted studies of cultural evolution based on archaeological data for a number of years before White published this essay. White, along with Steward, returned the evolutionary element to American cultural anthropology. The evolutionary materialism of these thinkers is reflected in much of American archaeology in the second half of this century.

ent with the herdsman and the farmer. These persons make plants and animals work for them.[13]

Living plants and animals are biochemical mechanisms which, of themselves, accumulate and store up energy derived originally from the sun. Under agriculture and animal husbandry these accumulations can be appropriated and utilized by man periodically in the form of milk, wool, eggs, fruits, nuts, seeds, sap, and so on. In the case of animals, energy generated by them may be utilized by man in the form of work, more or less continuously throughout their lifetime. Thus, when man domesticated animals and brought plants under cultivation, he harnessed powerful forces of nature, brought them under his control, and made them work for him just as he has harnessed rivers and made them run mills and dynamos, just as he has harnessed the tremendous reservoirs of solar energy that are coal and oil. Thus the difference between a wild plant and animal economy and a domestic economy is that in the former the return for an expenditure of human energy, no matter how large, is fixed, limited, whereas in agriculture and animal husbandry the initial return for the expenditure of human labor, augments itself indefinitely. And so it has come about that with the development and perfection of the arts of animal husbandry and agriculture — selective breeding, protection from their competitors in the Darwinian struggle for survival, feeding, fertilizer, irrigation, drainage, etc. — a given quantity of human labor produces much more than it could before these forces were harnessed. It is true, of course, that a given amount of human labor will produce more food in a wild economy under exceptionally favorable circumstances, — such, e.g., as in the Northwest Coast of America where salmon could be taken in vast numbers with little labor, or in the Great Plains of North America where, after the introduction of the horse and in favorable circumstances, a large quantity of bison meat could be procured with but little labor, — than could be produced by a feeble development of agriculture in unfavorable circumstances. But history and archaeology prove that, by and large, the ability of man to procure the first necessity of life, food, was tremendously increased by the domestication of animals and by the cultivation of plants. Cultural progress was extremely rapid after the origin of agriculture.[m] The great civilizations of China, India, Mesopotamia, Egypt, Mexico, and Peru sprang up quickly after the agricultural arts had attained to some degree of development and maturity. This was due, as we have already observed, to the fact that, by means of agriculture man was able to harness, control, and put to work for himself powerful forces of nature. With greatly augmented energy resources man was able to expand and develop his way of life, i.e., his culture.[14]

In the development of culture, agriculture is a much more important and powerful factor than animal husbandry.[n] This is because man's control over the forces of nature is more immediate and more complete in agriculture than in animal husbandry. In a pastoral economy man exerts control

---

[13] In these passages White, following Childe (1942) — who followed Morgan (see essay 3) — provides criteria for distinguishing savagery, barbarism, and civilization. Compare White's criteria with Childe's comment that "upper Paleolithic societies must be designated savage inasmuch as they relied for a livelihood on hunting, fishing, and collecting" (1942:37) or his statement that the development of agriculture was the first step in the Neolithic Revolution and distinguishes barbarism from savagery (1942:48).

[14] As these passages illustrate, for White, human cultural evolution was best understood as a process of increasing human control over the natural environment. This is a teleological vision of evolution, much like that of the nineteenth-century evolutionists. For White, cultural evolution has a single goal: virtually complete human control of the environment. This vision accords very well with the times in which White wrote. In the 1940s and (particularly) the 1950s, people foresaw a not-too-distant future of domed, climate-controlled cities. Childe, for example, wrote in 1942 that the development of agriculture turned humans into "active partners with nature instead of parasites on nature" (1942:48). Today, our understanding of human ability to exert control over nature, as well as its desirability, is considerably different. Would a modern textbook, for example, refer to hunters and gatherers as parasites on nature? The theories we produce today tend to emphasize the limits of human abilities and the impossibility of determining the direction of biological or cultural evolution. Perhaps our vision of the world is conditioned by the economics and politics of our own day just as White's was by events of his era.

over the animals only, he merely harnesses solar energy in animal form. But the animals themselves are dependent upon wild plants. Thus pastoral man is still dependent to a great extent upon the forces and caprices of nature. But in agriculture, his control is more intimate, direct, and, above all, greater. Plants receive and store up energy directly from the sun. Man's control over plants is direct and immediate. Further independence of nature is achieved by means of irrigation, drainage, and fertilizer. To be sure, man is always dependent upon nature to a greater or less extent; his control is never complete. But his dependence is less, his control greater, in agriculture than in animal husbandry. The extent to which man may harness natural forces in animal husbandry is limited. No matter how much animals are improved by selective breeding, no matter how carefully they are tended—defended from beasts of prey, protected from the elements—so long as they are dependent upon wild plant food, there is a limit, imposed by nature, to the extent to which man can receive profitable returns from his efforts expended on his herds. When this limit has been reached no further progress can be made. It is not until man controls also the growth of the plants upon which his animals feed that progress in animal husbandry can advance to higher levels. In agriculture, on the other hand, while there may be a limit to the increase of yield per unit of human labor, this limit has not yet been reached, and, indeed it is not yet even in sight. Thus there appears to be a limit to the return from the expenditure of a given amount of human labor in animal husbandry. But in agriculture this technological limit, if one be assumed to exist, lies so far ahead of us that we cannot see it or imagine where it might lie.

Added to all of the above, is the familiar fact that a nomadic life, which is customary in a pastoral economy, is not conducive to the development of advanced cultures. The sedentary life that goes with agriculture is much more conducive to the development of the arts and crafts, to the accumulation of wealth and surpluses, to urban life.

Agriculture increased tremendously the amount of energy per capita available for culture-building, and, as a consequence of the maturation of the agricultural arts, a tremendous growth of culture was experienced. Cultural progress was very slow during Eolithic and Paleolithic times. But after a relatively brief period in the Neolithic age, during which the agricultural arts were being developed, there was a tremendous acceleration of culture growth and the great cultures of China, India, Mesopotamia, Egypt, Mexico, and Peru, came rapidly into being.

The sequence of events was somewhat as follows: agriculture transformed a roaming population into a sedentary one. It greatly increased the food supply, which in turn increased the population. As human labor became more productive in agriculture, an increasing portion of society became divorced from the task of food-getting, and was devoted to other occupations. Thus society becomes organized into occupational groups: masons, metal workers, jade carvers, weavers, scribes, priests. This has the effect of accelerating progress in the arts, crafts, and sciences (astronomy, mathematics, etc.), since they are now in the hands of specialists, rather than jacks-of-all-trades. With an increase in manufacturing, added to division of society into occupational groups, comes production for exchange and sale (instead of primarily for use as in tribal society), mediums of exchange, money, merchants, banks, mortgages, debtors, slaves. An accumulation of wealth and competition for favored regions provoke wars of conquest, and produce professional military and ruling classes, slavery and serfdom. Thus agriculture wrought a profound change in the life-and-culture of man as it had existed in the human-energy stage of development.[15]

---

[15] In this passage, White presents an evolutionary model that derives from Childe (1942: chapters 3 and 4) but is ultimately based upon Spencer. He saw cultural evolution as a process of increasing differentiation and specialization. White's evolutionism, like that of other twentieth-century thinkers, lacks the explicit ethnocentrism and racism of nineteenth-century evolutionists. A key difference is probably the experience of World Wars I and II. (White fought in World War I.) It was, perhaps, easy for an English intellectual at the end of the nineteenth century to maintain that the Victorian Age represented the pinnacle of currently achieved evolution. To continue to hold this position after the carnage of battles like the Somme, where the British took 60,000 casualties on the first day of fighting and where there were a total of over 1.2 million casualties, however, required considerable mental gymnastics.

But the advance of culture was not continuous and without limit. Civilization had, in the main, reached the limit of its development on the basis of a merely agricultural and animal husbandry technology long before the next great cultural advance was initiated by the industrial revolution. As a matter of fact, marked cultural recessions took place in Mesopotamia, Egypt, Greece, Rome, perhaps in India, possibly in China. This is not to say that no cultural progress whatsoever was made; we are well aware of many steps forward from time to time in various places. But so far as general type of culture is concerned, there is no fundamental difference between the culture of Greece during the time of Archimedes and that of Western Europe at the beginning of the eighteenth century.

After the agricultural arts had become relatively mature, some six, eight or ten thousand years before the beginning of the Christian era, there was little cultural advance until the nineteenth century A.D. Agricultural methods in Europe and the United States in 1850 differed very little from those of Egypt of 2000 B.C. The Egyptians did not have an iron plow, but otherwise there was little difference in mode of production. Even today in many places in the United States and in Europe we can find agricultural practices which, the use of iron excepted, are essentially like those of dynastic Egypt. Production in other fields was essentially the same in western Europe at the beginning of the eighteenth (we might almost say nineteenth) century as in ancient Rome, Greece, or Egypt. Man, as freeman, serf, or slave, and beasts of burden and draft animals supplemented to a meager extent by wind and water power, were the sources of energy. The Europeans had gunpowder whereas the ancients did not. But gunpowder cannot be said to be a culture-builder.º There was no essential difference in type of social–political and economic–institutions. Banks, merchants, the political state, great landowners, guilds of workmen, and so on were found in ancient Mesopotamia, Greece, and Rome.

Thus we may conclude that culture had developed about as far as could upon the basis of an agricultural-animal husbandry economy, and that there were recessions from peaks attained in Mesopotamia, Egypt, Greece and Rome long before the beginning of the eighteenth century A.D. We may conclude further, that civilization would never have advanced substantially beyond the levels already reached in the great cultures of antiquity if a way had not been found to harness a greater magnitude of energy per capita per unit of time, by tapping a new source of energy: fuel.[16]

The invention of the steam engine, and of all subsequent engines which derive power from fuels, inaugurated a new era in culture history. When man learned to harness energy in the form of fuel he opened the door of a vast treasure house of energy. Fuels and engines tremendously increased the amount of energy under man's control and at his disposal for culture-building. The extent to which energy has been thus harnessed in the modern world is indicated by the eminent physicist, Robert A. Millikan[17] (1939:211) as follows:ᴾ

> In this country [the U.S.A.] there is now expended about 13.5 horsepower hours per day per capita—the equivalent of 100 human slaves for each of us; in England the figure is 6.7, in Germany 6.0, in France 4.5, in Japan 1.8, in Russia 0.9, China, 0.5.

---

[16] White's evolutionism was modified by his reading of Marx. Most nineteenth-century evolutionists saw evolution as a process of gradual incremental change without major breaks, but Marx saw cultural evolution as proceeding by revolution: long periods of relative stasis broken by cataclysmic upheaval. White's vision in these passages is close to this view: he saw long epochs without change broken by quantum changes in energy production and consumption.

[17] White had an interest in physics and would certainly have been aware of quantum mechanics. While there is no direct link between White's theories here and quantum theory, which developed in the late 1920s and the 1930s, the parallel is suggestive. Quantum mechanics described abrupt changes in the levels of energy of subatomic particles; White describes abrupt changes in the levels of energy available to cultures.

He quotes Robert Millikan twice in this article. Millikan (1868–1953) won the Nobel prize in 1923, primarily for his famous oil drop experiment. Using a simple but ingenious apparatus, Millikan determined the electrical charge of an electron and discovered that it was constant. The experiment is a classic of scientific literature, and its results were fundamental building blocks of quantum mechanics.

Let us return now, for a moment, to our basic principle — culture develops as (1) the amount of energy harnessed and put to work per capita per unit of time increases, and (2) as the efficiency of the means with which this energy is expended increases — and consider the evolution of culture from a slightly different angle. In the course of human history various sources of energy are tapped and harnessed by man and put to work at culture-living and culture-building. The original source of energy was, as we have seen, the human organism. Subsequently, energy has been harnessed in other forms — agriculture, animal husbandry, fire,[q] wind, water, fuel. Energy is energy, and from the point of view of technology it makes no difference whether the energy with which a bushel of wheat is ground comes from a free man, a slave,[r] an ox, the flowing stream or a pile of coal. But it makes a big difference to human beings where the energy comes from,[s] and an important index of cultural development is derived from this fact.

To refer once more to our basic equation: On the one hand we have energy expended; on the other, human-need-serving goods and services are produced. Culture advances as these two factors increase, hand in hand. But the energy component is resolvable into two factors: the human energy, and the non-human energy, factors. Of these, the human energy factor is a constant; the non-human energy factor, a variable. The increase in quantity of need-serving goods goes hand in hand with an increase in the amount of non-human energy expended. But, since the human energy factor remains constant, an increase in amount of goods and services produced means more goods and services per unit of human labor. Hence, we obtain the law: *Other things being equal, culture evolves as the productivity of human labor increases.*[18]

In Savagery (wild food economy) the productivity of human labor is low; only a small amount of human-need-serving goods and services are produced per unit of human energy. In Barbarism (agriculture, animal husbandry), this productivity is greatly increased. And in Civilization (fuels, engines) it is still further increased.

We must now consider another factor in the process of cultural development, and an important one it is, viz., *the social system within which energy is harnessed and put to work.*

We may distinguish two kinds of determinants in social organization, two kinds of social groupings.[19] On the one hand we have social groupings which serve those needs of man which can be fed by drawing upon resources within man's own organism: clubs for companionship, classes or castes in so far as they feed the desire for distinction, will serve as examples. On the other hand, social organization is concerned with man's adjustment to the external world; social organization is the way in which human beings organize themselves for the three great processes of adjustment and survival — food-getting, defense from enemies, protection from the elements. Thus, we may distinguish two factors in any social system, those elements which are *ends in themselves,* which we may call E; and elements which are *means to ends* (food, defense, etc.) which we may term M.

In any social system M is more important than E, because E is dependent upon M. There can be no men's clubs or classes of distinction unless food is provided and enemies guarded against. In the development of culture, moreover, we may regard E as a constant: a men's club is a men's club whether among savage or civilized peoples. Being a constant, we may ignore factor E in our consideration of cultural evolution and deal only with the factor M.

M is a variable factor in the process of cultural evolution.[20] It is, moreover, a dependent variable, dependent upon the technological way

---

[18] In *Capital* (1930), Marx argues that it is human labor that gives value to goods and services. White may have considered that as he wrote this passage.

[19] White distinguished three components in the analysis of culture: technological, sociological, and ideational-attitudinal. He gave priority to the technological. He saw social organization and beliefs as arising primarily from the constraints and possibilities of technology (1959:18–28). These ideas are variations on Marx's analytical divisions: forces of production, relations of production, base, and superstructure.

[20] Here, without crediting Marx, White lays out some principles of materialist thinking. Marx had written that the mode of economic production determines the general character of the social, political, and spiritual processes of life. White uses

which energy is harnessed and put to work. It is obvious, of course, that it is the technological activities of hunting people that determine, in general, their form of social organization (in so far as that social organization is correlated with hunting rather than with defense against enemies). We of the United States have a certain type of social system (in part) because we have factories, railroads, automobiles, etc.; we do not possess these things as a consequence of a certain kind of social system. Technological systems engender social systems rather than the reverse. Disregarding the factor E, social organization is to be regarded as the way in which human beings organize themselves to wield their respective technologies. Thus we obtain another important law of culture: *The social organization (E excluded) of a people is dependent upon and determined by the mechanical means with which food is secured, shelter provided, and defense maintained.* In the process of cultural development, *social evolution is consequence of technological evolution.*

But this is not the whole story. While it is true that social systems are engendered by, and dependent upon, their respective underlying technologies, it is also true that social systems condition the operation of the technological systems upon which they rest; the relationship is one of mutual, though not necessarily equal, interaction and influence. A social system may foster the effective operation of its underlying technology or it may tend to restrain and thwart it. In short, in any given situation the social system may play a progressive role or it may play a reactionary role.

We have noted that after the agricultural arts had attained a certain degree of development, the great civilizations of China, India, Egypt, the Near East, Central America and Peru came rapidly into being as a consequence of the greatly augmented energy resources of the people of these regions. But these great civilizations did not

continue to advance indefinitely. On the contrary they even receded from maximum levels in a number of instances. Why did they not continue progressively to advance? According to our law culture will advance, other things being equal, as long as the amount of energy harnessed and put to work per capita per unit of time increases. The answer to our question, Why did not these great cultures continue to advance? is, therefore, that the amount of energy per capita per unit of time, *ceased to increase,* and furthermore, the efficiency of the means with which this energy was expended *was not advanced beyond a certain limit.*[21] In short, there was no fundamental improvement in the agricultural arts from say 2000 B.C. to 1800 A.D.

The next question is, Why did not the agricultural arts advance and improve during this time? We know that the agricultural arts are still capable of tremendous improvement, and the urge of man for plenty, security and efficiency was as great then as now. Why, then, did agriculture fail to progress beyond a certain point in the great civilizations of antiquity? The answer is, The social system, within which these arts functioned, curbed further expansion, thwarted progress.

All great civilizations resting upon intensive agriculture are divided into classes: a ruling class and the masses who are ruled.[22] The masses produced the means of life. But the distribution of these goods is in accordance with rules which are administered by the ruling class. By one method of control or another—by levies, taxes, rents, or some other means—the ruling class takes a portion of the wealth produced by the masses from them, and consumes it according to their liking or as the exigencies of the time dictate.

In this sort of situation cultural advancement may cease at a certain point for lack of incentive. No incentive to progress came from the ruling class in the ancient civilizations of which we

---

American society in an example of precisely this sort of thinking. Marx believed that the ultimate result of the thwarting of technology by society was revolution and the emergence of new social structures. In the passages below, White echoes this belief.

[21] While many of White's theories stay close to Marx, his use of energy to explain social change is not found in Marx's work.

[22] Notice here and below, the direct use of class analysis. White does not quote Marx directly, but the Marxist view of history as class struggle is very much evident in these passages.

are speaking. What they appropriated from their subjects they consumed or wasted. To obtain more wealth the ruling class merely increased taxes, rents, or other levies upon the producers of wealth. This was easier, quicker, and surer than increasing the efficiency of production and thereby augmenting the total product. On the other hand, there was no incentive to progress among the masses — if they produced more by increasing efficiency it would only mean more for the tax-gatherers of the ruling class. The culture history of China during the past few centuries, or indeed, since the Han dynasty, well illustrates situations of this sort.

We come then to the following conclusion: *A social system may so condition the operation of a technological system as to impose a limit upon the extent to which it can expand and develop. When this occurs, cultural evolution ceases.* Neither evolution nor progress in culture is inevitable (neither Morgan nor Tylor ever said, or even intimated, that they are). When cultural advance has thus been arrested, it can be renewed only by tapping some new source of energy and by harnessing it in sufficient magnitude to burst asunder the social system which binds it. Thus freed the new technology will form a new social system, one congenial to growth, and culture will again advance until, perhaps, the social system once more checks it.[23]

It seems quite clear that mankind would never have advanced materially beyond the maximum levels attained by culture between 2000 B.C. and 1700 A.D. had it not tapped a new source of energy (fuel) and harnessed it in substantial magnitudes. The speed with which man could travel, the range of his projectiles, and many other things, could not have advanced beyond a certain point had he not learned to harness more energy in new forms. And so it was with culture as a whole.

The steam engine ushered in a new era. With it, and various kinds of internal combustion engines, the energy resources of vast deposits of coal and oil were tapped and harnessed in progressively increasing magnitudes. Hydroelectric plants contributed a substantial amount from rivers. Populations grew, production expanded, wealth increased. The limits of growth of the new technology have not yet been reached; indeed, it is probably not an exaggeration to say that they have not even been foreseen, so vast are the possibilities and so close are we still to the beginning of this new era. But already the new technology has come into conflict with the old social system.[24] The new technology is being curbed and thwarted. The progressive tendencies of the new technology are being held back by a social system that was adapted to pre-fuel technology. This fact has become commonplace today.

In our present society, goods are produced for sale at a profit. To sell one must have a market. Our market is a world market, but it is, nevertheless, finite in magnitude. When the limit of the market has been reached production ceases to expand: no market, no sale; no sale, no profit; no profit, no production. Drastic curtailment of production, wholesale destruction of surpluses follow. Factories, mills, and mines close; millions of men are divorced from industrial production and thrown upon relief. Population growth recedes. National incomes cease to expand. Stagnation sets in.

When, in the course of cultural development, the expanding technology comes into conflict with the social system, one of two things will happen: either the social system will give way, or technological advance will be arrested. If the latter occurs, cultural evolution will, of course, cease. The outcome of situations such as this is not preordained. The triumph of technology and

---

[23] Here White diverges critically from Marx. Marx believed that social evolution toward communism was inevitable, though its rate might be affected by human action. White claims that "neither evolution nor progress in culture is inevitable."

[24] White's distaste for capitalism is evident in passages such as this. When White wrote this essay in 1943, World War II was raging, and the memory of the Depression was still very fresh in people's minds. White believed that capitalism inevitably entailed a cycle of depression and destructive warfare. Although he was appalled by Stalin's policies in Russia and considered the members of the American Communist Party "a bunch of stooges for Stalin" (quoted in Peace 1998), he was a committed socialist.

the continued evolution and progress of culture are not assured merely because we wish it or because it would be better thus.[25] In culture as in mechanics, the greater force prevails. A force is applied to a boulder. If the force be great enough, the rock is moved. If the rock be large enough to withstand the force, it will remain stationary. So in the case of technology-institutions conflicts: if the force of the growing technology be great enough, the restraining institutions will give way; if this force is not strong enough to overcome institutional opposition, it must submit to it.

There was undoubtedly much institutional resistance to the expanding agricultural technology in late neolithic times. Such staunch institutions as the tribe and clan which had served man well for thousands of years did not give way to the political state without a fight; the "liberty, equality and fraternity" of primitive society were not surrendered for the class-divided, serf and lord, slave and master, society of feudalism without a struggle.[26] But the ancient and time-honored institutions of tribal society could not accommodate the greatly augmented forces of the agricultural technology. Neither could they successfully oppose these new forces. Consequently, tribal institutions gave way and a new social system came into being.

Similarly in our day, our institutions have shown themselves incapable of accommodating the vast technological forces of the Power Age. What the outcome of the present conflict between modern fuel technology and the social system of an earlier era will be, time alone will tell. It seems likely, however, that the old social system is now in the process of destruction. The tremendous forces of the Power Age are not to be denied. The great wars of the twentieth century derive their chief significance from this fact: they are the means by which an old social order is to be scrapped, and a new one to be brought into being.[27] The first World War wiped out the old ruling families of the Hapsburgs, Romanoffs, and Hohenzollerns, hulking relics of Feudalism, and brought Communist and Fascist systems into being. We do not venture to predict the social changes which the present war will bring about. But we may confidently expect them to be as profound and as far-reaching as those effected by World War I.

Thus, in the history of cultural evolution, we have witnessed one complete cultural revolution, and the first stage of a second. The technological transition from a wild food economy to a relatively mature agricultural and animal husbandry economy was followed by an equally profound institutional change: from tribal society to civil society. Thus the first fundamental and all-inclusive cultural change, or revolution, took place. At the present time we are entering upon the second stage of the second great cultural revolution of human history. The Industrial Revolution was but the first stage, the technological stage, of this great cultural revolution. The Industrial Revolution has run its course, and we are now entering upon the second stage, one of profound institutional change, of social revolution. Barring collapse and chaos, which is of course possible, a new social order will emerge. It appears likely that human race will occupy the earth for some million years to come. It seems probable, also, that man, after having won his way up through Savagery and Barbarism, is not likely to stop, when at last he finds himself upon the very threshold of Civilization.[28]

---

[25] White's absolute faith in the desirability of technological progress is characteristic of the era in which he wrote. Modern anthropologists have lost much of this faith.

[26] White again echoes Marx's dictum that change comes about through revolutionary struggle rather than gradual evolutionary progress.

[27] Remember that this essay was written during World War II. White had served in the Navy in World War I and was greatly shaken by his wartime experiences. He later wrote that these experiences inspired his move from the physical to the social sciences (Barnes 1960).

[28] Notice a strong utopian thread in White's writing here and later. Provided enough energy can be found, the destiny of humanity is civilization and a new social order. It follows from White's logic that the new social order, since it is better matched to technology, will be superior to the old. Progress is our most important product.

The key to the future, in any event, lies in the energy situation. If we can continue to harness as much energy per capita per year in the future as we are doing now, there is little doubt but that our old social system will give way to a new one, a new era of civilization. Should, however, the amount of energy that we are able to harness diminish materially, then culture would cease to advance or even recede. A return to a cultural level comparable to that of China during the Ming dynasty is neither inconceivable nor impossible. It all depends upon how man harnesses the forces of nature and the extent to which this is done.

At the present time "the petroleum in sight is only a twelve year supply, . . . and new discoveries [of oil] are not keeping pace with use."[t] Coal is more abundant. Even so, many of the best deposits in the United States—which has over half of the world's known coal reserves—will some day be depleted.[29] "Eventually, no matter how much we conserve, this sponging off past ages for fossil energy must cease . . . What then?"[u] The answer is, of course, that culture will decline unless man is able to maintain the amount of energy harnessed per capita per year by tapping new sources.

Wind, water, waves, tides, solar boilers, photochemical reactions, atomic energy, etc., are sources which might be tapped or further exploited. One of the most intriguing possibilities is that of harnessing atomic energy. When the nucleus of an atom of uranium (U235) is split it "releases 200,000,000 electron volts, the largest conversion of mass into energy that has yet been produced by terrestrial means."[v] Weight for weight, uranium (as a source of energy produced by nuclear fission) is 5,000,000 times as effective as coal.[w] If harnessing sub-atomic energy could be made a practical success, our energy resources would be multiplied a thousand fold. As Dr. R. M. Langer,[x] research associate in physics at California Institute of Technology, has put it:

> The face of the earth will be changed. . . . Privilege and class distinctions will become relics because things that make up the good life will be so abundant and inexpensive. War will become obsolete because of the disappearance of those economic stresses that immemorially have caused it. . . . The kind of civilization we might expect . . . is so different in kind from anything we know that even guesses about it are futile.

To be able to harness sub-atomic energy would, without doubt, create a civilization surpassing sober imagination of today. But not everyone is as confident as Dr. Langer that this advance is imminent. Some experts have their doubts, some think it a possibility. Time alone will tell.[30]

But there is always the sun, from which man has derived all of his energy, directly or indirectly, in the past. And it may be that it will become, directly, our chief source of power in the future. Energy in enormous amounts reaches the earth daily from the sun. "The average intensity of solar energy in this latitude amounts to about 0.1 of a horse power per square foot" (Furnas 1941:426). "Enough energy falls on about 200 square miles of an arid region like the Mojave Desert to supply the [present needs of the] United States" (Furnas 1941:427). But the problem is, of course, to harness it effectively and efficiently.[y] The difficulties do not seem insuperable. It will doubtless be done, and probably before a serious diminution of power from dwindling resources of oil and coal overtakes us. From a power standpoint the outlook for the future is not too dark for optimism.

We turn now to an interesting and important fact, one highly significant to the history of anthropology: The thesis set forth in the preceding

---

[29] Fears about limits of the world's energy supplies are nothing new. The estimates White cites here are similar to some of those given during the energy crisis thirty years later.

[30] White wrote this before the invention of the atomic bomb and the nuclear power plant. In the 1950s, his writing seemed almost prescient. Many people then believed that nuclear energy would result in electric power so inexpensive it would not be worth metering. White, and others, pointed out that such a development would have profound effects on social structure. Langer (quoted here) is perhaps disingenuous when he writes that guesses are futile; the type of society he describes is precisely that predicted by Marx.

pages is substantially the same as that advanced by Lewis H. Morgan and E. B. Tylor many decades ago.[31] We have expounded it in somewhat different form and words; our presentation is, perhaps, more systematic and explicit. At one point we have made a significant change in their theoretical scheme: we begin the third great stage of cultural evolution with engines rather than with writing. But essentially our thesis is that of the Evolutionist school as typified by Morgan and Tylor.

According to Morgan, culture developed as man extended and improved his control over his environment, especially with regard to the food supply.[32] The "procurement of subsistence" is man's "primary need" (p. 525).ᶻ

> The important fact that mankind commenced at the bottom of the scale and worked up, is revealed in an expressive manner by their successive arts of subsistence. Upon their skill in this direction, the whole question of human supremacy on the earth depended. Mankind are the only beings who may be said to have gained an absolute control over the production of food; which at the outset they did not possess above other animals. Without enlarging the basis of subsistence, mankind could not have propagated themselves into other areas not possessing the same kinds of food, and ultimately over the whole surface of the earth; and, lastly, without obtaining an absolute control over both its variety and amount, they could not have multiplied into populous nations. It is accordingly probable that the great epochs of human progress have

been identified, more or less directly, with the enlargement of the sources of subsistence (p. 19). When the great discovery was made that the wild horse, cow, sheep, ass, sow and goat might be tamed, and, when produced in flocks and herds, become a source of permanent subsistence, it must have given a powerful impulse to human progress (p. 534).

And

> the acquisition of farinaceous food by cultivation must be regarded as one of the greatest events in human experience (p. 42).

Morgan is much concerned with the significance of technology and its development:

> "The domestic animals supplementing human muscle with animal power, contributed a new factor of the highest value" (p. 26). The bow and arrow, "the first deadly weapon for the hunt, . . . must have given a powerful upward influence to ancient society," since it made man more effective in the food quest (pp. 21–22). "The plow drawn by animal power may be regarded as inaugurating a new art" (p. 26). The "production of iron gave the plow with an iron point and a better spade and axe" (p. 26). Many other inventions, such as pottery, adobe brick, metallurgy—when man "had invented the furnace, and produced iron from ore, nine tenths of the battle for civilization was won" (p. 43)—are emphasized as motive forces of cultural development. "The most advanced portion of the human race were halted, so to express it, at certain stages of progress, until

---

[31] You may have caught many references to Morgan's and Tylor's scheme of cultural evolution in the preceding passages. Here, White makes their contribution to his work explicit. White's detailed acknowledgment of Morgan and Tylor must be seen as an attack on most of American anthropology of his time—much of Boasian anthropology was a reaction against the evolutionism of nineteenth-century writers such as Morgan and Tylor. Boas and his students dismissed their work as logically flawed, insufficiently scientific, and implicitly racist. White's rehabilitation of Morgan and Tylor in the pages of *American Anthropologist* (where this essay first appeared) must have seemed audacious to his contemporaries. His repeated quotation of them in these passages was a goad to established anthropological opinion. White later wrote, "I was ridiculed and scoffed at. Everyone knew that evolutionism was dead." He quotes Ralph Linton (1893–1953), an eminent anthropologist of the time, as saying that he, White, "ought to be given the courtesy extended to suspected horse thieves and shady gamblers in the days of the Wild West, namely, to allow them to get out of town before sundown" (quoted in Carneiro 1981:229).

[32] White's first teaching post was at Buffalo, Morgan's hometown. While there, he read Morgan's work and was profoundly affected by it. He later edited Morgan's letters and journals and produced a definitive edition of Morgan's *Ancient Society*. He was certainly the greatest scholar of Morgan's work of his era. Harris has written, "In every respect, White's *The Evolution of Culture* is the modern equivalent of Morgan's *Ancient Society*" (1968:643).

some great invention or discovery, such as the domestication of animals or the smelting of iron ore, gave a new and powerful impulse forward" (pp. 39–40).

Morgan shows how technological advance brings about social change: technological evolution produces social evolution. In many places, but particularly in Part IV of *Ancient Society*, he shows how property, which accumulates through "an enlargement of the means of subsistence" and through a development of the individual arts, affects and changes the constitution of society. "Property and office were the foundations upon which aristocracy planted itself" (p. 551). Also,

> From . . . the increased abundance of subsistence through field agriculture, nations began to develop, numbering many thousands under one government. . . . The localization of tribes in fixed areas and in fortified cities, with the increase of the numbers of the people, intensified the struggle for the possession of the most desirable territories. It tended to advance the art of war, and to increase the rewards of individual prowess. These changes of condition and of the plan of life indicate the approach of civilization which was to overthrow gentile and establish political society (p. 540).

We find essentially the same ideas in Tylor. Like Morgan, Tylor declares that man's "first need is to get his daily food" (p. 206).[aa] Culture develops as man's control over his environment, especially over the food supply, increases. Mankind advanced from savagery to barbarism when they took to agriculture: "With the certain supply of food which can be stored until next harvest, settled village and town life is established, with immense results in the improvement of arts, knowledge, manners and government" (p. 24). "Those edible grasses," says Tylor, "which have been raised by cultivation into the cereals, such as wheat, barley, rye, and by their regular and plentiful supply have become the mainstay of human life and the *great moving power of civilization*" (p. 215; emphasis ours).

A pastoral economy, according to Tylor, is superior to that of a hunting and gathering (wild food) economy, but inferior to an agricultural economy. A combination of agriculture and animal husbandry is superior to either way of life by itself (pp. 24, 220).

Social evolution comes as a consequence of technological development: To this "change of habit [i.e., from a wild food economy to agriculture] may be plainly in great part traced the expansion of industrial arts and the creation of higher social and political institutions" (p. 118; article "Anthropology," in Encyclopaedia Britannica, 11th ed.).

With the development of agriculture and the industrial arts comes a struggle for the most desirable territories (as Morgan puts it) and warfare "for gain" rather than "for quarrel or vengeance" (Tylor, p. 225). The consequences of this warfare for gain are tremendous: ". . . captives, instead of being slain, are brought back for slaves, and especially set to till the ground. By this agriculture is much increased, and also a new division of society takes place . . . Thus we see how in old times the original equality of men broke up, a nation dividing into an aristocracy of warlike freemen, and an inferior laboring caste" (p. 225). "It was through slave labor that agriculture and industry increased, that wealth accumulated, and leisure was given to priests, scribes, poets, philosophers, to raise the level of men's minds" (p. 435). Furthermore, according to Tylor, warfare, among culturally advanced peoples, produces "two of the greatest facts in history—the organized army . . . and the confederation of tribes . . ." (pp. 432–433); tribes become states, primitive society gives way to civil society.

Tylor is much interested in the ways in which man harnesses the forces of nature and the extent to which energy is harnessed. "It was a great movement in civilization," he says, when man harnessed water power (p. 204). He speaks of the "civilized world . . . drawing an immense supply of power from a new source, the coal burnt in the furnace of the steam-engine, which is already used so wastefully that economists are uneasily calculating how long this stored-up fossil force will last, and what must be turned to next—tide force or sun's heat—to labor for us" (pp. 204–205).

Tylor clearly recognizes the problem we have dealt with in this essay when he speculates: "It is an interesting problem in political economy to reckon the means of subsistence in our country during the agricultural and pastoral period, and to compare them with the resources we now gain from coal, in doing home-work and manufacturing goods to exchange for foreign produce. Perhaps the best means of realizing what coal is to us, will be to consider, that of three Englishmen now [1881], one at least may be reckoned to live by coal, inasmuch as without it the population would have been so much less" (p. 272). The energy significance of modern civilization lies in the fact that "in modern times, man seeks more and more to change the laborer's part he played in early ages, for the higher duty of director or controller of the world's forces" (p. 205).

Thus, we see that our essay is substantially a systematic exposition of the ideas of Morgan and Tylor.[33] Man is an animal. His first and greatest need is food. Control over habitat in general and food supply in particular is effected by means of tools (of all kinds, weapons included). Through invention and discovery the technological means of control are extended and improved. Social evolution follows upon technological evolution.

At one point we have made an innovation. Both Morgan (p. 12) and Tylor (p. 24) use the origin of writing to mark the beginning of the third great era of cultural development, "Civilization." In our scheme, "civilization" begins with the invention of the steam engine as a practical means of harnessing energy.[34]

Although Morgan and Tylor both deal directly with the energy factor in cultural development, they lose sight of it when they consider writing. Writing is not a motive force. What change would writing have effected in the culture of the Arunta, or the Eskimo, or the Iroquois? It would not have altered their way of life in any essential respect. The culture of the ancient Peruvians, which lacked writing, was quite as advanced as that of the Aztecs who had writing. And in our own culture, writing has served to preserve and perpetuate—when it has not sanctified—the ignorance and superstitions of our barbaric ancestors quite as much as it has promoted progress and enlightenment.

But, if writing is not to be considered a motive force in cultural development, the human organism, domesticated animals, cultivated plants, water wheels, windmills, steam engines, etc., are motive forces (or the means of harnessing energy). What we have done is to reduce all specific, concrete motive forces in cultural development to a single, abstract, common term: energy. To classify cultures as "wild food, domestic food, and literate," as Morgan and Tylor did, is illogical; it is like classifying vehicles as "three-wheeled, four-wheeled, and pretty." We classify cultures according to the way, or ways, in which they harness energy and the manner in which it is put to work to serve human needs.

In the foregoing we have, we believe, a sound and illuminating theory of cultural evolution. We have hold of principles, fundamental principles, which are operative in all cultures at all times and places. The motive force of cultural evolution is laid bare, the mechanisms of development made clear. The nature of the relationship between social institutions on the one hand and technological instruments on the other is indicated. Understanding that the function of culture is to serve the needs of man, we find that we have an objective criterion for evaluating culture in terms of the extent to which, and the efficiency with which, human needs are satisfied by cultural means. We can measure the amounts of energy expended; we can calculate the efficiency of the expenditure of energy in terms of measurable quantities of goods and services produced. And,

---

[33] White's portrayal of Morgan and Tylor conceals a very important difference between their thinking and his own. Morgan and Tylor, like many other nineteenth-century evolutionists, generally saw social change as driven by psychic unity. While the material aspects of a society may indicate the level of evolution it had attained, progress was ultimately dependent on the organic unfolding of germs of thought. White, on the other hand, proposed that humans' biologically based need to make life secure was the force driving cultural evolution.

[34] White's appreciation of Morgan was enhanced by the importance given him by Marx and Engels, who saw Morgan's *Ancient Society* as providing independent confirmation of their model of social and historical development. For this reason, Soviet communists in the first half of this century often had an unusually detailed understanding of Morgan. White would have been exposed to this on his trip to the Soviet Union in 1929.

finally, as we see, these measurements can be expressed in mathematical terms.[35]

The theory set forth in the preceding pages was, as we have made clear, held by the foremost thinkers of the Evolutionist school of the nineteenth century, both in England and in America. Today they seem to us as sound as they did to Tylor and Morgan, and, if anything, more obvious. It seems almost incredible that anthropologists of the twentieth century could have turned their backs upon and repudiated such simple, sound, and illuminating generalization, one that makes the vast range of tens of thousands of years of culture history intelligible. But they have done just this.[bb] The anti-evolutionists, led in America by Franz Boas, have rejected the theory of evolution in cultural anthropology and have given us instead a philosophy of "planless hodge-podge-ism."[36]

It is not surprising, therefore, to find at the present time the most impressive recognition of the significance of technological progress in cultural evolution in the writings of a distinguished physicist, the Nobel prize winner, Robert A. Millikan:[cc]

> The changes that have occurred within the past hundred years not only in the external conditions under which the average man, at least in this western world, passes life on earth, but in his superstitions . . . his fundamental beliefs, in his philosophy, in his conception of religion, in his whole world outlook, are probably greater than those that occurred during the preceding four thousand years all put together. Life seems to remain static for thousands of years and then shoot forward with amazing speed. The last century has been one of those periods of extraordinary change, the most amazing in human history. If, then, you ask me to put into one sentence the cause of that recent rapid and enormous change I should reply: "It is found in the discovery and utilization of the means by which heat energy can be made to do man's work for him."

Tucked away in the pages of Volume II of a manual on European archeology, too, we find a similar expression from a distinguished American scholar, George G. MacCurdy:[dd]

> The *degree of civilization* of any epoch, people, or group of peoples *is measured by ability to utilize energy for human advancement or needs.* Energy is of two kinds, internal and external or free. Internal energy is that of the human body or machine, and its basis is food. External energy is that outside the human body and its basis is fuel. Man has been able to tap the great storehouse of external energy. Through his internal energy and that acquired from external sources, he has been able to overcome the opposing energy of his natural environment. *The difference between these two opposing forces is the gauge of civilization* (emphasis ours).

Thus, this view is not wholly absent in anthropological theory in America today although extremely rare and lightly regarded. The time will come, we may confidently expect, when the theory of evolution will again prevail in the science of culture as it has in the biological and the physical sciences. It is a significant fact that in cultural anthropology alone among the sciences is a philosophy of anti-evolutionism respectable — a fact we would do well to ponder.[37]

---

[35] Boas and most of his students believed that universal laws of the evolution of human culture could not be formulated and that thinkers such as Morgan and Tylor were ethnocentric. However, Boas' specific criticism of the evolutionists was based on flaws in their method – he claimed that they were insufficiently scientific. Here, White answers this criticism by showing what he believes are objective, empirical criteria for the comparison of cultures.

[36] The "planless hodge-podge-ism" refers to a frequently quoted passage in the work of Robert Lowie (1883–1957), a student of Boas. In the final paragraph of his widely read *Primitive Society,* Lowie wrote, "To that planless hodgepodge, that thing of shreds and patches called civilization, its historian can no longer yield superstitious reverence" (1920:441). While it stands at variance with much of Lowie's other work, this statement has often been used to caricature historical particularism.

[37] Despite his rejection by the Boasians, White had a profound effect on many younger scholars. He spent almost all of his forty-year academic career at the University of Michigan and was known as a brilliant and challenging teacher. Through his students, he had a powerful impact not only on cultural anthropology but on archaeology and physical anthropology

Notes

a. By "energy" we mean "the capacity for performing work."

b. Cf. Leslie A. White, *The Symbol: The Origin and Basis of Human Behavior* (Philosophy of Science, Vol. 7, October, 1940), pp. 451–463.

c. See Leslie A. White, *Science Is Sciencing* (Philosophy of Science, Vol. 5, October, 1938), pp. 369–389, for a discussion of this general point of view.

d. "Natural science" is a redundancy. All science is natural; if it is not natural it is not science.

e. Actually, of course, it is not wholly constant; there may be progress in music, myth-making, etc., regardless of technology. A men's club, however, is still a men's club, whether the underlying technology be simple and crude or highly developed. But, since the overwhelming portion of cultural development is due to technological progress, we may legitimately ignore that small portion which is not so dependent by regarding it a constant.

f. "There is only one cultural reality that is not artificial, to wit: the culture of all humanity at all periods and in all places," R. H. Lowie, *Cultural Anthropology: A Science* (American Journal of Sociology, Vol. 42, 1936), p. 305.

g. We say "per year" although "per unit of time" would serve as well, because in concrete cultural situations a year would embrace the full round of the seasons and the occupations and actions appropriate thereto.

h. The cultural evolutionists have been criticized for identifying progress with evolution by pointing out that these two words are not synonymous. It is as true as it is obvious that they are not synonymous — in the dictionary. But by and large, in the history of human culture, progress and evolution *have gone hand in hand.*

i. See Tylor, *Primitive Culture*, Vol. I, p. 14 (London, 1929 printing) for another respect in which, in the theory of evolution, "the student of the habits of mankind has a great advantage over the student of the species of plants and animals."

j. "Commencing probably with the dog . . . followed . . . by the capture of the young of other animals and rearing them, not unlikely, *from the merest freak of fancy,* it required time and experience to discover the utility of each . . ." (emphasis ours). Morgan, *Ancient Society*, p. 42 (Holt ed.).

k. *Introduction to Cultural Anthropology* (New York, 1940 ed.) pp. 51–52. In this argument Lowie leans heavily upon Eduard Hahn, whose work, incidentally, appeared many years after *Ancient Society* ("Subsistence," p. 303, in *General Anthropology*, F. Boas, ed., New York, 1938; *History of Ethnological Theory*, p. 112 ff., New York, 1937).

l. Following Morgan and Tylor, we use "savagery" to designate cultures resting upon a wild-food basis, "barbarism" for cultures with a domestic food basis. Our use of "civilization," however, differs from that of Tylor and Morgan (see p. 355).

m. "Finds in the Near East seem to indicate that the domestication of plants and animals in that region was followed by an extraordinary flowering of culture," Ralph Linton, *The Present Status of Anthropology* (Science, Vol. 87, 1938), p. 245.

n. But this does not mean that agriculture *must be preceded* by a pastoral economy in the course of cultural development. Contrary to a notion current nowadays, none of the major evolutionists ever maintained that farming must be preceded by herding.

o. It is true, of course, that powder is used in blasting in quarries, etc., and is to this extent a motive force in culture-building. But energy employed in this way is relatively insignificant quantitatively. The bow and arrow inaugurated cultural advance because in its economic context it provided man with food in greater quantity or with less effort. The gun, in its hunting context, has had the opposite effect, that of reducing the food supply by killing off the game. In their military contexts, neither the bow and arrow or the gun has been a culture-builder. The mere conquest or extermination of one tribe or nation by another, the mere change from one dynasty or set of office holders to another, is not culture-building.

p. *Science and the World Tomorrow* (Scientific Monthly, Sept. 1939) p. 211. These figures do not, however, tell the whole story for they ignore the vast amount of energy harnessed in the form of cultivated plants and domesticated animals.

q. We may be permitted thus to distinguish two different ways of harnessing energy although each involves fire and fuel. By "fire" we indicate such energy uses of fire which preceded the steam engine — clearing forests, burning logs to make dugout canoes, etc. By "fuel" we designate energy harnessed by steam, gasoline, etc., engines.

---

as well. His students include cultural anthropologists Robert Carneiro, David Kaplan, and Napoleon Chagnon; archaeologists Louis Binford and Jeffrey Parsons; and physical anthropologists Frank Livingston, George Armelagos, and Jack Kelso, as well as many others in each of these fields.

r. Technologically a freeman and a slave are equal, both being energy in homo sapiens form. Sociologically, there is, of course, a vast difference between them. Sociologically, a slave is not a human being; he is merely a beast of burden who can talk.

s. According to E. H. Hull, of the General Electric Research Laboratory, the power equivalent of "a groaning and sweating slave" is "75 watts of electricity, which most of us can buy at the rate of two-fifths of a cent an hour." *Engineering: Ancient and Modern* (Scientific Monthly, November, 1939), p. 463.

t. C. C. Furnas, *Future Sources of Power* (Science, Nov. 7, 1941), p. 425.

u. Ibid., p. 426.

v. Herbert L. Anderson, *Progress in Harnessing Power from Uranium* (Scientific Monthly, June 1940).

w. Robert D. Potter, *Is Atomic Power at Hand?* (Scientific Monthly, June, 1940), p. 573.

x. *Fast New World* (Collier's, July 6, 1940).

y. See C. C. Abbot, *Utilizing Heat from the Sun* (Smithsonian Miscellaneous Collections, Vol. 98, No. 5, March 30, 1939).

z. The page references are to Morgan's *Ancient Society*, Henry Holt edition.

aa. Page references are to Tylor's *Anthropology* (New York, Appleton & Co. edition of 1916).

bb. One distinguished anthropologist has gone so far as to declare that "the theory of cultural evolution [is] to my mind the most inane, sterile, and pernicious theory ever conceived in the history of science . . ." B. Laufer, in a review of Lowie's *Culture and Ethnology* (American Anthropologist, Vol. 20, 1918), p. 90.

cc. Op. cit., p. 211.

dd. *Human Origins* (New York, 1933), Vol. II, pp. 134–135.

20. Family Stability in Non-European Cultures

George Peter Murdock (1897–1985)

THIS PAPER PRESENTS THE CONCLUSIONS OF A special study of the stability of marriage in forty selected non-European societies undertaken in an attempt to place the family situation in the contemporary United States in cross-cultural perspective.[1] Eight societies were chosen from each of the world's major ethnographic regions — Asia, Africa, Oceania, and native North and South America. Within each region the samples were carefully selected from widely scattered geograph-

(1950)

ical locations, from different culture areas, and from levels of civilization ranging from the simplest to the most complex. The data were obtained from the collections in the Human Relations Area Files, formerly the Cross-Cultural Survey.[2] The selection was made in as random a manner as possible except that it was confined to cultures for which the descriptive literature is full and reliable. Once chosen, a particular society was rejected and another substituted only in a few instances where the sources failed to provide (1) information on the relative rights of the two

---

[1] One of Murdock's most famous publications is his 1949 book *Social Structure*, an extensive cross-cultural analysis of the relationship between environment, rules of residence, family and kin organization, and marriage patterns. This article, published just one year after *Social Structure*, is an extension of that work. It is also notable because it explicitly places family structure in the United States in a cross-cultural perspective, an unusual technique for the time he was writing.

[2] Murdock received his introduction to the social sciences from sociologist Albert Keller (1874–1956), one of his professors at Yale. To understand Murdock's work, it is useful to know a bit about Keller and Keller's predecessor at Yale, William Graham Sumner.

Sumner was an ordained Episcopal priest and a celebrated political economist and sociologist. He held a variety of teaching posts and religious offices before accepting a newly created chair in Political and Social Science at Yale in 1872, sexes in divorce, or (2) evidence permitting a solid judgment as to the degree of family stability relative to that in our own society.

SOCIETIES IN SAMPLE

The method, it is believed, comes as close to that of purely random sampling as is feasible today in comparative social science. The results, it must be admitted, contain a number of surprises—even to the writer, who has been steeped for years in the literature of world ethnography. The forty selected societies are listed and located below.[3]

Asia: the Chukchi of northeastern Siberia, the Japanese, the Kazak of Turkestan, the Kurd of Iraq, the Lakher of Assam, the Mongols of Outer Mongolia, the Semang Negritos of Malaya, and the Toda of southern India.

Africa: the Dahomeans of coastal West Africa, the Ganda of Uganda, the Hottentot of South-West Africa, the Jukun of Northern Nigeria, the Lamba of Northern Rhodesia, the Langa of Kenya, the Siwans of the oasis of Siwa in Egypt, and the Wolof of Senegal.

Oceania: the Atayal aborigines of interior Formosa, the Balinese of Indonesia, the Kalinga of the northern Philippines, the Kurtatchi of the Solomon Islands in Melanesia, the Kwoma of New Guinea, the Murngin of northern Australia, the Samoans of Polynesia, and the Trukese of Micronesia.

North America: the Aztecs of ancient Mexico, the Creek of Alabama, the Crow of the high plains in Montana, the Haida of northern British Columbia and southern Alaska, the Hopi pueblo dwellers of Arizona, the Iroquois of northern New York, the Klamath of interior Oregon, and the Yurok of coastal California.

South America: the Cuna of southern Panama, the Guaycuru or Mbaya of the Gran Chaco, the Incas of ancient Peru, the Kaingang of southern Brazil, the Macusi of Guiana, the Ona of Tierra del Fuego, the Siriono of lowland Bolivia, and the Witoto of the northwest Amazonian jungle.[4]

---

a position he held until retiring in 1909. Sumner was an avid disciple of Herbert Spencer and "denounced, often in scathing terms, . . . Socialism, and all forms of or approaches to state paternalism" (*The National Cyclopedia of American Biography,* 1967:9). He even successfully fought the president of Yale over the right to use Spencer's *Study of Sociology* as a textbook.

Sumner and Keller particularly admired Spencer's massive thirteen-volume work *Descriptive Sociology* (1873–1934), in which Spencer presented ethnographic material indexed to common categories. At the time of his death in 1910, Sumner was working on a treatise on the science and evolution of society, a project that Keller completed from Sumner's notes and published as *The Science of Society* in 1927. This four-volume catalog of ethnographic material continued Spencer's quest to present a total picture of world evolution. Volume 4 is composed of ethnographic cases linked to the other three volumes through a comprehensive index. This index provided a model for Murdock's attempt to create a universal catalog of ethnographic materials and illustrates his debt, through Keller and Sumner, to Spencer (Harris 1968:607–8).

Murdock initiated the Cross-Cultural Survey project in 1937. Within a decade, this ethnographic database had been expanded and its name changed to the Human Relations Area Files. Today, the HRAF comprise the largest cross-cultural database in the world, with information on over 360 societies. Originally produced as sets of typed index cards, the volume of material in the files today is so large (800,000 pages of text) that microfilm and CD-ROM copies are commonly used.

[3] Murdock is best known for his studies of social structure and for his quantitative cross-cultural approach. Other than Durkheim, who did so in *Suicide* (1951 [1897]), he is the first author in this volume to use statistical analysis of ethnographic data and random sampling. However, he did not invent quantitative comparative analysis. A statistical version of the comparative method had been previously outlined by Tylor in his 1889 essay "On a Method of Investigating the Development of Institutions; Applied to Laws of Marriage and Descent." This approach was further developed by Murdock in the HRAF.

[4] Because Murdock pioneered the development of cross-cultural quantitative analysis in anthropology, many consider him a principal force behind the emergence of "scientific" cultural analyses. However, quantitative analysis does not necessarily eliminate researcher subjectivity. There are over 700 categories of topics coded in the HRAF, but can any single set of categories capture human cultural diversity? Also, the data in the HRAF were first edited by individuals (often graduate students) who chose what information to include in their reports and how that data would be coded in the files. Further, Murdock states here that one of the criteria used to choose societies for this study was his ability to determine their

From these cases it emerges, as a first conclusion, that practically all societies make some cultural provision for the termination of marriage through divorce. The Incas stand isolated as the solitary exception; among them a marriage, once contracted in the presence of a high official representing the emperor, could not subsequently be dissolved for any reason. None of the other thirty-nine societies in our sample compels a couple to maintain their matrimonial relationship where there are reasons for separation that would impress most contemporary Americans as genuinely cogent.

DIVORCE RIGHTS — BY SEX

Perhaps the most striking conclusion from the study is the extraordinary extent to which human societies accord to both sexes an approximately equal right to initiate divorce. In thirty of the forty cultures surveyed it was impossible to detect any substantial difference in the rights of men and women to terminate an unsatisfactory alliance. The stereotype of the oppressed aboriginal woman proved to be a complete myth.[5]

The author expected, in line with general thought on the subject, that males would be found to enjoy superior, though perhaps not exclusive, rights in a substantial minority of the cultures surveyed, if not in a majority. They were discovered to possess such prerogatives, however, in only six societies — a bare 15 per cent of the total. In two of the Moslem societies, the Kurd and the Siwans, a husband can dismiss his wife with the greatest of ease, even for a momentary whim. He needs only to pick up three stones and drop them, uttering to his spouse a routine formula of divorce. She has no comparable right; she can only run away and hope that her male relatives will support her. Among the Japanese, divorce is very easy for the husband or by mutual consent, but can be obtained by a woman against the will of her spouse only for serious cause and with considerable legal difficulty. A Ganda man, too, is free to dismiss his wife for any cause, whereas she has no right to initiate a permanent separation. If severely mistreated she can only run away to her male relatives, to whom the husband must justify himself and make amends in order to get her back. For the Siriono it is reported that only men, never women, initiate divorce. A Guaycuru man who wants to terminate his marriage for any reason merely removes for a few days to another hut in the same village, until his wife takes the hint and returns to her family. Women rarely seek a divorce directly, but not infrequently they deliberately act in such a manner as to provoke their husbands into leaving them.

In four societies, or 10 per cent of the total sample, women actually possess superior privileges as regards divorce. Among the Kwoma a wife is relatively free to abandon her husband, but he has no right to dismiss her. His only recourse is to make life so miserable for her that she will leave of her own accord. In the stable form of Dahomean marriage, i.e., that characterized by patrilocal residence and the payment of a bride price, a woman can readily desert her husband for cause, but he cannot initiate divorce proceedings directly; he can only neglect his wife, insult her relatives, and subject her to petty annoyances until she takes matters into her own hands and departs. A Yurok marriage can be terminated at the initiative of either partner, but it

---

degree of family stability. He does not tell the reader what he defines as the family or the criteria by which they are judged stable or instable. Additionally, Murdock treats his data as if it is absolutely uniform and comparable even though the societies in his sample are diverse both geographically and temporally. The Aztec and Inca cultures, largely eradicated in the sixteenth century by conquest, are included with contemporary peoples such as the Japanese. Are historical and cultural contexts irrelevant? Is Murdock justified in drawing the conclusions he does about family stability in non-European cultures?

One final comment. Murdock, alone among the modern authors in this volume, provides absolutely no references to the sources of his data. Who wrote the studies of the Aztec and Japanese from which Murdock takes his data? Knowing the sources of information is typically very important to scholars — it is one way of judging the accuracy of reports.

[5] Murdock's study was written at a time when the social prohibitions on divorce in the United States were being eased. Most recent work on the subject supports his claim that the "stereotype of the oppressed aboriginal woman" is a myth, although Murdock reached this judgment on the basis of one criterion only.

involves the return of a substantial bride price. A wife is in a much better position to persuade her male relatives of the justice of her cause than is her husband. His claims are scrutinized with great skepticism, and are often rejected. While in theory he could still agree to an uncompensated separation, no male in his right mind in this highly pecuniary culture would think of incurring voluntarily such a financial loss. A Witoto woman can secure a divorce by merely running away. In such a case the husband is always blamed, because people assume that no woman would leave her male protector unless cruelly mistreated. A man can dismiss his wife for cause, but this makes him a target of damaging ridicule and gossip, and unless he is able to justify his action to the complete satisfaction of the local council of adult men, he becomes a virtual social outcast.

FREQUENCY OF DIVORCE— BY SOCIETY

Analysis of the relative frequency of divorce reveals that, in addition to the Incas, the stability of marital unions is noticeably greater than in our society among Atayal, Aztecs, Creek, Dahomeans, Ganda, Hopi, Hottentot, Jukun, Kazak, Lakher, Lango, Murngin, Ona, Siriono, and Witoto. In the remaining twenty-four societies, constituting 60 per cent of the total, the divorce rate manifestly exceeds that among ourselves. Despite the widespread alarm about increasing "family disorganization" in our own society, the comparative evidence makes it clear that we still remain well within the limits which human experience has shown that societies can tolerate with safety.[6]

In most of the societies with relatively infrequent divorce, the stability is achieved through the mores and the pressure of public opinion rather than through legal enactments and judicial obstacles. The Atayal, Aztecs, and Hottentot con-

stitute partial exceptions. In the first of these tribes divorce is freely allowed for childlessness, but petitions on any other grounds must receive a hearing before the chief. He may refuse or grant the divorce, but in the latter case he usually sentences the guilty party to punishment and may even forbid him or her to remarry. Any other separation is likely to precipitate a feud between the families of the estranged spouses. Among the Aztecs, divorce cases were heard before a special court, and the party adjudged guilty forfeited half of his property to the other. Among the Hottentot, adequate grounds for a divorce have to be proved to the satisfaction of a council consisting of all the adult men of the clan, which may order a runaway wife to return to her husband, or award the property of a deserting husband to his wife.

In only two of the societies with frequent divorce is separation effected by the action of constituted authorities—by village officials among the Balinese and by the courts in an action brought by a Japanese woman. Except in these five societies and the Incas, divorce is everywhere exclusively a private matter, and such restraints as are exercised are imposed by informal social pressures rather than by legal restrictions.

STABILIZING DEVICES

The cases reveal clearly some of the devices whereby different peoples have attempted to make marital unions more stable. One of the most common is the payment of a bride price, which comparative studies have shown to be customary among approximately half of the societies of the earth. Contrary to the popular impression, the bride price is almost never conceived as a payment for a purchased chattel. Its primary function nearly everywhere is that of providing an additional economic incentive to reinforce the

---

[6] This essay appeared during a time of rapid social change in America, when there was much concern over changes in family life. In fact, it was originally published in an issue of *The Annals of the American Academy of Political and Social Science* titled "Toward Family Stability." Murdock's point about the stability in American families is relevant today, when the fragmentation of the American family and the need to support "family values" are hotly debated. In the next passage, he emphasizes that divorce in most societies is a private matter not controlled by legal restrictions. Is he merely being descriptive, or is he trying to make a point about American divorce laws?

stability of marriage. In our sample, the sources on Dahomeans, Klamath, Lango, Mongols, Wolof, and Yurok reveal particularly clear evidence of the stabilizing effect of the bride price.[7]

An even more frequent device is to take the choice of a marital partner largely out of the hands of young men and women and vest it in their parents. Most cultures reflect a marked distrust of sexual attraction as a primary motive in marriage, as it is likely to be in the minds of young people, and it seems to be widely recognized that parents, with their greater worldly experience, are more likely to arrange matches on the basis of factors better calculated to produce a durable union. Having been responsible for a marriage, parents tend to feel humiliated when it shows signs of breaking up, and are likely to exert themselves to restore harmony and settle differences. This is attested very specifically for the Haida and the Iroquois, and the evidence shows that the influence of relatives is also a prominent stabilizing factor among Creek, Hopi, Jukun, Kalinga, Murngin, and Ona.

The lengths to which this precaution can be carried in cases of infidelity is well illustrated by the Jukun. A wife first attempts to persuade her husband to give up an adulterous relationship about which she has learned, whereas the husband in a similar situation merely requests a relative or friend to remonstrate with his wife. If the relationship still continues, the innocent spouse reports the matter to the father, uncle, or elder brother of the other, who exerts all the pressure in his power to bring the delinquency to an end. Only after these steps prove fruitless, and the infidelity continues, is a separation effected.

Occasionally, of course, relatives break up a union that is satisfactory to both the parties primarily concerned. Among the Chukchi, for example, the parents of the groom can send the bride home if they become dissatisfied with her at any time within a year or eighteen months after the wedding, and a woman's relatives attempt to break up her marriage if they become estranged from her husband's family at any time, even going to the extreme of carrying off the unwilling wife by force.

In one of the societies of the sample—the Crow Indians—public opinion, instead of exerting its usual stabilizing influence, actually tends to undermine the marital relationship. Divorce is exceedingly frequent, and a man subjects himself to ridicule if he lives too long with one woman. Rivalrous military societies make a sport of stealing wives from one another, and any husband feels ashamed to take back a wife thus abducted from him, however much against her will and his own.

INCIDENCE OF DIVORCE

The sources rarely give precise statistics on the incidence of divorce in societies where it occurs most frequently. All we have is fragmentary statements, for instance, that one-third of all adult Chukchi women have been divorced, or that the ethnographer encountered Cuna of both sexes who had lived through from seven to nine successive marriages or that it is not uncommon to meet a Siwan woman of forty who has been married and divorced more than ten times.[8]

It is nevertheless possible to segregate one group of societies in which the excessive frequency of divorce is confined to recently con-

---

[7] Like Steward and White, Murdock believed that social structure was created by forces external to social organization, principally economic factors. In *Social Structure* he wrote, "It is assumed herewith, for example, that the available sources of food and the techniques for procuring it affect the sex division of labor and the relative statuses of the sexes, predisposing peoples to particular rules of residence, which can eventuate in the formation of extended families, clans, and sibs ... and that these and other factors external to social structure can strongly influence rules of residence and marriage and through them the forms of social organization and kinship structure" (1949:137). Although the economic factors that influence various marriage and divorce patterns are not a part of Murdock's discussion here, it is useful to remember that he too was a materialist.

[8] By the time this article was written, Murdock had information on hundreds of societies, but his desire to draw statistical inferences from his data has a fundamental problem: his sources are almost exclusively qualitative. Murdock briefly addresses this problem here, but he really doesn't have much quantitative data upon which to base his work. For exam-

tracted marriages and dwindles to a rarity after a union has endured for a year or more, especially after children have been born. This is attested, for example, among the Japanese, the Kaingang, the Kalinga, and the Macusi. Among the Trukese, marriages are very brittle and shifting with people in their twenties, but by the end of this early period of trial and error the majority have found spouses with whom they are content to live in reasonable harmony for the rest of their lives.

In other societies, like the Semang, while the rate of divorce subsides markedly after the birth of children, it still remains high as compared with our own. All in all, the sample reveals nineteen societies, or nearly half of the total, in which permanent separations appear substantially to exceed the present rate in the United States throughout the lifetime of the individual. Among them, either spouse can terminate the union with little difficulty and for slight or even trivial reasons among Balinese, Chukchi, Crow, Cuna, Haida, Iroquois, Klamath, Kurtatchi, Lamba, Mongols, Samoans, Semang, Toda, and Wolof. In matrilocal communities like the Cuna or the Iroquois, the husband simply walks out, or the wife unceremoniously dumps his effects outside her door. It is more surprising to encounter an equal facility in divorce among patrilocal and even patriarchal peoples like the Mongols, who see no reason for moral censure in divorce and say in perfectly matter-of-fact manner that two individuals who cannot get along harmoniously together had better live apart.

GROUNDS FOR DIVORCE

The societies which condone separation for a mere whim are few. The great majority recognize only certain grounds as adequate. The Lamba, for whom the information is particularly full, consider a man justified in seeking a divorce if he has been continually harassed by his parents-in-law, if his wife commits adultery or theft, if she has contracted a loathsome disease, if she is quarrelsome or disrespectful, or if she refuses to remain at his home after he has taken a second wife. For a woman the recognized grounds are impotence or loathsome disease in her spouse, his failure to prepare a garden or provide her with adequate clothing, persistent wife-beating, or mere cessation of her affection for him. If the marriage produces no issue, husband and wife argue as to who is responsible, and usually agree to separate. If the woman then bears a child to her new husband whereas the man fails to produce offspring by his next wife, the former husband is so overcome with shame that he usually either commits suicide or leaves the community.

Particular societies recognize interesting special grounds as adequate. Thus the Aztecs, who strongly disapproved of divorce and required proof of substantial cause before a special court, readily granted separation to a woman if she showed that her husband had done less than his share in attending to the education of their children. In general, however, a few basic reasons recur repeatedly as those considered justifiable in a wide range of societies. These are incompatibility, adultery, barrenness or sterility, impotence or frigidity, economic incapacity or nonsupport, cruelty, and quarrelsomeness or nagging. Desertion rarely appears, because it is, of course, not usually a reason for divorce, but the actual means by which a permanent separation is effected. The degree to which the more widespread grounds are recognized as valid in the forty sample societies is shown in Table 1. In order to provide comparability, an entry is made under each heading for every society. Judgments that are merely inferred as probable from the general context, however, are distinguished from evidence specifically reported or unmistakably implied in the sources.[9]

---

ple, in the previous section, he asserts that in many cases parents arrange marriages. Consider the Haida he describes above. How often in that society do parents arrange marriages? How often do they act to keep troubled marriages together? Do parents often succeed? Murdock does not know, and neither do we.

[9] Examine Murdock's table and the collection of data presented in it. Murdock separates his data into three categories: specifically reported evidence, that which was "unmistakably implied," and that which was "inferred as probable." He

Table 1 — Reasons for Divorce (Forty Sample Societies)

Reasons	Permitted				Forbidden			
	Definitely		Inferentially		Definitely		Inferentially	
	To Man	To Wife	To Man	To Wife	To Man	To Wife	To Man	To Wife
Any grounds, even trivial	9	6	5	6	14	13	12	15
Incompatibility, without more specific grounds	17	17	10	10	6	7	7	6
Common adultery or infidelity	19	11	8	12	8	10	5	7
Repeated or exaggerated infidelity	27	23	8	10	5	5	0	2
Childlessness or sterility	12	4	15	18	7	7	6	11
Sexual impotence or unwillingness	9	12	24	21	3	4	4	3
Laziness, non-support, economic incapacity	23	22	11	9	4	5	2	4
Quarrelsomeness or nagging	20	7	7	12	6	11	7	10
Mistreatment or cruelty	7	25	19	9	3	4	11	2

The data in Table 1 reinforce the earlier comment concerning the extraordinary equality of the sexes in rights of divorce revealed by the present study. Where the table shows notable differences, these have relatively obvious explanations. That cruelty is recognized as an adequate ground for women far more often than for men merely reflects their comparative physical strength. The aggression of women toward their spouses is thus perforce directed more often into verbal channels, with the result that quarrelsomeness and nagging become an adequate justification for divorce much more commonly for the male sex.

CONCERN OVER DIVORCE PROBLEM

The demonstration that divorce tends to be easier and more prevalent in other societies than in our own does not warrant the conclusion that most peoples are indifferent to the stability of the marriage relationship and the family institution. In our sample, such a charge might be leveled with some justification at the Crow, the Kaingang, and the Toda, but for most of the rest the data explicitly reveal a genuine concern with the problem. The devices of the bride price and the arrangement of marriages by parents, already alluded to, represent only two of the most common attempts to reach a satisfactory cultural solution. Others, demonstrated by the author in a previous study (*Social Structure*, 1949), may be briefly summarized here.

One such device is the taboo on primary incest, which is absolutely universal. There is not a single society known to history or ethnography which does not prohibit and penalize, among the general run of its members, both sexual intercourse and marriage between father and daughter, mother and son, and brother and sister. These universal prohibitions are understandable only as

---

lumps the first two forms of evidence together, a procedure of questionable validity. Even if we accept that grouping, Table 1 tells us that 328 of the 720 entries in the table (46 percent) are "inferred as probable." On what basis are these inferences made? Would someone else make the same inferences? Does this affect the validity of his conclusions?

an adaptive provision, arrived at everywhere by a process of mass trial and error, by which sexual rivalry is inhibited within the nuclear family so that the unity and integrity of this basic institution are preserved for the performance of its crucial societal services—economic co-operation, sexual reproduction, and the rearing and education of children.[10]

Nearly as universal are prohibitions of adultery. A very large majority of all known societies permit relatively free sexual experimentation before marriage in their youth of both sexes, but this license is withdrawn when they enter into matrimony. In a world-wide sample of 250 societies, only five—a mere 2 per cent of the total—were found to condone adulterous extramarital liaisons. In many of the remaining 98 percent, to be sure, the ideal of marital fidelity is more honored in the breach than in the observance. Its very existence, nevertheless, can only reflect a genuine and widespread concern with the stability of marriage and the family, which are inevitably threatened by the jealousy and discord generated by infidelity.

It is clear that approximately as many peoples disapprove in theory of divorce as of adultery. They have learned through experience, however, that the reasons are commonly much more urgent for the former than for the latter, and they consequently allow it wider latitude. The vital functions of the family are not likely to be well performed where husband and wife have become genuinely incompatible. Children raised by stepparents, grandparents, or adoptive parents may frequently find their new social environment more conducive to healthy personality development than a home torn by bitter internal conflict. Even though less desirable than an ideal parental home, since this is unattainable divorce may represent for them, as for their parents, the lesser of two evils.[11]

No society in our sample, with the possible exception of the Crow, places any positive value on divorce. The general attitude is clearly that it is regrettable, but often necessary. It represents merely a practical concession to the frailty of mankind, caught in a web of social relationships and cultural expectations that often impose intolerable pressure on the individual personality. That most social systems work as well as they do, despite concessions to the individual that appear excessive to us, is a tribute to human ingenuity and resiliency.[12]

---

[10] In this paragraph, Murdock refers to the "universal taboo on primary incest." His explanation for the existence of universal cultural patterns was based on his belief in the principle of "limited possibilities," a concept introduced by Franz Boas' student Alexander Goldenweiser. This means that human nature and the physical and behavioral characteristics of animals and objects predetermine a limited number of evolutionarily possible responses to a given set of environmental conditions. Murdock characterizes the incest taboo as "an adaptive provision" and explicitly linked this idea with Steward's concept of multilinear evolution in his 1959 article "Evolution in Social Organization" (Harris 1968:627).

[11] Murdock was a pioneer in what today is called *behavioral science.* The work of his day in psychology, ethology, anthropology, and sociology convinced him that they were all part of a single discipline, and he worked to develop a theoretical approach that would unite them. This paragraph hints at his familiarity with sociological and psychological studies of family and child development.

[12] The benefit of Murdock's form of research is the ability to rapidly retrieve and correlate large amounts of cross-cultural data, but critics have pointed out several problems with Murdock's methods. Tabulating data demonstrates only that one can draw statistical correlations between different factors. Demonstrating the frequency with which factors are associated does not shed light on the causes of the cross-cultural phenomena he illustrates. Furthermore, when ethnographic information is stripped of cultural context, there is no means of accounting for the process of diffusion. How do we know that similar cases in different societies are not derived from the same source?

Murdock's work was well received by many anthropologists in the United States, but not all. One reaction to it was the developing field of ethnoscience, which became popular in the mid-1950s. Ethnoscientists asserted that since each society had its own way of classifying cultural phenomena, schemes such as Murdock's were inappropriate and ethnocentric. One of Murdock's own students, Ward Goodenough, a founding member of the ethnoscientific movement, implicitly attacked Murdock's approach in his seminal 1956 article, "Componential Analysis and the Study of Meaning."

AMERICAN FAMILY COMPARATIVELY STABLE

The cross-cultural evidence makes it abundantly clear that the modern American family is unstable in only a relative and not an absolute sense. From an absolute, that is, comparative, point of view, our family institution still leans quite definitely toward the stable end of the ethnographic spectrum. Current trends could continue without reversal for a considerable period before the fear of social disorganization would acquire genuine justification. Long before such a point is reached, however, automatic correctives, some of them already apparent, will have wrought their effect, and a state of relative equilibrium will be attained that will represent a satisfactory social adjustment under the changed conditions of the times.[13]

---

[13] Murdock's data are snapshots of societies at particular places and times. Consequently, like the functionalists before him, his research methods are unable to deal with cultural change. Like them, Murdock believed that societies remain in relative equilibrium because they are social adaptations to environmental and economic factors. In the 1960s and 1970s this view of society was strongly expressed by ecological functionalists and materialists such as Roy Rappaport and Marvin Harris, whose work appears in the next section.

Despite the problems with Murdock's data, you would have a difficult time finding an anthropologist who has not made similar cross-cultural comparisons and conclusions. At least in this case, his conclusions stand up reasonably well. Divorce *is* common in societies around the world, societies do have mechanisms to slow down or prevent divorce, and both women and men can initiate divorce in most societies (the equality he claims is perhaps a different matter). If it is true that many anthropologists reacted against Murdock's methods, it is also true that an equal number of anthropologists conduct cross-cultural research. The HRAF remain a popular and valuable tool for research.

Neomaterialism: Evolutionary, Functionalist, Ecological, and Marxist

*J*ulian Steward and Leslie White set the stage for ecological anthropology and materialist cultural analysis, but it was the next generation of anthropologists who really developed these fields of inquiry. By midcentury, two types of materialism were becoming popular in anthropology: ecological-materialist approaches and neo-Marxist approaches.

The ecological-materialist approach to anthropology was heavily influenced by general systems theory and the growing science of ecology (Orlove 1980). Ecological materialists also borrowed from cybernetics. They commonly assumed that societies were homeostatic—that is, that cultural institutions functioned as feedback mechanisms (like thermostats) to maintain a balance between energy production and expenditure and the productive capacity of the environment. Typically, ecological-materialist anthropologists examined culture using an equilibrium model that traced energy flow within an ecosystem. For example, a society might be analyzed in terms of its food production and the caloric expenditure of human energy required to maintain the society in equilibrium.

In addition, ecological-materialist studies differed from those of Steward and White in that the former tended to take local populations rather than cultures as their units of analysis. Ecological materialists examined the interactions between populations and environments rather than treating the environment as a passive background that shapes culture but is not influenced by it.

Ecological materialism can be subdivided into two different approaches: neoevolutionism and neofunctionalism (Orlove 1980). Like Lewis Henry Morgan (see essay 3), neoevolutionists were primarily interested in the origins of cultural phenomena. Examples of this work include Morton Fried's (1923–1986) *The Evolution of Political Society* (1967), Elman Service's (1915–1996) *Primitive Social Organization: An Evolutionary Perspective* (1962), and Kent Flannery's (1934–) "The Cultural Evolution of Civilizations" (1972). (Archaeological research has been a major part of this field as well but is beyond the scope of this book.)

The neoevolutionists were often concerned with the identification of stages through which cultural phenomena developed. For instance, the famous bands-tribes-chiefdoms-states sequence of cultural development was proposed by Service (1962), a student of both White and Steward.

The essay representing this school of thought is by Morton Fried. Fried was both a graduate student and a professor at Columbia University. He was deeply affected by classes he took from Julian Steward as well as by his fellow students, including Elman Service, Stanley Diamond (1922–1991), Eric Wolf (1923–1999), and Robert Manners (1913–1996). He also credited Leslie White and V. Gordon Childe with making major contributions to his understanding of social evolution (Service 1988). Fried's principal area of field research was China, and he made numerous trips to China as well as to Chinese communities in other parts of the world.

In his essay, Fried examines the role of social stratification in the evolution of society, an argument he develops more fully in *The Evolution of Political Society*. There, Fried examined the development of social inequality, proposing the evolutionary stages of egalitarian, ranked, stratified, and state societies.

Neofunctionalists, on the other hand, "took the position that social organization and culture were functional adaptations which permitted populations to exploit their environments successfully without exceeding the carrying capacity of their ecological resources" (Applebaum 1987:204). The dominant perspective within neofunctionalism is called cultural materialism, and Marvin Harris (1927–) is its leading proponent.

Harris did both his undergraduate and graduate training at Columbia University, and was a professor there from 1953 to 1980. His mentor was Charles Wagley (1913–1991), a student of Boas. Harris took courses from Steward, and was attracted by White's critique of the Boasians, but during his career as a student, these did not have very profound effects on him. He moved decisively toward materialism after his fieldwork in Mozambique. His experiences of Portuguese colonialism there convinced him that systems of production were fundamental to any understanding of culture (Harris 1994:75–76).

Harris' work follows the Marxist perspective resurrected by Leslie White. Recall that Marx (see essay 4) believed production played the primary role in social evolution, influencing the sociological and ideological levels of society. While rejecting Marxist dialectics, cultural materialists firmly insist on the primacy of modes of production and reproduction—what Harris (1979) calls "infrastructure"—in determining behaviors and beliefs within a society. The decisive influence of infrastructure "stems from the fact that human beings are subject to immutable natural laws governing the acquisition of life-sustaining energy" (Lett 1987:91).

Cultural materialism has been one of the most powerful and enduring theoretical positions within modern American anthropology, partly because Harris himself has been an extremely successful and indefatigable promoter of it. Generations of graduate students have read Harris' classic *The Rise of Anthropological Theory* (1968). As you have no doubt noticed, we frequently refer to it in this volume. Harris' book is one of the few comprehensive analyses of the history of anthropology, but it is also a polemic promoting cultural materialism.

In addition to copious work designed for professional consumption, Harris has written extensively for popular audiences. These books include *Cows, Pigs, Wars and Witches: The Riddles of Cul-*ture (1974), *Cannibals and Kings: The Origins of Culture* (1977), *Good to Eat: Riddles of Food and Culture* (1985), and many others. These books, which give cultural-materialist explanations of cultural phenomena, are written in an accessible and engaging style and have had enormous popular success.

Cultural-materialist analysis was popular in the 1970s and 1980s and continues to command a large following today. However, it is also frequently attacked as naive positivism, "rooted in a mechanical, naturalistic mode that fails to reckon with the fact that the mind is more than a *tabula rasa*" (Murphy 1994:58). Harris vehemently resists such charges, while insisting that an objective, positivist science of society is not only possible but necessary. His position is perhaps best summed up in the title of one of his recent essays: "Cultural Materialism Is Alive and Well and Won't Go Away Until Something Better Comes Along" (1994).

Our example of cultural materialism is Harris' 1966 article "The Cultural Ecology of India's Sacred Cattle." Writing for a technical audience, Harris argues that the Hindu prohibition on killing cattle should be understood in relation to the role that cattle play in the production of food crops, fuel, and fertilizer. He convincingly demonstrates the material and ecological importance of cattle to Indian society and argues that this, rather than Hindu religious doctrine, is the ultimate basis of India's ban on killing and eating cattle. In fact, following Marx's and Harris' lead, the sacredness of cattle can be seen as a result of the productive importance of cattle.

A second orientation in neofunctionalist materialism comes from the work of Roy Rappaport (1926–1997). While Fried and Harris drew their inspiration from Marx, Rappaport was more deeply affected by the work of ecological biologists. Like Fried and Harris, Rappaport was a student at Columbia. However, while he was influenced by White and notions of general evolution, he was more deeply affected by classes he took with Harold Conklin (1926–) and Conrad Arensburg (1912–1997), and by fieldwork seminars with Margaret Mead (Rappaport 1994:166). However, his deep reading in biological ecology led to dissertation work under Andrew P. Vayda (1931–), an anthropologist vitally interested in ecology. Rappaport and Vayda believed that general laws of biological ecology could be used to study human populations, and they put this belief to work in their fieldwork.

From cybernetics, Rappaport and other neofunctionalist anthropologists adopted the concept of feedback to explain cultural stability. In the essay reproduced here (23), Rappaport proposes that the sacrifice of pigs in the kaiko ritual of the Tsembaga of New Guinea is a feedback mechanism that regulates the ecological relationship between men, pigs, local food supplies, and warfare. He outlined this point of view in greater detail in his 1967 work *Pigs for the Ancestors.*

In addition to neoevolutionism and neofunctionalism, we distinguish the neo-Marxist approach. Neofunctionalism and neoevolutionism were primarily American theoretical developments, and though these schools relied on insights from Marxist scholarship, they rejected key elements of Marxist doctrine, particularly the dialectic. Neo-Marxism, on the other hand, was centered in Europe, where political conditions made strictly Marxist anthropology more feasible. There, a tradition of rigorously Marxist work already existed. Much of this was inspired by Soviet ethnographers, who generally reflected Stalinist and Leninist interpretations of Marx. However, in the 1960s, particularly in France, a group of Marxist thinkers emerged that challenged Soviet ethnographic hegemony. This group, including Claude Meillassoux (1925–) and Maurice Godelier (1925–), suggested that Marx's work provided the basic insights for the analysis of traditional society, but that because his writings had focused primarily on the development of capitalism in Europe, they could not be applied directly to ethnographic analysis. The neo-Marxists modified Marx's work to adapt it for this purpose. In particular, they described new modes of production and proposed new evolutionary sequences. Unlike almost all other anthropologists of their era, they had a keen critical eye for the effects of colonialism and international economic transfers.

While American materialists tended to focus on feedback mechanisms and stable adaptations, the neo-Marxists directed their attention to dialectical contradiction. They viewed society in terms of the struggle of different social groups (which they frequently insisted were classes) for control and power. They were frequently brutally critical of American materialist approaches that minimized the role of conflict or ignored the dialectic. A particularly good example of this criticism is the essay "Marxism, Structuralism, and Vulgar Materialism" (1974), in which Jonathan Friedman provides an extensive critique of Harris' ideas on Indian cattle worship and Rappaport's understanding of the ecological importance of pigs and ritual. Friedman argues that by ignoring the dialectic, American anthropologists transform subtle and sophisticated Marxist analysis to mechanistic "vulgar materialism." As a result, they misunderstand the insights Marxist analysis can provide.

We have provided two examples of neo-Marxist analysis. The first, essay 24 in this section, is by Philippe Bourgois (1956–). Bourgois received his B.A. from Harvard University and his graduate education at Stanford. He was particularly influenced by cultural production theory, a variety of Marxist thought centered on the ways in which class-based meaning is reproduced. His work is much more recent than that of the other scholars collected in this section. This emphasizes the fact that materialist thinking in anthropology is very much a part of the current landscape. Unlike any other essay in this volume, Bourgois' work focuses on inner-city America. From 1989 to 1991, Bourgois lived in the slums of East Harlem, New York, and his ethnography centers on issues of class and conflict. More recently, he has worked with street children in Bolivia as well as gang members and heroin addicts in San Francisco.

A second example of neo-Marxist thought can be found in the "Anthropology and Gender" section. There, in essay 34, we have reprinted Eleanor Leacock's essay "Interpreting the Origins of Gender Inequality: Conceptual and Historical Problems." Leacock and her work are described more fully in the introduction to that section.

21. On the Evolution of Social Stratification and the State

Morton H. Fried (1923–1986)

The evolutionists never discussed in detail—still less observed—what actually happened when a society in Stage A changed into a society at Stage B; it was merely argued that all Stage B societies must somehow have evolved out of the Stage A societies.

—E. R. Leach, 1954, p. 283

To SOME EXTENT E. R. LEACH'S CHARGE, WHICH relates to the evolution of political organization, is unfair. The climate in which pristine systems of state organization took shape no longer exists. The presence of numerous modern states and the efficiency of communications have converted all movements toward state level organization into acculturation phenomena of some degree. In fact, it seems likely that the only truly pristine states—those whose origin was *sui generis*,[1] out of local conditions and not in response to pressures emanating from an already highly organized but separate political entity—are those which arose in the great river valleys of Asia and Africa and the one or two comparable developments in the Western Hemisphere. Elsewhere the development of the state seems to have been "secondary" and to have depended upon pressures, direct or indirect, from existing states. Where such pressures exist, the process of development is accelerated, condensed, and often warped, so that a study of contemporary state formation is a murky

(1960)

mirror in which to discern the stages in the development of the pristine states.

Further, the conditions of emergence of rank and stratification as pristine phenomena are similarly obscured when the impetus to change is the introduction of aspects of a market economy, money as a medium of exchange, rationalization of production, and the transformation of labor into a commodity. It would be extremely gratifying to actually observe societies in transition from a "Stage A" (egalitarian organization) to a "Stage B" (rank society) and from there to a "Stage C" (stratification society) and finally from that stage to a "Stage D" (state society).[2] Indeed, some of these observations have been made, though no one has yet been able to follow a single society or even selected exemplars from a group of genetically related societies through all these stages. Instead a variety of unrelated societies are selected, each representing one or another of the several possible transitions. Mr. Leach himself has contributed one of the most valuable of the accounts dealing with this matter in his analysis of the movement from *gumlao* to *gumsa* organization among the Kachin of northern Burma.[3]

---

[1] *Sui generis:* Latin for "of its own kind," meaning unique or individual.

[2] In this article, Fried proposes an evolutionary model of society. Ever since Morgan, cultural evolutionary studies have tended to be synchronic—comparing contemporary societies at different levels of development to try to reconstruct the process by which simple societies evolved into more complex forms. (On the other hand, archaeological studies of cultural evolution tend to be diachronic—studying the development of one society in a specific area through time.) Fried posits that state-level societies are the final product of an evolutionary sequence that begins with egalitarian bands and progresses first to ranked and then to stratified societies. The mechanisms that propel societies through this evolutionary sequence are material factors such as economy, population, and environment. Fried also points out that the evolutionary sequence he is proposing has never actually been observed. Pristine traditional systems no longer exist.

[3] Fried cites Edmund Leach's (1911–1989) classic 1954 study *Political Systems of Highland Burma,* which describes the evolution of a political system. We have included a later study by Leach in this volume (essay 26) reflecting a structuralist perspective, but he started his career as a structural functionalist. A weakness of the functionalists was their tendency

Following leads supplied in the data of such accounts as that of Leach, just mentioned, of Douglas Oliver (1955), and others, it is our intention to discuss in detail the things which it seems to us must have occurred in order to make the previous transitions possible. Since the data are largely contemporary, the statements are to be viewed as hypotheses in their application to pristine situations beyond even archaeological recall.

Here then is what we seek to accomplish: (1) to suggest some specific institutional developments, the occurrences of which are normal and predictable in viable societies under certain conditions, and in the course of which the whole society perforce moves into a new level of sociocultural organization; (2) to suggest some of the conditions under which these institutional developments occurred and came to florescence; (3) to indicate as a by-product, that the movement occurs without conscious human intervention, the alterations taking place slowly enough and with such inevitability that the society is revolutionized before the carriers of the culture are aware of major changes.[4]

In approaching this task, it seems wise, if only to head off needless argument, to deny any intention of supplying a single master key to a lock that has defied the efforts of great talents from the time of the Classical civilizations to the present. It seems obvious that other sequences of events than those sketched here could, under proper circumstances, have had similar results. Indeed, the writer is eager to entertain other possibilities and hopes hereby to stimulate others to offer counter suggestions. It will also be obvious to the reader that substantial trains of thought herein stated are merely borrowed and not created by the writer. The recent strides in economic anthropology, and I refer primarily to the work of Polanyi, Arensberg, and Pearson (1957), the clarification of some basic concepts in the study of social organization, and the incentives provided by a seminal paper by Paul Kirchhoff (1935) have all been combined in the present effort.[5]

THE NON-RANK, NON-STRATIFIED SOCIETY

Every human society differentiates among its members and assigns greater or less prestige to individuals according to certain of their attributes. The simplest and most universal criteria of differential status are those two potent axes of the basic division of labor, age and sex. Beyond are a

---

to view cultures as static. *Political Systems of Highland Burma* was a structural-functionalist study, but Leach saw Kachin political structure as dynamic, alternating between egalitarian and stratified forms. His book emphasized the evolution of political systems in relation to ecology and subsistence. This work, coming just six years before Fried's, had a major impact on Fried's own analysis. The quotation at the opening of this article is from Leach's book, and Fried used Leach's data in formulating his own theory.

[4] Note the third goal listed in this paragraph. Fried's comments are reminiscent of the nineteenth-century Spencerian view of social evolution. Recall that Spencer described evolution as superorganic, occurring without the conscious awareness or intervention of the members of society. The evolutionary process was inevitable and resulted from the slow accumulation of social changes. The course of evolution was from simple undifferentiated societies to increasingly complex and specialized societies. Similarly, in Fried's evolutionary model, egalitarian bands evolve into increasingly complex societies with internal social differentiation.

[5] The 1957 work by Polanyi, Arensberg, and Pearson, *Trade and Market in the Early Empires,* was a seminal document in economic anthropology. Karl Polanyi (1886–1964), a historian, suggested that economies could be organized by ideas other than the market and that the rules of economic analysis developed for use in capitalist societies did not apply to other societies. This perspective came to be known as substantivism and was important in the economic anthropology of the 1960s. According to Polanyi, societies could be organized either by reciprocity, redistribution, or some form of market. Fried makes great use of this theory later in this article. You should also remember the principles of prestation Marcel Mauss outlined in *The Gift* (see essay 8) when reading Fried's discussion of Polanyi.

Paul Kirchhoff (1900–1972) was an ethnologist who studied theology, comparative religion, and psychology as well as anthropology. Kirchhoff spent the majority of his career working in Mexico. His primary work was on the Indians of North and South America, and he was a cofounder of the *Escuela Nacional de Antropología e Historia.* It was he who first coined the term *Mesoamerica.* The work Fried refers to is a manuscript called "The Principles of Clanship in Human Society."

host of others which are used singly or in combination to distinguish among the members of a category otherwise undifferentiated as to sex or age group. Most important of the characteristics used in this regard are those which have a visible relation to the maintenance of subsistence, such as strength, endurance, agility, and other factors which make one a good provider in a hunting and gathering setting. These characteristics are ephemeral; moreover, the systems of enculturation prevalent at this level, with their emphasis upon the development of subsistence skills, make it certain that such skills are well distributed among the members of society of the proper sex and age groups.

The major deviation from this system of subsistence-oriented statuses is associated with age. However, it makes no difference to the argument of this paper whether the status of the old is high or low since the basis of its ascription is universal. Anyone who is of the proper sex and manages to live long enough automatically enters into its benefits or disabilities.

Given the variation in individual endowment which makes a chimera[6] of absolute equality, the primitive societies which we are considering are sufficiently undifferentiated in this respect to permit us to refer to them as "egalitarian societies." An egalitarian society can be defined more precisely: it is one in which there are as many positions of prestige in any given age-sex grade as there are persons capable of filling them. If within a certain kin group or territory there are four big men, strong, alert, keen hunters, then there will be four "strong men"; if there are six, or three, or one, so it is. Eskimo society fits this general picture. So do many others. Almost all of these societies are founded upon hunting and gathering and lack significant harvest periods when large reserves of food are stored.

There is one further point I wish to emphasize about egalitarian society. It accords quite remarkably with what Karl Polanyi has called a reciprocal economy.[a]

Production in egalitarian society is characteristically a household matter. There is no specialization; each family group repeats essentially similar tasks. There may be individuals who make certain things better than do others, and these individuals are often given recognition for their skills, but no favored economic role is established, no regular division of labor emerges at this point, and no political power can reside in the status (Leacock, 1958). Exchange in such a society takes place between individuals who belong to different small-scale kin groups; it tends to be casual and is not bound by systems of monetary value based upon scarcity. Such exchanges predominate between individuals who recognize each other as relatives or friends, and may be cemented by such procedures as the provision of hospitality and the granting of sexual access to wives.

Within the local group or band the economy is also reciprocal, but less obviously so. Unlike the exchanges between members of different local groups which, over the period of several years, tend to balance, the exchanges within a group may be quite asymmetrical over time. The skilled and lucky hunter may be continually supplying others with meat; while his family also receives shares from the catch of others, income never catches up with the amounts dispensed. However, the difference between the two quantities is made up in the form of prestige, though, as previously mentioned, it conveys no privileged economic or political role. There frequently is a feeling of transience as it is understood that the greatest hunter can lose his luck or his life, thereby making his family dependent on the largesse of others.

In all egalitarian economies, however, there is also a germ of redistribution. It receives its simplest expression in the family but can grow no more complex than the pooling and redisbursing of stored food for an extended family. In such an embryonic redistributive system the key role is frequently played by the oldest female in the active generation, since it is she who commonly coordinates the household and runs the kitchen.

THE RANK SOCIETY

Since a truly egalitarian human society does not exist, it is evident that we are using the word "rank" in a somewhat special sense. The crux of

---

[6] *Chimera:* something unreal or imaginary.

the matter, as far as we are concerned, is the structural way in which differential prestige is handled in the rank society as contrasted with the way in which egalitarian societies handle similar materials. If the latter have as many positions of valued status as they have individuals capable of handling them, the rank society places additional limitations on access to valued status. The limitations which are added have nothing to do with sex, age group, or personal attributes. Thus, the rank society is characterized by having fewer positions of valued status than individuals capable of handling them. Furthermore, most rank societies have a fixed number of such positions, neither expanding them nor diminishing them with fluctuations in the populations, save as totally new segmented units originate with fission or disappear as the result of catastrophe or sterility.

The simplest technique of limiting status, beyond those already discussed, is to make succession to status dependent upon birth order. This principle, which is found in kinship-organized societies, persists in many more complexly organized societies. At its simplest, it takes the form of primogeniture or ultimogeniture on the level of the family, extended family, or lineage.[7] In more complex forms it may be projected through time so that only the first son of a first son of a first son enjoys the rights of succession, all others having been excluded by virtue of ultimate descent from a positionless ancestor. There are still other variants based on the theme: the accession to high status may be by election, but the candidates may come only from certain lineages which already represent selection by birth order.

The effects of rules of selection based on birth can be set aside by conscious action. Incompetence can be the basis for a decision to by-pass the customary heir, though it would seem more usual for the nominal office to remain vested in the proper heir while a more energetic person performed the functions of the status. A strategic murder could also accomplish the temporary voiding of the rule, but such a solution is much too dangerous and extreme to be practical on the level which we are considering. It is only in rather advanced cultures that the rewards associated with such statuses are sufficient to motivate patricide and fratricide.

Whether accomplished by a rule of succession or some other narrowing device, the rank society as a framework of statuses resembles a triangle, the point of which represents the leading status hierarchically exalted above the others. The hierarchy thus represented has very definite economic significance, going hand in hand with the emergence of a superfamilial redistributive network. The key status is that of the central collector of allotments who also tends to the redistribution of these supplies either in the form of feasts or as emergency seed and provender in time of need. Depending on the extent and maturity of the redistributive system, there will be greater or lesser development of the hierarchy. Obviously, small-scale networks in which the members have a face-to-face relationship with the person in the central status will have less need of a bureaucracy.[8]

In the typical ranked society there is neither exploitative economic power nor genuine political power. As a matter of fact, the central status closely resembles its counterpart in the embryonic redistributive network that may be found even in the simplest societies. This is not surprising, for the system in typical rank societies is actually based upon a physical expansion of the kin group and the continuation of previously known kinship rights and obligations. The kingpin of a redistributive network in an advanced hunting and gathering society or a simple agricultural one is as much the victim of his role as its manipulator. His special function is to collect, not to expropriate; to distribute, not to consume. In a conflict between personal accumulation and the

---

[7] *Primogeniture* is inheritance by the firstborn son; *ultimogeniture* is inheritance by the lastborn.

[8] In Fried's theory one can see Marx's idea that modes of production determine the ideological features of society. Fried believes that the force that drives political evolution is the control over production and distribution of resources. Egalitarian societies are marked by universal access to prestige and reciprocity of resources. A key feature of rank societies is that their members have unequal access to prestige that results from the power of high-prestige individuals to control the distribution of resources.

demands of distribution it is the former which suffers. Anything else leads to accusations of hoarding and selfishness and undercuts the prestige of the central status; the whole network then stands in jeopardy, a situation which cannot be tolerated. This, by the way, helps to explain that "anomaly" that has so frequently puzzled students of societies of this grade: why are their "chiefs" so often poor, perhaps poorer than any of their neighbors? The preceding analysis makes such a question rhetorical.[9]

It is a further characteristic of the persons filling these high status positions in typical rank societies that they must carry out their functions in the absence of political authority. Two kinds of authority they have: familial, in the extended sense, and sacred, as the redistributive feasts commonly are associated with the ritual life of the community. They do not, however, have access to the privileged use of force, and they can use only diffuse and supernatural sanctions to achieve their ends. Indeed, the two major methods by which they operate are by setting personal examples, as of industriousness, and by utilizing the principles of reciprocity to bolster the emergent redistributive economy.[b]

Despite strong egalitarian features in its economic and political sectors, the developing rank society has strong status differentials which are marked by sumptuary specialization and ceremonial function.[10] While it is a fact that the literature abounds in references to "chiefs" who can issue no positive commands and "ruling classes" whose members are among the paupers of the realm, it must be stated in fairness that the central redistributive statuses *are* associated with fuss, feathers, and other trappings of office. These people sit on stools, have big houses, and are consulted by their neighbors. Their redistributive roles place them automatically to the fore in the religious life of the community, but they are also in that position because of their central kinship status as lineage, clan,[c] or kindred heads.[11]

FROM EGALITARIAN TO RANK SOCIETY

The move from egalitarian to rank society is essentially the shift from an economy dominated by reciprocity to one having redistribution as a major device. That being the case, one must look for the causes of ranking (the limitation of statuses such that they are fewer than the persons capable of handling them) in the conditions which enable the redistributive economy to emerge from its position of latency in the universal household economy, to dominate a network of kin groups which extend beyond the boundaries of anything known on the reciprocal level.

Though we shall make a few suggestions relating to this problem, it should be noted that the focus of this paper does not necessitate immediate disposition of this highly complicated question. In view of the history of our topic, certain negative conclusions are quite significant. Most important of all is the deduction that the roots of ranking do not lie in features of human personality. The structural approach obviates, in this case, psychological explanations. To be precise, we need assume no universal human drive for power[d] in comprehending the evolution of ranking.[12]

---

[9] Fried, although strongly influenced by Marx, does not believe in revolutionary dialectical change. Instead, he says that the transition from egalitarian to rank societies is characterized by the continuation of previously known rights and obligations. Like Darwin and Spencer, Fried believed that evolutionary change occurred in slow incremental stages. Further, in his discussion of "mature" and "embryonic" redistributive networks, Fried's terminology hearkens back to the organic analogy of the nineteenth century.

[10] *Sumptuary specialization:* specialized clothing marking one's status.

[11] Max Weber conducted some of the early work on the distinction between types of authority and power. Fried's distinction between political versus familial and sacred authority is clearly part of the same tradition.

[12] Here Fried rejects all psychological explanations for the evolutionary shift from egalitarian to rank societies, pointing instead to the change from one form of economic distribution to another. By linking the evolution from egalitarian to rank society to the shift from a reciprocal economy to one dominated by redistribution, Fried echoes the Marxist-materialist perspective as interpreted in Polanyi's work.

It is unthinkable that we should lead a reader this far without indicating certain avenues whereby the pursuit of the problem may be continued. We ask, therefore, what are the circumstances under which fissioning kin or local groups retain active economic interdigitation,[13] the method of interaction being participation in the redistributive network?

In a broad sense, the problem may be seen as an ecological one. Given the tendency of a population to breed up to the limit of its resources and given the probably universal budding of kin and local groups which have reached cultural maxima of unit size, we look into different techno-geographical situations for clues as to whether more recently formed units will continue to interact significantly with their parent units, thereby extending the physical and institutional range of the economy. Such a situation clearly arises when the newer group moves into a somewhat different environment while remaining close enough to the parent group to permit relatively frequent interaction among the members of the two groups. Given such a condition, the maintenance of a redistributive network would have the effect of diversifying subsistence in both units and also providing insurance against food failures in one or the other. This is clearly something of a special case; one of its attractions is the amount of work that has been done upon it by another student of the problem (Sahlins, 1957, 1958).[14]

It is possible to bring to bear upon this problem an argument similar to that employed by Tylor in the question of the incest taboo (Tylor,

1888, p. 267; White, 1948), to wit: the redistributive network might appear as a kind of random social mutation arising out of nonspecific factors difficult to generalize, such as a great personal dependence of the members of the offspring unit upon those they have left behind. Whatever the immediate reason for its appearance, it would quickly show a superiority over simple reciprocal systems in (a) productivity, (b) timeliness of distribution, (c) diversity of diet, and (d) coordination of mundane and ceremonial calendars (in a loose cyclical sense). It is not suggested that the success of the institution depends upon the rational cognition of these virtues by the culture carriers; rather the advantages of these institutions would have positive survival value over a long period of time.[15]

We should not overlook one other possibility that seems less special than the first one given above. Wittfogel has drawn our attention on numerous occasions to the social effects of irrigation (see Wittfogel, 1957, for a summation of his latest thinking). The emergence of the superfamilial redistributive network and the rank society seem to go well with the developments he has discussed under the rubric "hydro-agriculture," in which some supervision is needed in order to control simple irrigation and drainage projects yet these projects are not large enough to call into existence a truly professional bureaucracy.

It may be wondered that one of the prime explanations for the emergence of ranking, one much favored by notable sociologists of the past, has not appeared in this argument. Reference is

---

[13] *Interdigitation:* interlocking, like the fingers of both hands.

[14] Fried attempts here to expand the scientific basis for his argument (which is essentially a hypothetical reconstruction) by incorporating the field of cultural ecology, which was relatively new at this time. Notice that the reader is taken from a discussion of kin groups, economies, and prestige to breeding populations and ecology. In particular, he cites Marshall Sahlins (1930–), a fellow evolutionist and a leading proponent of cultural ecology. See, for example, Sahlins' article "Culture and Environment: The Study of Cultural Ecology" (1964).

[15] Fried cannot definitively outline the rationale behind the transition from egalitarian to rank society, so he offers three possibilities. The first is the fissioning of related kin groups in expanded redistributive networks. The second is an argument borrowed from evolutionary biology: the development of ranking may be a random "social mutation" that conveyed a selective advantage or "positive survival value" on those who adopted the trait. The third is Wittfogel's hydro-agriculture hypothesis, which is discussed in the next paragraph. Karl A. Wittfogel (1896–1988) was an archaeologist who proposed that irrigation was a primary factor in the development of stratified societies. Briefly, Wittfogel felt that the origins of social stratification and the state lay in the formation of a body of ruler-managers who oversaw the construction and maintenance of large-scale irrigation systems necessary for intensive agriculture. As a universal explanation, this theory was refuted by Adams (1966) and Carneiro (1970).

to the effects of war upon a society. I would like in this article to take a deliberately extreme stand and assert that military considerations serve to institutionalize rank differences only when these are already implicit or manifest in the economy. I do not believe that pristine developments in the formalization of rank can be attributed to even grave military necessity.[16]

THE STRATIFIED SOCIETY

The differences between rank society and stratified society are very great, yet it is rare that the two are distinguished in descriptive accounts or even in the theoretical literature. Briefly put, the essential difference is this: the rank society operates on the principle of differential status for members with similar abilities, but these statuses are devoid of privileged economic or political power, the former point being the essential one for the present analysis. Meanwhile, the stratified society is distinguished by the differential relationships between the members of the society and its subsistence means — some of the members of the society have unimpeded access to its strategic resources[e] while others have various impediments in their access to the same fundamental resources.[17]

With the passage to stratified society man enters a completely new area of social life. Whereas the related systems of redistribution and ranking rest upon embryonic institutions that are as universal as family organization (*any* family, elementary or extended, conjugal or consanguineal, will

do equally well), the principles of stratification have no real foreshadowing on the lower level.

Furthermore, the movement to stratification precipitated many things which were destined to change society even further, and at an increasingly accelerated pace. Former systems of social control which rested heavily on enculturation, internalized sanctions, and ridicule now required formal statement of their legal principles, a machinery of adjudication, and a formally constituted police authority. The emergence of these and other control institutions were associated with the final shift of prime authority from kinship means to territorial means and describes the evolution of complex forms of government associated with the state. It was the passage to stratified society which laid the basis for the complex division of labor which underlies modern society. It also gave rise to various arrangements of socio-economic classes and led directly to both classical and modern forms of colonialism and imperialism.[18]

THE TRANSITION TO STRATIFIED SOCIETY

The decisive significance of stratification is not that it sees differential amounts of wealth in different hands but that it sees two kinds of access to strategic resources. One of these is privileged and unimpeded; the other is impaired, depending on complexes of permission which frequently require the payment of dues, rents, or taxes in labor or in kind. The existence of such a distinction en-

---

[16] The most notable of the sociologists referred to by Fried was Spencer, whose views on stratification and war he quotes several times in *The Evolution of Political Society.* The role of warfare in the evolution of society has long been a contentious issue among anthropologists. Here and in *The Evolution of Political Society* Fried argues emphatically that warfare was not a primary catalyst in the formation of stratified societies, an opinion based on his belief that primitive societies are not typically warlike. He cites several ethnographic examples supporting this view in his book. In contrast, Robert Carneiro (1927–) is one of the strongest advocates for the role of warfare in the origin of state-level societies (Carneiro 1970).

[17] The description Fried gives in this paragraph stands today as the standard definition of social stratification. It can be found virtually verbatim in most introductory cultural anthropology texts.

[18] For Fried, the development of stratification was a revolutionary step that defined the transition to state-level societies. The influence of nineteenth-century evolutionary thought is evident in this paragraph. Like the Spencerians, Fried focuses on increasing complexity, specialization, and the shift from autonomous individuals to interdependency of occupations and classes. The shift from kin-based to property-based authority is derived from Marx and Morgan. In Morgan's view, the modern state was founded on the notions of territory and property (see essay 3).

ables the growth of exploitation, whether of a relatively simple kind based upon drudge slavery or of a more complex type associated with involved divisions of labor and intricate class systems. The development of stratification also encourages the emergence of communities composed of kin parts and non-kin parts which, as wholes, operate on the basis of non-kin mechanisms.[19]

So enormous is the significance of the shift to stratification that previous commentators have found it essential that the movement be associated with the most powerful people in the society. Landtman, for example, says:

"It is in conjunction with the dissimilarity of individual endowments that inequality of wealth has conduced to the rise of social differentiation. As a matter of course the difference as regards property in many cases goes hand in hand with difference in personal qualities. A skillful hunter or fisher, or a victorious warrior, has naturally a better prospect of acquiring a fortune than one who is inferior to him in these respects" (Landtman 1938, p. 68).

If our analysis is correct, however, such is definitely not the case. The statuses mentioned by Landtman are not those which stand to make great accumulations but rather stand to make great give-aways. Furthermore, the leap from distribution to power is unwarranted by the ethnographic evidence.[20]

There are unquestionably a number of ways in which secondary conditions of stratification can emerge. That is, once the development of stratification proceeds from contact with and tutelage by cultures which are at the least already strati-fied and which may be the possessors of mature state organization, there are many specific ways in which simpler cultures can be transformed into stratified societies. The ways which come quickest to mind include the extension of the complex society's legal definitions of property to the simpler society, the introduction of all-purpose money and wage labor, and the creation of an administrative system for the operation of the simpler society on a basis which is acceptable to the superordinate state. Often the external provenance of these elements is obvious in their misfit appearance. A sharper look may reveal, indeed, that the stratified system is a mere facade operated for and often by persons who have no genuine local identities, while the local system continues to maintain informally, and sometimes in secrecy, the older organization of the society. Put more concretely, this means that "government" appointed chiefs are respected only in certain limited situations and that the main weight of social control continues to rest upon traditional authorities and institutions which may not even be recognized by the ruling power.[21]

An excellent climate for the development of stratification in a simple society can be supplied in a relatively indirect way by a society of advanced organization. Let us take the situation in which a culture has no concept of nuclear family rights to land. The economy is based upon hunting, trapping, and fishing, with the streams and forests being associated in a general way with weakly organized bands which have a decided tendency to fragment and reconstitute, each time with potentially different membership. Subvert this setup

---

[19] Although Fried, like most materialists at this time, did not cite Marx, the Marxist view of stratification and class exploitation is clearly expressed in this paragraph. This is particularly evident in his use of the term *exploitation,* the meaning of which is different for Marxists and non-Marxists. For non-Marxists, exploitation refers to receiving unfair returns for labor. To Marxists, exploitation is the appropriation of the surplus value of labor, which is inherently unfair. Fried is using the term in the Marxist sense.

[20] Fried explicitly rejects the claim that social stratification is founded on the differences between people's personal qualities and skills, an idea reminiscent of nineteenth-century social darwinism. He provides ethnographic evidence in his discussion of redistribution in rank societies to refute this doctrine.

[21] Remember that Fried is writing at the end of the period of European colonialism in the Pacific, Africa, and Asia and the beginning of the "development" of the Third World. His comments about local systems operating in secrecy and government-appointed chiefs refer to this situation. These remarks are an early example of the anthropological critique of colonialism; earlier theorists had often discussed how their work was useful to colonial administrators. Fried says that colonialism does not work.

with an external market for furs and a substantial basis for stratification has been laid. This system, like the direct intervention of a superordinate state, also seems to have certain limitations for there is ample evidence that the development of private property in such a system as that just mentioned is confined to trapping lines and does not extend to general subsistence hunting and fishing in the area (see Leacock, 1958).

Another situation that bears study is one in which important trade routes linking two or more advanced societies traverse marginal areas in which simple societies are located. Certain geographical conditions make it possible for the relatively primitive folk to enhance their economies with fruits derived from the plunder of this trade or, in a more mature system, by extorting tribute from the merchants who must pass by. The remoteness of these areas, the difficulty of the terrain and the extreme difficulties and costs of sending a punitive force to pacify the area often enables the simpler people to harass populations whose cultural means for organized violence far exceeds their own. Be this as it may, the combination of the examples of organization presented by the outposts of complexly organized societies and the availability of commodities which could not be produced in the simple culture may combine to lay the basis for an emergence of stratification. Precisely such conditions seem partially responsible for the political developments described for the Kachin (Leach, 1954, esp. pp. 235, 247 ff.).

None of this seems to apply to the pristine emergence of stratification. As a matter of fact, it is not even particularly suggestive. There is, however, one particular ecological condition that appears in highland Burma which also has been noted elsewhere, each time in association with rather basic shifts in social organization paralleling those already sketched in the previous section of this paper. We refer to the shift from rainfall to irrigation farming, particularly to the construction of terraced fields. This is admittedly a restricted ethnographic phenomenon and as such it cannot bear the weight of any general theory. It is the suggestive character of these developments and the possibility of extrapolating from them to hypothetical pristine conditions that makes them so interesting.[22]

In brief, the shift to irrigation and terracing is from swiddens or impermanent fields to plots which will remain in permanent cultivation for decades and generations. Whereas we have previously stressed the possible role of hydro-agriculture in the transition from egalitarian to rank society, we now note its possible role in the transition to stratification. This it could accomplish by creating conditions under which access to strategic resources, in this case land and water, would be made the specific prerogative of small-scale kin groups such as minimal lineages or even stem families. Through the emergence of hydro-agriculture a community which previously acknowledged no *permanent* association between particular component units and particular stretches of land now begins to recognize such permanent and exclusive rights. Incidentally, the evidence seems to indicate that the rank-forming tendencies of hydro-agriculture need not occur prior to the tendencies toward stratification: both can occur concomitantly. This in turn suggests that we must be cautious in constructing our theory not to make stratification emerge from ranking, though under particular circumstances this is certainly possible.[23]

A point of considerable interest about hydro-agriculture is that it seems to present the possibility of an emergence of stratification in the absence of a problem of overpopulation or resource limitation. We need a great deal of further thought on the matter. Studies of the last two decades, in which a considerably higher degree of agricultural expertise on the part of the fieldwork-

---

[22] The passage refers back to Wittfogel's hydraulic hypothesis discussed above. Fried wrote this article at a time when Wittfogel's hypothesis was popular, before major criticisms of the theory had been published.

[23] An important point is being made here. Although Fried has proposed a materialist analysis of the relationship between stratification (differential access to prestige and wealth) and ranking, he allows for the possibility that ranking precedes stratification. In other words, he hedges on a strictly Marxist interpretation. Do you see how nicely this statement ties into Julian Steward's views on multilinear evolution? In fact, Steward's *Theory of Culture Change: The Methodology of Multilinear Evolution* had been published in 1955, just five years before this article.

ers has been manifested than was formerly the case, have increasingly tended to show that hydro-agriculture does not invariably out-produce slash and burn and that, other things being equal, a population does not automatically prefer hydro-agriculture as a more rationalized approach to agricultural subsistence. Here we can introduce a factor previously excluded. The hydro-agricultural system invariably has a higher degree of settlement concentration than swiddens. Accordingly, it would seem to have considerable value in the maintenance of systems of defense, given the presence of extensive warfare. Here then, is a point at which military considerations would seem to play an important if essentially reinforcing role in the broad evolutionary developments which we are considering.

The writer is intrigued with another possibility for the emergence of stratification. Once again, the conditions involved seem a little too specific to serve the purpose of a single unified theory. It requires the postulation of a society with a fixed rule of residence, preferably one of the simpler ones such as patrilocality/virilocality or matrilocality/uxorilocality[f] and a fixed rule of descent, preferably one parallel to the residence rule.[24] It further postulates a condition of population expansion such that, given slash and burn agriculture, the society is very near the limits of the carrying capacity of the system. Such conditions are very likely to develop at varying speeds within an area of several hundred miles due to obvious imbalances in reproductive rates and to micro-ecological variation. Now, as long as there is no notable pressure of people on the land, deviation in residence and even in descent will be expectable though quite unusual and lacking in motiva-tion. As the situation grows grave in one area but remains relatively open in another, there may be a tendency for a slight readjustment in residence rules to occur. For example, in a normally virilocal society, the woman who brings her husband back to her natal group transgresses a few customary rules in doing so but presents her agnates with no basic problems in resource allocation since she, as a member of the agnatic group, has her own rights of access which may be shared by the spouse during her lifetime. The complication arises at her death when her husband and all of her children discover themselves to be in an anomalous position since they are not members of the kin community. Where local land problems are not severe and where such breaches of the residence pattern are yet uncommon, it is not unlikely that the aliens will be accepted as *de facto* members of the community with the expectation that future generations will revert to custom, the unorthodox switch of residence fading in memory with the passage of time. Here we have a crude and informal *ambil-anak*.[25] But as the local community enters worsening ecological circumstances and as the exceptional residence becomes more frequent, the residence and descent rules, particularly the latter, assume greater and greater importance. As the situation continues, the community is slowly altered, though the members of the community may be unable to state exactly what the changes are. The result, however, is clear. There are now two kinds of people in the village where formerly there was only one. Now there are kernel villagers, those who have unimpaired access to land, and those whose tenure rests upon other conditions, such as loyalty to a patron, or tribute, or even a precarious squatter's right.[26]

---

[24] *Virilocality:* customary residence with the husband's father's kin after marriage; *uxorilocality:* customary residence with the wife's kin after marriage.

[25] *Ambil-anak:* a form of marriage occurring among the otherwise patrilocal Batak people of Indonesia. There, under certain conditions, rather than paying bridewealth, a man may move in with his wife's family. The children of such a marriage will be members of the wife's father's lineage.

[26] In this paragraph Fried is trying to describe an ecological scenario where population pressure in an area of limited resources leads to the formation of stratification within a formerly egalitarian society. He proposes that stratification may evolve in a society of swidden horticulturalists when an expanding population taxes the carrying capacity of the local environment. The change is propelled by the potential conflict between the patrilineal inheritance of land and the demand for land by people who are related matrilineally to those in the village. This is a very Marxist view: a change in the structure of society is a result of this conflict.

THE STATE SOCIETY

> The word should be abandoned entirely . . . after this chapter the word will be avoided scrupulously and no severe hardship in expression will result. In fact, clarity of expression demands this abstinence (Easton, 1953, p. 108).

The word was "state" and the writer, a political scientist, was reacting to some of the problems in his own field in making this judgment, but it does look as if he was pushed to drastic action by the work of some anthropologists in whose hands the concept of state lost all character and utility, finally ending as a cultural universal. E. Adamson Hoe-bel, one of the few United States anthropologists to make a serious specialization in the field of law and the state, formerly introduced students to this question by remarking that

> where there is political organization there is a state. If political organization is universal, so then is the state. One is the group, the other an institutionalized complex of behavior (Hoebel, 1949, p. 376).[27]

In a revision of the same book after a few years, Hoebel's treatment of the subject seems to indicate that he is in the process of rethinking the matter. His summary words, however, repeat the same conclusion:

> Political organization is characteristic of every society. . . . That part of culture that is recognized as political organization is what constitutes the state (Hoebel, 1958, p. 506).

This is a far cry from the approach of evolutionists to the state as exemplified in Sumner and Keller (1927, I, p. 700):

> The term state is properly reserved for a somewhat highly developed regulative organization. . . . It is an organization with authority and discipline essential to large-scale achievements, as compared with the family, for example, which is an organization on the same lines but simpler and less potent.

Without making a special issue of the definition of the state (which would easily consume the entire space of this article, if not the volume) let me note one used by the jurist Léon Duguit which conveys the sense most useful to the point of view of this paper:

> En prenant le mot dans son sens le plus général, on peut dire qu'il y a un Etat toutes les fois qu'il existe dans une société donnée une différenciation politique, quelque rudimentaire ou quelque compliquée et developée qu'elle soit. Le mot Etat designe soit les gouvernants où le pouvoir politique, soit la société elle même, où existe cette différenciation entre gouvernants et gouvernés et où existe par là même une puissance politique (Duguit, 1921, p. 395).[28]

The difference between Hoebel and Duguit seems to be in the clear statement of power. Reviewing our own paper in the light of this difference we note our previous emphasis on the absence of coercive economic or political power in the egalitarian and rank societies. It is only in the stratified society that such power emerges

---

[27] E. Adamson Hoebel (1907–1993) was an American anthropologist who specialized in the study of politics and law in primitive societies. He was a student of Franz Boas, author of a famous ethnography of the Cheyenne, and president of the American Anthropology Association. Hoebel represents the Boasian relativism to which Fried is reacting. The source of the first quotation is the first edition of Hoebel's book *Man in the Primitive World* (1949); the quotation that follows is from a revised edition.

[28] Leon Duguit (1859–1928) was a French political scientist whose work focused on the government and the state. The translation of his quotation is

> Taking the word in its most general sense, one could say that there is a state every time a political disparity, however simple or however complex and well developed, exists within a given society. The word state can refer to governments and political power or the society itself where there is a difference between governors and governed, and where, likewise, political power exists.

from embryonic and universal foreshadowings in familial organization.[29]

The maturation of social stratification has manifold implications depending on the precise circumstances in which the developments take place. All subsequent courses, however, have a certain area of overlap; the new social order, with its differential allocation of access to strategic resources, must be maintained and strengthened. In a simple stratified society in which class differentials are more implicit than explicit the network of kin relations covers a sufficient portion of the total fabric of social relations so that areas not specifically governed by genuine kinship relations can be covered by their sociological extensions. The dynamic of stratification is such that this situation cannot endure. The stratified kin group emphasizes its exclusiveness: it erodes the corporative economic functions formerly associated with stipulated kinship and at every turn it amputates extensions of the demonstrated kin unit. The result of this pruning is that the network of kin relations fails more and more to coincide with the network of personal relations. Sooner or later the discrepancy is of such magnitude that, were non-kin sanctions and non-kin agencies absent or structured along customary lines only, the society would dissolve in uncomposable conflict.

The emergent state, then, is the organization of the power of the society on a supra-kin basis. Among its earliest tasks is the maintenance of general order but scarcely discernible from this is its need to support the order of stratification. The defense of a complete system of individual statuses is impossible so the early state concentrates on a few key statuses (helping to explain the tendency to convert any crime into either sacrilege or *lèse majesté*) and on the basic principles of organization, e.g., the idea of hierarchy, property, and the power of the law.

The implementation of these primary functions of the state gives rise to a number of specific and characteristic secondary functions, each of which is associated with one or more particular institutions of its own. These secondary functions include population control in the most general sense (the fixing of boundaries and the definition of the unit; establishment of categories of membership; census). Also a secondary function is the disposal of trouble cases (civil and criminal laws moving toward the status of codes; regular legal procedure; regular officers of adjudication). The protection of sovereignty is also included (maintenance of military forces; police forces and power; eminent domain). Finally, all of the preceding require fiscal support, and this is achieved in the main through taxation and conscription.[30]

In treating of this bare but essential list of state functions and institutions the idea of the state as a universal aspect of culture dissolves as a fantasy. The institutions just itemized may be made to appear in ones or twos in certain primitive societies by exaggeration and by the neglect of known history. In no egalitarian society and in no rank society do a majority of the functions enumerated appear regardless of their guise. Furthermore there is no indication of their appearance as a unified functional response to basic socio-cultural needs except in those stratified societies which are verging upon statehood.

THE TRANSITION TO STATE

Just as stratified society grew out of antecedent forms of society without the conscious awareness of the culture carriers, so it would seem that the state emerged from the stratified society in a similar, inexorable way.[31] If this hypothesis is correct, then such an explanation as the so-called "conquest theory" can be accepted only as a special

---

[29] Fried says that social stratification is foreshadowed in "familial organization"; that is, it lies in differential access to resources between small-scale kin groups.

[30] At the time Fried wrote this article there was a controversy over how to define a state. Archaeologists argued that features such as monumental architecture, urban populations, and large-scale public works were indicative of state-level societies. Here Fried is defining a state by complexity of social organization and stratification.

[31] When Fried talks about the inexorability of the emergence of the state, can there be any doubt about the influence of nineteenth-century evolutionism on his thinking?

case of "secondary-state" formation. The conquests discussed by such a theorist as Franz Oppenheimer (1914) established not stratification but super-stratification, either the conqueror or the conquered, or perhaps even both, already being internally stratified.[32]

The problem of the transition to state is so huge and requires such painstaking application to the available archaeological and historical evidence that it would be foolish to pursue it seriously here. Let us conclude, therefore, by harking back to statements made at the outset of this paper, and noting again the distinction between pristine and secondary states. By the former term is meant a state that has developed *sui generis* out of purely local conditions. No previous state, with its acculturative pressures, can be discerned in the background of a pristine state. The secondary state, on the other hand, is pushed by one means or another toward a higher form of organization by an external power which has already been raised to statehood.

The number of pristine states is strictly limited; several centuries, possibly two millennia, have elapsed since the last one emerged in Meso-America, and there seems to be no possibility that any further states of the pristine type will evolve, though further research may bring to light some of the distant past of which we yet have no positive information. In all, there seems to have been some six centers at which pristine states emerged, four in the Old World and two in the New: the Tigris-Euphrates area, the region of the lower Nile, the country drained by the Indus and the middle course of the Huang Ho where it is joined by the Han, Wei, and Fen. The separate areas of Peru-Bolivia and Meso-America complete the roster.

If there is utility in the concept of the pristine state and if history has been read correctly in limiting the designation to the six areas just enumerated, then we discover a remarkable correlation between areas demanding irrigation or flood control and the pristine state. Certainly this is no discovery of the author. It is one of the central ideas of Wittfogel's theory and has received extensive treatment from Julian Steward and others (see Steward, 1955, pp. 178–209; Steward *et al.*, 1955). The implication of the "hydraulic theory" for this paper, however, is that the development of the state as an internal phenomenon is associated with major tasks of drainage and irrigation. The emergence of a control system to ensure the operation of the economy is closely tied to the appearance of a distinctive class system and certain constelations of power in the hands of a managerial bureaucracy which frequently operates below a ruler who commands theoretically unlimited power.

It is an interesting commentary on nineteenth-century political philosophy that the starting point of so many theories was, of necessity, the Classical world of Greece and Rome. According to the present hypothesis, however, both of these great political developments of antiquity were not pristine but secondary formations which built on cultural foundations laid two thousand years and more before the rise of Greece. Furthermore, it would seem that the active commercial and military influences of the truly ancient pristine states, mediated through the earliest of the secondary states to appear in Asia Minor and the eastern Mediterranean littoral, were catalysts in the events of the northern and western Mediterranean.

CONCLUSION

The close of a paper like this, which moves like a gadfly from time to time, place to place, and subject matter to subject matter, and which never pauses long enough to make a truly detailed inquiry or supply the needed documentation, the close of such a paper requires an apology perhaps more than a conclusion.

I have been led to write this paper by my ignorance of any modern attempt to link up the contributions which have been made in many sub-disciplines into a single unified theory of the emergence of social stratification and the state. That the theory offered here is crude, often too special, and by no means documented seems less

---

[32] Franz Oppenheimer (1864–1943) was a German sociologist best known for his book *The State: Its History and Development Viewed Sociologically* (1914). In this essay Fried is concerned with the evolution of stratification in pristine states, not stratification imposed on a society through conquest. Thus he dismisses work like Oppenheimer's.

important than that it may be used as a sitting duck to attract the fire and better aim of others.[33]

Notes

a. The reader may object to crediting Polanyi with the concept of a reciprocal economy. While it is true that Thurnwald and Malinowski earlier expressed similar concepts, and Durkheim, with his distinction between segmental and organic societies, also foreshadows this development, it awaited Polanyi's analysis to place reciprocal economies into systematic harmony with other, more complex types of economy, such as the redistributive type discussed later on, and the market kind as well. For Polanyi's definitions of each of these types see Polanyi, Arensberg and Pearson, 1957, pp. 250–56.

b. For an ethnographic illustration of this point see Oliver, 1955, pp. 422 ff.

c. These, of course, would be ranked lineages or ranked clans. Cf. Fried, 1957, pp. 23–26.

d. As does Leach, 1954, p. 10.

e. Strategic resources are those things which, given the technological base and environmental setting of the culture, maintain subsistence. See Fried, 1957, p. 4.

f. Our residence terms follow usage suggested by J. L. Fischer, 1958.

---

[33] When Fried speaks of linking the contributions of many subdisciplines into a single unified theory, he refers, in particular, to the exchange between archaeology and cultural ecology and materialism. The transfer of ideas between these areas resulted in the publication of numerous works on cultural evolution for almost two decades.

---

22. The Cultural Ecology of India's Sacred Cattle

Marvin Harris (1927–)

IN THIS PAPER I ATTEMPT TO INDICATE CERTAIN puzzling inconsistencies in prevailing interpretations of the ecological role of bovine cattle in India. My argument is based upon intensive reading—I have never seen a sacred cow, nor been to India. As a non-specialist, no doubt I have committed blunders an Indianist would have avoided. I hope these errors will not deprive me of that expert advice and informed criticism which alone can justify so rude an invasion of unfamiliar territory.[1]

(1966)

I have written this paper because I believe the irrational, non-economic, and exotic aspects of the Indian cattle complex are greatly overemphasized at the expense of rational, economic, and mundane interpretations.

My intent is not to substitute one dogma for another, but to urge that explanation of taboos, customs, and rituals associated with management of Indian cattle be sought in "positive-functioned" and probably "adaptive" processes of the ecological system of which they are a part,[a] rather than in the influence of Hindu theology.[2]

Mismanagement of India's agricultural resources as a result of the Hindu doctrine of

---

[1] In the 1960s ethnographic experience was the cornerstone of authority in American anthropology (and to some extent still is today). Harris' upfront admission that he had never been to India was a challenge to this prevailing anthropological opinion and is related to his views on the emic-etic debate that was raging within the profession at this time. (For more on emics and etics, see footnote 5).

[2] Harris makes his materialist and neofunctionalist position clear in the opening paragraphs of this essay. As a materialist, Harris presumes that Indian beliefs about the sacredness of cattle have a rational economic explanation that takes precedence over references to Hindu theology. Additionally, Harris' statement that the explanation for Indian cattle

ahimsa,[b] especially as it applies to beef cattle, is frequently noted by Indianists and others concerned with the relation between values and behavior. Although different antirational, dysfunctional, and inutile aspects of the cattle complex are stressed by different authors, many agree that *ahimsa* is a prime example of how men will diminish their material welfare to obtain spiritual satisfaction in obedience to nonrational or frankly irrational beliefs.

A sample opinion on this subject is here summarized: According to Simoons (1961:3), "irrational ideologies" frequently compel men "to overlook foods that are abundant locally and are of high nutritive value, and to utilize other scarcer foods of less value." The Hindu beef-eating taboo is one of Simoons' most important cases. Venkatraman (1938:706) claims, "India is unique in possessing an enormous amount of cattle without making profit from its slaughter." The Ford Foundation (1959:64) reports "widespread recognition not only among animal husbandry officials, but among citizens generally, that India's cattle population is far in excess of the available supplies of fodder and feed . . . At least ⅓, and possibly as many as ½, of the Indian cattle population may be regarded as surplus in relation to feed supply." Matson (1933:227) writes it is a commonplace of the "cattle question that vast numbers of Indian cattle are so helplessly inefficient as to have no commercial value beyond that of their hides." Srinivas (1952:222) believes "Orthodox Hindu opinion regards the killing of cattle with abhorrence, even though the refusal to kill the vast number of useless cattle which exist in India today is detrimental to the nation."

According to the Indian Ministry of Information (1957:243), "The large animal population is more a liability than an asset in view of our land resources." Chatterjee (1960) calculates that Indian production of cow and buffalo milk involves a "heavy recurring loss of Rs 774 crores. This is equivalent to 6.7 times the amount we are annually spending on importing food grains." Knight (1954:141) observes that because the Hindu religion teaches great reverence for the cow, "there existed a large number of cattle whose utility to the community did not justify economically the fodder which they consumed." Das and Chatterji (1962:120) concur: "A large number of cattle in India are old and decrepit and constitute a great burden on an already impoverished land. This is due to the prejudice among the Hindus against cow killing." Mishra (1962) approvingly quotes Lewis (1955:106): "It is not true that if economic and religious doctrines conflict the economic interest will always win. The Hindu cow has remained sacred for centuries, although this is plainly contrary to economic interest." Darling (1934:158) asserts, "By its attitude to slaughter Hinduism makes any planned improvement of cattle breeding almost impossible." According to Desai (1959:36), "The cattle population is far in excess of the available fodder and feeds."[3]

[In a 400-word passage eliminated from this edition, Harris continues his catalog of experts and government agencies that have declared Indian cattle practices uneconomic.]

In spite of the sometimes final and unqualified fashion in which "surplus," "useless," "uneconomic," and "superfluous" are applied to part or all of India's cattle, contrary conclusions seem admissible when the cattle complex is viewed as part of an *eco-system* rather than as a sector of a national price market. Ecologically, it is doubtful that any component of the cattle complex is "useless," i.e., the number, type, and condition of Indian bovines

---

management can be found in the "adaptive processes of the ecological system of which they are a part" clearly demonstrates the influence of the cultural ecology of Julian Steward (see essay 18). His claim that he does not wish to substitute one dogma for another is disingenuous — Harris is brilliant, but he is one of the more polemic writers in anthropology.

[3] Harris' materialist point of view has been so successful in the last few decades that it should be noted that Westerners really used to think that Indian cattle usage was irrational. In fact, the view that non-Western people's traditional practices were irrational formed one of the cornerstones of colonial ethnocentrism. From the Western point of view, the irrationality of Indian culture was demonstrated by the failure of Indians to conform to European notions of animal husbandry, a failure that confirmed the British in their self-perceived civilizing mission. So, while Harris is doing a cultural-materialist analysis, he is also working in a form of analysis that would have made Franz Boas proud.

do not per se impair the ability of the human population to survive and reproduce. Much more likely the relationship between bovines and humans is symbiotic[c] instead of competitive. It probably represents the outcome of intense Darwinian pressures acting upon human and bovine population, cultigens, wild flora and fauna, and social structure and ideology. Moreover presumably the degree of observance of taboos against bovine slaughter and beef-eating reflect the power of these ecological pressures rather than *ahimsa*; in other words, *ahimsa* itself derives power and sustenance from the material rewards it confers upon both men and animals.[4] To support these hypotheses, the major aspects of the Indian cattle complex will be reviewed under the following heading: (1) Milk Production, (2) Traction, (3) Dung, (4) Beef and Hides, (5) Pasture, (6) Useful and Useless Animals, (7) Slaughter, (8) Anti-Slaughter Legislation, (9) Old-Age Homes, and (10) Natural Selection.

MILK PRODUCTION

In India the average yield of whole milk per Zebu cow is 413 pounds, compared with the 5,000-pound average in Europe and the U.S.[d] (Kartha 1936:607; Spate 1954:231). In Madhya Pradesh yield is as low as 65 pounds, while in no state does it rise higher than the barely respectable 1,445 pounds of the Punjab (Chatterjee 1960: 1347). According to the 9th Quinquennial Livestock Census (1961) among the 47,200,000 cows over 3 years old, 27,200,000 were dry and/or not calved (Chaudri and Giri 1963:598).

These figures, however should not be used to prove that the cows are useless or uneconomic, since milk production is a minor aspect of the sacred cow's contribution to the *eco-system*. Indeed, most Indianists agree that it is the buffalo, not the Zebu, whose economic worth must be judged primarily by milk production. Thus, Kartha (1959: 225) writes, "the buffalo, and not the Zebu, is the dairy cow." This distinction is elaborated by Mamoria (1953:255):

> Cows in the rural areas are maintained for producing bullocks rather than for milk. She-buffaloes, on the other hand, are considered to be better dairy animals than cows. The male buffaloes are neglected and many of them die or are sold for slaughter before they attain maturity.

Mohan (1962:47) makes the same point:

> For agricultural purposes bullocks are generally preferred, and, therefore, cows in rural areas are primarily maintained for the production of male progeny and incidentally only for milk.

It is not relevant to my thesis to establish whether milk production is a primary or secondary objective or purpose of the Indian farmer. Failure to separate emics from etics (Harris 1964) contributes greatly to confusion surrounding the Indian cattle question.[5] The significance of the preceding quotations lies in the agreement that cows contribute to human material welfare in more important ways than milk production. In this new context, the fact that U.S. cows produce

---

[4] Harris' debt to the cultural ecology of Steward is clear in this paragraph. Although Harris' materialism is derived from Karl Marx via Leslie White, his statement that the features of the cattle complex are the consequence of Darwinian pressures within an ecological system sounds very much like Steward's concept of the cultural core. Harris doesn't spell out exactly how these pressures operate, but the invocation of Darwin increases the scientific feel of the article by associating it with a well-established scientific position.

[5] The terms *emic* and *etic* were coined in 1954 by the missionary-linguist Kenneth Pike (1912 –). Emic statements refer to meaning as it is perceived by the natives of a culture, and emic anthropologists tried to outline the models by which natives understood their society. By definition, emic understanding is culture-bound. In contrast, etic meanings are those arrived at by empirical investigation. Etic anthropologists aim at producing generalizations that are cross-culturally valid using methods of investigation that can be verified and replicated by anyone using a similar investigative process. Etic analyses are typically perceived to be more scientific, and Harris' analysis of cattle in India is an etic study. Harris believes that many studies mix etic and emic data together, thus confounding the analysis. Here he says the same problem "contributes greatly to confusion surrounding the Indian cattle question." Harris claims that when the situation is examined from an etic perspective (energy contribution of cows versus energy expenditures of cows within an overall ecosystem), it is clear that the treatment of cattle in India is adaptive.

20 times more milk than Indian cows loses much of its significance. Instead, it is more relevant to note that, despite the marginal status of milking in the symbiotic syndrome, 46.7% of India's dairy products come from cow's milk (Chatterjee 1960:1347). How far this production is balanced by expenditures detrimental to human welfare will be discussed later.

TRACTION

The principal positive ecological effect of India's bovine cattle is in their contribution to production of grain crops, from which about 80% of the human calorie ration comes. Some form of animal traction is required to initiate the agricultural cycle, dependent upon plowing in both rainfall and irrigation areas. Additional traction for hauling, transport, and irrigation is provided by animals, but by far their most critical kinetic contribution is plowing.

Although many authorities believe there is an overall surplus of cattle in India, others point to a serious shortage of draught animals. According to Kothavala (1934:122), "Even with . . . overstocking, the draught power available for land operations at the busiest season of the year is inadequate. . . ." For West Bengal, the National Council of Applied Economic Research (1962:56) reports:

> However, despite the large number of draught animals, agriculture in the State suffers from a shortage of draught power. There are large numbers of small landholders entirely dependent on hired animal labour.

Spate (1954:36) makes the same point, "there are too many cattle in the gross, but most individual farmers have too few to carry on with." Gupta (1959:42) and Lewis and Barnouw (1958:102) say a pair of bullocks is the minimum technical unit for cultivation, but in a survey by Diskalkar (1960:87), 18% of the cultivators had only 1 bullock or none. Nationally, if we accept a low estimate of 60,000,000 rural households (Mitra 1963:298) and a high estimate of 80,000,000 working cattle and buffaloes (Government of India 1962:76), we see at once that the allegedly excess number of cattle in India is insufficient to

permit a large portion, perhaps as many as ⅓, of India's farmers to begin the agricultural cycle under conditions appropriate to their techno-environmental system.

Much has been made of India's having 115 head of cattle per square mile, compared with 28 per square mile for the U.S. and 3 per square mile for Canada. But what actually may be most characteristic of the size of India's herd is the low ratio of cattle to people. Thus, India has 44 cattle per 100 persons, while in the U.S. the ratio is 58 per 100 and in Canada, 90 (Mamoria 1953:256). Yet, in India cattle are employed as a basic instrument of agricultural production.

Sharing of draught animals on a cooperative basis might reduce the need for additional animals. Chaudhri and Giri point out that the "big farmer manages to cultivate with a pair of bullock a much larger area than the small cultivators" (1963:596). But, the failure to develop cooperative forms of plowing can scarcely be traced to *ahimsa*. If anything, emphasis upon independent, family-sized farm units follows intensification of individual land tenure patterns and other property innovations deliberately encouraged by the British (Bhatia 1963:18 on). Under existing property arrangements, there is a perfectly good economic explanation of why bullocks are not shared among adjacent households. Plowing cannot take place at any time of the year, but must be accomplished within a few daylight hours in conformity with seasonal conditions. These are set largely by summer monsoons, responsible for about 90% of the total rainfall (Bhatia 1963:4). Writing about Orissa, Bailey (1957:74) notes:

> As a temporary measure, an ox might be borrowed from a relative, or a yoke of cattle and a ploughman might be hired . . . but during the planting season, when the need is the greatest, most people are too busy to hire out or lend cattle.

According to Desai (1948:86):

> . . . over vast areas, sowing and harvesting operations, by the very nature of things, begin simultaneously with the outbreak of the first showers and the maturing of crops respectively, and especially the former has got to be put through quickly during the first phase of the

monsoon. Under these circumstances, reliance by a farmer on another for bullocks is highly risky and he has got, therefore, to maintain his own pair.

Dube (1955:84) is equally specific:

The cultivators who depend on hired cattle or who practice cooperative lending and borrowing of cattle cannot take the best advantage of the first rains, and this enforced wait results in untimely sowing and poor crops.

Wiser and Wiser (1963:62) describe the plight of the bullock-short farmer as follows, "When he needs the help of bullocks most, his neighbors are all using theirs." And Shastri (1960:1592) points out, "Uncertainty of Indian farming due to dependence on rains is the main factor creating obstacles in the way of improvements in bullock labor."

It would seem, therefore, that this aspect of the cattle complex is not an expression of spirit and ritual, but of rain and energy.[6]

DUNG

In India cattle dung is the main source of domestic cooking fuel. Since grain crops cannot be digested unless boiled or baked, cooking is indispensable. Considerable disagreement exists about the total amount of cattle excrement and its uses, but even the lowest estimates are impressive. An early estimate by Lupton (1922:60) gave the BTU equivalent of dung consumed in domestic cooking as 35,000,000 tons of coal or 68,000,000 tons of wood. Most detailed appraisal is by National Council of Applied Economic Research (1959: 3), which rejects H. J. Bhabha's estimate of 131,000,000 tons of coal and the Ministry of

Food and Agriculture's 112,000,000 tons. The figure preferred by the NCAER is 35,000,000 tons anthracite or 40,000,000 tons bituminous, but with a possible range of between 35–45,000,000 of anthracite dung-coal equivalent. This calculation depends upon indications that only 36% of the total wet dung is utilized as fuel (p. 14), a lower estimate than any reviewed by Saha (1956:923). These vary from 40% (Imperial Council on Agricultural Research) to 50% (Ministry of Food and Agriculture) to 66.6% (Department of Education, Health and Lands). The NCAER estimate of a dung-coal equivalent of 35,000,000 tons is therefore quite conservative; it is nonetheless an impressive amount of BTU's to be plugged into an energy system.

Kapp (1963:144 on), who discusses at length the importance of substituting tractors for bullocks, does not give adequate attention to finding cooking fuel after the bullocks are replaced. The NCAER (1959:20) conclusion that dung is cheaper than coke seems an understatement. Although it is claimed that wood resources are potentially adequate to replace dung the measures advocated do not involve *ahimsa* but are again an indictment of a land tenure system not inspired by Hindu tradition (NCAER 1959:20 on; Bansil 1958:97 on). Finally, it should be noted that many observers stress the slow burning qualities of dung and its special appropriateness for preparation of *ghi* and deployment of woman-power in the household (Lewis and Barnouw 1958:40; Mosher 1946:153).[7]

As manure, dung enters the energy system in another vital fashion. According to Mujumdar (1960:743), 300,000,000 tons are used as fuel, 340,000,000 tons as manure, and 160,000,000

---

[6] Harris was taking a fairly radical position at this time, therefore he presents quotation after quotation supporting his views when one or two would suffice. Note that he relies almost exclusively on statistical rather than ethnographic data. True to his etic perspective, Harris provides the reader with a statistical portrait of Indian society. It is also instructive to examine Harris' writing style. Although not as polemical an author as Marx, who called one of his opponents "Saint Max" (see essay 4), Harris undercuts his opponents through rhetorical style as well as scientific argument. Throughout this section—as he does here—Harris concludes points by saying, in effect, you do not need religion to explain this. The cumulative effect is to make the position he is opposing look silly.

[7] Harris' statement about "a land tenure system not inspired by Hindu tradition" is an allusion to British colonialism. As Friedman points out in his 1974 critique of Harris' analysis, Harris never really deals with the cultural context in which the traditions he analyzes take place—i.e., centuries of British colonial rule.

Ghi, or *ghee,* is clarified butter made from the butterfat of milk.

tons "wasted on hillsides and roads." Spate (1954:238) believes that 40% of dung production is spread on fields, 40% burned, and 20% "lost." Possibly estimates of the amount of dung lost are grossly inflated in view of the importance of "roads and hillsides" in the grazing pattern (see Pasture). Similarly artificial and culture- or even class-bound judgments refer to utilization of India's night soil. It is usually assumed that Chinese and Indian treatment of this resource are radically different, and that vast quantities of nitrogen go unused in agriculture because of Hindu inspired definitions of modesty and cleanliness. However, most human excrement from Indian villages is deposited in surrounding fields; the absence of latrines helps explain why such fields raise 2 and 3 successive crops each year (Mosher 1946:154, 33; Bansil 1958:104.) More than usual caution, therefore, is needed before concluding that a significant amount of cattle dung is wasted. Given the conscious premium set on dung for fuel and fertilizer, thoughtful control maintained over grazing patterns (see Pasture), and occurrence of specialized sweeper and gleaner castes, much more detailed evidence of wastage is needed than is now available. Since cattle graze on "hillsides and roads," dung dropped there would scarcely be totally lost to the *eco-system,* even with allowance for loss of nitrogen by exposure to air and sunlight. Also, if any animal dung is wasted on roads and hillsides it is not because of *ahimsa* but of inadequate pasturage suitable for collecting and processing animal droppings. The sedentary, intensive rainfall agriculture of most of the subcontinent is heavily dependent upon manuring. So vital is this that Spate (1954: 239) says substitutes for manure consumed as fuel "must be supplied, and lavishly, even at a financial loss to government." If this is the case, then old, decrepit, and dry animals might have a use after all, especially when, as we shall see, the dung they manufacture employs raw materials lost to the culture-energy system unless processed by cattle, and especially when many apparently moribund animals revive at the next monsoon and provide their owners with a male calf.[8]

BEEF AND HIDES[9]

Positive contributions of India's sacred cattle do not cease with milk-grazing, bullock-producing, traction, and dung-dropping. There remains the direct protein contribution of 25,000,000 cattle and buffalo which die each year (Mohan 1962: 54). This feature of the eco-system is reminiscent of the East African cattle area where, despite the normal taboo on slaughter, natural deaths and ceremonial occasions are probably frequent enough to maintain beef consumption near the ecological limit with dairying as the primary function (Schneider 1957:278 on). Although most Hindus probably do not consume beef, the *eco-system* under consideration is not confined to Hindus. The human population includes some 55,000,000 "scheduled" exterior or untouchable groups (Hutton 1961:vii), many of whom will consume beef if given the opportunity (Dube 1955:68–69), plus several million more Moslems and Christians. Much of the flesh on the 25,000,000 dead cattle and buffalo probably gets consumed by human beings whether or not the cattle die naturally. Indeed, could it be that without the orthodox Hindu beef-eating taboo, many marginal and depressed castes would be deprived of an occasional, but nutritionally critical, source of animal protein?

---

[8] Since the publication of Leslie White's "Energy and the Evolution of Culture" in 1943, energy has had a significant role in American anthropology. Harris' discussion of dung as an energy source is an early example of the type of analysis that became a mainstay of the ecological and evolutionary approaches in cultural anthropology.

[9] This section may be the weakest in Harris' argument. Notice the absence of statistical support in his discussion of beef eating and the leather industry. He writes, "The quality of India's huge leather industry – the world's largest – leaves much to be desired, but the problem is primarily outmoded tanning techniques and lack of capital, not *ahimsa.*" But one could easily argue that it is precisely *ahimsa* that keeps the industry outmoded since, because of *ahimsa,* no one with prestige or capital will invest in tanning. Treating hides is the domain of the lowest castes. This point does not really damage his argument, but it is typical of Harris' dogmatism: he will allow no explanatory power to *ahimsa* at all.

It remains to note that the slaughter taboo does not prevent depressed castes from utilizing skin, horns and hoofs of dead beasts. In 1956 16,000,000 cattle hides were produced (Randhawa 1962:322). The quality of India's huge leather industry—the world's largest—leaves much to be desired, but the problem is primarily outmoded tanning techniques and lack of capital, not *ahimsa*.

PASTURE

The principal positive-functioned or useful contributions of India's sacred cattle to human survival and well-being have been described. Final evaluation of their utility must involve assessment of energy costs in terms of resources and human labor input which might be more efficiently expended in other activities.

Direct and indirect evidence suggests that in India men and bovine cattle do not compete for existence. According to Mohan (1962:43 on):

> . . . the bulk of the food on which the animals subsist . . . is not the food that is required for human consumption, i.e., fibrous fodders produced as incidental to crop production, and a large part of the crop residues or byproducts of seeds and waste grazing.

On the contrary, "the bulk of foods (straws and crop residues) that are ploughed into the soil in other countries are converted into milk" (p. 45).

The majority of the Indian cattle obtain their requirements from whatever grazing is available from straw and stalk and other residues from human foodstuffs, and are starved seasonally in the dry months when grasses wither.

In Bengal the banks and slopes of the embankments of public roads are the only grazing grounds and the cattle subsist mainly on paddy straw, paddy husks and . . . coarse grass. . . . (Mamoria 1953:263–64).

According to Dube (1955:84, ". . . the cattle roam about the shrubs and rocks and eat what-

ever fodder is available there." This is confirmed by Moomaw (1949:96): "Cows subsist on the pasture and any coarse fodder they can find. Grain is fed for only a day or two following parturition." The character of the environmental niche reserved for cattle nourishment is described by Gourou (1963:123), based on data furnished by Dupuis (1960) for Madras:

> Il faut voir clairement que le faible rendement du bétail indien n'est pas un gaspillage: ce bétail n'entre pas en concurrence avec la consommation de produits agricoles . . . ils ne leur sacrifient pas des surfaces agricoles, ou ayant un potential agricole.[10]

NCAER (1961:57) confines this pattern for Tripura: "There is a general practice of feeding livestock on agricultural by-products such as straw, grain wastes and husks"; for West Bengal (NCAER 1962:59): "The state has practically no pasture or grazing fields, and the farmers are not in the habit of growing green fodders . . . livestock feeds are mostly agricultural by-products"; and for Andhra Pradesh (NCAER 1962:52): "Cattle are stall-fed, but the bulk of the feed consists of paddy straw. . . ."

The only exceptions to the rural pattern of feeding cattle on waste products and grazing them on marginal or unproductive lands involve working bullocks and nursing cows:

> The working bullocks, on whose efficiency cultivation entirely depends, are usually fed with chopped bananas at the time of fodder scarcity. But the milch cows have to live in a semi-starved condition, getting what nutrition they can from grazing on the fields after their rice harvest (Gangulee 1935:17). At present cattle are fed largely according to the season. During the rainy period they feed upon the grass which springs up on the *uncultivated* hillsides. . . . But in the dry season there is hardly any grass, and cattle wander on the *cropless* lands in an often halfstarved condition. True there is some fodder at these times in the

---

[10] The translation of this passage is "One needs to see clearly that the small return of Indian cattle is not waste: these beasts do not compete for the consumption of agricultural produce . . . neither fields nor areas that could be used for agriculture are sacrificed to them."

shape of rice-straw and dried copra, but it is not generally sufficient, and is furthermore given mainly to the animals actually *working* at the time (Mayer 1952:70, italics added).

There is much evidence that Hindu farmers calculate carefully which animals deserve more food and attention. In Madras, Randhawa, et al. (1961:117) report: "The cultivators pay more attention to the male stock used for ploughing and for draft. There is a general neglect of the cow and the female calf even from birth . . ." Similar discrimination is described by Mamoria (1953:263 on):

Many plough bullocks are sold off in winter or their rations are ruthlessly decreased whenever they are not worked in full, while milch cattle are kept on after lactation on poor and inadequate grazing. . . . The cultivator feeds his bullocks better than his cow because it pays him. He feeds his bullocks better during the busy season, when they work, than during the slack season, when they remain idle. Further, he feeds his more valuable bullocks better than those less valuable. . . . Although the draught animals and buffaloes are properly fed, the cow gets next to nothing of stall feeding. She is expected to pick up her living on the bare fields after harvest and on the village wasteland. . . .

The previously cited NCAER report on Andhra Pradesh notes that "Bullocks and milking cows during the working season get more concentrates. . . ." (1962:52). Wiser and Wiser (1963:71) sum up the situation in a fashion supporting Srinivas' (1958:4) observation that the Indian peasant is "nothing if he is not practical":

Farmers have become skillful in reckoning the minimum of food necessary for maintaining animal service. Cows are fed just enough to assure their calving and giving a little milk. They are grazed during the day on lands which yield very little vegetation, and are given a very sparse meal at night.

Many devout Hindus believe the bovine cattle of India are exploited without mercy by greedy Hindu owners. *Ahimsa* obviously has little to do with economizing which produces the famous *phooka* and *doom dev* techniques for dealing with dry cows.[11] Not to Protestants but to Hindus did Gandhi (1954:7) address lamentations concerning the cow:

How we bleed her to take the last drop of milk from her, how we starve her to emaciation, how we ill-treat the calves, how we deprive them of their portion of milk, how cruelly we treat the oxen, how we castrate them, how we beat them, how we overload them. . . . I do not know that the condition of the cattle in any other part of the world is as bad as in unhappy India.

USEFUL AND USELESS ANIMALS

How then, if careful rationing is characteristic of livestock management, do peasants tolerate the widely reported herds of useless animals? Perhaps "useless" means one thing to the peasant and quite another to the price-market-oriented agronomist. It is impossible at a distance to judge which point of view is ecologically more valid, but the peasants could be right more than the agronomists are willing to admit.

Since non-working and non-lactating animals are thermal and chemical factories which depend on waste lands and products for raw materials, judgment that a particular animal is useless cannot be supported without careful examination of its owner's household budget. Estimates from the cattle census which equate useless with dry or non-working animals are not convincing. But even if a given animal in a particular household is of less-than-marginal utility, there is an additional factor whose evaluation would involve long-range bovine biographies. The utility of a particular animal to its owner cannot be established simply by its performance during season or an animal cycle. Perhaps the whole system of Indian bovine management is alien to costing procedures of the West. There may be a kind of low-risk sweepstakes which drags on for 10 or 12 years before the losers and winners are separated.

---

[11] The "famous" *phooka* and *doom dev* techniques Harris refers to are procedures Indians use to stimulate a cow's flow of milk. As described by Harris in his 1974 book *Cows, Pigs, Wars, and Witches*, *phooka* is blowing air into the cow's uterus through a hollow pipe, while *doom dev* refers to stuffing the cow's tail into its vagina.

As previously observed, the principal function of bovine cows is not their milk-producing but their bullock-producing abilities. Also established is the fact that many farmers are short of bullocks. Cows have the function primarily to produce male offspring, but when? In Europe and America, cows become pregnant under well-controlled, hence predictable, circumstances and a farmer with many animals can count on male offspring in half the births. In India, cows become pregnant under quite different circumstances. Since cows suffer from malnutrition through restriction to marginal pasture, they conceive and deliver in unpredictable fashion. The chronic starvation of the inter-monsoon period makes the cow, in the words of Mamoria (1953:263), "an irregular breeder." Moreover, with few animals, the farmer may suffer many disappointments before a male is born. To the agriculture specialist with knowledge of what healthy dairy stock look like, the hot weather herds of walking skeletons "roaming over the bare fields and dried up wastes" (Leake 1923:267) must indeed seem without economic potential. Many of them, in fact, will not make it through to the next monsoon. However, among the survivors are an unknown number still physically capable of having progeny. Evidently neither the farmer nor the specialist knows which will conceive, nor when. To judge from Bombay city, even when relatively good care is bestowed on a dry cow, no one knows the outcome: "If an attempt is made to salvage them, they have to be kept and fed for a long time. Even then, it is not known whether they will conceive or not" (Nandra, *et al.* 1955:9).

In rural areas, to judge a given animal useless may be to ignore the recuperative power of these breeds under conditions of erratic rainfall and unpredictable grazing opportunities. The difference of viewpoint between the farmer and the expert is apparent in Moomaw's (1949) incomplete attempt to describe the life history of an informant's cattle. The farmer in question had 3 oxen,

2 female buffaloes, 4 head of young cattle and 3 "worthless" cows (p. 23). In Moomaw's opinion, "the three cows . . . are a liability to him, providing no income, yet consuming feed which might be placed to better use." Yet we learn, "The larger one had a calf about once in three years"; moreover 2 of the 3 oxen were "raised" by the farmer himself. (Does this mean that they were the progeny of the farmer's cows?) The farmer tells Moomaw, "The young stock get some fodder, but for the most part they pasture with the village herd. The cows give nothing and I cannot afford to feed them." Whereupon Moomaw's *non sequitur:* "We spoke no more of his cows, for like many a farmer he just keeps them, without inquiring whether it is profitable or not" (p. 25).

The difficulties in identifying animals that are definitely uneconomic for a given farmer are reflected in the varying estimates of the total of such animals. The Expert Committee on the Prevention of Slaughter of Cattle estimated 20,000,000 uneconomic cattle in India (Nandra, *et al.* 1953: 62). Roy (1955:14) settles for 5,500,000, or about 3.5%. Mamoria (1953:257), who gives the still lower estimate of 2,900,000, or 2.1%, claims most of these are males. A similarly low percentage— 2.5%—is suggested for West Bengal (NCAER 1962:56). None of these estimates appears based on bovine life histories in relation to household budgets; none appears to involve estimates of economic significance of dung contributions of older animals.[12]

Before a peasant is judged a victim of Oriental mysticism, might it not be well to indicate the devastating material consequences which befall a poor farmer unable to replace a bullock lost through disease, old age, or accident? Bailey (1957:73) makes it clear that in the economic life of the marginal peasantry, "Much the most devastating single event is the loss of an ox (or a plough buffalo)." If the farmer is unable to replace the animal with one from his own herd, he must borrow money at usurious rates. Defaults

---

[12] Harris' concern is for the economics of cattle at the level of the Indian peasant household, but the statistics he cites are national or state-level figures. Millions of starving cattle wandering around might present state-level problems not experienced by an individual farmer—the level at which a problem is examined affects one's analysis. Both Harris and the government figures he cites may be correct, but in different ways. The only macro-level view Harris takes is farther down, when he discusses the political significance of cattle slaughter bans.

on such loans are the principal causes of transfer of land titles from peasants to landlords. Could this explain why the peasant is not overly perturbed that some of his animals might turn out to be only dung-providers? After all, the real threat to his existence does not arise from animals but from people ready to swoop down on him as soon as one of his beasts falters. Chapekar's (1960:27) claim that the peasant's "stock serve as a great security for him to fall back on whenever he is in need" would seem to be appropriate only in reference to the unusually well-established minority. In a land where life expectancy at birth has only recently risen to 30 years (Black 1959:2), it is not altogether appropriate to speak of security. The poorest farmers own insufficient stock. Farm management studies show that holdings below ⅔ of average area account for ⅖ of all farms, but maintain only ¼ of the total cattle on farms. "This is so, chiefly because of their limited resources to maintain cattle" (Chaudhri and Giri 1963:598).

SLAUGHTER

Few, if any, Hindu farmers kill their cattle by beating them over the head, severing their jugular veins or shooting them. But to assert that they do not kill their animals when it is economically important for them to do so may be equally false. This interpretation escapes the notice of so many observers because the slaughtering process receives recognition only in euphemisms. People will admit that they "neglect" their animals, but will not openly accept responsibility for the *etic* effects, i.e., the more or less rapid death which ensues. The strange result of this euphemistic pattern is evidenced in the following statement by Moomaw (1949:96): "All calves born, however inferior, are allowed to live until they die of neglect." In the light of many similar but, by Hindu standards, more vulgar observations, it is clear that this kind of statement should read, "Most calves born are not allowed to live, but are starved to death."

This is roughly the testimony of Gourou (1963:125), "Le paysan conserve seulement les

veaux qui deviendront boeufs de labour ou vaches laitieres; les autres sont ecartes . . . et meurent d'epuisement."[13] Wiser and Wiser (1963:70) are even more direct:

> Cows and buffaloes too old to furnish milk are not treated cruelly, but simply allowed to starve. The same happens to young male buffaloes. . . . The males are unwanted and little effort is made to keep them alive.

Obviously, when an animal, undernourished to begin with, receives neither food nor care, it will not enjoy a long life (compare Gourou 1963:124). Despite claims that an aged and decrepit cow "must be supported like an unproductive relative, until it dies a natural death" (Mosher 1946:124), ample evidence justifies belief that "few cattle die of old age"[e] (Bailey 1957:75). Dandekar (1964:352) makes the same point: "In other words, because the cows cannot be fed nor can they be killed, they are neglected, starved and left to die a 'natural' death."

The farmer culls his stock by starving unwanted animals and also, under duress, sells them directly or indirectly to butchers. With economic pressure, many Indians who will not kill or eat cows themselves:

> are likely to compromise their principles and sell to butchers who slaughter cows, thereby tacitly supporting the practice for other people. Selling aged cows to butchers has over the centuries become an accepted practice along side the *mos* that a Hindu must not kill cattle (Roy 1955:15)

Determining the number of cattle slaughtered by butchers is almost as difficult as determining the number killed by starvation. According to Dandekar (1964:351), "Generally it is the useless animals that find their way to the slaughter house." Lahiry (n.d.:140) says only 126,900 or .9% of the total cattle population is slaughtered per year. Darling (1934:158) claims:

> All Hindus object to the slaughter and even to the sale of unfit cows and keep them indefi-

---

[13] The translation of this quotation is "The peasant only saves those cows that will become traction animals or milk cows. The others are taken away and die of starvation."

nitely. . . . rather than sell them to a cattle dealer, who would buy only for the slaughter house, they send them to a *gowshala* or let them loose to die. Some no doubt sell secretly, but this has its risks in an area where public opinion can find strong expression through the *panchayat.*[14]

Such views would seem to be contradicted by Sinha (1961:95): "A large number of animals are slaughtered privately and it is very difficult to ascertain their numbers." The difficulty of obtaining accurate estimates is also implied by the comment of the Committee on the Prevention of Slaughter that "90% of animals not approved for slaughter are slaughtered stealthily outside of municipal limits" (Nandra, *et. al.* 1955:11).[15]

An indication of the propensity to slaughter cattle under duress is found in connection with the food crisis of World War II. With rice imports cut off by Japanese occupation of Burma (Thirumalai 1954:38; Bhatia 1963:309 on), increased consumption of beef by the armed forces, higher prices for meat and foodstuffs generally, and famine conditions in Bengal, the doctrine of *ahimsa* proved to be alarmingly ineffectual. Direct military intervention was required to avoid destruction of animals needed for plowing, milking, and bullock-production:

> During the war there was an urgent need to reduce or to avoid the slaughter for food of animals useful for breeding or for agricultural work. For the summer of 1944 the slaughter was prohibited of: 1) Cattle below three years of age; 2) Male cattle between two and ten years of age which were being used or were likely to be used as working cattle; 3) All cows between three and ten years of age, other than

cows which were unsuitable for bearing offspring; 4) All cows which were pregnant or in milk (Knight 1954:141).

Gourou (1963:124–25), aware that starvation and neglect are systematically employed to cull Indian herds, nonetheless insists that destruction of animals through starvation amounts to an important loss of capital. This loss is attributed to the low price of beef caused by the beef-eating taboo, making it economically infeasible to send animals to slaughter. Gourou's appraisal, however, neglects deleterious consequences to the rural tanning and carrion-eating castes if increased numbers of animals went to the butchers. Since the least efficient way to convert solar energy into comestibles is to impose an animal converter between plant and man (Cottrell 1955), it should be obvious that without major technical and environmental innovations or drastic population cuts, India could not tolerate a large beef-producing industry. This suggests that insofar as the beef-eating taboo helps discourage growth of beef-producing industries, it is part of an ecological adjustment which maximizes rather than minimizes the calorie and protein output of the productive process.

ANTI-SLAUGHTER LEGISLATION AND GOWSHALAS[16]

It is evident from the history of anti-slaughter agitation and legislation in India that more than *ahimsa* has been required to protect Indian cattle from premature demise. Unfortunately, this legislation is misinterpreted and frequently cited as evidence of the anti-economic effect of Hinduism. I am unable to unravel all the tangled economic

---

[14] *Gowshala:* an "old age home" for cattle; *panchayat:* a village council.

[15] One thing to keep in mind while reading all these statements is that cattle slaughter is a sensitive political topic in India; those making the statements may be politically motivated to take one or another position. It is possible that such statements are more revealing of Indian politics than the conditions of Indian cattle. Currently, in most Indian states cattle slaughter is illegal.

[16] Having discussed the utility of *ahimsa* to Indian peasant farmers, Harris turns to a discussion of the social and political ramifications of the practice. Here he injects an element of class conflict into his argument. Discussing the disparity between wealthy landowners and the landless he writes, "To have one's cow eat other people's crops may be a very fine solution to the subsistence problem of those with no crops of their own." However, while Harris sees conflict, he doesn't make it the engine of cultural change. The system he describes is essentially static. A true Marxist would bring this conflict to the center of the analysis.

and political interests served by the recent anti-slaughter laws of the Indian states. Regardless of the ultimate ecological consequences of these laws, however, several points deserve emphasis. First it should be recalled that cow protection was a major political weapon in Gandhi's campaign against both British and Moslems. The sacred cow was the ideological focus of a successful struggle against English colonialism; hence the enactment of total anti-slaughter legislation obviously had a relational base, at least among politicians who seized and retained power on anti-English and anti-Moslem platforms. It is possible that the legislation will now backfire and upset the delicate ecological balance which now exists. The Committee on the Prevention of Slaughter claimed that it

> actually saw in Pepsu (where slaughter is banned completely) what a menace wild cattle can be. Conditions have become so desperate there, that the State Government have got to spend a considerable sum for catching and redomesticating wild animals to save the crops (Nandra, *et al.* 1955:11).

According to Mayadas (1954:29):

> The situation has become so serious that it is impossible in some parts of the country to protect growing crops from grazing by wandering cattle. Years ago it was one or two stray animals which could either be driven off or sent to the nearest cattle pound. Today it is a question of constantly being harassed day and night by herds which must either feed on one's green crops, or starve. How long can this state of affairs be allowed to continue?

Before the deleterious effects of slaughter laws can be properly evaluated, certain additional evolutionary and functional possibilities must be examined. For example, given the increasing growth rate of India's human population, the critical importance of cattle in the *eco-system,* and the absence of fundamental technical and environmental changes, a substantial increase in cattle seems necessary and predictable, regardless of slaughter legislation. Furthermore, there is some indication, admittedly incomplete but certainly worthy of careful inquiry, that many who protest most against destructiveness of marauding herds

of useless beasts may perceive the situation from very special vantage points in the social hierarchy. The implications of the following newspaper editorial are clear:

> The alarming increase of stray and wild cattle over wide areas of Northern India is fast becoming a major disincentive to crop cultivation. . . . Popular sentiment against cow slaughter no doubt lies at the back of the problem. People prefer to let their aged, diseased, and otherwise useless cattle live at the expense of *other people's crops* (Indian Express, New Delhi, 7 February 1959, italics added).

Evidently we need to know something about whose crops are threatened by these marauders. Despite post-independence attempts at land reform, 10% of the Indian agricultural population still owns more than ½ the total cultivated area and 15,000,000, or 22%, of rural households own no land at all (Mitra 1963:298). Thorner and Thorner (1962:3) call the land reform program a failure, and point out how "the grip of the larger holder serves to prevent the lesser folk from developing the land. . . ." Quite possibly, in other words, the anti-slaughter laws, insofar as they are effective, should be viewed as devices which, contrary to original political intent, bring pressure to bear upon those whose lands are devoted to cash crops of benefit only to narrow commercial, urban, and landed sectors of the population. To have one's cows eat other people's crops may be a very fine solution to the subsistence problem of those with no crops of their own. Apparently, in the days when animals could be driven off or sent to the pound with impunity, this could not happen, even though *ahimsa* reigned supreme then as now.

Some form of anti-slaughter legislation was required and actually argued for, on unambiguously rational, economic, and material grounds. About 4% of India's cattle are in the cities (Mohan 1962:48). These have always represented the best dairy stock, since the high cost of feeding animals in a city could be offset only by good milking qualities. A noxious consequence of this dairy pattern was the slaughter of the cow at the end of its first urban lactation period because it was too expensive to maintain while awaiting another pregnancy. Similarly, and by methods previously discussed, the author calf was killed after it had stimulated the cow to "let down." With the growth of urban milk consumption, the best of India's dairy cattle were thus systematically prevented from breeding, while animals with progressively poorer milking qualities were preserved in the countryside (Mohan 1962:48; Mayadas 1954:29; Gandhi 1954:13 on). The Committee on the Prevention of Slaughter of Cattle (Nandra, *et al.* 1955:2) claimed at least 50,000 high-yielding cows and she-buffaloes from Madras, Bombay, and Calcutta were "annually sent to premature slaughter" and were "lost to the country." Given such evidence of waste and the political potential of Moslems being identified as cow-butchers and Englishmen as cow-eaters (Gandhi 1954:16), the political importance of *ahimsa* becomes more intelligible. Indeed, it could be that the strength of Gandhi's *charisma* lay in his superior understanding of the ecological significance of the cow, especially in relation to the underprivileged masses, marginal low caste and out caste farmers. Gandhi (p. 3) may have been closer to the truth than many a foreign expert when he said:

> Why the cow was selected for apotheosis is obvious to me. The cow was in India the best companion. She was the giver of plenty. Not only did she give milk but she also made agriculture possible.

OLD-AGE HOMES

Among the more obscure aspects of the cattle complex are bovine old-age homes, variously identified as *gowshalas, pinjrapoles,* and, under the Five-Year Plans, as *gosadans.* Undoubtedly some of these are "homes for cows, which are supported by public charity, which maintain the old and derelict animals till natural death occurs" (Kothavala 1934:123). According to Gourou (1963:125), however, owners of cows sent to these religious institutions pay rent with the understanding that if the cows begin to lactate they will be returned. The economics of at least some of these "charitable" institutions is, therefore, perhaps not as quaint as usually implied. It is also significant that, although the 1st Five-Year Plan called for establishment of 160 *gosadans* to serve 320,000 cat-tle, only 22 *gosadans* servicing 8,000 cattle were reported by 1955 (Government of India Planning Commission 1956:283).

NATURAL SELECTION

Expert appraisers of India's cattle usually show little enthusiasm for the typical undersized breeds. Much has been made of the fact that 1 large animal is a more efficient dung, milk, and traction machine than 2 small ones. "Weight for weight, a small animal consumes a much larger quantity of food than a bigger animal" (Mamoria 1953:268). "More dung is produced when a given quantity of food is consumed by one animal than when it is shared by two animals" (Ford Foundation 1959:64). Thus it would seem that India's smaller breeds should be replaced by larger, more powerful, and better milking breeds. But once again, there is another way of looking at the evidence. It might very well be that if all of India's scrub cattle were suddenly replaced by an equivalent number of large, high-quality European or American dairy and traction animals, famines of noteworthy magnitude would immediately ensue. Is it not possible that India's cattle are undersized precisely because other breeds never could survive the atrocious conditions they experience most of the year? I find it difficult to believe that breeds better adapted to the present Indian *ecosystem* exist elsewhere.

> By nature and religious training, the villager is unwilling to inflict pain or to take animal life. But the immemorial grind for existence has hardened him to an acceptance of survival of the fittest (Wiser and Wiser 1963).

Not only are scrub animals well adapted to the regular seasonal crises of water and forage and general year-round neglect, but long-range selective pressures may be even more significant. The high frequency of drought-induced famines in India (Bhatia 1963) places a premium upon drought-resistance plus a more subtle factor: A herd of smaller animals, dangerously thinned by famine or pestilence, reproduces faster than an equivalent group of larger animals, despite the fact that the larger animal consumes less per pound than 2 smaller animals. This is because there are 2 cows in the smaller herd per equivalent large cow. Mohan (1962:45) is one of the few authorities to have grasped this principle, including it in defense of the small breeds:

> Calculations of the comparative food conversion efficiency of various species of Indian domestic livestock by the writer has revealed, that much greater attention should be paid to small livestock than at present, not only because of their better conversion efficiency for protein but also because of the possibilities of bringing about a rapid increase in their numbers.

CONCLUSION[17]

The probability that India's cattle complex is a positive-functioned part of a naturally selected *eco-system* is at least as good as that it is a negative-functioned expression of an irrational ideology. This should not be interpreted to mean that no "improvements" can be made in the system, nor that different systems may not eventually evolve. The issue is not whether oxen are more efficient than tractors. I suggest simply that many features of the cattle complex have been erroneously reported or interpreted. That Indian cattle are weak and inefficient is not denied, but there is doubt that this situation arises from and is mainly perpetuated by Hindu ideology. Given the techno-environmental base, Indian property relation-

ships, and political organization, one need not involve the doctrine of *ahimsa* to understand fundamental features of the cattle complex. Although the cattle population of India has risen by 38,000,000 head since 1940, during the same period, the human population has risen by 120,000,000. Despite the anti-slaughter legislation, the ratio of cattle to humans actually declined from 44:100 in 1941 to 40:100 in 1961 (Government of India 1962:74; 1963:6). In the absence of major changes in environment, technology or property relations, it seems unlikely that the cattle population will cease to accompany the rise in the human population. If *ahimsa* is negative-functioned, then we must be prepared to admit the possibility that all other factors contributing to the rapid growth of the Indian human and cattle populations, including the germ theory of disease, are also negative-functioned.[18]

Notes

a. The author (1960) suggested that the term "adaptive" be restricted to traits, biological or cultural, established and diffused in conformity with the principle of natural selection. Clearly, not all "positive functioned," i.e., useful, cultural traits are so established.

b. *Ahimsa* is the Hindu principle of unity of life, of which sacredness of cattle is principal sub-case and symbol.

c. According to Zeuner (1954:328), "Symbiosis includes all conditions of the living together of two different species, provided both derive advantages

---

[17] At the time Harris wrote this essay, an approach called ethnoscience, or the new ethnography, was very popular. With a focus on the emic perspective, an underlying assumption of ethnoscience was that culture was a mental model that people acted out. One goal of ethnoscience was to re-create these models so that anthropologists could understand the world in the same way as their informants. Harris, however, disagrees strongly with this view of culture, arguing against it in *The Rise of Anthropological Theory*. According to Harris, culture should be defined as behavior that is determined by techno-environmental factors. Harris' article is both an example of a materialist perspective and a challenge to ethnoscience.

[18] Harris is certainly one of the most colorful and polemical figures in contemporary anthropology. For the last thirty years, while other perspectives have come and gone, Harris has stood firm as one of the leading proponents of cultural materialism and the etic approach. Starting as an intellectual approach to cultural analysis, his advocacy of cultural materialism has taken on a moral-ideological dimension. For example, in the introduction to his book *America Now*, Harris writes

> The task of this book is to reassert the primacy of rational endeavor and objective knowledge in the struggle to save and renew the American dream.... Anthropologists regard it as their solemn duty to represent the hopes and fears, values and goals, beliefs and rituals of different groups and communities seen from within, the way people who belong to these groups and communities perceive them to be, and the way they want them to be seen by others. But that can be only half the job. The other half is to describe and explain what people are actually saying and doing from the standpoint of the objective study of culture and history (Harris 1981:15).

therefrom. Cases in which both partners benefit equally are rare." In the symbiosis under consideration, men benefit more than cattle.

d. The U.S. Census of Agriculture (1954) showed milk production averaging from a low of 3,929 pounds per cow in the Nashville Basin sub-region to 11,112 pounds per cow in the Southern California sub-region.

e. Srinivas (1962:126) declared himself properly skeptical in this matter: "It is commonly believed that the peasant's religious attitude to cattle comes in the way of the disposal of useless cattle. Here again, my experience of Rampura makes me skeptical of the general belief. I am not denying that cattle are regarded as in some sense sacred, but I doubt whether the belief is as powerful as it is claimed to be. I have already mentioned that bull-buffaloes are sacrificed to village goddesses. And in the case of the cow, while the peasant does not want to kill the cow or bull himself he does not seem to mind very much if someone else does the dirty job out of his sight."

23. Ritual Regulation of Environmental Relations Among a New Guinea People[a]

Roy A. Rappaport (1926–1997)

(1967)

MOST FUNCTIONAL STUDIES OF RELIGIOUS BEhavior in anthropology have as an analytic goal the elucidation of events, processes, or relationships occurring within a social unit of some sort.[1] The social unit is not always well defined, but in some cases it appears to be a church, that is, a group of people who entertain similar beliefs about the universe, or a congregation, a group of people who participate together in the performance of religious rituals. There have been exceptions. Thus Vayda,[2] Leeds, and Smith (1961) and O. K. Moore (1957) have clearly perceived that the functions of religious ritual are not necessarily confined within the boundaries of a congregation or even a church. By and large, however, I believe that the following statement by Homans (1941:172) represents fairly the dominant line of anthropological thought concerning the functions of religious ritual:

> Ritual actions do not produce a practical result on the external world—that is one of the reasons why we call them ritual. But to make this statement is not to say that ritual has no function. Its function is not related to the world external to the society but to the internal constitution of the society. It gives the members of the society confidence, it dispels their anxieties, it disciplines their social organization.

No argument will be raised here against the sociological and psychological functions imputed by Homans, and many others before him, to ritual. They seem to me to be plausible. Nevertheless, in some cases at least, ritual does produce, in Homans' terms, "a practical result on the world" external not only to the social unit composed of those who participate together in ritual performances but also to the larger unit composed of those who entertain similar beliefs concerning the

---

[1] In the opening passage of this essay, Rappaport critiques functionalism in much the same way Julian Steward did almost thirty years previously. That is, holistic functional explanations do not generally show causes, only interrelations among parts within a system. Functionalists suppose that social systems are only weakly connected with their environments. Rappaport, following the cultural-ecology model, wishes to show that religion, at least among those he studies, is articulated with, and has a profound effect upon, the natural world.

[2] Andrew P. Vayda (1931–) was Rappaport's dissertation advisor at Columbia and was in New Guinea with Rappaport when the fieldwork that formed the basis for this essay was done.

universe. The material presented here will show that the ritual cycles of the Tsembaga, and of other local territorial groups of Maring speakers living in the New Guinea interior, play an important part in regulating the relationships of these groups with both the nonhuman components of their immediate environments and the human components of their less immediate environments, that is, with other similar territorial groups.[3] To be more specific, this regulation helps to maintain the biotic communities existing within their territories, redistributes land among people and people over land, and limits the frequency of fighting. In the absence of authoritative political statuses or offices, the ritual cycle likewise provides a means for mobilizing allies when warfare may be undertaken. It also provides a mechanism for redistributing local pig surpluses in the form of pork throughout a large regional population while helping to assure the local population of a supply of pork when its members are most in need of high quality protein.

Religious ritual may be defined, for the purposes of this paper, as the prescribed performance of conventionalized acts manifestly directed toward the involvement of nonempirical or supernatural agencies in the affairs of the actors. While this definition relies upon the formal characteristics of the performances and upon the motives for undertaking them, attention will be focused upon the empirical effects of ritual performances and sequences of ritual performances. The religious rituals to be discussed are regarded as neither more nor less than part of the behavioral repertoire employed by an aggregate of organisms in adjusting to its environment.[4]

The data upon which this paper is based were collected during fourteen months of field work among the Tsembaga, one of about twenty local groups of Maring speakers living in the Simbai and Jimi Valleys of the Bismarck Range in the Territory of New Guinea. The size of Maring local groups varies from a little over 100 to 900. The Tsembaga, who in 1963 numbered 204 persons, are located on the south wall of the Simbai Valley. The country in which they live differs from the true highlands in being lower, generally more rugged, and more heavily forested. Tsembaga territory rises, within a total surface area of 3.2 square miles, from an elevation of 2,200 feet at the Simbai river to 7,200 feet at the ridge crest. Gardens are cut in the secondary forests up to between 5,000 and 5,400 feet, above which the area remains in primary forest. Rainfall reaches 150 inches per year.

The Tsembaga have come into contact with the outside world only recently; the first government patrol to penetrate their territory arrived in 1954.[5] They were considered uncontrolled by the Australian government until 1962, and they remain unmissionized to this day.

The 204 Tsembaga are distributed among five putatively patrilineal clans, which are, in turn, organized into more inclusive groupings on two hierarchical levels below that of the total local group.[b] Internal political structure is highly egali-

---

[3] One of the principal influences on Rappaport and many other social scientists of the 1960s was general systems theory. This approach, developed primarily by Austrian biologist Ludwig von Bertalanffy (1901–1972), was a way of providing a mathematical description of a physical system. It encouraged anthropologists to examine cultures as systems composed of both human and nonhuman elements. It presumed that the normal state of a system was equilibrium and described the various methods by which systems deviated from states of balance and were returned to them. In this essay, Rappaport describes Tsembaga culture as just such a system, highlighting the role of religious practices as mechanisms that return the system to equilibrium.

[4] Notice Rappaport's style—he writes in a scientific trope, frequently referring to those he studies as "biological organisms" rather than people or individuals. His goal is to analyze human behavior in a fashion analogous to that used by biologists examining animal behavior. Ethology, the study of animal behavior, was becoming an increasingly important field within biology at this time. Austrian ethologist Konrad Lorenz (1901–1989) published his popular account of animal behavior, *King Solomon's Ring,* in 1952. This had an important impact on many scholars in this era.

[5] A criticism sometimes made of this essay (and this style of analysis) is that it makes very little reference to history. This brief paragraph is virtually the only reference to the history of the Tsembaga or their relations with outside (European) powers.

tarian. There are no hereditary or elected chiefs nor are there even "big men" who can regularly coerce or command the support of their clansmen or co-residents in economic or forceful enterprises.

It is convenient to regard the Tsembaga as a population in the ecological sense, that is, as one of the components of a system of trophic[6] exchanges taking place within a bounded area. Tsembaga territory and the biotic community existing upon it may be conveniently viewed as an ecosystem. While it would be permissible arbitrarily to designate the Tsembaga as a population and their territory with its biota as an ecosystem, there are also nonarbitrary reasons for doing so.[7] An ecosystem is a system of material exchanges, and the Tsembaga maintain against other human groups exclusive access to the resources within their territorial borders. Conversely, it is from this territory alone that the Tsembaga ordinarily derive all of their foodstuffs and most of the other materials they require for survival. Less anthropocentrically, it may be justified to regard Tsembaga territory with its biota as an ecosystem in view of the rather localized nature of cyclical material exchanges in tropical rainforests.

As they are involved with the nonhuman biotic community within their territory in a set of trophic exchanges, so do they participate in other material relationships with other human groups external to their territory. Genetic materials are exchanged with other groups, and certain crucial items, such as stone axes, were in the past obtained from the outside. Furthermore, in the area occupied by the Maring speakers, more than one local group is usually involved in any process, either peaceful or warlike, through which people are redistributed over land and land redistributed among people.

The concept of the ecosystem, though it provides a convenient frame for the analysis of interspecific trophic exchanges taking place within limited geographical areas, does not comfortably accommodate intraspecific exchanges taking place over wider geographic areas. Some sort of geographic population model would be more useful for the analysis of the relationship of the local ecological population to the larger regional population of which it is a part, but we lack even a set of appropriate terms for such a model. Suffice it here to note that the relations of the Tsembaga to the total of other local human populations in their vicinity are similar to the relations of local aggregates of other animals to the totality of their species occupying broader and more or less continuous regions. This larger, more inclusive aggregate may resemble what geneticists mean by the term population, that is, an aggregate of interbreeding organisms persisting through an indefinite number of generations and either living or capable of living in isolation from similar aggregates of the same species. This is the unit which survives through long periods of time while its local ecological (*sensu stricto*)[8] subunits, the units more or less independently involved in interspecific trophic exchanges such as the Tsembaga, are ephemeral.

Since it has been asserted that the ritual cycles of the Tsembaga regulate relationships within what may be regarded as a complex system, it is necessary, before proceeding to the ritual cycle itself, to describe briefly, and where possible in quantitative terms, some aspects of the place of the Tsembaga in this system.[9]

All gardens are mixed, many of them containing all of the major root crops and many greens. Two named garden types are, however, distinguished

---

[6] *Trophic:* relating to nutrition.

[7] Notice that Rappaport again treats humans simply as organisms within an ecosystem. Given this, how would Rappaport define culture? See the epilogue to the second edition of Rappaport's book-length treatment of this material, *Pigs for the Ancestors* (1984:371–403).

[8] *Sensu stricto:* Latin for strictly speaking.

[9] Rappaport's description focuses on those aspects of Tsembaga life that are of direct concern to his theoretical approach, particularly gardening. Within this framework, he discusses the Tsembaga as calorie producers and consumers. Note also Rappaport's quantification of data, which reflects his desire to make his work scientifically rigorous. Subsistence activities form the basis of his analysis. Other cultural features arise as a result of this core or are historically particular and of less analytic importance. Rappaport's treatment is similar to Steward's idea of the culture core.

by the crops which predominate in them. "Taro-yam gardens" were found to produce, on the basis of daily harvest records kept on entire gardens for close to one year, about 5,300,000 calories[c] per acre during their harvesting lives of 18 to 24 months; 85 percent of their yield is harvested between 24 and 76 weeks after planting. "Sugar-sweet potato gardens" produce about 4,600,000 calories per acre during their harvesting lives, 91 percent being taken between 24 and 76 weeks after planting. I estimated that approximately 310,000 calories per acre is expended on cutting, fencing, planting, maintaining, harvesting, and walking to and from taro-yam gardens. Sugar-sweet potato gardens required an expenditure of approximately 290,000 calories per acre.[d] These energy ratios, approximately 17:1 on taro-yam gardens and 16:1 on sugar-sweet potato gardens, compare favorably with figures reported for swidden cultivation in other regions.[e]

Intake is high in comparison with the reported dietaries of other New Guinea populations. On the basis of daily consumption records kept for ten months on four households numbering in total sixteen persons, I estimated the average daily intake of adult males to be approximately 2,600 calories, and that of adult females to be around 2,200 calories.[10] It may be mentioned here that the Tsembaga are small and short-statured.[11] Adult males average 101 pounds in weight and approximately 58.5 inches in height; the corresponding averages for adult females are 85 pounds and 54.5 inches.[f]

Although 99 percent by weight of the food consumed is vegetable, the protein intake is high by New Guinea standards. The daily protein consumption of adult males from vegetable sources was estimated to be between 43 and 55 grams, of adult females 36 to 48 grams. Even with an adjustment for vegetable sources, these values are slightly in excess of the recently published WHO/FAO daily requirements (Food and Agriculture Organization of the United Nations 1964). The same is true of the younger age categories, although soft and discolored hair, a symptom of protein deficiency, was noted in a few children. The WHO/FAO protein requirements do not include a large "margin for safety" or allowance for stress; and, although no clinical assessments were undertaken, it may be suggested that the Tsembaga achieve nitrogen balance at a low level. In other words, their protein intake is probably marginal.[12]

Measurements of all gardens made during 1962 and of some gardens made during 1963 indicate that, to support the human population, between .15 and .19 acres are put into cultivation per capita per year. Fallows range from 8 to 45 years. The area in secondary forest comprises approximately 1,000 acres, only 30 to 50 of which are in cultivation any time. Assuming calories to be the limiting factor, and assuming an unchanging population structure, the territory could support—with no reduction in lengths of fallow and without cutting into the virgin forest from which the Tsembaga extract many important items—between 290 and 397 people if the pig population remained minimal. The size of the pig herd, however, fluctuates widely. Taking Maring pig husbandry procedures into consideration, I have estimated the human carrying capacity[13] of the

---

[10] Rappaport is giving many figures here, but they are based on observation of a small number of people: 16 in four families. In most studies in biology or ecology, this would be a very small sample indeed. What sort of questions does this raise about his conclusions? Despite the small numbers, it should be noted that, at the time this essay was published, it was probably the most detailed and comprehensive body of data ever collected on swidden agriculturalists. In keeping with the biological model on which he based this work, all of the data is available for inspection in the appendices to *Pigs for the Ancestors.*

[11] In *Pigs for the Ancestors* (1968), a picture shows the five-foot, ten-inch Rappaport towering over the Tsembaga.

[12] Rappaport's analysis, clearly materialist, is functionalist rather than Marxist; there is no reference to the evolution of culture in this essay. Further, for Marxists, conflict drives progressive change, but for Rappaport, conflict is a feature that returns the cultural system to an equilibrium state.

[13] Rappaport again uses a concept borrowed from biology—carrying capacity, which is the number of individuals of a species that a given ecosystem can support without suffering degradation. Notice that for humans, the technology of food production must be taken into account, a point also discussed by Steward.

Tsembaga territory at between 270 and 320 people.

Because the timing of the ritual cycle is bound up with the demography of the pig herd, the place of the pig in Tsembaga adaptation must be examined.[14]

First, being omnivorous, pigs keep residential areas free of garbage and human feces. Second, limited numbers of pigs rooting in secondary growth may help to hasten the development of that growth. The Tsembaga usually permit pigs to enter their gardens one and a half to two years after planting, by which time second-growth trees are well established there. The Tsembaga practice selective weeding; from the time the garden is planted, herbaceous species are removed, but tree species are allowed to remain. By the time cropping is discontinued and the pigs are let in, some of the trees in the garden are already ten to fifteen feet tall. These well-established trees are relatively impervious to damage by the pigs, which, in rooting for seeds and remaining tubers, eliminate many seeds and seedlings that, if allowed to develop, would provide some competition for the established trees. Moreover, in some Maring-speaking areas swiddens are planted twice, although this is not the case with the Tsembaga. After the first crop is almost exhausted, pigs are penned in the garden, where their rooting eliminates weeds and softens the ground, making the task of planting for a second time easier. The pigs, in other words, are used as cultivating machines.

Small numbers of pigs are easy to keep. They run free during the day and return home at night to receive their ration of garbage and substandard tubers, particularly sweet potatoes. Supplying the latter requires little extra work, for the substandard tubers are taken from the ground in the course of harvesting the daily ration for humans. Daily consumption records kept over a period of some months show that the ration of tubers received by the pigs approximates in weight that consumed by adult humans, i.e., a little less than three pounds per day per pig.

If the pig herd grows large, however, the substandard tubers incidentally obtained in the course of harvesting for human needs become insufficient, and it becomes necessary to harvest especially for the pigs. In other words, people must work for the pigs and perhaps even supply them with food fit for human consumption. Thus, as Vayda, Leeds, and Smith (1961:71) have pointed out, there can be too many pigs for a given community.

This also holds true of the sanitary and cultivating services rendered by pigs. A small number of pigs is sufficient to keep residential areas clean, to suppress superfluous seedlings in abandoned gardens, and to soften the soil in gardens scheduled for second plantings. A larger herd, on the other hand, may be troublesome; the larger the number of pigs, the greater the possibility of their invasion of producing gardens, with concomitant damage not only to crops and young secondary growth but also to the relations between the pig owners and garden owners.

All male pigs are castrated at approximately three months of age, for boars, people say, are dangerous and do not grow as large as barrows. Pregnancies, therefore, are always the result of unions of domestic sows with feral males. Fecundity is thus only a fraction of its potential. During one twelve-month period only fourteen litters resulted out of a potential 99 or more pregnancies. Farrowing generally takes place in the forest and mortality of the young is high. Only 32 of the offspring of the above mentioned fourteen pregnancies were alive six months after birth. This number is barely sufficient to replace the number of adult animals which would have died or been killed during most years without pig festivals.

---

[14] When Rappaport did his graduate training at Columbia, thinking there was dominated by the ideas of White and Steward. Rappaport thus went into the field with a background in cultural ecology. Once there, his experiences compelled him to take a position in some ways more extreme than these classic cultural ecologists. Steward had supposed that, though environment had a profound impact on human society, humans were, in fundamental ways, so different from other creatures that natural laws that applied to populations of other animals could not be applied to them. (This view was consistent with his training in historical particularism.) Rappaport, on the other hand, came to believe that while the human possession of culture does separate us from other animals, as biological organisms we are subject to the same fundamental laws. In this essay he repeatedly compares humans to other species.

The Tsembaga almost never kill domestic pigs outside of ritual contexts. In ordinary times, when there is no pig festival in progress, the rituals are almost always associated with misfortunes or emergencies, notably warfare, illness, injury, or death. Rules state not only the contexts in which pigs are to be ritually slaughtered, but also who may partake of the flesh of the sacrificial animals. During warfare it is only the men participating in the fighting who eat the pork. In cases of illness or injury, it is only the victim and certain near relatives, particularly his co-resident agnates and spouses, who do so.

It is reasonable to assume that misfortune and emergency are likely to induce in the organisms experiencing them a complex of physiological changes known collectively as "stress." Physiological stress reactions occur not only in organisms which are infected with disease or traumatized, but also in those experiencing rage or fear (Houssay et al. 1955:1096), or even prolonged anxiety (National Research Council 1963:53). One important aspect of stress is the increased catabolization of protein (Houssay et al. 1955:451; National Research Council 1963:49), with a net loss of nitrogen from the tissues (Houssay et al. 1955:450).[15] This is a serious matter for organisms with a marginal protein intake. Antibody production is low (Berg 1948:311), healing is slow (Large and Johnston 1948:352), and a variety of symptoms of a serious nature are likely to develop (Lund and Levenson 1948:349; Zintel 1964:1043). The status of a protein-depleted animal, however, may be significantly improved in a relatively short period of time by the intake of high quality protein, and high protein diets are therefore routinely prescribed for surgical patients and those suffering from infectious diseases (Burton 1959:231; Lund and Levenson 1948:350; Elman 1951:85ff.; Zintel 1964:1043ff.).

It is precisely when they are undergoing physiological stress that the Tsembaga kill and consume their pigs, and it should be noted that they limit the consumption to those likely to be experiencing stress most profoundly.[g] The Tsembaga, of course, know nothing of physiological stress. Native theories of the etiology and treatment of disease and injury implicate various categories of spirits to whom sacrifices must be made. Nevertheless, the behavior which is appropriate in terms of native understandings is also appropriate to the actual situation confronting the actors.

We may now outline in the barest of terms the Tsembaga ritual cycle. Space does not permit a description of its ideological correlates. It must suffice to note that the Tsembaga do not necessarily perceive all of the empirical effects which the anthropologist sees to flow from their ritual behavior. Such empirical consequences as they may perceive, moreover, are not central to their rationalizations of the performances. The Tsembaga say that they perform the rituals in order to rearrange their relationships with the supernatural world. We may only reiterate here that behavior undertaken in reference to their "cognized environment"—an environment which includes as very important elements the spirits of ancestors—seems appropriate in their "operational environment," the material environment specified by the anthropologist through operations of observation, including measurement.[16]

---

[15] One element of Rappaport's argument is that pig consumption is driven by exceptional demand for protein. This is based on the idea that humans in crisis situations or about to do strenuous work experience a physiological need for protein. Even when this article was written, in 1967, this was a controversial position, and there was evidence in the scientific literature pointing against it (see Keys 1943, 1946; Mayer and Bullen 1960). Today, most nutritionists would probably agree that what people in these conditions need is not protein but carbohydrates. Rappaport reconsidered the protein issue in the appendix of the 1984 edition of *Pigs for the Ancestors* and suggested that he was probably mistaken about protein intake, but for a different reason—further fieldwork revealed that the stressed person generally does not get to eat much of the pig sacrificed for him.

[16] The focus of much of Rappaport's work is the relationship between the cognized and operational environments. This distinction is similar to the one Marvin Harris and others have made between etic and emic analysis (see essay 22, footnote 5). While this essay focuses on describing the Tsembaga in ecosystem terms, *Pigs for the Ancestors* contains an extensive treatment of the Tsembaga understanding of their environment.

Since the rituals are arranged in a cycle, description may commence at any point.[17] The operation of the cycle becomes clearest if we begin with the rituals performed during warfare. Opponents in all cases occupy adjacent territories, in almost all cases on the same valley wall. After hostilities have broken out, each side performs certain rituals which place the opposing side in the formal category of "enemy." A number of taboos prevail while hostilities continue. These include prohibitions on sexual intercourse and on the ingestion of certain things—food prepared by women, food grown on the lower portion of the territory, marsupials, eels, and while actually on the fighting ground, any liquid whatsoever.

One ritual practice associated with fighting which may have some physiological consequences deserves mention. Immediately before proceeding to the fighting ground, the warriors eat heavily salted pig fat. The ingestion of salt, coupled with the taboo on drinking, has the effect of shortening the fighting day, particularly since the Maring prefer to fight only on bright sunny days. When everyone gets unbearably thirsty, according to informants, fighting is broken off.

There may formerly have been other effects if the native salt contained sodium (the production of salt was discontinued some years previous to the field work, and no samples were obtained). The Maring diet seems to be deficient in sodium. The ingestion of large amounts of sodium just prior to fighting would have permitted the warriors to sweat normally without a lowering of blood volume and consequent weakness during the course of the fighting. The pork belly ingested with the salt would have provided them with a new burst of energy two hours or so after the commencement of the engagement. After fighting was finished for the day, lean pork was consumed, offsetting, at least to some extent, the nitrogen loss associated with the stressful fighting (personal communications from F. Dunn, W. McFarlane, and J. Sabine, 1965).

Fighting could continue sporadically for weeks. Occasionally it terminated in the rout of one of the antagonistic groups, whose survivors would take refuge with kinsmen elsewhere. In such instances, the victors would lay waste their opponents' groves and gardens, slaughter their pigs, and burn their houses. They would not, however, immediately annex the territory of the vanquished. The Maring say that they never take over the territory of an enemy for, even if it has been abandoned, spirits of their ancestors remain to guard it against interlopers. Most fights, however, terminated in truces between the antagonists.

With the termination of hostilities a group which has not been driven off its territory performs a ritual called "planting the *rumbim*." Every man puts his hand on the ritual plant, rumbim (*Cordyline fruticosa* (L.), A. Chev; *C. terminalis*, Kunth), as it is planted in the ground. The ancestors are addressed, in effect, as follows:[18]

> We thank you for helping us in the fight and permitting us to remain on our territory. We place our souls in this *rumbim* as we plant it on our ground. We ask you to care for this *rumbim*. We will kill pigs for you now, but they are few. In the future, when we have many pigs, we shall again give you pork and uproot the *rumbim* and stage a *kaiko* (pig festival). But until there are sufficient pigs to repay you the *rumbim* will remain in the ground.

---

[17] The idea of a cycle is quite important and again relates to developments in biology in the 1960s. Biologists viewed ecosystems in terms of nutrient cycles. Rappaport applies the same sort of logic to the system he describes here. Note, however, that Rappaport was in the field for only fourteen months, from October 1962 to December 1963. He was thus unable to observe a single complete cycle, which takes place over a period of a decade or more.

[18] Notice that Rappaport does not report what people *said* on a particular occasion, but rather the kind of thing they are *likely to say*. He cannot report verbatim because he was not present at a *rumbim* planting. Anthropologists who view culture in primarily mentalistic terms, such as structuralists and ethnoscientists, would have trouble with such a reconstruction. They would most likely be concerned with the specifics of *rumbim* symbolism and would see such a reconstruction as doing violence to the data. Because Rappaport's view of culture is primarily materialistic, the reconstruction adds a bit of ethnographic interest and is largely irrelevant to the data.

This ritual is accompanied by the wholesale slaughter of pigs. Only juveniles remain alive. All adult and adolescent animals are killed, cooked, and dedicated to the ancestors. Some are consumed by the local group, but most are distributed to allies who assisted in the fight.

Some of the taboos which the group suffered during the time of fighting are abrogated by this ritual. Sexual intercourse is now permitted, liquids may be taken at any time, and food from any part of the territory may be eaten. But the group is still in debt to its allies and ancestors. People say it is still the time of the *bamp ku*, or "fighting stones," which are actual objects used in the rituals associated with warfare. Although the fighting ceases when *rumbim* is planted, the concomitant obligations, debts to allies and ancestors, remain outstanding; and the fighting stones may not be put away until these obligations are fulfilled. The time of the fighting stones is a time of debt and danger which lasts until the *rumbim* is uprooted and a pig festival (*kaiko*) is staged.

Certain taboos persist during the time of the fighting stones. Marsupials, regarded as the pigs of the ancestors of the high ground, may not be trapped until the debt to their masters has been repaid. Eels, the "pigs of the ancestors of the low ground," may neither be caught nor consumed. Prohibitions on all intercourse with the enemy come into force. One may not touch, talk to, or even look at a member of the enemy group, nor set foot on enemy ground. Even more important, a group may not attack another group while its ritual plant remains in the ground, for it has not yet fully rewarded its ancestors and allies for their

assistance in the last fight. Until the debts to them have been paid, further assistance from them will not be forthcoming. A kind of "truce of god" thus prevails until the *rumbim* is uprooted and a *kaiko* completed.[19]

To uproot the *rumbim* requires sufficient pigs. How many pigs are sufficient, and how long does it take to acquire them? The Tsembaga say that, if a place is "good," this can take as little as five years; but if a place is "bad," it may require ten years or longer. A bad place is one in which misfortunes are frequent and where, therefore, ritual demands for the killing of pigs arise frequently. A good place is one where such demands are infrequent. In a good place, the increase of the pig herd exceeds the ongoing ritual demands, and the herd grows rapidly. Sooner or later the substandard tubers incidentally obtained while harvesting become insufficient to feed the herd, and additional acreage must be put into production specifically for the pigs.

The work involved in caring for a large pig herd can be extremely burdensome. The Tsembaga herd just prior to the pig festival of 1962–63, when it numbered 169 animals, was receiving 54 percent of all the sweet potatoes and 82 percent of all the manioc harvested. These comprised 35.9 percent by weight of all root crops harvested. This figure is consistent with the difference between the amount of land under cultivation just previous to the pig festival, when the herd was at maximum size, and that immediately afterwards, when the pig herd was at minimum size. The former was 36.1 percent in excess of the latter.[20]

I have estimated, on the basis of acreage yield and energy expenditure figures, that about 45,000

---

[19] Rappaport's description of the relationship between ritual and environment is heavily influenced by cybernetics, which was considered an important new field at the time the essay was written. Cybernetics had begun in the 1940s and was concerned with environmental feedback to automatic devices, specifically antiaircraft guns. By the time Rappaport was writing, the principles of cybernetics were being applied to computers and the human nervous system as well. Here, the ritual planting of the *rumbim* is understood as a switch that turns hostilities off.

[20] Rappaport goes to lengths to prove that the Tsembaga hold festivals when the burden of caring for pigs becomes excessive. Critics ask why the Tsembaga don't control herd size simply by killing and eating pigs when they are too numerous. Rappaport does not address these issues here, preferring to concentrate on the functioning of the *kaiko* rather than its origin, but he did respond to such questions at length in the epilogue to the 1984 edition of *Pigs for the Ancestors*. Functionalism did, of course, have an important effect on Steward and other key thinkers in cultural ecology. They criticized it because it did not give enough attention to the relation between people and their environment (see essay 18) and because it did not produce empirically testable hypotheses. Rappaport's work is, in part, a functional analysis that attempts to respond to these problems.

calories per year are expended in caring for one pig 120–150 pounds in size. It is upon women that most of the burden of pig keeping falls. If, from a woman's daily intake of about 2,200 calories, 950 calories are allowed for basal metabolism, a woman has only 1,250 calories a day available for all her activities, which include gardening for her family, child care, and cooking, as well as tending pigs. It is clear that no woman can feed many pigs; only a few had as many as four in their care at the commencement of the festival; and it is not surprising that agitation to uproot the *rumbim* and stage the *kaiko* starts with the wives of the owners of large numbers of pigs.

A large herd is not only burdensome as far as energy expenditure is concerned; it becomes increasingly a nuisance as it expands. The more numerous pigs become, the more frequently are gardens invaded by them. Such events result in serious disturbances of local tranquility. The garden owner often shoots, or attempts to shoot, the offending pig; and the pig owner commonly retorts by shooting, or attempting to shoot, either the garden owner, his wife, or one of his pigs. As more and more such events occur, the settlement, nucleated when the herd was small, disperses as people try to put as much distance as possible between their pigs and other people's gardens and between their gardens and other people's pigs. Occasionally this reaches its logical conclusion, and people begin to leave the territory, taking up residence with kinsmen in other local populations.

The number of pigs sufficient to become intolerable to the Tsembaga was below the capacity of the territory to carry pigs. I have estimated that, if the size and structure of the human population remained constant at the 1962–1963 level, a pig population of 140 to 240 animals averaging 100 to 150 pounds in size could be maintained perpetually by the Tsembaga without necessarily inducing environmental degradation. Since the size of the herd fluctuates, even higher

cyclical maxima could be achieved. The level of toleration, however, is likely always to be below the carrying capacity, since the destructive capacity of the pigs is dependent upon the population density of both people and pigs, rather than upon population size. The denser the human population, the fewer pigs will be required to disrupt social life. If the carrying capacity is exceeded, it is likely to be exceeded by people and not by pigs.

The *kaiko* or pig festival, which commences with the planting of stakes at the boundary and the uprooting of the *rumbim*, is thus triggered by either the additional work attendant upon feeding pigs or the destructive capacity of the pigs themselves. It may be said, then, that there are sufficient pigs to stage the *kaiko* when the relationship of pigs to people changes from one of mutualism to one of parasitism or competition.[21]

A short time prior to the uprooting of the *rumbim*, stakes are planted at the boundary. If the enemy has continued to occupy its territory, the stakes are planted at the boundary which existed before the fight. If, on the other hand, the enemy has abandoned its territory, the victors may plant their stakes at a new boundary which encompasses areas previously occupied by the enemy. The Maring say, to be sure, that they never take land belonging to an enemy, but this land is regarded as vacant, since no *rumbim* was planted on it after the last fight. We may state here a rule of land redistribution in terms of the ritual cycle: *If one of a pair of antagonistic groups is able to uproot its rumbim before its opponents can plant their rumbim, it may occupy the latter's territory.*[22]

Not only have the vanquished abandoned their territory; it is assumed that it has also been abandoned by their ancestors as well. The surviving members of the erstwhile enemy group have by this time resided with other groups for a number of years, and most if not all of them have already had occasion to sacrifice pigs to their ancestors at their new residences. In so doing

---

[21] Here Rappaport again relies on the vocabulary of biology. *Mutualism* is a relationship between any two species in which both species benefit. *Parasitism* is such a relationship in which only one benefits.

[22] In this paragraph and below, Rappaport builds a formal model (or part of one) by stating a series of rules. This is similar to White's style of writing (see essay 19). Unlike White, whose rules are evolutionary and intended to apply to all cultures, however, Rappaport's rules are specific to Tsembaga culture and say nothing about the long-term direction of cultural change.

they have invited these spirits to settle at the new locations of the living, where they will in the future receive sacrifices. Ancestors of vanquished groups thus relinquish their guardianship over the territory, making it available to victorious groups. Meanwhile, the *de facto* membership of the living in the groups with which they have taken refuge is converted eventually into *de jure* membership.[23] Sooner or later the groups with which they have taken up residence will have occasion to plant *rumbim,* and the refugees, as co-residents, will participate, thus ritually validating their connection to the new territory and the new group. *A rule of population redistribution may thus be stated in terms of ritual cycles: A man becomes a member of a territorial group by participating with it in the planting of rumbim.*[24]

The uprooting of the *rumbim* follows shortly after the planting of stakes at the boundary. On this particular occasion the Tsembaga killed 32 pigs out of their herd of 169. Much of the pork was distributed to allies and affines outside of the local group.

The taboo on trapping marsupials was also terminated at this time.[25] Information is lacking concerning the population dynamics of the local marsupials, but it may well be that the taboo which had prevailed since the last fight—that against taking them in traps—had conserved a fauna which might otherwise have become extinct.

The *kaiko* continues for about a year, during which period friendly groups are entertained from time to time. The guests receive presents of vegetable foods, and the hosts and male guests dance together throughout the night.

These events may be regarded as analogous to aspects of the social behavior of many nonhuman animals. First of all, they include massed epigamic,[26] or courtship, displays (Wynne-Edwards 1962:17). Young women are presented with samples of the eligible males of local groups with which they may not otherwise have had the opportunity to become familiar. The context, moreover, permits the young women to discriminate amongst this sample in terms of both endurance (signaled by how vigorously and how long a man dances) and wealth (signaled by the richness of a man's shell and feather finery).

More importantly, the massed dancing at these events may be regarded as epideictic display,[27] communicating to the participants information concerning the size or density of the group (Wynne-Edwards 1962:16). In many species such displays take place as a prelude to actions which adjust group size or density, and such is the case among the Maring. The massed dancing of the visitors at a *kaiko* entertainment communicates to the hosts, while the *rumbim* truce is still in force, information concerning the amount of support they may expect from the visitors in the bellicose enterprises that they are likely to embark upon soon after the termination of the pig festival.

Among the Maring there are no chiefs or other political authorities capable of commanding the support of a body of followers, and the decision to assist another group in warfare rests with each individual male. Allies are not recruited by appealing for help to other local groups as such. Rather, each member of the groups primarily involved in the hostilities appeals to his cognatic and affinal kinsmen in other local groups. These men, in turn, urge other of their co-residents and kinsmen to "help them fight." The channels through which invitations to dance are extended

---

[23] *De facto* means in actuality, *de jure* means in law.

[24] In a personal communication Rappaport noted that participating in the planting of a *rumbim* is how the Tsembaga themselves understand becoming a member of a territorial group. What is important for Rappaport's approach, however, is that participation in this ceremony provides a clear operational and behavioral way of determining group membership, whether perceived that way by the Tsembaga or not.

[25] Notice that Rappaport suggests that other aspects of the system he has identified also serve ecological functions.

[26] *Epigamic:* related to the mating of animals and particularly the use of color to attract the opposite sex.

[27] *Epideictic:* in ornithology, this refers to collective displays and other conventional behavior, which are believed to have evolved from the need to control population.

are precisely those through which appeals for military support are issued. The invitations go not from group to group, but from kinsman to kinsman, the recipients of invitations urging their co-residents to "help them dance."

Invitations to dance do more than exercise the channels through which allies are recruited; they provide a means for judging their effectiveness. Dancing and fighting are regarded as in some sense equivalent. This equivalence is expressed in the similarity of some pre-fight and pre-dance rituals, and the Maring say that those who come to dance come to fight. The size of a visiting dancing contingent is consequently taken as a measure of the size of the contingent of warriors whose assistance may be expected in the next round of warfare.[28]

In the morning the dancing ground turns into a trading ground. The items most frequently exchanged include axes, bird plumes, shell ornaments, an occasional baby pig, and, in former times, native salt. The *kaiko* thus facilitates trade by providing a market-like setting in which large numbers of traders can assemble. It likewise facilitates the movement of two critical items, salt and axes, by creating a demand for the bird plumes which may be exchanged for them.

The *kaiko* concludes with major pig sacrifices. On this particular occasion the Tsembaga butchered 105 adult and adolescent pigs, leaving only 60 juveniles and neonates alive. The survival of an additional fifteen adolescents and adults was only temporary, for they were scheduled as imminent victims. The pork yielded by the Tsembaga slaughter was estimated to weigh between 7,000 and 8,500 pounds, of which between 4,500 and 6,000 pounds were distributed to members of other local groups in 163 separate presentations. An estimated 2,000 to 3,000 people in seventeen local groups were the beneficiaries of the redistribution. The presentations, it should be mentioned, were not confined to pork. Sixteen Tsembaga men presented bridewealth or child-wealth, consisting largely of axes and shells, to their affines at this time.[29]

The *kaiko* terminates on the day of the pig slaughter with the public presentation of salted pig belly to allies of the last fight. Presentations are made through the window in a high ceremonial fence built specially for the occasion at one end of the dance ground. The name of each honored man is announced to the assembled multitude as he charges to the window to receive his hero's portion. The fence is then ritually torn down, and the fighting stones are put away. The pig festival and the ritual cycle have been completed, demonstrating, it may be suggested, the ecological and economic competence of the local population. The local population would now be free, if it were not for the presence of the government, to attack its enemy again, secure in the knowledge that the assistance of allies and ancestors would be forthcoming because they have received pork and the obligations to them have been fulfilled.[30]

Usually fighting did break out again very soon after the completion of the ritual cycle. If peace still prevailed when the ceremonial fence had

---

[28] Notice that the flow of information is important in Rappaport's description. Information theory, developed in the 1950s, provided a way of expressing the transmission of certain types of information in energy terms. It was useful because, in principle, when combined with nutritional analysis, it provided a way of measuring the flow of both food and information through a cultural system in terms of energy. In practice, it proved extremely difficult to apply.

[29] Rappaport, here and above, briefly mentions the economic functions of the *kaiko,* but does not elaborate upon them, and below he mentions some specifics about how pork is distributed. Rappaport frequently supplies ethnographic details, like Steward, but they play a different role for each researcher. For Steward, details of ceremonies are generally secondary cultural features determined by the specific history of the group and therefore not meaningful for analysis. For Rappaport, they are part of the critical interface between culture and environment.

[30] The Tsembaga were under the administration of the Australian government when Rappaport worked among them, and the government had suppressed fighting among the different groups. Rappaport describes a *kaiko* festival he witnessed. However, he was unable to witness the cycle of warfare that led to it, which took place before his arrival. This element of his description is thus reconstructed from the memories of informants he interviewed.

rotted completely—a process said to take about three years, a little longer than the length of time required to raise a pig to maximum size—*rumbim* was planted as if there had been a fight, and all adult and adolescent pigs were killed. When the pig herd was large enough so that the *rumbim* could be uprooted, peace could be made with former enemies if they were also able to dig out their *rumbim*. To put this in formal terms: *If a pair of antagonistic groups proceeds through two ritual cycles without resumption of hostilities their enmity may be terminated.* [h]

The relations of the Tsembaga with their environment have been analyzed as a complex system composed of two subsystems. What may be called the "local subsystem" has been derived from the relations of the Tsembaga with the nonhuman components of their immediate or territorial environment. It corresponds to the ecosystem in which the Tsembaga participate. A second subsystem, one which corresponds to the larger regional population of which the Tsembaga are one of the constituent units and which may be designated as the "regional subsystem," has been derived from the relations of the Tsembaga with neighboring local populations similar to themselves. [31]

It has been argued that rituals, arranged in repetitive sequences, regulate relations both within each of the subsystems and within the larger complex system as a whole. The timing of the ritual cycle is largely dependent upon changes in the states of the components of the local subsystem. But the *kaiko,* which is the culmination of the ritual cycle, does more than reverse changes which have taken place within the local subsystem. Its occurrence also affects relations among the components of the regional subsys-

tem. During its performance, obligations to other local populations are fulfilled, support for future military enterprises is rallied, and land from which enemies have earlier been driven is occupied. Its completion, furthermore, permits the local population to initiate warfare again. Conversely, warfare is terminated by rituals which preclude the reinitiation of warfare until the state of the local subsystem is again such that a *kaiko* may be staged and completed. Ritual among the Tsembaga and other Maring, in short, operates as both transducer, "translating" changes in the state of one subsystem into information which can effect changes in a second subsystem, and homeostat, maintaining a number of variables which in sum comprise the total system within ranges of viability. To repeat an earlier assertion, the operation of ritual among the Tsembaga and other Maring helps to maintain an undegraded environment, limits fighting to frequencies which do not endanger the existence of the regional population, adjusts man-land ratios, facilitates trade, distributes local surpluses of pig throughout the regional population in the form of pork, and assures people of high quality protein when they are most in need of it. [32]

Religious rituals and the supernatural orders toward which they are directed cannot be assumed *a priori* to be mere epiphenomena. [33] Ritual may, and doubtless frequently does, do nothing more than validate and intensify the relationships which integrate the social unit, or symbolize the relationships which bind the social unit to its environment. But the interpretation of such presumably *sapiens*-specific phenomena as religious ritual within a framework which will also accommodate the behavior of other species shows, I think, that reli-

---

[31] In this paper, due to space limitations imposed by the original publication format, Rappaport tells us little about data collection. In his book-length treatment of this material, however, he includes a good deal of information on data collection and extensive appendices with raw data. Rappaport was unusual for his time. Most ethnographic work of this era did not include this sort of information and was strongly criticized on that basis by anthropologists in the 1970s and 1980s.

[32] When Rappaport's work on the Tsembaga was published in the late 1960s, it fell on fertile ground. It seemed to many to demonstrate the ecological soundness and wisdom of traditional society. This idea was appealing in the late 1960s and the 1970s, when many in academia were concerned with ecology and the value of traditional communities and folks were busy developing communes. As these ideas fell out of popularity and political conservatism became increasingly dominant, criticism of his work grew.

[33] *Epiphenomena:* secondary events.

gious ritual may do much more than symbolize, validate, and intensify relationships. Indeed, it would not be improper to refer to the Tsembaga and the other entities with which they share their territory as a "ritually regulated ecosystem," and to the Tsembaga and their human neighbors as a "ritually regulated population."[34]

Notes

a. The field work upon which this paper is based was supported by a grant from the National Science Foundation, under which Professor A. P. Vayda was principal investigator. Personal support was received by the author from the National Institutes of Health. Earlier versions of this paper were presented at the 1964 annual meeting of the American Anthropological Association in Detroit, and before a Columbia University seminar on Ecological Systems and Cultural Evolution. I have received valuable suggestions from Alexander Alland, Jacques Barrau, William Clarke, Paul Collins, C. Glen King, Marvin Harris, Margaret Mead, M. J. Meggitt, Ann Rappaport, John Street, Marjorie Whiting, Cherry Vayda, A. P. Vayda and many others, but I take full responsibility for the analysis presented herewith.

b. The social organization of the Tsembaga will be described in detail elsewhere.

c. Because the length of time in the field precluded the possibility of maintaining harvest records on single gardens from planting through abandonment, figures were based, in the case of both "taro-yam" and "sugar-sweet potato" gardens, on three separate gardens planted in successive years. Conversions from the gross weight to the caloric value of the yield were made by reference to the literature. The sources used are listed in Rappaport (1966: Appendix VIII).

d. Rough time and motion studies of each of the tasks involved in making, maintaining, harvesting, and walking to and from gardens were undertaken. Conversion to energy expenditure values was accomplished by reference to energy expenditure tables prepared by Hipsley and Kirk (1965:43) on the basis of gas exchange measurements made during the performance of garden tasks by the Chimbu people of the New Guinea highlands.

e. Marvin Harris, in an unpublished paper, estimates the ratio of energy return to energy input on Dyak

(Borneo) rice swiddens at 10:1. His estimates of energy ratios on Tepoltzlan (Meso-America) swiddens range from 13:1 on poor land to 29:1 on the best land.

f. Heights may be inaccurate. Many men wear their hair in large coiffures hardened with pandanus grease, and it was necessary in some instances to estimate the location of the top of the skull.

g. The possible significance of pork consumption by protein-short people during periods of physiological stress was unknown to me while I was in the field. I did not, therefore, investigate this matter in full detail. Georgeda Bick and Cherry Vayda, who visited the Maring area in 1966, have investigated the circumstances surrounding pork consumption further, and will publish their more detailed materials elsewhere.

h. After this article had gone to press in *Ethnology,* where it was originally published, I learned from A. P. Vayda, who spent the summer of 1966 in the Maring area, that he received somewhat different accounts of peace-making mechanisms, both from informants in other Maring local groups and from the Tsembaga man who had supplied me with the only full account which I was able to obtain (details of his account were, however, corroborated by information obtained from other Tsembaga men). According to Vayda's account, when the ceremonial fence had rotted away completely, some, but not all, adult and adolescent pigs were slain and offered to certain ancestral spirits to insure the health and fecundity of the remaining pigs, and no *rumbim* was planted. When the herds of the erstwhile antagonists again reached maximum size peace could be made.

It is important to note here that the other rituals treated in this paper were either observed by me or described by a number of informants who had participated in them, but none of either Vayda's informants or mine had ever participated in peace-making procedures, for none had taken place during the adult life of any of them. They were only reporting what they remembered from their childhood or what they had heard from their fathers or grandfathers. It is likely, therefore, that none of the informants are particularly well-versed in the details of the procedure. However, it is also important to note that all of the informants are in basic agreement upon what is in the present context the most important aspects of peace-making: that the rituals were not performed until pig herds of the erstwhile

---

[34] The functions Rappaport identifies for religion here fit well with those Bronislaw Malinowski noted in his work among the people of the Trobriand Islands. While Rappaport's work is limited to the Maring, it may suggest to readers that ecological, homeostatic functions be looked for in other religions as well.

antagonists had reached maximum size. The rule which I have proposed would seem to stand if it is understood that the second ritual cycle of the sequence may differ from the first in that *rumbim* might not be planted, and if it is understood that the truce may not be sanctified during the second cycle of the sequence.

References

Berg, C.
1948   Protein deficiency and its relation to nutritional anemia, hypoproteinemia, nutritional edema, and resistance to infection. *In* Protein and amino acids in nutrition, ed. M. Sahyun, pp. 290–317. New York: Reinhold.

Burton, B. T., ed.
1959   The Heinz handbook of nutrition. New York: McGraw-Hill.

Elman, R.
1951   Surgical Care. New York: Appleton-Century-Crofts.

Food and Agriculture Organization of the United Nations
1964   Protein: At the heart of the world food problem. World Food Problems 5. Rome: FAO.

Hipsley, E. and N. Kirk
1965   Studies of the dietary intake and energy expenditure of New Guineans. South Pacific Commission, Technical Paper 147. Noumea: South Pacific Commission.

Homans, G. C.
1941   Anxiety and ritual: The theories of Malinowski and Radcliffe-Brown. American Anthropologist 43:164–172.

Houssay, B. A. et al.
1955   Human physiology, 2nd ed. New York: McGraw-Hill.

Large, A., and C. G. Johnston
1948   Proteins as related to burns. *In* Proteins and amino acids in nutrition, ed. M. Sahyun, pp. 386–396. New York: Reinhold.

Lund, C. G., and S. M. Levenson
1948   Protein nutrition in surgical patients. *In* Proteins and amino acids in nutrition, ed. M. Sahyun, pp. 349–363. New York: Reinhold.

Moore, O. K.
1957   Divination—a new perspective. American Anthropologist 59:69–74.

National Research Council
1963   Evaluation of protein quality. National Academy of Sciences—National Research Council Publication 1100. Washington: NAS/NRC.

Rappaport, R. A.
1966   Ritual in the ecology of a New Guinea people. Unpublished doctoral dissertation. Columbia University.

Vayda, A. P., A. Leeds, and D. B. Smith
1961   The place of pigs in Melanesian subsistence. In proceedings of the 1961 Annual Spring Meeting of the American Ethnological Society, ed. V. E. Garfield, pp. 69–77. Seattle: University of Washington Press.

Wynne-Edwards V. C.
1962   Animal dispersion in relation to social behavior. Edinburgh and London: Oliver & Boyd.

Zintel, Harold A.
1964   Nutrition in the care of the surgical patient. *In* Modern nutrition in health and disease. ed. M. G. Wohl and R. S. Goodhart, pp. 1043–1064, 3rd ed. Philadelphia: Lea and Febiger.

24. From Jíbaro to Crack Dealer: Confronting the Restructuring of Capitalism in El Barrio

Philippe Bourgois (1956–)

FOLLOWING HIS YEAR AND A HALF OF FIELD work in a rural coffee-growing country in the central highlands of Puerto Rico from 1948 through 1949, Eric R. Wolf warned that even the small farmers and coffee pickers in the most isolated and traditional rural barrio that he was studying "in the future will supply many hundreds of hands to the coast, to the towns, and to the United States" (Wolf 1956b, 231). Macroeconomic and political forces proved Wolf's warning to be an understatement. American industrial capital was provided with extraordinary incentives and local agricultural development in Puerto Rico atrophied at the same time that emigration to the factories of New York City was actively promoted. The ensuing exodus over the next three and a half decades of almost a third of Puerto Rico's total population resulted proportionally in one of the larger labor migrations in modern history.[1]

STRUCTURAL CONSTRAINTS OF THE NUYORICAN EXPERIENCE

The majority of the immigrants found employment in New York City's most vulnerable subsector of light manufacturing. They arrived precisely on the eve of the structural decimation of factory

(1995)

production in urban North America. Indeed, the post-World War II Puerto Rican experience provides almost a textbook illustration of what Wolf in his later work refers to as "the growth of ever more diverse proletarian diasporas" that "capitalist accumulation . . . continues to engender" as it spreads across the globe (1982a, 383). Perhaps most interesting and relevant for understanding Nuyorican ethnicity—that is, the experience of New York City-born and raised Puerto Ricans— are the contradictory ways that the "changing needs of capital . . . continuously produce and re-create symbolically marked 'cultural' distinctions" among "the new working classes" who have crisscrossed oceans and continents in their struggle for survival and dignity (Wolf 1982a, 379–380).[2]

Depending upon one's formal definition, over the past three or four generations, the Puerto Rican people—especially those living in New York—have passed through almost a half dozen distinct modes of production: (1) from small land-owning semisubsistence peasantry or hacienda peons; (2) to export agricultural laborers on foreign-owned, capital-intensive plantations; (3) to factory workers in urban shantytowns; (4) to sweat-shop workers in ghetto tenements; (5) to service sector employees in high-rise inner-city housing projects; (6) to underground economy entrepreneurs homeless on the street.[3]

---

[1] This essay first appeared in *Articulating Hidden Histories* (Schneider and Rapp 1995), a collection of essays dedicated to exploring the legacy of Eric R. Wolf. Wolf (1923–1999) is generally considered one of the most important Marxist-influenced anthropologists of the midcentury. He is particularly interested in the ways in which the expansion of capitalism has affected cultures throughout the world. He explores this theme at length in *Europe and the People Without History* (1982), a book widely considered a classic of the neo-Marxist approach.

[2] One of Wolf's key contentions is that the histories of oppressed peoples and minority groups are fundamental to understanding culture and ourselves (Schneider and Rapp 1995:7). Wolf sees such people as fundamental actors driving culture change—a theme he explores in *Peasant Wars of the Twentieth Century* (1969). Bourgois, in dealing with people from the slums of New York, is acting very much in the tradition of Wolf.

[3] The *mode of production* is a fundamental Marxist concept. Unfortunately, Marx never provided a concise definition of it. Briefly, a mode of production is a pattern that combines labor, the machines and raw materials that workers use, and the social and technical relations under which they use them (Suchting 1983:76–77). Marx analyzed the history of Europe as a

This marathon sprint through economic history onto New York City's streets has been compounded ideologically by an overtly racist "cultural assault." Literally overnight the new immigrants — many of whom were enveloped in a *jíbaro* (hillbilly)-dominated culture emphasizing interpersonal webs of patriarchal *respeto* — found themselves transformed into "racially" inferior cultural pariahs. Ever since their arrival they have been despised and humiliated with that virulence so characteristic of America's history of polarized race relations in the context of massive labor migrations. Even though the Puerto Rican experience is extreme, it is by no means unique. On the contrary, peoples all through the world and throughout history have been forced to traverse multiple modes of production and have suffered social dislocation.[4]

The historic structural transformations imposed upon the Puerto Rican jíbaro translate statistically into a tragic profile of unemployment, substance abuse, broken families, and devastated health in U.S. inner cities. No other ethnic group except perhaps Native Americans fares more poorly in the official statistics than do mainland U.S. Puerto Ricans. This is most pronounced for the majority cohort living in New York City where Puerto Ricans have the highest welfare dependency and poverty rates, the lowest labor force participation rates, and the fastest growing HIV infection rates of any group (Falcon 1992; Lambert 1990).

THE ETHNOGRAPHIC SETTING

These contemporary expressions of historical dislocation formed the backdrop for my five years of participant-observation fieldwork on street culture in the "crack economy" during the late 1980s and early 1990s. For a total of approximately three and a half years I lived with my wife and young son in an irregularly heated, rat-filled tenement in East Harlem, better known locally as El Barrio or Spanish Harlem. This two-hundred-square-block neighborhood is visibly impoverished yet it is located in the heart of the richest city in the western hemisphere. Its vacant lots and crumbling abandoned tenements are literally a stone's throw from multimillion-dollar condominiums. Although one in three families survives on public assistance, the majority of El Barrio's 130,000 Puerto Rican and African-American residents comprise the ranks of the "working poor." They eke out an uneasy subsistence in entry-level service and manufacturing jobs in a city with one of the highest costs of living in the world.[5]

In my ethnographic research, I explored the ideologies (i.e., the power-charged belief systems) that organize "common sense" on the street — what I call "street culture." Consequently, over

---

series of successive modes of production. His modes were Asiatic, ancient, feudal, and modern bourgeois (Lichtheim 1973:151). Traditional Marxist analysis demanded that societies belong to one of these four modes. One of the neo-Marxists' critical innovations was to expand the mode of production concept to include many societies that did not fit easily into Marx's original modes. This, however, tended to result in a great proliferation of new modes of production. Here Bourgois delineates a number of modes of production, none of which are found in the works of Marx, but each of which describes a pattern of labor, material, equipment, social, and technical relationships that is found in the modern world.

[4] The Boasian tradition in anthropology has often emphasized the unique characteristics of cultures. Ethnoscientists (essays 28, 29) as well as some postmodernists (essays 38, 39) claim that cultures are essentially incommensurate and no attempt should be made to compare them. Marxism, on the other hand, is a universalizing theory. Marxists claim that fundamental hidden processes underlie all societies. As a result, these societies pass through similar stages and take similar forms. Thus, while much of anthropology emphasizes cultural variation, Marxist anthropologists tend to be more concerned with cultural similarities.

[5] Note that while Bourgois' essay is an analysis of Nuyorican culture, it is also a scathing critique of American capitalism. It is impossible to read this essay without asking yourself "what kind of a system allows this waste of human talent?" Marx, of course, held that capitalism was inherently oppressive and that it would inevitably give way to socialism and communism. In other words, he thought the rise of communism to be a scientific certainty. Most modern Marxists reject this theological notion. However, they generally continue to be harsh critics of capitalism. Bourgois continues to critique American capitalism throughout this essay. He is particularly caustic in its final paragraphs.

the years, I interacted with and befriended the addicts, thieves, dealers, and con artists who comprise a minority proportion of El Barrio residents but who exercise hegemony over its public space. Specifically, I focused on a network of some twenty-five street-level crack dealers who operated on and around my block.

On the one hand, such an intensive examination of street participants risks exoticizing the neighborhood and may be interpreted as reinforcing violent stereotypes against Puerto Ricans. On the other hand, case studies of the "worthy poor" risk "normalizing" the experience of class and racial segregation and can mask the depths of human suffering that accompanies rapid economic restructuring. Furthermore, the legally employed majority of El Barrio residents has lost control of the streets and has retreated from daily life in the neighborhood. To understand the experience of living in the community, the ideologies of violence, opposition, and material pursuit which have established hegemony over street life—much to the dismay of most residents—have to be addressed systematically. Furthermore, on a subtle theoretical level, the "caricatural" responses to poverty and marginalization that the dealers and addicts represent provide privileged insight into processes that may be experienced in one form or another by major sectors of any vulnerable working-class population experiencing rapid structural change anywhere in the world and at any point in history.[6] Once again, there is nothing structurally exceptional about the Puerto Rican experience except that the human costs involved are more clearly visible given the extent

and rapidity with which Puerto Rican society has been absorbed by the United States and the particularly persistent virulence of American ideologies around "race" and culture.[7]

My central concern is the relationship of the street dealers to the worlds of work—that is, the legal and illegal labor markets—that employ them and give meaning to their lives. The long-term structural transformation of New York from a manufacturing to a service economy is crucial to understanding this experience. Although economists, sociologists, and political scientists have argued extensively over the details of the statistics, most recognize that the dislocations caused by the erosion of the manufacturing sector are a driving force behind the economic polarization of urban America (Wilson 1987). They also specifically recognize that Puerto Ricans are the most vulnerable group in New York's structural adjustment because of their over-concentration in the least dynamic subsector within light manufacturing and because of their fragile incipient foothold in public sector and service employment (Rodriguez 1989).

Through my ethnographic data I hope to show the local-level implications of the global-level restructuring of capital and, in the process, give voice to some unrepentant victims. In a nutshell, I am arguing that the transformation from manufacturing to service employment—especially in the professional office work setting—is much more culturally disruptive than the already revealing statistics on reductions in income, employment, unionization, and worker's benefits would indicate. Low-level service sector employment

---

[6] As noted in footnote 4, Marxists tend to focus on cultural similarities in their analyses. However sympathetic we may be to the plight of those described here, we must still examine Bourgois' assumptions. Does studying the lives of dealers and addicts really provide an insight into vulnerable working-class populations at any point in history and anywhere in the world?

[7] This passage expresses several key concerns of current anthropology. The first is the notion of "exoticizing." To exoticize a group of people is to make them appear strange, foreign, and, ultimately, to allow their humanity to be diminished. A group that is exotic doesn't have to be taken seriously. A second key concept is "privilege." A privileged insight is one that is to be taken more seriously because of the position of those who offer it. The use of privilege in this manner is often derogatory. Thus, white males of European extraction are held to have privileged positions. That is, for historical reasons, they are the ones whose voices and interpretations are granted the most credibility. Much current anthropology makes an issue of resisting the privileged voices of these people. Here, Bourgois speaks of the privileged voice of the crack dealers, an extremely unprivileged group of people. They are to be taken more seriously because their control of public spaces in the neighborhood and their position in society gives them special insight.

engenders a humiliating ideological—or cultural—confrontation between a powerful corps of white office executives and their assistants versus a mass of poorly educated, alienated, "colored" workers.[8]

SHATTERED WORKING-CLASS DREAMS

All the crack dealers and addicts whom I have interviewed worked at one or more legal jobs in their early youth. In fact, most entered the labor market at a younger age than the typical American. Before they were twelve years old they were bagging groceries at the supermarket for tips, stocking beer off-the-books in local *bodegas,* or shining shoes. For example, Julio, the night manager at a video games arcade that sells five-dollar vials of crack on the block where I lived, pursued a traditional working-class dream in his early adolescence. With the support of his extended kin who were all immersed in a working-class "common sense," he dropped out of junior high school to work in a local garment factory:

> I was like fourteen or fifteen playing hooky and pressing dresses and whatever they were making on the steamer. They was cheap, cheap clothes.
>
> My mother's sister was working there first and then her son, my cousin Hector—the one who's in jail now—was the one they hired first, because his mother agreed: "If you don't want to go school, you gotta work."
>
> So I started hanging out with him. I wasn't planning on working in the factory. I was supposed to be in school; but it just sort of happened.

Ironically, little Julio actually became the agent who physically moved the factory out of the inner city. In the process, he became merely one more of the 445,900 manufacturing workers in New York City to lose their jobs as factory employment dropped 50 percent from 1963 to 1983 (Romo and Schwartz 1993). Of course, instead of understanding himself as the victim of a structural transformation, Julio remembers with pleasure and even pride the extra income he earned for clearing the machines out of the factory space:

> Them people had money, man. Because we helped them move out of the neighborhood. It took us two days—only me and my cousin, Hector. Wow! It was work. They gave us seventy bucks each.[9]

Almost all the crack dealers had similar tales of former factory jobs. For poor adolescents, the decision to drop out of school and become a marginal factory worker is attractive. It provides the employed youth with access to the childhood "necessities"—sneakers, basketballs, store-bought snacks—that sixteen-year-olds who stay in school cannot afford. In the descriptions of their first forays into legal factory-based employment, one hears clearly the extent to which they and their families subscribed to mainstream working-class ideologies about the dignity of engaging in "hard work" versus education.

Had these enterprising, early-adolescent workers from El Barrio not been confined to the weakest sector of manufacturing in a period of rapid job loss their teenage working-class dream might have stabilized. Instead, upon reaching their mid-twenties they discovered themselves to be unem-

---

[8] Notice two critical Marxist concerns in the previous two paragraphs. The first is the relationship of work and meaning. Marxists take production as the most basic patterning element of society. Marx (in this volume) wrote that ". . . [people] begin to distinguish themselves from animals as soon as they begin to produce their means of subsistence. . . ." Here, Bourgois takes it as axiomatic that people's lives are given meaning by their work, rather than, as might be possible, people choose their jobs because of meanings they acquire from religion or other aspects of social life. The second is the notion of conflict. Conflict is central to Marxist analysis. All societies (except the future communist utopia) are riven by conflicts. History and progress are the inexorable working out of these conflicts and the generation of new conflict.

[9] In Marxist analysis, the structural factors that drive cultural change are often hidden from cultural participants. In this passage we see Julio actively participating in the change that will lead to poverty for the people around him. Julio is unaware of the structural changes and forces of production that determine much of his life. It is only the analyst who can see the broader picture.

ployable high school dropouts. This painful realization of social marginalization expresses itself generationally as the working-class values of their families conflict violently with the reality of their hard-core lumpenization.[10] They are constantly accused of slothfulness by their mothers and even by friends who have managed to maintain legal jobs. They do not have a regional perspective on the dearth of adequate entry-level jobs available to "functional illiterates" in New York City and they begin to suspect that they might indeed be "vago bons" (lazy bums) who do not *want* to work hard and help themselves. Confused, they take refuge in an alternate search for career, meaning, and ecstasy in substance abuse.[11]

Formerly, when most entry-level jobs were found in factories the contradiction between an oppositional street culture and traditional working-class, shop-floor culture was less pronounced— especially when the worksite was protected by a union. Factories are inevitably rife with confrontational hierarchies; nevertheless, on the shop floor, surrounded by older union workers, high school dropouts who are well versed in the latest and toughest street-culture styles function effectively. In the factory, being tough and violently macho has high cultural value; a certain degree of opposition to the foreman and the "bossman" is expected and is considered appropriately masculine.

In contrast, this same oppositional street identity is nonfunctional in the service sector that has burgeoned in New York's finance-driven economy because it does not allow for the humble, obedient, social interaction — often across gender lines — that professional office workers impose on their subordinates. A qualitative change characterizes the tenor of social interaction in office-based service sector employment. Workers in a mailroom or behind a photocopy machine cannot publicly maintain their cultural autonomy. Most concretely, they have no union; more subtly, there are few fellow workers surrounding them to insulate them and to provide them with a culturally based sense of class solidarity.[a] Instead they are besieged by supervisors and bosses from the alien, hostile, and obviously dominant culture. When these office managers are not intimidated by street culture, they ridicule it. Workers like Willie and Julio appear inarticulate to their professional supervisors when they try to imitate the language of power in the workplace and instead stumble pathetically over the enunciation of unfamiliar words.

---

[10] The word *lumpenization* comes from Marx's notion of the *lumpenproletariat.* Marx described the lumpenproletariat as comprising "ruined and adventurous off-shoots of the bourgeoisie, vagabonds, discharged soldiers, discharged jailbirds . . . pickpockets, brothel keepers, rag-pickers, beggars," etc. (Bottomore 1991:327). Thus, the lumpenproletariat are the disinherited dregs of society. Their significance is twofold. First, since workers fear lumpenization, they will accept high levels of exploitation. Second, the lumpenproletariat are politically volatile. Since they are disaffected, they are easily drawn to political radicals and can be mobilized to challenge the power structure.

[11] The work of Antonio Gramsci (1891 – 1937) has been critical for many modern Marxists, and his effect is felt throughout this essay. Gramsci was a founder of the Italian Communist Party. Imprisoned from 1926 to 1937, he was released because of ill health and died shortly thereafter. Gramsci's key works are his prison notebooks which, since they were written in part to avoid detection by prison censors, are extremely difficult to understand. Gramsci's most important contribution to Marxism is the concept of hegemony, which he does not define with any precision. He most consistently uses *hegemony* to refer to a system of political and moral leadership. It describes the use by the leadership of a society of "intellectual devices to infuse its ideas of morality to gain the support of those who resist or may be neutral, to retain the support of those who consent to its rule . . ." (Kurtz 1996:106). In other words, hegemony is a system of ethical and political ideas propounded by a broad alliance of political and intellectual leaders and believed as "common sense" by the masses. The hegemony of a dominant class is created and reinforced in the institutions, social relations, and dominant ideas of a society (Sassoon 1991:230). In proposing a primary role for hegemony and intellectual leadership, Gramsci provides a counterbalance to the traditional Marxist emphasis on the fundamental importance of economic relations of production. The notion of hegemony has been attractive to Marxist anthropologists because it gives critical importance to the cultural realm. Gramsci's influence has been particularly felt in Cultural Studies and cultural-production theory (see footnote 23).

The concept of hegemony plays a crucial role in this essay. In this passage, the working-class families of the crack dealers accept the hegemonic ideology of America's power elites: "common sense" about "hard work." The dealers themselves are at least partially accepting of these same ideologies and suspect that they are "vago bons."

They cannot decipher the hastily scribbled instructions — rife with mysterious abbreviations — that are left for them by harried office managers. The "common sense" of white-collar work is foreign to them; they do not, for example, understand the logic for filing triplicate copies of memos or for postdating invoices. When they attempt to improvise or show initiative they fail miserably and instead appear inefficient — or even hostile — for failing to follow "clearly specified" instructions.

Their "social skills" are even more inadequate than their limited professional capacities. They do not know how to look at their fellow co-service workers — let alone their supervisors — without intimidating them. They cannot walk down the hallway to the water fountain without unconsciously swaying their shoulders aggressively as if patrolling their home turf. Gender barriers are an even more culturally charged realm. They are repeatedly reprimanded for harassing female co-workers.

The cultural clash between white "yuppie" power and inner-city "scrambling jive" in the service sector is much more than a difference of style. Service workers who are incapable of obeying the rules of interpersonal interaction dictated by professional office culture will never be upwardly mobile. In the high-rise office buildings of midtown Manhattan, newly employed inner-city high school dropouts suddenly realize that they look like idiotic buffoons to the men and women they work for. Once again, a gender dynamic exacerbates the confusion and sense of insult experienced by young, male inner-city employees because most supervisors in the lowest reaches of the service sector are women. Street culture does not allow males to be subordinate across gender lines.[12]

"GETTIN' DISSED"

On the street, the trauma of experiencing a threat to one's personal dignity has been frozen linguistically in the commonly used phrase "to diss" which is short for "to disrespect." Significantly, back in the coffee-hacienda highlands of Puerto Rico in 1949, Wolf had noted the importance of the traditional Puerto Rican concept of *respeto*: "The good owner 'respects' [*respeta*] the laborer." Wolf pointed specifically to the role "respect" plays in controlling labor power: "It is probably to the interest of the landowner to make concessions to his best workers, to deal with them on a respect basis, and to enmesh them in a network of mutual obligations" (Wolf 1956*b*, 235; see also Lauria 1964).[13]

Puerto Rican street dealers do not find "respect" in the entry-level service sector jobs that have increased twofold in New York's economy since the 1950s. On the contrary, they "get dissed" in their new jobs. Julio, for example, remembers the humiliation of his former work experiences as an "office boy," and he speaks of them in a race- and gender-charged idiom:

> I had a prejudiced boss. She was a fucking "ho'," Gloria. She was white. Her name was Christian. No, not Christian, Kirschman. I don't know if she was Jewish or not. When she was talking to people she would say, "He's illiterate."
>
> So what I did one day was, I just looked up the word, "illiterate," in the dictionary and

---

[12] This passage points up a crucial issue in Marxist analysis, and in much of anthropology. The individuals in Bourgois' study seem to be in "the iron grip of culture." Bourgois' subjects are frightening, but somewhat attractive. This comes from the sense that they might be decent individuals trapped by forces beyond their control. In this paragraph, workers are "incapable" of obeying the rules of office culture and forbidden by Puerto Rican street culture from being subordinate to women. Does culture really compel us to this degree?

[13] The theme of this section is the clash of cultures: the "street culture" of the crack dealers versus the office culture in which they seek employment. Although the subjects of his study are Puerto Rican Americans, Bourgois says their experience is not unique and has been reenacted all over the world throughout history. In this, he is focusing his analysis on class and economic conflict rather than race or ethnicity. Notice also that while Bourgois is sympathetic to his crack-dealer subjects, the cultures in question are not equal. The critical dimension of the relationship of crack-dealer culture to office culture is that the members of office-worker culture have power, and despite their demands for respect, crack dealers have none.

I saw that she's saying to her associates that I'm stupid or something!

Well, I am illiterate anyway.

The most profound dimension of Julio's humiliation was being obliged to look up in the dictionary the word used to insult him. In contrast, in the underground economy, he is sheltered from this kind of threat:

Big Pete [the crack house franchise owner] he would never disrespect me that way. He wouldn't tell me that because he's illiterate too. Plus I've got more education than him. I got a GED.

To succeed at Gloria Kirschman's magazine publishing company, Julio would have had to submit wholeheartedly to her professional cultural style but he was unwilling to compromise his street identity. He refused to accept her insults and he was unable to imitate her culture; hence, he was doomed to a marginal position behind a photocopy machine or at the mail meter. The job requirements in the service sector are largely cultural—that is, having a "good attitude"—therefore they conjugate powerfully with racism:

I wouldn't have mind that she said I was illiterate. What bothered me was that when she called on the telephone, she wouldn't want me to answer even if my supervisor who was the receptionist was not there. [Note how Julio is so low in the office hierarchy that his immediate supervisor is a receptionist.]

When she hears my voice it sounds like she's going to get a heart attack. She'd go, "Why are you answering the phones?"

That bitch just didn't like my Puerto Rican accent.

Julio's manner of resisting this insult to his cultural dignity exacerbated his marginal position in the labor hierarchy:

And then, when I did pick up the phone, I used to just sound *Porta'rrrican* on purpose.

In contrast to the old factory sweatshop positions, these just-above-minimum-wage office jobs require intense interpersonal contact with the middle and upper-middle classes. Proximal contact across class lines and the absence of a working-class autonomous space for eight hours a day in the office can be a claustrophobic experience for an otherwise ambitious, energetic, young inner-city worker.

Willie interpreted this requirement to obey white, middle-class norms as an affront to his dignity that specifically challenged his definition of masculinity:

I had a few jobs like that [referring to Julio's "telephone diss"] where you gotta take a lot of shit from bitches and be a wimp.

I didn't like it but I kept on working, because "Fuck it!" you don't want to fuck up the relationship. So you just be a punk [shrugging his shoulders dejectedly].

One alternative for surviving at a workplace that does not tolerate a street-based cultural identity is to become bicultural: to play politely by "the white woman's" rules downtown only to come home and revert to street culture within the safety of one's tenement or housing project at night. Tens of thousands of East Harlem residents manage this tightrope, but it often engenders accusations of betrayal and internalized racism on the part of neighbors and childhood friends who do not have—or do not want—these bicultural skills.

This is the case, for example, of Ray, a rival crack dealer whose black skin and tough street demeanor disqualify him from legal office work. He quit a "nickel-and-dime messenger job downtown" to sell crack full-time in his project stairway shortly after a white woman fled from him shrieking down the hallway of a high-rise office building. Ray and the terrified woman had ridden the elevator together and coincidentally Ray had stepped off on the same floor as her to make a delivery. Worse yet, Ray had been trying to act like a "debonair male" and suspected the contradiction between his inadequate appearance and his "chivalric" intentions was responsible for the woman's terror:

You know how you let a woman go off the elevator first? Well that's what I did to her but I may have looked a little shabby on the ends. Sometime my hair not combed. You know. So I could look a little sloppy to her maybe when I let her off first.

What Ray did not quite admit until I probed further is that he too had been intimidated by the lone white woman. He had been so disoriented by her tabooed, unsupervised proximity that he had forgotten to press the elevator button when he originally stepped on after her:

> She went in the elevator first but then she just waits there to see what floor I press. She's playing like she don't know what floor she wants to go to because she wants to wait for me to press my floor. And I'm standing there and I forgot to press the button. I'm thinking about something else—I don't know what was the matter with me. And she's thinking like, "He's not pressing the button; I guess he's following me!"

As a crack dealer, Ray no longer has to confront this kind of confusing humiliation. Instead, he can righteously condemn his "successful" neighbors who work downtown for being ashamed of who they were born to be:

> When you see someone go downtown and get a good job, if they be Puerto Rican, you see them fix up their hair and put some contact lens in their eyes. Then they fit in. And they do it! I seen it.
> They turnovers. They people who want to be white. Man, if you call them in Spanish, it wind up a problem.
> When they get nice jobs like that, all of a sudden, you know, they start talking proper.

SELF-DESTRUCTIVE RESISTANCE

Third- and second-generation Spanish Harlem residents born into working-class families do not tolerate high levels of "exploitation." In the new jobs available to them, however, there are no class-based institutions to channel their resistance. They are caught in a technological time warp. They have developed contemporary main-stream American definitions of survival needs and emotional notions of job satisfaction. In short, they are "made in New York"; therefore, they are not "exploitable" or "degradable." Both their objective economic needs as well as their personal cultural dignities have to be satisfied by their jobs. They resist inadequate working conditions. Finally, they are acutely aware of their relative depravation vis-à-vis the middle-level managers and wealthy executives whose intimate physical proximity they cannot escape at work.

At the same time that young men like Julio, Willie, and Ray recognize how little power they have in the legal labor market, they do not accept their domination passively. They are resisting exploitation from positions of subordination. They are living the unequal power struggle that a growing body of anthropological and ethnographic literature is beginning to address (Bourgois in press; Foley 1990; Fordham 1988; Willis 1977; Wolf 1990*b*, 590).

Unfortunately, for people like Julio and Willie, the traditional modes of powerless resistance—footdragging, disgruntlement, petty theft, and so forth—which might be appropriate in traditional peasant or even proletarian settings (see Scott 1985) contradict the fundamental "technological" requirement for enthusiastic "initiative" and "flexibility" that New York's finance-driven service sector demands. In manufacturing, resistance can be channeled through recognized institutions—unions—that often reinforce class consciousness. In fact, oppositionally defined cultural identities are so legitimate on the shop floor that they even serve to ritualize management/worker confrontation.[14]

In the service sector, however, there is no neutral way to express cultural nonconformity. Scowling on the way to brewing coffee for a su-

---

[14] Here Bourgois focuses on class conflict, a fundamental theme in Marxist analysis. While Durkheim and the functionalist thinkers saw society as fundamentally cooperative, Marx saw it as riven by conflict. This is illustrated in Bourgois' descriptions of factory workers. The functionalist approach to inequality, often credited to sociologists Kingsley Davis and Wilbert Moore, suggests that people work cooperatively at their level of competence and are rewarded appropriately for their efforts. The center of this model is consensus. We all work together, each doing his or her job, to produce a final product. In Marxist analysis, on the other hand, factory production seems almost secondary to the struggle between workers and overseers on the factory floor. Workers are in conflict with managers and owners. Unable, in most circumstances, to openly rebel, they protest their condition by theft and small acts of sabotage. If these are not excessive, such acts are tolerated by owners as a cost of doing business. In fact, tolerating small amounts of theft is one way owners can keep

pervisor results in an unsatisfactory end-of-year performance evaluation. Stealing on the job is just cause for instant job termination. Indeed, petty theft is the avenue for "powerless revenge" most favored by Willie and Julio. They both were skilled at manipulating the Pitney-Bowes postage meter machines and at falsifying stationery inventory to skim "chump change."

More subtle, however, was the damage to Julio's work performance due to his constant concern lest Gloria Kirschman once again catch him off guard and "disrespect" him without his being immediately aware of the gravity of the insult. Consequently, when he was ordered to perform mysteriously specific tasks such as direct mailings of promotional materials that required particular combinations of folding, stuffing, or clipping, he activated his defense mechanisms. Julio had rarely received direct mail advertisements in his project apartment mailbox; consequently, the urgency and the precision with which his supervisor oversaw the logistics of these mailings appeared overbearingly oppressive and insulting. Gloria appeared almost superstitious in the rigor and anxiety with which she supervised each detail and Julio refused to accept the "flexibility" that these delicate mailings required—that is, late-night binges of collating and recollating to make bulk-rate postage deadlines coincide with the magazine's printing and sales deadlines. Furthermore, to Julio, it was offensive to have to bring over the assembled promotional packets to Gloria's home for a last-minute late-night inspection:

> It would be late and I would be at the office to do these rush jobs: collate them, staple them, fold them in the correct way . . . whatever way she said. It was always different. And it had to be just the way she wanted it. I'd stuff them

just the right way [making frantic shuffling motions with his hands] and then seal the shit.

I used to hate that. I would box it and take it to the 38th Street Post Office at 10:30 at night.

But then sometimes she would call me from home and I would have to bring papers up to her house on 79th Street and 3rd Avenue [Manhattan's silk stocking district] to double check.

And she would try to offer me something to eat and I would say, "No, thank you," because she would try to pay me with that shit. 'Cause she's a cheap bitch.

She'd say, "You want pizza, tea, or cookies?" She had those Pepperidge Farm cookies [wrinkling his face with disgust].

But I wouldn't accept anything from her. I wasn't going to donate my time man.

She thought I was illiterate. She thought I was stupid. Not me boy, charge *every penny*. From the moment I leave the office that's overtime all the way to her house. That's time and a half.

I used to exaggerate the hours. If I worked sixteen, I would put eighteen or twenty to see if I could get away with it. And I would get away with it. I'm not going to do that kind of shit for free.

And that bitch was crazy. She used to eat baby food. I know cause I saw her eating it with a spoon right out of the jar.

If Julio appeared to be a scowling, ungrateful, dishonest worker to Gloria, then Gloria herself looked almost perverted to Julio. What normal middle-aged woman would invite her twenty-year-old employee into her kitchen late at night and eat baby food in front of him?[15]

Julio's victories over his employer, Gloria, were Pyrrhic.[16] In the cross-cultural confrontation taking place in the corridors of high-rise office

---

wages low. The critical issue for Bourgois' crack dealers is that in a factory, there is separation of the classes. Management and workers rarely meet face-to-face. This makes small acts of resistance possible. On the other hand, in an office, service workers are in constant contact with management. This means that they must suppress all insubordination or develop subtle ways of showing it.

[15] Like the story above about Ray and the elevator, this story emphasizes the overlap between class and culture. In both stories, attempts to show respect or friendship are misinterpreted. In the first story, Ray's attempt to show respect to a woman on an elevator goes awry when she interprets his actions as those of an assailant. In this story, Gloria almost certainly understands herself as proffering a minimal degree of friendship. Julio interprets this as an insult.

[16] A *Pyrrhic victory* is a victory at a cost so great it harms the victor.

buildings there is no ambiguity over who wields power. This unequal hierarchy is constantly reasserted through the mechanisms of cultural capital so foreign to participants in street culture. For example, when someone like Willie, Julio, or Ray is "terminated" for suspicion of theft, the personnel report registers an insulting notation: "lack of initiative," "inarticulate," or "no understanding of the purpose of the company." Julio correctly translates this information into street-English: "She's saying to her associates that I'm stupid!"

Willie and Julio have no frame of reference to guide them through service employment because their social network only has experience with factory work. In their first factory jobs, both Willie and Julio were guided by older family members who were producing the very same products they were making. Still today, for example, Julio's mother is a sweatshop/homework seamstress and Willie's uncle is a factory foreman in the Midwestern town where his metal-chroming company relocated. In contrast, the only socialization available to Willie and Julio in the service sector comes from equally isolated and alienated fellow workers. Willie, for example, who has always been precocious in everything he has done in life — from dropping out of school, to engaging in street violence, to burglarizing, to selling drugs, to abusing women, to becoming a crack addict — immediately understood the impossibility of his supervisor's maintaining an objective quality control in the mailroom where he worked prior to being hired by Julio at the crack house:

> I used to get there late, but the other workers wasn't never doing shit. They was *lazy* motherfuckers — even the supervisor.
>
> They all be sitting, asking each other questions over the phone, and fooling with video games on the computer. And that's all you do at a place like that. My boss, Bill, be drinking on the sneak cue, and eating this bad-ass sausage.

Finally, the precarious tenure of entry-level jobs in the service sector was the immediate precipitating factor in Willie's and Julio's retreat from the legal labor market. When they were not fired for "bad attitude," they were laid off due to economic retrenchment. The companies employing them fluctuated with the unpredictable whims of rapidly changing "yuppie fashions." Julio, for example, lost two different positions in fragile companies that folded: (1) Gloria Kirschman's trendy magazine, and (2) a desktop publishing house.

Surprisingly, in his accounts of being laid off Julio publicly admitted defeat and vulnerability. On repeated occasions I had seen Julio brave violence on the streets and in the crack house. I knew him capable of deliberate cruelty, such as refusing to pay for his fifteen-year-old girlfriend's abortion or of slowly breaking the wrist of an adolescent who had played a prank on him.[17] Downtown, however, behind the computer terminal where he had held his last job "in printing," he had been crushed psychologically by the personnel officers who fired him. Ironically, I registered on my tape recorder his tale of frustration, humiliation, and self-blame for losing his last legal job as a printer only a week after recording with him a bravado-laced account of how he mugged a drunken Mexican immigrant in a nearby housing project:

> I was with Rico and his girl, Daisy. We saw this Mexican. . . . He was just probably drunk. I grabbed him by the back of the neck, and put my 007 [knife] in his back [making the motion of holding someone in a choke hold from behind]. Right here [pointing to his own lower back]. And I was jigging him *HARD* [grinning for emphasis at me and his girlfriend, who was listening, rapt with attention]!
>
> I said: "*No te mueve cabron o te voy a picar como un pernil* [Don't move motherfucker or I'll stick you like a roast pork]." [More loud chuckles from Julio's girlfriend.] Yeah, yeah, like how you stab a pork shoulder when you want to put all the flavoring in the holes.
>
> I wasn't playing, either, I was serious. I would have jigged him. And I'd regret it later, but I was looking at that gold ring he had.

---

[17] To his credit, Bourgois does not romanticize the central characters in this essay. They are capable of great cruelty and violence. However, in the logic of Marxist analysis, they are victims of economic forces beyond their control. More specifically, their surroundings have made them who they are. Thus, despite their actions, these young men are depicted in a sympathetic light. Still, many thousands of people are subjected to the same conditions and virtually none of them sell drugs or break the wrists of children. Bourgois' argument is compelling, but is it complete?

[Chuckle.]

The Mexican panicked. So I put him to the floor, poking him hard, and Rico's girl started searching him.

I said, "Yo, take that asshole's fucking ring too!"

After she took the ring we broke out. We sold the ring and then we cut-out on Daisy. We left her in the park, she didn't get even a cent. She helped for nothing. [More chuckling.]

As a knife-wielding mugger on the street, Julio could not contrast more dramatically with the panic-stricken employee begging for a second chance that legal employment had reduced him to:

I was more or less expecting it. But still, when I found out, I wanted to cry, man. My throat got dry, I was like . . . [waves his hands, and gasps as if struck by a panic attack].

They called me to the office, I was like, "Oh *shit!*"

I couldn't get through to them. I even told them, "I'll let you put me back to messenger; I will take less pay; just keep me employed. I need the money; I need to work. I got a family."

But they said, "Nope, nope, nope." I left.

I just stood right outside the building; I was fucked, man. All choked up. *Me jodieron* [They jerked me].[18]

THE NEW IMMIGRANT ALTERNATIVE

The flooding of cocaine and then crack onto America's streets during the 1980s infused new energy into the underground economy, making drug dealing the most vibrant equal opportunity employer for Harlem youths. Normally, in order to fill jobs adequately in the expanding service sector, New York's legal economy should have to compete for the hearts and minds of the growing proportion of the inner city's "best and brightest" who are choosing to pursue more remunerative and culturally compatible careers in the underground economy. A wave of cheaper, more docile and disciplined new immigrant workers, however, is altering this labor power balance. These immigrants—largely undocumented—are key agents in New York's latest structural economic adjustment. Their presence allows low-wage employment to expand while social services retrench. This helps explain, for example, how the real value of the minimum wage could have declined by one-third in the 1980s while the federal government was able to decrease the proportion of its contribution to New York City's budget by over 50 percent (Berlin 1991, 10; Rosenbaum 1989, A1). The breakdown of the inner city's public sector is no longer an economic threat to the expansion of New York's economy because the labor force that these public subsidies maintain is increasingly irrelevant.[19]

Like the parents and grandparents of Julio and Willie, many of New York's newest immigrants are from remote rural communities or squalid shantytowns where meat is eaten only once a week, and where there is no running water or electricity. In downtown Manhattan many of these new immigrants are Chinese, but in East Harlem the vast majority are Mexicans from the rural states of Puebla and Guerrero. To them, New York's streets are still "paved in gold" if one works hard enough.

Half a century ago Julio's mother fled precisely the same living conditions these new immigrants

---

[18] These two stories are important because they demonstrate that, at some level, Julio understands the true nature of power. Julio is a violent and abusive individual capable of injuring another person without remorse. He is, however, easily defeated by people such as Gloria Kirschman, who would probably be terrified of him were they to meet on the streets of the barrio. The point is that ultimately power does not stem from the ability of individuals to threaten physical violence, but from the relations of production in which they are enmeshed. Management is able to demolish Julio because he realizes that, despite his bravado, they hold enormous power and he holds almost none. For Marxists, while physical violence may be terrible, the worst sort of violence is structural—that is, the violence done to human beings that stems from exploitative and oppressive relationships of production.

[19] The principle underlying this passage is the notion that in a capitalist society an individual's value is his or her contribution to capitalist production. Individuals who make no contribution have no value. Because they can be easily replaced by new immigrants, Julio and those like him have very little value, and society need not expend much on their support.

are only just struggling to escape. Her reminiscences about childhood in her natal village reveal the trajectory of improved material conditions, cultural dislocation, and crushed working-class dreams that is propelling her second-generation son into a destructive street culture:

> I loved that life in Puerto Rico, because it was a healthy, healthy, healthy life.
>
> We always ate because my father always had work, and in those days the custom was to have a garden in your patio to grow food and everything that you ate.
>
> We only ate meat on Sundays because everything was cultivated on the same little parcel of land. We didn't have a refrigerator, so we ate *bacalao* [salted codfish], which can stay outside, and a meat that they call old-meat, *carne de vieja*, and sardines from a can. But thanks to God, we never felt hunger. My mother made a lot of cornflour.
>
> Some people have done better by coming here, but many people haven't. Even people from my barrio, who came trying to find a better life [*buen ambiente*] just found disaster. Married couples right from my neighborhood came only to have the husband run off with another woman.
>
> In those days in Puerto Rico, when we were in poverty, life was better. Everyone will tell you life was healthier and you could trust people. Now you can't trust anybody.
>
> What I like best was that we kept all our traditions . . . our feasts. In my village, everyone was either an Uncle or an Aunt. And when you walked by someone older, you had to ask for their blessing. It was respect. There was a lot of respect in those days. [Original in Spanish][20]

Ironically, at sixty, Julio's monolingual Spanish-speaking mother is the only one of her family who can still compete effectively with the new immigrants who are increasingly filling Manhattan's entry-level labor market. She ekes out a living on welfare in her high-rise housing-project apartment by taking in sewing from undocumented garment industry subcontractors.

Rather than bemoaning the structural adjustment which is destroying their capacity to survive on legal wages, street-bound Puerto Rican youths celebrate their "decision" to bank on the underground economy and to cultivate their street identities. Willie and Julio repeatedly assert their pride in their street careers. For example, one Saturday night after they finished their midnight shift at the crack house, I accompanied them on their way to purchase "El Sapo Verde" (The Green Toad), a twenty-dollar bag of powder cocaine, sold by a reputable outfit three blocks away. While waiting for Julio and Willie to be "served" by the coke seller, I engaged three undocumented Mexican men drinking beer on a neighboring stoop in a conversation about finding work in New York. One of the new immigrants was already earning five hundred dollars a week fixing deep-fat-fry machines. He had a straightforward racist explanation for why Willie — who was standing next to me — was "unemployed":

> OK, OK I'll explain it to you in one word: Because the Puerto Ricans are brutes! [pointing at Willie] Brutes! Do you understand?
>
> Puerto Ricans like to make easy money. They like to leech off the other people. But not us Mexicans! No way! We like to work for our money. We don't steal. We came here to work and that's all. [Original in Spanish]

Instead of physically assaulting the employed immigrant for insulting him, Willie turned the racist tirade into the basis for a new, generational-based "American-born," urban cultural pride. In fact, in his response, he ridiculed what he interpreted to be the hillbilly naivete of the Mexicans who still believe in the "American Dream." He spoke slowly in street-English as if to mark sarcastically the contrast between his "savvy" Nuyorican identity versus the limited English proficiency of his detractor:

> That's right, m'a man! We is real vermin lunatics that sell drugs. We don't want no part of society. "Fight the Power!"[b]

---

[20] Marxists hold that capitalism is a system of maximal exploitation because under capitalism, the individual is stripped of everything except his or her labor. This has sometimes led Marxists to romanticize noncapitalist systems of production. In this passage, Julio's mother reminisces about the beauty of life in Puerto Rico, forgetting for the moment that it was most likely the crushing poverty and misery of that life that caused her family to emigrate to New York City. Bourgois uses this rather long quote as a rhetorical device to emphasize the misery of relations of production in New York.

What do we wanna be working for? We rather live off the system. Gain weight, lay women.

When we was younger, we used to break our asses too. [Gesturing toward the Mexican men who were straining to understand his English] I had all kinds of stupid jobs too . . . advertising agencies . . . computers.

But not no more! Now we're in a rebellious stage. We rather evade taxes, make quick money and just survive. But we're not satisfied with that either. Ha![21]

CONCLUSION: ETHNOGRAPHY AND OPPRESSION

America was built on racial hierarchy and on blame-the-victim justifications for the existence of poverty and class distinctions. This makes it difficult to present ethnographic data from inner-city streets without falling prey to a "pornography of violence" or a racist voyeurism. The public "common sense" is not persuaded by a structural economic understanding of Willie's and Julio's "self-destruction." Even the victims themselves psychologize their unsatisfactory lives. Most concretely, political will and public policy ignore the fundamental structural economic facts of marginalization in America (see Romo and Schwartz 1993). Instead the first priority of federal and local social "welfare" agencies is to change the psychological—or at best the "cultural"—orientations of misguided individuals (Katz 1989).[22]

Unfortunately researchers in America have allowed the gap to grow between their hegemonically "liberal" intellectual community and an overwhelmingly conservative popular political culture. From the late 1970s through most of the 1980s, inner-city poverty was simply ignored by all but right-wing academics who filled a popular

vacuum with scientifically flawed "best sellers" on the psychological and cultural causes of poverty in order to argue against the "poisonous" effect of public sector intervention (cf. Gilder 1982; Murray 1984). Their analyses coincide with the deep-seated individualistic, blame-the-victim values so cherished in American thought.

There is a theoretical and methodological basis for anthropology's reticence to confront devastating urban poverty in its front yard. Qualitative researchers prefer to avoid tackling taboo subjects such as personal violence, sexual abuse, addiction, alienation, self-destruction, and so forth, for fear of violating the tenets of cultural relativism and of contributing to popular racist stereotypes. Even the "new advocacy ethnography" which is confronting inner-city social crises—homelessness, AIDS, teen pregnancy—in an engaged manner tends to present its "subjects" in an exclusively sympathetic framework (Dehavenon n.d.). The pragmatic realities of a new advocacy anthropology require published data to be politically crafted. A complex critical perspective therefore is often stifled by the necessity of contributing effectively and responsibly to a "policy debate." Defining policy as a political arena for engagement can demobilize both theory and practice.

Regardless of the political, scholarly, or personal motivations, anthropology's cautious and often self-censored approaches to social misery have obfuscated an ethnographic understanding of the multifaceted dynamics of the experience of oppression and ironically sometimes even have served to minimize the depths of human suffering involved. At the same time, there is a growing body of ethnographic literature at the intersection of education and anthropology—sometimes referred to as cultural production theory—which

---

[21] Gramsci believed that subaltern populations, that is, those who are subordinate or held in positions of oppression and exploitation, produce intellectuals who develop counter-hegemonic ideas. In other words, the oppressed develop new notions of morality and leadership, as well as new alliances that redefine the cultural worlds in which they live. In Gramsci's thought, the organization of a counter-hegemony is critical to developing the revolutionary potential of the masses. In this passage the recent Mexican immigrants echo the hegemonic ideas of bourgeois American society. Willie, in ridiculing these ideas and defying the "hard work makes success" logic of the Mexicans, offers a counter-hegemonic response.

[22] In other words, social institutions serve to reinforce the hegemonic ideas of the power elites. The "cure" for Willie's radicalism, for instance, is to be found in social service organizations that will convince him of the virtues of "common sense" and "hard work."

provides insight into how contradictory and complicated forms of resistance often lead to personal self-destruction and community trauma (Foley 1990; Fordham 1988; MacLeod 1987; Willis 1977). Nevertheless, perhaps even these more self-consciously theoretical attempts to grapple with an unpleasant reality tend to glorify—or at least to overidentify with—the resistance theme in order to escape a "blame-the-victim" insinuation (see Bourgois 1989).[23]

Much of the problem is rooted in the nature of the ethnographic endeavor itself. Engulfed in an overwhelming whirlpool of personal suffering it is often difficult for ethnographers to see the larger relationships structuring the jumble of human interaction around them. Structures of power and history cannot be touched or talked to. Empirically this makes it difficult to identify the urgent political economy relationships shaping everyday survival—whether they be public sector breakdown or economic restructuring. For my own part, in the heat of daily life on the street in El Barrio, I often experienced a confusing anger with the victims, the victimizers, and the wealthy industrialized society that generated such a record toll of unnecessary human suffering. For example, when confronted with a pregnant friend frantically smoking crack—and condemning her fetus to a postpartum life of shattered emotions and dulled brain cells—it was impossible for me to remember the history of her people's colonial terror and humiliation or to contextualize her position in New York's changing economy. Living the inferno of what America calls its "underclass,"

I—like my neighbors around me and like the pregnant crack addicts themselves—often blamed the victim. To overcome such a partial perspective when researching painful human contexts it is especially important to develop a sensitive political economy analysis that "articulates the hidden histories" of the peoples raking themselves over the coals of the latest forms of capitalism.

Notes

The author would like to thank the following institutions for their support: The Russel Sage Foundation, the Harry Frank Guggenheim Foundation, the Social Science Research Council, the National Institute on Drug Abuse, the Wenner-Gren Foundation for Anthropological Research, the United States Bureau of the Census, and San Francisco State University. Helpful critical comments by Jane Schneider and Rayna Rapp changed the shape of the article. Finally, none of this could have been written without Harold Otto's moral support and typing, as well as final work on the keyboard by Henry Ostendorf and Charles Pearson.

a. Significantly, there are subsectors of the service industry that are relatively unionized—such as hospital work and even custodial work—where there is a limited autonomous space for street culture and working-class resistance.

b. "Fight for Power" is a song composed by the rap group Public Enemy.

References

Berlin, Gordon
  1991 "The Poverty among Families: A Service Decategorization Response." Photocopied report, Manpower Demonstration Research Corporation, New York.

---

[23] Cultural-production theory is part of the Cultural Studies approach to anthropology and sociology that is closely identified with the work of the Birmingham Centre for Contemporary Cultural Studies and French Marxist Louis Althusser. Cultural Studies scholars focus on studying popular culture expressed in the styles adopted by subcultures as well as in cinema and television aimed at mass audiences. Following Althusser, they believe popular culture expresses the structural relationships between classes and social groups. In addition to expressing this relationship, culture is an ideology that defines the relationship of individuals and groups to the world. This is similar to Gramsci's notion of hegemony and counterhegemony (see footnotes 11 and 21).

Paul Willis is perhaps the best-known cultural-production theorist. He locates his notion of cultural production within the general field of Cultural Studies. However, while Cultural Studies stresses the meanings and practices that individuals acquire as a result of their structural position in society, Willis emphasizes the meanings that individuals create in response to these positions. He claims that individuals are "active appropriators who produce meanings and cultural forms" (1983:114) and sees the production of culture as the active creation, by individuals, of new forms and styles that allow them to occupy (and often challenge) the structural positions capitalist society forces them into. Willis' theory has been widely criticized for political pessimism and romanticization of the oppressed (Walker 1986), hence Bourgois' attempt in the last sentence of this paragraph to distance himself from this theory.

Bourgois, Philippe
1989 "Crack in Spanish Harlem: Culture and Economy in the Inner City." *Anthropology Today* 5:6–11.
In press *In Search of Respect: Selling Crack in Spanish Harlem*. New York: Cambridge University Press.

Falcon, Angelo
1992 "Puerto Ricans and Other Latinos in New York City Today: A Statistical Profile." Pamphlet, Institute for Puerto Rican Policy, New York.

Foley, Doug
1990 *Learning Capitalist Culture: Deep in the Heart of Tejas*. Philadelphia: University of Pennsylvania.

Fordham, Signithia
1988 "Racelessness as a Factor in Black Students' School Success: Pragmatic Strategy or Pyrrhic Victory?" *Harvard Educational Review* 53:257–293.

Gilder, George
1982 *Wealth and Poverty*. New York: Bantam.

Katz, Michael
1989 *The Undeserving Poor: From the War on Poverty to the War on Welfare*. New York: Pantheon Press.

Lambert, Bruce
1990 "AIDS Travels New York-Puerto Rico 'Air Bridge,'" *New York Times* (15 June):B1.

Lauria, Anthony, Jr.
1994 "'Respeto,' 'Relajo,' and Inter-Personal Relations in Puerto Rico." *Anthropological Quarterly* 37(2):53–67.

MacLeod, Jay
1987 *Ain't No Makin' It: Leveled Aspirations in Low-Income Neighborhood*. Boulder, Colo.: Westview Press.

Murray, Charles
1984 *Losing Ground: American Social Policy 1950–1980*. New York: Basic Books.

Rodriguez, Clara E.
1989 *Puerto Ricans: Born in the U.S.A.* Winchester, Mass.: Unwin Hyman.

Romo, Frank, and Michael Schwartz
1993 "The Coming of Post-Industrial Society Revisited: Manufacturing and the Prospects for a Service Based Economy." In *Explorations in Economic Sociology*, Richard Swedburg, ed., 335–373. New York: Russell Sage Foundation.

Rosenbaum, David E.
1989 "Bush and Congress Reach Accord Raising Minimum Wage to $4.25." *New York Times* (1 November):A1–A2.

Scott, James C.
1985 *Weapons of the Weak: Everyday Forms of Peasant Resistance*. New Haven: Yale University Press.

Willis, Paul
1977 *Learning to Labor: How Working Class Kids Get Working Class Jobs*. New York: Columbia University Press.

Wilson, William Julius
1987 *The Truly Disadvantaged: The Inner City, the Underclass, and Public Policy*. Chicago: University of Chicago Press.

Wolf, Eric R.
1956b "San Jose: Subcultures of a Traditional Coffee Municipality." In *The People of Puerto Rico: A Study in Social Anthropology*, by Julian Steward et al., pt. 7, 171–264. Urbana: University of Illinois Press.
1982a *Europe and the People without History*. Berkeley, Los Angeles, London: University of California Press. (Translations: German, Italian, Spanish.)
1990b "Distinguished Lecture: Facing Power—Old Insights, New Questions." *American Anthropologist* 92:586–596.

Structuralism

Claude Lévi-Strauss (1908–) almost single-handedly founded the modern field of structuralism. In the 1940s, he proposed that the proper area of study for anthropologists is not how people categorize their world, but the underlying patterns of human thought that produce those categories. Pursuing this quest, he has spent the last half century conducting cross-cultural studies of kinship, myths, and religion in an attempt to understand the fundamental structure of human cognition.

Lévi-Strauss' theory of culture is based in psychology, but unlike Freud or the culture and personality theorists, he does not believe that the psychological structure he proposes determines culture. Instead, Lévi-Strauss believes that the underlying logical processes that structure all human thought operate within different cultural contexts. Consequently, cultural phenomena are not identical, but they are the products of an underlying universal pattern of thought. His anthropology centers on the search to uncover this pattern. For this reason, Kaplan and Manners describe Lévi-Strauss as "the ultimate logician of culture" (1972:176).

Lévi-Strauss' structuralism was heavily influenced by the great French scholars of the previous generation: Durkheim and Mauss. In fact, the title of his first major work, *The Elementary Structures of Kinship* (1969 [1949]), echoes the title of Durkheim's great work on religion *The Elementary Forms of the Religious Life* (1965 [1912]). The so-called Prague School of structural linguistics, organized in 1926, also played a major role in the formulation of Lévi-Strauss' theory. This group of scholars, founded by the linguists Roman Jakobson (1896–1982) and Nikolai Troubetzkoy (1890–1938), placed an emphasis on the synchronic (descriptive) rather than diachronic (historical) study of language and pro-

moted the theory that linguistic meaning was built upon contrasts between sounds, or phonemes. Members of the Prague School defined and characterized the phonemic study of languages. This provided Lévi-Strauss with the concept of binary contrasts that was fundamental in his formulation of structuralism.

Perhaps the simplest way to explain the theoretical basis of structuralism is to compare it to linguistics. All languages are composed of arbitrary groups of sounds called phonemes. Phonemes by themselves are meaningless. It is only when they are combined into larger units (morphemes, words, phrases, and so on) according to certain patterns (the rules of syntax and grammar) that phonemes form meaningful units (speech). Most speakers of a language cannot articulate the underlying rules that structure their use of phonemes and create meaningful communication, yet all are able to use language to communicate successfully with one another. Therefore, at a subconscious level, we must all "know" the rules that structure our use of language. The job of a linguist is to go beyond the outward use of language and discover these unconscious principles. In the same way, Lévi-Strauss tried to design a technique for studying the unconscious principles that structure human culture.

To Lévi-Strauss, culture, like language, is essentially a collection of arbitrary symbols. He is not interested in the specific meaning of the symbols any more than a linguist is interested in the phonemes of a language. Rather, he is concerned with the patterning of elements—the way cultural elements relate to one another to form the overall system (Lévi-Strauss 1963:208).

A key insight of the Prague School was that words were built upon contrasts (binary oppositions) between phonemes rather than simply being groups of sounds. Following this linguistic model, Lévi-Strauss proposed that the fundamental pattern of human thought also uses binary contrasts such as black-white, night-day, and hot-cold. This insight dovetailed nicely with Durkheim's and Hertz's proposition that distinctions such as sacred and profane and right and left were fundamental parts of the collective conscious.

In *The Elementary Structures of Kinship*, Lévi-Strauss analyzed kinship based on his notion of the binary structure of human thought, using the work of another of Durkheim's followers, Marcel Mauss. In *The Gift* (1967 [1925]), Mauss tried to demonstrate that exchange in primitive societies was not motivated by economic motives but instead by rules of reciprocity upon which the solidarity of society depended. In his book, Lévi-Strauss took Mauss' concept of reciprocity and applied it to marriage in primitive societies, arguing that women are a commodity that could be exchanged. Lévi-Strauss contended that one of the first and most important distinctions a human makes is between self and others. This "natural" binary distinction then leads to the formation of the incest taboo, which necessitates choosing spouses from outside your family. In this way, the binary distinction between kin and nonkin is resolved by the reciprocal exchange of women and the formation of kin networks in primitive societies.

Lévi-Strauss' interest in mythology lies in his belief that studying the mythologies of primitive peoples allows him to examine the unconscious universal patterning of human thought in its uncontaminated form. In Lévi-Strauss' view, the mythology of primitive peoples is closer to these universal principles than Western beliefs because the training we receive in Western society buries the logical structure he seeks under layers of "cultural interference" created by our social environment. In his work on myths, folktales, and religion, Lévi-Strauss expanded on the notion that human cognition was structured into binary oppositions. He proposed that a fundamental characteristic of human thought was the desire to find a midpoint between such oppositions.

In Lévi-Strauss' view, the elements of myth, like the phonemes of language, acquire meaning only when arranged according to certain structural relations. Consequently, the structuralist examines the rules that govern the relationships between myth elements. The task of structural analysis is to break the myth into its constituent elements and uncover the unconscious meaning found in the binary relationships between them. Uncovering this hidden structural core will reveal the essential elements of human thought.

The essays we have chosen for this part of the book are examples of the application of structural analysis to different areas of study over several decades. In "Structural Analysis," one of his classic early essays first published in 1945, Lévi-Strauss outlines his theory of kinship based on Mauss' notion of reciprocity.

Essay 26, "Genesis as Myth," is an example of the structural analysis of myth by the British anthropologist Edmund Leach (1910–1989). Leach's initial academic training had nothing to do with anthropology—he studied mathematics and engineering at Cambridge University. A meeting with Malinowski in 1937 resulted eventually in what he called a "conversion experience" (Leach 1984:2). Leach first encountered Lévi-Strauss through *The Elementary Structures of Kinship* while he was preparing his own book *The Political Systems of Highland Burma*. He became interested in structuralism after spending the academic year 1960–1961 at Stanford, where he worked with Jakobson. Until his death he was considered one of the foremost English authorities on structural analysis.

Our final selection in this section is a structural analysis of gender stratification by the American anthropologist Sherry Ortner (1941–). Although her first work was in symbolic anthropology, in the last few decades Ortner has become known for her contributions to the field of feminist anthropology. In particular, her volume *Sexual Meanings: The Cultural Constructions of Gender and Sexuality* (edited with Harriet Whitehead; 1981) is considered a classic in the field. In essay 27, which was originally published in 1974, Ortner examines the issue of gender inequality. Echoing Lévi-Strauss, she suggests that gender stratification is based on the fundamental opposition between nature and culture. Women, she proposes, because of pregnancy and childbirth, are universally associated with nature. Men, on the other hand, because they are unable to bear children, are cultural creators and are thus accorded higher status.

Structuralism had a profound effect on American anthropology. In particular, it influenced symbolic anthropology, which was popular in the 1970s; cognitive anthropology; and postmodernism, which achieved notoriety in the 1980s.

25. Structural Analysis in Linguistics and in Anthropology

Claude Lévi-Strauss (1908–)

LINGUISTICS OCCUPIES A SPECIAL PLACE AMONG the social sciences, to whose ranks it unquestionably belongs.[1] It is not merely a social science like the others, but, rather, the one in which by far the greatest progress has been made. It is probably the only one which can truly claim to be a science and which has achieved both the formulation of an empirical method and an understanding of the nature of the data submitted to its analysis. This privileged position carries with it several obligations. The linguist will often find scientists from related but different disciplines drawing inspiration from his example and trying to follow his lead. *Noblesse oblige.* A linguistic journal like *Word* cannot confine itself to the illustration of strictly linguistic theories and points of view. It must also welcome psychologists, sociologists, and anthropologists eager to learn from modern linguistics the road which leads to the empirical knowledge of social phenomena. As Marcel Mauss wrote already forty years ago: "Sociology would certainly have progressed much further if it had everywhere followed the lead of the linguists. . . ."[a] The close

(1963)

methodological analogy which exists between the two disciplines imposes a special obligation of collaboration upon them.

Ever since the work of Schrader[b] it has been unnecessary to demonstrate the assistance which linguistics can render to the anthropologist in the study of kinship. It was a linguist and a philologist (Schrader and Rose)[c] who showed the improbability of the hypothesis of matrilineal survivals in the family in antiquity, to which so many anthropologists still clung at that time.[2] The linguist provides the anthropologist with etymologies which permit him to establish between certain kinship terms relationships that were not immediately apparent. The anthropologist, on the other hand, can bring to the attention of the linguist customs, prescriptions, and prohibitions that help him to understand the persistence of certain features of language or the instability of terms or groups of terms. At a meeting of the Linguistic Circle of New York, Julien Bonfante once illustrated this point of view by reviewing the etymology of the word for uncle in several Romance languages. The Greek *Oeiox* corresponds in Italian, Spanish, and Portuguese to *zio* and *tio*; and he added that in certain

---

[1] Work in linguistics is one of the major sources of Lévi-Strauss' structural anthropology, and the original version of this essay appeared in 1945 in *Word, Journal of the Linguistic Circle of New York,* which is mentioned in the first paragraph. In the early 1900s, the work of Swiss linguist Ferdinand de Saussure (1857–1913) revolutionized that field. Studies in linguistics had been focused on the history of languages. Saussure studied language as a self-sufficient system existing at a given time. He distinguished between the set of abstract rules governing the production of a language, which he called *langue,* and the act of speech, which he termed *parole.*

[2] The issue of matrilineal survivals was crucial for many anthropologists at the turn of the century because Morgan and others had suggested that the family had followed a universal course of evolution from matrilineal to patrilineal. Some of the evidence used by both those who favored this argument and those who opposed it was linguistic. If the hypothesis was correct, anthropologists should be able to show survivals of matrilineal kin-terms in the language of modern patrilineal groups.

regions of Italy the uncle is called *barba*. The "beard," the "divine" uncle—what a wealth of suggestions for the anthropologist! The investigations of the late A. M. Hocart into the religious character of the avuncular relationship and the "theft of the sacrifice" by the maternal kinsmen immediately come to mind.[d] Whatever interpretation is given to the data collected by Hocart (and his own interpretation is not entirely satisfactory), there is no doubt that the linguist contributes to the solution of the problem by revealing the tenacious survival in contemporary vocabulary of relationships which have long since disappeared. At the same time, the anthropologist explains to the linguist the bases of etymology and confirms its validity. Paul K. Benedict, in examining, as a linguist, the kinship systems of Southeast Asia, was able to make an important contribution to the anthropology of the family in that area.[e]

But linguists and anthropologists follow their own paths independently.[3] They halt, no doubt, from time to time to communicate to one another certain of their findings; these findings, however, derive from different operations, and no effort is made to enable one group to benefit from the technical and methodological advances of the other. This attitude might have been justified in the era when linguistic research leaned most heavily on historical analysis. In relation to the anthropological research conducted during the same period, the difference was one of degree rather than of kind. The linguists employed a more rigorous method, and their findings were established on more solid grounds; the sociologists could follow their example in "renouncing consideration of the spatial distribution of contemporary types as a basis

for their classifications."[f] But, after all, anthropology and sociology were looking to linguistics only for insights; nothing foretold a revelation.[g]

The advent of structural linguistics completely changed this situation. Not only did it renew linguistic perspectives; a transformation of this magnitude is not limited to a single discipline. Structural linguistics will certainly play the same renovating role with respect to the social sciences that nuclear physics, for example, has played for the physical sciences. In what does this revolution consist, as we try to assess its broadest implications? N. Troubetzkoy, the illustrious founder of structural linguistics, himself furnished the answer to this question.[4] In one programmatic statement,[h] he reduced the structural method to four basic operations. First, structural linguistics shifts from the study of *conscious* linguistic phenomena to study of their *unconscious* infrastructure; second, it does not treat *terms* as independent entities, taking instead as its basis of analysis the *relations* between terms; third, it introduces the concept of *system*—"Modern phonemics does not merely proclaim that phonemes are always part of a system; it *shows* concrete phonemic systems and elucidates their structure";[i] finally, structural linguistics aims at discovering *general laws*, either by induction "or . . . by logical deduction, which would give them an absolute character."[j]

Thus for the first time, a social science is able to formulate necessary relationships. This is the meaning of Troubetzkoy's last point, while the proceeding rules show how linguistics must proceed in order to attain this end. It is not for us to show that Troubetzkoy's claims are justified. The vast majority of modern linguists seem sufficiently

---

[3] In this passage, Lévi-Strauss continues to build his case that linguistics presents a valuable model for anthropologists. He was convinced that the work of twentieth-century linguists, particularly those of the Prague School (more about this in footnote 4), was a scientific revolution to rival the Copernican or Einsteinian revolutions in physics.

[4] Nikolai Troubetzkoy (1890–1938) and Roman Jakobson (1896–1982) are the founders of the Prague School of linguistics. It was Jakobson who had the greatest impact upon Lévi-Strauss—they were colleagues at the New School for Social Research in the 1940s. The Prague School was characterized by a concern for the social functions of language. One of these functions is poetic, which concerns the form of an utterance rather than its meaning. This led Prague School theorists to emphasize the sounds of language, which they dubbed *phonemes*. The phoneme is the basic unit of sound in a language and can be characterized by the physiology required for its production (position of lips, tongue, and so on). Prague School theorists focused on how each language builds the system of phonemes of which it is composed. They discovered that such systems were built upon contrasts, binary oppositions, rather than simply being catalogues of sounds.

agreed on this point. But when an event of this importance takes place in one of the sciences of man, it is not only permissible for, but required of, representatives of related disciplines immediately to examine its consequences and its possible application to phenomena of another order.

New perspectives then open up. We are no longer dealing with an occasional collaboration where the linguist and the anthropologist, each working by himself, occasionally communicate those findings which each thinks may interest the other. In the study of kinship problems (and, no doubt, the study of other problems as well), the anthropologist finds himself in a situation which formally resembles that of the structural linguist. Like phonemes, kinship terms are elements of meaning; like phonemes, they acquire meaning only if they are integrated into systems. "Kinship systems," like "phonemic systems," are built by the mind on the level of unconscious thought. Finally, the recurrence of kinship patterns, marriage rules, similar prescribed attitudes between certain types of relatives, and so forth, in scattered regions of the globe and in fundamentally different societies, leads us to believe that, in the case of kinship as well as linguistics, the observable phenomena result from the action of laws which are general but implicit. The problem can therefore be formulated as follows: Although they belong to *another order of reality,* kinship phenomena are *of the same type* as linguistic phenomena. Can the anthropologist, using a method analogous *in form* (if not in content) to the method used in structural linguistics, achieve the same kind of progress in his own science as that which has taken place in linguistics?[5]

We shall be even more strongly inclined to follow this path after an additional observation has been made. The study of kinship problems is today broached in the same terms and seems to be in the throes of the same difficulties as was linguistics on the eve of the structuralist revolution. There is a striking analogy between certain attempts by Rivers and the old linguistics, which sought its explanatory principles first of all in history.[6] In both cases, it is solely (or almost solely) diachronic analysis which must account for synchronic phenomena. Troubetzkoy, comparing structural linguistics and the old linguistics, defines structural linguistics as a "systematic structuralism and universalism," which he contrasts with the individualism and "atomism" of former schools. And when he considers diachronic analysis, his perspective is a profoundly modified one: "The evolution of a phonemic system at any given moment is directed by the *tendency toward a goal.* This evolution thus has a direction, an internal logic, which historical phonemics is called upon to elucidate."[k] The "individualistic" and "atomistic" interpretation, founded exclusively on historical contingency, which is criticized by Troubetzkoy and Jakobson, is actually the same as that which is generally applied to kinship problems.[l] Each detail of terminology and each special marriage rule is associated with a specific custom as either its consequence or its survival. We thus meet with a chaos of discontinuity. No one asks how kinship systems, regarded as synchronic wholes, could be the arbitrary prod-

---

[5] The two key linguistic ideas that Lévi-Strauss seizes on and tries to apply are Saussure's distinction between *langue* and *parole* and Jakobson's idea of speech as a system formed of contrasting binaries. Saussure believed that the ultimate formal rules of *langue* could not be observed but could be inferred from *parole.* Similarly, Lévi-Strauss believes that the ultimate transcendant and universal laws of culture (equivalent to *langue*) can be inferred from the observations of cultures (equivalent to *parole).* However, in order for this to be possible, these analytic units used to describe culture must be similar to the units with which Jakobson described language. Jakobson analyzed speech as a system of contrasting basic elements (phonemes in his case) that exist independently of the specific meaning of any particular utterance. Using this method, he claimed to discover universal laws of the production of language. Lévi-Strauss wishes to analyze culture in the same way and with the same goals. He focuses on kinship as a system comparable to the system of phonemes.

[6] Lévi-Strauss critiques W. H. R. Rivers, who, in 1900, had proposed the genealogical method as a cornerstone of scientific research in anthropology. Lévi-Strauss points out that while Rivers had developed a scientific method for collecting genealogies, this had led simply to a proliferation of scientifically collected particular genealogies rather than the discovery of laws underlying the structures of kinship.

uct of a convergence of several heterogeneous institutions (most of which are hypothetical), yet nevertheless function with some sort of regularity and effectiveness.[m]

However, a preliminary difficulty impedes the transposition of the phonemic method to the anthropological study of primitive peoples. The superficial analogy between phonemic systems and kinship systems is so strong that it immediately sets us on the wrong track. It is incorrect to equate kinship terms and linguistic phonemes from the viewpoint of their formal treatment. We know that to obtain a structural law the linguist analyzes phonemes into "distinctive features," which he can then group into one or several "pairs of oppositions."[n] Following an analogous method, the anthropologist might be tempted to break down analytically the kinship terms of any given system into their components. In our own kinship system, for instance, the term father has positive connotations with respect to sex, relative age, and generation; but it has a zero value on the dimension of collaterality, and it cannot express an affinal relationship. Thus, for each system, one might ask what relationships are expressed and, for each term of the system, what connotation — positive or negative — it carries regarding each of the following relationships: generation, collaterality, sex, relative age, affinity, etc. It is at this "microsociological" level that one might hope to discover the most general structural laws, just as the linguist discovers his at the infra-phonemic level or the physicist at the infra-molecular or atomic level. One might interpret the interesting attempt of Davis and Warner in these terms.[o]

But a threefold objection immediately arises. A truly scientific analysis must be real, simplifying, and explanatory. Thus the distinctive features which are the product of phonemic analysis have

an objective existence from three points of view: psychological, physiological, and even physical; they are fewer in number than the phonemes which result from their combination; and, finally, they allow us to understand and reconstruct the system. Nothing of the kind would emerge from the preceding hypothesis. The treatment of kinship terms which we have just sketched is analytical in appearance only; for, actually, the result is more abstract than the principle; instead of moving toward the concrete, one moves away from it, and the definitive system — if system there is — is only conceptual. Secondly, Davis and Warner's experiment proves that the system achieved through this procedure is infinitely more complex and more difficult to interpret than the empirical data.[p] Finally, the hypothesis has no explanatory value; that is, it does not lead to an understanding of the nature of the system and still less to a reconstruction of its origins.[7]

What is the reason for this failure? A too literal adherence to linguistic method actually betrays its very essence. Kinship terms not only have a sociological existence; they are also elements of speech. In our haste to apply the methods of linguistic analysis, we must not forget that, as a part of vocabulary, kinship terms must be treated with linguistic methods in direct and not analogous fashion. Linguistics teaches us precisely that structural analysis cannot be applied to words directly, but only to words previously broken down into phonemes. *There are no necessary relationships at the vocabulary level.*[q] This applies to all vocabulary elements including kinship terms. Since this applies to linguistics, it ought to apply *ipso facto* to the sociology of language. An attempt like the one whose possibility we are now discussing would thus consist in extending the method of structural linguistics while ignoring its

---

[7] The first problem Lévi-Strauss encounters in his attempt to analyze kinship using a linguistic model is finding the unit of kinship that is analogous to the phoneme. To do this, he must separate the characteristics that lead to universal generalizations from those that merely describe the use of kin-terms in a particular culture. He critiques Davis and Warner, who attempted a structural analysis of kinship in the 1930s, for their failure to do this. Because of this failure, Lévi-Strauss claims that they have mistaken the historically particular for the universal. Their analysis suffers because it offers increased complication rather than sophistication. Lévi-Strauss here invokes Occam's razor: in scientific explanation, that which is simplest is best.

basic requirements. Kroeber prophetically fore-saw this difficulty in an article written many years ago.[r] And if, at that time, he concluded that a structural analysis of kinship terminology was im-possible, we must remember that linguistics itself was then restricted to phonetic, psychological, and historical analysis. While it is true that the social sciences must share the limitations of lin-guistics, they can also benefit from its progress.[8]

Nor should we overlook the profound differ-ences between the phonemic chart of a language and the chart of kinship terms of a society. In the first instance there can be no question as to func-tion; we all know that language serves as a means of communication. On the other hand, what the linguist did not know and what structural linguis-tics alone has allowed him to discover is the way in which language achieves this end. The function was obvious; the system remained unknown. In this respect, the anthropologist finds himself in the opposite situation. We know, since the work of Lewis H. Morgan, that kinship terms constitute systems; on the other hand, we still do not know their function. The misinterpretation of this initial situation reduces most structural analyses of kin-ship systems to pure tautologies. They demon-strate the obvious and neglect the unknown.

This does not mean that we must abandon hope of introducing order and discovering mean-ing in kinship nomenclature. But we should at least recognize the special problems raised by the sociology of vocabulary and the ambiguous char-acter of the relations between its methods and those of linguistics. For this reason it would be preferable to limit the discussion to a case where the analogy can be clearly established. Fortu-nately, we have just such a case available.

What is generally called a "kinship system" comprises two quite different orders of reality.[9]

First, there are terms through which various kinds of family relationships are expressed. But kinship is not expressed solely through nomenclature. The individuals or classes of individuals who em-ploy these terms feel (or do not feel, as the case may be) bound by prescribed behavior in their re-lations with one another, such as respect or fa-miliarity, rights or obligations, and affection or hostility. Thus, along with what we propose to call the *system of terminology* (which, strictly speak-ing, constitutes the vocabulary system), there is another system, both psychological and social in nature, which we shall call the *system of attitudes*. Although it is true (as we have shown above) that the study of systems of terminology places us in a situation analogous, but opposite, to the situation in which we are dealing with phonemic systems, this difficulty is "inversed," as it were, when we examine systems of attitudes. We can guess at the role played by systems of attitudes, that is, to in-sure group cohesion and equilibrium, but we do not understand the nature of the interconnec-tions between the various attitudes, nor do we perceive their necessity.[s] In other words, as in the case of language, we know their function, but the system is unknown.

Thus we find a profound difference between the *system of terminology* and the *system of atti-tudes,* and we have to disagree with A. R. Radcliffe-Brown if he really believed, as has been said of him, that attitudes are nothing but the expression or transposition of terms on the affective level.[t] The last few years have provided numerous exam-ples of groups whose chart of kinship terms does not accurately reflect family attitudes, and vice versa.[u] It would be incorrect to assume that the kinship system constitutes the principal means of regulating interpersonal relationships in all soci-eties. Even in societies where the kinship system

---

[8] Lévi-Strauss here makes the counterintuitive remark that the essence of linguistics is forsaken by taking it too literally. What he apparently means is that anthropologists must find the correct level at which to make the analogy between linguistic analysis using phonemes and kinship analysis. Once this basic unit of kinship is isolated, the description of a structural system of kinship can easily be made.

[9] In this passage, Lévi-Strauss begins to isolate the unit of kinship behavior that he believes analogous to the phoneme: it is found in psychology, the attitude of individuals toward their kin. In many respects, Lévi-Strauss' theory is psycholog-ical. That is, he sees cultures as primarily the manifestations of certain universal underlying patterns of brain structure and consciousness.

does function as such, it does not fulfill that role everywhere to the same extent. Furthermore, it is always necessary to distinguish between two types of attitudes: first, the diffuse, uncrystallized, and non-institutionalized attitudes, which we may consider as the reflection or transposition of the terminology on the psychological level; and second, along with, or in addition to, the preceding ones, those attitudes which are stylized, prescribed, and sanctioned by taboos or privileges and expressed through a fixed ritual.[10] These attitudes, far from automatically reflecting the nomenclature, often appear as secondary elaborations, which serve to resolve the contradictions and overcome the deficiencies inherent in the terminological system. This synthetic character is strikingly apparent among the Wik Munkan of Australia. In this group, joking privileges sanction a contradiction between the kinship relations which link two unmarried men and the theoretical relationship which must be assumed to exist between them in order to account for their later marriages to two women who do not stand themselves in the corresponding relationship.[v] There is a contradiction between two possible systems of nomenclature, and the emphasis placed on attitudes represents an attempt to integrate or transcend this contradiction.[11] We can easily agree with Radcliffe-Brown and assert the existence of "real relations of interdependence between the terminology and the rest of the system."[w] Some of his critics made the mistake of inferring, from the absence of a rigorous parallelism between attitudes and nomenclature, that the two systems were mutually independent. But this relationship of interdependence

does not imply a one-to-one correlation. The system of attitudes constitutes, rather, a dynamic integration of the system of terminology.

Granted the hypothesis (to which we wholeheartedly subscribe) of a functional relationship between the two systems, we are nevertheless entitled, for methodological reasons, to treat independently the problems pertaining to each system. This is what we propose to do here for a problem which is rightly considered the point of departure for any theory of attitudes — that of the maternal uncle. We shall attempt to show how a formal transposition of the method of structural linguistics allows us to shed new light upon this problem. Because the relationship between nephew and maternal uncle appears to have been the focus of significant elaboration in a great many primitive societies, anthropologists have devoted special attention to it. It is not enough to note the frequency of this theme; we must also account for it.

Let us briefly review the principal stages in the development of this problem.[12] During the entire nineteenth century and until the writings of Sydney Hartland,[x] the importance of the mother's brother was interpreted as a survival of matrilineal descent. This interpretation was based purely on speculation, and, indeed, it was highly improbable in the light of European examples. Furthermore, Rivers' attempt[y] to explain the importance of the mother's brother in southern India as a residue of cross-cousin marriage led to particularly deplorable results. Rivers himself was forced to recognize that this interpretation could not account for all aspects of the problem. He

---

[10] To begin his analysis, Lévi-Strauss must first show that attitudes are not merely the reflection of kin-terms, as he claims Radcliffe-Brown has asserted. If this were the case, the analytic separation of kin-terms from attitude proposed above would be meaningless. Lévi-Strauss here provides several examples to support his contention that this is not the case.

[11] Note the emphasis on attitude as a method of transcending contradiction, an echo of Marxist thought. Like Marx, but unlike the British structural-functionalists, Lévi-Strauss sees social systems as composed of inherently contradictory elements. For him, a key human cultural act is transcending these contradictions.

[12] In the next passage, Lévi-Strauss briefly surveys the history of anthropological attempts to treat the problem of the role of the mother's brother. He shows the inadequacy of early attempts to explain it as a survival of matrilineal descent or cross-cousin marriage. Lévi-Strauss credits Robert Lowie (1883–1957) with beginning the modern investigation of the avunculate and introducing what he terms the principle of "attitude qualification" — the idea that "there exists a general tendency to qualify attitudes, which constitutes the only empirical foundation for a theory of kinship systems." However, Lévi-Strauss points out that this begs the question of why only certain attitudes are associated with the avuncular relationship.

resigned himself to the hypothesis that several heterogeneous customs which have since disappeared (cross-cousin marriage being only one of them) were needed to explain the existence of a *single institution.*[z] Thus, atomism and mechanism triumphed. It was Lowie's crucial article on the matrilineal complex[aa] which opened what we should like to call the "modern phase" of the problem of the avunculate. Lowie showed that the correlation drawn or postulated between the prominent position of the maternal uncle and matrilineal descent cannot withstand rigorous analysis. In fact, the avunculate is found associated with patrilineal, as well as matrilineal, descent. The role of the maternal uncle cannot be explained as either a consequence or a survival of matrilineal kinship; it is only a specific application "of a very general tendency to associate definite social relations with definite forms of kinship regardless of maternal or paternal side." In accordance with this principle, introduced for the first time by Lowie in 1919, there exists a general tendency to qualify attitudes, which constitutes the only empirical foundation for a theory of kinship systems. But, at the same time, Lowie left certain questions unanswered. What exactly do we call an avunculate? Do we not merge different customs and attitudes under this single term? And, if it is true that there is a tendency to qualify all attitudes, why are only certain attitudes associated with the avuncular relationship, rather than just any possible attitudes, depending upon the group considered?

A few further remarks here may underline the striking analogy between the development of this problem and certain stages in the evolution of linguistic theory.[13] The variety of possible attitudes in the area of interpersonal relationships is almost unlimited; the same holds true for the variety of sounds which can be articulated by the vocal apparatus — and which are actually produced during the first months of human life. Each language, however, retains only a very small number among all the possible sounds, and in this respect linguistics raises two questions: Why are certain sounds selected? What relationships exist between one or several of the sounds chosen and all the others?[bb] Our sketch of the historical development of the avuncular problem is at precisely the same stage. Like language, the social group has a great wealth of psychophysiological material at its disposal. Like language too, it retains only certain elements, at least some of which remain the same throughout the most varied cultures and are combined into structures which are always diversified. Thus we may wonder about the reason for this choice and the laws of combination.

For insight into the specific problem of the avunculate we should turn to Radcliffe-Brown.[14] His well-known article on the maternal uncle in South Africa[cc] was the first attempt to grasp and analyze the modalities of what we might call the "general principle of attitude qualification." We shall briefly review the fundamental ideas of that now-classic study.

According to Radcliffe-Brown, the term *avunculate* covers two antithetical systems of attitudes. In one case, the maternal uncle represents family authority; he is feared and obeyed, and possesses certain rights over his nephew. In the other case, the nephew holds privileges of familiarity in relation to his uncle and can treat him more or less as his victim. Second, there is a correlation between the boy's attitude toward his maternal uncle and his attitude toward his father. We find the two systems of attitudes in both cases, but they are inversely correlated. In groups where familiarity characterizes the relationship between father and son, the relationship between maternal uncle and nephew is one of respect; and where the father stands as the austere representative of family authority, it is the uncle who is treated with familiarity. Thus the two sets of attitudes constitute (as the structural linguist would say) two pairs of oppositions. Radcliffe-Brown concluded his article

---

[13] Lévi-Strauss compares the development of theory about the avunculate with the development of linguistic theory, concluding that theory about the avunculate is at precisely the same stage as linguistic theory was before the advent of structural linguistics.

[14] The article referred to here appears as essay 14.

by proposing the following interpretation: In the final analysis, it is descent that determines the choice of oppositions. In patrilineal societies, where the father and the father's descent group represent traditional authority, the maternal uncle is considered a "male mother." He is generally treated in the same fashion, and sometimes even called by the same name, as the mother. In matrilineal societies, the opposite occurs. Here, authority is vested in the maternal uncle, while relationships of tenderness and familiarity revolve about the father and his descent group.

It would indeed be difficult to exaggerate the importance of Radcliffe-Brown's contribution, which was the first attempt at synthesis on an empirical basis following Lowie's authoritative and merciless criticism of evolutionist metaphysics. To say that this effort did not entirely succeed does not in any way diminish the homage due this great British anthropologist; but we should certainly recognize that Radcliffe-Brown's article leaves unanswered some fundamental questions.[15] First, the avunculate does not occur in all matrilineal or all patrilineal systems, and we find it present in some systems which are neither matrilineal nor patrilineal.[dd] Further, the avuncular relationship is not limited to two terms but presupposes four, namely, brother, sister, brother-in-law, and nephew. An interpretation such as Radcliffe-Brown's arbitrarily isolates particular elements of a global structure which must be treated as a whole. A few simple examples will illustrate this twofold difficulty.

The social organization of the Trobriand Islanders of Melanesia is characterized by matrilineal descent, free and familiar relations between father and son, and a marked antagonism between maternal uncle and nephew.[ee] On the other hand, the patrilineal Cherkess of the Caucasus place the hostility between father and son while the maternal uncle assists his nephew and gives him a horse when he marries.[ff] Up to this point we are still within the limits of Radcliffe-Brown's scheme. But let us consider the other family relationships involved. Malinowski showed that in the Trobriands husband and wife live in an atmosphere of tender intimacy and that their relationship is characterized by reciprocity. The relations between brother and sister, on the other hand, are dominated by an extremely rigid taboo. Let us now compare the situation in the Caucasus. There, it is the brother-sister relationship which is tender—to such an extent that among the Pschav an only daughter "adopts" a "brother" who will play the customary brother's role as her chaste bed companion.[gg] But the relationship between spouses is entirely different. A Cherkess will not appear in public with his wife and visits her only in secret. According to Malinowski, there is no greater insult in the Trobriands than to tell a man that he resembles his sister. In the Caucasus there is an analogous prohibition: It is forbidden to ask a man about his wife's health.

When we consider societies of the Cherkess and Trobriand types it is not enough to study the correlation of attitudes between *father / son* and *uncle / sister's son*. This correlation is only one aspect of a global system containing four types of relationships which are organically linked, namely: *brother / sister, husband / wife, father / son*, and *mother's brother / sister's son*. The two groups in our example illustrate a law which can be formulated as follows: In both groups, the relation between maternal uncle and nephew is to the relation between brother and sister as the relation between father and son is to that between husband and wife. Thus if we know one pair of relations, it is always possible to infer the other.[16]

---

[15] Lévi-Strauss' critique of Radcliffe-Brown is ultimately based on the same ideas he has used against Davis and Warner. In both cases, the works explain the particulars of the cases they mention but do not present a complete system. Therefore, they cannot be generalized to produce the universal laws of human behavior in which Lévi-Strauss is interested.

[16] Here, Lévi-Strauss completes the system, showing the additional relationships he believes necessary to an understanding of the avunculate: husband-wife and brother-sister. This is critical since Lévi-Strauss wishes to show pairs of binary relationships.

Thus, for the Trobriand example: uncle-nephew relations and brother-sister relations are both distant. Therefore, we expect father-son and husband-wife relations both to be close. As Lévi-Strauss explains on page 341, there must be one

Let us now examine some other cases.[17] On Tonga, in Polynesia, descent is patrilineal, as among the Cherkess. Relations between husband and wife appear to be public and harmonious. Domestic quarrels are rare, and although the wife is often of superior rank, the husband ". . . is nevertheless of higher authority in all domestic matters, and no woman entertains the least idea of rebelling against that authority."[hh] At the same time there is great freedom between nephew and maternal uncle. The nephew is *fahu,* or above the law, in relation to his uncle, toward whom extreme familiarity is permitted. This freedom strongly contrasts with the father-son relationship. The father is *tapu;* the son cannot touch his father's head or hair; he cannot touch him while he eats, sleep in his bed or on his pillow, share his food or drink, or play with his possessions. However, the strongest *tapu* of all is the one between brother and sister, who must never be together under the same roof.

Although they are also patrilineal and patrilocal, the natives of Lake Kutubu in New Guinea offer an example of the opposite type of structure. F. E. Williams writes: "I have never seen such a close and apparently affectionate association between father and son. . . ."[ii] Relations between husband and wife are characterized by the very low status ascribed to women and "the marked separation of masculine and feminine interests . . ."[jj] The women, according to Williams, "are expected to work hard for their masters . . . they occasionally protest, and protest may be met with a beating."[kk] The wife can always call upon her brother for protection against her husband, and it is with him that she seeks refuge. As for the relationship between nephew and maternal uncle, it is ". . . best summed up in the word 'respect' . . . tinged with apprehensiveness,[ll] for the maternal uncle has the power to curse his nephew and inflict serious illness upon him (just as among the Kipsigi of Africa).

Although patrilineal, the society described by Williams is structurally of the same type as that of the Siuai of Bougainville, who have matrilineal descent. Between brother and sister there is ". . . friendly interaction and mutual generosity. . . ."[mm] As regards the father-son relationship Oliver writes, ". . . I could discover little evidence that the word 'father' evokes images of hostility or stern authority or awed respect."[nn] But the relationship between the nephew and his mother's brother "appears to range between stern discipline and genial mutual dependence. . . ." However ". . . most of the informants agreed that all boys stand in some awe of their mother's brothers, and are more likely to obey them than their own fathers. . . ."[oo] Between husband and wife harmonious understanding is rare: ". . . there are few young wives who remain altogether faithful . . . most young husbands are continually suspicious and often give vent to jealous anger . . . marriages involve a number of adjustments, some of them apparently difficult. . . ."

The same picture, but sharper still, characterizes the Dobuans, who are matrilineal and neighbors of the equally matrilineal Trobrianders, while their structure is very different.[18] Dobuan marriages are unstable, adultery is widespread,

---

close relation and one distant relation in each generation. Thus this sort of system logically yields four possibilities (letting + equal a close relationship and − a distant one):

1	2	3	4
uncle-nephew: +	uncle-nephew: −	uncle-nephew: +	uncle-nephew: −
brother-sister: +	brother-sister: −	brother-sister: −	brother-sister: +
father-son: −	father-son: +	father-son: −	father-son: +
husband-wife: −	husband-wife: +	husband-wife: +	husband-wife: −

[17] Lévi-Strauss now tries to demonstrate that each of the possibilities presented in the previous footnote can be found in ethnography. The Cherkess example gives possibility one, the Trobriand example, possibility two. The Tonga example shows type three and the Kutubu type four. The Siuai, described in the next paragraph, are also type four, but while the Siuai are matrilineal, the Kutubu are patrilineal.

[18] The Dobuans, who are matrilineal like the Siuai, show the same pattern as the patrilineal Kutubu. As Lévi-Strauss notes later, this demonstrates that the phenomenon cannot be directly and simply linked to matrilineality or patrilineality.

and husband and wife constantly fear death induced by their spouse's witchcraft. Actually, Fortune's remark, "It is a most serious insult to refer to a woman's witchcraft so that her husband will hear of it"[qq] appears to be a variant of the Trobriand and Caucasian taboos cited above.

In Dobu, the mother's brother is held to be the harshest of all the relatives. "The mother's brother may beat children long after their parents have ceased to do so," and they are forbidden to utter his name. There is a tender relationship with the "navel," the mother's sister's husband, who is the father's double, rather than with the father himself. Nevertheless, the father is considered "less harsh" than the mother's brother and will always seek, contrary to the laws of inheritance, to favor his son at the expense of his uterine nephew. And, finally, "the strongest of all social bonds" is the one between brother and sister.[rr]

What can we conclude from these examples? The correlation between types of descent and forms of avunculate does not exhaust the problem. Different forms of avunculate can coexist with the same type of descent, whether patrilineal or matrilineal. But we constantly find the same fundamental relationship between the four pairs of oppositions required to construct the system. This will emerge more clearly from the diagrams which illustrate our examples. The sign + indicates free and familiar relations, and the sign − stands for relations characterized by hostility, antagonism, or reserve (Figure 1).[19] This is an oversimplification, but we can tentatively make use of it. We shall describe some of the indispensable refinements farther on.

The synchronic law of correlation thus suggested may be validated diachronically. If we summarize, after Howard,[ss] the evolution of family relationships during the Middle Ages, we find approximately this pattern: The brother's authority over his sister wanes, and that of the prospective husband increases. Simultaneously, the bond be-

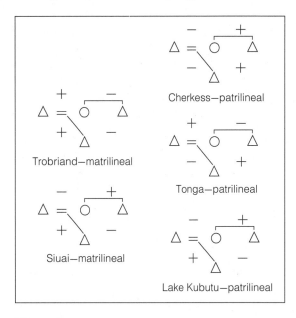

Figure 1.

tween father and son is weakened and that between maternal uncle and nephew is reinforced.[20]

This evolution seems to be confirmed by the documents gathered by Léon Gautier, for in the "conservative" texts (Raoul de Cambri, Geste des Loherains, etc.),[tt] the positive relationship is established chiefly between father and son and is only gradually displaced toward the maternal uncle and nephew.[uu]

Thus we see[vv] that in order to understand the avunculate we must treat it as one relationship within a system, while the system itself must be considered as a whole in order to grasp its structure. This structure rests upon four terms (brother, sister, father, and son), which are linked by two pairs of correlative oppositions in such a way that in each of the two generations there is always a positive relationship and a negative one. Now, what is the nature of this structure, and what is its function? The answer is as follows: This structure

---

[19] Lévi-Strauss' diagram illustrates the system of logical relations he described earlier and presents a different version of the relationship possibilities presented in footnote 16.

[20] There is a passing reference to historical change here. However, Lévi-Strauss is not an evolutionist. There is no suggestion that any one of these arrangements is better or more complex than another. He believes that all cultures are manifestations of the same underlying physiological and psychological causes.

is the most elementary form of kinship that can exist. It is, properly speaking, *the unit of kinship*.[21]

One may give a logical argument to support this statement. In order for a kinship structure to exist, three types of family relations must always be present: a relation of consanguinity, a relation of affinity, and a relation of descent—in other words, a relation between siblings, a relation between spouses, and a relation between parent and child. It is evident that the structure given here satisfies this threefold requirement, in accordance with the scientific principle of parsimony.[22] But these considerations are abstract, and we can present a more direct proof for our thesis.

The primitive and irreducible character of the basic unit of kinship, as we have defined it, is actually a direct result of the universal presence of an incest taboo. This is really saying that in human society a man must obtain a woman from another man who gives him a daughter or a sister.[23] Thus we do not need to explain how the maternal uncle emerged in the kinship structure: He does not emerge—he is present initially. Indeed, the presence of the maternal uncle is a necessary precondition for the structure to exist. The error of traditional anthropology, like that of traditional linguistics, was to consider the terms, and not the relations between the terms.

Before proceeding further, let us briefly answer some objections which might be raised. First, if the relationship between "brothers-in-law" is the necessary axis around which the kinship structure is built, why need we bring in the child of the marriage when considering the elementary structure? Of course the child here may be either born or yet unborn. But, granting this, we must understand that the child is indispensable in validating the dynamic and teleological character of the initial step, which establishes kinship on the basis of and through marriage.[24] Kinship is not a static phenomenon; it exists only in self-perpetuation. Here we are not thinking of the desire to perpetuate the race, but rather of the fact that in most kinship systems the initial disequilibrium produced in one generation between the group that gives the woman and the group that receives her can be stabilized only by counterprestations in following generations. Thus, even the most elementary kinship structure exists both synchronically and diachronically.

Second, could we not conceive of a symmetrical structure, equally simple, where the sexes would be reversed? Such a structure would involve a sister, her brother, brother's wife, and brother's daughter. This is certainly a theoretical possibility. But it is immediately eliminated on empirical grounds. In human society, it is the men who exchange the women, and not vice versa. It remains for further research to determine whether certain cultures have not tended to create a kind of fictitious image of this symmetrical structure. Such cases would surely be uncommon.

We come now to a more serious objection. Possibly we have only inverted the problem. Traditional anthropologists painstakingly endeavored to explain the origin of the avunculate, and we have brushed aside that research by treating the mother's brother not as an extrinsic element, but as an immediate given of the simplest family structure. How is it then that we do not find the avunculate at all times and in all places? For although the avunculate has a wide distribution, it

---

[21] Lévi-Strauss here returns to the center of his argument. He believes he has isolated a unit of kinship that is analogous to a phoneme, and therefore, the techniques of linguistic analysis can be fruitfully applied.

[22] Lévi-Strauss means that the kinship unit of husband, wife, wife's brother, and son is the smallest possible unit that has all the necessary family relationships.

[23] Lévi-Strauss' seminal *The Elementary Structures of Kinship* (1949) used Mauss' analysis of gift-giving (see essay 8) to describe the functions of the incest taboo. This essay was first published in 1945. Here and later, he presents many of the ideas that he will explore at greater length in his book. There he says that the key function of the incest taboo is to compel the reciprocal exchange of women (Harris 1968:490).

[24] When Lévi-Strauss speaks of teleological necessity, he means that a child must necessarily be returned to the group from which the wife has come. Thus, the child is implied in a marriage for logical reasons that transcend sexual desire or the perpetuation of humanity.

is by no means universal. It would be futile to explain the instances where it is present and then fail to explain its absence in other instances.

Let us point out, first, that the kinship system does not have the same importance in all cultures. For some cultures it provides the active principle regulating all or most of the social relationships. In other groups, as in our own society, this function is either absent altogether or greatly reduced. In still others, as in the societies of the Plains Indians, it is only partially fulfilled. The kinship system is a language; but it is not a universal language, and a society may prefer other modes of expression and action. From the viewpoint of the anthropologist this means that in dealing with a specific culture we must always ask a preliminary question: Is the system systematic? Such a question, which seems absurd at first, is absurd only in relation to language; for language is the semantic system par excellence; it cannot but signify, and exists only through signification. On the contrary, this question must be rigorously examined as we move from the study of language to the consideration of other systems which also claim to have semantic functions but whose fulfillment remains partial, fragmentary, or subjective, like, for example, social organization, art, and so forth.[25]

Furthermore, we have interpreted the avunculate as a characteristic trait of elementary structure. This elementary structure, which is the product of defined relations involving four terms, is, in our view, the true *atom of kinship*.[ww] Nothing can be conceived or given beyond the fundamental requirements of its structure, and, in addition, it is the sole building block of more complex systems.[26] For there are more complex systems; or, more accurately speaking, all kinship systems are constructed on the basis of this elementary structure, expanded or developed through the integration of new elements. Thus we must entertain two hypotheses: first, one in which the kinship system under consideration operates through the simple juxtaposition of elementary structures, and where the avuncular relationship therefore remains constantly apparent; second, a hypothesis in which the building blocks of the system are already of a more complex order. In the latter case, the avuncular relationship, while present, may be submerged within a differentiated context. For instance, we can conceive of a system whose point of departure lies in the elementary structure but which adds, at the right of the maternal uncle, his wife, and, at the left of the father, first the father's sister and then her husband. We could easily demonstrate that a development of this order leads to a parallel splitting in the following generation. The child must then be distinguished according to sex—a boy or a girl, linked by a relation which is symmetrical and inverse to the terms occupying the other peripheral positions in the structure (for example, the dominant position of the father's sister in Polynesia, the South African *nhlampsa*, and inheritance by the mother's brother's wife). In this type of structure the avuncular relationship continues to prevail but it is no longer the predominant one. In structures of still greater complexity, the avunculate may be obliterated or may merge with other relationships. But precisely because it is part of the elementary structure, the avuncular relationship re-emerges unmistakably and tends to become reinforced each time the system under consideration reaches a crisis—either because it is undergoing rapid transformation (as on the Northwest Coast), or because it is

---

[25] This first explanation is essentially a throwaway. While it is evident that family is not of equal importance in each culture, if Lévi-Strauss has indeed found the basic unit of kinship, it should still be present in these societies, though it will perhaps receive less cultural emphasis.

[26] The analysis presented here is very close to much of Lévi-Strauss' other work. His argument is ultimately that the avunculate is a basic feature of human cognition and is therefore present in all societies, although its presence may be camouflaged by elements that derive from the particular history of the culture under consideration. The structural anthropologist's task is to decode the kinship structure in such a way that the importance of its fundamental building block, the avunculate, is exposed. This is what Lévi-Strauss attempts to do in his discussion of the father's sister in Polynesia and the South African *nhlampsa* in this passage.

Figure 2.

a focus of contact and conflict between radically different cultures (as in Fiji and southern India) or, finally, because it is in the throes of a mortal crisis (as was Europe in the Middle Ages).

We must also add that the positive and negative symbols which we have employed in the above diagrams represent an oversimplification, useful only as a part of the demonstration. Actually, the system of basic attitudes comprises at least four terms: an attitude of affection, tenderness, and spontaneity; an attitude which results from the reciprocal exchange of prestations and counterprestations; and, in addition to these bilateral relationships, two unilateral relationships, one which corresponds to the attitude of the creditor, the other to that of the debtor.[27] In other words there are: mutuality (=), reciprocity (+−), rights (+), and obligations (−). These four fundamental attitudes are represented in their reciprocal relationships in Figure 2.

In many systems the relationship between two individuals is often expressed not by a single attitude, but several attitudes which together form, as it were, a "bundle" of attitudes (as in the Trobriands, where we find both mutuality *and* reci-

procity between husband and wife). This is an additional reason behind the difficulty in uncovering the basic structure.

We have tried to show the extent to which the preceding analysis is indebted to outstanding contemporary exponents of the sociology of primitive peoples. We must stress, however, that in its most fundamental principle this analysis departs from their teachings.[28] Let us cite as an example Radcliffe-Brown:

> The unit of structure from which a kinship is built up is the group which I call an "elementary family," consisting of a man and his wife and their child or children. . . . The existence of the elementary family creates three special kinds of social relationship, that between parent and child, that between children of the same parents (siblings), and that between husband and wife as parents of the same child or children. The three relationships that exist within the elementary family constitute what I call the first order. Relationships of the second order are those which depend on the connection of two elementary families through a common member, and are such as father's father, mother's brother, wife's sister, and so on. In the third order are such as father's brother's son and mother's brother's wife. Thus we can trace, if we have genealogical information, relationships of the fourth, fifth or nth order.[xx]

The idea expressed in the above passage, that the biological family constitutes the point of departure from which all societies elaborate their kinship systems, has not been voiced solely by Radcliffe-Brown. There is scarcely an idea which would today elicit greater consensus. Nor is there one more dangerous, in our opinion.[29] Of course

---

[27] Lévi-Strauss uses Mauss' terms *prestations* and *counterprestations.* Recall that these are gift exchanges between groups that appear "disinterested and spontaneous" but, in reality, are obligatory and enacted under a highly specific system of reciprocity.

[28] Lévi-Strauss' point here is to show that his conception of the basic unit of the family is different from Radcliffe-Brown's. The mother's brother, whom Lévi-Strauss sees as integral to the elementary unit of kinship, is assigned a secondary place by Radcliffe-Brown.

[29] To Lévi-Strauss, the appeal to biology implied in analyses stressing the primacy of the nuclear family is anathema. Lévi-Strauss sees culture as a product of the human mind: it is the mind's parsing of physical reality that is important, rather than that reality itself. Ultimately, Lévi-Strauss argues that the unit into which the human mind tends to parse kinship is the avunculate. This is not necessitated by the biology of reproduction, but by the sociology of human groups. Reproduction happens within the context of marriage, which because of the incest taboo is necessarily a relationship between groups rather than between individuals.

the biological family is ubiquitous in human society. But what confers upon kinship its sociocultural character is not what it retains from nature, but, rather, the essential way in which it diverges from nature. A kinship system does not consist in the objective ties of descent or consanguinity between individuals. It exists only in human consciousness; it is an arbitrary system of representations, not the spontaneous development of a real situation. This certainly does not mean that the real situation is automatically contradicted, or that it is to be simply ignored. Radcliffe-Brown has shown, in studies that are now classic, that even systems which are apparently extremely rigid and artificial, such as the Australian systems of marriage-classes, take biological parenthood carefully into account. But while this observation is irrefutable, still the fact (in our view decisive) remains that, in human society, kinship is allowed to establish and perpetuate itself only through specific forms of marriage. In other words, the relationships which Radcliffe-Brown calls "relationships of the first order" are a function of, and depend upon, those which he considers secondary and derived. The essence of human kinship is to require the establishment of relations among what Radcliffe-Brown calls "elementary families." Thus, it is not the families (isolated terms) which are truly "elementary," but rather the relations between those terms. No other interpretation can account for the universality of the incest taboo; and the avuncular relationship, in its most general form is nothing but a corollary, now covert, now explicit, of this taboo.

Because they are symbolic systems, kinship systems offer the anthropologist a rich field, where his efforts can almost (and we emphasize the "almost") converge with those of the most highly developed of the social sciences, namely, linguistics. But to achieve this convergence, from which it is hoped a better understanding of man will result, we must never lose sight of the fact that, in both

anthropological and linguistic research, we are dealing strictly with symbolism. And although it may be legitimate or even inevitable to fall back upon a naturalistic interpretation in order to understand the emergence of symbolic thinking, once the latter is given, the nature of the explanation must change as radically as the newly appeared phenomenon differs from those which have preceded and prepared it. Hence, any concession to naturalism might jeopardize the immense progress already made in linguistics, which is also beginning to characterize the study of family structure, and might drive the sociology of the family toward a sterile empiricism, devoid of inspiration.[30]

Notes

a. Marcel Mauss, "Rapports réels et pratiques de la psychologie et de la sociologie," *Journal de Psychologie Normale et Pathologique* (1924); reprinted in *Sociologie et Anthropologie* (Paris: 1951), p. 299.

b. O. Schrader, *Prehistoric Antiquities of the Aryan Peoples*, trans. F. B. Jevons (London: 1890), Chapter XII, Part 4.

c. *Ibid.* See also H. J. Rose, "On the Alleged Evidence for Mother-Right in Early Greece," *Folklore*, XXII (1911), and the more recent studies by George Thomson, which support the hypothesis of matrilineal survivals.

d. A. M. Hocart, "Chieftainship and the Sister's Son in the Pacific," *American Anthropologist*, n.s., XVII (1915); "The Uterine Nephew," *Man*, XXIII, No. 4 (1923); "The Cousin in Vedic Ritual," *Indian Antiquary*, LIV (1925); etc.

e. Paul K. Benedict, "Tibetan and Chinese Kinship Terms," *Harvard Journal of Asiatic Studies*, VI (1942); "Studies in Thai Kinship Terminology," *Journal of the American Oriental Society*, LXIII (1943).

f. L. Brunschvicg, *Le Progrés de la conscience dans la philosophie occidentale* (Paris: 1927), II, p. 562.

g. Between 1900 and 1920 Ferdinand de Saussure and Antoine Meillet, the founders of modern linguistics,

---

[30] Lévi-Strauss wrote this passage during an era when precisely the type of empirical research he attacks here was growing in importance, particularly in America. Its key proponents were evolutionary and ecological anthropologists such as Julian Steward and Leslie White and their students, as well as materialists such as Marvin Harris. Lévi-Strauss was bitterly attacked by anthropologists favoring empirical interpretations throughout the 1950s and 1960s. He defended himself in polemic that equaled that of his attackers. The echoes of this debate are still heard loudly today in the discourse between interpretive anthropologists and those favoring materialist approaches.

placed themselves determinedly under the wing of the anthropologists. Not until the 1920's did Marcel Mauss begin—to borrow a phrase from economics—to reverse this tendency.

h. N. Troubetzkoy, "La Phonologie actuelle," in *Psychologie du langage* (Paris: 1933).

i. *Ibid.*, p. 243.

j. Loc. cit.

k. *Ibid.*, p. 245; Roman Jakobson, "Principien der historischen Phonologie," *Travaux du Cercle linguistique de Prague*, IV (1931); and also Jakobson, "Remarques sur l'évolution phonologique du russe," *ibid.*, II (1929).

l. W. H. R. Rivers, *The History of Melanesian Society* (London: 1914), *passim*; *Social Organization*, ed. W. J. Perry (London: 1924), Chapter IV.

m. In the same vein, see Sol Tax, "Some Problems of Social Organization," in Fred Eggan (ed.), *Social Anthropology of North American Tribes* (Chicago: 1937).

n. Roman Jakobson, "Observations sur le classement phonologique des consonnes," *Proceedings of the Third International Congress of Phonetic Sciences.*

o. K. Davis and W. L. Warner, "Structural Analysis of Kinship," *American Anthropologist*, n.s., XXXVII (1935).

p. Thus at the end of the analysis carried out by these authors, the term husband is replaced by the formula: $C^{2a/2d}/^{0}$ SU^{la8}/Ego (*Ibid.*). There are now available two works which employ a much more refined logical apparatus and offer greater interest in terms both of method and of results. See F. G. Lounsbury, "A Semantic Analysis of the Pawnee Kinship Usage," *Language*, XXXII, No. 1 (1956), and W. H. Goodenough, "The Componential Analysis of Kinship," *ibid.*

q. As will be seen in Chapter V, I have now refined this formulation.

r. A. L. Kroeber, "Classificatory Systems of Relationship," *Journal of the Royal Anthropological Institute*, XXXIX (1909).

s. We must except the remarkable work of W. L. Warner, "Morphology and Functions of the Australian Murngin Type of Kinship," *American Anthropologist*, n.s., XXXII–XXXIII (1930–1931), in which his analysis of the system of attitudes, although fundamentally debatable, nevertheless initiates a new phase in the study of problems of kinship.

t. A. R. Radcliffe-Brown, "Kinship Terminology in California," *American Anthropologist*, n.s., XXXVII (1935); "The Study of Kinship Systems," *Journal of the Royal Anthropological Institute*, LXXI (1941).

u. M. E. Opler, "Apache Data Concerning the Relationship of Kinship Terminology to Social Classification," *American Anthropologist*, n.s., XXXIX (1937); A. M. Halpern, "Yuma Kinship Terms," *American Anthropologist*, n.s., XLIV (1942).

v. D. F. Thomson, "The Joking Relationship and Organized Obscenity in North Queensland," *American Anthropologist*, n.s., XXXVII (1935).

w. Radcliffe-Brown, "The Study of Kinship Systems," *op. cit.*, p. 8. This later formulation seems to us more satisfactory than his 1935 statement that attitudes present "a fairly high degree of correlation with the terminological classification" (*American Anthropologist*, n.s., XXXVII [1935], p. 53).

x. Sydney Hartland, "Matrilineal Kinship and the Question of its Priority," *Memoirs of the American Anthropological Association*, No. 4 (1917).

y. W. H. R. Rivers, "The Marriage of Cousins in India," *Journal of the Royal Asiatic Society* (July, 1907).

z. *Ibid.*, p. 624.

aa. R. H. Lowie, "The Matrilineal Complex," *University of California Publications in American Archaeology and Ethnology*, XVI, No. 2 (1919).

bb. Roman Jakobson, *Kindersprache, Aphasie und allgemeine Lautgesetze* (Uppsala: 1941).

cc. A. R. Radcliffe-Brown, "The Mother's Brother in South Africa," *South African Journal of Science*, XXI (1924).

dd. As among the Mundugomor of New Guinea, where the relationship between maternal uncle and nephew is always familiar, although descent is alternately patrilineal or matrilineal. See Margaret Mead, *Sex and Temperament in Three Primitive Societies* (New York: 1935), pp. 176–185.

ee. B. Malinowski, *The Sexual Life of Savages in Northwestern Melanesia* (London: 1929), 2 vols.

ff. Dubois de Monpereux (1839), cited in M. Kovalevski, "La Famille matriarcale au Caucase," *L'Anthropologie*, IV (1893).

gg. *Ibid.*

hh. E. W. Gifford, "Tonga Society," *Bernice P. Bishop Museum Bulletin*, No. 61 (Honolulu: 1929), pp. 16–22.

ii. F. E. Williams, "Group Sentiment and Primitive Justice," *American Anthropologist*, n.s., XLIII, No. 4, Part 1 (1941), p. 523.

jj. F. E. Williams, "Natives of Lake Kutubu, Papua," *Oceania*, XI (1940–1941), p. 266.

kk. *Ibid.*, p. 268.

ll. *Ibid.*, p. 280. See also *Oceania*, XII (1941–1942).

mm. Douglas L. Oliver, *A Solomon Island Society: Kinship and Leadership among the Siuai of Bougainville* (Cambridge, Mass.: 1955), p. 255.

nn. *Ibid.,* p. 251.

oo. *Ibid.,* p. 257.

pp. *Ibid.,* pp. 168–9.

qq. R. F. Fortune, *The Sorcerers of Dobu* (New York: 1932), p. 45.

rr. *Ibid.,* pp. 8, 10, 62–4.

ss. G. E. Howard, *A History of Matrimonial Institutions,* 3 vols. (Chicago: 1904).

tt. [Translator's note: The "Chansons de Geste," which survive in manuscript versions of the twelfth to the fifteenth century, are considered to be remodelings of much earlier originals, dating back to the age of Charlemagne. These poems of heroic and often legendary exploits also constitute a source of information on the family life of that period.]

uu. Leon Gautier, *La Chevalerie* (Paris: 1980). See also: F. B. Gummere, "The Sister's Son," in *An English Miscellany Presented to Dr. Furnivall* (London: 1901); W. O. Farnsworth, *Uncle and Nephew in the Old French Chanson de Geste* (New York: 1913).

vv. The preceding paragraphs were written in 1957 and substituted for the original text, in response to the judicious remark by my colleague Luc de Heusch of the Université Libre of Brussels that one of my examples was incorrect. I take this opportunity to thank him.

ww. It is no doubt superfluous to emphasize that the atomism which we have criticized in Rivers refers to classical philosophy and has nothing to do with the structural conception of the atom developed in modern physics. A. R. Radcliffe-Brown, "The Study of Kinship Systems," *op. cit.,* p. 2.

xx. A. R. Radcliffe-Brown, "The Study of Kinship Systems," *op. cit.,* p. 2.

26. Genesis as Myth[a]

Edmund Leach (1910–1989)

A DISTINGUISHED GERMAN THEOLOGIAN HAS defined myth as "the expression of unobservable realities in terms of observable phenomena." All stories which occur in the Bible are myths for the devout Christian, whether they correspond to historical fact or not. All human societies have myths in this sense, and normally the myths to which the greatest importance is attached are those which are the least probable. The non-rationality of myth is its very essence, for religion requires a

(1962)

demonstration of faith by the suspension of critical doubt.[1]

But if myths do not mean what they appear to mean, how do they come to mean anything at all? What is the nature of the esoteric mode of communication by which myth is felt to give "expression to unobservable realities"?

This is an old problem which has lately taken on a new shape because, if myth be a mode of communication, then a part of the theory which is embodied in digital computer systems ought to be relevant.[2] The merit of this approach is that it

---

[1] We have chosen Leach's analysis of Genesis as an example of the structural analysis of myth because it illustrates aspects of Lévi-Strauss' theory that are not exemplified in the first reading in this section. If you are not familiar with the first four chapters of Genesis or have not read them recently, we recommend you pause to read them before starting this essay.

[2] In the introduction and notes to essay 25, we explained that members of the Prague School of linguistics influenced the formation of structuralism. They theorized that words were built upon contrasts (binary oppositions) between phonemes rather than simply being groups of sounds. Structural anthropologists used this insight to look for the deep coding of culture. Like Lévi-Strauss, Leach believed that myths contained binary opposites. Thus, he saw them as similar to the digital computer systems, which run on binary programs.

draws special attention to precisely those features of myth which have formerly been regarded as accidental defects. It is common to all mythological systems that all important stories recur in several different versions. Man is created in Genesis (i.27) and then he is created all over again (ii.7). And, as if two first men were not enough, we also have Noah in chapter viii. Likewise in the New Testament, why must there be four gospels each telling the "same" story yet sometimes flatly contradictory on details of fact? Another noticeable characteristic of mythical stories is their markedly binary aspect; myth is constantly setting up opposing categories: "In the beginning God created the heaven and the earth"; "They crucified Him and two others with him, on either side one, and Jesus in the midst"; "I am the Alpha and the Omega, the beginning and the end, saith the Lord." So always it is in myth—God against the world and the world itself for ever dividing into opposites on either side: male and female, living and dead, good and evil, first and last. . . .

Now, in the language of communication engineers, the first of these common characteristics of myth is called *redundancy,* while the second is strongly reminiscent of the unit of information—the *bit.* "Information" in this technical sense is a measure of the freedom of choice in selecting a message.[3] If there are only two messages and it is arbitrary which you choose, then "information is unity," that is = 1 bit.[b]

Communication engineers employ these concepts for the analysis of problems which arise when a particular individual (the sender) wishes to transmit a coded message correctly to another individual (the receiver) against a background of interference (noise). "Information" refers on the one hand to the degrees of choice open to the sender in encoding his transmission, and on the other to the degrees of choice open to the receiver in interpreting what he receives (which will include noise in addition to the original transmitted signal). In this situation a high level of redundancy makes it easy to correct errors introduced by noise.

Now in the mind of the believer, myth does indeed convey messages which are the Word of God. To such a man the redundancy of myth is a very reassuring fact. Any particular myth in isolation is like a coded message badly snarled up with noisy interference. Even the most confident devotee might feel a little uncertain as to what precisely is being said. But, as a result of redundancy, the believer can feel that, even when the details vary, each alternative version of a myth confirms his understanding and reinforces the essential meaning of all the others.[4]

The anthropologist's viewpoint is different. He rejects the idea of a supernatural sender. He observes only a variety of possible receivers. Here redundancy increases information—that is the uncertainty of the possible means of decoding the message. This explains what is surely the most striking of all religious phenomena—the passionate adherence to sectarian belief. The whole of Christendom shares a single corpus of mythology so it is surely very remarkable that the members of each particular Christian sect are able to convince themselves that they alone possess the secret of revealed truth. The abstract propositions of communication theory help us to understand this paradox.

But if the true believer can interpret his own mythology in almost any way he chooses, what principle governs the formation of the original myth? Is it random chance that a myth assumes one pattern rather than another? The binary structure of myth suggests otherwise.

---

[3] Leach's comment about freedom of choice in selecting a message and the use of the word *bit* derive from communications theory, a mathematical field that discusses information in terms of bits of knowledge lost or gained. Communications theory was first developed in the 1940s and was fundamental to the rapid growth of telecommunications and television. Shannon's "A Mathematical Theory of Communication" (1948) and Brillouin's *Science and Information Theory* (1956) are seminal works in the development of this field. Just as Kroeber used a radio metaphor in his discussion of fashion (essay 11), Leach utilized a telephone and television metaphor in his analysis of myth as a form of communication.

[4] The idea that myths are transmitting a message from generation to generation is central to Lévi-Strauss' theory of myth; consequently, the concept of redundancy from communications theory is important. The difference is that communications engineers think of redundancy in terms of transmitting messages across distances; Lévi-Strauss thinks of it in terms of transmitting messages through time. In both cases, redundancy helps ensure that the message is transmitted accurately.

Binary oppositions are intrinsic to the process of human thought. Any description of the world must discriminate categories in the form "p is what not-p is not." An object is alive or not alive and one could not formulate the concept "alive" except as the converse of its partner "dead." So also human beings are male or not male, and persons of the opposite sex are either available as sexual partners or not available. Universally these are the most fundamentally important oppositions in all human experience.[5]

Religion everywhere is preoccupied with the first, the antinomy of life and death. Religion seeks to deny the binary link between the two words; it does this by creating the mystical idea of "another world," a land of the dead where life is perpetual. The attributes of this other world are necessarily those which are not of this world; imperfection here is balanced by perfection there. But this logical ordering of ideas has a disconcerting consequence—God comes to belong to the other world. The central "problem" of religion is then to reestablish some kind of bridge between Man and God.

This pattern is built into the structure of every mythical system; the myth first discriminates between gods and men and then becomes preoccupied with the relations and intermediaries which link men and gods together. This much is already implicit in our initial definition.

So too with sex relations. Every human society has rules of incest and exogamy. Though the rules vary they always have the implication that for any particular male individual all women are divided by at least one binary distinction, there are women of *our kind* with whom sex relations would be incestuous and there are women of the *other kind* with whom sex relations are allowed. But here again we are immediately led into paradox. How was it in the beginning? If our first parents were persons of two kinds, what was that other kind? But if they were both of our kind, then their relations must have been incestuous and we are all born in sin. The myths of the world offer many different solutions to this childish intellectual puzzle, but the prominence which it receives shows that it entails the most profound moral issues. The crux is as before. If the logic of our thought leads us to distinguish we from they, how can we bridge the gap and establish social and sexual relations with "the others" without throwing our categories into confusion?[6]

So, despite all variations of theology, this aspect of myth is a constant. In every myth system we will find a persistent sequence of binary discriminations as between human/superhuman, mortal/immortal, male/female, legitimate/illegitimate, good/bad . . . followed by a "mediation" of the paired categories thus distinguished.[7]

"Mediation" (in this sense) is always achieved by introducing a third category which is "abnormal" or "anomalous" in terms of ordinary "rational" categories. Thus myths are full of fabulous

---

[5] Structuralists accept the binary nature of human thought as a given; Leach calls it "intrinsic" to human thought without offering any evidence. Do you think that is really true? While most anthropologists accept that we do, in fact, commonly make binary distinctions, they also assert that humans conceptualize the world in other ways.

[6] Leach here is referring to Lévi-Strauss' theory of kinship as outlined in *The Elementary Structures of Kinship* and described to an extent in essay 25. Leach's initial familiarity with Lévi-Strauss' work on kinship came while he was preparing his own book *The Political Systems of Highland Burma*. Leach first became interested in Lévi-Strauss because the Burmese people he was studying, the Kachin, were used by Lévi-Strauss as a model of a generalized exchange marriage system. Leach writes

> I was intrigued by the fact that while his theory, in an odd sort of way, fitted some of the facts on the ground (with which I was intimately familiar and Lévi-Strauss was not), there was a very wide discrepancy between the details of the ethnography and what Lévi-Strauss had supposed to be the case. Afterward I was shocked to discover that he himself was in no way put out by these discrepancies; he blandly assured his readers that my ethnography must be wrong! (1984:18)

[7] Here Leach outlines Lévi-Strauss' dialectical model. Although Lévi-Strauss was influenced by Marxism and Hegelian thought, his analysis is neither. In the work of both Marx and Hegel the dialectic is firmly linked to progress and change, but progress is not an element in Lévi-Strauss' analysis. Further, Marx's idea of the dialectic is fundamentally materialistic and historical, but Lévi-Strauss believes he is uncovering universal, unchanging truths that arise from the structure of the human mind. He uses the idea of opposition and mediation, but is decidedly nonmaterialistic.

Figure 1.

monsters, incarnate gods, virgin mothers. This middle ground is abnormal, non-natural, holy. It is typically the focus of all taboo and ritual observance.

This approach to myth analysis derives originally from the techniques of structural linguistics associated with the name of Roman Jakobson but is more immediately due to Claude Lévi-Strauss, one of whose examples may serve to illustrate the general principle.[8]

Certain Pueblo Indian myths focus on the opposition between life and death. In these myths we find a threefold category distinction: agriculture (means to life), war (means to death), and hunting (a mediating category since it is means to life for men but means to death for animals). Other myths of the same cluster deploy a different triad: grass-eating animals (which live without killing), predators (which live by killing), and carrion-eating creatures (mediators, since they eat meat but do not kill in order to eat). In accumulation this total set of associated symbols serves to imply that life and death are not just the back and the front of the same penny, that death is not the necessary consequence of life.

My Fig. 1 has been designed to display an analogous structure for the case of the first four chapters of Genesis. The three horizontal bands of the diagram correspond to (i) the story of the seven-day creation, (ii) the story of the Garden of Eden, and (iii) the story of Cain and Abel. The diagram can also be read vertically: column 1 in band (ii) corresponds to column 1 in band (i) and so on. The detailed analysis is as follows:—

UPPER BAND

First Day. (i.1–5; not on diagram). Heaven distinguished from Earth; Light from Darkness; Day from Night; Evening from Morning.

Second Day. (i.6–8; col. 1 of diagram). (Fertile) water (rain) above; (infertile) water (sea) below. Mediated by firmament (sky).

Third Day. (i.9–10; col. 2 and i.11–12; col. 3). Sea opposed to dry land. Mediated by "grass, herb-yielding seed (cereals), fruit trees." These grow on dry land but need water. They are classed as things "whose seed is in itself" and thereby contrasted with bisexual animals, birds, etc.

The creation of the world as a static (that is, dead) entity is now complete and this whole phase of the creation is opposed to the creation of moving (that is, living) things.

Fourth Day. (i.13–18; col. 4). Mobile sun and moon are placed in the fixed firmament of col. 1. Light and darkness become alternations (life and death become alternates).

Fifth Day. (i.20–3; col. 5). Fish and birds are living things corresponding to the sea/land opposition of col. 2 but they also mediate the col. 1 oppositions between sky and earth and between salt water and fresh water.

Sixth Day. (i.24–5; col. 6). Cattle (domestic animals), beasts (wild animals), creeping things. These correspond to the static triad of col. 3. But only the grass is allocated to the animals. Everything else, including the meat of the animals, is for Man's use (i.29–30). Later at Leviticus xi creatures which do not fit this exact ordering of the world—for instance water creatures with no fins, animals and birds which eat meat or fish, etc.—are classed as "abominations." Creeping Things are anomalous with respect to the major categories, Fowl, Fish, Cattle, Beast, and are thus abominations *ab initio*[9] (Leviticus xi.41–2). This classification in turn leads to an anomalous contradiction. In order to allow the Israelites to eat locusts the author of Leviticus xi had to introduce a special qualification to the prohibition against eating creeping things: "Yet these ye *may* eat: of every flying creeping thing

---

[8] Jakobson is particularly remembered for his work on language acquisition and the relationship of language to culture. For more information on Jakobson and the Prague School, see footnotes 4 and 5 of essay 25.

[9] *Ab initio:* Latin for from the beginning.

that goeth on all four which have legs above their feet, to leap withal upon the earth" (v.21). The procedures of binary discrimination could scarcely be carried further!

(i.26–7; col. 7). Man and Woman are created simultaneously.

The whole system of living creatures is instructed to "be fruitful and multiply," but the problems of Life versus Death, and Incest versus Procreation are not faced at all.

CENTRE BAND

The Garden of Eden story which now follows tackles from the start these very problems which have been evaded in the first version. We start again with the opposition Heaven versus Earth, but this is mediated by a fertilizing mist drawn from the dry infertile earth (ii.4–6). This theme, which blurs the distinction life/death, is repeated. Living Adam is formed from the dead dust of the ground (ii.7); so are the animals (ii.19); the garden is fertilized by a river which "went out of Eden" (ii.10); finally fertile Eve is formed from a rib of infertile Adam (ii.22–3).

The opposition Heaven/Earth is followed by further oppositions — Man/Garden (ii.15); Tree of Life/Tree of Death (ii.9, 17); the latter is called the tree of the "knowledge of good and evil" which means the knowledge of sexual difference.[10]

Recurrent also is the theme that unity in the other world (Eden, Paradise) becomes duality in this world. Outside Eden the river splits into four and divides the world into separate lands (ii.10–14). In Eden, Adam can exist by himself, Life can exist by itself; in this world, there are men and women, life and death. This repeats the contrast between monosexual plants and bisexual animals which is stressed in the first story.

The other living creatures are now created specifically because of the loneliness of Man in Eden (ii.18). The categories are Cattle, Birds, Beasts. None of these are adequate as a helpmeet

for Man. So finally Eve is drawn from Adam's rib . . . "they are of one flesh" (ii.18–24).

Comparison of Band 1 and Band 2 at this stage shows that Eve in the second story replaces the "Creeping Things" of the first story. Just as Creeping Things were anomalous with respect to Fish, Fowl, Cattle and Beast so Eve is anomalous to the opposition Man versus Animal. And, as a final mediation (chapter iii), the Serpent, a creeping thing, is anomalous to the opposition Man versus Woman.

Christian artists have always been sensitive to this fact; they manage to give the monster a somewhat hermaphrodite appearance while still indicating some kind of identification between the Serpent and Eve herself. Hugo Van der Goes, in "The Fall" at the Kunsthistorisches Museum, Vienna, puts Eve and the Serpent in the same posture. Michaelangelo makes Adam and Eve both gaze with loving adoration on the Serpent, but the Serpent has Eve's face.

Adam and Eve eat the forbidden fruit and become aware of sexual difference; death becomes inevitable (iii.3–8). But now for the first time pregnancy and reproduction become possible. Eve does not become pregnant until after she has been expelled from Paradise (iv.1).

LOWER BAND

Cain the Gardener and Abel the Herdsman repeat the antithesis between the first three days of the Creation and the last three days in the first story. Abel's living world is more pleasing to God (iv.4–5). Cain's fratricide compares with Adam's incest and so God's questioning and cursing of Cain (iv.9–12) has the same form and sequence as God's questioning and cursing of Adam, Eve and the Serpent (ii.9–19). The latter part of iii.16 is later repeated exactly (iv.7), so Cain's sin was not only fratricide but also incestuous homosexuality. In order that immortal monosexual existence in Paradise may be exchanged for fertile heterosexual existence in reality, Cain, like Adam, must acquire

---

[10] Leach's statement that the tree of knowledge refers to knowledge of sexual difference is typical of his interpretation and points to a fundamental problem in structuralism. He speaks as if there is a universally agreed upon interpretation of the trees of Eden, but no such accord exists. This is a point of theological debate rather than an obvious and established interpretation.

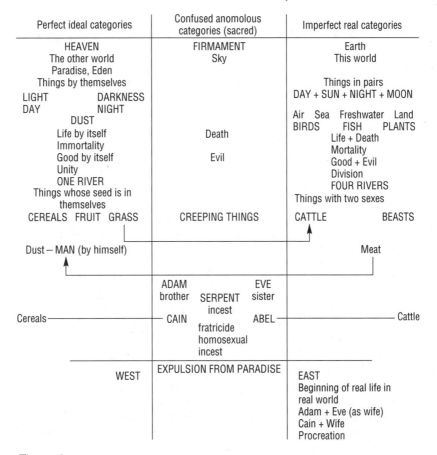

Perfect ideal categories	Confused anomolous categories (sacred)	Imperfect real categories
HEAVEN The other world Paradise, Eden Things by themselves	FIRMAMENT Sky	Earth This world
LIGHT DARKNESS DAY NIGHT DUST		Things in pairs DAY + SUN + NIGHT + MOON Air Sea Freshwater Land BIRDS FISH PLANTS
Life by itself Immortality Good by itself Unity ONE RIVER Things whose seed is in themselves	Death Evil	Life + Death Mortality Good + Evil Division FOUR RIVERS Things with two sexes
CEREALS FRUIT GRASS	CREEPING THINGS	CATTLE BEASTS

Dust — MAN (by himself)   Meat

	ADAM brother SERPENT EVE sister	
Cereals	incest CAIN ABEL fratricide homosexual incest	Cattle

WEST	EXPULSION FROM PARADISE	EAST Beginning of real life in real world Adam + Eve (as wife) Cain + Wife Procreation

Figure 2.

a wife (iv.17). To this end Adam must eliminate a sister: Cain a brother. The symmetry is complete.

The issue here is the logical basis of incest categories and closely analogous patterns must occur in all mythologies regardless of their superficial content. Cross-cultural comparison becomes easier if we represent the analysis as a systematic pattern of binary discriminations as in Fig. 2.[11]

Adam/Eve and Cain/Abel are then seen to be variants of a theme which can also occur in other forms, as in the well-known myth of Oedipus.

The actual symbolism in these two cases is nearly identical. Oedipus, like Adam and Cain, is initially earthbound and immobile. The conclusion of the Athenian version of the Oedipus story is that he is an exiled wanderer, protected by the gods. So also is Cain (iv.14–15). The Bible also includes the converse of this pattern. In Genesis xxviii Jacob is a lonely exile and wanderer under God's protection, but (xxxii.24–32) he is renamed Israel and thus given the status of a first ancestor with a territorial autochthonous[12] base, and he is tamed by God. Although Jacob dies

---

[11] This passage is a nice example of structuralist thought: Leach says the superficial content of myth is irrelevant, it is the deep structure the analyst pursues. But note that Leach's reasoning is deductive. According to his theory, deep structural patterns must occur; he then proceeds in his analysis to find what he believes must exist in his data.

[12] *Autochthonous:* originating in the earth. This is a common theme in mythology and generally applied to the original inhabitants of a locale.

abroad in Egypt he is buried on his own ancestral soil in Israel (xl.29–32; l.5–7).

In the Oedipus story, in place of Eve's Serpent we have Jocasta's Sphinx. Like Jocasta the Sphinx is female, like Jocasta the Sphinx commits suicide, like the Serpent the Sphinx leads men to their doom by verbal cunning, like the Serpent the Sphinx is an anomalous monster. Eve listens to the Serpent's words and betrays Adam into incest; Oedipus solves the Sphinx riddle and is led into incest. Again, Oedipus's patricide replaces Cain's fratricide — Oedipus, incidentally, meets Laius "at a cross roads."

Parallels of this kind seem too close to be accidental, but this kind of algebra is unfamiliar and more evidence will be needed to convince the skeptical. Genesis contains several further examples of first ancestors.

Firstly, Noah survived the destruction of the world by flood together with three sons and their wives. Prior to this the population of the world had included three kinds of being — "sons of God," "daughters of men" and "giants" who were the offspring of the union of the other two (vi.1–4). Since the forbears of Noah's daughters-in-law have all been destroyed by the Flood, Noah becomes a unique ancestor of all mankind without the implication of incest. Chapter ix.1–7 addressed to Noah is almost the duplicate of i.27–30 addressed to Adam.

Though heterosexual incest is evaded, the theme of homosexual incest in the Cain and Abel story recurs in the Noah saga when drunken Noah is seduced by his own son Ham (ix.21–5). The Canaanites, descendants of Ham, are for this reason accursed. (That a homosexual act is intended is evident from the language "Ham saw the nakedness of his father." Compare Leviticus xviii.6–19, where "to uncover the nakedness of" consistently means to have sexual relations with.)

In the second place Lot survives the destruction of the world by fire together with two nubile daughters. Drunken Lot is seduced by his own daughters (xix.30–8). The Moabites and the Ammonites, descendants of these daughters, are for this reason accursed. In chapter xix the men of Sodom endeavour to have homosexual relations with two angels who are visiting Lot. Lot offers his nubile daughters instead but they escape unscathed. The implication is that Lot's incest is

less grave than heterosexual relations with a foreigner, and still less grave than homosexual relations.

Thirdly, the affair of the Sodomites and the Angels contains echoes of "the sons of God" and "the daughters of men" but links superficially with chapter xviii where Abraham receives a visit from God and two angels who promise that his ageing and barren wife Sarah shall bear a son. Sarah is Abraham's half-sister by the same father (xx.12) and his relations with her are unambiguously incestuous (Leviticus xviii.9). Abraham loans Sarah to Pharaoh saying that she is his sister (xii.19). He does the same with King Abimelech (xx.2). Isaac repeats the game with Abimelech (xxvi.9–11) but with a difference. Isaac's wife Rebekah is his father's brother's son's daughter (second cousin) and the relation is *not* in fact incestuous. The barrenness of Sarah is an aspect of her incest. The supernatural intervention which ultimately ensures that she shall bear a child is evidence that the incest is condoned. Pharaoh and Abimelech both suffer supernatural penalties for the lesser offence of adultery, but Abraham, the incestuous husband, survives unscathed.

There are other stories in the same set. Hagar, Sarah's Egyptian slave, bears a son Ishmael to Abraham whose descendants are wanderers of low status. Sarah's son Isaac is marked out as of higher status than the sons of Abraham's concubines, who are sent away to "the east country" (c.f. wandering Cain who made his home in Nod "eastward of Eden"). Isaac marries a kinswoman in preference to a Canaanite woman. Esau's marriage to a Hittite woman is marked as a sin. In contrast his younger brother Jacob marries two daughters of his mother's brother who is in turn Jacob's father's father's brother's son's son.

All in all, this long tale asserts:

a. the overriding virtue of close kin endogamy;

b. that the sacred hero-ancestor Abraham can carry this so far that he marries his paternal half-sister (an incestuous relationship). Abraham is thus likened to Pharaoh, for the Pharaohs of Egypt regularly married their paternal half-sisters; and

c. that a rank order is established which places the tribal neighbours of the Israelites in varying degrees of inferior status depending upon the nature of the defect in their original ancestry as compared with the pure descent of Jacob (Israel).

The myth requires that the Israelites be descended unambiguously from Terah the father of Abraham. This is achieved only at the cost of a breach of the incest rule; but by reciting a large number of similar stories which entail even greater breaches of sexual morality the relations of Abraham and Sarah finally stand out as uniquely virtuous. Just as Adam and Eve are virtuous as compared to Cain and Abel, so Abraham's incest can pass unnoticed in the context of such outrageous characters as Ham, Lot's daughters, and the men of Sodom.

I have concentrated here upon the issue of sexual rules and transgressions so as to show how a multiplicity of repetitions, inversions and variations can add up to a consistent "message." I do not wish to imply that this is the only structural pattern which these myths contain.

The novelty of the analysis which I have presented does not lie in the facts but in the procedure. Instead of taking each myth as a thing in itself with a "meaning" peculiar to itself it is assumed, from the start, that every myth is one of a complex and that any pattern which occurs in one myth will recur, in the same or other variations, in other parts of the complex. The structure that is common to all variations becomes apparent when different versions are "superimposed" one upon the other.[13]

Whenever a corpus of mythology is recited in its religious setting such structural patterns are "felt" to be present, and convey meaning much as poetry conveys meaning. Even though the ordinary listener is not fully conscious of what has been communicated, the "message" is there in a quite objective sense. If the labour of programming could be performed the actual analysis could be done by a computer far better than by any human. Furthermore it seems evident that much the same patterns exist in the most diverse kinds of mythology. This seems to me to be a fact of great psychological, sociological and scientific significance. Here truly are observable phenomena which are the expression of unobservable realities.[14]

Notes

a. References such as (iv.3) refer to the third verse of the fourth chapter of the book of Genesis (English Authorized Version) unless otherwise stated.

b. Bit stands for "binary digit."

---

[13] In this paragraph, Leach says, "The novelty of the analysis which I have presented does not lie in the facts but in the procedure," implying that the procedure can be replicated. One of the most serious critiques of structural analysis revolves around the likelihood that the patterns discovered in the analysis are, to a great degree, found in the imagination of the interpreter. It is clear that although Leach's analysis is elegant, his choice of oppositions is subjective, as is his interpretation of what the pattern of oppositions means.

[14] Leach claims that his analysis is scientific; if the myth were programmed into a computer, the machine would generate the same analysis. Given that a computer is a machine that processes data according to its programming, we have no doubt that Leach's claim is true—but does that make structural analysis scientific? Judged by Karl Popper's standards for science, which include falsifiability, the answer must be no.

Lévi-Strauss has done anthropology a tremendous service by outlining a methodology for the sorting of anthropological data. As a method of analysis, structuralism can lead to valuable interpretive insights where other theoretical perspectives may fail. But as a means for proving the binary structure of the mind, structuralism has failed. Lévi-Strauss is no closer to proving his hypothesis about the unconscious structure of human thought than Freud had been almost a century ago. In spite of the dialectical nature of Lévi-Strauss' theory and his self-professed allegiance to Marxist thought, materialists have provided some of the most telling critiques of structuralism. Those who view anthropology as a science generally discount Lévi-Strauss' structuralism because the reality he claims to present is an unconscious one, and thus unverifiable (Malefijt 1974:330). Harris, for example, says that a "paralysis of reality" spreads over his entire work (1968:497). And even though he was one of Lévi-Strauss' greatest admirers, Leach says

I am ready to concede that the structures which he displays are products of an unconscious mental process, but I can see no reason to believe that they are human universals. Bereft of Lévi-Strauss' resourceful special pleading they appear to be local, functionally determined attributes of particular individuals or of particular cultural groups. (1976:126)

27. Is Female to Male as Nature Is to Culture?

Sherry B. Ortner (1941–)

MUCH OF THE CREATIVITY OF ANTHROPOLOGY derives from the tension between two sets of demands: that we explain human universals, and that we explain cultural particulars. By this canon, woman provides us with one of the more challenging problems to be dealt with. The secondary status of woman in society is one of the true universals, a pan-cultural fact. Yet within that universal fact, the specific cultural conceptions and symbolizations of woman are extraordinarily diverse and even mutually contradictory. Further, the actual treatment of women and their relative power and contribution vary enormously from culture to culture, and over different periods in the history of particular cultural traditions. Both of these points—the universal fact and the cultural variation—constitute problems to be explained.[1]

My interest in the problem is of course more than academic: I wish to see genuine change

(1974)

come about, the emergence of a social and cultural order in which as much of the range of human potential is open to women as is open to men. The universality of female subordination, the fact that it exists within every type of social and economic arrangement and in societies of every degree of complexity, indicates to me that we are up against something very profound, very stubborn, something we cannot rout out simply by rearranging a few tasks and roles in the social system, or even by reordering the whole economic structure. In this paper I try to expose the underlying logic of cultural thinking that assumes the inferiority of women; I try to show the highly persuasive nature of the logic, for if it were not so persuasive, people would not keep subscribing to it. But I also try to show the social and cultural sources of that logic, to indicate wherein lies the potential for change.[2]

It is important to sort out the levels of the problem. The confusion can be staggering. For

---

[1] Early feminist critiques assumed the universal subordination of women; for instance, in her opening paragraph, Ortner states that the secondary status of women is a "pan-cultural fact." The purpose of the article is to formulate a theory that explains this universal gender asymmetry.

Feminist scholars dealt with the question of gender asymmetry in a variety of ways. Leacock (essay 33 in this volume), for example, approached the issue from a Marxist perspective, claiming that gender subordination was a product of external factors—namely, the introduction of capitalism and men's control of the forces of production in society. Ortner's answer to this issue turns inward. Rather than finding the answer to her questions in the material factors of society, she looks for the answer in the structure of human thought.

Structuralists believe that cultural phenomena are the product of universal logical processes that organize human thought. And a fundamental characteristic of human thought, according to structuralists, is to sort data into binary oppositions. Therefore, one should be able to identify cross-cultural patterns of oppositions associated with men and women. This is exactly what Ortner sets out to do in this essay.

A decade later, theorists abandoned the view that women were everywhere and always subordinate to men in favor of a more sophisticated view that examined the cultural construction of relationships between men and women. But in the 1970s, within the political context of the women's movement, the domination of women by men was accepted doctrine for feminist anthropologists.

[2] Most anthropological theory, while influenced by prevailing political events or philosophies, is not written with an openly political objective. With rare exceptions, such as Gorer and Rickman's *The People of Great Russia* (1962 [1949]), it was not until the 1970s, when college campuses were extremely politicized, that anthropologists such as Ortner started writing politically charged work.

Ortner talks about exposing the "underlying logic of cultural thinking." The notion that a hidden logic underlies human thought is basic to structuralism. The fundamental dichotomy she has constructed for analysis is male-power versus example, depending on which aspect of Chinese culture we look at, we might extrapolate any of several entirely different guesses concerning the status of women in China. In the ideology of Taoism, *yin*, the female principle, and *yang*, the male principle, are given equal weight; "the opposition, alternation, and interaction of these two forces give rise to all phenomena in the universe" (Siu, 1968:2). Hence we might guess that maleness and femaleness are equally valued in the general ideology of Chinese culture.ª Looking at the social structure, however, we see the strongly emphasized patrilineal descent principle, the importance of sons, and the absolute authority of the father in the family. Thus we might conclude that China is the archetypal patriarchal society. Next, looking at the actual roles played, power and influence wielded, and material contributions made by women in Chinese society—all of which are, upon observation, quite substantial— we would have to say that women are allotted a great deal of (unspoken) status in the system. Or again, we might focus on the fact that a goddess, Kuan Yin, is the central (most worshiped, most depicted) deity in Chinese Buddhism, and we might be tempted to say, as many have tried to say about goddess-worshiping cultures in prehistoric and early historical societies, that China is actually a sort of matriarchy. In short, we must be absolutely clear about *what* we are trying to explain before explaining it.

We may differentiate three levels of the problem:

1. The universal fact of culturally attributed second-class status of woman in every society. Two questions are important here. First, what do we mean by this; what is our evidence that this is a universal fact? And second, how are we to explain this fact, once having established it?

2. Specific ideologies, symbolizations, and socio-structural arrangements pertaining to women that vary widely from culture to culture. The problem at this level is to account for any particular cultural complex in terms of factors specific to that group— the standard level of anthropological analysis.

3. Observable on-the-ground details of women's activities, contributions, powers, influence, etc., often at variance with cultural ideology (although always constrained within the assumption that women may never be officially preeminent in the total system). This is the level of direct observation, often adopted now by feminist-oriented anthropologists.

This paper is primarily concerned with the first of these levels, the problem of the universal devaluation of women. The analysis thus depends not upon specific cultural data but rather upon an analysis of "culture" taken generically as a special sort of process in the world. A discussion of the second level, the problem of cross-cultural variation in conceptions and relative valuations of women, will entail a great deal of cross-cultural research and must be postponed to another time. As for the third level, it will be obvious from my approach that I would consider it a misguided endeavor to focus only upon women's actual though culturally unrecognized and unvalued powers in any given society, without first understanding the overarching ideology and deeper assumptions of the culture that render such powers trivial.[3]

---

female-subordination. Ortner's argument is based directly on the work of Lévi-Strauss, whose books *The Elementary Structures of Kinship* (1969 [1949]) and *The Raw and the Cooked* (1969) are cited in her paper. In fact, the title of one section of her essay ("Nature and Culture") is a direct reference to Lévi-Strauss' proposition that a fundamental opposition through which humans conceptualize the world is between nature and culture.

[3] Ortner's choice of level follows from her structuralist theoretical position. A basic principle of structuralism is that a single universal cultural patterning underlies all individual cultures. Therefore, structuralism should be a good method for explaining universal cultural characteristics. It would be less effective at explaining the specifics of cultural symbols (Ortner's second level). In fact, structuralists do not generally consider the meanings of individual symbols important. It is their pattern that is critical. The third level is of even less interest for structuralists. Since they believe that culture is a mental model, structuralists are much more concerned with what people think and say than what they do.

THE UNIVERSALITY
OF FEMALE SUBORDINATION

What do I mean when I say that everywhere, in every known culture, women are considered in some degree inferior to men? First of all, I must stress that I am talking about *cultural* evaluations; I am saying that each culture, in its own way and on its own terms, makes this evaluation. But what would constitute evidence that a particular culture considers women inferior?

Three types of data would suffice: (1) elements of cultural ideology and informants' statements that *explicitly* devalue women, according them, their roles, their tasks, their products, and their social milieux less prestige than are accorded men and the male correlates; (2) symbolic devices, such as the attribution of defilement, which may be interpreted as *implicitly* making a statement of inferior valuation; and (3) social structural arrangements that exclude women from participation in or contact with some realm in which the highest powers of the society are felt to reside.[b] These three types of data may all of course be interrelated in any particular system, though they need not necessarily be. Further, any one of them will usually be sufficient to make the point of female inferiority in a given culture. Certainly, female exclusion from the most sacred rite or the highest political council is sufficient evidence. Certainly, explicit cultural ideology devaluing women (and their tasks, roles, products, etc.) is sufficient evidence. Symbolic indicators such as defilement are usually sufficient, although in a few cases in which, say, men and women are equally polluting to one another, a further indicator is required—and is, as far as my investigations have ascertained, always available.

On any or all of these counts, then, I would flatly assert that we find women subordinated to men in every known society.[4] The search for a genuinely egalitarian, let alone matriarchal, culture has proved fruitless. An example from one society that has traditionally been on the credit side of this ledger will suffice. Among the matrilineal Crow, as Lowie[5] (1956) points out, "Women . . . had highly honorific offices in the Sun Dance; they could become directors of the Tobacco Ceremony and played, if anything, a more conspicuous part in it than the men; they sometimes played the hostess in the Cooked Meat Festival; they were not debarred from sweating or doctoring or from seeking a vision" (p. 61). Nonetheless, "Women [during menstruation] formerly rode inferior horses and evidently this loomed as a source of contamination, for they were not allowed to approach either a wounded man or men starting on a war party. A taboo still lingers against their coming near sacred objects at these times" (p. 44). Further, just before enumerating women's rights of participation in the various rituals noted above, Lowie mentions one particular Sun Dance Doll bundle that was not supposed to be unwrapped by a woman (p. 60). Pursuing this trail we find: "According to all Lodge Grass informants and most others, the doll owned by Wrinkled-face took precedence not only of other dolls but of all other Crow medicines whatsoever. . . . This particular doll was not supposed to be handled by a woman" (p. 229).[c]

In sum, the Crow are probably a fairly typical case. Yes, women have certain powers and rights, in this case some that place them in fairly high positions. Yet ultimately the line is drawn: menstruation is a threat to warfare, one of the most valued institutions of the tribe, one that is central to their self-

---

[4] In this paragraph, Ortner sets out the basic criteria that she believes prove a culture considers women inferior. Below, she provides examples of these different classes of evidence from different societies. However, she doesn't give the reader all three types of evidence for any single society. Ortner says that although the three types of data may all be found in one system, any single one of them is sufficient to prove female inferiority in a given culture.

If one accepts the structuralist premise that cultural patterns originate in the way the brain processes information, this is an acceptable methodological technique. However, her methods seem little different from those of the nineteenth-century evolutionists who validated their cross-cultural comparative analyses using the concept of psychic unity.

[5] Austrian-born anthropologist Robert Lowie (1883–1957) was a student of Franz Boas. Lowie wrote extensively on the Crow as well as other Plains Indians. Be sure to read Ortner's footnote "c" (page 368) about Lowie and his doll.

definition; and the most sacred object of the tribe is taboo to the direct sight and touch of women.

Similar examples could be multiplied ad infinitum, but I think the onus is no longer upon us to demonstrate that female subordination is a cultural universal; it is up to those who would argue against the point to bring forth counter examples. I shall take the universal secondary status of women as a given, and proceed from there.[6]

NATURE AND CULTURE[d]

How are we to explain the universal devaluation of women? We could of course rest the case on biological determinism. There is something genetically inherent in the male of the species, so the biological determinists would argue, that makes them the naturally dominant sex; that "something" is lacking in females, and as a result women are not only naturally subordinate but in general quite satisfied with their position, since it affords them protection and the opportunity to maximize maternal pleasures, which to them are the most satisfying experiences of life. Without going into a detailed refutation of this position, I think it fair to say that it has failed to be established to the satisfaction of almost anyone in academic anthropology. This is to say, not that biological facts are irrelevant, or that men and women are not different, but that these facts and differences only take on significance of superior/inferior within the framework of culturally defined value systems.[7]

If we are unwilling to rest the case on genetic determinism, it seems to me that we have only one way to proceed. We must attempt to interpret female subordination in light of other universals, factors built into the structure of the most generalized situation in which all human beings, in

whatever culture, find themselves. For example, every human being has a physical body and a sense of nonphysical mind, is part of a society of other individuals and an inheritor of a cultural tradition, and must engage in some relationship, however mediated, with "nature," or the nonhuman realm in order to survive. Every human being is born (to a mother) and ultimately dies, all are assumed to have an interest in personal survival, and society/culture has its own interest in (or at least momentum toward) continuity and survival, which transcends the lives and deaths of particular individuals. And so forth. It is in the realm of such universals of the human condition that we must seek an explanation for the universal fact of female devaluation.

I translate the problem, in other words, into the following simple question. What could there be in the generalized structure and conditions of existence, common to every culture, that would lead every culture to place a lower value upon women? Specifically, my thesis is that woman is being identified with—or, if you will, seems to be a symbol of—something that every culture devalues, something that every culture defines as being of a lower order of existence than itself. Now it seems that there is only one thing that would fit that description, and that is "nature" in the most generalized sense. Every culture, or, generically, "culture," is engaged in the process of generating and sustaining systems of meaningful forms (symbols, artifacts, etc.) by means of which humanity transcends the givens of natural existence, bends them to its purposes, controls them in its interest. We may thus broadly equate culture with the notion of human consciousness, or with the products of human consciousness (i.e., systems of thought and technology), by means of which humanity attempts to assert control over nature.[8]

---

[6] Ortner says that even in societies in which women may hold high status and powerful positions, one can still find evidence indicating that they are inferior to men. She declares her case to be proven and places the burden of disproof on those who disagree. Are you convinced? Does the Crow example she provides bear this out?

[7] The reference to biological determinism in this paragraph is an allusion to theories popular at the time this essay was written. Additionally, books such as Ardrey's 1961 *African Genesis,* which emphasized the aggressive nature of men, had captured the popular imagination.

[8] The idea that all humans make a fundamental distinction between culture and nature, and that in every society, culture is believed to be superior to nature, is basic to the work of Lévi-Strauss. In the two paragraphs you have just read, Ortner paraphrases him. In *The Elementary Structures of Kinship* Lévi-Strauss wrote

Now the categories of "nature" and "culture" are of course conceptual categories—one can find no boundary out in the actual world between the two states or realms of being. And there is no question that some cultures articulate a much stronger opposition between the two categories than others—it has even been argued that primitive peoples (some or all) do not see or intuit any distinction between the human cultural state and the state of nature at all. Yet I would maintain that the universality of ritual betokens an assertion in all human cultures of the specifically human ability to act upon and regulate, rather than passively move with and be moved by, the givens of natural existence. In ritual, the purposive manipulation of given forms toward regulating and sustaining order, every culture asserts that proper relations between human existence and natural forces depend upon culture's employing its special powers to regulate the overall processes of the world and life.[9]

One realm of cultural thought in which these points are often articulated is that of concepts of purity and pollution. Virtually every culture has some such beliefs, which seem in large part (though not, of course, entirely) to be concerned with the relationship between culture and nature

(see Ortner, 1973, n.d.). A well-known aspect of purity/pollution beliefs cross-culturally is that of the natural "contagion" of pollution; left to its own devices, pollution (for these purposes grossly equated with the unregulated operation of natural energies) spreads and overpowers all that it comes in contact with. Thus a puzzle—if pollution is so strong, how can anything be purified? Why is the purifying agent not itself polluted? The answer, in keeping with the present line of argument, is that purification is effected in a ritual context; purification ritual, as a purposive activity that pits self-conscious (symbolic) action against natural energies, is more powerful than those energies.[10]

In any case, my point is simply that every culture implicitly recognizes and asserts a distinction between the operation of nature and the operation of culture (human consciousness and its products); and further, that the distinctiveness of culture rests precisely on the fact that it can under most circumstances transcend natural conditions and turn them to its purposes. Thus culture (i.e., every culture) at some level of awareness asserts itself to be not only distinct from but superior to nature, and that sense of distinctiveness and superiority rest precisely on the

---

. . . it is easy to recognize universality as the criterion of nature, for what is constant in man falls necessarily beyond the scope of customs, techniques, and institutions . . . Let us suppose that everything universal in man relates to the natural order . . . and that everything subject to a norm is cultural and is both relative and particular. (quoted in Boyne 1966:200)

Ortner's comments here directly reflect Lévi-Strauss' statement. She reasons from this passage that if everything universal relates to nature, and if female subordination is universal, then female subordination must relate to nature.

[9] A critical element of structuralist thought is expressed in this passage. Ortner notes that there is no boundary in the physical world between nature and culture. The boundary is a product of human thinking. Structuralists believe that the human mind imposes order by *parsing,* or breaking down, the world into culturally meaningful bits. Structuralists try to discover the fundamental principles by which humans accomplish this parsing.

[10] Having rejected biological foundations for the universal subordination of women, Ortner must formulate a cultural explanation. Following Lévi-Strauss, she chooses ritual as the focus of her analysis, as the place where cultures attempt to regulate and sustain order. Lévi-Strauss authored two studies of mythology—*The Raw and the Cooked* (1969) and *From Honey to Ashes* (1973)—based on what he claimed to be a fundamental opposition between nature and culture. Following Lévi-Strauss, Ortner states that humans transcend and control nature through the use of symbols. In particular, we distinguish ourselves from the natural world and regulate it through the use of ritual. It is through ritual that the natural, dangerous, and unacceptable is transformed into the cultural, acceptable, and safe.

The focus on ritual symbols and their power is not new for Ortner. In 1973, the year before the publication of this essay, Ortner published an article in *American Anthropologist* called "On Key Symbols," in which she discusses how symbols operate in ritual thought and action. Ortner is also not a strict structuralist. A year after this essay she published another analysis titled "Gods' Bodies, Gods' Food: A Symbolic Analysis of Sherpa Ritual," which was inspired by the work of Clifford Geertz (see essay 37).

ability to transform — to "socialize" and "culturalize" — nature.[11]

Returning now to the issue of women, their pan-cultural second-class status could be accounted for, quite simply, by postulating that women are being identified or symbolically associated with nature, as opposed to men, who are identified with culture. Since it is always culture's project to subsume and transcend nature, if women were considered part of nature, then culture would find it "natural" to subordinate, not to say oppress, them. Yet although this argument can be shown to have considerable force, it seems to oversimplify the case. The formulation I would like to defend and elaborate on in the following section, then, is that women are seen "merely" as being *closer* to nature than men. That is, culture (still equated relatively unambiguously with men) recognizes that women are active participants in its special processes, but at the same time sees them as being more rooted in, or having more direct affinity with, nature.

The revision may seem minor or even trivial, but I think it is a more accurate rendering of cultural assumptions. Further, the argument cast in these terms has several analytic advantages over the simpler formulation; I shall discuss these later. It might simply be stressed here that the revised argument would still account for the pan-cultural devaluation of women, for even if women are not equated with nature, they are nonetheless seen as representing a lower order of being, as being less transcendental of nature than men are. The next task of the paper, then, is to consider why they might be viewed in that way.[12]

WHY IS WOMAN SEEN AS CLOSER TO NATURE?

It all begins of course with the body and the natural procreative functions specific to women alone. We can sort out for discussion three levels at which this absolute physiological fact has significance: (1) woman's *body and its functions,* more involved more of the time with "species life," seem to place her closer to nature, in contrast to man's physiology, which frees him more completely to take up the projects of culture; (2) woman's body and its functions place her in *social roles* that in turn are considered to be at a lower order of the cultural process than man's; and (3) woman's traditional social roles, imposed because of her body and its functions, in turn give her a different *psychic structure,* which, like her physiological nature and her social roles, is seen as being closer to nature. I shall discuss each of these points in turn, showing first how in each instance certain factors strongly tend to align woman with nature, then indicating other factors that demonstrate her full alignment with culture, the combined factors thus placing her in a problematic intermediate position. It will become clear in the course of the discussion why men seem by contrast less intermediate, more purely "cultural" than women. And I reiterate that I am dealing only at the level of cultural and human universals. These arguments are intended to apply to generalized humanity; they grow out of the human condition, as humanity has experienced and confronted it up to the present day.

---

[11] Lévi-Strauss' ideas, like those of other theorists, were not uniformly accepted. Anthropologist Carol MacCormack (1934–1997), for example, criticized Lévi-Strauss' nature-culture formulation. While he saw the nature-culture contrast as timeless and value-free, MacCormack concluded that such ideas were culturally specific. MacCormack wrote

> There is no way to absolutely verify that the nature-culture opposition exists as an essential feature of universal unconscious structure, and there is ethnographic evidence to suggest that in the form in which Europeans now conceive it, the contrast is not a universal feature of consciously-held folk models. (1980:10)

[12] Ortner's distinction between women as identified with nature and women as "merely" closer to nature is subtle and performs two tasks in this essay. First, it makes her case more compelling but less amenable to testing. If Ortner said that women were identified wholly with nature, one or two counterexamples could easily disprove her point. However, she suggests that women are merely closer to nature than men. This means that in every case where anthropologists find women associated with culture rather than nature, they must ask, "Well, are men even more associated with culture?" This is a difficult proposition to test. Second, it opens the possibility that women mediate between culture and nature. This is discussed further below.

1. *Woman's physiology seen as closer to nature.*
This part of my argument has been anticipated,
with subtlety, cogency, and a great deal of hard
data, by De Beauvoir (1953).[13] De Beauvoir reviews the physiological structure, development,
and functions of the human female and concludes that "the female, to a greater extent than
the male, is the prey of the species" (p. 60). She
points out that many major areas and processes
of the woman's body serve no apparent function
for the health and stability of the individual; on
the contrary, as they perform their specific organic functions, they are often sources of discomfort, pain, and danger. The breasts are irrelevant
to personal health; they may be excised at any
time of a woman's life. "Many of the ovarian secretions function for the benefit of the egg, promoting its maturation and adapting the uterus to
its requirements; in respect to the organism as a
whole, they make for disequilibrium rather than
for regulation—the woman is adapted to the
needs of the egg rather than to her own requirements" (p. 24). Menstruation is often uncomfort-
able, sometimes painful; it frequently has negative
emotional correlates and in any case involves
bothersome tasks of cleansing and waste disposal;
and—a point that De Beauvoir does not mention—in many cultures it interrupts a woman's
routine, putting her in a stigmatized state involving various restrictions on her activities and social
contacts. In pregnancy many of the woman's vitamin and mineral resources are channeled into
nourishing the fetus, depleting her own strength
and energies. And finally, childbirth itself is
painful and dangerous (pp. 24–27 *passim*). In
sum, De Beauvoir concludes that the female "is
more enslaved to the species than the male, her
animality is more manifest" (p. 239).

While De Beauvoir's book is ideological, her
survey of woman's physiological situation seems
fair and accurate. It is simply a fact that propor-
tionately more of woman's body space, for a
greater percentage of her lifetime, and at some—

sometimes great—cost to her personal health,
strength, and general stability, is taken up with
the natural processes surrounding the reproduction of the species.

De Beauvoir goes on to discuss the negative
implications of woman's "enslavement to the
species" in relation to the projects in which humans engage, projects through which culture is
generated and defined. She arrives thus at the
crux of her argument (pp. 58–59):

> Here we have the key to the whole mystery.
> On the biological level a species is maintained
> only by creating itself anew; but this creation
> results only in repeating the same Life in more
> individuals. But man assures the repetition of
> Life while transcending Life through Existence
> [i.e., goal-oriented, meaningful action]; by this
> transcendence he creates values that deprive
> pure repetition of all value. In the animal,
> the freedom and variety of male activities are
> vain because no project is involved. Except
> for his services to the species, what he does is
> immaterial. Whereas in serving the species,
> the human male also remodels the face of the
> earth, he creates new instruments, he invents,
> he shapes the future.

In other words, woman's body seems to doom
her to mere reproduction of life; the male, in
contrast, lacking natural creative functions, must
(or has the opportunity to) assert his creativity
externally, "artificially," through the medium of
technology and symbols. In so doing, he creates
relatively lasting, eternal, transcendent objects,
while the woman creates only perishables—human beings.

This formulation opens up a number of important insights. It speaks, for example, to the
great puzzle of why male activities involving the
destruction of life (hunting and warfare) are often
given more prestige than the female's ability to
give birth, to create life. Within De Beauvoir's
framework, we realize it is not the killing that is
the relevant and valued aspect of hunting and

---

[13] Simone de Beauvoir (1908–1986) was a French existentialist author of plays and novels and the companion of the philosopher Jean Paul Sartre (1905–1980). The de Beauvoir reference is from her 1949 book *The Second Sex*, which an-alyzes women's inferior positions in society. In *The Second Sex*, de Beauvoir used existential argument and ethnographic data to compare women to oppressed minorities and proposed that women's status was the result of social conditions rather than biological factors. Today, *The Second Sex* is considered a fundamental document of modern feminism.

warfare; rather, it is the transcendental (social, cultural) nature of these activities, as opposed to the naturalness of the process of birth: "For it is not in giving life but in risking life that man is raised above the animal; that is why superiority has been accorded in humanity not to the sex that brings forth but to that which kills" (*ibid.*).

Thus if male is, as I am suggesting, everywhere (unconsciously) associated with culture and female seems closer to nature, the rationale for these associations is not very difficult to grasp, merely from considering the implications of the physiological contrast between male and female. At the same time, however, woman cannot be consigned fully to the category of nature, for it is perfectly obvious that she is a full-fledged human being endowed with human consciousness just as a man is; she is half of the human race, without whose cooperation the whole enterprise would collapse. She may seem more in the possession of nature than man, but having consciousness, she thinks and speaks; she generates, communicates, and manipulates symbols, categories, and values. She participates in human dialogues not only with other women but also with men. As Lévi-Strauss says, "Woman could never become just a sign and nothing more, since even in a man's world she is still a person, and since insofar as she is defined as a sign she must [still] be recognized as a generator of signs" (1969a:496).[14]

Indeed, the fact of woman's full human consciousness, her full involvement in and commitment to culture's project of transcendence over nature, may ironically explain another of the great puzzles of "the woman problem"—woman's nearly universal unquestioning acceptance of her own devaluation. For it would seem that, as a conscious human and member of culture, she has followed out the logic of culture's arguments and has reached culture's conclusions along with the men. As De Beauvoir puts it (p. 59):

> For she, too, is an existent, she feels the urge to surpass, and her project is not mere repetition but transcendence towards a different future—in her heart of hearts she finds confirmation of the masculine pretensions. She joins the men in the festivals that celebrate the successes and victories of the males. Her misfortune is to have been biologically destined for the repetition of Life, when even in her own view Life does not carry within itself its reasons for being, reasons that are more important than life itself.

In other words, woman's consciousness—her membership, as it were, in culture—is evidenced in part by the very fact that she accepts her own devaluation and takes culture's point of view.

I have tried here to show one part of the logic of that view, the part that grows directly from the physiological differences between men and women. Because of woman's greater bodily involvement with the natural functions surrounding reproduction, she is seen as more a part of nature than man is. Yet in part because of her consciousness and participation in human social dialogue, she is recognized as a participant in culture. Thus she appears as something intermediate between culture and nature, lower on the scale of transcendence than man.[15]

2. *Woman's social role seen as closer to nature.* Woman's physiological functions, I have argued,

---

[14] Lévi-Strauss' comments on women and signs are from his 1949 book *The Elementary Structures of Kinship.* There, he uses the notion of sign taken from the turn-of-the-century Swiss structural linguist Ferdinand de Saussure (1857–1913). Contrary to the popular views of his time, Saussure argued that the meanings of the majority of words in a language are derived from the arbitrary association of sound and meaning. Each idea in language is arbitrarily associated with a sound. The sound, Saussure called the "signifier"; the idea, the "signified." Together they form, in Saussure's terminology, a linguistic "sign." So, Ortner is saying that although devalued, women are still "generators of signs."

[15] Although Lévi-Strauss proposed that human thinking always parsed the world into binary oppositions, he also believed that the mind was dissatisfied with such oppositions and always searched for a mediator for them. A mediating category was a category that was not subsumed by either part of the binary but somehow transcended them. He argued that this mediator was always problematic. It was privileged, special, or ambiguous. In positioning women as "merely" closer to nature than men, and in insisting that women, while identified with nature, are in truth part of society's cultural project, Ortner is beginning to build a case that women are the mediating element in the culture-nature binary.

may tend in themselves to motivate[e] a view of woman as closer to nature, a view she herself, as an observer of herself and the world, would tend to agree with. Woman creates naturally from within her own being, whereas man is free to, or forced to, create artificially, that is, through cultural means, and in such a way as to sustain culture. In addition, I now wish to show how woman's physiological functions have tended universally to limit her social movement, and to confine her universally to certain social contexts which *in turn* are seen as closer to nature. That is, not only her bodily processes but the social situation in which her bodily processes locate her may carry this significance. And insofar as she is permanently associated (in the eyes of culture) with these social milieux, they add weight (perhaps the decisive part of the burden) to the view of woman as closer to nature. I refer here of course to woman's confinement to the domestic family context, a confinement motivated, no doubt, by her lactation processes.

Woman's body, like that of all female mammals, generates milk during and after pregnancy for the feeding of the newborn baby. The baby cannot survive without breast milk or some similar formula at this stage of life. Since the mother's body goes through its lactation processes in direct relation to a pregnancy with a particular child, the relationship of nursing between mother and child is seen as a natural bond, other feeding arrangements being seen in most cases as unnatural and makeshift. Mothers and their children, according to cultural reasoning, belong together. Further, children beyond infancy are not strong enough to engage in major work, yet are mobile and unruly and not capable of understanding various dangers; they thus require supervision and constant care. Mother is the obvious person for this task, as an extension of her natural nursing bond with the children, or because she has a new infant and is already involved with child-oriented activities. Her own activities are thus circumscribed by the limitations and low levels of her children's strengths and skills:[f] she is confined to the domestic family group; "woman's place is in the home."[16]

Woman's association with the domestic circle would contribute to the view of her as closer to nature in several ways. In the first place, the sheer fact of constant association with children plays a role in the issue; one can easily see how infants and children might themselves be considered part of nature. Infants are barely human and utterly unsocialized; like animals they are unable to walk upright, they excrete without control, they do not speak. Even slightly older children are clearly not yet fully under the sway of culture. They do not yet understand social duties, responsibilities, and morals; their vocabulary and their range of learned skills are small. One finds implicit recognition of an association between children and nature in many cultural practices. For example, most cultures have initiation rites for adolescents (primarily for boys; I shall return to this point below), the point of which is to move the child ritually from a less than fully human state into full participation in society and culture; many cultures do not hold funeral rites for children who die at early ages, explicitly because they are not yet fully social beings. Thus children are likely to be categorized with nature, and woman's close association with children may compound her potential for being seen as closer to nature herself. It is ironic that the rationale for boys' initiation rites in many cultures is that the boys must be purged of the defilement accrued from being around mother and other women so much of the time, when in fact much of the woman's defilement may derive from her being around children so much of the time.[17]

The second major problematic implication of women's close association with the domestic

---

[16] Ortner, like all authors, writes within a historical and political context. Her remarks on mother-child bonds and mother's nursing are an interesting reflection of this. American middle-class women "rediscovered" breast-feeding in the 1970s. Nursing became part of a political movement that included campaigns against corporations such as Nestle, which sold infant formula, especially in poor nations. There was also much popular writing on the importance of mother-infant bonding. Ortner may have had these things in mind as she wrote these passages.

[17] Ortner has constructed an elegant argument, but like Lévi-Strauss before her, has based her logic on a set of arbitrary assumptions. Why, for example, is the link between women and nature assumed as fact? As she herself states, women

context derives from certain structural conflicts between the family and society at large in any social system. The implications of the "domestic/public opposition" in relation to the position of women have been cogently developed by Rosaldo (1974), and I simply wish to show its relevance to the present argument. The notion that the domestic unit—the biological family charged with reproducing and socializing new members of the society—is opposed to the public entity—the superimposed network of alliances and relationships that is the society—is also the basis of Lévi-Strauss's argument in the *Elementary Structures of Kinship* (1969a). Lévi-Strauss argues not only that this opposition is present in every social system, but further that it has the significance of the opposition between nature and culture. The universal incest prohibition[g] and its ally, the rule of exogamy (marriage outside the group), ensure that "the risk of seeing a biological family become established as a closed system is definitely eliminated; the biological group can no longer stand apart, and the bond of alliance with another family ensures the dominance of the social over the biological, and of the cultural over the natural" (p. 479). And although not every culture articulates a radical opposition between the domestic and the public as such, it is hardly contestable that the domestic is always subsumed by the public; domestic units are allied with one another through the enactment of rules that are logically at a higher level than the units themselves; this creates an emergent unit—society—that is logically at a higher level than the

domestic units of which it is composed.[18]

Now, since women are associated with, and indeed are more or less confined to, the domestic context, they are identified with this lower order of social/cultural organization. What are the implications of this for the way they are viewed? First, if the specifically biological (reproductive) function of the family is stressed, as in Lévi-Strauss's formulation, then the family (and hence woman) is identified with nature pure and simple, as opposed to culture. But this is obviously too simple; the point seems more adequately formulated as follows: the family (and hence woman) represents lower-level, socially fragmenting, particularistic sort of concerns, as opposed to interfamilial relations representing higher-level, integrative, universalistic sorts of concerns. Since men lack a "natural" basis (nursing, generalized to child care) for a familial orientation, their sphere of activity is defined at the level of interfamilial relations. And hence, so the cultural reasoning seems to go, men are the "natural" proprietors of religion, ritual, politics, and other realms of cultural thought and action in which universalistic statements of spiritual and social synthesis are made. Thus men are identified not only with culture, in the sense of all human creativity, as opposed to nature; they are identified in particular with culture in the old-fashioned sense of the finer and higher aspects of human thought—art, religion, law, etc.[19]

Here again, the logic of cultural reasoning aligning woman with a lower order of culture

---

socialize children into cultural beings and turn raw substances into edible meals. So why are women not closer to culture? She answers by saying that socialization activities are taken over by men in adolescence. But why should this time period be inherently more important than earlier childhood in determining the relation of men and women to culture? Further, Ortner does not deal with activities that seem to place men close to nature. Shouldn't adult men, who are presumably out in nature hunting and killing, be closer to nature than women?

[18] Ortner is referring here to Lévi-Strauss' contention that one of the most basic of binary oppositions is between us and them, kin and nonkin. This relates to the nature-culture opposition because of the universal rules of incest (see essay 25).

Additionally, Ortner mentions Michelle Rosaldo's (1944–1981) article on gender inequality. There, Rosaldo presented a structuralist argument, but one that relied on a sociocultural rather than a biological explanation. She focused on the domestic-public opposition between men and women. She argued that men are typically associated with higher prestige public activities, while women, because they raise children, are limited to less prestigious domestic tasks.

Michelle Rosaldo, the wife of Renato Rosaldo, was killed in an accident during field research in October 1981. Renato Rosaldo's attempt to deal with his wife's death forms the core of his article "Grief and a Headhunter's Rage" (essay 38).

[19] When Ortner talks of culture in the old-fashioned sense, the is referring to Tylor's nineteenth-century definition of culture (arts, laws, morals, etc.; see essay 2) as opposed to a Boasian notion of culture.

than man is clear and, on the surface, quite compelling. At the same time, woman cannot be fully consigned to nature, for there are aspects of her situation, even within the domestic context, that undeniably demonstrate her participation in the cultural process. It goes without saying, of course, that except for nursing newborn infants (and artificial nursing devices can cut even this biological tie), there is no reason why it has to be mother — as opposed to father, or anyone else — who remains identified with child care. But even assuming that other practical and emotional reasons conspire to keep woman in this sphere, it is possible to show that her activities in the domestic context could as logically put her squarely in the category of culture.

In the first place, one must point out that woman not only feeds and cleans up after children in a simple caretaker operation; she in fact is the primary agent of their early socialization. It is she who transforms newborn infants from mere organisms into cultured humans, teaching them manners and the proper ways to behave in order to become fullfledged members of the culture. On the basis of her socializing functions alone, she could not be more a representative of culture. Yet in virtually every society there is a point at which the socialization of boys is transferred to the hands of men. The boys are considered, in one set of terms or another, not yet "really" socialized; their entree into the realm of fully human (social, cultural) status can be accomplished only by men. We still see this in our own schools, where there is a gradual inversion in the proportion of female to male teachers up through the grades: most kindergarten teachers are female; most university professors are male.[h]

Or again, take cooking. In the overwhelming majority of societies cooking is the woman's work. No doubt this stems from practical considerations — since the woman has to stay home with the baby, it is convenient for her to perform the chores centered in the home. But if it is true, as Lévi-Strauss has argued (1969b), that transforming the raw into the cooked may represent, in many systems of thought, the transition from nature to culture, then here we have woman aligned with this important culturalizing process, which could easily place her in the category of culture,

triumphing over nature. Yet it is also interesting to note that when a culture (e.g. France or China) develops a tradition of *haute cuisine* — "real" cooking, as opposed to trivial ordinary domestic cooking — the high chefs are almost always men. Thus the pattern replicates that in the area of socialization — women perform lower-level conversions from nature to culture, but when the culture distinguishes a higher level of the same functions, the higher level is restricted to men.

In short, we see once again some sources of woman's appearing more intermediate than man with respect to the nature/culture dichotomy. Her "natural" association with the domestic context (motivated by her natural lactation functions) tends to compound her potential for being viewed as closer to nature, because of the animal-like nature of children, and because of the infrasocial connotation of the domestic group as against the rest of society. Yet at the same time her socializing and cooking functions within the domestic context show her to be a powerful agent of the cultural process, constantly transforming raw natural resources into cultural products. Belonging to culture, yet appearing to have stronger and more direct connections with nature, she is once again seen as situated between the two realms.

[We have omitted most of the last two sections of Ortner's article, about 3,000 words, called "Woman's Psyche Seen as Closer to Nature" and "The Implications of Intermediacy." In the first section she argues that women not only have a different body and a different social importance than men but also a different psychic structure. In support of this view she relies mainly on an argument developed by Chodorow (1974), who claimed that men are more objective than women and communicate in terms of relatively abstract categories whereas women are subjective and relate in terms of relatively concrete phenomena. She argued that these differences are not innate but are due to the fact that "women, universally, are largely responsible for early care and for (at least) later female socialization" (1974:43).

The last section, "The Implications of Intermediacy," summarizes the essay's main points and discusses the implications of women's mediation between nature and culture. Ortner says that women are universally seen as occupying a middle status on a hierarchy of being from culture to nature. As a result they are lower than men and less capable of achieving transcendence of nature. Ortner believes that this position assigns them greater symbolic ambiguity. She says

> *Thus we can account easily for both the subversive feminine symbols (witches, evil eye, menstrual pollution, castrating mothers) and the feminine symbols of transcendence (mother goddesses, merciful dispensers of salvation, female symbols of justice, and the strong presence of feminine symbolism in the realms of art, religion, ritual, and law). Feminine symbolism, far more often than masculine symbolism, manifests this propensity toward polarized ambiguity— sometimes utterly exalted, sometimes utterly debased, rarely within the normal range of human possibilities."*

Ortner concludes this section as follows:]

In short, the postulate that woman is viewed as closer to nature than man has several implications for further analysis, and can be interpreted in several different ways. If it is viewed simply as a *middle* position on a scale from culture down to nature, then it is still seen as lower than culture and thus accounts for the pan-cultural assumption that woman is lower than man in the order of things. If it is read as a *mediating* element in the culture-nature relationship, then it may account in part for the cultural tendency not merely to devalue woman but to circumscribe and restrict her functions, since culture must maintain control over its (pragmatic and symbolic) mechanisms for the conversion of nature into culture. And if it is read as an *ambiguous* status between culture and nature, it may help account for the fact that, in specific cultural ideologies and symbolizations, woman can occasionally be aligned with culture, and in any event is often assigned polarized and contradictory meanings within a single symbolic system. Middle status, mediating functions, ambiguous meaning—all are different

readings, for different contextual purposes, of woman's being seen as intermediate between nature and culture.

CONCLUSIONS

Ultimately, it must be stressed again that the whole scheme is a construct of culture rather than a fact of nature. Woman is not "in reality" any closer to (or further from) nature than man—both have consciousness, both are mortal. But there are certainly reasons why she appears that way, which is what I have tried to show in this paper. The result is a (sadly) efficient feedback system: various aspects of woman's situation (physical, social, psychological) contribute to her being seen as closer to nature, while the view of her as closer to nature is in turn embodied in institutional forms that reproduce her situation. The implications for social change are similarly circular: a different cultural view can only grow out of a different social actuality; a different social actuality can only grow out of a different cultural view.

It is clear, then, that the situation must be attacked from both sides. Efforts directed solely at changing the social institutions—through settings quotas on hiring, for example, or through passing equal-pay-for-equal-work laws—cannot have far-reaching effects if cultural language and imagery continue to purvey a relatively devalued view of women. But at the same time efforts directed solely at changing cultural assumptions—through male and female consciousness-raising groups, for example, or through revision of educational materials and mass-media imagery—cannot be successful unless the institutional base of the society is changed to support and reinforce the changed cultural view. Ultimately, both men and women can and must be equally involved in projects of creativity and transcendence. Only then will women be seen as aligned with culture, in culture's ongoing dialectic with nature.[20]

---

[20] In the final paragraph Ortner seems to be caught on the horns of a dilemma. She advocates political action to end what she considers the universal subordination of women but cannot accommodate this notion within structuralism. Structuralism is designed to find consistencies within different cultures in order to reconstruct fundamental patterns of human thought. Because of this, culture change is irrelevant to structuralist analysis. Additionally, Ortner has located the source

Notes

The first version of this paper was presented in October 1972 as a lecture in the course "Women: Myth and Reality" at Sarah Lawrence College. I received helpful comments from the students and from my co-teachers in the course: Joan Kelly Gadol, Eva Kollisch, and Gerda Lerner. A short account was delivered at the American Anthropological Association meetings in Toronto, November 1972. Meanwhile, I received excellent critical comments from Karen Blu, Robert Paul, Michelle Rosaldo, David Schneider, and Terence Turner, and the present version of the paper, in which the thrust of the argument has been rather significantly changed, was written in response to those comments. I, of course, retain responsibility for its final form. The paper is dedicated to Simone De Beauvoir, whose book *The Second Sex* (1953), first published in French in 1949, remains in my opinion the best single comprehensive understanding of "the woman problem."

a. It is true of course that *yin,* the female principle, has a negative valence. Nonetheless, there is an absolute complementarity of *yin* and *yang* in Taoism, a recognition that the world requires the equal operation and interaction of both principles for its survival.

b. Some anthropologists might consider this type of evidence (social-structural arrangements that exclude women, explicitly or de facto, from certain groups, roles, or statuses) to be a subtype of the second type of evidence (symbolic formulations of inferiority). I would not disagree with this view, although most social anthropologists would probably separate the two types.

c. While we are on the subject of injustices of various kinds, we might note that Lowie secretly bought this doll, the most sacred object in the tribal repertoire, from its custodian, the widow of Wrinkled-face. She asked $400 for it, but this price was "far beyond [Lowie's] means," and he finally got it for $80 (p. 300).

d. With all due respect to Lévi-Strauss (1969a,b, and *passim*).

e. Semantic theory uses the concept of motivation of meaning, which encompasses various ways in which a meaning may be assigned to a symbol because of certain objective properties of that symbol, rather than by arbitrary association. In a sense, this entire paper is an inquiry into the motivation of the mean-

ing of woman as a symbol, asking why woman may be unconsciously assigned the significance of being closer to nature. For a concise statement on the various types of motivation of meaning, see Ullman (1963).

f. A situation that often serves to make her more childlike herself.

g. David M. Schneider (personal communication) is prepared to argue that the incest taboo is not universal, on the basis of material from Oceania. Let us say at this point, then, that it is virtually universal.

h. I remember having my first male teacher in the fifth grade, and I remember being excited about that—it was somehow more grown up.

References

Bakan, David. 1966. *The Duality of Human Existence.* Boston.

Carlson, Rae. 1971. "Sex Differences in Ego Functioning: Exploratory Studies of Agency and Communion," *Journal of Consulting and Clinical Psychology,* 37:267–77.

De Beauvoir, Simone. 1953. *The Second Sex.* New York.

Ingham, John M. 1971. "Are the Sirionó Raw or Cooked?" *American Anthropologist,* 73:1092–99.

Lévi-Strauss, Claude. 1969a. *The Elementary Structures of Kinship.* Trans. J. H. Bell and J. R. von Sturmer; ed. R. Needham. Boston.

———. 1969b. *The Raw and the Cooked.* Trans. J. and D. Weightman. New York.

Lowie, Robert. 1956. *The Crow Indians.* New York. Originally published in 1935.

Ortner, Sherry B. 1973. "Sherpa Purity," *American Anthropologist,* 75:49–63.

———. n.d. "Purification Beliefs and Practices," *Encyclopedia Britannica,* forthcoming.

Pitt-Rivers, Julian. 1961. *People of the Sierra.* Chicago.

Siu, R. G. H. 1968. *The Man of Many Qualities.* Cambridge, Mass.

Ullman, Stephen. 1963. "Semantic Universals," in Joseph H. Greenberg, ed., *Universals of Language.* Cambridge, Mass.

of female oppression in the fact that members of societies universally parse their worlds into nature and culture and universally assign women to a mediating category between them. One can easily imagine political action designed to improve the conditions of women in a society, but how can one ever change a culturally universal pattern of thought?

Ethnoscience and Cognitive Anthropology

It has long been evident that a major weakness in anthropology is the underdeveloped condition of ethnographic method. Typologies and generalizations abound, but their descriptive foundations are insecure. Anthropology is in the natural history stage of development rather than the "stage of deductively formulated theory" (Northrop 1947).

What is needed is the improvement of ethnographic method, to make cultural descriptions replicable and accurate, so that we know what we are comparing. Ethnoscience shows promise as the New Ethnography required to advance the whole of cultural anthropology (Sturtevant 1964:100–101).

*B*eginning in the mid-1950s, ethnographers constructed a new methodological program for conducting fieldwork: ethnoscience, or the new ethnography. Ethnoscience was based on a critique of traditional fieldwork. Ethnoscientists claimed that traditional ethnography was unscientific, that it forced Western conceptual classifications on data and thus distorted the data. To make anthropology more scientific and ethnographic descriptions more accurate, ethnoscientists argued that anthropologists should attempt to reproduce cultural reality as it was perceived and lived by members of society. Thus, they insisted that cultural descriptions should be emic rather than etic. To this end, they urged that descriptions of culture be couched in terms of native thought. Understanding native conceptual categories was key to this task. The ideal ethnoscientific ethnography would include all the rules, principles, and categories that natives must know in order to understand and act appropriately in social situations within their cultures.

The underlying theoretical assumption of ethnoscience was that a culture was a set of mental models. It was the job of ethnographers to duplicate the features of those cognitive models so that they could "think" like a native. An ethnog-

rapher's model was presumed correct if it allowed him or her to replicate the way a native categorized phenomena.

Because no one has direct access to another person's mind, the cognitive principles and codes drawn by ethnographers were based on what informants told them. Thus, the new ethnography drew heavily on the techniques of linguistic analysis. In particular, ethnoscientists adopted the methodology developed in the 1920s by members of the Prague School of linguistics. Members of the Prague School such as Jakobson and Troubetzkoy were interested in the structure of languages, in particular, phonology. They studied the phonetic structure of languages by contrasting sounds in order to analyze the features that made sounds distinct. Ethnoscientists incorporated this idea into their research by creating diagrams in which contrasts of meaning could be outlined and the features of native conceptual categories distinguished.

Another set of linguistic principles upon which ethnoscience was based can be traced to the 1930s and the work of anthropologists Edward Sapir and Benjamin L. Whorf. Sapir was Franz Boas' student, and Whorf was Sapir's student. Sapir worked as a professional in anthropology, but

Whorf earned his living working for the Hartford Fire Insurance Company. Both were interested in the relationship between language and thought. Together they formulated the Sapir-Whorf hypothesis, which postulated that language not only provided a means of communication but also shaped peoples' perceptions of the world. Whorf wrote

> We dissect nature along lines laid down by our native languages. . . . We cut nature up, organize it into concepts, and ascribe significances as we do, largely because we are parties to an agreement to organize it in this way—an agreement that holds throughout our speech community and is codified in the patterns of our language. (Whorf 1956:213)

Sapir and Whorf's emphasis on the linguistic determinism of perception was one element that led the ethnoscientists to view culture as very closely connected with language. They reasoned that replicating the classification system of any language would allow them to view the world in the same way as native speakers of that language.

William Sturtevant outlined the fundamental principles of this new approach in his 1964 article "Studies in Ethnoscience," published in *American Anthropologist*. However, other ethnoscientists were already outlining the new research methodologies. Individuals such as Ward Goodenough (1956) and Charles Frake (1962) described specific ways to conduct fieldwork and analyze data. The key instrument to be used in fieldwork was the highly structured interview, aimed specifically at eliciting native conceptual categories, which ethnoscientists called domains. They then used a technique called componential analysis to determine the definitive characteristics by which the objects and ideas in each domain were sorted. Ethnoscientists believed that the members of domains (and domains themselves) were organized following one of several logical possibilities. These included the paradigm, the taxonomy, the congerie, and the type-token. In theory, data collected in this manner was more systematic and replicable and thus more scientific. Once the appropriate model was selected, the ethnographer could classify information according to native conceptual categories. Some ethnoscientists claimed that this allowed them to

think like a native member of that culture. Early attempts at this form of classification, such as Lounsbury's (1956), concentrated on kin terminologies, but the methodology was easily applicable to other areas and soon applied in a variety of research situations. Notable examples of this are Conklin's study of Hanunóo color categories (reprinted in this section); Metzger and Williams' study of Tzeltal Maya categories of firewood (1966); Berlin, Breedlove, and Raven's 1974 analysis of Tzeltal Maya plant terminology; and a more contemporary example, Holland and Skinner's 1987 study of the cultural models behind American gender types.

The ethnoscientists' focus on the native point of view was not new. In the introduction to *Argonauts of the Western Pacific,* Bronislaw Malinowski had written that the final goal of ethnography was "to grasp the native's point of view, his relation to life, to realise *his* vision of *his* world" (1922:25, emphasis in original). The search for the native viewpoint also had strong resonances with Boasian historical particularism. Franz Boas and his students insisted on the uniqueness of each culture. They collected masses of physical data on the material and behavioral existence of the people they studied and made the doctrine of cultural relativism an item of faith among American anthropologists. Ethnoscientists continued the Boasian insistence on culture *sui generis* and extended the search for data from the material to the mental, something Boas had first suggested half a century previously.

Ethnoscience, like Boasian anthropology, implied an extreme cultural relativism, and this presented problems. Critics maintained that the approach made cross-cultural comparison impossible. If each culture had a unique way of conceptualizing the world and could only be described in its own terms, how could cultures be compared? Levi-Strauss' structuralism was seen by some as the answer to this dilemma, but skeptics argued that it was impossible for either ethnoscientists or structuralists to get inside other peoples' heads and see how they think or what they believe. A further problem concerned individual variation within society. When ethnoscientists said they were trying to re-create cultural reality from a native's point of view, an obvious question to ask was, "Which native?" (Kaplan and Manners 1972:185). Despite these criticisms, ethnoscience was an important factor in the development of at least two other theoretical approaches — cognitive anthropology and symbolic anthropology — both of which achieved major prominence in the following decades.

In the late 1960s and early 1970s, the focus of ethnoscientific work shifted. Instead of simply outlining native categories of thought, anthropologists proposed that by analyzing these, one could learn how the human mind functioned. They called this approach cognitive anthropology. Like structuralists and some linguists (Noam Chomsky, for example), cognitive anthropologists of the 1970s believed that there are universal cognitive processes that reflect an innate structure of the human brain. Taking their cue from the ethnoscientists, they proposed that linguistic analysis was the best way to understand these structures and gain insight into human thought and culture. Cognitive anthropologists attempted to understand the abstract thinking patterns of people in various cultures, studying not only the content of cognition but also the mental processes by which ideas and symbols were related (Applebaum 1987:407).

Anthropologists have long debated the nature of their field. Many believe that anthropology is a material and empirical science similar to biology or physics and want to be as methodologically similar to these fields as possible. Cognitive anthropologists such as Stephen A. Tyler (1932 –) conceptualized culture as a mental model and consequently focused on the rules by which things were categorized rather than material culture. They believed that anthropology should be more like philosophy or mathematics, with anthropologists searching for formal logical models (Applebaum 1987:409).

Although cognitive anthropology never achieved the prominence hoped for by its practitioners — and some, like Tyler, abandoned this area of research to pursue other interests — the anthropological study of cognition remains an active field of research that has advanced far from its ethnoscientific beginnings. By the mid-1970s, advances in anthropology, psychology, and the field of artificial intelligence had made it apparent that human cognition was much more complex than the models of native classification derived from componential analysis. The earlier focus on taxonomies and paradigms has given way to work in schema theory and connectionism. For example, a fundamental part of ethnoscience and early cognitive anthropology was the idea that people classified by checking off a mental list of essential features (apple = red, round, stem). Cognitive anthropologists today argue that people conceptualize by reference to general mental prototypes called schema. Cognitive psychologist George Mandler described schema in the following manner:

> The schema that is developed as a result of prior experiences with a particular kind of event is not a carbon copy of that event; schemas are abstract representations of environmental regularities. We comprehend events in terms of the schemas they activate.
>
> Schemas are also processing mechanisms; they are active in selecting evidence, in parsing the data provided by our environment, and in providing appropriate general or specific hypotheses. Most, if not all, of the activation processes occur automatically and without awareness on the part of the perceiver-comprehender. (quoted in D'Andrade 1995:122)

Thus, a child will recognize an object that is green, round, and has no stem as an apple because it fits the general schema of "appleness," rather than because it matches an exact list of traits.

Contrary to the view assumed by Tyler in essay 29 in this volume, it is now understood that much knowledge is nonlinguistic and is not governed by the linear logic of language. Thinking, in the view of Tyler (1969) and his contemporaries, involved a process whereby one element followed another in a linear sequence much like a computer. However, this model does not account for the speed and efficiency with which we process information and perform tasks. To explain nonsequential thought processes in areas where thinking is nonlinguistic, contemporary cognitive anthropologists and psychologists have turned to the theory of connectionism. Connectionism suggests that knowledge is linked, networked, and widely distributed by "processing units" that work like neurons (Strauss and Quinn 1994:286) and that we access and analyze information through these processing units. Because these units are connected and work simultaneously, we can process information much faster than any computer.

Looking at thinking and knowledge using the connectionist model has two advantages over the old ethnoscientific view. First, it acknowledges that information and knowledge do not have to be language based, and second, it is compatible with our ability to perform commonplace but complex actions rapidly and without conscious thought.

The experience of learning to drive a car illustrates the difference between language-based rule learning and nonverbal connectionist learning based on the networking of schemas (D'Andrade 1995). Driving involves both connectionist networks and verbally based knowledge. One can be told the brake pedal is on the left, gas pedal on the right, and in the United States one drives on the right side of the road. This type of learning is rapid and easy to change. However, verbal instruction is very different from the physical process of driving. It may require hundreds of driving experiences to make basic driving actions such as shifting gears smooth and automatic. The automatic driving reactions that come from practice and experience are based on schema networks that are set down and interconnected through observation and trial-and-error practice, not verbal instruction. If you learned to drive as McGee did, in a car with a manual transmission, you remember the practice it took to shift smoothly—something that no amount of verbal instruction could help. It is connectionist networks based on experience that allow you to drive without conscious thought, and to react quickly and automatically to situations around you. For example, if a child runs out into the street in front

of your car, you do not go through a thought process that ends with the conclusion that it would be logical in this situation to slow your vehicle. You simply, automatically apply the brakes.

A major consequence of the development of schema and connectionist theories of cognition was a shift in how cognitive anthropologists looked at the concept of culture. For the ethnoscientists of the 1950s and 1960s, culture was a mental model in the heads of native informants that could be diagrammed and replicated using the proper interviewing techniques. But connectionist theory demonstrates that a great deal of what goes on in the minds of human beings is certainly cultural, but not verbal, not conscious, and not possible to elicit through questioning. Thus the old definition of culture is inadequate. A solution to this problem, proposed by Hutchins (1994), is to define culture as a process. In this view, culture is not simply mental content; rather it involves the process of thinking and interacting in and with the physical world. These interactions build the schemas and create the mental connections in the brain that make cognition possible.

The essays chosen for this section reflect the development of ethnoscientific and cognitive anthropological thought through the 1960s and illustrate the close relationship between them. Essay 28, Harold C. Conklin's 1955 study, is a classic piece of ethnoscientific work in which he outlines the features by which the Hanunóo categorize colors. In Tyler's 1969 introduction to cognitive anthropology (essay 29), he outlines some of the conceptual models that he proposes underlie human thought. In particular, Tyler discusses what at the time he believed to be fundamental processes by which people classified information.

28. Hanunóo Color Categories[a]

Harold C. Conklin (1926–)

IN FOLLOWING BRIEF ANALYSIS OF A SPECIFIC Philippine color system I shall attempt to show how various ethnographic field techniques may be combined profitably in the study of lexical sets relating to perceptual categorization.[1]

Recently, I completed more than a year's field research on Hanunóo folkbotany.[b] In this type of work one soon becomes acutely aware of problems connected with understanding the local system of color categorization because plant determinations so often depend on chromatic differences in the appearance of flowers or vegetative structures—both in taxonomic botany and in popular systems of classification. It is no accident that one of the most detailed accounts of native color terminology in the Malayo-Polynesian area was written by a botanist.[c] I was, therefore, greatly concerned with Hanunóo color categories during the entire period of my ethnobotanical research. Before summarizing the specific results of my analysis of the Hanunóo material, however, I should like to draw attention to several general considerations.[2]

1. Color, in a western technical sense, is not a universal concept and in many languages such as Hanunóo there is no unitary terminological equivalent. In our technical literature definitions state that color is the evaluation of the visual sense of

(1955)

that quality of light (reflected or transmitted by some substance) which is basically determined by its spectral composition. The spectrum is the range of visible color in light measured in wave lengths (400 [deep red] to 700 [blue-violet] millimicrons).[d] The total color sphere—holding any set of external and surface conditions constant— includes two other dimensions, in addition to that of spectral position or hue. One is saturation or intensity (chroma), the other brightness or brilliance (value). These three perceptual dimensions are usually combined into a coördinate system as a cylindrical continuum known as the color solid. Saturation diminishes toward the central axis which forms the achromatic core of neutral grays from the white at the end of greatest brightness to black at the opposite extremity. Hue varies with circumferential position. Although technically speaking *black* is the absence of any "color," *white*, the presence of all visible color wave lengths, and neutral *grays* lack spectral distinction, these achromatic positions within the color solid are often included with spectrally-defined positions in the categories distinguished in popular color systems.

2. Under laboratory conditions, color *discrimination* is probably the same for all human populations, irrespective of language; but the manner in which different languages classify the millions[e] of "colors" which every normal individual can

---

[1] The focus of ethnoscientific studies were usually domains, which are patterns of classification of objects in a society. For example, sofas, chairs, and desks fall within the domain of furniture. Most of the early ethnoscientific studies concentrated on outlining the domains of limited phenomena such as native conceptions of disease or ethnobotany. Conklin's essay is a classic example of such a study.

[2] In the two numbered paragraphs, Conklin is setting up the framework on which he is going to build his presentation of Hanunóo color categories. He first provides a scientific definition of color, states that all humans are equally able to discriminate between colors, and postulates that color vocabulary influences the perception of color. Note here that Conklin is not saying that color vocabularies determine color perception, an implication of the Sapir-Whorf hypothesis described in the introduction to this section. Rather, he sets out to prove that color vocabularies influence color classification and thus the criteria by which people define colors. He wants to show the culturally specific criteria by which the Hanunóo classify color.

discriminate *differ*. Many stimuli are classified as equivalent, as extensive, cognitive — or perceptual — screening takes place.[f] Requirements of specification may differ considerably from one culturally-defined situation to another. The largest collection[g] of English color names runs to over 3,000 entries, yet only eight of these occur very commonly.[h] Recent testing by Lenneberg and others[i] demonstrates a high correlation in English and in Zuñi between ready color vocabulary and *ease in recognition of colors*. Although this is only a beginning it does show how the structure of a lexical set may affect color perception. It may also be possible to determine certain nonlinguistic correlates for color terminology. Color terms are a part of the vocabulary of particular languages and only the intracultural analysis of such lexical sets and their correlates can provide the key to their understanding and range of applicability. The study of isolated and assumed translations in other languages can lead only to confusion.[j]

In the field I began to investigate Hanunóo color classification in a number of ways, including the eliciting of linguistic responses from a large number of informants to painted cards, dyed fabrics, other previously prepared materials,[k] and the recording of visual-quality attributes taken from descriptions of specific items of the natural and artificial surroundings. This resulted in the collection of a profusion of attributive words of the nonformal — and therefore in a sense "color" — type. There were at first many inconsistencies and a high degree of overlap for which the controls used did not seem to account. However, as the work with plant specimens and minute floristic differentiation progressed, I noted that in *contrastive* situations this initial confusion and incongruity of informants' responses did not usually occur. In such situations, where the "nonformal (i.e. not spatially organized) visible quality"[1] of one substance (plant part, dyed thread, or color card) was to be related to and contrasted with that of another, both of which were either at hand or well known, terminological agreement was reached with relative ease. Such a defined situation seemed to provide the frame necessary for establishing a known level of specification. Where needed, a greater degree of specification (often employing different root morphemes) could be and was made. Otherwise, such finer distinctions were ignored. This hint of terminologically significant levels led to a reexamination of all color data and the following analysis emerged.[3]

Color distinctions in Hanunóo are made at two levels of contrast. The first, higher, more general level consists of an all-inclusive, coordinate, four-way classification which lies at the core of the color system. The four categories are mutually exclusive in contrastive contexts, but may overlap slightly in absolute (i.e., spectrally, or in other measurable) terms. The second level, including several sublevels, consists of hundreds of specific color categories, many of which overlap and interdigitate. Terminologically, there is "unanimous agreement"[m] on the designations for the four Level I categories, but considerable lack of unanimity — with a few explainable exceptions — in the use of terms at Level II.[4]

---

[3] Ethnoscience is primarily based on linguistic analysis of information elicited from informants in highly structured interviews. The data is then subjected to componential analysis. In componential analysis one identifies the defining attributes of a cultural category (in Conklin's case, colors) by discovering and describing contrasts within the category (Spradley 1980:133). In the following pages, Conklin describes the criteria used by the Hanunóo to classify different colors.

[4] Conklin says that the Hanunóo classify colors at two levels. The more general level of classification, upon which there is a high level of agreement, is a set of four terms – darkness, lightness, redness, and greenness – that are mutually exclusive contrasts. At the second level, hundreds of specific color names can overlap, and there is a lack of exact agreement. We have found an analogous situation during tests in our large classes. We color-code exams, asking students to identify the color of their exam on their answer sheets. Students easily distinguish between red, green, yellow, and blue (Conklin's Level I categorization) because these terms are mutually exclusive contrasts – if something is red, it cannot be blue. On the other hand, there is a great deal of disagreement about softer pastel colors. For example, students typically do not differentiate well between gold and orange. While all agree they are different colors, where does gold end and orange begin? This situation is analogous to Conklin's Level II Hanunóo color distinctions.

The four Level I terms are:

1. *(ma) biru*^{n} "relative darkness (of shade of color); blackness" (black)

2. *(ma) lagti*$^?$ "relative lightness (or tint of color); whiteness" (white)

3. *(ma) rara*$^?$ "relative presence of red; redness" (red)

4. *(ma) latuy* "relative presence of light greenness; greenness" (green).

The three-dimensional color solid is divided by this Level I categorization into four unequal parts; the largest is *mabiru*, the smallest *malatuy*. While boundaries separating these categories cannot be set in absolute terms, the focal points (differing slightly in size, themselves) within the four sections, can be limited more or less to black, white, orange-red, and leaf-green respectively. In general terms, *mabiru* includes the range usually covered in English by black, violet, indigo, blue, dark green, dark gray, and deep shades of other colors and mixtures; *malagti*$^?$, white and very light tints of other colors and mixtures; *marara*$^?$, maroon, red, orange, yellow, and mixtures in which these qualities are seen to predominate; *malatuy*, light green, and mixtures of green, yellow, and light brown. All color terms can be reduced to one of these four but none of the four is reducible. This does not mean that other color terms are synonyms, but that they designate color categories of greater specification within four recognized color realms.

The basis of this Level I classification appears to have certain correlates beyond what is usually considered the range of chromatic differentiation, and which are associated with nonlinguistic phenomena in the external environment. First, there is the opposition between light and dark, obvious in the contrasted ranges of meaning of *lagti*$^?$ and *biru*. Second, there is an opposition between dryness or desiccation and wetness or freshness (succulence) in visible components of the natural environment which are reflected in the terms *rara*$^?$ and *latuy* respectively. This distinction is of particular significance in terms of plant life. Almost all living plant types possess some fresh, succulent, and often "greenish" parts. To eat any kind of raw, uncooked food, particularly fresh fruits or vegetables, is known as *pag-laty-un* (< *latuy*). A shiny, wet, *brown*-colored section of newly-cut bamboo is *malatuy* (not *marara*$^?$). Dried-out or matured plant material such as certain kinds of yellowed bamboo or hardened kernels of mature or parched corn are *marara*$^?$. To become desiccated, to lose all moisture, is known as *mamara*$^?$ (< *para*$^?$ "desiccation"; and parenthetically, I might add that there are morphological and historical reasons—aside from Hanunóo folk etymologizing—to believe that at least the final syllables of these two forms are derived from a common root). A third opposition, dividing the two already suggested, is that of deep, unfading, indelible, and hence often more desired material as against pale, weak, faded, bleached, or "colorless" substance, a distinction contrasting *mabiru* and *marara*$^?$ with *malagti*$^?$ and *malatuy*. This opposition holds for manufactured items and trade goods as well as for some natural products (e.g., red and white trade beads, red being more valuable by Hanunóo standards; indigo-dyed cotton sarongs, the most prized being those dyed most often and hence of the deepest indigo color—sometimes obscuring completely the designs formed originally by *white* warp yarns; etc.). Within each of these Level I categories, increased esthetic value attaches as the focal points mentioned above are approached. There is only one exception: the color which is most tangibly visible in their jungle surroundings, the green (even the focal point near light- or yellow-green) of the natural vegetation, is *not* valued decoratively. Green beads, for example, are "unattractive," worthless. Clothing and ornament are valued in proportion to the sharpness of contrast between, and the intensity (lack of mixture, deep quality) of "black," "red," and "white."[5]

---

[5] Ethnoscientists asserted that their method of analysis helped anthropologists see how people in different cultures conceptualize their world. Hanunóo color categories incorporate distinctions that are not made in the American definition of color. For example, a factor that influences Hanunóo color identification is the perceived moisture content of the object. Conklin says the Hanunóo also pay attention to the texture and shine of the object's surface.

Level II terminology is normally employed only when greater specification than is possible at Level I is required, or when the name of an object referred to happens also to be a "color" term (e.g., *bulawon* "gold; golden [color]"). Level II terms are of two kinds: relatively specific color words like *(ma)dapug* "gray" (< *dapug* "hearth; ashes"), *(ma)ʔarum* "violet," *(ma)dilaw* "yellow" (< *dilaw* "tumeric"); and constructions, based on such specific terms—or on Level I names—but involving further derivations, such as *mabirubiru* "somewhat *mabiru*" (more specific than *mabiru* alone only in that a color which is *not* a solid, deep, black is implied, i.e., a color classed within the *mabiru* category at Level I, but not at or near the focal point), *mabiru (gid)* "very *mabiru*" (here something close to the focal center of jet black is designated), and *madilawdilaw* "weak yellow." Much attention is paid to the texture of the surface referred to, the resulting degree and type of reflection (iridescent, sparkling, dull), and to admixture of other nonformal qualities. Frequently these noncolorimetric aspects are considered of primary importance, the more spectrally-definable qualities serving only as secondary attributes. In either case polymorphemic descriptions are common.

At Level II there is a noticeable difference in the ready color vocabulary of men as compared to women. The former excel (in the degree of specification to which they carry such classification terminologically) in the ranges of "reds" and "grays" (animals, hair, feather, etc.); the latter, in "blues" (shades of indigo-dyed fabrics). No discernible similar difference holds for the "greens" or "whites."

In short, we have seen that the apparent complexity of the Hanunóo color system can be reduced at the most generalized level to four basic terms which are associated with lightness, darkness, wetness, and dryness. This intracultural analysis demonstrates that what appears to be color "confusion" at first may result from an inadequate knowledge of the internal structure of a color system and from a failure to distinguish sharply between sensory reception on the one hand and perceptual categorization on the other.[6]

Notes

a. Fieldwork among the Hanunóo on Mindoro Island (1952–1954) was supported by grants from the Social Science Research Council, the Ford Foundation, and the Guggenheim Foundation.

b. Conklin, 1954a, 1954b.

c. Bartlett, 1929.

d. Estimates range from 7,500,000 to more than 10,000,000 (Optical Society of America, 1953; Evans, 1948, p. 230).

e. Estimates range from 7,500,000 to more than 10,000,000 (Optical Society of America, 1953; Evans, 1948, p. 230).

f. Lounsbury, 1953.

g. Maerz and Paul, 1930.

h. Thorndike and Lorge, 1944.

i. Lenneberg, 1953, pp. 468–471; Lenneberg and Roberts, 1954; Brown and Lenneberg, 1954.

j. Lenneberg, 1953, pp. 464–466; Hjelmslev, 1953, p. 33.

k. Cf. Ray, 1952, 1953.

l. The lack of a term similar in semantic range to our word "color" makes abstract interrogation in Hanunóo about such matters somewhat complicated. Except for leading questions (naming some visual-quality attribute as a possibility), only circumlocutions such as *kabitay tida nu pagbantayun?* "How is it to look at?" are possible. If this results in a description of spatial organization or form, the inquiry may be narrowed by the specification *bukun kayʔ anyuʔ* "not its shape (or form)."

m. Lenneberg, 1953, p. 469.

n. These forms occur as attributes with the prefix *ma* "exhibiting, having" as indicated above in parentheses, or as free words (abstracts).

References

Bartlett, Harley Harris
   1929   *Color Nomenclature in Batak and Malay.* (Papers, Michigan Academy of Science, Arts, and Letters, vol. 10, pp. 1–52, Ann Arbor).

---

[6] Conklin's conclusion is a classic ethnoscientific statement: what researchers had considered "color confusion" by the Hanunóo is actually a lack of understanding of the criteria by which the Hanunóo distinguish colors. Although ethnoscientists soon realized that complete descriptions of all the domains of a society would be impossible to achieve, studies such as Conklin's, though limited in scale, provided valuable information about the beliefs of people in other societies. Ethnoscientists believed they had developed a method for the analysis of society that provided scientific results that could be replicated. One can see how much promise the first ethnoscientists saw in their method and why they called it the new ethnography.

Brown, Roger W., and Eric H. Lenneberg
1954 A Study in Language and Cognition. (*Journal of Abnormal and Social Psychology*, vol. 49, pp. 454–462).

Conklin, Harold C.
1954a *The Relation of Hanunóo Culture to the Plant World* (Doctoral dissertation, Yale University, New Haven).
1954b *An Ethnoecological Approach to Shifting Agriculture* (Transactions, New York Academy of Sciences, ser. II, vol. 17, pp. 133–142, New York).

Evans, Ralph M.
1948 *An Introduction to Color* (New York: Wiley).

Hjelmslev, Louis
1953 *Prolegomena to a Theory of Language* (Indiana University Publications in Anthropology and Linguistics, Memoir 7 of the International Journal of American Linguistics [translated by Francis J. Whitfield], Bloomington).

Lenneberg, Eric H.
1953 *Cognition in Ethnolinguistics* (Language, vol. 29, pp. 463–471, Baltimore).

———, and John M. Roberts
1954 *The Language of Experience, a Case Study* (Communications Program, Center of International Studies, Massachusetts Institute of Technology, Cambridge: hectographed, 45 pp. and 9 figs.).

Lounsbury, Floyd G.
1953 "Introduction" [section on Linguistics and Psychology] (in *Results of the Conference of Anthropologists and Linguists*, pp. 47–49, Memoir 8, International Journal of American Linguistics, Baltimore).

Maerz, A., and M. R. Paul
1930 *A Dictionary of Color* (New York: McGraw-Hill).

Optical Society of America, Committee on Colorimetry
1953 *The Science of Color* (New York: Crowell).

Osgood, Charles E.
1953 *Method and Theory in Experimental Psychology* (New York: Oxford University Press).

Ray, Verne F.
1952 *Techniques and Problems in the Study of Human Color Perception* (*Southwestern Journal of Anthropology*, vol. 8, pp. 251–259).
1953 *Human Color Perception and Behavioral Response* (Transactions, New York Academy of Sciences, ser. II, vol. 16, pp. 98–104, New York).

Thorndike, E. L., and I. Lorge
1944 *The Teacher's Word Book of 30,000 Words* (Teacher's College, Columbia University, New York).

29. Introduction

Stephen A. Tyler (1932–)

THE OLD AND THE NEW[a]

THE HISTORY OF ALL SCIENTIFIC DISCIPLINES IS marked by periods of intense theoretical innovation followed by relatively quiescent periods of consolidation and refinement. When the descriptive facts of science no longer fit the older explanatory models, it becomes necessary to discover new theories which will more adequately explain the accumulated data. Anthropology is currently in one of these periods of innovation.

Cognitive Anthropology (1969)

On every hand, the various subdisciplines of anthropology are astir with new formulations challenging and supplementing established concepts and methods. The very lexicon of anthropology reflects this ferment. The journals are full of articles on *formal analysis, componential analysis, taxonomy, ethnoscience, ethnosemantics,* and *sociolinguistics,* to list but a few. Nearly all of these topics have appeared in the brief span of approximately ten years, with increasing frequency in the last three or four years.[1]

Assessment of such new departures is always difficult. What are their historical antecedents and

---

[1] The model of science that Tyler outlines here probably comes from Thomas Kuhn's *The Structure of Scientific Revolutions*. This book, which first appeared in 1962, had a substantial impact on American science and social science. Kuhn proposed that paradigms—models used to describe the natural world—shifted when scientific explanation no longer

what do they augur for the future of anthropology? Are these genuinely viable reformulations or are they simply short-lived fads and blind alleys, detrimental in the long run to significant research?

Enough has been presented in symposia and journals for us to feel that we are witnessing a quiet revolution in anthropology—quiet because the new departures are firmly rooted in the past. Formal analysis derives in part from the work of such anthropological titans as Radcliffe-Brown, Lévi-Strauss, and Nadel. Folk taxonomies are foreshadowed in the writings of Mauss, Boas, and Evans-Pritchard.[2] That great ethnographer Malinowski would have been no stranger to recent developments in sociolinguistics. The concern for psychological validity is congruent with much of Sapir's work and, to a lesser extent, with some of Kroeber's. And, perhaps, most relevant of all is the work of Bateson.[3]

Yet, these developments constitute more than a disconnected reworking of disparate themes from out of the past. These new formulations contrast sharply with many of the aims, assumptions, goals, and methods of an earlier anthropology. Previous theoretical orientations in anthropology can in a very general way be classed into two types—those concerned primarily with change and development and those concerned with static descriptions. Thus, the evolutionists and the dif-

fusionists concentrated on patterns of change, while the functionalists eschewed this work as mere "speculative history," and focused on the internal organization and comparison of systems, hoping thereby to discover general laws of society. Some culture and personality studies attempted to characterize whole cultures with such concepts as "national character" and "modal personality type," while other culture and personality studies utilized a comparative approach in an attempt to correlate psychological and cultural features.

These formulations were attempts to construct universal organizational types which were linked either by similar processes of change or by similarities of internal structure. In order to achieve this goal, only certain kinds of information were accepted as relevant, and concrete ethnographic data had to be elevated to more abstract forms such as index variables and typological constructs. Consequently, abstract definitions of these features were necessary, and much of the discussion in books and journals concerned the adequacy of these definitions.[4] Once a corporate lineage, for example, had been defined in a particular way, it was only a matter of time before some fieldworker returned to his desk and elatedly reported that his tribe did not conform to the received definition. One way around this problem was to construct more types and subtypes, and

accounted accurately for data. Tyler suggests that such a paradigm shift was happening in anthropology. The "scientific" approach he takes throughout this essay evokes Kuhn's ideas.

[2] Later in the essay, Tyler will elaborate on formal analysis. A formal analysis is a set of logical principles. A good example would be a set of postulates and their implications applied to a proof in geometry.

[3] While Tyler positions his work as a logical extension of many strands of theory in anthropology, most of the theorists he mentions here, some of whom have essays in this volume, would probably not have supported his ideas. Tyler gives particular credit to Gregory Bateson, calling his ideas "most relevant of all." Bateson studied anthropology at Cambridge under Alfred Cort Haddon and did fieldwork in New Guinea. *Naven* (1958 [1936]), an important anthropological study of the religion and culture of the Iatmul of New Guinea, came from this fieldwork. *Naven* is crucial to Tyler because Bateson proposed a definition of culture very close to the one Tyler uses in this essay. Bateson defined culture as "a collective term for the coherent 'logical' system which may be constructed by the scientist, fitting together the various premises of the culture" (1958:218). He further specified that "we must expect to find different systems of logic, different modes of building together of premises, in different cultures" (1958:219).

[4] Ethnoscientists and cognitive anthropologists were concerned with problems of classification. Their critique of earlier anthropology was really much like Boas' attack on unilineal evolution half a century earlier. Boas had criticized evolutionists for theorizing in advance of data; the ethnoscientists criticized the methods by which anthropological data was obtained. The cornerstone of their critique was that the ethnographic method was fundamentally subjective because anthropologists applied their own classification systems to the societies they studied. Therefore, the categories used in traditional ethnographic analysis were incommensurate. The proliferation of categories Tyler mentions here is an artifact of that problem—evidence, to him, that anthropological theories no longer fit the data being collected.

broader, more abstract definitions. It was generally accepted that neither the types nor the definitions actually corresponded to anything in the "real world." They were merely convenient methods of ordering the data at hand. Proliferation of types, however, was dangerous, for as the types proliferated, so did the processes linking the types and their constituents. Contrary to expectations, anthropology became more and more particularistic rather than more general and universal.

This concern with typology and definition is an index to another feature characteristic of this period in anthropology. Anthropologists were really much more concerned with discovering what anthropology was than, for example, what an Eskimo was.[5] In a sense anthropologists were studying only one small culture—the culture of anthropology.

Aside from the diffusionists, these earlier theories can be characterized as attempts to construct monolithic, unitary systems which purported to either explain cultures or their development. Such concepts as cultural core, cultural norm, structure, modal structure, pattern, and others were used to describe these systems. These ideas are symptomatic of a quest for the typical, the normal, the usual, for those definitely bounded phenomena which would systematically differentiate one culture from another. In fact the very concept of culture is but another of these labels for some arbitrarily bounded unit within which certain types of behavior, norms, artifacts, and emotions are typical (cf. Sapir 1932:515; 1934: 593–595). The atypical, especially as expressed in patterns of variation, were either simply dismissed or artificially worked into the scheme as indices of change, diffusion, survival, innovation, dysfunction, abnormality, cultural disintegration, opportunities for the exercise of social control and the like. The only important variations were variations between cultures.

In contrast to these approaches, cognitive anthropology constitutes a new theoretical orientation. It focuses on *discovering* how different people organize and use their cultures. This is not so much a search for some generalized unit of behavioral analysis as it is an attempt to understand the *organizing principles underlying* behavior. It is assumed that each people has a unique system for perceiving and organizing material phenomena—things, events, behavior, and emotions (Goodenough 1957). The object of study is not these material phenomena themselves, but the way they are organized in the minds of men. Cultures then are not material phenomena; they are cognitive organizations of material phenomena.[b] Consequently cultures are neither described by mere arbitrary lists of anatomical traits and institutions such as house type, family type, kinship type, economic type and personality type, nor are they necessarily equated with some over-all integrative pattern of these phenomena. Such descriptions may tell us something about the way an anthropologist thinks about a culture, but there is little, if any, reason to believe that they tell us anything of how the people of some culture think about their culture.[6]

In essence, cognitive anthropology seeks to answer two questions: What material phenomena are significant for the people of some culture; and,

---

[5] The idea that traditional ethnology is really anthropology studying itself rather than making objective statements about others is a crucial insight of postmodern theorists. Many of them see themselves as direct descendants of the ethnoscientists. In his critique Tyler explains that in traditional ethnography culture is a creation of the anthropologists rather than the people they are studying. By defining some aspects of behavior as culture core (a term from Julian Steward and the cultural ecologists) or modal culture (a term from the culture and personality theorists), anthropologists inappropriately classify behavior according to their own idiosyncratic standards.

[6] Although Tyler does not use the term, ethnoscientists and cognitive anthropologists proposed an emic approach to anthropology. The critical distinction between emics and etics was first made by the linguist Kenneth Pike in 1954 based on the use of the words *phonetics* and *phonemics* in linguistics. Phonetics is the study of the production and transmission of language sounds in general. Phonemics, on the other hand, is the study of the ways in which sounds are organized within a language – that is, it analyzes units of sound that are psychologically distinct for speakers of a language. In anthropology, those studying emics strive to reproduce the meanings and understandings of the members of a culture. Those studying etics strive to analyze culture in terms meaningful to the scientific community though not necessarily to the members of the culture under observation. Cognitive anthropologists and ethnoscientists thus viewed culture as a mental construct

how do they organize these phenomena? Not only do cultures differ among one another in their organization of material phenomena, they differ as well in the kinds of material phenomena they organize. The people of different cultures may not recognize the same kinds of material phenomena as relevant, even though from an outsider's point of view the same material phenomena may be present in every case. For example, we distinguish between dew, fog, ice, and snow, but the Koyas of South India do not. They call all of these *mancu*. Even though they can perceive the differences among these if asked to do so, these differences are not significant to them. On the other hand, they recognize and name at least seven different kinds of bamboo, six more than I am accustomed to distinguish. Similarly, even though I know that my cousin George is the son of my mother's sister, while my cousin Paul is the son of my mother's brother, this objective difference is irrelevant to my system of classification. They are both "cousins." If I were a Koya, however, this difference would be highly important. I would call my mother's brother's son *baaTo* and my mother's sister's son *annaal*. Even though the same material phenomena are objectively present, they are subjectively perceived and organized differently by Koyas than they are by Americans.[c] Furthermore, there is no apparent over-all integrative pattern which relates the classification of bamboo to the classification of relatives. These are separate classes of phenomena with distinctive and unrelated principles of organization.

Not only may the same phenomena be organized differently from culture to culture, they may also be organized in more than one way in the same culture. There is, then, *intracultural* variation as well as *intercultural* variation. Some intracultural variations may be idiosyncratic, but more important from the anthropologist's point of view are those variations which are used by different classes of people and/or occur in different situations and contexts (cf. Goodenough 1963: 257–264). For example, if we are interested in describing the way people classify colors we may discover that there are variant patterns dependent upon the sex or age of our informant as well as his general experience with colors. Thus, females in our culture can generally discriminate and name more colors than males. Or, to take another example, the classification of relatives may be partially dependent on the social statuses of the people talking about relatives, the relationship between them, and the social context in which they are conversing. A Telugu refers to his younger sister as *celli* when talking to another member of his family, but when speaking to a person outside his family group, he uses the term *cellelu*, which may mean younger sister, or mother's sister's daughter, or father's brother's daughter.[7]

A consequence of this interest in variation is the idea that cultures are not unitary phenomena, that is, they cannot be described by only one set of organizing principles. For each class of relevant phenomena there may be several alternative organizations. The realization or choice of one alter-

---

or template. The principal tool they used to examine culture was linguistic analysis. They based their use of language on the work of Edward Sapir, a student of Boas best known for his work on Native American languages and cognition. Sapir argued that language determined those things people habitually noticed and, by extension, the manner in which they organized their worlds. An analysis of language could then be used to examine how people understood their worlds. In the later passages, Tyler points out several examples of distinctions between linguistic classification and empirical reality.

[7] Tyler's discussion of variation within cultures reflects the concern of ethnoscientists and their descendants with describing the precise nature of a culture. That culture is not a unitary phenomenon is a critical insight that distinguishes cognitive anthropology from many traditional approaches. However, it also leads to several logical problems. If culture is a mental template and can be approached through linguistic classification, then in what sense can individuals who have different systems of classification be said to be members of the same culture? Additionally, can one draw valid conclusions about a culture based on data from only a few informants?

These sorts of problems could lead to two distasteful possibilities. On the one hand, since no two people have exactly the same system of classification, each person may be a culture unto himself. On the other hand, if we look for the "average" system of classification, that shared by most people, we are back once again with a modal culture, precisely what Tyler says cognitive anthropology avoids.

native to the exclusion of some other is dependent upon a variety of factors. For example, some people have more or less knowledge of some phenomena, or certain alternatives may be acceptable only in particular contexts (cf. Hymes 1964b:41). If these variants are used only in certain identified situations, or if there is a hierarchy of choice so that variants are ordered on the basis of their relative desirability, we can say that they are in complementary distribution and do not conflict with one another. In such a situation it is possible for a large number of variants to coexist. But, if the variants conflict in their organization and the situations in which they occur, there must be some means of harmonizing the contrast. This can be achieved by some change in the principles of organization or in the situation in which they occur. For example, among the Koyas, the pig is classed as an edible animal, but among neighboring Muslims the pig is classed as inedible and defiling. Suppose a Koya woman were married to a Muslim man.[8] While in her husband's home she could not act on her classification of pig as an edible by eating pork; while visiting her parents in the absence of her husband she could. So long as the two systems of classification can be realized in these isolated contexts there is no necessary conflict between them, and both may persist. If these contexts were not in complementary distribution, some rearrangement of the two contrasting systems of classification would have to take place if the marriage were to persist.[d]

In fact, this is an argument for a different kind of unitary description which sees unity as emerging from the ordered relations between variants and contexts. Variants are not mere deviations from some assumed basic organization; with their rules of occurrence *they are the organization.*

(Wallace 1961:29–41; Hymes 1964a:386–387). It must be emphasized, however, that such a unitary description can be achieved only by the anthropologist. It is highly unlikely that the members of a culture ever see their culture as *this kind of* unitary phenomenon. Each individual member may have a unique unitary model of his culture, but is not necessarily cognizant of all unique, unitary models held by other members of his culture. He will be aware of and use some, but it is only the anthropologist who completely transcends these particular models and constructs a single, unitary model.[9] This cognitive organization exists solely in the mind of the anthropologist (cf. Bateson 1958:294). Yet, to the extent that it will generate concept models used by the people of a particular culture, it is a model of their cognitive systems.[e]

The "theory" here is not so much a THEORY OF CULTURE as it is *theories of cultures,* or a theory of descriptions. The aim of such a theory is to provide answers to the questions: How would the people of some other culture expect me to behave if I were a member of their culture; and what are the rules of appropriate behavior in their culture? Answers to these questions are provided by an adequate description of the rules used by people in that culture. Consequently, this description itself constitutes "theory" for that culture, for it represents the conceptual model of organization used by its members. Such a theory is validated by our ability to predict how these people would expect us to behave if we were members of the culture.

ORDER OUT OF CHAOS

In a sense, cognitive anthropology is not a new departure. Many anthropologists have expressed an interest in how the natives see their world. Yet,

---

[8] Another problem Tyler faces is that a single person, such as the Koya woman mentioned here, might hold more than one system of classification. This presents a problem because ethnoscience, as a logical system, should have no inconsistencies. Tyler deals with this by suggesting that an individual may hold differing systems of classification as long as these are used in different situations, but a person may not hold two conflicting classification systems in the same situation. However, it is worth asking if people *do* simultaneously hold conflicting ideas.

[9] Tyler is extremely equivocal about the ability of cognitive anthropologists to think like natives. In this passage he first states that models generated by cognitive anthropologists exist only in their own minds. This would seem to suggest that an anthropologist might learn to speak and behave as a native but not actually think like one. However, Tyler then asserts that to the extent that such a model generates concept models used by the people of a culture, it is a model of *their* (emphasis added) cognitive systems. This claim comes perilously close to claiming to think like the natives.

there is a difference of focus between the old and the new. Where earlier anthropologists sought categories of description in their native language, cognitive anthropologists seek categories of description in the language of their natives.[f] Ultimately, this is the old problem of what do we describe and how do we describe it? Obviously, we are interested in the mental codes of other peoples, but how do we infer these mental processes? Thus far, it has been assumed that the easiest entry to such processes is through language, and most of the recent studies have sought to discover codes that are mapped in language.[10] Nearly all of this work has been concerned with how other peoples "name" the "things" in their environment and how these names are organized into larger groupings. These names are thus both an index to what is significant in the environment of some other people, and a means of discovering how these people organize their perceptions of the environment. Naming is seen as one of the chief methods for imposing order on perception.[g]

In a very real sense, the anthropologist's problem is to discover how other people create order out of what appears to him to be utter chaos. Imagine, for a moment, a being from another planet equipped with all our sensory apparatus who perceives for the first time the infinite variety of sight and sound in which we live. Suppose further that he is attempting to describe this world in a scientific report for his colleagues at home. At first, everything would be chaotic. Each sound and object would seem to be unlike any other. His experience would be similar to what we feel the first time we hear a language we have never heard before. But, with infinite time and patience, let us assume that he is able to describe everything he perceives — that is, the total environment of earth. Probably he would eventually be able to organize his report around concepts acceptable to his world or devise new ones as he saw fit. Yet, would anyone of us accept his report as an accurate account of the world as we see and live in it? If he in fact describes everything, we would not. Nor would we accept his organization of the things he perceived, for they would almost certainly not fit our own system of organization. Unlike this mythical creature, we do not live in a world in which we discriminate among all the possible sensory stimuli in our environment, nor do we react to each stimulus as if it were totally new and foreign. In effect, we choose to ignore many of those perceptual differences which make each object unique. In large part, we do this by naming. By naming we classify and put objects which to us are similar into the same category, even though we can perceive differences among them (cf. Boas 1938:208–214). For example, the chair in which I sit has a nick in the left leg, yet I class it as a "straight chair" no different from others like it in the room.[11]

We classify because life in a world where nothing was the same would be intolerable. It is through naming and classification that the whole rich world of infinite variability shrinks to manipulable size and becomes bearable. Our methods

---

[10] At the core of ethnoscience and cognitive anthropology is an analogy between culture and language. One key source of this insight was Sapir, who has already been mentioned. Another was the work of Lévi-Strauss and, through him, that of the Prague School linguistic theorists, described in the notes to essay 25. Many social scientists working in the 1950s and 1960s considered linguistics to be the most advanced of all social sciences and believed that it could provide a model for other social sciences.

[11] A key insight of cognitive anthropology, derived from Sapir and Lévi-Strauss (who in his turn was inspired by Durkheim and Mauss), was that humans order their world through classification. The world presents us with chaos. We make sense of it by noticing some phenomena and ignoring others or by grouping some things together and excluding others. Both French and American thinkers arrived at this conclusion, but it implied different things to each of them. Working in the tradition of Durkheim and the evolutionists, Lévi-Strauss and his followers understood classification as reflecting underlying universal principles of organization, perhaps rooted in human biology.

Working in the tradition of Boasian cultural relativism, ethnoscientists and cognitive anthropologists attempted no such search for universal laws or generalizations. Instead, they viewed the classification system of each culture as more or less unique, reflecting that culture's specific history. Thus, as Tyler noted earlier, cognitive anthropology produces not a theory of culture, but essentially incommensurate theories of culture. Cognitive anthropologists proposed that ultimately,

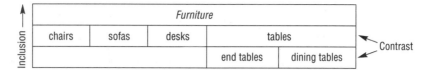

Figure 1. Taxonomy of furniture

of classification are entirely arbitrary and subjective. There is nothing in the external world which demands that certain things go together and others do not. It is our perception of similarities and differences together with a set of hierarchical cues that determine which things go together. We not only react to certain discriminable stimuli as if they were the same, we name them and organize them into groupings. Thus, for example, there are objects with a seat, a back and four legs which we label *chairs,* even though no two of these objects are exactly alike. The word *chair* then stands as a sign for a whole class of objects with a seat, a back, and four legs. This sign, too, is arbitrary— we might as well call these objects *argoboos.* Just as there is no inherent quality in an object that forces us to perceive it in exactly one way, neither is there an intrinsic characteristic associating an object with its name. Consequently, with the passage of time, a class of objects may be renamed, but the class of objects denoted by this name does not change, or, conversely, the class of objects denoted by a name may change, but the name does not.

Thus, we subjectively group the phenomena of our perceptual world into named classes. These classes are not disparate and singular. They are organized into larger groupings.[12] To the extent that these groupings are hierarchically arranged by a process of inclusion, they form a taxonomy. To continue the example of chairs, there are other objects in our homes which are not chairs. There are sofas, tables, desks, cabinets, and the like. Each of these constitutes a separate class, some with many subclasses. For example there are end tables, dining tables, and coffee tables, but each of these is also a member of some more inclusive class—the class of things called "furniture." A portion of this taxonomy is shown in Fig. 1.

Figure 1 illustrates two processes characteristic of taxonomies: (1) items at the same level contrast with one another; (2) items at different levels are related by inclusion. At the bottom level are the more highly discriminated classes, at the top is the most inclusive class. Thus, end tables are kinds of tables as tables are kinds of furniture; end tables are not the same as dining tables just as tables are not the same as chairs. These relationships could also be represented in a branching diagram as in Fig. 2.

This particular taxonomy constitutes one *semantic domain* in our culture. A semantic domain consists of a class of objects all of which share at least one feature in common which differentiates them from other semantic domains. Chairs, sofas,

---

universal laws of culture might be derived from their work; but like Boas, they believed that this goal required massive data collection and could only be attained in the distant future. Moreover, they presented no logical framework in which to move from such theories of culture to one overarching theory.

[12] The work of ethnoscience has generally consisted of describing domains—categories of cultural meaning that include other, smaller categories. Tyler, as he notes later, conceives of culture as consisting of a collection of domains. One has described a culture completely when one has outlined all of its domains.

A domain must be organized by some logical principle. Here and in later passages, Tyler sets out three different examples of this: taxonomy, paradigm, and tree. These are the best-known principles of organization, but elsewhere Tyler lists many more, including key, partonomy, congeries, type-token, and several others (Tyler 1978:255).

Note that when Tyler uses these terms (particularly taxonomy and paradigm), he is assigning new meanings to them that are specific to cognitive anthropology.

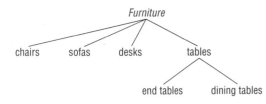

Figure 2. Branching diagram

Table 1 — Taxonomy of "Livestock"

Animal			
Livestock			
cattle	horse	sheep	swine
cow	mare	ewe	sow
bull	stallion	ram	boar
steer	gelding	wether	barrow
heifer	filly	lamb	gilt
calf	colt		shoat
	foal		piglet

desks, end tables, and dining tables have in common the designation *furniture*.

Note that Fig. 2 tells us nothing of the things which distinguish a chair from a table. It tells us only that they are different. Suppose you had to tell someone how you know that one object is a chair and the other is a table. In the process of doing this, you might describe certain underlying features, some of which both chairs and tables share and some of which they do not. For example, you might say a chair has four legs, a seat, and a back, but a table has four legs and a top. Chairs would thus differ from tables by the presence of two features — a seat and a back, and the absence of one feature — a top. These underlying features are *components* or *features* of meaning. They are some of the dimensions of meaning underlying the general domain of *furniture*. That these are not the only dimensions is apparent in the contrasts between desk and table. Both pieces of furniture have four legs and a top. Using only the two features you have isolated, it is not possible to say how a table differs from a desk. Should you wish to show how each of these items differs from the other you would have to discover other features of meaning.[13]

Semantic features, like labels, are also organized. A part of the taxonomy of "animals" in American English consists of the following lexemes: cow, bull, heifer, calf, steer, mare, stallion, filly, foal, colt, gelding, sow, boar, gilt, barrow,

shoat, piglet, ewe, ram, wether, lamb, livestock, cattle, swine, horse, sheep. This taxonomy is arranged in Table 1.

On even casual examination the items occurring in the lowest level of Table 1 seem to be related in some way. Closer inspection reveals that similar distinctions are made under each major category of livestock. The contrast between cow and bull, for example, is the same as the contrast between boar and sow; ram and ewe; stallion and mare. We can readily identify this contrast as one of sex or gender, male versus female. Similarly, there is an identical contrast between bull and steer; ram and wether; stallion and gelding; boar and barrow. Again, we would identify this as a contrast between male animals versus neutered animals. In addition to this sex contrast there is a further contrast between mature and immature animals. A calf is an immature cow or bull and a heifer is an "adolescent" cow. All the lexemes in the lowest level of Table 1 reflect the two semantic features of sex and maturity. Each of these has three values: sex (male, female, neuter); maturity (adult, adolescent, child). Note, however, that horse and pig have an additional feature of maturity denoting "newborn" or "baby" (piglet and foal).

Using symbols: δ — male; φ — female; $\varnothing$ — neuter; M^{-1} adult; M^{-2} adolescent; M^{-3} child;

---

[13] Once a domain has been identified, ethnoscientists and cognitive anthropologists attempted to perform componential analyses, which James P. Spradley (1933–1982) defined as "the systematic search for the attributes (components of meaning) associated with cultural categories" (1980:130). To do componential analysis, ethnoscientists search for how items in a domain systematically differ from each other. They construct a series of categories on which elements of the domain contrast. Tyler uses the example of horse and swine below. The contrasting categories are related to the sex of the animal. He calls the diagrams showing these contrasts *paradigms*.

		Sex		
		male ♂	female ♀	neuter ∅
Maturity	adult M-1	stallion boar	mare sow	gelding barrow
	adolescent M-2		filly gilt	
	child M-3	colt shoat		
	baby M-4	foal piglet		

Figure 3. Paradigm of features for "horse" and "swine." For cattle and sheep the contrast between baby and child would be omitted. Sheep also omits the adolescent distinction. There is however an archaic form for newborn sheep *viz.* "Yeanling."

M^{-4} baby; H—horse; P—swine; C—cattle; S—sheep; the distribution of features for each label can be stated in formulae as follows:

stallion	H ♂ M^{-1}	boar	P ♂ M^{-1}
mare	H ♀ M^{-1}	sow	P ♀ M^{-1}
gelding	H ∅ $M^{-1}M^{-2}$	barrow	P ∅ $M^{-1}M^{-2}$
filly	H ♀ M^{-2}	gilt	P ♀ M^{-2}
colt	H ♂♀ M^{-3}	shoat	P ♂♀ M^{-3}
foal	H ♂♀ M^{-4}	piglet	P ♂♀ M^{-4}

The first formula reads: a stallion is a horse, male, adult, or more appropriately, a stallion is an adult male horse. Such formulae are simply expressions of the distribution of features for each separate label. A box figure shows how these features distribute across the whole set of labels.

Reading from the diagram, a stallion is an adult male horse and a mare is an adult female horse. The features "adult" and "male" *intersect* at the space containing the label "stallion," while the features "adult" and "female" intersect at the space containing the label "mare." Since this diagram has two major features (maturity and sex) which cut across (intersect) one another, it is a *paradigm*. Features are paradigmatically arranged when they are: (1) multiple; (2) intersect.[h]

Paradigms and taxonomies are different kinds of semantic arrangements. In contrast to a paradigm, a taxonomy orders its labels by contrast and inclusion. A taxonomy typically asserts that items in lower levels are *kinds* of items in higher levels. A horse, for example, is a *kind* of livestock. A paradigm makes no such assertion. In Fig. 3 for example, a shoat is not necessarily a kind of boar.[14]

In addition to taxonomies and paradigms semantic features may be arranged on a branching diagram called a *tree*.[15] Features in a tree are ordered by sequential contrast of only one feature at a time. Trees are thus based on successive choices between only two alternatives. Such a semantic arrangement is most frequently encountered in zoological or botanical texts. Figure 4 is a simplified example of a tree.

---

[14] Although paradigms and taxonomies are different, they are not mutually exclusive. The same lexical elements may be arranged into both paradigms and taxonomies.

[15] Binary distinctions underlie many forms of organization but are most evident in trees. This emphasis on duality and opposition reflects the influence of Prague School linguistics, perhaps largely as filtered by Lévi-Strauss (see essay 25), a powerful influence on ethnoscientists.

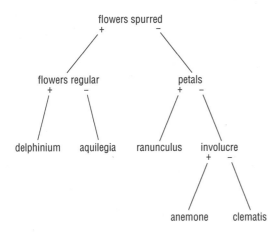

Figure 4. A tree arrangement. Plus (+) indicates presence of the feature, minus (–) its absence. Thus, if a flower is not spurred, has no petals, and no involucre, it is a clematis.

A reading of Fig. 4 would be: Are the flowers spurred? If yes, are the flowers regular? If they are regular, then this is a delphinium. Unlike a paradigm, the features of a tree do not intersect, and unlike a taxonomy items at lower levels are not included in higher levels. Consequently, paradigms, taxonomies and trees are fundamentally different kinds of semantic arrangements. Each semantic domain of a culture may be ordered by one or more of these arrangements.

A culture consists of many semantic domains organized around numerous features of meaning, and no two cultures share the same set of semantic domains or features of meaning, nor do they share the same methods of organizing these features. The problem for the anthropologist is to discover these semantic domains and their fea-

tures, for an anthropologist in the field is much like our interplanetary visitor. There is no familiar order to the way these strange people organize their world. But, unlike our visitor, the anthropologist must avoid imposing his own semantic categories on what he perceives. He must attempt to discover the semantic world in which these people live. There are, then, two ways of bringing order out of apparent chaos—*impose* a preexisting order on it, or *discover* the order underlying it.[i] Nearly all of earlier anthropology was characterized by the first method. By contrast, cognitive anthropology seeks to develop methods which can be used for discovering and describing these principles of organization.[16]

Since such semantic systems are implicit in our use of language, they constitute one of the most significant features of human communication. Yet, what can be communicated and how it is communicated is not solely determined by this kind of semantic feature. Other semantic features deriving from the context of communication are equally important. Context includes the manner of communication (for example, verbal and written), the social setting, and the linguistic repertories of speaker and hearer. Contextual semantic features and their mutual interdependence are as much a part of the cognitive system as taxonomies and semantic domains.

There still remains the question of how we discover features in cultures other than our own. If you will attempt to complete the statement of semantic features for the taxonomy of furniture, you will see that the discovery of these features is difficult enough in your native language. It is even more difficult in a strange language. As a consequence, new fieldwork techniques and methods

---

[16] The ethnoscientists' key critique of earlier anthropology was that it artificially imposed order on the data. Interestingly, at the same time that ethnoscience was emerging, George Peter Murdock (see essay 20) was developing the Human Relations Area Files (HRAF). Begun in 1937, the HRAF project was (and continues to be) a massive effort to provide a universal index to anthropological literature. Using the HRAF, a researcher may look up a single topic, say friendship, and find information indexed as friendship in ethnographies on many different societies. Murdock's statistical comparative approach was favored by materialists such as Marvin Harris and modern evolutionists such as Morton Fried.

Ethnoscientists and cognitive anthropologists were very critical of Murdock's approach on two levels: First, it was not clear that a classification such as friendship has the same meaning from culture to culture. Second, it was not clear that the various people who indexed the work had the same ideas about the meaning of friendship. Thus, critics claimed that the index compared apples to oranges, which meant that reliable generalizations could not be drawn.

have had to be devised. Most important among these are techniques of *controlled eliciting* and methods of *formal analysis*.[17]

Controlled eliciting utilizes sentence frames derived from the language of the people being studied. The aim of such eliciting is to enable the ethnographer to behave linguistically in ways appropriate to the culture he is studying. This involves the use of linguistically correct questions which relate concepts meaningful in that culture. Suppose you are a foreigner attempting to learn something about American culture. On seeing an object for which you do not know an English term, one possible sequence of related questions and responses might be:

Q: What is this?

A: This is a sow.

Q: Is that a sow, too?

A: No, that's a boar.

Q. Is a boar a kind of sow?

A: No, a boar is a kind of livestock.

Q: Is a sow a kind of livestock?

A: Yes.

Q: How many kinds of livestock are there?

A: There are pigs, horses, mules, sheep, goats, and others.

This sequence indicates that sows and boars are conceptually linked and that there are numerous other things grouped with them in the taxonomy of livestock. Note that decisions concerning the inclusion of items within this taxonomy are made by the informant, not by the investigator. Contrast this procedure with a familiar questionnaire technique derived from handbooks on social science methodology. Is the cow ____ very like; ____ somewhat like; ____ only a little like; ____ not at all like a god (check one). Aside from the spurious scaling, this question would be meaningful only in societies of English speakers in which there were: (a) cows, (b) gods, (c) some evidence that gods and cows were conceptually linked, or (d) sociologists. In this technique, the investigator has already made all the decisions about conceptual relevance. The informant's responses can only be replications in one way or another of the investigator's judgments about conceptual relevance. In a sense, such a method merely tells you what you already know. Controlled eliciting, on the other hand, is designed to provide the ethnographer with not only the answers, but also to assist him in discovering the relevant questions. It clearly derives from the fact that the questioning process is itself the dominant factor in scientific investigation (Collingwood 1929:29–43). Where the procedures and results of controlled eliciting are contained in the report, two things are achieved: (1) there is an explicit record of how the data were gathered; (2) a public record of the results is available.

Formal analysis is simply one method of stating the results of such controlled eliciting. It differs from other methods in its emphasis on

---

[17] Ethnoscientists and cognitive anthropologists criticized early anthropology in general and Murdock in particular for their lack of systematic methods of data collection.

It is certainly true that, until recently, graduate level texts or courses that dealt with field methods were few and far between. Michael Agar (1980) tells the story of a student of Kroeber who went to ask the grand old man for advice on the ways to do fieldwork. "After several passes by the open door, she entered and nervously cleared her throat. Kroeber was typing (naturally) and did not look up for a minute or so. When he did, the student . . . asked for advice. 'Well,' said Kroeber, returning to his typing, 'I suggest that you buy a notebook and a pencil.'"

The key point made by cognitive anthropologists and ethnoscientists was that since ethnographers did not use consistent data collection techniques, and since they used categories from their own cultures that they defined imprecisely, they could neither accurately reflect native understandings of the world nor make useful generalizations across cultures. They claimed that Murdock's HRAF was meaningless because it implied the existence of "natural" domains, that is, domains that have the same boundaries in every culture. Ethnoscientists and cognitive anthropologists believed that such things were theoretically possible but not likely to exist. Their position mirrors Boas' ideas on natural laws pertaining to cultures.

internal consistency, completeness, and form. A particular set of data relating to some semantic domain must be explained by the relationship between units comprising that domain—not by determinants outside it.[18] The problem of external determinants is delayed until internal determinants are analyzed. For example, the question of whether I call my mother's sister's son "cousin" because he is outside my nuclear family cannot be determined until I know the system of relations between cousin, brother, and all the other kin terms in the English system. A formal analysis is complete when the relations among all the units comprising a semantic domain are described.

THE NEW ORDER

The aims and methods of cognitive anthropology have important implications for cultural anthropology. They entail a rethinking of the culture concept, the comparative method, and of ethnography.

In this discussion culture has been identified with cognition. This must strike some cultural anthropologists as a truncated version of the culture concept, for it neglects many of their traditional interests. They might well ask, What about process? What about behavior? What about motivation? Implicit in these questions is an assumption that in addition to cognitive systems a theory of culture must explain cultures as systems emerging from patterned frequencies of observed behavior and processes of development and change (cf. Goodenough 1964). *As a general statement of anthropological goals, these are relevant considerations, but they are not relevant to a theory of culture.* There is no necessity to assume that the cognitive order is either systematically a derivative of or a predictor of substantive actions.[19] Just as the grammar of a language provides no information on what all individual speakers will say on any given occasion, so too a cognitive description of a culture does not pretend to predict the actual behavior of any individual. The formal analysis of culture, like a grammar, is concerned only with what is expected and appropriate. And just as an adequate grammar is neither contingent upon prior assumptions concerning developmental processes nor necessarily explains them, a grammar of culture need make no assumptions about nor attempt to explain these processes. So construed, neither prediction of actual events nor specification of developmental process is a necessary component of a theory of culture.[j] To paraphrase Collingwood (1956:217), cultural anthropology is not a description of events or an account of change. The cultural anthropologist is only concerned with those events which are expressions of underlying thoughts. His aim is to penetrate beyond mere material representation to the logical nexus of underlying concepts.

Culture, conceived as the totality of human behavior, ideas, history, institutions and artifacts has never been particularly useful as a meaningful method of explaining ethnographic facts.[20] Such a conception merely asserts that culture is equivalent to the whole of human knowledge. As a device which purports to explain all of man's learned behavior, motivations, prehistoric record,

---

[18] In many ways, cognitive anthropology and ethnoscience represent an extreme logical end of Boasian thinking. In this paragraph, for example, notice the restatement of Boasian cultural relativism in ethnoscientific terms: semantic domains may only be explained with reference to themselves. Like Boasian culture, they are *sui generis.*

[19] The theoretical battles of the 1950s and 1960s crystallized a profound division in American anthropology—that between materialist and idealist thinkers. This division had been present in anthropology from the beginning but is probably best seen in this era. Tyler and the cognitive and ethnoscientific anthropologists, who represent one extreme, conceive of culture in purely mentalistic terms. It is created *sui generis* and has no predictable effect on the "real world." The other pole is represented by Harris and the functional materialists and ecologists, who view culture as adaptive. They were concerned with observable behavior and generally less interested in the underlying thoughts of the actors.

[20] Tyler here takes aim at E. B. Tylor's classic definition of culture (see essay 2). What he proposes is, in fact, similar to what Boas proposed; that is, detailed descriptions of individual cultures rather than any single overarching analysis of culture. The difference is that Boas did not propose a specific methodology, and Tyler does. In theory, this means that Tyler's theories of culture will be expressed in a consistent manner that might allow a general theory to emerge.

ecological adaptations, biological limitations, and evolution it attempts too much. What we need is a more limited notion of culture which stresses *theories of culture*. Rather than attempt to develop a general THEORY OF CULTURE, the best we can hope for at present is particular theories of cultures. These theories will constitute complete, accurate descriptions of particular cognitive systems. Only when such particular descriptions are expressed in a single metalanguage with known logical properties will we have arrived at a general theory of culture. Such a general theory will be equivalent to the language in which we describe cultures (Kay 1965:112). In effect we already have a pseudometalanguage. It is for this reason that nearly all ethnographies have similar chapter headings. The problem with this metalanguage is that is assumes universality without prior demonstration.[21] Its universality inheres in the language of description and not necessarily in the object being described.[k]

At issue here are two contrasting views of cultural anthropology. The central issue is, is cultural anthropology a *natural* or *formal* science? Traditional cultural anthropology is based on the assumption that its data are discrete material phenomena which can be analyzed like the material phenomena of any other natural science. Cognitive anthropology is based on the assumption that its data are mental phenomena which can be analyzed by formal methods similar to those of mathematics and logic.[l] Each particular culture consists of a set of logical principles which order relevant material phenomena. To the cognitive anthropologist these logical principles rather than the material phenomena are the object of investigation. For the cognitive anthro-

pologist cultural anthropology is a formal science. It seems likely that the logical operations underlying principles of ordering are finite and universal, but capable of generating an infinite number of possible specific orderings (cf. Lévi-Strauss 1966:268). In this limited sense, cognitive anthropology constitutes a return to Bastian's search for the "psychic unity of mankind."[22]

The implications for the comparative method follow directly from the above. The central issue in comparative analysis is, What is the unit of comparison? There have been many attempts to specifically delimit the unit of comparison. Yet most so-called cross-cultural comparisons have really been nothing more than cross-tribal or cross-community comparisons. Obviously, if a culture is the unit of comparison, then we must compare whole systems which are bounded in space and time or demonstrate that the parts of systems we are comparing are justifiably isolable (cf. Boas 1940:275). Since most ethnographies are not sufficiently complete for either of these possibilities, the whole comparative approach based on substantive variables must be abandoned if our aim is indeed cultural comparison.[23] Those who insist that no fact has meaning except by comparison are right, but the implication that comparison can occur only between similar facts from different systems does not follow. It is much more pertinent to compare similar, but not identical facts within the same system. This is not so much a total abandonment of the comparative method; it is a matter of priorities. Comparisons between systems can only be useful if the facts compared are truly comparable, and we cannot know what facts are comparable until the facts themselves are adequately described. When

---

[21] The metalanguage Tyler refers to here is the language that would describe the structure of the domains outlined by cognitive anthropology and ethnoscience. He claims that current metalinguistic categories, such as kinship, religion, political system, and so on are inadequate because it has not been shown that they describe cross-culturally consistent domains. He calls these *pseudometalanguage.*

[22] Tyler here describes anthropology as a formal science, not only like math and logic but also like structural linguistics. He opens the possibility that some of the logical principles that will be discovered by cognitive anthropology are universals.

[23] In this passage, Tyler returns to his critique of traditional ethnography. He touches on a topic that became crucial to anthropologists in the late 1980s—defining the boundaries of cultural groups or subgroups. Tyler suggests that traditional ethnography has not done this in a consistent way that would make comparison possible. Some anthropologists in the 1980s suggested that such definition was by nature an impossible task.

this is achieved, the units of comparison will be formal features rather than substantive variables.

PROBLEMS AND PROSPECTS

[Tyler concludes his essay with a 2,000-word discussion of the problems and prospects of his approach. He discusses research problems in the following areas: arrangements, perception and conception, discourse analysis, propositional analysis, metamessages, historical linguistics, and semantic ontogenesis. Tyler views the problems he has identified as indicative of the vitality of cognitive anthropology rather than as fatal flaws in its theory. He closes with the following passage.]

These comments are intended as speculations on the possible areas of future development in cognitive anthropology. They do not pretend to be exhaustive nor even representative. Nonetheless, they do indicate that cognitive anthropology has moved into a secondary stage of development. We have a few tentative answers, some new questions, and a host of old questions still unanswered. Fresh ground has been broken and new areas occupied, but still more remote territories have opened up for further research.

Explicit here is a view of culture derived from a kind of ethnography in which the methods of description are public and replicable, and the results predictive of expectations of appropriate behavior.[24] Implicit is the cognitive reorganization of our categories of description and analysis. Cognitive anthropology entails an ethnographic technique which describes cultures from the inside out rather than from the outside in. Categories of description are initially derived from relevant features in a culture rather than from the lexicon of anthropology.

Cognitive reorganization is a familiar process in the history of anthropology — in fact of any scientific discipline. The history of science is but the record of constant reexamination of assumptions, methods, and data. Such new developments in science do not take place in a vacuum. Innovations in one branch of science are complemented by convergent developments in other branches.[25]

The psychologist's renewed interest in cognition, the linguist's rediscovery of semantics, the biologist's recent emphasis on taxonomy and species specific behavior, and the sociologist's concern with the presentation of the self all reflect a set of recent developments complementary to one another and to those in anthropology. To be sure, among these disciplines there are differences in emphasis and method, yet each shares with the other a common orientation — the discovery of the organizing principles used by individuals, cultures, and species in manipulating and adapting to their particular life-space.

Notes

a. I wish to thank the following people who commented on previous versions of this paper: Brent Berlin, Mary Black, Charles Frake, John Gumperz, Dell Hymes, Paul Kay, Floyd Lounsbury, Ronald Rohner, George and Louise Spindler. I hope it is evident that the views in this chapter are those of the editor and do not necessarily represent a consensus of opinion among the above nor among those whose papers comprise subsequent chapters.

b. In this, and in much of what follows, there is a pronounced neo-Kantian flavor.

c. For an instance of a similar distinction between "objective environment" and "perceived life-space," see von Uexküll (1957).

d. The processes involved in this example are related to theories of cognitive dissonance (cf. Festinger 1957).

---

[24] Tyler emphasizes that, in his view, anthropology is a scientific and not an interpretive discipline (though a formal and not a natural science). Its goal is to produce logical, consistent, and public descriptions of culture that will withstand what Tyler considers rigorous testing.

[25] In closing, Tyler returns once again to Kuhn's idea of paradigm shift. He views cognitive anthropology and ethnoscience as new paradigms that will revolutionize anthropology. This assessment of the place of cognitive anthropology was overoptimistic, however. It certainly did not have a revolutionary effect that rendered competing paradigms obsolete. In fact Tyler later abandoned this approach in favor of postmodernism. Nevertheless, ethnoscience and cognitive anthropology did have powerful impacts on anthropology in the 1960s and 1970s and were crucial to the development of postmodernist thinking in the 1980s.

e. The line of argument here derives mainly from Russell (1929:92–98), but see also Bateson (1958:294) and Sapir (1932:515–519).

f. The most notable exception to this statement is Boas.

g. It is probably not true that all named things are significant, just as it is not the case that all significant things are named. Yet, as a point of departure, named categories are of primary importance.

h. Note the two empty spaces in Fig. 3. These indicate that this is not a perfect paradigm. The empty spaces are the result of incomplete combination of semantic components. The combinations δ M^{-2}; $\varnothing$ M^{-3}; $\varnothing$ M^{-4} do not occur. In a perfect paradigm all possible combinations would be realized. Perfect paradigms occur less frequently than imperfect paradigms. It should also be noted that in some contexts the lexemes "boar" and "stallion" denote not only δ M^{-1} but δ M^{-1} M^{-2}. For "horse" the lexeme "yearling" may sometimes denote δ M^{-2}; φ M^{-2}; $\varnothing$ M^{-2}. Historically it is interesting to note that all the lexemes denoting "newborn" ($\delta \varphi M^{-4}$) except piglet are derived from verbs denoting "to give birth to." A cow "calves," a mare "foals," a ewe "lambs," or "yeans," but a sow "farrows." As might be expected the archaic term for a newborn pig is "farrow." The lexeme piglet is recent. Also relevant is the fact that the "wild animal" category denoted by the lexeme "deer" has, except for the neuter category, the same semantic features as the category denoted by cattle. Formerly deer denoted "animal." Finally the features male, female, neuter correspond to the generalized Indo-European classification of nouns as masculine, feminine, neuter.

i. This distinction between a priori and a posteriori models is difficult to maintain, for it impinges directly on the philosophical problem of "other minds." If the mind imposes its own order on the disorderly happenings of the universe, then the investigator of necessity imposes his own logical constructs on the world he believes he is exploring. From this point of view there is no evidence for a belief in the existence of other minds except by analogy. Yet, granted the existence of other minds it is possible to assume that since the logical constructs of an informant and of an investigator are both products of a mind, these constructs are knowable insofar as they are communicable. Hence, the cognitive anthropologist's emphasis on language as both a method of discovery and an object of investigation (cf. Russell 1929:99–103).

j. This is not to imply that such a theory is incompatible with the study of change and development. The point is that a theory of description constitutes a different order of theory than that required for processes of change (for a discussion of this point, see Bateson 1958:296–300). A theory of change emphasizing cognitive organization would probably demonstrate that most anthropological data on change relate not to cultural change, but merely to epiphenomenal fluctuations.

k. This is misleading. Scientific laws are of necessity statements of universals in the language of description. All talk of "objects" and an hypothesized relation between "objects" and the language of description is symptomatic of a pernicious kind of dualism. The point is that our current language of description is inadequate either for the description of particular cultures or the development of universals simply because its assumptions are implicit and its operations (when specified) are contradictory. The continuing argument in descent "theory" is a classic example of the inadequacy of our current "metalanguage." The misleading statement reflects my own vacillation between an "intuitionist" (conceptualist) and "logicist" (realist) point of view (cf. Quine 1952). In general, this chapter is intuitionist with occasional logicist lapses. The lapses create problems like the one referred to above. My assertion that the description of a culture is really a description of the anthropologist's cognitive ordering is pure intuitionism which does not square directly with the Lévi-Straussian quest for a universal pan-human logic expressed in other sections. In a sense, the psychological reality problem is a confrontation between intuitionism and realism or perhaps formalism (nominalism). My belief in the relevance of relevance as an aspect of cognitive anthropology is probably creeping realism.

l. Leach (1961:6–21) makes a similar point, but with different emphasis. For two discussions of the distinction between formal and factual or natural sciences, see Carnap (1953) and Quine (1960: 270–276). The distinction may be somewhat overdrawn, but this should not obscure the fact that cultural anthropology has traditionally emulated a model of scientific method derived from a rather naive nineteenth century scientific materialism. Harris's (1962) quest for elementary units of cultural "matter" is a recent example of this attitude.

References

Bateson, Gregory. 1958. *Naven*, 2d ed. Stanford: Stanford University Press.

———, D. D. Jackson, J. Haley, and J. H.-Weakland. (1956). Toward a theory of schizophrenia. *Behavioral Science* 1:250–264.

Boas, Franz. 1938. *The Mind of Primitive Man*. London: Macmillan.

———. 1940. *Race, language and culture.* New York: Macmillan.

Carnap, Rudolf. 1953. Formal and factual science. In H. Feigl and M. Brodbeck, eds., *Readings in the philosophy of science.* New York: Appleton.

Church, Joseph. 1961. *Language and the Discovery of Reality.* New York: Random House.

Collingwood, R. G. 1939. *An Autobiography.* New York: Oxford University Press.

———. 1956. *The Idea of History.* New York: Oxford University Press.

D'Andrade, Roy G., N. Quinn, S. B. Nerlove, and A. K. Romney. 1966. Categories of disease in American-English and Mexican-Spanish. Unpublished manuscript.

Festinger, Leon. 1957. *A Theory of Cognitive Dissonance.* New York: Harper and Row.

Goodenough, Ward H. 1957. Cultural anthropology and linguistics. In Paul Garvin, ed., Report of the seventh annual round table meeting on linguistics and language study. Georgetown University Monograph Series on Language and Linguistics No. 9.

———. 1963. *Cooperation in Change.* New York: Russell Sage.

———. 1964. Introduction. In W. H. Goodenough, ed., *Explorations in Cultural Anthropology.* New York: McGraw-Hill.

Gregg, John R. 1954. *The Language of Taxonomy: An Application of Symbolic Logic to the Study of Classificatory Systems.* New York: Columbia University Press.

Harris, Marvin. 1964. *The Nature of Cultural Things.* New York: Random House.

Harris, Zellig. 1952. Discourse analysis. *Language* 28:1–30.

Hymes, Dell, ed. 1964a. *Language in Culture and Society.* New York: Harper and Row.

———. 1964b. Directions in (ethno-) linguistic theory. *American Anthropologist* 66 Pt. 2, No. 3:656.

Kay, Paul. 1965. Does anthropology need a metalanguage? Paper presented at the Southwestern Anthropological Association Annual Meeting, 1965.

———. 1966. Ethnography and theory of culture. *Bucknell Review* 14:106–113.

Lamb, Sydney. 1964. The sememic approach to structural semantics. *American Anthropologist* 66 Pt. 2, No. 3:57–78.

Leach, E. R. 1961. *Rethinking anthropology.* London School of Economics Monographs on Social Anthropology No. 22. London: University of London Press.

Lévi-Strauss, Claude. 1966. *The Savage Mind.* Chicago: University of Chicago Press.

Porter, C. L. 1967. *Taxonomy of Flowering Plants.* San Francisco: Freeman.

Quine, Willard Van Orman. 1960. *Word and Object.* New York: Wiley.

———. 1952. On what there is. In L. Linsky, ed., *Semantics and the Philosophy of Language.* Urbana: University of Illinois Press.

Russell, Bertrand. 1929. *Our Knowledge of the External World.* New York: Norton.

Sapir, Edward. 1932. Cultural anthropology and psychiatry. In D. G. Mandelbaum, ed., *Selected Writings of Edward Sapir.* Berkeley: University of California Press.

———. 1934. The emergence of the concept of personality in a study of cultures. In D. G. Mandelbaum, ed., *Selected Writings of Edward Sapir.* Berkeley: University of California Press.

Tyler, Stephen A. 1965. Proto-central Dravidian kinship terminology. Paper presented at a symposium on kinship in India at the American Association for the Advancement of Science Annual Meeting, 1965.

Uexküll, Jakob Von. 1957. A stroll through the world of animals and men: A picture book of invisible worlds. In C. H. Schiller and K. S. Lashley, eds., *Instinctive Behavior: The Development of a Modern Concept.* New York: International Universities.

Voorhees, Thomas. 1959. The formal analysis and comparison of Yuman kinship systems. Unpublished MA thesis, Stanford University.

Wallace, A. F. C. 1961. *Culture and Personality.* New York: Random House.

Woodger, J. H. 1952. *Biology and Language: An Introduction to the Methodology of the Biological Sciences Including Medicine.* Cambridge: University Press.

Sociobiology, Evolutionary Psychology, and Behavioral Ecology

$\mathcal{U}$nlike most other twentieth-century anthropological perspectives, sociobiology seeks to explain human behavior in terms of Darwinian evolutionary theory. Just as Charles Darwin proposed the theory of natural selection to account for the biological evolution of physical characteristics, sociobiologists propose that differential reproductive success shapes the evolution of social behavior of all organisms, including humans. The basis of Darwinian evolution is that individuals with those variations best adapted to their environment reproduce more than those lacking such variations. As a result, each subsequent generation will include a higher percentage of such individuals. Sociobiologists argue that because humans are biological organisms, they are subject to the same evolutionary laws as other life forms. Given that there is a genetic component to behavior, they say, those behavior patterns that increase an organism's adaptiveness to its environment will be selected for and reproduced in future generations.

Cultural analogies to evolution are not new in anthropology. As outlined in the first section of this text, many nineteenth-century thinkers viewed human culture in such terms and tried to delineate what they viewed as the evolutionary progress of culture through a series of stages. Their work differs from that of the sociobiologists in several fundamental ways, however. The nineteenth-century evolutionists were concerned with overall patterns of culture; sociobiologists concentrate on specific human behaviors. The nineteenth-century thinkers used Darwinian or Lamarckian evolution as a metaphor but were not particularly concerned with the details of transmission of cultural traits; sociobi-

ologists focus on specific Darwinian and genetic mechanisms of transmission. Finally, nineteenth-century evolutionism was teleological—the authors were firmly convinced that the processes of evolution created increasingly perfect societies. Sociobiologists see no such teleology and view change in terms of adaptation and reproductive success rather than progress toward perfection.

Sociobiology grew out of the work of evolutionary biologists, geneticists, ethologists, and anthropologists studying primate behavior. The animal behavior specialists Konrad Lorenz (1901–1989), Karl Von Frisch (1906–1982), and Nikolas Tinbergen (1907–1988) were particularly influential. These three published widely in the 1950s and 1960s and shared a Nobel prize in 1973. However, the publications that brought sociobiology to the critical attention of anthropologists were two books published in 1975 and 1976—Harvard biologist E. O. Wilson's (1929–) *Sociobiology: The New Synthesis* and *The Selfish Gene* by Richard Dawkins (1941–). These authors adopted an approach that focused on the level of the gene. They saw social behavior as controlled, in principle, by particular genes, and they saw evolution as occurring at this level because reproductive success amounted to increasing the frequency of certain genes in future generations. In effect, they proposed that humans are little more than the vehicles genes use to reproduce themselves.

The notion that human cultural behavior was reducible to genetics violated the fundamental tenants of Boasian anthropology and produced enormous hostility among cultural anthropologists. There were many criticisms, but most focused on two points: First, sociobiological studies looked at behavior in terms of reproductive success and population genetics but ignored the effects of culture and learning, which most anthropologists claim are powerful influences on human society. Second, virtually all sociobiological research was conducted on animals and insects rather than humans. Wilson's own work, for example, was concerned with ants. Anthropologists doubted that research findings based on animal behavior were applicable to human behavior (Sahlins 1976, Montagu 1980).

Even though many flaws of the early work have been corrected, sociobiology remains one of the most contentious areas within anthropology — so contentious that several reviewers of this volume suggested that the section on sociobiology be entirely eliminated. You are reading this over their objections. Part of the hostility is a continuing reaction to the extreme claims sociobiologists made in the 1970s and early 1980s, when they frequently asserted that sociobiology would render all forms of social science obsolete. Today, it would be hard to find a sociobiologist who would support such a radical position. Beyond this, sociobiology is inimical to some of the most dearly held principles of American cultural anthropology. The insistence of sociobiologists on grounding at least some behavior in universal human genetic predispositions runs contrary to cultural anthropologists' emphasis on the primacy of culture itself as the determinant of human social life.

Because of the high level of hostility, the word *sociobiology* has been almost entirely dropped from anthropological discourse, and much of the study of the relationship between biology and human behavior has moved into other academic disciplines. Psychology, in particular, has captured much of the field; and sociobiology remains strong in biology, where it has few pejorative connotations.

Several distinct approaches can be identified in contemporary sociobiology. These are evolutionary psychology, human behavioral ecology, and the study of human universals. Evolutionary psychology is concerned primarily with the analysis of the mind as a device formed by natural selection. Evolutionary psychologists hypothesize that the mind is composed of a large number of functionally specialized neural circuits. These circuits were designed by natural selection to solve adaptive problems faced by our hunter-gatherer ancestors. Evolutionary psychologists attempt to describe brain circuits, show how they work, what information they are designed to process, and what they were designed to accomplish in a hunter-gatherer context (Cosmides and Tooby 1997).

A second focus, human behavioral ecology, looks to the integration of earlier forms of cultural ecology with more recent understandings of biological ecology. It emphasizes populations rather than cultures, human population biology, as well as evolutionary ecology (Kormondy and Brown 1998). However, rather than focusing on the mind, human behavioral ecologists focus on testing the hypothesis that culturally patterned traits actually enhance fitness.

A third current approach involves the search for human universals (Brown 1991). Followers of this approach concentrate on discovering the characteristics found in all human societies. They presume that ultimately such traits must be primarily based in human evolutionary biology and adaptation but do not focus their studies there.

The essays selected for this section show some of the evolution of the sociobiological approach. The first selection — from E. O. Wilson's classic *Sociobiology: The New Synthesis* — is an example of what we call the "selfish gene" approach. The second essay (31), by Jerome H. Barkow (1944 –), takes a more sophisticated view of the interaction between genetics and culture, studying the possible effects of cultural information on fitness. It belongs to the more recent evolutionary psychology approach.

While sociobiology in all of its forms continues to be rejected by most cultural anthropologists, it has increased in popularity, both among anthropologists and the general public, in the last several years. At least two factors help to explain this increasing acceptance. First, recent medical successes and high-profile research such as the Human-Genome Project have generally focused attention on the role of genetic inheritance in human life. As evidence emerges that things as diverse as cancers and homosexuality have genetic and biochemical bases, people are more willing to examine the connection between biology and behavior. Second, many anthropologists have reacted vehemently against postmodernism and the notion that no objective description of culture (or anything else) is possible. They turn to sociobiology as the branch of anthropology that most resembles the natural sciences. A good example of this is James Lett, whose recent book, *Science, Reason, and Anthropology,* is largely an attack on postmodernism. Lett takes postmodern anthropologists to task for their polemic approach to debate and goes on to define anthropology as "the scientific study of human evolution" (1997:121).

30. The Morality of the Gene

Edward O. Wilson (1929–)

CAMUS SAID THAT THE ONLY SERIOUS PHILO-sophical question is suicide. That is wrong even in the strict sense intended. The biologist, who is concerned with questions of physiology and evolutionary history, realizes that self-knowledge is constrained and shaped by the emotional control centers in the hypothalamus and limbic system of the brain. These centers flood our consciousness with all the emotions—hate, love, guilt, fear, and others—that are consulted by ethical philosophers who wish to intuit the standards of good and evil. What, we are then compelled to ask, made the hypothalamus and limbic system? They evolved by natural selection. That simple biological statement must be pursued to explain ethics and ethical philosophers, if not epistemology and epistemologists, at all depths. Self-existence, or the suicide that terminates it, is not the central question of philosophy. The hypothalamic-limbic complex automatically denies such logical reduction by countering it with feelings of guilt and altruism. In this one way the philosopher's own emotional control centers are wiser than his solipsist consciousness, "knowing" that in evolutionary time the individual organism counts for almost

From *Sociobiology: The New Synthesis* (1975)

nothing. In a Darwinist sense the organism does not live for itself. Its primary function is not even to reproduce other organisms; it reproduces genes, and it serves as their temporary carrier. Each organism generated by sexual reproduction is a unique, accidental subset of all the genes constituting the species. Natural selection is the process whereby certain genes gain representation in the following generations superior to that of other genes located at the same chromosome positions. When new sex cells are manufactured in each generation, the winning genes are pulled apart and reassembled to manufacture new organisms that, on the average, contain a higher proportion of the same genes. But the individual organism is only their vehicle, part of an elaborate device to preserve and spread them with the least possible biochemical perturbation. Samuel Butler's famous aphorism, that the chicken is only an egg's way of making another egg, has been modernized: the organism is only DNA's way of making more DNA. More to the point, the hypothalamus and limbic system are engineered to perpetuate DNA.[1]

In the process of natural selection, then, any device that can insert a higher proportion of certain genes into subsequent generations will come to characterize the species. One class of such

---

[1] This electrifying paragraph, which opens the first chapter of Wilson's book, makes immediately clear why it caused such a stir. Wilson begins by quoting Albert Camus (1913–1960), the French existential philosopher and novelist, and then immediately reduces the philosopher's statement to a biological issue. In *Sociobiology,* Wilson proposes a theory in which all human social activity is reducible to evolutionary genetics. The book's opening is a powerful rhetorical device. Wilson's

devices promotes prolonged individual survival. Another promotes superior mating performance and care of the resulting offspring. As more complex social behavior by the organism is added to the genes' techniques for replicating themselves, altruism becomes increasingly prevalent and eventually appears in exaggerated forms. This brings us to the central theoretical problem of sociobiology: how can altruism, which by definition reduces personal fitness, possibly evolve by natural selection? The answer is kinship: if the genes causing the altruism are shared by two organisms because of common descent, and if the altruistic act by one organism increases the joint contribution of these genes to the next generation, the propensity to altruism will spread through the gene pool. This occurs even though the altruist makes less of a solitary contribution to the gene pool as the price of its altruistic act.[2]

To his own question, "Does the Absurd dictate death?" Camus replied that the struggle toward the heights is itself enough to fill a man's heart. This arid judgment is probably correct, but it makes little sense except when closely examined in the light of evolutionary theory. The hypothalamic-limbic complex of a highly social species, such as man, "knows," or more precisely it has been programmed to perform as if it knows, that its underlying genes will be proliferated maximally only if it orchestrates behavioral responses that bring into play an efficient mixture of personal survival, reproduction, and altruism. Consequently, the centers of the complex tax the conscious mind with ambivalences whenever the organisms encounter stressful situations. Love joins hate; aggression,

fear; expansiveness, withdrawal; and so on; in blends designed not to promote the happiness and survival of the individual, but to favor the maximum of the controlling genes.

The ambivalences stem from counteracting pressures of natural selection. Their genetic consequences will be explored formally later in this book. For the moment suffice it to note what is good for the individual can be destructive to the family; what preserves the family can be harsh on both the individual and the tribe to which its family belongs; what promotes the tribe can weaken the family and destroy the individual; and so on upward through the permutations of levels of organization. Counteracting selection on these different units will result in certain genes being multiplied and fixed, others lost, and combinations of still others held in static proportions. According to the present theory, some of the genes will produce emotional states that reflect the balance of counteracting selection forces at the different levels.

I have raised a problem in ethical philosophy in order to characterize the essence of sociobiology. Sociobiology is defined as the systematic study of the biological basis of all social behavior. For the present it focuses on animal societies, their population structure, castes, and communication, together with all of the physiology underlying the social adaptations. But the discipline is also concerned with the social behavior of early man and the adaptive features of organization in the more primitive contemporary human societies. Sociology *sensu stricto,*[3] the study of human societies at all levels of complexity, still stands apart from sociobiology because of its largely

---

attempt to tackle what Camus believed was the ultimate problem of human existence is intended to grab the reader's attention by phrasing the problem in the most controversial terms possible. Most of its remaining pages are filled with technical arguments about animal and insect behavior, and little more is said about human life or philosophy.

[2] Altruism was a problem for sociobiology. If behavior is dictated by natural selection, how can altruistic acts (which may cost the organism food, reproductive potential, living space, and even its life) exist? The answer is called *kin selection theory,* which Wilson explains in this paragraph. The question of altruism came into focus for Wilson through his study of ant colonies. Only queen ants reproduce, and the vast majority of individuals are workers who give up their reproductive potential to support the queen and the colony. Why should these workers forgo reproduction to facilitate that of the queen? Wilson discovered that a worker ant actually passes on a greater percentage of its genetic material to future generations by supporting the queen, with whom it shares genetic material, rather than by reproducing itself.

[3] *Sensu stricto:* Latin for in a strict sense.

structuralist and nongenetic approach. It attempts to explain human behavior primarily by empirical description of the outermost phenotypes and by unaided intuition, without reference to evolutionary explanations in the true genetic sense. It is most successful, in the way descriptive taxonomy and ecology have been most successful, when it provides a detailed description of particular phenomena and demonstrates first-order correlations with features of the environment. Taxonomy and ecology, however, have been reshaped entirely during the past forty years by integration into neo-Darwinist evolutionary theory—the "Modern Synthesis," as it is often called—in which each phenomenon is weighed for its adaptive significance and then related to the basic principles of population genetics. It may not be too much to say that sociology and the other social sciences, as well as the humanities, are the last branches of biology waiting to be included in the Modern Synthesis. One of the functions of sociobiology, then, is to reformulate the foundations of the social sciences in a way that draws these subjects into the Modern Synthesis. Whether the social sciences can be truly biologicized in this fashion remains to be seen.[4]

This book makes an attempt to codify sociobiology into a branch of evolutionary biology and particularly of modern population biology. I believe that the subject has an adequate richness of detail and aggregate of self-sufficient concepts to be ranked as coordinate with such disciplines as molecular biology and developmental biology. In the past its development has been slowed by too close an identification with ethology and behavioral physiology. In the view presented here, the new sociobiology should be compounded of roughly equal parts of invertebrate zoology, vertebrate zoology, and population biology. Figure 1 shows the schema

with which I closed *The Insect Societies*, suggesting how the amalgam can be achieved.[5] Biologists have always been intrigued by comparisons between societies of invertebrates, especially insect societies, and those of vertebrates. They have dreamed of identifying the common properties of such disparate units in a way that would provide insight into all aspects of social evolution, including that of man. The goal can be expressed in modern terms as follows: when the same parameters and quantitative theory are used to analyze both termite colonies and troops of rhesus macaques, we will have a unified science of sociobiology. This may seem an impossibly difficult task. But as my own studies have advanced, I have been increasingly impressed with the functional similarities between invertebrate and vertebrate societies and less so with the structural differences that seem, at first glance, to constitute such an immense gulf between them. Consider for a moment termites and monkeys. Both are formed into cooperative groups that occupy territories. The group members communicate hunger, alarm, hostility, caste status or rank, and reproductive status among themselves by means of something on the order of 10 to 100 nonsyntactical signals.[6] Individuals are intensely aware of the distinction between groupmates and nonmembers. Kinship plays an important role in group structure and probably served as a chief generative force of sociality in the first place. In both kinds of society there is a well-marked division of labor, although in the insect society there is a much stronger reproductive component. The details of organization have been evolved by an evolutionary optimization process of unknown precision, during which some measure of added fitness was given to individuals with cooperative tendencies—at least toward relatives. The fruits of cooperativeness depend upon the particular

---

[4] To emphasize his biological perspective, Wilson characterizes sociology as describing "phenotypes"—in other words, behavior is no more than the visible expression of genetic information. Just as Freud tried to unite the social sciences under his theory of psychoanalysis, Wilson states that the social sciences and humanities can be incorporated into the field of biology.

[5] *The Insect Societies,* published in 1971, was Wilson's exhaustive study of the behavior of ants. It was from his study of insects that he derived many of the insights he brought to his work in sociobiological theory.

[6] *Nonsyntactical signals:* nonlinguistic signals, or communications that are not language. Primate call systems, for example, are aural signals but not language.

Evolutionary and Ecological Parameters

Figure 1. The connections that can be made between phylogenetic studies, ecology, and sociobiology

conditions of the environment and are available to only a minority of animal species during the course of their evolution.[7]

This comparison may seem facile, but it is out of such deliberate oversimplification that the beginnings of a general theory are made. The formulation of a theory of sociobiology constitutes, in my opinion, one of the great manageable problems of biology for the next twenty or thirty years. The prolegomenon of Figure 1 guesses part of its

future outline and some of the directions in which it is most likely to lead animal behavior research. Its central precept is that the evolution of social behavior can be fully comprehended only through an understanding, first, of demography, which yields the vital information concerning population growth and age structure, and, second, of the genetic structure of the populations, which tells us what we need to know about effective population size in the genetic sense, the coefficients of

---

[7] Wilson's focus on similarities between different species is typical of sociobiological studies. One could, no doubt, find more differences than similarities between termites and monkeys if one chose to look. It is probably no exaggeration to say that most anthropologists would find this list of similarities trivial and the differences one could think of profound. In fact, most cultural anthropologists probably believe that the sorts of behavior that sociobiologists study are relatively trivial and that any genetic universals underlying human behavior are limited and far less interesting than human cultural diversity.

relationship within the societies, and the amounts of gene flow between them. The principal goal of a general theory of sociobiology should be an ability to predict features of social organization from a knowledge of these population parameters combined with information on the behavioral constraints imposed by the genetic constitution of the species. It will be a chief task of evolutionary ecology, in turn, to derive the population parameters from a knowledge of the evolutionary history of the species and of the environment in which the most recent segment of that history unfolded. The most important feature of the prolegomenon, then, is the sequential relation between evolutionary studies, ecology, population biology, and sociobiology.[8]

In stressing the tightness of this sequence, however, I do not wish to underrate the filial relationship that sociobiology has had in the past with the remainder of behavioral biology. Although behavioral biology is traditionally spoken of as if it were a unified subject, it is now emerging as two distinct disciplines centered on neurophysiology and on sociobiology, respectively. The conventional wisdom also speaks of ethology, which is the naturalistic study of whole patterns of animal behavior, and its companion enterprise, comparative psychology, as the central, unifying fields of behavioral biology. They are not; both are destined to be cannibalized by neurophysiology and sensory physiology from one end and sociobiology and behavioral ecology from the other (see Figure 2).[9]

I hope not too many scholars in ethology and psychology will be offended by this vision of the future of behavioral biology. It seems to be indicated both by the extrapolation of current events and by consideration of the logical relationship behavioral biology holds with the remainder of science. The future, it seems clear, cannot be with the ad hoc terminology, crude models, and curve fitting that characterize most of contemporary ethology and comparative psychology. Whole patterns of animal behavior will inevitably be explained within the framework, first, of integrative neurophysiology, which classifies neurons and reconstructs their circuitry, and, second, of sensory physiology, which seeks to characterize the cellular transducers at the molecular level. Endocrinology will continue to play a peripheral role, since it is concerned with the cruder tuning devices of nervous activity. To pass from this level and reach the next really distinct discipline, we must travel all the way up to the society and the population. Not only are the phenomena best described by families of models different from those of cellular and molecular biology, but the explanations become largely evolutionary. There should be nothing surprising in this distinction. It is only a reflection of the larger division that separates the two greater domains of evolutionary biology and functional biology. As Lewontin[10] (1972a) has truly said: "Natural selection of the character states themselves is the essence of Darwinism. All else is molecular biology."[11]

References

Lewontin, R. C. 1972a. Testing the theory of natural selection. (Review of R. Creed, ed., *Ecological genetics and Evolution.* Blackwell Scientific Publications, Oxford, 1971.) *Nature*, London, 236 (5343): 181–182.

---

[8] Since sociobiology focuses on natural selection and reproductive success as the mechanisms for determining behavior, such factors as population growth, gene flow, and demography are important to it. Behaviors must be analyzed in terms of these factors. Notice that Wilson sees the key issues as entirely within the traditional hard sciences. Anthropology, sociology, economics – not to mention the humanities – are not on the list. This is because sociobiologists, at the time this essay was written, perceived the subject materials of these disciplines as epiphenomenal: they were secondary manifestations of biologically based phenomena and therefore of no interest.

[9] Wilson was profoundly reductionist. He was in search of a few unifying principles that would explain all behavior. According to Wilson, even the fields that gave rise to sociobiology, such as psychology, were due to be subsumed by it or neurophysiology.

[10] Richard Lewontin (1929–) is a geneticist and evolutionary biologist.

[11] Wilson's worldview is evident in this passage. He invokes parsimony as one of his guiding principles – explanations must be neat, concise, and leave no loose ends. The vision behind this hearkens back to the science of the nineteenth century

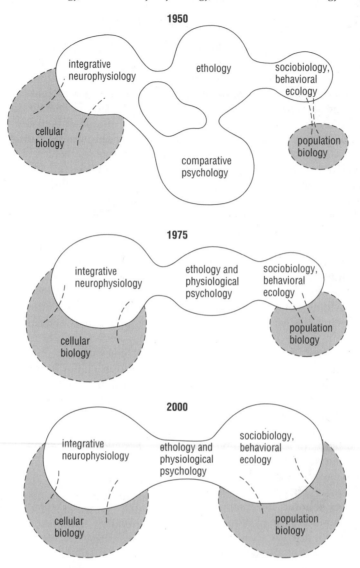

1950

integrative neurophysiology

ethology

sociobiology, behavioral ecology

cellular biology

population biology

comparative psychology

1975

integrative neurophysiology

ethology and physiological psychology

sociobiology, behavioral ecology

cellular biology

population biology

2000

integrative neurophysiology

ethology and physiological psychology

sociobiology, behavioral ecology

cellular biology

population biology

Figure 2. A subjective conception of the relative number of ideas in various disciplines in and adjacent to behavioral biology to the present time and as it might be in the future

and the belief that the world is a rational and orderly place. This view is rejected by most current anthropologists, and many in the hard sciences as well, who see complexity at all levels.

Twenty-five years have passed since the publication of this essay, and the progress that Wilson predicted for "the next twenty or thirty years" has not taken place. Sociobiology may be a useful theoretical perspective for understanding some aspects of culture, but even its most fervent supporters probably no longer believe that it has the potential to replace the social sciences. By the mid-1980s, Wilson himself adopted a more moderate and sophisticated line on the distinction between evolutionary biology and culture. See, for example, his 1984 book *Biophilia*.

31. The Elastic Between Genes and Culture[a]

Jerome H. Barkow (1944–)

SUMMARY OF THE ARGUMENT AND MAJOR CONCEPTS

IF THE COSTS OF LEARNING ENTIRELY BY ONE-self are sufficiently high, suggest Boyd and Richerson (1985), and if the environment is sufficiently homogeneous and stable to keep the costs of doing what others around one are doing sufficiently low, then selection will favor a reliance on socially transmitted information.[1] For Boyd and Richerson, it was in just such circumstances that the human dependence on socially transmitted information — on culture — may have begun. This paper suggests that there are grounds for expecting such a dependence on culture, when it is carried to the extreme typical of our species, to at times have genetically maladaptive consequences. We should therefore expect at least some socially transmitted information to be fitness-reducing for all or some segments of a local population. Although precise data are lacking, that does appear to be what we find. If socially transmitted information does at times tend to be fitness-reducing, then under certain circumstances we may expect selection to favor individual-level mechanisms that permit the individual not only to perform functions analogous to the editing and revising of received information, but to create new information as well. The question of why culture presum-

(1989)

ably is *not* (on the whole) maladaptive may be of theoretical significance equal only to the problem of why culture often *is* adaptive.

Two basic concepts in this paper are "culture" and "maladaptation." Culture, for present purposes, is conceptualized as a pool of at least somewhat organized information of various kinds,[2] socially transmitted within and across generations.[b]

The psychological (i.e., individual-level) processes involved in this transmission (usually termed "socialization" or "enculturation") are not well understood.[c] "Maladaptation" here means "tending to lower genetic fitness." A maladaptive culture trait is socially transmitted information that tends to lead to behavior likely to lower the fitness of those who accept it. There is no requirement that the trait be universally accepted or that it have the same effects on fitness for all segments of the population.

The present article stresses the genetically maladaptive, though the bias of evolutionary theorists has been so strongly in the opposite direction that the topic has been somewhat neglected. "Maladaptation" is a complex concept with implications having to do with gain, with net benefits, and with measurement. The measurement problem is the simplest, conceptually: There are only practical, not theoretical answers to the question of how many generations we must take into account before we decide whether a given trait is adaptive, maladaptive, or neutral.[3] In practice,

---

[1] In this paper, Barkow tackles one of the key problems facing sociobiologists. Following in the footsteps of the cultural ecologists and other materialists, sociobiologists viewed culture as adaptation. They suggested that humans adapt to their environments and increase their reproductive potential through behavioral changes driven by evolutionary pressures. These behaviors may ultimately be genetically encoded. The problem that Barkow tackles — one inherent in this approach — is that people clearly exhibit some behaviors that do not lead to reproductive success and may inhibit it.

[2] Sociobiologists conceive of culture in behavioral terms. Here Barkow speaks of it as a pool of information that affects behavior. This definition is the opposite of that used by ethnoscientists and cognitive anthropologists, who analyze culture as a mental model separate from individual behavior.

[3] In biological evolution, ultimately the only meaningful criterion of fitness (or adaptation) is reproductive success. A trait is adaptive if it results in greater numbers of fertile offspring, maladaptive if it results in fewer. In theory, the same criterion can be applied to human beings, but in practice, there are enormous difficulties in doing so. First, success or failure

we very often cannot even observe the individuals for a single generation, and we are forced to use measures such as copulatory success. When we speak of "maladaptive" or "fitness-reducing" *culture* traits, we are forced to use very indirect measures of lowered fitness, such as the prevalence of illness or the depletion of soil or of a fishery. The use of indirect measures would appear to be an unavoidable problem in any discussion of maladaptive culture traits.

Difficulties in measurement are further complicated by the recurring theoretical problem of the "unit of selection."[d] Whether we consider a trait "adaptive" or "maladaptive" may depend upon the scale of our analysis. This ambiguity reflects the fact that, when we measure fitness, we are actually measuring *net effect* on fitness. Any trait, from the level of a pleiotropic gene to the level of cultural capacity itself, will be selected for in terms of its (on-balance) net effect on fitness. An adaptive trait is simply one for which benefits outweigh costs. However, what is considered a cost of an (on-balance) adaptive trait at a molar scale may be considered a maladaptive trait on a more molecular scale. For example, arboreal adaptation in howler monkeys presumably *is* an adaptation, i.e., the benefits of relative freedom from predation and access to food are greater than the costs of, e.g., falls from trees. If we move to a finer scale, the tendency to fall from trees itself becomes a (maladaptive) trait. Similarly, in this paper I will be arguing for the existence of genetically maladaptive culture traits, even though it is possible to move upwards in scale and so to redefine them as costs of adaptive traits.[e]

Why should socially transmitted information at times be fitness reducing?[4] Such maladaptation might occur due to four processes: 1) *Environments alter.* Natural change may make previously useful practices deleterious, as when a reduction in mean annual rainfall causes a traditional cultivar to fail repeatedly. 2) *Expenses emerge.* Techniques may be fitness enhancing in the short term, fitness reducing in the long term. For example, deleterious environmental changes may be human-created, as when fisheries or soil fertility are exhausted, or when goats contribute to desertification. Alternatively, apparently beneficial traits may have more immediate but still unperceived costs. A grain may be replaced by a root crop because the latter yields more calories for the same amount of effort: Much less apparent is that this higher yield comes at the expense of protein. 3) *Errors accumulate.* Incorrect data get transmitted. For example, people may come to believe that a potentially important nutriment, such as the tomato, is poisonous. 4) *Elites appropriate.* Wealth and power are unequally distributed, and the teachings of a dominant group may tend to enhance the relative fitness of its members at the expense of that of others. It can be argued that culture is an arena for social conflict, and deception and misinformation are powerful weapons.

If the tendency for culture to move in fitness-reducing directions is real and has resulted in selection for psychological mechanisms to counter this tendency, what are those mechanisms? These mechanisms, I would hypothesize, are *not* separate and distinct from those associated with our tendencies to enhance our fitness more directly.[5]

---

can only be seen over several generations, but anthropologists rarely have the opportunity to do work spanning that amount of time. Second, there is the crucial issue of scale that Barkow discusses here. There is much debate among sociobiologists over the level at which adaptation takes place. Many sociobiologists, particularly those of the 1970s, presumed that selection occurred at the level of the individual. For them, culture is essentially the sum of these individual, genetically driven behaviors. Barkow offers the possibility that selection occurs at the group or population level. If so, then cultural traits become crucial.

[4] Note the language used here and in the paragraph above. Barkow is writing in a scientific idiom. He borrows freely from the hard sciences, using words such as *molecular* and *molar.* His use of *molar,* for example, has nothing to do with Avogadro's number, which determines the number of molecules in a mole, but gives his writing a scientific feel. By the way, a *pleiotropic* gene is one that is attached to another and may be selected because the other is selected. It goes along for the ride.

[5] Although culture is fundamentally adaptive, maladaptive characteristics tend to accumulate in culture over time. If this movement is allowed to proceed unchecked, it will reduce fitness. Thus, there must be a mechanism to counter the buildup of such traits.

Selection to counter genetically maladaptive culture traits seems most likely not to have generated special-purpose mechanisms that do nothing but revise all socially transmitted information. Rather, mechanisms that already revise socially transmitted information specifically in our own fitness interest would also tend to revise culture, often eliminating fitness-reducing information. For example, the stereotyped "rebellious" adolescent may be questioning both received culture and personal position in society. Other likely dual-purpose psychological characteristics may include our tendency to imitate the successful and the prestigious (in place of, at times, our own kin); political rebellion and revolution; and the deliberate socialization of children by parents wishing to transmit a revised culture to their offspring. This paper will largely ignore the individual fitness aspects of such psychological mechanisms and emphasize their effects on culture.

Cultural information is not homogeneous, and selection has presumably favored our tending to revise some categories of socially transmitted information more readily than others. Communicational and other cognitive structures, for example, are probably relatively stable, while culturally provided strategies associated with prestige and social identity may often be examined and revised.

Central to this article's arguments is a conception of culture transmission and of biological evolution as *intimately linked yet conceptually distinct*. I view culture transmission and biological evolution as the two ends of an elastic band. Each pulls on the other. Processes at one end tend to generate fitness-reducing, socially transmitted information; processes at the other tend to eliminate such information. Because both the "stretching" and the "pulling back" take place continually, at no time is any culture likely to be entirely fitness enhancing for all of its participants, nor is any culture likely to be entirely genetically maladaptive.[6] I will refer to culture's tendency to move in fitness-reducing directions as *culture stretch*. Processes tending to alter culture in fitness-enhancing ways will be termed *culture revision*.[f]

WHY SHOULD CULTURES TEND TO MOVE IN FITNESS-REDUCING DIRECTIONS (STRETCH)?

Four processes may cause stretch: environments alter, errors accumulate, elites appropriate, and expenses emerge.

Environments Alter

Imagine a static culture, one not being modified by interaction among individuals. That culture's physical environment, like any other, alters with time. One result is that some of the information of which the culture is composed becomes fitness reducing because it is no longer relevant to the altered external environment. Previously fitness-enhancing, culturally ordered behaviors now become fitness reducing. The relationship between the local population and its environment has altered. An ice age occurs or ends, annual rainfall declines, or new diseases develop. A static culture in a changing environment must eventually stretch. We need not wait for natural environmental deterioration to render our cultural adaptation obsolete: We can do it ourselves. Hardin's (1968) "Tragedy of the Commons" situations abound, in which unmitigated pursuit of private gain in the end makes all poorer: We can deplete our fisheries, wipe out our forests, or simply populate beyond the ability of our culture's resources and technology to support us.[7] For example, the Mayans may have contributed to the collapse of their civilization by

---

[6] Barkow is suggesting an important principle of relationship between individual fitness and cultural fitness. He suggests that the mechanisms that allow us to modify behavior to promote our own fitness can also result in modifications of culture that enhance its general fitness. He sees human behavior, and ultimately the direction of human evolution, as the result of dialectical tension between the tendency of cultures to accumulate misinformation and individuals' genetically based drive to increase their reproductive fitness (thus, the title of this essay).

[7] Garret Hardin (1915–), a biologist, published his original paper on the tragedy of the commons in 1968. It had an important impact on materialist anthropology because it showed the logic behind seemingly illogical cultural actions. Hardin argued that when a resource is held in common and is unregulated, individuals will exploit it to their advantage. Any gain from

reducing the lengthy fallow period their slash-and-burn horticulture required, until severe malnutrition affected all but the nobility (Wood 1979, pp. 180–186).

Many of the fitness strategies used by human beings are inherently likely to fail once they become common because of the nature of their "frequency-dependency." For such strategies, the probability of success decreases as the number of people following the strategy increases (Foley 1985, p. 358). For example, suppose a population grows, and pressure increases on pasturage, or on firewood supply, or perhaps on the fishery. An effective individual short-term strategy is to fish more. As more people fish more, the fish supply is depleted. A previously adaptive cultural strategy for resource acquisition—when you need more fish, fish more—is no longer successful. The culture has stretched. The local population may now crash, emigrate, or develop alternative resource strategies. The last possibility represents a form of culture revision.[g]

Errors Accumulate

There is a limiting feature common to all information systems: errors occur.[8] The errors discussed here are those that are inadvertent, i.e., not misinformation deliberately and self-servingly introduced by others. Errors can accumulate because any individual is likely to be in a position to test or verify only a small fraction of received culture. Indeed, much of cultural knowledge is in principle unverifiable (e.g., cosmology and eschatology.) Most of such unproven, socially transmitted knowledge has little direct bearing on genetic fitness, but some does,

as the two medical anthropology examples presented below (taken from my own fieldwork) are intended to illustrate. In these two cases, the information affects physical health but goes largely unchallenged.[h]

The *mayye*, in the Hausa-speaking regions of northern Nigeria and southern Niger, eats souls. *Mayyu* (the plural of *mayye*) have something like "hailstones" in the stomach that enable them to see your soul. They crave it. If one of them is overcome by lust and begins to eat your soul, you will sicken and die unless he or she is forced to release it. When asked about whether there really was such a thing as a *mayye*, informants would respond (when they responded at all, to what to them were silly questions) in about this manner: "Oh, you are skeptical, are you? Do not people frequently sicken and die for no good reason? The *mayye* does that. Don't you see people sickening and dying like that?" The existence of the "soul-eater" is self-evident. Ordinary people rarely get to actually see a soul being eaten: but *everyone* knows soul-eaters exist.

In much of the English-speaking world, tiny, invisible monsters eat people. They attack by the millions and billions. When they do, you will sicken and may die unless the *emdee* provides the right substances to be ingested or injected at prescribed intervals in prescribed quantities. When questioned, an informant is likely to reply in this manner: "You are skeptical? Do not people sicken and die, for no good reason? The existence of the *germ* is self-evident." Ordinary people rarely get to actually see a germ attacking a person: but *everyone* knows germs exist.

The point of this pair of parables is not that such beliefs are necessarily fitness reducing, but

---

the commons accrues to the individual while the costs of deterioration of commonly held property are borne by all. As a result, the logic that compels exploitation of the commons remains unchanged, even when the resource is badly depleted.

Hardin originally applied his argument to population growth, becoming an advocate for "lifeboat ethics," the notion that we should make conscious choices as to whose life should be supported and who should be left to die. More recently he has expanded it to include many aspects of the cultural use of resources. The core of Hardin's argument is that what is good for the individual may not be good for society. Consider the effect of this principle relative to Barkow's emphasis on the tensions between individual fitness and the cultural selection of behavior.

[8] One powerful continuity between ecological anthropology and sociobiology is that they both accord a powerful role to systems theory and information theory. Here Barkow treats culture as an information system. When he says that errors occur in such systems, he is stating a fundamental mathematical law that he believes can be applied equally to cultural systems and to the transmission of a digitized conversation over telephone wires.

that much of culture is unverified and often unverifiable. Medical anthropology readily provides additional examples of culturally transmitted, potentially fitness-reducing misinformation. Thus, for centuries "cupping" or "bleeding" was standard medical practice in large portions of the world.

Analysis of the medical practices and pharmacopoeias of the cultures of the world reveals both highly effective curative techniques and ones likely to be both ineffective and dangerous. There is a general consensus that non-Western systems tend to be efficacious at the psychosocial level. Controversy exists, however, over their clinical utility and safety. For example, Taylor et al. (1973, p. 208) point to the dangerousness of the mercury and other heavy metal compounds used both in Ayurvedic[9] and Islamic medicine. MacLean (1971, p. 84) points out that the Yoruba practice of treating convulsions in children with a medicine containing a strong solution of nicotine depresses brain activity dangerously, often to the point of "deep unconsciousness."

Nutrition and food are other areas in which cultures may include potentially fitness-reducing misinformation. For example, prior to 1820 the tomato was considered by North Americans to be poisonous (Sebrell et al. 1967, p. 149). (By dramatically eating a tomato on the courthouse steps of Salem, New Jersey, in that year, a single brave individual [Robert G. Johnston] revised his culture's classification of that fruit, moving it from "poisonous" to "edible.") Another example involves colostrum.[10] In a number of the world's cultures, the premilk secretion colostrum, with its important immunity-conferring properties, is denied to the child. There is substantial evidence, reviewed in Barkow and Hallett (1989), that this practice is deleterious to health, but it is unclear why it should occur. There is no evidence of any other mammal denying its young the colostrum.

Here is a typical account of colostrum denial, taken from Berland's (1982, p. 115) study of rural Pakistan:

> A mother's breast milk is believed to be safra ["hot"] for seven days following birth, so the baby is fed a mixture of water and brown sugar by dipping a twisted cloth into an open cup of the *gurpani* (sweet water or *sherbet*). Because the cup is exposed to flies, newborn babies frequently develop intestinal infections, and many die of marasmus and dehydration within two to three weeks. Between 60 and 65 percent of all babies die within the first month to six weeks of life. Because of the high infant mortality rate, babies are often not given a name until they are a year or more old. . . .

Berland goes on to document the sharp food restrictions on the pregnant woman and the new mother. Such restrictions are quite common cross-culturally, often involve foods high in protein, and constitute examples of what are quite likely to be fitness-reducing nutritional practices. (For a review of cultural restrictions on the nutrition of women and children, considered by some to be a major Third World health problem, see Rosenberg [1980].)

To return to theory, it has been argued that some fitness-reducing cultural information may be self-perpetuating in a manner analogous to the continuity of the genes themselves. Ball (1984) accepts Dawkins's (1976, 1982) argument that it is useful to think of culture as consisting of "memes" or replicators analogous to genes.[11] A "parasitic meme," for Ball (p. 147), "promotes behavior that is adaptive for itself but maladaptive for its organism." His example is "Praise the Lord, send money; tell your friends." The Shakers, an American religious group of the last century that enjoined strict celibacy upon its members, ceased to exist when its rate of recruitment fell below its

---

[9] Ayurvedic medicine is the traditional medical practice of India.

[10] Colostrum is the clear liquid that precedes milk production in lactating women.

[11] Richard Dawkins coined the word *meme* in his 1976 book *The Selfish Gene,* one of the works that defined sociobiology. The word derives from the Greek root for imitation. The connection is that memes are transmitted through one individual imitating the behavior of another. The meme is, in some ways, the holy grail of sociobiology — it is the unit of culture upon which evolution can act. It is also one of the difficulties of current sociobiological theory. Whereas a gene is a biological unit with scientifically measurable boundaries, no agreed-upon measurement is currently available for the meme.

old members' death rate (Alexander 1977). For Ball, "parasitic memes" ordinarily are expunged when natural selection results in psychological traits causing individuals to resist them. From the present perspective, such "memes" would be culturally transmitted misinformation in that they reduce fitness. They are stretch factors. Their elimination through natural selection would be a "genetic response."

Elites Appropriate

Social inequality may well be a major source of fitness-reducing culture traits. Hunter-gatherer (some prefer "foraging") societies are generally highly egalitarian: all individuals enjoy approximately the same standard of living, the same diet, and the same comforts.[12] Everywhere else, to varying degrees, inequality reigns. The high in status are likely to use their position to promote culture traits directly or indirectly in their own fitness interests. But discussion of social inequality first requires emphasizing the distinction between "society" and "culture."

A *society* refers to an actual group of people and how they order their social relations. A *culture,* as was noted previously, refers to a body of socially transmitted information and is therefore a broader term than "society." Because small-scale societies are usually culturally homogeneous, the terms are often used interchangeably. Larger scale societies, however, generally include diverse cultures or subcultures. Even where they do not, they exhibit social stratification.

Inequalities and conflicts among the components of a society are ubiquitous. Indeed, for sociology's "conflict theorists" (e.g., Marxists), conflict is the key to social process.[13] But a sociobiological theory of society too is, necessarily, a conflict theory. In sociobiological terms, the ultimate goal of the competition is not power, wealth, or control over the means of production: However often these are sought, they are not seen as ends in themselves but rather as instruments for the attainment of *reproductive advantage.*[i]

There is continuing discussion over the extent to which wealth, power, and prestige are indeed associated with reproductive advantage (e.g., Barkow 1977; Barkow and Burley 1980; Irons 1979; Vining 1986). Clearly, there is at least some reason to believe that, in our own zero-population growth North American and Western European societies, the association is not inevitable. For nonindustrial societies, however, the case is clearer for power equalling reproductive advantage. Betzig's (1986) cross-cultural survey, for example, establishes that, in such societies, there is a strong association between physical power over the lives of others and number of wives and children.

It seems reasonable to suggest that powerful elites are likely to manipulate culture traits in the interests of maintaining their status and, therefore indirectly, their possible reproductive advantage. Thus, much of ideology and religion can arguably be interpreted as reflecting efforts by elites to buttress their position. The resulting socially transmitted information may have to do with the powerful having much *mana* as in parts of Oceania, having

---

[12] Modern evolutionists and sociobiologists point out that if human biology is particularly suited to any lifestyle, it must be hunting and gathering. It is the only lifestyle that has existed for long enough for biological evolution to take place. This is a new twist on a very old idea. Recall that nineteenth-century evolutionary theorists supposed that primitive societies were "living fossils." Sociobiologists say that modern hunter-gatherers may not be living fossils in the nineteenth-century sense, but they replicate in part the lifestyle of early humans. The argument is important in the context of social inequality since it suggests that human society was, by evolutionary design, egalitarian. Therefore social inequality may be an important source of "stretch."

[13] Barkow mentions Marx, but as he points out, sociobiology is not in any meaningful way a Marxist theory. Marxism has nothing to do with reproductive advantage (in fact, Marx rejected Darwin's view of evolution and accepted that of Lamarck).

Despite the fact that the link between sociobiology and Marxism is weak, the argument presented here is powerfully similar to Marx's analysis of religion. Marx and Barkow agree that the role of religion is to reinforce the position of elites. However, for Marxists the goal is the maintenance of control over resources; for sociobiologists, it is reproductive advantage.

the approval of a personified supernatural being ("by god anointed"), or ruling in the name of a "dictatorship of the proletariat." In general, elites strive to convince the rest of the population that what is in the interests of the elite is also in the interests of the non-elite. For example, *droit de seigneur*[14] is typically defined as an "honor" for the bridegroom (MacDonald 1983). Of course, elites may at times accidentally undermine their own positions and often enough fail to prevail. However, to the extent that the elite succeed in introducing information into the culture that reaffirms their high position and leads to their reproductive advantage, they are acting in a manner likely to be contrary to the fitness interests of the rest of the society (since the interests of the non-elite presumably lie either in egalitarianism or in themselves becoming members of the elite).

Because children actively engage in cognitive mapping of physical and social reality, they are likely to be especially vulnerable to such manipulation of cultural information in the interests of others. If this reasoning is accurate, then we would expect children to be readily persuaded, for example, to enlist in "holy wars" and "children's crusades" that, in fact, are more in the interests of an older elite than in their own.

Not just secular but much of religious ideology, as well, it has been argued, represents manipulative misinformation disseminated by those whose fitness interests are thereby served (Alexander 1974; van den Berghe 1979; Lumsden and Wilson 1985, p. 350). Christianity is not the only Nietzschean "slave religion": any belief system that teaches acceptance and forbearance in order to achieve supernatural reward after death may be in effect supporting existing inequalities.[15] Hinduism, too, for example, with its concepts of the transmigration of the soul and accumulated karmic burden, also potentially serves to support existing political systems. The same can be said of the much smaller-scale religion of the Migili (or Koro) of Nigeria's Middle Belt, where the senior age-grade's monopoly of supernatural authority certainly buttressed this gerontocracy (Barkow 1982).

On the other hand, the politically less powerful are not necessarily powerless. In the area of religion, for example, they may succeed in spreading the belief that they are morally superior or even supernaturally more powerful than are those who rule: Moral authority can channel discontent into revolution, as the Shah of Iran discovered.[16] Alternatively, the ruler may find himself so hedged about with ritual restrictions and taboos as to find his actual power curtailed. And, of course, the weak of one year may be the powerful in the next. None of this lessens the reality of an unequal division of political power, within most societies.

Social inequality may thus be a major cause of stretch. Relative reproductive advantage is just that: relative. Advantage for one component of a society (whether a class or a cultural group) means disadvantage for another. The culture's pool of information can arguably be viewed as an arena for conflict as each faction or stratum struggles to revise the common culture for its own advantage. The victors rewrite the history books, revise the genealogies, and recreate the religion. From their perspective, the result is culture revision; from the perspective of the losers, the result is culture stretch. The transmission of culture involves conflict over information.[17]

---

[14] The *droit de seigneur* referred to here is the right of the medieval lord to have sex with the wives of his serfs.

[15] Friedrich Wilhelm Nietzsche (1844–1900) was a German philosopher who believed in the emergence of a new sort of person. Nietzsche, like Marx, believed that Christianity was a tool of domination and therefore a "slave religion." Barkow suggests that domination is one of the functions of many religions.

[16] The American-supported Shah of Iran, Mohammed Reza Shah Pahlavi (1919–1980), controlled a large modern military and secret police, but was overthrown by a conservative Moslem movement led by Ayatollah Ruhollah Khomeini (1902–1989).

[17] Implicit here is the question of scale. This sort of stretch operates at the group level, but how can that group be defined, and does such a group act consistently? Interestingly, Barkow provides insights here with which postmodernists, who are generally extremely critical of sociobiology, would feel at home. History and political power involve conflict over control of the narrative.

Advantages Entail Expenses: Trade-offs

Pharmaceuticals have both intended and unintended (or "side-") effects. Culture traits are similar. Like a new drug, a new culture trait is likely to be adopted when the benefits outweigh the costs. But "costs" and "benefits" in this case have to do with fitness. The costs to fitness of a cultural innovation may be considerable.

For example, Brothwell and Brothwell (1969, p. 181) argue that vitamin C deficiency probably was unknown, prior to the Neolithic. A forager's diet is likely to include a sufficient variety of fruits and vegetables to supply this nutrient. The Neolithic meant urban life, farming and animal husbandry, and a greatly narrowed diet. Unlike foragers, cultivators tend to limit the range of foods consumed and eventually to develop "superfoods," staples (such as maize, rice, bread, etc.) that loom so large in the daily diet that they become synonymous with the idea of "food": a meal without them is no meal but a mere snack. Malnutrition is often the result, because the smaller the range of foods consumed, the less likely the diet is to be balanced. It is reasonable to assume that the Neolithic on the whole meant fitness-enhancing cultural traits, such as craft specialists and the production of surpluses. But its cost may, if the Brothwells are correct, have been a greater risk of nutritional deficiency diseases.

In similar fashion, irrigation, while obviously enhancing fitness by improving the food supply, has had unanticipated negative consequences in many parts of the world. For example, irrigation provides breeding places for the respective vectors of malaria and schistosomiasis (Cockburn

1971). Without my wishing to espouse the cause of the Luddites, it is nevertheless likely that every technological innovation carries with it some deleterious consequences: Costs as well as benefits exist, even when the latter outweigh the former.[18] If one keeps in mind the earlier discussion of inequality, it is also common for the benefits of an innovation to be enjoyed by one segment of a society and the costs carried by another. In short, the adoption of "beneficial" culture traits may be a cause of fitness-reducing culture stretch.

I have now reviewed four processes, each of which may contribute to culture stretch, i.e., may add fitness-reducing information to the culture. But we also know (if only because our culture-bearing species continues to exist) that there must be countervailing, stretch-reducing processes. In the next section, I will argue that it is the psychological traits of our species that generate these stretch-reducing processes, so that we continually revise our cultures.

MECHANISMS OF CULTURE REVISION

I will assume that culture transmission and revision constitute a single set of processes with a single set of underlying mechanisms responsible for both.[19] Unfortunately, our understanding of these processes and mechanisms is preliminary. The mechanisms possibly vary with the age of the individual, so that children, for example, may acquire cultural information in a manner different from that of adults (an assumption that is relatively uncontroversial, if restricted to language acquisition, at least). I will also assume that cul-

---

[18] Luddites are against technological innovation. The term refers to members of an early nineteenth-century English working-class movement who opposed the Industrial Revolution out of fear that it would destroy their livelihoods. The movement was named after Ned Ludd, a rebellious eighteenth-century worker, who was, perhaps, fictional.

[19] Barkow here proposes a sociobiological theory of cultural change. His essential claim is that cultural revision will occur in the general direction of increased fitness and will take place as part of the transmission of cultural information from one individual or group to another.

This formulation is powerful for sociobiologists for two reasons. First, it enables them to frame their discussion in terms of memes, the units of social behavior that reproduce. Second, by phrasing the issue as one of transmission, mathematical concepts, such as information theory, can be applied to the passing of cultural information. From the sociobiological perspective, the problem is that much of the literature on the issue of enculturation comes from psychology (or culture and personality) and cannot be easily reformulated to fit the sociobiological model.

ture transmission/revision varies with the category of cultural information involved.[j]

No theory of culture transmission/revision of which I am aware deals with the interaction between age-of-individual and type-of-cultural information being transmitted/revised. What we do have, currently, are unintegrated theories that focus on the child, usually under the headings of socialization, personality development, cognitive development, and education (LeVine 1982). There are also approaches to culture transmission/revision that take population genetics as their model (e.g., Pulliam and Dunford 1980; Lumsden and Wilson 1981; Boyd and Richerson 1985). These theories focus on factors that are assumed to affect the relative frequencies of cultural units believed to be analogous to genes. By their very nature, transmission theories must abridge and simplify precisely the ground covered by the child-centered theories (i.e., personality development, cognitive development, socialization practices, and education), while paying little or no attention to social processes involving conflict. Thus, while they are intriguing, these efforts represent only a point of departure, and it can be anticipated that they will become far more complex in the future. Richerson and Boyd [1989] present transmission models that do appear to be moving in the direction of incorporating more complex psychological-level mechanisms in their models.

Unfortunately, the discussion that follows will not rectify the lack of a comprehensive theory of culture transmission/revision. It will only focus on several probable mechanisms with which such a theory is likely to deal.

Imitation and Prestige

Children do not imitate indiscriminately — they imitate some people more than others. The more important, powerful, successful,

and liked the other people are, the more a child will imitate them. Also, the people they see most often are the ones they imitate most. Parents fit all these criteria and they are the primary models for a child during the early years. (Sears et al. 1985, p. 270)

This quotation, from a widely used American social psychology textbook, indirectly explains much about both culture revision and culture stability. Human beings tend to give esteem to those who succeed in gaining or maintaining control over resources.[20] The acquisition of cultural goals and plans depends heavily on the relative standing of those who model them. Thus, effective strategies for resource control will tend to proliferate in the culture, at the expense of ineffective strategies. The prestigious hunter in his foraging society will be imitated by the children. The "many-mother" in the society with great esteem for fertility will be a role model. Yet, suppose the game is gone or it is the parents of the educated rather than of the numerous who are most respected: The prestige of the hunter and of the perpetually pregnant will fall. In their place may be the fur trapper or the woman who sends her children to school. The child will now learn from these others, and the culture will be revised. Here is a less hypothetical account of the relationship among imitation, prestige, and culture change.

The Migili (Koro) of Nigeria's Middle Belt were until recently a gerontocracy organized in terms of age-grades. The senior age-grade held most of the political and religious power. The age-grade of vigorous younger men (roughly 18–35) did most of the heavy physical labor required by this yam-growing society. Preparing hills in which to plant yams is an arduous task and the younger men did it for the senior men, for all the women, and for each other.

In the early 1960s, missionaries and a new road ended their isolation and changed the society

---

[20] One criticism of sociobiology is that it tends to be profoundly politically conservative. Sociobiologists often argue that what the most successful want for society must be the right thing because they are the most successful. Barkow's argument might be perceived in this way in that he suggests that imitation of the successful increases personal fitness. But Barkow's position is more complex. Nineteenth-century evolutionists saw evolution as a process that would result in ever more perfect forms. It was therefore morally correct. Modern evolutionists make no claims about the ends of evolution. Bear in mind that Barkow, unlike the Spencerians, believes that on a cultural level imitation of the successful might be maladaptive.

radically and quickly. Younger Migili men and women were taught that their respected elders lied to them and that the gods they worshiped were not real gods. The Migili were exposed to other groups (including the missionaries), groups that could marshal far more in power and wealth than could their own elders. They learned that their people, including their elders, were despised as ignorant, dirty "bush" people whose purple *galura* pigment (with which they dyed their clothing) and their distinctive hair styles were symbols of inferiority. In 1967, some of the younger men, along with some Migili members of the Nigerian army who were home on leave, forcibly seized several elders in the market place and cut off their hair. The younger men now began to refuse to work for the elders, instead putting their labor into their own fields. The value of produce had increased greatly, shortly before this time, and the young men discovered how much money yams were now worth, and what that money could buy. The age-graded gerontocracy collapsed, the people converted almost *en masse* to Roman Catholicism, and the elders and women had to rely on neighbors and close kin to help in the most strenuous tasks — tasks that now were performed for them only when and if the young men were finished with their own work.

When the elders had been perceived as high in status and as being in control of key resources, they were imitated and the culture perpetuated itself. Once a change in scale showed the elders to be low in prestige and power in the wider society, they were no longer considered worthy of being learned from. Young men and women looked elsewhere, particularly to Christians of other Nigerian ethnic groups, for models[21] (based on Barkow [1982] and on unpublished field notes).[k]

Similar tales can be garnered from the literature of ethnicity and assimilation. Immigrant children often perceive their parents as low in status and power and model themselves after dominant individuals. They may reject the parental language and values. More self-aware, as adults, they may seek their lost "roots," possibly reflecting a new and higher evaluation of the relative standing of their ethnic group. But groups are not equally subject to the "melting pot" process. If children's experiences are shaped such that they never cease to see their home culture as of high standing, then they should be resistant to acculturation.[l]

Child and Adolescent Rebelliousness

The extent to which child and adolescent rebelliousness is stretch correcting is an important but unstudied question. This gap seems odd, in view of the immense literature on child and adolescent cognitive, emotional and social development, and on parent-child attachment. Little if any of that literature, however, concerns itself with culture transmission and change *per se*. For example, some reports suggest that fathers who play little or no role in child rearing tend to have physically aggressive sons (Whiting and Whiting 1975), but we do not know how this factor affects culture transmission or how it is linked to social learning. It seems likely that it is so linked, because the emotional warmth of models affects what we learn from them (Bandura 1977). One of the "tasks" of adolescence is that of establishing an "identity." Elsewhere, I have argued that "identity" in this context closely equates with being a member of a social group (1975). Membership involves a young person's "weighing" the status of the various groups and categories into which he

---

[21] The mainstream of Boasian anthropolgy might view events among the Migili in very different terms — as the domination of an isolated tribal people by outsiders and their resulting acculturation. For most anthropologists, it might be a moral issue — with morality resting on the side of the shorn elders. Sociobiology, however, imposes its own morality, sometimes dubbed the "morality of the gene." In its extreme form, this morality suggests that whatever increases fitness is, by definition, good. Ethics have no place in scientific inquiry. However, it is also possible to take the view that while nature is beyond morality, humans are not. Sociobiology merely shows certain trends in human society. Individuals and societies can and, on occasion must, move in directions opposite these trends. For example, while the sociobiological trend in the case described here is toward acculturation, it may be that there is a moral case against it. Perhaps the conclusion to be drawn is that those concerned about Migili acculturation have much work to do. Sociobiology does not suggest that such action would be wrong, simply that it will be difficult.

or she might be accepted. Note that such weighing of social identities and group memberships is itself a revising of culture in that the frequencies of particular sets of roles and statuses are affected. Thus, the winning-a-position and revising-the-culture processes for the adolescent appear to be at least somewhat coincident. Note, too, that the sensitivity to peer-group pressure and to social status often characteristic of adolescents favors both of these processes.[22]

Oppression and Rebellion

Resistance to oppression appears to be an evolved social psychological trait of our species (see also Wilson 1975). Recalling the earlier discussion of "elites appropriate," low-power social groups occasionally seek to alter their society and revise their culture through physical violence. A detailed discussion of the factors that determine whether revolution actually takes place is beyond the scope of this paper. Presumably, each individual involved in effect weighs the relative costs and benefits of the status quo versus revolution.[23] Presumably, too, the balance between individual and collective solutions is of importance. So long as each individual as an individual believes it possible that he/she (or at least his/her children) may escape the situation through personal effort, the rebellion is probably unlikely. Stable systems of oppression are probably those in which there is always reason to hope, and the most stable of all are those that appear to permit the upward mobility of the most able of the oppressed (thereby depriving the remainder of the oppressed of capable leadership). Caste systems depending heavily on physical ("racial") features thus seem likely to be more unstable than are others because they presumably make it difficult for the low castes to believe in the promise of upward mobility. Where caste systems do succeed in attaining stability, they appear to rely heavily on religions that teach the oppressed that the reward for accepting their situation comes after death.[24]

Another evolved constellation of stretch-reducing social psychological traits involves our apparent readiness to revise culture in the face of external threats. This tendency appears to be related to the "ethnocentrism syndrome" (LeVine and Campbell 1972). In their view, ingroup solidarity usually increases in the face of external threat. So, presumably, does the strength of ideologies justifying ingroup solidarity.

Deliberate Socialization

Culture revision involves conscious, deliberate decision-making as well as nonvolitional processes. These points can be illustrated by parental child-training *decisions*.

In 1968, a thoughtful Maguzawa father (a member of a historically resistant-to-Islam Hausa group of northern Nigeria) confided to me that he was giving one of his sons to the Christian missionaries to be educated, another to the Moslem teachers (*mallams*). He did not know which path was best for the future, but he was convinced that there was no future in his traditional religion. Soon, he explained, everyone would have to be a Christian or a Moslem. His mien was sad, as we discussed the future, but he was doing what he felt was best for his children.

Thoughtfully trying "to do what is best for the children" may not be universal, but it does seem

---

[22] Barkow's analysis of adolescent rebellion seems to be more of a suspicion than a demonstration. It might be appropriate to ask in what ways the peer-group identity choices he mentions in this passage are different from the prestige-based imitation described and documented in the preceding section.

[23] Note that Barkow assumes extreme rationality – people actually calculate where their best interests lie. Is this the case? What about the power of crowd psychology? Psychologists and sociologists have argued that the essence of crowd behavior is its lack of rationality.

[24] Here again sociobiological thinking runs curiously close to Marxist thought, although there is a critical difference between them. Barkow and Edward O. Wilson (and here Barkow is citing Wilson's seminal work *Sociobiology: The New Synthesis*) suggest that a desire for egalitarianism is built into human genetics due to the evolutionary development of hunter-gatherer society. Marxists claim that oppression and resistance to it are built into social organization. They claim that rebellion against oppression is part of the historical process of the dialectic.

quite widespread. Assuming that this tendency does arise frequently among parents, then it would appear to help to move culture in fitness-enhancing directions. Many parents do not simply attempt to replicate themselves in their children: They try to prepare them for the future. During times of change, that may mean deliberately socializing them in a new manner or deliberately exposing them to socializing influences absent during their own youth.[m]

THE REVISION OF MALADAPTIVE CULTURE TRAITS

We have seen that, in theory, our cultures may include some fitness-reducing traits. What are the likely consequences of socially transmitted information that tends to lead to behavior that reduces genetic fitness? Four possibilities will be discussed.

1. If the information is stably transmitted for a sufficient number of generations while continuing to be maladaptive, then, assuming sufficient relevant genetic variance in the gene pool and assuming at least partial genetic isolation of the local population, natural selection will tend to eliminate the information.[25] Presumably, there will be selection for some kind of learning bias against the information (what Boyd and Richerson [1985] would term a "direct bias"). It has not, however, been established that the population structure and long-term cultural stability necessary for this process have ever existed, in modern hominid populations.[n] A genetically based revision therefore is probably the least likely consequence of a maladaptive culture trait.

2. Suppose the maladaptive trait is of a type that has frequently recurred in the course of our evolution. Let us take the example of the labelling of a potential nutriment as a nonfood. In such a

case, selection might long ago have resulted in a revision mechanism or (more likely) in the strengthening of an existing individual fitness-enhancing tendency that also revises this type of culture stretch. In the mislabeled nutriment case, one can conjecture that the mechanism might be the child's tendency to sample indiscriminately or, alternatively, that the mechanism is the tendency for those stricken by famine to be relatively unselective in their choice of food. Such mechanisms appear to have both individual fitness-enhancing and culture-revising consequences. For example, the adults might be lying to the child about favored foods in order to keep them for themselves, or simply be wrong about what is edible—while the starving have little to lose and much to gain by experimenting with new foods. Either mechanism might both enhance individual fitness and at the same time revise culture by correcting the mislabeling of a nutriment. These examples illustrate how, when appropriate psychological mechanisms already exist, fitness-reducing information may be eliminated quickly.

If, on the other hand, the maladaptive trait is quite novel and is not affected by existing psychological mechanisms, then the trait may endure. The medical system and colostrum-denial examples presented earlier appear to be of this nature. Contraception plus the female's control over her own fertility may be another novel and (at least at times) fitness-reducing trait, as Barkow and Burley (1980) have argued. Decoupling copulation from gravidity has left people free to seek the former without risk of the latter. The frequency with which individuals in our own society are choosing to have one or no children suggests that our species lacks a psychological mechanism that is to fertility reduction what the tendency of the starving to sample anything is to the mislabeling of nutriments.[26]

---

[25] The presupposition here is that given enough time, cultural behavior, which Barkow defines in the first section of this essay, could be directly coded in genes. However, among humans, this has not happened because no population has ever been isolated for enough time to permit it.

[26] Effective human control of pregnancy is a new trait, and though it might be fitness reducing, it has not been around long enough for evolution to respond to it.

3. Suppose the maladaptive trait has negative consequences only for the less powerful but is adaptive for the powerful, in a society marked by great social inequality. All things being equal, it seems reasonable to expect the information in question to endure longer than it would were its respective effects on the powerful and powerless reversed.

4. There is little reason to expect "advantages entail expenses" culture traits to be revised because until the long-term expenses actually arrive, these traits are not maladaptive, but adaptive. The only mechanism likely to correct such traits early is that of "deliberate socialization," as when parents predict that the fishery will eventually be depleted and train their offspring for other kinds of economic activity.[27]

MALADAPTATION VERSUS COLLECTIVE GOOD: A CAVEAT

Cultural traits apparently maladaptive at the level of the individual may be adaptive for the group, perhaps helping maintain the high level of human cooperativeness and sociality. Such traits might include (nonkin, nonreciprocal) altruism, patriotism, and willingness to accept a lower social rank than one might otherwise achieve. Campbell (1975) and Boyd and Richerson (1985) argue for the possibility of group selection at the cultural level. In their view, the more internally cooperative cultures may have been more likely qua cultures to survive and reproduce, in spite of the depressed genetic fitness of particularly norm-observing individuals. Campbell (1972, 1975, 1982, 1983) has repeatedly emphasized the role of internalized norms, morality and religion in restraining individual "self-

ishness" (including genetic selfishness) for the benefit of the collectivity.[o]

CONCLUSIONS AND RESEARCH IMPLICATIONS

The Individual and Looseness of Fit

Culture transmission has been presented here as a highly problematic process, with each individual in each generation being the revisor, editor, and often, innovator, of socially transmitted information. Though the individual may revise culture in fitness-enhancing ways, he or she is also capable of error, the culture-revision psychological mechanisms being very approximate.[28] We are very far indeed from the old anthropological notion of an automatic process of "enculturation" during which individuals served only as successive generations of passive pitchers for the storing and pouring of the unchanging waters of culture.

If this paper's arguments for socially transmitted information readily moving in fitness-reducing directions are at all valid, and if it is correct that the revision process is not necessarily successful, then we should expect some culture traits to be maladaptive. The relationship between genetic fitness and culture is apparently loose and not always predictable. This looseness has implications for research strategies in human sociobiology, the most important of which is that the testing of whether culturally ordered behaviors do or do not optimize fitness is an inherently weak research strategy. Elsewhere (footnote [f] and Barkow and Burley 1980), I have argued that a culture trait may for the moment enhance fitness purely as an epiphenomenon, with no implications for either past or future selection. We now see that cultural

---

[27] This again references the tragedy of the commons, which is called tragic because, for economic reasons, the behavior that leads to it is unlikely to be revised until disaster occurs.

[28] Traditionally, sociobiologists assumed that traits were fitness enhancing by virtue of existence. Barkow raises the likelihood that maladaptive traits are common. Thus, sociobiologists must prove that traits are adaptive. This task is quite difficult since the success or failure of a particular trait can only be seen over a long time – a longer time than that for which anthropologists generally observe culture. As a result, conclusions about the adaptive value of human cultural characteristics, Barkow suggests, are weak and often premature. This is a curious parallel to the Boasian position that theorizing about general laws of culture is premature.

traits may also at times reduce fitness. Thus, without detailed specification of the particular, individual-level evolved mechanisms involved, adaptationist interpretations of culture traits are unconvincing (Barkow 1984). Moreover, even the strongest confirmation that culturally patterned behavior is consistent with a fitness optimization model begs the question of process: What are the underlying mechanisms, what is the nature of the social interaction that generates this fitness?

An alternative and perhaps complementary strategy to that of attempting to match fitness optimization model and culture trait is to focus on the psychological-level mechanisms. This latter strategy can exist on its own, or it can complement research on the match between optimization models and culture traits by seeking the intervening processes. In any event, it is difficult to see how we can arrive at a full sociobiological theory of culture and culture transmission and change until the individual-level psychological mechanisms affecting socially transmitted information are better known.

Notes

a. This article is in part based on Chapter XII of Barkow (1989). I wish to thank Colin Irwin, Robert Boyd, and Peter Richerson for their comments on an earlier draft, and Michael McGuire for editing and pruning. Received April 1, 1987; revised July 25, 1987. Address reprint requests to: Jerome H. Barkow, Ph.D., Department of Sociology and Social Anthropology, Dalhousie University, Halifax, Nova Scotia, Canada B3H 1T2.

b. I am begging the question of whether culture is or is not "particulate." There are many kinds of cultural information, and it may be useful to treat some categories as particulate, for certain purposes (e.g., the mathematics of transmission models), while for other purposes, such as understanding how a political system works, the particulate approach would be pointless. See Barkow (1989) for further discussion. See that reference, too, for an explanation of why the definition of culture given here includes the phrase at least somewhat organized. For me, species that socially transmit unconnected items of information are best considered as having not culture but protoculture.

c. Throughout this paper, the term "psychological" is used as a synonym for "at the level of the individual" and contrasts with sociological rather than, e.g., with neurophysiological. Thus, the phrase "psy-

chological mechanism" is intended to be entirely agnostic as to the precise nature of the mechanism in question, asserting only that a specified mechanism exists and that it is an attribute of an individual rather than of a collectivity.

d. See Brandon and Burian (1984) for discussions of this problem.

e. Indeed, if one is willing to speak of a global capacity for culture, then one can argue that there are no maladaptive culture traits, only costs of our (on-balance) adaptive cultural capacity. The distinction between "cost-of-an-adaptation" and "maladaptive trait" often appears arbitrary, particularly when we deal with culture. Nevertheless, it is important, because we expect selection pressure against maladaptive, not adaptive, traits. The lesson may be that the more molecular our view, the more likely we are to find maladaptation.

f. The "stretch" metaphor should not make invisible the possibility that culture will for short periods lead us to enhance genetic fitness for reasons having nothing to do with previous evolution. Thus, as Barkow and Burley (1980) point out, peasants have large families and thereby enhance their genetic fitness. But they have these families because they need the work force and also the security for old age that children bring and not because past genetic selection has created some kind of unconscious "drive" for large families.

g. Richerson and Boyd ([1989], Boyd and Richerson 1985) would argue that this kind of tragedy of the commons situation can be overcome by cultural group selection.

h. By "challenge," I mean examine with a view towards revision.

i. Nonsociobiological conflict theories take these instrumental goals for ultimate goals but are otherwise far more consonant with sociobiology than are such consensus-oriented social theories as, say, structural-functionalism.

j. For a discussion of some suggested categories of cultural information and the different selection pressures involved with each, see Chapter VII of Barkow (1989).

k. Did these young people thereby increase their fitness? For some sociobiologists this question is crucial. From my own perspective, however, it is of only slight interest, since the Migili case would be only one case, one quite likely very different from the situations obtaining earlier in our evolution, when the imitate-the-high-in-status mechanism presumably evolved. For me, the crucial questions have to do with whether the mechanism can account for the ways in which Migili culture has been changing and whether it is consistent with more general theories of culture change and with broader psychological and social psychological theories. See the section headed "Conclusions and Research Implications" for further discussion along these lines.

l. If this hypothesis fits events in the world, then one would predict that culturally conservative, resistant-to-acculturation groups such as the Masai or Hutterites succeed in conveying to their children a perception of the home culture as superior to competing peoples in prestige and in control over vital resources.

m. Such deliberate socialization often is unsuccessful (LeVine 1982), given that parents are not perfect behavioral engineers and their predictions may be inaccurate: but presumably at times it does succeed, and, in any event, it alters the culture.

n. Long-term cultural stability may, however, have occurred during the Paleolithic, given the immense duration of the Oldowan and Chellean-Acheulean lithic traditions.

o. This view is in contrast to the conflict theory approach presented in my earlier discussion of how "elites appropriate."

References

Alexander, Richard D. The evolution of social behavior. *Annual Review of Systematics* 5:325–383, 1974.

———. Natural selection and the analysis of human sociality. In *Changing Scenes in the Natural Sciences, 1776–1976*, C. E. Gouden (Ed.) Special Publication 12 of the Academy of Natural Sciences. Philadelphia: Academy of Natural Sciences, 1977, pp. 283–337.

Ball, John A. Memes as replicators. *Ethology and Sociobiology* 5:145–161, 1984.

Bandura, W. *Social Learning Theory.* Englewood Cliffs, N.J.: Prentice-Hall, 1977.

Barkow, Jerome H. Prestige and culture: A biosocial approach. *Current Anthropology* 16:553–572, 1975.

———. Conformity to ethos and reproductive success in two Hausa communities: An empirical evaluation. *Ethos* 5:409–425,1977.

———. Return to nepotism: The collapse of a Nigerian gerontocracy. *International Journal of Political Science Review* 3:33–49, 1982.

———. *Joinings: An Evolutionary Frame for Self and Culture.* Toronto: University of Toronto Press, 1989. Forthcoming.

———, and Burley, Nancy. Human fertility, evolutionary biology, and the demographic transition. *Ethology and Sociobiology* 1:163–180, 1980.

———, and Hallett, Angela L. *The Denial of Colostrum.* Focus I of Chapter XII of Barkow (1989).

Berland, J. C. *No Five Fingers Are Alike. Cognitive Amplifiers in Social Context.* Cambridge, Mass: Harvard University Press, 1982.

Betzig, L. L. *Despotism and Differential Reproduction. A Darwinian View of History.* New York: Aldine, 1986.

Boyd, R., and Richerson, P. J. *Culture and the Evolutionary Process.* Chicago: University of Chicago Press, 1985.

Brandon, Robert N., and Burian, Richard M. (eds). *Genes, Organisms, Populations, Controversies over the Units of Selection.* Boston: Bradford/MIT Press, 1984.

Brothwell, D., and Brothwell, P. *Food in Antiquity.* A Survey of the Diet of Early Peoples. London: Thames and Hudson, 1969.

Campbell, D. T. On the genetics of altruism and the counter-hedonic components in human culture. *Journal of Social Issues* 28:21–37, 1972.

———. On the conflicts between biological and social evolution and between psychology and moral tradition. *American Psychology* 30:1103–1126, 1975.

———. Legal and primary-group social controls. *Journal of Social Biological Structures* 5:431–438, 1982.

———. The two distinct routes beyond kin selection to ultrasociality. Implications for the humanities and social sciences. In *The Nature of Prosocial Development: Interdisciplinary Theories and Strategies*, D. L. Bridgemen (Ed.) New York: Academic Press, 1983.

Cockburn, T. Aidan. Infectious diseases in ancient populations. *Current Anthropology* 12:45–62, 1971.

Dawkins, Richard. *The Selfish Gene.* Oxford: Oxford University Press, 1976.

———. *The Extended Phenotype: The Gene as the University of Selection.* Oxford and San Francisco: W. H. Freeman, 1982.

Foley, Robert. Optimality theory in anthropology. *Man* 20:222–242, 1985.

Hardin, G. The tragedy of the commons. *Science* 162: 1243, 1968. *Reprinted in Population, Evolution, and Birth Control, A Collage of Controversial Ideas*, G. Hardin (Ed.). San Francisco: Freeman, 1969, p. 367. Also reprinted in *Managing the Commons*, G. Hardin and J. Baden (Eds). San Francisco: W. H. Freeman, 1977.

Irons, William. Natural selection, adaptation, and human social behavior. In *Evolutionary Biology and Human Social Behavior: An Anthropological Perspective*, N. A. Chagnon and W. Irons (Eds). North Scituate: Duxbury, 1979, pp. 4–38.

LeVine, Robert A., and Campbell, D. T. *Ethnocentrism: Theories of Conflict, Ethnic Attitudes and Group Behavior.* New York: Wiley, 1972.

———. *Culture, Behavior, and Personality.* 2nd ed. Chicago: Aldine, 1982.

Lumsden, Charles J., and Wilson, Edward O. *Genes, Mind, and Culture.* Cambridge, Mass.: Harvard University Press, 1981.

———. The relation between biological and cultural evolution. *Journal of Social and Biological Structures* 8: 343–359, 1985.

MacDonald, K. Production, social controls, and ideology: Toward a sociobiology of the phenotype. *Journal of Social and Biological Structures* 6:297–317, 1983.

MacLean, U. *Magical Medicine: A Nigerian Case-Study.* Harmondsworth, Middlesex: Penguin Books, 1971.

Pulliam, H. R., and Dunford, C. *Programmed to Learn.* New York: Columbia University Press, 1980.

Rosenberg, E. M. Demographic Effects of Sex-Differential Nutrition. In *Nutritional Anthropology. Contemporary Approaches to Diet and Culture,* N. W. Jerome, R. F. Kandel, and G. H. Pelto, (Eds). Pleasantville, N.Y.: Redgrave, 1980, pp. 181–204.

Sears, D. O., Freedman, J. L., and Peplau, L. A. *Social Psychology.* 5th ed. Englewood Cliffs, N.J.: Prentice-Hall, 1985.

Sebrell, William H., Jr., Haggerty, James H., and the Editors of Life. *Food and Nutrition.* New York: Time, 1967.

Taylor, Carl E., et al. Asian medical systems: A symposium on the role of comparative sociology in improving health care. *Social Science and Medicine* 7:307–318, 1973.

van den Berghe, P., *Human Family Systems.* New York: Elsevier, 1979.

Vining, Daniel R., Jr. Social versus reproductive success: The central theoretical problem of human sociobiology. *Behavioral and Brain Sciences* 9:187–216, 1986.

Whiting, J. W. M, and Whiting, B. B. Aloofness and intimacy between husbands and wives. *Ethos* 3:183–207, 1975.

Wilson, Edward O. *Sociobiology: The New Synthesis.* Cambridge, Mass.: Belknap Press of Harvard University Press, 1975.

Wood, Corinne Shear. *Human Sickness and Health: A Biocultural View.* Fullerton, California: Mayfield, 1979.

Anthropology and Gender: The Feminist Critique

Unlike many disciplines, in anthropology women have reached high levels of professional achievement and gained popular recognition for their work. In this century, women such as Ruth Benedict and Margaret Mead have become household names, while others such as Mary Douglas (1921–), Laura Bohannon (1922–), Sherry Ortner (1941–), Michelle Rosaldo (1944?–1981), Peggy Reeves Sanday (1937–), Louise Lamphere (1940–), Lila Abu-Lughod (1952–), and Marilyn Strathern (1941–) are widely known to scholars outside of anthropology.

Despite the achievements of women within the discipline, until recently, discussions of women in the anthropological literature were usually limited to introductory textbook chapters on marriage, family, and kinship. Beginning in the 1970s, however, women anthropologists began to question some of the male-centered assumptions within anthropology and to focus their research specifically on women's statuses and roles in societies around the world. Since that time, interest in the study of gender roles and focus on gender and sexuality in a cross-cultural perspective has increased, and some of the basic assumptions of anthropology have been called into question. Many feminist anthropologists have documented the failure of the discipline to fully explore human experience because it has neglected women and gender as significant dimensions of social life (Morgen 1989:1).

Much of the research by feminist anthropologists in the early 1970s was concerned with documenting women's lives and their roles in societies around the world. Virtually all of these early studies assumed universal sexual asymmetry—that is, the worldwide subordination of women—and sought to explain this situation through various theoretical perspectives. For example, Freidl (1975) attempted to explain the position of women from a materialist perspective by focusing on women's subsistence roles. Chodorow (1974) examined the issue of subordination from a psychological view, emphasizing the role of childhood socialization in the formation of sex roles. In particular, Michelle Rosaldo and Louise Lamphere's 1974 volume *Women, Culture, and Society* and Reyna Reiter's 1975 anthology *Toward an Anthropology of Women* were two of the defining works in this era of feminist anthropology.

At the same time that feminist cultural anthropologists focused on gender inequality, research on women and gender by feminist archaeologists and physical anthropologists challenged the "man the hunter" version of human evolution. Work on this issue, such as the 1975 essay by physical anthropologist Sally Slocum (1939–) in this volume (32), charged that women's roles in human evolution had been ignored because scholars focused on hunting rather than gathering. For instance, Slocum challenges the popular idea that hunting by men, because it implied toolmaking, communication, and the development of complex cognitive skills (Washburn and Lancaster 1968), played a pivotal role in our evolutionary past. She stresses that women's gathering and child care also demanded complex communication, cooperation, and toolmaking. Slocum argues that evidence indicates foraging, not hunting, was the principal economic strategy throughout most of human evolutionary history (Lamphere 1987:16). This "woman the gatherer" approach inspired scholars to revise the standard views on human evolution. One particularly significant study was Tanner and Zihlman's (1976) on the evolutionary role of females.

At this time, scholars in archaeology also increasingly began to see gender as an important component of their research and started to question some of the androcentric assumptions of their discipline. Conkey and Spector's 1984 article "Archaeology and the Study of Gender" is a good example of the feminist impact on archaeology from this period.

In the 1980s, feminist anthropological research moved away from the previous decade's blanket assumptions of gender asymmetry. Research and analysis in the 1980s followed three principal trends. The first of these focused on the social construction of gender. Work such as Yanagisako and Collier's *Gender and Kinship* (1987) and Sanday and Goodenough's 1990 volume *Beyond the Second Sex* fall into this class of study.

Another direction in feminist research and analysis explored a materialist perspective. Materialist feminists used cross-cultural analysis to explain differences in women's status, roles, and power. These researchers were relatively unconcerned with describing the ways in which gender is defined in different societies. They concentrated on research that analyzed gender-related activities using measures of social, economic, and political power (Morgen 1989:4). Many scholars in this area focused on gender as it relates to class, the social relations of power, and changes in modes of production. Essay 33, by Eleanor Leacock (1922–1987), falls into this category of study. In this 1983 work, she presents an analysis of the oppression of women from a Marxist perspective. Leacock argues that in societies prior to Western contact, gender relations were typically egalitarian because men and women participated equally in the processes of production. She argues that the unequal place of women in societies today is the result of the subjugation of these societies by Europeans and the imposition of capitalist forms of production.

Overall, feminist anthropology of the 1980s demonstrated that gender is an important analytical concept and that the definition of gender changes historically and cross-culturally. Along with this initial insight, women of different class and ethnic backgrounds made feminist anthropologists increasingly aware that their interests did not necessarily coincide with those of the white middle-class women who had popularized feminism in anthropology. Micaela di Leonardo writes that feminist scholars were forced to confront ". . . the question of 'difference'—the multiple racial, ethnic, class, sexual, age, regional, and national identities of women—as they noted their own restricted demographic representation and research interests" (1991:18).

Scholars following this third trend have emphasized the cultural specificity of women's identities. They have moved away from the earlier theorizing about "woman" as a general concept to focus on the different ways in which race, class, and gender structure cultural institutions. Essay 34, by Ann Stoler (1949–), is an example of this type of research. There she outlines the ways in which sexual behavior, rules sanctioning or forbidding sexual relationships and marriage between colonists and indigenous women, and laws prohibiting immigration of European women were used to define and enforce class and racial boundaries in the European colonies of Africa and Asia.

The work of feminist anthropologists in the 1980s led to a much greater multicultural focus in the 1990s. In this decade feminist anthropologists have led the discipline in developing new, experimental forms of ethnographic writing. In particular, current feminist writing follows three new trends. First, feminist theorists have called the anthropological canon into question. In the introduction to *Women Writing Culture*, for example, Ruth Behar writes

> Why is it that the legacy of what counts as social theory is traced back only to Lewis Henry Morgan, Karl Marx, Émile Durkheim, Max Weber, Michael Foucault and Pierre Bourdieu? Why is there not a parallel matrilineal genealogy taking off from say, the turn-of-the-century work of Charlotte Perkins Gilman? . . . Why is the culture concept in anthropology only traced through Sir Edward Tylor, Franz Boas, Bronislaw Malinowski, Claude Lévi-Strauss, and Clifford Geertz? Could the writing of culture not be traced, as the essays in this volume suggest, through Elsie Clews Parsons, Ruth Benedict, Margaret Mead, Ella Deloria, Zora Neale Hurston, Ruth Landes, and Barbara Myerhoff to Alice Walker? (1995:11–12)

Second, some feminist anthropologists have led the discipline in emphasizing multivocality—that is, giving voice to a variety of viewpoints in their ethnographic writing. They question the objectivity of science and argue that anthropologists are not uniquely qualified interpreters of culture. They claim that traditional anthropological writing distanced authors from their subjects. To counter this, feminist authors have encouraged women of color to write about their cultures for themselves and challenged anthropologists to take into account ". . . the discriminations of racism, homophobia, sexism, and classism" they claim are a part of traditional anthropology (Behar and Gordon 1995:7).

Finally, some feminist anthropologists in the 1990s have emphasized experimentation with nontraditional forms of anthropological writing. Claiming that all ways of knowing are subjective, some authors have offered works of poetry and fiction as new forms of ethnography. Other authors experiment with the epistemological assumptions of anthropology by introducing their own thoughts and experiences into their research. One form this work has taken is the "autoethnography"—works that combine autobiographical information with anthropological analyses. In "A Tale of Two Pregnancies" (1995), for example, Lila Abu-Lughod discusses her experience of pregnancy and compares it with the pregnancies of Bedouin women with whom she conducted research.

Despite the continued efforts of feminist scholars, gender remains incompletely integrated into anthropology. A good index of this is the treatment it receives in introductory textbooks. The best-selling introductory cultural anthropology textbook (Haviland's *Cultural Anthropology*) does not have a chapter on gender. Other texts do include such a chapter, and women are also included in chapters on marriage, family, and childbearing. However, in most cases, coverage ends there. There is only cursory treatment of gender in chapters on economics, social stratification, or politics. Yet, twenty-five years ago, in "Women in Politics" (1974), Collier demonstrated that in many societies women were heavily involved in the political process at the household rather than public level and were central to political processes such as the formation or breakup of kin groups.

The theoretical myopia of looking only in the areas of kinship and marriage may reflect the dominant ideas about the place of women in Western society. It is surprising that women have so frequently been marginalized and gender issues ignored in a discipline whose subject matter is supposed to be humans and their cultures.

32. Woman the Gatherer: Male Bias in Anthropology

Sally Slocum (1939–)

LITTLE SYSTEMATIC ATTENTION HAS BEEN GIVEN in our discipline to an "anthropology of knowledge."[1] While some anthropologists have concerned themselves with knowledge in general, as

(1975)

seen through the varieties of human cultures, few have examined anthropological knowledge itself. An anthropology of knowledge would have several parts. First is what Peter Berger (1967:1–18) has called "philosophical anthropology": a study of the nature of the human species. This has always been

---

[1] The 1960s and 1970s were an era of radical rethinking within anthropology, with many strands contributing to a broad critique of positivist anthropology. The feminist critique was one of the most powerful since it attacked what feminists viewed as fundamental biases in a field that prided itself on being relatively bias free. This essay is taken from one of several groundbreaking anthologies of feminist essays in anthropology to appear in the 1970s, *Toward an Anthropology of Women*, edited by Rayna Reiter (1975).

a legitimate concern of anthropology, but too often we become so concerned with minute differences that we forget we are studying a single species. Second is how we "know" anything—what is accepted as "proof," what is reality, what are the grounds for rationality (Garfinkel, 1960), what modes are used in gathering knowledge, what are the effects of differences in culture and world view on what we "know." Third is a close examination of the questions asked in anthropology, for questions always determine and limit answers.

It is the third point, the nature of anthropological questions, to which I wish to speak in this paper. We are human beings studying other human beings, and we cannot leave ourselves out of the equation. We choose to ask certain questions, *and not others*. Our choice grows out of the cultural context in which anthropology and anthropologists exist. Anthropology, as an academic discipline, has been developed primarily by white Western males, during a specific period in history. Our questions are shaped by the particulars of our historical situation, and by unconscious cultural assumptions.[2]

Given the cultural and ethnic background of the majority of anthropologists, it is not surprising that the discipline has been biased. There are signs, however, that this selective blindness is beginning to come under scrutiny. For example, in the exchange in the journal *Current Anthropology* (1968), anthropologists like Kathleen Gough and Gerald Berreman point out the unconscious efforts of American political and economic assumptions on our selection of problems and populations to be studied. Restive minority groups in this country are pointing to the bias inherent in an-

thropological studies of themselves through books such as Vine Deloria's *Custer Died for Your Sins*. We have always encouraged members of American minority groups, and other "foreigners," to take up anthropology because of the perspective on the world that they can supply. The invitation is increasingly being accepted. As we had both hoped and feared, repercussions from this new participation are being felt in theory, method, interpretation, and problem choice, shaking anthropology to the roots.[3]

The perspective of women is, in many ways, equally foreign to an anthropology that has been developed and pursued primarily by males. There is a strong male bias in the questions asked, and the interpretations given. This bias has hindered the full development of our discipline as "the study of the human animal" (I don't want to call it "the study of man" for reasons that will become evident). I am going to demonstrate the Western male bias by reexamining the matter of evolution of Homo sapiens from our nonhuman primate ancestors. In particular, the concept of "Man the Hunter" as developed by Sherwood Washburn and C. Lancaster (1968) and others is my focus. This critique is offered in hopes of transcending the male bias that limits our knowledge by limiting the questions we ask.[4]

Though male bias could be shown in other areas, hominid evolution is particularly convenient for my purpose because it involves speculations and inferences from a rather small amount of data. In such a case, hidden assumptions and premises that lie behind the speculations and inferences are more easily demonstrated. Male bias

---

[2] One of the key questions of current anthropology is whether the fact that anthropology is generally done by a specific group of people fundamentally prejudices its results. Feminists were among the first to pose the question in these terms.

[3] The feminist critique was, of course, part of a broader revision of the social sciences and humanities that has continued in American intellectual culture. This change has been powerfully influenced by popular politics, especially the civil rights and women's movements of the 1960s. Several books aimed at popular rather than scholarly audiences were crucial. *Custer Died* (1969) was one of these. Dee Brown's 1971 *Bury My Heart at Wounded Knee* and Wallenchinsky and Wallace's 1975 *The People's Almanac* were others. All of these books became best-sellers. *Bury My Heart,* first published in January 1971, had gone through thirteen printings by October of that year.

[4] To some it seemed curious that anthropology should be accused of male bias. After all, several key early figures in anthropology had been women, and the best-known anthropologist in America in the 1960s was Margaret Mead. However, statistically, anthropology was overwhelmingly dominated by men. Moreover, the institutions anthropologists frequently considered most worthy of study were those controlled by males.

exists not only in the ways in which the scanty data are interpreted, but in the very language used. All too often the word "man" is used in such an ambiguous fashion that it is impossible to decide whether it refers to males or to the human species in general, including both males and females. In fact, one frequently is led to suspect that in the minds of many anthropologists, "man," supposedly meaning the human species, is actually exactly synonymous with "males."

This ambiguous use of language is particularly evident in the writing that surrounds the concept of Man the Hunter.[5] Washburn and Lancaster make it clear that it is specifically males who hunt, that hunting is much more than simply an economic activity, and that most of the characteristics which we think of as specifically human can be causally related to hunting. They tell us that hunting is a whole pattern of activity and way of life: "The biology, psychology, and customs that separate us from the apes—all these we owe to the hunters of time past" (1968:303). If this line of reasoning is followed to its logical conclusion, one must agree with Jane Kephart when she says:

> Since only males hunt, and the psychology of the species was set by hunting, we are forced to conclude that females are scarcely human, that is, do not have built-in the basic psychology of the species: to kill and hunt and ultimately to kill others of the same species.

The argument implies built-in aggression in human males, as well as the assumed passivity of human females and their exclusion from the mainstream of human development. (1970:5)

To support their argument that hunting is important to human males, Washburn and Lancaster point to the fact that many modern males still hunt, though it is no longer economically necessary. I could point out that many modern males play golf, play the violin, or tend gardens: these, as well as hunting, are things their culture teaches them. Using a "survival" as evidence to demonstrate an important fact of cultural evolution can be accorded no more validity when proposed by a modern anthropologist than when proposed by Tylor.

Regardless of its status as a survival, hunting, by implication as well as direct statement, is pictured as a male activity to the exclusion of females. This activity, on which we are told depends the psychology, biology, and customs of our species, is strictly male. A theory that leaves out half the human species is unbalanced. The theory of Man the Hunter is not only unbalanced; it leads to the conclusion that the basic human adaptation was the desire of males to hunt and kill.[6] This not only gives too much importance to aggression, which is after all only one factor of human life, but it derives culture from killing. I am going to suggest a less biased reading of the

---

[5] The feminist critique of the specific language used by anthropologists was particularly powerful because it referenced the Sapir-Whorf hypothesis that language shaped worldview, an idea that had been common since the 1930s and one to which most American anthropologists subscribed to one degree or another.

The idea of primitive "man" and "man" the hunter was a particularly apt target. Washburn and Lancaster had theorized that hunting was the most critical activity for early humans and that the most important human adaptations, bipedalism and language, arose as a result of it. This idea found its way into popular culture (where it is still common today). However, research in the 1960s had shown that male hunting played a relatively small role in supplying the nutritional needs of modern hunter-gatherers.

[6] In addition to Washburn and Lancaster, popular theory in ethology and evolution in the 1960s gave a very important place to aggression. Ethologist Konrad Lorenz's *On Aggression* (1966) and author Robert Ardrey's *African Genesis* (1961) were popular works that promoted this viewpoint. These works argued for the primacy of hunting and aggression in the evolutionary formation of humanity and more or less ignored the role played by women.

It is interesting to note that most of the primate ethology of the 1960s, particularly that on which Ardrey's popular works were based, was fundamentally flawed. It was derived largely from the work of Sir Solly Zuckerman (1904–1993) and Raymond Dart (1893–1988). Zuckerman drew his conclusions from watching an artificially assembled colony of hamadryas baboons in the London zoo in the 1920s. However, the behavior of these animals in the wild is very different from that of the London zoo colony. Dart, an anatomy professor and fossil hunter, on the basis of minimal evidence, proposed that early hominids had a murderous culture based on bone and wooden weaponry.

evidence, which gives a more valid and logical picture of human evolution, and at the same time a more hopeful one. First I will note the evidence, discuss the more traditional reading of it, and then offer an alternative reconstruction.

The data we have to work from are a combination of fossil and archaeological materials, knowledge of living nonhuman primates, and knowledge of living humans. Since we assume that the protohominid ancestors of Homo sapiens developed in a continuous fashion from a base of characteristics similar to those of living nonhuman primates, the most important facts seem to be the ways in which humans differ from nonhuman primates, and the ways in which we are similar. The differences are as follows: longer gestation period; more difficult birth; neoteny, in that human infants are less well developed at birth; long period of infant dependency; absence of body hair; year-round sexual receptivity of females, resulting in the possibility of bearing a second infant while the first is still at the breast or still dependent; erect bipedalism; possession of a large and complex brain that makes possible the creation of elaborate symbolic systems, languages, and cultures, and also results in most behavior being under cortical control; food sharing; and finally, living in families. (For the purposes of this paper I define families as follows: a situation where each individual has defined responsibilities and obligations to a specific set of others of both sexes and various ages. I use this definition because, among humans, the family is a *social* unit, regardless of any biological or genetic relationship which may or may not exist among its members.)

In addition to the many well-known close physiological resemblances, we share with nonhuman primates the following characteristics: living in social groups; close mother-infant bonds; affectional relationships; a large capacity for learning and a related paucity of innate behaviors; ability to take part in dominance hierarchies;

a rather complex nonsymbolic communication system which can handle with considerable subtlety such information as the mood and emotional state of the individual, and the attitude and status of each individual toward the other members of the social group.[7]

The fossil and archaeological evidence consists of various bones labeled Ramapithecus, Australopithecus, Homo habilis, Homo erectus, etc.; and artifacts such as stone tools representing various cultural traditions, evidence of use of fire, etc. From this evidence we can make reasonable inferences about diet, posture and locomotion, and changes in the brain as shown by increased cranial capacity, ability to make tools, and other evidences of cultural creation. Since we assume that complexity of material culture requires language, we infer the beginnings of language somewhere between Australopithecus and Homo erectus.

Given this data, the speculative reconstruction begins. As I was taught anthropology, the story goes something like this. Obscure selection pressures pushed the protohominid in the direction of erect bipedalism—perhaps the advantages of freeing the hands for food carrying or for tool use. Freeing the hands allowed more manipulation of the environment in the direction of tools for gathering and hunting food. Through a hand-eye-brain feedback process, coordination, efficiency, and skill were increased. The new behavior was adaptive, and selection pressure pushed the protohominid further along the same lines of development. Diet changed as the increase in skill allowed the addition of more animal protein. Larger brains were selected for, making possible transmission of information concerned with tool making, and organizing cooperative hunting. It is assumed that as increased brain size was selected for, so also was neoteny—immaturity of infants at birth with a corresponding increase in their period of dependency, allowing more time for learning at the same time

---

[7] Part of Slocum's argument comes from redefining differences between humans and nonhuman primates. In traditional anthropology and popular culture, the key differences between the two were brain size and language. She presents this image below. By 1970 it became clear that anatomical features such as bipedalism preceded language and increases in brain size, and thus were more important in differentiating between hominids and other primates. Notice that the first factors mentioned by Slocum in the previous paragraph all concern women exclusively. She places brain size and language well down the list.

as this learning became necessary through the further reduction of instinctual behaviors and their replacement by symbolically invented ones.[8]

Here is where one may discover a large logical gap. From the difficult-to-explain beginning trends toward neoteny and increased brain size, the story jumps to Man the Hunter. The statement is made that the females were more burdened with dependent infants and could not follow the rigorous hunt. Therefore they stayed at a "home base," gathering what food they could, while the males developed cooperative hunting techniques, increased their communicative and organizational skills through hunting and brought the meat back to the dependent females and young. Incest prohibitions, marriage, and the family (so the story goes) grew out of the need to eliminate competition between males for females. A pattern developed of a male hunter becoming the main support of "his" dependent females and young (in other words, the development of the nuclear family for no apparent reason). Thus the peculiarly human social and emotional bonds can be traced to the hunter bringing back the food to share. Hunting, according to Washburn and Lancaster, involved "cooperation among males, planning, knowledge of many species and large areas, and technical skill" (1968:296). They even profess to discover the beginnings of art in the weapons of the hunter. They point out that the symmetrical Acheulian biface tools are the earliest beautiful man-made objects. Though we don't know what these tools were used for, they argue somewhat tautologically that the symmetry indicates they may have been swung, because symmetry only makes a difference when irregularities might lead to deviations in the line of flight. "It may well be that it was the attempt to produce efficient high-speed weapons that first produced beautiful, symmetrical objects" (1968:298).

So, while the males were out hunting, developing all their skills, learning to cooperate, inventing language, inventing art, creating tools and weapons, the poor dependent females were sitting back at the home base having one child after another (many of them dying in the process), and waiting for the males to bring home the bacon. While this reconstruction is certainly ingenious, it gives one the decided impression that only half the species—the male half—did any evolving. In addition to containing a number of logical gaps, the argument becomes somewhat doubtful in the light of modern knowledge of genetics and primate behavior.

The skills usually spoken of as being necessary to, or developed through, hunting are things like coordination, endurance, good vision, and the ability to plan, communicate, and cooperate. I have heard of no evidence to indicate that these skills are either carried on the Y chromosome, or are triggered into existence by the influence of the Y chromosome. In fact, on just about any test we can design (psychological, aptitude, intelligence, etc.) males and females score just about the same. The variation is on an individual, not a sex, basis.

Every human individual gets half its genes from a male and half from a female; genes sort randomly. It is possible for a female to end up

<hr>

[8] Despite the popular interest in the social and behavioral aspects of early humans, physical anthropology was, at the time this article was written, relatively unconcerned with it. Most physical anthropologists focused on recovering and identifying fossils. While the version of evolution Slocum describes here was taught and generally accepted when she was writing, it was an area that had been relatively unstudied. Research since the 1970s has all but completely discredited this version of human evolution.

Slocum here is intentionally drawing a caricature of Washburn and Lancaster's position, presenting a version that can easily be demolished. Note the polemic tone of her writing. She both describes and ridicules Washburn and Lancaster's theory by using such phrases as "so the story goes" or "poor dependent females." Slocum's use of polemic language was, presumably, intentional. However, some of those she is critiquing, perhaps unintentionally, used language that seems equally polemic, which reinforces her point about bias in the literature. An example of this is an essay by Robin Fox that describes a theory by Chance, another researcher. According to Fox, Chance shows that "the whole process of enlarging the neo-cortex to take-off point was based on a competition between the dominant and sub-dominant males" (1972:373). Fox criticized Chance's view but was wildly condescending. In pointing out problems with the theory, he noted that it "would apply only to the male neo-cortex, and much as we may be mystified at the use made of this organ by the female of the species, she undoubtedly possesses it" (1972:373).

with all her genes from male ancestors, and for a male to end up with all his genes from female ancestors. The logic of the hunting argument would have us believe that all the selection pressure was on the males, leaving the females simply as drags on the species. The rapid increase in brain size and complexity was thus due entirely to half the species; the main function of the female half was to suffer and die in the attempt to give birth to their large-brained male infants. An unbiased reading of the evidence indicates there was selection pressure on both sexes, and that hunting was not in fact the basic adaptation of the species from which flowed all the traits we think of as specifically human. Hunting does not deserve the primary place it has been given in the reconstruction of human evolution, as I will demonstrate by offering the following alternate version.

Picture the primate band: each individual gathers its own food, and the major enduring relationship is the mother-infant bond.[9] It is in similar circumstances that we imagine the evolving protohominids. We don't know what started them in the direction of neoteny and increased brain size, but once begun the trends would prove adaptive. To explain the shift from the primate individual gathering to human food sharing, we cannot simply jump to hunting. Hunting cannot explain its own origin. It is much more logical to assume that as the period of infant dependency began to lengthen, *the mothers would begin to increase the scope of their gathering to provide food for their still-dependent infants.* The already strong primate mother-infant bond would begin to extend over a longer time period, increasing the depth and scope of social relationships, and giving rise to the first sharing of food.

It is an example of male bias to picture these females with young as totally or even mainly dependent on males for food. Among modern hunter-gatherers, even in the marginal environments where most live, the females can usually gather enough to support themselves and their families. In these groups gathering provides the major portion of the diet, and there is no reason to assume that this was not also the case in the Pliocene or early Pleistocene. In the modern groups women and children both gather and hunt small animals, though they usually do not go on the longer hunts. So, we can assume a group of evolving protohominids, gathering and perhaps beginning to hunt small animals, with the mothers gathering quite efficiently both for themselves and for their offspring.

It is equally biased, and quite unreasonable, to assume an early or rapid development of a pattern in which one male was responsible for "his" females(s) and young. In most primate groups when a female comes into estrus she initiates coitus or signals her readiness by presenting. The idea that a male would have much voice in "choosing" a female, or maintain any sort of individual, long-term control over her or her offspring, is surely a modern invention which could have had no place in early hominid life. (Sexual control over females through rape or the threat of rape seems to be a

---

[9] The picture of the primate band that Slocum draws here is much closer to that held by current physical anthropologists than the version she presented and ridiculed above. It was, however, only one of several feminist versions of human evolution offered in the early 1970s. The version that was probably most popular with nonprofessionals at that time was the aquatic hypothesis. This view was presented by Elaine Morgan in her 1972 book *The Descent of Woman.* Like Ardrey (who was originally a playwright), Morgan was a writer rather than an anthropologist, and her book was aimed at a popular rather than a professional audience.

Morgan argued that the fundamental human characteristics of bipedalism, language, and tool use resulted from adaptation to living in coastal environments and that the crucial evolutionary pressures were on females rather than males. Morgan's original work was polemic in tone. She published a more technical version of it called *The Aquatic Ape* in 1982. The aquatic hypothesis enjoyed great popularity among feminists and some cultural anthropologists, but it has been rejected by physical anthropologists as incompatible with the fossil evidence.

Unlike Morgan or Ardrey, Slocum is a physical anthropologist; she did her doctoral work on rhesus monkeys. Thus, her argument comes from within physical anthropology and demonstrates a much greater technical command of the field than Morgan's or Ardrey's work. Despite her background, the essay is aimed at an audience of cultural rather than physical anthropologists.

modern human invention. Primate females are not raped because they are willing throughout estrus, and primate males appear not to attempt coitus at other times, regardless of physiological ability.) In fact, there seems to me no reason for suggesting the development of male-female adult pair-bonding until much later. Long-term monogamy is a fairly rare pattern even among modern humans— I think it is a peculiarly Western male bias to suppose its existence in protohuman society. An argument has been made (by Morris, 1967, and others) that traces the development of male-female pair-bonding to the shift of sexual characteristics to the front of the body, the importance of the face in communication, and the development of face-to-face coitus. This argument is insufficient in the first place because of the assumption that face-to-face coitus is the "normal," "natural," or even the most common position among humans (historical evidence casts grave doubt on this assumption). It is much more probable that the coitus position was invented *after* pair-bonding had developed for other reasons.

Rather than adult male-female sexual pairs, a temporary consort-type relationship is much more logical in hominid evolution. It is even a more accurate description of the modern human pattern: the most dominant males (chief, headman, brave warrior, good hunter, etc.), mate with the most dominant females (in estrus, young and beautiful, fertile, rich, etc.), for varying periods of time. Changing sexual partners is frequent and common. We have no way of knowing when females began to be fertile year-round, but this change is not a necessary condition for the development of families. We need not bring in any notion of paternity, or the development of male-female pairs, or any sort of marriage in order to account for either families or food sharing.

The lengthening period of infant dependency would have strengthened and deepened the mother-infant bond; the earliest families would have consisted of *females and their children*. In such groups, over time, the sibling bond would have increased in importance also. The most universal, and presumably oldest, form of incest prohibition is between mother and son.[10] There are indications of such avoidance even among modern monkeys. It could develop logically from the mother-children family: as the period of infant dependency lengthened, and the age of sexual maturity advanced, a mother might no longer be capable of childbearing when her son reached maturity. Another factor which may have operated is the situation found in many primates today where only the most dominant males have access to fertile females. Thus a young son, even after reaching sexual maturity, would still have to spend time working his way up the male hierarchy before gaining access to females. The length of time it would take him increases the possibility that his mother would no longer be fertile.

Food sharing and the family developed from the mother-infant bond. The techniques of hunting large animals were probably much later developments, after the mother-children family pattern was established. When hunting did begin, and the adult males brought back food to share, the most likely recipients would be first their mothers, and second their siblings. In other words, a hunter would share food *not* with a wife or sexual partner, but with those who had shared food with him: his mother and siblings.

It is frequently suggested or implied that the first tools were, in fact, the weapons of the hunters.[11] Modern humans have become so accustomed to the thought of tools and weapons that it is easy for us to imagine the first manlike

---

[10] Here, in passing, Slocum makes a stab at the origins of the incest taboo, one of the oldest problems in anthropology and one that is still not solved to general satisfaction. In fact, her case here is very weak since females do not have to be fertile to have sex. However, just as theorists such as Washburn tried to link the evolution of an enormous number of traits to male hunting, Slocum tries to link a wide range of characteristics to particular aspects of female-led evolution.

[11] As Slocum attacked male bias in beliefs about evolution, she took on many commonly accepted themes in popular culture. The idea that early tools were offensive weapons came from Dart's work. Compare her analysis here to the story presented in Stanley Kubrick's *2001: A Space Odyssey,* an extremely popular film that appeared in the late 1960s. The opening scenes of the film show the discovery of tools: one apeman picks up a large bone, stares at it, and then uses it to beat a companion over the head.

creature who picked up a stone or club. However, since we don't really know what the early stone tools such as hand-axes were used for, it is equally probable that they were not weapons at all, but rather *aids in gathering*. We know that gathering was important long before much animal protein was added to the diet, and continued to be important. Bones, sticks, and hand-axes could be used for digging up tubers or roots, or to pulverize tough vegetable matter for easier eating. If, however, instead of thinking in terms of tools and weapons, we think in terms of *cultural inventions*, a new aspect is presented. I suggest that two of the *earliest and most important* cultural inventions were containers to hold the products of gathering, and some sort of sling or net to carry babies.[12] The latter in particular must have been extremely important with the loss of body hair and the increasing immaturity of neonates, who could not cling and had less and less to cling to. Plenty of material was available—vines, hides, human hair. If the infant could be securely fastened to the mother's body, she could go about her tasks much more efficiently. Once a technique for carrying babies was developed, it could be extended to the idea of carrying food, and eventually to other sorts of cultural inventions— choppers and grinders for food preparation, and even weapons. Among modern hunter-gatherers, regardless of the poverty of their material culture, food carriers and baby carriers are always important items in their equipment.

A major point in the Man the Hunter argument is that cooperative hunting among males demanded more skill in social organization and communication, and thus provided selection pressure for increased brain size. I suggest that longer periods of infant dependency, more difficult births, and longer gestation periods also demanded more skills in social organization and communication— creating selective pressure for increased brain size

without looking to hunting as an explanation. The need to organize for feeding after weaning, learning to handle the more complex social-emotional bonds that were developing, the new skills and cultural inventions surrounding more extensive gathering—all would demand larger brains. Too much attention has been given to the skills required by hunting, and too little to the skills required for gathering and the raising of dependent young. The techniques required for efficient gathering include location and identification of plant varieties, seasonal and geographical knowledge, containers for carrying the food, and tools for its preparation. Among modern hunting-gathering groups this knowledge is an extremely complex, well-developed, and important part of their cultural equipment. Caring for a curious, energetic, but still dependent human infant is difficult and demanding. Not only must the infant be watched, it must be taught the customs, dangers, and knowledge of its group. For the early hominids, as their cultural equipment and symbolic communication increased, the job of training the young would demand more skill. Selection pressure for better brains came from many directions.

Much has been made of the argument that cooperation among males demanded by hunting acted as a force to reduce competition for females. I suggest that competition for females has been greatly exaggerated.[13] It could easily have been handled in the usual way for primates—according to male status relationships already worked out—and need not be pictured as particularly violent or extreme. The seeds of male cooperation already exist in primates when they act to protect the band from predators. Such dangers may well have increased with a shift to savannah living, and the longer dependency of infants. If biological roots are sought to explain the greater aggressiveness of males, it would be more fruitful to look toward their function as protectors, rather than any

---

[12] Here and later Slocum is engaging in pure speculation. Like the sociobiologists, she is arguing by analogy to modern hunting-gathering bands, using them as "living fossils"—a method that hearkens back to the nineteenth century.

[13] Early theories about protohuman social organization tended to emphasize violent competition among males for essentially passive females. (Freud's essay, number 5 in this volume, is a good example.) The popular image is of the caveman dragging the cavewoman off by the hair. More modern theory, however, tends to emphasize the role of females in sexual selection, diminishing the importance of male aggression.

supposedly basic hunting adaptation. The only division of labor that regularly exists in primate groups is the females caring for infants and the males protecting the group from predators. The possibilities for both cooperation and aggression in males lies in this protective function.

The emphasis on hunting as a prime moving factor in hominid evolution distorts the data. It is simply too big a jump to go from the primate individual gathering pattern to a hominid co-operative hunting-sharing pattern without some intervening changes. Cooperative hunting of big game animals could only have developed *after* the trends toward neoteny and increased brain size had begun. Big-game hunting becomes a more logical development when it is viewed as growing out of a complex of changes which included sharing the products of gathering among mothers and children, deepening social bonds over time, increase in brain size, and the beginnings of cultural invention for purposes such as baby carrying, food carrying, and food preparation. Such hunting not only needed the prior development of some skills in social organization and communication, it probably also had to await the development of the "home base." It is difficult to imagine that most or all of the adult primate males in a group would go off on a hunting expedition, leaving the females and young exposed to the danger of predators, without some way of communicating to arrange for their defense, or at least a way of saying, "Don't worry, we'll be back in two days." Until that degree of communicative skill developed, we must assume either that the whole band traveled *and hunted* together, or that the males simply did not go off on large cooperative hunts.

The development of cooperative hunting requires, as a prior condition, an increase in brain size. Once such a trend is established, hunting skills would take part in a feedback process of selection for better brains just as would other cultural inventions and developments such as gathering skills. By itself, hunting fails to explain any part of human evolution and fails to explain itself.

Anthropology has always rested on the assumption that the mark of our species is our ability to *symbol*, to bring into existence forms of behavior and interaction, and material tools with which to adjust and control the environment. To explain human nature as evolving from the desire of males to hunt and kill is to negate most of anthropology.[14] Our species survived and adapted through the invention of *culture*, of which hunting is simply a part. It is often stated that hunting *must* be viewed as the "natural" species' adaptation because it lasted as long as it did, nine-tenths of all human history. However:

> Man the Hunter lasted as long as "he" did from no natural propensity toward hunting any more than toward computer programming or violin playing or nuclear warfare, but because that was what the historical circumstances allowed. We ignore the first premise of our science if we fail to admit that "man" is no more natural a hunter than "he" is naturally a golfer, for after symboling became possible our species left forever the ecological niche of the necessity of any one adaptation, and made all adaptations possible for ourselves. (Kephart, 1970:23)

That the concept of Man the Hunter influenced anthropology for as long as it did is a reflection of male bias in the discipline. This bias can be seen in the tendency to equate "man," "human," and "male"; to look at culture almost entirely from a male point of view; to search for examples of the behavior of males and assume that this is sufficient for explanation, ignoring almost totally the female half of the species; and to filter this male bias through the "ideal" modern Western pattern of one male supporting a dependent wife and minor children.[15]

---

[14] As you read these passages, recall again that this essay first appeared in 1971, close to the height of the movement protesting the Vietnam War. Slocum's suggestion that the hunting hypothesis negates most anthropology seems rash, but the idea that humans did not innately desire to kill was extremely popular in this era and, whether it followed logically or not, increased the emotional appeal of Slocum's argument.

[15] Slocum's suggestion that, even within anthropology, there was a tendency to equate man and human was certainly no exaggeration. Consider C. F. Hockett's 1973 anthropology text called *Man's Place in Nature* with chapters titled "Man the Tinkerer," "Man the Chatterer," "Man the Worshiper," "Man the Owner," and so on.

The basis of any discipline is not the answers it gets, but the questions it asks. As an exercise in the anthropology of knowledge, this paper stems from asking a simple question: what were the females doing while the males were out hunting? It was only possible for me to ask this question after I had become politically conscious of myself as a woman. Such is the prestige of males in our society that a woman, in anthropology or any other profession, can only gain respect or be attended to if she deals with questions deemed important by men. Though there have been women anthropologists for years, it is rare to be able to discern any difference between their work and that of male anthropologists. Learning to be an anthropologist has involved learning to think from a male perspective, so it should not be surprising that women have asked the same kinds of questions as men. But political consciousness, whether among women, blacks, American Indians, or any other group, leads to reexamination and reevaluation of taken-for-granted assumptions. It is a difficult process, challenging the conventional wisdom, and this paper is simply a beginning. The male bias in anthropology that I have illustrated here is just as real as the white bias, the middle-class bias, and the academic bias that exist in the discipline. It is our task, as anthropologists, to create a "study of the human species" in spite of, or perhaps because of, or maybe even by means of, our individual biases and unique perspectives.[16]

References

Berger, Peter, and T. Luckmann
1967 *The Social Construction of Reality.* Garden City, N.Y.: Doubleday Anchor.

Current Anthropology
1968 Social Responsibilities Symposium. Reprint from December 1968 issue.

Garfinkel, Harold
1960 "The Rational Properties of Scientific and Common Sense Activities." *Behavioral Science* 5, no. 1:72–83.

Kephart, Jane
1970 "Primitive Woman as Nigger, or, The Origin of the Human Family as Viewed Through the Role of Women." M.A. Dissertation, University of Maryland.

Morris, Desmond
1967 *The Naked Ape.* New York: McGraw-Hill.

Washburn, Sherwood, and Lancaster, C.
1968 "The Evolution of Hunting." In *Man the Hunter* edited by R. B. Lee and Irven DeVore. Chicago: Aldine.

---

[16] Notice the layering of political change, personal change, and theoretical perspective in this final paragraph. Slocum's perception that a change in her political consciousness caused a change in her theoretical position prefigures postmodern anthropology. Compare it to some of Renato Rosaldo's insights in essay 38 in this volume. However, Slocum is certainly no postmodernist, and feminist writers of this era did not make the leap to extreme relativism that characterizes some postmodern writing.

33. Interpreting the Origins of Gender Inequality: Conceptual and Historical Problems

Eleanor Leacock (1922–1987)

FOR SOME TIME I HAVE ARGUED THAT THE analysis of women's oppression and its origins calls for clarification along two lines, historical and conceptual.*[1] The historical dimension requires that the myth of the "ethnographic present" be totally eradicated, and that anthropologists deal fully with the fact that the structure of gender relations among the people they study does not follow from pre-capitalist production relations as such, but from the ways in which these have been affected by particular histories of colonization. The conceptual dimension requires a complete break with the tendency to interpret all cultures in terms of categories derived from capitalist society. Such categories distort the structure of primitive communist relations and thereby obscure the sources of hierarchy. Equally critical, as consistently pointed out by feminist scholars, is the need to root out the pervasive assumption that women are not actors on the scene of human history to the same degree as are men. There is still a widespread failure to recognize that correcting the anthropological distortion of women's roles in society has profound implications for the

(1983)

interpretation of social structure generally. In particular, the fact that the French Marxists have not launched a thorough-going criticism of Lévi-Strauss' assumption that the exchange of women by men inaugurated human society has served to weaken their analyses of pre-capitalist production modes.[2]

ANTHROPOLOGY AND HISTORY

The importance of paying constant attention to history was impressed upon me as a graduate student at Columbia University when I was fortunate enough to take part in Wm. Duncan Strong's seminar on "Time Perspective and the Plains." Strong drew on archaeology and ethnohistory to demonstrate that "typical" Plains culture, as then conceived, was not aboriginal, but had developed in the 18th century when formerly diverse tribes, some agricultural, some hunting-gathering, took advantage of the horse and either moved out onto, or spent more of the year on the prairies. I would add that a greatly expanded market for buffalo hides plus land pressure resulting from European intrusion to the east and south were also important reasons for the move out onto the

---

[1] Leacock's original essay contained ninety-six notes. Space limitations prevent us from reproducing them here, but asterisks have been included to show where they were placed.

[2] Leacock's feminist Marxist perspective is immediately apparent in this opening paragraph. Here she touches on a number of issues that were central to feminists and Marxists in the late 1970s and early 1980s. These included a critique of the notion of the ethnographic present (see footnote 4) as well as a declaration that not only are women of equal importance to men in society but also relationships between men and women are fundamental elements that pattern society.

The notion of primitive communism is very important in this essay. Marx and Engels proposed that early societies were communistic. This idea was given force by Lewis Henry Morgan's description of early societies as having communistic living arrangements and possessing liberty and equality (1871, 1877). These descriptions provided data for Marx and Engels.

In the last sentence of the paragraph, Leacock refers to Lévi-Strauss' work *The Elementary Structures of Kinship,* in which he argues that the fact that women are commodities exchanged by men is one of the fundamental patterning elements of society. You can find a more thorough discussion of Lévi-Strauss' theory in the introduction to the "Structuralism" section in this book. Lévi-Strauss had a critical impact on the development of Marxist thought because many leading French Marxists of the 1960s and 1970s were his students.

plains. In a fairly short time, social, ritual, and material traits were borrowed, developed, and/or elaborated upon by different peoples who integrated them into a relatively uniform culture.[3]

Strong's ethnohistorical orientation influenced a number of dissertations, some on Plains peoples,* and some on other areas.* Subsequently, extensive studies of native American social-economic organization and land use were undertaken in connection with the Indian Claims actions initiated in the 1950s.* This work revealed a fact of major significance for understanding the unstratified societies that existed in most of what was to become the United States: bands, villages, and towns were only loosely grouped into what are called tribes; politically, however, they functioned as fully autonomous units. The point was made explicit by Kroeber,* and it has been elaborated upon by Fried in his critique of the concept "tribe"*. Kroeber wrote:

> The more we review aboriginal America, the less certain does any consistently recurring phenomenon become that matches our usual conventional concept of tribe; and the more largely does this concept appear to be a White man's creation of convenience for talking about Indians, negotiation with them, administering them . . . It was infinitely more convenient and practicable for us to deal with representatives of one large group than with these of ten, twenty, or thirty tiny and shifting ones whose very names and precise habitat often were not known. This was equally so whether treaties were being negotiated for trade, traverse, settlement or resettlement, land cession, peace, subsidy or rationing, administration on a reservation, or abrogating and opening up a reservation. Generally we treated the nationality-"tribes" as if they were sovereign state-tribes, and by sheer pressure of greater strength forced the Indians to submit to our classification of them.*

Kroeber's point that tribes as commonly defined were a product of colonization requires the qualification that tribal organization and leadership were not only imposed from without. They also arose. among native Americans as necessary for resisting white invasion. Such warfare as had existed in pre-colonial times usually took the form of petty raiding by young men (and such women as occasionally chose to participate) who tested their mettle in a coup-counting system that deemed it more prestigious to touch enemies than kill them. When warfare for survival became necessary, strong leaders emerged to unite one or more tribes and meet the need.

In any case, Kroeber wrote that the "larger nationalities," i.e. the culturally affiliated groups known as tribes, were "ethnic" but "non-political" in the sense that they held no power over their constituents. It was the "smaller units, whether they be called villages, bands, towns, tribelets, lineages, or something else . . . that were independent, sovereign, and held and used a territory."* However, these smaller units should not be considered miniature tribes in the sense of stable, bonded groups subject to the authority of a chief and/or council. Such a formulation violates the reality of communally organized societies, in which movement among groups was easy and frequent; rights to lands were not viewed as exclusive; decisions about individual activities were made by those who would carry them out; and decisions about group activities, arrived at through consensus, did not bind those who did not agree.* Such a formulation also distorts the working structure of relations among bands and villages and the complex social and ceremonial forms that affirmed cooperation and friendship or ritualized and contained potential animosity.

Kroeber's and Fried's discussions of changing political forms demonstrate how unjustifiable it is to consider the cultures that have been recon-

---

[3] The archaeologist William Duncan Strong (1899–1962) was a student of A. L. Kroeber and a classmate of Julian Steward. Strong was a major influence on Leacock during her years at Columbia. He conducted extensive research in the western United States, in Labrador, and with his student, Gordon Wiley (1913–), in Peru. While not a Marxist, Strong emphasized the role of history in anthropology and critiqued both evolutionism without adequate historical research and functionalist approaches that ignored history, such as those of A. R. Radcliffe-Brown (Solecki and Wagley 1963). After Strong's death, Leacock edited the journals he kept during his fieldwork among the Naskapi Indians. Although she began this project in the early 1960s, the resulting book, *Labrador Winter: The Ethnographic Journals of William Duncan Strong, 1927–1928,* was not published until 1994, seven years after her death.

structed from the memories of late 19th and early 20th century elders as "traditional" in the sense of pre-Columbian. To do so is to gloss over the active participation of native Americans in almost 500 years of post-colonial history. It is to present them as cardboard figures, living according to a congeries of "culture traits" within "culture areas," traits that did not change but were "lost" through "acculturation."*4

GENDER IN NATIVE NORTH AMERICA

With regard to the position of women, it is equally unjustifiable to make generalizations about one or another Indian culture without consideration of the historical dimension. During the colonial period, male authority was being encouraged by Euro-Americans in their political and military dealings with native Americans at the same time as Indian women were becoming dependent in individual households on wage-earning and trading husbands. For example, after documenting the full social equality of Cherokee women revealed by colonial accounts, Reid, an historian of law, wrote:

> The decline of hunting and the adoption of American ways during the nineteenth century, with the substitution of factory-made for home-made goods . . . freed the Cherokee woman from outdoor labor, placing her in the

kitchen and her husband in the fields, but it also deprived her of economic independence, making her politically and legally more like her white sisters.*

A second example of changes in women's position following the colonization of native North America is afforded by the contrast between Lafitau and Morgan on the Iroquois.5 In his 18th century account, Lafitau stated that Iroquois and/or Huron women were "the souls of the Councils, the arbiters of peace and war," in whom "all real authority is vested."* In Morgan's 19th century description, despite reference to women's decision-making powers in Iroquois households, he wrote that Iroquois men considered women as "inferior, the dependent, and the servant of men," and that a woman, "from nurture and habit, . . . actually considered herself to be so."* Although the flatness of the latter statement can well be questioned, it was written at the time when Iroquois women had lost their role as major producers and the control over the products of their labor that had insured them personal autonomy and public authority. Their situation was no longer that of 1791, when elder Seneca women informed Colonel Proctor, an envoy from George Washington,

> you ought to hear and listen to what we, women, shall speak, as well as to the sachems; for we are the owners of this land—and it is ours. It is we that plant it for our and their

---

4 Throughout this section, Leacock shows her concern with the historical background of Native America and attacks the notion of the ethnographic present. Through the first half of the twentieth century, most ethnographies did not pay any particular attention to history. Societies were described either in their current state or as they were remembered by their elder members. For the purposes of their writing, many anthropologists assumed that the societies they studied were relatively isolated from external forces of change, and internally driven change was extremely slow. Thus, notions of history were largely irrelevant to ethnography. Additionally, two prominent schools of thought in the 1960s and 1970s were structuralism and ethnoscience (or new ethnography). Members of these schools focused on what they believed to be the fundamental ways in which members of a society understood their world. They held that the effects of history on such understandings were of little importance. Marxism, on the other hand, is fundamentally concerned with history: Marxists see societies developing as their internal contradictions are worked out. Thus, a feminist Marxist approach must be vitally concerned with showing the importance of history for understanding the position of women in society.

5 In this section Leacock begins to build the case that the gender relations reported in most twentieth-century ethnographies are the result of contact with Europeans rather than structural elements of non-European society. Some of the important names Leacock mentions in this section are the Wyandot, Powell, and Lafitau. The Wyandot are better known as the Huron. Powell refers to John Wesley Powell (1834–1902), the founder of the Bureau of American Ethnology. Additional information on Powell can be found in the introduction to "Historical Particularism." Joseph-Francois Lafitau (1681–1746), author of *American Savages Compared with Those of Earliest Times* (1724), was a Jesuit missionary who worked among the Iroquois from 1711 to 1717. He wrote on Iroquois kinship systems one hundred years before Morgan.

use. Hear us, therefore, for we speak of things that concern us while our men shall say more to you; for we have told them.*

The changing relationship between women's economic role and their decision-making powers among the Iroquois and the Huron is further illuminated by a little known paper on the Wyandot by the early anthropologist Powell. Powell wrote:

> Cultivation is communal; that is, all of the able-bodied women of the gens take part in the cultivation of each household tract in the following manner:

> The head of the household sends her brother or son into the forest or to the stream to bring in game or fish for a feast; then the able-bodied women of the gens are invited to assist in the cultivation of the land, and when this work is done a feast is given.*

Powell stated that women were family heads among the Wyandot, and that four family heads, plus a man of their choosing, made up the clan council. The clan councils together made up the tribal council that was responsible for dividing Wyandot lands among the clans. The women councilors of each clan were in turn responsible for dividing it among the clan households, as well as for matters such as giving personal names and discussing and consenting to marriages. Apparently the entire council, that is, including the male member, handled certain transgressions while others were brought before the tribal council. Warfare was the responsibility of the men; all "able-bodied men" made up what Powell called a "military council" headed by a "military chief." The fact that women were not members of these councils has led to a serious underestimation of their authority in societies organized, as many North American societies were, along lines roughly similar to the Wyandot Huron. First, accounts of military negotiations between the outsiders and "military councils" and "military chiefs" do not recognize the formal structure of women's power which can therefore be interpreted as indirect and "behind the scene."* Second, the imminence of conquest increased the responsibility and power of "military councils." Subsequent economic developments, along with policies such as the Dawes (General Allotment) Act of 1887 (designed to divide all Indian lands into family-owned plots), undercut the collective economic activities traditionally controlled by women. As among the Cherokee and the Iroquois, the egalitarian and reciprocal structure of decision-making among the Huron was destroyed.

CONCEPTUALIZING PRIMITIVE COMMUNISM AND ITS TRANSFORMATION

As the above discussion suggests, the egalitarian relations that obtained in most foraging and many horticultural societies around the world at the time of European expansion rested on the fact that all mature individuals participated directly in the full process of production. By "full process" I refer to Marx's concept of production, distribution, exchange, and consumption as "members of one entity, different aspects of one unit,"* as opposed to formulations that limit their emphasis to either work processes or the allocation of produce. The control that all individuals had over the conditions of their labor, over the skills as well as the resources necessary to perform it, and over the disposition and use of its products, distinguishes egalitarian from hierarchically ordered structures.[6]

A Marxist conceptual baseline for analysing egalitarian society, interpreted in these terms, sharpens the fact that the transformation from egalitarian to hierarchical relations was qualitative and not merely quantitative. Such a view contrasts with the common practice of describing

---

[6] In Marxist thought, there is a close link between production and power. Since social relations flow primarily from relations of production, the greater the contribution of an individual to production, the greater that individual's power should be. Leacock is arguing that her reading of the ethnography shows that women and men participated fully in production before their societies were profoundly affected by Europeans. If they did so, then, from a Marxist viewpoint, it would be a logical necessity that both men and women participated fully in political decision making as well.

egalitarian society in terms of the same features that characterize class society. In formulations of this type, differential access to land and other resources, hereditary authority, and social-economic hierarchies are treated as incipient—as weakly developed tendencies that only needed strengthening to become predominant. Despite caveats to the contrary, history is thereby implied to be unilineal and teleological, with Western society as its ultimate purpose and measure. Alternatives for the future are obscured by the implication that there was no real alternative in the past.[7]

The widely held assumption that female subordination is a universal of human society derives from, and in turn supports, the assumption that primitive communal society was ultimately ordered by the same constraints and compulsions that order class society.* Where institutionalized hostility between the sexes exists, it is interpreted as a variant of a universal battle between the sexes, rather than as evidence of emerging status differentiations among men and among women, as well as between men and women. The critical relationship between the development of ranking and the attempt to subvert women's public and autonomous status (such as in the so-called big men societies of Melanesia) is seldom recognized.

In sum, gender hierarchy is all too often taken for granted, and both the structure of primitive communism and the basis for its transformation are thereby mystified.[8]

There is much talk of paradigms these days, and much emphasis on process. Nonetheless, cross-cultural analyses still rely heavily on states or essences as categories, rather than processes or relationships. The mid-century admission that the regularities of social evolution as broadly outlined by Engels and Morgan approximated historical reality, opened the way in anthropology for a dialectical analysis of human history in terms of basic transformations in the ways people interrelated as they reproduced themselves and their social structures. In particular, given the focus on relations between individual and society that characterized the personality and culture school, and its successors in psychological anthropology, the significance of Marx's sixth thesis on Feuerbach could have been explored in terms of how individual behavior and societal processes interrelate.[9]

"The essence of man is no abstraction inherent in each separate individual," Marx wrote. "In its reality it is the *ensemble* (aggregate) of social relations."* To Marx and Engels people did not

---

[7] Although Leacock does not provide any references for what she describes as a common practice—seeing egalitarian societies as incipient states—she is probably thinking of Morton Fried's *The Evolution of Political Society* (1967). Fried's book was published several years before this essay, and she cites it repeatedly later in the work.

[8] Many 1970s feminists understood female subordination as a human universal. Ortner, for example, says that female subordination "exists within every type of social and economic arrangement and in societies of every degree of complexity" (see essay 27). When a practice is universal, there is at least the strong suspicion that it is rooted in human nature. However, for a Marxist, there can be no such thing. Human nature is not fixed and universal, but created in the process of production. Therefore, explanations that rely upon human nature cannot be sustained. Leacock makes this point repeatedly in the next several paragraphs.

[9] When Leacock refers to the midcentury admission that Engels and Morgan were approximately correct, she is probably thinking of Leslie White's work on cultural evolution and his editing of Morgan's work (see essay 19). Marx's *Theses on Feuerbach* is a short work written in 1845. It was published as an appendix to Engels' *Ludwig Feuerbach and the End of Classical German Philosophy* (1949 [1888]). It consists of eleven brief points that, in Marx's opinion, separated his own work from Feuerbach's. The sixth thesis, in its entirety, is

Feuerbach resolves the religious essence into the human essence. But the human essence is no abstraction inherent in each single individual. In its reality it is the ensemble of the social relations. Feuerbach, who does not enter upon a criticism of this real essence, is consequently compelled: 1) To abstract from the historical process and to fix the religious sentiment as something by itself and to presuppose an abstract—isolated—human individual. 2) Essence, therefore, can be comprehended only as "genus," as an internal, dumb generality which naturally unites the many individuals.

In the following paragraph, Leacock explains the significance of Marx's point for her own argument.

have an intrinsic nature apart from society, but neither were they mere reflections of their society. In a number of oft-quoted passages, Marx and Engels stressed that "men make their own history,"* although the circumstances under which they do so are inherited from the past. Furthermore, the independent unfolding of social forces means that people's actions do not necessarily lead to the intended results. Instead the "simplest determinations," the relations of production, ways people relate to one another as they produce, distribute, exchange, and consume the necessities of life, set processes in motion that lie beyond the wills of the actors.* On the one hand, social structures are created by the behavior of individuals; "the social structure and the State are continually evolving out of the life-processes of definite individuals." On the other hand, however, these life-processes are themselves structured by production relations, as people "are effective, produce materially, and are active under definite material limits, presuppositions and conditions independent of their will."*[10]

Marxist dialectics, then, opened the way for examining the series of interlocking processes—the different levels of integration—that constitute human history. At the individual physiological level, human nature is not a given but a mix of potentials and propensities that are expressed differently under different conditions; at the societal level, social-historical processes are of an altogether different order; in between, mediating the two, at the individual psycho-social or behavioral level, the person operates as a nexus of social-economic relationships; and at the ideological level, people's perceptions of their relations to each other and to nature are patterned by traditional concepts, in part spontaneous and in part manipulated, and with a certain lawfulness of their own that arises from the nature of language as a symbol system.*

Such a line of thinking has been followed through only minimally. Instead, anthropology has been plagued by ever more radically reductionist and anti-historical formulations. In structuralist theory, and more recently in sociobiology, social determinants are defined in terms of behavioral outcomes and ultimately reduced to psychobiologically fixed entities. Whether these be such grotesque notions as Wilson's "conformer" and other behavior-specific genes, or Lévi-Strauss's more elegant, since undefined, deep structures, or Laughlin and d'Aquili's more scientifically couched, if less euphonious "neuroanatomical-neurophysiological relationships," their inventors all reduce human history and society to mere projections of individual biological propensities, with the environment the only independently interacting factor.*[11]

The result of ruling out a level of societal process entirely separate from individual propensities is like attempting to explain the movements of the solar system as flowing from the properties of the atomic particles (or processes) that make it up. To be sure, planetary movements are in a superficial sense the sum total of all movements of subatomic particles, just as social processes are in a trivial sense the sum total of individual behav-

---

[10] In this and the following paragraph, Leacock is describing a Marxist dialectic. She is saying that society is not simply a reflection of the structure of production (that is a position that Marxists call "vulgar materialism") but rather emerges from the relations of production and how people think about these relations.

[11] When this essay was written, French structuralism and sociobiology were extremely popular in the United States. In this paragraph, Leacock takes aim at both, particularly sociobiologist E. O. Wilson's *Sociobiology: The New Synthesis*. (The introduction to Wilson's book is reprinted as essay 30.) Wilson's notion that genes were responsible for much of human nature was anathema to most anthropologists. Behind the notion of the "conformer gene" is the idea that hunting required a high degree of coordination and conformity. Laughlin (mentioned in this paragraph) called hunting the "master behavior pattern of the human species" (cited in Barash 1979:186). Thus, the tendency of humans to conform is genetically based—the result of the fact that, over the millennia, there was strong evolutionary pressure for conformity.

Leacock criticizes French structuralism as reductionist and antihistorical. For Lévi-Strauss, the underlying meaning of myths and other cultural phenomena involves a few universal themes such as resolving humans' relations to nature. The outward form of the stories and the historical circumstances that produced them have no meaning. This perspective is anathema to Leacock.

iors. Scientifically, however, it would be absurd not to recognize that the lawful movements of planetary bodies have their own history of development, and operate at a level of integration independent from the internal processes that characterize their constituent parts. With respect to society, few would argue directly that social processes do not also operate at a level of their own. In effect, however, this is precisely what reductionist formulations imply.

Anthropologists have long been sensitive to biological reductionism with regard to physical variations of a racial order, and somewhat aware that reductionist formulations serve as ideological rationalizations of oppression. Unfortunately, this is not the case with respect to physical variations of a sexual order. Although the fact that physiological sex and social gender are far from isometric is well established and documented in anthropology, cross-cultural discussions of sex roles commonly fall into reductionism in their formulations.[12] Many Marxists, as well as other scholars, translate the gender structure of the hierarchical exploitative society with which they are familiar into innate predispositions and the practice is encouraged by the recent worldwide spread of Western norms, at least on a superficial level. The assumption remains prevalent that physiological differences between the sexes embody hints of female subordination only slightly expressed in egalitarian cultures but that come to full flower in class-based state-organized urban societies. Instead of being treated as an historical development, hierarchy becomes written into human physiology. Despite much citation from Marx and Engels on the part of those who do this, they contradict a fully Marxist view of human nature as

informed by the last hundred years of social science research. Their entanglement with male supremacist ideology feeds into and is fed by the failure to deal rigorously with both history and theory in the interpretation of primitive communist society and the source of its transformation.[13]

THE ORIGINS OF HIERARCHY

The two sets of relations defined by Marx and Engels as critical to the emergence of exploitation are: first, the loss of control over the production process (i.e., production, exchange, distribution, and consumption) through the division of labor beyond that by sex; and second, the emergence of dyadic relations[14] of dependency within individual families as a public/private dichotomy developed in economic and political life, making families separate economic units rather than parts of encompassing communal groups. The fundamental historical development analysed at length in Marx's opening section of *Capital* and central to Engels' reworking of Morgan's evolutionary hypothesis in *The Origin of the Family, Private Property and the State,* was the transformation from production for use to production for exchange. The emergence of production for exchange meant that value as an attribute of goods began to supersede use as the feature of primary social significance. As a consequence "abstract labor," the labor time represented in an exchangeable object, became separable from concrete work, a development that eventually made it possible for those who controlled exchange to regulate and exploit the productivity of others. Finally, money developed in various forms as a

---

[12] *Isometric:* of equal measure.

Here, Leacock says that although sex and gender are not equivalent, many scholars still believe that the physiological differences between men and women are the basis for gender inequality. One example of this type of work is Ortner's structural analysis in this volume (essay 27).

[13] In the paragraphs above, Leacock has condemned the sociobiologists and structuralists. Here she takes aim at unnamed Marxists who fail to fully apply Marxist analysis to their subject because they accept the Western ideology of male supremacy. Neo-Marxist authors are well known for attacking one another's positions, and Leacock does not spare those who share her theoretical outlook.

[14] A dyadic relationship is one with two parts. Leacock argues here that the emergence of dyadic relations of dependency within individual families was a second factor explaining the origins of exploitation.

medium of exchange, as a pure commodity. Marx stressed that the money form allowed the fetishistic absurdity whereby relations among people appeared to them as relations among things; thus the structure of exploitation was mystified and the existence of class differences rationalized.[15]

In *The Evolution of Political Society,* Fried raised the question why people accepted control by others over the products of their work and allowed the loss of their independence.[16] Whatever the answer, Fried stated, people did not realize the magnitude of the changes they were bringing about.* To be sure, they did not, since, through exchange and the division of labor, people were simply enriching their lives and cementing interpersonal and intergroup bonds, innocent of the processes thereby set in motion. As Engels put it, "the more a social activity, a series of social processes . . . appears a matter of pure chance, then all the more surely within this chance the laws peculiar to it and inherent in it assert themselves." Commodity production and the division of labor that accompanied it slowly but inexorably led to class stratification; they raised up "incorporeal alien powers . . . too powerful for men's conscious control."*[17]

Simple barter does not separate the producer from control over exchange and distribution. As barter develops in importance, however, it leads to a contradiction between the material benefits to be derived from specialized production for trade and the structure of full egalitarianism. Fried suggested that the elaboration of redistribution was important to the emergence of ranking, the first form of stratification.* The focus should be sharpened and emphasis placed on the significance of redistribution for the emergence of commodity production with all its consequences. Goods produced for exchange rather than for use create new interest groups. For a long time, egalitarian relationships prevent persons in pivotal positions in networks of exchange and redistribution from exploiting the economic possibilities of their position. Nonetheless, the conflict between egalitarian relations sharpens and, in what are called ranking societies, people begin to accept dependent positions in relation to "big men" and other chiefly people in order to benefit from the hand-outs associated with them. Eventually, unequal appropriation among and within competitively structured lineages is institutionalized, and the conflict between egalitarian distribution and consumption on the one hand, and the potential afforded by exchange and increasing specialization of labor on the other, is partially resolved. New contradictions are already crystallizing, however, between the potentials created by increasingly farflung economic ties and social forms attuned to autonomous kin and village groupings, in turn to be resolved by full stratification and political organization and the familiar conflicts of class society.[18]

---

[15] In this paragraph, Leacock is trying to briefly recount Marx's theory of the origins of hierarchy. The first step is a movement from producing things simply to use them (for their "use value") to producing things as commodities that can be sold. Marx argues that this movement allows people in capitalist societies to think of the amount of labor that goes into the production of an object as equivalent to the value of that object. However, capitalist society makes a fetish of the commodity, valuing it over the labor that produced it. Marx's notion is sometimes referred to as the labor theory of value and is one of the most controversial aspects of his philosophy.

　　The Origin of the Family, Private Property, and the State (1972 [1884]) is a book that Engels wrote based on notes Marx had taken as he read Morgan's *Ancient Society.* Engels' analysis is based on Morgan's notion that families were originally matrilineal. He ties the historic shift from matrilineality to patrilineality to the emergence of private property. Leacock was very familiar with Engels' work. In fact, she wrote an introduction to the 1972 edition.

[16] In this section, Leacock leans heavily on the theory of stratification advanced by Morton Fried in *The Evolution of Political Society* (1967). The essay by Fried in this volume (21) was published seven years before his book and is a summary of the principal arguments he advanced there.

[17] In this section, "The Origins of Hierarchy," Leacock points out that social processes are qualitatively different from the actions of individuals. Here, individuals simply pursue their own benefit, but the net result is a social shift to hierarchy that results in their loss of independence. She argues that this same shift also results in the emergence of gender hierarchy.

[18] In Marxist thinking, it is the resolution of conflict that creates change between social forms. However, each such resolution contains the germs of a new conflict and, hence, progress to new social forms. In this paragraph, Leacock points

To return to the second component of exploitation and stratification, it is in conjunction with the above developments that a public/private dichotomy emerges and dyadic relations of dependence within families as economic units begin to take shape. Lévi-Strauss posits to the contrary, in egalitarian societies, women are not exchanged by men; instead they exchange goods and services with men.* Direct exchange between the sexes, like single barter, does not separate either sex from control over its own production. Instead, alienation develops in tandem with the development of exchange systems, as individuals use lineage and extended family units to compete for ranking positions in relation to control over the production and distribution of valued goods. Gender responsibilities for marketing and exchange vary according to how different environments and histories have patterned the sex division of labor, and women's position in decision-making structures varies correspondingly.* Yet the question remains: when ranking begins to undermine the equal prerogatives of people generally, why is it that the autonomy and authority of women as a sex are threatened rather than those of men? Aside from various formulations of male superiority, it is usually argued that the physical limitations of childbirth and suckling are critical. Yet these do not hinder women in egalitarian societies.* In keeping with my reading of dialectical materialist theory as outlined above, I would say that the significance of women's childbearing ability is transformed by new social relations when they become the producers, not only of people as individuals, but also of what is becoming "abstract"—i.e., exploitable—labor. The origins of gender hierarchy, then, are inextricably meshed with the origins of exploitation and class stratification.*[19]

Engels posed a sharp contrast between the status of women among the egalitarian Iroquois and that in the patriarchal societies of the classical Middle East and Mediterranean where control over female sexuality was important for the inheritance of status and property. In his view, the family as an economic unit was of primary importance within the upper class although it had ramifications throughout society. It remained for mid-20th century Marxist-feminist scholarship to add a further dimension to these ramifications. Female subordination within the family as an economic unit also enabled an upper class to squeeze more surplus from workers, serfs and slaves. The fact that domestic work could be separated from a public sphere and assigned to women as the wards of men assured to an upper class the reproduction and maintenance of workers through socially unremunerated—i.e., slave—labor. This

---

first to a conflict between egalitarian social forms and specialization. Since no two specializations are likely to be entirely equal, it is impossible to maintain egalitarian social relations once specialization begins. This is resolved in rank societies through a hierarchical ranking of kin groups. This, however, creates new contradictions because nonkin relations are now available through trade with distant people.

[19]Leacock argues that in egalitarian societies based on barter economics, gender relations are relations of equality. Making a fetish of commodities and making labor a commodity are part of the formation of hierarchical societies, and it is only when egalitarian societies become rank societies that women lose rights and men gain them. This leaves her with a difficult question: why are women, rather than men, the ones who lose the rights? She rejects explanations rooted in either biology or "human nature" and instead asserts that women are disadvantaged because they are associated with the production of labor power rather than of commodities themselves. Thus, women produce labor, men produce commodities. Commodities are more valued in hierarchical societies than is labor, therefore men are more highly valued than women. Note that the accuracy of this claim rests wholly on acceptance of Marx's notion of the labor theory of value and the notion of making a fetish of the commodity. Without these ideas, there is no reason why producing labor should be intrinsically more or less valuable than producing commodities.

Interestingly, Leacock's analysis here bears a superficial resemblance to Ortner's notions in "Is Female to Male as Nature Is to Culture?" (essay 27). In that essay, Ortner contends that women are seen as inferior because nature is seen as inferior to culture. Women's production of children ties them to nature while men's production of material ties them to culture. The critical difference between Ortner's structural analysis and Leacock's Marxist analysis is that Ortner sees the relative positions of nature and culture as fundamental features of human consciousness in all societies. Leacock, on the other hand, believes that the position of labor relative to its products is a specific, historical development in capitalist societies.

is not to say that the arrangement was thought through in advance any more than other major historical developments of the past. However, given the records of women's steady decline in legal and social rights in classical antiquity, it remains to trace some of the steps whereby the household subordination of women was buttressed by ideological and social sanctions as its economic advantages were realized.*[20]

All of this, however, pertains to the final stages of women's subordination. The majority of societies with which anthropology deals involve the most preliminary stages—points at which women's autonomy began to be threatened and a certain hostility between the sexes began to be institutionalized, but that were very far indeed from the legal and political reduction of women to the status of ward that accompanied full-scale stratification. I am suggesting that the structure of gender in such societies needs to be interpreted in relation to: the structure of exchange and the division of labor; the structure of ranking and the degree to which some sections of the society are gaining control over the labor of others; the structure of kinship and the extent to which lineages have become competing sodalities rather than the means for organizing production and distribution in communal villages; the degree to which the well-being of one segment of a society is not merely relative but is actually at the expense of other segments; and, in the light of all this, the structure of marriage in relation to control over children as exploitable labor or as exploiters of labor.[21]

In what are called ranking societies, women's position begins to shift from valued people who cement networks of reciprocal relations and who have access to various publically recognized mechanisms for adjudicating their interests as women, into that of service workers in the households of husbands and their kin groups. Bride wealth begins to take the form of purchasing a woman's children, rather than of gift exchange. Sacks has explored the relation of such developments to the emergence of status difference among women as well as between women and men.* She has demonstrated the usefulness of separating the status of women as wives from that as sisters in order to appreciate the extent to which women exercise publically recognized authority through the manipulation of kin ties in societies where economic stratification and gender hierarchy are emerging. Sanday has stressed the fact that women may protect and maintain their public authority well into the conditions of stratification, a fact attested to by extensive data on West African societies and suggested by the case of ancient Crete.* All told, a focus on the above developments and the particularities of their unfolding in different historical, cultural and environmental contexts, makes clear that changes in women's position are neither secondary phenomena, as some imply, nor prior to economic hierarchy, as argued by others. They are at the core of, and inseparable from, profound transformations that take place in conjunction with the development of exchange and the division of labor.

The social and economic subordination of women was established in some parts of the world millenia ago; it was unfolding in other parts of the world at the time of European exploration

---

[20] Leacock is arguing that men were able to reproduce their superior social position by relying on the unpaid domestic work of women. Her argument comes substantially from Engels' *Origin of the Family*. In that work, Engels argues that property was key to marriage among the bourgeoisie, and he likened marriage to prostitution. Women in such marriages traded domestic and sexual service for economic support. Engels argued that after the communist revolution, marriage would be egalitarian since each partner would be equally involved in production.

[21] In this passage, Leacock cites two other prominent feminist anthropologists: Peggy Sanday (1937–) and Karen Sacks (1941–). When this essay was written, Sanday had recently published *Female Power and Male Dominance: On the Origins of Sexual Inequality* (1981). There, she argued that in "inner oriented" societies—those with abundant food supplies and little threat of outside aggression—people lived in harmony with nature and each other. Gender relations were egalitarian. But in "outer oriented" societies, characterized by food scarcity and warfare, men dominated women. She reported that the number of "outer oriented" societies increased with colonialism. Karen Sacks is also concerned with issues of gender equality and, when this essay was written, had recently published *Sisters and Wives: The Past and Future of Sexual Equality* (1979).

and conquest; and it has been developing in yet others in the context of Western colonialism and imperialism.* I am here arguing that in order to interpret this development correctly, it is essential, first: to have a clear concept of primitive communism, divested of stereotypical assumptions that female subordination is a natural rather than historical phenomenon, and second: to place any society under study clearly in the context of its particular history, pre- and post-colonial. I now return to the second point.

THE HISTORICAL CONTEXT OF ANTHROPOLOGICAL ANALYSIS

The actual people contemporary anthropologists study are not autonomous gatherer-hunters or horticulturalists or whatever. In one way or another the relations of capitalism have impinged upon them for a long time. Whatever the specific nature of a people's involvement with capitalism, the *ultimate* direction of change is the same: the individualization and alienation of labor, the individualization of the nuclear family, and the relegation of women both to unrecompensed domestic labor and to public labor as an unstable and underpaid work force. People lose what control over the process and products of their labor they previously had, and their labor itself becomes increasingly transformed into a commodity to be

bought, if not outright commandeered. The responsibility for rearing the new generation is progressively transferred from some larger kin or band grouping to individual families. Idealized by missionary teachings as loving care for husband and children, women's labor in the household becomes for all practical purposes a gift to the plantation or mine owner, manufacturer or trader, who draws profits from the work of husbands and sons and then buys women's additional labor at a marginal price.*[22]

Untidy details like plantation labor and commercial transactions have too commonly been ignored when data on so-called traditional societies are codified and punched on IBM cards for cross-cultural comparison.[23] Not surprisingly, a recent analysis concludes that there are no consistent correlations between women's position in a society and other factors.* Luckily, however, ethnohistorical and archaeological reconstruction of pre-colonial and colonial culture histories is proceeding apace, and it is possible to throw light on puzzling cases where there seems to be little relation between female subordination and economic inequality.[24]

I have already made reference to North America, which, north of Mexico, constitutes the largest world area that was inhabited by egalitarian peoples at the time of European expansion. Ranking was elaborated in coastal areas, especially along the Gulf of Mexico and the northern

---

[22] Leacock's critical point is that women's domestic labor is essential to the reproduction of the workforce. Without domestic labor, families cannot be maintained and workers cannot be produced. However, the owners of capital (the factory owners or mine owners) pay their workers (usually male) but do not pay the women whose work enables the production of these workers. Thus, from Leacock's perspective, women's domestic work is a gift to capitalists.

[23] Leacock is attacking George Peter Murdock's Human Relations Area Files project (see essay 20). Murdock's project was a descendant of the large-scale cross-cultural studies started by Herbert Spencer. Thus it has a history that places it squarely in the anti-Marxist camp. The "Outline of Cultural Materials" Murdock devised to code the HRAF is decidedly non-Marxist, giving little attention to conflict, imperialism, class consciousness, or other interests central to Marxist analysis.

[24] Leacock makes the point in the second half of this essay that European expansion, from the fifteenth century on, had critical effects on people throughout the world. In particular, as capitalist relations of production were imposed on indigenous groups, the social and political position of women suffered. Previously egalitarian societies, in which women enjoyed either full equality with men or very substantial rights, were subverted, and men came to dominate women. Leacock argues that most ethnographic writing simply fails to take the effects of European colonialism into account. Thus ethnographies that showed the oppression of women among indigenous peoples were generally in error. The authors of these monographs, writing in the ethnographic present, fail to realize that the practices they assume to be "traditional" date only from the transformation of these societies by capitalism. If these societies could be seen before the advent of European expansion, the equality of gender relations in egalitarian and early ranked societies would be apparent. In making

Pacific, but the vast majority of native North Americans had retained egalitarian socio-economic structures. The Iroquois are the best known example of the gender equality common in North America, and, contrary to the opinion of Lévi-Strauss,* are not an anomaly. Instead, they afford a well-documented example of the economic and political reciprocity that accompanied the matrilineal-matrilocal organization widespread among North American horticulturalists.* Among hunting-gathering peoples, the Inuit (Eskimo) are commonly cited as an example of masculine brutality toward women in an otherwise egalitarian society, an example seemingly paralleled by accounts of female subordination among the Chipewyan.* However, ethnographic accounts of women's independence and assertiveness among the Inuit indicate that ethnohistorical analysis, long overdue, will reveal the latter-day character of male abusiveness as following from the demoralization and drunkenness suffered in many Inuit communities.* As for the Chipewyan case, it is based on an account of middlemen in the fur trade, the "gang" that collected around the unusually dedicated worker for the Hudson's Bay Company, and not on independent Chipewyan hunters. The quality of relations therein described contrasts sharply with the 17th century Jesuit accounts of gender equality among the Montagnais-Naskapi.*

Australia

Aboriginal Australia has furnished ample grounds for arguments that male dominance is a psychosocial or psychobiological universal rather than an historical development. Male control of women's marriage, male inheritance of land, virilocal residence, male brutality towards women, and male exclusion of women from important rituals in a non-stratified society form an imposing package and have been documented again and again. To be sure, data modifying these generalizations are beginning to assert themselves. Older women have a say in marriages along with older men, while young men, like young women, have little say. Just as young women are commonly married the first time to elder men, so are young men often married to elder women. Women have clubs with which they not only defend themselves, but with which they beat men for misbehavior; they are not cowed by men. Furthermore, if wrongfully hit, a woman may simply leave, or may take up residence in the women's section of the camp, taboo to men. Women are important in the conduct of some male rituals, and are indifferent to their exclusion from others; their own, from which men are excluded, hold more interest for them.* Tindale has pointed out that among the Pitjandara of western Australia, women call male rituals to a close if they find themselves walking too far for food and wish to move camp.* Bell worked in a north-central Australian settlement where "the maintenance of law and order . . . is still a co-operative venture between men and women who turn to each other for assistance on some issues and assert their independent rights on others."*

However, while such data qualify the picture of male dominance claimed for Australian gatherer-hunters, the historical setting in which 20th cen-

---

this argument Leacock is strongly influenced by World Systems Theory, a popular neo-Marxist position of the 1960s and 1970s. While notions of dependency have been around for a long time, World Systems Theory was promoted by the work of Andre Gunder-Frank (1929–) and Immanuel Wallerstein (1930–). In his most famous essay, "The Development of Underdevelopment" (1966), Gunder-Frank argued that the nations of Latin America were not poor because they failed to industrialize. Rather, the processes of the expansion of capitalism in the wealthy nations, particularly in North America and in northern Europe, had drawn wealth out of Latin America. Thus, the poverty of southern nations was directly linked to the wealth of northern capitalist societies. In 1974 Wallerstein published *The Modern World-System,* in which he traced the development of global capitalism from its origins in the early seventeenth century, emphasizing its deleterious effects on noncapitalist cultures around the world. As with Gunder-Frank, the principal thesis Wallerstein advanced was that the wealth of nations and the poverty of nations are interlinked. Today's wealthy nations became rich by expropriating the wealth of today's poor nations. Although Leacock focuses on gender relations rather than wealth, the fundamental argument is the same. She insists that it was the expansion of capitalist power that undermined the position of women in society after society.

tury Aboriginal society has been functioning must be understood if this image is to be contradicted in its entirety. First and foremost, not to evaluate the effects of the brutal genocide native Australians have suffered is as unscientific as it is unethical. Brutality against native Australians has been practiced from the earliest forays by Malays; to the sporadic explorations by Europeans and the 1788 convict settlement at what is now Sydney; through the steady encroachment on Australian lands and the accompanying shooting, poisoning, beating and enslaving, along with disastrous disease; into the brutal policing and racist restrictions of the present. One cannot talk of men hitting women as if apart from a pattern of frontier violence where demoralization is compounded by alcohol.*

Second, it is — or should be — inexcusable to analyse land rights in Australia without considering the impact of forced movements away from coastal areas and the resulting land pressure in interior regions to which many Aborigines fled. Some early meetings between Europeans and Australians were friendly, but the Europeans were over-ready to use their guns, and apparently the Australians sometimes retaliated with the unambiguous act of treating their foes as food. For the most part, therefore, early explorers from Europe were glad to leave the Australians alone, once it was decided that there was no ready gold or other easy wealth on their lands. Then the arrival of the first merino sheep in New South Wales in 1797 was followed in 1813 by the discovery, west of the Blue Mountains, of the immense grasslands that were to make Australia the largest producer of fine wool in the world.* The push was on. The rich southeast, where 400 to 600 people were

wont to gather at certain seasons to socialize and live on seafood and crayfish, was soon depopulated of Aborigines. Some were killed, some moved west, and a few married into the white community. The herders too pushed west, enslaving the Aborigines, or pressing them into labor, and brutally suppressing their resistance.* Driven westward and inland, away from expanding centers of white settlement and onto each other's traditional homelands, different peoples turned against each other, fighting and quarrelling. As among native Americans, the recognition of a common identity as Aborigines, with a common history and common struggle, took time to emerge. White Australians of course took advantage of and exacerbated divisiveness among the Aborigines, favoring "pacified" groups and using them to enslave or control others.

The demoralization found among displaced Aboriginal survivors is documented by Daisy Bates, who over a period of some forty years publicized the Aboriginal condition from her isolated camp in South Australia.* Despite the patronization and misinterpretations of her account, many incidents she reports parallel the macabre bitterness of collective suicide described by Turnbull for the Ik.* A particularly bizarre scene ensues when Bates accompanied Radcliffe-Brown to the grim hospital island where sick and fearful Aborigines, separated from their own people, are taken only to die. She describes Radcliffe-Brown asking the old men to sing ritual songs into his phonograph and playing them Tannhauser and Egmont in return.*25

By the 20th century, disease and genocide in its various forms had reduced an estimated 300,000 or more people of aboriginal Australia to

---

25 This paragraph contains references to several notorious characters. Daisy Bates (1861–1951) was an Irishwoman who lived among the Aborigines for thirty years, beginning in about 1913. Bates wrote several books about her experience. It is impossible to doubt that horrific things happened to the Aborigines, but Daisy Bates might not be the best source. Julia Blackburn, author of *Daisy Bates in the Desert: A Woman's Life Among the Aborigines* (1994), writes that Bates fabricated her life history and that she was unable to separate her experiences from her imagination.

Colin Turnbull was the author of *The Forest People* (1961) and *The Mountain People* (1972). The first of these describes the idyllic life of the Mbuti of the Ituri Forest and the second, the horrific life of the Ik of Uganda. Both portraits have been heavily critiqued as romantic (or antiromantic).

A. R. Radcliffe-Brown lived in Australia from 1926 to 1931. The image Bates and Leacock present here is a compelling one, and it may well have happened. It is clear that Radcliffe-Brown had little interest in history and believed that the social structures he studied had been relatively little affected by colonialism.

less than 40,000.* By mid-century, with the "sta-bilization" of native reserves, and the dispensa-tion of minimal food supplies and medical care by government or mission stations, the Aboriginal population began to rise again. Ritual life, too, began to revive and expand, although serving a new function as a focus for the assertion of iden-tity and self-respect by a people robbed of their independence. Anthropologists also expanded in numbers, typically wishing to study the lives of pristine hunter-gatherers. They usually took care to interview people living a distance from mission stations or cattle ranches, rather than the service workers directly attached to such enterprises. Sel-dom, however, did they inquire deeply into a peo-ple's history, nor even inquire about existing official regulations for Aborigines, such as those that prohibit marriage off of a reserve.*

The point should be clear. To ignore the his-torical, economic, and political realities of Abo-riginal life is to gloss over the effects of conquest and oppression, and therefore to misconstrue the social relations that obtained when Aborigines were autonomous gatherers and hunters in con-trol of their own social world. With respect to re-lations between the sexes, when one scrapes the surface of ethnohistorical materials, one finds suggestions of women's former importance, such as Howitt's reference to influential elder women in southeastern Australia. Only recently, however, have these begun to be followed up.* As long ago as a hundred years, Spencer and Gillin note a three-day women's section of an initiation cere-mony among the Arunta and comment that "there was a time when women played a more important part in regard to such ceremonies than they do at the present time."* Unfortunately, they give no further information except that they personally find the ceremony boring. In his recently repub-lished *Australian Religion*, Mircea Eliade makes ample reference to male high gods, but nowhere mentions the important mythological personage who keeps reappearing in the pages of Spencer and Gillin, the female Sun. Eliade writes that ini-tiation for Australian girls is simpler than for boys, and flatly contradicts ethnographic fact by stating, "as everywhere in the world."*

Hart and Pilling raise the need for ethno-historical work in their account of the Tiwi.*

They describe how missionary influences as well as prostitution encouraged male control over women's sexuality in the early 20th century, and then go on to consider earlier influences on the politics of wife-trading. Archival research is needed, they write, to determine the extent of slave raiding by the Portuguese in the 18th century. Since it was probably the younger men who were taken off to Timor, they suggest the slaving may have encouraged the dominance of old Tiwi men and their monopolization of wives.

Leacock provides three additional ethnographic examples, but space considerations prevent us from reprinting them here. We summarize them below.

In a 1,100-word section with 12 notes entitled "The Amazon," Leacock first divides Amazonian history into five periods. The first of these is pre-colonial, but in the others she dwells on the effects of colonization. She then moves to a discussion of the Yanomamo, asserting that their portrayal as "the fierce people" serves to rational-ize the destruction of the Amazon forests. Citing geographer William J. Smole (1976), Leacock argues that the Yanomamo studied by Chagnon were made fierce by their contacts with Portu-guese and Spanish invaders. Smole also reports that the position of women among the highland Yanomamo he studied was very much better than that reported by Chagnon. Leacock concludes this section by claiming that Chagnon's failure to deal with the Yanomamo history and politics cast doubt on his portrayal of the male aggressiveness and dominance among a virtually pristine egali-tarian people.

In an 830-word section with 6 notes entitled "Melanesia," Leacock suggests that the societies of New Guinea are often used as evidence for the subordination of women in egalitarian societies. This, however, is incorrect since ancient irriga-tion works and trade connections suggest that stratification had already begun in this area. Fur-ther, trade connections with Malays, Chinese, and Europeans may have badly compromised egalitarian relations. The hostility often expressed between men and women is highly suggestive of a society in which rank is being asserted and women are losing control over their production.

The fact that in New Guinea women often respond to their subordination with open anger rather than passive acceptance is strongly suggestive of societies in which the process of stratification is only beginning. These relations may have been further exacerbated by European conquest, which increased conflict between tribes.

A 2,000-word section with 19 notes titled "Africa" includes a substantial critique of the work of French neo-Marxists Claude Meillassoux and Emanuel Terray. Their work was critical in the development of Marxist thought in anthropology during the 1960s and 1970s, and both worked in Africa. The French neo-Marxists broke from Soviet-style Marxist anthropology. Soviet ethnographers insisted on the primacy of the modes of production outlined by Marx and Morgan's scheme for the evolution of society. The French neo-Marxists expanded the notion of mode of production to include new modes germane to the societies anthropologists studied. They were also largely trained by Lévi-Strauss and were deeply influenced by his notions on exchange and the role of women.

Leacock begins by noting that African history is extremely complex but often ignored. Despite some exceptions, the ethnography of African societies portrays women as firmly under male authority. Ethnohistorical work, however, shows that the position of African women deteriorated with the advent of colonial rule. Before colonialism, they often had important public political roles. Although in African hierarchical societies, women's autonomy was undermined, it was not destroyed, except in later Moslem states. Leacock faults the French neo-Marxists for failing to use Engels' notion that the subjugation of women was central to the development of hierarchy in analyzing the emergence of ranked societies in Africa. Because they agree with Lévi-Strauss on the universal subjugation of women, they tend to condense egalitarian and beginning rank societies into a single mode of production. This obscures the critical processes of the emergence of hierarchy. The problem is evident in Terray's work on
the Gayman. Terray sees kin relations among the Gayman as exploiting women and youth. These relations were eventually dominated by relations based on slavery. Terray does not, however, look for a reason why women are exploited in the first place. Leacock, however, finds the answer in Terray's own work. She notes that he says the lineage structure is related to the political structure and did not come before it; further, "youth" was a rank that could include older men. Finally, captive labor was used in the lineage mode of production. Thus, Terray fails to realize that the exploitation of women and youth in the lineage mode of production is integral to the existence of hierarchical society and did not precede it. Terray also fails to consider that the ranked urban portion of society could have affected the more egalitarian rural part of society. His analysis is also weakened by failure to consider changes brought about by exposure to European slaving.

CONCLUSION

Across the disciplines, research on the economic and social activities of women has been shaking up some established assumptions about society and history. I have argued that only when gender hierarchy is taken as an historical problematic, rather than a psycho-biological given, can the structure of primitive communist relations be properly understood, and the part played by exchange in the transformation of these relations clearly formulated. The need for an effective theory of exchange in pre-capitalist societies is well recognized by Marxist anthropologists,* but ironically it is associated, especially for those working in the structuralist tradition, with the wholly anti-Marxist concept of woman exchange as basic in primitive communist society.[26] Only when such a formulation is stringently challenged can the first phases of the process whereby women actually became exchanged be understood, for these were inseparable from initial steps in the transformation of use to value, work to abstract labor, and cooperative production to exploitation.

---

[26] Here, Leacock is once again attacking the French Marxists she has discussed in her analysis of Africa. We have edited this portion of the essay from the text, but be sure to read our condensation of it.

An effective theory of exchange is necessary both for analysing pre-capitalist societies and for interpreting the effects on these societies of colonization and imperialism. Only when the genders in primitive communist societies are understood as economically independent exchangers of goods and services, can the full force of capitalist relations in subverting the labor of women, and therefore transforming the entire structure of relationships in such societies, be appreciated. Until such time, the myth of the ethnographic present will continue to support the assumption, so prevalent in pop-science and the mass media, that the widespread normative ideal of men as household heads who provision dependent women and children reflects some human need or drive. And until such time, the unique and valued culture history and tradition of each Third World people will continue to be distorted, twisted to fit the interests of capitalist exploitation.

34. Making Empire Respectable: The Politics of Race and Sexual Morality in Twentieth-Century Colonial Cultures

Ann L. Stoler (1949–)

THE SHIFT AWAY FROM VIEWING COLONIAL elites as homogeneous communities of common interest marks an important trajectory in the anthropology of empire, signaling a major rethinking of gender relations within it. More recent attention to the internal tensions of colonial enterprises has placed new emphasis on the quotidian[1] assertion of European dominance in the colonies, on imperial interventions in domestic life, and thus on the cultural prescriptions by which European women and men lived (Callan and Ardener 1984; Knibiehler and Goutalier 1985; Reijs, et. al 1986; Callaway 1987; Strobel 1987). Having focused on how colonizers have viewed the indigenous Other, we are beginning to sort out how Europeans in the colonies imagined themselves and constructed communities built on asymmetries of race, class and gender—entities significantly at odds with the European models on which they were drawn.

These feminist attempts to engage the gender politics of Dutch, French and British imperial

(1989)

cultures converge on some strikingly similar observations; namely that European women in these colonies experienced the cleavages of racial dominance and internal social distinctions very differently than men precisely because of their ambiguous positions, as both subordinates in colonial hierarchies and as active agents of imperial culture in their own right. Concomitantly, the majority of European women who left for the colonies in the late 19th and early 20th centuries confronted profoundly rigid restrictions on their domestic, economic and political options, more limiting than those of metropolitan Europe at the time and sharply contrasting the opportunities open to colonial men.

In one form or another these studies raise a basic question: in what ways were gender inequalities essential to the structure of colonial racism and imperial authority? Was the strident misogyny of imperial thinkers and colonial agents a byproduct of receiving metropolitan values ("they just brought it with them"), a reaction to contemporary feminist demands in Europe ("women need to be put back in their breeding place"), or a

---

[1] *Quotidian:* daily. A quotidian assertion is an everyday assertion.

novel and pragmatic response to the conditions of conquest? Was the assertion of European supremacy in terms of patriotic manhood and racial virility an expression of imperial domination or a defining feature of it?[2]

In this paper I examine some of the ways in which colonial authority and racial distinctions were fundamentally structured in gendered terms. I look specifically at the administrative and medical discourse and management of European sexual activity, reproduction and marriage as it articulated with the racial politics of colonial rule. Focusing on French Indochina and the Dutch East Indies in the early 20th century, but drawing on other contexts, I suggest that the very categories of "colonizer" and "colonized" were secured through forms of sexual control which defined the domestic arrangements of Europeans and the cultural investments by which they identified themselves.*[3]

Gender specific sexual sanctions demarcated positions of power by refashioning middle-class conventions of respectability, which, in turn, prescribed the personal and public boundaries of race.[4]

Colonial authority was constructed on two powerful, but false, premises. The first was the notion that Europeans in the colonies made up an easily identifiable and discrete biological and social entity; a "natural" community of common class interests, racial attributes, political affinities and superior culture. The second was the related notion that the boundaries separating colonizer from colonized were thus self-evident and easily drawn (Stoler 1989). Neither premise reflected colonial realities (see for example, Cooper 1980; Drooglever 1980; Ridley 1983; Prochaska 1989; Comaroff (this volume)). Internal divisions developed out of conflicting economic and political

---

[2] In the 1970s and 1980s, feminist scholars tended to view women as a more-or-less homogenous group and focused their analysis on the social position of women in general. In the late 1980s and 1990s, the notion that women share common positions in society or face common problems has come under sharp attack. Women from poor nations and from minority groups in wealthy nations have led the charge. They argue that the feminist movement of the 1970s and 1980s was led by middle-class white scholars and reflected their concerns and opinions. The movement failed to recognize the privileged position of wealthy white women with respect to poor women of color. It failed to see that there were as many divisions among women as between women and men. Further, it failed to note that these divisions were often oppressive. Scholars in the late 1980s and 1990s have moved to address this situation and have often focused their work on the divisions among women and the ways in which the social positions and attitudes of wealthy women supported the social system and buttressed the oppression of poor women. Nowhere was this issue more apparent than in the anthropology of colonialism. In colonialism, women from colonizing societies, who were often quite brutally oppressed themselves, participated in and supported the oppression of women from colonized societies. Thus, examination of the colonial experience is ideal for exploring the complex ways in which notions of gender and ideas about class intersect and support one another.

[3] Stoler's original essay contained 29 notes totaling approximately 2,000 words. Space limitations prevent us from reproducing them here, but asterisks have been included to show where they were placed.

[4] Following a trend set in the 1980s (see Leacock, essay 33), Stoler argues that understanding the position of women in colonial society is central to any analysis of that society. Despite a myriad of different theoretical positions, a critical element that holds current feminist theorists together is the idea that gender relations are the fundamental, organizing principle of society.

Stoler's concern in this essay is understanding how men and women in colonial societies understood gender roles and classified the people around them. In one sense, this brings her close to the concerns of the ethnoscientists discussed in essays 28 and 29. However, Stoler's interests in history and in the relationship of systems of knowledge to systems of power clearly differentiate her from the ethnoscientists. The work of Michel Foucault is probably one of the most important influences on her.

Michel Foucault (1926–1984), a French philosopher, was vitally concerned with the relationship between systems of knowledge and systems of power and social control. Foucault's early work (1965 [1961]) focused on the ways in which mental institutions create languages of inclusion and exclusion that reflect and support the social order. He characterized his later work as "genealogical." For Foucault, this meant tracing the histories of the systems of knowledge used by the powerful in order to understand the relationship between power and knowledge and its connection with actual agendas, frictions over appropriate methods for safeguarding European privilege and power, competing criteria for reproducing a colonial elite and for restricting its membership.[5]

This latter, the colonial politics of exclusion, was contingent on constructing categories, legal and social classifications designating who was "white," who was "native," who could become a citizen rather than a subject, which children were legitimate progeny and which were not. What mattered were not only one's physical properties but who counted as "European" and by what measure.* Skin shade was too ambiguous; bank accounts were mercurial; religious belief and education were crucial but never enough. Social and legal standing derived not only from color, but from the silences, acknowledgments, and denials of the social circumstances in which one's parents had sex (Martinez-Alier 1974; Ming 1983; Taylor 1983). Sexual unions in the context of con-

cubinage, domestic service, prostitution or church marriage derived from the hierarchies of rule; but these were negotiated and contested arrangements, bearing on individual fates and the very structure of colonial society. Ultimately inclusion or exclusion required regulating the sexual, conjugal and domestic life of *both* Europeans in the colonies and their colonized subjects.[6]

Colonial observers and participants in the imperial enterprise appear to have had unlimited interest in the sexual interface of the colonial encounter (Malleret 1934:216; Pujarniscle 1931:106; Loutfi 1970:36). Probably no subject is discussed more than sex in colonial literature and no subject more frequently invoked to foster the racist stereotypes of European society. The tropics provided a site of European pornographic fantasies long before conquest was underway, but with a sustained European presence in colonized territories, sexual prescriptions by class, race and gen-

---

practices. One place he tried to apply this method was in *The History of Sexuality* (1978). There, he argued that the notion that sexuality has been repressed in Western society is erroneous. In fact, a discussion of sexuality has been central to how Europeans understand their society as well as to defining membership in sexual minorities. In particular, Foucault argued that until the late eighteenth century, people who had sexual relations with members of their own sex were not considered homosexuals. However, in the eighteenth and nineteenth centuries, along with the emergence of science, the discourse on sexuality changed. Homosexuals began to be identified as a group possessing specific characteristics. In other words, homosexuality changed from something a person did to something a person was.

Although Stoler does not cite Foucault in this essay, his influence on her work is evident. Foucault saw discourse on sexuality as central to understanding social structure and power relations within Western society. Tracing the historical changes of this discourse was fundamental to his project. Stoler sees gender as essential in understanding power relations in colonial societies and tries to trace the history of gender-related discourse and actual practices.

Feminist thinkers have had a deeply ambivalent relationship with the work of Foucault. The ideas that our understandings are socially constructed discourses, that these are related to power structures, and that the meanings of sexuality are historically situated all have powerful resonances for feminists. However, feminists have also been critical of Foucault for what they see as his narrowly masculine vision, his pessimistic outlook, and his denial of the possibilities for political change (Sawicki 1991). Beyond this, Foucault has often been criticized for lacking interest in gender. Foucault's work focuses on the relationship of individuals to worlds of knowledge, but he was less interested in the relationship of people to one another. His work does not consider how "the deployment of sexuality has affected the relations between men and women" (Bell 1993:27), a central issue for feminists.

[5] Race is a critical item on the agenda for many contemporary feminists. Late nineteenth-century and early twentieth-century American anthropology was vitally concerned with the issue of race. There was fierce debate over the equality of races. For cultural anthropologists, the debate ended with Boas' insistence on the biopsychological equality of all humans. Human differences, most cultural anthropologists believed, were entirely cultural, and the issue of race could be disposed of altogether. The result of accepting this doctrine was that discussion of race as an important organizing principle of society is absent from most cultural anthropology between the time of Boas and the 1980s. However, as greater numbers of women and men of color became anthropologists, the issue of race began once again to be important. These anthropologists insisted that even though race was not viable as a biological concept, it had frequently been a major organizing principle of European-dominated society. Understanding how race could have no biological existence and yet be a fundamental element of society became central to their concerns.

der became increasingly central to the politics of rule and subject to new forms of scrutiny by colonial states (Loutfi 1971; Gilman 1985:79).*

While anthropologists have attended to how European, and particularly Victorian, sexual mores affected *indigenous* gendered patterns of economic activity, political participation and social knowledge, less attention has been paid to the ways in which sexual control affected the very nature of colonial relations themselves (Tiffany and Adams 1985). In colonial scholarship more generally, sexual domination has figured as a social metaphor of European supremacy. Thus, in Edward Said's treatment of orientalist discourse, the sexual submission and possession of Oriental women by European men *"stands for* the pattern of relative strength between East and West" (1979:6). In this "male power-fantasy," the Orient is penetrated, silenced and possessed (ibid:207). Sexuality illustrates the iconography of rule, not its pragmatics; sexual assymetries are tropes to depict other centers of power.[7]

Such a treatment begs some basic questions. Was sexuality merely a graphic substantiation of who was, so to speak, on the top? Was the medium the message, or did sexual relations always "mean" something else, stand in for other relations, evoke the sense of *other* (pecuniary, political, or some possibly more subliminal) desires? This analytic slippage between the sexual symbols of power and the politics of sex runs throughout

the colonial record and contemporary commentaries upon it. Certainly some of this is due to the polyvalent quality of sexuality; symbolically rich and socially salient at the same time. But sexual control was more than a "social enactment"—much less a convenient metaphor—for colonial domination (Jordan 1968:141); it was, as I argue here, a fundamental class and racial marker implicated in a wider set of relations of power (Ballhatchet 1980).

The relationship between gender prescriptions and racial boundaries still remains unevenly unexplored. While we know that European women of different classes experienced the colonial venture very differently from one another and from men, we still know relatively little about the distinct investments they had in a racism they shared (Van Helten and Williams 1983; Knibielher and Goutalier 1985; Callaway 1987). New feminist scholarship has begun to sort out the unique colonial experience of European women as they were incorporated into, resisted and affected the politics of their men. But the emphasis has tended to be on the broader issue of gender subordination and colonial authority, not more specifically on how sexual control figured in the construction of racial boundaries per se.*

The linkage between sexual control and racial tensions is both obvious and elusive at the same time. While sexual fear may at base be a racial anxiety, we are still left to understand why it is

---

[6]In this passage, Stoler focuses on the intersection of race, class, and gender. Briefly, her point is that colonialism required maintaining the fiction that there was a clear racial difference between the colonized and the colonizer. Since the colonizers were more powerful than the subjects, this race difference was also a class difference. However, race is linked to sex and reproduction. Sex between members of different race/class groups creates progeny that are not easily classified and threaten the distinctions on which colonialism is based. Therefore, gender in general and control of sexuality in particular is a fundamental element of colonialism.

The notions of contested arrangements and negotiation appear in this passage as well. These ideas have become common in current anthropology. A contested arrangement is the idea that people are not satisfied with inferior social positions and invariably fight against them. Negotiation covers the idea that individual or group identity is not a fixed essence but is determined by a process of give-and-take with other individuals and groups.

[7] Edward Said (pronounced "sa-*eed*") (1935–), a professor of comparative literature and cultural critic, has been an important figure in the development of current anthropology. Said's breakthrough book was *Orientalism* (1978). In this work, Said argues that scholars constructed an exotic, sensual Middle East that had little to do with the realities of the actual nations and powers of that region. However, since these exotic and sensual images were held and promoted by wealthy and powerful interests, they became widely accepted. Stoler is invoking the notion that the way the wealthy and powerful think, speak, and write about people and place has a critical influence on policies affecting those places and thus realities in them.

through sexuality that such anxieties are expressed (Takaki 1977). If, as Sander Gilman (1985) claims, sexuality is the most salient marker of Otherness, organically representing racial difference, then we should not be surprised that colonial agents and colonized subjects expressed their contests — and vulnerabilities — in these terms (see Chatterjee this volume).

An overlapping set of discourses has provided the psychological and economic underpinnings for colonial distinctions of difference, linking fears of sexual contamination, physical danger, climatic incompatibility, and moral breakdown to a European colonial identity with a racist and class-specific core. Colonial scientific reports and the popular press are laced with statements and queries varying on a common theme: "native women bear contagions"; "white women become sterile in the tropics"; "colonial men are susceptible to physical, mental and moral degeneration when they remain in their colonial posts too long." To what degree are these statements medically or politically grounded? We need to unpack what is metaphor, what is perceived as dangerous (is it disease, culture, climate, or sex?) and what is not.[8]

In the sections that follow I look at the relationship between the domestic arrangements of colonial communities and their wider political structures. Part I examines the colonial debates over European family formation, over the relationship between subversion and sex in an effort to trace how evaluations of concubinage, morality and white prestige more generally were altered by new tensions within colonial cultures and by new challenges to imperial rule.

Part II examines what I call the "cultural hygiene" of colonialism. Focusing on the early 20th century as a break point, I take up the convergent metropolitan and colonial discourses on health hazards in the tropics, race-thinking and social reform as they related to shifts in the rationalization of colonial management. In tracing how fears of "racial degeneracy" were grounded in

class-specific sexual norms, I return to how and why biological and cultural distinctions were defined in gender terms.

THE DOMESTIC POLITICS OF COLONIALISM: CONCUBINAGE AND THE RESTRICTED ENTRY OF EUROPEAN WOMEN

The regulation of sexual relations was central to the development of particular kinds of colonial settlements and to the allocation of economic activity within them. Who bedded and wedded with whom in the colonies of France, England, Holland and Iberia was never left to chance. Unions between Annamite women and French men, between Javanese women and Dutch men, between Spanish men and Inca women produced offspring with claims to privilege, whose rights and status had to be determined and prescribed. From the early 1600s through the 20th century the sexual sanctions and conjugal prohibitions of colonial agents were rigorously debated and carefully codified. In these debates over matrimony and morality, trading and plantation company officials, missionaries, investment bankers, military high commands and agents of the colonial state confronted one another's visions of empire, and the settlement patterns on which it would rest.

In 1622 the Dutch East Indies Company (VOC) arranged for the transport of six poor but marriageable young Dutch women to Java, providing them with clothing, a dowry upon marriage and a contract binding them to five years in the Indies (Taylor 1983:12). Aside from this and one other short-lived experiment, immigration of European women to the East Indies was consciously restricted for the next 200 years. Enforcing the restriction by selecting bachelors as their European recruits, the VOC legally and financially made concubinage the most attractive domestic option for its employees (Blussé 1986:173; Ming 1983:69; Taylor 1983:16).

---

[8] The notion of unpacking is another common hallmark of current anthropology. To unpack an issue is to explore its various elements and levels of meaning. In this respect, the term updates Geertz's notion of "thick description," popular in the 1970s and 1980s.

It was not only the VOC which had profited from such arrangements. In the 19th and early 20th centuries, salaries of European recruits to the colonial armies, bureaucracies, plantation companies and trading enterprises were kept artificially low because local women provided domestic services for which new European recruits would otherwise have had to pay. In the mid-1800s, such arrangements were *de rigueur* for young civil servants intent on setting up households on their own (Ritter 1856:21). Despite some clerical opposition, at the end of the century concubinage was the most prevalent living arrangement for European colonials in the Indies (Ming 1983:70; Taylor 1983:16; van Marle 1952:486).[9]

Referred to as *nyai* in Java and Sumatra, *congai* in Indochina, and *petite épouse* throughout the French empire, the colonized woman living as a concubine to a European man formed the dominant domestic arrangement in colonial cultures through the early 20th century. Unlike prostitution, which could and often did result in a population of syphilitic and therefore nonproductive European men, concubinage was considered to have a stabilizing effect on political order and colonial health—a relationship that kept men in their barracks and bungalows, out of brothels and less inclined to perverse liaisons with one another.[10]

In Asia and Africa corporate and government decision makers invoked the social services which local women supplied as "useful guides to the language and other mysteries of the local societies" (Malleret 1934:216; Cohen 1971:122). Handbooks for incoming plantation employees bound for Tonkin, Sumatra and Malaya urged men to find local "companions" as a prerequisite for quick acclimatization, as insulation from the ill-health that sexual abstention, isolation and boredom were thought to bring (Butcher 1979:200, 202; Hesselink 1987:208; Braconier 1933:922; Dixon 1913:77). Although British and Dutch

colonial governments officially banned concubinage in the early 20th century, such measures were only selectively enforced. It remained tacitly condoned and practiced long after (Hyam 1986; Callaway 1987:49). In Sumatra's plantation belt newly opened in the late 19th century, for example, Javanese and Japanese *huishoudsters* (householders) remained the rule rather than the exception through the 1920s (Clerkx 1961:87–93; Stoler 1985a:31–34; Lucas 1986:84).

Concubinage was a contemporary term which referred to the cohabitation outside of marriage between European men and Asian women; in fact, it glossed a wide range of arrangements which included sexual access to a non-European woman as well as demands on her labor and legal rights to the children she bore (Pollman 1986:100; Lucas 1986:86).* Native women (like European women in a later period) were to keep men physically and psychologically fit for work, marginally content, not distracting or urging them out of line, imposing neither the time consuming nor financial responsibilities that European family life was thought to demand (Chivas-Baron 1929:103).*

To say that concubinage reinforced the hierarchies on which colonial societies were based is not to say that it did not make those distinctions more problematic at the same time. Grossly uneven sex ratios on North Sumatran estates made for intense competition among male workers and their European supervisors, with *vrouwen perkara* (disputes over women) resulting in assaults on whites, new labor tensions and dangerous incursions into the standards deemed essential for white prestige (Stoler 1985a:33; Lucas 1986:90–91). In the Netherlands Indies more generally an unaccounted number of impoverished Indo-European women moving between prostitution and concubinage further disturbed the racial sensibilities of the Dutch-born elite (Hesselink 1987:216). Metropolitan critics were particularly disdainful of such domestic arrangements on moral grounds—

---

[9] Note how Stoler draws attention to the fact that European colonials are not a homogenous group. They are divided not only by gender but also by social position. In this passage we learn that company owners encouraged the use of concubines because it allowed them to pay lower salaries and increase profits.

[10] In *The History of Sexuality* (1978), Foucault also links changing understandings of sexuality in the nineteenth century to ideas about health.

all the more so when these unions *were* sustained and personally significant relationships, thereby contradicting the racial premise of concubinage as an emotionally unfettered convenience.* But perhaps most important, the tension between concubinage as a confirmation and compromise of racial hierarchy was realized in the progeny that it produced, "mixed-bloods," poor "indos," and abandoned "*métis*" children who straddled the divisions of ruler and ruled threatened to blur the colonial divide.[11]

In an 1,100-word conclusion to this section, with 3 notes, Stoler writes that while authors often claimed few European women lived in the colonies because of poor living conditions, in general, this was not true. European women were discouraged from emigrating. Concubinage remained the preferred form of relationship long after the colonies became stable, secure, and medically upgraded. One result of these policies was that European men far outnumbered European women in most colonies. Because they could control the immigration of European women and the sorts of sexual relations their employees were permitted, states and corporations could fix the conditions under which European populations and privileges could be reproduced. The involvement of states and corporations in intimate matters shows that sexuality was tightly tied to state security and corporate profit. Improper sexual relations were thought to subvert security and profit while "normal" relations supported them. Stoler demonstrates this principle using an example from Northern Sumatra, where tobacco and rubber companies employed only single European workers. After the workers protested, the rule was changed and marriage permitted after five years' service. Some workers could get around this rule, but wages of new and low-level workers were kept too low to pay for a European family.

Various considerations led government and company officials to pursue different policies in different places and at different times. Sometimes, as in Malaya in the 1920s, concubinage was fa-

vored because officials believed that allowing the immigration of European women would create a class of poor whites that would threaten European prestige. But earlier, in Java, concubinage itself was condemned as a source of poor whites, but the use of brothels was condoned. The difference between the two cases was political. Where European supremacy was clearly established, concubinage could be allowed. When European dominance was threatened, European women or prostitution were used to increase the distance between colonizer and colonized. In the next sections, Stoler traces some common gendered issues shared by different colonial societies, focusing on how the positioning of European women promoted racial distinctions and colonial control.

RACIST BUT MORAL WOMEN: INNOCENT BUT IMMORAL MEN

Perhaps nothing is as striking in the sociological accounts of colonial communities as the extraordinary changes which are said to accompany the entry of European-born women. These adjustments shifted in one direction; toward European lifestyles accentuating the refinements of privilege and the etiquettes of racial difference. Most accounts agree that the presence of these women put new demands on the white communities to tighten their ranks, clarify their boundaries, and mark out their social space. The material culture of French settlements in Saigon, outposts in New Guinea, and estate complexes in Sumatra were retailored to accommodate the physical and moral requirements of a middle-class and respectable feminine contingent (Malleret 1934; Gordon and Meggitt 1985; Stoler 1989). Housing structures in Indochina were partitioned, residential compounds in the Solomon Islands enclosed, servant relations in Hawaii formalized, dress codes in Java altered, food and social taboos in Rhodesia and the Ivory Coast became more strict. Taken together, the changes encouraged new kinds of consumption and new social services

---

[11] Thus, concubinage was a two-edged sword for European colonizers. On the one hand, the use of local women kept wages low and may have enabled rapid integration into local culture. On the other hand, it produced mixed-race children whose existence threatened the racial hierarchy on which colonialism rested.

catering to these new demands (Boutilier 1982; Spear 1963; Woodcock 1969; Cohen 1971).

The arrival of large numbers of European women thus coincided with an embourgeoisment of colonial communities and with a significant sharpening of racial lines. European women supposedly required more metropolitan amenities than men and more spacious surroundings to allow it; their more delicate sensibilities required more servants and thus suitable quarters—discrete and enclosed. In short, white women needed to be maintained at elevated standards of living, in insulated social spaces cushioned with the cultural artifacts of "being European." Whether women or men set these new standards is left unclear. Who exhibited "overconcern" and a "need for" segregation (Beidelman 1982:13)? Male doctors advised French women in Indochina to have their homes built with separate domestic and kitchen quarters (Grall 1908:74). Segregationist standards were what women "deserved," and more importantly what white male prestige required that they maintain.[12]

Colonial rhetoric on white women was riddled with contradictions. At the same time that new female immigrants were chided for not respecting the racial distance of local convention, an equal number of colonial observers accused these women of being more avid racists in their own right (Spear 1963; Nora 1961). Allegedly insecure and jealous of the sexual liaisons of European men with native women, bound to their provincial visions and cultural norms, European women in Algeria, the Indies, Madagascar, India, and West Africa were uniformly charged with constructing the major cleavages on which colonial stratification rested (Spear 1963:140; Nora 1961:174; Mannoni 1964[1950]:115; Gan and Duignan 1978:242; Kennedy 1947:164; Nandy 1983:9).

What is most startling here is that women, otherwise marginal actors on the colonial stage, are charged with dramatically reshaping the face of colonial society, imposing their racial will on African and Asian colonies where "an iron curtain of ignorance" replaced "relatively unrestrained social intermingling" in earlier years (Vere Allen 1970:169; Cohen 1971:122). European women were not only the bearers of racist beliefs, but hardline operatives who put them into practice, encouraging class distinctions among whites while fostering new racial antagonisms, no longer muted by sexual access (Vere Allen 1970:168).* Are we to believe that sexual intimacy with European men yielded social mobility and political rights for colonized women? Or, even less likely, that because British civil servants bedded with Indian women, somehow Indian men had more "in common" with British men and enjoyed more parity? Colonized women could sometimes parlay their positions into personal profit and small rewards, but these were *individual* negotiations with no social, legal, or cumulative claims.[13]

Male colonizers positioned European women as the bearers of a redefined colonial morality. But to suggest that women fashioned this racism out of whole cloth is to miss the political chronology in which new intensities of racist practice

---

[12] Stoler's point in this section is that it is incorrect to believe that separation between natives and colonials increased because of the arrival of European women who required European surroundings. In fact, threatened by challenges to European superiority, colonial leaders moved to increase the separation between rulers and subjects. The arrival of European women was the mechanism used to justify and enable the social disengagement of ruler and ruled.

[13] Stoler is arguing that colonial authorities were following a policy of blaming the victim. Immigration of European women was encouraged to increase the separation of ruler and subject. The attitudes of these same women were then blamed for misunderstandings between colonials and their subjects as well as for any new problems that resulted in increased social distance.

Stoler belittles the notion that concubinage had beneficial effects. However, her ridicule actually misses its mark and, in fact, contradicts her main point. If increased contact between colonials and their subjects or increased knowledge of local cultures by colonial officials was beneficial to the colonized, then concubinage had positive effects. If colonial authorities did not at least believe that concubinage had some political benefit to their subjects, they would have no motivation to replace it. In other words, in order for colonial officials to feel threatened by concubinage (as Stoler argues they did), they must have believed that it increased the power of their subjects.

arose. In the African and Asian contexts already mentioned, the arrival of large numbers of European wives, and particularly the fear for their protection, followed from new terms and tensions in the colonial encounter. The presence and protection of European women was repeatedly invoked to clarify racial lines. It coincided with perceived threats to European prestige (Brownfoot 1984:191), increased racial conflict (Strobel 1987:378), covert challenges to the colonial order, outright expressions of nationalist resistance, and internal dissension among whites themselves (Stoler 1989:147).

If white women were the primary force behind the decline of concubinage as is often claimed, they did so as participants in a broader racial realignment and political plan (Knibiehler and Goutalier 1985:76). This is not to suggest that European women were passive in this process, as the dominant themes in their novels attest (Taylor 1977:27). Many European women did oppose concubinage not because of their inherent jealousy of native women, but, as they argued, because of the double standard it condoned for European men (Clerkx 1961; Lucas 1986:94–95).* The voices of European women, however, had little resonance until their objections coincided with a realignment in racial and class politics.

DEALING WITH TRANSGRESSIONS: POLICING THE PERIL

The gender-specific requirements for colonial living, referred to above, were constructed on heavily racist evaluations which pivoted on the heightened sexuality of colonized men (Tiffany and Adams 1985). Although European women were absent from men's sexual reveries in colonial literature, men of color were considered to see them as desired and seductive figures. European women needed protection because men of color had "primitive" sexual urges and uncontrollable lust, aroused by the sight of white women (Strobel 1987:379; Schmidt 1987:411). In some colonies, that sexual threat was latent; in others it was given a specific name.

In southern Rhodesia and Kenya in the 1920s and 1930s, preoccupations with the "Black Peril"

(referring to the professed dangers of sexual assault on white women by black men) gave rise to the creation of citizens' militias, ladies' riflery clubs and investigations as to whether African female domestic servants would not be safer to employ than men (Kirkwood 1984:158; Schmidt 1987:412; Kennedy 1987:128–147). In New Guinea the White Women's Protection Ordinance of 1926 provided "the death penalty for any person convicted for the crime of rape or attempted rape upon a European woman or girl" (Inglis 1975:vi). And as late as 1934, Solomon Islands authorities introduced public flogging as punishment for "criminal assaults on [white] females" (Boutilier 1984:197).

What do these cases have in common? The rhetoric of sexual assault and the measures used to prevent it had virtually no correlation with the incidence of rape of European women by men of color. Just the contrary: there was often no evidence, *ex post facto* or at the time, that rapes were committed or that rape attempts were made (Schmidt 1987; Inglis 1975; Kirkwood 1984; Kennedy 1987; Boutilier 1984). This is not to suggest that sexual assaults never occurred, but that their incidence had little to do with the fluctuations in anxiety about them. Secondly, the rape laws were race-specific; sexual abuse of black women was not classified as rape and therefore was not legally actionable, nor did rapes committed by white men lead to prosecution (Mason 1958:246–247). If these accusations of sexual threat were not prompted by the fact of rape, what did they signal and to what were they tied?

Allusions to political and sexual subversion of the colonial system went hand in hand. Concern over protection of white women intensified during real and perceived crises of control—provoked by threats to the internal cohesion of the European communities or by infringements on their borders. While the chronologies differ, we can identify a patterned *sequence* of events in which Papuan, Algerian, and South African men heightened their demands for civil rights and refused the constraints imposed upon their education, movements, or dress (Inglis 1975:8,11; Sivan 1983:178). Rape charges were thus based on perceived transgressions of political and social space. "Attempted rapes" turned out to be "incidents" of a Papuan man "discovered" in the vicinity of a white residence, a Fijian man who entered a European patient's room, a male servant poised at the bedroom door of a European woman asleep or in half-dress (Boutilier 1984:197; Inglis 1975:11; Schmidt 1987:413). With such a broad definition of danger, all colonized men of color were potential aggressors.

Accusations of sexual assault frequently followed upon heightened tensions within European communities—and renewed efforts to find consensus within them. In South Africa and Rhodesia, the relationship between reports of sexual assault and strikes among white miners and railway workers is well documented (van Onselen 1982:51; Kennedy 1987:138). Similarly, in the late 1920s when labor protests by Indonesian workers and European employees were most intense, Sumatra's corporate elite expanded their vigilante organizations, intelligence networks and demands for police protection to ensure their women were safe and their workers "in hand" (Stoler 1985b). In this particular context where the European community had been blatantly divided between low-ranking estate employees and the company elite, common interests were emphasized and domestic situations were rearranged.[14]

In an 800-word conclusion to this section, with 3 notes, Stoler notes that in Sumatra, in the 1920s, policies were enacted to favor European families. This undercut some European workers' opposition to colonial administration. New laws and policies curtailed native transgression of social and sexual boundaries, and women became responsible for guarding this separation. Despite this, European women were frequently blamed for overfamiliarity and provocation of native sexuality. They too were under constant surveillance and often had to obey rigid codes of chivalry. Nonetheless, women did frequently work in the colonies, but their work supported rather than contested colonial power structures. Some French feminists encouraged

European women to go to the colonies, but in general, colonial administrators discouraged this. Colonial administrations feared that single or widowed working women would become a class of poor whites and their presence would damage European prestige. Stoler concludes that colonial policies were designed to exclude the many European women who fell outside of the rigorously assigned categories of custodians of family welfare and respectability. In the next section she aims to show "how a European family life and bourgeois respectability became increasingly tied to notions of racial survival, imperial patriotism and the political strategies of the colonial state."

WHITE DEGENERACY, MOTHERHOOD AND THE EUGENICS OF EMPIRE

de·gen·er·ate (adj.) [L. *degeneratus*, pp. of *degenerare*, to become unlike one's race, degenerate < *degener*, not genuine, base < *de-*, from + *genus*, race, kind: see genus]. 1. having sunk below a former or normal condition, character, etc.; deteriorated. 2. morally corrupt; depraved n.   (a degenerate person, esp. one who is morally depraved or sexually perverted) vi   -at´ed, -at´ing 1. to decline or become debased morally, culturally, etc. 3. Biol. to undergo degeneration; deteriorate

[Webster's New World Dictionary 1972:371].

European women were essential to the colonial enterprise and the solidification of racial boundaries in ways that repeatedly tied their supportive and subordinate posture to community cohesion and colonial peace. These features of their positioning within imperial politics were powerfully reinforced at the turn of the century by a metropolitan bourgeois discourse (and an eminently anthropological one) intensely concerned with notions of "degeneracy" (Le Bras 1981:77).

---

[14] In this section, Stoler continues to rely heavily on Foucault's notions about the meaning of discourse on sex. Foucault's main point is that when people discuss sexuality they are centrally concerned with society, relations of power, and defining group membership. Here, discussions of rape by native men and laws about it do not refer to actual instances of rape (though Stoler says these did occur) but to political fears. The fact that native men threatened the colonial system was discussed in terms of native men sexually threatening European women.

Middle-class morality, manliness and motherhood were seen as endangered by the intimately linked fears of "degeneration" and miscegenation in scientifically construed racist beliefs (Mosse 1978:82).* Due to environmental and/or inherited factors, degeneracy could be averted positively by eugenic selection, or negatively by eliminating the "unfit" (Mosse 1978:87; Kevles 1985:70–84). Eugenic arguments used to explain the social malaise of industrialization, immigration and urbanization in the early 20th century derived from the notion that acquired characteristics were inheritable and thus that poverty, vagrancy and promiscuity were class-linked biological traits, tied to genetic material as directly as nightblindness and blonde hair.[15]

Appealing to a broad political and scientific constituency at the turn of the century, eugenic societies included advocates of infant welfare programs, liberal intellectuals, conservative businessmen, Fabians,[16] and physicians with social concerns. By the 1920s, however, it contained an increasingly vocal number of those who called for and put into law, if not practice, the sterilization of significant numbers in the British, German and American working-class populations (Mosse 1978:87; 1982:122).* Negative eugenics never gained the same currency in Holland as it did elsewhere, nevertheless, it seems clear from the Dutch and Dutch Indies scientific and popular press that concerns with hereditary endowment and with "Indo degeneracy" were grounded in a cultural racism that rivaled its French variant, if in a somewhat more muted form.*

Feminists attempted to appropriate this rhetoric for their own birth control programs, but eugenics was essentially elitist, racist and misogynist in principle and practice (Gordon 1976:395; Davin 1978;

Hammerton 1979). Its proponents advocated a pronatalist policy toward the white middle and upper classes, a rejection of work roles for women that might compete with motherhood, and "an assumption that reproduction was not just a function but the purpose . . . of a woman's life" (Gordon 1976:134). In France, England, Germany, and the United States, positive eugenics placed European women of "good stock" as "the fountainhead of racial strength" (Ridley 1983:91), exalting the cult of motherhood while subjecting it to more thorough scientific scrutiny (Davin 1978:12).

As part of metropolitan class politics, eugenics reverberated in the colonies in predictable as well as unexpected forms. The moral, biological and sexual referents of the notion of degeneracy (distinct in the dictionary citation above) came together in how the concept was actually deployed. The "colonial branch" of eugenics embraced a theory and practice concerned with the vulnerabilities of white rule and new measures to safeguard European superiority. Designed to control the procreation of the "unfit" lower orders, eugenics targeted "the poor, the colonized, or unpopular strangers" (Hobsbawm 1987:253). It was, however, also used by metropolitan observers against colonials, and by colonial elites against "degenerate" members among themselves (Koks 1931:179–189). While studies in Europe and the U.S. focused on the inherent propensity of the poor for criminality, in the Indies delinquency among "European" children was biologically linked to the amount of *native blood* among children of poor Indo-Europeans (Braconier 1918:11). Eugenics provided not so much a new vocabulary as it did a medical and moral basis for anxiety over white prestige which reopened debates over segregated residence and ed-

---

[15] The notions of eugenics fit nicely with Spencer's idea of evolution. Recall that Spencer saw evolution occurring through struggle both between and within societies. Struggle for survival led to a constant bettering of a society's stock of people. Darwin's cousin, Sir Frances Galton (1822–1911), extended this argument to matters of intelligence. In his 1869 work *Hereditary Genius,* Galton proposed that intelligence is inheritable and that societies should take steps to assure the reproduction of their most fit members. He coined the term *eugenics* in *Inquiries into Human Faculty* (1883) to describe the process of selectively breeding humans for intelligence and other forms of exceptionality. As Stoler reports, this notion became extremely popular in the late nineteenth and early twentieth centuries. Eugenics societies sprang up in many industrialized nations, including the United States.

[16] The Fabian society was an organization dedicated to establishing a democratic socialist state in England. It was the forerunner of the current British Labour Party.

ucation, new standards of morality, sexual vigilance and the rights of certain Europeans to rule.

Eugenic influence manifested itself, not in the direct importation of metropolitan practices such as sterilization, but in a translation of the political *principles* and the social values which eugenics implied. In defining what was unacceptable, eugenics also identified what constituted a "valuable life": "a gender-specific work and productivity, described in social, medical and psychiatric terms" (Bock 1984:274). Applied to European colonials, eugenic statements pronounced what kind of people should represent Dutch or French rule, how they should bring up their children and with whom they should socialize. Those concerned with issues of racial survival and racial purity invoked moral arguments about the national duty of French, Dutch, British, and Belgian colonial women to stay at home.[17]

If in Britain racial deterioration was conceived to be a result of the moral turpitude and the ignorance of working-class mothers, in the colonies, the dangers were more pervasive, the possibilities of contamination worse. Formulations to secure European rule pushed in two directions: on the one hand, away from ambiguous racial genres and open domestic arrangements, and on the other hand, toward an upgrading, homogenization, and a clearer delineation of European standards; away from miscegenation toward white endogamy, away from concubinage toward family formation and legal marriage; away from, as in the case of the Indies, mestizo customs and toward metropolitan norms (Taylor 1983; van Doorn 1985). As stated in the bulletin of the Netherlands Indies' Eugenic Society, "eugenics is nothing other than belief in the possibility of preventing degenerative symptoms in the body of our beloved *moedervolken,* or in cases where they may already be present, of counteracting them" (Rodenwaldt 1928:1).

Like the modernization of colonialism itself, with its scientific management and educated technocrats with limited local knowledge, colonial communities of the early 20th century were rethinking the ways in which their authority should be expressed. This rethinking took the form of asserting a distinct colonial morality, explicit in its reorientation toward the racial and class markers of "Europeanness," emphasizing transnational racial commonalities despite national differences—distilling a *homo europeaus* of superior health, wealth and intelligence as a white man's norm. As one celebrated commentator on France's colonial venture wrote: "one might be surprised that my pen always returns to the words *blanc* [white] or "European" and never to "*Français*" . . . in effect colonial solidarity and the obligations that it entails allies all the peoples of the white races" (Pujarniscle 1931:72; also see Delavignette 1946:41).

Such sensibilities colored imperial policy in nearly all domains with fears of physical contamination merging with those of political vulnerability. To guard their ranks, whites had to increase their numbers and to ensure that their members neither blurred the biological nor political boundaries on which their power rested.* In the metropole[18] the socially and physically "unfit," the poor, the indigent and the insane were either to be sterilized or prevented from marriage. In the British and Belgian colonies, among others, it was these very groups among Europeans who were either excluded from entry or institutionalized while they were there and when possible were sent home (Arnold 1979; see also Vellut 1987:97).

Thus, whites in the colonies adhered to a politics of exclusion that policed their members as well as the colonized. Such concerns were not new to the 1920s (Taylor 1983; Sutherland 1982). As early as the mid-18th century, the Dutch East Indies Company had already taken "draconian measures" to control pauperism among "Dutchmen of mixed blood" (*Encyclopedie van Nederland-Indie*

---

[17] Stoler's analysis of eugenics relies once again on Foucault's exposition of these ideas in *The History of Sexuality*. Foucault sees eugenics in terms of a discourse of degeneracy that becomes increasingly dominated by scientific themes (1978:118–19). In eugenics, issues of power and control are couched in the scientific language of breeding and genetics, purity and contamination.

[18] The metropole refers to the colonizing country.

1919:367). In the same period, the British East Indies Company legally and administratively dissuaded lower-class European migration and settlement, with the argument that it might destroy Indian respect for "the superiority of the European character" (quoted in Arnold 1983:139). Patriotic calls to populate Java in the mid-1800s with poor Dutch farmers were also condemned, but it was with new urgency that these possibilities were rejected in the following century as challenges to European rule were more profoundly felt.

Measures were taken both to avoid poor white migration and to produce a colonial profile that highlighted the vitality, colonial patriotism, and racial superiority of European men (Loutfi 1971: 112–113; Ridley 1983:104).* Thus, British colonial administrators were retired by the age of 55, ensuring that "no Oriental was ever allowed to see a Westerner as he aged and degenerated, just as no Westerner needed ever to see himself . . . as anything but a vigorous, rational, ever-alert young Raj" (Said 1978:42). In the 20th century, these "men of class" and "men of character" embodied a modernized and renovated colonial rule; they were to safeguard the colonies against physical weakness, moral decay and the inevitable degeneration that long residence in the colonies encouraged and the temptations that interracial domestic situations had allowed.

Given this ideal, it is not surprising that colonial communities strongly discouraged the presence of nonproductive men. Dutch and French colonial administrators expressed a constant concern with the dangers of unemployed or impoverished Europeans. During the succession of economic crises in the early 20th century, relief agencies in Sumatra, for example, organized fund raisers, hill station retreats and small-scale agricultural schemes to keep "unfit" Europeans "from roaming around" (Kroniek 1917:49). The colonies were neither open for retirement nor tolerant of the public presence of poor whites. During the 1930s depression when tens of thousands of Europeans in the Indies found themselves without jobs, government and private resources were quickly mobilized to ensure that they were not "reduced" to native living standards (Veerde 1931; Kantoor van Arbeid 1935). Subsidized

health care, housing and education complemented a rigorous affirmation of European cultural standards in which European womanhood played a central role in keeping men *civilisé*.

In a 600-word section with 3 notes titled "On Cultural Hygiene: The Dynamics of Degeneration," Stoler reports that in twentieth-century Europe, medical and sociological work began to identify Europeans who stayed too long in the colonies as a distinct degenerate type. Colonials were believed to acquire physical and psychological faults from prolonged contact with native populations. Colonial medicine backed the notion that moral and cultural degeneracy produced by long stays in the colonies was associated with physical disease. Neurasthenia, a nervous disorder caused by exhaustion and overwork, was a common diagnosis. While in Europe, neurasthenia was associated with "modern civilization," in colonies it was believed to be caused by separation from civilization. One response to this was a proliferation of colonial "hill stations"—places that simulated European environments. Some doctors prescribed return to Europe while others insisted that a stable, European-style family life would reduce neurasthenia. They denounced the lifestyle of the "old colonists" as unhealthy.

CULTURAL CONTAMINATION, CHILDREN AND THE DANGERS OF METISSAGE

> [Young colonial men] are often driven to seek a temporary companion among women of color; this is the path by which, as I shall presently show, contagion travels back and forth, contagion in all senses of the word [Maunier 1932:171].

Racial degeneracy was thought to have social causes and political consequences, both tied to the domestic arrangements of colonialism in specific ways. *Metissage* (interracial unions) generally, and concubinage in particular, represented the paramount danger to racial purity and cultural identity in all its forms. It was through sexual contact with women of color that French men "contracted" not only disease but debased senti-

ments, immoral proclivities and extreme suscep-
tibility to decivilized states (Dupuy 1955:198).

By the early 20th century, concubinage was
denounced for undermining precisely those things
that it was charged with fortifying decades earlier.
Local women who had been considered protectors
of men's well-being, were now seen as the bearers of ill health and sinister influences; adaptation
to local food, language, and dress, once prescribed
as healthy signs of acclimatization, were now
sources of contagion and loss of (white) self. The
benefits of local knowledge and sexual release
gave way to the more pressing demands of respectability, the community's solidarity and its
mental health. Increasingly French men in Indochina who kept native women were viewed as
passing into "the enemy camp" (Pujarniscle 1931:
107). Concubinage became the source not only
of individual breakdown and ill-health, but the biological and social root of racial degeneration and
political unrest. Children born of these unions
were "the fruits of regrettable weakness" (Mazet
1932:8), physically marked and morally marred
with "the defaults and mediocre qualities of their
[native] mothers" (Douchet 1928:10).[19]

Concubinage was not as economically tidy
and politically neat as colonial policy makers had
hoped. It concerned more than sexual exploitation and unpaid domestic work; it was about children—many more than official statistics often
revealed—and who was to be acknowledged as a
European and who was not. Concubine children
posed a classification problem, impinging on political security and white prestige. The majority of
such children were not recognized by their fathers, nor were they reabsorbed into local communities as authorities often claimed. Although
some European men legally acknowledged their
progeny, many repatriated to Holland, Britain or
France and cut off ties and support to mother and
children (Brou 1907; Ming 1983:75). Native
women had responsibility for, but attenuated
rights over, their own offspring. They could nei-

ther prevent their children from being taken from
them nor contest paternal suitability for custody.
While the legal system favored a European upbringing, it made no demands on European men
to provide it; many children became wards of the
state, subject to the scrutiny and imposed charity
of the European-born community at large.

Concubine children were invariably counted
among the ranks of the European colonial poor,
but European paupers in the late 19th century
Netherlands Indies came from a far wider strata
of colonial society than that of concubines alone
(Rapport der Pauperisme-Commissie 1903). Many
Indo-Europeans had become increasingly marginalized from strategic political and economic
positions in the early 20th century despite new
educational opportunities encouraged at the turn
of the century. In the 1920s and 1930s Indies-
born and educated youth were uncomfortably
squeezed between an influx of new colonial recruits from Holland and the educated *inlander*
("native") population with whom they were in direct competition for jobs (Mansvelt 1932:295).*
At the turn of the century, volumes of official reports were devoted to documenting and alleviat-
ing the proliferation on Java of a "rough" and
"dangerous pauper element" among (Indo) European clerks, low-level officials and vagrants (*Encyclopedie van Nederland-Indie* 1919:367).

European pauperism in the Indies reflected
broad inequalities in colonial society, underscoring
the social heterogeneity of the category "European" itself. Nonetheless, as late as 1917, concubinage was still seen by some as its major cause
and as the principal source of *"blanken-haters"*
(white-haters) (Braconier 1917:298). Concubinage became equated with a progeny of "malcon-
tents," or "parasitic" whites, idle and therefore
dangerous. The fear of concubinage was carried
yet a step further and tied to the political fear that
such Eurasians would demand economic access,
political rights and express their own interests
through alliance with (and leadership of) organized

---

[19] In this section on concubinage, Stoler makes a firm connection between race and gender. Mixed-race children were a
special problem in colonial possessions because they blurred the definition of superior and inferior races on which colonial rule was based.

opposition to Dutch rule (Mansvelt 1932; Blumberger 1939).*

Racial prejudice against *métis* was often, as in the Belgian Congo, "camouflaged under protestations of 'pity' for their fate, as if they were '*malheureux*' [unhappy] beings by definition" (Vellut 1982:103). As objects of charity, their protection in Indochina was a cause célèbre of European women—feminists and staunch colonial supporters—at home and abroad (Knibiehler and Goutalier 1985:37). European colonial women were urged to oversee their "moral protection," to develop their "natural" inclination toward French society, to turn them into "partisans of French ideas and influence" instead of revolutionaries (Chenet 1936:8; Sambuc 1931:261). The gender breakdown is clear: moral instruction reflected fears of sexual promiscuity in *métisse* girls and the political threat of *métis* boys turned militant men.

Orphanages for abandoned European and Indo-European children were not new features of 20th century colonial cultures; however, their importance increased vastly as an ever larger number of illegitimate children of mixed parentage populated grey zones along colonial divides. In the Netherlands Indies by the mid-18th century, state orphanages for Europeans were established to prevent "neglect and degeneracy of the many free-roaming poor bastards and orphans of Europeans" (quoted in Braconier 1917:293). By the 19th century, church, state and private organizations had become zealous backers of orphanages, providing some education but stronger doses of moral instruction. In India, civil asylums and charity schools cared for European and Anglo-Indian children in "almost every town, cantonment and hill-station" (Arnold 1979:108). In French Indochina in the 1930s virtually every colonial city had a home and society for the protection of abandoned *métis* youth (Chenet 1936; Sambuc 1931:256–272; Malleret 1934:220).

Whether these children were in fact "abandoned" by their Asian mothers is difficult to establish; the fact that *métis* children living in native homes were often *sought out* by state and private organizations and placed in these institutions to protect them against the "demoralised and sinister" influences of native kampung life suggests another interpretation (Taylor 1983). Public assistance in India, Indochina and the Netherlands Indies was designed not only to keep fair skinned children from running barefooted in native villages but to ensure that the proliferation of European pauper settlements was curtailed and controlled.* The preoccupation with creating a patriotic loyalty to French and Dutch culture among children was symptomatic of a more general fear; namely, that there were *already* patricides of the colonial fatherland in the making; that as adult women these children would fall into prostitution; that as adult men with emotional ties to native women and indigenous society they would join the enemies of the state, *verbasterd* (degenerate) and *décivilisé* (Braconier 1917:293; Pouvourville 1926; Sambuc 1931:261; Malleret 1934).[20]

EUROPEAN MOTHERHOOD AND MIDDLE-CLASS MORALITY

"A man remains a man as long as he is under the watch of a woman of his race" [George Hardy quoted in Chivas-Baron 1929:103].

Rationalization of imperial rule and safeguards against racial degeneracy in European colonies merged in the emphasis on particular moral themes. Both entailed a reassertion of European conventions, middle-class respectability, more frequent ties with the metropole and a restatement of what was culturally distinct and superior about how colonials ruled and lived. For

---

[20] Stoler's analysis of orphanages here bears resemblance to Foucault's analysis of insane asylums in *Madness and Civilization* (1965 [1961]). In that work he argued, among other things, that modern horror of madness is based on moral disapproval of the values implicit in it. He saw treatment of the insane as a way to bring them back to bourgeois moral values. Stoler is arguing here that colonial Europeans in the twentieth century had a horror of the values implicit in children of mixed race. Orphanages were aimed at forcing the children to adopt the values of the colonizer rather than simply taking care of them.

those women who came to join their spouses or to find husbands, the prescriptions were clear. Just as new plantation employees were taught to manage the natives, women were schooled in colonial propriety and domestic management. French manuals, such as those on colonial hygiene in Indochina, outlined the duties of colonial wives in no uncertain terms. As "auxiliary forces" in the imperial effort they were to "conserve the fitness and sometimes the life of all around them" by ensuring that "the home be happy and gay and that all take pleasure in clustering there" (Grall 1908:66; Chailley-Bert 1897). Practical guides to life in the Belgian Congo instructed (and indeed warned) *la femme blanche* that she was to keep "order, peace, hygiene and economy" (Favre 1938:217), "perpetuate a vigorous race," while preventing any "laxity in our administrative mores" (Favre 1938:256; Travaux du Groupe d'Etudes coloniales 1910:10).

This "division of labor" contained obvious asymmetries. Men were considered more susceptible to moral turpitude than women who were thus held responsible for the immoral states of men. European women were to create and protect colonial prestige, insulating their men from cultural and sexual contact with the colonized (Travaux . . . coloniales 1910:7). Racial degeneracy would be curtailed by European women charged with regenerating the physical health, the metropolitan affinities and the imperial purpose of their men (Hardy 1929:78).

At its heart was a reassertion of racial difference which harnessed nationalistic rhetoric and markers of middle-class morality to its cause (Delavignette 1946:47; Loutfi 1971:112; Mosse 1978:86). George Mosse describes European racism in the early 20th century as a "scavenger ideology," annexing nationalism and bourgeois respectability such that control over sexuality was central to all three (1985:10, 133–152). If the European middle class sought respectability "to maintain their status and self-respect against the lower-classes, and the aristocracy," in the colonies respectability was a defense against the colonized, and a way of more clearly defining themselves (Mosse 1985:5). Good colonial living now meant hard work, no sloth, and physical exercise rather than sexual release, which had been one rationale

for condoning concubinage and prostitution in an earlier period. The debilitating influences of climate could be surmounted by regular diet and meticulous personal hygiene over which European women were to take full charge. Manuals on how to run a European household in the tropics provided detailed instructions in domestic science, moral upbringing and employer-servant relations. Adherence to strict conventions of cleanliness and cooking occupied an inordinate amount of women's time (Hermans 1925; Ridley 1983:77). Both activities entailed a constant surveillance of native nursemaids, laundrymen and live-in servants, while reinforcing the domestication of European women themselves (Brink 1920:43).

In an 1,200-word conclusion to this section, with 1 note, Stoler writes that it now became a European woman's duty to provide the happy family life seen as basic to colonial stability. The emphasis on women's duty to provide children and happy homes was also prevalent in Europe. This led to improvements in health care facilities but also to increased social control over reproduction.

The belief that health conditions in the colonies were poor for women and children made childrearing a "conflicted endeavor" for colonial women. Doctors reported a wide range of grave medical conditions for women in the colonies, especially high infant mortality. In some cases doctors suggested that over generations, white women in the tropics would become sterile. In other cases prolonged residence would lead to reduced fertility or racial degeneration of offspring. Like the fear of degeneration, fears of sterility were linked to political issues. Such fears were greatest during the depression, when discussions about resettling poor whites in the colonies were often couched in terms of sex and the ability of white women to reproduce in the tropics.

Childrearing manuals used by colonial women warned against contact with natives. European children were perceived to be in danger from both native caretakers and native children. Even where medical conditions were excellent, experts frequently claimed that European children could not thrive and should be sent back to Europe to be raised. Assuring the moral upbringing of children — that is, an upbringing free from contact with native people and ideas — became the principal focus of European women's associations. Women were caught between their responsibilities to raise their children in Europe and to be with their husbands in the colonies. These contrasting duties affected women's "social space" and economic possibilities.

SHIFTING STRATEGIES OF RULE AND SEXUAL MORALITY

> Though sex cannot of itself enable men to transcend racial barriers, it generates some admiration and affection across them, which is healthy, and which cannot always be dismissed as merely self-interested and prudential. On the whole, sexual interaction between Europeans and non-Europeans probably did more good than harm to race relations; at any rate, I cannot accept the feminist contention that it was fundamentally undesirable [Hyam 1986a:75].

The political etymology of colonizer and colonized was gender and class specific. The exclusionary politics of colonialism demarcated not just external boundaries but interior frontiers, specifying internal conformity and order among Europeans themselves. I have tried to show that the categories of colonizer and colonized were secured through notions of racial difference constructed in gender terms. Redefinitions of sexual protocol and morality emerged during crises of colonial control precisely because they called into question the tenuous artifices of rule *within* European communities and what marked their borders. Even from the limited cases we have reviewed, several patterns emerge. First and most obviously, colonial sexual prohibitions were racially assymetric and gender specific. Thus racial attributes were rarely discussed in nongendered terms; one was always a black *man*, an Asian *woman*. Secondly, interdictions against interracial unions were rarely a primary impulse in the strategies of rule. Interracial unions (as opposed to marriage) between European men and colonized women aided the long-term settlement of European men in the colonies while ensuring that colonial patrimony

stayed in limited and selective hands. In India, Indochina and South Africa in the early centuries — colonial contexts usually associated with sharp social sanctions against interracial unions — "mixing" was systematically tolerated and even condoned.*

Changes in sexual access and domestic arrangements have invariably accompanied major efforts to reassert the internal coherence of European communities and to redefine the boundaries of privilege between the colonizer and the colonized. Sexual union in itself, however, did not automatically produce a larger population legally classified as "European." On the contrary, miscegenation signaled neither the absence nor presence of racial prejudice in itself; hierarchies of privilege and power were written into the *condoning* of interracial unions, as well as into their condemnation.

While the chronologies vary from one colonial context to another, we can identify some parallel shifts in the strategies of rule and in sexual morality. Concubinage fell into moral disfavor at the same time that new emphasis was placed on the standardization of European administration. While this occurred in some colonies by the early 20th century and in others later on, the correspondence between rationalized rule, bourgeois respectability and the custodial power of European women to protect their men seems strongest during the interwar years when Western scientific and technological achievements were then in question, and native nationalist and labor movements were hard pressing their demands.* Debates concerning the need to systematize colonial management and dissolve the provincial and personalized satraps of "the old-time *colon*" in the French empire invariably targeted and condemned the unseemly domestic arrangements in which they lived. British high colonial officials in Africa imposed new "character" requirements on their subordinates, designating specific class attributes and conjugal ties that such a selection implied (Kuklick 1979). Critical to this restructuring was a new disdain for colonials too adapted to local custom, too removed from the local European community, and too encumbered with intimate native ties. As in Sumatra, this hands-off policy distanced Europeans in more than one sense: it forbade European staff both from personal confrontations with their Asian fieldhands and from the limited local knowledge they gained through sexual ties.

At the same time, medical expertise confirmed the salubrious benefits of European comradery and frequent home leaves, of a *cordon sanitaire*, not only around European enclaves, but around each home. White prestige became defined by this rationalized management and by the moral respectability and physical well-being of its agents, with which European women were charged. Colonial politics locked European men and women into a routinized protection of their physical health and social space in ways which bound gender prescriptions to class conventions, thereby fixing the racial cleavages between "us" and "them."

I have focused here on the multiple levels at which sexual control figured in the substance, as well as the iconography, of racial policy and imperial rule. But colonial politics was obviously not just about sex; nor did sexual relations reduce to colonial politics. On the contrary, sex in the colonies was about sexual access and reproduction, class distinctions and racial privileges, nationalism and European identity in different measure and not all at the same time. These major shifts in the positioning of women were not signaled by the penetration of capitalism per se but by more subtle changes in class politics, imperial morality and as responses to the vulnerabilities of colonial control. As we attempt broader ethnographies of empire, we may begin to capture how European culture and class politics resonated in colonial settings, how class and gender discriminations not only were translated into racial attitudes, but themselves reverberated in the metropole as they were fortified on colonial ground. Such investigations should help show that sexual control was both an instrumental image for the body politic, a salient part standing for the whole, and itself fundamental to how racial policies were secured and how colonial projects were carried out.[21]

References

Abatucci

1910 Le milieu africain considéré au point de vue de ses effets sur le système nerveux de l'européen. *Annales d'Hygiène et de Médecine Coloniale* 13:328–335.

Adas, Michael

1989 *Machines as the Measure of Men: Scientific and Technological Superiority and Ideologies of Western Dominance.* Ithaca: Cornell University Press.

Arnold, David

1979 European Orphans and Vagrants in India in the Nineteenth Century. *Journal of Imperial and Commonwealth History* 7:2:104–127.

1983 White Colonization and Labour in Nineteenth-Century India. *Journal of Imperial and Commonwealth History* 11:2:133–158.

Bajema, Carl, ed.

1976 *Eugenics Then and Now.* Stroudsburg, PA: Dowden, Hutchinson & Ross.

Ballhatchet, Kenneth

1980 *Race, Sex and Class under the Raj: Imperial Attitudes and Policies and Their Critics, 1793–1905.* New York: St. Martin's.

Baroli, Marc

1967 *La vie quotidienne des Francais en Algérie.* Paris: Hachette.

Baudin, D. C. M.

1941 [1927] *Het Indische Leven.* S'Gravenhage: H. P. Leopolds.

Beidelman, Thomas

1982 *Colonial Evangelism.* Bloomington: Indiana University Press.

Berenger-Feraud, L.

1875 *Traité Clinique des Maladies des Europèens au Sénégal.* Paris: Adrien Delahaye.

Blumberger, J. Th. Petrus

1939 *De Indo-Europeesche Beweging in Nederlandsch-Indie.* Haarlem: Tjeenk Willink.

---

[21] Stoler presents a compelling argument; however, it is a point of view largely derived from her studies of historical documents and secondary analysis. The voices of the colonial subjects themselves are conspicuously absent. Given the current emphasis on multivocality in feminist anthropology, it is curious that Stoler does not allow colonial subjects, some of whom are still alive, to speak for themselves. We wonder what they would say.

Blussé, Leonard

1986 *Strange Company: Chinese Settlers, Mestizo Women and the Dutch in VOC Batavia*. Dordrecht: Foris.

Bock, Gisela

1984 Racism and Sexism in Nazi Germany: Motherhood, Compulsory Sterilization, and the State. In *When Biology Became Destiny: Women in Weimar and Nazi Germany*, pp. 271–296. New York: Monthly Review Press.

Boutilier, James

1984 European Women in the Solomon Islands, 1900–1942. In *Rethinking Women's Roles: Perspectives from the Pacific*, Denise O'Brien and Sharon Tiffany, eds, pp. 173–199. Berkeley: University of California Press.

Braconier, A. de

1913 Het Kazerne-Concubinaat in Ned-Indie. *Vragen van den Dag* 28:974–995.

1917 *Het Pauperisme onder de in Ned. Oost-Indie levende Europeanen*. In *Nederlandsch-Indie* (1st yr.), 291–300.

1918 *Kindercriminaliteit en de verzorging van misdadig aangelegde en verwaarloosde minderjarigen in Nederlandsch Indie*. Baarn: Hollandia-Drukkerij.

1933 Het Prostitutie-vraagstuk in Nederlandsch-Indie. *Indisch Gids* 55:2:906–928.

Brink, K. B. M. Ten

1920 *Indische Gezondheid*. Batavia: Nillmij.

Brou, A. M. N.

1907 Le Métis Franco-Annamite. *Revue Indochinois* (July):897–908.

Brownfoot, Janice N.

1984 Memsahibs in Colonial Malaya: A Study of European Wives in a British Colony and Protectorate 1900–1940. In *The Incorporated Wife*, Hilary Callan and Shirley Ardener, eds. London: Croom Helm.

Butcher, John

1979 *The British in Malaya, 1880–1941: The Social History of a European Community in Colonial Southeast Asia*. Kuala Lumpur: Oxford University Press.

Callan, Hilary, and Shirley Ardener, eds.

1984 *The Incorporated Wife*. London: Croom Helm.

Callaway, Helen

1987 *Gender, Culture and Empire: European Women in Colonial Nigeria*. London: Macmillan Press.

Chailley-Bert, M. J.

1897 L'Emigration des femmes aux colonies. Union Coloniale Francaise-conférence, 12 January. Paris: Armand Colin.

Chatterjee, Partha

1989 Colonialism, nationalism, and colonialized women: the content in India. *American Ethnologist* 16(4):622–633.

Chenet, Ch.

1936 Le role de la femme française aux Colonies: Protection des enfants métis abandonnés. *Le Devoir des Femmes* (15 February):8.

Chivas-Baron, Clotide

1929 *La femme française aux colonies*. Paris: Larose.

Clerkx, Lily

1961 Mensen in Deli. Amsterdam: Sociologisch-Historisch Seminarium voor Zuidoost-Azie. Publication no. 2.

Cock, J.

1980. *Maids and Madams*. Johannesburg: Raven Press.

Cohen, William

1971 *Rulers of Empire: The French Colonial Service in Africa*. Stanford: Hoover Institution Press.

1980 *The French Encounter with Africans. White Response to Blacks, 1530–1880*. Bloomington: Indiana University Press.

Comaroff, John L.

1989 Images of Empire, Contests of Conscience: Models of Colonial Domination in South Africa. *American Ethnologist* 16(4):661–685.

Cool, F.

1938 De Bestrijding der Werkloosheidsgevolgen in Nederlandsch-Indie gedurende 1930–1936. *De Economist*, 135–147; 217–243.

Cooper, Frederick

1980 *From Slaves to Squatters*. New Haven: Yale University Press.

Corneau, Grace

1900 *La femme aux colonies*. Paris: Librairie Nilsson.

Courtois, E.

1900 Des Régles Hygiéniques que doit suivre l'Européen au Tonkin. *Revue Indo-chinoise* 83:539–541; 564–566; 598–601.

Davin, Anna

1978 Imperialism and Motherhood. *History Workshop* 5:9–57.

Degler, Carl

1971 *Neither Black nor White*. New York: Macmillan.

Delavignette, Robert

1946 *Service Africain*. Paris: Gallimard.

Dixon, C. J.

1913 *De Assistent in Deli*. Amsterdam: J. H. de Bussy.

Douchet

1928 Métis et congaies d'Indochine. Hanoi.

Dowd Hall, Jacquelyn

1984 "The Mind that Burns in Each Body": Women, Rape, and Racial Violence. *Southern Exposure* 12:6:61–71.

Drooglever, P.

1980 *De Vaderiandse Club, 1929–42*. Franeker: T. Wever.

Dupuy, Aime

1955 La personnalité du colon. *Revue d'Histoire Economique et Sociale* 33:1:77–103.

Encyclopedie van Nederland-Indie

1919 S'Gravenhage Nijhoff and Brill.

Etienne, Mona, and Eleanor Leacock, eds.

1980 *Women and Colonization: Anthropological Perspectives*. New York: Praeger.

Fannon, Franz

1967 [1952] *Black Skin, White Masks*. New York: Grove Press.

Favre, J. L.

1938 *La Vie aux Colonies*. Paris: Larose.

Feuilletau de Bruyn, W.

1938 Over de Economische Mogelijkheid van een Kolonisatie van Blanken op Nederlandsch Nieuw-Guinea. In *Comptes Rendus du Congres International de Geographie, Amsterdam*, pp. 21–29. Leiden: Brill.

Fredrickson, George

1981 *White Supremacy*. New York: Oxford University Press.

Gaitskell, Deborah

1983 Housewives, Maids or Mothers: Some Contradictions of Domesticity for Christian Women in Johannesburg, 1903–39. *Journal of African History* 24:241–256.

Gann, L. H., and Peter Duignan

1978 *The Rulers of British Africa, 1870–1914*. Stanford: Stanford University Press.

Gantes, Gilles de

1981 *La population française au Tonkin entre 1931 et 1938. Memoire*. Aix-en-Provence: Institut d'Histoire des Pays d'Outre Mer.

Gartrell, Beverley

1984 Colonial Wives: Villains or Victims? In *The Incorporated Wife*, H. Callan and S. Ardener, eds., pp. 165–185. London: Croom Helm.

Gilman, Sander L.

1985 *Difference and Pathology*. Ithaca: Cornell University Press.

Gordon, Linda

1976 *Woman's Body, Woman's Right*. New York: Grossman.

Gordon, R., and M. Meggitt

1985 *Law and Order in the New Guinea Highlands*. Hanover: University Press of New England.

Grall, Ch.

1908 *Hygiéne Coloniale Appliquée*. Paris: Bailliere.

Grimshaw, Patricia

1983 Christian Woman, Pious Wife, Faithful Mother, Devoted Missionary: Conflicts in Roles of American Missionary Women in Nineteenth-Century Hawaii. *Feminist Studies* 9:3:489–521.

Hammerton, James

1979 *Emigrant Gentlewomen*. London: Croom Helm.

Hansen, Karen Tranberg

1986 Household Work as a Man's Job: Sex and Gender in Domestic Service in Zambia. *Anthropology Today* 2:3:18–23.

Hardy, George

1929 *Ergaste ou la Vocation Coloniale*. Paris: Armand Colin.

Hartenberg

1910 *Les Troubles Nerveux et Mentaux chez les coloniaux*. Paris.

Harwood, Dorothy

1938 The Possibility of White Colonization in the Tropics. In *Comptes Rendu du Congrès Int'l de Géographie*, pp. 131–140. Leiden: Brill.

Hermans, E. H.

1925 *Gezondscheidsleer voor Nederlandsch-Indie*. Amsterdam: Meulenhoff.

Hesselink, Liesbeth

1987 Prostitution: A Necessary Evil, Particularly in the Colonies: Views on Prostitution in the Netherlands Indies. In *Indonesian Women in Focus*, E. Locher-Scholten and A. Niehof, pp. 205–224. Dordrecht: Foris.

Het Pauperisme Commissie

1901 *Het Pauperisme onder de Europeanen*. Batavia: Landsdrukkerij.

1903 *Rapport der Pauperisme-Commissie*. Batavia: Landsdrukkerij.

Hobsbawn, Eric

1987 *The Age of Empire, 1875–1914*. London: Weidenfeld and Nicholson.

Hunt, Nancy

1988 Le bébé en brousse: European women, African Birth Spacing and Colonial Intervention in Breast Feeding in the Belgian Congo. *International Journal of African Historical Studies* 21:3.

Hyam, Ronald

1986a Empire and Sexual Opportunity. *Journal of Imperial and Commonwealth History* 14:2:34–90.

1986b Concubinage and the Colonial Service: The Crewe Circular (1909). *Journal of Imperial and Commonwealth History* 14:3:170–186.

Inglis, Amirah

1975 *The White Women's Protection Ordinance: Sexual Anxiety and Politics in Papua*. London: Sussex University Press.

Jaurequiberry

1924 *Les Blancs en Pays Chauds*. Paris: Maloine.

Jordan, Winthrop

1968 *White over Black: American Attitudes Toward the Negro, 1550–1812*. Chapel Hill: University of North Carolina Press.

Joyeux, Ch., and A. Sice

1937 *Affections exotiques du système nerveux. Précis de Médecine Coloniale*. Paris: Masson.

Kantoor van Arbeid

1935 *Werkloosheid in Nederlandsch-Indie*. Batavia: Landsdrukkerij.

Kennedy, Dane

1987 *Islands of White*. Durham: Duke University Press.

Kennedy, Raymond

1947 *The Ageless Indies*. New York: John Day.

Kevles, Daniel

1985 *In the Name of Eugenics*. Berkeley: University of California Press.

King, Anthony

1976 *Colonial Urban Development*. London: Routledge & Kegan Paul.

Kirkwood, Deborah

1984 Settler Wives in Southern Rhodesia: A Case Study. In *The Incorporated Wife*, H. Callan and S. Ardener, eds. London: Croom Helm.

Knibiehler, Y., and R. Goutalier

1985 *La femme au temps des colonies*. Paris: Stock.

1987 *Femmes et Colonisation: Rapport Terminal au Ministère des Relations Extérieures et de la Coopération*. Aix en-Provence: Institut d'Historie des Pays d'Outre-Mer.

Koks, Dr. J. Th.

1931 *De Indo*. Amsterdam: H. J. Paris.

Kroniek

1917 *Oostkust van Sumatra-Instituut*. Amsterdam: J. H. de Bussy.

Kuklick, Henrika

1979 *The Imperial Bureaucrat: The Colonial Administrative Service in the Gold Coast, 1920–1939*. Stanford: Hoover Institution Press.

Le Bras, Hervé

1981 Historie secrète de la fécondité. *Le Debat* 8:76–100.

Loutfi, Martine Astier

1971 *Littérature et Colonialisme*. Paris: Mouton.

Lucas, Nicole

1986 Trouwverbod, inlandse huishousdsters en Europese vrouwen. In *Vrouwen in de Nederlandse Kolonien*, J. Reijs, et al., eds., 78–97. Nijmegen: SUN.

Mackinnon, Murdoch

1920 European Children in the Tropical Highlands. *Lancet* 199:944–945.

Malleret, Louis

1934 *L'Exotisme Indochinois dans la Littérature Française depuis 1860*. Paris: Larose.

Mannoni, Octavio

1964 *Prospero and Caliban*. New York: Praeger.

Mansvelt, W.

1932 De Positie der Indo-Europeanen. *Kolonial Studien*, 290–311.

Martinez-Alier, Verena

1974 *Marriage, Class and Colour in Nineteenth Century Cuba*. Cambridge: Cambridge University Press.

Mason, Philip

1958 *The Birth of a Dilemma: The Conquest and Settlement of Rhodesia*. New York: Oxford University Press.

Maunier, M. René

1932 *Sociologie Coloniale*. Paris: Domat-Montchrestien.

Mazet, Jacques

1932 *La Condition Juridique des Métis*. Paris: Domat-Montchrestien.

Mercier, Paul

1965 The European Community of Dakar. In *Africa: Social Problems of Change and Conflict*, Pierre van den Berghe, ed., pp. 284–304. San Francisco: Chandler.

Ming, Hanneke

1983 Barracks-Concubinage in the Indies, 1887–1920. *Indonesia* 35 (April):65–93.

Moore-Gilbert, B. J.

1986 *Kipling and "Orientalism"*. New York: St. Martin's.

Mosse, George

1978 *Toward the Final Solution*. New York: Fertig.

1985 *Nationalism and Sexuality*. Madison: University of Wisconsin Press.

Muller, Hendrik

1912 De Europeesche Samenleving. Neerlands Indie. Amsterdam: Elsevier: 371–384.

Nandy, Ashis

1983 *The Intimate Enemy: Loss and Recovery of Self under Colonialism*. Delhi: Oxford University Press.

Nash, June

1980 Aztec Women: The Transition from Status to Class in Empire and Colony. In *Woman and Colonization: Anthropological Perspectives,* Mona Etienne and Eleanor Leacock, eds., pp. 134–148. New York: Praeger.

Nieuwenhuys, Roger

1959 *Tussen Twee Vaderlanden*. Amsterdam: Van Oorschot.

Nora, Pierre

1961 *Les Français d'Algerie*. Paris: Julliard.

O'Brien, Rita Cruise

1972 *White Society in Black Africa: The French in Senegal*. London: Faber & Faber.

Pollmann, Tessel

1986 Bruidstraantjes: De Koloniale roman, de njai en de apartheid. In *Vrouwen in de Nederlandse Kolonien,* J. Reijs, et al., eds., pp. 98–125. Nijmegen: SUN.

Pourvourville, Albert de

1926 Le Métis. Le Mal d'Argent. Paris: Monde Moderne, 97–114.

Price, Grenfell A.

1939 *White Settlers in the Tropics*. New York: American Geographical Society.

Prochaska, David

1989 *Making Algeria French: Colonialism in Bone, 1870–1920*. Cambridge: Cambridge University Press.

Pujarniscle, E.

1931 *Philoxène ou de la litterature coloniale*. Paris.

Raptschinsky, B.

1941 *Kolonisatie van blanken in de tropen*. Den Haag: Bibliotheek van weten en denken.

Reijs, J., E. Kloek, U. Jansz, A. de Wildt, S. van Norden, and M. de Baar

1986 *Vrouwen in de Nederlandse Kolonien*. Nijmegen: SUN.

Ridley, Hugh

1983 *Images of Imperial Rule*. New York: Croom & Helm.

Ritter, W. L.

1856 *De Europeaan in Nederlandsch Indie*. Leyden: Sythoff.

Rodenwalt, Ernest

1928 Eugenetische Problemen in Nederlandsch-Indie. *Ons Nageslacht,* 1–8.

Said, Edward W.

1978 *Orientalism*. New York: Vintage.

Sambuc

1931 Les Métis Franco-Annamites en Indochine. *Revue du Pacifique,* 256–272.

Schmidt, Elizabeth

1987 Ideology,. Economics and the Role of Shona Women in Southern Rhodesia, 1850–1939. Ph.D. dissertation, University of Wisconsin.

Schneider, William

1972 Toward the Improvement of the Human Race: The History of Eugenics in France. *Journal of Modern History* 54:269–291.

Schoevers, T.

1913 Het leven en werken van den assistant bij de Tabakscultuur in Deli. Jaarbock der Vereeniging "Studiebelangen." Wageningen: Zomer, 3–43.

Simon, Jean-Pierre

1981 *Rapatriés d'Indochine*. Paris: Harmattan.

Sivan, Emmanuel

1983 *Interpretations of Islam*. Princeton: Darwin Press.

Smith-Rosenberg, Carroll, and Charles Rosenberg

1973 The Female Animal: Medical and Biological Views of Woman and Her Role in Nineteenth-Century America. *Journal of American History* 60(2):332–356.

Spear, Percival

1963 *The Nabobs*. London: Oxford University Press.

Stepan, Nancy

1982 *The Idea of Race in Science*. London: Macmillan.

Stoler, Ann

1985a *Capitalism and Confrontation in Sumatra's Plantation Belt, 1870–1979*. New Haven: Yale University Press.

1985b Perceptions of Protest. *American Ethnologist* 12:4:642–658.

1989 Rethinking Colonial Categories: European Communities and the Boundaries of Rule. *Comparative Studies in Society and History* 13(1):134–161.

Strobel, Margaret

1987 Gender and Race in the 19th and 20th Century British Empire. In *Becoming Visible: Women in European History,* R. Bridenthal et al., eds., pp. 375–396. Boston: Houghton Mifflin.

Stuurman, Siep

1985 *Verzuiling, Kapitalisme en Patriarchaat.* Nijrnegen: SUN.

Sutherland, Heather

1982 Ethnicity and Access in Colonial Macassar. In *Papers of the Dutch-Indonesian Historical Conference,* pp. 250–277. Leiden: Bureau of Indonesian Studies.

Takaki, Ronald

1977 *Iron Cages.* Berkeley: University of California Press.

Taylor, Jean

1977 The World of Women in the Colonial Dutch Novel. *Kabar Seberang* 2:26–41.

1983 *The Social World of Batavia.* Madison: University of Wisconsin Press.

Tiffany, Sharon, and Kathleen Adams

1985 *The Wild Woman: An Inquiry into the Anthropology of an Idea.* Cambridge, MA: Schenkman.

Tirefort, A.

1979 'Le Bon Temps': La Communauté Francaise en Basse Cote d'Ivoire pendant L'Entre-Deux Guerres, 1920–1940. Troisième Cycle, Centre d'Etudes Africaines, Paris.

Travaux du Groupe d'Etudes Coloniales

1910 *La Femme Blanche au Congo.* Brussels: Misch & Thron.

Van Doom, Jacques

1983 *A Divided Society: Segmentation and Mediation in Late-Colonial Indonesia.* Rotterdam: CASPA.

1985 Indie als Koloniale Maatschappy. In *De Nederlandse samenleving sinds 1815,* F. L. van Holthoon, ed. Assen: Maastricht.

Van Helten, J., and K. Williams

1983 'The Crying Need of South Africa': The Emigration of Single British Women in the Transvaal, 1901–1910. *Journal of South African Studies* 10:1:11–38.

Van Heyningen, Elizabeth B.

1984 The Social Evil in the Cape Colony 1868–1902: Prostitution and the Contagious Disease Acts. *Journal of Southern African Studies* 10:2:170–197.

Van Marle, A.

1952 De group der Europeanen in Nederlands-Indie. *Indonesie,* 5:2:77–121; 5:3:314–341; 5:5:481–507.

Van Onselen, Charles

1982 *Studies in the Social and Economic History of the Witwatersrand 1886–1914.* Vol. I. New York: Longman.

Veerde, A. G.

1931 Onderzoek naar den omvang der werkloosheid op java, November 1930–Juni 1931. *Koloniale Studien,* 242–273; 503–533.

Vellut, Jean-Luc

1982 Materiaux pour une image du Blanc dans la société coloniale du Congo Belge. In *Stéréotypes Nationaux et Préjudés Raciaux aux XIXe et XXe Siècles,* Jean Pirotte, ed. Leuven: Editions Nauwelaerts.

Vere Allen, J. de

1970 Malayan Civil Service, 1874–1941: Colonial Bureaucracy Malayan Elite. *Comparative Studies in Society and History* 12:149–178.

Wanderken, P.

1943 Zoo leven onze kinderen. In *Zoo Leven Wij in Indonesia,* pp. 172–187. Deventer: Van Hoever.

Wertheim, Willem

1959 *Indonesian Society in Transition.* The Hague: Van Hoeve.

Winckel, Ch. W. F.

1938 The Feasibility of White Settlements in the Tropics: a Medical Point of View. In *Comptes Rendus de Congrès International de Géographie Amsterdam,* pp. 345–356. Leiden: Brill.

Woodcock, George

1969 *The British in the Far East.* New York: Atheneum.

Symbolic and Interpretive Anthropology

*B*eginning in the 1960s and reaching its fullest expression in the 1970s, symbolic or interpretive anthropology was part of a general reevaluation of cultural anthropology as a scientific enterprise. Cultural materialists insisted that the analysis of culture follow a model from the physical sciences and focus on empirical material phenomena. In contrast, symbolic anthropologists treated culture as a mental phenomenon. But unlike ethnoscientists or cognitive anthropologists, symbolic anthropologists rejected the notion that culture could be modeled like mathematics or logic. Instead they used a variety of analytical tools drawn from psychology, history, and literature to study symbolic action within culture. Their fundamental interest was in examining how people formulated their reality. Dolgin, Kemnitzer, and Schneider (1977), for example, write "Our concern is not with whether or not the views a people hold are accurate in any 'scientific' sense of the term. . . . In social action, that which is thought to be real is treated as real" (quoted in Lett 1987:111).

The practice of symbolic analysis was influenced by the work of Benjamin L. Whorf and Edward Sapir in linguistics and ethnoscientific studies, which gained popularity in the 1950s. Linguistics was particularly influential because human knowledge and communication are based on language, a shared system of symbols that is meaningful within a particular historical and social context. Symbolic anthropologists believe that culture does not exist apart from individuals but rather lies in their interpretations of events and the things around them. In other words, symbolic anthropologists believe we construct our cultural reality. Consequently, symbolic anthropologists such as David Schneider and Clifford Geertz take what is called a semiotic approach,

that is, they focus on the analysis of meaning. As Geertz writes:

> Believing, with Max Weber, that man is an animal suspended in webs of significance he himself has spun, I take cultures to be those webs, and the analysis of it to be therefore not an experimental science in search of law but an interpretive one in search of meaning. (1973:5)

The term *symbolic anthropology* covers a variety of forms of analysis, but two dominant trends in the field are represented by the work of Clifford Geertz (1926–) and Victor Turner (1920–1983). Although both are concerned with the interpretation of symbolic action in non-Western societies, their approaches are very different. Geertz's emphasis on culture as an organized collection of symbolic systems is typically American in flavor. Turner's work, on the other hand, is in the British structural-functionalist style and is concerned with the operation of symbols in the maintenance of society.

Lett (1987:111) calls Clifford Geertz the "principal architect of symbolic anthropology." Breaking with ethnoscience and cognitive anthropology, Geertz argues that culture is not a model inside people's heads but rather is embodied in public symbols and actions. He writes, "Whatever sense we have of how things stand with someone else's inner life, we gain it through their expressions, not through some magical intrusion into their consciousness" (1986:373).

To Geertz, symbols are means of transmitting meaning. But, unlike Turner (discussed below), he is not interested in how symbols perform cultural functions such as healing or killing through witchcraft. His focus is on how symbols affect the way people think about their world, how "symbols operate as vehicles of culture" (Ortner 1984: 129). Thus, in "Notes on a Balinese Cockfight" (see essay 37), Geertz deciphers the various symbolic meanings of the cockfight for the Balinese who engage in the sport and how these various levels of meaning influence their lives.

In contrast to Claude Lévi-Strauss' structuralism, Geertz is also concerned with symbolic analysis from the actor's point of view. Geertz believes the proper method of symbolic analysis to be "thick description," which is what anthropologists do when they break ethnographic information down, sorting through layers of significance to derive the meaning from the native's perspective (see Geertz 1973:6–10). Geertz does not advocate that we get inside the heads of native informants but that anthropologists try to position themselves within the same cultural context as their informants. As the article reprinted here shows, this actor-centered perspective is fundamental to Geertz's form of analysis.

Victor Turner approached symbolic analysis from a different angle. Trained in British structural-functionalism, he examined symbols as mechanisms for the maintenance of society. Geertz studies cultural symbols to examine the worldview of people in a society. Turner, however, viewed symbols as "operators in the social process, things that, when put together in certain arrangements in certain contexts (especially rituals), produce essentially social transformations" (Ortner 1984:131). Turner argued that social solidarity had to be continually maintained. Ritual symbols, in his view, were the primary tools through which social order was renewed. Turner also made a major contribution to the conceptual vocabulary of symbolic analysis by outlining various properties of symbols such as multivocality, condensation, the unification of disparate significata, and polarization of meaning (Turner 1967:28). These are discussed in essay 36.

Unlike Geertz's "thick description," Turner followed a more formal program that combined emic and etic descriptions. He believed that the interpretation of ritual symbols could be derived from three classes of data: (1) external form and observable characteristics, (2) the interpretations of specialists and laymen within the society,

and (3) deduction from specific contexts by the anthropologist.

Turner viewed his work as a contrast to Lévi-Strauss' structuralism and to the psychoanalytic analysis of cultural symbols. In particular, he emphasized study of the context in which symbols were expressed. He wrote

> I found that I could not analyze ritual symbols without studying them in a time series in relation to other "events," for symbols are essentially involved in social process. I came to see performances of rituals as distinct phases in the social process whereby groups became adjusted to internal changes and adapted to their external environment. From this standpoint the ritual symbol becomes a factor in social action, a positive force in an activity field. (Turner 1967:20)

One of the great shortcomings of symbolic analysis is that it is primarily descriptive and does not lend itself to general theoretical or methodological formulations. Like Boasians, symbolic anthropologists claim to search for universals of human understanding through the collection of locally particular data. However, much of what symbolic anthropologists know is derived through imaginative insight into particular cultures or events within those cultures. As a result, their knowledge does not provide a theoretical basis for understanding culture as a universal phenomenon.

Mary Douglas (1921–) is one symbolic anthropologist whose work defies this generalization. She has attempted to analyze universal patterns of symbolism, focusing on beliefs about pollution and hygiene as they are expressed in religions. In her two most famous works—*Purity and Danger* (1966) and *Natural Symbols* (1970) — Douglas contends that universal patterns of purity-pollution symbolism exist and are based on reference to the human body. She argues her case from a Durkheimian perspective, suggesting that shared symbols "create a unity in experience" (1966:2) and that religious ideas about purity and pollution symbolize beliefs about social order. In the introduction to *Purity and Danger* she writes

> I believe that some pollutions are used as analogies for expressing a general view of the social order. For example, there are beliefs

that each sex is a danger to the other through contact with sexual fluids. . . . Such patterns of sexual danger can be seen to express symmetry or hierarchy. It is implausible to interpret them as suggesting something about the actual relation of the sexes. I suggest that many ideas about sexual dangers are better interpreted as symbols of the relation between parts of society, as mirroring designs of hierarchy or symmetry which apply in the larger social system. . . . Sometimes bodily orifices seem to represent points of entry or exit to social units, or bodily perfection can symbolise an ideal theocracy. (1966:3–4)

Symbolic anthropology is concerned with studying the process by which people give meaning to their world and how this world is expressed in cultural symbols. Geertz writes that "Cultural analysis is (or should be) guessing at meanings, assessing the guesses, and drawing explanatory conclusions from the better guesses" (1973:20). However, symbolic anthropologists have never specifically explained a methodology for "guessing at meaning." Anthropologists who do not share Geertz's view find this to be a fundamental flaw in symbolic anthropology. Critics claim that the credibility of symbolic interpretation is based on the explanatory skills of the anthropologist and argue that such anthropology often seems closer to literary criticism than social science.

35. External Boundaries

Mary Douglas (1921–)

THE IDEA OF SOCIETY IS A POWERFUL IMAGE. IT is potent in its own right to control or to stir men to action. This image has form; it has external boundaries, margins, internal structure. Its outlines contain power to reward conformity and repulse attack. There is energy in its margins and unstructured areas. For symbols of society any human experience of structures, margins or boundaries is ready to hand.[1]

Van Gennep shows how thresholds symbolise beginnings of new statuses. Why does the bridegroom carry his bride over the lintel? Because the step, the beam and the door posts make a frame which is the necessary everyday condition of entering a house. The homely experience of going through a door is able to express so many kinds of entrance. So also are cross roads and arches, new seasons, new clothes and the rest. No experience is too lowly to be taken up in ritual and given a lofty meaning. The more personal and intimate the source of ritual symbolism, the more telling its message. The more the symbol is drawn from the common fund of human experience, the more wide and certain its reception.[2]

The structure of living organisms is better able to reflect complex social forms than door

From *Purity and Danger* (1966)

---

[1] Trained by Evans-Pritchard at Oxford in the British structural-functionalist school, Mary Douglas was influenced by Durkheim's notions of society and social cohesion. Durkheim argued that religion was essentially a model of society that served to promote social cohesion (see essay 7); Douglas believes that shared symbols promote social solidarity and provide mechanisms for social control. She opens this article with a powerful image of society as a coherently organized whole. Her comment that human experiences of structures or boundaries can serve as symbols of society hints at one of her fundamental ideas – that the human body is a symbol of society.

[2] Douglas, interested in discovering universals of symbolism, suggests that the most potent symbols are found in the realm of the mundane. Because the form of the human body may be the most common human experience, her analysis centers on the body and its products.

posts and lintels. So we find that the rituals of
sacrifice specify what kind of animal shall be
used, young or old, male, female or neutered, and
that these rules signify various aspects of the situation which calls for sacrifice. The way the animal is to be slaughtered is also laid down. The
Dinka cut the beast longitudinally through the
sexual organs if the sacrifice is intended to undo
an incest; in half across the middle for celebrating a truce; they suffocate it for some occasions
and trample it to death for others. Even more direct is the symbolism worked upon the human
body. The body is a model which can stand for
any bounded system. Its boundaries can represent any boundaries which are threatened or precarious. The body is a complex structure. The
functions of its different parts and their relation
afford a source of symbols for other complex
structures. We cannot possibly interpret rituals
concerning excreta, breast milk, saliva and the
rest unless we are prepared to see in the body a
symbol of society, and to see the powers and dangers credited to social structure reproduced in
small on the human body.[3]

It is easy to see that the body of a sacrificial
ox is being used as a diagram of a social situation.
But when we try to interpret rituals of the human
body in the same way the psychological tradition
turns its face away from society, back towards the
individual. Public rituals may express public concerns when they use inanimate door posts or animal sacrifices: but public rituals enacted on the
human body are taken to express personal and
private concerns. There is no possible justification for this shift of interpretation just because
the rituals work upon human flesh. As far as I
know the case has never been methodically
stated. Its protagonists merely proceed from un-

challenged assumptions, which arise from the
strong similarity between certain ritual forms and
the behavior of psychopathic individuals. The assumption is that in some sense primitive cultures
correspond to infantile stages in the development
of the human psyche. Consequently such rites
are interpreted as if they express the same preoccupations which fill the mind of psychopaths or
infants.[4]

Let me take two modern attempts to use primitive cultures to buttress psychological insights.
Both stem from a long line of similar discussions,
and both are misleading because the relation between culture and individual psyche are not made
clear.

Bettelheim's *Symbolic Wounds* is mainly an
interpretation of circumcision and initiation rites.
The author tries to use the set rituals of Australians and Africans to throw light on psychological phenomena. He is particularly concerned to
show that psychoanalysts have overemphasized
girls' envy of the male sex and overlooked the importance of boys' envy of the female sex. The idea
came to him originally in studying groups of
schizophrenic children approaching adolescence.
It seems very likely that the idea is sound and important. I am not at all claiming to criticize his insight into schizophrenia. But when he argues that
rituals which are explicitly designed to produce
genital bleeding in males are intended to express
male envy of female reproductive processes, the
anthropologist should protest that this is an inadequate interpretation of a public rite. It is
inadequate because it is merely descriptive. What
is being carved in human flesh is an image of society. And in the moiety- and section-divided
tribes he cites, the Murngin and Arunta, it seems
more likely that the public rites are concerned to

---

[3] Douglas treats the symbolism of blood, breast milk, and other products of the human body as symbols of society.
Ultimately, this argument is based on the organic analogy, a nineteenth-century model of society generally associated
with Spencer. But whereas Spencer argued by direct analogy—telegraph wires are the nerves of society, for instance—
Douglas' argument is symbolic—society is not a body, but it can be symbolically represented by a body. In the next essay,
on Ndembu symbolism, Victor Turner makes a similar point.

[4] Douglas here criticizes psychological interpretations of symbolism, particularly psychoanalytic interpretations, which
tended to treat non-Western peoples as childlike or mentally ill. One line of psychoanalytic thought equated the trancing
of shamans or other religious specialists in primitive societies with the acts of psychiatric patients in Western hospitals.
See, for example, Kroeber's "Psychotic Factors in Shamanism" (1940) or Devereux's "Shamans as Neurotics" (1961).

create a symbol of the symmetry of the two halves of society.[5]

The other book is *Life Against Death,* in which Brown outlines an explicit comparison between the culture of "archaic man" and our own culture, in terms of the infantile and neurotic fantasies which they seem to express. Their common assumptions about primitive culture derive from Roheim (1925): primitive culture is autoplastic, ours is alloplastic.[6] The primitive seeks to achieve his desires by self-manipulation, performing surgical rites upon his own body to produce fertility in nature, subordination in women or hunting success. In modern culture we seek to achieve our desires by operating directly on the external environment, with the impressive technical results that are the most obvious distinction between the two types of cultures. Bettelheim adopts this summing up of the differences between the ritual and the technical bias in civilization. But he supposes that the primitive culture is produced by inadequate, immature personalities, and even that the psychological shortcomings of the savage accounts for his feeble technical achievements:

> If preliterate peoples had personality structures as complex as those of modern man, if their defenses were as elaborate and their con-

sciences as refined and demanding; if the dynamic interplay between ego, superego and id were as intricate and if their ego's were as well adapted to meet and change external reality—they would have developed societies equally complex, though probably different. Their societies have, however, remained small and relatively ineffective in coping with the external environment. It may be that one of the reasons for this is their tendency to try to solve problems by autoplastic rather than alloplastic manipulation. (p. 87)

Let us assert again, as many anthropologists have before, that there are no grounds for supposing that primitive culture as such is the product of a primitive type of individual whose personality resembles that of infants or neurotics. And let us challenge the psychologists to express the syllogisms on which such a hypothesis might rest. Underlying the whole argument is the assumption that the problems which rituals are intended to solve are personal psychological problems. Bettelheim actually goes on to compare the primitive ritualist with the child who hits his own head when frustrated. This assumption underlies his whole book.

Brown makes the same assumption, but his reasoning is more subtle.[7] He does not suppose that the culture's primitive condition is caused by

---

[5] Bruno Bettelheim (1903–1990) was an Austrian student of Sigmund Freud who emigrated to the United States in 1939 and spent virtually his whole career at the University of Chicago. Bettelheim was best known for his work with emotionally disturbed children. He was also recognized for his psychoanalytic analysis of ethnographic material, particularly his 1955 work *Symbolic Wounds.*

[6] Geza Roheim (1892–1953) was a Hungarian anthropologist. Early in his career he became a follower of Freud. Roheim spent several years conducting fieldwork in Australia, Africa, and Melanesia and was one of the leading proponents of the psychoanalytic analysis of ethnographic material. When Malinowski attacked Freud's excursions into anthropology, Roheim was one of Freud's staunchest defenders. In his 1925 book *Australian Totemism,* he characterized primitive cultures as autoplastic and Western society as alloplastic. These are medical terms. *Autoplastic* refers to the surgical repair of defects with tissue from another part of the patient's body. *Alloplasty* is replacing a diseased or damaged body part with synthetic material. Using Bettelheim's example from *Symbolic Wounds* that Douglas cites in the paragraph above, Australian Aborigines are autoplastic because a man performs a ritual subincision of his penis in order to simulate the flow of a woman's menstrual blood. Ritual use of a blood substitute, say a red vegetable dye, would be considered alloplastic.

[7] The Brown discussed here is the Oxford-educated American scholar Norman O. Brown (1913–), best known for his book *Life Against Death* (1959), a psychoanalytic reinterpretation of human history. Today, works such as *Life Against Death* and *Symbolic Wounds* are considered artifacts of a bygone era; even at the time of publication these works were never widely popular among American anthropologists. But Douglas is English, and Freudian theory was taken much more seriously by European anthropologists. When she wrote this book in 1966, she was attacking a view that was still popular among European scholars.

individual personal traits: he allows very properly for the effect of cultural conditioning on the individual personality. But he proceeds to consider the total culture as if it, in its totality, could be compared to an infant or a retarded adult. The primitive culture resorts to bodily magic to achieve its desires. It is in a stage of cultural evolution comparable to that of infantile anal eroticism. Starting from the maxim: "Infantile sexuality is autoplastic compensation for the loss of the Other; sublimation is alloplastic compensation for loss of Self" (p. 170) he goes on to argue that "archaic" culture is directed to the same ends as infantile sexuality, that is escape from the hard realities of loss, separation and death. Epigrams are, by their nature, obscure. This is another approach to primitive culture which I would like to see fully spelt out. Brown develops the theme only briefly, as follows:

> Archaic man is preoccupied with the castration complex, the incest taboo and the desexualisation of the penis, that is, the transference of the genital impulses into that aim-inhibited libido which sustains the kinship systems in which archaic life is embedded. The low degree of sublimation, corresponding to the low level of technology, means by our previous definitions, a weaker ego, an ego which has not yet come to terms (by negation) with its own pregenital impulses. The result is that all the fantastic wishes of infantile narcissism express themselves in unsublimated form so that archaic man retains the magic body of infancy. (p. 298–9)

These fantasies suppose that the body itself could fulfill the infant's wish for unending, self-replenishing enjoyment. They are a flight from reality, a refusal to face loss, separation and death. The ego develops by sublimating these fantasies. It mortifies the body, denies the magic of excrement and to that extent faces reality. But sublimation substitutes another set of unreal aims and ends by providing the self with another kind of false escape from loss, separation and death. This is how I understand the argument to run. The more material that an elaborate technology imposes between ourselves and the satisfaction of our infantile desires, the more busily has sublimation been at work. But the converse seems questionable. Can we argue that the less the material basis of civilization is developed, the less sublimation has been at work? What precise analogy with infantile fantasy can be valid for a primitive culture based on a primitive technology? How does a low level of technology imply "an ego which has not yet come to terms (by negation) with its own pregenital impulses"? In what sense is one culture more sublimated than another?[8]

[We have omitted a 1,000-word discussion in which Douglas refutes the psychoanalytic interpretation of excremental magic using an example of what she considers to be Brown's bias in his discussion of a Winnebago Indian trickster myth. She also cites an ethnographic example of how body substances such as blood and spittle may be considered as both polluting or sacred substances. Douglas concludes her discussion of what she calls "body dirt" with a reference to the ritual use of royal corpses. We rejoin the text at the beginning of her discussion of why products of the body are symbols of danger and power.]

But now we are ready to broach the central question. Why should bodily refuse be a symbol of danger and of power? Why should sorcerers be thought to qualify for initiation by shedding blood or committing incest or anthropophagy?[9] Why, when initiated, should their art consist largely of manipulating powers thought to inhere in the margins of the human body? Why should bodily margins be thought to be specially invested with power and danger?

First, we can rule out the idea that public rituals express common infantile fantasies. These erotic desires which it is said to be the infant's dream to satisfy within the body's bounds are presumably

---

[8] Douglas' central argument is that bodily substances are symbols of danger or power because they symbolize relations within a society. Consequently, she strongly argues against the psychoanalytic notion that the ritualized use of body refuse, such as excrement, is a psychiatric phenomena based on infantile fantasies.

[9] *Anthropophagy:* the eating of human flesh.

common to the human race. Consequently body symbolism is part of the common stock of symbols, deeply emotive because of the individual's experience. But rituals draw on this common stock of symbols selectively. Some develop here, others there. Psychological explanations cannot of their nature account for what is culturally distinctive.

Second, all margins are dangerous. If they are pulled this way or that the shape of fundamental experience is altered. Any structure of ideas is vulnerable at its margins. We should expect the orifices of the body to symbolise its specially vulnerable points. Matter issuing from them is marginal stuff of the most obvious kind. Spittle, blood, milk, urine, faeces or tears by simply issuing forth have traversed the boundary of the body. So also have bodily parings, skin, nail, hair clippings and sweat. The mistake is to treat bodily margins in isolation from all other margins. There is no reason to assume any primacy for the individual's attitude to his own bodily and emotional experience, any more than for his cultural and social experience. This is the clue which explains the unevenness with which different aspects of the body are treated in the rituals of the world. In some, menstrual pollution is feared as a lethal danger; in others not at all (see Chapter 9). In some, death pollution is a daily preoccupation; in others not at all. In some, excreta is dangerous, in others it is only a joke. In India cooked food and saliva are pollution-prone, but Bushmen collect melon seeds from their mouths for later roasting and eating (Marshall-Thomas, p. 44).[10]

Each culture has its own special risks and problems. To which particular bodily margins its beliefs attribute power depends on what situation the body is mirroring. It seems that our deepest fears and desires take expression with a kind of witty aptness. To understand body pollution we should try to argue back from the known dangers of society to the known selection of bodily themes and try to recognize what appositeness[11] is there.

In pursuing a last-ditch reduction of all behavior to personal preoccupations of individuals with their own bodies the psychologists are merely sticking to their last.

> The derisive remark was once made against psychoanalysis that the unconscious sees a penis in every convex object and a vagina or anus in every concave one. I find that this sentence well characterises the facts. (Ferenczi, *Sex in Psychoanalysis*, p. 227, quoted by Brown)[12]

It is the duty of every craftsman to stick to his last. The sociologists have the duty of meeting one kind of reductionism with their own. Just as it is true that everything symbolizes the body, so it is equally true (and all the more so for that reason) that the body symbolizes everything else. Out of this symbolism, which in fold upon fold of interior meaning leads back to the experience of the self with its body, the sociologist is justified in trying to work in the other direction to draw out some layers of insight about the self's experience in society.

If anal eroticism is expressed at the cultural level we are not entitled to expect a population of anal erotics. We must look around for whatever it is that has made appropriate any cultural analogy

---

[10] At the start of this essay, Douglas referred to the work of Arnold Van Gennep (1873–1957), a folklorist, and his influence is evident in this passage. His best-known work is *Rites of Passage* (1960 [1909]). Every rite of passage marking a person's change from one status to another, in his view, was outlined by the stages of separation, transition, and incorporation. During the transition phase one is in a liminal state, outside the margins of society, no longer one thing, but not yet another. Thus, separation from the group is necessary because, in the stage of transition, one may be ritually impure or dangerous. Douglas applies this same principle to the human body. She writes that "all margins are dangerous" and that matter issuing from the body's orifices, because it has traversed the boundary of the body, may be dangerous. One of the classic discussions of liminal states in rites of passage is Victor Turner's "Betwixt and Between: The Liminal Period in Rites of Passage," first published in 1964 and then revised in 1967, in which he referred to this essay by Douglas.

[11] *Appositeness:* suitability or pertinence.

[12] Sandor Ferenczi was a professor of psychoanalysis and a colleague of Sigmund Freud. For more information on Ferenczi, see note 19 in essay 5.

with anal eroticism. The procedure in a modest way is like Freud's analysis of jokes. Trying to find a connection between the verbal form and the amusement derived from it he laboriously reduced joke interpretation to a few general rules. No comedian script-writer could use the rules for inventing jokes, but they help us to see some connections between laughter, the unconscious, and the structure of stories. The analogy is fair for pollution is like an inverted form of humour. It is not a joke for it does not amuse. But the structure of its symbolism uses comparison and double meaning like the structure of a joke.[13]

Four kinds of social pollution seem worth distinguishing. The first is danger pressing on external boundaries; the second, danger from transgressing the internal lines of the system; the third, danger in the margins of the lines. The fourth is danger from internal contradiction, when some of the basic postulates are denied by other basic postulates, so that at certain points the system seems to be at war with itself. In this chapter I show how the symbolism of the body's boundaries is used in this kind of unfunny wit to express danger to community boundaries.[14]

The ritual life of the Coorgs (Srinivas) gives the impression of a people obsessed by the fear of dangerous impurities entering their system. They treat the body as if it were a beleaguered town, every ingress and exit guarded for spies and traitors. Anything issuing from the body is never to be re-admitted, but strictly avoided. The most dangerous pollution is for anything which has once emerged gaining re-entry. A little myth, trivial by other standards, justifies so much of their behavior and system of thought that the ethnographer has to refer to it three or four times. A Goddess in every trial of strength or cunning defeated her two brothers. Since future precedence depended on the out-

come of these contests, they decided to defeat her by a ruse. She was tricked into taking out of her mouth the betel that she was chewing to see if it was redder than theirs and into popping it back again. Once she had realized she had eaten something which had once been in her own mouth and was therefore defiled by saliva, though she wept and bewailed she accepted the full justice of her downfall. The mistake canceled all her previous victories, and her brothers' eternal precedence over her was established as of right.

The Coorgs have a place within the system of Hindoo castes. There is good reason to regard them as not exceptional or aberrant in Hindoo India (Dumont and Peacock). Therefore they conceive status in terms of purity and impurity as these ideas are applied throughout the regime of castes. The lowest castes are the most impure and it is they whose humble services enable the higher castes to be free of bodily impurities. They wash clothes, cut hair, dress corpses and so on. The whole system represents a body in which by the division of labour the head does the thinking and praying and the most despised parts carry away waste matter. Each sub-caste community in a local region is conscious of its relative standing in the scale of purity. Seen from ego's position the system of caste purity is structured upwards. Those above him are more pure. All the positions below him, be they ever so intricately distinguished in relation to one another, are to him polluting. Thus for any ego within the system the threatening non-structure against which barriers must be erected lies below. The sad wit of pollution as it comments on bodily functions symbolizes descent in the caste structure by contact with faeces, blood and corpses.[15]

The Coorgs shared with other castes this fear of what is outside and below. But living in their

---

[13] Douglas is referring to Freud's *Jokes and Their Relation to the Unconscious* (1960 [1905]), which explored the relationship between dreams and jokes. In this book he outlined different types of jokes and the literary and psychological mechanisms that he believed made them amusing.

[14] Using the example of an Indian caste called the Coorgs, Douglas shows that the four types of bodily purity-pollution practices she outlines are symbolic models of larger social relationships.

[15] In the caste system of India, the purest individuals are leaders and priests; those who are most polluted have tasks dealing with the disposal of human waste and refuse. This association of pollution with human refuse is an extension of body symbolism, a key metaphor in Hindu belief. In the Vedas (sacred Hindu texts), the creation of the world is described as the result of the gods sacrificing a divine being named Purusha. From Purusha's mouth came the priests, from his arms

mountain fastness they were also an isolated community, having only occasional and controllable contact with the world around. For them the model of the exits and entrances of the human body is a doubly apt symbolic focus of fears for their minority standing in the larger society. Here I am suggesting that when rituals express anxiety about the body's orifices the sociological counterpart of this anxiety is a care to protect the political and cultural unity of a minority group. The Israelites were always in their history a hard-pressed minority. In their beliefs all the bodily issues were polluting, blood, pus, excreta, semen, etc. The threatened boundaries of their body politic would be well mirrored in their care for the integrity, unity and purity of the physical body.

The Hindoo caste system, while embracing all minorities, embraces them each as a distinctive, cultural sub-unit. In any given locality, any sub-caste is likely to be a minority. The purer and higher its caste status, the more of a minority it must be. Therefore the revulsion from touching corpses and excreta does not merely express the order of caste in the system as a whole. The anxiety about bodily margins expresses danger to group survival.[16]

That the sociological approach to caste pollution is much more convincing than a psychoanalytic approach is clear when we consider what the Indian's private attitudes to defecation are. In the ritual we know that to touch excrement is to be defiled and that the latrine cleaners stand in the lowest grade of the caste hierarchy. If this pollu-

tion rule expressed individual anxieties we would expect Hindoos to be controlled and secretive about the act of defecation. It comes as a considerable shock to read that slack disregard is their normal attitude, to such an extent that pavements, verandahs and public places are littered with faeces until the sweeper comes along.[17]

> Indians defecate everywhere. They defecate, mostly, beside the railway tracks. But they also defecate on the beaches — they defecate on the streets; they never look for cover. . . . These squatting figures — to the visitor, after a time, as eternal and emblematic as Rodin's Thinker — are never spoken of; they are never written about; they are not mentioned in novels or stories; they do not appear in feature films or documentaries. This might be regarded as part of a permissible prettifying intention. But the truth is that Indians do not see these squatters and might even with complete sincerity, deny that they exist. (Naipaul, chapter 3)

Rather than oral or anal eroticism it is more convincing to argue that caste pollution represents only what it claims to be. It is a symbolic system, based on the image of the body, whose primary concern is the ordering of a social hierarchy.

It is worth using the Indian example to ask why saliva and genital excretions are more pollution-worthy than tears. If I can reverently drink his tears, wrote Jean Genet, why not the so limpid drop on the end of his nose?[18] To this we can reply: first that nasal secretions are not so limpid as tears. They are more like treacle than water.

---

the warriors, from his thighs the merchants, and from his feet the laborers. In other words, the caste divisions were created by the division of Purusha's body. This Hindu myth is a poetic example of the body-society symbolism with which Douglas began the essay.

[16] Douglas suggests that anxiety about one's minority status in a society is typically reflected in rituals concerning the body's orifices. Just as Hindus must be careful about what goes into their body and the disposal of what comes out, the Coorgs, living isolated in the mountains, controlled who came into their communities and who left. The care taken to avoid pollution to their physical bodies is a symbolic manifestation of their desire to protect their political and social integrity as well. Note here that Douglas is outlining a principle she believes is universal; the Coorgs are simply an example.

[17] Douglas' comment that she was shocked to read that Indians defecate in public serves as a reminder that she is conducting cross-cultural comparative research in the tradition of Lévi-Strauss or Radcliffe-Brown. Though she does not make an issue of it, as Harris does in essay 22 on the uses of cattle in India, her interpretations are based on her reading of ethnographic material rather than personal field research.

[18] Jean Genet (1910–1986) was a French novelist, playwright, and protégé of the existentialist philosopher Jean Paul Sartre. Genet was best known for his plays. His works are contributions to the theater of the absurd, a form of drama in which the impossible routinely happens in order to make philosophical points.

When a thick rheum oozes from the eye it is no more apt for poetry than nasal rheum.[19] But admittedly clear, fast-running tears are the stuff of romantic poetry: they do not defile. This is partly because tears are naturally preempted by the symbolism of washing. Tears are like rivers of moving water. They purify, cleanse, bathe the eyes, so how can they pollute? But more significantly tears are not related to the bodily functions of digestion or procreation. Therefore their scope for symbolizing social relations and social processes is narrower. This is evident when we reflect on caste structure. Since place in the hierarchy of purity is biologically transmitted, sexual behavior is important for preserving the purity of caste. For this reason, in higher castes, boundary pollution focuses particularly on sexuality. The caste membership of an individual is determined by his mother, for though she may have married into a higher caste, her children take their caste from her. Therefore women are the gates of entry to the caste. Female purity is carefully guarded and a woman who is known to have had sexual intercourse with a man of lower caste is brutally punished. Male sexual purity does not carry this responsibility. Hence male promiscuity is a lighter matter. A mere ritual bath is enough to cleanse a man from sexual contact with a low caste woman. But his sexuality does not entirely escape the burden of worry which boundary pollution attaches to the body. According to Hindoo belief a sacred quality inheres in semen, which should not be wasted. In a penetrating essay on female purity in India (1963) Yalman says:

> While caste purity must be protected in women and men may be allowed much greater freedom, it is, of course, better for the men not to waste the sacred quality contained in their semen. It is well-known that they are exhorted not merely to avoid low-caste women, but all women (Carstairs 1956, 1957; Gough 1956).

For the loss of semen is the loss of this potent stuff . . . it is best never to sleep with women at all.

Both male and female physiology lend themselves to the analogy with the vessel which must not pour away or dilute its vital fluids. Females are correctly seen as, literally, the entry by which the pure content may be adulterated. Males are treated as pores through which the precious stuff may ooze out and be lost, the whole system being thereby enfeebled.

A double moral standard is often applied to sexual offenses. In a patrilineal system of descent wives are the door of entry to the group. In this they hold a place analogous to that of sisters in the Hindoo caste. Through the adultery of a wife impure blood is introduced to the lineage. So the symbolism of the imperfect vessel appropriately weighs more heavily on the women than on the men.[20]

If we treat ritual protection of bodily orifices as a symbol of social preoccupations about exits and entrances, the purity of cooked food becomes important. I quote a passage on the capacity of cooked food to be polluted and to carry pollution (in an unsigned review article on Pure and Impure, *Contributions to Indian Sociology*, III, July 1959, p. 37).

> When a man uses an object it becomes part of him, participates in him. Then, no doubt, this appropriation is much closer in the case of food, and the point is that appropriation precedes absorption, as it accompanies the cooking. Cooking may be taken to imply a complete appropriation of the food by the household. It is almost as if, before being "internally absorbed" by the individual, food was, by cooking, collectively predigested. One cannot share the food prepared by people without sharing in their nature. This is one aspect of the situation. Another is that cooked food is extremely permeable to pollution.

---

[19] *Limpid:* clear or transparent; *treacle:* molasses or syrup; *rheum:* a watery mucous discharge from the eyes or nose.

[20] Douglas says that rules of body purity and pollution are symbolic of a group's place in society as well as the preservation of that group. It follows that because caste membership is transmitted through women, the rules of sexual purity and pollution are more strict for women than for men. Just as sexual restrictions can be symbolic of anxiety about caste membership, the polluting qualities of menstrual blood, semen, or other body products can be symbolic of lineage membership. Yalman's discussion of sexuality and male and female purity is actually a second issue – not the preservation of a social group such as a caste, but the maintenance of gender boundaries.

This reads like a correct transliteration of Indian pollution symbolism regarding cooked food. But what is gained by proffering a descriptive account as if it were explanatory? In India the cooking process is seen as the beginning of ingestion, and therefore cooking is susceptible to pollution, in the same way as eating. But why is this complex found in India and in parts of Polynesia and in Judaism and other places, but not wherever humans sit down to eat? I suggest that food is not likely to be polluting at all unless the external boundaries of the social system are under pressure.[21] We can go further to explain why the actual cooking of the food in India must be ritually pure. The purity of the castes is correlated with an elaborate hereditary division of labour between castes. The work performed by each caste carries a symbolic load: it says something about the relatively pure status of the caste in question. Some kinds of labour correspond with the excretory functions of the body, for example that of washermen, barbers, sweepers, as we have seen. Some professions are involved with bloodshed or alcoholic liquor, such as tanners, warriors, toddy tappers. So they are low in the scale of purity in so far as their occupations are at variance with Brahminic ideals. But the point at which food is prepared for the table is the point at which the interrelation of the purity structure and the occupational structure needs to be set straight. For food is produced by the combined efforts of several castes of varying degrees of purity: the blacksmith, carpenter, ropemaker, the peasant. Before being admitted to the body some clear symbolic break is needed to express food's separation from necessary but impure contacts. The cooking process, entrusted to pure hands, provides this ritual break. Some such break we would expect to find whenever the production of food is in the hands of the relatively impure.

These are the general lines on which primitive rituals must be related to the social order and the culture in which they are found. The examples I have given are crude, intended to exemplify a broad objection to a certain current treatment of ritual themes. I add one more, even cruder, to underline my point. Much literature has been expended by psychologists on Yurok pollution ideas (Erikson, Posinsky). These North Californian Indians who lived by fishing for salmon in the Klamath River, would seem to have been obsessed by the behavior of liquids, if their pollution rules can be said to express an obsession. They are careful not to mix good water with bad, not to urinate into rivers, not to mix sea and fresh water, and so on. I insist that these rules cannot imply obsessional neuroses, and they cannot be interpreted unless the fluid formlessness of their highly competitive social life be taken into account (Dubois).

To sum up. There is unquestionably a relation between individual preoccupations and primitive ritual. But the relation is not the simple one which some psychoanalysts have assumed. Primitive ritual draws upon individual experience, of course. This is a truism. But it draws upon it so selectively that it cannot be said to be primarily inspired by the need to solve individual problems common to the human race, still less explained by clinical research. Primitives are not trying to cure or prevent personal neuroses by their public rituals. Psychologists can tell us whether the public expression of individual anxieties is likely to solve personal problems or not. Certainly we must suppose that some interaction of the kind is probable. But that is not at issue. The analysis of ritual symbolism cannot begin until we recognize ritual as an attempt to create and maintain a particular culture, a particular set of assumptions by which experience is controlled.

Any culture is a series of related structures which comprise social forms, values, cosmology, the whole of knowledge and through which all experience is mediated. Certain cultural themes are expressed by rites of bodily manipulation. In this very general sense primitive culture can be said to be autoplastic. But the objective of these rituals

---

[21] Douglas refers to the prohibition of eating beef in India, the principles of mana and taboo in traditional Polynesian societies, and the dietary rules about kosher food in Judaism. She suggests that if a society or class feels the need to protect itself from outsiders or foreign influences, this will be symbolized through rules of behavior and eating. For example, in Polynesia, commoners were forbidden to touch anything associated with the noble classes because these objects contained mana, a power that could harm them. According to Douglas, protecting the body from pollution by guarding the orifices, in this case restricting the diet, symbolizes the protection of traditional beliefs.

is not negative withdrawal from reality. The assertions they make are not usefully to be compared to the withdrawal of the infant into thumb-sucking and masturbation. The rituals enact the form of social relations and in giving these relations visible expression they enable people to know their own society. The rituals work upon the body politic through the symbolic medium of the physical body.[22]

References

Bettelheim, B. 1955. *Symbolic Wounds.* Glencoe, IL.

Brown, Norman O. 1959. *Life Against Death.* London.

Dubois, Cora. 1936. "The Wealth Concept as an Integrative Factor in Tolowa-Tututni Culture." Chapter in *Essays in Anthropology, Presented to A. L. Kroeber.*

Dumont, L. and Peacock, D. 1959. *Contributions to Indian Sociology.* Vol. III.

Marshall-Thomas, E. 1959. *The Harmless People.* New York.

Naipaul, V. S. 1964. *An Area of Darkness.* London.

Posinky. 1956. *Psychiatric Quarterly* XXX, p. 598.

Roheim, G. 1925. *Australian Totemism.*

Yalman, N. 1963. "The Purity of Women in Ceylon and Southern India." *Journal of the Royal Anthropological Institute.*

---

[22] Douglas' conclusion reflects the strong influence of Durkheim on her work. Durkheim was concerned with demonstrating that society was a separate phenomenon from individual psychology and that social actions could not be reduced to the sum total of individual actions. In other words, he tried very hard to separate sociology from psychology. Douglas attempts to do the same thing. She insists that the rules of ritual and pollution are what Durkheim called *social facts.* They are not reducible to manifestations of individual psychology. Whatever effects they may have on the individual, they reflect the ways society maintains its structure and solidarity. The essay is profoundly symbolic – a materialist's analysis of the caste system, for example, would have focused on the political and economic inequalities inherent in it, which Douglas ignores. With some modification we could imagine this essay appearing as a chapter in Durkheim's *Elementary Forms of the Religious Life.* For example, in the last sentence of the paragraph above, she characterizes ritual as the attempt to create and maintain a particular culture.

36. Symbols in Ndembu Ritual

Victor Turner (1920–1983)

AMONG THE NDEMBU OF ZAMBIA (FORMERLY Northern Rhodesia), the importance of ritual in the lives of the villagers in 1952 was striking. Hardly a week passed in a small neighborhood without a ritual drum being heard in one or another of its villages.

By "ritual" I mean prescribed formal behavior for occasions not given over to technological routine having reference to beliefs in mystical beings or powers. The symbol is the smallest unit of ritual which still retains the specific properties of ritual behavior; it is the ultimate unit of specific structure in a ritual context. Since this essay is in the main a description and analysis of the structure and properties of symbols, it will be enough to state here, following the *Concise Oxford Dictionary,* that a "symbol" is a thing regarded by general consent as naturally typifying or representing or recalling something by possession of analogous qualities or by association in fact or thought. The symbols I observed in the field were, empirically, objects, activities, relationships, events, gestures, and spatial units in a ritual situation.[1]

From *The Forest of Symbols* (1967)

---

[1] This essay, first presented as a paper at a professional meeting in 1958, is one of Turner's most famous works. In it he outlines some basic properties of symbols and contrasts his method of symbolic analysis with psychoanalytic thought using examples from his fieldwork with the Ndembu.

Following the advice and example of Professor Monica Wilson, I asked Ndembu specialists as well as laymen to interpret the symbols of their ritual. As a result, I obtained much exegetic[2] material. I felt that it was methodologically important to keep observational and interpretative materials distinct from one another. The reason for this will soon become apparent.[3]

I found that I could not analyze ritual symbols without studying them in a time series in relation to other "events," for symbols are essentially involved in social process. I came to see performances of ritual as distinct phases in the social processes whereby groups became adjusted to internal changes and adapted to their external environment. From this standpoint the ritual symbol becomes a factor in social action, a positive force in an activity field. The symbol becomes associated with human interests, purposes, ends, and means, whether these are explicitly formulated or have to be inferred from the observed behavior. The structure and properties of a symbol become those of a dynamic entity, at least within its appropriate context of action.[4]

STRUCTURE AND PROPERTIES OF RITUAL SYMBOLS

The structure and properties of ritual symbols may be inferred from three classes of data: (1) external form and observable characteristics; (2) interpretations offered by specialists and by laymen; (3) significant contexts largely worked out by the anthropologist.[5]

Here is an example. At *Nkang'a,* the girl's puberty ritual, a novice is wrapped in a blanket and laid at the foot of a *mudyi* sapling. The *mudyi* tree *Diplorrhyncus condylocarpon* is conspicuous for its white latex, which exudes in milky beads if the thin bark is scratched. For Ndembu this is its most important observable characteristic, and therefore I propose to call it "the milk tree" henceforward.[6] Most Ndembu women can attribute several meanings to this tree. In the first place, they say that the milk tree is the "senior" (*mukulumpi*) tree of the ritual. Each kind of ritual has this "senior" or, as I will call it, "dominant" symbol. Such symbols fall into a special class which I will discuss more fully later. Here it

---

[2] *Exegetic:* the adjectival form of *exegesis,* an interpretation or explanation.

[3] Turner was a student of Monica H. Wilson (1908–1982), a Cambridge-educated South African social anthropologist. In the 1930s, most anthropologists in the structural-functionalist tradition were writing about African societies as static traditions. Wilson, however, focused on economic, political, and social change in African societies, particularly among the Nyakyusa. She is best known for her detailed fieldwork and ethnographies.

Turner speaks of keeping observational and interpretive materials separate from one another because he wrote this article at a time when symbolic interpretation was controversial and because of the training he received from Wilson. The care with which he outlines his argument is in part a reaction to the controversy caused by Freudian interpretations of ethnographic material. Psychoanalytic analysis relies heavily on the interpreter's explication of the unconscious meaning of a ritual or other symbols. In the British structural-functionalist tradition, Turner considers symbols to be empirically verifiable units and is interested in the laws by which they are used.

[4] Contrary to the psychoanalytic approach, Turner maintains that because ritual symbols are a part of social action they must be analyzed within the social and temporal contexts in which they are expressed. Turner's structural-functionalist roots are also apparent in this paragraph in that he sees rituals as the mechanism by which groups adjust to changes in their social and external environment.

[5] Reacting to the ethnoscientists' critique of ethnography, Turner refuses to get drawn into a conflict over the validity of different forms of interpretation. Here he says that observed data, informants' interpretations, and the anthropologist's analysis are all legitimate. In the following paragraph he demonstrates how the symbolism of the *mudyi* tree can be viewed from all three perspectives.

[6] Turner says Ndembu women attribute several symbolic meanings to the *mudyi* tree. The fact that a single symbol can represent many things is called *multivocality,* and it is one of Turner's key ideas. He first defined the term in his 1965 article "Ritual Symbolism, Morality, and Social Structure among the Ndembu." Note that Turner proposes to call the tree the milk tree, thus imposing a symbolic image of his own. What do the Ndembu call the *mudyi* tree? Is milk tree the English translation of *mudyi*?

is enough to state that dominant symbols are regarded not merely as means to the fulfillment of the avowed purposes of a given ritual, but also and more importantly refer to values that are regarded as ends in themselves, that is, to axiomatic values. Secondly, the women say with reference to its observable characteristics that the milk tree stands for human breast milk and also for the breasts that supply it. They relate this meaning to the fact that *Nkang'a* is performed when a girl's breasts begin to ripen, not after her first menstruation, which is the subject of another and less elaborate ritual. The main theme of *Nkang'a* is indeed the tie of nurturing between mother and child, not the bond of birth. This theme of nurturing is expressed at *Nkang'a* in a number of supplementary symbols indicative of the act of feeding and of foodstuff. In the third place, the women describe the milk tree as "the tree of a mother and her child." Here the reference has shifted from description of a biological act, breast feeding, to a social tie of profound significance both in domestic relations and in the structure of the widest Ndembu community. This latter meaning is brought out most clearly in a text I recorded from a male ritual specialist. I translate literally.

> The milk tree is the place of all mothers of the lineage (*ivumu*, literally "womb" or "stomach"). It represents the ancestress of women and men. The milk tree is where our ancestress slept when she was initiated. To initiate here means the dancing of women round and round the milk tree where the novice sleeps. One ancestress after another slept there down to our grandmother and our mother and ourselves the children. That is the place of our tribal custom (*muchidi*)[a] where we began, even men just the same, for men are circumcised under a milk tree.

This text brings out clearly those meanings of the milk tree which refer to principles and values of social organization. At one level of abstraction

the milk tree stands for matriliny, the principle on which the continuity of Ndembu society depends. Matriliny governs succession to office and inheritance of property, and it vests dominant rights of residence in local units. More than any other principle of social organization it confers order and structure on Ndembu social life. Beyond this, however, "*mudyi*" means more than matriliny, both according to this text and according to many other statements I have collected. It stands for tribal custom (*muchidi wetu*) itself. The principle of matriliny, the backbone of Ndembu social organization, as an element in the semantic structure of the milk tree, itself symbolizes the total system of interrelations between groups and persons that makes up Ndembu society. Some of the meanings of important symbols may themselves be symbols, each with its own system of meanings. At its highest level of abstraction, therefore, the milk tree stands for the unity and continuity of Ndembu society. Both men and women are components of that spatiotemporal continuum. Perhaps that is why one educated Ndembu, trying to cross the gap between our cultures, explained to me that the milk tree was like the British flag above the administrative headquarters. "*Mudyi* is our flag," he said.[7]

When discussing the milk tree symbolism in the context of the girls' puberty ritual, informants tend to stress the harmonizing, cohesive aspects of the milk tree symbolism. They also stress the aspect of dependence. The child depends on its mother for nutriment; similarly, say the Ndembu, the tribesman drinks from the breasts of tribal custom. Thus nourishment and learning are equated in the meaning content of the milk tree. I have often heard the milk tree compared to "going to school"; the child is said to swallow instruction as a baby swallows milk and *kapudyi*, the thin cassava gruel Ndembu liken to milk. Do we not ourselves speak of "a thirst for knowledge"? Here the milk tree is a shorthand for the

---

[7] Like Douglas, Turner inherited the Durkheimian perspective implicit in British structural functionalism. Here you see this perspective expressed in his statement that the *mudyi* tree represents not only breast milk, but at its most abstract level of meaning, Ndembu society. Turner was also influenced by Raymond Firth (1901–). A student of Malinowski, Firth was interested in linking the interpretation of symbolism to social structures and social events (Firth 1973:25). Note the symbolic tie between the *mudyi* tree and matrilineality. Here Turner makes the link between kinship and symbolism. In classic functionalist style, Turner focuses on the harmonious, integrative functions of symbols.

process of instruction in tribal matters that follows the critical episode in both boys' and girls' initiation—circumcision in the case of the boys and the long trial of lying motionless in that of the girls. The mother's role is the archetype, of protector, nourisher, and teacher. For example, a chief is often referred to as the "mother of his people," while the hunter-doctor who initiates a novice into a hunting cult is called "the mother of huntsmanship (*mama dawuyang'a*)." An apprentice circumciser is referred to as "child of the circumcision medicine" and his instructor as "mother of the circumcision medicine." In all the senses hitherto described, the milk tree represents harmonious, benevolent aspects of domestic and tribal life.

However, when the third mode of interpretation, contextual analysis, is applied, the interpretations of informants are contradicted by the way people actually behave with reference to the milk tree. It becomes clear that the milk tree represents aspects of social differentiation and even opposition between the components of a society which ideally it is supposed to symbolize as a harmonious whole. The first relevant context we shall examine is the role of the milk tree in a series of action situations within the framework of the girls' puberty ritual. Symbols, as I have said, produce action, and dominant symbols tend to become focuses in interaction. Groups mobilize around them, worship before them, perform other symbolic activities near them, and add other symbolic objects to them, often to make composite shrines. Usually these groups of participants themselves stand for important components of the secular social system, whether these components consist of corporate groups, such as families and

lineages, or of mere categories of persons possessing similar characteristics, such as old men, women, children, hunters, or widows. In each kind of Ndembu ritual a different group or category becomes the focal social element. In *Nkang'a* this focal element is the unity of Ndembu women. It is the women who dance around the milk tree and initiate the recumbent novice by making her the hub of their whirling circle. Not only is the milk tree the "flag of the Ndembu"; more specifically, in the early phases of *Nkang'a*, it is the "flag" of Ndembu women. In this situation it does more than focus the exclusiveness of women; it mobilizes them in opposition to the men. For the women sing songs taunting the men and for a time will not let men dance in their circle. Therefore, if we are to take account of the operational aspect of the milk tree symbol, including not only what Ndembu say about it but also what they do with it in its "meaning," we must allow that it distinguishes women as a social category and indicates their solidarity.[8]

The milk tree makes further discriminations. For example, in certain action contexts it stands for the novice herself. One such context is the initial sacralization of a specific milk tree sapling. Here the natural property of the tree's immaturity is significant. Informants say that a young tree is chosen because the novice is young. A girl's particular tree symbolizes her new social personality as a mature woman. In the past and occasionally today, the girl's puberty ritual was part of her marriage ritual, and marriage marked her transition from girlhood to womanhood. Much of the training and most of the symbolism of *Nkang'a* are concerned with making the girl a sexually accomplished spouse, a fruitful woman, and a mother

---

[8] Anthropologist Max Gluckman (1911–1975) was a major influence on Turner. Gluckman, a structural-functionalist, focused on the socially integrative effects of ritual expressions of conflict (Gluckman 1956). Famous for his formulation of the concept of "rituals of rebellion," Gluckman proposed that the ritual enactment of conflict (such as that between women and men in the *Nkang'a* rite) is a form of catharsis that allows the expression of hostility without endangering the established social order. Having discussed the role that *mudyi* tree symbolism plays in tribal life, Turner tells us that the milk tree also represents differentiation and opposition in a situation that should be harmonious. In the *Nkang'a* ritual the *mudyi* is the "flag" of Ndembu women as they highlight their opposition to men, taunting them and denying them access to their dance circle. This contradiction is explained in Gluckman's terms. Marxist analysts also placed emphasis on conflict, but used the concept very differently. For structural-functionalists, ritualized forms of conflict prevent social disruption and maintain a society's stability. For Marxists, conflict is the key force propelling revolution and, thus, social evolution.

able to produce a generous supply of milk. For each girl this is a unique process. She is initiated alone and is the center of public attention and care. From her point of view it is *her Nkang'a*, the most thrilling and self-gratifying phase of her life. Society recognizes and encourages these sentiments, even though it also prescribes certain trials and hardships for the novice, who must suffer before she is glorified on the last day of the ritual. The milk tree, then, celebrates the coming-of-age of a new social personality, and distinguishes her from all other women at this one moment in her life. In terms of its action context, the milk tree here also expresses the conflict between the girl and the moral community of adult women she is entering. Not without reason is the milk tree site known as "the place of death" or "the place of suffering," terms also applied to the site where boys are circumcised, for the girl novice must not move a muscle throughout a whole hot and clamant[9] day.

In other contexts, the milk tree site is the scene of opposition between the novice's own mother and the group of adult women. The mother is debarred from attending the ring of dancers. She is losing her child, although later she recovers her as an adult co-member of her lineage. Here we see the conflict between the matricentric family and the wider society which, as I have said, is dominantly articulated by the principle of matriliny. The relationship between mother and daughter persists throughout the ritual, but its content is changed. It is worth pointing out that, at one phase in *Nkang'a*, mother and daughter interchange portions of clothing. This may perhaps be related to the Ndembu custom whereby mourners wear small portions of a dead relative's clothing. Whatever the interchange of clothing may mean to a psychoanalyst—and here we arrive at one of the limits of our present anthropological competence—it seems not unlikely that Ndembu intend to symbolize the termination for both mother and daughter of an important aspect of their relationship. This is one of the symbolic actions—one of very few—about which I found it impossible to elicit any interpretation in the puberty ritual. Hence it is legitimate to infer, in my opinion, that powerful unconscious wishes, of a kind considered illicit by Ndembu, are expressed in it.[10]

Opposition between the tribeswomen and the novice's mother is mimetically represented at the milk tree towards the end of the first day of the puberty ritual. The girl's mother cooks a huge meal of cassava and beans—both kinds of food are symbols in *Nkang'a*, with many meanings—for the women visitors, who eat in village groups and not at random. Before eating, the women return to the milk tree from their eating place a few yards away and circle the tree in procession. The mother brings up the rear holding up a large spoon full of cassava and beans. Suddenly she shouts: "Who wants the cassava of *chipwampwilu?*" All the women rush to be first to seize the spoon and eat from it. "*Chipwampwilu*" appears to be an archaic word and no one knows its meaning. Informants say that the spoon represents the novice herself in her role of married woman, while the food stands both for her reproductive power (*lusemu*) and her role as cultivator and cook. One woman told my wife: "It is lucky if the person snatching the spoon comes from the novice's own village.[11] Otherwise, the mother believes that her child will go far away from her to

---

[9] *Clamant:* noisy.

[10] Elements of both Gluckman and Freud appear in this paragraph. First, Turner explains that the ritual allows the symbolic expression of hostility between the initiate's mother and the larger group of adult women in this matrilineal society. Then, because Turner was unable to elicit any explanation for a mother and daughter's exchange of apparel during the *Nkang'a* rite, he assumes the symbolism of the exchange indicates unconscious feelings that the Ndembu censor from conscious expression.

[11] Turner mentions the presence of his wife in this paragraph. Although she accompanied him into the field and helped him conduct research, Edith Turner (1921–) is rarely mentioned in his works. She is an accomplished anthropologist in her own right, with several books to her credit. Some of her recent works are *The Spirit and the Drum: A Memoir of Africa* (1987) and *Experiencing Ritual: A New Interpretation of African Healing* (1992).

a distant village and die there. The mother wants her child to stay near her." Implicit in this statement is a deeper conflict than that between the matricentric family and mature female society. It refers to another dominant articulating principle of Ndembu society, namely virilocal marriage according to which women live at their husbands' villages after marriage. Its effect is sometimes to separate mothers from daughters by considerable distances. In the episode described, the women symbolize the matrilineal cores of villages. Each village wishes to gain control through marriage over the novice's capacity to work. Its members also hope that her children will be raised in it, thus adding to its size and prestige. Later in *Nkang'a* there is a symbolic struggle between the novice's matrilineal kin and those of her bridegroom, which makes explicit the conflict between virilocality and matriliny.

Lastly, in the context of action situation, the milk tree is sometimes described by informants as representing the novice's own matrilineage. Indeed, it has this significance in the competition for the spoon just discussed, for women of her own village try to snatch the spoon before members of other villages. Even if such women do not belong to her matrilineage but are married to its male members, they are thought to be acting on its behalf. Thus, the milk tree in one of its action aspects represents the unity and exclusiveness of a single matrilineage with a local focus in a village against other such corporate groups. The conflict between yet another subsystem and the total system is given dramatic and symbolic form.[12]

By this time, it will have become clear that considerable discrepancy exists between the interpretations of the milk tree offered by informants and the behavior exhibited by Ndembu in situations dominated by the milk tree symbolism. Thus, we are told that the milk tree represents the close tie between mother and daughter. Yet the milk tree separates a daughter from her mother. We are also told that the milk tree stands for the unity of Ndembu society. Yet we find that in practice it separates women from men, and some categories and groups of women from others. How are these contradictions between principle and practice to be explained?

SOME PROBLEMS OF INTERPRETATION

I am convinced that my informants genuinely believed that the milk tree represented only the linking and unifying aspects of Ndembu social organization. I am equally convinced that the role of the milk tree in action situations where it represents a focus of specified groups in opposition to other groups, forms an equally important component of its total meaning. Here the important question must be asked, "meaning for whom?" For if Ndembu do not recognize the discrepancy between their interpretation of the milk tree symbolism and other behavior in connection with it, does this mean that the discrepancy has no relevance for the social anthropologist? Indeed some anthropologists claim, with Nadel (1954, 108), that "uncomprehended symbols have no part in social enquiry, their social effectiveness lies in their capacity to indicate, and if they indicate nothing to the actors, they are, from our point of view, irrelevant, and indeed no longer symbols (whatever their significance for the psychologist or psychoanalyst)."[13] Professor Monica Wilson (1957, 6) holds a similar point of view. She writes that she stresses "Nyakyusa interpretations of their own rituals, for anthropological literature is bespattered with symbolic guessing, the ethnographer's interpretations of the rituals of other people." Indeed, she goes so far as to base her whole analysis of Nyakyusa ritual on "the Nyakyusa translation or interpretation of the symbolism." In

---

[12] Turner's analysis is clearly similar to the work on kinship conducted by Radcliffe-Brown a generation earlier (see essay 14). He states that the ritual actions refer to sociostructural elements of the society as well as express the conflict between matrilineality and virilocality.

[13] S. F. Nadel (1903–1956) received a doctoral degree in psychology and philosophy from the University of Vienna and studied anthropology at the London School of Economics with Malinowski and Seligman. He is best known for his work with the Nupe in northern Nigeria and the Nuba in Sudan.

my view, these investigators go beyond the limits of salutary caution and impose serious, and even arbitrary, limitations on themselves. To some extent, their difficulties derive from their failure to distinguish the concept of symbol from that of a mere sign. Although I am in complete disagreement with his fundamental postulate that the collective unconscious is the main formative principle in ritual symbolism, I consider that Carl Jung (1949, 601) has cleared the way for further investigation by making just this distinction. "A sign," he says, "is an analogous or abbreviated expression of a *known* thing. But a symbol is always the best possible expression of a relatively *unknown* fact, a fact, however, which is none the less recognized or postulated as existing." Nadel and Wilson, in treating most ritual symbols as signs, must ignore or regard as irrelevant some of the crucial properties of such symbols.[14]

FIELD SETTING AND STRUCTURAL PERSPECTIVE

How, then, can a social anthropologist justify his claim to be able to interpret a society's ritual symbols more deeply and comprehensively than the actors themselves? In the first place, the anthropologist, by the use of his special techniques and concepts, is able to view the performance of a given kind of ritual as "occurring in, and being interpenetrated by, a totality of coexisting social entities such as various kinds of groups, sub-groups, categories, or personalities, and also barriers between them, and modes of interconnexion" (Lewin 1949, 200). In other words, he can place this ritual in its significant field setting and describe the structure and properties of that field. On the other hand, each participant in the ritual views it from his own particular corner of obser-

vation. He has what Lupton has called his own "structural perspective." His vision is circumscribed by his occupancy of a particular position, or even of a set of situationally conflicting positions, both in the persisting structure of his society, and also in the role structure of the given ritual. Moreover, the participant is likely to be governed in his actions by a number of interests, purposes, and sentiments, dependent upon his specific position, which impair his understanding of the total situation. An even more serious obstacle against his achieving objectivity is the fact that he tends to regard as axiomatic and primary the ideals, values, and norms that are overtly expressed or symbolized in the ritual. Thus, in the *Nkang'a* ritual, each person or group in successive contexts of action, sees the milk tree only as representing her or their own specific interests and values at those times. However, the anthropologist who has previously made a structural analysis of Ndembu society, isolating its organizational principles, and distinguishing its groups and relationships, has no particular bias and can observe the real interconnections and conflicts between groups and persons, in so far as these receive ritual representation. What is meaningless for an actor playing a specific role may well be highly significant for an observer and analyst of the total system.[15]

On these grounds, therefore, I consider it legitimate to include within the total meaning of a dominant ritual symbol, aspects of behavior associated with it which the actors themselves are unable to interpret, and indeed of which they may be unaware, if they are asked to interpret the symbol outside its activity context. Nevertheless, there still remains for us the problem of the contradiction between the expressed meanings of the milk tree symbol and the meaning of the stereo-

---

[14] Here Turner attempts to deal with the argument that symbolic meaning not recognized by native informants is invalid. Although Turner does not use the terms, this is the same emic-etic debate that was conducted in the United States between ethnoscientists and materialists.

[15] Turner says that anthropologists are privileged observers without bias who can view symbolic actions in a wider social context than a ritual participant. Do you agree? Are anthropologists really impartial observers with no particular bias, or do they have their "own particular corner of observation" too? This is a central question for the postmodernists, who claim that an observer cannot be impartial. But even if that is true, an important question remains: can anthropologists accurately see some things invisible to a culture's participants?

typed forms of behavior closely associated with it. Indigenous interpretations of the milk tree symbolism in the abstract appear to indicate that there is no incompatibility or conflict between the persons and groups to which it refers. Yet, as we have seen, it is between just such groups that conflict is mimed at the milk tree site.

THREE PROPERTIES OF RITUAL SYMBOLS

Before we can interpret, we must further classify our descriptive data, collected by the methods described above. Such a classification will enable us to state some of the properties of ritual symbols.[16] The simplest property is that of *condensation*. Many things and actions are represented in a single formation. Secondly, a dominant symbol is a *unification of disparate significata*. The disparate *significata* are interconnected by virtue of their common possession of analogous qualities or by association in fact or thought. Such qualities or links of association may in themselves be quite trivial or random or widely distributed over a range of phenomena. Their very generality enables them to bracket together the most diverse ideas and phenomena. Thus, as we have seen, the milk tree stands for, *inter alia*, women's breasts, motherhood, a novice at *Nkang'a*, the principle of matriliny, a specific matrilineage, learning, and the unity and persistence of Ndembu society. The themes of nourishment and dependence run through all these diverse *significata*.

The third important property of dominant ritual symbols is *polarization of meaning*. Not only the milk tree but all other dominant Ndembu symbols possess two clearly distinguishable poles of meaning. At one pole is found a cluster of *significata* that refer to components of the moral and social orders of Ndembu society, to principles of social organization, to kinds of corporate grouping, and to the norms and values inherent in structural relationships. At the other pole, the *significata* are usually natural and physiological phenomena and processes. Let us call the first of these the "ideological pole," and the second the "sensory pole." At the sensory pole, the meaning content is closely related to the outward form of the symbol. Thus one meaning of the milk tree — breast milk — is closely related to the exudation of milky latex from the tree. One sensory meaning of another dominant symbol, the *mukula* tree, is blood; this tree secretes a dusky red gum.[17]

At the sensory pole are concentrated those *significata* that may be expected to arouse desires and feelings; at the ideological pole one finds an arrangement of norms and values that guide and control persons as members of social groups and categories. The sensory, emotional *significata* tend to be "gross" in a double sense. In the first place, they are gross in a general way, taking no account of detail or the precise qualities of emotion. It cannot be sufficiently stressed that such symbols are social facts, "collective representations," even though their appeal is to the lowest common denominator of human feeling. The second sense of "gross" is "frankly, even flagrantly, physiological." Thus, the milk tree has the gross meanings of breast milk, breasts, and the process of breast feeding. These are also gross in the sense that they represent items of universal Ndembu experience. Other Ndembu symbols, at their sensory poles of meaning, represent such themes as blood, male and female genitalia, semen, urine, and feces. The same symbols, at their ideological poles

---

[16] Earlier, Turner defined "dominant symbols" as those referring to "axiomatic," or self-evident, values. In this section, he further explains dominant symbols and describes three of their most important properties: condensation, unification of disparate significata, and polarization of meaning. These principles help explain how symbols can have various and conflicting meanings.

[17] Turner here imposes a scheme of classification that strongly resembles Lévi-Strauss' nature-culture binary opposition. The poles of meaning that Turner labels ideological and sensory could almost as easily be labeled culture and nature. Why, given that he considers these poles of meaning universal, did Turner not turn to structuralism? In the 1960s and 1970s a structural-functionalist interested in symbolic analysis could turn to Lévi-Strauss or Freud. Like Douglas, who studied the symbolism of body wastes and social boundaries, Turner chose to derive his symbolic meanings from Freud.

of meaning, represent the unity and continuity of social groups, primary and associational, domestic, and political.[18]

[*A 569-word section of Turner's article called "Reference and Condensation" has been omitted. In this section, Turner discusses Edward Sapir's discussion of the means by which ritual symbols stimulate emotional responses.*]

DOMINANT AND INSTRUMENTAL SYMBOLS

Certain ritual symbols, as I have said, are regarded by Ndembu as dominant. In rituals performed to propitiate ancestor spirits who are believed to have afflicted their living kin with reproductive disorders, illness, or bad luck at hunting, there are two main classes of dominant symbols. The first class is represented by the first tree or plant in a series of trees or plants from which portions of leaves, bark, or roots are collected by practitioners or adepts in the curative cult. The subjects of ritual are marked with these portions mixed with water, or given them, mixed in a potion, to drink. The first tree so treated is called the "place of greeting" (*ishikenu*), or the "elder" (*mukulumpi*). The adepts encircle it several times to sacralize it. Then the senior practitioner prays at its base, which he sprinkles with powdered white clay. Prayer is made either to the named spirit, believed to be afflicting the principal subject of ritual, or to the tree itself, which is in some way identified with the afflicting spirit. Each *ishikenu* can be allotted several meanings by adepts. The second class of dominant symbols in curative rituals consists of shrines where the subjects of such rituals sit while the practitioners wash them with vegetable substances mixed with water and perform actions on their behalf of a symbolic or ritualistic nature. Such shrines are often composite, consisting of several objects in configuration. Both classes of dominant symbols are closely associated with nonempirical beings. Some are regarded as their repositories; others, as being identified with them; others again, as representing them. In life-crisis rituals, on the other hand, dominant symbols seem to represent not beings but nonempirical powers or kinds of efficacy. For example, in the boys' circumcision ritual, the dominant symbol for the whole ritual is a "medicine" (*yitumbu*), called "*nfunda*," which is compounded from many ingredients, e.g., the ash of the burnt lodge which means "death," and the urine of an apprentice circumciser which means "virility." Each of these and other ingredients have many other meanings. The dominant symbol at the camp where the novices' parents assemble and prepare food for the boys is the *chikoli* tree, which represents, among other things, an erect phallus, adult masculinity, strength, hunting prowess, and health continuing into old age. The dominant symbol during the process of circumcision is the milk tree, beneath which novices are circumcised. The dominant symbol in the immediate postcircumcision phase is the red *mukula* tree, on which the novices sit until their wounds stop bleeding. Other symbols are dominant at various phases of seclusion. Each of these symbols is described as "*mukulumpi*" (elder, senior). Dominant symbols appear in many different ritual contexts, sometimes presiding over the whole procedure, sometimes over particular phases. The meaning-content of certain dominant symbols possesses a high degree of constancy and consistency throughout the total symbolic system, exemplifying Radcliffe-Brown's proposition that a symbol recurring in a cycle of rituals is likely to have the same significance in each. Such symbols also possess considerable autonomy with regard to the

---

[18] Turner is concerned not only with interpreting symbols, but also with explaining why they affect people the way they do. He states that blood, genitals, semen, urine, and feces are all represented by basic Ndembu symbols at their sensory and ideological poles of meaning, thus relying on both Durkheim and Freud. He sees symbols as social facts and notes that at the ideological pole these symbols represent "unity and continuity of social groups," which draws on Durkheim. His identification of the sensory pole of meaning as being "flagrantly physiological" shows the influence of Freud, who believed that such physiological symbolism was universal because the experience of these elements in infancy was universal.

aims of the rituals in which they appear. Precisely because of these properties, dominant symbols are readily analyzable in a cultural framework of reference. They may be regarded for this purpose as what Whitehead would have called "eternal objects."[b] They are the relatively fixed points in both the social and cultural structures, and indeed constitute points of junction between these two kinds of structure. They may be regarded irrespective of their order of appearance in a given ritual as ends in themselves, as representative of the axiomatic values of the widest Ndembu society. This does not mean that they cannot also be studied, as we have indeed studied them, as factors of social action, in an action frame of reference, but their social properties make them more appropriate objects of morphological study than the class of symbols we will now consider.

These symbols may be termed "instrumental symbols." An instrumental symbol must be seen in terms of its wider context, i.e., in terms of the total system of symbols which makes up a given kind of ritual. Each kind of ritual has its specific mode of interrelating symbols. This mode is often dependent upon the ostensible purposes of that kind of ritual. In other words, each ritual has its own teleology.[19] It has its explicitly expressed goals, and instrumental symbols may be regarded as means of attaining those goals. For example, in rituals performed for the overt purpose of making women fruitful, among the instrumental symbols used are portions of fruit-bearing trees or of trees that possess innumerable rootlets. These fruits and rootlets are said by Ndembu to represent children. They are also thought of as having efficacy to make the woman fruitful. They are means to the main end of the ritual. Perhaps such symbols could be regarded as mere signs or referential symbols, were it not for the fact that the meanings of each are associated with powerful conscious and unconscious emotions and wishes. At the psychological level of analysis, I suspect that these symbols too would approximate to the condition of condensation symbols, but here we touch upon the present limits of competence of anthropological explanation, a problem we will now discuss more fully.

THE LIMITS OF ANTHROPOLOGICAL INTERPRETATION

We now come to the most difficult aspect of the scientific study of ritual symbolism: analysis. How far can we interpret these enigmatic formations by the use of anthropological concepts? At what points do we reach the frontiers of our explanatory competence? Let us first consider the case of dominant symbols. I have suggested that these have two poles of meaning, a sensory and an ideological pole. I have also suggested that dominant symbols have the property of unifying disparate *significata*. I would go so far as to say that at both poles of meaning are clustered disparate and even contradictory *significata*. In the course of its historical development, anthropology has acquired techniques and concepts that enable it to handle fairly adequately the kind of data we have classified as falling around the ideological pole. Such data, as we have seen, include components of social structure and cultural phenomena, both ideological and technological. I believe that study of these data in terms of the concepts of three major subdivisions of anthropology—cultural anthropology, structuralist theory, and social dynamics—would be extremely rewarding. I shall shortly outline how I think such analyses might be done and how the three frameworks might be interrelated, but first we must ask how far and in what respects is it relevant to submit the sensory pole of meaning to intensive analysis, and, more importantly, how far are we, as anthropologists, qualified to do so? It is evident, as Sapir has stated, that ritual symbols, like all condensation symbols, "strike deeper and deeper roots in the unconscious." Even a brief acquaintance with

---

[19] What Turner means is that each ritual has its own design and purpose. An instrumental symbol must be analyzed in terms of the specific ritual context in which it occurs. Dominant symbols are "axiomatic," that is, self-evidently true. The implication here is that, within a culture, dominant symbols are constant in meaning, while the meaning of instrumental symbols is dependent on their context.

depth psychology is enough to show the investigator that ritual symbols, with regard to their outward form, to their behavioral context, and to several of the indigenous interpretations set upon them, are partially shaped under the influence of unconscious motivations and ideas. The interchange of clothes between mother and daughter at the *Nkang'a* ritual; the belief that a novice would go mad if she saw the milk tree on the day of her separation ritual; the belief that if a novice lifts up the blanket with which she is covered during seclusion and sees her village her mother would die; all these are items of symbolic behavior for which the Ndembu themselves can give no satisfactory interpretation. For these beliefs suggest an element of mutual hostility in the mother-daughter relationship which runs counter to orthodox interpretations of the milk tree symbolism, in so far as it refers to the mother-daughter relationship. One of the main characteristics of ideological interpretations is that they tend to stress the harmonious and cohesive aspect of social relationships. The exegetic idiom feigns that persons and groups always act in accordance with the ideal norms of Ndembu society.

[We have omitted a 700-word section of Turner's article called "Depth Psychology and Ritual Symbolism," in which he discusses the psychoanalytic interpretation of ritual symbols such as the work of Bruno Bettelheim, which was discussed in the previous essay, by Mary Douglas. In this section, Turner claims that psychoanalysts generally reject the ideological pole of meaning and focus on the sensory meanings. He writes that psychoanalysts regard indigenous explanations of symbols as identical to the justifications that neurotics provide for their behavior. Further, Turner says that psychoanalysts look on ritual symbols as being identical with symptoms of neurosis or psychosis or as dream symbols of Western Europeans. Turner, of course, disagrees with this point of view. He states that symbols are partly influenced by unconscious motivations and ideas, but his is not a psychoanalytic interpretation. He ends the

section in an almost comic manner, referring to "hapless anthropologists" having to choose between competing psychoanalytic interpretations.]

PROVINCES OF EXPLANATION

I consider that if we conceptualize a dominant symbol as having two poles of meaning, we can more exactly demarcate the limits within which anthropological analysis may be fruitfully applied. Psychoanalysts, in treating most indigenous interpretations of symbols as irrelevant, are guilty of a naive and one-sided approach. For those interpretations that show how a dominant symbol expresses important components of the social and moral orders are by no means equivalent to the "rationalizations," and the "secondary elaborations" of material deriving from endopsychic conflicts. They refer to social facts that have an empirical reality exterior to the psyches of individuals. On the other hand, those anthropologists who regard only indigenous interpretations as relevant, are being equally one-sided. This is because they tend to examine symbols within two analytical frameworks only, the cultural and the structural. This approach is essentially a static one, and it does not deal with processes involving temporal changes in social relations.

Nevertheless, the crucial properties of a ritual symbol involve these dynamic developments. Symbols instigate social action. In a field context they may even be described as "forces," in that they are determinable influences inclining persons and groups to action.[20] It is in a field context, moreover, that the properties we have described, namely, polarization of meanings, transference of affectual quality, discrepancy between meanings, and condensations of meanings, become most significant. The symbol as a unit of action, possessing these properties, becomes an object of study both for anthropology and for psychology. Both disciplines, in so far as they are concerned with human actions must conceptualize the ritual symbol in the same way.

---

[20] The influence of Durkheim on Turner's analysis is strongly manifested in this section. Turner's description of symbols as forces that incline people to action is quite similar to Durkheim's description of social facts (see essay 6). Turner also refers to Durkheim's *The Elementary Forms of the Religious Life* in this section.

The techniques and concepts of the anthropologist enable him to analyze competently the interrelations between the data associated with the ideological pole of meaning. They also enable him to analyze the social behavior directed upon the total dominant symbol. He cannot, however, with his present skills, discriminate between the precise sources of unconscious feeling and wishing, which shape much of the outward form of the symbol; select some natural objects rather than others to serve as symbols; and account for certain aspects of the behavior associated with symbols. For him, it is enough that the symbol should evoke emotion. He is interested in the fact that emotion is evoked and not in the specific qualities of its constituents. He may indeed find it situationally relevant for his analysis to distinguish whether the emotion evoked by a specific symbol possesses the gross character, say, of aggression, fear, friendliness, anxiety, or sexual pleasure, but he need go no further than this. For him the ritual symbol is primarily a factor in group dynamics, and, as such, its references to the groups, relationships, values, norms, and beliefs of a society are his principal items of study. In other words, the anthropologist treats the sensory pole of meaning as a constant, and the social and ideological aspects as variables whose interdependencies he seeks to explain.

The psychoanalyst, on the other hand, must, I think, attach greater significance than he now does to social factors in the analysis of ritual symbolism. He must cease to regard interpretations, beliefs, and dogmas as mere rationalizations when, often enough, these refer to social and natural realities. For, as Durkheim wrote (1954, 2–3), "primitive religions hold to reality and express it. One must learn to go underneath the symbol to the reality which it represents and which gives it its meaning. No religions are false, all answer, though in different ways, to the given conditions of human existence." Among those given conditions,

the arrangement of society into structured groupings, discrepancies between the principles that organize these groupings, economic collaboration and competition, schism within groups and opposition between groups—in short, all those things with which the social aspect of ritual symbolism is concerned—are surely of at least equal importance with biopsychical drives and early conditioning in the elementary family. After all, the ritual symbol has, in common with the dream symbol, the characteristic, discovered by Freud, of being a compromise formation between two main opposing tendencies. It is a compromise between the need for social control, and certain innate and universal human drives whose complete gratification would result in a breakdown of that control. Ritual symbols refer to what is normative, general, and characteristic of unique individuals. Thus, Ndembu symbols refer among other things, to the basic needs of social existence (hunting, agriculture, female fertility, favourable climatic conditions, and so forth), and to shared values on which communal life depends (generosity, comradeship, respect for elders, the importance of kinship, hospitality, and the like). In distinguishing between ritual symbols and individual psychic symbols, we may perhaps say that while ritual symbols are gross means of handling social and natural reality, psychic symbols are dominantly fashioned under the influence of inner drives. In analyzing the former, attention must mainly be paid to relations between data external to the psyche; in analyzing the latter, to endopsychic data.[21]

For this reason, the study of ritual symbolism falls more within the province of the social anthropologist than that of the psychologist or psychoanalyst, although the latter can assist the anthropologist by examining the nature and interconnections of the data clustered at the sensory pole of ritual symbolism. He can also, I believe, illuminate certain aspects of the stereotyped behavior associated with symbols in field

---

[21] Here Turner distinguishes between cultural symbols and individual psychological symbols. He argues that the former are the province of anthropology while the latter are that of psychology. This concern with distinguishing anthropology and sociology from psychology is similar to that expressed by Durkheim at the turn of the century. Both Turner and Durkheim argued that collective phenomena are the subjects of anthropology, while individual consciousness belongs in psychology.

contexts, which the actors themselves are unable to explain. For as we have seen, much of this behavior is suggestive of attitudes that differ radically from those deemed appropriate in terms of traditional exegesis. Indeed, certain conflicts would appear to be so basic that they totally block exegesis.

THE INTERPRETATION OF OBSERVED EMOTIONS

Can we really say that behavior portraying conflict between persons and groups, who are represented by the symbols themselves as being in harmony, is in the full Freudian sense unconscious behavior? The Ndembu themselves in many situations outside *Nkang'a*, both secular and ritual, are perfectly aware of and ready to speak about hostility in the relationships between particular mothers and daughters, between particular sublineages, and between particular young girls and the adult women in their villages. It is rather as though there existed in certain precisely defined public situations, usually of a ritual or ceremonial type, a norm obstructing the verbal statement of conflicts in any way connected with the principle and rules celebrated or dramatized in those situations. Evidences of human passion and frailty are just not spoken about when the occasion is given up to the public commemoration and reanimation of norms and values in their abstract purity.

Yet, as we have seen, recurrent kinds of conflict may be acted out in the ritual or ceremonial form. On great ritual occasions, common practice, as well as highest principle, receives its symbolic or stereotyped expression, but practice, which is dominantly under the sway of what all societies consider man's "lower nature," is rife with expressions of conflict. Selfish and factional interests, oath breaking, disloyalty, sins of omission as well as sins of commission, pollute and disfigure those ideal prototypes of behavior which in precept, prayer, formula, and symbol are held up before the ritual assembly for its exclusive attention. In the orthodox interpretation of ritual it is pretended that common practice has no efficacy and that men and women really are as they ideally should be. Yet, as I have argued above, the "energy" required to reanimate the values and norms enshrined in dominant symbols and expressed in various kinds of verbal behavior is "borrowed," to speak metaphorically in lieu at the moment of a more rigorous language, from the miming of well-known and normally mentionable conflicts. The raw energies of conflict are domesticated into the service of social order.[22]

I should say here that I believe it possible, and indeed necessary, to analyze symbols in a context of observed emotions. If the investigator is well acquainted with the common idiom in which a society expresses such emotions as friendship, love, hate, joy, sorrow, contentment, and fear, he cannot fail to observe that these are experienced in ritual situations. Thus, in *Nkang'a* when the women laugh and jeer at the men, tease the novice and her mother, fight one another for the "porridge of *chipwampwilu*," and so on, the observer can hardly doubt that emotions are really aroused in the actors as well as formally represented by ritual custom. ("What's Hecuba to him or he to Hecuba, that he should weep for her?")[23]

These emotions are portrayed and evoked in close relation to the dominant symbols of tribal cohesion and continuity, often by the performance of instrumentally symbolic behavior. However, since they are often associated with the mimesis[24] of interpersonal and intergroup conflict, such emotions and acts of behavior obtain no place

---

[22] For Turner, apparent conflict reinforces social order, once again illustrating Gluckman's perspective. Although he does not specifically call the *Nkang'a* a ritual of rebellion, it is clear that he has this in mind.

[23] Turner says that it is important for one to analyze symbols in the context of observed emotions. The quotation is from Hamlet, Act II, scene 2, where Hamlet, writing a play in which his father's murder will be re-created, comments on the power of emotion that can be expressed by an actor.

[24] *Mimesis:* imitation.

among the official, verbal meanings attributed to such dominant symbols.[25]

THE SITUATIONAL SUPPRESSION OF CONFLICT FROM INTERPRETATION

Emotion and praxis,[26] indeed, give life and coloring to the values and norms, but the connection between the behavioral expression of conflict and the normative components of each kind of ritual, and of its dominant symbols, is seldom explicitly formulated by believing actors. Only if one were to personify a society, regarding it as some kind of supra-individual entity, could one speak of "unconsciousness" here. Each individual participant in the *Nkang'a* ritual is well aware that kin quarrel most bitterly over rights and obligations conferred by the principle of matriliny, but that awareness is situationally held back from verbal expression: the participants must behave as if conflicts generated by matriliny were irrelevant.

[Several paragraphs totaling about 560 words were omitted from the text. These contained a discussion of the situational suppression of conflict in the ritual expression of dominant symbols.]

For example, in the frequently performed *Nkula* ritual, the dominant symbols are a cluster of red objects, notably red clay (*mukundu*) and the *mukula* tree mentioned previously. In the context of *Nkula*, both of these are said to represent menstrual blood and the "blood of birth," which is the blood that accompanies the birth of a child. The ostensible goal of the ritual is to co-agulate the patient's menstrual blood, which has been flowing away in menorrhagia, around the fetus in order to nourish it. A series of symbolic acts are performed to attain this end. For example, a young *mukula* tree is cut down by male doctors and part of it is carved into the shape of a baby, which is then inserted into a round calabash medicated with the blood of a sacrificed cock, with red clay, and with a number of other red ingredients. The red medicines here, say the Ndembu, represent desired coagulation of the patient's menstrual blood, and the calabash is a symbolic womb. At the ideological pole of meaning, the *mukula* tree and the medicated calabash both represent (as the milk tree does) the patient's matrilineage and, at a higher level of abstraction, the principle of matriliny itself. This is also consistent with the fact that *ivumu*, the term for "womb," also means "matrilineage."[27] In this symbolism the procreative, rather than the nutritive, aspect of motherhood is stressed. However, Ndembu red symbolism, unlike the white symbolism of which the milk tree symbolism is a species, nearly always has explicit reference to violence, to killing, and, at its most general level of meaning, to breach, both in the social and natural orders. Although informants, when discussing this *Nkula* ritual specifically, tend to stress the positive, feminine aspects of parturition and reproduction, other meanings of the red symbols, stated explicitly in other ritual contexts, can be shown to make their influence felt in *Nkula*. For example, both red clay and the *mukula* tree are dominant symbols in the hunter's cult, where they mean the blood of animals, the red meat of game, the inheritance through either parent of

---

[25] Turner's emphasis on interpreting behavior rather than thought appears repeatedly in this essay, highlighting the difference between him and the American ethnoscientists of this period. His focus on behavior largely collapsed the emic-etic distinctions so important in American anthropology.

[26] *Praxis:* practice, as distinguished from theory.

[27] Earlier in the article Turner stated that psychoanalytic interpretations typically focus on the sensory pole of meaning. Here, in his description of the *Nkula* ritual, the symbolism of the calabash as womb and red clay as menstrual blood is very Freudian. At the ideological pole of meaning the same symbols refer to the patient's matrilineage. This is a structural interpretation in the tradition of Radcliffe-Brown. The characteristics of symbols that Turner described earlier in this article — condensation, polarization of meaning, and the unification of disparate significata — allow him to reconcile these seemingly contradictory interpretations.

hunting prowess, and the unity of all initiated hunters. It also stands for the hunter's power to kill.[28] The same red symbols, in the context of the *Wubanji* ritual performed to purify a man who has killed a kinsman or a lion or leopard (animals believed to be reincarnated hunter kin of the living), represent the blood of homicide. Again, in the boys' circumcision ritual, these symbols stand for the blood of circumcised boys. More seriously still, in divination and in antiwitchcraft rituals, they stand for the blood of witches' victims, which is exposed in necrophagous feasts.[29]

Most of these meanings are implicit in *Nkula*. For example, the female patient, dressed in skins like a male hunter and carrying a bow and arrow, at one phase of the ritual performs a special hunter's dance. Moreover, while she does this, she wears in her hair, just above the brow, the red feather of a lourie bird. Only shedders of blood, such as hunters, man-slayers, and circumcisers, are customarily entitled to wear this feather.[30] Again, after the patient has been given the baby figurine in its symbolic womb, she dances with it in a style of dancing peculiar to circumcisers when they brandish aloft the great *nfunda* medicine of the circumcision lodge. Why then is the woman patient identified with male bloodspillers? The field context of these symbolic objects and items of behavior suggests that the Ndembu feel that the woman, in wasting her menstrual blood and in failing to bear children, is actively renouncing her expected role as a mature married female. She is behaving like a male killer, not like a female nourisher. The situation is analogous, though modified by matriliny, to the following pronouncement in the ancient Jewish Code of Qaro: "Every man is bound to marry a wife in order to beget children, and he who fails of this duty is as one who sheds blood."

One does not need to be a psychoanalyst, one only needs sound sociological training, acquaintance with the total Ndembu symbolic system, plus ordinary common sense, to see that one of the aims of the ritual is to make the woman accept her lot in life as a childbearer and rearer of children for her lineage. The symbolism suggests that the patient is unconsciously rejecting her female role, that indeed she is guilty; indeed, "*mbayi*," one term for menstrual blood, is etymologically connected with "*ku-baya*" (to be guilty). I have not time here to present further evidence of symbols and interpretations, both in *Nkula* and in cognate rituals, which reinforce this explanation. In the situation of *Nkula*, the dominant principles celebrated and reanimated are those of matriliny, the mother-child bond, and tribal continuity through matriliny. The norms in which these are expressed are those governing the behavior of mature women, which ascribe to them the role appropriate to their sex. The suppressed or submerged principles and norms, in this situation, concern and control the personal and corporate behavior deemed appropriate for man.

The analysis of *Nkula* symbolism throws into relief another major function of ritual. Ritual adapts and periodically readapts the biopsychical individual to the basic conditions and axiomatic values of human social life. In redressive rituals, the category to which *Nkula* belongs, the eternally rebellious individual is converted for a while into a loyal citizen. In the case of Nkula, a female individual whose behavior is felt to demonstrate her rebellion against,

---

[28] Earlier, Turner characterized instrumental symbols as those that have a ritually specific meaning; here he gives an example. The *mukula* tree represents menstrual blood and the matrilineage in the women's *Nkula* rite, but it also represents the blood of animals and the hunter's power to kill, among other meanings, in men's hunting rites.

[29] *Necrophagy* is the eating of the dead.

[30] The role reversals in the *Nkula* ceremony—women dressing in hunter's garb and dancing a hunter's dance—are other aspects of the rituals of rebellion that Gluckman described in his research. See for example, his *Custom and Conflict in Africa* (1956). Gluckman's central idea was that while the ritualized reversing of established roles (the poor mock the wealthy, women dress as men) seemed to challenge the established order, in fact, these symbolic reversals reinforced it. Similarly, Turner identifies Ndembu women's ceremonial cross-dressing as a demonstration of male and female roles. He sees the ritual as a symbolic means of forcing women to accept their place as childbearers and not challenge male gender roles.

or at least her reluctance to comply with, the biological and social life patterns of her sex, is both induced and coerced by means of precept and symbol to accept her culturally prescribed destiny.[31]

MODES OF INFERENCE IN INTERPRETATION

Each kind of Ndembu ritual, like *Nkula,* has several meanings and goals that are not made explicit by informants, but must be inferred by the investigator from the symbolic pattern and from behavior. He is able to make these inferences only if he has previously examined the symbolic configurations and the meanings attributed to their component symbols by skilled informants, of many other kinds of ritual in the same total system. In other words, he must examine symbols not only in the context of each specific kind of ritual, but in the context of the total system. He may even find it profitable, where the same symbol is found throughout a wide culture area, to study its changes of meaning in different societies in that area.[32]

There are two main types of contexts, irrespective of size. There is the action-field context, which we have discussed at some length. There is also the cultural context in which symbols are regarded as clusters of abstract meanings. By comparing the different kinds and sizes of contexts in which a dominant symbol occurs, we can often see that the meanings "officially" attributed to it in a particular kind of ritual may be mutually consistent. However, there may be much discrepancy and even contradiction between many of the meanings given by informants, when this dominant symbol is regarded as a unit of the total symbolic system. I do not believe that this discrepancy is the result of mere carelessness and ignorance

or variously distributed pieces of insight. I believe that discrepancy between *significata* is a quintessential property of the great symbolic dominants in all religions. Such symbols come in the process of time to absorb into their meaning-content most of the major aspects of human social life, so that, in a sense, they come to represent "human society" itself.[33] In each ritual they assert the situational primacy of a single aspect or of a few aspects only, but by their mere presence they suffuse those aspects with the awe that can only be inspired by the human total. All the contradictions of human social life, between norms, and drives, between different drives and between different norms, between society and the individual, and between groups, are condensed and unified in a single representation, the dominant symbols. It is the task of analysis to break down this amalgam into its primary constituents.

[The 350-word section called "The Relativity of Depth" was omitted from this text. In it, Turner criticizes the notion that psychoanalytic interpretations of symbolism are "deeper" than anthropological analyses and characterizes symbols as a "force in a field of social action."]

CONCLUSION: THE ANALYSIS OF SYMBOLS IN SOCIAL PROCESSES

Let me outline briefly the way in which I think ritual symbols may fruitfully be analyzed. Performances of ritual are phases in broad social processes, the span and complexity of which are roughly proportional to the size and degree of differentiation of the groups in which they occur. One class of ritual is situated near the apex of a whole hierarchy of redressive and regulative

---

[31] The paragraph concluding Turner's description of the *Nkula* rite highlights the structural-functionalist background that he brings to his analysis. Ritual compels a woman who rebels against her assigned role to "accept her culturally prescribed destiny," thus preserving the stability of Ndembu society.

[32] Note again Turner's view of the anthropologist as neutral omniscient observer—anthropologists can interpret, he says, because they see the total system. The individual immersed in the system does not possess this clarity of vision. Compare this point of view with that of the postmodernists in essays 38 and 39.

[33] Remember Durkheim's contention that Australian Aboriginal religious beliefs were a model of their own society. Here Turner makes a similar claim, not just for Ndembu symbolism, but for the dominant symbols of any society.

institutions that correct deflections and deviations from customarily prescribed behavior. Another class anticipates deviations and conflicts. This class includes periodic rituals and life-crisis rituals. Each kind of ritual is a patterned process in time, the units of which are symbolic objects and serialized items of symbolic behavior.

The symbolic constituents may themselves be classed into structural elements, or "dominant symbols," which tend to be ends in themselves, and variable elements, or "instrumental symbols," which serve as means to the explicit or implicit goals of the given ritual. In order to give an adequate explanation of the meaning of a particular symbol, it is necessary first to examine the widest action-field context, that, namely, in which the ritual itself is simply a phase. Here one must consider what kinds of circumstances give rise to a performance of ritual, whether these are concerned with natural phenomena, economic and technological processes, human life-crises, or with the breach of crucial social relationships. The circumstances will probably determine what sort of ritual is performed. The goals of the ritual will have overt and implicit reference to the antecedent circumstances and will in turn help to determine the meaning of the symbols. Symbols must now be examined within the context of the specific ritual. It is here that we enlist the aid of indigenous informants. It is here also that we may be able to speak legitimately of "levels" of interpretation, for laymen will give the investigator simple and esoteric meanings, while specialists will give him esoteric explanations and more elaborate texts. Next, behavior directed towards each symbol should be noted, for such behavior is an important component of its total meaning.[34]

We are now in a position to exhibit the ritual as a system of meanings, but this system acquires additional richness and depth if it is regarded as itself constituting a sector of the Ndembu ritual system, as interpreted by informants and as observed in action. It is in comparison with other sectors of the total system, and by reference to the dominant articulating principles of the total system, that we often become aware that the overt and ostensible aims and purposes of a given ritual conceal unavowed, and even "unconscious," wishes and goals. We also become aware that a complex relationship exists between the overt and the submerged, and the manifest and latent patterns of meaning. As social anthropologists we are potentially capable of analyzing the social aspect of this relationship. We can examine, for example, the relations of dependence and independence between the total society and its parts, and the relations between different kinds of parts, and between different parts of the same kind. We can see how the same dominant symbol, which in one kind of ritual stands for one kind of social group or for one principle of organization, in another kind of ritual stands for another kind of group or principle, and in its aggregate of meanings stands for unity and continuity of the widest Ndembu society, embracing its contradictions.[35]

THE LIMITS OF CONTEMPORARY ANTHROPOLOGICAL COMPETENCE

Our analysis must needs be incomplete when we consider the relationship between the normative elements in social life and the individual. For this

---

[34] Note Turner's comment that different people will interpret symbols differently. A decade later, postmodern writers emphasized this point. They used the term *positioning* and claimed that one's point of view was influenced by social, economic, and political factors. One important difference between Turner's view and that of the postmodernists was that these latter were more influenced by Marxism: they tended to see positioning in terms of conflict and domination of one group over another. Turner notes that positioning exists, but he does not question its effect. He insists that anthropologists occupy a privileged position and are impartial observers.

[35] In the two paragraphs above, Turner provides an outline of his methods of analysis. The sophistication that he brought to symbolic analysis becomes apparent when you compare his work with studies of ritual or religion from the first part of the century such as Sir James Frazer's *Golden Bough* (1911–1915 [1890]) and Freud's *Moses and Monotheism* (1939). Turner's analysis of the different types of symbols and their properties stands today as one of the seminal works in symbolic anthropology.

relationship, too, finds its way into the meaning of ritual symbols. Here we come to the confines of our present anthropological competence, for we are now dealing with the structure and properties of psyches, a scientific field traditionally studied by other disciplines than ours. At one end of the symbol's spectrum of meanings we encounter the individual psychologist and the social psychologist, and even beyond them (if one may make a friendly tilt at an envied friend), brandishing his Medusa's head, the psychoanalyst, ready to turn to stone the foolhardy interloper into his caverns of terminology.

We shudder back thankfully into the light of social day. Here the significant elements of a symbol's meaning are related to what it does and what is done to it by and for whom. These aspects can only be understood if one takes into account from the beginning, and represents by appropriate theoretical constructs, the total field situation in which the symbol occurs. This situation would include the structure of the group that performs the ritual we observe, its basic organizing principles and perdurable relationships, and, in addition, its extant division into transient alliances and factions on the basis of immediate interest and ambitions, for both abiding structure and recurrent forms of conflict and selfish interest are stereotyped in ritual symbolism. Once we have collected informants' interpretations of a given symbol, our work of analysis has indeed just begun. We must gradually approximate to the action-meaning of our symbol by way of what Lewin calls (1949, 149) "a stepwise increasing specificity" from widest to narrowest significant action context. Informants' "meanings" only become meaningful as objects of scientific study in the course of this analytical process.[36]

Notes

Read at a meeting of the Association of Social Anthropologists of the Commonwealth in London, March 1958. First published in *Closed Systems and Open Minds: The Limits of Naivety in Social Science*, M. Gluckman, ed. (Edinburgh: Oliver and Boyd, 1964).

a. *Muchidi* also means "category," "kind," "species," and "tribe" itself.

b. I.e., objects not of indefinite duration but to which the category of time is not applicable.

References

Bettelheim, Bruno. 1954. *Symbolic Wounds: Puberty Rites and the Envious Male*. Glencoe, Ill: Free Press.

Durkheim, E. 1954. *Elementary Forms of the Religious Life*. London: Allen and Unwin.

Fenichel, Otto. 1946. *The Psychoanalytic Theory of Neuroses*. London: Routledge and Kegan Paul.

Jung, Carl G. 1949. *Psychological Types*. London: Routledge and Kegan Paul.

Lewin, K. 1949. *Field Theory in Social Science*. London: Tavistock Publications.

Nadel, S. F. 1954. *Nupe Religion*. London: Routledge and Kegan Paul.

Sapir, E. "Symbols," *Encyclopedia of the Social Sciences*, XIV. New York: Macmillan.

Wilson, M. 1957. *Rituals of Kinship Among the Nyakyusa*. London: Oxford University Press, for the International African Institute.

---

[36] The role of symbols in culture and individual psychology is a complex question that has defied definitive explication since it first arose at the turn of the century. In the final paragraphs, Turner, like Durkheim and Douglas, focuses on the intellectual division between anthropology-sociology and psychology.

37. Deep Play: Notes on the Balinese Cockfight

Clifford Geertz (1926–)

THE RAID

EARLY IN APRIL OF 1958, MY WIFE AND I ARRIVED, malarial and diffident, in a Balinese village we intended, as anthropologists, to study.[1] A small place, about five hundred people, and relatively remote, it was its own world. We were intruders, professional ones, and the villagers dealt with us as Balinese seem always to deal with people not part of their life who yet press themselves upon them: as though we were not there. For them, and to a degree for ourselves, we were nonpersons, specters, invisible men.

We moved into an extended family compound (that had been arranged before through the provincial government) belonging to one of the four major factions in village life. But except for our landlord and the village chief, whose cousin and brother-in-law he was, everyone ignored us in a way only a Balinese can do. As we wandered around, uncertain, wistful, eager to please, people seemed to look right through us with a gaze focused several yards behind us on some more actual stone or tree. Almost nobody greeted us; but nobody scowled or said anything unpleasant to us

From *The Interpretation of Cultures* (1973)

either, which would have been almost as satisfactory. If we ventured to approach someone (something one is powerfully inhibited from doing in such an atmosphere), he moved, negligently but definitely, away. If, seated or leaning against a wall, we had him trapped, he said nothing at all, or mumbled what for the Balinese is the ultimate nonword—"yes." The indifference, of course, was studied; the villagers were watching every move we made, and they had an enormous amount of quite accurate information about who we were and what we were going to be doing. But they acted as if we simply did not exist, which, in fact, as this behavior was designed to inform us, we did not, or anyway not yet.

This is, as I say, general in Bali. Everywhere else I have been in Indonesia, and more latterly in Morocco, when I have gone into a new village, people have poured out from all sides to take a very close look at me, and, often an all-too-probing feel as well. In Balinese villages, at least those away from the tourist circuit, nothing happens at all. People go on pounding, chatting, making offerings, staring into space, carrying baskets about while one drifts around feeling vaguely disembodied. And the same thing is true on the individual level. When you first meet a Balinese, he seems

---

[1] The work of symbolic anthropologists like Victor Turner and Mary Douglas was concerned with demonstrating what Devons and Gluckman (1964) called the "logic of the irrational" (quoted in Kaplan and Manners 1972:121). One motive underlying their work was to demonstrate how institutions that seemed irrational to the observer are actually rational, even if the natives themselves are unaware of the cultural logic behind their behavior. Turner and Douglas accounted for this hidden rationality by penetrating the surface behavior and explanations to look for concealed layers of meaning. This form of inquiry ultimately led analysts to resort to psychological explanations of behavior, or semimetaphysical concepts such as social facts or the collective conscience. Geertz, although he too is concerned with the interpretation of cultural symbolism, follows a very different approach: he wishes to provide the reader with an empathic understanding of another society. Geertz believes that culture is acted out in public symbols such as the cockfight and is the mechanism by which members of a society communicate their worldview. He is not trying to uncover the hidden symbolic meaning of the Balinese cockfight, for he believes the Balinese understand the symbolism of the contest as well as anyone. Instead, in this analysis Geertz attempts to situate readers of the essay within the Balinese system in order to facilitate their understanding of the meaning of the cockfight. This is not, in any sense, a scientific goal. His observations are not replicable. Someone else trying to do the same work might well have a very different set of insights.

Geertz's original article is accompanied by 43 voluminous footnotes, which space limitations do not allow us to reprint. Asterisks have been used to show readers the placement of his footnotes in the text.

virtually not to relate to you at all; he is, in the term Gregory Bateson and Margaret Mead made famous, "away."* Then—in a day, a week, a month (with some people the magic moment never comes)—he decides, for reasons I have never quite been able to fathom, that you *are* real, and then he becomes a warm, gay, sensitive, sympathetic, though, being Balinese, always precisely controlled, person. You have crossed, somehow, some moral or metaphysical shadow line. Though you are not exactly taken as a Balinese (one has to be born to that), you are at least regarded as a human being rather than a cloud or a gust of wind. The whole complexion of your relationship dramatically changes to, in the majority of cases, a gentle, almost affectionate one—a low-keyed, rather playful, rather mannered, rather bemused geniality.

My wife and I were still very much in the gust-of-wind stage, a most frustrating, and even, as you soon begin to doubt whether you are really real after all, unnerving one, when, ten days or so after our arrival, a large cockfight was held in the public square to raise money for a new school.

Now, a few special occasions aside, cockfights are illegal in Bali under the Republic (as, for not altogether unrelated reasons, they were under the Dutch), largely as a result of the pretensions to puritanism radical nationalism tends to bring with it. The elite, which is not itself so very puritan, worries about the poor, ignorant peasant gambling all his money away, about what foreigners will think, about the waste of time better devoted to building up the country. It sees cockfighting as "primitive," "backward," "unprogressive," and generally unbecoming an ambitious nation. And, as with those other embarrassments—opium smoking, begging, or uncovered breasts—it seeks, rather unsystematically, to put a stop to it.

Of course, like drinking during Prohibition or, today, smoking marihuana, cockfights, being a part of "The Balinese Way of Life," nonetheless go on happening, and with extraordinary frequency. And, as with Prohibition or marihuana, from time to time the police (who, in 1958 at least, were almost all not Balinese but Javanese) feel called upon to make a raid, confiscate the cocks and spurs, fine a few people, and even now and then expose some of them in the tropical sun

for a day as object lessons which never, somehow, get learned, even though occasionally, quite occasionally, the object dies.

As a result, the fights are usually held in a secluded corner of a village in semisecrecy, a fact which tends to slow the action a little—not very much, but the Balinese do not care to have it slowed at all. In this case, however, perhaps because they were raising money for a school that the government was unable to give them, perhaps because raids had been few recently, perhaps, as I gathered from subsequent discussion, there was a notion that the necessary bribes had been paid, they thought they could take a chance on the central square and draw a larger and more enthusiastic crowd without attracting the attention of the law.

They were wrong. In the midst of the third match, with hundreds of people, including, still transparent, myself and my wife, fused into a single body around the ring, a superorganism in the literal sense, a truck full of policemen armed with machine guns roared up. Amid great screeching cries of "pulisi! pulisi!" from the crowd, the policemen jumped out, and, springing into the center of the ring, began to swing their guns around like gangsters in a motion picture, though not going so far as actually to fire them. The superorganism came instantly apart as its components scattered in all directions. People raced down the road, disappeared headfirst over walls, scrambled under platforms, folded themselves behind wicker screens, scuttled up coconut trees. Cocks armed with steel spurs sharp enough to cut off a finger or run a hole through a foot were running wildly around. Everything was dust and panic.

On the established anthropological principle, "When in Rome," my wife and I decided, only slightly less instantaneously than everyone else, that the thing to do was run too. We ran down the main village street, northward, away from where we were living, for we were on that side of the ring. About halfway down another fugitive ducked suddenly into a compound—his own, it turned out—and we, seeing nothing ahead of us but rice fields, open country, and a very high volcano, followed him. As the three of us came tumbling into the courtyard, his wife, who had apparently been through this sort of thing before, whipped out a table, a tablecloth, three chairs, and three cups of tea, and we all, without any explicit communication whatsoever, sat down, commenced to sip tea, and sought to compose ourselves.

A few moments later, one of the policemen marched importantly into the yard, looking for the village chief. (The chief had not only been at the fight, he had arranged it. When the truck drove up he ran to the river, stripped off his sarong, and plunged in so he could say, when at length they found him sitting there pouring water over his head, that he had been away bathing when the whole affair had occurred and was ignorant of it. They did not believe him and fined him three hundred rupiah, which the village raised collectively.) Seeing me and my wife, "White Men," there in the yard, the policeman performed a classic double take. When he found his voice again he asked, approximately, what in the devil did we think we were doing there. Our host of five minutes leaped instantly to our defense, producing an impassioned description of who and what we were, so detailed and so accurate that it was my turn, having barely communicated with a living human being save my landlord and the village chief for more than a week, to be astonished. We had a perfect right to be there, he said, looking the Javanese upstart in the eye. We were American professors; the government had cleared us; we were there to study culture; we were going to write a book to tell Americans about Bali. And we had all been there drinking tea and talking about cultural matters all afternoon and did not know anything about any cockfight. Moreover, we had not seen the village chief all day; he must have gone to town. The policeman retreated in rather total disarray. And, after a decent interval, bewildered but relieved to have survived and stayed out of jail, so did we.

The next morning the village was a completely different world for us. Not only were we no longer invisible, we were suddenly the center of all attention, the object of a great outpouring of warmth, interest, and most especially, amusement. Everyone in the village knew we had fled like everyone else. They asked us about it again and again (I must have told the story, small detail by small detail, fifty times by the end of the day), gently,

affectionately, but quite insistently teasing us: "Why didn't you just stand there and tell the police who you were?" "Why didn't you just say you were only watching and not betting?" "Were you really afraid of those little guns?" As always, kinesthetically minded and, even when fleeing for their lives (or, as happened eight years later, surrendering them), the world's most poised people, they gleefully mimicked, also over and over again, our graceless style of running and what they claimed were our panic-stricken facial expressions. But above all, everyone was extremely pleased and even more surprised that we had not simply "pulled out our papers" (they knew about those too) and asserted our Distinguished Visitor status, but had instead demonstrated our solidarity with what were now our covillagers. (What we had actually demonstrated was our cowardice, but there is fellowship in that too.) Even the Brahmana priest, an old, grave, halfway-to-heaven type who because of its associations with the underworld would never be involved, even distantly, in a cockfight, and was difficult to approach even to other Balinese, had us called into his courtyard to ask us about what had happened, chuckling happily at the sheer extraordinariness of it all.

In Bali, to be teased is to be accepted. It was the turning point so far as our relationship to the community was concerned, and we were quite literally "in." The whole village opened up to us, probably more than it ever would have otherwise (I might actually never have gotten to that priest, and our accidental host became one of my best informants), and certainly very much faster. Getting caught, or almost caught, in a vice raid is perhaps not a very generalizable recipe for achieving that mysterious necessity of anthropological field work, rapport, but for me it worked very well. It led to a sudden and unusually complete acceptance into a society extremely difficult for outsiders to penetrate. It gave me the kind of immediate, inside-view grasp of an aspect of "peasant mentality" that anthropologists not fortunate enough to flee headlong with their subjects from armed authorities normally do not get. And, perhaps most important of all, for the other things might have come in other ways, it put me very quickly on to a combination emotional explosion, status war, and philosophical drama of central significance to the society whose inner nature I desired to understand. By the time I left I had spent about as much time looking into cockfights as into witchcraft, irrigation, caste, or marriage.[2]

OF COCKS AND MEN

Bali, mainly because it is Bali, is a well-studied place. Its mythology, art, ritual, social organization, patterns of child rearing, forms of law, even styles of trance, have all been microscopically examined for traces of that elusive substance Jane Belo called "The Balinese Temper."* But, aside from a few passing remarks, the cockfight has barely been noticed, although as a popular obsession of consuming power it is at least as important a revelation of what being a Balinese "is really like" as these more celebrated phenomena.* As much of America surfaces in a ball park, on a golf links, at a race track, or around a poker table, much of Bali surfaces in a cock ring. For it is only apparently cocks that are fighting there. Actually, it is men.

To anyone who has been in Bali any length of time, the deep psychological identification of Balinese men with their cocks is unmistakable. The double entendre here is deliberate. It works in exactly the same way in Balinese as it does in English, even to producing the same tired jokes, strained puns, and uninventive obscenities. Bateson and Mead have even suggested that, in line with the Balinese conception of the body as a set of separately animated parts, cocks are viewed as detachable, self-operating penises, ambulant genitals with a life of their own.* And while I do not have the kind of unconscious material either to confirm or disconfirm this intriguing notion, the fact that they are masculine symbols par excellence is about as indubitable, and to the Balinese about as evident, as the fact that water runs downhill.

The language of everyday moralism is shot through, on the male side of it, with roosterish imagery. *Sabung*, the word for cock (and one which appears in inscriptions as early as A.D. 922), is used metaphorically to mean "hero," "warrior," "champion," "man of parts," "political candidate," "bachelor," "dandy," "lady-killer," or "tough guy." A pompous man whose behavior presumes above his station is compared to a tailless cock who struts about as though he had a large, spectacular one. A desperate man who makes a last, irrational effort to extricate himself from an impossible situation is likened to a dying cock who makes one final lunge at his tormentor to drag him along to a common destruction. A stingy man, who promises much, gives little, and begrudges that, is compared to a cock which, held by the tail, leaps at another without in fact engaging him. A marriageable young man still shy

---

[2] This is one of the most famous stories in anthropology and almost any anthropologist in the United States could tell it to you. Why? First, it is an adventure and a fieldworker's fantasy: confused anthropologists find empathy and acceptance. Second, it highlights the strength of Geertz's writing style. Not only is it interesting because it is self-revealing, but Geertz is one of the finest writers in anthropology today. The essay is full of action and humor. Interestingly, the essay was first published in *Daedalus,* a literary journal; it is aimed at a highly educated audience but not one composed exclusively of anthropologists.

Geertz's self-relevatory style was unusual for ethnographic writing at this time. (See the introduction to Evans-Pritchard's *The Nuer* (1940) for an early example of self-relevatory ethnographic writing.) Although the style is common now, compare his descriptions of the police raid with earlier ethnographic work. Can you imagine Kroeber or Radcliffe-Brown writing an account of their escape from the police? This story is not only fun to read, but Geertz's writing helps a reader visualize the events. He addresses the reader directly: "You have crossed, somehow, some oral or metaphysical shadow line. Though you are not exactly taken as Balinese. . . . you are at least regarded as a human being" (1973:413).

The story with which Geertz begins this essay is crucial to his analysis as well. Due to a more or less chance occurrence, Geertz gained a particular position in Balinese society that enabled him to make certain kinds of observations. A decade before postmodernism became a serious endeavor within anthropology, Geertz, in this article, discussed his position within Balinese society and the insights it afforded him.

with the opposite sex or someone in a new job anxious to make a good impression is called "a fighting cock caged for the first time."* Court trials, wars, political contests, inheritance disputes, and street arguments are all compared to cockfights.* Even the very island itself is perceived from its shape as a small, proud cock, poised, neck extended, back taut, tail raised, in eternal challenge to large, feckless, shapeless Java.*

But the intimacy of men with their cocks is more than metaphorical. Balinese men, or anyway a large majority of Balinese men, spend an enormous amount of time with their favorites, grooming them, feeding them, discussing them, trying them out against one another, or just gazing at them with a mixture of rapt admiration and dreamy self-absorption. Whenever you see a group of Balinese men squatting idly in the council shed or along the road in their hips down, shoulders forward, knees up fashion, half or more of them will have a rooster in his hands, holding it between his thighs, bouncing it gently up and down to strengthen its legs, ruffling its feathers with abstract sensuality, pushing it out against a neighbor's rooster to rouse its spirit, withdrawing it toward his loins to calm it again. Now and then, to get a feel for another bird, a man will fiddle this way with someone else's cock for a while, but usually by moving around to squat in place behind it, rather than just having it passed across to him as though it were merely an animal.

In the houseyard, the high-walled enclosures where the people live, fighting cocks are kept in wicker cages, moved frequently about so as to maintain the optimum balance of sun and shade. They are fed a special diet, which varies somewhat according to individual theories but which is mostly maize, sifted for impurities with far more care than it is when mere humans are going to eat it, and offered to the animal kernel by kernel. Red pepper is stuffed down their beaks and up their anuses to give them spirit. They are bathed in the same ceremonial preparation of tepid water, medicinal herbs, flowers, and onions in which infants are bathed, and for a prize cock just about as often. Their combs are cropped, their plumage dressed, their spurs trimmed, and their legs massaged, and they are inspected for flaws with the squinted concentration of a diamond merchant. A man who has a passion for cocks, an enthusiast in the literal sense of the term, can spend most of his life with them, and even those, the overwhelming majority, whose passion though intense has not entirely run away with them, can and do spend what seems not only to an outsider, but also to themselves, an inordinate amount of time with them. "I am cock crazy," my landlord, a quite ordinary *afficionado* by Balinese standards, used to moan as he went to move another cage, give another bath, or conduct another feeding. "We're all cock crazy."

The madness has some less visible dimensions, however, because although it is true that cocks are symbolic expressions or magnifications of their owner's self, the narcissistic male ego writ out in Aesopian terms, they are also expressions — and rather more immediate ones — of what the Balinese regard as the direct inversion, aesthetically, morally, and metaphysically, of human status: animality.

The Balinese revulsion against any behavior regarded as animal-like can hardly be overstressed. Babies are not allowed to crawl for that reason. Incest, though hardly approved, is a much less horrifying crime than bestiality. (The appropriate punishment for the second is death by drowning, for the first being forced to live like an animal.)* Most demons are represented — in sculpture, dance, ritual, myth — in some real or fantastic animal form. The main puberty rite consists in filing the child's teeth so they will not look like animal fangs. Not only defecation but eating is regarded as a disgusting, almost obscene activity, to be conducted hurriedly and privately, because of its association with animality. Even falling down or any form of clumsiness is considered to be bad for these reasons. Aside from cocks and a few domestic animals — oxen, ducks — of no emotional significance, the Balinese are aversive to animals and treat their large number of dogs not merely callously but with a phobic cruelty. In identifying with his cock, the Balinese man is identifying not just with his ideal self, or even his penis, but also, and at the same time, with what he most fears, hates, and ambivalence being what it is, is fascinated by — "The Powers of Darkness."

The connection of cocks and cockfighting with such Powers, with the animalistic demons that threaten constantly to invade the small, cleared-off space in which the Balinese have so carefully built their lives and devour its inhabitants, is quite explicit. A cockfight, any cockfight, is in the first instance a blood sacrifice offered, with the appropriate chants and oblations, to the demons in order to pacify their ravenous, cannibal hunger. No temple festival should be conducted until one is made. (If it is omitted, someone will inevitably fall into a trance and command with the voice of an angered spirit that the oversight be immediately corrected.) Collective responses to natural evils — illness, crop failure, volcanic eruptions — almost always involve them. And that famous holiday in Bali, "The Day of Silence" (*Njepi*), when everyone sits silent and immobile all day long in order to avoid contact with a sudden influx of demons chased momentarily out of hell, is preceded the previous day by large-scale cockfights (in this case legal) in almost every village on the island.

In the cockfight, man and beast, good and evil, ego and id, the creative power of aroused masculinity and the destructive power of loosened animality fuse in a bloody drama of hatred, cruelty, violence, and death. It is little wonder that when, as is the invariable rule, the owner of the winning cock takes the carcass of the loser — often torn limb from limb by its enraged owner — home to eat, he does so with a mixture of social embarrassment, moral satisfaction, aesthetic disgust, and cannibal joy. Or that a man who has lost an important fight is sometimes driven to wreck his family shrines and curse the gods, an act of metaphysical (and social) suicide. Or that in seeking earthly analogues for heaven and hell the Balinese compare the former to the mood of a man whose cock has just won, the latter to that of a man whose cock has just lost.[3]

THE FIGHT

Cockfights (*tetadjen; sabungan*) are held in a ring about fifty feet square. Usually they begin toward late afternoon and run three or four hours until sunset. About nine or ten separate matches (*sehet*) comprise a program. Each match is precisely like the others in general pattern: there is no main match, no connection between individual matches, no variation in their format, and each is arranged on a completely ad hoc basis. After a fight has ended and the emotional debris is cleaned away — the bets have been paid, the curses cursed, the carcasses possessed — seven, eight, perhaps even a dozen men slip negligently into the ring with a cock and seek to find there a logical opponent for it. This process, which rarely takes less than ten minutes, and often a good deal longer, is conducted in a very subdued, oblique, even dissembling manner. Those not immediately involved give it at best but disguised, sidelong attention; those who, embarrassedly, are, attempt to pretend somehow that the whole thing is not really happening.[4]

A match made, the other hopefuls retire with the same deliberate indifference, and the selected cocks have their spurs (*tadji*) affixed — razor-sharp, pointed steel swords, four or five inches long. This is a delicate job which only a small proportion of men, a half-dozen or so in most villages, know how to do properly. The man who attaches the spurs also provides them, and if the rooster he assists wins, its owner awards him the spur-leg of the victim. The spurs are affixed by winding a long length of string around the foot of the spur and the leg of the cock. For reasons I shall come to presently, it is done somewhat differently from case to case, and is an obsessively

---

[3] Although Geertz is attempting a very different kind of symbolic analysis than Freud or Lévi-Strauss, the influence of their work is apparent here. The symbolic link between the fighting birds, genitals, and male status is obviously Freudian. Although Geertz is not a structuralist, the binary constructions — man-beast, good-evil, creation-destruction — are based on Lévi-Strauss' nature-culture dichotomy. The human cultural world is repulsed by the animal-natural world, but the two spheres of existence meet in cocks and the cockfight.

[4] Geertz describes the cockfight and patterns of betting that take place in great detail. He attempts to re-create the context in which the action takes place in order that the reader may share, as much as possible, in the context in which Balinese cultural meaning is created. Geertz describes this form of analysis as "thick description" (1973:6), which he identifies as uncovering the layers of meaning surrounding an event.

deliberate affair. The lore about spurs is extensive — they are sharpened only at eclipses and the dark of the moon, should be kept out of the sight of women, and so forth. And they are handled, both in use and out, with the same curious combination of fussiness and sensuality the Balinese direct toward ritual objects generally.

The spurs affixed, the two cocks are placed by their handlers (who may or may not be their owners) facing one another in the center of the ring.* A coconut pierced with a small hole is placed in a pail of water, in which it takes about twenty-one seconds to sink, a period known as a *tjeng* and marked at beginning and end by the beating of a slit gong. During these twenty-one seconds the handlers (*pengangkeb*) are not permitted to touch their roosters. If, as sometimes happens, the animals have not fought during this time, they are picked up, fluffed, pulled, prodded, and otherwise insulted, and put back in the center of the ring and the process begins again. Sometimes they refuse to fight at all, or one keeps running away, in which case they are imprisoned together under a wicker cage, which usually gets them engaged.

Most of the time, in any case, the cocks fly almost immediately at one another in a wing-beating, head-thrusting, leg-kicking explosion of animal fury so pure, so absolute, and in its own way so beautiful, as to be almost abstract, a Platonic concept of hate. Within moments one or the other drives home a solid blow with his spur. The handler whose cock has delivered the blow immediately picks it up so that it will not get a return blow, for if he does not the match is likely to end in a mutually mortal tie as the two birds wildly hack each other to pieces. This is particularly true if, as often happens, the spur sticks in its victim's body, for then the aggressor is at the mercy of his wounded foe.

With the birds again in the hands of their handlers, the coconut is now sunk three times after which the cock which has landed the blow must be set down to show that he is firm, a fact he demonstrates by wandering idly around the ring for a coconut sink. The coconut is then sunk twice more and the fight must recommence.

During this interval, slightly over two minutes, the handler of the wounded cock has been working frantically over it, like a trainer patching a mauled boxer between rounds, to get it in shape for a last, desperate try for victory. He blows in its mouth, putting the whole chicken head in his own mouth and sucking and blowing, fluffs it, stuffs its wounds with various sorts of medicines, and generally tries anything he can think of to arouse the last ounce of spirit which may be hidden somewhere within it. By the time he is forced to put it back down he is usually drenched in chicken blood, but, as in prize fighting, a good handler is worth his weight in gold. Some of them can virtually make the dead walk, at least long enough for the second and final round.

In the climactic battle (if there is one; sometimes the wounded cock simply expires in the handler's hands or immediately as it is placed down again), the cock who landed the first blow usually proceeds to finish off his weakened opponent. But this is far from an inevitable outcome, for if a cock can walk, he can fight, and if he can fight, he can kill, and what counts is which cock expires first. If the wounded one can get a stab in and stagger on until the other drops, he is the official winner, even if he himself topples over an instant later.

Surrounding all this melodrama — which the crowd packed tight around the ring follows in near silence, moving their bodies in kinesthetic sympathy with the movement of the animals, cheering their champions on with wordless hand motions, shiftings of the shoulders, turnings of the head, falling back en masse as the cock with the murderous spurs careens toward one side of the ring (it is said that spectators sometimes lose eyes and fingers from being too attentive), surging forward again as they glance off toward another — is a vast body of extraordinarily elaborate and precisely detailed rules.[5]

---

[5] One criticism of Geertz's work is that his interpretation is intuitive, making it difficult for others to replicate. Indeed, one could say that the power of Geertz's analysis is based on his compelling writing style. For example, you may not have noticed that Geertz is not presenting us with a description of one cockfight but rather with a literary construct based on his experience of at least fifty-seven matches (see Crapanzano's essay 39).

These rules, together with the developed lore of cocks and cockfighting which accompanies them, are written down in palm-leaf manuscripts (*lontar; rontal*) passed on from generation to generation as part of the general legal and cultural tradition of the villages. At a fight, the umpire (*saja komong; djuru kembar*)—the man who manages the coconut—is in charge of their application and his authority is absolute. I have never seen an umpire's judgment questioned on any subject, even by the more despondent losers, nor have I ever heard, even in private, a charge of unfairness directed against one, or, for that matter, complaints about umpires in general. Only exceptionally well trusted, solid, and, given the complexity of the code, knowledgeable citizens perform this job, and in fact men will bring their cocks only to fights presided over by such men. It is also the umpire to whom accusations of cheating, which, though rare in the extreme, occasionally arise, are referred; and it is he who in the not infrequent cases where the cocks expire virtually together decides which (if either, for, though the Balinese to not care for such an outcome, there can be ties) went first. Likened to a judge, a king, a priest, and a policeman, he is all of these, and under his assured direction the animal passion of the fight proceeds within the civic certainty of the law. In the dozens of cockfights I saw in Bali, I never once saw an altercation about rules. Indeed, I never saw an open altercation, other than those between cocks, at all.

This crosswise doubleness of an event which, taken as a fact of nature, is rage untrammeled and, taken as a fact of culture, is form perfected, defines the cockfight as a sociological entity. A cockfight is what, searching for a name for something not vertebrate enough to be called a group and not structureless enough to be called a crowd, Erving Goffman has called a "focused gathering"—a set of persons engrossed in a common flow of activity and relating to one another in terms of that flow.* Such gatherings meet and disperse; the participants in them fluctuate; the activity that focuses them is discrete—a particulate process that reoccurs rather than a continuous one that endures. They take their form from the situation that evokes them, the floor on which they are placed, as Goffman puts it; but it is a form, and an articulate one, nonetheless. For the situation, the floor is itself created, in jury deliberations, surgical operations, block meetings, sit-ins, cockfights, by the cultural preoccupations—here, as we shall see, the celebration of status rivalry—which not only specify the focus but, assembling actors and arranging scenery, bring it actually into being.[6]

In classical times (that is to say, prior to the Dutch invasion of 1908), when there were no bureaucrats around to improve popular morality, the staging of a cockfight was an explicitly societal matter. Bringing a cock to an important fight was, for an adult male, a compulsory duty of citizenship; taxation of fights, which were usually held on market day, was a major source of public revenue; patronage of the art was stated responsibility of princes; and the cock ring, or *wantilan,* stood in the center of the village near those other monuments of Balinese civility—the council house, the origin temple, the marketplace, the signal tower, and the banyan tree. Today, a few special occasions aside, the newer rectitude makes so open a statement of the connection between the excitements of collective life and those of blood sport impossible, but, less directly expressed, the connection itself remains intimate and intact. To expose it, however, it is necessary to turn to the aspect of cockfighting around which all the others pivot, and through which they exercise their force, an aspect I have thus far studiously ignored. I mean, of course, the gambling.

---

[6] In this paragraph, you get a sense of Geertz's definition of culture: a shared code of meaning that is acted out publically. Unlike the ethnoscientists, Geertz believes that culture is not a mental model, but exists between people, created by their social actions. Additionally Geertz was interested in the sociology of religion. His reference to Erving Goffman (1922–1982), an important sociologist of the 1960s, gives a clue to the sociological influence on his work. Goffman viewed individual actions as performances and was concerned with delineating the rules governing nonverbal interaction. You can see Goffman's influence in these paragraphs, as Geertz describes people's actions at cockfights.

[We have omitted a 2,200-word section with 7 footnotes called "Odds and Even Money," in which Geertz gives a detailed explanation of cockfight betting patterns. He identifies two types of bets in a cockfight, the main bet between the principals who own the fighting cocks and peripheral bets between members of the audience. The principal bets are large collective wagers involving coalitions of bettors; they are quietly arranged with the umpire in the center of the ring. The second type of bet is typically small and is arranged impulsively by individuals shouting back and forth across the ring.

Because center bets are always for even money, participants typically arrange fair matches. The more evenly matched the cocks, the higher the center bets. The side bets vary wildly according to the odds individual bettors are willing to give. The larger the center bet, the more frenzied the side betting. These fights are considered more interesting because more is at stake in them. In a high-stakes fight, men are risking money and social prestige, as well as valuable fighting cocks. When a match ends, all bets are immediately paid.

We return to Geertz's narrative at the last paragraph in the section, where he introduces the notion of "depth" in the analysis of culture.]

The Balinese attempt to create an interesting, if you will, "deep," match by making the center bet as large as possible so that the cocks matched will be as equal and as fine as possible, and the outcome, thus, as unpredictable as possible.[7] They do not always succeed. Nearly half the matches are relatively trivial, relatively uninteresting—in my borrowed terminology, "shallow"—affairs. But that fact no more argues against my interpretation than the fact that most painters, poets, and playwrights are mediocre argues against the view that

artistic effort is directed toward profundity and, with a certain frequency, approximates it. The image of artistic technique is indeed exact: the center bet is a means, a device, for creating "interesting," "deep" matches, *not* the reason, or at least not the main reason, *why* they are interesting, the source of their fascination, the substance of their depth. The question of why such matches are interesting—indeed, for the Balinese, exquisitely absorbing—takes us out of the realm of formal concerns into more broadly sociological and social-psychological ones, and to a less purely economic idea of what "depth" in gaming amounts to.*

PLAYING WITH FIRE

Bentham's concept of "deep play" is found in his *The Theory of Legislation*.* By it he means play in which the stakes are so high that it is, from his utilitarian standpoint, irrational for men to engage in it at all. If a man whose fortune is a thousand pounds (or ringgits) wages five hundred of it on an even bet, the marginal utility of the pound he stands to win is clearly less than the marginal disutility of the one he stands to lose. In genuine deep play, this is the case for both parties. They are both in over their heads. Having come together in search of pleasure they have entered into a relationship which will bring the participants, considered collectively, net pain rather than net pleasure. Bentham's conclusion was, therefore, that deep play was immoral from first principles and, a typical step for him, should be prevented legally.[8]

But more interesting than the ethical problem, at least for our concerns here, is that despite the logical force of Bentham's analysis men do engage in such play, both passionately and often, and even in the face of law's revenge. For Bentham and those who think as he does (nowadays

---

[7] For Geertz, the secret of decoding the cockfight lies in viewing it as a representation of Balinese society. The long discussion of cockfight betting in the next section leads to a discussion of how betting patterns recapitulate the divisions of the larger society. This insight hearkens back to Durkheim and the structural functionalists, but Geertz does not use his analysis for their purposes.

[8] Jeremy Bentham (1748–1832) was an English philosopher and social theorist best known for his doctrine of Utilitarianism, the principles of which are outlined in his 1789 book *An Introduction to the Principles of Morals and Legislation*. Utilitarianism is the belief that the aim of society should be to create the greatest level of happiness for the greatest number

mainly lawyers, economists, and a few psychiatrists), the explanation is, as I have said, that such men are irrational—addicts, fetishists, children, fools, savages, who need only to be protected against themselves. But for the Balinese, though naturally they do not formulate it in so many words, the explanation lies in the fact that in such play, money is less a measure of utility, had or expected, than it is a symbol of moral import, perceived or imposed.

It is, in fact, in shallow games, ones in which smaller amounts of money are involved, that increments and decrements of cash are more nearly synonyms for utility and disutility, in the ordinary, unexpanded sense—for pleasure and pain, happiness and unhappiness. In deep ones, where the amounts of money are great, much more is at stake than material gain: namely, esteem, honor, dignity, respect—in a word, though in Bali a profoundly freighted word, status.* It is at stake symbolically, for (a few cases of ruined addict gamblers aside) no one's status is actually altered by the outcome of a cockfight; it is only, and that momentarily, affirmed or insulted. But for the Balinese, for whom nothing is more pleasurable than an affront obliquely delivered or more painful than one obliquely received—particularly when mutual acquaintances, undeceived by surfaces, are watching—such appraisive drama is deep indeed.

This, I must stress immediately, is *not* to say that the money does not matter, or that the Balinese is no more concerned about losing five hundred ringgits than fifteen. Such a conclusion would be absurd. It is because money *does*, in this hardly unmaterialistic society, matter and matter very much that the more of it one risks, the more of a lot of other things, such as one's pride, one's poise, one's dispassion, one's masculinity, one also risks, again only momentarily but again very publicly as well. In deep cockfights an owner and his collaborators, and, as we shall see, to a lesser but still quite real extent also their backers on the outside, put their money where their status is.

It is in large part *because* the marginal disutility of loss is so great at the higher levels of betting that to engage in such betting is to lay one's public self, allusively and metaphorically, through the medium of one's cock, on the line. And though to a Benthamite this might seem merely to increase the irrationality of the enterprise that much further, to the Balinese what it mainly increases is the meaningfulness of it all. And as (to follow Weber[9] rather than Bentham) the imposition of meaning on life is the major end and primary condition of human existence, that access of significance more than compensates for the economic costs involved.* Actually, given the even-money quality of the larger matches, important changes in material fortune among those who regularly participate in them seem virtually nonexistent, because matters more or less even out over the long run. It is, actually, in the smaller, shallow fights, where one finds the handful of more pure, addict-type gamblers involved—those who *are* in it mainly for the money—that "real" changes in social position, largely downward, are affected. Men of this sort, plungers, are highly dispraised by "true cockfighters" as fools who do not understand what the sport is all about, vulgarians who simply miss the point of it all. They are, these addicts, regarded as fair game for the genuine enthusiasts, those who do understand, to take a little money away from—something that is easy enough to do by luring them, through the force of their greed, into irrational bets on mismatched cocks. Most of them do indeed manage

---

of people. Bentham believed that correct conduct was determined by the balance of pleasure over pain that a given act would produce, and that pain and pleasure could be quantitatively measured. Thus legislative decision making could be reduced to a quasimathematical science. Among Bentham's best-known intellectual followers were John Stuart Mill (1806–1873) and Herbert Spencer.

When Bentham died, his body was embalmed and his head removed and replaced with a wax replica. His corpse was then dressed and placed on display at University College, London, where it remains to this day.

[9] Geertz claims Max Weber as one of the major influences in his intellectual development. He was first exposed to Weber by one of his professors, Talcott Parsons (1902–1979), while a graduate student at Harvard University. For more information on Geertz's career and academic life, see Handler's 1991 interview with Geertz in *Current Anthropology*.

to ruin themselves in a remarkably short time, but there always seems to be one or two of them around, pawning their land and selling their clothes in order to bet, at any particular time.*

This graduated correlation of "status gambling" with deeper fights and, inversely, "money gambling" with shallower ones is in fact quite general. Bettors themselves form a sociomoral hierarchy in these terms. As noted earlier, at most cockfights there are, around the very edges of the cockfight area, a large number of mindless, sheer-chance-type gambling games (roulette, dice throw, coin-spin, pea-under-the-shell) operated by concessionaires. Only women, children, adolescents, and various other sorts of people who do not (or not yet) fight cocks—the extremely poor, the socially despised, the personally idiosyncratic—play at these games, at, of course, penny ante levels. Cockfighting men would be ashamed to go anywhere near them. Slightly above these people in standing are those who though they do not themselves fight cocks, bet on the smaller matches around the edges. Next, there are those who fight cocks in small, or occasionally medium matches, but have not the status to join in the large ones, though they may bet from time to time on the side in those. And finally, there are those, the really substantial members of the community, the solid citizenry around whom local life revolves, who fight in the larger fights and bet on them around the side. The focusing element in these focused gatherings, these men generally dominate and define the sport as they dominate and define the society. When a Balinese male talks, in that almost venerative way, about "the true cockfighter," the *bebatoh* ("bettor") or *djuru kurung* ("cage keeper"), it is this sort of person, not those who bring the mentality of the pea-and-shell game into the quite different, inappropriate context of the cockfight, the driven gambler (*potét*, a word which has the secondary meaning

of thief or reprobate), and the wistful hanger-on, that they mean. For such a man, what is really going on in a match is something rather closer to an *affaire d'honneur* (though, with the Balinese talent for practical fantasy, the blood that is spilled is only figuratively human) than to the stupid, mechanical crank of a slot machine.[10]

What makes Balinese cockfighting deep is thus not money in itself, but what, the more of it that is involved the more so, money causes to happen: the migration of the Balinese status hierarchy into the body of the cockfight.[11] Psychologically an Aesopian representation of the ideal/demonic, rather narcissistic, male self, sociologically it is an equally Aesopian representation of the complex fields of tension set up by the controlled, muted, ceremonial, but for all that deeply felt, interaction of those selves in the context of everyday life. The cocks may be surrogates for their owners' personalities, animal mirrors of psychic form, but the cockfight is—or more exactly, deliberately is made to be—a simulation of the social matrix, the involved system of cross-cutting, overlapping, highly corporate groups—villages, kingroups, irrigation societies, temple congregations, "castes"—in which its devotees live.* And as prestige, the necessity to affirm it, defend it, celebrate it, justify it, and just plain bask in it (but not, given the strongly ascriptive character of Balinese stratification, to seek it), is perhaps the central driving force in the society, so also—ambulant penises, blood sacrifices, and monetary exchanges aside—is it of the cockfight. This apparent amusement and seeming sport is, to take another phrase from Erving Goffman, "a status bloodbath."*

The easiest way to make this clear, and at least to some degree to demonstrate it, is to invoke the village whose cockfighting activities I observed the closest—the one in which the raid occurred and from which my statistical data are taken.

---

[10] The cockfight is not about winning or losing money; it is a simulation of the social interactions between various groups in the community. Geertz contends that this is why the matches are so "deep" to the Balinese.

[11] For Geertz, the cockfight is a symbolic key to Balinese personality because it is the ritual through which the Balinese express their values. Geertz uses the phrase the "migration of the Balinese status hierarchy into the body of the cockfight" to characterize his idea that one can observe the stratification of Balinese society in the organization of people within and around the cockfight area.

Like all Balinese villages, this one—Tihingan, in the Klungkung region of southeast Bali— is intricately organized, a labyrinth of alliances and oppositions. But, unlike many, two sorts of corporate groups, which are also status groups, particularly stand out, and we may concentrate on them, in a part-for-whole way, without undue distortion.

First, the village is dominated by four large, patrilineal, partly endogamous descent groups which are constantly vying with one another and form the major factions in the village. Sometimes they group two and two, or rather the two larger ones versus the two smaller ones plus all the unaffiliated people; sometimes they operate independently. There are also subfactions within them, subfactions within the subfactions, and so on to rather fine levels of distinction. And second, there is the village itself, almost entirely endogamous, which is opposed to all the other villages round about in its cockfight circuit (which, as explained, is the market region), but which also forms alliances with certain of these neighbors against certain others in various supravillage political and social contexts. The exact situation is thus, as everywhere in Bali, quite distinctive; but the general pattern of a tiered hierarchy of status rivalries between highly corporate but various based groupings (and, thus, between the members of them) is entirely general.

Consider, then, as support of the general thesis that the cockfight, and especially the deep cockfight, is fundamentally a dramatization of status concerns, the following facts, which to avoid extended ethnographic description I shall simply pronounce to be facts though the concrete evidence, examples, statements, and numbers that could be brought to bear in support of them, is both extensive and unmistakable:[12]

1. A man virtually never bets against a cock owned by a member of his own kingroup. Usually he will feel obliged to bet for it, the more so the closer the kin tie and the deeper the fight. If he is certain in his mind that it will not win, he may just not bet at all, particularly if it is only a second cousin's bird or if the fight is a shallow one. But as a rule he will feel he must support it and, in deep games, nearly always does. Thus the great majority of the people calling "five" or "speckled" so demonstratively are expressing their allegiance to their kinsman, not their evaluation of his bird, their understanding of probability theory, or even their hopes of unearned income.

2. This principle is extended logically. If your kingroup is not involved you will support an allied kingroup against an unallied one in the same way, and so on through the very involved networks of alliances which, as I say, make up this, as any other, Balinese village.

3. So, too, for the village as a whole. If an outsider cock is fighting any cock from your village, you will tend to support the local one. If, what is a rarer circumstance but occurs every now and then, a cock from outside your cockfight circuit is fighting one inside it, you will also tend to support the "home bird."

4. Cocks which come from any distance are almost always favorites, for the theory is the man would not have dared to bring it if it was not a good cock, the more so the further he has come. His followers are, of course, obliged to support him, and when the more grand-scale legal cockfights are held (on holidays, and so on) the people of the village take what they regard to be the best cocks in the village, regardless of ownership, and go off to support them, although they will almost

---

[12] Geertz's discussion is reminiscent of Mauss' analysis of the potlatch (see essay 8). The potlatch was a competition for status between individuals representing their kin groups and communities. In the same way, the Balinese cockfight is a competition for status, with men always betting on the birds owned by kinsmen or men of their communities who are competing with people from other communities. A major difference between Geertz and Mauss, however, is that Mauss thought the potlatch was a real competition for status—a defeat in a potlatch meant the loss of a position of leadership. On the other hand, Geertz's point is that the cockfight does not really change anything. In fact, status in Bali is ascribed and cannot change. Although Geertz's analysis is interpretive, the discussion of betting and kin are structural-functionalist in tone. Durkheim or Radcliffe-Brown would have said that the function of the cockfight is to create and reinforce solidarity between these competing kin groups.

certainly have to give odds on them and to make large bets to show that they are not a cheapskate village. Actually, such "away games," though infrequent, tend to mend the ruptures between village members that the constantly occurring "home games," where village factions are opposed rather than united, exacerbate.

5. Almost all matches are sociologically relevant. You seldom get two outsider cocks fighting, or two cocks with no particular group backing, or with group backing which is mutually unrelated in any clear way. When you do get them, the game is very shallow, betting very slow, and the whole thing very dull, with no one save the immediate principals and an addict gambler or two at all interested.

6. By the same token, you rarely get two cocks from the same group, even more rarely from the same subfaction, and virtually never from the same sub-subfaction (which would be in most cases one extended family) fighting. Similarly, in outside village fights two members of the village will rarely fight against one another, even though, as bitter rivals, they would do so with enthusiasm on their home grounds.

7. On the individual level, people involved in an institutionalized hostility relationship, called *puik,* in which they do not speak or otherwise have anything to do with each other (the causes of this formal breaking of relations are many: wife-capture, inheritance arguments, political differences) will bet very heavily, sometimes almost maniacally, against one another in what is a frank and direct attack on the very masculinity, the ultimate ground of his status, of the opponent.[13]

8. The center bet coalition is, in all but the shallowest games, *always* made up by structural allies—no "outside money" is involved. What is "outside" depends upon the context, of course, but given it, no outside money is mixed in with the main bet; if the principals cannot raise it, it is not made. The center bet, again especially in deeper games, is thus the most direct and open expression of social opposition, which is one of the reasons why both it and matchmaking are surrounded by such an air of unease, furtiveness, embarrassment, and so on.

9. The rule about borrowing money—that you may borrow *for* a bet but not *in* one—stems (and the Balinese are quite conscious of this) from similar considerations: you are never at the *economic* mercy of your enemy that way. Gambling debts, which can get quite large on a rather short-term basis, are always to friends, never to enemies, structurally speaking.

10. When two cocks are structurally irrelevant or neutral so far as *you* are concerned (though, as mentioned, they almost never are to each other) you do not even ask a relative or a friend whom he is betting on, because if you know how he is betting and he knows you know, and you go the other way, it will lead to strain. This rule is explicit and rigid; fairly elaborate, even rather artificial precautions are taken to avoid breaking it. At the very least you must pretend not to notice what he is doing, and he what you are doing.

11. There is a special word for betting against the grain, which is also the word for "pardon me" (*mpura*). It is considered a bad thing to do, though if the center bet is small it is sometimes all right as long as you do not do it too often. But the larger the bet and the more frequently you do it, the more the "pardon me" tack will lead to social disruption.

---

[13] The discussion of *puik* is a good place to make another point about Geertz's analysis. Because his work is interpretive, Geertz is often criticized by anthropologists who work in materialist traditions. However, some of Geertz's earlier work was concerned with economics, religion, and ecology. See, for example, his books *Agricultural Involution: The Processes of Ecological Change in Indonesia* (1963a) and *Peddlers and Princes: Social Development and Economic Change in Two Indonesian Towns* (1963b). Here, in one of his most famous works, Geertz does not rule out materialist interpretations, he just is not interested in them. Geertz repeatedly insists that nothing really happens at a cockfight—the conflicts, alliances, wins, and losses are all symbolic of things that happen elsewhere. *Puik,* for example, are not caused by cockfight bets; rather, they signal deeper-level conflicts. In the cockfight, all action is symbolic. The real causes lie elsewhere, presumably in material circumstances.

12. In fact, the institutionalized hostility relation, *puik,* is often formally initiated (though its causes always lie elsewhere) by such a "pardon me" bet in a deep fight, putting the symbolic fat in the fire. Similarly, the end of such a relationship and resumption of normal social intercourse is often signalized (but, again, not actually brought about) by one or the other of the enemies supporting the other's bird.

13. In sticky, cross-loyalty situations, of which in this extraordinarily complex social system there are of course many, where a man is caught between two more or less equally balanced loyalties, he tends to wander off for a cup of coffee or something to avoid having to bet, a form of behavior reminiscent of that of American voters in similar situations.*

14. The people involved in the center bet are, especially in deep fights, virtually always leading members of their group—kinship, village, or whatever. Further, those who bet on the side (including these people) are, as I have already remarked, the more established members of the village — the solid citizens. Cockfighting is for those who are involved in the everyday politics of prestige as well, not for youth, women, subordinates, and so forth.

15. So far as money is concerned, the explicitly expressed attitude toward it is that it is a secondary matter. It is not, as I have said, of no importance; Balinese are no happier to lose several weeks' income than anyone else. But they mainly look on the monetary aspects of the cockfight as self-balancing, a matter of just moving money around, circulating it among a fairly well-defined group of serious cockfighters. The really important wins and losses are seen mostly in other terms, and the general attitude toward wagering is not any hope of cleaning up, of making a killing (addict gamblers again excepted), but that of the horseplayer's prayer: "Oh, God, please let me break even." In prestige terms, however, you do not want to break even, but, in a momentary, punctuate sort of way, win utterly. The talk (which goes on all the time) is about fights against such-and-such a cock of So-and-So which your cock demolished, not on how much you won, a fact people, even for large bets, rarely re-

member for any length of time, though they will remember the day they did in Pan Loh's finest cock for years.

16. You must bet on cocks of your own group aside from mere loyalty considerations, for if you do not people generally will say, "What! Is he too proud for the likes of us? Does he have to go to Java or Den Pasar [the capital town] to bet, he is such an important man?" Thus there is a general pressure to bet not only to show that you are important locally, but that you are not so important that you look down on everyone else as unfit even to be rivals. Similarly, home team people must bet against outside cocks or the outsiders will accuse them — a serious charge — of just collecting entry fees and not really being interested in cockfighting, as well as again being arrogant and insulting.

17. Finally, the Balinese peasants themselves are quite aware of all this and can and, at least to an ethnographer, do state most of it in approximately the same terms as I have. Fighting cocks, almost every Balinese I have ever discussed the subject with has said, is like playing with fire only not getting burned. You activate village and kingroup rivalries and hostilities, but in "play" form, coming dangerously and entrancingly close to the expression of open and direct interpersonal and intergroup aggression (something which, again, almost never happens in the normal course of ordinary life), but not quite, because, after all, it is "only a cockfight."

More observations of this sort could be advanced, but perhaps the general point is, if not made, at least well-delineated, and the whole argument thus far can be usefully summarized in a formal paradigm:

The more a match is . . .

1. Between near status equals (and/or personal enemies)
2. Between high status individuals

   The deeper the match.

The deeper the match . . .

1. The closer the identification of cock and man (or, more properly, the deeper the

match the more the man will advance his best, most closely-identified-with cock).

2. The finer the cocks involved and the more exactly they will be matched.

3. The greater the emotion that will be involved and the more the general absorption in the match.

4. The higher the individual bets center and outside, the shorter the outside bet odds will tend to be, and the more betting there will be overall.

5. The less an "economic" and the more a "status" view of gaming will be involved, and the "solider" the citizens who will be gaming.*

Inverse arguments hold for the shallower the fight, culminating, in a reversed-signs sense, in the coin-spinning and dice-throwing amusements. For deep fights there are no absolute upper limits, though there are of course practical ones, and there are a great many legendlike tales of great Duel-in-the-Sun combats between lords and princes in classical times (for cockfighting has always been as much an elite concern as a popular one), far deeper than anything anyone, even aristocrats, could produce today anywhere in Bali.

Indeed, one of the great culture heroes of Bali is a prince, called after his passion for the sport, "The Cockfighter," who happened to be away at a very deep cockfight with a neighboring prince when the whole of his family—father, brothers, wives, sisters—were assassinated by commoner usurpers. Thus spared, he returned to dispatch the upstart, regain the throne, reconstitute the Balinese high tradition, and build its most powerful, glorious, and prosperous state. Along with everything else that the Balinese see in fighting cocks—themselves, their social order, abstract hatred, masculinity, demonic power—they also see the archetype of status virtue, the arrogant, resolute, honor-mad player with real fire, the ksatria prince.*[14]

FEATHERS, BLOOD, CROWDS, AND MONEY

"Poetry makes nothing happen," Auden says in his elegy of Yeats, "it survives in the valley of its saying . . . a way of happening, a mouth."[15] The cockfight too, in this colloquial sense, makes nothing happen. Men go on allegorically humiliating one another and being allegorically humiliated by one another, day after day, glorying quietly in the experience if they have triumphed, crushed only slightly more openly by it if they have not. *But no one's status really changes.* You cannot ascend the status ladder by winning cockfights; you cannot, as an individual, really ascend it at all. Nor can you descend it that way.* All you can do is enjoy and savor, or suffer and withstand, the concocted sensation of drastic and momentary movement along an aesthetic semblance of that ladder, a kind of behind-the-mirror status jump which has the look of mobility without its actuality.[16]

Like any art form—for that, finally, is what we are dealing with—the cockfight renders ordinary, everyday experience comprehensible by presenting it in terms of acts and objects which have had their practical consequences removed and been reduced (or, if you prefer, raised) to the level of sheer appearances, where their meaning can be more powerfully articulated and more exactly

---

[14] Despite the skill with which Geertz draws his picture of Balinese culture, the feminist critique of ethnographic writing applies here. In his footnote, Geertz writes that the cockfight is unusual in that it is a single-sex activity, yet he talks about cockfighting as a key to Balinese society. Perhaps it is a key only for male Balinese society.

[15] W. H. Auden (1907–1973) was a British-born American poet. William Butler Yeats (1865–1939) was an Irish poet and nationalist.

[16] In a recent interview (Handler 1991), Geertz stated that a weakness of anthropology before the 1960s was that anthropologists read only other anthropologists. His point was that intellectual development in anthropology is based on knowledge in a wide range of fields. As you read, look at the diversity of literature that Geertz ties into his work: Balinese sources, poetry, sociology, psychology, mythology, art, and philosophy, to name just a few, all have a place in his thought. Conversely, Geertz is one of the few anthropological theorists widely read by scholars of literature and history.

perceived. The cockfight is "really real" only to the cocks—it does not kill anyone, castrate anyone, reduce anyone to animal status, alter the hierarchical relations among people, or refashion the hierarchy; it does not even redistribute income in any significant way. What it does is what, for other peoples with other temperaments and other conventions, *Lear* and *Crime and Punishment* do; it catches up these themes—death, masculinity, rage, pride, loss, beneficence, chance—and, ordering them into an encompassing structure, presents them in such a way as to throw into relief a particular view of their essential nature. It puts a construction on them, makes them, to those historically positioned to appreciate the construction, meaningful—visible, tangible, graspable—"real," in an ideational sense. An image, fiction, a model, a metaphor, the cockfight is a means of expression; its function is neither to assuage social passions nor to heighten them (though, in its playing-with-fire way it does a bit of both), but, in a medium of feathers, blood, crowds, and money, to display them.

The question of how it is that we perceive qualities in things—paintings, books, melodies, plays—that we do not feel we can assert literally to be there has come, in recent years, into the very center of aesthetic theory.* Neither the sentiments of the artist, which remain his, nor those of the audience, which remain theirs, can account for the agitation of one painting or the serenity of another. We attribute grandeur, wit, despair, exuberance to strings of sounds; lightness, energy, violence, fluidity to blocks of stone. Novels are said to have strength, buildings eloquence, plays momentum, ballets repose. In this realm of eccentric predicates, to say that the cockfight, in its perfected cases at least, is "disquietful" does not seem at all unnatural, merely, as I have just denied it practical consequence, somewhat puzzling.

The disquietfulness arises, "somehow," out of a conjunction of three attributes of the fight: its immediate dramatic shape; its metaphoric content; and its social context. A cultural figure against a social ground, the fight is at once a convulsive surge of animal hatred, a mock war of symbolical selves, and a formal simulation of status tensions, and its aesthetic power derives from its capacity to force together these diverse realities. The reason it is disquietful is not that it has material effects (it has some, but they are minor); the reason that it is disquietful is that, joining pride to selfhood, selfhood to cocks, and cocks to destruction, it brings to imaginative realization a dimension of Balinese experience normally well-obscured from view. The transfer of a sense of gravity into what is in itself a rather blank and unvarious spectacle, a commotion of beating wings and throbbing legs, is effected by interpreting it as expressive of something unsettling in the way its authors and audience live, or, even more ominously, what they are.[17]

As a dramatic shape, the fight displays a characteristic that does not seem so remarkable until one realizes that it does not have to be there: a radically atomistical structure.* Each match is a world unto itself, a particulate burst of form. There is the matchmaking, there is the betting, there is the fight, there is the result—utter triumph and utter defeat—and there is the hurried, embarrassed passing of money. The loser is not consoled. People drift away from him, look around him, leave him to assimilate his momentary descent into nonbeing, reset his face, and return, scarless and intact, to the fray. Nor are winners congratulated, or events rehashed; once a match is ended the crowd's attention turns totally to the next, with no looking back. A shadow of the experience no doubt remains with the principals, perhaps even with some of the witnesses of a deep fight, as it remains with us when we leave the theater after seeing a powerful play well-performed; but it quite soon fades to become at most a schematic memory—a diffuse glow or an abstract shudder—and usually not even that.

---

[17] Geertz views culture as shared codes of meaning that are publicly acted out, which makes his analysis a method of dramatic interpretation. The cockfight is like a play the Balinese perform for themselves, and its importance is artistic. Geertz says it has "aesthetic power" because it forces layers of significance, what he calls "diverse realities," together. It expresses what the Balinese are in a way that is "normally well obscured from view."

Any expressive form lives only in its own present—the one it itself creates. But, here, that present is severed into a string of flashes, some more bright than others, but all of them disconnected, aesthetic quanta. Whatever the cockfight says, it says in spurts.

But, as I have argued lengthily elsewhere, the Balinese live in spurts.* Their life, as they arrange it and perceive it, is less a flow, a directional movement out of the past, through the present, toward the future than an on-off pulsation of meaning and vacuity, an arrhythmic alternation of short periods when "something" (that is, something significant) is happening, and equally short ones where "nothing" (that is, nothing much) is—between what they themselves call "full" and "empty" times, or, in another idiom, "junctures" and "holes." In focusing activity down to a burning-glass dot, the cockfight is merely being Balinese in the same way in which everything from the monadic encounters of everyday life, through the clanging pointillism of *gamelan*[18] music, to the visiting-day-of-the-gods temple celebrations are. It is not an imitation of the punctuateness of Balinese social life, nor a depiction of it, nor even an expression of it; it is an example of it, carefully prepared.*[19]

If one dimension of the cockfight's structure, its lack of temporal directionality, makes it seem a typical segment of the general social life, however, the other, its flat-out, head-to-head (or spur-to-spur) aggressiveness, makes it seem a contradiction, a reversal, even a subversion of it. In the normal course of things, the Balinese are shy to the point of obsessiveness of open conflict. Oblique, cautious, subdued, controlled, masters of indirection and dissimulation—what they call

alus, "polished," "smooth"—they rarely face what they can turn away from, rarely resist what they can evade. But here they portray themselves as wild and murderous, with manic explosions of instinctual cruelty. A powerful rendering of life as the Balinese most deeply do not want it (to adapt a phrase Frye has used of Gloucester's blinding)[20] is set in the context of a sample of it as they do in fact have it.* And, because the context suggests that the rendering, if less than a straightforward description, is nonetheless more than an idle fancy; it is here that the disquietfulness—the disquietfulness of the *fight,* not (or, anyway, not necessarily) its patrons, who seem in fact rather thoroughly to enjoy it—emerges. The slaughter in the cock ring is not a depiction of how things literally are among men, but, what is almost worse, of how, from a particular angle, they imaginatively are.*

The angle, of course, is stratificatory. What, as we have already seen, the cockfight talks most forcibly about is status relationships, and what it says about them is that they are matters of life and death. That prestige is a profoundly serious business is apparent everywhere one looks in Bali—in the village, the family, the economy, the state. A peculiar fusion of Polynesian title ranks and Hindu castes, the hierarchy of pride is the moral backbone of the society. But only in the cockfight are the sentiments upon which that hierarchy rests revealed in their natural colors. Enveloped elsewhere in a haze of etiquette, a thick cloud of euphemism and ceremony, gesture and allusion, they are here expressed in only the thinnest disguise of an animal mask, a mask which in fact demonstrates them far more effectively than it conceals them. Jealousy is as much a part of Bali

---

[18] *Gamelan* is a type of Southeast Asian music using chimes and gongs.

[19] Geertz has led us back from the details of the cockfight to his definition of culture. He stresses that culture does not exist apart from individuals; instead, it is created in peoples' interpretations of events around them and bound up in public symbols and communication (Applebaum 1987:485). Here he says the cockfight is not a depiction, expression, or example of Balinese life; rather, it *is* Balinese life.

[20] Northrop Frye (1912–1991) was an influential literary critic who was particularly concerned with the relationship of literature to myth and society. Gloucester's blinding occurs in Shakespeare's *King Lear,* where the Earl of Gloucester is punished for aiding Lear by having his eyes gouged out. Frye says that the audience does not want to see a real experience (a man's eyes put out); they want a vicarious experience from the point of view of the imagination. The fact that the blinding does not really happen is crucial to the psychological experience (Frye 1964:98–99).

as poise, envy as grace, brutality as charm; but without the cockfight the Balinese would have a much less certain understanding of them, which is, presumably, why they value it so highly.

Any expressive form works (when it works) by disarranging semantic contexts in such a way that properties conventionally ascribed to certain things are unconventionally ascribed to others, which are then seen actually to possess them. To call the wind a cripple, as Stevens does, to fix tone and manipulate timbre, as Schoenberg does, or, closer to our case, to picture an art critic as a dissolute bear, as Hogarth does, is to cross conceptual wires;[21] the established conjunctions between objects and their qualities are altered, and phenomena—fall weather, melodic shape, or cultural journalism—are clothed in signifiers which normally point to other referents.* Similarly, to connect—and connect, and connect— the collision of roosters with the divisiveness of status is to invite a transfer of perceptions from the former to the latter, a transfer which is at once a description and a judgment. (Logically, the transfer could, of course, as well go the other way; but, like most of the rest of us, the Balinese are a great deal more interested in understanding men than they are in understanding cocks.)

What sets the cockfight apart from the ordinary course of life, lifts it from the realm of everyday practical affairs, and surrounds it with an aura of enlarged importance is not, as functionalist sociology would have it, that it reinforces status discriminations (such reinforcement is hardly necessary in a society where every act proclaims

them), but that it provides a metasocial commentary upon the whole matter of assorting human beings into fixed hierarchical ranks and then organizing the major part of collective existence around that assortment. Its function, if you want to call it that, is interpretive: it is a Balinese reading of Balinese experience, a story they tell themselves about themselves.[22]

SAYING SOMETHING OF SOMETHING

To put the matter this way is to engage in a bit of metaphorical refocusing of one's own, for it shifts the analysis of cultural forms from an endeavor in general parallel to dissecting an organism, diagnosing a symptom, deciphering a code, or ordering a system—the dominant analogies in contemporary anthropology—to one in general parallel with penetrating a literary text. If one takes the cockfight, or any other collectively sustained symbolic structure, as a means of "saying something of something" (to invoke a famous Aristotelian tag), then one is faced with a problem not in social mechanics but social semantics.* For the anthropologist, whose concern is with formulating sociological principles, not with promoting or appreciating cockfights, the question is, what does one learn about such principles from examining culture as an assemblage of texts?[23]

Such an extension of the notion of a text beyond written material, and even beyond verbal, is, though metaphorical, not, of course, all that

---

[21] Wallace Stevens (1879–1955) was an American poet, Arnold Schoenberg (1874–1951) an Austrian composer, and William Hogarth (1697–1764) an English painter and lithographer.

[22] Although rarely discussed in this light, Geertz's article is an attack on structural functionalism. A young generation of American anthropologists including Geertz, David Schneider, and Eric Wolf butted heads with a group of British anthropologists, including Max Gluckman and Meyer Fortes, at a conference in Cambridge, England, in 1963. In this essay, Geertz has performed an analysis that could have come straight from the pen of a British structural-functionalist ethnographer. In the last few sections, however, he turns the structural-functionalist position upside down, saying that functionalist conclusions are meaningless for the Balinese. Instead he points to an existentialist conclusion. That is, the cockfight is not about social divisions, it is about understanding what it means to be human in Bali and the being and nothingness that are its temporary results.

[23] In this final section, Geertz summarizes his argument and explains how the cockfight attains personal significance for Balinese participants. Up to now the analysis has been very particular, but his conclusions try to say something universal about the nature of culture: that cultures are a form of text.

novel. The *interpretatio naturae* tradition of the middle ages, which, culminating in Spinoza, attempted to read nature as Scripture, the Nietzschean effort to treat value systems as glosses on the will to power[24] (or the Marxian one to treat them as glosses on property relations), and the Freudian replacement of the enigmatic text of the manifest dream with the plain one of the latent, all offer precedents, if not equally recommendable ones.* But the idea remains theoretically undeveloped; and the more profound corollary, so far as anthropology is concerned, that cultural forms can be treated as texts, as imaginative works built out of social materials, has yet to be systematically exploited.*

In the case at hand, to treat the cockfight as a text is to bring out a feature of it (in my opinion, the central feature of it) that treating it as a rite or a pastime, the two most obvious alternatives, would tend to obscure: its use of emotion for cognitive ends. What the cockfight says it says in a vocabulary of sentiment—the thrill of risk, the despair of loss, the pleasure of triumph. Yet what it says is not merely that risk is exciting, loss depressing, or triumph gratifying, banal tautologies of affect, but that it is of these emotions, thus exampled, that society is built and individuals are put together. Attending cockfights and participating in them is, for the Balinese, a kind of sentimental education. What he learns there is what his culture's ethos and his private sensibility (or, anyway, certain aspects of them) look like when spelled out externally in a collective text; that the two are near enough alike to be articulated in the symbolics of a single such text; and—the disquieting part—that the text in which this revelation is accomplished consists of a chicken hacking another mindlessly to bits.

Every people, the proverb has it, loves its own form of violence. The cockfight is the Balinese re-

flection on theirs: on its look, its uses, its force, its fascination. Drawing on almost every level of Balinese experience, it brings together themes—animal savagery, male narcissism, opponent gambling, status rivalry, mass excitement, blood sacrifice—whose main connection is their involvement with rage and the fear of rage, and, binding them into a set of rules which at once contains them and allows them play, builds a symbolic structure in which, over and over again, the reality of their inner affiliation can be intelligibly felt. If, to quote Northrop Frye again, we go to see *Macbeth* to learn what a man feels like after he has gained a kingdom and lost his soul, Balinese go to cockfights to find out what a man, usually composed, aloof, almost obsessively self-absorbed, a kind of moral autocosm, feels like when, attacked, tormented, challenged, insulted, and driven in result to the extremes of fury, he has totally triumphed or been brought totally low. The whole passage, as it takes us back to Aristotle (though to the *Poetics* rather than the *Hermeneutics*), is worth quotation:

> But the poet [as opposed to the historian], Aristotle says, never makes any real statements at all, certainly no particular or specific ones. The poet's job is not to tell you what happened, but what happens: not what did take place, but the kind of thing that always does take place. He gives you the typical, recurring, or what Aristotle calls universal event. You wouldn't go to *Macbeth* to learn about the history of Scotland—you go to it to learn what a man feels like after he's gained a kingdom and lost his soul. When you meet such a character as Micawber in Dickens, you don't feel that there must have been a man Dickens knew who was exactly like this: you feel that there's a bit of Micawber in almost everybody you know, including yourself. Our impressions of human life are picked up one by one, and remain for most of us loose and disorganized. But we con-

---

[24] Baruch Spinoza (1632–1677) was an influential philosopher in the rationalist tradition. In one of his best-known works, *Ethics,* he set out a geometrical program of definitions, axioms, postulates, and theorems that he proposed was a systematic procedure for the perfection of human nature. His work influenced many later scholars, including Georg Wilhelm Friedrich Hegel.

Friedrich Nietzsche was a German philosopher whose work was influential in the development of existentialism. His book *The Birth of Tragedy* (1956 [1872]) was important in the work of Ruth Benedict and is discussed in essay 16. Geertz's comment concerning the "will to power" refers to a concept Nietzsche developed in his most famous work, *Thus Spake Zarathustra* (1954 [1883–1885]).

stantly find things in literature that suddenly coordinate and bring into focus a great many such impressions, and this is part of what Aristotle means by the typical or universal human event.*

It is this kind of bringing of assorted experiences of everyday life to focus that the cockfight, set aside from that life as "only a game" and reconnected to it as "more than a game," accomplishes, and so creates what, better than typical or universal, could be called a paradigmatic human event—that is, one that tells us less what happens than the kind of thing that would happen if, as is not the case, life were art and could be as freely shaped by styles of feeling as *Macbeth* and *David Copperfield* are.

Enacted and re-enacted, so far without end, the cockfight enables the Balinese, as, read and reread, *Macbeth* enables us, to see a dimension of his own subjectivity. As he watches fight after fight, with the active watching of an owner and a bettor (for cockfighting has no more interest as a pure spectator sport than does croquet or dog racing), he grows familiar with it and what it has to say to him, much as the attentive listener to string quartets or the absorbed viewer of still life grows slowly more familiar with them in a way which opens his subjectivity to himself.*

Yet, because—in another of those paradoxes, along with painted feelings and unconsequenced acts, which haunt aesthetics—that subjectivity does not properly exist until it is thus organized, art forms generate and regenerate the very subjectivity they pretend only to display. Quartets, still lifes, and cockfights are not merely reflections of a pre-existing sensibility analogically represented; they are positive agents in the creation and maintenance of such a sensibility. If we see ourselves as a pack of Micawbers, it is from reading too much Dickens (if we see ourselves as unil-

lusioned realists, it is from reading too little); and similarly for Balinese, cocks, and cockfights. It is in such a way, coloring experience with the light they cast it in, rather than through whatever material effects they may have, that the arts play their role, as arts, in social life.*

In the cockfight, then, the Balinese forms and discovers his temperament and his society's temper at the same time. Or, more exactly, he forms and discovers a particular facet of them. Not only are there a great many other cultural texts providing commentaries on status hierarchy and self-regard in Bali, but there are a great many other critical sectors of Balinese life besides the stratificatory and the agonistic that receive such commentary. The ceremony consecrating a Brahmana priest, a matter of breath control, postural immobility, and vacant concentration upon the depths of being, displays a radically different, but to the Balinese equally real, property of social hierarchy—its reach toward the numinous[25] transcendent. Set not in the matrix of the kinetic emotionality of animals, but in that of the static passionlessness of divine mentality, it expresses tranquillity not disquiet. The mass festivals at the village temples, which mobilize the whole local population in elaborate hostings of visiting gods—songs, dances, compliments, gifts—assert the spiritual unity of village mates against their status inequality and project a mood of amity and trust.* The cockfight is not the master key to Balinese life, any more than bullfighting is to Spanish. What it says about that life is not unqualified nor even unchallenged by what other equally eloquent cultural statements say about it. But there is nothing more surprising in this than in the fact that Racine and Moliere were contemporaries, or that the same people who arrange chrysanthemums cast swords.*[26]

The culture of a people is an ensemble of texts, themselves ensembles, which the anthropologist

---

[25] *Numinous:* mysterious, surpassing comprehension.

[26] This paragraph is important because it shows that Geertz was moving away from the popular image of culture as an organic whole toward the postmodern vision of culture as the intersection of competing views and interests. Geertz emphasizes that rather than presenting a consistent, integrated message, culture is full of competing voices and messages that are at odds with each other. Jean Racine (1639–1699) and Jean-Baptiste Molière (1622–1673) were French playwrights: the first a great writer of tragedies, the latter famous for his comedies. The last line of the paragraph refers to Ruth Benedict's study of Japanese national character, *The Chrysanthemum and the Sword* (1946).

strains to read over the shoulders of those to whom they properly belong. There are enormous difficulties in such an enterprise, methodological pitfalls to make a Freudian quake, and some moral perplexities as well. Nor is it the only way that symbolic forms can be sociologically handled. Functionalism lives, and so does psychologism. But to regard such forms as "saying something of something," and saying it to somebody, is at least to open up the possibility of an analysis which attends to their substance rather than to reductive formulas professing to account for them.

As in more familiar exercises in close reading, one can start anywhere in a culture's repertoire of forms and end up anywhere else. One can stay, as I have here, within a single, more or less bounded form, and circle steadily within it. One can move between forms in search of broader unities or informing contrasts. One can even compare forms from different cultures to define their character in reciprocal relief. But whatever the level at which one operates, and however intricately, the guiding principle is the same: societies, like lives, contain their own interpretations. One has only to learn how to gain access to them.[27]

---

[27] The notion that a culture is a collection of texts that anthropologists read over the shoulders of those who live them had a powerful impact on the next generation of anthropological theorists. In particular, this idea led anthropologists to borrow some of the tools of textual analysis from literary criticism. Geertz's work provided part of the foundation for postmodernism, which is dealt with in the next section.

This essay was published at a time when the works of modern French critical thinkers such as Roland Barthes (1915–1980) and Jacques Derrida (1930–) were becoming available in English. Among their critical insights is the notion that texts are systems of symbols that reveal the assumptions of particular cultures at particular times. As Geertz was writing this essay, the whole idea of deconstructing texts, or culture, was transforming the field of literary criticism. This essay is a critical bridge between literature and anthropological theory.

Postmodernism and Its Critics

McGee: "I'm having trouble getting started on this introduction to postmodernism."
Warms: "Why don't you write about the process of writing the introduction?"

$\mathcal{R}$ich Warms responded to Jon McGee's difficulty in a classic postmodernist fashion, trying to convince him to write it in a postmodern style. We hope that what makes Warms' (unsuccessful) response postmodern will become clear as you read.

Modernism is a term drawn from the study of literature and art. Applied to anthropology, it broadly refers to the years between the 1920s and the mid-1970s (Manganaro 1990). Analysts suggest that some of the attributes of modernist writing in anthropology were detachment, the assumption of a position of scientific neutrality, and rationalism (Rabinow 1986). Postmodernists challenge these assertions. They maintain that such claims are distorted or, at best, true in only a very limited sense. They believe that objective, neutral knowledge of another culture (or any aspect of the world) is impossible. The postmodernist challenge has led anthropologists to examine the basis of their discipline and to engage in a rancorous debate between the two points of view.

Although the authors represented in this section are all Americans, the roots of the postmodern approach to anthropology lie in Europe, particularly in the work of the hermeneutic philosophers and post–World War II French social theorists Jacques Derrida (1930–) and Michel Foucault (1926–1984).

Hermeneutics—the study of the interpretation of meanings—has been an intellectual concern in Europe for most of the twentieth century, but it was largely ignored by American anthropologists until the cognitive research of the 1960s and 1970s. Those who take the hermeneutic perspective do not accept the view that observers can derive neutral and objective knowledge about the world. Rather, following the philosopher Martin Heidegger (1889–1976), they believe humans cannot have knowledge about the world that is not tinged by a particular perspective or bias. Knowledge is conditioned by culture, context, and history. Hermeneuticist Hans-Georg Gadamer (1900–), for example, wrote that the sciences did not allow humans to see beyond their culturally shaped contexts (Applebaum 1987:486). According to this philosophy, because we cannot separate our ways of knowing from our language and culture, it is impossible for us to interpret the world in a truly detached, objective manner. We all interpret the world around us in our own way, based on our language, cultural background, and personal experiences.

Layton divides the European postmodernists into the "hard" or extreme postmodernists such as Derrida, and the "soft" or moderate postmodernists such as Foucault (1997:186). Derrida is considered one of the fathers of deconstruction in European thought (Lilla 1998:36). He argued that all cultures construct autonomous self-contained worlds of meaning. Thus ethnographic descriptions distort native understandings by forcing them into our own society's ways of conceptualizing the world. In other words, meaning can never be accurately translated.

Foucault is best known in the United States for his discussion of "discourses of power." He argued that social relations between people are characterized by dominance and subjugation. Dominating people or classes control the ideological conditions under which knowledge, truth, and reality are defined. "Because modernity is viewed, alongside other configurations of knowledge, as the product of power, the objective character of scientific knowledge is shown to be an historical construct" (Erickson 1998:142). In the United States, anthropologists such as George Marcus (1946–), Michael Fischer (1946–), Steven Tyler (1932–), and James Clifford (1945–) were profoundly affected by Derrida and Foucault.

Throughout the history of our discipline, anthropologists have claimed to be authorities on other cultures. They have fortified this claim by emphasizing the mystique of fieldwork and by explaining other cultures to their audiences through written descriptions. The hermeneutic and deconstructionist approaches led many American anthropologists to ask a variety of questions about their own work and the work of other (often prominent) anthropologists. Some of the most important of these issues involve the conduct of fieldwork, the literary techniques used in the writing of ethnographies, and the validity of the author's interpretations over competing alternatives.

The conduct of fieldwork is a critical issue to postmodernists because traditionally most ethnography has contained very little information on the actual process of research. Postmodernists argue that it is precisely this process that is crucial in the creation of ethnographic texts. They believe that anthropologists can never be unbiased observers of all that goes on in a culture. Fieldworkers must, of necessity, be in specific places at specific times. As a result, they see some things and not others. The particular circumstances of fieldwork—the political context in which it occurs, the investigator's preferences and predilections, and the people met by chance or design—all condition the understanding of society that results. Ethnography has traditionally been written as if the anthropologist was a neutral, omniscient observer. Postmodernists claim, however, that because the collection of anthropological data is subjective, it is not possible to analyze the data objectively (Taylor 1979). Essay 38 in this section dramatically illustrates this point. In this essay, "Grief and a Headhunter's Rage," Renato Rosaldo (1941–) describes his almost unbearable sorrow after the accidental death of his wife in the field. He then tells us how this experience led him to a visceral understanding of why Ilongot men take heads after the death of loved ones, something he could not comprehend through intellectual study of the custom.

Writing ethnography is the primary means by which anthropologists convey their interpretations of other cultures, and ethnographies have traditionally followed some basic literary conventions, which Marcus and Cushman (1982) have described in detail. Even if you are not a student of ethnographic writing, you will immediately recognize several of these forms. One of the most obvious characteristics of ethnographic writing is that rather than saying, "I am writing my interpretation of what the natives were doing," authors claim to represent the native point of view. Of course, an anthropologist cannot possibly present the point of view of everyone in a society; he or she works with selected informants. So the anthropologist chooses who speaks for the society, and in his or her translation of the native language decides what words are presented to the audience.

Another common rhetorical device of Anglo-American ethnography is that writers claim to describe completely other cultures or societies, even though anthropologists actually know only the part of a culture that they personally experience. One of the more insidious writing conventions is that of the omniscient narrator—the authoritative third-person observer who replaces the fallible first person. Instead of writing "I saw my informant pour ketchup on his ice cream," which is the result of direct observation, many ethnographies contain statements such as "The people of San Marcos pour ketchup on their ice cream." The use of the omniscient narrator heightens the sense of scientific objectivity projected by the text, but it also severs the relationship between what the ethnographer knows and how he or she came to know it (Marcus and Cushman 1982:32).

One result of these understandings was the more revealing style in which some anthropologists began to write ethnographies. There has always been some self-revelation in ethnography, but in the late 1960s and early 1970s, anthropologists such as Chagnon (1968), Briggs (1970), Geertz (1973), and Rabinow (1977) began to write ethnographies in which their recounting of their own experiences and feelings takes a prominent role. For postmodern writers in the 1980s and 1990s, this self-reflectiveness is not simply a more straightforward form of reportage. The recounting of field experiences can become the narrative device by which anthropological understanding is conveyed. Rosaldo, for example, says that the writing of his essay was an act of catharsis that helped him deal with his grief as well as giving him new insight into the Ilongot custom of head-hunting.

"Hermes' Dilemma," by Vincent Crapanzano (1939–), is a different style of postmodern writing—one that deals with textual analysis (see essay 39). Crapanzano examines the construction of ethnographies as literary texts and deconstructs three different ethnographic accounts. The hermeneutic premise behind Crapanzano's work is that while data of themselves are mute, anthropologists construct meaning by writing ethnographies. Because one must write according to certain literary conventions (tense, voice, and so on), the act of writing is a literary construction of the writer. Readers in turn impose their own interpretation on the author's text. In other words, the writing and reading of ethnographic texts involves the piling of layer upon layer of interpretation. In his analysis, Crapanzano deconstructs the literary devices (peels back some of the layers) used by the authors in order to better understand the biases that influenced their writing.

A final critical issue that underlies almost all postmodern writing lies in the area of interpretation. Postmodernists maintain that if a text is an author's interpretation and if that author's work is taken as an authoritative account, then all other voices and interpretations are silenced. Because everything is an interpretation in the postmodern view, the only way authors can generate an interpretation that is accepted as true is to "delicense" all other interpretations. But can one person's interpretation be more valid than another's? Postmodernists maintain that it cannot. They insist that the acceptance of an interpretation is ultimately an issue of power and wealth. Historically, they say, the interpretations voiced by white Protestant males in Western industrialized nations have delicensed all others and silenced them. They ask why the Anglo-American view of events is the only acceptable interpretation and

claim that deconstructing this mainstream work allows other opinions to be expressed. Postmodernists assert that in history, literature, and politics, the voices of women, minorities, and the poor are finally being heard.

The question of whose voice gets heard is a contentious political issue in America today. Insisting that the voices of minorities, women, and others be heard results in the teaching of unpopular viewpoints and in the promotion of heightened sensitivity toward those who are not part of what is traditionally considered mainstream culture. This has often resulted in backlash from members of mainstream culture who feel their understandings and prerogatives are threatened.

While covering postmodernism in our theory class one year, a student toppled over into a nihilistic funk. "Why should I have spent all this time and money getting an anthropology degree," he asked, "if it is all just interpretations of interpretations, and there is no objective knowledge to be gained in anthropology? Why shouldn't I just go be an English major?" Good questions.

What does this line of thought have to do with the writing of ethnography? How does postmodernism and the deconstructing of texts help us understand the anthropological endeavor? We have a couple of answers, but first, we must make a critical point. Postmodernism is not the logical culmination of all anthropology. While it is popular, only a minority of anthropologists working today would identify themselves as postmodernists, and most of those would probably have reservations. The final essay in this section, by Roy D'Andrade (1931–), shows that opposition to postmodernism in anthropology can be strident and vociferous.

Taken to its logical extreme, postmodernism comes very close to turning anthropology into a subfield of literature: if all writing is nothing more than interpretations of interpretations, then ethnography is fiction, and no conclusions can be ultimately reached about anything. However, postmodernism is a logical part of the interpretive tendency in anthropology that goes back to the Boasians. Recall that Boas and his students first advanced the perspective of cultural relativism in the early part of the twentieth century.

Also recall that Kroeber had a masters degree in literature, and Ruth Benedict was a published poet. Postmodernism has not replaced positivism in anthropology. From cultural materialism to neo-Marxism, the positivist tradition is alive and well. Postmodernism can be seen as part of a continuing dialectic between scientific and humanistic approaches to the discipline. It is not the end of anthropology, but part of the field's continuing history.

Even the most ardent opponents of postmodernism would agree that postmodern theorists have made important contributions to anthropology. They would agree, for example, that as writers of ethnographies, anthropologists should be aware of rhetorical issues. This awareness can inform and enrich our own writing and help us evaluate both our own and others' claims to objectivity.

Hermeneutic philosophers remind us that ethnographies are literary creations, so it becomes possible to think of cultures as the poetic interplay of voices and performances. Cultures, instead of being read as texts, can be viewed as performances in which the anthropologist participates. Understanding this can allow ethnographers greater insight into the complexities of cultures and invites them to consciously consider their specific effect on those they study. It may aid them in seeing individual differences, conflict, and fragmentation within cultures. Of course, this approach can also lead ethnographers to deny cultural unity. They may fail to see the forest for the trees.

Rather than throwing anthropology into a relativistic black hole, as imagined by our student, the postmodern critique demands that we ask new and challenging questions and thus opens new realms for ethnographic research. For example, anthropologists must now ask how new forms of authority and voices other than their own can be included in ethnography. Furthermore, anthropologists must determine what kind of information can be counted as knowledge. In particular, we think the recognition and incorporation of gender and class issues can revolutionize the anthropological enterprise.

The conflict between postmodernists and those who view anthropology as a science stems largely from their differing opinions of the purpose of anthropology. If we agree that the goal of anthropology is to describe and explain human affairs and teach a reader the subjective meaning of human experience, then the scientific and postmodern goals of anthropology are complementary.

Postmodernism has been one of the most controversial developments in anthropology, and its critics also raise telling points. Many scholars vigorously defend anthropology as an empirical science. They argue that although some aspects of ethnographic data collection are subjective, it is possible to do empirically objective anthropology. O'Meara (1989), for example, systematically explores and refutes the primary arguments that postmodernists give to support their claim that anthropology is not a science. Additionally, many scholars critical of the postmodernist view argue that this position, pursued to its logical extreme, must result in nihilism. If all voices should be heard, they say, does that mean fascist voices and the voices of white supremacists or neo-Nazis are no less worthy of respect than others? As Todorov, a key postmodern thinker, has pointed out, "It is not possible without inconsistency, to defend human rights on one hand and deconstruct the idea of humanity with the other" (1987:190). Indeed, during World War II, hermeneuticist Martin Heidegger was an apologist for the Nazis, and Paul de Man, who later became a prominent deconstructionist, was a Nazi journalist (Lehman 1992).

Our final essay in this volume, by Roy D'Andrade, is a strong critique of the postmodernist perspective. D'Andrade argues that postmodernists have misrepresented the notion of objectivity, and he presents a defense of objectivity and science. He argues that science has advanced knowledge and that the postmodern critique of anthropology is based on an implicit moral, rather than objective, model of the world. D'Andrade contends that the postmodernist critique of science—that it has led to oppression and Western hegemony—is not supported by any data and that the difference between moral and objective models should be recognized.

38. Grief and a Headhunter's Rage

Renato Rosaldo (1941–)

IF YOU ASK AN OLDER ILONGOT MAN OF NORTH-ern Luzon, Philippines, why he cuts off human heads, his answer is brief, and one on which no anthropologist can readily elaborate: He says that rage, born of grief, impels him to kill his fellow human beings. He claims that he needs a place "to carry his anger." The act of severing and toss-ing away the victim's head enables him, he says, to vent and, he hopes, throw away the anger of his bereavement. Although the anthropologist's job is to make other cultures intelligible, more questions fail to reveal any further explanation of this man's pithy statement.[1] To him, grief, rage, and headhunting go together in a self-evident manner. Either you understand it or you don't. And, in fact, for the longest time I simply did not.

In what follows, I want to talk about how to talk about the cultural force of emotions.[a] The *emotional force* of a death, for example, derives less from an abstract brute fact than from a particular intimate relation's permanent rupture. It refers to the kinds of feelings one experiences on learning, for example, that the child just run over by a car is one's own and not a stranger's. Rather than speak-ing of death in general, one must consider the sub-

From *Culture and Truth* (1989)

ject's position within a field of social relations in order to grasp one's emotional experience.[b]

My effort to show the force of a simple state-ment taken literally goes against anthropology's classic norms, which prefer to explicate culture through the gradual thickening of symbolic webs of meaning. By and large, cultural analysts use not *force* but such terms as *thick description, multivo-cality, polysemy, richness,* and *texture.*[2] The notion of force, among other things, opens to question the common anthropological assumption that the greatest human import resides in the densest for-est of symbols and that analytical detail, or "cul-tural depth," equals enhanced explanation of a culture, or "cultural elaboration." Do people al-ways in fact describe most thickly what matters most to them?

THE RAGE IN ILONGOT GRIEF

Let me pause a moment to introduce the Ilon-gots, among whom my wife, Michelle Rosaldo, and I lived and conducted field research for thirty months (1967–69, 1974). They number about 3,500 and reside in an upland area some 90 miles northeast of Manila, Philippines.[c] They subsist

---

[1] From the opening, it is evident that Rosaldo is writing a different sort of anthropology than most of the authors in this book. Most anthropological writing has been built on a scientific model. Essays are written as reports, almost always in the third person. This essay, on the other hand, is conversational in tone, and much of it is in the first and second per-son. Beyond this, Rosaldo seems, in his opening, to deny the possibility of meaningful anthropological explanation of Ilon-got head-hunting. The idea of emotional force is not so much explanation as a statement that no further description or explanation is possible.

[2] By invoking the concepts of thick description and multivocality, Rosaldo is referring especially to Clifford Geertz and Vic-tor Turner. The important difference between Rosaldo and Geertz can be seen in two different possible interpretations of the following story recounted by Geertz: "There is an Indian story—at least I heard it as an Indian story—about an En-glishman who, having been told that the world rested on a platform which rested on the back of an elephant which rested in turn on the back of a turtle, asked (perhaps he was an ethnographer; it is the way they behave), what did the turtle rest on? Another turtle. And that turtle? 'Ah Sahib, after that it is turtles all the way down.'" (1973:28–29).

Geertz goes on to say that "cultural analysis is intrinsically incomplete"—meaning that there is always another layer of meaning. His parable can also be interpreted to mean that there is no meaning other than that expressed. It is all just turtles and nothing beyond that. This, perhaps, is the meaning that Rosaldo would prefer.

by hunting deer and wild pig and by cultivating rain-fed gardens (swiddens) with rice, sweet potatoes, manioc, and vegetables. Their (bilateral) kin relations are reckoned through men and women. After marriage, parents and their married daughters live in the same or adjacent households. The largest unit within the society, a largely territorial descent group called the *bertan,* becomes manifest primarily in the context of feuding. For themselves, their neighbors, and their ethnographers, headhunting stands out as the Ilongots' most salient cultural practice.

When Ilongots told me, as they often did, how the rage in bereavement could impel men to headhunt, I brushed aside their one-line accounts as too simple, thin, opaque, implausible, stereotypical, or otherwise unsatisfying. Probably I naively equated grief with sadness. Certainly no personal experience allowed me to imagine the powerful rage Ilongots claimed to find in bereavement. My own inability to conceive the force of anger in grief led me to seek out another level of analysis that could provide a deeper explanation for older men's desire to headhunt.[3]

Not until some fourteen years after first recording the terse Ilongot statement about grief and a headhunter's rage did I begin to grasp its overwhelming force. For years I thought that more verbal elaboration (which was not forthcoming) or another analytical level (which remained elusive) could better explain older men's motives for headhunting. Only after being reposi-

tioned through a devastating loss of my own could I better grasp that Ilongot older men mean precisely what they say when they describe the anger in bereavement as the source of their desire to cut off human heads. Taken at face value and granted its full weight, their statement reveals much about what compels these older men to headhunt.

In my efforts to find a "deeper" explanation for headhunting, I explored exchange theory, perhaps because it had informed so many classic ethnographies. One day in 1974, I explained the anthropologist's exchange model to an older Ilongot man named Insan. What did he think, I asked, of the idea that headhunting resulted from the way that one death (the beheaded victim's) canceled another (the next of kin). He looked puzzled, so I went on to say that the victim of a beheading was exchanged for the death of one's own kin, thereby balancing the books, so to speak. Insan reflected a moment and replied that he imagined somebody could think such a thing (a safe bet, since I just had), but that he and other Ilongots did not think any such thing.[4] Nor was there any indirect evidence for my exchange theory in ritual, boast, song, or casual conversation.[d]

In retrospect, then, these efforts to impose exchange theory on one aspect of Ilongot behavior appear feeble.[5] Suppose I had discovered what I sought? Although the notion of balancing the ledger does have a certain elegant coherence, one wonders how such bookish dogma could inspire

---

[3] Rosaldo and other postmodern authors share a great deal of concern with the idea of the privileged position. In social science, to privilege a position is to give special credence to certain types of explanation and discount others. Postmodernists argue that Western social science has privileged a particular type of analysis: that which follows the model used in the physical sciences. The closer an explanation is to this model, the more "true" the information it generates, and the higher the prestige of the field that uses it.

[4] The "deeper" explanation of head-hunting for which Rosaldo searched was some sort of accounting modeled on a natural law (here, a mathematical formula, one death cancels another). However, in describing this theory to the Ilongot, Rosaldo faces a problem: even if the theory explains observed behavior, how can Rosaldo grant it any explanatory power when the idea is utterly unintelligible to the Ilongot themselves?

[5] In some ways, the idea of privileged position is a recasting of the emic-etic dichotomy. A principal source of postmodern thought is ethnoscience and cognitive anthropology, but there is a powerful difference between postmodern thought and ethnoscience. Earlier debate on emics and etics was about the privileging of one or the other of these two positions. Postmodernism confronts the specific interests and positioning of both the anthropologists and their informants. Part of the reason for Rosaldo's misunderstanding of Ilongot head-hunting comes from his attempt to apply a Western scientific model to it.

any man to take another man's life at the risk of his own.

My life experience had not as yet provided the means to imagine the rage that can come with devastating loss. Nor could I, therefore, fully appreciate the acute problem of meaning that Ilongots faced in 1974. Shortly after Ferdinand Marcos declared martial law in 1972, rumors that firing squads had become the new punishment for headhunting reached the Ilongot hills. The men therefore decided to call a moratorium on taking heads. In past epochs, when headhunting had become impossible, Ilongots had allowed their rage to dissipate, as best it could, in the course of everyday life. In 1974, they had another option; they began to consider conversion to evangelical Christianity as a means of coping with their grief.[6] Accepting the new religion, people said, implied abandoning their old ways, including headhunting. It also made coping with bereavement less agonizing because they could believe that the deceased had departed for a better world. No longer did they have to confront the awful finality of death.

The force of the dilemma faced by the Ilongots eluded me at the time. Even when I correctly recorded their statements about grieving and the need to throw away their anger, I simply did not grasp the weight of their words. In 1974, for example, while Michelle Rosaldo and I were living among the Ilongots, a six-month-old baby died, probably of pneumonia. That afternoon we visited the father and found him terribly stricken. "He was sobbing and staring through glazed and bloodshot eyes at the cotton blanket covering his baby."[e] The man suffered intensely, for this was the seventh child he had lost. Just a few years be-

fore, three of his children had died, one after the other, in a matter of days. At the time, the situation was murky as people present talked both about evangelical Christianity (the possible renunciation of taking heads) and their grudges against lowlanders (the contemplation of headhunting forays into the surrounding valleys).[7]

Through subsequent days and weeks, the man's grief moved him in a way I had not anticipated. Shortly after the baby's death, the father converted to evangelical Christianity. Altogether too quick on the inference, I immediately concluded that the man believed that the new religion could somehow prevent further deaths in his family. When I spoke my mind to an Ilongot friend, he snapped at me, saying that I had missed the point: what the man in fact sought in the new religion was not the denial of our inevitable deaths but a means of coping with his grief. With the advent of martial law, headhunting was out of the question as a means of venting his wrath and thereby lessening his grief. Were he to remain in his Ilongot way of life, the pain of his sorrow would simply be too much to bear.[f] My description from 1980 now seems so apt that I wonder how I could have written the words and nonetheless failed to appreciate the force of the grieving man's desire to vent his rage.

Another representative anecdote makes my failure to imagine the rage possible in Ilongot bereavement all the more remarkable. On this occasion, Michelle Rosaldo and I were urged by Ilongot friends to play the tape of a headhunting celebration we had witnessed some five years before. No sooner had we turned on the tape and heard the boast of a man who had died in the intervening years than did people abruptly tell us to

---

[6] Although postmodern anthropology draws on ethnoscience, it is critically different in many ways, one of which is shown here. Ethnoscientists viewed culture as a more or less unchanging mental template. For postmodernists, culture is always historically contingent. The actions of individuals and the derivation of meaning within cultures cannot be explained without reference to specific sociohistorical circumstances.

[7] A key source of the emphasis on history in postmodernism is Marxism, particularly as filtered by the French Marxist anthropologists and political radicals of the 1960s and 1970s (when most postmodernists were doing their graduate training). Marxists, of course, see culture as part of a historical process that will ultimately result in communism. Postmodernists do not see any end to history, but they do view cultural action as dependent on historical circumstances. It is, for example, critical to the story Rosaldo is telling here that the action takes place in 1974, when head-hunting was made impossible and evangelical Christianity was available as an alternative.

shut off the recorder. Michelle Rosaldo reported on the tense conversation that ensued:[8]

> As Insan braced himself to speak, the room again became almost uncannily electric. Backs straightened and my anger turned to nervousness and something more like fear as I saw that Insan's eyes were red. Tukbaw, Renato's Ilongot "brother," then broke into what was a brittle silence, saying he could make things clear. He told us that it hurt to listen to a headhunting celebration when people knew that there would never be another. As he put it: "The song pulls at us, drags our hearts, it makes us think of our dead uncle." And again: "It would be better if I had accepted God, but I still am an Ilongot at heart; and when I hear the song, my heart aches as it does when I must look upon unfinished bachelors whom I know that I will never lead to take a head." Then Wagat, Tukbaw's wife, said with her eyes that all my questions gave her pain, and told me: "Leave off now, isn't that enough? Even I, a woman, cannot stand the way it feels inside my heart."[g]

From my present position, it is evident that the tape recording of the dead man's boast evoked powerful feelings of bereavement, particularly rage and the impulse to headhunt. At the time I could only feel apprehensive and diffusely sense the force of the emotions experienced by Insan, Tukbaw, Wagat, and the others present.

The dilemma for the Ilongots grew out of a set of cultural practices that, when blocked, were agonizing to live with.[9] The cessation of headhunting called for painful adjustments to other modes of coping with the rage they found in bereavement. One could compare their dilemma with the notion that the failure to perform rituals can create anxiety.[h] In the Ilongot case, the cultural notion that throwing away a human head also casts away the anger creates a problem of meaning when the headhunting ritual cannot be performed. Indeed, Max Weber's classic problem of meaning in *The Protestant Ethic and the Spirit of Capitalism*[10] is precisely of this kind.[i] On a logical plane, the Calvinist doctrine of predestination seems flawless: God has chosen the elect, but his decision can never be known by mortals. Among those whose ultimate concern is salvation, the doctrine of predestination is as easy to grasp conceptually as it is impossible to endure in everyday life (unless one happens to be a "religious virtuoso"). For Calvinists and Ilongots alike, the problem of meaning resides in practice, not theory. The dilemma for both groups involves the practical matter of how to live with one's beliefs, rather than the logical puzzlement produced by abstruse doctrine.

HOW I FOUND THE RAGE IN GRIEF

One burden of this introduction concerns the claim that it took some fourteen years for me to grasp what Ilongots had told me about grief, rage, and headhunting. During all those years I was not yet in a position to comprehend the force of anger possible in bereavement, and now I am. Introducing myself into this account requires a certain

---

[8] This extended quotation, presumably originally from field notes, is typical of the self-revealing style of postmodernism. Michelle Rosaldo's *Knowledge and Passion* (1980) makes extensive use of such quotations. In traditional ethnography, information from the field is presented in abstract, scientific fashion. Names are rarely mentioned; in fact, pains are sometimes taken to ensure the anonymity of the speakers. Here the opposite is done. Since all knowledge is contingent on the positioning of observers and informants, the fact that specific people are speaking is critical.

[9] Another aspect of Marxist theory absorbed by postmodernists is the emphasis on conflict. Functionalists and ethnoscientists looked for logically consistent systems. Postmodernists believe society to be beset by conflict between social groups (here, the Ilongot versus the government) or between theory and practice (the Calvinist example that follows). The contradictions are not abnormalities that would be eliminated in a smoothly functioning society, but rather a fundamental part of any social system.

[10] The book by Weber to which Rosaldo refers in this paragraph was extremely influential in anthropology and sociology. In it, Weber argued that the beliefs encouraged by Calvinist theology, particularly individualism and the work ethic, contributed directly to the rise of capitalism.

hesitation both because of the discipline's taboo and because of its increasingly frequent violation by essays laced with trendy amalgams of continental philosophy and autobiographical snippets. If classic ethnography's vice was the slippage from the ideal of detachment to actual indifference, that of present-day reflexivity is the tendency for the self-absorbed Self to lose sight altogether of the culturally different Other. Despite the risks involved, as the ethnographer I must enter the discussion at this point to elucidate certain issues of method.[11]

The key concept in what follows is that of the positioned (and repositioned) subject.[j] In routine interpretive procedure, according to the methodology of hermeneutics, one can say that ethnographers reposition themselves as they go about understanding other cultures. Ethnographers begin research with a set of questions, revise them throughout the course of inquiry, and in the end emerge with different questions than they started with. One's surprise at the answer to a question, in other words, requires one to revise the question until lessening surprises or diminishing returns indicate a stopping point. This interpretive approach has been most influentially articulated within anthropology by Clifford Geertz.[k]

Interpretive method usually rests on the axiom that gifted ethnographers learn their trade by preparing themselves as broadly as possible. To follow the meandering course of ethnographic inquiry, field-workers require wide-ranging theoretical capacities and finely tuned sensibilities. After all, one cannot predict beforehand what one will encounter in the field. One influential anthropologist, Clyde Kluckhohn, even went so far as to recommend a double initiation: first, the ordeal of psychoanalysis, and then that of fieldwork. All too often, however, this view is extended until certain prerequisites of field research appear to guarantee an authoritative ethnography. Eclectic book knowledge and a range of life experiences, along with edifying reading and self-awareness, supposedly vanquish the twin vices of ignorance and insensitivity.[12]

Although the doctrine of preparation, knowledge, and sensibility contains much to admire, one should work to undermine the false comfort that it can convey. At what point can people say that they have completed their learning or their life experience? The problem with taking this mode of preparing the ethnographer too much to heart is that it can lend a false air of security, an authoritative claim to certitude and finality that our analyses cannot have. All interpretations are provisional; they are made by positioned subjects who are prepared to know certain things and not others.[13] Even when knowledgeable, sensitive, fluent in the language, and able to move easily in an alien cultural world, good ethnographers still have their limits, and their analyses always are incomplete. Thus, I began to fathom the force of

---

[11] The fundamental implication of Rosaldo's position is that the accounts produced by ethnographers depend upon their positioning, that is, the vantage point from which they view and analyze society. Their positioning is, in turn, contingent on their life experiences rather than being derived from any uniform application of scientific method. The logical extension of this is that postmodern ethnographies are often highly introspective. They become tales about the ethnographer's experiences. The subject of such work is generally the ethnographer's increasing understanding of himself or herself and the people with whom he or she is living. Rather than writing conventional anthropological reports, postmodernists tend to write about the process of doing fieldwork. While Rosaldo criticizes the worst excesses of this sort of ethnography, he uses this approach himself.

[12] Anthropologists in the 1960s were very concerned with the methodology of data gathering. Ethnoscientists and cognitive anthropologists, reacting to the lack of preparation of most fieldworkers, prescribed very specific types of training and interviewing, such as controlled eliciting, to attempt to produce scientifically valid, replicable results. If, on the other hand, anthropology is about the interpretation of culture, then it is dependent on the life experiences of the anthropologist, and training can never be adequate and can never produce scientific, replicable results. Postmodernists insist on good training in language and ethnography, but they do not believe that such skills will result in a scientific anthropology.

[13] Rosaldo's argument is that interpretation changes with positioning. To understand Ilongot head-hunting, he had to experience grief and loss himself. In this paragraph and later, he describes those personal experiences. Personal revelation is very rare in traditional ethnography, but has become commonplace in recent ethnographic accounts. Traditional

what Ilongots had been telling me about their losses through my own loss, and not through any systematic preparation for field research.

My preparation for understanding serious loss began in 1970 with the death of my brother, shortly after his twenty-seventh birthday. By experiencing this ordeal with my mother and father, I gained a measure of insight into the trauma of a parent's losing a child. This insight informed my account, partially described earlier, of an Ilongot man's reactions to the death of his seventh child. At the same time, my bereavement was so much less than that of my parents that I could not then imagine the overwhelming force of rage possible in such grief. My former position is probably similar to that of many in the discipline. One should recognize that ethnographic knowledge tends to have the strengths and limitations given by the relative youth of field-workers who, for the most part, have not suffered serious losses and could have, for example, no personal knowledge of how devastating the loss of a long-term partner can be for the survivor.

In 1981 Michelle Rosaldo and I began field research among the Ifugaos of northern Luzon, Philippines. On October 11 of that year, she was walking along a trail with two Ifugao companions when she lost her footing and fell to her death some 65 feet down a sheer precipice into a swollen river below. Immediately on finding her body I became enraged. How could she abandon me? How could she have been so stupid as to fall? I tried to cry. I sobbed, but rage blocked the tears. Less than a month later I described this moment in my journal: "I felt like in a nightmare, the whole world around me expanding and contracting, visually and viscerally heaving. Going down I

find a group of men, maybe seven or eight, standing still, silent, and I heave and sob, but no tears." An earlier experience, on the fourth anniversary of my brother's death, had taught me to recognize heaving sobs without tears as a form of anger. This anger, in a number of forms, has swept over me on many occasions since then, lasting hours and even days at a time. Such feelings can be aroused by rituals, but more often they emerge from unexpected reminders (not unlike the Ilongots' unnerving encounter with their dead uncle's voice on the tape recorder).

Lest there be any misunderstanding, bereavement should not be reduced to anger, neither for myself nor for anyone else.[1] Powerful visceral emotional states swept over me, at times separately and at other times together. I experienced the deep cutting pain of sorrow almost beyond endurance, the cadaverous cold of realizing the finality of death, the trembling beginning in my abdomen and spreading through my body, the mournful keening that started without my willing, and frequent tearful sobbing. My present purpose of revising earlier understandings of Ilongot headhunting, and not a general view of bereavement, thus focuses on anger rather than on other emotions in grief.

Writings in English especially need to emphasize the rage in grief. Although grief therapists routinely encourage awareness of anger among the bereaved, upper-middle-class Anglo-American culture tends to ignore the rage devastating losses can bring.[14] Paradoxically, this culture's conventional wisdom usually denies the anger in grief at the same time that therapists encourage members of the invisible community of the bereaved to talk in detail about how angry their losses make

---

ethnography does contain occasional glimpses of the fieldworker. For example, Evans-Pritchard, in the introduction to *The Nuer* (1940), tells about his personal experience of Nuer land and his problems living there. However, the reader learns nothing of his background or family life. Here, and later, Rosaldo touches on experiences that are so personal they may make the reader uneasy (because of our own positioning, Michelle Rosaldo is a real person to us in a way that the dead Ilongot uncle described earlier is not). The difference is that Evans-Pritchard did not believe that his background had a critical bearing on his understanding of the Nuer. Rosaldo is convinced that only his personal experiences allow him to understand the Ilongot.

[14] Rosaldo's understanding is conditioned not only by his experiences but by his own culture. Here, he points to the "Anglo-American" understanding of grief. One of the principal motivations for postmodern interpretive anthropology is culture critique. For the postmodernist, anthropology allows the opportunity to reflect upon and analyze the culture of our own society as much as it allows for the analysis of the other. Here and later, in order for Rosaldo to examine and explain Ilongot practices, he must also examine and explain American practices. Anthropology then becomes a dialogue – a negotiation of interpretation between ethnographers and the cultures they purport to study.

them feel. My brother's death in combination with what I learned about anger from Ilongots (for them, an emotional state more publicly celebrated than denied) allowed me immediately to recognize the experience of rage.[m]

Ilongot anger and my own overlap, rather like two circles, partially overlaid and partially separate. They are not identical. Alongside striking similarities, significant differences in tone, cultural form, and human consequences distinguish the "anger" animating our respective ways of grieving. My vivid fantasies, for example, about a life insurance agent who refused to recognize Michelle's death as job-related did not lead me to kill him, cut off his head, and celebrate afterward. In so speaking, I am illustrating the discipline's methodological caution against the reckless attribution of one's own categories and experiences to members of another culture. Such warnings against facile notions of universal human nature can, however, be carried too far and harden into the equally pernicious doctrine that, my own group aside, everything human is alien to me. One hopes to achieve a balance between recognizing wide-ranging human differences and the modest truism that any two human groups must have certain things in common.

Only a week before completing the initial draft of an earlier version of this introduction, I rediscovered my journal entry, written some six weeks after Michelle's death, in which I made a vow to myself about how I would return to writing anthropology, if I ever did so, "by writing Grief and a Headhunter's Rage. . . ." My journal went on to reflect more broadly on death, rage, and headhunting by speaking of my "wish for the Ilongot solution; they are much more in touch with reality than Christians. So, I need a place to carry my anger—and can we say a solution of the

imagination is better than theirs? And can we condemn them when we napalm villages? Is our rationale so much sounder than theirs?" All this was written in despair and rage.[15]

Not until some fifteen months after Michelle's death was I again able to begin writing anthropology. Writing the initial version of "Grief and a Headhunter's Rage" was in fact cathartic, though perhaps not in the way one would imagine.[16] Rather than following after the completed composition, the catharsis occurred beforehand. When the initial version of this introduction was most acutely on my mind, during the month before actually beginning to write, I felt diffusely depressed and ill with a fever. Then one day an almost literal fog lifted and words began to flow. It seemed less as if I were doing the writing than that the words were writing themselves through me.

My use of personal experience serves as a vehicle for making the quality and intensity of the rage in Ilongot grief more readily accessible to readers than certain more detached modes of composition. At the same time, by invoking personal experience as an analytical category one risks easy dismissal. Unsympathetic readers could reduce this introduction to an act of mourning or a mere report on my discovery of the anger possible in bereavement. Frankly, this introduction is both and more. An act of mourning, a personal report, *and* a critical analysis of anthropological method, it simultaneously encompasses a number of distinguishable processes, no one of which cancels out the others. Similarly, I argue in what follows that ritual in general and Ilongot headhunting in particular form the intersection of multiple coexisting social processes.[17] Aside from revising the ethnographic record, the paramount claim made here concerns how my own mourning and consequent reflection on Ilongot bereavement,

---

[15] Notice the important role that empathy plays in Rosaldo's analysis. He warns against false attribution of our character traits to the other, but his essential insight into Ilongot head-hunting occurs only after he has personal experiences that allow him to identify with them in a visceral way.

[16] Postmodernists remind us that most of what anthropologists do, we do for our own purposes. Here, Rosaldo's anthropological insights come either as revelation or therapy. As he reports later, writing this essay was a cathartic act and an enormously personal one.

[17] Turner's idea of multivocality runs deeply through Rosaldo's work. Just as symbols do not necessarily have single meanings, cultural action does not have discrete, unique causes. Instead, causation is always multiple. Rosaldo's essay is no exception: it is "an act of mourning, a personal report, and an analysis of anthropological method."

rage, and headhunting raise methodological issues of general concern in anthropology and the human sciences.

DEATH IN ANTHROPOLOGY

Anthropology favors interpretations that equate analytical "depth" with cultural "elaboration."[18] Many studies focus on visibly bounded arenas where one can observe formal and repetitive events, such as ceremonies, rituals, and games. Similarly, studies of word play are more likely to focus on jokes as programmed monologues than on the less scripted, more free-wheeling improvised interchanges of witty banter. Most ethnographers prefer to study events that have definite locations in space with marked centers and outer edges. Temporally, they have middles and endings. Historically, they appear to repeat identical structures by seemingly doing things today as they were done yesterday. Their qualities of fixed definition liberate such events from the untidiness of everyday life so that they can be "read" like articles, books, or, as we now say, *texts*.

Guided by their emphasis on self-contained entities, ethnographies written in accord with classic norms consider death under the rubric of ritual rather than bereavement. Indeed, the subtitles of even recent ethnographies on death make the emphasis on ritual explicit. William Douglas's *Death in Murelaga* is subtitled *Funerary Ritual in a Spanish Basque Village;* Richard Huntington and Peter Metcalf's *Celebrations of Death* is subtitled *The Anthropology of Mortuary Ritual;* Peter Metcalf's *A Borneo Journey into Death* is subtitled *Berawan Eschatology from Its Rituals.*[n] Ritual itself is defined by its formality and routine; under

such descriptions, it more nearly resembles a recipe, a fixed program, or a book of etiquette than an open-ended human process.

Ethnographies that in this manner eliminate intense emotions not only distort their descriptions but also remove potentially key variables from their explanations. When anthropologist William Douglas, for example, announces his project in *Death in Murelaga,* he explains that his objective is to use death and funerary ritual "as a heuristic device with which to approach the study of rural Basque society."[o] In other words, the primary object of study is social structure, not death, and certainly not bereavement. The author begins his analysis by saying, "Death is not always fortuitous or unpredictable."[p] He goes on to describe how an old woman, ailing with the infirmities of her age, welcomed her death. The description largely ignores the perspective of the most bereaved survivors, and instead vacillates between those of the old woman and a detached observer.

Undeniably, certain people do live a full life and suffer so greatly in their decrepitude that they embrace the relief death can bring. Yet the problem with making an ethnography's major case study focus on "a very easy death"[q] (I use Simone de Beauvoir's title with irony, as she did) is not only its lack of representativeness but also that it makes death in general appear as routine for the survivors as this particular one apparently was for the deceased. Were the old woman's sons and daughters untouched by her death? The case study shows less about how people cope with death than about how death can be made to appear routine, thereby fitting neatly into the author's view of funerary ritual as a mechanical programmed unfolding of prescribed acts.[19] "To

---

[18] Rosaldo's analysis of anthropological interpretations of mourning is actually a general attack on traditional anthropological method. In some ways, it is an extension of the reasoning of ethnoscience. Ethnoscientists and cognitive anthropologists criticized traditional anthropologists for using their own systems of classification rather than those of the natives. Rosaldo suggests that the problem goes further: the ways that events are bounded and the way ethnography is written is, in itself, the imposition of a certain sort of reality upon ethnographic material. Events may be bounded by time, actors, physical location, and so on. To postmodernists, such boundaries are artificial, the products of specific observers or specific individuals involved. To report on an event, the ethnographer draws discrete boundaries around it. The type of boundary drawn around the event critically influences its interpretation.

[19] Rosaldo here shows an example of how the preconceptions of the investigator can exert a powerful influence over the ethnography produced. Notice that Rosaldo is not accusing Douglas of misreporting but rather of choosing a point of view within Basque society that confirms his own understanding of that society.

the Basque," says Douglas, "ritual is order and order is ritual."[r]

Douglas captures only one extreme in the range of possible deaths. Putting the accent on the routine aspects of ritual conveniently conceals the agony of such unexpected early deaths as parents losing a grown child or a mother dying in childbirth. Concealed in such descriptions are the agonies of the survivors who muddle through shifting, powerful emotional states. Although Douglas acknowledges the distinction between the bereaved members of the deceased's domestic group and the more public ritualistic group, he writes his account primarily from the viewpoint of the latter. He masks the emotional force of bereavement by reducing funerary ritual to orderly routine.[20]

Surely, human beings mourn both in ritual settings *and* in the informal settings of everyday life. Consider the evidence that willy-nilly spills over the edges in Godfrey Wilson's classic anthropological account of "conventions of burial" among the Nyakyusa of South Africa:[21]

> That some at least of those who attend a Nyakyusa burial are moved by grief it is easy to establish. I have heard people talking regretfully in ordinary conversation of a man's death; I have seen a man whose sister had just died walk over alone towards her grave and weep quietly by himself without any parade of grief; and I have heard of a man killing himself because of his grief for a dead son.[s]

Note that all the instances Wilson witnesses or hears about happen outside the circumscribed sphere of formal ritual. People converse among themselves, walk alone and silently weep, or more impulsively commit suicide. The work of grieving, probably universally, occurs both within obligatory ritual acts and in more everyday settings where people find themselves alone or with close kin.

In Nyakyusa burial ceremonies, powerful emotional states also become present in the ritual itself, which is more than a series of obligatory acts. Men say they dance the passions of their bereavement, which includes a complex mix of anger, fear, and grief:

> "This war dance (*ukukina*)," said an old man, "is mourning, we are mourning the dead man. We dance because there is war in our hearts. A passion of grief and fear exasperates us (*ilyyojo likutusila*)." . . . *Elyojo* means a passion or grief, anger or fear; *ukusila* means to annoy or exasperate beyond endurance. In explaining *ukusila* one man put it like this: "If a man continually insults me then he exasperates me (*ukusila*) so that I want to fight him." Death is a fearful and grievous event that exasperates those men nearly concerned and makes them want to fight.[t]

Descriptions of the dance and subsequent quarrels, even killings, provide ample evidence of the emotional intensity involved. The articulate testimony by Wilson's informants makes it obvious that even the most intense sentiments can be studied by ethnographers.

Despite such exceptions as Wilson, the general rule seems to be that one should tidy things up as much as possible by wiping away the tears and ignoring the tantrums. Most anthropological studies of death eliminate emotions by assuming the position of the most detached observer.[u] Such studies usually conflate the ritual process with the process of mourning, equate ritual with the obligatory, and ignore the relation between ritual and everyday life. The bias that favors formal ritual risks assuming the answers to questions

---

[20] One element of Rosaldo's critique of anthropology is a recurring theme first expressed in Boas' attack on the evolutionists. According to Rosaldo, Douglas is not producing ethnography driven by observation but using specific case examples to back his theoretical position. To some degree, this is also true of the symbolic anthropologists, with whom Rosaldo has great sympathy. Symbolic anthropologists tended to concentrate on the analysis of ceremony and other symbolically complex behavior. They saw these events as the points at which culture displays its greatest richness, therefore making interpretive analysis more productive.

[21] Godfrey Wilson (?–1944), whom Rosaldo quotes here, was the husband of Monica Wilson. The Wilsons worked together in Tanganyika (now Tanzania) and Northern Rhodesia (now Zambia) in the 1930s and 1940s. Victor Turner was a student of Monica Wilson and refers extensively to her work in essay 36 in this volume.

that most need to be asked. Do rituals, for example, always reveal cultural depth?[22]

Most analysts who equate death with funerary ritual assume that rituals store encapsulated wisdom as if it were a microcosm of its encompassing cultural macrocosm. One recent study of death and mourning, for example, confidently begins by affirming that rituals embody "the collective wisdom of many cultures."[v] Yet this generalization surely requires case-by-case investigation against a broader range of alternative hypotheses.[23]

At the polar extremes, rituals either display cultural depth or brim over with platitudes. In the former case, rituals indeed encapsulate a culture's wisdom; in the latter instance, they act as catalysts that precipitate processes whose unfolding occurs over subsequent months or even years. Many rituals, of course, do both by combining a measure of wisdom with a comparable dose of platitudes.

My own experience of bereavement and rituals fits the platitudes and catalyst model better than that of microcosmic deep culture. Even a careful analysis of the language and symbolic action during the two funerals for which I was a chief mourner would reveal precious little about the experience of bereavement.[w] This statement, of course, should not lead anyone to derive a universal from somebody else's personal knowledge. Instead, it should encourage ethnographers to ask whether a ritual's wisdom is deep or conventional, and whether its process is immediately transfor-mative or but a single step in a lengthy series of ritual and everyday events.

In attempting to grasp the cultural force of rage and other powerful emotional states, both formal ritual and the informal practices of everyday life provide crucial insight. Thus, cultural descriptions should seek out force as well as thickness, and they should extend from well-defined rituals to myriad less circumscribed practices.

GRIEF, RAGE, AND ILONGOT HEADHUNTING

When applied to Ilongot headhunting, the view of ritual as a storehouse of collective wisdom aligns headhunting with expiatory sacrifice.[24] The raiders call the spirits of the potential victims, bid their ritual farewells, and seek favorable omens along the trail. Ilongot men vividly recall the hunger and deprivation they endure over the days and even weeks it takes to move cautiously toward the place where they set up an ambush and await the first person who happens along. Once the raiders kill their victim, they toss away the head rather than keep it as a trophy. In tossing away the head, they claim by analogy to cast away their life burdens, including the rage in their grief.

Before a raid, men describe their state of being by saying that the burdens of life have made them heavy and entangled, like a tree with vines clinging to it. They say that a successfully com-

---

[22] The notion that great symbolic complexity does not necessarily indicate great meaning to the people involved is critical to Rosaldo's concept of force. If this is true, exhaustive interpretive treatments of ceremony may not aid much in understanding culture. Great cultural depth may be present in the Nyakyusa ceremonies described in this passage, but as Rosaldo notes later, despite great symbolism there was little depth in the ceremonies he attended for his brother and wife.

[23] Cultural force, though it may not be present in ritual, frequently appears where powerful emotional states such as rage, anger, fear, or love are expressed. However, traditional ethnography, modeled on scientific writing, deals only very poorly with these. The scientific trope in writing demands that reporting be dispassionate and that writers adopt an emotionally neutral stance toward their subjects. Paul Stoller (1947) contends that "vivid descriptions of the sensoria of ethnographic situations have been largely overshadowed by a dry analytic prose" (1989:8). While it may be relatively easy to describe a ritual in such prose, Stoller claims that characterizations of others as they lead their social lives are lost in this sort of writing. He argues for an anthropology that relies more on descriptions of nonvisual sensory information.

[24] In this relatively brief section of the essay, Rosaldo gives an analysis of Ilongot head-hunting that is sensitive to the issues he raises throughout the paper. Rosaldo attempts to break through the boundaries imposed by the act of analysis. For many postmodernists, anthropology is, above all, the acts of observing and writing, which necessarily impose boundaries upon events. Because of this, anthropologists tend to write about self-contained events. To escape from this type of analysis, Rosaldo proposes instead that Ilongot head-hunting results from the intersection of three more or less independent processes.

pleted raid makes them feel light of step and ruddy in complexion. The collective energy of the celebration with its song, music, and dance reportedly gives the participants a sense of well-being. The expiatory ritual process involves cleansing and catharsis.

The analysis just sketched regards ritual as a timeless, self-contained process. Without denying the insight in this approach, its limits must also be considered. Imagine, for example, exorcism rituals described as if they were complete in themselves, rather than being linked with larger processes unfolding before and after the ritual period. Through what processes does the afflicted person recover or continue to be afflicted after the ritual? What are the social consequences of recovery or its absence? Failure to consider such questions diminishes the force of such afflictions and therapies for which the formal ritual is but a phase. Still other questions apply to differently positioned subjects, including the person afflicted, the healer, and the audience. In all cases, the problem involves the delineation of processes that occur before and after, as well as during, the ritual moment.

Let us call the notion of a self-contained sphere of deep cultural activity the *microcosmic view,* and an alternative view *ritual as a busy intersection.* In the latter case, ritual appears as a place where a number of distinct social processes intersect. The crossroads simply provides a space for distinct trajectories to traverse, rather than containing them in complete encapsulated form. From this perspective, Ilongot headhunting stands at the confluence of three analytically separable processes.

The first process concerns whether or not it is an opportune time to raid. Historical conditions determine the possibilities of raiding, which range from frequent to likely to unlikely to impossible.[25] These conditions include American colonial efforts at pacification, the Great Depression, World War II, revolutionary movements in the surrounding lowlands, feuding among Ilongot groups, and the declaration of martial law in 1972. Ilongots use the analogy of hunting to speak of such historical vicissitudes. Much as Ilongot huntsmen say they cannot know when game will cross their path or whether their arrows will strike the target, so certain historical forces that condition their existence remain beyond their control. My book *Ilongot Headhunting, 1883–1974* explores the impact of historical factors on Ilongot headhunting.

Second, young men coming of age undergo a protracted period of personal turmoil during which they desire nothing so much as to take a head. During this troubled period, they seek a life partner and contemplate the traumatic dislocation of leaving their families of origin and entering their new wife's household as a stranger. Young men weep, sing, and burst out in anger because of their fierce desire to take a head and wear the coveted red hornbill earrings that adorn the ears of men who already have, as Ilongots say, arrived (*tabi*). Volatile, envious, passionate (at least according to their own cultural stereotype of the young unmarried man [*buintaw*]), they constantly lust to take a head. Michelle and I began fieldwork among the Ilongots only a year after abandoning our unmarried youths; hence our ready empathy with youthful turbulence. Her book on Ilongot notions of self explores the passionate anger of young men as they come of age.

Third, older men are differently positioned than their younger counterparts. Because they have already beheaded somebody, they can wear the red hornbill earrings so coveted by youths. Their desire to headhunt grows less from chronic adolescent turmoil than from more intermittent acute agonies of loss. After the death of somebody to whom they are closely attached, older men

---

[25] The idea of positioning is again crucial. Rosaldo has spoken earlier of the positioning of the anthropologist; here the positioning of the Ilongot becomes the main object of analysis. Rosaldo does not see Ilongot society as timeless, harmonious, and undifferentiated (as Durkheim, for example, might) but as fixed in historical time and composed of diverse individuals and groups with different interests. Head-hunting happens when historical circumstances make it possible and when the emotional states of young and old men coincide.

often inflict on themselves vows of abstinence, not to be lifted until the day they participate in a successful headhunting raid. These deaths can cover a range of instances from literal death, whether through natural causes or beheading, to social death where, for example, a man's wife runs off with another man. In all cases, the rage born of devastating loss animates the older men's desire to raid. This anger at abandonment is irreducible in that nothing at a deeper level explains it. Although certain analysts argue against the dreaded last analysis, the linkage of grief, rage, and headhunting has no other known explanation.[26]

My earlier understandings of Ilongot headhunting missed the fuller significance of how older men experience loss and rage. Older men prove critical in this context because they, not the youths, set the processes of headhunting in motion. Their rage is intermittent, whereas that of youths is continuous. In the equation of headhunting, older men are the variable and younger men are the constant. Culturally speaking, older men are endowed with knowledge and stamina that their juniors have not yet attained, hence they care for (*saysay*) and lead (*bukur*) the younger men when they raid.

In a preliminary survey of the literature on headhunting, I found that the lifting of mourning prohibitions frequently occurs after taking a head. The notion that youthful anger and older men's rage lead them to take heads is more plausible than such commonly reported "explanations" of headhunting as the need to acquire mystical "soul stuff" or personal names.[x] Because the discipline correctly rejects stereotypes of the "bloodthirsty savage," it must investigate how headhunters create an intense desire to decapitate their fellow humans. The human sciences must explore the cultural force of emotions with a view to delineating the passions that animate certain forms of human conduct.

SUMMARY

The ethnographer, as a positioned subject, grasps certain human phenomena better than others. He or she occupies a position or structural location and observes with a particular angle of vision. Consider, for example, how age, gender, being an outsider, and association with a neocolonial regime influence what the ethnographer learns.[27] The notion of position also refers to how life experiences both enable and inhibit particular kinds of insight. In the case at hand, nothing in my own experience equipped me even to imagine the anger possible in bereavement until after Michelle Rosaldo's death in 1981. Only then was I in a position to grasp the force of what Ilongots had repeatedly told me about grief, rage, and headhunting. By the same token, so-called natives are also positioned subjects who have a distinctive mix of insight and blindness. Consider the structural positions of older versus younger Ilongot men, or the differing positions of chief mourners versus those less involved during a funeral. My discussion of anthropological writings on death often achieved its effects simply by shifting from the position of those least involved to that of the chief mourners.

Cultural depth does not always equal cultural elaboration. Think simply of the speaker who is filibustering. The language used can sound elaborate as it heaps word on word, but surely it is not deep. Depth should be separated from the presence or absence of elaboration. By the same token, one-line explanations can be vacuous or pithy. The concept of force calls attention to an enduring intensity in human conduct that can

---

[26] In analyzing the head-hunting of the older men, Rosaldo applies his notion of force. He insists that there is no meaningful way to analyze Ilongot rage other than to record it. His insistence that there can be no other explanation of the linkage of grief, rage, and head-hunting is extremely provocative. Many anthropologists find it difficult to accept.

[27] Postmodern anthropology collapses many of the distinctions upon which more traditional anthropology is based. There is no longer an observer and an observed. Instead there are individuals prepared to know certain things and not others. These are both anthropologists and members of the cultures the anthropologists are analyzing. Accepting Rosaldo's critique renders the distinction between emic and etic meaningless.

occur with or without the dense elaboration conventionally associated with cultural depth. Although relatively without elaboration in speech, song, or ritual, the rage of older Ilongot men who have suffered devastating losses proves enormously consequential in that, foremost among other things, it leads them to behead their fellow humans. Thus, the notion of force involves both affective intensity and significant consequences that unfold over a long period of time.

Similarly, rituals do not always encapsulate deep cultural wisdom. At times they instead contain the wisdom of Polonius.[28] Although certain rituals both reflect and create ultimate values, others simply bring people together and deliver a set of platitudes that enable them to go on with their lives. Rituals serve as vehicles for processes that occur both before and after the period of their performance. Funeral rituals, for example, do not "contain" all the complex processes of bereavement. Ritual and bereavement should not be collapsed into one another because they neither fully encapsulate nor fully explain one another. Instead, rituals are often but points along a number of longer processual trajectories; hence, my image of ritual as a crossroads where distinct life processes intersect.[y]

The notion of ritual as a busy intersection anticipates the critical assessment of the concept of culture developed in the following chapters. In contrast with the classic view, which posits culture as a self-contained whole made up of coherent patterns, culture can arguably be conceived as a more porous array of intersections where distinct processes crisscross from within and beyond its borders. Such heterogeneous processes often derive from differences of age, gender, class, race, and sexual orientation.

This book argues that a sea change in cultural studies has eroded once-dominant conceptions of truth and objectivity. The truth of objectivism—absolute, universal, and timeless—has lost its monopoly status. It now competes, on more nearly equal terms, with the truths of case studies that are embedded in local contexts, shaped by local interests, and colored by local perceptions. The agenda for social analysis has shifted to include not only eternal verities and lawlike generalizations but also political processes, social changes, and human differences. Such terms as *objectivity, neutrality,* and *impartiality* refer to subject positions once endowed with great institutional authority, but they are arguably neither more nor less valid than those of more engaged, yet equally perceptive, knowledgeable social actors. Social analysis must now grapple with the realization that its objects of analysis are also analyzing subjects who critically interrogate ethnographers—their writings, their ethics, and their politics.[29]

Notes

An earlier version of this chapter appeared as "Grief and a Headhunter's Rage: On the Cultural Force of Emotions," in *Text, Play, and Story: The Construction and Reconstruction of Self and Society,* ed. Edward M. Bruner (Washington, D.C.: American Ethnological Society, 1984), pp. 178–95.

a. In contrasting Moroccan and Javanese forms of mysticism, Clifford Geertz found it necessary to distinguish the "force" of cultural patterning from its "scope" (Clifford Geertz, *Islam Observed* [New Haven, Conn: Yale University Press, 1968]). He distinguished force from scope in this manner: "By 'force' I mean the thoroughness with which such a pattern is internalized in the personalities of the individuals who adopt it, its centrality or marginality

---

[28] Polonius, a character in *Hamlet,* is minister to the king and Ophelia's father. Although he is the king's advisor, he dispenses greeting-card wisdom.

[29] In closing his essay, Rosaldo makes several important points. He refers to the fact that in a world where education in Western languages is increasingly widespread, people who were traditionally the subjects of ethnography are increasingly reading it, and sometimes writing their own. A traditional anthropologist such as Evans-Pritchard did not have to worry about how the Nuer were going to react to his description of them. Current anthropologists write with the knowledge that some of their informants will read and critique their work. This has changed the nature of anthropology.

More controversially, Rosaldo asserts that the interpretations of anthropologists must be judged as neither more nor less valid than those of other astute observers. By extension, this implies that anthropological training confers no particular authority. If this is the case, what should be the role of the "human sciences," among which Rosaldo has included anthropology?

in their lives" (p. 111). "By 'scope,' on the other hand, I mean the range of social contexts within which religious considerations are regarded as having more or less direct relevance" (p. 112). In his later works, Geertz developed the notion of scope more than that of force. Unlike Geertz, who emphasizes processes of internalization within individual personalities, my use of the term force stresses the concept of the positioned subject.

b. Anthropologists have long studied the vocabulary of the emotions in other cultures (see, e.g., Hildred Geertz, "The Vocabulary of Emotion: A Study of Javanese Socialization Processes," *Psychiatry* 22 [1959]: 225–37). For a recent review essay on anthropological writings on emotions, see Catherine Lutz and Geoffrey M. White, "The Anthropology of Emotions," *Annual Review of Anthropology* 15 (1986): 405–36.

c. The two ethnographies on the Ilongots are Michelle Rosaldo, *Knowledge and Passion: Ilongot Notions of Self and Social Life* (New York: Cambridge University Press, 1980), and Renato Rosaldo, *Ilongot Headhunting, 1883–1974: A Study in Society and History* (Stanford, Calif: Stanford University Press, 1980). Our field research among the Ilongots was financed by a National Science Foundation predoctoral fellowship, National Science Foundation Research Grants GS–1509 and GS–40788, and a Mellon Award for junior faculty from Stanford University. A Fulbright Grant financed a two-month stay in the Philippines during 1981.

d. Lest the hypothesis Insan rejected appear utterly implausible, one should mention that at least one group does link a version of exchange theory to headhunting. Peter Metcalf reports that, among the Berawan of Borneo, "Death has a chain reaction quality to it. There is a considerable anxiety that, unless something is done to break the chain, death will follow upon death. The logic of this is now plain: The unquiet soul kills, and so creates more unquiet souls" (Peter Metcalf, *A Borneo Journey into Death: Berawan Eschatology from Its Rituals* [Philadelphia: University of Pennsylvania Press, 1982], p. 127).

e. R. Rosaldo, *Ilongot Headhunting, 1883–1974,* p. 286.

f. Ibid., p. 288.

g. M. Rosaldo, *Knowledge and Passion,* p. 33.

h. See A. R. Radcliffe-Brown, *Structure and Function in Primitive Society* (London: Cohen and West, Ltd., 1952), pp. 133–52. For a broader debate on the "functions" of ritual, see the essays by Bronislaw Malinowski, A. R. Radcliffe-Brown, and George C. Homans, in *Reader in Comparative Religion: An Anthropological Approach* (4th ed.), ed. William A. Lessa and Evon Z. Vogt (New York: Harper and Row, 1979), pp. 37–62.

i. Max Weber, *The Protestant Ethic and the Spirit of Capitalism* (New York: Charles Scribner's Sons, 1958).

j. A key antecedent to what I have called the "positioned subject" is Alfred Schutz, *Collected Papers,* vol. 1, *The Problem of Social Reality,* ed. and intro. Maurice Natanson (The Hague: Martinus Nijhoff, 1971). See also, e.g., Aaron Cicourel, *Method and Measurement in Sociology* (Glencoe, Ill.: The Free Press, 1964) and Gerald Berreman, *Behind Many Masks: Ethnography and Impression Management in a Himalayan Village,* Monograph No. 4 (Ithaca, N.Y.: Society for Applied Anthropology, 1962). For an early anthropological article on how differently positioned subjects interpret the "same" culture in different ways, see John W. Bennett, "The Interpretation of Pueblo Culture," *Southwestern Journal of Anthropology* 2 (1946): 361–74.

k. Clifford Geertz, *The Interpretation of Cultures* (New York: Basic Books, 1974) and *Local Knowledge: Further Essays in Interpretive Anthropology* (New York: Basic Books, 1983).

l. Although anger appears so often in bereavement as to be virtually universal, certain notable exceptions do occur. Clifford Geertz, for example, depicts Javanese funerals as follows: "The mood of a Javanese funeral is not one of hysterical bereavement, unrestrained sobbing, or even of formalized cries of grief for the deceased's departure. Rather, it is a calm, undemonstrative, almost languid letting go, a brief ritualized relinquishment of a relationship no longer possible" (Geertz, *The Interpretation of Cultures,* p. 153). In cross-cultural perspective, the anger in grief presents itself in different degrees (including zero), in different forms, and with different consequences.

m. The Ilongot notion of anger (*liget*) is regarded as dangerous in its violent excesses, but also as life-enhancing in that, for example, it provides energy for work. See the extensive discussion in M. Rosaldo, *Knowledge and Passion.*

n. William Douglas, *Death in Murelaga: Funerary Ritual in a Spanish Basque Village* (Seattle: University of Washington Press, 1969); Richard Huntington and Peter Metcalf, *Celebrations of Death: The Anthropology of Mortuary Ritual* (New York: Cambridge University Press, 1979); Metcalf, *A Borneo Journey into Death.*

o. Douglas, *Death in Murelaga,* p. 209.

p. Ibid., p. 19.

q. Simone de Beauvoir, *A Very Easy Death* (Harmondsworth, United Kingdom: Penguin Books, 1969).

r. Douglas, *Death in Murelaga,* p. 75.

s. Godfrey Wilson, *Nyakyusa Conventions of Burial* (Johannesburg: The University of Witwatersrand Press, 1939), pp. 22–23. (Reprinted from Bantu Studies.)

t. Ibid., p. 13.

u. In his survey of works on death published during the 1960s, for example, Johannes Fabian found that the four major anthropological journals carried only nine papers on the topic, most of which "dealt only with the purely ceremonial aspects of death" (Johannes Fabian, "How Others Die: Reflections on the Anthropology of Death," in *Death in American Experience,* ed. A. Mack [New York: Schocken, 1973], p. 178).

v. Huntington and Metcalf, *Celebrations of Death,* p. 1.

w. Arguably, ritual works differently for those most afflicted by a particular death than for those least so. Funerals may distance the former from overwhelm-ing emotions whereas they may draw the latter closer to strongly felt sentiments (see T. J. Scheff, *Catharsis in Healing, Ritual, and Drama* [Berkeley: University of California Press, 1979]). Such issues can be investigated through the notion of the positioned subject.

x. For a discussion of cultural motives for headhunting, see Robert McKinley, "Human and Proud of It! A Structural Treatment of Headhunting Rites and the Social Definition of Enemies," in *Studies in Borneo Societies: Social Process and Anthropological Explanation,* ed. G. Appell (DeKalb, Ill.: Center for Southeast Asian Studies, Northern Illinois University, 1976), pp. 92–126; Rodney Needham, "Skulls and Causality," *Man* 11 (1976): 71–88; Michelle Rosaldo, "Skulls and Causality," *Man* 12 (1977): 168–70.

y. Pierre Bourdieu, *Outline of a Theory of Practice* (New York: Cambridge University Press, 1977), p. 1.

39. Hermes' Dilemma: The Masking of Subversion in Ethnographic Description

Vincent Crapanzano (1939–)

"ALL TRANSLATION," WALTER BENJAMIN (1969: 75) wrote, "is only a somewhat provisional way of coming to terms with the foreignness of languages." Like translation, ethnography is also a somewhat provisional way of coming to terms with the foreignness of languages—of cultures and societies. The ethnographer does not, however, translate texts the way the translator does. He must first produce them. Text metaphors for

(1986)

culture and society notwithstanding, the ethnographer has no primary and independent text that can be read and translated by others. No text survives him other than his own. Despite its frequent ahistorical—its synchronic—pretense, ethnography is historically determined by the moment of the ethnographer's encounter with whomever he is studying.[1]

The ethnographer is a little like Hermes: a messenger who, given methodologies for uncovering the masked, the latent, the unconscious, may

---

[1] Walter Benjamin (1892–1940) was a leading German literary and art critic whose work first appeared in English translation in the 1960s and 1970s along with that of other major European postmodern thinkers.

Crapanzano's opening paragraph immediately identifies this work as a postmodern analysis. Clifford Geertz viewed culture as a text read by anthropologists. But as Crapanzano points out, when we read Geertz's account of cockfighting in Bali we are not looking at Balinese culture, we are reading Geertz's written interpretation of the cockfight. Crapanzano begins this way to set us up for the type of analysis he is about to present: an investigation of the literary devices used in the writing of three ethnographic texts, including Geertz's essay. One of the key insights of the postmodern perspective is that anthropological texts, despite their claims to objectivity, are influenced by the political and social contexts within which they are written.

even obtain his message through stealth. He presents languages, cultures, and societies in all their opacity, their foreignness, their meaninglessness; then like the magician, the hermeneut, Hermes himself, he clarifies the opaque, renders the foreign familiar, and gives meaning to the meaningless. He decodes the message. He interprets.[2]

The ethnographer conventionally acknowledges the provisional nature of his interpretations. Yet he assumes a final interpretation—a definitive reading. "I have finally cracked the Kariera section system," we hear him say. "I finally got to the root of all their fuss about the *mudyi* tree." He resents the literary critic's assertion that there is never a final reading. He simply has not got to it yet.

The ethnographer does not recognize the provisional nature of his presentations. They are definitive. He does not accept as a paradox that his "provisional interpretations" support his "definitive presentations." (It is perhaps for this reason that he insists on a final reading.) Embedded in interpretation, his presentations limit reinterpretation. Ethnography closes in on itself. It is even possible that the more general theories the ethnologist generates from ethnography are only refractions, distorted repetitions in another register, of the provisional interpretations that support the presentation of data. The possibility must be entertained. Hermes was the tutelary god of speech and writing, and speech and writing, we know, are themselves interpretations.[3]

Hermes, etymologically "he of the stone heap," was associated with boundary stones (Nilsson 1949; Brown 1969). The herm, a head and a phallus on a pillar, later replaced the stone heap. The ethnographer, if I may continue my conceit, also marks a boundary: his ethnography declares the limits of his and his readers' culture. It also attests to his—and his culture's—interpretive power. Hermes was a phallic god and a god of fertility. Interpretation has been understood as a phallic, a phallic-aggressive, a cruel and violent, a destructive act, and as a fertile, a fertilizing, a fruitful, and a creative one. We say a text, a culture even, is pregnant with meaning. Do the ethnographer's presentations become pregnant with meaning because of his interpretive, his phallic fertilizations? (I have insisted here on using the masculine pronoun to refer to the ethnographer, despite his or her sexual identity, for I am writing of a stance and not of the person.)[4]

The ethnographer is caught in a second paradox. He has to make sense of the foreign. Like Benjamin's translator, he aims at a solution to the problem of foreignness, and like the translator (a point missed by Benjamin) he must also communicate the very foreignness that his interpreta-

---

[2] Although postmodern, Crapanzano's essay is very different from Renato Rosaldo's essay (essay 38) on Ilongot head-hunting. Two strands of postmodern analysis are reflexivity and deconstruction. Rosaldo's essay is reflexive, that is, personal in style; he wrote a great deal about the process through which he arrived at an understanding of Ilongot head-hunting. Crapanzano's essay, on the other hand, focuses on deconstruction. He takes apart and examines the rhetorical devices that other authors used in constructing their ethnographic accounts. By using this procedure, Crapanzano proposes to tell us something about the background thoughts and motives of the authors. With this knowledge, we can look at the texts with a different, more critical, perspective. Because of the tropes assumed in the act of writing ethnography, Crapanzano implies that ethnographers, like Hermes, may unconsciously transmit messages through stealth.

[3] Crapanzano here reminds us of the postmodern contention that all ethnographic work is interpretation. Because interpretations are formed in certain specific times and contexts, which are constantly changing, all interpretations are necessarily provisional. With his reference to the *mudyi* tree earlier, Crapanzano is criticizing the work of well-known anthropologists, such as Victor Turner, who claim to make definitive interpretations of cultural phenomena. Postmodernists insist there is no definitive understanding of a culture, just various readings set in certain personal, social, and temporal contexts.

[4] Crapanzano's previous work was built on psychological interpretations of ethnographic data, and you will see a psychological influence in much of what he writes here. This is an important paragraph for Crapanzano, demonstrating one of the fundamental principles he argues—the power of an author's voice to control a text. The use of Hermes, the phallic associations, and the masculine pronoun are not sexist in intent. Rather they demonstrate his power, as the author, to control the discourse and interpretation presented in a text.

tions (the translator's translations) deny, at least in their claim to universality. He must render the foreign familiar and preserve its very foreignness at one and the same time. The translator accomplishes this through style, the ethnographer through the coupling of a presentation that asserts the foreign and an interpretation that makes it all familiar.

Hermes was a trickster: a god of cunning and tricks. The ethnographer is no trickster. He, so he says, has no cunning and no tricks. But he shares a problem with Hermes. *He must make his message convincing.* It treats of the foreign, the strange, the unfamiliar, the exotic, the unknown — that, in short, which challenges belief. The ethnographer must make use of all the persuasive devices at his disposal to convince his readers of *the* truth of his message, but, as though these rhetorical strategies were cunning tricks, he gives them scant recognition. His texts assume a truth that speaks for itself — a whole truth that needs no rhetorical support. His words are transparent. He does not share Hermes' confidence. When Hermes took the post of messenger of the gods, he promised Zeus not to lie. He did not promise to tell the whole truth. Zeus understood. The ethnographer has not.[5]

In this paper I shall present a reading of three ethnographic texts, only one of which was written by an anthropologist, to look at some of the ways the ethnographer tries to make his message convincing. They are George Catlin's (1841; 1867) account of the Mandan Indians' O-Kee-Pa ceremony, Johann Wolfgang von Goethe's (1976a; 1982) description of the Roman carnival in his *Italienische Reise* of 1789, and Clifford Geertz's (1973) study of the Balinese cockfight. The events described in the three texts are explosive, teasing if not the performers' then the authors' assumptions of meaning and order. The authors are challenged, and all make use of many different rhetorical strategies for convincing the reader, and presumably themselves, of the accuracy of their descriptions (see Marcus 1980).

Foremost among these strategies is the constitution of the ethnographer's authority: his presence at the events described, his perceptual ability, his "disinterested" perspective, his objectivity, and his sincerity (see Clifford 1983a). In all three cases, the ethnographer's place in his text is purely rhetorical. It is deictically, or better perhaps pseudo-deictically, constructed.[6] It is impossible to fix his vantage point. His is a roving perspective, necessitated by his "totalistic" presentation of the events he is describing. His presence does not alter the way things happen or, for that matter, the way they are observed or interpreted. He assumes an invisibility that, unlike Hermes, a god, he cannot, of course, have. His "disinterest," his objectivity, his neutrality are in fact undercut by his self-interest — his need to constitute his authority, to establish a bond with his readers, or, more accurately, his interlocutors, and to create an appropriate distance between himself and the "foreign" events he witnesses.

Aside from the devices the ethnographer uses to constitute his authority, he uses others to establish the validity of his ethnographic presentations directly. I single out three of these, which are used to various extents and with variable success by Catlin, Goethe, and Geertz. In Catlin it is

---

[5] Crapanzano is concerned with the rhetorical devices ethnographers use to convince the audience that what they write is true: what postmodernists call the "authority of the text." Crapanzano claims this authority is provided by the use of rhetorical devices contained in the ethnographer's writing style. Note that Crapanzano's analysis is completely divorced from field data. For postmodernists, the data for analysis is the ethnography itself. Many believe the reality that ethnographic texts attempt to analyze is ultimately beyond objective description.

[6] Crapanzano's first criticism of these texts is their lack of reflexivity. He says the authors' presence in the texts is only "pseudo-deictic," in that the accounts only pretend to identify their temporal, spatial location. The writers present a total description of cultures or events in ways which were impossible for them to have personally experienced. They act as if they were invisible and their presence did not influence the surroundings. Crapanzano says that the claim to objectivity is undercut by their need to convince the readers of their authority. It is this need to construct scientific authority that inhibits the reflexivity for which postmodern ethnographers strive.

a hypotyposis[7] that predominates. In Goethe it is an external (nonmetaphorical) theatrical narrativity. Geertz depends primarily on interpretive virtuosity. In all three cases, as we shall see, the very figures the authors use to convince their readers — and themselves — of their descriptions in fact render them suspect, and in all three cases this failure to convince is covered by an institutionally legitimated concern for "meaning." Catlin and Goethe give the ceremonies they describe an allegorical (moral) significance. Geertz claims a phenomenological-hermeneutical perspective on meaning that is, at least rhetorically, insufficient. His essay becomes exemplary, and the cockfight itself takes on not only metaphorical but methodological significance. The O-Kee-Pa, the carnival, and the cockfight all become figures of disorder — of arbitrary violence, unruliness, and meaninglessness — in a transcending story in which precisely this disorder, this violence, unruliness, and meaninglessness are overcome. The ceremonies are shown to have, if not order and meaning, then at least significance. But, ironically, as figures that mask an initial rhetorical subversion — a failure to convince — the descriptions are again subverted. The O-Kee-Pa, the Roman carnival, and the Balinese cockfight become the "O-Kee-Pa," the "Roman carnival," and the "Balinese cockfight."[8]

> With this very honourable degree which had just been conferred upon me, I was standing in front of the medicine-lodge early in the morning, with my companions by my side, endeavouring to get a peep, if possible, into its sacred interior; when the *master of ceremonies,* guarding and conducting its secrets, as I before described, came out of the door and taking me with a firm *professional* affection by the arm, led me into this *sanctum sanctorum,* which was strictly guarded from, even a peep or a gaze from the vulgar, by a vestibule of eight or ten feet in length, guarded with a double screen or door, and two or three dark and frowning centinels with spears or war clubs in their hands. I gave the wink to my companions as I was passing in, and the potency of my *medicine* was such as to gain them quiet admission, and all of us were comfortably placed on elevated seats, which our conductor soon prepared for us.

With these words, George Catlin (1841: 161–62), the romantic-realist painter of the American Indians, describes his entrance into a medicine lodge in which he was to witness what is surely one of the most sanguinary rites in the annals of ethnography, the Mandan O-Kee-Pa — "an ordeal of privation and torture" in which young Mandan men, "emaciated with fasting, and thirsting, and waking, for nearly four days and nights," were hung by rawhide passed through the skewered flesh of their shoulders and breasts from the lodge's roof until they were "lifeless." The O-Kee-Pa was celebrated annually, according to Catlin, to commemorate the subsiding of a great flood that the Mandan believed once covered the world, to ensure the coming of the buffalo, and to initiate the young men of the tribe into manhood through an ordeal "which, while it is supposed to harden their muscles and prepare them for extreme endurance, enables the chiefs who are spectators to the scene to decide upon their comparative bodily strength and ability to endure the extreme privations and sufferings that often fall to the lots of Indian warriors" (1841: 157).[9]

---

[7] *Hypotyposis:* the lifelike description of a thing or scene. Terms such as deictic and hypotyposis come from literary criticism rather than anthropology, and their use points to the debt that postmodernism owes to the study of literature.

[8] Crapanzano believes that all three authors' accounts fail to be convincing because of the rhetorical devices they use to justify their authority. He also claims that this failure is covered up by the authors' attempts to interpret the meaning of the events they describe. Catlin attributes moral significance to the O-Kee-Pa rite, while Geertz finds Western-style dramatic meaning in the Balinese cockfight. In both cases, physical events become literary works. Crapanzano uses a classic deconstructionist technique in his analysis. A basic deconstructionist assumption is that all texts contain gaps, alternative voices, and suppressed meanings. According to this point of view, understanding is furthered by giving these suppressed perspectives their voice.

[9] O-Kee-Pa, the Sun Dance, and other Native American spiritual traditions have, to some degree, become popular icons. The Hollywood version of Catlin's description of the O-Kee-Pa can be found in the movie *A Man Called Horse.*

It was the summer of 1832—six years before the Mandan were decimated by an epidemic of smallpox. Catlin had spent several weeks with them. He found that "they are a people of decidedly a different origin from that of any other tribe in these regions," and later he argued that they were descendents of Welsh sailors who under the direction of Prince Madoc had set sail in the fourteenth century (actually in the twelfth century) and were thought to have settled somewhere in North America (Catlin 1867; Ewers 1967). The day before his admission to the medicine lodge, Catlin painted the master of ceremonies and so pleased was this great magician with his portrait—"he could see its eyes move"—that he and the other "doctors" unanimously elevated Catlin to a "respectable rank in the craft" of magic and mysteries and gave him the name "White Medicine Painter." It was this honor that allowed him to enter the lodge, and it was his reputed medicine that enabled his companions—J. Kipp, an agent of the American fur trade who had long been familiar with the Mandan and spoke their language; L. Crawford, Kipp's clerk; and Abraham Bogard, whose identity I have not been able to determine—to accompany him. They were apparently the first white men to witness the O-Kee-Pa, and Catlin was the first to describe it: on January 10, 1833 (though written on August 12, 1832), in the *New-York Commercial Advertiser*; then in 1841 in his *Manners, Customs, and Conditions of the North American Indians*; and, finally, in 1867 in a little book (with a *Folium Reservatum* for scholars) entirely devoted to the ceremony.[10]

Catlin asserts melodramatically that he shudders and even shrinks from the task of reciting what he has seen. "I entered the *medicine-house* of these scenes," he writes as I would have entered a church, and expected to see something extraordinary and strange, but yet in the form of worship or devotion, but, alas! little did I expect to see the interior of their holy temple turned into a *slaughterhouse*, and its floor strewed with the blood of its fanatic devotees. Little did I think that I was entering a house of God, where His blinded worshippers were to pollute its sacred interior with their blood, and propitiatory suffering and tortures—surpassing, if possible, the cruelty of the rack or the inquisition; but such the scene has been, and as such I will endeavour to describe it" (1841: 156).[11]

Despite all of Catlin's shuddering and shrinking, he and his companions managed to watch the spectacle from the seats they were assigned. "We were then in full view of everything that transpired in the lodge, having before us the scene exactly, which is represented in the first of the four pictures [that Catlin painted of the ceremony and that illustrated his second and third accounts]. To this seat we returned every morning until sundown for four days, the whole time which these strange scenes occupied" (1841: 162). They were not even permitted to move from their assigned places. Once when Catlin got up to take a closer look at what he calls the central mystery of the rite—"the *sanctissimus sanctorum*, from which seemed to emanate all the sanctity of their proceedings"—he was sent back to his seat.

I started several times from my seat to approach it, but all eyes were instantly upon me, and every mouth in the assembly sent forth a hush—sh—! which brought me back to my seat again; and I at length quieted my stifled curiosity as well as I could, upon learning the fact, that so sacred was that object, and so important its secrets or mysteries, that not *I*

---

[10]Just as Crapanzano deconstructs Catlin, Crapanzano's work too can be deconstructed. He mentions smallpox among the Mandan and Catlin's theory that the Mandan were descended from fourteenth-century Welsh sailors, but these two pieces of information are not developed further in this essay. What do you think are Crapanzano's motives for mentioning them? Could he be trying to make Catlin appear ridiculous and the Mandan tragic? The *Folium Reservatum* mentioned at the end of the paragraph was a collection of graphic drawings and a description of the more prurient aspects of the ceremony. Does the fact that Catlin thought the Mandan were Welsh and made drawings of them that Victorians thought obscene mean his description of the O-Kee-Pa is not accurate?

[11] While trying to show how Catlin constituted his authority in his description of the O-Kee-Pa, Crapanzano uses satire to discredit Catlin. For example, in the next paragraph, he capitalizes on the fact that Catlin is a nineteenth-century writer whose language sounds stilted to late twentieth-century ears.

alone, but even the young men, who were passing the ordeal, and all the village, save the conductor of the mysteries, were stopped from approaching it, or knowing what it was. (1841: 162)

Like an artist standing before his easel, Catlin's vantage point is fixed. So at least he asserts. *And yet,* he is in fact no objectivist, no Robbe-Grillet, describing the ceremony laboriously, metonymous step by metonymous step,[12] from the fixed position of his consciousness. His vision is larger, constructed, exaggerated, uneven—metaphorical. His eye constantly betrays itself. He describes the arrival of the evil one, O-kee-hee-de.

> But alas! in the last of these dances, on the fourth day, in the midst of all their mirth and joy, and about noon, and in the height of all these exultations, an instant scream burst forth from the tops of the lodges!—men, women, dogs and all, seemed actually to howl and shudder with alarm, as they fixed their glaring eyeballs upon the prairie bluff, about a mile in the west, down the side of which a man was seen descending at full speed toward the village. This strange character darted about in a zig-zag course in all directions on the prairie like a boy in pursuit of a butterfly, until he approached the piquets of the village, when it was discovered that his body was entirely naked, and painted as black as a negro, with pounded charcoal and bear's grease. . . . (1841: 166)

Catlin rambles, repeats, generalizes, simplifies, exaggerates, and embellishes. He refers indiscriminately to what he has seen before or learned afterward. Amidst a purportedly realistic description, masked here as elsewhere in *Manners, Customs, and Conditions* by measurement ("about a

mile in the west," "a vestibule of eight or ten feet"), are metaphorical turns of phrase, similes in the above example ("like a boy in pursuit of a butterfly," "painted as black as a negro") that seem as inappropriate to the event he describes as the colors—Baudelaire (1846) called them terrifying, mysterious—of his Indian paintings.[a] They ring true neither to his presumed experience of the event nor to that of the Mandan participants. The two experiences are stylistically blurred—sacrificed ultimately to the experience Catlin wishes to engender in his readers. This pathopoetic sacrifice of the participant's subjectivity to that of his readers occurs even when Catlin claims to take the participant's point of view. He describes, for example, one of the hanging victims of torture, a condensation apparently of several.

> Surrounded by imps and demons as they appear, a dozen or more, who seem to be concerting and devising means for his exquisite agony, gather around him, when one of the number advances toward him in a sneering manner, and commences turning him around with a pole which he brings in his hand for the purpose. This is done in a gentle manner at first; but gradually increased, when the brave fellow, whose proud spirit can control its anger no longer, burst out in the most lamentable and heart rendering cries that the human voice is capable of producing, crying forth a prayer to the Great Spirit to support and protect him in this dreadful trial; and continually repeating his confidence in his protection. In this condition he is continued to be turned, faster and faster—and there is no hope of escape from it, nor chance for the slightest relief, until by fainting, his voice falters, and his struggling ceases, and he hangs, apparently, a still and lifeless corpse! (1841: 171)[13]

---

[12] *Metonymy:* a figure of speech in which an idea is evoked by referring to an associated term, such as the use of "to put to the sword" to refer to execution.

    The French author and filmmaker Alain Robbe-Grillet (1922–) is a powerful spokesperson for objectivism. Objectivism in art and poetry insists on the primacy of visual information. Things, and sometimes actions, exist in and of themselves, stripped of context.

[13] Crapanzano points out that one of the devices Catlin uses to establish his authority is to take the participant's point of view. It is a dramatic literary device, but in reality, Catlin could not have known the thoughts or feelings of the men hanging from the roof of the lodge. On the other hand, Catlin's description tells us little more than pain hurts, which is not too radical an assumption. What is the basis for Crapanzano's judgment that Catlin's work is not accurate? Was Crapanzano there? Is Crapanzano guilty of the same mistake when he tries to read Catlin's psychological motives?

Here Catlin moves from his (objectifying) metaphorical perspective to that of the tortured; despite this move, his intention is not phenomenological, but rhetorical: He does not describe either the Indian's or his own experience of the torture. The "imps and demons as they appear" (to whom? to Catlin? to the Mandan?) is stylistically equivalent to "there is no hope of escape from it." They are directed to the reader and it is the reader's reaction that will guarantee Catlin's perceptions.

In these passages and throughout his *Manners, Customs, and Conditions of the North American Indians*, Catlin's principal stylistic figure is hypotyposis. His aim is to impress his experience of what he has *seen* so strongly, so vividly, on his readers that they cannot doubt its veracity. It is the visual that gives authority. The realistic tradition, Alexander Gelley (1979: 420) observes, "sought to reenforce the description of things and places by making the object of the description coincide with the object of a specular act, image, or process." Catlin's assertion of a fixed vantage point, of an assigned seat—there are similar assertions elsewhere in *Manners, Customs, and Conditions*—must be understood rhetorically. It attests deictically to his presence. It gives him the authority of the painter before his easel. It enables him to lead his readers into the visualized scene and to convince them (and himself) of its truth.[b]

Catlin's vision is not, however, secure. Unlike today's social scientists whose theories (regardless of their merit) serve their ethnographic credibility, Catlin's credibility has ultimately to rest on the power of his descriptions. Just as his painting is not particularly believable, nor is his prose. It undermines itself. His intention is realistic, but his style is romantic. Through metaphor, often extravagant metaphor, ecphonesis, the promiscuous use of the vocative, hyperbole, pathopoeia, apoplanesis,[14] interruption, suspense, subjectivism—to name only a few of his stylistic strategies—Catlin tries to give to his descriptions a compelling veracity, but it is precisely these strategies that subvert his intention. Realism demands stylistic sobriety.[15] For Catlin such sobriety precludes the hypotyposis upon which his credibility rests.

In *Manners, Customs, and Conditions* he begins the letter in which he describes the O-Kee-Pa ceremony with these words:

> Oh! *"horrible visu—et mirabile dictu!"* Thank God, it is over, that I have seen it, and am able to tell it to the world. (1841: 155)

But why see it? why tell it to the world? Catlin has no framework for his experience—no justification for his reportage. His intention is documentary, but does this intention justify witnessing and describing a "shocking and disgusting custom" that "sickens the heart and even the stomach of a traveller in the country" (182–83) and yet that fills such a traveler with pity?[16]

Catlin rationalizes his description in a confused manner. (He was never a systematic thinker.) He writes that the ceremony "will be

---

[14] Crapanzano refers to various rhetorical devices—*ecphonesis* is an exclamation or exclamatory phrase; the *vocative* is used in calling, specifying, or addressing; *pathopoeia* is a scene or passage intended to arouse feelings; *apoplanesis* is the use of digression to evade an issue. Deconstructionist authors often use the specialized jargon of literary criticism to establish their own authority. Those who are not specialists in literary criticism could not possibly be expected to know these words no matter what their level of education. The effect is to make much deconstructionist writing impenetrable to nonspecialists. Comparatively speaking, Crapanzano's writing is quite accessible. Much postmodern writing is extraordinarily dense.

[15] Crapanzano claims that "realism demands stylistic sobriety," but was that true in Catlin's day? A problem of deconstructionists is that they impose today's standards on actions and events in the past. Is Crapanzano imposing modern standards on Catlin's work?

Also note that Crapanzano has found what he believes is a critical disjunction in the text: the rhetorical tools that Catlin uses. Crapanzano argues that Catlin's writing style subverts the realistic visual imagery (which he also impugns) on which his claim for authenticity rests. We are entitled to ask why, if this is the case, has Catlin's work been widely accepted as accurate.

[16] Crapanzano believes Catlin's account is further weakened because he has no real justification for the work and does not bother to describe the Mandan justification ("native exegesis") for their ceremony. However, Catlin lived in a world

new to the civilized world, and therefore worth knowing" (157). He suggests that parts of the ceremony are grotesque and amusing and others, having to do with the deluge, are "harmless and full of interest" (177). He has no theoretical justification. Native exegesis is not satisfactory. The ceremony cannot be historically situated. He argues that even if he had time to elaborate a disquisition on the ceremony, he would probably fail because simple people like the Mandan "have no history to save facts and systems from falling into the most absurd and disjointed fable and ignorant fiction" (177).

Catlin shares here the distinctly nineteenth-century conviction that explanation is embedded in origin. In *Manner, Customs, and Conditions* he relates Mandan beliefs and tales to biblical stories of the flood, Eve's transgression, and the birth and death of Christ. (Such an equation puts a stop fundamentalistically to the quest for both origins and meaning.) Noting the Mandans' distinctive ("white") appearance, noting too that their culture hero is white, Catlin assumes Christian contact, and, as we have seen, twenty-six years later, he argued that the Mandan were descended from the Welsh. But to acknowledge Christian influence or, for that matter, Welsh descent hardly explains the O-Kee-Pa tortures. Catlin shifts abruptly—his informal letter style permits this[c]—and he discusses the Mandans' potential for salvation. "I deem it not folly nor idle to say that these people *can be saved*," he concludes his letter,

> nor officious to suggest to some of the very many excellent and pious men, who are almost throwing away the best energies of their lives along the debased frontier, that if they would introduce the ploughshare and their prayers amongst these people, who are so far separated from the taints and contaminating vices of the frontier, they would soon see their most ardent desires accomplished and be able to solve to the world the perplexing enigma, by presenting a nation of savages, civilized and Christianized (and consequently *saved*), in the heart of the American wilderness. (1841: 184).

Catlin's ultimate justification—a justification that runs through American anthropology—is pragmatic; applied, as we say; evangelical in the case in point. The pragmatic, the applied, and the evangelical must also be understood rhetorically.

Despite his figurative language, his speculations about meaning, and his concern for the Indians' salvation, Catlin was in fact haunted by this problem of credibility. "I took my sketch-book with me," he writes toward the beginning of his description of the O-Kee-Pa ceremony,

> and have made many and faithful drawings of what we saw, and full notes of everything as translated to me by the interpreter; and since the close of that horrid and frightful scene, which was a week ago or more, I have been closely ensconced in an earthcovered wigwam, with a fine sky-light over my head, with my pallette and brushes, endeavouring faithfully to put the whole of what we saw upon canvas, which my companions all agree to be critically correct, and of the fidelity of which they have attached their certificates to the backs of the paintings. (1841: 155)

As if prophetically, Catlin also had Kipp, Crawford, and Bogard attach a certificate of authenticity to his account of the ceremony in *Manners, Customs, and Conditions*; for his report was to be questioned by no less a figure in American ethnology than Henry Rowe Schoolcraft. In the third volume of his *Historical and Statistical Information Respecting the History, Condition and Prospects of the Indian Tribes of the United States*, Schoolcraft (1851–57) included a two-page article on the Mandan by David D. Mitchell, then superintendent of Indian affairs in St. Louis, who had been in the Indian trade in Mandan territory in upper Missouri in the 1830s. Mitchell's article concluded: "Information about their [the Mandans'] peculiar customs can be found in the Journal of Lewis and Clark. The scenes described by Catlin, existed almost entirely in the fertile imagination of that gentleman" (254). When he was in South America, Catlin learned of Schoolcraft's and Mitchell's repudiation of his work in a letter from Alexander von Humboldt, who urged him to

---

where exploration and description was its own rationale, where the scientific model was based on natural history more than deductive reasoning. Although Crapanzano's analysis is an elegant demonstration of deconstructionist method, he is saying that Catlin's work would not pass modern peer review by anthropologists. Is this a relevant criticism?

write to Prince Maximilian of Neuwied, who had also spent a winter among the Mandan. Before Catlin was able to obtain a letter of vindication from the prince—he eventually did in 1866—both Schoolcraft and Mitchell died. Although Catlin's description is now more or less accepted as an accurate portrayal of the O-Kee-Pa ceremony (Bowers 1950; see also Matthews 1873), Catlin himself was plagued by the doubt cast on the accuracy of his accounts for the rest of his life.[17]

[Crapanzano's 3,800-word discussion of Johann Wolfgang von Goethe's description of the Roman carnival has been omitted from this essay. The essay resumes at the beginning of Crapanzano's analysis of Clifford Geertz's "Deep Play: Notes on a Balinese Cockfight." The deleted section contains 7 footnotes.]

The title of Clifford Geertz's essay "Deep Play: Notes on a Balinese Cockfight," written about the time the film *Deep Throat* was all the rage, announces a series of erotic puns—puns, Geertz maintains, the Balinese themselves would understand—used throughout his essay.[18] Puns are frequent in ethnography. They position the ethnographer between his world of primary orientation, his reader's world, and the world of those others, the people he has studied, whom at some

level I believe, he is also addressing (Crapanzano 1977a). Through the pun he appeals collusively to the members of one or the other world, usually the world of his readership, thereby creating a hierarchical relationship between them. He himself, the punster, mediates between these worlds.

Geertz's essay is divided into seven sections, and the titles of these sections—"The Raid," "Of Cocks and Men," "The Fight," "Odds and Even Money," "Playing with Fire," "Feathers, Blood, Crowds, and Money," and "Saying Something of Something"—are all suggestive of a distinctly urban environment, of a sex-and-violence whodunit, something out of Mickey Spillane, perhaps, which, unlike Geertz's erotic puns, the villagers could not possibly have understood, at least in 1958. The titles do little to characterize the ethos of a Balinese village or cockfight, but, like puns, they create a collusive relationship between the ethnographer and, in this case, his readers. They also attest to the ethnographer's stylistic virtuosity. He and his readers come out on top of the hierarchy of understanding.

Geertz's essay begins with a humorous tale of entry—by now, in its own right, a genre or subgenre of ethnography.[19] The hero, the anthropologist, is cast stereotypically as a *naïf*, an awkward simpleton, not at all sure of his identity,

---

[17] Although Catlin's description of the O-Kee-Pa is generally accepted as accurate today, in his lifetime it was questioned by several authorities on the Mandan. From a postmodern perspective this is not surprising: different people in different contexts will interpret events around them in different ways. This is a common situation in anthropology, with the Mead-Freeman controversy being one example. Interestingly, Catlin received support from no less a figure than Alexander von Humboldt, one of the great scientists and explorers of the nineteenth century. Humboldt (1769–1859) traveled extensively in the Americas and Asia. He was an eclectic scholar whose most famous work, *Kosmos* (1845–1862), combined elements of cosmology, history, astronomy, and anthropology. Humboldt's works were widely read by European and American intellectuals. Alexander von Humboldt's brother, Karl Wilhelm von Humboldt, was also an illustrious figure in nineteenth-century science and is discussed in Tylor's essay (essay 2, footnote 24).

[18] It is important to separate Crapanzano's use of postmodern deconstructionist method from his more personal criticism of Geertz's work. Geertz describes the word play surrounding *cock,* which has a double meaning for people in Bali as it does for American readers of his essay. But there is no reference to cheesy detective stories. The equation of Mickey Spillane and Balinese cocks in the following paragraph is Crapanzano's, not Geertz's. Balinese villagers understand the cock pun, but the collusive relationship that Crapanzano sees created here is his own rhetorical invention. "Of Cocks and Men" might also be intended to remind readers of John Steinbeck's novel *Of Mice and Men* as well as making reference to sexual organs.
  Deep Throat was a pornographic film that achieved notoriety in the early 1970s.

[19] The tale of entry has become a genre of ethnographic writing today. This increased reflexivity is a method for making ethnography more approachable for a popular audience. Alternatively, a critic of postmodernism might see the tale of entry as a stylistic requirement of modern anthropology because it is now widely assumed that positioning has an important effect on data. It is important to bear in mind, however, that when Geertz's essay appeared, the tale of entry was a radical departure from standard practice.

often suffering from some sort of exotic malady, who is caught in a betwixt and between world. We could see him at Goethe's Roman Carnival. He is no longer in his own world, and he has not yet mastered his new world—the world he will constitute through his ethnography.

> Early in April of 1958, my wife and I arrived, malarial and diffident, in a Balinese village we intended, as anthropologists, to study. A small place, about five hundred people, and relatively remote, it was its own world. We were intruders, professional ones, and the villagers dealt with us as Balinese seem always to deal with people not part of their life who yet press themselves upon them: as though we were not there. For them, and to a degree for ourselves, we were nonpersons, specters, invisible men. (1973: 412)

Here in the first paragraph of "Deep Play," Geertz establishes an opposition between himself and his wife and the Balinese who live in their own remote little world. Geertz and his wife are "anthropologists," "professionals," and "intruders." The tale of entry is, as I have noted, called "The Raid," referring manifestly to a police raid of a village cockfight. It may also reflect Geertz's attitude toward his and his wife's presence, their mission, in the village.[20] He claims dramatically that he and his wife were "nonpersons, specters, invisible men" for the villagers and "to a degree for ourselves"—that is, until like the other villagers attending the cockfight, they fled the police. Then they were recognized. Geertz offers no evidence for this contention, and in the very next paragraph he contradicts himself.

> But except for our landlord and the village chief, whose cousin and brother-in-law he was, everyone ignored us only as the Balinese can

do. As we wandered around, uncertain, wistful, eager to please, people seemed to look right through us with a gaze focused several yards behind us on some more actual stone or tree. Almost nobody greeted us; but nobody scowled or said anything unpleasant to us either which would have been almost as satisfactory. . . . The indifference, of course, was studied; the villagers were watching every move we made, and they had an enormous amount of quite accurate information about who we were and what we were going to be doing. But they acted as if we simply did not exist, which, in fact, as this behavior was designed to inform us, we did not, or anyway not yet. (412–13)

There is of course a difference between being a nonperson, a specter, an invisible man—a collection of nonequivalent statuses in any case—and being treated with "studied indifference." The Geertzes may have been treated as though they were not there, but they were surely there. How else could they be informed of their "nonexistence"?

I call attention here to what might simply be dismissed as a not altogether successful storytelling ruse, were it not indicative of a more serious problem that flaws Geertz's essay. Here, at a descriptive level, he blurs his own subjectivity—his experience of himself in those early Balinese days—with the subjectivity and the intentionality of the villagers.[21] (His wife's experience presents still another problem as well as something of a conceptual embarrassment: she is dismissed from this tale of men and cocks—a dismissal already heralded in the first paragraph by the use of "men" in the phrase "invisible men.") Later, at the level of interpretation, we discover the same confusion (see Crapanzano 1981a; Lieberson 1984). We must ask whether this interpretive confusion is facilitated by Geertz's particular descriptive tack.

---

[20] Notice how Crapanzano delves into the psychological motives behind Geertz's writing, whereas he had criticized Geertz for similar delving into Balinese psychology.

[21] Crapanzano makes an important point here, highlighting a common problem in ethnographic writing. Just because Geertz felt like a nonperson does not mean the Balinese thought of him that way. It is not unusual for ethnographers to commingle what they believe natives think with how natives actually feel. Because the ethnographer's voice is the only one we hear in an ethnography, this distinction is important. Whether or not Geertz is guilty of committing this particular error is an open question. Crapanzano may err by taking Geertz's essay (which is full of irony, humor, and double entendre) at face value. A common problem of much postmodern criticism is its tendency to literalism and lack of humor.

Through puns, titles, subtitles, and simple declarations, the "anthropologist" and his "Balinese" are separated from one another. In the opening section of "Deep Play" Geertz and his wife are cast, however conventionally, as individuals. The Balinese are not. They are generalized. Turns of phrase like "as Balinese always do," reminiscent if not of superficial travel accounts, then of national character studies, run through "Deep Play": "in a way only a Balinese can do" (412); "the deep psychological identification of Balinese men with their cocks" (417); "the Balinese never do anything in a simple way when they can contrive to do it in a complicated way" (425); "the Balinese are shy to the point of obsessiveness of open conflict" (446). The "Balinese"—surely not the Balinese—becomes a foil for Geertz's describing, interpreting, and theorizing—for his self-presenting.[22]

Geertz likens his nonpersonhood to being "a cloud or a gust of wind": "My wife and I were still very much in the gust of wind stage, a most frustrating, and even, as you begin to doubt whether you are really real after all, unnerving one when . . ." (413). And he goes on to describe the police raid through which he achieved his "personhood." This passage is significant not so much because of what Geertz has to say about himself and his wife as because of a pronoun switch from "I/we," or more accurately from "I + noun" ("my wife and I") to "you." This switch anticipates his disappearance in the sections to come. The "you" serves as more, I suggest, than an appeal to the reader to empathize with him. It decenters the narrator in the space of intersubjective understanding. He engages in dialogue with his reader in a way, at least in his presentation, that he does not engage with the Balinese. *They* remain cardboard figures.[23]

Despite popular grammatical understanding that a pronoun is simply a noun substitute, there is, as Emile Benveniste (1966) and others have observed, a fundamental difference between first and second person personal pronouns ("I" and "you" and their plurals) and third person pronouns ("he," "she," "it," "they"). The first and second are properly indexical: they "relate" to the context of utterance. The third person pronouns refer back anaphorically[24] to an antecedent, a noun, often enough a proper noun, in the text. They are liberated, so to speak, from the context of utterance, but they are embedded in the textual context. They are intratextual and derive their meaning from their textually described antecedents. Thus, in Geertz's essay, and in most ethnography, the "I/you" of the ethnographer and the "I/you" of the ethnographer's interlocutors in the field are converted asymmetrically into an anaphorically free "I" and an anaphoric—a cumulative "they." Indeed, in most ethnographic texts, including Geertz's, the "I" itself disappears except in conventional tales of entry or in text evaluation shifters and becomes simply a stylistically borne "invisible" voice.[d] Symptomatically, "we" seldom occurs in ethnography.

"The Raid" represents a delicate, unstable moment. Geertz, the author/narrator, is an "I." The Balinese are referentially described: a "they." Just as the Balinese recognize Geertz after his flight from the police, he, at least as an I, flees

---

[22] Another typical convention of ethnographic writing is that anthropologists make generalizations about whole populations based on their experience with groups of informants. Crapanzano, reflecting postmodern thought, critiques Geertz's claims to describe Balinese character in general, based on his experience with his informants. But is this trope *necessarily* invalid? Deconstructing Geertz's text does not automatically disprove his portrayal of the Balinese. For a discussion of this issue see Sangren (1988:414–416).

[23] Crapanzano is remarkably adept at bringing taken-for-granted conventions of writing to the forefront. For example, Geertz begins his article with a first-person account of his experiences. He then disappears from the text during his examination of the cockfight as he slips into the third person, a trope that readers accept as scientific writing. As a reader, one of your jobs is to judge the validity of Geertz's analysis. Does the fact that he moved from first- to third-person writing bother you?

[24] *Anaphora:* the use of a word as a regular grammatical substitute for a preceding word or group of words. For example, the use of *it* and *does* in the phrase, "I know it, and he does, too." Pronouns are used anaphorically.

from the text in a section revealingly entitled "Of Cocks and Men." Does the lingering "I" of "The Raid" compensate for Geertz's nonpersonhood in those first days of fieldwork he is describing?

Throughout the remainder of "Deep Play" there is continual blurring of Geertz's understanding and the understanding of the Balinese as he describes them. Without any evidence he attributes to the Balinese all sorts of experiences, meanings, intentions, motivations, dispositions, and understandings. He writes, for example:

> In the cockfight man and beast, good and evil, ego and id, the creative power of aroused masculinity and the destructive power of loosened animality fuse in a bloody drama of hatred, cruelty, violence, and death. It is little wonder that when, as is the invariable rule, the owner of the winning cock takes the carcass of the loser—often torn limb from limb by its enraged owner—home to eat, he does so with a mixture of social embarrassment, moral satisfaction, aesthetic disgust, and cannibal joy. (430–31)

We must not be carried away by Geertz's Grand Guignol[25] sensibility. We must ask: on what grounds does he attribute "social embarrassment," "moral satisfaction," "aesthetic disgust" (whatever that means), and "cannibal joy" to the Balinese? to all Balinese men? to any Balinese man in particular? Clearly Geertz's aim, like Catlin's, is to render the moment vivid, but unlike Catlin, who makes no pretense of uncovering the subjective meaning—the experience—of the O-Kee-Pa ceremony for the Mandan, Geertz does make such a claim of the Balinese.

Toward the end of his essay, as though pulling a rabbit out of a hat, Geertz suddenly declares the cockfight to be an art form, which he understands in a very Western way: "As any art form—for that, finally, is what we are dealing with—the cockfight renders ordinary, everyday experience comprehensible by presenting it in terms of acts and objects which have had their practical consequences removed and been reduced (or, if you prefer, raised) to the level of sheer appearance,

where their meaning can be more powerfully articulated and more exactly perceived" (443). We must ask: for whom does the cockfight articulate everyday experience—the experience of status hierarchy—and render it more perceptible? After likening the cockfight to *King Lear* and *Crime and Punishment,* Geertz goes on to assert that it

> catches up these themes—death, masculinity, rage, pride, loss, beneficence, change—and ordering them into an encompassing structure, presents them in such a way as to throw into relief a particular view of their essential nature. It puts a construction on them, makes them, to those historically positioned to appreciate the construction, meaningful—visible, tangible, graspable—"real" in an ideational sense. An image, fiction, a model, a metaphor, the cockfight is a means of expression; its function is neither to assuage social passions nor to heighten them (though, in its playing-with-fire way it does a bit of both), but, in a medium of feathers, blood, crowds, and money, to display them. (443–44)

We must ask: who is historically positioned to appreciate the construction? Geertz completely ignores the fact that *King Lear* and *Crime and Punishment* are culturally and linguistically marked as a tragedy and a novel; as representations of a particular order; as fictions to be read in a special way—indeed, to be read. He offers no proof anywhere that the cockfight is so marked for his Balinese. Piling image on image—"image," "fiction," and "metaphor"—may assuage Geertz's own theoretical anxiety, but it hardly gets rid of the problem. (Image, fiction, model, and metaphor are of course no more equivalent than nonperson, specter, and invisible man). Cockfights are surely cockfights for the Balinese—and not images, fictions, models, and metaphors. They are not marked as such, though they may be read as such by a foreigner for whom "images, fictions, models, and metaphors" have interpretive value.[e] It is perhaps no accident that in a following paragraph Geertz describes the cockfight as "disquietful": "The reason it is disquietful is that, joining

---

[25] *Grand Guignol:* a short drama stressing horror and sensationalism.

pride to selfhood, selfhood to cocks, and cocks to destruction, it brings to imaginative realization a dimension of Balinese experience normally well-obscured from view" (444). We must ask yet again: for whom is the cockfight disquietful?[26]

In the final pages of "Deep Play" Geertz likens the cockfight to a text. He also refers to it as "a Balinese reading of Balinese experience," "a story they tell the natives about themselves," a "meta-commentary." "It is a means of saying something about something." It requires the anthropologist to "penetrate" it, just as a critic "penetrates" a text. For Geertz the interpreted text, the cock-fight, is a drama of status hierarchy, and in bla-tantly intentional language he suggests that is why Balinese go to cockfights: "Balinese go to cockfights to find out what a man, usually com-posed, aloof, almost obsessively self-absorbed, a kind of moral autocosm, feels like when attacked, tormented, challenged, insulted, and driven in re-sult to the extremes of fury, he has totally tri-umphed or been brought low" (450).

Elsewhere, he asserts Balinese subjectivity at cockfights.

> Enacted and re-enacted, so far without end the cockfight enables the Balinese, as, read and reread, *Macbeth* enables us, to see a dimension of his own subjectivity. As he watches fight after fight, with the active watching of an owner and a bettor (for cockfighting has no more interest as a pure spectator sport than does croquet or dog-racing), he grows familiar with it and what it has to say to him much as the attentive listener to a string quartet or the absorbed viewer of still life grows slowly more familiar with them in a way which opens his objectivity to himself. (450–51)

Who told Geertz? How can a whole people share a single subjectivity? Are there not differences be-tween texts, commentaries, metacommentaries, dramas, sports, string quartets, and still lifes? Has Professor Geertz abandoned all of the analytic distinctions that have characterized the success (and the failure) of his civilization? Like Catlin's colorful, concrete metaphors, Geertz's colorless, abstract metaphors subvert both his description and his interpretation. Indeed, they subvert his authority. His message is simply not convincing.[27]

Despite his phenomenological-hermeneutical pretensions, there is in fact in "Deep Play" no un-derstanding of the native from the native's point of view. There is only the constructed under-standing of the constructed native's constructed point of view. Geertz offers no specifiable evidence for his attributions of intention, his assertions of subjectivity, his declarations of experience. His constructions of constructions of constructions appear to be little more than projections, or at least blurrings, of his point of view, his subjectiv-ity, with that of the native, or, more accurately, of the constructed native.

Finally, as if to give his, or any anthropologist's, constructions a certain, if you will, substantialized authority, Geertz refers in "Deep Play" to culture "as an ensemble of texts, themselves ensembles, which the anthropologist strains to read over the shoulder of those to whom they properly belong" (452–53).[f] The image is striking: sharing and not sharing a text. It represents a sort of asymmetri-cal we-relationship with the anthropologist behind and above the native, hidden but at the top of the hierarchy of understanding. It reflects, I believe, the indexical drama of "The Raid" in which the parties to the ethnographic encounter are brought

---

[26] Crapanzano's analysis demonstrates that ethnographic writing can tell as much about the author as it does about its subjects. As he explains, Geertz offers no evidence that the cockfight moves the Balinese in the same way that an artistic performance affects a Western audience. Geertz may be right, but he may also be projecting his feelings about the cock-fight onto his Balinese subjects. Drama is the metaphor by which Geertz understands the cockfight, and he passes his un-derstanding to us. We don't really know how the Balinese feel.

[27] It is, of course, Crapanzano and not Geertz who has abandoned "the analytic distinctions that have characterized the success" of his civilization. By building a theoretical model, Geertz is in the mainstream of scientific tradition. By implicitly challenging the authority of any text, Crapanzano is outside of the positivist tradition of modern science. Crapanzano claims that Geertz is not convincing, but "Notes on a Balinese Cockfight" has proven to be one of the most durable and compelling essays in anthropology.

together in the narration as they are separated through style. There is never an I-you relationship, a dialogue, two people next to each other reading the same text and discussing it face-to-face, but only an I-they relationship. And, as we have seen, even the I disappears — replaced by an invisible voice of authority who declares what the you-transformed-to-a-they experience.[28]

In traditional ethnography the ethnographer's encounter with the people he has studied is rarely described. Often, as in the case of Geertz's "Deep Play," hardly a traditional ethnography, even the activity that is described and interpreted — a cockfight, a carnival, a test of prowess, or, for that matter, the weaving of a basket or the preparation of a meal — is not presented in its particularity as a single, and in some ways unique, performance. We are usually given a general picture. Presumably many observations, taken from many vantage points, are conflated into a single, constructed performance, which becomes a sort of ideal, a Platonic performance. Catlin and Goethe describe a single performance, but, despite deictic and other particularizing locutions, they do it in a generalizing way. Geertz, who apparently attended many cockfights, never describes a specific cockfight. He constructs the Balinese cockfight and interprets his construction: "the Balinese cockfight." His conventional tale of entry serves a deictic function not that different from Catlin's assigned place or Goethe's "here's" and "now's." It gives the illusion of specificity when there is no specific temporal or spatial vantage point. It attests to the ethnographer's having been there and gives him whatever authority arises from that presence.[29]

In "Deep Play" the problem of the ethnographer's authoritative constructions is further complicated by the author's phenomenological and hermeneutical pretentions. Neither Catlin nor Goethe make any sustained effort to describe the experience for the participants of the ceremonies they observed. Catlin assumes the perspective of the Mandan only rhetorically. For him, the O-Kee-Pa was a "shocker" ("This part of the ceremony [the torture], as I have just witnessed it, is truly shocking to behold, and will stagger the belief of the world when they read of it" [1867: 157]); and he struggled unsuccessfully to give it meaning. He could find no familiar story in which to fit it in more than a fragmented way. The Roman carnival became for Goethe an allegory of individual destiny. It was of course not *that* unfamiliar. He was able to organize it along familiar theatrical — *commedia dell'arte* — lines and to synchronize his descriptive rhythm with the carnival's rhythm. We may find Goethe's allegory arch, moribund even, but it is subsuming. For Geertz, the cockfight itself becomes a grand metaphor for Balinese social organization, and, as such, closes in on itself. Despite Geertz's ostensible concern for the understanding of the native's point of view, his essay is less a disquisition on Balinese cockfighting, subjectively or objectively understood, than on interpreting — reading — cultural data. His analysis is exemplary, and this exemplary quality, Geertz's interpretive virtuosity, helps render it ethnographically convincing. Its ultimate significance is not moral but methodological. Catlin makes a plea for the salvation of the Mandan; Goethe for the full appreciation of fleeting moments of joy; Geertz for hermeneutics. In all three instances the events described are subverted by the transcending stories in which they are cast. They are sacrificed to their rhetorical function in a literary discourse that is far removed from the indigenous discourse of their occurrence. The sacrifice, the subversion of the event described, is in the final analysis masked neither by rhetoric, hypotyposis, theatricality, and interpretive virtuosity nor by their metaphorization — salvation, life, society — but by the au-

---

[28] Crapanzano has a good point here. But is it possible to write an ethnography that includes all perspectives?

[29] In this passage Crapanzano presents the crux of the postmodern critique of ethnographic writing: ethnography is a literary creation. Geertz does not present us with a Balinese cockfight, he has constructed a cockfight and interpreted his construction. Crapanzano claims that Geertz's analysis is exemplary because of the methodological tool Geertz employed, using the cockfight as a window through which Balinese society may be seen. However, he believes Geertz's account is a literary fiction, albeit one made palatable by the skill with which Geertz writes.

thority of the author, who, at least in much ethnography, stands above and behind those whose experience he purports to describe. All too often, the ethnographer forgets that the native, like Eduard in Goethe's *Elective Affinities,* cannot abide someone reading over his shoulder. If he does not close his book, he will cast his shadow over it. Of course, the ethnographer will also cast his shadow over it. It is perhaps for this reason, if I may conclude with the conceit of my own tale of entry into this paper, that Zeus understood when Hermes promised to tell no lies but did not promise to tell the whole truth.[30]

Notes

a. In his commentaries on the Salon of 1846, Baudelaire (1846: 634), who admired Catlin's work, wrote: "Le rouge, la couleur de la vie, abondait tellement dans ce sombre musée, que c'était une ivresse; quant aux paysages, —montagnes boisées, savanes immenses, rivières desertes, —ils étaient monotonement, éternellement verts, le rouge, cette couleur si obscure, si épaisse, plus difficile à pénétrer que les yeux d'un serpent—le vert, cette couleur calme et gaie et souriante de la nature, je les retrouve chantant leur antithèse mélodique." There is of course something of this melodic antithesis in Catlin's prose.

b. Gelley (1979: 420) argues that ways of seeing in the realist novel can be understood "as a type of deictic at a phenomenological level, a sign important not so much on account of its content but because it is capable of identifying the instance of observation and tracing its modifications."

c. There is a revealing parallel between Catlin's disjunctive style and his jumpy speculations about the meaning of the ceremony.

d. I am simplifying here. The ethnographer's "I" must be carefully examined in its specific occurrences, for

---

[30] Crapanzano outlines the tropes by which Catlin and Geertz created ethnographic authority for their texts, but one can apply the same method of analysis to his own work. By questioning the legitimacy of other's opinions, Crapanzano attempts to create ethnographic authority for his own. The methodology that Crapanzano uses to criticize Catlin and Geertz can also demonstrate the rhetorical devices that he disingenuously uses to convince readers of *his authority.* As Sangren says, "Any announcement of the demise of the authority of traditional forms of knowledge inevitably amounts to an assertion of a rival authority" (1988:422).

Crapanzano has assumed the voice of the dispassionate observer and critic, but as postmodernists point out, no one is unbiased. He also uses another literary device, which we might call "implication by association." Several times in the text Crapanzano attacks individuals or ethnographies by associating them with negative ideas, but he does not directly state the criticism implied by the association. For instance, look at the following sentence from near the beginning of this essay:

The ethnographer must make use of all the persuasive devices at his disposal to convince his readers of *the* truth of his message, but, as though these rhetorical strategies were cunning tricks, he gives them scant recognition.

The implication of the sentence is that in order to be convincing, ethnographers consciously deceive their audience, but Crapanzano does not say this directly.

While Crapanzano's essay can be deconstructed, some parts of his critique of Geertz are apt. Geertz's essay *is* a literary construction based on his view of fifty-seven cockfights, and Geertz's skill as a writer makes his essay convincing. However, the following three points seem true of all ethnographic writing: (1) Ethnographers must establish their authority, otherwise there is no point in reading their work. (2) By its very nature, all ethnography constructs the other for readers, whether this is done through verbatim quotations, statistical analysis, or the paradigms of cognitive anthropologists. (3) Beyond this construction lie other constructions, since just as the ethnographer constructs the subject for the reader, so too the subject, to some degree, constructs itself for the ethnographer and readers construct their own understandings of the text. The permutations of interpretation are probably endless.

By choosing to write on Catlin, Goethe, and Geertz, Crapanzano blurs the distinction between travel writing, literature, and ethnography. This is not problematical for him, since to postmodernists, a positivist, scientific anthropology is impossible. Deconstruction reduces anthropological analysis to a text within a text within a text. Anthropology collapses into literary analysis.

Deconstructionist anthropology had its heyday in the 1980s. Today, many anthropologists use the insights of the postmodernists to inform the writing of their ethnographies, making them more sensitive to issues of power and voice.

You may have noticed that we have been much more critical of deconstruction than of other methods of analysis. This is because deconstruction always lends itself to further deconstruction. Astute readers can easily deconstruct our commentary but will find their own analyses subject to further deconstruction.

it can serve multiple functions, even simultaneously. It may, for example, be descriptive, referring to a grammatically distorted interlocution ("I said"/"he said" or "I observed") or it may in fact refer to the context of writing. There is also, as I have argued elsewhere (1981b), an anaphoric potential to first and second person indexicals, particularly in "authored" texts.

e. One would ultimately have to consider the ontological status of Balinese equivalents (if there are any) of these Western categories.

f. See my discussion (Crapanzano 1981c) of text and text metaphors. I argue that despite a certain literary critical penchant to view texts abstractly, their rhetorical force rests on the concreteness, the tangible existence, of the text.

References

Baudelaire, Charles. 1846. "Salon de 1846." In *Oeuvres complètes,* edited by Y. G. le Dantec and Claude Pichois, 605–80. Paris: Edition de la Pléiade, 1954.

Benveniste, Emile. 1966. *Problèmes de linguistique générale.* Paris: Gallimard.

Benjamin, Walter. 1969. *Illuminations.* New York: Shocken.

Bowers, Alfred W. 1950. *Mandan Social and Ceremonial Organization.* Chicago: University of Chicago Press.

Catlin, George. 1841. *Letters and Notes on the Manners, Customs, and Conditions of the North American Indians.* 2 vols. New York: Dover Publications, 1973.

1867. *O-Kee-Pa: A Religious Ceremony and Other Customs of the Mandan.* New Haven, Conn.: Yale University Press, 1967.

Clifford, James. 1983a. "On Ethnographic Authority." *Representations* 1, no. 2: 118–46.

Crapanzano, Vincent. 1977a. "The Writing of Ethnography." *Dialectical Anthropology* 2: 69–73.

1981a. Review of *Meaning and Order in Moroccan Society: Three Essays in Cultural Analysis,* by C. Geertz, H. Geertz, and L. Rosen. *Economic Development and Culture Change* 29: 851–60.

1981b. "The Self, The Third, and Desire." In *Psychosocial Theories of the Self,* edited by B. Lee, 179–206. New York and London: Plenum.

1981c. "Text, Transference, and Indexicality." *Ethos* 9, no. 2: 122–48.

Ewers, John C. 1967. *Introduction to O-Kee-Pa: A Religious Ceremony and Other Customs of the Mandan,* by George Catlin. New Haven, Conn.: Yale University Press.

Geertz, Clifford. 1973. *The Interpretation of Cultures.* New York: Basic Books.

Gelley, Alexander. 1979. "The Represented World: Toward a Phenomenological Theory of Description in the Novel." *Journal of Aesthetics and Art Criticism* 37: 415–22.

Goethe, J. W. von. 1976a. *Italienische Reise.* 2 vols. Frankfurt am Main: Insel Verlag.

1982. *Italian Journey 1786–1788.* Translated by W. H. Auden and Elizabeth Mayer. San Francisco: North Point Press.

Lieberson, Jonathon. 1984. Review of *Local Knowledge: Further Essays in Interpretive Anthropology,* by C. Geertz. *New York Review of Books* 31: 39–46.

Marcus, George. 1980. "Rhetoric and the Ethnographic Genre in Anthropological Research." *Current Anthropology* 21: 507–510.

Matthews, Washington. 1873. *Grammer and Dictionary of the Language of the Hidatsa.* New York: Shea's American Linguistics, series 2, no. 1.

Nilsson, M. P. 1949. *History of Greek Religion.* 2nd ed. Oxford: Oxford University Press.

Schoolcraft, H. R. 1851–1857. *Historical and Statistical Information Respecting the History, Condition, and Prospects of the Indian Tribes of the United States.* Washington, D.C.: Bureau of Indian Affairs.

40. Moral Models in Anthropology

Roy D'Andrade (1931–)

FOR OVER A DECADE THERE HAVE BEEN CON-certed attacks in anthropology on objectivity (Rosaldo 1989), science (Scheper-Hughes 1991), the notion of truth (Tyler 1986), making generalizations of any kind (Abu-Lughod 1991), doing ethnography (Dwyer 1982), and anthropology itself as a type of Western colonialism (Asad 1973). These attacks come not from some fringe group but from well-known and established anthropologists. Why should so many anthropologists attack the very foundations of their discipline? Originally, I thought these attacks came from people who had the same agenda I did, just different assumptions about how to accomplish that agenda. I now realize that an entirely different agenda is being proposed—that anthropology be transformed from a discipline based upon an *objective* model of the world to a discipline based upon a *moral* model of the world.

By a "model" I mean a set of cognitive elements used to understand and reason about something. The term "moral" is used here to refer to the primary *purpose* of this model, which is to identify what is *good* and what is *bad* and to allocate *reward* and *punishment*. In the usual language of philosophy, goodness and badness, like beauty and taste, are considered subjective, not objective things; the beauty of a human baby may not be beauty to an ostrich and the badness of killing one's lover may not be badness to a praying mantis. An objective description tells about the thing described, not about the agent doing the description, while a subjective description

(1995)

tells how the agent doing the description *reacts* to the object. "He is a good guy" is a subjective description of someone; "He helps his friends" would be a more objective description of the same person.

The distinction between object and subject is one of the basic human cognitive accomplishments. Normal people are expected to be able to recognize the difference between their response to an object and the object itself. Despite the cognitive salience of the objective/subjective distinction, in ordinary talk the two are often blended. To say someone is a "crook" is to refer to more than the objective fact that something was intentionally taken by someone who had no legal right to it; part of the meaning of "crook" is that the person who did this did something *bad* and is a *bad person*. Many of the terms of natural language blend the way the world is and our reaction to it, perhaps because in this way we can tell others how we want them to respond also ("respond as *I* do"). Although it may be impossible to present an entirely objective account, when we want to understand something outside ourselves we use terms that, so far as possible, tell about *that thing* so we can understand *that thing*, rather than our *response* to that thing. One tries to be objective if one wants to tell others about the *object*, not about oneself.[1]

It should be noted that an objective account is not necessarily value-free. For example, the statement "X cures cancer" is not free of positive value for most people. Nor are objective accounts necessarily unbiased. One well-known way of producing a biased account is to report only those

---

[1] D'Andrade opens his essay with a seemingly commonsensical account of the difference between objectivity and subjectivity. But common sense is not so common, and there may be no such thing as sense. Much of the postmodern anthropology of the 1980s and 1990s has been aimed at dissolving the distinction between the objective and subjective. Postmodernists typically claim that because observations can never exist independently of the observer, all observations are necessarily subjective. Thus, the claim of Western physical and social scientists that they produce objective observations is inaccurate. It reflects the privileged position of science rather than anything "real" about the world. To a postmodernist, D'Andrade's claim that objective science exists seems anachronistic, possibly even quaint.

facts which reflect badly on something. As used here, *objectivity* refers just to the degree to which an account gives information about the object being described. Finally, it should be noted that trying to be objective does not preclude investigating other people's subjective worlds. One can be as objective about what people think as one can be about the crops they grow.[2]

One result of the attempt to be objective—to talk about the thing, not oneself—is that it is more likely that what one says can be tested to see if it is true or false. And because it is more likely that an objective account can be tested, an objective account can be attempted again by someone else and the replicability of the account assessed. For knowledge to accumulate, accounts must be objective, but they must also be testable and replicable. What Pons and Fleischmann said about cold fusion was objective enough, but unfortunately what they described seems to be unreplicable.[3]

In contrast to an objective model, which tries to describe the object, the aim of a moral model is to identify what is good and bad, to allocate praise and blame, and also to explain how things not in themselves good or bad come to be so. Typically, this is done using words that Kenneth Burke (1945) calls "god" terms, words that stand for things that are an *ultimate* good or an *ultimate* evil and which are the source of further good or evil.[4] Thus, in the current moral model in anthropology, *oppression* is an ultimate evil; nothing can make oppression good, and it is assumed that most of the bad things in the world are the result of oppression. The truth of the badness of *oppression* is not an empirical matter. If you lack moral sense, no recounting of the facts can explain it to you. And given the ultimate badness of oppression, anything that creates or maintains oppressions must also be bad. Thus colonialism is bad because it necessarily involves the use of oppression. Power is bad because it is an instrument of oppression. The hegemony of Western culture is bad because it supports and maintains Western colonialist oppression. Silencing and violence are bad because they are typical means of oppression. And so on.[a]

Every moral model must contain at least partially objective terms if it is to apply to things in the world. Thus "oppression" is not totally subjective; like the term "crook," it refers to something objective—the use of power by some individuals or groups to affect other individuals or groups in ways not to their liking. The subjective part of the term "oppression" is the evaluation built into it that defines this use of power as

---

[2] D'Andrade defines objectivity as ". . . the degree to which an account gives information about the object being described." By defining objectivity this way, he tries to avoid the postmodern critique that objectivity is impossible to achieve because ethnographic writing reflects the background of the author. D'Andrade claims that an objective account does not have to be value free.

[3] The allusion to Pons and Fleischmann and cold fusion refers to a scientific controversy in 1989–90. B. Stanley Pons and Martin Fleischmann are two chemists. Pons was at the University of Utah and Fleischmann at the University of Southampton in England. In March 1989 they held a news conference and announced that they had successfully initiated a cold fusion nuclear reaction in a tabletop device they had constructed for a few thousand dollars. Their announcement triggered a frenzy of activity. Scientists in physics labs all over the world rushed to replicate Pons and Fleischmann's experiment. The two were called to Washington to make a presentation before members of the House Committee on Science, Space, and Technology. However, when all attempts to replicate their work failed or were inconclusive, the accuracy of Pons and Fleischmann's work was challenged and their professional reputations called into question. They resigned their university posts and went to work in a privately funded research facility in France.

[4] Kenneth Burke (1897–1993) was a poet, literary theorist, and critic whose major philosophical and critical work was concerned with the nature of knowledge and his view of literature as symbolic action. Burke attempted to integrate scientific and philosophical concepts with his perspectives on literature. This resulted in numerous scholarly publications, including the 1945 volume *A Grammar of Motives* cited here by D'Andrade. Burke had an incredibly diverse career. He worked for the New York Bureau of Social Hygiene, was a music critic for the *Nation,* and held a variety of academic posts at such institutions as the New School for Social Research, University of Chicago, Princeton, Indiana University, and Pennsylvania State University.

something bad and as something that brings about things that are bad.[5]

In most moral models there is some way to correct evil. In the current moral model in anthropology this is done by unmasking the symbolic hegemony that hides and legitimates oppression. The morally corrective act is *denunciation*. One can also act morally by giving voice to those who resist oppression; this at least identifies the oppression and the oppressors. Nowadays, one can have a moral career in anthropology; having a moral career in anthropology is being known for what one has denounced.[6]

Nancy Scheper-Hughes's "Hungry Bodies, Medicine, and the State: Toward a Critical Psychological Anthropology" (1992a) is a good illustration of the use of the current moral model in anthropology.[7] In her paper, Scheper-Hughes explicitly says that she wants to redirect psychological anthropology toward the new model. According to Scheper-Hughes (1992a:229):

> The essential insight, derived from European critical theory, is that the given world or the "commonsense reality" may be false, illusory, and oppressive. It is an insight shared with all contemporary critical epistemologies including modern psychoanalysis, feminism and Marxism. All variants of modern critical theory work at the essential task of stripping away the surface forms of reality in order to expose concealed and buried truths. Their aim, then, is to "speak truth" to power and domination, both in individuals and submerged social groups or classes.

Demystification—"exposing concealed and buried truths"—is thus seen as a necessary remedy for the domination of individuals, groups, and classes. And the "critical theories" which do this are different from "objective" theories.

> [Critical theories] are reflexive rather than objective epistemologies. Critical theories differ radically in their epistemology from positivist theories derived from the natural sciences. All theories in the "natural" sciences presuppose an "objective" structure of reality knowable by minds that are likewise understood as sharing uniform cognitive structure. Critical theories assert the subjectivity of knowable phenomena and propose "reflection" as a valid category and method of discovery.[8]

The problem Scheper-Hughes is addressing here, I think, involves the term "truth." Immediately before, she has said that the goal is to "speak truth to power." But isn't finding out the truth what science—old-fashioned anthropology—does? She claims that "critical theories" do something else—they know in a "subjective" way, not just an "objective" way, by "reflection." Scheper-Hughes is not explicit about how reflection works as a method of discovery, but she is clear that it is different from "positivism" and "natural science." In her view, "The objectivity of science and of medicine is always a phantom objectivity, a mask that conceals

---

[5] D'Andrade believes that even subjective judgments have an objective foundation that can be exposed to empirical examination. Thus he is able to answer the postmodernist claim that there is no such thing as objectivity.

[6] Although D'Andrade's tone here sounds sarcastic, the call to fight oppression and give a voice to oppressed peoples has long been a goal for many anthropologists. Boas, for example, was an outspoken pacifist and supporter of human rights. More recently, Harvard anthropologist David Maybury-Lewis (1929–) founded the organization Cultural Survival in 1972, with the specific goal of campaigning for the rights of indigenous peoples and oppressed ethnic minorities around the world.

[7] D'Andrade's essay is one of a pair of works featured in a 1995 issue of *Current Anthropology* under the title "Objectivity and Militancy: A Debate." Nancy Scheper-Hughes (1944–), who features so prominently in D'Andrade's essay, is the author of the second essay—the "militancy" side of the debate. Scheper-Hughes is currently a professor of anthropology at the University of California Berkeley. Two of her best-known works are *Saints, Scholars, and Schizophrenics: Mental Illness in Rural Ireland* (1979) and *Death Without Weeping: The Violence of Everyday Life in Brazil* (1992).

[8] Critical theory is a broad term generally used to designate neo-Marxist, post-structuralist, and deconstructionist theories. A principal aspect of critical theory is that it is overtly political. Epistemology, which is of central concern to postmodernists, is the investigation of the origin and nature of knowledge. What Scheper-Hughes is saying in this paragraph is that critical theories are reflexive rather than objective ways of knowing.

more than it reveals" (p. 229). Thus, positivistic natural science is a *bad* way to find out about the world because it is part of the process of mystification. Objectivity turns out to be a mask for domination. One of the most salient characteristics of the current moral model is exactly this attack on objectivity.

Scheper-Hughes continues (p. 229):

> At the heart of all critical theories and methods is a critique of ideology and power. Ideologies (whether political, economic, or religious) can mystify reality, obscure relations of power and domination, and prevent people from grasping their situation in the world. Specific forms of consciousness may be called ideological when they are invoked to sustain or legitimate particular institutions or social practices. When these institutional arrangements reproduce inequality, domination, and human suffering, the aims of critical theory are broadly emancipatory.

This repeats some of the ideas already presented: reality gets mystified to obscure relations of domination; the goal is to emancipate by revealing the ideologies which mystify such relations (pp. 229–30):

> The process of liberation is complicated, however, by the unreflexive complicity and identification of people with the very ideologies and practices that are their own undoing. Here is where Antonio Gramsci's notion of hegemony is useful. Gramsci . . . recognized that the dominant classes exercised power both directly and forcefully through the state, and also indirectly by merging with the civil society and identifying their own class-based interests

with broad cultural ideas and aims, making them appear indistinguishable from each other.

Here Scheper-Hughes begins to specify how mystification works—by the identification of the interests of the dominant classes with "broad" cultural ideas and aims. The state is the power that acts to create this mystification (p. 230):

> Increasingly in modern bureaucratic states technicians and professionals—laboratory scientists, geneticists, doctors, psychologists, teachers, social workers, sociologists, criminologists and so forth—come to play the role of the "traditional intellectuals" in sustaining "commonsense" definitions of reality through their highly specialized and validating forms of discourse. Gramsci anticipated Foucault (see Foucault 1972) in his understanding of the diffuse power circuits in modern states and of the role of "expert" forms of power/knowledge in sustaining the "common sense" order of things.[9]

Scheper-Hughes makes the case that in Northeast Brazil people suffer from a disorder called *nervos* that involves weakness, sleeplessness, heart palpitations, shaking, headache, fainting, etc., and that this disorder "is a primary idiom through which hunger and hunger-anxiety are expressed" (1992a:231). For this disorder, minor tranquilizers are considered by the Brazilian medical establishment to be an appropriate treatment. This treatment, according to Scheper-Hughes, by *not* recognizing the problems of hunger that underlie *nervos*, deflects the underlying rage against domination and mystifies the source of the problem (p. 230):

---

[9] Scheper-Hughes is strongly influenced by the work of Michel Foucault, and she cites his 1972 text *The Archaeology of Knowledge*. In this work, Foucault argues that all knowledge is conditioned by its historical context. Further, critical symbols and ideas serve the purposes of the powerful, thereby controlling and dominating people's understanding of the world. Foucault's ideas are described more fully in footnote 4 of essay 34.

Antonio Gramsci (1891–1937) was an Italian scholar and politician who founded the Italian Communist party in 1921, then left to spend two years in Russia. When he returned to Italy, he was elected head of the Communist Party and was elected to the Italian parliament. In 1926 his party was outlawed, and Gramsci was arrested and imprisoned for eleven years. Gramsci's health deteriorated badly while in prison, and he died in a Roman hospital soon after his release. He is best known for the series of letters he wrote from prison, which were published posthumously in 1947 as *Lettere dal carcere* or *Prison Notebooks* (1994). Although a Communist, Gramsci turned away from Marx's emphasis on materialism and focused on the concept of symbolic hegemony. That is to say, the political and intellectual leaders of a society create a system of beliefs and ideas that are accepted by the common people and which help maintain the power of the ruling class. Additional information on Gramsci can be found in essay 24, footnote 11.

In the context of this discussion, doctors occupy the pivotal role of "traditional" intellectuals whose function is, in part, to fail to see the secret indignation of the hungry poor expressed in their inchoate folk idiom of "*nervos.*" But anthropologists, too, often play the role of the "traditional" intellectual in their unconscious collusions with hegemonic interpretations of social reality fostered by powerful local interests.[10]

The specification of the immoral agents moves from the state to bureaucracy technicians to doctors to teachers and social workers and finally to anthropologists. All are in complicity with oppression, although they may not know it. So—"What is to be done?" According to Scheper-Hughes (p. 229),

> As social scientists (and not social revolutionaries) critical practice implies an epistemological struggle in which the contested domain is anthropology itself. The struggle concerns the way knowledge is generated, the class interests that it serves, and the challenge is to make our discipline more relevant and non-oppressive to the people we study. Finally, it is addressed to clinical practitioners as a challenge to reintegrate the social and political dimension in their practice so as to put themselves squarely on the side of human suffering.

The call to action is clear. Anthropology has been part of the process of mystification, serving interests that oppress others. The moral thing to do is to denounce those who maintain this mystification and transform anthropology from an objective natural science, which is just a charade and a means of continuing oppression, into a *critical anthropology* which will help change the world.

It is important to keep in mind that one can also use an objective model for moral purposes, as for example, in investigating the biochemical basis of schizophrenia in order to make possible better medicine for schizophrenics. The separation between moral models and objective models is not based on the motives or biases of the investigator. In most scientific fields which aim to help people, there are both moral and objective models, linked together. For example, in medicine, there is an objective language of physiology and biochemistry that describes what various pathogens do and how the body reacts to them. This biological model describes how things work, not whether viruses or antibodies are good or bad. Linked to this objective model is a less formal model concerning what is healthy, what is safe, what is medically ethical, etc., in which, for example, melanoma is considered a *bad* cancer while warts are usually considered *benign*. This language of health and ethics is carefully kept separate from the objective language of biological processes. One of my colleagues calls this the "separation of church and state." You can have both, but they should be kept separate and distinct.

The separation of moral models and objective models is a crucial issue. It is exactly this separation that is explicitly attacked by anthropology's current moralists. For example, Rabinow[11] (1983:68–70, emphasis added) offers what he calls a "schematization of relations of truth and power" as follows:

> In the first position, that represented by Boas, the role of the anthropologist as a scientist was to speak truth to power. Boas was a profoundly political man: a typical secular, emancipated, German, Jewish liberal with a strong faith in the force of reason as a functional tool of political emancipation and as

---

[10] It is hard to read the works of Scheper-Hughes and not be moved by her call to action. As a young woman in the mid-1960s, Scheper-Hughes worked as a Peace Corps volunteer among the urban poor of northeastern Brazil. She later returned to the same area to conduct fieldwork that resulted in a number of publications (1989, 1992). In these she vividly describes the horrible conditions under which children and adults live and die.

[11] Paul Rabinow (1944–), like Scheper-Hughes, is a professor in the Department of Anthropology at the University of California Berkeley. Rabinow was one of the early voices in the postmodern movement in anthropology. In *Reflections on Fieldwork in Morocco* (1977), Rabinow discusses the process of doing fieldwork and the ways in which his position as a young outsider anthropologist affected the people he talked to and the data he collected. The book is widely considered a classic of reflexive ethnography.

an absolute value in its own right. The calling of the intellectual, for Boas, consisted of the advancement of reason through science and the conquest of tradition, irrationality, and injustice.

The dignity and achievements of Boas and his students are not in question—they were centrally responsible for making antiracism an accepted part of the American academic agenda—but neither are their limits and contradictions. The position of speaking truth to power, opposing humanism to nihilism, is still with us; and it is by no means the worst alternative. But ultimately *this position has not proved sufficiently hardy,* either intellectually or politically, to have spawned a science or politics which lives up to the standards of coherence and efficacy by which these individuals wished to be judged.

In an important sense, the second position, that represented by Geertz, *has no politics at all.* The ascetic imperative of Boas or Weber, who sought to separate truth and politics, still entailed an active vigilance lest these two realms fuse. It never occurred to these European intellectuals that political concerns were not central to the life of an intellectual—they saw them as so central they had to be kept in check. The sacrifice demanded of the scientist was not the loss of political passions but only that they be kept clearly distinct from scientific activities qua science. Over the time of two generations, the tension between these two callings, and hence the potential threat they posed for each other's autonomy, was gradually dissipated. In its place an ethics of scientific comportment became a code of civility. As this code took center stage, the more directly political concerns were weakened.

I am not advocating that we jettison the moral and intellectual achievements of the aggressively antiracist anthropology of Boas, nor that we discard what has been constructed and made to function as a civility which allows for dispute within a community of shared

discourse. The main conclusion I draw from the analysis presented in this paper is that *it is the dogged separation of truth and power in order to construct a science which has had the most deleterious effects on anthropology;* it is the conception of a humanist activity which has unwittingly pushed these anthropologists into a kind of nihilism which is the exact opposite of their intent.

Rabinow is clear that in his opinion the separation of moral models from objective models is a mistake resulting in an anthropology without morality ("politics" is a code word for "morality"). He presumes that anthropology *should* be moral and that the failure of anthropologists to maintain Boas's moral passion condemns the idea of separating moral and objective models; Geertz has failed us because he has no politics.[b]

Rabinow asserts that all anthropologists must have Boas's moral passion. I do not agree. In my moral universe, one can be an anthropologist simply because one is interested in human life and still be a good person. However, whether or not one has politics, or believes that all anthropologists should have politics, I argue that anthropology's claim to moral authority rests on knowing *empirical* truths about the world and that moral models should be kept separate from objective models because moral models are counterproductive in discovering how the world works. This is not an argument that anthropologists should have no politics; it is an argument that they should keep their politics separate from the way they do their science.

Without attempting to meet all attacks, I will first take up some of the most egregious arguments against objectivity.

1. *Objective models are dehumanizing.*

According to Rorty[12] (1983:164), "Foucault is doubtless right that the social sciences have

---

[12] Richard Rorty (1931–) is a prominent American philosopher. In his breakthrough work, *Philosophy and the Mirror of Nature* (1979), he promoted a style of thinking he called pragmatism. Rorty argued that philosophy cannot be a science and that the scientific method itself was invalid. Instead, beliefs about the world are supported by appeals to the conventional means through which a culture justifies its beliefs. Such a system of justification does not have any necessary foundation in empirical reality. Apart from specific social and cultural traditions of justification, there can be no general account of what makes a proposition true.

coarsened the moral fiber of our rulers. Something happens to politicians who are exposed to endless tabulations of income levels, rates of recidivism, cost-effectiveness of artillery fire, and the like—something like what happens to concentration camp guards." Here is complete fantasy. No evidence besides a mention of Foucault is cited. Certainly I know of no research that shows that social science research findings have a dehumanizing effect on people. What seem to be operating here are the assumptions of the current moral model; objectivity is part of science, science is used in the domination of others, domination is the inhuman treatment of others, hence objectivity is dehumanizing. All this follows from first principles and need not be proved.[13]

2. *The distinctions between objectivity and subjectivity, fact and language, knowledge and opinion, depend on a realist conception of the world and the correspondence theory of truth. This theory is flawed, and therefore the distinctions which grow out of it are confusing and unnecessary.*

The realist conception of science argues that science "works" because it corresponds in some degree and in some manner to the "way the world really is." That is, science tries to find out the "truth," and "truth" consists of statements that correspond to "reality." It is this correspondence to reality that explains why science is successful at prediction and control. The argument of Rorty (1991) and others, who call themselves "relativists," or "antirealists" or "antirationalists," is that the "correspondence" between statements and the world is not an obvious matter. Various conventions about what counts as evidence are needed in order to decide the truth or falsity of statements; in a mature science these conventions are quite complex. For example, in psychology, the value of experimental evidence depends on a variety of statistical considerations involving reliability, control cases, proportion of the variance accounted for, type 1 and type 2 errors, etc. But where do these conventions come from? They are conventions agreed upon by a commu-

nity. Thus truth depends on the consensus of the community, and objectivity reduces to social solidarity (Rorty 1991:22).

This argument has also been put forward by a number of individuals working in the history of science and the sociology of knowledge. Latour (1988), Latour and Woolgar (1979), Shapin and Schaffer (1985), and others have presented specific case histories which they argue show that scientific debate is determined not by the winners' being closer to some abstract truth but by their having more social and cultural power. Philip Kitcher, a philosopher of science who is a vigorous defender of the rationality of science, summarizes the position of the antirationalists, among whom he explicitly includes Feyerabend, Barnes, Bloor, Shapin, Schaffer, Collins and Latour, as follows (1993:198):

[1] The community decision is reached when sufficiently many sufficiently powerful subgroups within the community have arrived at decisions (possibly independent, possibly coordinated) to modify their practices in a particular way.

[2] Scientists are typically moved by nonepistemic as well as epistemic goals.

[3] There is significant cognitive variation within scientific communities, in terms of individual practices, underlying propensities, and exposure to stimuli.

[4] During all phases of scientific debate, the processes undergone by the ultimate victors are no more well designed for promoting cognitive progress than those undergone by the ultimate losers.

[5] Scientific debates are closed when one group musters sufficient power to exclude its rival(s) from the community; the subsequent articulation and development of the successful modification of practice absorb all available resources, so that later comparisons can be made between a highly developed tradition and an underdeveloped rival. . . .

---

[13] D'Andrade refers to arguments from *first principles*. Such an argument starts with a basic, universal, verifiable statement with which everybody can agree, and goes on to produce larger truths such as the existence of God, or the scientific method.

Kitcher points out that the first three points are not central to the antirationalist argument; the crucial points are 4 and 5, which deny that, over the long term, correspondence with the "truth," or with "the way the world really is," tips the battle so that scientific knowledge progresses. All five points are empirical generalizations; if they are true it is a matter not of first principles but of fact. Kitcher argues that a more empirically accurate characterization would modify points 4 and 5 as follows:

> [4] During the early phases of scientific debate, the processes undergone by the ultimate victors are (usually) no more well designed for promoting cognitive progress than those undergone by the ultimate losers.

> [5] Scientific debates are closed when, as a result of conversations among peers and encounters with nature that are partially produced by early decisions to modify individual practices, there emerges in the community a widely shared argument, encapsulating a process for modifying practice which, when judged by [an external standard] is markedly superior in promoting cognitive progress than other processes undergone by protagonists in the debate: power accrues to the victorious group principally in virtue of the integration of this process into the thinking of members of the community and recognition of its virtues.[14]

There is probably no "knock-down" argument from first principles to demonstrate that the correspondence theory of truth is right (or wrong) or that scientific knowledge has advanced (or not advanced). Whether the correspondence theory of truth is right and whether scientific knowledge has advanced are empirical questions, and I think that the empirical answers are reasonably clear. As Gellner (1992:60–61) has said:

> One particular style of knowledge [scientific knowledge] has proved so overwhelmingly powerful, economically, militarily, administratively, that all societies have had to make their peace with it and adopt it. Some have done it more successfully than others, and some more willing or more quickly than others; but all of them have had to do it, or perish. Some have retained more, and some less, of their previous culture.

That is, the empirical support for the hypothesis that science advances is simply the strong evidence that scientific knowledge about the world *has* advanced. Whether, on balance, scientific knowledge has been used for good or evil is another question. My own unoriginal conclusion is that, on balance, the world is considerably better off because of science. However, those who disagree on this point would, I believe, still have to agree that scientific *knowledge* has advanced. Given the obvious success of science as a way of finding out about the world, it is remarkable that many anthropologists are attracted to philosophers and historians who flirt with the idea that there is no true progress in scientific knowledge and no way of knowing what is true.c [15]

The antirationalists further argue that there are no independent criteria for explaining the success of science (Rorty 1991). My own opinion is that the success of science is due primarily both to the norm of presenting generalizations in a form that makes it possible to dispute them with

---

[14] The difference between D'Andrade's argument and that of the critical theorists is well summed up in the comparison of this version of point 5 with the version above. In the first version, the critical issue is not how well a theory maps reality but whether those who promote the theory have political and economic power. If a theory is promoted by the powerful, it is accepted. In the version of point 5 presented here, it is the degree of explanatory power of a theory that determines its acceptance. If a theory is a powerful device to explain empirical reality, then it will be accepted by members of the scientific community. Both of these positions are extreme, but how you feel about them is probably a good indication of your own position in the debate between postmodernists and their detractors. If you lean toward the first point 5, you favor postmodern interpretations. If you prefer the second, you will be more comfortable in the empiricist camp.

[15] Although D'Andrade makes a strong case for the advancement of knowledge through science, it is also true that other ways of knowing may be equally valid. If one's goal is to describe the world or the cultural understandings of members of a society, art, literature, myth, and other modes of interpretation may offer insights as powerful as those generated by science.

evidence and to the norm of carrying out extensive tests of other people's generalizations. The testability of statements and the constant testing of statements ward off the very strong tendency of humans to believe what they *want* to believe. It is these two norms that give the scientific enterprise its power.[16]

Finally, there is something inconsistent about the statements made by Rorty and others about the badness of the subject/object, language/fact, and knowledge/opinion distinctions. For example, according to Rorty (1991:41, emphasis added);

> On the pragmatist view, the contrast between "relations of ideas" and "matters of fact" is a special case of the bad seventeenth-century contrasts between being "in us" and being "out there," between subject and object, between our beliefs and what those beliefs (moral, scientific, theological, etc.) are trying to get right. . . . [The pragmatist] is suggesting that instead of invoking anything like the idea-fact, or language-fact, or mind-world, or subject-object distinctions to explicate our intuition that *there is something out there to be responsible to,* we just drop the intuition.

Imagine a lazy student in one of Rorty's classes who complains that he only got a D. Professor Rorty says, "That is what you deserve." The student replies, "You are invoking the intuition that there is something out there [my performance, objectively viewed] *to be responsible to.* You should drop that intuition. Subjectively, I *feel* I did quite well, and although I said that I would turn in a paper, the *fact* that I did not simply reinvokes the language/fact distinction, which depends on the flawed correspondence theory of truth." Of course, Rorty would explain that he bases his judgments on the normal consensus about what counts as true (the professor's judgment) rather than some ultimate correspondence of the professor's judgment with reality. What

Rorty means by "objectivity" and "truth" is not what the student means; Rorty is talking about ultimate truth and complete objectivity, not ordinary judgments about course performance and broken promises. Rorty does not mean (I think) that in ordinary life the distinctions between object and subject, mind and world, idea and fact, etc., should be dispensed with (that would make an odd world). It is only in certain kinds of philosophic discourse that these distinctions are not to be made. However, in my opinion this speaks badly for such kinds of philosophic discourse.

3. *The idea that people can be objective is illusory; people construct the reality that suits them best. Hence an objective model is impossible, and any pretense that such a model can be achieved is simply hegemonic mystification.*

Scheper-Hughes's statement "The objectivity of science and of medicine is always a phantom objectivity, a mask that conceals more than it reveals" (1992:229) is one example of this position. It should be noted that the meaning of "objective" in these arguments is shifted from "an account which describes the object, not the describer" to "an account given without bias or self-interest." This is a secondary sense of the term; literally, "objective" glosses as "pertaining to the object." The secondary sense of the term "unbiased" is an extension based on the notion that those who have no axe to grind give a more objective account. By shifting from the primary sense to the secondary sense one can make the case that, since people are always biased to some degree, an "objective" account is impossible. Then, since "objectivity" (not having any interests) is impossible, any claim to objectivity must be a "mask," a mystification. However, the accusation depends on the trick of substituting a secondary for a primary meaning. Besides, who ever claimed that

---

[16] Note the shift of style in this paragraph. D'Andrade shies away from making a bold statement about the reasons for the success of science. Instead he offers us his opinion, which may be right or wrong, but in any event is only an opinion. He is wise in this since he is entering an area where there is much disagreement and he has told us just above that there is no way to argue from first principles to scientific truth. Nonetheless, what he suggests here is far from radical. The notion that the strength of science comes from public attempts to falsify hypotheses comes primarily from the work of Karl Popper (see essay 26, footnote 14) and is widely accepted.

scientists are unbiased? A brief acquaintanceship with the history of science would certainly disabuse anyone of that notion. Science works not because it produces unbiased accounts but because its accounts are objective enough to be proved or disproved no matter what anyone wants to be true.[17]

While I am objecting to the rhetorical tricks that are used to identify objectivity and science with badness, I should also note that similar tricks are used to identify objectivity and science with goodness. The methods of science and the use of objective accounts are the best way to find out about the world (I would argue), but the method has no *guarantee* of working. Employment of the term "science" as an honorific to give weight to unreplicated and often unsound generalizations, sometimes constructed with considerable bias, is a continuing abuse. One could even argue that there is so much positive mystification around the term "science" that some negative mystification is needed as a balance. Fine, if the result is intellectual balance—the recognition that, on both sides, rhetoric is not evidence and that "fact" is always a probability, not an absolute.[18]

It might be thought that I am claiming that science should be value-free and outside politics. This is not the case. Science is an institutionalized activity—a means, not an end. It can be used for all sorts of ends—to create engines of war, to make new products, to cure physical and mental ills, and even just to discover things. The determination of the ends of scientific activity in the United States has long been a political matter in which Congress and a variety of interest groups, including those who want to do science just for the sake of enlightenment, contend for

the money. Science demystified is not intrinsically good or bad.

4. *Objectivity is part of the general hegemony of Western culture, and is authoritarian and oppressive.*

Abu-Lughod (1991:150–51) writes:

> Generalization, the characteristic model of operation and style of writing of the social sciences, can no longer be regarded as neutral description. . . . There are two reasons for anthropology to be wary of generalization. The first is that, as part of a professional discourse of "objectivity" and expertise, it is inevitably a language of power. On the one hand, it is the language of those who seem to stand apart from and outside of what they are describing. . . . On the other hand, even if we withhold judgment on how closely the social sciences can be associated with the apparatuses of management, we have to recognize how all professional discourses by nature assert hierarchy.

Here the contagious badness-of-oppression continues to spread like a plague; oppression's badness infects power, power's badness infects objectivity ("standing apart"), and objectivity's badness infects generalizations. Again, the badness is asserted on the basis of first principles, not demonstrated. In opposition to Abu-Lughod, I claim that it is *not* bad to make generalizations about people and that ethnographic generalizations do *not* damage people. *Nor* does objectivity. *Nor* do power differences. This is another fantasy. What damages people is the way power is *used* and the way generalizations are *used*. And what *helps* people is the way power is *used* and the way generalizations are *used*. It is irrational to hold that power as such is bad. The

---

[17] The distinction D'Andrade makes here is important. It is clear that the types of questions scientists ask and the reasons for which they ask them are set by their personal backgrounds, cultures, histories, and desires. Scientific questions are always in this sense subjective, and scientific observers are human and always have axes to grind. However, does that necessarily mean their results are invalid? D'Andrade says observers don't have to be objective in order for observations to be objective.

[18] Here D'Andrade discusses the use of *science* as an honorific. In so doing he is acknowledging that in our society, to designate a field of study as science is to privilege it. When he talks about using the term science to support unsound generalizations, he is probably thinking of "creation science," or Erik Von Daniken's theory that archaeological remains can only be explained by extraterrestrial landings, and other such pseudoscientific endeavors. In these cases, the term science is clearly used to lend an air of legitimacy to otherwise nonscientific investigations.

D'Andrade calls for intellectual balance—that identifying science with goodness or badness is equally absurd. He says rhetoric is not evidence and "fact" is always probability.

result is a spreading pollution that makes it bad to say that the Bedouin are polygynous (Abu-Lughod 1991:153).[19]

One effect of the current ban on objectivity is the substitution of stories and narratives for generalizations. Abu-Lughod says, "For these reasons I propose that we experiment with *narrative ethnographies of the particular* in a continuing tradition of fieldwork-based writing" (1991:153, emphasis added). By telling a story about someone, the ethnographer does not have to make any generalizations and thereby appears to avoid the danger of hegemonic discourse. However, the appearance is deceptive; quite the reverse happens in fact. It is a natural assumption of the reader that any narrative is, in some important sense, typical of what happens in that place, unless told otherwise. Kenneth Burke (1945) calls this rhetorical strategy that of the "reductive anecdote" — the world is "summarized by" and "reduces to" the story one tells about it. *Presenting an anecdote is just as essentializing and totalizing as stating a generalization.* Consider, for example, the well-known anecdote about George Washington and the cherry tree: it acts just like the generalization "Washington was honest" but hides the claim. Hence Burke's comment on the rhetorical use of anecdotes: beware of people just telling stories.[20]

It is striking that these attacks on objective models do not present any evidence of the damage done by objectivity. In the same vein, evidence about the good done by science is ignored. A major reason for the unimportance of evidence, I believe, is what is being asserted is not a set of empirical facts but whether one's first allegiance is to morality or to truth. My hypothesis that what is being expressed is allegiance to a set of moral principles explains another rather odd aspect of many of the attacks — their loose adherence to the laws of logic. A number of scholars who have critiqued various postmodernist positions (e.g., Spiro 1986, Bailey 1991, Gellner 1992) have commented on the internal contradictions, principle begging, and appeals to authority found in much of this writing. These objections have not been answered; the usual response I have heard is that they are "beside the point." And, if the point is that relativism is the correct *moral* response to cultural differences, then, indeed, logic and evidence are not relevant.

One might say, "Well, some of these moral concerns may be overdone, but why not use the current moral model? Isn't it a reasonable model of reality as well as a model which shows what is right? Can't one blend together objectivity and morality in a single model?" So far as I know, a mixed model would not violate any principle of logic. However, there are reasonably well-understood problems with trying to graft moral and objective models together if one wants to find out about the world. It may need to be repeated that the argument here is not against anthropologists' having moral models. Indeed, I believe that anthropologists should work to develop more coherent, clearly articulated moral models. These moral models should, I think, describe both the anthropologist's responsibilities and a vision of what the good society and the good culture would look like. The point has often been made that if anthropologists do not try to

---

[19] D'Andrade's use of Abu-Lughod's work is particularly apt. An important feminist anthropologist and postmodernist, Abu-Lughod has led the field in presenting narrative accounts of women she worked with in her study of Bedouin society. However, it is important to point out that although Abu-Lughod is a radical postmodernist who has pioneered the use of genres such as "auto-ethnography" (she writes extensively about her own pregnancy, for example [1995]), she is not quite as radical as D'Andrade portrays her. In the passage he cites here, she does not say that all anthropology should become narrative stories, but that such stories should "complement rather than replace a range of other types of anthropological projects . . ." She does not say we should completely avoid the use of the term polygyny but rather discuss the ways in which particular individuals "live the 'institution' that we call polygyny."

[20] In this passage, D'Andrade makes an ironic point, turning one of the basic insights of the postmodernists against them. The notion that authors build authority through the conventions and styles of writing is fundamental to deconstructionist theory. Crapanzano explores this theme in great detail in essay 39. Here D'Andrade notes that postmodern attempts to discuss the particular through narrative stories are doomed because, whether they desire it or not, such stories are bound to be understood as generalizations. He backs his point with a quote from Burke, but it could easily be supported with reference to Derrida or other postmodern philosophers.

influence the ends to which the knowledge they produce is used, others will do it for them. But— the point I am arguing—these moral models should be kept separate from the objective models with which we debate what is.

The first problem with blended models is *identification*. To use the current moral model, with its emphasis on the badness of oppression, to understand the world, one must be able to identify when something is or is not oppression. But what makes something oppression? Is taking away the freedom of serial murderers oppression? Most people would say that it is not—that they deserve to have their freedom taken away, and that it is prudent to do so as well. It is not oppression, then, if the people being dominated deserve to be dominated or need to be dominated for the common good. But who is to say who deserves to be dominated? And who is to say what the common good is? Serbs believe that Croats should be dominated for a variety of reasons. Badness and goodness are not simple properties of things but complex interactions between events and human intentions and welfare. It becomes very difficult to define what oppression is except by one's *reaction* to the situation—whenever it seems to be a bad use of power call it "oppression," and whenever it is a good use call it "justice" or something else. This is a central doctrine of subjectivity; what one truly feels is bad *is* bad. Of course, one can say that this is just quibbling, and that everyone—or almost everyone— can tell a good from a bad use of power. However, because of the complexity of human life we often find ourselves vehemently disagreeing even with people we respect about exactly this. The experience of people trying to find out about how the world works is that you find out more when you avoid the use of evaluative terms—otherwise you spend all your time arguing about the use of these terms, trying to make the bad things get the bad words and the good things get the good words.

A second problem in trying to meld together moral and objective models is that the objective world comes in many shades of grey but the moral world tends toward black and white. Op-

pression, for example, is not an all-or-none state; it varies in degree. Not every use of power is equally bad. To make a model account for what happens in the world, one usually needs to distinguish *more* from *less*. But morality does not seem to like to do this; each case of oppression must be treated as an equal horror because they are all *wrong*. Sin is sin, and if one sets up a scale of greater and lesser sins one quickly finds out that lesser sins are no longer considered *real* sins. Thus the pragmatics of morality and the pragmatics of finding out about the world pull in different directions.

A third problem is the powerful tendency to believe that good things produce good results and bad things produce bad results: "By their fruits ye shall know them." But the complexities of causality do not respect our human wish for the good to produce good and the bad to produce bad. Furthermore, the pragmatics of morality tend strongly toward a unicausal view of events; for every bad event there is a single bad thing that caused it. This makes assignment of blame much easier. But the world tends to be strongly multicausal. When a fire burns down a building, who is to blame? Why, the man who threw the match in the wastepaper basket. But for a physicist the match would not have lit the material in the wastepaper basket if it had a higher combustion point or if there had been no oxygen in the air or if the building had been made entirely of stone. We *blame* a knowing and intentional agent, but almost always what happens is the result not *just* of a knowing intentional act but a complex web of causes. Use of the notion that "bad causes bad" results in the kind of conclusion that Abu-Lughod reaches about generalizations: power brings about oppression, therefore power is bad. Science gives people power, therefore science is bad. Objectivity is part of science, therefore objectivity is bad. Generalizations are produced by objective science, therefore generalizations are bad. And some would take it further: generalizations are based on fieldwork, therefore fieldwork is, if not bad, at least a situation that places one in very grave moral jeopardy.[21]

---

[21]This is probably D'Andrade's weakest point. While it is certainly true that since the early 1970s anthropologists have often condemned fieldwork as supporting oppression (see footnote 24), it is less clear that they believe there is a single

A fourth pragmatic problem in trying to meld moral and objective models is that whereas an objective model can—at least sometimes—be changed by new data, new arguments, new theories, moral models are very hard to change. The history of the current moral model is interesting in this regard. So far as I have been able to ascertain, the present moral model was first outlined by Jeremy Bentham, a late-18th-century English philosopher and one of the founders of utilitarianism. Bentham said that those who govern use symbols which serve the interests of the governing class. These symbols are fictions; there is no such thing as the "Crown" or the "Church," for example. Bentham's interest was in revealing the rhetorical fictions and phantoms used to hide what he termed "sinister interests" (Bentham 1952). His goal was explicitly moral: to demystify and thereby denounce these fictions so that there could be clarification of the "common good."[22]

Marx, who read Bentham and commented on his notions of sinister interests and fictions, added Bentham's ideas about mystification to his own model of social conflict and its resolution through socialism. He disclaimed ethical and humanitarian reasons for preferring socialism. For him it was historically determined that socialism would overthrow capitalism. The important causal machinery in Marx's model concerns class conflict and material conditions. Symbolic hegemony might have some effect in slowing down the revolution, since false consciousness could interfere temporarily with the necessary recognition of class interests on the part of workers, but it was not a primary force. The Benthamite model

was, however, often used by Marxists in their intellectual battles with other political philosophies and in their battles with each other. The standard argument was that the ideas of other philosophies were nothing more than expressions of class interests and attempts at symbolic hegemony; Marxism alone had an "objective" basis. Later, in Gramsci's writings, the complex machinery of the Marxist model, involving forces of production, relations of production, material conditions, etc., was replaced by the role of symbols, culture, and intellectuals in the maintenance and legitimation of the status quo (Femia 1981). The material parts of the Marxist model were eliminated, and what remained was the claim that governments were able to stay in power because the state controlled ideology which became part of the common sense of the common culture. The model moved back from Marx to Bentham, except that the state remained the primary source of oppression.[23]

By the late 1960s the current oppression model was a well-entrenched part of the ideology of the American intellectual radical left in the social sciences and the humanities. The main outlines of this model were presented in a collection of essays, edited by Dell Hymes, titled *Reinventing Anthropology*.[24] Much of the moral stirring in anthropology at that time was a result of the Vietnam war, and *Reinventing Anthropology* reflects the conflicts of that time. But beyond discussion of issues relating to Vietnam, the contributors were clear that anthropology should be permanently changed. In the essays in this volume (Hymes 1972), Berreman called for an end to the pervasive hypocrisy of academic anthropology,

---

cause for evil in the world. In fact, it would probably be more accurate to say that postmodernists emphasize complexity of both cause and effect.

[22] Jeremy Bentham is less well noted for these positions than for the utilitarian principle that good can be defined as that which provides the greatest benefit to the greatest number of people. A more complete note on Bentham can be found in essay 37, footnote 8.

[23] D'Andrade's interpretation of Gramsci is extreme. Although Gramsci does give a more prominent place to the power of ideology (which he terms hegemony) than Marx, he never completely abandons materialism.

[24] In the 1970s, anthropologists started to cast a critical eye on their discipline. First, anthropologists who worked for government agencies or received government funding were severely criticized because of popular sentiment against U.S. government actions in Southeast Asia. Second, because many anthropologists worked in countries that were former colonial possessions of European nations, and worked with the approval of those governments in a context of coercion, their research was seen as supporting the colonial oppression of those governments. Dell Hymes' 1972 book *Reinventing Anthropology* and Talal Asad's *Anthropology and the Colonial Encounter* (1973) were particularly vigorous in their

William Willis defined anthropology as the study of dominated people done in aid of imperialism, Minna Caulfield discussed cultural exploitation in terms of its effect on the colonialized culture and individuals sharing it, Richard Clemmer discussed the development of resistance among American Indians, Norman Klein speculated about the effect of the 1960 counterculture on American cultural hegemony, Robert Jay described how he had come to feel that anthropological theory and anthropological fieldwork involve serious moral problems because of their dehumanizing effects on society and on anthropologists, and Bob Scholte presented an agenda for anthropology based on a reflexive and critical epistemology in contrast to "value-free" social science.

All of this was stated clearly in the 1960s. However, unlike the current moralists, the moralists of the 1960s and 1970s were, with some exceptions, young and relatively unknown and also not epistemological relativists. What seems to have happened next is that this model went "tacit" and then reemerged in full voice in the 1980s as a part of the postmodernist movement.[d] Postmodernism, with its concerns about the authority of representation and its interest in the deconstruction of the verities, gave the moral model a much more resplendent vocabulary and greater epistemological bite. *Writing Cultures* (Clifford and Marcus 1986) was ostensibly about a new way of writing ethnography. Behind the discussion of modes of presentation was the presupposition that the old way of writing was the expression of the old objective (realist/hegemonic) model and therefore had to be replaced. The language used in the essays in *Writing Cultures* made strong claims to upper-middle-class sensibility in esthetic matters

but did not modify the basics of the moral model. It did, however, make it possible to claim that concern with writing and representation counted as a serious moral pursuit. In any case, the moral model, as developed during the later part of the 18th century, has changed very little because, I believe, of its usefulness in moral argument by intellectuals against other intellectuals.[25]

So far, I have discussed four general problems with the use of moral models as a means of finding out about the world: the difficulty in getting reliable identifications for basic terms, the tendency towards all-or-none thinking, the tendency towards monocausality and evaluative contagion, and the difficulty of changing a moral model. There are also a number of problems with the *particular* moral model of oppression current in anthropology.

First, in my opinion, this particular moral model is not a very good representation of the way the world is. As an explanation of what is happening globally, the model in its Gramscian form made most sense in the 1950s and '60s, when the cold war was at its height. At that time two powerful empires, one capitalist, the other communist, held sway over much of the world. The difference between the two empires was not a matter of material conditions; both were modern industrial economies. What happened to make the difference was ideology. That is, to explain how the world could be so divided, it made sense to postulate that the division was due to differences in belief and that the commitment to belief was the result of the rhetoric produced by mystifiers who managed the flow of symbols and information that created the common sense of ordinary people. The Gramscian worldview is

---

condemnation of the discipline. A more recent critique of anthropology in this vein is Faye Harrison's *Decolonizing Anthropology: Moving Further Toward an Anthropology for Liberation,* published in 1991.

[25] Clifford and Marcus' 1986 volume *Writing Culture: The Poetics and Politics of Ethnography* was a decisive volume, bringing together a collection of essays by several leading American postmodernists, including James Clifford, Vincent Crapanzano, Renato Rosaldo, Stephen Tyler, Tala Asad, George Marcus, Michael Fischer, and Paul Rabinow. The point of *Writing Culture* was to argue that ethnographic writing was a cross between fiction, memoir, scientific report, and travelogue. Therefore, anthropological writing should be subjected to literary and political analysis.

Ironically, this volume was severely attacked by feminist anthropologists for the lack of women authors in the work (there is only one – a literary critic named Pratt) and for Clifford's dismissal of feminist anthropology in the volume's introduction. Clifford wrote clearly inadequate, however, to account for the breakup of the Soviet Union and the current world disorder in which nation-states are unable to contain ethnic conflicts. The present problem for any macrosocial theory is not identifying oppression but accounting for the failure of current governments to maintain order.[26]

It can be argued that the moral model still has some representational adequacy in accounting for oppression within particular countries. However, in my opinion, oppression in China, Brazil, or the United States can be better understood by recourse to theoretical models about the privileged access of special-interest groups to governmental functions, the operation of political parties, the lack of civil society, and other standard kinds of political analysis than by explanation based on a model of mass mystification. The only situation to which the oppression/mystification/denunciation model seems to have a reasonable degree of fit is to discrimination—racism and sexism. However, even with respect to racism and sexism the moral model does not explain much; it simply condemns discrimination as oppression. It does not tell us why discrimination is worse at some times and in some places.

A number of other problems with the current moral model may be considered briefly. The moral model has no theory of *good* power or *good* inequality and so must simply condemn without understanding much of the operation of any social system. Also, the model is almost entirely

negative in character; it creates a climate of denunciation and rage. Further, while those who use the model are reflexive in asking, "Am *I* acting oppressively?" they are not at all reflexive on other points; they do not ask, "What is there about *me* that makes *me* see oppression as bad?" or "Why should others believe *my* assertions when *I* do not believe theirs?" or "Why have *I* been blessed with the knowledge of good and evil that *others* do not seem to have?" Overall, there is the unreflexive assumption that one is a member of an elect that by natural grace knows what is right, and this elect consists of those who hold the current moral model. All others are to be driven out of anthropology by "epistemological struggle," as Scheper-Hughes puts it.

Another limitation of the current model is that it does not seem likely that it will bring about very much good in the world. It does not lead one to do anything positive about bad conditions. Instead it leads to denunciations of various social practitioners, such as social workers, doctors, psychiatrists, economists, civil servants, bureaucrats, etc., and especially other anthropologists. Isn't it odd that the true enemy of society turns out to be that guy in the office down the hall? But the intellectual destruction of these mystifiers, however desirable within the framework of the model, is unlikely to help the truly oppressed very much. Steven Sangren, in his article "Rhetoric and the Authority of Anthropology" (1988), pointed to the will to power expressed by postmodernist

---

Feminist ethnography has focused either on setting the record straight about women or revising anthropological categories (for example the nature/culture opposition). It has not produced either unconventional forms of writing or a developed reflection on ethnographic textuality as such. (1986: 20–21)

Behar and Gordon edited a volume in 1995 called *Women Writing Culture* specifically in response to Clifford's challenge.

[26] Note that once again, D'Andrade shifts to a writing style that emphasizes opinion. Here he argues that Gramscian notions are ill-suited to account for the breakup of the Soviet Union and the problems of the maintenance of order in the world today. However, this relies on a gross oversimplification of Gramsci's work consistent with D'Andrade's notion that Gramsci was not a materialist. Gramsci did not propose that hegemony existed devoid of material circumstances or opposition. In fact, he proposed the existence of counterhegemonies within societies and saw politics as a battleground between economic forces and contesting hegemonic and counterhegemonic systems. As a result, followers of Gramsci do not have any particular difficulty accounting for recent events. However, it does not follow that Gramsci's model is the best one, and D'Andrade is certainly entitled to his opinions.

The idea that the fundamental problem for current theories is to account for the failure of current governments to maintain order is a popular notion promoted in the works of Robert Kaplan. Kaplan sees understanding the collapse of state authority as basic to any appreciation of the world's current condition or its future. He has written frequently on this advocates of the moral model. The current moral model is a good instrument for intellectual battle within the university; it hardly seems likely, even on its own terms, to accomplish much else. This is what Bentham created it for, and this has been its most important use in Marxist thought.

The best part of the model is the analysis of different kinds of mystification; these do tell us something about the world. Much weaker is the assertion that these mystifications are effective in maintaining oppression—that ordinary people do not rise to overthrow the capitalists or colonialists or sexists because of the power of these mystifications. This is undemonstrated though in some cases plausible. More often it appears to be the case that people do not revolt either because (1) they face overwhelming force, (2) they are receiving satisfaction from their lives as lived, or (3) the persons, groups, or institutions that the social scientist has identified as the source of the oppression are not the true source of oppression—the source being more diffuse and less amenable to solution than the social scientist thinks and the social scientist's explanation in fact being the one that is mystifying.

Finally, the current moral model is ethnocentric. It is strong for equality (the escape from inequality) and freedom (the release from oppression). In my opinion these are not bad values, but they are very American. These are not the predominant values of modern Japan, India, China, the Middle East, or Southeast Asia, but they are the predominant values in the United States and much of Europe. It is ironic that these moralists should be so colonialist in their assumption about what is evil.

However, even if the moral model were a more adequate representation of what is going on in the world, included a theory of good power and good inequality, were less negative in character, more reflexive about matters of moral belief, and more oriented toward doing something positive in the world, gave better explanations for why people do not revolt, and were much less ethnocentric, it would still be a mistake to try to make such a model also serve as the model for understanding how things work. The driving force of a moral model is the allocation of praise and blame, reward and punishment, and this goal *will* shape its cognitive character. The driving force of an objective model is the goal of obtaining a surer understanding of how things work, of what is happening "out there." It is nice to believe that one can have both in a single model, but the evidence is strong that one cannot. The current moral model is a case in point.

It comes down to a choice: whatever one wants in the way of political change, will the first priority be to understand how things work? That would be my choice. I believe that anthropology can maintain its moral authority only on the basis of empirically demonstrable truths. But I am afraid that my choice may be in the minority. A large and growing number of American anthropologists appear to believe that the moral agenda of anthropology should take priority over the scientific agenda. An even larger number appear to believe that the scientific agenda of anthropology is in deservedly bad repute because of its association with oppression. "Science" has become a bad word in anthropology.[e] Can we at least hold on to "objectivity?"

I do not know how this will turn out. Perhaps after another few years of continued moral suasion, the internal bickering of the moralists will begin to be more interesting than their message, and the current wave of moral righteousness will be followed by a period of cynicism and disillusionment. This seems to be what happened after the French Revolution, after Cromwell in England, and after Stalin in Russia. In five or ten years the New Young Turks will probably flaunt their cynicism and find the moral pretensions of their elders unbearably hypocritical. In any case, let us hope that anthropology, as a science, will survive. As estheticized journalism

---

subject. One of his most important essays, "The Coming Anarchy," appeared in early 1994.

D'Andrade argues that the moral model is ill-equipped to deal with current conditions. Below he issues a scathing condemnation of the postmodern viewpoint, arguing that this moral model has no explanatory value, is good for little but condemnation with no understanding, and is unlikely to bring about the positive change it seeks.

and moralistic pamphleteering it can easily be replaced.[27]

Notes

a. A reviewer of an earlier draft of this article disagreed with my characterization of the "oppression model" as moral, arguing that the current "postmodern" position derives from the work of Nietzsche, Derrida, DeMan, and Foucault, all in the reviewer's opinion "amoral relativists." Whatever the merits of this reviewer's position, it is nevertheless the case that the anthropologists cited here—Rosaldo, Scheper-Hughes, Rabinow, Dwyer, Abu-Lughod, and others—are principled moralists who wish to make this world better.

b. In his Distinguished Lecture to the American Anthropological Association "Anti Anti-Relativism," Geertz (1984) protests Rabinow's characterization. Geertz makes the point that *his* politics of tolerance and understanding—of fighting against provincialism and ethnocentrism—are just as moral as other positions and that it is unfair to be labeled "without politics" by those who have *other* politics.

c. Bruno Latour (1993) appears to have moved to a realist position not substantially different from that of Kitcher. For example, in discussing Shapin and Schaffer's account of the controversy between Boyle and Hobbes about vacuum pumps and the role of experimentation, Latour (1993:28 emphasis added) says, "Boyle . . . invents the laboratory within which artificial machines create phenomena out of whole cloth. Even though they are artificial, costly, and hard to reproduce, and despite the small number of trained reliable witnesses, *these facts indeed represent nature as it is. . . . Scientists are scrupulous representatives of the facts.* Who is speaking when they speak? The facts themselves beyond all question, but also their authorized spokespersons."

d. A reviewer of an earlier draft points out that during this period there were extensive criticisms by feminist, Third World, and minority scholars of the biases in social science writing and research. The influence of these critiques on anthropology has been very powerful, and in many cases they have been used to support a blanket rejection of objectivity and a commitment to the kind of moral model described here. However, many feminist, minority, and Third World scholars do not reject the idea of objectivity and in fact find that the epistemological relativism typical of much postmodernist writing undercuts attempts to identify what has actually happened in the world and what needs to be changed.

e. Laura Nader has a good point with respect to the conception of "science." She says, "One question that should interest all of us has to do with clarifying the meaning of the *human* sciences qua science. In order to do this there needs to be recognition of

---

[27] In his final comments D'Andrade issues a devastating critique of the moral model upon which postmodernism is based and turns the postmodern attack upon itself. He concludes

1. The moral model is good for intellectual fighting but little else.

2. The postmodern focus on oppression may, in fact, obscure the real reasons people do not attempt to change their lives.

3. The moral model is ethnocentric, assuming Western moral values and goals.

4. The objective model attempts to discover how things work, but the moral model focuses on assigning blame and punishment.

Like much anti-postmodernist writing, D'Andrade's conclusion is alarmist in tone. He positions himself as a minority voice arguing against an overwhelming tide of antiscience and irrationality. In the last line, he goes as far as to suggest that if the forces of darkness—the postmodernists—win, the existence of the discipline of anthropology itself will be threatened. But it is important to note that the debate between those who view anthropology as the description of culture and those who view it as a science of culture designed to produce generalizable laws is as old as the discipline itself and unlikely to abate . . . ever.

It is not much of an exaggeration to say that this debate is one of the basic forces that drives anthropological theory. To grossly oversimplify: In American anthropology, Boas' inductive methodology was a reaction to the generalizations of nineteenth-century thinkers. Steward's and White's generalizations about cultural evolution were a reaction to the Boasians' insistence on the *sui generis* nature of culture. Ethnoscientists produced highly particularistic accounts of culture in reaction to cultural ecology. Ecological and cultural materialists, in their turn, reacted to the accounts of ethnoscientists, urging a generalizable, empirically based anthropology; and postmodernists, reacting to this, call for highly particular, narrative accounts of culture. What's next?

plurality in science. . . . A recognition of many kinds of science as applied to anthropology forces us to consider that the study of the human condition requires a division of labor in the research process. . . . how do anthropologists escape from dogmatic orthodoxy? They are driven by the research question" (Nader 1989:154).

References

Abu-Lughod, Lila. 1991. "Writing against culture," in *Recapturing Anthropology.* Edited by Richard G. Fox, pp. 37–62. Santa Fe: School of American Research Press.

Asad, Talal. 1973. *Anthropology and the colonial encounter.* London: Ithaca Press.

Bailey, F. G. 1991. *The prevalence of deceit.* Ithaca: Cornell University Press.

Bentham, Jeremy. 1952. *Bentham's handbook of political fallacies.* Baltimore: Johns Hopkins Press.

Burke, Kenneth. 1945. *A grammar of motives.* New York: Prentice-Hall.

Clifford, James, and George Marcus. 1986. *Writing culture: The poetics and politics of ethnography.* Berkeley: University of California Press.

Dwyer, Kevin. 1986. *Moroccan dialogues: Anthropology in question.* Baltimore: Johns Hopkins University Press.

Femia, Joseph V. 1981. *Gramsci's political thought: Hegemony, consciousness, and the revolutionary process.* Oxford: Clarendon Press.

Geertz, Clifford. 1984. Anti anti-relativism. *American Anthropologist.* 86: 263–78.

Gellner, Ernest. 1992. *Postmodernism, reason, and religion.* New York: Routledge.

Hymes, Dell. 1972. *Reinventing anthropology.* New York: Random House.

Kitcher, Philip. 1993. *The advancement of science.* Oxford: Oxford University Press.

Latour, Bruno. 1988. *The Pasteurization of France.* Cambridge: Harvard University Press.

———. 1993. *We have never been modern.* Cambridge: Harvard University Press.

Latour, Bruno, and Steve Woolgar. 1979. *Laboratory life.* Princeton: Princeton University Press.

Nadar, L. 1989. Post-interpretive anthropology. *Anthropological Quarterly* 62: 149–59.

Rabinow, Paul. 1983. "Humanism as nihilism: The bracketing of truth and seriousness in American cultural anthropology," in *Social science as moral inquiry.* Edited by R. Bellah, P. Rabinow, and W. Sullivan, pp. 33–51. New York: Columbia University Press.

Rorty, Richard. 1983. "Method and morality," in *Social science as moral inquiry.* Edited by R. Bellah, P. Rabinow, and W. Sullivan, pp. 52–75. New York: Columbia University Press.

———. 1991. *Objectivity, relativism, and truth: Philosophical papers.* Vol. 1. Cambridge: Cambridge University Press.

Rosaldo, Renato. 1989. *Culture and truth: The remaking of social analysis.* Boston: Beacon Press.

Scheper-Hughes, Nancy. 1992. "Hungry bodies, medicine, and the state: Toward a critical psychological anthropology," in *New directions in psychological anthropology.* Edited by T. Schwartz, G. White, and C. Lutz, pp. 221–47. New York: Cambridge University Press.

Shapin, Steven, and Simon Schaffer. 1982. *Leviathan and the air-pump.* Princeton: Princeton University Press.

Spiro, Melford E. 1986. Cultural relativism and the future of anthropology. *Cultural Anthropology* 1259–89.

Tyler, Stephen A. 1986. "Post-modern ethnography: From the document of occult to occult document," in *Writing cultures.* Edited by J. Clifford and G. Marcus, pp. 122–40. Berkeley: University of California Press.

Bibliography

GENERAL REFERENCES

A wide variety of reference works were used to fill in definitions, dates, and details of biography. The following books were among the most useful.

Edwards, Paul, ed.
1967 The *Encyclopedia of Philosophy*. New York: Macmillan.

Gacs, Ute, Aisha Khan, Jerry McIntyre, and Ruth Weinberg, eds.
1988 *Women Anthropologists: A Biographical Dictionary*. New York: Greenwood Press.

Sills, David L.
1968 *International Encyclopedia of the Social Sciences*. New York: Macmillan.

Winters, Christopher, ed.
1991 *International Dictionary of Anthropologists*. New York: Garland.

Abu-Lughod, Lila
1995 A Tale of Two Pregnancies. In *Women Writing Culture*, Ruth Behar and Deborah A. Gordon, eds., pp. 339–349. Berkeley: University of California Press.

Adams, R. M.
1966 *The Evolution of Urban Society*. Chicago: Aldine.

Agar, Michael H.
1980 *The Professional Stranger: An Informal Introduction to Ethnography*. New York: Academic Press.

Applebaum, Herbert, ed.
1987 *Perspectives in Cultural Anthropology*. Albany: State University of New York Press.

Ardrey, Robert
1961 *African Genesis*. New York: Atheneum

Asad, Talal
1973 *Anthropology and the Colonial Encounter*. London: Ithaca Press.

Atkinson, J. J.
1903 *Primal Law*. London, New York, and Bombay: Longman, Green.

Bachofen, Johann Jakob
1992 [1861] *Das Mutterrecht*. In *Myth, Religion and Mother Right: Selected Writings of J. J. Bachofen*, Ralph Manheim, trans. Princeton, N.J.: Princeton University Press.

Barash, D.
1979 *The Whisperings Within*. New York: Harper & Row.

Barnes, Harry E.
1960 Foreword. In *Essays in the Science of Culture in Honor of Leslie A. White*, Gertrude E. Dole and Robert L. Carneiro, eds., pp. xi–xvi. New York: Crowell.

Bateson, Gregory
1958 [1936] *Naven*. Palo Alto, Calif.: Stanford University Press.

Bateson, Gregory, and Margaret Mead
1942 *Balinese Character: A Photographic Analysis*. New York: New York Academy of Sciences.

Bateson, M. C.
1984 *With a Daughter's Eye: A Memoir of Margaret Mead and Gregory Bateson*. New York: William Morrow.

Beardsley, Richard K.
1976 An Appraisal of Leslie A. White's Scholarly Influence. *American Anthropologist* 78(3): 617–620.

Behar, Ruth
1995 Introduction: Out of Exile. In *Women Writing Culture*, Ruth Behar and Deborah A. Gordon, eds., pp. 1–29. Berkeley: University of California Press.

Behar, Ruth, and Deborah A. Gordon
1995 *Women Writing Culture*. Berkeley: University of California Press.

Bell, V.
1993 *Interrogating Incest: Feminism, Foucault, and the Law*. London: Routledge.

Benedict, Ruth Fulton
1930 Psychological Types in the Cultures of the Southwest. In *Proceedings of the Twenty-Third International Congress of Americanists* (held in New York, September 17–22, 1928), pp. 572–581. Lancaster, Pa.: Science Press Printing.

1934a Anthropology and the Abnormal. *Journal of General Psychology* 10(2): 59–82.
1934b *Patterns of Culture*. Boston, New York: Houghton Mifflin.
1946 *The Chrysanthemum and the Sword: Patterns of Japanese Culture*. Boston: Houghton Mifflin.
1948 Anthropology and the Humanities. *American Anthropologist* 50: 585–593.

Bentham, Jeremy
1789 *An Introduction to the Principles of Morals and Legislation*. London.

Berlin, Brent O., Dennis Breedlove, and Peter Raven
1974 *Principles of Tzeltal Plant Classification*. New York: Academic.

Bettelheim, Bruno
1955 *Symbolic Wounds: Puberty Rites and the Envious Male*. London: Thames and Hudson.

Blackburn, J.
1994 *Daisy Bates in the Desert: A Woman's Life Among the Aborigines*. London: Secker & Warburg.

Boas, Franz
1896 The Limitations of the Comparative Method in Anthropology. *Science*, n.s., 4: 901–908.
1974 [1938] The Background of My Early Thinking. In *The Shaping of American Anthropology 1883–1911: A Franz Boas Reader*. G. Stocking, pp. 41–42. New York: Basic Books.

Bock, Phillip K.
1988 *Rethinking Psychological Anthropology*. New York: W. H. Freeman.

Borofsky, Robert, ed.
1994 *Assessing Cultural Anthropology*. New York: McGraw-Hill.

Bottomore, T.
1991 Lumpenproletariat. In *A Dictionary of Marxist Thought*, T. Bottomore, ed., p. 327. Oxford: Basil Blackwell.

Bourgois, Philippe
1995 From Jíbaro to Crack Dealer: Confronting the Restructuring of Capitalism in El Barrio. In *Articulating Hidden Histories: Exploring the Influence of Eric R. Wolf*, Jane Schneider and Rayna Rapp, eds., pp. 125–141. Berkeley: University of California Press.

Boyne, Roy
1966 Structuralism. In *The Blackwell Companion to Social Theory*, Bryan S. Turner, ed., pp. 194–220. Oxford: Blackwell.

Briggs, Jean L.
1970 *Never in Anger: Portrait of an Eskimo Family*. Cambridge, Mass.: Harvard University Press.

Brillouin, Leon
1956 *Science and Information Theory*. New York: Academic.

Brown, D. E.
1991 *Human Universals*. New York: McGraw-Hill.

Brown, Dee
1971 *Bury My Heart at Wounded Knee*. New York: Holt, Rinehart, and Winston.

Brown, Norman O.
1959 *Life Against Death: The Psychoanalytical Meaning of History*. Middleton, Conn.: Wesleyan University Press.

Bücher, Carl
1968 [1901] *Industrial Evolution*. New York: Augustus M. Kelley.

Buffon, Georges Louis Leclerc
1752–1799 *Histoire naturelle, generale et particulier*. Paris: De l'Imprimerie Royale.

Carneiro, Robert L.
1970 A Theory of the Origin of the State. *Science* 169: 733–738.
1981 Leslie White. In *Totems and Teachers: Perspectives on the History of Anthropology*. New York: Columbia University Press.

Carneiro, Robert L., ed.
1967 *The Evolution of Society: Selections from Herbert Spencer's Principles of Sociology*. Chicago: University of Chicago Press.

Chagnon, Napoleon
1968 *The Fierce People*. New York: Holt, Rinehart, and Winston.

Childe, V. Gordon
1942 *What Happened in History*. Baltimore: Penguin.

Chodorow, Nancy
1974 Family Structure and Feminine Personality. In *Woman, Culture, and Society*, Michelle Rosaldo and Louise Lamphere, eds., pp. 43–66. Palo Alto, Calif.: Stanford University Press.

Clifford, James, and George E. Marcus, eds.
1986 *Writing Culture: The Poetics and Politics of Ethnography*. Berkeley: University of California Press.

Collier, Jane F.
1974 Women in Politics. In *Woman, Culture, and Society*, Michelle Rosaldo and Louise Lamphere, eds., pp. 89–96. Palo Alto, Calif.: Stanford University Press.

Collier, Jane F., and Sylvia Yanagisako, eds.
1987 *Gender and Kinship*. Palo Alto, Calif.: Stanford University Press.

Condorcet, Jean-Antoine-Nicholas
1902 [1794] *Esquisse d'un tableau historique des progres de l'esprit humain*. Paris: Bibliotheque Nationale.

Conkey, Margaret, and Janet Spector
1984   Archaeology and the Study of Gender. *Advances in Archaeological Method and Theory* 7: 1–38.

Copeland, Lennie
1985   *Going International: How to Make Friends and Deal Effectively in the Global Marketplace.* New York: Random House.

Coquery-Vidrovitch, Catherine
1978   Researches on an African Mode of Production. In *Relations of Production: Marxist Approaches to Economic Anthropology,* David Sedden, ed., pp. 261–288. London: Frank Cass.

Cosmides, L., and J. Tooby
1997   Evolutionary Psychology: A Primer. http://www.psych.ucsb.edu/research/cep/primer/htm, retrieved October 20, 1998.

Crapo, Richard H.
1993   *Cultural Anthropology: Understanding Ourselves and Others.* Guilford, Conn.: Dushkin Publishing.

Crocker, J. Christopher
1977   My Brother the Parrot. In *The Social Use of Metaphor: Essays on the Anthropology of Rhetoric,* J. David Sapir and J. Christopher Crocker, eds., pp. 164–192. Philadelphia: University of Pennsylvania Press.

Crosby, Alfred W.
1989   *America's Forgotten Pandemic: The Influenza of 1918.* Cambridge: Cambridge University Press.

D'Andrade, Roy
1995a   *The Development of Cognitive Anthropology.* Cambridge: Cambridge University Press.
1995b   Moral Models in Anthropology. *Current Anthropology* 36(3): 399–408.

Darwin, Charles
1858   On the Tendency of Species to Form Varieties; and on the Perpetuation of Varieties and Species by Natural Means of Selection. *Journal of the Linnean Society* 3: 45–62.
1871   *The Descent of Man and Selection in Relation to Sex.* London: John Murray.
1988 [1859]   *On the Origin of Species.* New York: New York University Press.

Davis, Kingsley, and Wilbert E. Moore
1945   Some Principles of Stratification. *American Sociological Review* 10: 242–249.
1953   Replies to Tumin. *American Sociological Review* 18: 394–396.

Dawkins, Richard
1976   *The Selfish Gene.* New York: Oxford University Press.

de Beauvoir, Simone
1952   *The Second Sex,* H. M. Parshley, ed. and trans. New York: Knopf.

Deloria, Vine, Jr.
1969   *Custer Died for Your Sins: An Indian Manifesto.* New York: Macmillan.

Devereux, G.
1961   Shamans as Neurotics. *American Anthropologist* 63: 1088–1090.

Devons, Ely, and Max Gluckman
1964   Conclusion: Modes and Consequences of Limiting a Field of Study. In *Closed Systems and Open Minds,* Max Gluckman, ed., pp. 254–259. Chicago: Aldine.

di Leonardo, Micaela
1991   Introduction: Gender, Culture, and Political Economy Feminist Anthropology in Historical Perspective. In *Gender at the Crossroads of Knowledge,* Micaela di Leonardo, ed., pp. 1–48. Berkeley: University of California Press.

Dolgin, Janet L., David S. Kemnitzer, and David M. Schneider
1977   *Symbolic Anthropology.* New York: Columbia University Press.

Douglas, Mary
1966   *Purity and Danger: An Analysis of the Concepts of Pollution and Taboo.* London: Routledge and Kegan Paul.
1970   *Natural Symbols: Explorations in Cosmology.* New York: Pantheon.

Durkheim, Émile
1933 [1893]   *The Division of Labor in Society,* George Simpson, trans. New York: Macmillan.
1951 [1897]   *Suicide: A Study in Sociology,* Jon A. Spaulding and George Simpson, trans. New York: Free Press.
1965 [1912]   *The Elementary Forms of the Religious Life,* Joseph Swain, trans. New York: Free Press.

Durkheim, Émile, and Marcel Mauss
1963 [1903]   *Primitive Classification,* Rodney Needham, trans. Chicago: University of Chicago Press.

Eiseley, Loren
1961   *Darwin's Century: Evolution and the Men Who Discovered It.* New York: Anchor Books.

Engels, Friedrich
1949 [1888]   *Ludwig Feuerbach and the End of Classical German Philosophy.* Moscow: Foreign Languages Publishing House.
1972 [1884]   *The Origin of the Family, Private Property, and the State.* New York: Pathfinder Press.

Erickson, P. A. W., and L. D. Murphy
1998   A History of Anthropological Theory. Peterborough, Ontario: Broadview.

Evans-Pritchard, E. E.
1940   The Nuer: A Description of the Modes of Livelihood and Political Institutions of a Nilotic People. Oxford: Oxford University Press.
1951a   Kinship and Marriage Among the Nuer. Oxford: Clarendon Press.
1951b   Social Anthropology. New York: Free Press.
1956   Nuer Religion. Oxford: Clarendon Press.

Fagan, Brian M.
1989   People of the Earth: An Introduction to World Prehistory. Glenview, Ill.: Scott Foresman.

Firth, Raymond
1964   The Place of Malinowski in the History of Economic Anthropology. In Man and Culture: An Evaluation of the Work of Bronislaw Malinowski, Raymond Firth, ed., pp. 209–227. New York: Harper & Row.
1973   Symbols, Public and Private. Ithaca, N.Y.: Cornell University Press.

Flannery, Kent V.
1972   The Cultural Evolution of Civilizations. Annual Review of Ecological Systems 3: 399–426.

Fortes, Meyer, and E. E. Evans-Pritchard
1967 [1940]   African Political Systems. London: Oxford University Press.

Foucault, Michel
1965 [1961]   Madness and Civilization. New York: Pantheon.
1972   The Archaeology of Knowledge, A. M. Sheridan Smith, trans. New York: Harper Colophon.
1978   The History of Sexuality, Volume I: An Introduction. New York: Pantheon.

Fox, Robin
1972   In the Beginning: Aspects of Hominid Behavioral Evolution. In Perspectives on Human Evolution, Sherwood L. Washburn and Phyllis Dolhinow, eds., pp. 358–381. New York: Holt, Rinehart, and Winston.

Frake, Charles
1962   The Ethnographic Study of Cognitive Systems. In Anthropology and Human Behavior, Thomas Gladwin and William D. Sturtevant, eds., pp. 72–85. Washington, D.C.: The Anthropological Society of Washington.

Frank, G.
1997   Jews, Multiculturalism, and Boasian Anthropology. American Anthropologist 99(4): 731–745.

Frazer, James George
1911–1915 [1890]   The Golden Bough: A Study in Magic and Religion, 3rd ed. London: Macmillan.

Freidl, Ernestine
1975   Women and Men: An Anthropologist's View. New York: Holt, Rinehart, and Winston.

Freud, Sigmund
1939   Moses and Monotheism, Katherine Jones, trans. London: Hogarth Press.
1950 [1913]   Totem and Taboo: Some Points of Agreement Between the Mental Lives of Savages and Neurotics, James Strachey, trans. New York: W. W. Norton.
1960 [1905]   Jokes and Their Relation to the Unconscious, James Strachey, trans. New York: W. W. Norton.
1961a [1930]   Civilization and Its Discontents, James Strachey, trans. New York: W. W. Norton.
1961b [1928]   The Future of an Illusion, James Strachey, trans. New York: W. W. Norton.
1963 [1900]   On Dreams, James Strachey, trans. New York: W. W. Norton.

Fried, Morton
1967   The Evolution of Political Society. New York: Random House.

Friedman, Jonathan
1974   Marxism, Structuralism, and Vulgar Materialism. Man 9(3): 444–469.

Frye, Northrop
1964   The Educated Imagination. Bloomington: Indiana University Press.

Gadamer, Hans-Georg
1975   Truth and Method, Garren Burden and John Cumming, trans. New York: Seabury Press.

Galton, F., Sr.
1869   Hereditary Genius: An Inquiry into Its Laws and Consequences. London: Macmillan.
1883   Inquiries into Human Faculty and Its Development. New York: Macmillan.

Garbarino, Merwyn S.
1977   Sociocultural Theory in Anthropology. New York: Holt, Rinehart, and Winston.

Geertz, Clifford
1963a   Agricultural Involution: The Processes of Ecological Change in Indonesia. Berkeley: University of California Press.
1963b   Peddlers and Princes: Social Development and Economic Change in Two Indonesian Towns. Chicago: University of Chicago Press.
1973   The Interpretation of Cultures. New York: Basic Books.
1975   On the Nature of Anthropological Understanding. American Scientist 63(1): 47–53.
1986   Making Experience Authoring Selves. In The Anthropology of Experience, Victor W. Turner and Ed-

ward M. Bruner, eds., pp. 373–380. Urbana: University of Illinois Press.

Gennep, Arnold van
1960 [1909] *The Rites of Passage,* Monica Vizedom and Gabrielle L. Caffee, trans. Chicago: University of Chicago Press.

Gerth, H. H., and C. Wright Mills
1946 Introduction: The Man and His Work. In *From Max Weber: Essays in Sociology,* H. H. Gerth and C. Wright Mills, eds., pp. 1–74. New York: Oxford University Press.

Gibbon, Edward
1942 [1776–1788] *The Decline and Fall of the Roman Empire.* New York: E. P. Dutton.

Gluckman, Max
1956 *Custom and Conflict in Africa.* Glencoe, Ill.: Free Press.
1967 [1956] The Peace and the Feud. In *Custom and Conflict in Africa,* pp. 2–26. New York: Barnes and Noble.

Goldenweiser, Alexander
1910 Totemism: An Analytical Study. *Journal of American Folklore* 23: 179.

Goodenough, Ward
1956 Componential Analysis and the Study of Meaning. *Language* 32: 195–216.

Goody, Jack
1995 *The Expansive Moment: Anthropology in Britain and Africa 1918–1970.* Cambridge: Cambridge University Press.

Gorer, Geoffrey, and John Rickman
1962 [1949] *The People of Great Russia: A Psychological Study.* New York: W. W. Norton.

Gould, Stephen Jay
1981 *The Mismeasure of Man.* New York: W. W. Norton.
1994 Cabinet Museums Revisited. *Natural History* 103(1): 12–20.

Graebner, F.
1911 *Die Methode der Ethnologie.* Heidelberg: C. Winter.

Gramsci, Antonio
1994 *Letters From Prison,* Frank Rosengarten, ed.; Raymond Rosenthal, trans. New York: Columbia University Press.

Graves, Robert
1948 *The White Goddess.* New York: Vintage.

Gunder-Frank, A.
1966 The Development of Underdevelopment. *Monthly Review* 18(4): 17–31.

Handler, Richard
1991 An Interview with Clifford Geertz. *Current Anthropology* 32(5): 603–613.

Hardin, Garrett
1968 The Tragedy of the Commons. *Science* 162(13 December): 1243–1248.

Harris, Marvin
1968 *The Rise of Anthropological Theory.* New York: Thomas Y. Crowell.
1974 *Cows, Pigs, Wars and Witches: The Riddles of Culture.* New York: Random House.
1977 *Cannibals and Kings: The Origins of Culture.* New York: Random House.
1979 *Cultural Materialism: The Struggle for a Science of Culture.* New York: Random House.
1981 *America Now: The Anthropology of a Changing Culture.* New York: Simon & Schuster.
1985 *Good to Eat: Riddles of Food and Culture.* New York: Simon & Schuster.
1994 Cultural Materialism Is Alive and Well and Won't Go Away Until Something Better Comes Along. In *Assessing Cultural Anthropology,* R. Borofsky, ed., pp. 62–76. New York: McGraw-Hill.

Harrison, Faye V., ed.
1991 *Decolonizing Anthropology: Moving Further Toward an Anthropology for Liberation.* Washington, D.C.: American Anthropological Association, Association of Black Anthropologists.

Harrison, Lawrence E.
1992 *Who Prospers? How Cultural Values Shape Economic and Political Success.* New York: Basic Books.

Haviland, William A.
1999 *Cultural Anthropology,* 9th ed. New York: Harcourt Brace.

Hertz, Robert
1973 [1909] The Pre-eminence of the Right Hand: A Study in Religious Polarity. In *Right and Left: Essays on Dual Symbolic Classification,* Rodney Needham, ed., pp. 3–31. Chicago: University of Chicago Press.

Hobbes, Thomas
1983 [1651] *Leviathan.* London: Dent.

Hockett, Charles F.
1973 *Man's Place in Nature.* New York: McGraw-Hill.

Hoebel, E. Adamson
1949 *Man in the Primitive World: An Introduction to Anthropology.* New York: McGraw-Hill.

Hoernle, Agnes Winifred
1925 The Social Organization of the Nama Hottentots of Southwest Africa. *American Anthropologist* 27(1): 1–24.

Holland, Dorothy, and Debra Skinner
1987   Prestige and Intimacy, the Cultural Models Behind Americans' Talk about Gender Types. In *Cultural Models in Language and Thought*, D. Holland and N. Quinn, eds., pp. 78–111. New York: Cambridge University Press.

Holmes, G.
1914   Areas of American Culture Characterization Tentatively Outlined as an Aid in the Study of Antiquities. *American Anthropologist* 16: 413–416.

Hsu, Francis L. K.
1980   Margaret Mead and Psychological Anthropology. *American Anthropologist* 82(2): 349–353.

Humboldt, Alexander von
1874 [1845–1862]   *Kosmos*. Stuttgart: J. G. Cotta.

Humboldt, Wilhelm von
1963   *Humanist Without a Portfolio: An Anthology of the Writings of Wilhelm von Humboldt*, Marianne Cowen, trans. Detroit: Wayne State University Press.

Hutchins, Edwin
1994   *Cognition in the Wild*. Cambridge: MIT Press.

Hyatt, Marshall
1990   *Franz Boas, Social Activist: The Dynamics of Ethnicity*. New York: Greenwood Press.

Hymes, Dell
1972   *Reinventing Anthropology*. New York: Pantheon.

Jung, Carl Gustave
1971 [1923]   *Psychological Types*. Princeton, N.J.: Princeton University Press.

Kaplan, David, and Robert A. Manners
1972   *Cultural Theory*. Englewood Cliffs, N.J.: Prentice-Hall.

Kaplan, Robert
1994   The Coming Anarchy. *Atlantic Monthly* 273(2): 44–76.

Karp, Ivan, and Kent Maynard
1983   Reading the Nuer. *Current Anthropology* 24(4): 481–503.

Kenyatta, Jomo
1979 [1938]   *Facing Mount Kenya: The Traditional Life of the Gikuyu*. London: Heinemann.

Keys, Ancel
1943   Physical Performance in Relation to Diet. *Federation Proceedings*. 2: 164–187.
1946   Nutrition and Capacity for Work. *Occupational Medicine* 2: 536–545.

Kirchhoff, Paul
1935   Principles of Clanship in Human Society (ms.; cf. *Davidson Journal of Anthropology* 1 [1955]).

Kormondy, E. J., and D. E. Brown
1998   *Fundamentals of Human Ecology*. Upper Saddle River: Prentice-Hall.

Kottak, Conrad Phillip
1994   *Cultural Anthropology*. New York: McGraw-Hill.

Kroeber, A. L.
1901   Decorative Symbolism of the Arapaho. *American Anthropologist* 3: 308–336.
1917   The Superorganic. *American Anthropologist* 19: 163–213.
1939   *Cultural and Natural Areas of Native North America*. Berkeley: University of California Press.
1940   Psychotic Factors in Shamanism. *Character and Personality* 8: 204–215.

Kuhn, Thomas S.
1962   *The Structure of Scientific Revolutions*. Chicago: University of Chicago Press.

Kuklick, H.
1991   *The Savage Within: The Social History of British Anthropology, 1885–1945*. Cambridge: Cambridge University Press.

Kurtz, Donald V.
1996   Hegemony and Anthropology: Gramsci, Exegesis, Reinterpretations. *Critique of Anthropology* 16(2): 103–135.

Lacoste, Yves
1984   *Ibn Khaldoun: The Birth of History and the Past of the Third World*. London: Verso.

Lamphere, Louise
1987   The Struggle to Reshape Our Thinking about Gender. In *The Impact of Feminist Research in the Academy*, Christie Farnham, ed., pp. 11–33. Bloomington: Indiana University Press.

Langness, L. L.
1987   *The Study of Culture*. Novato, Calif.: Chandler and Sharp.

Layton, Robert
1997   *An Introduction to Theory in Anthropology*. Cambridge: Cambridge University Press.

Le Bon, Gustave
1977 [1895]   *The Crowd: A Study of the Popular Mind*. New York: Penguin.

Leach, Edmund R.
1954   *Political Systems of Highland Burma: A Study of Kachin Social Structure*. London: London School of Economics and Political Science.
1976   *Claude Lévi-Strauss*. New York: Penguin.
1984   Glimpses of the Unmentionable in the History of British Social Anthropology. In *Annual Review of Anthropology*, Bernard Siegel, Alan Beals, and Stephen

Tyler, eds., vol. 13, pp. 1–23. Palo Alto, Calif.: Annual Reviews.

Leacock, Eleanor
1983 Interpreting the Origins of Gender Inequality: Conceptual and Historical Problems. *Dialectical Anthropology* 7(4): 263–284.

Leaf, Murray J.
1979 *Man, Mind, and Science: A History of Anthropology.* New York: Columbia University Press.

Lehman, David
1992 Paul de Man: The Plot Thickens. *New York Times Book Review,* May 24.

Lett, James
1987 *The Human Enterprise: A Critical Introduction to Anthropological Theory.* Boulder, Colo.: Westview Press.
1997 *Science, Reason and Anthropology: the Principles of Rational Inquiry.* Lanham, Rowman & Littlefield.

Lévi-Strauss, Claude
1963a The Effectiveness of Symbols. In *Structural Anthropology,* pp. 186–205. New York: Basic Books.
1963b Structural Analysis in Linguistics and in Anthropology. In *Structural Anthropology,* pp. 31–54. New York: Basic Books.
1969a [1949] *The Elementary Structures of Kinship,* rev. ed. Boston: Beacon Press.
1969b *The Raw and the Cooked.* New York: Harper & Row.
1973 *From Honey to Ashes.* Chicago: University of Chicago Press.

Levy-Bruhl, Lucien
1966 [1910] *How Natives Think,* Lillian A. Clare, trans. New York: Washington Square Press.

Lichtheim, G.
1973 Marx and the "Asiatic Mode of Production." In *Karl Marx,* T. Bottomore, ed., pp. 151–171. Englewood Cliffs, N.J.: Prentice-Hall.

Lilla, Mark
1998 The Politics of Jacques Derrida. *The New York Review of Books,* XLV(11): 36–41.

Locke, John
1939 [1690] An Essay Concerning the True Original Extent and End of Civil Government. In *The English Philosophers from Bacon to Mill,* Edwin A. Burtt, ed. New York: Modern Library.

Lorentz, Konrad
1952 *King Solomon's Ring: New Light on Animal Ways,* Marjorie Kerr Wilson, trans. New York: Crowell.
1966 *On Aggression.* New York: Harcourt, Brace and World.

Lounsbury, Floyd
1956 A Semantic Analysis of the Pawnee Kinship Usage. *Language* 32: 158–194.

Lowie, Robert H.
1913 Military Societies of the Crow Indians. *Anthropological Papers of the American Museum of Natural History* 11: 145–217.
1920 *Primitive Society.* New York: Liveright.
1937 *The History of Ethnological Theory.* New York: Holt, Rinehart, and Winston.

Lubbock, Sir John
1865 *Prehistoric Times: As Illustrated by Ancient Remains and the Manners and Customs of Modern Savages.* London: William and Norgate.
1870 *The Origin of Civilization and the Primitive Condition of Man: Mental and Social Condition of Savages.* London: Longman, Green.

Lutkehaus, N. C.
1995 Margaret Mead and the "Rustling-of-the-wind-in-the-palm-trees-school" of Ethnographic Writing. In *Women Writing Culture,* R. Behar and D. A. Gordon, eds., pp. 186–201. Berkeley: University of California Press.

Lyell, Sir Charles
1863 *The Geological Evidences of the Antiquity of Man.* Philadelphia: G. W. Childs.

MacCormack, Carol P.
1980 Nature, Culture, and Gender: A Critique. In *Nature, Culture, and Gender,* Carol P. MacCormack and Marilyn Strathern, eds., pp. 1–24. Cambridge: Cambridge University Press.

Macintosh, Sir James
1828 [1799] *A Discourse on the Study of the Law of Nature and Nations.* London: H. Goode.

McDowell, Nancy
1980 The Oceanic Ethnography of Margaret Mead. *American Anthropologist* 82(2): 278–303.

McLennan, John Ferguson
1865 *Primitive Marriage: An Inquiry into the Origin of the Form of Capture in Marriage Ceremonies.* Edinburgh: A. and C. Black.

Maillet, Benoit de
1748 *Telliamed, ou, Entretiens d'un philosophe indien avec un missionaire francois sur le diminution de la mer, la formation de la terre, l'origine de l'homme etc.* Amsterdam: L'honore.

Maine, H. S.
1963 *Ancient Law: Its Connection with the Early History of Society and Its Relation to Modern Ideas.* Boston: Beacon Press.

Malefijt, Annemarie de Waal
1974 *Images of Man: A History of Anthropological Thought.* New York: Alfred A. Knopf.
1989 *Religion and Culture: An Introduction to Anth-ropology of Religion.* Prospect Heights, Ill.: Waveland Press.

Malinowski, Bronislaw
1922 *Argonauts of the Western Pacific.* New York: E. P. Dutton.
1955 [1927] *Sex and Repression in Savage Society.* New York: Harcourt, Brace.
1929a Practical Anthropology. *Africa* 2: 22–38.
1929b *The Sexual Life of Savages in Northwestern Melanesia.* London: Routledge.
1935 *Coral Gardens and Their Magic.* New York: American Book Company.
1939 The Group and the Individual in Functional Analysis. *American Journal of Sociology* 44: 938–964.
1954 [1925] *Magic, Science and Religion and Other Essays.* New York: Doubleday.
1967 *A Diary in the Strict Sense of the Term.* New York: Harcourt, Brace and World.

Malthus, Thomas Robert
1926 [1798] *An Essay on the Principles of Population as It Affects the Future Improvement of Society with Remarks on the Speculations of Mr. Godwin, M. Condorcet, and Other Writers.* London: Macmillan.

Manganaro, Marc, ed.
1990 *Modernist Anthropology: From Fieldwork to Text.* Princeton, N.J.: Princeton University Press.

Marcus, George E., and Dick Cushman
1982 Ethnographies as Texts. *Annual Reviews of Anthropology* 11: 25–69.

Marx, Karl
1930 [1867] *Capital: A Critique of Political Economy,* 4th ed., Paul Eden and Paul Ceder, trans. New York: E. P. Dutton.
1963 [1844] On the Jewish Question. In *Karl Marx: Early Writings,* T. B. Bottomore, ed., pp. 3–40. New York: McGraw-Hill.

Marx, Karl, and Friedrich Engels
1970 [1846] *The German Ideology: Part One with Selections from Parts Two and Three, Together with Marx's Introduction to a Critique of Political Economy,* C. J. Arthur, ed. New York: International Publishing.
1972 [1848] The Communist Manifesto. In *Karl Marx: Essential Writings,* Fredrick L. Bender, ed., pp. 240–263. New York: Harper & Row.
1975 [1845] *The Holy Family: Or Critique of Critical Criticism: Against Bruno Bauer and Company.* Moscow: Progress Publishers.

Mason, Otis
1895 Similarities in Culture. *American Anthropologist* 8: 101–117.

Mauss, Marcel
1967 [1925] *The Gift: Forms and Functions of Exchange in Archaic Societies,* Ian Cunnison, trans. New York: W. W. Norton.

Mayer, Jean, and Beverly Bullen
1960 Nutrition and Athletic Performance. *Physiological Reviews* 40(3): 369–397.

Mead, Margaret
1928 *Coming of Age in Samoa: A Psychological Study of Primitive Youth for Western Civilization.* New York: William Morrow.
1930 *Growing Up in New Guinea: A Comparative Study of Primitive Education.* New York: William Morrow.
1935 *Sex and Temperament in Three Primitive Societies.* New York: William Morrow.
1949 *Male and Female: A Study of the Sexes in a Changing World.* New York: William Morrow.

Metzger, Duane, and G. Williams
1966 Some Procedures and Results in the Study of Native Categories: Tzeltal "Firewood." *American Anthropologist* 68: 389–407.

Modell, Judith Schachter
1983 *Ruth Benedict: Patterns of a Life.* Philadelphia: University of Pennsylvania Press.

Montagu, Ashley
1980 *Sociobiology Examined.* Oxford: Oxford University Press.

Morgan, Elaine
1972 *The Descent of Woman.* New York: Stein and Day.
1982 *The Aquatic Ape.* New York: Stein and Day.

Morgan, Lewis Henry
1871 Systems of Consanguinity and Affinity of the Human Family. *Smithsonian Contributions to Knowledge* no. 218, vol. 17. Washington, D.C.: Smithsonian.
1985 [1877] *Ancient Society.* Tucson: University of Arizona Press.

Morgen, Sandra
1989 Gender and Anthropology: Introductory Essay. In *Gender and Anthropology — Critical Reviews for Research and Teaching,* Sandra Morgan, ed., pp. 1–20. Washington, D.C.: American Anthropological Association.

Morgan, Samuel G.
1839 *Crania Americana.* Philadelphia: J. Dobson.
1844 *Crania Aegyptiaca.* Philadelphia: J. Penington.

Müller, F. Max
1977 [1856] *Comparative Mythology.* New York: Arno Press.

Murdock, George P.
1959   Evolution in Social Organization. In *Evolution and Anthropology*, B. Meggers, ed., pp. 126–145. Washington, D.C.: Anthropological Society of Washington.
1960 [1949]   *Social Structure*. New York: Macmillan.

Murphy, R. F.
1994   The Dialectics of Deeds and Words. In *Assessing Cultural Anthropology*, R. Borofsky, ed., pp. 55–61. New York: McGraw-Hill.

Murray, Margaret Alice
1921   *The Witch-Cult in Western Europe: A Study in Anthropology*. Oxford: Clarendon Press.

Nadel, S. F.
1954   *Nupe Religion*. London: Routledge and Kegan Paul.

National Cyclopedia of American Biography
1967   William Graham Sumner, vol. 25, pp. 8–9. Clifton, N.J.: J. T. White.

Nietzsche, Friedrich
1954 [1883–1885]   *Thus Spake Zarathustra*. New York: Modern Library.
1956 [1872]   *The Birth of Tragedy and the Genealogy of Morals*. Garden City, N.Y.: Doubleday.

Obeyesekere, Gananath
1981   *Medusa's Hair: An Essay on Personal Symbols and Religious Experience*. Chicago: University of Chicago Press.

O'Laughlin, Bridget
1975   Marxist Approaches in Anthropology. In *Annual Review of Anthropology*, Bernard Siegel, Alan Beals, and Stephen Tyler, eds., vol. 4, pp. 341–370. Palo Alto, Calif.: Annual Reviews.

O'Meara, J. Tim
1989   Anthropology as Empirical Science. *American Anthropologist* 91: 354–369.

Oppenheimer, Franz
1914   *The State: Its History and Development Viewed Sociologically*, John M. Gitterman, trans. Indianapolis: Bobbs-Merrill.

Orlove, Benjamin S.
1980   Ecological Anthropology. In *Annual Review of Anthropology*, Bernard Siegel, Alan Beals, and Stephen Tyler, eds., vol. 9, pp. 235–273. Palo Alto, Calif.: Annual Reviews.

Ortner, Sherry B.
1973   On Key Symbols. *American Anthropologist* 75: 1338–1346.
1975   Gods' Bodies, Gods' Food: A Symbolic Analysis of Sherpa Ritual. In *The Interpretation of Symbolism*, Ray Willis, ed., pp. 133–167. New York: John Wiley and Sons.

1984   Theory in Anthropology since the Sixties. *Comparative Studies in Society and History* 26(1): 126–166.

Ortner, Sherry B., and Harriet Whitehead
1981   *Sexual Meanings: The Cultural Construction of Gender and Sexuality*. Cambridge: Cambridge University Press.

Peace, W. J.
1998   Bernhard Stern, Leslie A. White, and an Anthropological Appraisal of the Russian Revolution. *American Anthropologist* 100(1): 84–93.

Pike, Kenneth
1954   *Language in Relation to a Unified Theory of the Structure of Human Behavior*, vol. 1. Glendale, Calif.: Summer Institute of Linguistics.

Plato
1993   *Republic*, Robin Waterfield, trans. Oxford: Oxford University Press.

Polanyi, Karl, Conrad M. Arensberg, and Harry W. Pearson
1957   *Trade and Market in the Early Empires: Economies in History and Theory*. Glencoe, Ill.: Free Press.

Quetelet, Adolphe
1848   *Du Système Social et des Lois qui le Régissent*. Paris: Guillaumin.
1968 [1835]   *A Treatise on Man and the Development of His Faculties*. New York: B. Franklin.

Rabinow, Paul
1977   *Reflections on Fieldwork in Morocco*. Berkeley: University of California Press.
1986   Representations Are Social Facts: Modernity and Postmodernism in Anthropology. In *Writing Culture: The Poetics and Politics of Ethnography*, James Clifford and George Marcus, eds., pp. 234–261. Berkeley: University of California Press.

Radcliffe-Brown, A. R.
1924   The Mother's Brother in South Africa. *South African Journal of Science* 21: 542–555.
1935   On the Concept of Function in Social Science. *American Anthropologist* 37: 392–402.
1964 [1922]   *The Andaman Islanders*. New York: Free Press.
1965 [1940]   On Joking Relationships. In *Structure and Function in Primitive Society*, A. R. Radcliffe-Brown, ed., pp. 90–104. New York: Free Press.

Radin, Paul
1911   Description of a Winnebago Funeral. *American Anthropologist* 13(3): 437–444.
1924   Ojibwa Ethnological Chit Chat. *American Anthropologist* 26(4): 491–530.
1926   *Crashing Thunder: The Autobiography of an American Indian*. New York: Appleton.

1957 [1927] *Primitive Man as Philosopher*, 2nd ed. New York: Dover.

Rappaport, Roy A.
1967 *Pigs for the Ancestors*. New Haven: Yale University Press.
1984 *Pigs for the Ancestors*. New Haven: Yale University Press.
1994 Humanity's Evolution and Anthropology's Future. In *Assessing Cultural Anthropology*, R. Borofsky, ed., pp. 153–167. New York, McGraw-Hill.

Reiter, Rayna, ed.
1975 *Toward an Anthropology of Women*. New York: Monthly Review Press.

Resek, Carl
1960 *Lewis Henry Morgan: American Scholar*. Chicago: University of Chicago Press.

Ritzer, George
1992 *Sociological Theory*, 3rd ed. New York: McGraw-Hill.

Rivers, W. H. R.
1900 A Genealogical Method of Collecting Social and Vital Statistics. *Journal of the Anthropological Institute*, n.s., 3: 74–82.
1910 The Genealogical Method of Anthropological Inquiry. *The Sociological Review* 3: 1–12.

Roheim, Geza
1971 [1925] *Australian Totemism: A Psychoanalytic Study in Anthropology*. New York: Humanities Press.

Rorty, Richard
1979 *Philosophy and the Mirror of Knowledge*. Princeton, N.J.: Princeton University Press.

Rosaldo, Michelle
1974 Women, Culture, and Society: A Theoretical Overview. In *Women, Culture, and Society*, Michelle Rosaldo and Louise Lamphere, eds., pp. 14–42. Palo Alto, Calif.: Stanford University Press.
1980 *Knowledge and Passion: Ilongot Notions of Self and Social Life*. Cambridge: Cambridge University Press.

Rosaldo, Michelle, and Louis Lamphere, eds.
1974 *Women, Culture, and Society*. Palo Alto, Calif.: Stanford University Press.

Rousseau, Jean-Jacques
1974 [1762] *Emile*, Barbara Foxley, trans. New York: E. P. Dutton.

Sacks, K.
1979 *Sisters and Wives: The Past and Future of Sexual Equality*. Westport, Conn.: Greenwood Press.

Sahlins, Marshall D.
1964 Culture and Environment: The Study of Cultural Ecology. In *Horizons of Anthropology*, Sol Tax, ed., pp. 132–147. Chicago: Aldine.

1976 *The Use and Abuse of Biology: An Anthropological Critique of Sociobiology*. Ann Arbor: University of Michigan Press.

Sahlins, Marshall D., and Elman R. Service
1960 *Evolution and Culture*. Ann Arbor: University of Michigan Press.

Said, E.
1978 *Orientalism*. New York: Pantheon.

Sanday, Peggy Reeves
1980 Margaret Mead's View of Sex Roles in Her Own and Other Societies. *American Anthropologist* 82(2): 340–348.
1981 *Female Power and Male Dominance: On the Origins of Sexual Inequality*. New York: Cambridge University Press.

Sanday, Peggy Reeves, and Ruth Gallagher Goodenough, eds.
1990 *Beyond the Second Sex: New Directions in the Anthropology of Gender*. Philadelphia: University of Pennsylvania Press.

Sangren, Steven P.
1988 Rhetoric and the Authority of Ethnography. *Current Anthropology* 29(3): 405–435.

Sassoon, A. S.
1991 Hegemony. In *A Dictionary of Marxist Thought*, T. Bottomore, ed., pp. 229–231. Oxford: Basil Blackwell.

Sawicki, J.
1991 *Disciplining Foucault: Feminism, Power, and the Body*. New York: Routledge.

Scheper-Hughes, Nancy
1979 *Saints, Scholars, and Schizophrenics: Mental Illness in Rural Ireland*. Berkeley: University of California Press.
1989 Death Without Weeping. *Natural History* 98: 8–16.
1922 *Death Without Weeping: The Violence of Everyday Life in Brazil*. Berkeley: University of California Press.
1995 The Primacy of the Ethical: Propositions for a Militant Anthropology. *Current Anthropology* 36(3): 409–420.

Schneider, Jane, and Reyna Rapp, eds.
1995 *Articulating Hidden Histories: Exploring the Influences of Eric R. Wolf*. Berkeley: University of California Press.

Seligman, Charles G.
1910 *The Melanesians of British New Guinea*. Cambridge: Cambridge University Press.

Service, Elman R.
1962 *Primitive Social Organization: An Evolutionary Perspective*. New York: Random House.

1976 Leslie Alvin White, 1900–1975. *American Anthropologist* 78(3): 612–617.
1988 Morton Herbert Fried (1923–1986). *American Anthropologist* 90(1): 148–152.

Shannon, Claude
1948 A Mathematical Theory of Communication. *Bell System Technical Journal* 27: 379–423.

Silverman, J.
1967 Shamanism and Acute Schizophrenia. *American Anthropologist* 69: 21–31.

Smith, Adam
1976 [1776] *An Inquiry into the Nature and Causes of the Wealth of Nations.* Oxford: Clarendon Press.

Smith, Grafton Elliot
1928 *In the Beginning: The Origin of Civilization.* New York: Morrow.

Smole, William J.
1976 *The Yanoama Indians: A Cultural Geography.* Austin: University of Texas Press.

Solecki, R., and C. Wagley
1963 William Duncan Strong (1899–1962). *American Anthropologist* 65(5): 1102–1111.

Spencer, Herbert
1859 What Knowledge Is of Most Worth? *Westminster Review* 72: 1–41.
1860 The Social Organism. *Westminster Review,* new series, 17: 51–68.
1873 *The Study of Sociology.* Boston: Routledge and Kegan Paul.
1873–1934 *Descriptive Sociology,* 13 vols. New York: Appleton-Century-Crofts.
1885 *The Principles of Sociology,* 2 vols. New York: Appleton-Century-Crofts.
1967 *The Evolution of Society: Selections from Herbert Spencer's Principles of Sociology,* Robert L. Carneiro, ed. Chicago: University of Chicago Press.

Spinoza, Baruch
1930 [1677] *Ethics.* London: Oxford University Press.

Spradley, James P.
1980 *Participant Observation.* New York: Holt, Rinehart, and Winston.

Spradley, James P., ed.
1987 *Culture and Cognition.* New York: Waveland Press.

Steward, Julian
1955 *Theory of Culture Change: The Methodology of Multilinear Evolution.* Urbana: University of Illinois Press.

Stirner, Max
1918 [1844] *The Ego and His Own.* Steven T. Byington, trans. New York: Boni and Liveright.

Stocking, G.
1968 The Scientific Reaction Against Cultural Anthropology, 1917–1920. In *Race, Culture, and Evolution: Essays in the History of Anthropology,* G. Stocking, ed., pp. 270–307. New York: The Free Press.
1974 *The Shaping of American Anthropology 1883–1911.* New York: Basic Books.
1987 *Victorian Anthropology.* New York: Free Press.
1992 Ideas and Institutions in American Anthropology: Thoughts Toward a History of the Interwar Years. The Ethnographer's Magic and Other Essays. In *The History of Anthropology,* G. Stocking, ed., pp. 114–177. Madison: University of Wisconsin.

Stoler, Ann Laura
1989 Making Empire Respectable: the Politics of Race and Sexual Morality in 20th Century Colonial Cultures. *American Ethnologist* 16(4): 634–660.

Stoller, Paul
1989 *The Taste of Ethnographic Things: The Senses in Anthropology.* Philadelphia: University of Pennsylvania Press.

Strauss, Claudia, and Naomi Quinn
1994 A Cognitive/Cultural Anthropology. In *Assessing Cultural Anthropology,* Robert Borofsky, ed., pp. 284–300. New York: McGraw-Hill.

Strauss, David Friedrich
1892 *The Life of Jesus,* 2nd ed., George Eliot, trans. London: Swan and Sonnenschein.

Strong, W. D.
1994 *Labrador Winter: The Ethnographic Journals of William Duncan Strong, 1927–1928.* Washington, D.C.: Smithsonian Institution.

Sturtevant, William C.
1964 Studies in Ethnoscience. *American Anthropologist* 66: 99–131.

Suchting, W. A.
1983 *Marx: An Introduction.* New York: New York University Press.

Sumner, William Graham
1914 The Concentration of Wealth: Its Economic Justification. In *The Challenge of Facts and Other Essays,* Albert G. Keller, ed., pp. 79–90. New Haven: Yale University Press.

Sumner, William Graham, and Albert G. Keller
1927 *The Science of Society.* New Haven, Conn.: Yale University Press.

Tanner, Nancy, and Adrienne Zihlman
1976 Women in Evolution. Part I: Innovation and Selection in Human Origins. *Signs* 2(3): 585–608.

Taylor, Charles
1979 Interpretation and the Sciences of Man. In *Interpretive Social Science: A Reader,* Paul Rabinow and W. M. Sullivan, eds., pp. 25–71. Berkeley: University of California Press.

Taylor, William Cooke
1841 *The Natural History of Society in the Barbarous and Civilized State.* New York: Appleton.

Todorov, Tzvetzn
1987 *Literature and Its Theorists: A Personal View of Twentieth-Century Criticism,* Catherine Porter, trans. Ithaca, N.Y.: Cornell University Press.

Tooker, Elizabeth
1992 Lewis H. Morgan and His Contemporaries. *American Anthropologist* 94(2): 357–375.

Turgot, Anne-Robert-Jacques
1973 [1750] *Turgot on Progress, Sociology and Economics: A Philosophical Review of the Successive Advances of the Human Mind, on Universal History (and) Reflections on the Formation and the Distribution of Wealth,* Roland L. Meek, trans. Cambridge: Cambridge University Press.

Turnbull, C.
1961 *The Forest People.* New York: Simon and Schuster.
1972 *The Mountain People.* New York: Simon and Schuster.

Turner, Bryan S., ed.
1966 *The Blackwell Companion to Social Theory.* Oxford: Blackwell.

Turner, Edith
1987 *The Spirit and the Drum: A Memoir of Africa.* Tucson: University of Arizona Press.
1992 *Experiencing Ritual: A New Interpretation of African Healing.* Philadelphia: University of Pennsylvania Press.
1965 Ritual Symbolism, Morality, and Social Structure among the Ndembu. In *African Systems of Thought,* M. Fortes and G. Dieterlen, eds., pp. 48–58. London: Oxford University Press.

Turner, Victor
1967 *The Forest of Symbols: Aspects of Ndembu Ritual,* pp. 93–111. Ithaca, N.Y.: Cornell University Press.

Tyler, Stephen
1969 *Cognitive Anthropology.* New York: Holt, Rinehart, and Winston.
1978 *The Said and the Unsaid: Mind, Meaning, and Culture.* New York: Academic Press.

Tylor, Sir Edward Burnett
1861 *Anahuac: Or Mexico and the Mexicans, Ancient and Modern.* London: Longman, Green, Longman and Roberts.
1871 *Primitive Culture.* London: John Murray.
1889 On a Method of Investigating the Development of Institutions; Applied to Laws of Marriage and Descent. *Journal of the Royal Anthropological Institute* 18: 245–269.
1920 *Primitive Culture,* 2nd ed. London: John Murray.

Veblen, Thorstein
1912 [1899] *The Theory of the Leisure Class: An Economic Study of Institutions.* New York: Viking Press.

Vico, Giambattista
1984 [1725] *The New Science of Giambattista Vico,* Thomas Goddard Bergin and Max Harold Fisch, trans. Ithaca, N.Y.: Cornell University Press.

Walker, J. C.
1986 Romanticizing Resistance, Romanticizing Culture: Problems in Willis's Theory of Cultural Production. *British Journal of Sociology of Education* 7(1): 59–80.

Wallenchinsky, David, and Irving Wallace, eds.
1975 *The People's Almanac.* Garden City, N.Y.: Doubleday.

Wallerstein, I.
1974 *The Modern World-System; Capitalist Agriculture and the Origins of the European World-Economy in the Sixteenth Century (by) Immanuel Wallerstein.* New York: Academic Press.

Washburn, Sherwood, and C. Lancaster
1968 The Evolution of Hunting. In *Man the Hunter,* R. B. Lee and Irven DeVore, eds., pp. 293–303. Chicago: Aldine.

Weber, Max
1958 [1904–1905] *The Protestant Ethic and the Spirit of Capitalism,* Talcott Parsons, trans. New York: Charles Scribner's Sons.
1978 *Economy and Society: An Outline of Interpretive Sociology,* Guenther Roth and Claus Wittich, eds.; Ephraim Fischoff, trans. Berkeley: University of California Press.
1993 [1920] Collected Essays in *The Sociology of Religion.* Boston: Beacon Press.

White, Leslie A.
1943 Energy and the Evolution of Culture. *American Anthropologist* 43: 335–356.
1949 Ikhnaton: The Great Man vs. the Culture Process. In *The Science of Culture: A Study of Man and Civilization,* pp. 233–281. New York: Farrar, Straus and Company.
1959 *The Evolution of Culture.* New York: McGraw-Hill.
1975 *The Concept of Cultural Systems: A Key to Understanding Tribes and Nations.* New York: Columbia University Press.

Whorf, Benjamin Lee
1956 *Language Thought and Reality.* Cambridge, Mass., MIT Press.

Willis, P.
1983 Cultural Production and Theories of Reproduction. In *Race, Class and Education,* L. Barton and S. Walker, eds., pp. 107–138. London: Croom Helm.

Wilson, Edward O.
1971 *The Insect Societies.* Cambridge, Mass.: Harvard University Press.
1975 *Sociobiology: The New Synthesis.* Cambridge, Mass.: Belknap Press of Harvard University Press.
1984 *Biophilia.* Cambridge, Mass.: Harvard University Press.

Wissler, Clark
1917 *The American Indian: An Introduction to the Anthropology of the New World.* New York: D. C. McMurtrie.
1926 *The Relation of Nature to Man in Aboriginal America.* New York: Oxford University Press.

Wolf, E. R.
1969 *Peasant Wars of the Twentieth Century.* New York: Harper & Row.
1981 *Totems and Teachers: Perspectives on the History of Anthropology,* Sydel Silverman, ed. New York: Columbia University Press.
1982 *Europe and the People Without History.* Berkeley: University of California Press.

Wundt, Wilhelm Max
1904 [1874] *Principles of Physiological Psychology,* Edward Bradford Titchener, trans. New York: Macmillan.
1916 [1912] *Elements of Folk Psychology: Outlines of a Psychological History of the Development of Mankind.* New York: Macmillan.

Yanagisako, Sylvia, and Jane Collier
1987 Toward a Unified Analysis of Gender and Kinship. In *Gender and Kinship: Essays Toward a Unified Analysis,* J. Collier and S. Yanagisako, eds., pp. 14–50. Palo Alto, Calif.: Stanford University Press.

Credits

JEROME H. BARKOW, "The Elastic Between Genes and Culture" from *Ethnology and Sociobiology,* vol. 10, 1989, 111–129. Copyright © 1989 by Elsevier Science Inc. Reprinted with permission of the publisher.

RUTH FULTON BENEDICT, "Psychological Types in the Cultures of the Southwest" from the Proceedings of the Twenty-Third International Congress of Americanists, New York, September 17–22, 1928. Courtesy of the Institute for Intercultural Studies, Inc., New York.

FRANZ BOAS, "The Methods of Ethnology" from *American Anthropologist* 22:4, October–November 1920.

PHILIPPE BOURGOIS, "From Jíbaro to Crack Dealer: Confronting the Restructuring of Capitalism in El Barrio," *Articulating Hidden Histories: Exploring the Influence of Eric R. Wolf,* Jane Schneider and Rayna Rapp, eds., University of California Press, 1995. Reprinted with permission from the author.

HAROLD C. CONKLIN, "Hanunoo Color Categories" from *Southwestern Journal of Anthropology,* vol. 11, 1955, 339–344. Reprinted with permission from the publisher.

VINCENT CRAPANZANO, "Hermes' Dilemma: The Masking of Subversion in Ethnographic Description," *Writing Culture: Poetics and Politics of Ethnography,* James Clifford and George Marcus. Copyright © 1986 The Regents of the University of California. Reprinted by permission of the University of California Press.

ROY D'ANDRADE, "Moral Models in Anthropology," *Current Anthropology,* vol. 36, No. 3, June 1995. Reprinted with permission from The University of Chicago Press.

MARY DOUGLAS, "External Boundaries," *Purity and Danger,* Routledge, 1966. Reprinted with permission from Routledge, Inc., United Kingdom.

ÉMILE DURKHEIM, "What Is a Social Fact?" Reprinted with the permission of The Free Press, a division of Simon & Schuster, Inc. from *The Rules of Sociological Method* by Émile Durkheim. Translated by Sarah A. Solovay and John H. Mueller. Edited by George E. G.

Catlin. Copyright © 1938 by George E. G. Catlin; copyright renewed 1966 by Sarah A. Solovay, John H. Mueller, and George E. G. Catlin. "The Cosmological System of Totemism and the Idea of Class." Reprinted with the permission of The Free Press, a division of Simon & Schuster, Inc. from *The Elementary Forms of the Religious Life* by Émile Durkheim. Translated by Joseph Ward Swain. Copyright © 1915 by George Allen & Unwin; 1965 by The Free Press. Also with permission from International Thomson Publishing Services, Ltd.

E. E. EVANS-PRITCHARD, "The Nuer of the Southern Sudan" from *The Nuer* by E. E. Evans-Pritchard, 1940. Reprinted by permission of Oxford University Press.

SIGMUND FREUD, "The Return of Totemism in Childhood," from *Totem and Taboo* by Sigmund Freud, translated by James Strachey. Translation copyright 1950 by Routledge & Kegan Paul, Ltd. Reprinted by permission of W.W. Norton & Company, Inc. and Routledge, Inc.

MORTON H. FRIED, "On the Evolution of Social Stratification and the State," from *Culture in History: Essays in Honor of Paul Radin* by Stanley Diamond. Copyright © 1960 Columbia University Press. Reprinted with permission of the publisher.

CLIFFORD GEERTZ, "Deep Play: Notes on the Balinese Cockfight" from "Myth, Symbol, and Culture," *Daedalus,* Journal of the American Academy of Arts and Sciences, Winter 1972, vol. 101, no. 1. Reprinted with permission from the publisher.

MARVIN HARRIS, "The Cultural Ecology of India's Sacred Cattle," from *Current Anthropology* 7, no. 1 (1966), 51–59. Reprinted with permission from The University of Chicago Press.

ALFRED L. KROEBER, "On the Principle of Order in Civilizations as Exemplified by Changes of Fashion" from *American Anthropologist* 21, 1919.

EDMUND LEACH, "Genesis as Myth" first appeared in *Discovery,* incorporated into *Science Journal,* vol. XXIII, May 1962, Jonathan Cape. Reprinted with permission from Random House, United Kingdom Ltd.

Index